June 13–15, 2011
Athens, Greece

 Association for Computing Machinery

Advancing Computing as a Science & Profession

PODS'11

Proceedings of the 30th Symposium on
Principles of Database Systems

Sponsored by:
ACM SIGMOD, ACM SIGACT, & ACM SIGART

Supported by:
EMC², Microsoft, Oracle, Google, IBM Research, SAP, Sybase, Yahoo! Labs, AsterData, HP, Intrasoft International, Kosmix, MarkLogic, Twitter, Virtualtrip, Greenplum, & NEC

Association for
Computing Machinery

Advancing Computing as a Science & Profession

The Association for Computing Machinery
2 Penn Plaza, Suite 701
New York, New York 10121-0701

Notice to Past Authors of ACM-Published Articles
ACM intends to create a complete electronic archive of all articles and/or other material previously published by ACM. If you have written a work that has been previously published by ACM in any journal or conference proceedings prior to 1978, or any SIG Newsletter at any time, and you do NOT want this work to appear in the ACM Digital Library, please inform permissions@acm.org, stating the title of the work, the author(s), and where and when published.

ISBN: 978-1-4503-0660-7

Additional copies may be ordered prepaid from:

ACM Order Department
PO Box 30777
New York, NY 10087-0777, USA

Phone: 1-800-342-6626 (USA and Canada)
+1-212-626-0500 (Global)
Fax: +1-212-944-1318
E-mail: acmhelp@acm.org
Hours of Operation: 8:30 am – 4:30 pm ET

ACM Order Number: 415112

Printed in the USA   Cover Image Credit: Rainer Sturm / pixelio.de

PODS'11 General Chair's Welcome Message

It is our great pleasure to welcome you to the *2011 ACM Symposium on Principles of Database Systems – PODS'11*. This year's symposium continues its tradition of being the premier international conference on the theoretical aspects of data management. PODS papers are distinguished by a rigorous approach to widely diverse problems in databases, often bringing to bear techniques from a variety of different areas, including computational logic, finite model theory, computational complexity, algorithm design and analysis, programming languages, and artificial intelligence. The first PODS conference was held in Los Angeles (CA) in 1982, with Jeffrey D. Ullman as General Chair. Since that time, virtually all new ideas, methods and techniques for data management have been investigated and presented in subsequent PODS conferences (see http://www09.sigmod.org/sigmod/pods/ for various information on the conference series).

To celebrate the 30th anniversary of the Symposium, the PODS Executive Committee has organized the PODS 30th Anniversary Colloquium, a special event held in June 12, 2011, with the goal of providing a retrospective on the role of database theory, and outlining a picture of the future directions of the discipline. The Colloquium featured five invited presentations from distinguished leaders in the field, namely:

Moshe Y. Vardi: "The rise, fall, and rise of dependency theory: Part 1, the rise and fall",

Ronald Fagin: "The rise, fall, and rise of dependency theory: Part 2, the rise from the ashes",

Jeffrey D. Ullman: "Deductive Databases",

Serge Abiteboul: "Trees, semistructured data, and other strange ways to go beyond tables",

Victor Vianu: "Database Theory: Back to the Future".

The PODS Executive Committee is grateful to the speakers for their participation in the event, and to Frank Neven for organizing a lively discussion session ending the Colloquium.

As usual, putting together *PODS'11* was a team effort. We are particularly grateful to the Program Chair, Thomas Schwentick, and to the whole program committee, who worked very hard in reviewing papers and providing feedback for authors. Finally, we thank the PODS proceedings and publicity Chair, Wim Martens, the hosting organization, and all our sponsors, in particular the ACM Special Interest Groups on Management of Data, for its invaluable support.

We hope that you will find the PODS'11 program interesting and thought provoking, in the best tradition of the PODS Symposium.

Maurizio Lenzerini
PODS'11 General Chair

PODS'11 Program Chair's Message

This volume contains the proceedings of the Thirtieth ACMSI GMOD-SIGACT-SIGART Symposium on Principles of Database Systems (PODS 2011), held in Ath ens, Greece, on June 13-15, 2011, in conjunction with the 2011 ACM SIGMOD International Conference on Management of Data.

The proceedings include a paper by Daniel Deutch and Tova Milo based on the keynote address by Tova Milo and two papers, the first by Marcelo Arenas and Jorge Pérez, based on t he tutorial by Marcelo Arenas, and t he second based on the tutorial by S. M uthu Muthukrishnan, and 2 5 contributed papers that were selected by the Program Committee from 113 submissions. Most of these papers are prel iminary reports on work in progress. While they have been read by program committee members, they have not been for mally refereed. Many of them will probably appear in more polished and detailed form in scientific journals.

The program committee selected the paper *Data Exchange beyond Complete Data* by Marcelo Arenas, Jorge Pérez and Juan L. Reutter for the *PODS 2011 Best Paper Award*. In ad dition, the announcement of the *2011 ACM PODS Alberto O. Mendelzon Test-of-Time Award* appears in the proceedings. This ye ar, the award is given to *Optimal Aggregation Algorithms for Middleware* by Ronald Fagin, Amnon Lotem, and Moni Naor. The paper ori ginally appeared in the proceedings of PODS 2001. Warmest congratulations to the authors of these papers.

I thank all authors who submitted papers to the symposium, the members of the program committee and the many external referees for t he enormous amount of work they have done. I am parti cularly grateful to Peter Widmayer for han dling the papers for which I h ad a co nflict of interest. The program committee did not meet in person, b ut carried out extensive discussions during the electronic PC meeting. I am grateful to Andrei Voronkov for his EasyChair system which made it so easy to manage and coordinate the discussion of the submitted papers.

I thank Maurizio Lenzerini, the PODS Gen eral Chair, for hi s constant help with so many details related to the organization of the symposium, to Wim Martens who served as the PODS Proceedings Chair and as PODS Publ icity Chair, to Dirk van Gucht, the previous PODS Program Chair, and to Jan Paredaens, t he previous PODS General Chair, for useful suggestions on several issues, to the members of the PODS E xecutive Committee, particularly to Jian wen Su as an im portant link between SIGMOD and PODS and to Renée J. Miller, the SIGMOD Program Chair, for the excellent collaboration.

I thank many colleagues involved in the organization of t he conference for fruitful collaboration: Timos Sellis (SIGMOD General Chair); Lisa Singh (SIGMOD/PODS coordinator); Yannis Stavrakas (Web/Information Chair); Yannis Kot idis (Local Arrangements Chair) & Lisa Toll es (Sheridan Printing Company). Finally, I thank the SIGMOD/PODS sponsors for their support.

Thomas Schwentick
PODS'11 Program Chair
Technische Universität Dortmund

Table of Contents

Session 1: Keynote Address

Session 2: Streaming & Sampling

Session 3: Incomplete Information & Awards

Session 4: Index Structures & External Memory

Session 5: Provenance

PODS 2011 Symposium Organization

Executive Committee: Maurizio Lenzerini *(Sapienza University of Rome, Italy)*
Phokion G. Kolaitis *(Univ. of California, Santa Cruz & IBM Research, USA)*
Jan Paredaens *(University of Antwerp, Belgium)*
Thomas Schwentick *(TU Dortmund University, Germany)*
Jianwen Su *(University of California, Santa Barbara, USA)*
Dirk Van Gucht *(Indiana University, USA)*

General Chair: Maurizio Lenzerini *(Sapienza University of Rome, Italy)*

Program Chair: Thomas Schwentick *(TU Dortmund University, Germany)*

Program Committee: Sara Cohen *(Hebrew University of Jerusalem, Israel)*
Alin Deutsch *(University of California, San Diego, USA)*
Thomas Eiter *(Vienna University of Technology, Austria)*
Wenfei Fan *(University of Edinburgh & Bell Labs, UK & USA)*
Sudipto Guha *(University of Pennsylvania, USA)*
Claudio Gutierez *(University of Chile, Chile)*
Peter Haas *(IBM Almaden Research Center, USA)*
Ravi Kumar *(Yahoo! Research, Silicon Valley, USA)*
Domenico Lembo *(University of Rome La Sapienza, Italy)*
Thomas Lukasiewicz *(Oxford University, UK)*
Filip Murlak *(Warsaw University, Poland)*
Dan Olteanu *(Oxford University, UK)*
Rafail Ostrovsky *(University of California Los Angeles, USA)*
Thomas Schwentick *(TU Dortmund University, Germany)*
Cristina Sirangelo *(ENS Cachan, France)*
Stijn Vansummeren *(Université Libre de Bruxelles, Belgium)*
Gerhard Weikum *(MPI Saarbrücken, Germany)*
Peter Widmayer *(ETH Zürich, Switzerland)*
Ke Yi *(Hong Kong University of Science and Technology, China)*

Proceedings & Publicity Chair: Wim Martens *(TU Dortmund University, Germany)*

PODS'11 External Reviewers

Pankaj Agarwal
Shun'ichi Amano
Marcelo Arenas
Lars Arge
Diego Arroyuelo
Vince Bárány
Jérémy Barbay
Pablo Barceló
Tugkan Batu
Michael Benedikt
Leopoldo Bertossi
Vladimir Braverman
Gerth Stølting Brodal
Toon Calders
Andrea Calì
Diego Calvanese
James Cheney
Flavio Chierichetti
Rada Chirkova
Jan Chomicki
Francisco Claude
Nilesh Dalvi
Anirban Dasgupta
Claire David
Giuseppe De Giacomo
Daniel Deutch
Tommaso Di Noia
Yanlei Diao
Xiaoyong Du
Georges Dupret
Thomas Erlebach
Alexandre Evfimievski
Arash Farzan
Diego Figueira
Michael Fink
George H. L. Fletcher

Minos Garofalakis
Olivier Gauwin
Stephen Hegner
Joseph Hellerstein
André Hernich
Alexander Hinneburg
Hendrik Jan Hoogeboom
Tomas Hruz
Tomasz Idziaszek
Riko Jacob
Wojciech Jaworski
Benny Kimelfeld
Solmaz Kolahi
Leszek Kołodziejczyk
David Koop
Lukasz Kowalik
John Langford
Kasper Green Larsen
Silvio Lattanzi
Lap-Kei Lee
Dirk Leinders
Maurizio Lenzerini
Leonid Libkin
Anthony Widjaja Lin
Alejandro López-Ortiz
Maria Vanina Martinez
Frank McSherry
Massimo Mecella
Ulrich Meyer
Matúš Mihal'ák
Mohamed Mokbel
Jelani Nelson
Frank Neven
Evdokia Nikolova
Werner Nutt
Rodrigo Paredes

Paweł Parys
Jorge Pérez
Jeff Phillips
Reinhard Pichler
Lucian Popa
Gabriele Puppis
Leonardo Querzoni
Vibhor Rastogi
Juan Reutter
Riccardo Rosati
Sudeepa Roy
Michael Schmidt
Marcel Schöngens
Bernhard Seeger
Gerardo Simari
Yannis Sismanis
D. Sivakumar
Adam Smith
Eljas Soisalon-Soininen
Jacek Sroka
Heiner Stuckenschmidt
Tony Tan
Yufei Tao
Nikolaj Tatti
Bernhard Thalheim
Srikanta Tirthapura
David Toman
Denis Turdakov
Alejandro Vaisman
Sergei Vassilvitskii
Millist Vincent
Wei Wang
Jef Wijsen
David Woodruff
Norbert Zeh
Guido Zuccon

PODS 2011 Sponsor & Supporters

Sponsor:

Platinum Supporters:

Gold Supporters:

Silver Supporters:

Additional supporters: NEC Greenplum

The ACM PODS Alberto O. Mendelzon Test-of-Time Award 2011

In 2007, the PODS Executive Committee decided to establish a Test-of-Time Award, named after the late Alberto O. Mendelzon, in recognition of his scientific legacy, and his service and dedication to the database community. Mendelzon was an international leader in database theory, whose pioneering and fundamental work has inspired and influenced both database theoreticians and practitioners, and continues to be applied in a variety of advanced settings. He served the database community in many ways; in particular, he served as the General Chair of the PODS conference, and was instrumental in bringing together the PODS and SIGMOD conferences. He also was an outstanding educator, who guided the research of numerous doctoral students and postdoctoral fellows. The Award is to be awarded each year to a paper or a small number of papers published in the PODS proceedings ten years prior, that had the most impact (in terms of research, methodology, or transfer to practice) over the intervening decade. The decision was approved by SIGMOD and the ACM. The funds for the Award were contributed by IBM Toronto.

The PODS Executive Chair has appointed us to serve as the Award Committee for 2011. After careful consideration, we have decided to select the following paper as the award winner for 2011:

> Ronald Fagin, Amnon Lotem, and Moni Naor.
> *Optimal Aggregation Algorithms for Middleware*

The paper investigates a very important problem that originates in multimedia databases: Given a set of objects with grades (rankings) on many attributes, find the objects with the best overall combined grades under some monotone combining function such as min or average. The paper presents a very simple algorithm, called Threshold Algorithm, and proves that it is essentially optimal (in finding the best overall grades) for all monotone functions and over every database. Furthermore, the algorithm only requires a small constant-size buffer. The paper also gives adaptation of the algorithm for situations such as no random accesses. The Threshold Algorithm has been used in a wide range of applications where the problem naturally occurs, from databases with traditional and non-traditional types of data (music, video, text, uncertain data, etc.) to social networks, sensor networks, etc. The paper is among the most highly cited papers in PODS 2001, and perhaps all time. The paper has clearly had a major influence on the database and other research communities. Hence, the committee found it to be entirely worthy of this award.

Peter Buneman
University of Edinburgh
UK

Meral Ozsoyoglu
Case Western Reserve University
USA

Jianwen Su (Chair)
UC Santa Barbara
USA

The Alberto O. Mendelzon Test-of-Time Award Committee for 2011

A Quest for Beauty and Wealth
(or, Business Processes for Database Researchers) *

Daniel Deutch
Ben Gurion University
deutchd@cs.bgu.ac.il

Tova Milo
Tel Aviv University
milo@cs.tau.ac.il

ABSTRACT

While classic data management focuses on the data itself, research on Business Processes considers also the *context* in which this data is generated and manipulated, namely the processes, the users, and the goals that this data serves. This allows the analysts a better perspective of the organizational needs centered around the data. As such, this research is of fundamental importance.

Much of the success of database systems in the last decade is due to the beauty and elegance of the relational model and its declarative query languages, combined with a rich spectrum of underlying evaluation and optimization techniques, and efficient implementations. This, in turn, has lead to an economic wealth for both the users and vendors of database systems. Similar beauty and wealth are sought for in the context of Business Processes. Much like the case for traditional database research, elegant modeling and rich underlying technology are likely to bring economic wealth for the Business Process owners and their users; both can benefit from easy formulation and analysis of the processes. While there have been many important advances in this research in recent years, there is still much to be desired: specifically, there have been many works that focus on the processes behavior (flow), and many that focus on its data , but only very few works have dealt with both. We will discuss here the important advantages of a holistic flow-and-data framework for Business Processes, the progress towards such a framework, and highlight the current gaps and research directions.

Categories and Subject Descriptors

H.2.3 [**Database Management**]: [Languages]; F.4.3 [**Theory of Computation**]: [Formal Languages]

---

*This work has been partially funded by the Israel Science Foundation, by the US-Israel Binational Science Foundation, by the EU grant MANCOOSI and by the ERC grant Webdam, agreement 226513.

General Terms

Algorithms, Languages, Theory

1. INTRODUCTION

Recent years have seen s shift in data management research. While research on stand-alone database management continues to be foundational, increasing attention is directed towards the *context* in which this data is generated and manipulated, namely *the processes, the users, and the goals* that this data serves. In a nutshell, this is what research on Business Processes is all about.

A Business Process (BP for short) consists of a group of business activities undertaken by one or more organizations in pursuit of some particular goal. Such Business Processes describe the operational logic of applications, including the possible *application flow* and the *data* that is manipulated by it. Research in this direction involves marrying ideas and concepts from database management, with ideas from workflow and process flow management, that previously have been mostly studied separately. This combined flow-and-data management in Business Processes is the focus of this paper. We note that we use here the term "Business Processes" in a very broad sense and the problems and solutions that we will consider are applicable to many other contexts that involve data and flow, such as scientific workflows, Web applications and services, e-government and electronic patient records.

Consider a classic example of an inventory management of a company, say one that sells computer parts. Research that focuses only on the inventory data, its storage and manipulation (perhaps in a distributed setting, or even in the cloud) can tell us how to design the database, and how to query it in an optimal way. However, in the broader perspective of the company, the inventory database is only a tool that is used in the company *Business Process*, which, to the company, is itself of no less interest than the data. For instance, the company may provide an online interface for ordering computer parts. In this case, the interaction with the database may be initiated by an order made by an online user; the process in charge of processing of this order will query the database to find the required product, and if absent will issue an order from the mainline factory. If the product does not exist, the process may issue other queries on the products database, possibly to recommend the user other alternative products. The user may then choose one of these options or ask for more recommendations, which will be computed using a refined query, and so on.

Knowledge about the operation of such a Business Process is thus of tremendous importance to both the company (or application) owners and their users. First, the process specification, and its possible executions flows, are themselves a valuable data; their analysis can be used by the application owners for detecting bugs or optimizing the process. For instance, in our computers company example, the company owners may wish to verify that whenever a user asks for a product that is not available, the appropriate actions are taken. Similarly, the application users may wish to infer the optimal ways of using the process, e.g. shortest (click-wise) navigation in the web-site to buy a computer with some specified features, or one that leads to minimal cost. Second, execution traces (logs) of Business Processes, detailing (parts of) the course of past execution, are another extremely valuable source of data. For example, logs analysis can reveal that customers are unsatisfied with the alternative products that are recommended to them, (as they typically navigate away from the store interface when presented with the suggestions), thereby helping to improve the application design. A combined analysis that uses both the process specification and its execution traces may also be extremely valuable. Tt may allow, for instance, to obtain answers to questions such as "what other alternative actions could users whose request failed take, but didn't". This may be used to improve the UI and make these options more apparent.

We observe that in the Business Process settings there is an inherent coupling of application *data* and *logic* (also referred to as *flow*): the flow affects the data and vice versa. This attracted the attention of database researchers (e.g. [10, 61, 46, 43, 32, 42]), that attempt to extend the good principles of data management (declarative specifications, optimization, etc.), to the broader perspective that includes not only the database itself but also the process surrounding it. Specifically, much of the success of database systems in the last decade is due to the beauty and elegance and of the relational model and its declarative query languages, combined with a rich spectrum of underlying evaluation and optimization techniques, and efficient implementations. This, in turn, has lead to an economic wealth for both the users and vendors of database systems. Similar beauty and wealth are sought for in the context of Business Processes. What is desired for Business Processes is an equivalently elegant formal model and query languages, that will allow easy formulation, readability and seamless optimizations, while at the same time will be expressively rich and comprehensive enough to capture intricate processes flow and their manipulation of data. Much like the case for database research, such beauty and richness of the model are also likely to result in economic wealth, for both the owners and the users of the processes.

While there have been many important advances in this research in recent years, there is still much to be desired. Specifically, there are several good models and techniques for capturing and analyzing the processes flow, and several good models and techniques for capturing and analyzing the data they manipulate. But the former often consider data only in a limited way while the latter typically capture the flow only in an implicit, data driven, manner. We are still missing a satisfactory, comprehensive solution for the *explicit* modeling and analyzing the processes flow *and* data, and their interactions.

We next briefly review the main tasks that are required towards achieving this goal, in the order considered in the rest of this paper. These tasks include *modeling* the processes, *generating* an instance of the chosen model, for a given Business Process, and *analyzing* (*querying*) process specifications and executions. The goal of the present paper is to highlight some of the main challenges in this area, review the state-of-the-art of research that tackles these challenges, and pinpoint several current research directions and challenges.

As always with such problems, the first challenge is *modeling*. One difficulty that rise when attempting an effective management of Business Processes is the typical complexity of their representations. Business processes usually operate in a cross-organizational, distributed environment and the software implementing them is fairly complex. For instance, our computer components company may interact in intricate ways with various suppliers of components, with the users that are placing orders, etc. But much like in the case of data management, effective Business Process management needs to rely on an abstract model for the Business Process. To answer this need, many different abstract representation models have been suggested (e.g. [5, 11, 12, 27, 10, 50, 33] and many others), that combine, to some extent, "classic" flow models such as state machines and context free systems with models that describe the underlying databases of the application and their interaction with flow. We review such models in Section 2.

Clearly, for Business Processes implemented in a language such as Java, their representation in such abstract models is not an easy task. Luckily, this gap is slowly being bridged by *declarative standards* that facilitate the design, deployment, and execution of BPs. In particular, the recent BPEL [14] standard (Business Process Execution Language), provides an XML-based language to describe the interface between the participants in a process, as well as the full operational logic of the process and its execution flow. The BPEL standard is relatively declarative, and it is much easier to abstract it further, to fit the model; there are also many graphical interfaces and editors that allow for a relatively simple, intuitive design of BPEL specifications.

Graphical interfaces are very useful in promoting a high-level (formal) specification of a Business Process. Still, in many cases, the specification of the Business Process is partially or completely unknown. In such cases, the abstract model needs to be *mined* [61, 66, 46] automatically, e.g. from a set of observed executions. In Section 3, we review both facets (graphical design interfaces and mining techniques) of obtaining instances of process specifications.

Once a process model is given, it may be used for *process querying and analysis*. Two kinds of analysis are of interest: the first is analysis of the possible *future* executions of a given process specification and the second is the analysis of *past* execution, stored in *execution logs*.

First, consider analysis of possible future executions (also referred to as *static analysis*). The idea is that we are given a specification of the Business Process (that is considered as our input data), and we wish to verify that some property (query) holds for *all* possible executions of the process. For instance, for our computer components company example, we may be interested in verifying that no customer can place an order without paying; or that whenever an order is processed, the system checks for the existence of the product in the database before asking an external vendor. Alternatively, we also be interested in computing the probability that some property holds in a random execution, e.g. what is the probability for a user to ask for a component that is not in stock. The results of such analysis are of interest for both the process owners, as well as their users: the former may optimize their business processes, reduce operational costs, and ultimately increase competitiveness. The latter may allow users to make an optimal use of it (e.g. find out what is the most popular way of buying a computer?). Importantly, the results of such an analysis, that is aware not only of the company database, but also to the applications that manipulate it, can be very useful in improving the Database design, and in optimizing the data accesses (queries) made in the course of the Business Processes.

Next, let us consider the analysis of past executions. Execution logs detailing such past executions are of tremendous importance for companies, since they may reveal *patterns* in the behavior of the users (e.g. "users that buy a specific brand of RAM also tend to buy a specific brand of Motherboard"), may allow to identify run-time bugs that occurred, or a breach of the company policy etc. But the challenges are that typical repositories of such execution logs are of very large size, and that the patterns that are of interest are those that occur frequently but are not always known in advance. Consequently, various works considered data mining and OLAP (On-line Analytical Process) techniques for querying logs repositories; but there are also some works that introduce query languages for execution traces. Continuing the analogy with Databases, what is required for specifying the analysis tasks is a *declarative query language*, supported by efficient *query evaluation mechanisms*.

One particular challenge in the context of Business Processes and workflows is that of *security / privacy* [27, 59]. While the application owner may wish to disclose some of the process specification / logs (or parts of them) of the Business Processes, some (parts of) logs must be kept confidential, such as the credit card details of users performing a computer components purchase, or part of her interaction with the company interface, etc. Privacy/security have been studies (separately) for workflows and Databases. But what is desired is *combined* flow-and-data privacy/security mechanisms. In Section 4 we consider the analysis and querying of Business Processes, including all of the above aspects.

Personal Perspective. In a series of works (see e.g. [10, 28, 29, 30, 31]), the authors of this paper and collaborators have studied a particular model for Business Processes, its properties and the means for querying and analyzing it. Wherever in this paper we use the term "Our model", we refer to this model, initially defined in [10] and extended in further works.

2. MODELING

There are various models for Business Processes that may be found in the literature. Similarly to process models in verification and model checking (see e.g. [37, 20, 55, 53, 21, 58, 15] and many others), these models differ in their expressive power, i.e. in which sets of possible executions they can represent. But unlike works on verification, research on Business Processes further incorporates an explicit modeling of the *data* that underly the process. However, as we show below, in the vast majority of the models that consider data, the flow description is either implicit, or lacks expressive power. *In our opinion, what is critically missing is an*

integrated, expressive and intuitive (explicit) model for both the flow and the underlying data. Such a model, accompanied with appropriate analysis tools / query languages, can allow process analysts to deduce important knowledge on the process, and ultimately improve its performance.

We start our review by considering some common flow models that are considered in verification; we then show how research on Business Processes extends these models to account for underlying data, of two kinds: relational and semi-structured. Finally, we will highlight the main challenges still remaining in modeling Business Processes. We will demonstrate the models using our running example of a company that sells computer components.

2.1 Control Flow Models

In the context of verification, the focus is typically on modeling (and analyzing; see section 4) the *flow* of applications. The simplest model that is studied is that of a *Finite State Machine* (FSM) [48]; the FSM states model the logical states of the application, and transitions are dictated by (typically external) input. For instance, the logical flow of our computer components company may be modeled by a Finite State Machine where some of the states may e.g. be "wait for user order", "processing user order", "search database for product", etc. But finite state models have a quite limited expressive power from a theoretical perspective, and furthermore modeling real-life systems with them may be cumbersome, and require a large number of states. The latter problem is somewhat alleviated by using the model of Hierarchial State Machine (HSM) [11]. HSMs allow to define hierarchy of Finite State Machines, in a way resembling "function calls". That is, an HSM consists of a set of state machines, and one state machine may "invoke" another, meaning that the control flow moves to the invoked machine; while the execution in this machine reaches an accepting state, the control returns to the invoking location [1]. For our example, the processing of orders may be modeled as a "function", itself represented by a Finite State Machine, encapsulating all states in the sub-process of order management.

The hierarchy of state machines gives conciseness in representation, but not a stronger expressive power. In real-life processes, there is often the need to represent (context-free) *recursion*. For instance, our specification should enable recursive invocations of the ordering sub-process, to account for more and more orders. A more expressive model that accommodates recursion is that of *Recursive State Machine* (RSM) [8]. Like for HSMs, in RSMs state machines may invoke each other, but they can furthermore do so in a *recursive* manner. RSMs have strictly more expressive power than HSMs, and in particular can capture context free languages [8]. There are multiple variants of RSMs, differing in the number of *entries* (initial states) and *exits* (final states) of the state machines. The class of RSMs where the state machines have multiple exits is strictly more expressive than the class of single exit recursive state machine [8].

Most of the process models, while modeling parallelism at the specification level, consider every single execution as a sequence (path) of events. There are however some explicit formal models for parallel executions, such as Petri Nets

---

[1]We mention in this context that the notion of hierarchy, along with additional constructs, lies at the core of the StateCharts [47].

[58]. In the context of Business Processes, our model [10] captures parallelism in the executions, as follows. The specification of a process in this model is a set of DAGs, connected through (possibly recursive) implementation relation, which is a notion similar to that of invocation in Recursive State Machines. The implementation relation is one-to-many, i.e. for every activity there are many possible implementations, and one is chosen at run-time, dictating the course of execution. The possible choices of implementation are annotated by *guarding formulas*. These are logical formulas on external effects such as user choices, network state, server response time etc., that may dictate the course of execution. For instance, a guarding formula may have the form $UserChoice = "ShowRAMs"$, and this formula will hold if the user chose to view the brand of RAMs suggested by the computer components store. At run-time the truth value of these formulas will determine the chosen implementation for every activity. For instance, depending on the user choice (and thus the satisfaction of the above formula), the user will be presented with the available RAM brands. Nodes in these DAGs correspond to business activities, while the edges reflect their ordering. Unlike RSMs, executions are defined as the entire graph (in this case DAG) that is obtained. This allows to capture *parallelism* in the execution, reflected by its DAG structure: activities that have no directed path between them are assumed to occur in parallel. For instance, the business logic underlying the web-based interface of our company may dictate that in parallel to having the system wait for users orders, *advertisements* are injected to the screen. Using a DAG structure for the execution it is much easier to capture such parallelism.

We also mention that our model in [10] for BPs has strong connections with that of Context Free Graph Grammars (CFGGs) [60, 52, 26]. CFGGs, similarly to "classic" context free (string) grammars (CFGs), CFGGs are composed of non-terminals, terminals, and derivation rules. But unlike string CFGs, with CFGGs the righthand side of the derivation rules contain *graphs*, and consequently a grammar define a family of graphs, that are derived by the grammar. There are many variants of this model, different in the definition of whether the non-terminals correspond to nodes or (hyper)edges of the graph, in how the derived sub-graph is connected (referred to as the "connection relation" [52]), etc. Our model may be considered as specific, restricted case of CFGGs, where all graphs are DAGs; the counterpart of derivation rules is the possibly recursive implementation relation described above.

Probabilistic Variants. In the context of Business Processes, it is important to model the uncertainty that is inherent in the external effects that govern the executions. For example, the course of execution of our computers store Business Process depends on the choices of users, submitted through its web interface. The choices that users will make are unknown at the time of analyzing the process, but we may have some probabilistic knowledge on the behavior of users. The above mentioned models all have *probabilistic* counterparts, where the possible executions (derivations) are associated with probabilities of occurring in practice. The probabilistic counterpart of Finite State Machines is Markov Chains [57], where every transition is associated with a probability of occurring in practice. These probabilities are assumed to be independent (the Markovian assump-

tion is that the probability of taking a transition in a given state is independent on the previously made transitions), thus the probability of an execution is simply the multiplication of the probabilities along its transitions. Similar extensions were studied for probabilistic context free grammars (see e.g. [54]), and Recursive Markov Chains (RMCs) [39] that are the counterpart of Recursive State Machines; in these extensions the Markovian property is also assumed.

While the independence assumption simplifies the models and allow for a more efficient analysis (See section 4), it is in some cases unrealistic when modeling Business Processes. In particular, when the transitions are governed by external effects such as user choices, the state of the network, server response time etc., it is unreasonable to assume their independence: for instance, users that choose a particular computer component is more likely to later choose compatible components. Consequently, our model for *Probabilistic Business Processes* [30] (which extends the non-probabilistic variant) allows to associate the guarding formulas dictating the execution course with probabilistic events, and these events may be inter-dependent to some bounded extent. More specifically, a choice may depend on the n previous choices for some constant n. The value of n is typically small in real-life Business Processes (e.g. the choices of users depend on their previous choices, but only on a small number of such choices).

A Little Bit of Data. Before considering full fledged modeling of data in Business Processes, we consider flow models that capture data but only to a small extent. One such example is in our own Business Process model where the *guarding formulas* that "guard" the possible implementations use data variable. The value of these variables determines the formulas satisfaction and thus the choice of implementation for each activity. This, in turn, dictates the course of execution. However the use of data here is limited: guarding formulas may ask for the value of a specific data item, but cannot e.g. issue full-fledged SQL queries on the underlying Database to decide on the choice of implementation.

Another example is *scientific workflows* where the interaction between flow and data is given an interesting twist. Scientific workflows are processes that are executed by scientists and composed of modules. Each module performs some scientific task and the modules interact by passing data between them. The workflow specification may be hierarchical, in the sense that a module may be composite and itself implemented as a workflow. The data that is modeled here includes the input and output of every module, but not the internal database or the way it is manipulated / queried by the modules.

2.2 Underlying Relational Data

The models that we have mentioned so far mainly focused on the *flow*, i.e. they allow to capture the control flow of a given process, but the data that is manipulated by the process was only modeled to a limited extent. A complementary line of research, in the databases area, resulted in the development of a variety of process models that are centered around data. Such models have appeared even before the term Business Processes emerged in research, such as the model of Relational Transducers [5] (and the follow-up work on ASM transducers [64]), that was shown to be very effective in capturing e-commerce applications. In relational

$$
\begin{aligned}
Ord(user, prod) \quad & + : - \quad InOrd(user, prod) \\
PayedOrd(user, prod) \quad & + : - \quad InPayment(user, prod) \\
UnpaidOrd(user, prod) \quad & + : - \quad Ord(user, prod) \textbf{ AND} \\
& \qquad\quad \textbf{NOT } PayedOrd(user, prod) \\
OutReceipt(user, prod) \quad & + : - \quad PayedOrd(user, prod) \textbf{ AND} \\
& \qquad\quad InStock(prod)
\end{aligned}
$$

Figure 1: Relational Transducer Example

$$
\begin{aligned}
ArtifactClass \quad & : \quad ComputerOrder \\
componentName \quad & : \quad string \\
componentType \quad & : \quad "RAM" \\
processed \quad & : \quad bool \\
PaidFor \quad & : \quad bool
\end{aligned}
$$

Figure 2: Artifact Example

transducers, the state of the application is modeled as a relational database and the database state is modified using the repeated activation of queries (in the spirit of active databases [3]). The database is used to model not only the internal database state, but also the interaction of the transducer with the external environment: these are modeled via a set of input and output relations. There is thus no clear distinction between the *flow* and the *underlying data* - the database stores it all. A Datalog-like program is used to query and update the state, input and output relations. For instance, the rules in Figure 1 can be used to (partially) specify the business logic of our computers company. Relation names starting with "In" stand for input relations, those with "Out" for output relations, and the rest are state relations. Here the semantics of the rules is like in inflationary Datalog, that is, a satisfying assignment to the righthand side leads to an addition of a corresponding tuple for the relation whose name appears on the rule left hand side.

Note the process flow that is implicit in the above description: the input orders made by the user change the state of the orders, and user payments change the order status from unpaid to payed. *The difficulty is that the underlying flow is not easily observable from the process specification, especially in the common case when the number of state relations is large and inter-dependent.* As a consequence, the process designers and analysts may have difficulty grasping the causality and temporal relationship between actions/data, e.g. which part of the data is influencing other parts, which is updated before the other and how, etc. This is in contrast to case of the flow models mentioned above, where the execution flow is immediately observable from the specification.

A similar approach is taken in the works on Business Process artifacts [50, 42, 68, 2]. The model focuses on the data received, generated and manipulated by the process (e.g. purchase orders, sales invoices, etc.). The data structures encapsulating this information are referred to in this context as *artifacts*. An example for such an artifact, for a user order of a computer component is given in Figure 2.2. Artifact states are queried and modified by *services*, which are defined by declarative rules, accompanied by pre-and post conditions for their invocation. Again, there is an implicit modeling of flow, since the state of the order (artifact) reflects whether or not it was processed, and whether or not it was paid for, etc. and this information is updated as the flow evolves. But similarly to the case of relational transducers, the description of flow is somewhat implicit.

Last, we mention that the modeling of data-centered Web Applications have also received a significant attention in recent years. One notable model in this context is the one of data-driven, interactive Web Applications [32, 34] which are essentially implicitly specified *infinite-state machines* in which the state (database) is shared across various applications, each of which may read/write its contents. The interaction of web services, and specifically the data passed between them, were studied also in the context of [16].

2.3 Underlying Semi-structured Data

Before we conclude, we mention another class of works in this context that considers data which is not relational, but rather semi-structured, and specifically XML. Here again, there are works with an underlying flow model of a finite state machine or context free languages, as well as some probabilistic models. We next review them briefly. The Active XML model [1, 7] extends XML with Web Service calls, whose results are embedded back in the document, allowing to make additional calls etc. In a recent work [2] the authors suggest an artifacts model that combines a simple flow model of Finite State Machine, with the data model of Active XML. Also, recent works have studied models for probabilistic XML documents that is based on a generative process modeled by a Recursive State Machine [12]. In our opinion, these works are important steps towards rich models that combine flow and data; but more work is required to further find the correct balance between the models expressiveness, and the efficiency of query evaluation they allow (see Section 4).

2.4 Research Directions and Open Problems

We conclude this section by listing a few aspects that are absent in the current Business Processes and workflow models, yet we believe are important.

- Arguably the biggest challenge in Business Process modeling is the combination of rich flow model with rich model for underlying database manipulation. As we will see in the next section, high complexity or even undecidability of analysis is difficult to avoid whenever such rich models are considered. We note that the recent work of [2] has made a progress in this area by designing an artifact model for Active XML [7] with an underlying, explicitly modeled, Finite State Machines. But there is still a long way to go, extending the model expressivity within the boundaries of decidability.

- In [25] the authors state that no model is likely to be "the best" for all needs, and consequently that there is a need for the development of a theory (and practical implementations) of *views* on Business Processes and a practical mapping between them. We concur and believe that this is even more true for rich, combined flow and data model. Recently, there have been a few advancements in this respect. In [2] the authors suggest the notion of a workflow view and use it as a way of comparing expressive power of workflow specification languages. We believe that there are important research challenges in the efficient computation and maintenance of such views.

3. GENERATION OF A MODEL INSTANCE

In the previous section we have considered the modeling of Business Processes, and discussed various possible choices for such models. Once such a model is chosen, we need to create an instance of this model for the given business process. Ideally, this would be done as part of the process specification, with the actual software that implements the process being automatically generated following the specification (and thus matching precisely the model). In this case, the challenge lies in suggesting effective specification tools, and in particular convenient visual interfaces for the designer. Alternatively, the process model can be defined manually, describing as close as possible the (already existing) Business Process, or be automatically mined from the available execution logs.

In recent years there has been significant effort in all these directions, in both industry and the academia. However, here too there is still much to be desired. We next review the state-of-the-art in these directions: we first consider manual model design, and then automatic mining tools.

3.1 (Manual) Instance Design

The increasing interest in high-level Business Process specifications has triggered research and development geared towards *User Interfaces* that will allow such process design. Many of these interfaces are based on process *visualization*. This has many advantages: it allows the designer to easily formulate and modify the process logic, allows users to easily understand the process logic and how to use it, and allows analyzers to easily pose analysis tasks. One standard class of such visual interfaces uses *UML (Unified Modeling Language) [13] state diagrams*. These are essentially StateCharts [47] with standardized notation. Such state diagrams allow to represent the process flow (using hierarchical states), along with the process interaction with its environment and other processes (i.e. events that affect the flow, messages that are emitted by the process during the flow, etc.) guarding the different transitions. While StateCharts (and consequently UML state diagrams) are highly successful as a user-friendly, graphical model for designers of process *flow*, the incorporation of *data* and its *interaction with flow* in this model may be quite intricate. In principal, this can come as part of the description of events actions that guard the transitions. But unlike the case for flow, the UML state diagrams standard does not dictate any syntax for the exact formulation of events and actions, and *the common practice is to use "structured English", or high-level programming languages such as C or Java (but not database query languages) for expressing the conditions and actions* [36].

Another standard for specifying Business Processes that has emerged in the last decade is the *BPEL (Business Process Execution language) standard*. This standard, developed jointly by BEA Systems, IBM, and Microsoft, combines and replaces IBMŠs WebServices Flow Language (WSFL) and MicrosoftŠs XLANG. It provides an XML-based language to describe, *in a declarative way*, the interface between the participants in a process, as well as the full operational logic of the process and its execution flow. Commercial vendors offer systems that allow to design BPEL specification via a visual interface, using a conceptual, intuitive view of the process as a graph; these designs are automatically converted to BPEL specifications, *and can further be automatically compiled into executable code that implements the described process*. Unlike StateCharts, BPEL specifications do allow some explicit representation of data. However this representation is mainly geared towards the modeling of the *interaction* of different processes (and more specifically web-services). It includes an XML schema for sent and received data (captured by variables), and an XPath interface for accessing these variables. But it has no explicit modeling of full-fledged database manipulation.

Figure 3 depicts an example BPEL specification, edited through a Graphical User Interface. The specification given here describes the operational logic of a fictive travel agency called "AlphaTours" (as may be observed from the property nodes on the upper righthand side of the figure). Observe that the *control flow* of the agency is captured via a DAG, appearing in the "behavior" tab; also for every activity, the *input data* type required by the activity and the *output data* type that it generates are depicted as nodes in the "Data" tab; these nodes are connected to the corresponding flow activities through unique "data edges". For instance, the input of the "searchTrip" activity is a trip request, and its output ("tripResults") is fed as input to the "reserveTrip" activity, etc.

Another line of tools that allows for declaratively specifying Business Processes / Web Applications flow and their underlying database include WebML and Web Ratio [22], WAVE [33], Hilda [70], Siena [24], and others. Here however the representation of flow is only implicit, and an intuitive flow visualization in the style described above is not available. *What is desired, and is the subject of an intriguing research is an interface for explicit visualizing of both the processes flow and manipulation of data*. Of course, there may be parts of the specification (both in terms of flow and data manipulation) which are complicated and difficult to visualize in a user-friendly form. However, it is still worthwhile to intuitively visualize those parts that are simpler, and perhaps suggest simplified "views" on the more complicated part.

3.2 Mining Model Instance

Even the best interface for process design requires a designer that will use it to specify the logic of the process. Works on *process mining* take an orthogonal approach. It tries to infer the process structure from a set of observed (perhaps partial) executions. Even if we consider only flow, this is clearly a challenge: consider a set of logs containing many different operations, occurring in different orders among different logs. Inferring a process model here includes deciding which of these operations are defined to occur in "parallel" (i.e. in an arbitrary order), and which of them are in order. But it may be the case that for two activities which may actually be parallel in the process specification, there exists some consistent ordering in the given set of logs - simply because the number of "sampled" (observed) logs is not big enough to exhibit all orderings. More generally, identifying the causality relationship between the invocation of activities is a major challenge in this context.

There are several approaches for process mining, attempt-

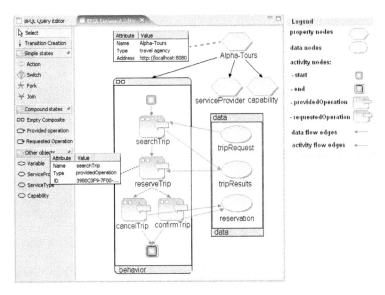

Figure 3: A process example modeled using BPEL Editor

ing to alleviate these difficulties. Some of these approaches use techniques such as Neural networks and Association rules mining for learning the process structure. This includes the Process mining tools in the Business (Process) Intelligence (BPI) suite [46]. While these approaches have some experimentally proven successful, it is difficult to provide any formal guarantees on their results. Other approaches [62, 54] are based on statistics, and try to maximize the likelihood of the observed sequence given the model. These approaches are rooted in works on formal models, such as those on inference of a best fit (i.e. maximizing the likelihood of observations, given the model) Markov Chain [62], or a Probabilistic Context Free Grammar [54] for a given set of observations. However these models typically do not model *parallelism*, which is inherent in process models. Moreover, to the best of our knowledge, these approaches all pertain to the application structure and flow, some of them in the broader context of the organization and the interaction of the process with it and with other processes, *but not the manipulated data.*

3.3 Research Directions and Open Problems

To conclude this section, we consider some open questions and promising research directions in this context of the works presented above.

- Similarly to the case with process modeling (and thus not surprisingly), visual interfaces for designing processes flow hardly provide tools for modeling the data that is manipulated. Of course, one can design externally a database schema and simply annotate the flow with SQL queries. But still, for instance, visualizing (even some part of) the effect of the data on the flow, and vice versa, is an intriguing and non-trivial task. What is required for that is an holistic model and visual interface for both flow and data. The lack of treatment of data is even more noticable in the works on process mining, as observed above; any advance towards this end would be very important.

- The declarative nature of some interfaces for process design, such as BPEL, opens the way for dedicated *optimization* techniques, improving the performance of the processes. There have been works on optimization of the execution of declaratively described processes, in various contexts (e.g. [69, 63]). However, there is currently no theory of declarative Business Process optimization, that is comparable to the comprehensive theory on database query optimizations.

- Due to the difficulty of process mining, one can consider an hybrid approach, where some parts of (or "clues about") the process specification are given, but other parts need to be inferred from the observed executions. This could model relatively well real-life scenarios.

4. QUERYING

As exemplified in the Introduction, Business Processes serve as an important mine of information for the processes owners as well as their users. There are (at least) two kinds of analysis that are of interest in this context: first, the analysis of possible (and, perhaps, probable) *future* executions of the process. This can be e.g. used to preempt possible bugs or breach of policies in future executions. Second, querying logs of *past* executions can also reveal important information, such as problems that occurred at runtime, trends in the process usage, etc. To support such an analysis, what is desired is a formal *query language*.

Desiderata. We next list some of the desired features of such a query language.

- It is desired that such query language will be, like the Business Process specification itself, *declarative, intuitive* and *graphical*, allowing the process designer to specify the analysis tasks side by side with the design of the process specification.

- The same query language will preferably allow uniformly for the analysis of future as well as past execution. Such uniformity will have several advantages: it will require analysts to only master a single language, it will allow to combine specification analysis with log querying, it may allow for uniform development of query optimization techniques, etc.

- We have stressed the importance of models that describe both the process flow and its underlying data. Correspondingly, the query language that is used to analyze the modeled Business Processes should allow to query *both the process flow and the data*, and the interactions between them.

- The query language should allow to pose queries at different levels of granularity, specified by the analysts. For instance, one may wish to ask coarse-grain queries that consider certain process components as black boxes and allow for high level abstraction, as well as fine-grained queries that "zoom-in" on all or some of the process components, querying there innerworkings.

- The query language should allow to specify "boolean" verification queries, pertaining to the existence of bugs, the enforcement of policies etc, as well as "selection" and "projection" queries that allow to retrieve some parts of the process or its executions, that are relevant for the analysis. For instance, we may not only be interested in the boolean existence of a bug, but if it exists we wish to know in which part of the process it occurred / may occur, under what circumstances, what is may affect, etc.

- Naturally, to make things practical, the query language should allow for efficient query evaluation algorithms and optimizations.

We next review the state-of-the-art in works on querying future and past executions of Business Processes, highlighting which of these desired properties were (partially) achieved, and which still remain as challenges.

4.1 Querying Future Executions

Given a Business Process specification, analysts are typically interested in testing/querying properties of its possible future executions. The property may be some constraint that is expected to hold in every execution, such as "a user can not place an order without giving her credit card details" or "a user must have a positive balance in her account before placing an order". It may also be the probability that some situation occurs in a random execution, such as "what is the probability that a user chooses to order a Motherboard given that she ordered a RAM?".

The analysis of possible future executions of a process, also referred to as *static analysis*, was extensively studied for formal flow models (Finite State Machines, Pushdown automata, Context Free Grammars, etc.). The dominant approach for such analysis is to use a *temporal logic* formalism [37] to query the possible executions of a given process. In temporal logic, formulas are constructed from predicates and temporal quantifiers such as "before" (B), "always" (A), "until" (U) etc. For instance, a query of the sort "a user must login *before* placing an order" can be expressed by a formula of the form *Login B Order*, where *Login* and *Order* are predicates that can be checked locally on a given flow state.

While temporal logic is very useful, it fails to satisfy many of the desiderata in the context of Business Processes. The main difficulties in using it for analysis of Business Processes executions are the following. First, similarly to the case of First Order Logic, the design of temporal logic formulas for complicated properties may be cumbersome, and the outcome may be difficult to read. Second, in temporal logic there is no explicit reference to underlying process data, and the properties it allows to capture pertain only to the process flow. Third, it allows only to verify boolean properties, and cannot express any counterpart of selection and projection database queries, and in particular does not allow to retrieve paths that are of interest.

The shortcoming of explicit constructs for referring to both the flow and data was alleviated by the work of [32], suggesting a query language called LTL-FO (for Linear Temporal Logic-First Order). The idea is that temporal logic is used for querying the execution flow, while First Order constructs may be used inside the predicates, for querying not only the execution flow state, but rather the *database* state at the current point of the execution. For instance, the following formula specifies that whenever a user orders any product, its balance must be positive (we assume that Order and Balance are database relations. A is the temporal operator "Always" and user, sum, product are used as bound variables in the formula).

- $\forall user, product. A(Order(user, product) \Rightarrow \exists sum > 0.balance(user, sum))$

LTL-FO is an important step in the direction of querying Business Processes. We also mention in this context the work on querying Active XML documents [4], introducing tree-LTL, where temporal operators are used over tree patterns. But these languages still lack some of the above desiderata: they do not allow to specify non-boolean queries, do not allow controlled levels of granularity, and they are hard to formulate for non (logic) experts.

Some of the desiderata that are not achieved by the different variants of temporal logic (with or without constructs for querying data), are satisfied by our query language BPQL (Business Process Querying Language) [10], allowing to pose queries on our Business Process model. BPQL is based on abstraction of the BPEL formalism, along with a graphical user interface that allows for simple formulation of queries on BPEL specifications. At the core of the BPQL language are Business Process *patterns* that allow users to describe the pattern of activities/data flow that are of interest. Business Process patterns are similar to the tree and graph-patterns offered by query languages for XML and graph-shaped data, but include two novel features designed to address the above desiderata. First, BPQL supports navigation along two axis: (1) the standard path-based axis, that allows to navigate through, and query, paths in process graphs, and (2) a novel zoom-in axis, that allows to navigate (transitively) inside process components and query them at any depth of nesting. Second, paths are considered first class objects in BPQL and can be retrieved, and represented compactly. An example for such an execution pattern, designed using the BPQL Graphical User Interface, is depicted in Figure 4.

Figure 4: A query example modeled using BPQL Editor

This query looks for a login activity, followed, after some sequence (path) of choices, by a searchFlights activity.

Recall however that our Business Processes model does not allow explicit modeling of data, and correspondingly BPQL does not have explicit constructs for underlying data, but rather focuses on querying the execution flow of the process. More work is required in combining the desired features of BPQL, with the ability to formulate data-aware queries.

Complexity Results. We briefly review some main complexity results for the query formalisms described above. First, the complexity of evaluation of Linear Temporal Logic (LTL) queries (as well as branching-time logic CTL^* [37]) on Finite State Machines is known to be linear in the state machine size but exponential in the size of the formula. In [8] the authors show the same complexity results for context free processes, and equivalently for Single Exit RSMs [38]. Similarly, for BPQL, the complexity of query evaluation was shown to be polynomial in the process specification size, with the exponent depending on the query size. We have mentioned above the query language LTL-FO for querying both flow and data. In [35] the authors show that evaluating LTL-FO queries on their process model is *PSPACE-complete* under some restrictive assumptions on the input process, and is undecidable in general (although they describe in [32] a practical implementation based on strong heuristics). It is observable that the blowup in the complexity of query evaluation is difficult to avoid when querying flow and data together. Finding a framework that will satisfy all of the above listed desiderata, and will in particular allow for efficient query evaluation, is an important research challenge.

4.2 Querying Past Executions

We have discussed the analysis of future executions of a given process specification. Equally important is the analysis of executions that took place in the past, and are recorded in a repository. Execution logs are of tremendous importance for companies, since they may reveal *patterns* in the behavior of the users (e.g. "users that buy a specific brand of RAM also tend to buy a specific brand of Motherboard"), may allow to identify run-time errors that occurred, or a

breach of the company policy. In the context of scientific workflows (see section 2), these execution logs are referred to as *provenance*. They represent instances of the scientific process that was used in practice, and they are in fact the main object that is analyzed in this context. This analysis can verify the correctness of experiments represented by the workflow, identify the different tools that were used, with which parameters, etc. Another application of log analysis is inference of probabilities, based on past observations, for the probabilistic process models discussed in section 2.

Contents of the Log. One basic question in this context is what is recorded in execution logs. One option is to record only the execution flow, i.e. the activities (functions, web-services, modules..) that were used at run-time, along with their order of occurrence. But in many cases what is also of interest is the record of *data* that was manipulated / transmitted throughout the execution, and the interaction of data with the execution flow. This entails "marrying" workflow provenance (that includes record of the activities or modules that occurred at run-time), with the notion of *data* provenance (e.g. [45, 40, 67, 17, 44, 41, 23, 19, 18, 71, 49]) - the management of fine-grained record on the course of databases queries evaluation.

There are two challenges in this context: first, keeping a complete record of all activities that occurred at run-time, and all data that was manipulated, may be infeasible in terms of the *required storage resources*. Second, while parts of the logs may be essential for analysis purposes, it is often the case that other parts of the logs should be kept confidential. How do we decide what to record?

There are various works that suggest partial solutions to (different aspects of) this challenge. In [28], we have suggested a selective tracing systems for Business Processes execution flows, that uses a *renaming function* for activities, to mask the real names of the recorded activities, and a *deletion set* for activities, allowing the deletion of all record of some activities from the execution logs. In the context of scientific workflows, there are recent works [6, 51] that suggest frameworks for keeping track of both the activated modules and their internal manipulation of data. But the provenance that is tracked there is not fine-grained "enough", in the sense that it does not keep track of the exact transformations performed on each data item (in contrast to the case of provenance management in "standard" databases, see e.g. [45]). In [27] the authors distinguish three types of workflow privacy: module privacy, data privacy, and provenance privacy. The first refers to hiding the functionality of one or more modules in a workflow, the second refers to hiding the internal data of a module, and the third refers to hiding the way a data item is manipulated and transmitted between the modules of the workflow. There are still many open challenges in workflow security, as described in [27].

What Formalisms to Use for Analysis. Ideally, the same query language used for querying future executions could be used for querying past executions, with the appropriate adaptation of the query evaluation algorithms. This may allow analysts to only master a single language, allow to combine specification analysis with log querying and allow a uniform development of query optimization techniques. Such uniformity may be challenging to achieve, since queries that can be evaluated on a given log (or a database of logs) may become undecidable when evaluated statically over (potentially infinite number of) possible future executions. These challenges can possibly be addressed by a careful choice of the query formalism. For instance, we have shown in [28] that BPQL, originally designed for querying future executions, can be used also as query language for execution logs. LTL-FO, mentioned above in the context of querying future executions, can also be adapted for querying past executions. There are also other works (e.g. [56]) that show how to use temporal logic for analysis of execution logs. The similarities of solutions entail also similarities in the remaining challenges described above, and in particular the design of a user friendly (graphical) query language, that will allow to query both the flow and data of execution logs.

Challenges and (Partial) Solutions in Query Evaluation. One challenge in querying log repositories is that their typical size is very large (perhaps distributed among many locations, for complex distributed systems), as logs are collected over a long period. A first thing to observe is that process logs may be abstractly viewed as graphs that record the execution flow. Much research has been dedicated to query evaluation over graphs, developing various index structures and labeling schemes for the graph nodes to speed up query processing. There is naturally also large body of work on standard database query optimization. But, to our knowledge, the problem of efficient combined analysis of flow-and-data has not yet been addressed.

In the context of Business Processes, information about the process structure (derived from its specification) may be used to further improve performance. For example, in [28] we have presented a framework for type-based optimization of query evaluation on execution logs, based on the observation that the specification reveals useful information on the kinds of flow that can (and cannot) appear in the execution logs, and this information can be used to optimize query evaluation. Similarly, we have shown in a recent paper [9] that, using the process specification, one may derive compact labels for the graph nodes, thereby allowing for efficient processing of reachability queries. These works however focus on the flow and extending them to handle data aspects is intriguing.

An additional challenge is that in many cases what is sought for in these logs is vaguely defined as "interesting patterns", and is difficult to express formally. For these reasons, a dominating approaches is to use *data mining* and OLAP techniques for analyzing log repositories. Indeed, many works adapt "classic" data mining techniques such as clustering, associating rule mining and various sorts of statistical analysis [46]. One issue that appears uniquely in execution logs (in contrast to "general" data mining) is the *temporal* nature of events. To that end, there are dedicated data mining techniques such as *Sequential Patterns* and *Complex Event Processing* that account for the order in which events occur and find patterns in the sequence of events. But these works focus mainly on the execution flow, rather than on data. Here again what is missing is an effective processing accounting for both flow and data.

Run-time Monitoring. To conclude this section we briefly consider a third axis of analysis, namely that of *run-time monitoring* of the process execution. For instance, the owners of the computer store in our running example may be interested in being notified whenever a user places orders for five or more different products in, say, less than ten seconds (because this may indicate that a malicious automated process in fact placed these orders).

There have been several approaches to the runtime monitoring of Business Processes. One approach [46] is to use pre-defined templates (such as a process P was at a state S for more than X seconds), that can be instantiated (i.e. fed with concrete values) by analysts via a form. The instantiated tasks are internally implemented using e.g. SQL statements. But the templates are fixed and are intended to be designed only by the system administrator, and not by the analyst. This approach is effective in some cases, but fails to satisfy the desiderata we listed above. More in the spirit of our desiderata are works that lift the same formalisms used for static analysis of executions, and use them in the context of monitoring. Specifically, [56] showed how to use LTL for effective monitoring of distributed systems; this is an interesting direction but it suffers from the same problems discussed above regarding temporal logic. In [10] we show how to adapt BPQL for monitoring tasks, but again, the focus is on the process flow rather than its data. As before, we believe that what is missing is a comprehensive flow-and-data monitoring solutions, that will preferably be employed uniformly with a solution for the analysis of past and future executions.

4.3 Research Directions and Open Problems

To conclude, we list several research directions and open questions in the context of querying Business Processes.

- We have presented many different formalisms for querying processes, however most of them focus only on flow and not on data, and those that allow to query flow-and-data are computationally expensive in terms of worst case complexity. Further studying the tradeoff between expressivity and complexity of query evaluation in this context is an intriguing research direction.

- One specifically important benefit of declarative query languages is a seamless optimization. The development of dedicated optimization techniques for the analysis of past, present and future executions, perhaps based on the information given by the Business Process specification, is an important challenge.

- We have mentioned the work on provenance for scientific workflows and for database queries. As described above, maintaining fine-grained (i.e. flow and data) provenance for scientific (and other) workflows is useful, but may require a lot of storage space. Finding efficient ways of storing fine-grained provenance, and then utilizing it for analysis tasks, is the subject of an on-going research. We note in this context that economical storage of temporal databases has been extensively studied (see [65]), but the additional challenges here are due to the possibly intricate structure of the process *flow* that is absent from temporal databases, and entails intricate causality relations between process activities and data items.

5. CONCLUSION

We provide in this paper a database perspective to Business Processes. Research in this area considers the context (processes) in which data is generated and manipulated, the users interacting with the data and the goals that the data serves. We have exemplified the importance of such a holistic approach to process and data management and its benefits. We have discussed the state-of-the-art research in this direction and highlighted the remaining gaps. We argue that similarly to the case of "conventional" database research, elegant modeling and rich underlying technology are likely to bring economic wealth for the Business Process owners and their users. Consequently, we believe that Business Processes constitute a very promising area for research and that Database researchers are best equipped to lead a breakthrough in this field.

6. REFERENCES

[1] Serge Abiteboul, Pierre Bourhis, Alban Galland, and Bogdan Marinoiu. The axml artifact model. In *TIME*, 2009.

[2] Serge Abiteboul, Pierre Bourhis, and Victor Vianu. Comparing workflow specification languages: a matter of views. In *ICDT*, 2011.

[3] Serge Abiteboul, Richard Hull, and Victor Vianu. *Foundations of Databases*. Addison-Wesley, 1995.

[4] Serge Abiteboul, Luc Segoufin, and Victor Vianu. Static analysis of active xml systems. *ACM Trans. Database Syst.*, 34(4), 2009.

[5] Serge Abiteboul, Victor Vianu, Brad Fordham, and Yelena Yesha. Relational transducers for electronic commerce. In *PODS*, 1998.

[6] Umut Acar, Peter Buneman, James Cheney, Jan Van Den Bussche, Natalia Kwasnikowska, and Stijn Vansummeren. A graph model of data and workflow provenance. In *TaPP*, 2010.

[7] Active XML. http://activexml.net/.

[8] R. Alur, M. Benedikt, K. Etessami, P. Godefroid, T. Reps, and M. Yannakakis. Analysis of recursive state machines. *ACM Trans. Program. Lang. Syst.*, 27(4), 2005.

[9] Zhuowei Bao, Susan B. Davidson, Sanjeev Khanna, and Sudeepa Roy. An optimal labeling scheme for workflow provenance using skeleton labels. In *SIGMOD*, 2010.

[10] C. Beeri, A. Eyal, T. Milo, and A. Pilberg. Monitoring business processes with queries. In *Proc. of VLDB*, 2007.

[11] M. Benedikt, P. Godefroid, and T. Reps. Model checking of unrestricted hierarchical state machines. In *ICALP*, 2001.

[12] Michael Benedikt, Evgeny Kharlamov, Dan Olteanu, and Pierre Senellart. Probabilistic XML via Markov chains. *PVLDB*, 3(1), September 2010.

[13] Grady Booch, James Rumbaugh, and Ivar Jacobson. *The Unified Modeling Language user guide*. Addison Wesley Longman Publishing Co., Inc., 1999.

[14] Business Process Execution Language for Web Services. http://www.ibm.com/developerworks/library/ws-bpel/.

[15] Daniel Brand and Pitro Zafiropulo. On communicating finite-state machines. *J. ACM*, 30, 1983.

[16] T. Bultan, J. Su, and X. Fu. Analyzing conversations of web services. *IEEE Internet Computing*, 10(1), 2006.

[17] P. Buneman, J. Cheney, and S. Vansummeren. On the expressiveness of implicit provenance in query and update languages. *ACM Trans. Database Syst.*, 33(4), 2008.

[18] Peter Buneman, James Cheney, and Stijn Vansummeren. On the expressiveness of implicit provenance in query and update languages. In *ICDT*, 2007.

[19] Peter Buneman, Sanjeev Khanna, and Wang Chiew Tan. Why and where: A characterization of data provenance. In *Proc. of ICDT*, 2001.

[20] J. R. Burch, E. M. Clarke, K. L. McMillan, D. L. Dill, and L. J. Hwang. Symbolic model checking: 1020 states and beyond. *Inf. Comput.*, 98(2), 1992.

[21] O. Burkart and B. Steffen. Model checking for context-free processes, 1992.

[22] S. Ceri, P. Fraternali, A. Bongio, S. Comai M. Brambilla, and M. Matera. *Designing data-intensive Web applications*. Morgan-Kaufmann, 2002.

[23] James Cheney, Stephen Chong, Nate Foster, Margo I. Seltzer, and Stijn Vansummeren. Provenance: a future history. In *Proc. of OOPSLA*, 2009.

[24] David Cohn, Pankaj Dhoolia, Fenno Heath, Iii, Florian Pinel, and John Vergo. Siena: From powerpoint to web app in 5 minutes. In *ICSOC*, 2008.

[25] David Cohn and Richard Hull. Business artifacts: A data-centric approach to modeling business operations and processes. *IEEE Data Eng. Bull.*, 32(3):3–9, 2009.

[26] B. Courcelle. Recognizable sets of graphs, hypergraphs and relational structures : a survey. In *DLT '04*, volume 3340 of *LNCS*, 2004.

[27] Susan B. Davidson, Sanjeev Khanna, Sudeepa Roy, and Sarah Cohen Boulakia. Privacy issues in scientific workflow provenance. In *WANDS*, 2010.

[28] D. Deutch and T. Milo. Type inference and type checking for queries on execution traces. In *Proc. of VLDB*, 2008.

[29] D. Deutch and T. Milo. Evaluating top-k queries over business processes (short paper). In *Proc. of ICDE*, 2009.

[30] D. Deutch and T. Milo. Top-k projection queries for probabilistic business processes. In *Proc. of ICDT*, 2009.

[31] D. Deutch, T. Milo, N. Polyzotis, and T. Yam. Optimal top-k query evaluation for weighted business processes. In *Proc. of VLDB*, 2010.

[32] A. Deutsch, M. Marcus, L. Sui, V. Vianu, and D. Zhou. A verifier for interactive, data-driven web applications. In *Proc. of SIGMOD*, 2005.

[33] A. Deutsch, M. Marcus, L. Sui, V. Vianu, and D. Zhou. A verifier for interactive, data-driven web applications. In *Proc. of SIGMOD*, 2005.

[34] A. Deutsch, L. Sui, V. Vianu, and D. Zhou. Verification of communicating data-driven web services. In *Proc. of PODS*, 2006.

[35] Alin Deutsch, Liying Sui, and Victor Vianu. Specification and verification of data-driven web services. In *PODS*, 2004.

[36] Bruce Powel Douglass. Uml statecharts. *Embedded Systems Programming*, 1999.

[37] E. A. Emerson. Temporal and modal logic. In J. van Leeuwen, editor, *Handbook of Theoretical Computer Science: Volume B: Formal Models and Semantics*. Elsevier, 1990.

[38] K. Etessami and M. Yannakakis. Algorithmic verification of recursive probabilistic state machines. In *TACAS*, 2005.

[39] K. Etessami and M. Yannakakis. Recursive markov chains, stochastic grammars, and monotone systems of nonlinear equations. *JACM*, 56(1), 2009.

[40] J. N. Foster, T. J. Green, and V. Tannen. Annotated xml: queries and provenance. In *PODS*, 2008.

[41] J.N. Foster, T.J. Green, and V. Tannen. Annotated XML: queries and provenance. In *PODS*, 2008.

[42] C. Fritz, R. Hull, and J. Su. Automatic construction of simple artifact-based business processes. In *ICDT*, 2009.

[43] W. Gaaloul and C. Godart. Mining workflow recovery from event based logs. In *Business Process Management*, 2005.

[44] T.J. Green, G. Karvounarakis, Z. Ives, and V. Tannen. Update exchange with mappings and provenance. In *VLDB*, 2007.

[45] Todd J. Green, Gregory Karvounarakis, and Val Tannen. Provenance semirings. In *Proc. of PODS*, 2007.

[46] D. Grigori, F. Casati, M. Castellanos, M.Sayal U .Dayal, and M. Shan. Business process intelligence. *Computers in Industry*, 53, 2004.

[47] D. Harel. Statecharts: A visual formalism for complex systems. *Science of Comp. Programming*, 8:231–274, 1987.

[48] J.E. Hopcroft and J.D. Ullman. *Introduction To Automata Theory, Languages, And Computation*. Addison-Wesley Longman Publishing Co., Inc., 1990.

[49] J. Huang, T. Chen, A. Doan, and J. F. Naughton. On the provenance of non-answers to queries over extracted data. *Proc. VLDB*, 1, 2008.

[50] R. Hull and J. Su. Tools for composite web services: a short overview. *SIGMOD Rec.*, 34(2), 2005.

[51] Robert Ikeda, Hyunjung Park, and Jennifer Widom. Provenance for generalized map and reduce workflows. In *CIDR*, 2011.

[52] D. Janssens and G. Rozenberg. Graph grammars with node-label controlled rewriting and embedding. In *Proc. of COMPUGRAPH*, 1983.

[53] Antonín Kucera, Javier Esparza, and Richard Mayr. Model checking probabilistic pushdown automata. *Logical Methods in Computer Science*, 2(1), 2006.

[54] K. Lary and S. J. Young. The estimation of stochastic context-free grammars using the inside-outside algrithm. *Computer, Speech and Language*, 4:35–56, 1990.

[55] Z. Manna and A. Pnueli. *The temporal logic of reactive and concurrent systems*. Springer-Verlag, 1992.

[56] Thierry Massart, Cédric Meuter, and Laurent Van Begin. On the complexity of partial order trace model checking. *Inf. Process. Lett.*, 106(3):120–126, 2008.

[57] S. P. Meyn and R. L. Tweedie. *Markov Chains and Stochastic Stability*. Springer-Verlag, 1993.

[58] T. Murata. Petri nets: Properties, analysis and applications. *Proceedings of the IEEE*, 77(4), 1989.

[59] Martin S. Olivier, Reind P. van de Riet, and Ehud Gudes. Specifying application-level security in workflow systems. In *DEXA*, 1998.

[60] T. Pavlidis. Linear and context-free graph grammars. *J. ACM*, 19(1), 1972.

[61] D. M. Sayal, F. Casati, U. Dayal, and M. Shan. Business Process Cockpit. In *Proc. of VLDB*, 2002.

[62] R. Silva, J. Zhang, and J. G. Shanahan. Probabilistic workflow mining. In *Proc. of KDD*, 2005.

[63] Alkis Simitsis, Panos Vassiliadis, and Timos Sellis. State-space optimization of etl workflows. *IEEE Transactions on Knowledge and Data Engineering*, 17:1404–1419, 2005.

[64] Marc Spielmann. Verification of relational transducers for electronic commerce. *Journal of Computer and Systems Sciences (JCSS)*, 66, 2003.

[65] Abdullah Uz Tansel, James Clifford, Shashi Gadia, Sushil Jajodia, Arie Segev, and Richard Snodgrass, editors. *Temporal databases: theory, design, and implementation*. Benjamin-Cummings Publishing Co., Inc., 1993.

[66] W. M. P. van der Aalst, B. F. van Dongen, J. Herbst, L. Maruster, G. Schimm, and A. J. M. M. Weijters. Workflow mining: a survey of issues and approaches. *Data Knowl. Eng.*, 47(2), 2003.

[67] Stijn Vansummeren and James Cheney. Recording provenance for sql queries and updates. *IEEE Data Eng. Bull.*, 30(4):29–37, 2007.

[68] Victor Vianu. Automatic verification of database-driven systems: a new frontier. In *ICDT*, pages 1–13, 2009.

[69] Marko Vrhovnik, Holger Schwarz, Oliver Suhre, Bernhard Mitschang, Volker Markl, Albert Maier, and Tobias Kraft. An approach to optimize data processing in business processes. In *VLDB*, pages 615–626, 2007.

[70] Fan Yang, Nitin Gupta, Nicholas Gerner, Xin Qi, Alan Demers, Johannes Gehrke, and Jayavel Shanmugasundaram. A unified platform for data driven web applications with automatic client-server partitioning. In *WWW*, 2007.

[71] W. Zhou, M. Sherr, T. Tao, X. Li, B. T. Loo, and Y. Mao. Efficient querying and maintenance of network provenance at internet-scale. In *SIGMOD Conference*, 2010.

Get the Most out of Your Sample:
Optimal Unbiased Estimators using Partial Information

Edith Cohen
AT&T Labs–Research
180 Park Avenue
Florham Park, NJ 07932, USA
edith@research.att.com

Haim Kaplan
School of Computer Science
Tel Aviv University
Tel Aviv, Israel
haimk@cs.tau.ac.il

ABSTRACT

Random sampling is an essential tool in the processing and transmission of data. It is used to summarize data too large to store or manipulate and meet resource constraints on bandwidth or battery power. Estimators that are applied to the sample facilitate fast approximate processing of queries posed over the original data and the value of the sample hinges on the quality of these estimators.

Our work targets data sets such as request and traffic logs and sensor measurements, where data is repeatedly collected over multiple *instances*: time periods, locations, or snapshots. We are interested in operations, like quantiles and range, that span multiple instances. Subset-sums of these operations are used for applications ranging from planning to anomaly and change detection.

Unbiased low-variance estimators are particularly effective as the relative error decreases with aggregation. The Horvitz-Thompson estimator, known to minimize variance for subset-sums over a sample of a single instance, is not optimal for multi-instance operations because it fails to exploit samples which provide partial information on the estimated quantity.

We present a general principled methodology for the derivation of optimal unbiased estimators over sampled instances and aim to understand its potential. We demonstrate significant improvement in estimate accuracy of fundamental queries for common sampling schemes.

Categories and Subject Descriptors: G.3 [**Probability and Statistics**] : Statistical Computing

General Terms: Algorithms, Measurement, Performance

1. INTRODUCTION

Random sampling had become an essential tool in the handling of data. It is used to accommodate resource constraints on storage, bandwidth, battery power, and processing power. Massive data sets can be too large to be stored for long term or transmitted. Sensor nodes collecting measurements are subject to energy limitations. Even if the data is available, but dispersed across locations, computation of exact aggregates may require gleaning information across different times and locations.

The sample is used as a summary of the original data sets that is small enough to store, transmit, and manipulate in a single location. It is used to approximate aggregates defined over the original data and is suitable also when queries are not a priori known. [22, 28, 4, 3, 7, 18, 19, 1, 16, 1, 20, 10, 17, 8, 11].

Commonly, data has the form of multiple *instances* which are *dispersed* in time or location. Each instance corresponds to an assignment of values to a set of identifiers (keys). The universe of key values is shared between instances but the values change. This data can be modeled as a numeric matrix of instances × keys. Instances can be snapshots of a database that is modified over time, measurements from sensors or of parameters taken in different time periods, or number of requests for resources processed at multiple servers. Clearly, any scalable summarization algorithm of dispersed data must decouple the processing of different instances: the processing of one instance must not depend on values in other instances.

An important class of query primitives are functions with arguments that span values assumed by a key in multiple instances, such as quantiles (maximum, minimum, median) or the *range* (difference between maximum and minimum). *Sum aggregates* of such primitives over selected subsets of keys [23, 15, 6, 14, 12] include difference norms such as the L_1 distance and are used for change or anomaly detection, similarity-based clustering, monitoring, and planning. See example in Figure 1.

Common sampling-based summarization methods of a single instance are Poisson – where keys are sampled independently, bottom-k (order) [25, 9, 17, 10, 11] – where keys are assigned random rank values and the k smallest ranked keys are selected (as in weighted sampling without replacement and priority sampling), and VAROPT [8, 5] . Samples of multiple dispersed instances can be independent or coordinated. Coordination, achieved using random hash function, means that a key getting sampled in one instance is more likely to get sampled in another. Coordination was proposed in the Statistics [2, 26, 24, 25] and CS literature [4, 3, 7, 18, 19, 1, 10, 20, 11, 12] and can boost estimation quality of multi-instance functions [12, 13].

The Horvitz Thompson (HT) estimator [21], based on inverse-probability weights, is a classic method for estimating subset-sums over a single instance: The estimate on the weight of a key is 0 if it is not included in the sample and the ratio of its true weight and the inclusion probability otherwise. The estimate on the weight of a subset of keys is the sum of estimates over sampled keys that are members of the subset. This estimator is unbiased and has minimum variance amongst unbiased nonnegative estimators. A variant of HT is used for bottom-k sampling [17, 27, 12].

Previous estimators we are aware of for multi-instance functions are based on an adaptation of HT: a positive estimate is provided only on samples that revealed sufficient information to compute the exact value of the estimated quantity. We observe that such estimators may not be optimal for multi-instance functions. The reason is that samples which provide partial information on the estimated value are not exploited. We aim to understand the form and potential performance gain of better estimators.

Contribution: A key idea behind our design of better estimators is the use of partial information, which we motivate by the following simple scenario. Consider estimating the maximum of two values, v_1 and v_2, sampled independently with respective probabilities p_1 and p_2. We can be certain about the value $\max(v_1, v_2)$ only when both values are sampled, which happens with probability $p_1 p_2$. The inverse-probability weight is $\max(v_1, v_2)/(p_1 p_2)$ when both values are sampled and 0 otherwise and is an unbiased estimate. We now observe that when exactly one of the values is sampled, we know that the maximum is at least that value, that is, we have meaningful partial information in the form of a positive lower bound on the maximum. We will show how to exploit that and obtain a nonnegative and unbiased estimator with lower variance than the inverse-probability weight.

Our work broadly applies to all common sampling methods. The sample of each instance can be Poisson, VARopt, or bottom-k. Sampling can be weighted (inclusion probability in the sample depends on the value)) or weight-oblivious. Samples of different instances can be *independent* or *coordinated*.

Our main contribution is a principled methodology for the derivation of optimal estimators. For multi-instance functions, there may not be a single estimator with minimum variance on all data and we therefore consider *dominant* estimators which are such that any other estimator with lower variance on some data must have higher variance on some other data. Our methods also apply to queries for which inverse-probability weighting is not applicable.

We explicitly derive dominant estimators for basic aggregations over common sampling distributions and demonstrate significant gain, in terms of lower variance, over state-of-the-art estimators.

We capture the limitations on sampling dispersed instances by characterizing all joint sample distributions that can be realized under the constraint that sampling of one instance may not depend on values of another. Our characterization is general in that we do not limit the size of the representation of random hash functions.

We distinguish between two models of independent weighted samples according to the "reproducibility" of the randomization used in the sampling. *Known (unknown) seeds* model a situation where the random hash functions used in sampling each instance are (are not) available to the estimator. We show that there is a gap between the power of the estimator in these two models. When seeds are unknown, there is no nonnegative unbiased estimator for basic primitives including the maximum of two values. With known seeds, *any* query that has an unbiased nonnegative estimator over some sample distribution over instances can be estimated over independent samples.

Overview. Section 2 characterizes all sample distributions that are consistent with the constraints on summarization of dispersed values. Our model covers common sample distributions: Independent and coordinated sampling of instances, weighted versus weight-oblivious, and known versus unknown seeds. Section 3 proposes methods to obtain dominant estimators. Sections 4-6 focus on independent (Poisson) sampling of instances. We provide example derivations of dominant estimators and evaluate their performance. Weight-oblivious sampling is studied in Section 4, weighted sampling with known seeds in Section 5, and finally, negative results are established in Section 6 for weighted sampling with unknown seeds.

2. SAMPLING DISPERSED VALUES

In terms of an instances $\times$ keys data matrix (top table of Figure 1), we focus on functions over the values $\mathbf{v} = (v_1, \ldots, v_r)$ of a *single* key (i.e., column) in r instances. To estimate sum aggregates over multiple selected keys, we sum individual estimates for

keys: $K = \{1,\ldots,6\}$, **Instances:** $1, 2, 3$						
Instance/key	1	2	3	4	5	6
1	15	0	10	5	10	10
2	20	10	12	20	0	10
3	10	15	15	0	15	10
Multi-instance functions f						
$\max(v_1, v_2, v_3)$	20	15	15	20	15	10
$\min(v_1, v_2)$	15	0	10	0	0	10
$\mathrm{RG}(v_2, v_3)$	10	5	3	20	15	0
$\mathrm{RG}_2(v_2, v_3)$	100	25	9	400	225	0

Sum aggregates: on selected keys and instances
L_1 distance: $\sum_{i \in \{2,4,6\}} \mathrm{RG}(v_2, v_3)$
L_2 distance: $\sqrt{\sum_{i \in \{2,4,6\}} \mathrm{RG}_2(v_2, v_3)}$
max: $\sum_{i \leq 4} \max(v_1, v_2, v_3)$

Figure 1: Example data set with 3 instances and 6 keys.

the selected keys. For example, to estimate the L_1 difference, we apply a range estimator for each key and sum these estimates.

The data is represented by a vector $\mathbf{v} = (v_1, \ldots, v_r)$ where $v_i \in V_i$ and $\mathbf{V} = V_1 \times \cdots \times V_r$. We are interested in a function $f(\mathbf{v})$ of the data such as ith entry value: v_i, quantiles: maximum $\max(\mathbf{v}) = \max_{i \in [r]} v_i$, minimum $\min(\mathbf{v}) = \min_{i \in [r]} v_i$, and ℓth largest entry $\ell^{\text{th}}(\mathbf{v})$, range: $\mathrm{RG}(\mathbf{v}) = \max(\mathbf{v}) - \min(\mathbf{v})$, and $\mathrm{RG}(\mathbf{v})_d \equiv \mathrm{RG}(\mathbf{v})^d$ for $d > 0$. Example domains $\mathbf{V}$ are the nonnegative quadrant of $\mathbb{R}^r$ or $\{0, 1\}^r$.

For a subset $V' \subset \mathbf{V}$ of data vectors we define $\underline{f}(V') = \inf\{f(v) \mid v \in V'\}$ and $\overline{f}(V') = \sup\{f(v) \mid v \in V'\}$, the lowest and highest values of f on V'.

We see a random sample $S \subset [r]$ of the entries of $\mathbf{v}$. The sample distribution is subjected to the constraint that the inclusion of i in S is independent of the values v_j for $j \neq i$. This is formalized as follows: There is a probability distribution $\mathcal{T}$ over a sample space Ω of predicates $\boldsymbol{\sigma} = (\sigma_1, \ldots, \sigma_r)$, where σ_i has domain V_i. The sample $S \equiv S(\boldsymbol{\sigma}, \mathbf{v})$ is a function of the predicate vector $\boldsymbol{\sigma}$ and the data vector $\mathbf{v}$ and includes $i \in [r]$ if and only if $\sigma_i(v_i)$ is true: $i \in S \Leftrightarrow \sigma_i(v_i)$.

To simplify presentation, we treat Ω as finite and $\mathcal{T}$ as a discrete distribution. The extension to infinite domains (which we also use here) is straightforward.

Weighted and weight-oblivious sampling. Sampling is *weight-oblivious* when inclusion of i in S is independent of v_i, that is, σ is a boolean vector and entry i is sampled if and only if $\sigma_i = 1$, which happens with probability $p_i = \mathsf{E}[\sigma_i]$. Sampling is *weighted* if i is more likely to be sampled when v_i is larger. In particular, if $v_i = 0$ then $i \notin S$. Weighted sampling is important when summarizing sparse datasets, as dominant "0" entries need not be processed or represented in the sample. It is also critical for accuracy when functions increase with the data values. With weighted sampling, the random predicate vector $\boldsymbol{\sigma}$ can be replaced with a random numeric *threshold* vector $\boldsymbol{\tau}$ such that

$$i \in S \iff \sigma_i(v_i) \iff v_i \geq \tau_i .$$

Weighted sampling is *IPPS* (Inclusion Probability Proportional to Size) when $\tau_i = u_i \tau_i^*$, where $\boldsymbol{\tau}^*$ is a fixed vector and u_i are drawn uniformly at random from $[0, 1]$. We refer to the random vector $\mathbf{u}$ as the *seed* vector. With IPPS sampling of instances, i is sampled with probability $\min\{1, v_i/\tau_i^*\}$.

Poisson (independent) sampling. Entries are sampled independently: $\mathcal{T}$ is a product distribution so that σ_i is independent of all σ_j for $j \neq i$. With IPPS Poisson sampling, u_i are independent.

Shared-seed sampling: For $i \in [r]$, $\tau_i(u)$ is a non-decreasing function of a seed $u \in [0, 1]$ selected uniformly at random. This captures shared-seed coordinated sampling of instances. With shared-seed IPPS sampling, $u_i = u$ for all $i \in [r]$.

2.1 Estimators

An estimator $\hat{f}$ of a function $f(\mathbf{v})$ is a function applied to the outcome S. The outcome contains $\{i \mid \sigma_i(v_i)\}$ and their values. The estimator can use knowledge of the domain $\mathbf{V}$ and the distribution $\mathcal{T}$. When sampling is weight-oblivious, σ is a boolean vector that can be inferred from the sample. Otherwise, we say that seeds are *(not) known* when the random predicate vector σ is (not) available to the estimator (included with the outcome). When inclusion of an entry depends on its value, knowing σ allows us to obtain information on values of entries that are not included in the sample: If $i \notin S$, we know that $v_i \in \sigma_i^{-1}(0)$.

With an outcome S, we associate a set $V^*(S) \subset \mathbf{V}$ of all data vectors consistent with this outcome: $V^*(S) = \{\mathbf{v} \in \mathbf{V} \mid \mathrm{PR}[S \mid \mathbf{v}] > 0\}$. When seeds are not known, $V^*(S)$ contains $\mathbf{v}$ if and only if there exists $\sigma \in \Omega$ such that $S(\sigma, \mathbf{v})$ matches our outcome. With known seeds, the outcome also includes σ, hence $\mathbf{v} \in V^*(S)$ if and only if the outcome matches $S(\sigma, \mathbf{v})$.

We seek estimators with some or all of the following properties:

unbiased: for all $\mathbf{v}$, $\mathsf{E}[\hat{f} \mid \mathbf{v}] = f(\mathbf{v})$.

nonnegative: $\hat{f} \geq 0$.

bounded variance: $\forall \mathbf{v}$, $\mathrm{VAR}[\hat{f} \mid \mathbf{v}] < \infty$.

dominance: We say that an estimator $\hat{f}^{(1)}$ *dominates* $\hat{f}^{(2)}$ if for all data vectors $\mathbf{v}$, $\mathrm{VAR}[\hat{f}^{(1)} \mid \mathbf{v}] \leq \mathrm{VAR}[\hat{f}^{(2)} \mid \mathbf{v}]$. An estimator $\hat{f}$ is *dominant* if there is no other unbiased nonnegative estimator $\hat{f}'$ that dominates $\hat{f}$.

monotone: Nonnegative and non-decreasing with information. If $V^*(S) \subset V^*(S')$, then $\hat{f}(S) \geq \hat{f}(S')$.

Unbiasedness is particularly desirable when estimating sums (summing estimates). When unbiased and independent (or non-positively correlated) estimates are combined, the relative error decreases. Nonnegativity is desirable when estimating a nonnegative function $f \geq 0$, ensuring an estimate from the same domain as the estimated quantity. Dominance is a notion of optimality. If there is an estimator that dominates all others, it is the optimal one and the only dominant one. If there isn't, we instead aim for a dominant estimator. Monotonicity is an intuitive smoothness requirement.

2.2 Horvitz Thompson estimator

Suppose we are interested in estimating a function $f(v) \geq 0$ of a single entry ($r = 1$). When the entry is sampled, we know the value v and from the distribution $\mathcal{T}$, we can obtain the probability $p = \mathsf{E}[\sigma(v)]$ that the entry is sampled. The HT estimator [21] $\hat{f}^{(HT)}$ of $f(v)$ applies *inverse probability weighting*: $\hat{f} = 0$ if the entry is not sampled and $\hat{f} = f(v)/p$ if sampled. This estimator is clearly nonnegative, monotone, and unbiased: $\mathsf{E}[\hat{f}] = (1 - p) * 0 + p\frac{f(v)}{p} = f(v)$. The variance is

$$\mathrm{VAR}[\hat{f}] = f(v)^2 \left(\frac{1}{p} - 1\right). \tag{1}$$

The HT estimator is optimal when we do not get any useful information on $f(v)$ when the entry is not sampled. Formally, when it is possible that $f(v) = 0$ if entry is not sampled. Under these conditions, the HT estimator minimizes $\mathrm{VAR}[\hat{f}]$ for all $\mathbf{v}$ over all unbiased nonnegative estimators. This is because any nonnegative

unbiased estimator must have $\hat{f} = 0$ if entry is not sampled and variance is minimized when the estimate has a fixed value when it is sampled.

Multi-entry f. The application of inverse-probability weights on multi-entry functions is more delicate. We can use the set $\mathcal{S}^*$ of outcomes with all entries sampled $S \in \mathcal{S}^* \iff S = [r]$. For these outcomes we know the data $\mathbf{v}$ and from $\mathcal{T}$, can determine $\mathrm{PR}[\mathcal{S}^* \mid \mathbf{v}]$. The estimator is $f(\mathbf{v})/\mathrm{PR}[\mathcal{S}^* \mid \mathbf{v}]$ for $S \in \mathcal{S}^*$ and 0 otherwise. This estimator is defined when $\mathrm{PR}[\mathcal{S}^* \mid \mathbf{v}] > 0$. With weighted sampling, however, "0" valued entries are never sampled, so we may have $\mathrm{PR}[S = [r]] = 0$ when $f(\mathbf{v}) > 0$.

A broader definition of inverse-probability estimators [12, 13] is with respect to a subset $\mathcal{S}^*$ of all possible outcomes (over Ω and $\mathbf{V}$). The outcomes $\mathcal{S}^*$ are those on which the estimator is positive. The estimator is defined for $\mathcal{S}^*$ if there exist two functions f^* and p^* with domain $\mathcal{S}^*$ that satisfy the following:

- for any outcome $S \in \mathcal{S}^*$, for all $\mathbf{v} \in V^*(S)$, $f(\mathbf{v}) = f^*(S)$ and $\mathrm{PR}[\mathcal{S}^* \mid \mathbf{v}] = p^*(S)$.

- for all $\mathbf{v} \in \mathbf{V}$ with $f(v) > 0$, $\mathrm{PR}[\mathcal{S}^* \mid \mathbf{v}] > 0$.

The estimate is $\hat{f}(S) = 0$ if $S \notin \mathcal{S}^*$ and $\hat{f}(S) = f^*(S)/p^*(S)$ otherwise. These functions and hence the estimator are unique for $\mathcal{S}^*$ if they exist. When $\mathcal{S}^*$ is more inclusive, the respective estimator has lower (or same) variance on all data. We use the notation $\hat{f}^{(HT)}$ for the estimator corresponding to the most inclusive $\mathcal{S}^*$. A sufficient condition for optimality of $\hat{f}^{(HT)}$ is that for all outcomes $S \notin S^*$, $\underline{f}(V^*(S)) = 0$.

2.3 Necessary conditions for estimation

Inverse-probability estimators are unbiased, nonnegative (when f is), and monotone. They are clearly bounded, that is, the set of estimates produced for each data vector is bounded. Since bounded, they also have bounded variance. An inverse-probability estimator, however, is possible only if for all data such that $f(\mathbf{v}) > 0$, there is positive probability of recovering $f(\mathbf{v})$ from the outcome. An example where this is not the case, and hence there is no inverse-probability estimator, is RG_d under weighted sampling: When the data has at least one positive and one zero entry, there is zero probability of recovering the exact value of $\mathrm{RG}_d(\mathbf{v})$ from the outcome. We identify weaker properties necessary for the existence of an estimator with these properties.

For a set of outcomes, determined by a portion $\Omega' \subset \Omega$ of the sample space and data vector $\mathbf{v}$, we define

$$V^*(\Omega', \mathbf{v}) = \bigcap_{\sigma \in \Omega'} V^*(S(\sigma, \mathbf{v}))$$

the set of all vectors that are consistent with all outcomes determined by Ω' and $\mathbf{v}$.
For $\mathbf{v}$ and ϵ, we define

$$\underline{\Delta}(\mathbf{v}, \epsilon) = 1 - \max \left\{ \mathrm{PR}[\Omega'] \mid \Omega' \subset \Omega, \underline{f}(V^*(\Omega', \mathbf{v})) \leq f(\mathbf{v}) - \epsilon \right\} \tag{2}$$

We look for Ω' of maximum size such that if we consider all vectors $\mathbf{v}' \in V^*(\Omega', \mathbf{v})$ that are consistent with $\mathbf{v}$ on Ω', the infimum of f over $V^*(\Omega', \mathbf{v})$ is at most $f(\mathbf{v}) - \epsilon$. We define $\underline{\Delta}(\mathbf{v}, \epsilon)$ as the probability $\mathrm{PR}[\Omega \setminus \Omega']$ of not being in that portion.

LEMMA 2.1. *A function f has an estimator that is*

- *unbiased and nonnegative* ⇒:

$$\forall \mathbf{v}, \forall \epsilon > 0, \underline{\Delta}(\mathbf{v}, \epsilon) > 0 \qquad (3)$$

- *unbiased, nonnegative, and bounded variance* ⇒:

$$\forall \mathbf{v}, \underline{\Delta}(\mathbf{v}, \epsilon) = \Omega(\epsilon^2) . \qquad (4)$$

- *unbiased, nonnegative, and bounded* ⇒:

$$\forall \mathbf{v}, \underline{\Delta}(\mathbf{v}, \epsilon) = \Omega(\epsilon) . \qquad (5)$$

PROOF. The contribution of Ω' to the expectation of $\hat{f}$ must not exceed $\underline{f}(V^*(\Omega', \mathbf{v}))$. Because if it does, then $\hat{f}$ must assume negative values for $\mathbf{v}' \in V^*(\Omega', \mathbf{v})$ with minimum $f(\mathbf{v}')$. Considering a maximum Ω' with $\underline{f}(V^*(\Omega', \mathbf{v})) \leq f(\mathbf{v}) - \epsilon$, its contribution to the expectation is at most $f(\mathbf{v}) - \epsilon$ and the contribution of the complement, which has probability $\underline{\Delta}(\mathbf{v}, \epsilon)$, must be at least ϵ.

If $\underline{\Delta}(\mathbf{v}, \epsilon) = 0$ then this is not possible, so (3) follows. The expectation of the estimator over the complement is at least $\frac{\epsilon}{\underline{\Delta}(\mathbf{v}, \epsilon)}$, thus (5) is necessary. The contribution to the variance of that complement is at least

$$\underline{\Delta}(\mathbf{v}, \epsilon) \left(\frac{\epsilon}{\underline{\Delta}(\mathbf{v}, \epsilon)} - f(\mathbf{v}) \right)^2$$

which implies (4) is necessary. □

3. DOMINANT ESTIMATORS

We present constructive definitions of dominant estimators which we use to derive estimators and establish their dominance.

The first construction, Algorithm 1, uses an order $\prec$ over the set V of all possible data vectors. The estimator minimizes variance in an order-respecting way: The variance of the estimator for a data vector $\mathbf{v}$ is minimized conditioned on values it assigned to outcomes consistent with vectors that precede $\mathbf{v}$.

The algorithm defines $\hat{f}$ through sequential processing of data vectors in increasing $\prec$ order. When $\mathbf{v}$ is processed, the estimate value $\hat{f}(S)$ is determined on all outcomes S that are consistent with $\mathbf{v}$ but not with any preceding vector, that is, all outcomes S such that $\min_\prec V^*(S) = \mathbf{v}$. When this holds, we say that S is *determined* by the data vector $\mathbf{v}$ and that $\mathbf{v}$ is the *determining vector* of S. An outcome S precedes $\mathbf{v}$ if it is determined by $\mathbf{u} \prec \mathbf{v}$.

The algorithm processes $\mathbf{v}$ considering the values of $\hat{f}$ on the outcomes $\mathcal{S}_0 \subset \mathcal{S}$ assigned when processing the vectors V_0 that precede $\mathbf{v}$. It computes the contribution f_0 of the outcomes $\mathcal{S}_0$ to the expectation of the estimate of $f(\mathbf{v})$. The estimate on outcomes $S \in \mathcal{S}'$ that are consistent with $\mathbf{v}$ and do not precede $\mathbf{v}$ is as follows: If $\text{PR}[\mathcal{S}'|\mathbf{v}] = 0$ and $f(\mathbf{v}) = f_0$, $\hat{f}(S) \leftarrow 0$. If $\text{PR}[\mathcal{S}'|\mathbf{v}] = 0$ and $f(\mathbf{v}) \neq f_0$, we declare failure. Else, $\hat{f}(S) \leftarrow \frac{f(\mathbf{v}) - f_0}{\text{PR}[\mathcal{S}'|\mathbf{v}]}$. Applying the inverse-probability weights principle, this minimizes variance $\text{VAR}[\hat{f}|\mathbf{v}]$ conditioned on $\hat{f}: \mathcal{S}_0$.

LEMMA 3.1. *If Algorithm 1 terminates successfully, the estimator $\hat{f}$ is dominant and unbiased.*

PROOF. Dominance: Consider an estimator $\hat{f}' \neq \hat{f}$. Let $\mathbf{v}$ be $\prec$-minimal such that the estimators differ when data is $\mathbf{v}$. Let $\mathcal{S}_0$ and $\mathcal{S}'$ be as in Algorithm 1 when processing $\mathbf{v}$. We must have $\hat{f}: \mathcal{S}_0 = \hat{f}': \mathcal{S}_0$ and hence $\hat{f}: \mathcal{S}' \neq \hat{f}': \mathcal{S}'$. The setting of $\hat{f}$ on the outcomes $\mathcal{S}'$ is the *unique* choice which minimizes the variance of $\mathbf{v}$ subject to $\hat{f}: \mathcal{S}_0$. Hence, $\text{VAR}[\hat{f}'|\mathbf{v}] > \text{VAR}[\hat{f}|\mathbf{v}]$ and thus $\hat{f}'$ can not dominate $\hat{f}$. Unbiasedness: follows from the choice of $\hat{f}$ on the outcomes $\mathcal{S}'$ in line 13: $\text{E}[\hat{f}] = \text{E}[\hat{f}|\mathcal{S}']\text{PR}[\mathcal{S}'] + \text{E}[\hat{f}|\mathcal{S}_0]\text{PR}[\mathcal{S}_0] = f(\mathbf{v})$. □

Algorithm 1 DOMEST($\prec$)

Require: $\prec$ is an order on V
1: $\mathcal{S}_0 \leftarrow \emptyset$ ▷ set of processed outcomes
2: $V_0 \leftarrow \emptyset$ ▷ set of processed data vectors
3: **while** $V_0 \neq V$ **do**
4:    $\mathbf{v} \leftarrow \min_\prec(V \setminus V_0)$ ▷ A minimum unprocessed vector
5:    $f_0 \leftarrow \sum_{S \in \mathcal{S}_0} \hat{f}(S)\text{PR}[S|\mathbf{v}]$ ▷ Contribution of processed outcomes to the estimate of $f(\mathbf{v})$
6:    $\mathcal{S}' \leftarrow \{S | \mathbf{v} \in V^*(S)\} \setminus \mathcal{S}_0$ ▷ Unprocessed outcomes consistent with $\mathbf{v}$
7:    **if** $\text{PR}[\mathcal{S}'|\mathbf{v}] = 0$ **then**
8:      **if** $f(\mathbf{v}) \neq f_0$ **then return** "failure"   ▷ No unbiased estimator
9:      **else**
10:        $\forall S \in \mathcal{S}', \hat{f}(S) \leftarrow 0$
11:      **end if**
12:    **end if**
13:    $\forall S \in \mathcal{S}', \hat{f}(S) \leftarrow \frac{f(\mathbf{v}) - f_0}{\text{PR}[\mathcal{S}'|\mathbf{v}]}$
14:    $V_0 \leftarrow V_0 \cup \{\mathbf{v}\}$
15:    $\mathcal{S}_0 \leftarrow \mathcal{S}_0 \cup \mathcal{S}'$
16: **end while**

A concise way to specify an estimator obtained using Algorithm 1 is as a function of the determining vector of the outcome: Slightly abusing notation, we define $\hat{f}(\min_\prec V^*(S)) \equiv \hat{f}(S)$.

The ordering $\prec$ uniquely defines the estimator but different orderings may result in the same estimator. If a *partial* order $\prec$ has the property that for all outcomes S, $\min_\prec V^*(S)$ is unique, then all applications of Algorithm 1 to a linearization of $\prec$ yield the same estimator.

LEMMA 3.2. *The estimator $\hat{f}$ computed by Algorithm 1 is monotone if and only if for any outcome S and $\mathbf{v} \in V^*(S)$, the estimate on outcomes determined by $\mathbf{v}$ is at least $\hat{f}(S)$:*

$$\hat{f} \text{ is monotone} \iff \forall S, \forall \mathbf{v} \in V^*(S) \ \hat{f}(\mathbf{v}) \geq \hat{f}(S) .$$

PROOF. An outcome S' with $V^*(S') = \{\mathbf{v}\}$ has $V^*(S') \subset V^*(S)$ and is determined by $\mathbf{v}$. From monotonicity, we must have $\hat{f}(\mathbf{v}) \geq \hat{f}(S)$. Conversely, consider two outcomes S and S' such that $V^*(S) \subset V^*(S')$. Let $\mathbf{v}'$ be the determining vector of S' and $\mathbf{v}$ be the determining vector of S. We have that $\mathbf{v} \in S'$, hence $\hat{f}(\mathbf{v}) = \hat{f}(S) \geq \hat{f}(S')$. □

Algorithm 1 may produce negative estimates. When processing a data vector $\mathbf{v}$, the contribution f_0 to the estimate of previously processed outcomes may already exceed $f(\mathbf{v})$, resulting in a negative value in line 13. This can be remedied by constraining the setting of $\hat{f}: \mathcal{S}'$ to ensure that nonnegativity is not violated on successive vectors:

$$\min \sum_{S \in \mathcal{S}'} \text{PR}[S|\mathbf{v}](\hat{f}(S) - f(\mathbf{v}))^2 \qquad (6)$$

$$\sum_{S \in \mathcal{S}'} \text{PR}[S|\mathbf{v}]\hat{f}(S) = f(\mathbf{v}) - f_0 \qquad (7)$$

$$\forall \mathbf{v}' \succ \mathbf{v} \quad \sum_{S \in \mathcal{S}' \cup \mathcal{S}_0} \hat{f}(S)\text{PR}[S|\mathbf{v}'] \leq f(\mathbf{v}') . \qquad (8)$$

We minimize variance (6) subject to unbiasedness (7) and not violating nonnegativity to any $\mathbf{v}' \succ \mathbf{v}$ (8). The resulting estimator is dominant (is not dominated by any nonnegative estimator) if the solution of the system is unique.

This modification increases the sensitivity of the estimator computed by algorithm 1 to the order $\prec$: even when the sets of unprocessed outcomes consistent with two vectors $\mathbf{v}$ and $\mathbf{v}''$ are disjoint, a vector may have lower variance if processed earlier. This is because when $\mathbf{v}$ is processed before $\mathbf{v}''$, the constraints (8) due to vectors $\mathbf{v}'$ that succeed both $\mathbf{v}$ and $\mathbf{v}''$ are less tight.

Algorithm 2 defines a more flexible construction, where vectors are processed in batches. The algorithm allows us to "balance" the variance between vectors that are members of the same batch. We use a partition $U_0, U_1, \ldots$ of V, where at step i we process U_i, setting the estimator on all outcomes consistent with U_i and not consistent with any vector in U_j for $j < i$. Step i computes a *locally dominant* estimator for U_i: given $\hat{f} : \mathcal{S}_0$, unbiasedness (7) for all $\mathbf{v} \in U_i$ and nonnegativity (8) for all $\mathbf{v}' \in U_{>i}$. That is, under these constraints, there is no other setting of $\hat{f}$ on $\mathcal{S}'$ with smaller or equal variance for all vectors in U_i, and a strictly smaller variance for at least one vector. The estimator $\hat{f}$ is dominant if at each step h, when fixing the variance of all vectors in U_h, the solution is unique.

Algorithm 2 PartDom

Require: $U_0, U_1, \ldots$ is a partition of $\mathbf{V}$
1: $\mathcal{S}_0 \leftarrow \emptyset$ $\triangleright$ set of processed outcomes
2: **for** $h = 0, 1, 2, \ldots$ **do** $\triangleright$ h is the index of current part to process
3:     $\mathcal{S}' \leftarrow \{S | U_h \cap V^*(S) \neq \emptyset\} \setminus \mathcal{S}_0$ $\triangleright$ Unprocessed outcomes consistent with U_h
4:     Compute a locally dominant estimator for U_h, extending $\hat{f}$ on $\mathcal{S}_0$, and satisfying

$$\forall \mathbf{v}', \quad \sum_{S \in \mathcal{S}' \cup \mathcal{S}_0} \hat{f}(S) \mathrm{PR}[S | \mathbf{v}'] \leq f(\mathbf{v}') .$$

5:     $\mathcal{S}_0 \leftarrow \mathcal{S}_0 \cup \mathcal{S}'$
6: **end for**

The variance on a vector is lower when it is processed earlier and therefore we can choose the order $\prec$ (in Algorithm 1) or the ordered partition (in Algorithm 2) so that vectors that are more likely to occur as data appear earlier. Symmetry (invariance to permutation of entries) can be achieved in Algorithm 2 by including all symmetric data vectors in the same part and using a symmetric locally dominant estimator.

4. POISSON: WEIGHT-OBLIVIOUS

We now consider estimating $f(\mathbf{v})$ when sampling of entries is weight-oblivious and Poisson: entry $i \in [r]$ is sampled independently with probability $p_i > 0$.

The inverse-probability weights are $\hat{f}^{(HT)}(S) = f(\mathbf{v}) / \prod_{i \in [r]} p_i$, when $S \equiv [r]$ (all entries are sampled), and $\hat{f}^{(HT)}(S) = 0$ otherwise. This estimator is defined for all f and from (1) has variance

$$\mathrm{VAR}[\hat{f}^{(HT)}] = f(\mathbf{v})^2 \left(\frac{1}{\prod_{i \in [r]} p_i} - 1 \right) . \quad (9)$$

This is the optimal inverse probability estimator for quantiles and range[1]. Moreover, the estimators $\mathrm{RG}^{(HT)}$ ($r = 2$) and $\hat{\min}^{(HT)}$

---

[1] $\mathcal{S}^*$ which contains all outcomes with $|S| = r$ is the most inclusive set for which we can determine both the value $f(\mathbf{v})$ and $\mathrm{PR}[\mathcal{S}^* | \mathbf{v}]$ (see Section 2.2)

---

are dominant[2]. $\hat{f}^{(HT)}$ is not dominant, however, for all other quantiles (ℓ^{th} when $\ell < r$) or RG when $r > 2$. We present dominant estimators for max and boolean OR: $\hat{\max}^{(L)}$ and $\hat{\mathrm{OR}}^{(L)}$ which are monotone and prioritize dense data vectors and $\hat{\max}^{(U)}$ and $\hat{\mathrm{OR}}^{(U)}$ which prioritize sparse vectors.

4.1 Estimator $\hat{\max}^{(L)}$

We apply Algorithm 1 using the following partial order $\prec$: The minimum element is $\mathbf{v} = \mathbf{0}$, that is $\forall \mathbf{v} \in V$, $\mathbf{0} \prec \mathbf{v}$. Otherwise, $\prec$ corresponds to the numeric order on $L(\mathbf{v}) \equiv |\{j \in [r] | v_j < \max_{i \in [r]} v_i\}|$ (the number of entries strictly lower than the maximum one): $\mathbf{v} \prec \mathbf{w} \iff L(\mathbf{v}) < L(\mathbf{w})$.

The determining vector $\mathbf{v}' = \min_{\prec} V^*(S)$ of an outcome S is $\mathbf{0}$ if $\forall i \in S$, $v_i = 0$ (In particular if $S = \emptyset$). If $S \neq \emptyset$, $v'_h \equiv v_h$ if $h \in S$ and $v'_h = \max_{i \in S} v_i$ otherwise. As $\min_{\prec} V^*(S)$ is well defined, the partial order $\prec$ uniquely defines the estimator. Because $\prec$ is invariant to permutation of entries, the estimator is symmetric.

Our choice of $\prec$ is geared to yield "conservative" estimates in order to obtain a monotone estimator. The estimate value assigned to an outcome S is optimized for vectors in $V^*(S)$ where all unseen entries are equal to the maximum $\max_{i \in S} v_i$. This means that we assume that a higher lower bound $f(V^*(S'))$ applies in other parts of the sample space resulting in higher estimate values "elsewhere" which imply more conservative value for our outcome. More informative outcomes on the same data vector either reveal a higher maximum (by including an entry with a higher value) or reveal that entries have value lower than the maximum, in which case, we compensate for smaller-than-assumed estimates by using larger estimates on these more informative samples.

Processing the minimum vector $\mathbf{0}$, the estimator is $\hat{\max}^{(L)} = 0$ on all outcomes S such that $\forall i \in S$, $v_i = 0$. The estimator can then be determined for all outcomes S such that the determining vector has $L(\mathbf{v}) = 0$, that is, outcomes where at least one entry is sampled, has positive value, and all other sampled entries have the same value: $\forall_{i \in S}$, $v_i = \max_{i \in S} v_i > 0$. The probability of such an outcome given data vector $\mathbf{v}$ with $L(\mathbf{v}) = 0$ is the probability that at least one entry is sampled: $1 - \prod_{i \in [r]}(1 - p_i)$ and the estimate value is accordingly

$$\hat{\max}^{(L)} = \frac{\max_{i \in S} v_i}{1 - \prod_{i \in [r]}(1 - p_i)} . \quad (10)$$

Estimator for $r = 2$. We have $\hat{\max}^{(L)} = 0$ on outcomes consistent with data $(0, 0)$ and from (10) $\hat{\max}^{(L)} = \frac{\max_{i \in S} v_i}{p_1 + p_2 - p_1 p_2}$ for outcomes consistent with data with two equal positive entries ($S = \{1\}$, $S = \{2\}$, or $S = \{1, 2\}$ and $v_1 = v_2 = v$). We now consider data vectors where $v_2 < v_1$ (other case $v_1 < v_2$ is symmetric). The estimate is already determined on outcomes where exactly one entry is sampled. These and the empty outcome are in $\mathcal{S}_0$. The outcomes $\mathcal{S}'$ are those where both entries are sampled, and hence $\mathrm{PR}[\mathcal{S}'] = p_1 p_2$. To be unbiased, the estimate x must satisfy the linear equation (line 13 of Algorithm 1):

$$\max\{v_1, v_2\} = p_1 p_2 x + \\ + p_1 (1 - p_2) \frac{v_1}{p_1 + p_2 - p_1 p_2} + p_2 (1 - p_1) \frac{v_2}{p_1 + p_2 - p_1 p_2} .$$

Solving and summarizing we obtain:

---

[2] Any nonnegative estimator must have $\hat{f}(S) = 0$ on outcomes consistent with data vectors with $f(\mathbf{v}) = 0$, which includes all outcomes with $|S| < r$. Considering all estimators that assume positive values only when $|S| = r$, variance is minimized when using a fixed value.

Outcome S		$\text{m\^ax}^{(L)}(S)$
$S = \emptyset$	:	0
$S = \{1\}$	:	$\frac{v_1}{p_1 + p_2 - p_1 p_2}$
$S = \{2\}$	:	$\frac{v_2}{p_1 + p_2 - p_1 p_2}$
$S = \{1, 2\}$	:	$\frac{\max(v_1, v_2)}{p_1 p_2} - \frac{(1/p_2 - 1)v_1 + (1/p_1 - 1)v_2}{p_1 + p_2 - p_1 p_2}$.

A convenient way to express the estimator is as a function of the determining vector. Assuming $v_1 \geq v_2$ (other case is symmetric),

$$\text{m\^ax}^{(L)}(\mathbf{v}) = v_1 \frac{1}{p_1(p_1 + p_2 - p_1 p_2)} - v_2 \frac{1 - p_1}{p_1(p_1 + p_2 - p_1 p_2)} \quad (11)$$

LEMMA 4.1. *The estimator* $\text{m\^ax}^{(L)}$ *is dominant, monotone, nonnegative, and dominates the estimator* $\text{m\^ax}^{(HT)}$.

PROOF. Dominance follows from applying Algorithm 1. For monotonicity, we observe that determining vectors of more informative outcomes have an equal-or-larger v_1 or an equal-or-smaller v_2, which clearly holds as the coefficient of v_1 in(11) is positive and that of v_2 is negative. Nonnegativity follows from monotonicity and that the estimate is 0 when $S = \emptyset$.

The estimator $\text{m\^ax}^{(HT)}$ assumes values 0 or $\frac{\max(v_1, v_2)}{p_1 p_2}$ and thus maximizes variance amongst all unbiased estimators with values in the same range. Hence, to establish dominance over $\text{m\^ax}^{(HT)}$, it suffices to show that on data $\mathbf{v}$, $\text{m\^ax}^{(L)} \leq \frac{\max(v_1, v_2)}{p_1 p_2}$, which is immediate from (11). □

$\text{m\^ax}^{(L)}$ **for** $r \geq 2$.

Expressing the estimator as a function of the determining vector of the outcome when entries are ordered in decreasing order (entries of $\mathbf{p}$ are permuted accordingly), we obtain that the estimator is a contiguous function of the form

$$\text{m\^ax}^{(L)}(v_1, v_2, \ldots, v_r) = \sum_{i \in [r]} \alpha_i v_i , \quad (12)$$

where the coefficients α_i depend on the permuted vector $\mathbf{p}$.

This is established inductively on the steps of the algorithm. It clearly holds for the determining vector $\mathbf{0}$, which has the estimate $\text{m\^ax}^{(L)} = 0$. When processing a vector $\mathbf{v}$ we consider all determining vectors that are different than $\mathbf{v}$ and have outcomes consistent with $\mathbf{v}$. The probability distribution over these vectors depends only on the relative order of entry values. Assuming the estimator is contiguous and has a linear form for preceding vectors, and substituting in line 13, the solution also has these properties. Because the estimator is contiguous, the coefficients obtained for determining vectors with all entries distinct holds for all determining vectors.

We conjecture that $\text{m\^ax}^{(L)}$ is monotone, nonnegative, and dominates $\text{m\^ax}^{(HT)}$. We verified these properties for $r \leq 4$ with uniform $\mathbf{p}$, using the following Lemma and explicit computation of the coefficients.

LEMMA 4.2. *To establish monotonicity, nonnegativity, and dominance of* $\text{m\^ax}^{(L)}$ *over* $\text{m\^ax}^{(HT)}$ *it suffices to show that* $\alpha_i < 0$ *for* $i > 1$ *and that* $\alpha_1 \leq 1/\prod_{i \in [r]} p_i$.

PROOF. By substituting $\mathbf{v}$ with all entries equal in (12) and using (10), we obtain $\sum_{i \in [r]} \alpha_i = 1/(1 - \prod_{i \in [r]}(1 - p_i))$. To establish monotonicity, consider two types of manipulations of a determining vector: increasing the maximum entries or decreasing an entry which is not the unique maximum one. Now, for any data $\mathbf{v}$ and outcomes $S_1 \subset S_2$, the determining vector of S_2 can be obtained from that of S_1 using such operations. For monotonicity, we need to show that the estimate value obtained for $\mathbf{v}$ on outcome

S_2 is at least that of S_1, equivalently, that these manipulations can only increase $\text{m\^ax}^{(L)}$. For the second manipulation, it suffices to show that $\alpha_i < 0$ for $i > 1$. For the first manipulation, we need to show that $\sum_{j=1}^{i} \alpha_j > 0$ for all $i \geq 1$. Since we know that $\sum_{i \in [r]} \alpha_i > 0$, this is implied by $\alpha_i < 0$ $i > 1$. Nonnegativity follows from monotonicity and the base case of estimate value 0 when there are no sampled entries.

To establish dominance over $\text{m\^ax}^{(HT)}$, given monotonicity, it suffices to show that $\alpha_1 \leq 1/\prod_{i \in [r]} p_i$. This means that all $\text{m\^ax}^{(L)}$ estimates on a given data vector $\mathbf{v}$ are at most $\frac{\max(\mathbf{v})}{\prod_{i \in [r]} p_i}$, which is the $\text{m\^ax}^{(HT)}$ estimate. The HT estimate has maximum variance amongst all unbiased estimators that assume values in the range $\left[0, \frac{\max(\mathbf{v})}{\prod_{i \in [r]} p_i}\right]$. Hence, $\text{VAR}[\text{m\^ax}^{(L)}] \leq \text{VAR}[\text{m\^ax}^{(HT)}]$. □

Uniform $\mathbf{p}$. When $p = p_1 = p_2 = \ldots = p_r$, the coefficients $\boldsymbol{\alpha}$ in (12) depend on p. We define the matrix P such that P_{ij} is the probability that the jth largest entry of the determining vector is equal to the ith largest entry in the data vector (assuming for the definition that values in the data vector are distinct).

If $j < i$, this is the probability that i is the largest sampled entry. If $j \geq i$, this is the probability that i is sampled, at least one entry $< i$ is sampled, and exactly $j - i$ entries $> i$ are not sampled or that i is the largest sampled entry and that there are at least $j - i$ of the $> i$ entries are not sampled.

To summarize,

	P_{ij}
$j < i$	$p(1-p)^{i-1}$
$j \geq i$	$p(1 - (1-p)^{i-1})\binom{r-i}{j-i}(1-p)^{j-i}p^{r-j} +$ $+ p(1-p)^{i-1}\sum_{h=j-i}^{r-i}\binom{r-i}{h}(1-p)^h p^{r-i-h}$

LEMMA 4.3. *The coefficients vector* $\boldsymbol{\alpha}$ *of the estimator is a solution of the system*

$$P\boldsymbol{\alpha} = (1, 0, 0 \ldots, 0)^T .$$

PROOF. Consider a data vector $\mathbf{v}$, with entries sorted to be in decreasing order. The unbiasedness constraint of the estimator when expressed in the form (12) is

$$v_1 = \sum_{i \in [r], j \in [r]} \alpha_j P_{ij} v_i . \quad (13)$$

(13) must hold for all vectors. Substituting $\mathbf{v} = (1, 0, 0 \ldots)$ we obtain the equation $\sum_{j \in [r]} \alpha_j P_{1j} = 1$. We next substitute $\mathbf{v} = (1, 1, 0 \ldots)$ in (13) and subtract the first equation, obtaining $\sum_{j \in [r]} \alpha_j P_{2j} = 0$. Similarly, we obtain that for all $h > 1$, $\sum_{j \in [r]} \alpha_j P_{hj} = 0$. Summarizing, we obtain the system $P\boldsymbol{\alpha} = (1, 0, 0 \ldots)^T$. □

The matrix P and coefficients $\boldsymbol{\alpha}$ for $r = 2, 3$ are

$$P = \begin{pmatrix} p & p(1-p) \\ p(1-p) & p \end{pmatrix}$$

$$\boldsymbol{\alpha} = \left(\frac{1}{p^2(2-p)}, -\frac{1-p}{p^2(2-p)} \right)$$

$$P = \begin{pmatrix} p & p(1-p^2) & p(1-p)^2 \\ p(1-p) & p(p^2+1-p) & 2p(1-p) \\ p(1-p)^2 & p(1-p)^2 & p \end{pmatrix}$$

$$\boldsymbol{\alpha} = \left(\frac{2 - 2p + p^2}{p^3(2-p)(3-3p+p^2)}, \right.$$
$$\left. -\frac{1-p}{p^3(3-3p+p^2)}, -\frac{(1-p)^2}{p^2(2-p)(3-3p+p^2)} \right)$$

4.2 Estimator $\hat{\mathrm{max}}^{(U)}$

We now seek a dominant estimator which favors "sparse" vectors, optimizing for the case where all "unseen" entries in the outcome are 0. The construction is guided by a partial order according to $L(\mathbf{v}) \equiv |\{j \in [r] | v_j > 0\}|$ (the number of positive entries). This order specifies a partition, where part U_h includes all vectors with $L(\mathbf{v}) = h$. We derive estimators for $r = 2$ while demonstrating issues with the different constructions.

U_0 contains only the vector $\mathbf{0}$. An outcome S is consistent with $\mathbf{0}$ if and only if $\forall i \in S, v_i = 0$ and we set $\hat{\mathrm{max}}^{(U)}(S) \leftarrow 0$. This setting must be the same for all nonnegative unbiased estimators.

As a first attempt, we extend the estimator using Algorithm 1. The determining vector of an outcome is obtained by substituting 0 values for all entries $i \notin S$. The estimator is invariant to the order in which vectors in U_1 are processed and we obtain the estimate $\hat{\mathrm{max}}^{(U)}(S) = v_i/p_i$ on all outcomes with one positive entry $v_i > 0$ amongst $i \in S$. It remains to process vectors U_2. The outcomes S' have $S = \{1, 2\}$ with $v_1, v_2 > 0$ and hence a determining vector with two positive entries. The estimate is the solution of the linear equation $p_1 p_2 \hat{\mathrm{max}}^{(U)}(S) + p_1(1-p_2)\frac{v_1}{p_1} + p_2(1-p_1)\frac{v_2}{p_2} = \max((v_1, v_2))$. The solution, $\frac{\max(v_1, v_2) - (1-p_1)v_2 - (1-p_2)v_1}{p_1 p_2}$, however, may be negative (e.g., when $v_1 = v_2$ and $p_1 + p_2 < 1$).

We next attempt to process the vectors U_1 sequentially while enforcing the nonnegativity constraints (8). Now the result is sensitive to the particular order of processing vectors in U_1: Suppose vectors of the form $(v_1, 0)$ are processed before vectors of the form $(0, v_2)$. The vector $(v_1, 0)$ is the determining vector of all outcomes with the first entry sampled. That is, all outcomes with both entry sampled and values are (v_1, v_2) and outcomes with only the first entry sampled and has value v_1. The probability of such outcome given data $(v_1, 0)$ is p_1. To minimize variance, we would like to set the estimate to v_1/p_1 on these outcomes, which we can do because this setting does not violate nonnegativity (8) for other vectors. We next process vectors of the form $(0, v_2)$. They are determining vectors for outcomes S'_1 with both entries sampled and values are $(0, v_2)$ and outcomes S'_2 with only the second entry sampled and value is v_2. The outcomes S'_1 are not consistent with any other data, and are not constrained by (8). The outcomes S'_2 are also consistent with data vectors with two positive entries (v'_1, v_2) and therefore we need to ensure that we do not violate (8) for these vectors. To minimize the variance on $(0, v_2)$, we seek $\hat{\mathrm{max}}(S_1) \geq \hat{\mathrm{max}}(S_2)$ with $\hat{\mathrm{max}}(S_2)$ being as large as possible without violating (8). Lastly, we process vectors with two positive entries. The outcomes determined by these vectors have both entries sampled and are not consistent with any other data vector. Summarizing, we obtain the estimator

Outcome S		$\hat{\mathrm{max}}^{(Uas)}(S)$
$S = \emptyset$	:	0
$S = \{1\}$	:	$\frac{v_1}{p_1}$
$S = \{2\}$	:	$\frac{v_2}{\max\{1-p_1, p_2\}}$
$S = \{1, 2\}$	:	$\frac{\max(v_1, v_2) - \frac{p_2(1-p_1)}{\max\{1-p_1, p_2\}} v_2 - (1-p_2)v_1}{p_1 p_2}$

This estimator is dominant and nonnegative, but is asymmetric: the estimate changes if the entries of $\mathbf{v}$ (and $\boldsymbol{p}$) are permuted.

To obtain a symmetric estimator, we apply Algorithm 2 processing U_1 and U_2 in batches, searching for a symmetric locally dominant estimator for U_1 and then for U_2. We obtain:

Outcome S		$\hat{\mathrm{max}}^{(U)}(S)$
$S = \emptyset$	:	0
$S = \{1\}$	:	$\frac{v_1}{p_1(1+\max\{0, 1-p_1-p_2\})}$
$S = \{2\}$	:	$\frac{v_2}{p_2(1+\max\{0, 1-p_1-p_2\})}$
$S = \{1, 2\}$	:	$\frac{\max(v_1, v_2) - \frac{v_1(1-p_2)+v_2(1-p_1)}{1+\max\{0, 1-p_1-p_2\}}}{p_1 p_2}$

The estimator $\hat{\mathrm{max}}^{(U)}$ dominates $\hat{\mathrm{max}}^{(HT)}$ – this is easy to see as $\hat{\mathrm{max}}^{(U)}$ for data (v_1, v_2) is always at most $\max(\mathbf{v})/(p_1 p_2)$.

Figure 2 shows the estimators $\hat{\mathrm{max}}^{(L)}$, $\hat{\mathrm{max}}^{(U)}$, and $\hat{\mathrm{max}}^{(HT)}$ and their variance for data vectors of the form $\mathbf{v} = (v_1, v_2)$ where each entry is sampled independently with probability $1/2$. The plot shows the ratios $\frac{\mathrm{VAR}[\hat{\mathrm{max}}^{(L)}]}{\mathrm{VAR}[\hat{\mathrm{max}}^{(HT)}]}$ and $\frac{\hat{\mathrm{max}}^{(U)}}{\mathrm{VAR}[\hat{\mathrm{max}}^{(HT)}]}$ as a function of $\min(v_1, v_2)/\max(v_1, v_2)$. We can see that $\hat{\mathrm{max}}^{(HT)}$ is dominated by $\hat{\mathrm{max}}^{(L)}$ and $\hat{\mathrm{max}}^{(U)}$ and that the two dominant estimators $\hat{\mathrm{max}}^{(L)}$ and $\hat{\mathrm{max}}^{(U)}$ are incomparable: on inputs where one of the values is 0, $\mathrm{VAR}[\hat{\mathrm{max}}^{(U)}] = \frac{3}{4} \max(\mathbf{v})^2$ whereas $\mathrm{VAR}[\hat{\mathrm{max}}^{(L)}] = (11/9) \max(\mathbf{v})^2$. On inputs where $v_1 = v_2$, $\mathrm{VAR}[\hat{\mathrm{max}}^{(L)}] = (1/3) \max(\mathbf{v})^2$ whereas $\mathrm{VAR}[\hat{\mathrm{max}}^{(U)}] = \frac{3}{4} \max(\mathbf{v})^2$.

4.3 Boolean OR

We now consider $\mathrm{OR}(\mathbf{v}) = v_1 \vee v_2 \vee \cdots \vee v_r$ over the domain $\mathbf{V} = \{0, 1\}^r$. The optimal inverse probability estimator is $\hat{\mathrm{OR}}^{(HT)} = 1/\prod_{i=1}^r p_i$ when $|S| = r$ and $\bigvee_{i \in S} v_i = 1$ and $\hat{\mathrm{OR}}^{(HT)} = 0$ otherwise. By specializing $\hat{\mathrm{max}}^{(L)}$ and $\hat{\mathrm{max}}^{(U)}$, we obtain the estimators $\hat{\mathrm{OR}}^{(L)}$ and $\hat{\mathrm{OR}}^{(U)}$, which turn out to be dominant as well. The estimator $\hat{\mathrm{OR}}^{(L)}$ is dominant because it can be obtained by applying Algorithm 1 using the order $\prec$ satisfying: $\forall \mathbf{v} \in V \setminus \{\mathbf{0}\}, \mathbf{0} \prec \mathbf{v}$ and for $\mathbf{v}, \mathbf{v}' \neq \mathbf{0}$,

$$\mathbf{v} \prec \mathbf{v}' \iff L(\mathbf{v}) < L(\mathbf{v}'),$$

where $L(\mathbf{v}) = |\{i | v_i = 0\}|$ is the number of zero entries in $\mathbf{v}$. The determining vector of an outcome S is obtained by setting, for $i \notin S$, $v_i \leftarrow \bigvee_{j \in S} v_j$. For $r = 2$, the estimator as a function of the determining vector is

$$\hat{\mathrm{OR}}^{(L)}(v_1, v_2) = \frac{\mathrm{OR}(v_1, v_2)}{p_1 p_2} - \frac{(1/p_2 - 1)v_1 + (1/p_1 - 1)v_2}{p_1 + p_2 - p_1 p_2}.$$

Similarly, $\hat{\mathrm{OR}}^{(U)}$ can be obtained by mimicking the derivation of $\hat{\mathrm{max}}^{(U)}$ on the binary domain.

The estimators $\hat{\mathrm{OR}}^{(HT)}$, $\hat{\mathrm{OR}}^{(L)}$, and $\hat{\mathrm{OR}}^{(U)}$ are always 0, and hence have zero variance, when $\mathbf{v} = \mathbf{0}$. When $\mathrm{OR}(\mathbf{v}) = 1$, using (1):

$$\mathrm{VAR}[\hat{\mathrm{OR}}^{(HT)}] = \frac{1}{\prod_{i \in [r]} p_i} - 1. \quad (14)$$

The estimate $\hat{\mathrm{OR}}^{(L)}$ on data vector $(1, 1)$ is $1/p$ with probability $p = p_1 + p_2 - p_1 p_2$ and 0 otherwise and hence, using (1):

$$\mathrm{VAR}[\hat{\mathrm{OR}}^{(L)}|(1, 1)] = \frac{1}{p_1 + p_2 - p_1 p_2} - 1. \quad (15)$$

The estimate for data vector $(1, 0)$ is 0 with probability $1 - p_1$ (entry 1 is not sampled), $\frac{1}{p_1 + p_2 - p_1 p_2}$ with probability $p_1(1 - p_2)$ ($S = \{1\}$) and $\frac{1}{p_1(p_1 + p_2 - p_1 p_2)}$ when $S = \{1, 2\}$. Therefore,

$$\mathrm{VAR}[\hat{\mathrm{OR}}^{(L)}|(1, 0)]$$
$$= (1 - p_1) + p_1(1 - p_2)\left(\frac{1}{p_1 + p_2 - p_1 p_2} - 1\right)^2$$
$$+ p_1 p_2 \left(\frac{1}{p_1(p_1 + p_2 - p_1 p_2)} - 1\right)^2$$

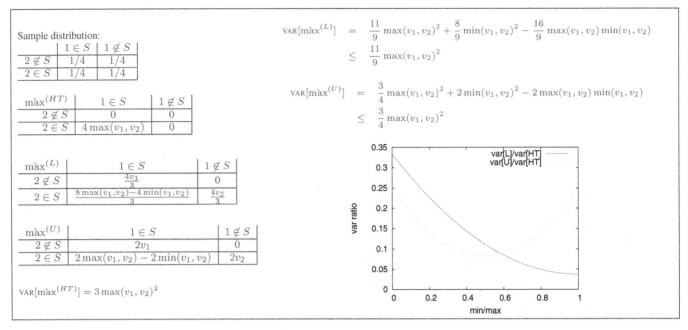

Figure 2: Estimators for $\max\{v_1, v_2\}$ **over Poisson samples (weight-oblivious) with** $p_1 = p_2 = 1/2$.

Figure 3 shows the variance of the estimators $\hat{OR}^{(HT)}$, $\hat{OR}^{(L)}$ and $\hat{OR}^{(U)}$ as a function of $p = p_1 = p_2$. The estimators $\hat{OR}^{(L)}$ and $\hat{OR}^{(U)}$ dominate $\hat{OR}^{(HT)}$. The estimator $\hat{OR}^{(L)}$ has minimum variance on $(1,1)$ and $\hat{OR}^{(U)}$ is the symmetric estimator with minimum variance on $(1,0)$ and $(0,1)$ (over all nonnegative unbiased estimators).

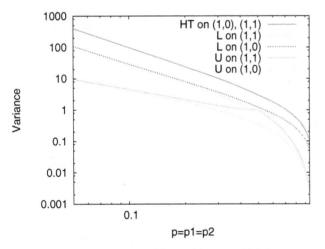

Figure 3: Variance of $\hat{OR}^{(HT)}$, $\hat{OR}^{(L)}$ **and** $\hat{OR}^{(U)}$ **when** $p_1 = p_2 = p$, **on data vectors** $(1,1)$ **and** $(1,0)$, **as a function of** p.

Asymptotically, when $p \rightarrow 0$, $\text{VAR}[\hat{OR}^{(HT)}] \approx 1/p^2$ for data vectors $(1,0)$, $(0,1)$, and $(1,1)$. $\text{VAR}[\hat{OR}^{(L)}]$, $\text{VAR}[\hat{OR}^{(U)}] \approx 1/(4p^2)$ for data $(1,0)$ and $(0,1)$ and $\text{VAR}[\hat{OR}^{(L)}]$, $\text{VAR}[\hat{OR}^{(U)}] \approx 1/(2p)$ for data $(1,1)$. This means that for data $(1,1)$ ("no change"), variance is the square root of half of the variance of $\hat{OR}^{(HT)}$. For data $(1,0)$ or $(0,1)$ ("change") variance is $1/4$ of the variance of $\hat{OR}^{(HT)}$.

5. POISSON: WEIGHTED, KNOWN SEEDS

We turn our attention to weighted Poisson sampling with known seeds, starting with binary domains and estimating OR and then consider estimators for max over the nonnegative reals.

For the purpose of deriving estimators over *binary domains* ($\mathbf{V} = \{0,1\}^r$), Poisson weighted sampling with known seeds is equivalent to Poisson weight-oblivious sampling (Section 4). This relation holds only for binary domains and is established through a 1-1 mapping between outcomes in terms of the information we can glean from the outcome.

The sample distribution of weighted sampling over binary domains is as follows: there is a seed vector $\mathbf{u} \in [0,1]^r$ where u_i are independent and selected uniformly at random from the interval $[0,1]$. Defining $p \in [0,1]^r$ such that $p_i = \text{PR}[\tau_i \leq 1]$,

$$i \in S \iff v_i = 1 \wedge u_i \leq p_i .$$

p_i is the probability that the ith entry is sampled if $v_i = 1$. The entry is never sampled if $v_i = 0$ but since we know $\mathbf{u}$, if $u_i \leq p_i$ and $i \notin S$ we know that $v_i = 0$.

We now map an outcome S of weighted sampling with known seeds to outcome S' of weight-oblivious sampling with vector p

$$
\begin{aligned}
i \in S &\iff i \in S' \text{ and } v_i = 1 \\
i \notin S \text{ and } u_i \leq p_i &\iff i \in S' \text{ and } v_i = 0 \\
i \notin S \text{ and } u_i > p_i &\iff i \notin S' .
\end{aligned}
$$

It is easy to see that $\text{PR}[S] = \text{PR}[S']$ and that $V^*(S) \equiv V^*(S')$.

Observe that the weighted sample S is smaller than the corresponding weight-oblivious one S' since entries with 0 values are not represented in the sample. Knowledge of seeds, however, compensates for this. We use knowledge of the seeds in a more elaborate way in the (significantly more involved) derivations of estimators for $\max(\mathbf{v})$.

5.1 Boolean OR

We state the estimators $\hat{OR}^{(HT)}$, $\hat{OR}^{(L)}$, and $\hat{OR}^{(U)}$ by mapping the respective estimators obtained in the weight-oblivious setting (Section 4.3).

The optimal inverse-probability estimator uses the set of outcomes $\mathcal{S}^*$ such that $\forall i \in [r], u_i \leq p_i$. This corresponds to $S = [r]$ in the weight-oblivious setting. If $\forall i \in [r], u_i \leq p_i$ and $\text{OR}(\mathbf{v}) = 1$, $\hat{\text{OR}}^{(HT)} = 1/\prod_{i \in [r]} p_i$. Otherwise, $\hat{\text{OR}}^{(HT)} = 0$.

Estimator $\hat{\text{OR}}^{(L)}$.

Outcome S		$\hat{\text{OR}}^{(L)}$
$S = \emptyset$	:	0
$(S = \{1\} \wedge u_2 > p_2) \vee$		
$(S = \{2\} \wedge u_1 > p_1) \vee$		
$S = \{1, 2\}$	:	$\frac{1}{p_1 + p_2 - p_1 p_2}$
$S = \{1\} \wedge u_2 \leq p_2$	:	$\frac{1}{p_1(p_1 + p_2 - p_1 p_2)}$
$S = \{2\} \wedge u_1 \leq p_1$	:	$\frac{1}{p_2(p_1 + p_2 - p_1 p_2)}$

Estimator $\hat{\text{OR}}^{(U)}$.

Outcome S		$\hat{\text{OR}}^{(U)}$
$S = \emptyset$	:	0
$S = \{1\} \wedge u_2 > p_2$	:	$\frac{1}{p_1(1 + \max\{0, 1 - p_1 - p_2\})}$
$S = \{2\} \wedge u_1 > p_1$	:	$\frac{1}{p_2(1 + \max\{0, 1 - p_1 - p_2\})}$
Else	:	$\frac{1 - \frac{v_1(1-p_2) + v_2(1-p_1)}{1 + \max\{0, 1 - p_1 - p_2\}}}{p_1 p_2}$

Section 4.3 (and Figure 3) shows the performance of these estimators. In applications where a binary instance designates a set (a key is a member if and only if value is 1), a sum aggregate using the OR primitive is the size of the union of the sets. We can therefore apply these estimators to estimate the size of the union of sampled sets, when the sampling of each sets is Poisson or bottom-k with known seeds and sets are independently sampled. Variance is smaller when an item is a member of both sets, and thus the variance of the union estimate depends on the Jaccard coefficient – the more similar the sets, the smaller is the variance of the union estimate. Figure 4 shows the sample size s as a function of the input size n for a coefficient of variation $cv = 0.1$ when estimating the size of the union of two sets of size n with Jaccard similarity J using $\text{OR}^{(HT)}$ and $\text{OR}^{(L)}$, demonstrating significant improvements over the HT estimator.

5.2 Maximum over nonnegative reals

We study estimating max under Poisson IPPS weighted sampling. The seed vector $\mathbf{u} \in [0,1]^r$ has entries drawn independently and uniformly from $[0,1]$. $\boldsymbol{\tau}^*$ is a fixed vector and an entry i is included in S iff $v_i \geq u_i \tau_i^*$, that is, with probability $\min\{1, v_i/\tau_i^*\}$.

Recall that both $\boldsymbol{\tau}^*$ and the seed vector $\mathbf{u}$ are available to the estimator. Therefore, when $i \notin S$, we know that $v_i < u_i \tau_i^*$.

Estimator $\hat{\text{max}}^{(HT)}$ [12, 13]

Consider the set of outcomes $\mathcal{S}^*$ such that

$$S \in \mathcal{S}^* \iff \max_{i \notin S} u_i \tau_i^* \leq \max_{i \in S} v_i .$$

This set includes all outcomes from which $\max(\mathbf{v})$ can be determined: For $S \in \mathcal{S}^*$, $\max(\mathbf{v}) = \max_{i \in S} v_i$. For any data vector $\mathbf{v}$, the probability that the outcome is in $\mathcal{S}^*$

$$\text{PR}[\mathcal{S}^* | \mathbf{v}] = \prod_{i \in [r]} \min\{1, \frac{\max_{i \in S} v_i}{\tau_i^*}\} ,$$

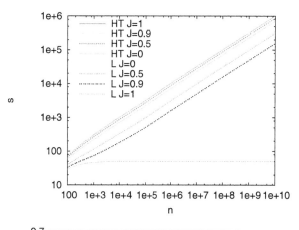

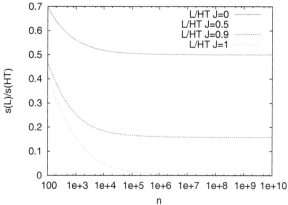

Figure 4: Required sample size s as a function of the instance size n for coefficient of variation $cv = 0.1$ when estimating union of two sets I_1, I_2 using $\text{OR}^{(HT)}$ and $\text{OR}^{(L)}$ where each set is sampled using bottom-k or Bernoulli sampling with known seeds and $J = |I_1 \cap I_2|/|I_1 \cup I_2|$ is the Jaccard coefficient.

can be computed from the outcome, for any outcome in $\mathcal{S}^*$. The inverse-probability estimator is therefore:

$$\hat{\text{max}}^{(HT)} = \begin{cases} \max_{i \notin S} u_i \tau_i^* \leq \max_{i \in S} v_i & : \frac{\max_{i \in S} v_i}{\prod_{i \in [r]} \min\left\{1, \frac{\max_{i \in S} v_i}{\tau_i^*}\right\}} \\ \text{otherwise} & : 0 \end{cases}$$

This is the optimal inverse-probability estimator since $\mathcal{S}^*$ is the most inclusive set possible.

Estimator $\hat{\text{max}}^{(L)}$

We apply Algorithm 1 using a partial order $\prec$ with $\mathbf{0}$ preceding all other vectors, and otherwise the order corresponds to an increasing lexicographic order on the lists $L(\mathbf{v})$ that is the sorted multiset of differences $\{\max(\mathbf{v}) - v_i | i \in [r]\}$.

The determining vector $\mathbf{v}' = \min_{\prec} V^*(S)$ of an outcome S is $\mathbf{0}$ if $S = \emptyset$. For an outcome S, $V^*(S)$ contains all vectors with v_h as in S for $h \in S$ and $v_h \leq u_h \tau_h^*$ otherwise. Therefore, $v'_h = v_h$ if $h \in S$ then and $v'_h = \min\{\max_{i \in S} v_i, u_h \tau_h^*\}$ if $h \notin S$.

The estimator $\hat{\text{max}}^{(L)}$ for $r = 2$ is presented in Figure 5 using two tables. The first table shows a mapping of outcomes to determining vectors, the second states the estimator as a function of the determining vector. See Appendix for an outline of the derivation. Monotonicity can be easily verified for $r = 2$ and is conjectured

outcome S	determining vector $\mathbf{v}' = \min_{\prec} V^*(S)$	
	v_1'	v_2'
$S = \emptyset$:	0	0
$S = \{1\}$:	v_1	$\min\{u_2 \tau_2^*, v_1\}$
$S = \{2\}$:	$\min\{u_1 \tau_1^*, v_2\}$	v_2
$S = \{1,2\}$:	v_1	v_2

$\mathbf{v} = (v_1, v_2),\ v_1 \geq v_2$	$\widehat{\mathrm{max}}^{(L)}(\mathbf{v})$
$\mathbf{v} = (0,0)$:	0
$v_1 \geq v_2 \geq \tau_2^*$:	$v_2 + \dfrac{v_1 - v_2}{\min\{1, \frac{v_1}{\tau_1^*}\}}$
$v_1 \geq \tau_1^*,\ v_2 \leq \min\{\tau_2^*, v_1\}$:	v_1
$v_2 \leq v_1 \leq \min\{\tau_1^*, \tau_2^*\}$:	$\dfrac{\tau_1^* \tau_2^*}{\tau_1^* + \tau_2^* - v_1} + \dfrac{\tau_1^* \tau_2^* (\tau_1^* - v_1)}{v_1(\tau_1^* + \tau_2^*)} \ln\left(\dfrac{(\tau_1^* + \tau_2^* - v_2)v_1}{v_2(\tau_1^* + \tau_2^* - v_1)}\right) + \dfrac{(v_1 - v_2)\tau_1^* \tau_2^* (\tau_1^* - v_1)}{v_1(\tau_1^* + \tau_2^* - v_2)(\tau_1^* + \tau_2^* - v_1)}$
$v_2 \leq \tau_2^* \leq v_1 \leq \tau_1^*$:	$\tau_1^* + \tau_2^* - \dfrac{\tau_1^* \tau_2^*}{v_1} + \dfrac{(\tau_1^* \tau_2^*)(\tau_1^* - v_1)}{v_1(\tau_1^* + \tau_2^*)} \ln\left(\dfrac{(\tau_1^* + \tau_2^* - v_2)\tau_1^*}{\tau_2^*(\tau_1^* + \tau_2^* - v_1)}\right) + \dfrac{\tau_2^* (\tau_1^* - v_1)(\tau_2^* - v_2)}{(\tau_1^* + \tau_2^* - v_2)v_1}$

Figure 5: Estimator $\widehat{\mathrm{max}}^{(L)}$. The top table maps each outcome S to the determining data vector of S. The bottom table presents the estimator as a function of the determining data vector $\mathbf{v}$ with $v_1 \geq v_2$. The symmetric expressions when $v_2 \geq v_1$ are omitted.

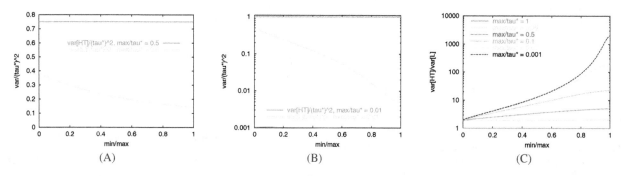

(A) (B) (C)

Figure 6: Estimators $\widehat{\mathrm{max}}^{(L)}$ and $\widehat{\mathrm{max}}^{(HT)}$ for two independent ipps samples with $\tau_1^* = \tau_2^* = \tau^*$. (A) and (B) show the normalized variance $(\mathrm{VAR}[\widehat{\mathrm{max}}]/(\tau^*)^2$ for $\rho = \max(v_1, v_2)/\tau^* \in \{0.01, 0.5\}$, as a function of $\min(v_1, v_2)/\max(v_1, v_2)$. (C) shows the variance ratio $\mathrm{VAR}[\widehat{\mathrm{max}}^{(HT)}]/\mathrm{VAR}[\widehat{\mathrm{max}}^{(L)}]$ as a function of $\min(v_1, v_2)/\max(v_1, v_2)$ for different values of ρ.

for $r > 2$. The estimator has bounded variance. Figure 6 illustrates the relation between $\mathrm{VAR}[\widehat{\mathrm{max}}^{(L)}]$ and $\mathrm{VAR}[\widehat{\mathrm{max}}^{(HT)}]$ when $\tau_1^* = \tau_2^* = \tau^*$. The estimator $\widehat{\mathrm{max}}^{(L)}$ dominates $\widehat{\mathrm{max}}^{(HT)}$. We show the variance (divided by $(\tau^*)^2$) as a function of the ratio $\min(\mathbf{v})/\max(\mathbf{v})$. When $\max(\mathbf{v}) \geq \tau^*$ or $\mathbf{v} = \mathbf{0}$, $\mathrm{VAR}[\widehat{\mathrm{max}}^{(HT)}|\mathbf{v}] = \mathrm{VAR}[\widehat{\mathrm{max}}^{(L)}|\mathbf{v}] = 0$, and these are the only cases where there is no advantage to $\widehat{\mathrm{max}}^{(L)}$ over $\widehat{\mathrm{max}}^{(HT)}$. In all other cases,

$$\frac{\mathrm{VAR}[\widehat{\mathrm{max}}^{(HT)}|\mathbf{v}]}{\mathrm{VAR}[\widehat{\mathrm{max}}^{(L)}|\mathbf{v}]} \geq \frac{1+\rho}{\rho} \geq 2 ,$$

where $\rho = \max(\mathbf{v})/\tau^*$. The variance ratio is at least 2 and asymptotically $O(1/\rho)$ when ρ is small. Fixing ρ, the inverse-probability weight is positive with probability $p = \left(\frac{\max(\mathbf{v})}{\tau^*}\right)^2 = \rho^2$. Hence, $\frac{\mathrm{VAR}[\widehat{\mathrm{max}}^{(HT)}|\mathbf{v}]}{(\tau^*)^2} = \rho^2(1/p - 1) = 1 - \rho^2$ and is independent of $\min(\mathbf{v})$. The variance $\mathrm{VAR}[\widehat{\mathrm{max}}^{(L)}]$ increases with $\min(\mathbf{v})$. For a fixed ρ, it is minimized when $\min(\mathbf{v}) = 0$ and is maximized when $\min(\mathbf{v}) = \max(\mathbf{v})$ ($\mathbf{v} = (\rho\tau^*, \rho\tau^*)$), where

$$\frac{\mathrm{VAR}[\widehat{\mathrm{max}}^{(L)}|(\rho\tau^*, \rho\tau^*)]}{(\tau^*)^2} = \rho^2(1/\rho - 1) = \rho - \rho^2 .$$

The maximum variance ratio (realized when $\mathbf{v} = (\rho\tau^*, \rho\tau^*)$) is accordingly

$$\frac{\mathrm{VAR}[\widehat{\mathrm{max}}^{(HT)}]}{\mathrm{VAR}[\widehat{\mathrm{max}}^{(L)}]} = \frac{1 - \rho^2}{\rho - \rho^2} = \frac{1 + \rho}{\rho} .$$

The variance ratio $\mathrm{VAR}[\widehat{\mathrm{max}}^{(L)}]/\mathrm{VAR}[\widehat{\mathrm{max}}^{(HT)}]$ is smaller when entry values are closer and with higher sampling rates (larger τ^*).

Figure 7 shows an application of $\widehat{\mathrm{max}}^{(L)}$ and $\widehat{\mathrm{max}}^{(HT)}$ to estimate $\sum \max$ of two instances that are independently sampled using Poisson IPPS with known seeds (results are the same for priority sampling). Each instance corresponds to an hour of IP traffic containing approximately 2.45×10^4 distinct destination IP addresses (keys) each, with a total of 3.8×10^4 distinct destinations. The value associated with each destination in each instance was the number of IP flows to that destination. The total number of flows in each instance was approximately 5.5×10^5 and the sum of the maximum values was 7.47×10^5. The figure shows the normalized variance $\frac{\mathrm{VAR}[\sum \widehat{\mathrm{max}}]}{(\sum \max)^2} \equiv \frac{\sum \mathrm{VAR}[\widehat{\mathrm{max}}]}{(\sum \max)^2}$ as a function of percentage of sampled keys. The ratio $\frac{\mathrm{VAR}[\sum \widehat{\mathrm{max}}^{(HT)}]}{\mathrm{VAR}[\sum \widehat{\mathrm{max}}^{(L)}]}$ varied from 2.45 to 2.7.

6. POISSON: WEIGHTED, UNKNOWN SEEDS

We show that when seeds are not available to the estimator, it is not possible to obtain a nonnegative unbiased estimator for $\ell^{\text{th}}(\mathbf{v})$ where $\ell < r$ with weighted Poisson sampling. This also holds over binary domains and for estimating OR in particular.

This result completes the picture on existence of nonnegative unbiased quantile estimators under Poisson sampling. Inverse-probability weight estimators exist when sampling is weight-oblivious (Section 4), when weighted and seeds are known ([12, 13] and Section 5) and when weighted with unknown seeds for estimating min

22

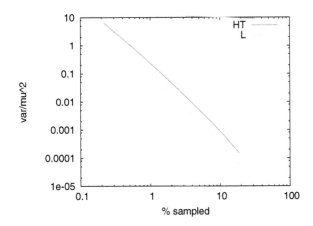

Figure 7: Variance (normalized) for estimating max **dominance using the** HT **and L estimators over two independently-sampled instances with known seeds (Poisson IPPS or priority sampling).**

$(\ell = r)$ (we obtain inverse-probability weights with respect to $\mathcal{S}^*$ that includes all outcomes with $S = [r]$).

THEOREM 6.1. *For any $\ell < r$, there is no unbiased nonnegative estimator for $\ell^{\text{th}}(\mathbf{v})$ over independent weighted samples with unknown seeds.*

PROOF. Recall that with weighted sampling, an entry where $v_i = 0$ is never sampled. As seeds are not available, we do not have any information from the outcome on values of entries that are not sampled. Therefore, the set $V^*(S)$ of data vectors consistent with S includes all vectors in $\mathbf{V}$ that agree with S on sampled entries.

We first establish the claim for $r = 2$. Since our arguments use values restricted to $\{0, 1\}$, they also hold for $\text{OR}(v_1, v_2)$. Let p_i be the inclusion probability of entry i when $v_i = 1$. We show that when $p_1 + p_2 < 1$, there is no unbiased estimator that is simultaneously correct for the four data vectors $(1, 1), (1, 0), (0, 1), (0, 0)$.

On outcome $S = \emptyset$, we must have $\hat{\text{OR}}(S) \equiv 0$ to ensure nonnegative estimates on data $(0, 0)$. When $S = \{i\}$ ($v_i = 1$) the estimator must have expected value $1/p_i$ in order to be unbiased for $(1, 0)$ or $(0, 1)$. When the data is $(1, 1)$, the contribution to the expectation from outcomes with exactly one sampled entry is $p_1(1 - p_2)/p_1 + p_2(1 - p_1)/p_2 = 2 - p_1 - p_2 > 1$. In order to be unbiased, the estimator must have negative expectation on outcome $S = \{1, 2\}$, which contradicts nonnegativity.

Lastly, we extend the argument for $\ell^{\text{th}}(\mathbf{v})$ and general r. We consider the four data vectors where $v_3 = \cdots = v_{\ell+1} = 1$, $v_{\ell+2} = \cdots = v_r = 0$, and $(v_1, v_2) \in \{0, 1\}^2$. Let $p_i > 0$ be the sampling probability of entry i when $v_i = 1$ and assume that $p_1 + p_2 < 1$. On these vectors, $\ell^{\text{th}}(\mathbf{v}) = \text{OR}(v_1, v_2)$. if neither 1 or 2 are sampled, we have $\ell - 1$ positive sampled entries and the estimate must be 0. On outcomes with exactly one $i \in \{1, 2\}$ sampled, the expectation of the estimator must be $\frac{1}{p_i \prod_{h=3}^{\ell+1} p_h}$ to be unbiased for data vectors $(v_1, v_2) = (1, 0), (0, 1)$. The contribution of the estimator from these outcomes for data with $v_1 = v_2 = 1$ is $\frac{2 - p_1 - p_2}{\prod_{h=3}^{\ell+1} p_h} > 1$, a contradiction. $\square$

Conclusion

Our work laid the foundations for deriving optimal estimators for queries spanning multiple sampled instances. We demonstrated

significant improvements over existing estimators for example queries over common sampling schemes. We plan to explore in detail further applications to coordinated samples and L_p distance queries. In the longer run, we hope that sometimes tedious derivations can be replaced by automated tools.

Another contribution of our work is highlighting the benefit of *reproducible randomization* when the independent weighted samples we collect might be used post hoc for estimates of multi-instance queries. Reproducible randomization is achieved through random hash functions and makes the randomization used for sampling available to the estimator applied to the sample. We demonstrated that this provides critical information on values that are not sampled and facilitates better estimators. While reproducible randomization was extensively used as a means to coordinate samples, we believe that its value to enhance the usefulness of independent weighted samples was not previously properly understood.

7. REFERENCES

[1] K. S. Beyer, P. J. Haas, B. Reinwald, Y. Sismanis, and R. Gemulla. On synopses for distinct-value estimation under multiset operations. In *ACM SIGMOD*, 2007.

[2] K. R. W. Brewer, L. J. Early, and S. F. Joyce. Selecting several samples from a single population. *Australian J. of Statistics*, 14(3):231–239, 1972.

[3] A. Z. Broder. On the resemblance and containment of documents. In *IEEE Compression and Complexity of Sequences*, 1997.

[4] A. Z. Broder. Identifying and filtering near-duplicate documents. In *Proc. of the 11th Ann. Symp. on Combinatorial Pattern Matching*, *LLNCS* vol 1848, pages 1–10. Springer, 2000.

[5] M. T. Chao. A general purpose unequal probability sampling plan. *Biometrika*, 69(3):653–656, 1982.

[6] M. S. Charikar. Similarity estimation techniques from rounding algorithms. In *ACM STOC*. 2002.

[7] E. Cohen. Size-estimation framework with applications to transitive closure and reachability. *J. Comput. System Sci.*, 55:441–453, 1997.

[8] E. Cohen, N. Duffield, H. Kaplan, C. Lund, and M. Thorup. Stream sampling for variance-optimal estimation of subset sums. In *ACM-SIAM SODA*. 2009.

[9] E. Cohen and H. Kaplan. Summarizing data using bottom-k sketches. In *ACM PODC'*, 2007.

[10] E. Cohen and H. Kaplan. Tighter estimation using bottom-k sketches. In *VLDB*, 2008.

[11] E. Cohen and H. Kaplan. Leveraging discarded samples for tighter estimation of multiple-set aggregates. In *ACM SIGMETRICS*, 2009.

[12] E. Cohen, H. Kaplan, and S. Sen. Coordinated weighted sampling for estimating aggregates over multiple weight assignments. *VLDB*, 2009.

[13] E. Cohen, H. Kaplan, and S. Sen. Coordinated weighted sampling for estimating aggregates over multiple weight assignments. arXiv:0906.4560, 2009.

[14] G. Cormode and S. Muthukrishnan. Estimating dominance norms of multiple data streams. In *ESA*. Springer-Verlag, 2003.

[15] G. Cormode and S. Muthukrishnan. What's new: finding significant differences in network data streams. *IEEE/ACM Tran. on Networking*, 13(6):1219–1232, 2005.

[16] T. Dasu, T. Johnson, S. Muthukrishnan, and V. Shkapenyuk. Mining database structure; or, how to build a data quality browser. In *ACM SIGMOD*, 2002.

[17] N. Duffield, M. Thorup, and C. Lund. Priority sampling for estimating arbitrary subset sums. *J. ACM*, 54(6), 2007.

[18] P. Gibbons and S. Tirthapura. Estimating simple functions on the union of data streams. In *ACM SPAA*. 2001.

[19] P. B. Gibbons. Distinct sampling for highly-accurate answers to distinct values queries and event reports. In *VLDB*, 2001.

[20] M. Hadjieleftheriou, X. Yu, N. Koudas, and D. Srivastava. Hashed samples: Selectivity estimators for set similarity selection queries. In *VLDB*, 2008.

[21] D. G. Horvitz and D. J. Thompson. A generalization of sampling without replacement from a finite universe. *J. of the American Stat. Assoc.*, 47(260):663–685, 1952.

[22] D.E. Knuth. *The Art of Computer Programming, Vol. 2: Seminumerical Algorithms.* Addison-Wesley, 1969.

[23] B. Krishnamurthy, S. Sen, Y. Zhang, and Y. Chen. Sketch-based change detection: Methods, evaluation, and applications. In *ACM IMC*, 2003.

[24] E. Ohlsson. Coordination of pps samples over time. In *Int. Conf. on Establishment Surveys*, pages 255–264. American Stat. Assoc., 2000.

[25] B. Rosén. Asymptotic theory for order sampling. *J. Statistical Planning and Inference*, 62(2):135–158, 1997.

[26] P. J. Saavedra. Fixed sample size pps approximations with a permanent random number. In *Proc. of the Section on Survey Research Methods*, pages 697–700. American Stat. Assoc., 1995.

[27] M. Szegedy. The DLT priority sampling is essentially optimal. In *ACM STOC*. 2006.

[28] J.S. Vitter. Random sampling with a reservoir. *ACM Trans. Math. Softw.*, 11(1):37–57, 1985.

APPENDIX

$\hat{\max}^{(L)}$ for independent weighted samples with known seeds

The minimum element of $\prec$ is $\mathbf{0}$, and hence $\mathbf{0}$ is the determining vector of all outcomes consistent with $\mathbf{0}$, which are all outcomes with $S = \emptyset$. Hence, on empty outcomes, $\hat{\max}^{(L)}(S) = 0$. We next process vectors with two equal entries (v, v). The outcomes determined by (v, v) are: $S = \{1, 2\}$ and $v_1 = v_2 = v$, $S = \{1\}$ $v_1 = v$, and $u_2 \geq v_1/\tau_2^*$, or $S = \{2\}$, $v_2 = v$, and $u_1 \geq v_2/\tau_1^*$. That is, outcomes where both entries are sampled and have the same value v or when exactly one entry is sampled, its value is v, and the upper bound on the value of the other entry is at least v. The probability of an outcome determined by (v, v) for data (v, v) is $\min\{1, \frac{v}{\tau_1^*}\} + (1 - \min\{1, \frac{v}{\tau_1^*}\}) \min\{1, \frac{v}{\tau_2^*}\}$. The estimate is therefore

$$\hat{\max}^{(L)}(v, v) = \frac{v}{\min\{1, \frac{v}{\tau_1^*}\} + (1 - \min\{1, \frac{v}{\tau_1^*}\}) \min\{1, \frac{v}{\tau_2^*}\}} . \quad (16)$$

It remains to define the estimator on outcomes that are consistent with data vectors with two different valued entries and not consistent with data vectors with two identical entries: When $|S| = 2$ and $v_1 \neq v_2$, when $S = \{1\}$ and $u_2\tau_2^* < v_1$ or when $S = \{2\}$ and $u_1\tau_1^* < v_2$. We formulate a system of equations relating the estimate value for determining vectors of the form $(v, v - \Delta)$ $(\Delta \geq 0)$ to the estimate value on determining vectors of the same form and smaller values of Δ. The case of determining vectors of the form $(v - \Delta, v)$ is symmetric.

case: $v - \Delta \geq \tau_2^*$: Outcomes consistent with $(v, v - \Delta)$ are $S = \{1, 2\}$, in which case the determining vector is $(v, v - \Delta)$, or $S = \{2\}$ and $u_1\tau_1^* > v \geq v - \Delta$, in which case the determining vector is $(v - \Delta, v - \Delta)$. The probability of $S = \{1, 2\}$ when the data is $(v, v - \Delta)$ is $\min\{1, \frac{v}{\tau_1^*}\}$. The probability of $S = \{2\}$ is $1 - \min\{1, \frac{v}{\tau_1^*}\}$. From Line 13

$$v = \hat{\max}^{(L)}(v, v - \Delta) \min\{1, \frac{v}{\tau_1^*}\} + $$
$$\hat{\max}^{(L)}(v - \Delta, v - \Delta)(1 - \min\{1, \frac{v}{\tau_1^*}\}) .$$

Using (16), $\hat{\max}^{(L)}(v - \Delta, v - \Delta) = v - \Delta$: Substituting and solving for $\hat{\max}^{(L)}(v, v - \Delta)$ we obtain

$$\hat{\max}^{(L)}(v, v - \Delta) = v - \Delta + \frac{\Delta}{\min\{1, \frac{v}{\tau_1^*}\}} . \quad (17)$$

case: $v \geq \tau_1^*$: Outcomes consistent with data $(v, v - \Delta)$ have $S = \{1, 2\}$ or $S = \{1\}$. Outcomes with $S = \{1, 2\}$ have determining vector $(v, v - \Delta)$ and probability $\min\{1, \frac{v - \Delta}{\tau^*}\}$. Outcomes with $S = \{1\}$ and $u_2\tau_2^* \geq v$ have determining vector (v, v), estimate value v (using (16)), and probability $(1 - \min\{1, \frac{v}{\tau_2^*}\})$. Outcomes with $S = \{1\}$ and $v - \Delta \leq u_2\tau_2^* \leq v$ have determining vector $(v, u_2\tau_2^*)$, and probability $\frac{\min\{\tau_2^*, v\} - v + \Delta}{\tau_2^*}$.

The equation in Line 13 is

$$v = \hat{\max}^{(L)}(v, v)(1 - \min\{1, \frac{v}{\tau_2^*}\}) + $$
$$\frac{1}{\tau_2^*} \int_{v - \Delta}^{\min\{v, \tau_2^*\}} \hat{\max}^{(L)}(v, y) dy + $$
$$\min\{1, \frac{v - \Delta}{\tau_2^*}\} \hat{\max}^{(L)}(v, v - \Delta) .$$

Substituting $\hat{\max}^{(L)}(v, v) = v$, we obtain that $\hat{\max}^{(L)}(v, y) = v$ for all $0 \leq y \leq v$ is a solution.

case: $\tau_2^* > v - \Delta$, $\tau_1^* > v$

$$v = \hat{\max}^{(L)}(v, v - \Delta) \frac{v}{\tau_1^*} \frac{v - \Delta}{\tau_2^*} + \quad (18)$$
$$\hat{\max}^{(L)}(v, v) \frac{v}{\tau_1^*} (1 - \min\{1, \frac{v}{\tau_2^*}\}) + $$
$$\hat{\max}^{(L)}(v - \Delta, v - \Delta)(1 - \frac{v}{\tau_1^*}) \frac{v - \Delta}{\tau_2^*} + $$
$$\frac{v}{\tau_1^*} \frac{1}{\tau_2^*} \int_{v - \Delta}^{\min\{v, \tau_2^*\}} \hat{\max}^{(L)}(v, y) dy + $$

The first term is for outcomes with $S = \{1, 2\}$. The determining vector is $(v, v - \Delta)$ and the probability given data vector $(v, v - \Delta)$ is $\frac{v}{\tau_1^*} \frac{v - \Delta}{\tau_2^*}$. The second is when $S = \{1\}$ and $u_2\tau_2^* \geq v$, that is, the upper bound on v_2 is at least v. The determining vector of these outcomes is (v, v). The third is when $S = \{2\}$ and $u_1\tau_1^* \geq v$, that is, the upper bound on the first entry is at least v. The determining vector of these outcomes is $(v - \Delta, v - \Delta)$. The fourth is when $S = \{1\}$ and the upper bound on the second entry is $y \in [v - \Delta, \min\{v, \tau_2^*\}]$. The determining vector is v, y. The second term is zero if $\tau_2^* < v$. To solve, we apply (16) and obtain an integral equation for the estimator. For the subcase $\tau_1^*, \tau_2^* \geq v$:

$$v = \hat{\max}^{(L)}(v, v - \Delta) \frac{v(v - \Delta)}{\tau_1^*\tau_2^*} + $$
$$\frac{v(\tau_2^* - v)}{\tau_1^* + \tau_2^* - v} + \frac{(\tau_1^* - v)(v - \Delta)}{\tau_1^* + \tau_2^* - v + \Delta} + $$
$$\frac{v}{\tau_1^*\tau_2^*} \int_{v - \Delta}^{v} \hat{\max}^{(L)}(v, y) dy$$

And for subcase $\tau_1^* > v > \tau_2^* > v - \Delta$:

$$v = \hat{\max}^{(L)}(v, v - \Delta) \frac{v(v - \Delta)}{\tau_1^*\tau_2^*} + $$
$$\frac{(\tau_1^* - v)(v - \Delta)}{\tau_1^* + \tau_2^* - v + \Delta} + \frac{v}{\tau_1^*\tau_2^*} \int_{v - \Delta}^{\tau_2^*} \hat{\max}^{(L)}(v, y) dy + $$
$$(\tau_1^* + \tau_2^* - \frac{\tau_1^*\tau_2^*}{v}) \frac{v - \tau_2^*}{\tau_2^*}$$

To solve we take a partial derivative with respect to Δ and obtain an expression for $\frac{\partial \hat{\max}^{(L)}(v, v - \Delta)}{\partial \Delta}$. We integrate and use the boundary values $\hat{\max}^{(L)}(v, v)$ and $\hat{\max}^{(L)}(v, \tau_2^*)$ respectively in the two subcases. The estimator is provided in Figure 5. Details will be provided in the full version.

FIFO Indexes for Decomposable Problems

Cheng Sheng
CUHK
Hong Kong
csheng@cse.cuhk.edu.hk

Yufei Tao
CUHK
Hong Kong
taoyf@cse.cuhk.edu.hk

ABSTRACT

This paper studies *first-in-first-out* (FIFO) *indexes*, each of which manages a dataset where objects are deleted in the same order as their insertions. We give a technique that converts a static data structure to a FIFO index for all decomposable problems, provided that the static structure can be constructed efficiently. We present FIFO access methods to solve several problems including *half-plane search*, *nearest neighbor search*, and *extreme-point search*. All of our structures consume linear space, and have optimal or near-optimal query cost.

Categories and Subject Descriptors

F2.2 [**Analysis of algorithms and problem complexity**]: Nonnumerical algorithms and problems; H3.1 [**Information storage and retrieval**]: Content analysis and indexing—*indexing methods*

General Terms

Algorithms, theory

Keywords

Index, half-plane search, nearest neighbor search, extreme-point search

1. INTRODUCTION

Given a set D of objects, a (searching) *problem* Π is to construct a data structure for D so that the result $\Pi(q, D)$ of any legal query q can be computed efficiently. If D never needs to be updated, the structure on D is *static*. In this paper, we are interested in that D is dynamically changing according to some *update scheme*. For instance, if only new objects can be added to D while existing ones are never removed, the structure on D is required to support only insertions, and is hence *insertion only*. If both insertions and deletions are possible, the structure is *fully dynamic*.

We consider the *online* setting, where a query must be answered (i.e., having its result reported in entirety) before handling the next operation, no matter whether that operation is an insertion, a deletion, or a query. We will denote by N the problem size, and by K the output size, i.e., $N = |D|$ and $K = |\Pi(q, D)|$.

1.1 FIFO update scheme and its applications

We introduce the notion of *first-in-first-out* (FIFO) *index*. As with fully-dynamic indexes, a FIFO structure must handle both insertions and deletions. However, deletions are restricted — only the *oldest* object, namely the one inserted the longest time ago (among the objects still in the index), can be removed. This scheme is useful in several areas, as explained below, that have been actively studied in the last decade.

Spatio-temporal databases. With the proliferation of intelligent location-aware devices (e.g., mobile phones, GPS devices, etc.), it is nowadays feasible to support spatial queries (such as range searching, nearest neighbor retrieval, and so on) on a large set of continuously moving objects [25, 31]. A simple, effective, way to keep track of object locations[1] is to have every object report its position periodically at an appropriate interval [31] (e.g., 1 minute). In other words, each location stored at the server automatically expires in a minute, at which time it is replaced by a fresh update. Therefore, locations expire in the same order that they are inserted, making FIFO indexes the key to query processing in these environments.

Sliding windows over data streams. By definition, sliding windows, which have been extensively studied since the pioneering paper of Babcock et al. [11], are well-known examples of the FIFO update scheme. There are two common types of sliding windows. The first one, *tuple-based sliding window*, simply covers the N most recently-received records for a fixed parameter N. The second one, *time-based sliding window*, includes all the records that arrived at the system within t timestamps from now, for a fixed parameter t. The number of tuples in the window varies, as it depends on the data's arrival rate during the past t timestamps.

---

[1]We consider objects whose future locations cannot be accurately predicted by simple motion functions, which makes the update schemes of [3, 26] inapplicable. Examples of such objects are vehicles in urban areas, pedestrians, etc. See [25] and the references therein for more discussion.

PODS'11, June 13–15, 2011, Athens, Greece.
Copyright 2011 ACM 978-1-4503-0660-7/11/06 ...$10.00.

Evolving databases. Massive transaction records are generated on a daily basis in various businesses (such as supermarkets, banks, stock exchanges, etc.) to support analytical report generation and decision making. For these purposes, user queries are biased towards recent records, such that data older than a certain past timestamp are no longer interesting and hence, can be discarded from the system. Coining the concept of *evolving databases* for such systems, Shivakumar and Garcia-Molina [28] presented a detailed coverage on the importance of the so-called *wave indexes* to answering queries efficiently. Such an index is in fact a FIFO structure by our definition. It is worth mentioning that an evolving database is similar to a *transaction time database* [27] but with the oldest data gradually purged (in their insertion order).

1.2 Technical motivations

A problem Π under the FIFO scheme can obviously be settled by a fully dynamic structure for Π. However, since FIFO is no harder than the fully-dynamic update scheme, we may be able to find a FIFO structure that is better than the fully-dynamic state of the art, in terms of the space, query, and/or update performance. This benefits the applications mentioned in Section 1.1 because it allows the practitioners there to improve their implementation without having to wait for a new fully-dynamic structure to come out.

A prominent example is *half-plane search* (its formal definition will appear in Section 1.3), whose static version can be solved with linear space and logarithmic query time [19] in the RAM model. Dynamization, however, appears to be rather difficult. The best known result [6] uses $O(N^{1+\epsilon})$ space, processes a query in $O(\log N + K)$ time, and requires $O(N^\epsilon)$ time for both an insertion and a deletion. We will show that, under the FIFO scheme, the problem can be solved with a structure that consumes linear space, answers a query in $O(\log N + K)$ time, and supports an update with $O(\log^2 N)$ cost.

At a higher level, a more ambitious goal is to develop a generic framework of designing FIFO structures. In particular, assuming that we already know how to solve the *static* version of a problem, is it possible to utilize *just* that solution for FIFO indexing? Proving a positive answer to this question, which we manage to do in this work, gives us a good starting point to approach some FIFO problems, as will be demonstrated later.

1.3 Problems, computation models, and basic notations

In the sequel, we define several problems to be discussed in detail. The purposes of studying these problems are twofold. First, they will be utilized to demonstrate how to apply the proposed generic framework to derive FIFO indexes. Second, all of them are well-known problems in the database literature. At the end of the subsection, we will clarify the computation models for our complexity analysis.

- *Half-plane search:* the dataset D is a set of 2-d points, a query q is a half-plane, and its result $\Pi(q, D) = q \cap D$, i.e., all the points of D falling in q. This problem is fundamental to, for example, non-isothetic range searching [29] and searching with linear constraints [4].

- *Nearest neighbor* (NN) *search:* D is again a set of

points in the plane, q is also a point, and $\Pi(q, D)$ is the data point $p \in D$ minimizing the Euclidean distance $\|q, p\|$. This problem has been extensively investigated on moving objects; see [25] and its bibliography.

- *Extreme-point search:* D is still a planar point set, q is a linear function $q((x, y)) = ax + by$, and $\Pi(q, D)$ is the point $p \in D$ maximizing $q(p)$. This is equivalent to *top-1 search*, which is crucial to multi-criteria optimization [15, 23].

See Figure 1 for some illustrations.

The above problems share the common property of being *decomposable*. Specifically, a problem Π is decomposable if, for any dataset D and query q, $\Pi(q, D)$ can be computed efficiently from $\Pi(q, D_1)$ and $\Pi(q, D_2)$, where D_1 and D_2 form a *partition* of D, namely, $D_1 \cup D_2 = D$ and $D_1 \cap D_2 = \emptyset$. The proposed indexing framework can be applied to all decomposable problems.

We are interested in both main-memory and I/O-efficient data structures. For the former, our analysis is under the standard *unit-cost RAM model*. For the latter, we adopt the *external memory* (EM) *model* [7], which has been successful in capturing the characteristics of database algorithms [30]. In this model, a computer has a memory of M words, and a disk of unbounded size that has been formatted into *blocks* of size B. An I/O operation transfers a block of information between the memory and the disk. Space complexity is measured in the number of blocks occupied, while time complexity is gauged in the number of I/Os performed. We make the *tall cache* assumption[2] [5, 10] that $M \geq B^2$. Note that, a *linear* complexity should be understood as $O(N/B)$ in the EM model, instead of $O(N)$ as in RAM. Furthermore, *poly-logarithmic* should be interpreted as $O(\log_B^c N)$ for some constant c in EM, as opposed to $O(\log^c N)$ in RAM. All complexities are worst-case unless specifically stated otherwise.

In RAM, we characterize the performance of a *static* structure by three functions (assuming that the dataset has size N):

- $S(N)$ which bounds from above its space consumption;

- $Q(N)$ which bounds from above the time of answering a query;

- $U(N)$ such that $N \cdot U(N)$ bounds from above the time of constructing the structure. In other words, $U(N)$ can be understood as the amount of preprocessing cost amortized over each object.

Similarly, in EM, a static structure is also characterized by $S(N)$, $Q(N)$ and $U(N)$, except that the construction time is bounded above by $(N/B) \cdot U(N)$. Note that, strictly speaking, the query cost should include the overhead of outputting the query result. However, since the output overhead is *always* linear (i.e., $O(K)$ and $O(K/B)$ in RAM and EM, respectively) for all the algorithms discussed in this paper, we omit the term from $Q(N)$.

---

[2] A typical value of B in practice is 1024 words, in which case $M \geq B^2$ means that the memory should have size at least 1 mega words. Most computers today (even those in smart phones) have memory larger than this.

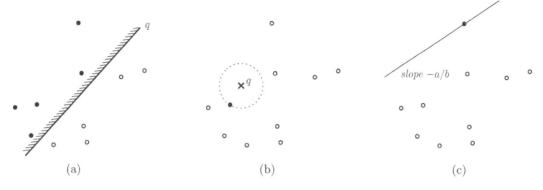

Figure 1: Illustrations of the problems studied: (a) half-plane search, (b) nearest neighbor search, and (c) extreme-point search. In each case, the query result includes the black dot(s). For (c), note that the answer to an extreme-point query with parameters (a, b) is the first data point hit as we move a line with slope $-a/b$ from infinity gradually towards the dataset.

For example, a binary tree uses $O(N)$ space, solves a 1-d range query in $O(\log N + K)$ time, and can be built in $O(N \log N)$ time. We have $S(N) = O(N), Q(N) = O(\log N)$, and $U(N) = O(\log N)$. Similarly, regarding the B-tree and 1-d range searching, $S(N) = O(N/B)$, $Q(N) = O(\log_B N)$, and $U(N) = O(\log_B N)$. In particular, note that the $U(N)$ indicates that the B-tree can be constructed in $O((N/B) \log_B N)$ I/Os.

We need to impose some constraints on $S(N)$, $Q(N)$, and $U(N)$ for our technique to work:

- All of them should be non-decreasing with N.

- $S(N)$ should grow at least linearly. Following [12], in RAM this means that $S(N)/N$ is non-decreasing. Accordingly, in EM, we require that $S(N)/(N/B)$ be non-decreasing with N.

- $U(N)$ needs to satisfy:

$$U(O(N)) = O(U(N)) \qquad (1)$$

which is fulfilled by a wide range of $U(N)$, including all the standard functions (e.g., constant, poly-logarithmic, polynomial, etc.).

- Both $Q(N)$ and $U(N)$ need to be $\Omega(1)$.

1.4 Previous results

Next, we survey the existing results related to our work. Our discussion consists of three parts. The first one describes the known general techniques for designing FIFO (or insertion-only) structures. The second clarifies the differences between FIFO and the *semi-online* update scheme of Dobkin and Suri [20]. Finally, the third part reviews the efficiency of the previous solutions to the problems listed in Section 1.3.

General techniques. Bentley and Saxe [12] initialized the research of developing general techniques to dynamize static structures for decomposable problems. They proposed several methods to convert static indexes to insertion-only structures (which can be regarded as special FIFO indexes

where deletions never happen). The basic idea of their methods is to partition a dataset D into several subsets, each managed by a dedicated static structure. An insertion is handled by reorganizing some subsets and reconstructing their structures respectively. By the definition of decomposability, a query q can be correctly answered by issuing q on every subset, and then combining all results.

Bentley and Saxe presented three methods achieving various tradeoffs. Given a static structure with performance characterized by $S(N)$, $Q(N)$ and $U(N)$, their *binary transformation*, perhaps better known as the *logarithmic method* [10], yields an insertion-only index with $O(S(N))$ space, $O(Q(N) \log N)$ query cost, and $O(U(N) \log N)$ amortized insertion time. The other two transformations are less interesting for our purposes, as they yield either $O(Q(N)N^\epsilon)$ query time or $O(U(N)N^\epsilon)$ update time, where the multiplicative term N^ϵ is too expensive when $Q(N)$ and $U(N)$ are poly-logarithmic.

Arge and Vahrenhold [10] extended the logarithmic method to the EM model, achieving similar performance bounds. Specifically, the resulting insertion-only index consumes $O(S(N))$ space, answers a query in $O(Q(N) \log_B N)$ I/Os, and supports an insertion in $O(U(N) \log_B N)$ amortized cost.

Arasu and Manku [8] described a method we refer to as the *dyadic approach* for query processing on sliding windows. Although not explicitly mentioned in [8], this method can be modified to convert a static structure to a FIFO index in internal memory. The rationale is to index the *sequence number* of every object in D with a binary tree, and associate each node of the tree with a secondary, static, structure on all the objects in the node's subtree. Rebuilding of the secondary structures can be carried out in a manner that amortizes only a small amount of cost on every update. In general, the FIFO structure produced by the dyadic approach occupies $O(S(N) \log N)$ space, and supports a query in $O(Q(N) \log N)$ time, and an update in $O(U(N) \log N)$ amortized time. Note that there is an $O(\log N)$ blow-up in the space complexity. It is worth noting that this approach is not designed for the EM model. Naive adaptation will lead to the gigantic query cost of $O(Q(N) \cdot B \log_B N)$, with

	Model	Space	Query	Insertion	Deletion
logarithmic method [12]	RAM	$S(N)$	$Q(N) \log N$	$U(N) \log N$	no support
external logarithmic method [10]	EM		$Q(N) \log_B N$	$U(N) \log_B N$	
dyadic approach [8]	RAM	$S(N) \log N$	$Q(N) \log N$	$U(N) \log N$	$U(N) \log N$
external dyadic approach (adapted from [8])	EM	$S(N) \log_B N$	$B \cdot Q(N) \log_B N$	$U(N) \log_B N$	$U(N) \log_B N$
ours RAM	**RAM**	$S(N)$	$Q(N) \log N$	$U(N) \log N$	$U(N) \log N$
EM	**EM**		$Q(N) \log_B N$	$U(N) \log_B N$	$U(N) \log_B N$

Table 1: Comparison of the general techniques for deriving FIFO indexes. All complexities are in big-O. The update results are amortized while the others are worst case.

Problem	Model	Fully-dynamic				FIFO (by Theorem 1.1)			**FIFO (our best)**		
		Space	Query	Update	Ref	Space	Query	Update	**Space**	**Query**	**Update**
half-plane	RAM	$N^{1+\epsilon}$	$\log N + K$	N^ϵ	[6]	N	$\log^2 N + K$	$\log^2 N$	N	$\log N + K$	$\log^2 N$
nearest	RAM	N	$\log^2 N$	$\log^6 N$	[14]	N	$\log^2 N$	$\log^2 N$	N	$\log^2 N$	$\log N$
neighbor	EM		?			N/B	$\log_B^3 N$	$\log_B^2 N$	N/B	$\log_B^3 N$	$\log_B^2 N$
extreme-	RAM	N	$\log N$	$\log N$	[13]	N	$\log^2 N$	$\log^2 N$	N	$\log N$	$\log N$
point	EM		?			N/B	$\log_B^2 N$	$\log_B^2 N$	N/B	$\log_B N$	$\log_B N$

? = we are not aware of any published result.

Table 2: Comparison of fully-dynamic and FIFO indexes. All complexities are in big-O. The update results are amortized while the others are worst case.

the space and update complexities being $O(S(N) \log_B N)$ and $O(U(N) \log_B N)$, respectively.

Semi-online. Dobkin and Suri [20] proposed a framework to convert a static structure to a dynamic one under a *semi-online* update scheme. Specifically, in that scheme, at the moment an object is inserted, we are told when the object will be deleted in the future. In particular, the future deletion time is given as the number of updates, *as opposed to* an absolute timestamp (e.g., by specifying 10, it means that the object will be deleted after 10 subsequent updates). This scheme is more general than FIFO in an *offline* setting, where all the update and query operations are given in advance, so that an algorithm can first scan the dataset once to attach each deletion time to its corresponding insertion.

In the online setting, however, the semi-online scheme does *not* subsume FIFO. Recall that, in this setting, every query must be answered before the algorithm can process the next operation. In other words, when answering a query q, the algorithm is not allowed to peek into the updates after q, and thus in general, cannot determine when an object o currently in the dataset will be removed – noticing that there can be an arbitrary number of insertions between q and the deletion of o. Unfortunately, knowledge of objects' deletion time is vital to the semi-online technique of [20], which thus becomes inapplicable. A FIFO algorithm, on the other hand, must work without knowing when objects will be deleted.

Concrete problems. For each problem in Section 1.3, we summarize below the performance of the best known static and fully-dynamic structures (if they exist, to our knowledge), under the computation model(s) where we will solve the problem in the FIFO scheme.

- Half-plane search: As mentioned in Section 1.2, in RAM, Chazelle et al. [19] gave a static solution that uses linear space and solves a query in $O(\log N + K)$ time. Their structure can be constructed in $O(N \log N)$ time. The dynamic state of the art is due

to Agarwal and Matousek [6], having space, query, and update cost $O(N^{1+\epsilon})$, $O(\log N + K)$, and amortized $O(N^\epsilon)$, respectively.

- NN search: In RAM, the static version can be settled in linear space and logarithmic query time, by combining a Voronoi diagram with a point-location structure. Its dynamization had been a long-standing open problem until recently Chan [14] proposed an index that occupies linear space (combining with ideas due to Af-shni and Chan [1]), achieves $O(\log^2 N)$ query cost, and demands $O(\log^3 N)$ and $O(\log^6 N)$ amortized time to handle an insertion and deletion respectively.

  In EM, Goodrich et al. [21] showed that the Voronoi diagram of N points can be constructed in $O((N/B) \log_B N)$ I/Os. Agarwal et al. [2] presented a point-location structure that requires linear space, answers a query in $O(\log_B^2 N)$ I/Os, and can be built in $O((N/B) \log_B N)$ I/Os. Combining these results gives a static index for NN search[3].

- Extreme-point search. In RAM, for static data, an extreme-point query can be answered in logarithmic time utilizing a linear-space index. This can be achieved by first computing the dataset's convex hull in $O(N \log N)$ time (with, for example, *Graham scan* [22]), and then, building a binary tree on the points of the hull. The dynamic case has been solved by Brodal and Jacob [13], whose structure achieves linear space and logarithmic query and amortized update time. Their data structure is rather complex such that the authors themselves listed a practical solution with the same complexity as an open problem.

  In EM, replacing the binary tree with a B-tree gives a static structure that occupies linear space and an-

---

[3]Arge et al. [9] gave an alternative linear-size index that solves a point-location query in $O(\log_B N)$ I/Os. Unfortunately, their structure is expensive to construct, and thus is not suitable as the base structure for FIFO conversion.

swers a query in $O(\log_B N)$ cost. The structure can be constructed in $O((N/B)\log_B N)$ I/Os by externalizing Graham scan [21].

1.5 Our results

Our first main result is a generic framework that converts a static solution of any decomposable problem Π into an index for solving the FIFO version of Π:

THEOREM 1.1 (THE FIFO THEOREM). *Assume that there is a static structure solving a decomposable problem Π in RAM that consumes no more than $S(N)$ space, answers a query within $Q(N)$ time, and can be built within $N \cdot U(N)$ time. Then, there is a FIFO index for Π with the following performance guarantees:*

If the dataset currently has N objects, the index consumes $O(S(N))$ space, solves a query in $O(Q(N)\log N)$ time, and supports an update in $O(U(N)\log N)$ amortized time.

The same result holds in EM except that (i) the construction time of the static index should be bounded above by $(N/B) \cdot U(N)$, and (ii) each $\log N$ should be replaced with $\log_B N$.

Our technique extends the logarithmic method of Bentley and Saxe [12] with a *2-phase-indexing* idea. More specifically, we partition the dataset D into $2\log N$ subsets with different sizes, based on objects' insertion times. Among these subsets, $\log N$ of them contain objects ready for deletion — these objects are in the *deletion phase*. The rest of the objects are in the *insertion phase*. We give algorithms to merge and split the subsets, so that the amortized cost of an update can be minimized. The performance bounds are derived through an analysis that is substantially different from that of [12].

Table 1 compares the FIFO indexes produced by Theorem 1.1 to those by the existing frameworks. In particular, regarding the dyadic approach [8], the proposed technique (i) reduces the space by a logarithmic factor in both RAM and EM, and (ii) improves the query efficiency by a factor of $O(B)$ in EM.

Theorem 1.1 immediately gives non-trivial FIFO indexes for all the problems in Section 1.3, by combining with the state-of-the-art static structures surveyed in Section 1.4. Each of those FIFO indexes treats the underlying static structure as a *black box*. Our second contribution is to show that we can sometimes obtain more efficient FIFO access methods by *hacking* into those black boxes. More specifically, in RAM, the objective of hacking is to achieve a query bound of $o(Q(N)\log N)$ and/or an update bound of $o(U(N)\log N)$, thus improving the results in Theorem 1.1. An analogous objective exists in EM as well.

Table 2 summarizes our results. It also includes the performance of the best corresponding fully-dynamic structure, to echo the motivation mentioned in Section 1.2 that better solutions may be derived by leveraging the special properties of the FIFO scheme. For extreme-point search in RAM, although having the same performance as that of [13], our structure is simpler, and amenable to practical implementation. All logarithmic query cost (with linear output time) in Table 2 is optimal in the comparison model of computation.

2. MAKING A STATIC STRUCTURE FIFO

Given a static structure for settling a decomposable problem with performance characterized by $S(N)$, $Q(N)$ and $U(N)$, we will present a generic framework to obtain a FIFO index. Section 2.1 describes the framework for the RAM model, which will be extended to the EM model in Section 2.2.

2.1 The RAM model

We say that an object is *active* if it has been inserted but not deleted yet. At any moment, we assign a *phase* to every object o. Specifically, when o is inserted, it enters the *insertion phase*. Sometime later, we will switch o into the *deletion phase*, in which the object stays until its deletion.

Denote by D the set of all objects currently active. Set $N = |D|$. The objects of D can be naturally ordered by their insertion timestamps. We say that an object is *newer (older)* than another, if the former one has greater (lower) insertion time. Let D^+ (D^-) be the subset of D that includes all the objects in the insertion (deletion) phase. We partition D^+ (D^-) into subsets with the following properties:

- D^+ is divided into D_0^+, D_1^+, ..., $D_{h^+}^+$, where h^+ is an integer that is $O(\log N)$ and varied by our algorithm. The size of D_i^+ ($0 \le i \le h^+$) is either 0 or 2^i. Furthermore, for any $i < j$, each object in D_i^+ is newer than all the objects in D_j^+.

- D^- is divided into $D_{h^-}^-$, ..., D_1^-, D_0^-, where $h^- = O(\log N)$ is also varied by our algorithm. The size of D_i^- ($0 \le i \le h^-$) is either 0 or 2^i. For any $i < j$, each object in D_i^- is older than all objects in D_j^-.

- $h^+ \le h^-$.

See Figure 2 for an illustration. We say that a subset is *older (newer)* than another if the objects in the former subset are older (newer). Each of the $h^+ + h^- + 2$ subsets is indexed with a static structure. Furthermore, for each subset, we keep a chronological list of its objects.

At the beginning (when D is empty), both h^+ and h^- equal 0. Next, we explain how to perform updates efficiently.

Insertion. Our insertion algorithm is the same as in the logarithmic method [12]. Given an object o, we identify the smallest $i \le h^+$ such that D_i^+ is empty. In case such an i does not exist (i.e., D_0^+, ..., $D_{h^+}^+$ are all non-empty), increment h^+ by 1 and set i to the new h^+. We empty all of D_0^+, ..., D_{i-1}^+, discard the structures on them, add all the objects therein together with o to D_i^+, and create a new static index on D_i^+. Note that the total number of migrated objects is

$$1 + \sum_{j=0}^{i-1} |D_j^+| = 1 + \sum_{j=0}^{i-1} 2^j = 2^i,$$

which is exactly the desired size of D_i^+. The construction takes $O(2^i \cdot U(2^i))$ time. If now h^+ has exceeded h^-, we simply rename $D_{h^+}^+$ as $D_{h^-+1}^-$, after which h^- is increased by 1, and h^+ is reset to 0.

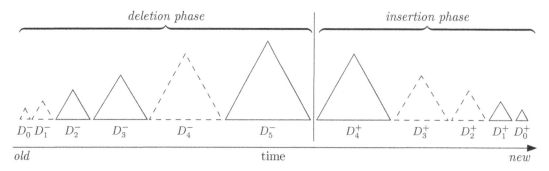

Figure 2: Illustration of 2-phase indexing: Solid triangles represent non-empty structures while dashed triangles represent empty ones; $h^+ = 4$ and $h^- = 5$.

Deletion. To remove the oldest object o in D, we find the smallest $i \leq h^-$ such that D_i^- is non-empty. Find and discard o from the chronological list of D_i^- in constant time. The remaining objects of D_i^- are then broken into D_0^-, ..., D_{i-1}^- in $O(|D_i^-|) = O(2^i)$ time, observing the time-ordering and cardinality constraints mentioned earlier. Build a static structure on each of D_0^-, ..., D_{i-1}^- in totally

$$\sum_{j=0}^{i-1} |D_j^-| \cdot U(|D_j^-|) = \sum_{j=0}^{i-1} 2^j \cdot U(2^j)$$
$$= O(2^i \cdot U(2^i))$$

time. If $i = h^-$, we decrease h^- by 1. It is possible that h^- now drops below h^+. In this case, rename $D_{h^+}^+$ as $D_{h^-+1}^-$, increase h^- by 1, and decrease h^+ to the greatest j such that D_j^+ is non-empty (if no such j exists, $h^+ = 0$).

Query. We answer a query by simply searching the indexes of all subsets and combining their results. Correctness is obvious as the underlying problem is decomposable. The query time is

$$\sum_{i=0}^{h^+} Q(2^i) + \sum_{i=0}^{h^-} Q(2^i) = O\left((h^+ + h^-)Q(N)\right)$$
$$= O\left(Q(N)\log N\right). \quad (2)$$

Analysis. If no deletion ever happens, our 2-phase framework degenerates into the logarithmic method [12]. Unfortunately, the analysis of [12] cannot be extended to prove the performance guarantees (in particular, the update time) of our technique. In fact, in the absence of deletions, the value of N monotonically increases with time, thus allowing an insertion to use more time than each of the earlier insertions. This property can be leveraged to simplify the analysis significantly. In the FIFO context, N can vary *arbitrarily* with time, which necessitates a more delicate discussion, as presented below.

The query cost of 2-phase indexing is already given in Equation 2. Clearly all the $h^+ + h^- + 2$ structures consume

$$\sum_{i=0}^{h^+} S(|D_i^+|) + \sum_{i=0}^{h^-} S(|D_i^-|) = O(S(N))$$

space, where the equality used the fact that function $S(N)$ grows at least linearly.

Next, we focus on bounding the update overhead. Initially, D is empty. Consider a FIFO update sequence SEQ with n updates, each of which can be an insertion or a deletion. Denote by N_i ($i \leq n$) the size of D after the i-th update. Our objective is to show that the total cost of handling all the updates is bounded by

$$cost(SEQ) = O\left(\sum_{i=0}^{n} U(N_i)\log N_i\right). \quad (3)$$

This is what is needed to prove that the i-th update has amortized cost $O(U(N_i)\log N_i)$.

Let n_{del} be the number of deletions in SEQ. It follows that $n_{ins} = n - n_{del}$ objects are inserted. After processing the entire SEQ, the oldest n_{del} objects have been removed from D. We say that they are *short-term* objects. The other $n_{ins} - n_{del}$ objects are *long-term*.

We define the *timestamp* of an update in SEQ as its sequence number (i.e., the first update is at time 1, the second at time 2, and so on). If o is a short-term object, denote by $t^+(o)$ and $t^-(o)$ the timestamps at which o is inserted and deleted, respectively. If o is long-term, we still use $t^+(o)$ to represent its insertion time, and assume a *virtual* deletion of o at time:

$$t^-(o) = n + i \quad (4)$$

where i is such that o is the i-th oldest long-term object in SEQ. Remember that $cost(SEQ)$, as in Equation 3, does not include the cost of virtual deletions. Regardless of whether o is long- or short-term, we define its *lifespan* as $[t^+(o), t^-(o))$. Note that a lifespan is close on the left and open on the right.

If o is short-term, let $\Delta^+(o)$ be the number of insertions during the lifespan of o, excluding the insertion of o itself. Similarly, let $\Delta^-(o)$ be the number of deletions during the lifespan. If o is long-term, the semantics of $\Delta^+(o)$ is the same, while $\Delta^-(o)$ is defined as:

Figure 3: Illustration of the notations of a long-term object: each black (white) dot represents an insertion (deletion) in SEQ. Let o be the object as shown, which is the 2nd oldest long-term object. We have: $t^+(o) = 7$, $t^-(o) = 10 + 2 = 12$, $s(o) = 5$, $\Delta^+(o) = 2$, $\Delta^-(o) = 1 + 2 - 1 = 2$.

$$\Delta^-(o) = c + i - 1 \qquad (5)$$

where c counts the number of deletions in SEQ after the insertion of o, and i is the same as in Equation 4. Finally, no matter whether o is short- or long-term, we define its *spread* as

$$s(o) = t^-(o) - t^+(o).$$

which is essentially the number of timestamps in the lifespan of o. By the definitions of $\Delta^+(o)$ and $\Delta^-(o)$, it is not hard to observe:

$$s(o) = \Delta^+(o) + \Delta^-(o) + 1. \qquad (6)$$

Figure 3 illustrates the above notations for a long-term o.

Some useful observations can be made:

- Property 1: $N_{t^+(o)} = \Delta^-(o) + 1$. When o is inserted, D contains only those objects inserted earlier but not deleted yet. All and only such objects have deletion timestamps in the lifespan of o, by definition of FIFO updating.

- Property 2: for a short-term object o, $N_{t^-(o)} = \Delta^+(o)$. This is because only the objects (not counting o itself) inserted during the lifespan of o can still remain in D right after o is deleted.

- Property 3: for a short-term object o, $s(o) = N_{t^+(o)} + N_{t^-(o)}$, which immediately follows the previous two properties and Equation 6.

- Property 4: $N_i \leq s(o)$ for all i satisfying $t^+(o) < i < t^-(o)$. The reason is that, if another object o' co-exists with o in D at any moment, their lifespans must intersect. Hence, either $t^+(o')$ or $t^-(o')$ falls within the lifespan of o, making $\Delta^+(o) + \Delta^-(o)$ an upper bound of the size of $D - \{o\}$ for all D containing o.

Lemma 2.1.
$$cost(SEQ) = \sum_{i=1}^{n_{ins}} O\Big(U\big(s(o_i)\big) \log s(o_i)\Big)$$

where o_i is the i-th oldest object ever inserted.

Proof. Every time a static structure in the insertion (deletion) phase is constructed (destroyed), the cost of processing SEQ increases by at most $x \cdot U(x)$, where x is the number of objects in the structure. We charge $O(U(x))$ on every object o in the structure. By Property 4, $x \leq s(o)$; hence, $O(U(x))$ is bounded above by $O(U(s(o)))$. Every time o is charged, it migrates to an older subset. Since o cannot appear in a D with more than $s(o)$ objects (otherwise, N would be greater than $s(o)$), it can only be charged $O(\log s(o))$ times. Therefore, the total cost of processing the whole SEQ that is amortized over o is bounded by $O\big(U(s(o)) \log s(o)\big)$. $\square$

We are finally ready to establish Equation 3.

Lemma 2.2.
$$\sum_{i=1}^{n_{ins}} U\big(s(o_i)\big) \log s(o_i) = O\left(\sum_{i=0}^{n} U(N_i) \log N_i\right) \qquad (7)$$

Proof. Introduce $f(x) = U(x) \log x$. From Equation 1, we have $f(O(x)) = O(f(x))$. Therefore, it holds that:

$$f(x + y) = \Theta(f(x) + f(y)) \qquad (8)$$

To prove this, assume, without loss of generality, $x \leq y$. Hence, $f(x+y) = f(O(y)) = O(f(y)) = O(f(x)+f(y))$. On the other hand, since function f is non-decreasing, $f(x) + f(y) \leq 2f(x+y) = O(f(x+y))$.

Let $\mathcal{S}$ ($\mathcal{L}$) be the set of short- (long-) term objects. Each object o ever inserted by SEQ contributes a term $f(s(o))$ in the left hand side (LHS) of Equation 7. On the other hand, every object in $\mathcal{S}$ and $\mathcal{L}$ contributes two and one term in the right hand side (RHS), respectively.

For each object $o \in \mathcal{S}$, we have

$$f(s(o)) = O\bigg(f\big(N_{t^+(o)}\big) + f\big(N_{t^-(o)}\big)\bigg) \qquad (9)$$

To see this, notice that Property 3 implies that either $N_{t^+(o)}$ or $N_{t^-(o)}$ is $\Omega(s(o))$. Without loss of generality, suppose that $N_{t^+(o)} \leq N_{t^-(o)}$. Then, $f(s(o)) = f(O(N_{t^-(o)})) = O(f(N_{t^-(o)}))$, validating Equation 9.

There are $n_{ins} - n_{del}$ long-term objects, among which let o_i be the i-th oldest. In the sequel, we will show

$$\sum_{i=1}^{n_{ins}-n_{del}} f\big(s(o_i)\big) = \sum_{i=1}^{n_{ins}-n_{del}} O\bigg(f\big(N_{t^+(o_i)}\big)\bigg) \qquad (10)$$

Let δ_i be the number of *short-term* objects deleted after the insertion of o_i. We observe:

$$N_{t^+(o_i)} = i + \delta_i$$

which is because, right after o_i is inserted, D consists of exactly i *long-term* objects and δ_i short-term objects. We also observe:

$$s(o_i) = n_{ins} - n_{del} + \delta_i$$

due to the fact that the lifespan of o_i covers (i) either the insertion or deletion time of every long-term object, and (ii) the deletion timestamps of δ_i short-term objects.

Therefore:

$$\text{LHS of (10)} = \sum_{i=1}^{n_{ins}-n_{del}} f\big(n_{ins} - n_{del} + \delta_i\big)$$

$$= \sum_{i=1}^{n_{ins}-n_{del}} O\left(f\big(n_{ins} - n_{del} - i\big) + f(i) + f(\delta_i)\right)$$

$$= \sum_{i=1}^{n_{ins}-n_{del}} O\left(2f(i) + f(\delta_i)\right)$$

$$= \sum_{i=1}^{n_{ins}-n_{del}} O\left(f(i + \delta_i)\right) = \text{RHS of (10)}$$

where the 2nd and 4th equalities used Equation 8.

From Inequalities 9 and 10, we know that

$$\text{LHS of (7)} = \sum_{o \in \mathcal{S}} f(s(o)) + \sum_{o \in \mathcal{L}} f(s(o))$$

$$= \sum_{o \in \mathcal{S}} O\left(f\big(N_{t^+(o)}\big) + f\big(N_{t^-(o)}\big)\right) +$$

$$\sum_{o \in \mathcal{L}} O\left(f\big(N_{t^+(o)}\big)\right) = \text{RHS of (7)}$$

thus completing the proof. □

This proves the part of Theorem 1.1 in the RAM model.

2.2 The EM model

In external memory, our 2-phase indexing divides D into $D_0^+, ..., D_{h^+}^+, D_{h^-}^-, ..., D_0^-$ in the same manner as in the RAM model, except for two differences:

- Both h^+ and h^- are $O(\log_B N)$.

- For each $i \le h^+$ or h^-, $|D_i^+|$ or $|D_i^-|$ should
  - be either 0 or
  - fall in the range $[B^i/2, B^{i+1}]$.

Insertion of an object o is similar to that in the external logarithmic method [10]. We first find the smallest i such that the union of all D_j^+ ($0 \le j \le i$) has less than B^{i+1} objects. Then, empty $D_0^+, ..., D_i^+$, collect all their objects together with o into D_i^+, and construct a static index on D_i^+. In case the requirement $h^+ \le h^-$ is violated, carry out renaming and adjust h^- and h^+ as in the RAM model.

To delete an object o, we identify the lowest i such that D_i^- is non-empty, and discard o from D_i^-. The remaining objects of D_i^- are then divided into $D_0^-, D_1^-, ..., D_i^-$ (obeying the time-ordering constraint) such that D_j^- ($0 \le j \le i-1$) gets exactly $B^{j+1}/2$ objects. If there are not enough objects to achieve the purpose, we allow D_{i-1}^- to include less than $B^i/2$ objects; otherwise, the outstanding objects are put back in D_i^-. In any case, let $k \le i$ be the maximum integer such that that D_k^- is non-empty (k must be either $i-1$ or i). In case $|D_k^-| \le B^k/2$, empty D_k^- and move all its objects to D_{k-1}^-, whose size is now $B^k/2 + |D_k^-| \le B^k$. Construct a static index on $D_0^-, ...,$

D_{k-1}^- respectively, and also on D_k^- if it is non-empty. If h^+ now exceeds h^-, fix it in the same way as in the RAM model

The query algorithm is identical to the RAM counterpart.

Analysis. We discuss only the update complexity as the space and query cost can be derived easily. All the notations in the analysis of the RAM model can be re-used here. The following is the EM version of Lemma 2.1.

LEMMA 2.3.

$$cost(SEQ) = \sum_{i=1}^{n_{ins}} O\left(U\big(s(o_i)\big) \log_B s(o_i)\right)$$

where o_i is the i-th oldest object ever inserted.

PROOF. In the insertion (deletion) algorithm, every time the static structure on a D_i^+ (D_i^-) is constructed (destroyed), the cost of processing SEQ grows by at most $(x/B) \cdot U(x)$ I/Os, where x is the number of objects in the structure. Note that $(x/B) \cdot U(x) = O(B^i \cdot U(x))$. Next, we will show that $\Omega(B^i)$ objects will migrate to an older subset. This allows us to charge $O(U(x))$ I/Os over each of those objects, which will complete the proof as an object o can be charged $O(\log_B s(o))$ times.

For the insertion case, all the objects in $D_0^+, ..., D_{i-1}^+$ will migrate to D_i^+. The selection of i ensures that there are at least B^i such objects. For the deletion case, consider the situation after the deletion has finished. If D_i^- becomes empty, all the $|D_i^-| \ge B^i/2$ objects in D_i^- have migrated to older subsets. Otherwise, at least $B^i/2$ objects have migrated to D_{i-1}^-. □

Changing each log to $\log_B$, Lemma 2.2 still holds (in fact, the proof directly applies after the changes). This indicates that the i-th update is handled with $O(U(N_i) \log_B N_i)$ I/Os amortized. We thus conclude the proof of Theorem 1.1.

3. SOLVING CONCRETE PROBLEMS

In this section, we present FIFO indexes for the problems defined in Section 1.3. Integration of Theorem 1.1 and the static solutions reviewed in Section 1.4 immediately gives the results in the fourth column of Table 2. The subsequent discussion will show how to obtain the results in the last column of that table. Towards this, We will first give two general techniques for improving the FIFO structures yielded by Theorem 1.1, and then, apply them to solve each individual problem.

FIFO fractional cascading. Recall that our 2-phase indexing framework divides the set D of N active objects into $h^+ + h^- + 2$ subsets $D_0^+, ..., D_{h^+}^+, D_{h^-}^-, ..., D_0^-$. Each subset is managed by a static structure. Next, we consider the following problem. Let G_i^+ ($0 \le i \le h^+$) be a set of $O(|D_i^+|)$ real values. G_i^+ has the property that it can be retrieved from D_i^+ into the sorted order using linear time. Define G_i^- ($0 \le i \le h^-$) similarly on D_i^-. Given a real value q, a *combined predecessor query* returns, from each possible G_i^+ (G_i^-), the predecessor of q, namely, the greatest value in G_i^+ (G_i^-) not exceeding q.

LEMMA 3.1. *In RAM, a FIFO index can be augmented such that a combined predecessor query can be answered* in $O(\log N)$ time. *The augmentation does not alter the space, query, and update complexities of the original index. The same result holds in EM by replacing $O(\log N)$ with $O(\log_B N)$.*

PROOF. We achieve this with a manipulation of *fractional cascading* (FC) [18]. In RAM, we build two FC structures F^+ and F^-, where the former indexes $G_0^+, ..., G_{h^+}^+$, and the latter indexes $G_0^-, ..., G_{h^-}^-$. Specifically, F^+ has $h^+ + 1$ sorted lists $H_0^+, ..., H_{h^+}^+$ where

- $H_{h^+}^+$ includes a value out of every 4 consecutive values in $G_{h^+}^+$;

- for each $i = h^+ - 1, ..., 0$, H_i^+ includes a value out of every 4 consecutive values in the sorted list of $G_i^+ \cup H_{i+1}^+$.

Note that an H_i^+ can be non-empty even if G_i^+ is empty, as H_i^+ may contain values from G_j^+ with $j > i$. We refer to the constant 4 as the *sample interval*. An analogous definition applies to F^-. By standard techniques [18], F^+ and F^- can be deployed to answer a combined predecessor query in $O(\log N + h^+ + h^-) = O(\log N)$ time.

The two FC structures occupy linear space. In fact, regarding F^+, the following holds for any i satisfying $0 \le i \le h^+ - 1$:

$$|H_i^+| \le \left(|H_{i+1}^+| + |G_i^+|\right)/4 \le |H_{i+1}^+|/4 + c2^{i-2} \quad (11)$$

for some constant c. Obviously, $|H_{h^+}^+| \le c2^{h^+-2}$. In general, given $H_{i+1}^+ < c2^i$, Equation 11 shows:

$$|H_i^+| < c2^i/4 + c2^{i-2} < c2^{i-1}.$$

Hence, we can create H_i^+ from G_i^+ and H_{i+1}^+ in $O(|G_i^+| + |H_{i+1}^+|) = O(2^i)$ time. Similar arguments apply to F^- as well.

To maintain the FC structures, we extend our insertion algorithm in Section 2.1 as follows. Consider the moment when the index on D_i^+ has been rebuilt (for some legal i), namely, $D_0^+, ..., D_{i-1}^+$ have been emptied. We derive the new G_i^+ in $O(|D_i^+|)$ time, compute H_i^+ in $O(2^i)$ time, and then create the new $H_{i-1}^+, ..., H_0^+$ (in this order) using $\sum_{j=0}^{i-1} O(2^j) = O(2^i)$ time. Hence, the total insertion cost is the same as before if the requirement $h^+ \le h^-$ is not violated. In case h^+ exceeds h^-, denote by x the number of objects currently in $D_{h^+}^+$. We perform renaming and adjust h^+, h^- as in the original algorithm. This is followed by rebuilding both F^+ and F^- from scratch. As all G_i^+ and G_i^- are sorted, F^+ and F^- can be constructed in $O(N)$ time. We amortize the cost over the x objects that just migrated from the insertion phase to the deletion phase. As $x = \Omega(N)$, each object bears only constant time. Since every object is charged at most once this way, the amortized update cost is unaffected. The deletion algorithm in Section 2.1 can be modified based on analogous ideas without any extra overhead asymptotically.

A similar approach also works in EM, using a sample interval of $2B$. Adapting the above analysis in a straightforward

manner, we can show that the resulting FC structures occupy linear space, answer a combined predecessor query in $O(\log_B N)$ I/Os, and their maintenance demands no extra cost on top of the original update overhead. $\square$

Linear reorganization. Let S be a set of active objects. Consider a *chronological partition* S_1, S_2 of S, namely, (i) S_1, S_2 form a partition of S, and (ii) every object in S_1 is older than all objects in S_2. We say that the underlying static structure is *linearly reorganizable* if it satisfies both conditions below:

- given a structure on S, we can create the structures on S_1 and S_2 respectively in total time linear to $|S|$.

- given the structures on S_1 and S_2 respectively, we can create the structure on S in time linear to $|S|$.

LEMMA 3.2. *If the underlying static structure is linearly reorganizable, the update cost of 2-phase indexing is $O(\log N)$ and $O(\log_B N)$ amortized in RAM and EM, respectively.*

PROOF. We prove the lemma only in RAM because the discussion extends to external memory easily. The key is to accelerate each insertion and deletion by a factor of $O(U(N))$, compared to the algorithms in Section 2.1.

Recall that insertion requires constructing the index of a D_i^+ on the union of D_j^+ for all $0 \le j \le i - 1$. This can be done in $O(2^i)$ time (as opposed to $O(2^i \cdot U(2^i))$ in Section 2.1) as follows. First, build an index T from the structures on D_0^+ and D_1^+. Then, incrementally, create a new T from the previous T and the structure on D_j^+, for $j = 2, ..., i - 1$. The final T is the index on D_i^+. By the definition of linear reorganizable, this process takes

$$\sum_{j=1}^{i-1} O(2^j + 2^{j-1}) = O(2^i)$$

time. A similar, but reverse, approach works for deletion to achieve the claimed efficiency. $\square$

Applications. The above techniques serve different purposes. Specifically, FIFO fractional cascading may be leveraged for reducing the query overhead, whereas linear reorganization for lowering the update cost. They are independent in the sense that sometimes they can be applied together to enhance query and update efficiency simultaneously. Next, we demonstrate this by improving the FIFO indexes directly obtained from Theorem 1.1.

- Half-plane search: In RAM, Chazelle et al. [19] showed that a half-plane query can be reduced to finding the predecessor of a value (computed based on the original query) in a set G of real numbers, such that $|G|$ is no greater than the cardinality of the dataset. Once the predecessor is found, all the result objects can be reported in $O(K)$ time. G can be extracted into a sorted order in linear time after constructing the (static) index of [19]. In 2-phase indexing, query processing boils down finding the predecessors of a query value, in $h^+ + h^- + 2$ sets of real values respectively, i.e., one for each of $D_0^+, ..., D_{h^+}^+, D_{h^-}^-, ..., D_0^-$. By Lemma 3.1, the query cost is $O(\log N + K)$.

- NN search: In RAM, the static version of the problem can be settled by constructing a point-location structure on the Voronoi diagram (VD) of the dataset. One such structure is due to Kirkpatrick [24]. Given a VD, his structure can be built in linear time. In the FIFO context, let S be a set of points, and S_1, S_2 a chronological partition of it. Using the techniques of Chazelle [16] and Chazelle et al. [17], we can (i) create the VDs of S_1 and S_2 respectively from that of S in $O(|S|)$ expected time, and (ii) create the VD of S from those of S_1 and S_2 also in $O(|S|)$ time. Therefore, the static NN structure is linearly reorganizable. By Lemma 3.2, the update cost can be lowered to $O(\log N)$ amortized.

- Extreme-point search: In RAM, the static structure is merely a binary tree indexing the points on the convex hull of the dataset, sorted in clockwise order. A query can be reduced to predecessor search on the tree. To make the structure linearly reorganizable, we keep a separate *x-list* that sorts *all* data points by their x-coordinates. By feeding the x-list to Graham scan, we can compute the convex hull in time linear to the dataset size. Now, consider a set S of points, and a chronological partition S_1, S_2. To obtain the structure of S_1 (the case of S_2 is similar) from S, we scan the x-list of S once to generate the x-list of S_1 in $O(|S|)$ time, after which the structure on S_1 can be built in $O(|S_1|)$ time. Conversely, to create the structure of S from those of S_1, S_2, we obtain the x-list of S by merging those of S_1 and S_2 in $O(|S|)$ time, after which the index on S is constructed with linear cost.

Given the FIFO index from Theorem 1.1, extreme-point search is performed by first retrieving the predecessors of a query value in $h^+ + h^- + 2$ sets of numbers, and then returning the best one among the $O(\log N)$ objects corresponding to those predecessors. By Lemma 3.1, this can be done in $O(\log N)$ time overall. Finally, Lemma 3.2 allows us to improve the update time to $O(\log N)$ amortized. A similar approach works in the EM model to achieve logarithmic query and amortized update cost.

4. CONCLUSIONS

We have presented a general framework of designing FIFO data structures for decomposable problems, provided that an index solving the static version of the underlying problem is available. Furthermore, as long as the static index can be efficiently constructed, the resulting FIFO structure is simple enough for practical use. We have utilized our framework to develop FIFO indexing solutions with nontrivial performance guarantees to half-plane search, nearest neighbor search, and extreme-point search (all in 2-d space).

5. ACKNOWLEDGEMENTS

This work was supported by grants GRF 4173/08, GRF 4169/09, and GRF 4166/10 from HKRGC. We are grateful to the anonymous reviewers for their comments on how to improve the paper.

6. REFERENCES

[1] P. Afshani and T. M. Chan. Optimal halfspace range reporting in three dimensions. In *Proceedings of the Annual ACM-SIAM Symposium on Discrete Algorithms (SODA)*, pages 180–186, 2009.

[2] P. K. Agarwal, L. Arge, G. S. Brodal, and J. S. Vitter. I/O-efficient dynamic point location in monotone planar subdivisions. In *Proceedings of the Annual ACM-SIAM Symposium on Discrete Algorithms (SODA)*, pages 11–20, 1999.

[3] P. K. Agarwal, L. Arge, and J. Erickson. Indexing moving points. *Journal of Computer and System Sciences (JCSS)*, 66(1):207–243, 2003.

[4] P. K. Agarwal, L. Arge, J. Erickson, P. G. Franciosa, and J. S. Vitter. Efficient searching with linear constraints. *Journal of Computer and System Sciences (JCSS)*, 61(2):194–216, 2000.

[5] P. K. Agarwal, L. Arge, J. Yang, and K. Yi. I/O-efficient structures for orthogonal range-max and stabbing-max queries. In *Proceedings of European Symposium on Algorithms (ESA)*, pages 7–18, 2003.

[6] P. K. Agarwal and J. Matousek. Dynamic half-space range reporting and its applications. *Algorithmica*, 13(4):325–345, 1995.

[7] A. Aggarwal and J. S. Vitter. The input/output complexity of sorting and related problems. *Communications of the ACM (CACM)*, 31(9):1116–1127, 1988.

[8] A. Arasu and G. S. Manku. Approximate counts and quantiles over sliding windows. In *Proceedings of ACM Symposium on Principles of Database Systems (PODS)*, pages 286–296, 2004.

[9] L. Arge, A. Danner, and S.-M. Teh. I/O-efficient point location using persistent B-trees. *ACM Journal of Experimental Algorithmics*, 8, 2003.

[10] L. Arge and J. Vahrenhold. I/O-efficient dynamic planar point location. *Computational Geometry*, 29(2):147–162, 2004.

[11] B. Babcock, S. Babu, M. Datar, R. Motwani, and J. Widom. Models and issues in data stream systems. In *Proceedings of ACM Symposium on Principles of Database Systems (PODS)*, pages 1–16, 2002.

[12] J. L. Bentley and J. B. Saxe. Decomposable searching problems I: Static-to-dynamic transformation. *Journal of Algorithms*, 1(4):301–358, 1980.

[13] G. S. Brodal and R. Jacob. Dynamic planar convex hull. In *Proceedings of Annual IEEE Symposium on Foundations of Computer Science (FOCS)*, pages 617–626, 2002.

[14] T. M. Chan. A dynamic data structure for 3-d convex hulls and 2-d nearest neighbor queries. *Journal of the ACM (JACM)*, 57(3), 2010.

[15] Y.-C. Chang, L. D. Bergman, V. Castelli, C.-S. Li, M.-L. Lo, and J. R. Smith. The Onion technique:

Indexing for linear optimization queries. In *Proceedings of ACM Management of Data (SIGMOD)*, pages 391–402, 2000.

[16] B. Chazelle. An optimal algorithm for intersecting three-dimensional convex polyhedra. *SIAM Journal of Computing*, 21(4):671–696, 1992.

[17] B. Chazelle, O. Devillers, F. Hurtado, M. Mora, V. Sacristan, and M. Teillaud. Splitting a delaunay triangulation in linear time. *Algorithmica*, 34(1):39–46, 2002.

[18] B. Chazelle and L. J. Guibas. Fractional cascading: I. a data structuring technique. *Algorithmica*, 1(2):133–162, 1986.

[19] B. Chazelle, L. J. Guibas, and D. T. Lee. The power of geometric duality. *BIT Numerical Mathematics*, 25(1):76–90, 1985.

[20] D. P. Dobkin and S. Suri. Maintenance of geometric extrema. *Journal of the ACM (JACM)*, 38(2):275–298, 1991.

[21] M. T. Goodrich, J.-J. Tsay, D. E. Vengroff, and J. S. Vitter. External-memory computational geometry. In *Proceedings of Annual IEEE Symposium on Foundations of Computer Science (FOCS)*, pages 714–723, 1993.

[22] R. L. Graham. An efficient algorithm for determining the convex hull of a finite planar set. *Information Processing Letters (IPL)*, 1(4):132–133, 1972.

[23] V. Hristidis and Y. Papakonstantinou. Algorithms and applications for answering ranked queries using ranked views. *The VLDB Journal*, 13(1):49–70, 2004.

[24] D. G. Kirkpatrick. Optimal search in planar subdivisions. *SIAM Journal of Computing*, 12(1):28–35, 1983.

[25] K. Mouratidis, M. Hadjieleftheriou, and D. Papadias. Conceptual partitioning: An efficient method for continuous nearest neighbor monitoring. In *Proceedings of ACM Management of Data (SIGMOD)*, pages 634–645, 2005.

[26] S. Saltenis, C. S. Jensen, S. T. Leutenegger, and M. A. Lopez. Indexing the positions of continuously moving objects. In *Proceedings of ACM Management of Data (SIGMOD)*, pages 331–342, 2000.

[27] B. Salzberg and V. J. Tsotras. Comparison of access methods for time-evolving data. *ACM Computing Surveys*, 31(2):158–221, 1999.

[28] N. Shivakumar and H. Garcia-Molina. Wave-indices: Indexing evolving databases. In *Proceedings of ACM Management of Data (SIGMOD)*, pages 381–392, 1997.

[29] S. Sioutas, D. Sofotassios, K. Tsichlas, D. Sotiropoulos, and P. Vlamos. Canonical polygon queries on the plane: A new approach. *Journal of Computers*, 4(9):913–919, 2009.

[30] J. S. Vitter. Algorithms and data structures for external memory. *Foundation and Trends in Theoretical Computer Science*, 2(4):305–474, 2006.

[31] O. Wolfson, L. Jiang, A. P. Sistla, S. Chamberlain, N. Rishe, and M. Deng. Databases for tracking mobile units in real time. In *Proceedings of International Conference on Database Theory (ICDT)*, pages 169–186, 1999.

Pan-private Algorithms Via Statistics on Sketches

Darakhshan Mir, S. Muthukrishnan, Aleksandar Nikolov, Rebecca N. Wright
Department of Computer Science
Rutgers University, Piscataway, NJ 08854
$\{$mir, muthu, anikolov, rebecca.wright$\}$@cs.rutgers.edu

ABSTRACT

Consider fully dynamic data, where we track data as it gets inserted and deleted. There are well developed notions of private data analyses with dynamic data, for example, using differential privacy. We want to go beyond privacy, and consider privacy together with security, formulated recently as *pan-privacy* by Dwork et al. (ICS 2010). Informally, pan-privacy preserves differential privacy while computing desired statistics on the data, *even if the internal memory of the algorithm is compromised* (say, by a malicious break-in or insider curiosity or by fiat by the government or law).

We study pan-private algorithms for basic analyses, like estimating distinct count, moments, and heavy hitter count, with fully dynamic data. We present the first known pan-private algorithms for these problems in the fully dynamic model. Our algorithms rely on sketching techniques popular in streaming: in some cases, we add suitable noise to a previously known sketch, using a novel approach of calibrating noise to the underlying problem structure and the projection matrix of the sketch; in other cases, we maintain certain statistics on sketches; in yet others, we define novel sketches. We also present the first known lower bounds explicitly for pan privacy, showing our results to be nearly optimal for these problems. Our lower bounds are stronger than those implied by differential privacy or dynamic data streaming alone and hold even if unbounded memory and/or unbounded processing time are allowed. The lower bounds use a noisy decoding argument and exploit a connection between pan-private algorithms and data sanitization.

Categories and Subject Descriptors

K.4.1 [**Computers and Society**]: Privacy; H.2.8 [**Database Applications**]: Statistical Databases

General Terms

Algorithms, Security, Theory

Keywords

Differential Privacy, Pan-Privacy

1. INTRODUCTION

Consider the following simple, motivating example. Say we keep track of visitors that enter or leave a large facility (offline sites like a corporate or government office or online like websites). When queried, we wish to determine how many different visitors are on-site. This is a *distinct count* query. Unlike a data publication scenario where data is static after it is published, here the data is dynamic, varying over time, and the distinct count query may be posed any time, or even multiple times.

Our focus is first on privacy. Known methods for instance would be able to maintain the list of all IDs currently on site, and when queried, compute the precise answer D but return $D + \alpha$ for some suitable α that balances utility of the approximate distinct count against compromising the privacy of any particular ID. This intuitive approach has been formalized and a rich theory of (differential) privacy now exists for limitations and successes of answering this and many other queries privately.

Now, we go beyond privacy, and consider security. In particular, suppose the program—that tracks the data and answers the query—is compromised. Of course, this may happen because a malicious intruder hacks the system. But more subtly, this may happen because an insider with access, such as a systems administrator, may turn curious or crooked; data analysis may be outsourced to far away countries where people and laws are less stringent; or the contents of the registers may be subpoenaed by law or security officials. How can distinct count query processing be done securely, as well as with privacy? Maintaining a list of IDs on-site will not work, since it compromises all such IDs when a breach occurs. A natural idea is to hash (or encrypt) IDs into a new space that hides the identity. On a closer look, this too will not work since a breach will reveal the hash function or the encrypting key, and the intruder can exhaustively enumerate potential visitors to a site and determine the identity of all visitors currently on-site; this is known as a *dictionary attack*. (Notice that we are not limiting the intruder to have any computational constraints; however, even for computationally bounded adversaries, no cryptographic guarantees are known when the adversary has full access to the private key).

Maintaining a random sample of the IDs too will not work since it compromises the sampled IDs, and further, sample-based solutions are not known for estimating D with dynamic data when visitors arrive and depart, only for *partly dynamic* case when departure of visitors is not recorded. One can be principled and use well-known *sketches* since they only keep aggregate information (like counts, projections), rather than explicit IDs, and therefore afford natural obfuscation. While such solutions approximate distinct count well with dynamic data, they also do not work because they rely on hash functions to aggregate IDs: during the breach, the intruder obtains access to the hash functions, and can carry out a dictionary attack, compromising some of the IDs.

This example illustrates the issues involved when one seeks privacy and security simultaneously: even if we rely on cryptography and use exponential space or time to process the dynamic data, there are no known methods for even simple queries like distinct count. Of course, in reality, the dynamic data may have more attributes and many queries are of interest from estimating statistics like averages, to data mining tasks like finding heavy hitters, anomalies and others.

In this paper, we address such problems and develop both algorithmic and lower bound techniques. In order to do that, we need to formalize security and privacy. Typically, this is done by defining the limitations of an adversary and proving methods to be secure against one. In contrast, we are inspired by the information-theoretic approach of *differential privacy* and its recent extension *pan-privacy*, where the adversary has no computational or storage limitations.

We consider the *fully dynamic* setting in which for each user, represented by an ID i, (drawn from a universe $\mathcal{U}$), we maintain a *state* a_i, which consists of cumulative updates to i until time t. At each time step, the state of a single user is modified by incrementing or decrementing updates (in arbitrary integral values). In *partly dynamic* data, only increments are allowed. In addition, we call this *fully* or *partly streaming*, respectively, if the algorithms use sublinear space (typically, space polylogarithmic in various parameters).

We adopt the notion of differential privacy [5]. Informally, a randomized function f is *differentially private* with respect to the IDs if the probability distribution on the range of f is not sensitive to changing the state of any single user ID. To add security to privacy, Dwork et al. [7, 4] formalized the notion of *pan-privacy*. Informally, both the distribution of the internal states of the algorithm and the distribution of outputs should be insensitive to changing the state of a single user. This addresses privacy even in the case when there is one unannounced memory breach by the adversary. We study this model henceforth, and later, comment on variants of the model. Without some "secret state" (such as a secret set of hash or cryptographic keys), it might seem impossible to estimate statistics privately, but, surprisingly, Dwork et al. [7] showed that several interesting statistics on streams can be estimated accurately on *partly dynamic data*. Their algorithms are based on the technique of randomized response [16] and sampling.

1.1 Our Contributions

We design the first known pan-private algorithms for *distinct count*, *cropped first moment* and *heavy hitters count* for fully dynamic data. Our algorithms rely on *sketches* widely useful in streaming: in some cases, we add suitable noise using a novel approach of calibrating noise to the underlying problem structure and the projection matrix of the sketch; in other cases, we maintain certain statistics on sketches,

and in yet others, we define novel sketches. In what follows, m is the size of the universe of IDs. These statistics, in one form or the other, have a long history, and are considered basic in data analysis tasks over dynamic data in the past few decades and different streaming solutions are known for these problems:

1. *Distinct Count D*: Given a sequence of updates, D is the number of user IDs with nonzero state: $D = |\{i \in \mathcal{U} : a_i \neq 0\}|$. We present an algorithm that is ε-pan private and outputs an estimate $(1+\alpha)D \pm \text{polylog}$ with probability at least $1 - \delta$, where polylog is a polylogarithmic function of various input parameters and m is the size of the universe. It directly uses a sketch known before based on stable distributions for estimating distinct count [1, 10], but maintains noisy versions based on a new method of adding noise tailored to the sketch and the underlying problem. What is surprising is that without the constraints of pan-privacy, this approach yields approximations for higher frequency moments $F_k = \sum_i a_i^k$ for $k = 1$ and 2 [10], but while we are able to derive pan-private distinct counts (related to F_0) using the same approach, it does not work for pan-private cropped moments such as $T_1(\tau) = \sum_i \min(a_i, \tau)$ or $T_2(\tau) = \sum_i \min(a_i, \tau)^2$ or other cropped moments.

   We complement this result by showing lower bounds. Let $\mathcal{A}$ be an online (not necessarily streaming) algorithm that outputs $D \pm o(\sqrt{m})$ with small constant probability. Then we show that $\mathcal{A}$ is not ε-pan private for any constant ε. This is the first known lower bound explicitly for pan-private algorithms and the best such bound for the distinct count problem. In fact, we develop an approach to showing lower bounds that takes a copy of the memory by breaching the algorithm once, and then simulating the algorithm with random inputs in parallel with this seed memory like noisy decoding [3]. Our lower bound holds irrespective of the memory used by $\mathcal{A}$—even if the memory is $\Omega(m)$. Further, we show a lower bound of $(1+\alpha)D \pm \text{polylog}(1/\delta)$ for algorithms that succeed with probability $1 - \delta$, essentially tight up to additive polylog terms with our pan-private algorithm.

2. *Cropped first moment $T_1(\tau)$*: We present a fully dynamic algorithm that is ϵ-pan private and outputs an estimate in $[1/2 T_1(\tau) - O(\tau\sqrt{m}/\epsilon), 2T_1(\tau) + O(\tau\sqrt{m}/\epsilon)]$. Using a prior technique, this guarantee can be improved to an estimate in $[1/2(1+\alpha)T_1 - O(\tau \log m/\epsilon), 2(1+\alpha)T_1 + O(\tau \log m/\epsilon)]$. Our solution is a new sketch for this problem that is linear *modulo 2τ*, an approach that is unusual in the streaming literature but helps reduce the error of our pan-private algorithm.

   The lower bounds for distinct counts above imply that no ϵ-pan private algorithm can estimate $T_1(\tau)$ to within $o(\tau\sqrt{m})$ additive error with small constant probability.

3. *Heavy Hitters Count $\text{HH}(k)$* is defined as $\text{HH}(k) = |\{i : a_i \geq F_1/k\}|$. It is the number of IDs that have state that is at least a $1/k$ fraction of the total state over all IDs. We present a fully dynamic pan-private algorithm that returns an estimate in $[(1 - \alpha)\text{HH}(k) - O(\sqrt{k}), \text{HH}(O(k^2)) + O(\sqrt{k})]$ (that is no worse than $O(k)$ approximation, up to additive errors). We obtain this algorithm by first observing that using our T_1 estimator and with $O(m)$ space, we can provide an

estimate $\mathrm{HII}(k) \pm O(\sqrt{m})$, and then using this on the space of all buckets in the Count-Min sketch [2] which uses much smaller space.

Once again a reduction from distinct counts establishes that no ϵ-pan private algorithm can estimate the k-heavy hitters count to within $o(\sqrt{k})$ additive error, even if it is allowed to output the count of arbitrarily light IDs with nonzero state.

We emphasize that all our algorithms work on fully dynamic data which has not been considered in pan-privacy before. Dwork et al. [7] provide pan-private algorithms for problems (1)-(3) for partly dynamic data. Our definitions of the problems we consider differ slightly from those in [7]: we consider distinct count instead of density, cropped sum instead of cropped mean, and a more standard definition of heavy hitters count. In all cases our definitions specify problems that are at least as hard to approximate as those in [7].

The algorithms presented in [7] are based on sampling and randomized response and do not work with fully dynamic data. This is why we had to develop alternative techniques based on maintaining statistics over sketches. Surprisingly, for both distinct counts and cropped sums, our algorithms provide estimates for fully dynamic data that match the best bounds from [7] for partly dynamic data (up to additive polylog factors for distinct counts, and multiplicative factor 2 for cropped sum). The hashing technique used in [7] to obtain a constant multiplicative approximation for distinct count and cropped sum has an implicit additive factor of $O(\log m)$ because of adding Laplacian noise linear in $\log m$, giving an approximation of $(1 \pm \alpha)D \pm O(\log m)$. In fact a pure multiplicative approximation of $1 \pm \alpha$, for any constant α, is prohibited by our lower bounds on distinct counts.

The pan-private estimation of heavy hitters count in [7] outputs an estimate $[\mathrm{HH}((1 + \rho)k) - \alpha m, \mathrm{HH}(k/(1 + \rho)) + \alpha m]$. The hashing technique in [7] discussed above cannot be directly applied to this problem because it could both decrease or increase the number of heavy hitters in different hash levels. In fact, our algorithm is based on a precise analysis of how hashing affects the heavy hitters count. We thus give the first constant additive error approximation for heavy hitters count for either partly or fully dynamic data.

No explicit lower bounds were previously known for pan-private algorithms with a single intrusion. Independent of our work, [12] study lower bounds for two-party differential privacy, where two parties performing an analysis on their joint data, want to keep each party's view of the protocol a differentially private function of the other's input. In this model, they show a lower bound of $\Omega(\sqrt{n}/\log n)$ for computing the Hamming distance of two n-bit vectors. This lower bound implies a lower bound on multi-pass pan-private algorithms for distinct count (as well as for related statistics), allowing a single intrusion in each of the multiple passes over the data. Developed independently of their work, our lower bounds use different methods, hold for algorithms for fully dynamic data that may be thought of as single pass algorithms with just one intrusion, and are stronger than the bounds implied by their work for the single pass scenario.

Finally, we make an intriguing observation. Pan-privacy does not require algorithms to have any computational or storage constraints; it only requires differential privacy and security against intrusion. In fact, our lower bounds hold against algorithms that can use unbounded storage and per-form arbitrary computations per update. On the other hand, the pan-private algorithms for distinct count and heavy hitters we present here are actually streaming algorithms that use only polylogarithmic time per update and polylogarithmic space. This may be an artifact of the techniques we use. We leave it open to find problems for which pan-private algorithms exist that necessarily use large (say polynomial) space.

We start in Section 2 by introducing relevant definitions and notation. In Section 3, we present our pan-private algorithms by keeping statistics on sketches. In Section 4, we present our lower bounds. We conclude with additional discussion in Section 5.

2. BACKGROUND

In this section we introduce notation and definitions and recapitulate earlier work that we build on.

2.1 Model and Notation

We are given a universe $\mathcal{U}$, where $|\mathcal{U}| = m$. An *update* is defined as an ordered pair $(i, d) \in \mathcal{U} \times \mathbb{Z}$. Consider a semi-infinite sequence of updates $(i_1, d_1), (i_2, d_2), \ldots$; the *input* for all our algorithms consists of the first t updates, denoted $S_t = (i_1, d_1), \ldots, (i_t, d_t)$. The *state vector* after t updates is an m-dimensional vector $\mathbf{a}^{(t)}$, indexed by the elements in $\mathcal{U}$. (We omit the superscript when it is clear from the context.) The elements of the vector state vector $\mathbf{a} = \mathbf{a}^{(t)}$, store the cumulative updates to i: $a_i = \sum_{j:i_j=i} d_j$. Each a_i is referred to as the state of ID i. In the *partly dynamic* model, all updates are positive, i.e. $\forall j : d_j \geq 0$; in the *fully dynamic* model, updates can be both positive (*inserts*), i.e. $d_j \geq 0$, and negative (*deletes*), i.e. $d_j < 0$, but at any time, $a_i \geq 0$ (since deletes cannot exceed inserts). We assume an upper bound Z on the maximum absolute value of the state of any $i \in \mathcal{U}$, i.e. $a_i \leq Z$ at any time step.

2.2 Differential Privacy

Dwork et al. [5] define the notion of differential privacy that provides a guarantee that the probability distribution on the outputs of a mechanism is "almost the same," irrespective of whether or not an individual is present in the data set. Such a guarantee incentivizes participation of individuals in a database by assuring them of incurring very little risk by such a participation. To capture the notion of a user opting in or out, the sameness condition is defined to hold with respect to a neighbor relation; intuitively, two inputs are neighbors if they differ only in the participation of a single individual. For example, Dwork et al. defined datasets to be neighbors if they differ in a single row. Formally,

DEFINITION 1. *[5] A randomized function f provides ε-differential privacy with respect to a binary neighbor relation $\sim$, if for input data sets D, D' such that $D \sim D'$, and for all $Y \subseteq Range(f)$, $\Pr[f(D) \in Y] \leq \exp(\varepsilon) \times \Pr[f(D') \in Y]$.*

One mechanism that Dwork et al. [5] use to provide differential privacy is the *Laplacian noise method* which depends on the *global sensitivity* of a function:

DEFINITION 2. *[5] For $f : \mathcal{D} \to \mathbb{R}^d$, the global sensitivity of f is $GS_f = \max_{D \sim D'} ||f(D) - f(D')||_1$.*

THEOREM 1. *[5] For $f : \mathcal{D} \to \mathbb{R}$, mechanism $\mathcal{M}$ that adds independently generated noise drawn from $Lap(GS_f/\varepsilon)$ to the output preserves ε-differential privacy.*

Another, more general (though, not always computationally efficient) method of providing differential privacy is the so called *exponential mechanism* proposed by McSherry and Talwar [13]. This mechanism is parametrized by a "quality function" $q(\mathbf{x}, r)$ that maps a pair of an input data set $\mathbf{x}$ (a vector over some arbitrary real-valued domain) and candidate output r (again over an arbitrary range R) to a real valued "score." The mechanism selects an output with exponential bias in favor of high scoring outputs by sampling from the following *exponential distribution*: $\mu_\varepsilon(r) \propto \exp(\varepsilon q(\mathbf{x}, r))$. For discrete ranges, Gupta et al. [9] provide an analog of a theorem of McSherry and Talwar [13]. Let $\Delta_q = \max_{\mathbf{x} \sim \mathbf{y}, r} |q(\mathbf{x}, r) - q(\mathbf{y}, r)|$.

THEOREM 2. *[13] The exponential mechanism, when used to select an output $r \in R$, gives $2\varepsilon\Delta_q$-differential privacy. Let R^* be the subset of R achieving $q(\mathbf{x}, r) = \max_r q(\mathbf{x}, r)$, and $\mathcal{E}_q^\varepsilon$ be a value drawn from the exponential mechanism, then:*

$$\Pr[q(\mathbf{x}, \mathcal{E}_q^\varepsilon) < \max_r q(\mathbf{x}, r) - \ln(|R| / |R^*|)/\varepsilon - t/\varepsilon] \leq e^{-t}$$

We will use the exponential mechanism to design a new mechanism, which will help us derive pan-private estimates of norms from sketches (see Section 3.1).

Part of the usefulness of differential privacy lies in its resilience to various notions of composition. Next we present two composition theorems due to Dwork et al. [5] that will be useful in the remainder of this paper. The first composition result concerns the privacy of computing multiple differentially private functions of the same input.

THEOREM 3. *[5] Given mechanisms $\mathcal{M}_i$, $i \in [r]$ each of which provide ε_i-differential privacy, then the overall mechanism $\mathcal{M}$ that executes these r mechanisms with independent randomness and outputs the vector of their outputs, provides $\left(\sum_{i \in [r]} \varepsilon_i\right)$-differential privacy.*

The second composition result concerns composition of the neighbor relation. First we define the notion of ℓ-neighborhood, which is a binary relation induced by the neighbor relation.

DEFINITION 3. *Given a neighbor relation $\sim$, the ℓ-neighbor relation $\sim_\ell$ is defined as follows. Two input datasets D, D' are said to be 1-neighbors—i.e. $D \sim_1 D'$, if $D \sim D'$. For a natural number $\ell > 1$, D, D' are said to be ℓ-neighbors—i.e. $D \sim_\ell D'$ if $D \sim_{\ell-1} D'$ or there exists a dataset $D''\sim D'$ such that $D'' \sim_{\ell-1} D$.*

Another way to think of ℓ-neighbors is as inputs that are linked by a path of length at most ℓ in the graph induced by the neighbor relation. Next we present a theorem of Dwork et al. formally showing that differential privacy is resilient to composition of the neighbor relation.

THEOREM 4. *[5] If a function f provides ε-differential privacy with respect to $\sim$, then f provides $\ell\varepsilon$-differential privacy with respect to $\sim_\ell$.*

2.3 Pan privacy

Pan privacy guarantees a participant that his/her risk of being identified by participating in a data set is very little even if there is an external intrusion on the internal state of the analyzing algorithm. Formally, consider two online sequences of updates $S = ((i_1, d_1), \ldots, (i_t, d_t))$ and $S' = ((i'_1, d'_1), \ldots, (i'_{t'}, d'_{t'}))$ associated with state vectors $\mathbf{a}$ and $\mathbf{a}'$ respectively.

DEFINITION 4 (USER-LEVEL NEIGBORS). *S and S' are said to be (user-level) neighbors if there exists a (multi)set of updates in S indexed by $K \subseteq [t]$ that update the same ID $i \in \mathcal{U}$, and there exists a (multi)set of updates in S' indexed by $K' \subseteq [t']$ that updates some $j(\neq i) \in \mathcal{U}$ such that $\sum_{k \in K} d_k = \sum_{k \in K'} d'_k$ and for all other updates in S and S' indexed by $Q = [t] - K$ and $Q' = [t'] - K'$ respectively,*

$$\forall i \in \mathcal{U} \sum_{k \in Q, s.t.\ i_k = i} d_k = \sum_{k \in Q', s.t.\ i'_k = i} d'_k.$$

Notice that in the definition above t and t' do not have to be equal because we allow the d_i's to be integers. The definition ensures that two inputs are neighbors if some of the occurrences of an ID in S is replaced by some other ID in S' and everything else stays the same except (a) the order may be arbitrarily different and (b) the updates can be arbitrarily broken up since they are not constrained to be 1's. The neighbor relation preserves the first frequency moment of the sequence of updates, considered to be public information. Also, the graph induced by the neighbor relation on any set of sequences with the same first frequency moment is connected.

Our notion of neighborhood is slightly different the definition of Dwork et al. [7] definition, where any two data streams S and S' are neighbors if they differ only in the presence or absence of any number of occurrences of any element $i \in \mathcal{U}$ (i.e. $\mathbf{a}$ and $\mathbf{a}'$ have hammind distance at most 1). Our definition ensures that two neighboring sequences of updates are of the same "length," in the sense that the sum of the updates over all items is the same for both S and S', that is, $\sum_{i=1}^t d_k = \sum_{i=1}^{t'} d'_k$. For this purpose, we constrain the sum of the updates of the occurrences of item i in S to be conserved when they are replaced by item j in S'. In our definition, the total weight of updates is public, but, still, an adversary cannot distinguish between appearances of ID i or ID j, even if the adversary knows all other appearances of all other IDs. This modified definition of neighborhood (with its modified notion of privacy) is necessary to make the sensitivity of the k-heavy hitters count bounded. Such a modification was not necessary in [7], as they used a non-standard (and easier to approximate) notion of k-heavy hitters. We emphasize that except for our heavy hitters algorithm, all our other algorithms are private both according to the definition of Dwork et al. and according to our definition of neighborhood.

We comment on the composability of our definition of neighborhood. Applying definition 3, we see that two sequences S and S' will be ℓ-neighbors if there exist (possibly multi) sets of ID's of cardinality ℓ: $\{i_1, i_2 \ldots i_\ell\}$ and $\{j_1, j_2, \ldots, j_\ell\}$ all from $\mathcal{U}$, such that some occurrences of each $i_k, 1 \leq k \leq \ell$ in S are replaced by some occurrences of $j_k \neq i_k, 1 \leq k \leq \ell$ in S'. There is no other restriction on the j'_ks; they may be all equal, different or any subset of these may be equal. Hence Theorem 4 is applicable to our definition of ℓ-neighbors.

DEFINITION 5 (USER-LEVEL PAN PRIVACY [7]). *Let $\mathbf{Alg}$ be an algorithm. Let I denote the set of internal states of the algorithm, and let σ the set of possible output* *sequences. Then algorithm* **Alg** *mapping input prefixes to the range* $I \times \sigma$, *is pan-private (against a single intrusion) if for all sets* $I' \subseteq I$ *and* $\sigma' \subseteq \sigma$, *and for all pairs of user-level neighboring data stream prefixes* S *and* S'

$$\Pr[\mathbf{Alg}(S) \in (I', \sigma')] \leq e^{\varepsilon} \Pr[\mathbf{Alg}(S') \in (I', \sigma')]$$

where the probability spaces are over the coin flips of the algorithm **Alg**.

2.4 Sketches and Stable Distributions

In this section we discuss previous work in sketch-based streaming.

DEFINITION 6. *[15] A distribution* $\mathcal{S}(p)$ *over* $\mathbb{R}$ *is said to be p-stable if there exists* $p \geq 0$ *such that for any n real numbers* $b_1, \ldots, b_m$ *and i.i.d. variables* $Y_1, \ldots, Y_m$ *with distribution* $\mathcal{S}(p)$, *the random variable* $\sum_i b_i Y_i$ *has the same distribution as the random variable* $(\sum_i |b_i|^p)^{1/p} Y$, *where* Y *is a random variable with distribution* $\mathcal{S}(p)$.

Examples of p-stable distributions are the Gaussian distribution, which is 2-stable, and the Cauchy distribution, which is 1-stable. Stable distributions have been used to compute the L_p norms of vectors ($L_p = (\sum_i a_i^p)^{1/p}$) in the streaming model [10, 1].

Let X be a matrix of random values of dimension $m \times r$, where each entry of the matrix $X_{i,j}$, $1 \leq i \leq m$, and $1 \leq j \leq r$, is drawn independently from $\mathcal{S}(p)$, with p as small as possible. The *sketch vector* $\mathrm{sk}(\mathbf{a})$ is defined as the dot product of matrix X^T with $\mathbf{a}$, so $\mathrm{sk}(\mathbf{a}) = X^T \cdot \mathbf{a}$. From the property of stable distributions we know that each entry of $\mathrm{sk}(\mathbf{a})$ is distributed as $(\sum_i |a_i|^p)^{1/p} X_0$, where X_0 is a random variable chosen from a p-stable distribution. The sketch is used to compute $\sum_i |a_i|^p$ for $0 < p < \alpha / \log Z$, from which we can approximate $D^{(t)}$ up to a $(1 + \alpha)$ factor(See [1] for details). By construction, any $\mathrm{sk}(\mathbf{a})_j$ can be used to estimate L_p^p. Cormode et al. [1] and Indyk [10] obtain a low-space good estimator for $(\sum_i |a_i|^p)$ by taking the median of all entries $\left| \mathrm{sk}(\mathbf{a})_j \right|^p$ over j:

THEOREM 5. *If the continuous stable distribution is approximated by discretizing it to a grid of size* $(\frac{mZ}{\alpha \delta})^{O(1)}$, *the support of the distribution* $\mathcal{S}(p)$ *from which the values* $X_{i,j}$ *are drawn is truncated beyond* $(mZ)^{O(1)}$, *and* $r = O(1/\alpha^2 \cdot \log(1/\delta))$, *then with probability* $1 - \delta$,

$$(1 - \alpha)^p \mathrm{median}_j \left| \mathrm{sk}(\mathbf{a})_j \right|^p \leq \mathrm{median} |X_0|^p \left(\sum_i |a_i|^p \right)$$

$$\leq (1 + \alpha)^p \mathrm{median}_j \left| \mathrm{sk}(\mathbf{a})_j \right|^p$$

where $\mathrm{median} |X_0|^p$ *is the median of absolute values (raised to the power p) from a (truncated, discretized) p-stable distribution.*

We will use these details in Algorithm 1 in Section 3.1 to propose a pan-private algorithm for distinct counts.

3. PAN-PRIVATE ALGORITHMS FOR FULLY DYNAMIC DATA

In this section we present our pan-private algorithms that work for fully dynamic data. Our algorithms follow the outline:

- initialize a sketch to a noisy vector chosen from an appropriate distribution;
- update the sketch linearly (linearity may be over the real field, or modulo a real number); and
- compute a global statistic of the sketch.

The fact that, for all the algorithms, the state of the algorithm is a linear function of its input and the noisy initialization allows us to characterize the distribution of the state of the algorithm at any time step; this property is essential to both the privacy and utility analyses of our algorithms. While particular entries in the sketches may not be accurate approximations of the states of the user IDs, the global statistic computed at the end can be shown to be an accurate estimate of the desired value.

3.1 Distinct count

We use sketching based on stable distributions outlined in Section 2.4 to design an algorithm for pan-private estimation of the distinct count statistic $D^{(t)}$. We exploit the linearity property of the sketches by maintaining a noisy version of the sketch in order to achieve pan-privacy. Because the sketch is a linear function of the state vector, it is enough to add an initial noise vector drawn from the appropriate distribution. To do so without adding too much noise, we develop a new technique of adding noise calibrated to the underlying random projection matrix and the nature of the statistic we are computing, using the exponential mechanism of McSherry and Talwar [13]. As a consequence, while this mechanism, in general, is not computationally efficient, it provides us with a new framework for adding noise that is not "function oblivious." The established Laplace mechanism [5], that adds noise calibrated to the *global sensitivity* of the function, beyond being aware of the global sensitivity of the function is oblivious of the underlying structure of the problem. This is important for our application as the sensitivity of the stable distribution sketch can be very high due to the heavy tails of p-stable distributions for small p.

Next we describe the mechanism we use to draw the noise vector.

An initializing noise vector: We use the exponential distribution to generate a random noise vector that initializes the sketch. The sketch vector has dimension r; let us denote the i-th row of X as X_{i*} and the j-th column of X as X_{*j}.

We use the exponential mechanism of McSherry and Talwar with the following quality function q. If the true sketch vector is $\mathrm{sk}(\mathbf{a})$, then

$$q\left(\mathrm{sk}(\mathbf{a}), \mathrm{sk}(\mathbf{a})^{\mathrm{priv}}\right) = -d\left(\mathrm{sk}(\mathbf{a}) - \mathrm{sk}(\mathbf{a})^{\mathrm{priv}}\right),$$

where d is defined as:

$$d(\mathbf{z}) := \min \|\mathbf{c}\|_0 \quad \text{s.t.}$$
$$\mathbf{z} = X^T \mathbf{c}$$
$$\forall i \in [m] : c_i \in [-2Z, 2Z].$$

If the above program is infeasible, then $d(\mathbf{z}) = \infty$.

Given sketch vector $\mathrm{sk}(\mathbf{a})$, the mechanism picks a sketch $\mathrm{sk}(\mathbf{a})^{\mathrm{priv}}$ from a distribution, μ_ϵ given by

$$\mu_\epsilon(\mathrm{sk}(\mathbf{a})^{\mathrm{priv}}) \propto \exp\left(\frac{\epsilon}{4} q(\mathrm{sk}(\mathbf{a}), \mathrm{sk}(\mathbf{a})^{\mathrm{priv}})\right).$$

Intuitively, the distance function d roughly measures the minimum number of items in the state vector $\mathbf{a}$, whose entries need to be changed in order to get from $sk(\mathbf{a})$ to $sk(\mathbf{a})^{priv}$. This is used in the utility analysis.

Next, we need to compute the sensitivity Δ_q of q defined as $\Delta_q = \max_{\mathbf{x} \sim \mathbf{z}, \mathbf{y}} |d(\mathbf{x}, \mathbf{y}) - d(\mathbf{z}, \mathbf{y})|$.

LEMMA 1. *For q as defined above, $\Delta_q \leq 2$.*

PROOF. If $sk(\mathbf{a})$ and $sk(\mathbf{a}')$ are the true sketch vectors for neighboring sequences of updates corresponding to state vectors $\mathbf{a}$ and $\mathbf{a}'$ respectively, then for some $i, j \in \mathcal{U}$, $i \neq j$, $sk(\mathbf{a}') = sk(\mathbf{a}) + c_i X_{i*} + c_j X_{j*}$, for some $c_i, c_j \in [-2Z, 2Z]$. Therefore,

$$\Delta_q \leq \max_{sk(\mathbf{a}), sk(\mathbf{a}'), \mathbf{y}} |d(sk(\mathbf{a}) - \mathbf{y}) - d(sk(\mathbf{a}') - \mathbf{y})|$$
$$\leq \max_{sk(\mathbf{a}), c_i, c_j, \mathbf{y}} |d(sk(\mathbf{a}) - \mathbf{y})$$
$$- d(sk(\mathbf{a}) - \mathbf{y} + c_i X_{i*} + c_j X_{j*})|$$
$$\leq 2.$$

$\square$

Let $B = \mathbf{poly}(m, Z)$ be large enough so that: (1) Theorem 5 holds, (2) for any $c \in [-2Z, 2Z]^m$, $X^T c \in [-B, B]^r$. We pick an initializing vector $\mathbf{y}$ using the exponential distribution with quality function q from the range $\mathcal{R} = [-B, B]^r \cap \langle X_{1*}, \ldots, X_{m*} \rangle$, discretized to within $\mathbf{poly}(m, Z, 1/\alpha, 1/\delta)$ precision, again so Theorem 5 holds. Notice that $\log \mathcal{R} = O(r \cdot \log(\mathbf{poly}(m, Z, 1/\alpha, 1/\delta)))$, which implies that $\log \mathcal{R} = \mathbf{poly}(\log m, \log Z, 1/\varepsilon, 1/\alpha, \log(1/\delta))$.

The Algorithm: After initializing, we update and decode the sketch as in the non-private algorithm. Before outputting the final answer, we draw another vector using the exponential mechanism with the same parameters. The algorithm is shown below as Algorithm 1.

Since updates are linear, and $q(sk(\mathbf{a}), sk(\mathbf{a})^{priv})$ is a function of $sk(\mathbf{a}) - sk(\mathbf{a})^{priv}$, initializing the sketch to a vector picked using the exponential mechanism with quality function $q(\mathbf{y}, 0) = -d(\mathbf{y})$ ensures that any state is $2\frac{\epsilon}{4}\Delta_q$-differentially private. More formally, from Theorems 2 and 3, and Definition 5:

LEMMA 2. *At any step in Algorithm 1, the state of the algorithm is a sketch and the distribution over states is given by the exponential mechanism with quality function*

$$q(sk(\mathbf{a}), sk(\mathbf{a})^{priv}) = -d(sk(\mathbf{a}) - sk(\mathbf{a})^{priv}).$$

Hence the algorithm is ϵ-pan private.

Also, by simple application of Theorem 2:

LEMMA 3. *The initializing vector $\mathbf{y}$ has $d(\mathbf{y}) \leq 4\frac{\log |\mathcal{R}|}{\epsilon} + \frac{4}{\epsilon} \log 1/\delta \leq \text{polylog}(m, Z, 1/\epsilon, \log(1/\delta), 1/\alpha)$ with probability $1 - \delta$. The same holds for $\mathbf{y}'$*

THEOREM 6. *With probability $1 - \delta$, Algorithm 1 outputs an estimate in $(1 \pm \alpha)D^{(t)} \pm \mathbf{poly}(\log m, \log Z, \frac{1}{\varepsilon}, \frac{1}{\alpha}, \log \frac{1}{\delta})$.*

PROOF. Follows by the previous lemma, the definition of d, the fact that $\|\mathbf{a}\|_0 - \|\mathbf{c}\|_0 \leq \|\mathbf{a} + \mathbf{c}\|_0 \leq \|\mathbf{a}\|_0 + \|\mathbf{c}\|_0$, Theorem 5 and the linearity property of sketches: $sk(\mathbf{a}) \pm sk(\mathbf{b}) = sk(\mathbf{a} \pm \mathbf{b})$. $\square$

Algorithm 1 is a streaming algorithm since it uses space polylogarithmic in m and takes time polylogarithmic in m per new update.

Algorithm 1 Pan-private approximation of $D^{(t)}$

INPUT: privacy parameter ε, $0 < p < \alpha/Z < 1$, matrix X computed off-line See [1] for converting this to the on-line setting using seeded pseudorandom constructions., $\text{sf}(p) = \text{median} |X_0|^p$ also computed off-line numerically.

Initialize the r-dimensional sketch vector $sk(\mathbf{a})^{priv}$ to $\mathbf{y}$, by picking $\mathbf{y}$ from μ_ε
for all tuples (i, d_t) **do**
  for all $j = 1$ to r **do**
    $sk(\mathbf{a})^{priv}_j \leftarrow sk(\mathbf{a})^{priv}_j + d_t * X_{ij}$
  end for
end for

OUTPUT: Draw r-dimensional vector $\mathbf{y}'$ from μ_ε, assign $sk(\mathbf{a})^{priv} \leftarrow sk(\mathbf{a})^{priv} + \mathbf{y}'$.
return $\tilde{\mathcal{D}} = \text{median}_j \left(\left| sk(\mathbf{a})^{priv}_j \right|^p \right) \cdot \text{sf}(p)$

Since we use the exponential mechanism, our techniques are not efficient in general. We need to sample from a space of 2^S different possible sketches, where S is the maximum bit size of a sketch. When S is polylogarithmic, we need to sample from a quasipolinomial set of objects. Note that a noise vector is only drawn during the preprocessing and postprocessing phases of the algorithm. While these phases take time 2^s, the time per update is only polylogarithmic.

A general noise-calibrating technique for sketches. The construction above gives a more general "recipe." Assume that a function f from state vectors to the reals ($f : [-Z, Z]^\mathcal{U} \to \mathbb{R}$) with $f(0) = 0$ can be approximated by a sketch. More precisely, the sketch is given by a linear map L and there exists a procedure that given the sketch outputs $\tilde{f}(\mathbf{a}) \in [\gamma_1 f(\mathbf{a}), \gamma_2 f(\mathbf{a})]$. Then we can use the technique above with $d(\mathbf{z}) = \min\{f(\mathbf{c}) : L\mathbf{c} = \mathbf{z}\}$, where the minimum is over valid differences of state vectors, i.e. $\mathbf{c} \in [-2Z, 2Z]^\mathcal{U}$. By identical proofs to the ones above, the algorithm is $\epsilon/2\Delta_q$-pan private and computes an approximation of f in $[\gamma_1 f(\mathbf{a}) - O(S), \gamma_2 f(\mathbf{a}) + O(S)]$, where S is a bound on the bitsize of a sketch, provided that $f(\mathbf{a} + \mathbf{y}) \in f(\mathbf{a}) \pm f(\mathbf{y})$. Note also that $\Delta_q = \max_{\mathbf{y}: \|\mathbf{y}\|_0 = 1} |f(\mathbf{y})|$, where $\mathbf{y}$ has one nonzero component, and that component is bounded in $[-2Z, 2Z]$.

In particular, a variant of Theorem 6 can be easily achieved for pan-private computation of L_1 and L_2. However, for both L_1 and L_2, this results in an additive factor that is linear in Z, the upper bound on each $|a_i|$. This is because for L_1 or L_2, the sensitivity of the quality function is $\Delta_q = 2Z$ (where d minimizes $\|c\|_1$ and $\|c\|_2$, respectively, instead of $\|c\|_0$) and we need to sample the noise vector from $\mu_{\varepsilon'}$, where $\varepsilon' = \varepsilon/2Z$. In turn, this results in linear dependence on Z in the bound on $d(\mathbf{y})$. The linear dependence is inherent in trying to estimate L_1 and L_2, due to their high sensitivity.

3.2 Cropped First Moment

In this section, we approximate $T_1(\tau)$ using sketches that are linear modulo an appropriately chosen parameter, to be specified later. The difficulty in approximating $T_1(\tau)$ for fully dynamic data is the apparent need to keep counters with range $[0, Z]$ for items, where Z is an upper bound on a_i (because the counters can race up to Z during intermediate stages and later get decremented to less than τ, so one has to keep track of the counter even when it goes far past τ for fully dynamic data). Such an approach results in error that scales linearly with Z, while the sensitivity of $T_1(\tau)$ is only τ, i.e. independent of Z. A natural workaround is to use modular counters, for example to use counters that estimate $a_i \bmod \tau$. However, such counters cannot distinguish between $a_i = 1$ and $a_i = \tau + 1$, and result in an estimate that is no better than a random guess. We show that if we scale a_i randomly between a_i and $2a_i$, then in expectation the modular counters provide an accurate approximation to $T_1(\tau)$. To the best of our knowledge, this approach to modular sketching is new, being motivated by the challenges of pan-private approximation in the fully dynamic data model. The modular counter technique allows us to show accuracy guarantees that are independent of Z.

For any $i \in \mathcal{U}$, let w_i be a real number independently and uniformly sampled from the interval $[1, 2]$. Define:

$$T'(\tau) = \sum_{i \in \mathcal{U}} w_i a_i \bmod 2\tau.$$

In analyzing the relation of $T'(\tau)$ to $T(tau)$, the following technical claim is useful:

CLAIM 1. *Let $a \geq \tau$ and let w be uniformly distributed in $[1, 2]$. Then $\mathbb{E}[wa \bmod 2\tau] \geq \tau/2$.*

PROOF SKETCH. Intuitively, because a is large, wa is supported on a constant fraction of the range $[0, 2\tau]$. Therefore, $\mathbb{E}[wa]$ is high. The full proof appears in Appendix A.1. $\square$

LEMMA 4. *Assume that $\forall i \in \mathcal{U} : a_i \geq 0$. It follows that,*

$$\frac{1}{2} T_1(\tau) \leq \mathbb{E}[T'(\tau)] \leq 2 T_1(\tau). \tag{1}$$

PROOF. Let us break down $T_1(\tau)$ and $T'(\tau)$ into partial sums. Define $A = \sum_{i:a_i < \tau} a_i$, $A' = \sum_{i:a_i < \tau} w_i a_i \bmod 2\tau$, $B = \sum_{i:a_i \geq \tau} \tau = |i : a_i > \tau| \tau$, and $B' = \sum_{i:a_i \geq \tau} w_i a_i \bmod 2\tau$. By definition, $T_1(\tau) = A + B$ and $T'(\tau) = A' + B'$.

Note that for $0 \leq a_i < \tau$, $w_i a_i \bmod 2\tau = w_i a_i$ since $w_i a_i < 2\tau$. Therefore, $\mathbb{E}[A'] = 3/2 A$.

Next we compute $\mathbb{E}[B']$ and compare it to B. Notice first that $w_i a_i \bmod 2\tau < 2\tau$, and, therefore, $B' \leq 2B$.

Claim 1 provides a lower bound B' in terms of B. In particular, Claim 1 implies that $\mathbb{E}[B'] \geq 1/2B$.

The lemma follows from the bounds on $\mathbb{E}[A']$ and $\mathbb{E}[B']$.

$\square$

Since $T'(\tau)$ is the sum of bounded independent random variables, Hoeffding's bound can be used to show that $T'(\tau) = (1 \pm \frac{1}{2}) T_1(\tau) \pm O(\tau\sqrt{m})$ with high constant probability.

The next step is to estimate $T'(\tau)$ pan-privately. First, for technical reasons related to the noise distribution, we need to prove a variation of Lemma 4.

LEMMA 5.

$$\mathbb{E}\left[T'(\tau) - \sum_{w_i a_i \bmod 2\tau > 2\tau - 1} w_i a_i \bmod 2\tau \right]$$
$$\geq \left(\frac{1}{2} - \frac{1}{\tau} \right) T_1(\tau).$$

PROOF SKETCH. We show that only the contribution of items i with $a_i \geq \tau$ is reduced and we bound the reduction. $\square$

We are now ready to describe and analyze the algorithm. We first describe the noise distribution we use. Let $\mathcal{N}$ be the distribution given by the following density function:

$$f(x) = \begin{cases} \frac{e^\varepsilon}{2\tau - 1 + e^\varepsilon} & x \in [0, 1] \\ \frac{1}{2\tau - 1 + e^\varepsilon} & x \in (1, 2\tau) \end{cases} \tag{2}$$

This distribution corresponds to the following experiment: with probability $e^\varepsilon/(2\tau - 1 + e^\varepsilon)$ pick a uniform random value from $[0, 1]$; with probability $(2\tau - 1)/(2\tau - 1 + e^\varepsilon)$ pick a uniform random value from $(1, 2\tau)$.

The algorithm is shown as Algorithm 2.

Algorithm 2 Pan-private approximation of $T_1(\tau)$

INPUT: privacy parameter α, cropping parameter τ

for all $i \in \mathcal{U}$ **do**
    pick c_i independently from $\mathcal{N}$
    pick w_i independently and uniformly from $[1, 2]$
end for

for all tuples (i, d_t) **do**
    set $c_{i_t} := (c_{i_t} + w_{i_t} d_t) \bmod 2\tau$
end for

OUTPUT:
Set $\sigma = \sum_i c_i$, and $\tilde{\sigma} = \sigma + \mathrm{Lap}(2\tau/\epsilon)$
Set:

$$\tilde{T}_1(\tau) := \left(\tilde{\sigma} - \frac{\tau^2 m}{2\tau - 1 + e^\varepsilon} \right) \frac{2\tau - 1 + e^\varepsilon}{e^\varepsilon - 1} - \frac{m}{2}$$

return $\tilde{T}_1(\tau)$

THEOREM 7. *Algorithm 2 is 2ϵ-pan private. Further, with probability at least $2/3$,*

$$\left(\frac{1}{2} - \frac{1}{\tau} \right) T_1 - O(\tau\sqrt{m}/\varepsilon) \leq \tilde{T}_1(\tau) \leq 2 T_1 + O(\tau\sqrt{m}\varepsilon).$$

PROOF SKETCH. Since the state of Algorithm 2 is a linear function of the input and the initial noise, to prove both privacy and utility, it is enough to consider the noise distribution when the state vector at query time is $\mathbf{a}$. Namely, observe that for any i with state a_i, c_i is distributed as $(\mathcal{N} + w_i a_i) \bmod 2\tau$. It can be shown that this distribution provides pan-privacy and has expectation bounded above by $T'(\tau)$ and below by $T'(\tau) - \sum_{w_i a_i \bmod 2\tau > 2\tau - 1} w_i a_i \bmod 2\tau$. Then Lemma 4, Lemma 5, and a Hoeffding bound finish the proof. $\square$

Using the technique of multiple levels of hashing [7], the additive error can be reduced to $\tau \, \mathbf{poly}(\log m, \frac{1}{\varepsilon})$ at the cost of slightly increasing the multiplicative approximation factor. Also, Algorithm 2 can be used to approximate distinct counts by setting τ to a small constant greater than 2. However, this method provides a worse approximation than the one we achieve using stable distribution sketches.

43

3.3 Heavy Hitter Counts

We present a pan-private algorithm for heavy hitter count estimation with fully dynamic data by using the T_1 statistic over a structure inspired by the well known CM sketches [2]. We use the T_1 algorithm from Subsection 3.2 as a black box; in fact, any T_1 estimator that works with fully dynamic data suffices.

Recall that our T_1 estimator incurs a multiplicative approximation factor of 2 and an additive error $O(\sqrt{m}/\epsilon)$. As $HH(k)$ is bounded by k, which can be assumed to be constant, the additive error term is prohibitive. The key step in our algorithm is to project the input S onto S' over a much smaller universe, so that S' has approximately the same k-heavy hitters count. In fact, we are able to reduce the universe size to a constant that depends only on k and the desired approximation guarantee. The reduced universe size directly implies a more accurate T_1 estimate and, hence, a more accurate estimate of the number of k-heavy hitters. Next we present our algorithm.

Assume the value $F_1 = F_1^{(t_0)}$, where t_0 is the time step when the algorithm is queried, is known ahead of time (this value is public by our definition of neighborhood). Assume also oracle access to a random function $f : [m] \rightarrow [h]$. Given a sequence of updates S, let $f(S)$ be the sequence $(f(i_1), d_1), \dots, (f(i_t), d_t)$, and let $T_k(\tau|f)$ and $\tilde{T}_k(\tau|f)$ be, respectively, $T_k(\tau)$ and $\tilde{T}_k(\tau)$ computed on the stream $f(S)$. Note that $f(S)$ is a stream over the universe $[h]$ and can easily be simulated online given the oracle for f. Our algorithm is shown as Algorithm 3.

Algorithm 3 Pan-private approximation of $HH(k)$

INPUT: privacy parameter ε, parameter k

Choose a random function $f : \mathcal{U} \rightarrow [h]$
Compute $x_1 = \tilde{T}_1(F_1/k|f)$ and $x_2 = \tilde{T}_1(F_1/ck|f)$ using Algorithm 2

OUTPUT: return

$$\tilde{HH}(k) := (x_1 - x_2)\left(\frac{F_1}{k} - \frac{F_1}{ck}\right)^{-1}$$

Algorithm 3 is accurate provided that the function f approximately preserves the number of heavy hitters. Lemma 6 shows that a random f satisfies this condition with high probability.

LEMMA 6. *Let $f : \mathcal{U} \rightarrow [h]$ be a random function. Also, let $\tilde{k} = |\{j : \exists i \in h^{-1}(j) \text{ s.t. } a_i \geq t/k\}|$. With probability $1 - \delta$,*

$$\frac{\tilde{k}}{HH(k)} \geq 1 - \frac{k}{\delta h}.$$

PROOF SKETCH. The proof is a standard balls-and-bins analysis. $\square$

Lemma 7 shows that we can project the universe onto a significantly smaller universe without creating "new" heavy hitters.

LEMMA 7. *Let $A \subseteq \mathcal{U}$ be set of items s.t. $\forall i \in A : a_i \leq F_1\delta/2k^2$. Also, let $f : \mathcal{U} \rightarrow [h]$ be a pairwise-independent*

hash function. There exists an $h_0 = \Theta(k)$, s.t. for any $h \geq h_0$ with probability at least $1 - \delta$

$$\forall j \in [h] : \sum_{i \in A \cap f^{-1}(j)} a_i \leq F_1/k.$$

PROOF SKETCH. The proof follows from a variance computation and Chebyshev's bound. $\square$

We are now ready to analyze $\tilde{HH}(k)$.

THEOREM 8. *$\tilde{HH}(k)$ can be computed while satisfying 2ϵ-pan privacy. Moreover, for large enough $h = \Omega(k)$, with constant probability the following holds:*

$$\frac{1-\beta}{2} HH(k) - O(\sqrt{k}/\varepsilon) \leq 2\tilde{HH}(O(k^2)) + O(\sqrt{k}/\varepsilon)$$

PROOF. The privacy guarantee follows by the ϵ-pan privacy of the cropped sum estimators and the composition theorem. Next we analyze utility.

Let $N_j = \sum_{i \in f^{-1}(j)} a_i$. Computing $T_1(\tau)$ at two levels of τ provides an approximation of the number of heavy hitters:

$$T_1(F_1/k) - T_1(F_1/ck)$$
$$= \sum_{j : N_j \geq F_1/ck} \min(N_j, F_1/k) - F_1/ck$$
$$= \sum_{j : N_j \geq F_1/k} (F_1/k - F_1/ck)$$
$$+ \sum_{j : F_1/ck \geq N_j \geq F_1/k} (N_j - F_1/ck)$$

It immediately follows that $|\{j : N_j \geq F_1/k\}| < \mathbb{E}[\tilde{HH}(k)] \leq |\{j : N_j \geq F_1/ck\}|$. By Lemma 6, $|\{j : N_j \geq F_1/k\}| \geq (1 - \beta) HH(k)$ except with probability δ. Lemma 7 can be applied with $A = \{i : a_i \leq F_1\delta/2c^2k^2\}$. By the lemma, for every $j \in [h]$, it holds that $N_j \geq F_1/ck \Rightarrow \exists i \in f^{-1}(j)$ s.t. $a_i \geq F_1\delta/(2c^2k^2)$, except with probability δ. Therefore, $|\{j : N_j \geq F_1/ck\}| \leq HH(c^2k^2/\delta)$. The proof then follows by the guarantees for $\tilde{T}_1$. $\square$

As described, Algorithm 3 keeps only constantly many counters. However, the space complexity is at least linear, as the algorithm needs to keep $O(n \log k)$ random bits in order to evaluate a truly random function f. The number of random bits can be decreased by picking a function f from a family of bounded independence. Kane et al. [11] show that if f is picked from an r-wise independent family, where $r = \Omega(\log(k/\beta)/\log\log(k/\beta))$, then the lower bound on the ratio $\tilde{k}/HH(k)$ from Lemma 6 decreases by at most a multiplicative factor of $1 - \beta$, with high probability. Notice also that for Lemma 7 only pairwise independence is required. Since a function from $\mathcal{U}$ to $[h]$ from an r-wise independent family can be represented by $O(r \log m + r \log k)$ bits and r only needs to be logarithmic in k, Algorithm 3 can be implemented using $O(k + \log k \log m / \log\log k)$ words.

4. LOWER BOUNDS

We present the first known lower bounds against pan-private algorithms that allow a single intrusion. We emphasize that these are the first lower bounds explicitly for pan-privacy with a single intrusion. The lower bounds were developed independently of the work of McGregor et al. [12] and use different methods. The lower bounds of McGregor et al. imply lower bounds for pan-private algorithms that make multiple passes over the data and allow one intrusion in each pass. We consider only single pass algorithms, but our lower bounds are stronger than those of McGregor et al. in the single pass model. We present a more concrete comparison at the end of this section. Our lower bounds hold even for partly dynamic data, and therefore also for fully dynamic data. We show that if only an additive approximation is allowed, the full space extension of prior work [7] for distinct count estimation is optimal. Thus, the multiplicative approximation factor in the analysis of our algorithm is necessary. Furthermore, our new noisy decoding theorem shows that our sketching algorithm gives an almost optimal bi-approximation guarantee. Interestingly, our lower bounds make no assumptions on the space or time complexity of the algorithm, and yet the (almost) optimal algorithm biapproximation happens to use polylogarithmic space.

Dinur-Nissim Style Decoding. Our lower bounds utilize a decoding algorithm of the style introduced in a privacy context by Dinur and Nissim [3]. Informally, we argue that the (private) state of an accurate pan-private algorithm can be thought of as a sanitization of the part of the input that was already processed. We then employ the noisy decoding results to show that if this sanitization is very accurate, then most of the input of the algorithm can be recovered by an adversary.

Next, we introduce the decoding results we will use.

THEOREM 9 ([3]). *Let $\mathbf{x} \in \{0,1\}^n$. For any ϵ and $n \geq n_\epsilon$, the following holds. Given $O(n \log^2 n)$ random strings $\mathbf{q}_1, \ldots, \mathbf{q}_t \in_R \{0,1\}^n$, and approximate answers $\tilde{\mathbf{a}}_1, \ldots, \tilde{\mathbf{a}}_t$ s.t. $\forall i \in [t] : |\mathbf{x} \cdot \mathbf{q}_i - \tilde{\mathbf{a}}_i| = o(\sqrt{n})$, there exists an algorithm that outputs a string $\tilde{\mathbf{x}} \in \{0,1\}^n$ and except with negligible probability $||\mathbf{x} - \tilde{\mathbf{x}}||_0 \leq \epsilon n$.*

In follow up work, [6] strengthened the above and showed that decoding is possible even when a constant fraction of the queries are inaccurate.

THEOREM 10 ([6]). *Given $\rho < \rho^*$, where $\rho*$ is a constant approximately equal to 0.239, there exists a constant ϵ s.t. the following holds. Let $\mathbf{x} \in \{0,1\}^n$. There exists a matrix $A \in \{-1,1\}^{n \times m}$ for some $m = O(n)$ and an efficient algorithm $\mathcal{A}$, s.t. on input $\tilde{b} \in \mathbb{N}^m$, satisfying $|\{i : |(A\mathbf{x} - \tilde{b})_i| > \alpha\}| \leq \rho$, $\mathcal{A}$ outputs $\tilde{\mathbf{x}} \in \{0,1\}^n$ and with probability $1 - e^{-O(m)}$, $||\mathbf{x} - \tilde{\mathbf{x}}||_0 \leq \epsilon \alpha^2$*

Next, we prove a result that is similar to Dinur and Nissim's but uses "union queries" rather than dot product queries.

THEOREM 11. *Let $\mathbf{x} \in \{0,1\}^n$, $||\mathbf{x}||_0 \leq L$ for some $L = L(n)$. For any ϵ and $n \geq n_\epsilon$, there exist $n^{O(L)}$ binary strings $\mathbf{q}_1, \ldots, \mathbf{q}_t \in \{0,1\}^n$ and an algorithm $\mathcal{A}$ such that given answers $\tilde{\mathbf{a}}_1, \ldots, \tilde{\mathbf{a}}_1$ satisfying*

$$\forall i : (1-\alpha_1)||\mathbf{x} + \mathbf{q}_i||_0 - \alpha_2 \leq \tilde{\mathbf{a}}_i \leq (1+\alpha_1)||\mathbf{x} + \mathbf{q}_i||_0 + \alpha_2$$

for $\alpha_2 = o(L)$, $\mathcal{A}$ outputs $\tilde{\mathbf{x}}$ with $||\mathbf{x} - \tilde{\mathbf{x}}||_0 \leq \frac{16(\alpha_1 + \epsilon)}{1 - \alpha_1} L$.

PROOF SKETCH. The proof follows the outline of Dinur and Nissim's arguments for lower bounds against exponentially many queries [3]. □

Lower Bounds from Noisy Decoding. Our approach is to consider pan-private algorithms as sanitization algorithms that respect specific restrictions. The private state

revealed to the adversary at the time of intrusion can be thought of as a sanitization of the part of the input that was processed before the time of intrusion. The adversary is then allowed to ask any query that can be encoded as adding more input and asking for the final answer of the function computed by the algorithm on the concatenated inputs. Using noisy decoding results, we can give noise lower bounds for this sanitization setting which then imply lower bounds for pan-private algorithms.

Another point of view is that the sanitization setting with restricted queries described above can be seen as a one-way two-party differentially private protocol, i.e. a one-way restriction of the model defined by Mironov et al. [14]. Then our lower bounds can be thought of as lower bounds for one-way two-party differential privacy. Since pan-private algorithms give one-way two-party differentially private protocols in the same way in which streaming algorithms give one-way communication protocols in the communication complexity setting, the lower bounds for pan-private algorithms follow.

We introduce our approach using the most direct argument first: a lower bound for the dot product problem.

PROBLEM 1. *Input is a sequence S_t of updates followed by a sequence S'_t.*
Output: Let $\mathbf{a}$ be the state of sequence S_t, and let $\mathbf{a}'$ be the state of S'_t. Output $\mathbf{a} \cdot \mathbf{a}' \pm \alpha = \sum_{i \in \mathcal{U}} a_i a'_i \pm \alpha$, where α is an approximation factor.

THEOREM 12. *Let $\mathcal{A}$ be a streaming algorithm that on input streams S_t, S'_t outputs $\mathbf{a} \cdot \mathbf{a}' \pm o(\sqrt{m})$ with probability at least $1 - O(m^{-2})$. Then $\mathcal{A}$ is not ϵ-pan private for any constant ϵ.*

PROOF. Fix an input sequence S_t s.t. $\forall i \in \mathcal{U} : a_i \in \{0,1\}$. Let X be the internal state of the algorithm $\mathcal{A}$ after processing S_t. By the definition of pan privacy, X is ϵ-differentially private with respect to S_t. Fix some constants δ and η. We will show that for all large enough m, any algorithm $\mathcal{Q}$ that takes as input X and a stream S'_t and outputs $\mathbf{a} \cdot \mathbf{a}' \pm o(\sqrt{m})$ with probability at least $1 - O(m^{-2})$ can be used to compute a vector $\tilde{\mathbf{a}}$ such that $\tilde{a}_i = a_i$ for all but an η fraction of $i \in \mathcal{U}$ with probability $1 - \delta$. Therefore, the existence of such an algorithm $\mathcal{Q}$ implies that X cannot be ϵ-differentially private for any fixed ϵ. Indeed, assume for the sake of contradiction that an algorithm with the given properties exists and X is ϵ-differentially private. Since $\mathcal{Q}$ depends only on X and not on S_t, the output of $\mathcal{Q}$ is also ϵ-differentially private. This is a contradiction, since the output of $\mathcal{Q}$ can be used to guess a bit of the binary vector $\mathbf{a}$ accurately with probability at least $(1 - \delta - \eta)$, where δ and η can be chosen arbitrarily small. More formally, choose a component i of $\mathbf{a}$ uniformly at random. The event $E = \{\tilde{a}_i = a_i\}$ happens with probability at least $1 - \delta - \eta$ by a union bound. Now consider an input sequence S''_t which is a neighbor of S_t and $a''_i \neq a_i$. If S''_t were the input to $\mathcal{A}$, the event E would happen only if the vector $\tilde{\mathbf{a}}''$ computed from the output of $\mathcal{Q}$ disagrees with $\mathbf{a}''$ on i. By a union bound this happens with probability at most $\eta + \delta$. We get a contradiction with pan privacy as long as $(1 - \delta - \eta)/(\delta + \eta) \geq e^\epsilon$.

To finish the proof we show that an algorithm $\mathcal{Q}$ with the specified properties can be used to recover all but an η fraction of $\mathbf{a}$ with probability $1 - \delta$. To see this, observe that $\mathcal{Q}$ can be used to answer queries $\mathbf{a} \cdot \mathbf{q}$ for any arbitrary

q to within $o(\sqrt{m})$ additive error. In particular, to answer queries $\mathbf{a} \cdot \mathbf{q}_1, \ldots, \mathbf{a} \cdot \mathbf{q}_r$, run $\mathcal{Q}(X, S_t^{(1)}), \ldots, \mathcal{Q}(X, S_t^{(r)})$ in parallel, where $S_t^{(i)}$ is a stream with state $\mathbf{q}_i$. If $r = o(n^2)$, then, by the union bound, with probability $1 - \delta$ for any constant δ, $\mathcal{Q}(X, S_t^{(i)}) = \mathbf{a} \cdot \mathbf{q}_i \pm o(\sqrt{m})$ for all i. By Theorem 9, there exists an algorithm that, given the output of $\mathcal{Q}(X, S_t^{(1)}), \ldots, \mathcal{Q}(X, S_t^{(r)})$, outputs $\tilde{\mathbf{a}}$ s.t. except with negligible probability $\tilde{\mathbf{a}}$ agrees with $\mathbf{a}$ on all but η fraction of the coordinates. $\square$

For the same problem, a recent and independently proved result by McGregor et al. [12] for two-party differential privacy, when interpreted to apply to dynamic data, would imply a lower bound on the additive error of $\Omega(\sqrt{m}/\log m)$. Thus, our lower bound improves the asymptotic additive term by a factor of $\log m$, and, unlike their bound, is tight, even for partly dynamic data.

We have the following corollary.

COROLLARY 1. *Let $\mathcal{A}$ be an online algorithm that on input S_t outputs $D^{(t)} \pm o(\sqrt{m})$ with probability at least $1 - O(m^{-2})$. Then $\mathcal{A}$ is not ϵ-pan private for any constant ϵ. Moreover, the same conclusion holds for $\mathcal{A}$ that outputs $T_1(\tau) \pm \tau o(\sqrt{m})$ with probability $1 - O(m^{-2})$.*

PROOF. Notice that the proof of Theorem 12 goes through if we restrict the instances to be binary, i.e. if we require that $\forall i \in \mathcal{U} : a_i, a_i' \in \{0, 1\}$. The corollary follows by a reduction from this restricted dot-product problem to the distinct elements problem. Given binary streams S_t', S_t'', let $S_t = (S_t', S_t'')$ be their concatenation. By a simple application of inclusion-exclusion, $D^{(t)} = D^{(t)}(S') + D^{(t)}(S'') - \mathbf{a} \cdot \mathbf{a}'$. Therefore, an ϵ-pan private algorithm for $D^{(t)}$ that achieves additive approximation α with probability $1 - \delta$ implies a 3ϵ-pan private algorithm for dot product on binary instances that achieves additive approximation 3α with probability $1 - 3\delta$.

The statement for T_1 holds by the same reduction, but substituting binary instances with instances for which $\forall i \in \mathcal{U} : a_i, a_i' \in \{0, \tau\}$. $\square$

A similar corollary holds for heavy hitters. Recall that $\mathrm{HH}(k)$ is the number of items i such that for which $a_i \geq F_1/k$.

COROLLARY 2. *Let $\mathcal{A}$ be an online algorithm that on input S_t outputs an estimate $\tilde{\mathrm{H}}\mathrm{H}(k) \in [\mathrm{HH}(k) - o(\sqrt{k}), \mathrm{HH}(k') + o(\sqrt{k})]$ for some $k' \leq F_1$ with probability at least $1 - O(m^{-2})$. Then $\mathcal{A}$ is not ϵ-pan private for any constant ϵ*

PROOF IDEA. The proof is a reduction from the distinct count problem on sequences of updates with items drawn from the universe $[k]$, to the k-Heavy Hitters problem on sequences with items drawn from $\mathcal{U}$. The full details can be found in Appendix B. $\square$

The next theorems follow by arguments identical to the one used to prove Theorem 12, but using, respectively, Theorem 10 and Theorem 11 in place of Theorem 9.

THEOREM 13. *Let $\mathcal{A}$ be an online algorithm that on inputs S_t, S_t' outputs $\mathbf{a} \cdot \mathbf{a}' \pm o(\sqrt{m})$ with probability at least $1 - \delta$. If $\delta < \rho^*/2(1 + \eta)$ for any η, then $\mathcal{A}$ is not ϵ-pan private for any constant ϵ.*

PROOF. The proof is analogous to the proof of Theorem 12. Note first that the $\{-1, 1\}$ queries of Theorem 10 can be simulated as the difference of two $\{0, 1\}$ queries, which gives $o(\sqrt{m})$ additive error with probability at most $1 - 2\delta$. In order to apply Theorem 10, we need to guarantee that at most $\rho < \rho^*$ fraction of the queries answered by $\mathcal{Q}$ have error $\Omega(\sqrt{m})$. Call such queries *inaccurate*. In expectation, there are at most 2δ inaccurate queries. Since the statement of Theorem 10 holds when the queries are independent, an application of a Chernoff bound with a large enough number of queries shows that except with negligible probability there are at most ρ^* inaccurate queries. After applying Theorem 10, the proof can be finished analogously to the proof of Theorem 12. $\square$

COROLLARY 3. *Let $\mathcal{A}$ be an online algorithm that on input S outputs $D^{(t)}(S) \pm o(\sqrt{m})$ with probability at least $1 - \delta$. If $\delta < \rho^*/6(1 + \eta)$, then $\mathcal{A}$ is not ϵ-pan private for any constant ϵ. Moreover, the same conclusion holds for $\mathcal{A}$ that outputs $T_1(\tau) \pm \tau o(\sqrt{m})$ with probability $1 - \delta$, for $\delta < \rho^*/(6(1 + \eta))$.*

This corollary implies the optimality of the full-space extensions of the *partly dynamic* algorithms for distinct count and $T_1(\tau)$ of Dwork et al. [7]. Furthermore, it establishes that the our fully dynamic (full space) $T_1(\tau)$ algorithm presented in Section 3.2 is almost optimal, except for a constant multiplicative factor.

The corresponding lower bound for k-Heavy Hitters follows by the reduction from distint counts problem in the proof of Corollary 2.

COROLLARY 4. *Let $\mathcal{A}$ be an online algorithm that on input S_t outputs an estimate $\tilde{\mathrm{H}}\mathrm{H}(k) \in [\mathrm{HH}(k) - o(\sqrt{k}), \mathrm{HH}(k') + \sqrt{k}]$ for some $k' \leq F_1$ with probability at least $1 - O(\delta)$. If $\delta < \rho^*/6(1 + \eta)$, then $\mathcal{A}$ is not ϵ-pan private for any constant ϵ.*

This result implies that our k-Heavy Hitters algorithm in Section 3.3 is almost optimal, up to an arbitrarily small multiplicative factor.

Using similar arguments and utilizing Theorem 11, we can show the following (proof omitted).

THEOREM 14. *Let $\mathcal{A}$ be a streaming algorithm that on input a stream S_t and any constant α outputs $(1 \pm \alpha)D^{(t)} \pm o(\log \frac{1/\delta}{\log m})$ with probability at least $1 - \delta$. Then $\mathcal{A}$ is not ϵ-pan private for any constant ϵ. Moreover, the same conclusion holds for $\mathcal{A}$ that for any constant α outputs $(1 \pm \alpha)T_1(\tau) \pm \tau o(\log \frac{1/\delta}{\log m})$ with probability at least $1 - \delta$.*

For small enough δ (for example, $\delta < m^{\log m}$), the theorem establishes that when an arbitrarily small multiplicative approximation factor is allowed, an additive polylogarithmic error is unavoidable for the problem of estimating distinct count. In particular, our lower bound matches the logarithmic dependence of the additive error on the probability of failure of our fully streaming (i.e. fully dynamic sublinear space) algorithm for distinct count estimation. The non-private sketch based algorithm for distinct count, gives an $(1 + \alpha)$ ([1]) multiplicative approximation. Hence, the theorem also implies that a pan-private algorithm for the distinct count problem necessarily incurs error larger than a small space streaming algorithm for the problem by an additive factor. This is the first known separation between the two models, namely between pan-private algorithms (with unbounded space) and polylogarithmic space streaming algorithms.

5. DISCUSSION

We focus not only on privacy of data analysis, but also security, formulated as pan-privacy in [7]. Informally, pan-private algorithms guarantee differential privacy of data analyses even when the internal memory of the algorithm may be compromised by an unannounced intrusion. We present the first pan-private algorithms on fully dynamic data for various useful statistics (distinct count, cropped sum, and heavy hitter count), and also present matching and almost matching lower bounds for these problems—the first such lower bounds explicitly for pan-privacy.

Privacy with security is an important issue, and pan-privacy [7] is an effective and interesting formulation of this problem. A number of extensions are of interest.

Other Security Models. In the bulk of the paper, we focus on security against a single unannounced intrusion. A natural extension is to protect against multiple intrusions. If the occurence of an intrusion is announces before or immediately after the intrusion, such as in applications where they are legally mandated or are detected by the system, then our results will still hold, with the simple fix to randomize anew after each intrusion. If the intrusions are unannounced, there are extreme cases when differential privacy cannot be ensured even with partly dynamic data [7]. We leave it open to formulate a realistic model of multiple unannounced intrusions and investigate tradeoffs between privacy and accuracy guarantees.

In a dynamic data scenario, it is often desirable to *continuously monitor* some set of statistics in order to detect trends in the data in a timely manner [4]. Our results can also be used to provide *continual event-level pan-privacy* [8, 4]—i.e., to provide the ability to monitor the statistics we have considered while ensuring privacy and security. *Event-level pan-privacy* can be defined analogously as in Definition 5 by considering event-level neighbors instead. Two sequences S and S' are said to be event-level neighbors if some "event" (i_k, d_k) in S is replaced by some other event (j, d_k), where $j \neq i_k$ in S'. While the notion of user-level privacy offers protection to a user, event-level privacy seeks to protect an "event,"—i.e., a particular update. Continual event-level pan privacy addresses the problem of providing continual outputs over dynamic data (over time $1 \leq t \leq T$), that are event-level pan-private with respect to one intrusion. As further evidence of the utility of linear sketches (and linear measurements of data, in general), we notice that along with L_p sketches, our noise adding technique of Section 3.1 can easily be extended to provide a continual event-level pan-private data structure for computing the number of distinct elements in a dynamic stream by a simple extension of the results in [8]. They propose a counter that within a bounded time period of T provides an accurate estimate of the number of ones in a binary stream, with an additive error term scaled by $O(\log(T)^{2.5})$. A key ingredient in their construction is the linearity of the binary count operation; since operations on sketches are also linear, essentially the same construction (replaced by linear sketch updates) works for our case. The same observation can also be made for our sketches for cropped sum and k-heavy hitters.

Other Data Models. We studied the fully dynamic data where items may be inserted or deleted. In such applications, at all times, for all i, $a_i \geq 0$ since one does not delete an item or copy that was not inserted. Still, there are applications with for example, distributed data, which may be modeled by dynamic data where some a_i's may be negative. Our algorithm for distinct count from Section 3.1 still works and provides the same guarantees, but we need new algorithms for estimating cropped sum and heavy hitter count in such a data model.

Other Queries. We studied basic statistical queries in this paper. Many richer queries are of interest, including estimating the entropy of dynamic data, join size estimation for dynamic relations, graph quantities on dynamic graphs, rank and compressibility of dynamic matrices and so on.

Other Lower Bound Techniques. In the cases above, we may also need new lower bound techniques beyond the one based on noisy decoding that we introduced in this paper. Developing a collection of lower bounds for problems in the one-way two-party differential privacy model will be useful for showing lower bounds for pan-private algorithms.

We believe that there is a rich theory of pan-private algorithms that needs to be developed, inspired by recent work on differential privacy and streaming algorithms, but already quite distinct as we know from [7] and this paper.

Acknowledgments

The authors would like to thank the anonymous reviewers for many insightful comments and Kobbi Nissim and Graham Cormode for helpful discussions.

Darakhshan Mir was supported by NSF Awards No. CCF-0728937 and CCF-1018445 and U.S. DHS Award No. 2009-ST-061-CCI002, S. Muthukrishnan was supported by NSF Awards No. DMS-0354690, IIS-0414852 and CCF-916782, and U.S. DHS Award No. 2009-ST-061-CCI002. Aleksandar Nikolov was supported by NSF Award No. CCF-1018445. Rebecca N. Wright was supported by NSF Award No. CCF-1018445.

6. REFERENCES

[1] G. Cormode, M. Datar, P. Indyk, and S. Muthukrishnan. Comparing data streams using hamming norms (how to zero in). *TKDE*, 2003.

[2] G. Cormode and S. Muthukrishnan. An improved data stream summary: The count-min sketch and its applications. *Journal of Algorithms*, 2005.

[3] I. Dinur and K. Nissim. Revealing information while preserving privacy. In *PODS*, 2003.

[4] C. Dwork. Differential privacy in new settings. In *SODA*, 2010.

[5] C. Dwork, F. Mcsherry, K. Nissim, and A. Smith. Calibrating noise to sensitivity in private data analysis. In *TCC*, 2006.

[6] C. Dwork, F. McSherry, and K. Talwar. The price of privacy and the limits of lp decoding. In *STOC*, 2007.

[7] C. Dwork, M. Naor, T. Pitassi, G. Rothblum, and S. Yekhanin. Pan-Private streaming algorithms. In *ICS*, 2010.

[8] C. Dwork, T. Pitassi, M. Naor, and G. Rothblum. Differential privacy under continual observation. In *STOC*, 2010.

[9] A. Gupta, K. Ligett, F. McSherry, A. Roth, and

K. Talwar. Differentially private combinatorial optimization. In *SODA*, 2010.

[10] P. Indyk. Stable distributions, pseudorandom generators, embeddings, and data stream computation. In *Journal of ACM*, 2006.

[11] D. Kane, J. Nelson, and D. Woodruff. An optimal algorithm for the distinct elements problem. In *PODS*, 2010.

[12] A. McGregor, I. Mironov, T. Pitassi, O. Reingold, K. Talwar, and S. Vadhan. Limits of two-party differential privacy. In *FOCS*, 2010.

[13] F. Mcsherry and K. Talwar. Mechanism design via differential privacy. In *FOCS*, 2007.

[14] I. Mironov, O. Pandey, O. Reingold, and S. Vadhan. Computational differential privacy. In *CRYPTO*, 2009.

[15] J. P. Nolan. *Stable Distributions - Models for Heavy Tailed Data*. Birkhäuser, 2010. In progress, Chapter 1 online at academic2.american.edu/~jpnolan.

[16] S. Warner. Randomized response: A survey technique for eliminating evasive answer bias. *Journal of American Statistical Association*, 1965.

APPENDIX

A. PROOFS FOR SECTION 3

A.1 Proofs for Subsection 3.2

Here we prove the following technical claim, used in the proof of Lemma 4.

CLAIM 2. *Let $a \geq \tau$ and let w be uniformly distributed in $[1, 2]$. Then $\mathbb{E}[wa \bmod 2\tau] \geq \tau/2$.*

PROOF. Let $a \bmod 2\tau = j$. Assume that $a = 2x\tau + y$, for x, y positive integers, $y \leq 2\tau - 1$. We consider two cases.

Case I. Assume that $y < 2\tau - j$. Then conditioned on the event $w \in [1, 1 + 2x\tau/a]$, wa is uniformly distributed in $[0, 2\tau)$; conditioned on the event $w \in [1 + 2x\tau/a, 2]$, wa is uniformly distributed in $[j, j + y]$. By the law of total expectation,

$$\mathbb{E}[wa \bmod 2\tau] = \frac{2x\tau}{a}\tau + \frac{y}{a}(j + \frac{1}{2}y)$$

If $x \geq 1$, $2x\tau/a > 1/2$; then $\mathbb{E}[wa \bmod 2\tau] > \tau/2$. If $x = 0$, then $y \geq \tau$, and $\mathbb{E}[wa \bmod 2\tau] \geq j + \tau/2 \geq \tau/2$.

Case II. Assume that $y \geq 2\tau - j$. Again, conditioned on $w \in [1, 1 + 2x\tau/a]$, wa is uniformly distributed in $[0, 2\tau)$. Conditioned on $w \in [1 + 2x\tau/a, 2]$, wa is uniformly distributed in $[j, 2\tau) \cup [0, y - 2\tau + j)$. By the law of total expectation,

$$\mathbb{E}[wa \bmod 2\tau] = \frac{2x\tau}{a}\tau + \frac{2\tau - j}{a}(j + \frac{2\tau - j}{2}) + \frac{y - 2\tau + j}{a}\frac{y - 2\tau + j}{2}.$$

Once again, if $x \geq 1$, $\mathbb{E}[wa \bmod 2\tau] > \tau/2$. If $x = 0$, then $y = a \geq \tau$. Let $(2\tau - j)/a = f$. Then we have,

$$\mathbb{E}[wa \bmod 2\tau] = f(j + \frac{fa}{2}) + (1 - f)\frac{(1 - f)a}{2} \geq \frac{a}{2} \geq \tau/2.$$

□

B. PROOFS FOR SECTION 4

B.1 Noisy Decoding

B.2 Heavy Hitters Lower Bound

Next, we present the details of the reduction that establishes a lower bound for the heavy hitters problem (Corollary 2). Once again, recall that $\mathrm{HH}(k)$ is the number of items i such that $a_i \geq F_1/k$.

COROLLARY 5. *Let $\mathcal{A}$ be an online algorithm that outputs an estimate $\tilde{\mathrm{HH}}(k) \in [\mathrm{HH}(k) - o(\sqrt{k}), \mathrm{HH}(k') + o(\sqrt{k})]$ for some $k' \leq F_1$ with probability at least $1 - O(m^{-2})$. Then $\mathcal{A}$ is not ϵ-pan private for any constant ϵ*

PROOF. Given a sequence $S_t = \{(i_1, d_1), (i_2, d_2), \ldots\}$ with state vector $\mathbf{a}$ and $i_j \in [k]$ for all j, we can construct a sequence $S'_t = \{(i'_1, d'_1), (i'_2, d'_2), \ldots\}$ with state vector $\mathbf{a}'$ and $i'_j \in \mathcal{U}$ in the following way. Select an arbitrary set $J \in \binom{\mathcal{U}}{k}$, a mapping $\phi : [k] \to J$, and a real number W. If $a_i > 0$, construct S'_t so that $a'_{\phi(i)} = W/k$; otherwise, let $a'_{\phi(i)} = 0$. For our lower bound it is enough to assume that $\mathbf{a}$ is binary and to show a contradiction with the definition of differential privacy on a neighbor of S_t which is also binary, i.e. has the same hamming weight but one 1 was "moved" to a different coordinate. The reason this is sufficient for a lower bound is that for the proof of Corollary 1 it is sufficient to consider binary instances and binary neighbors. Observe then that for binary instances and binary neighbors with the same weight the following hold:

- two neighboring sequences on universe $[k]$ give rise to two neighboring sequences on universe $\mathcal{U}$; therefore, an algorithm that is ϵ-pan-private with respect to the transformed input is also ϵ-pan-private with respect to the original input;

- the number of k-heavy hitters in S'_t is equal to the distinct counts for S_t, as each item with nonzero state in S_t maps to an item with state WF_1/k in S'_t, and $F'_1 \leq WF_1$;

- since each item in S'_t is either a k-heavy hitter or has state 0, $HH(k) = HH(k')$ for any $k' \leq F'_1$.

As a consequence, an algorithm that is ε-pan private and outputs $\tilde{\mathrm{HH}}(k) \in [\mathrm{HH}(k) - o(\sqrt{k}), \mathrm{HH}(k') + o(\sqrt{k})]$ with probability $1 - \delta$ can be used to approximate $D^{(t)}$ to within $o(\sqrt{k})$ additive error with probability $1 - \delta$ on sequences of updates with items drawn from $[k]$, while satisfying ϵ-pan-privacy. By Corollary 1, this is a contradiction. □

Tight Bounds for Lp Samplers, Finding Duplicates in Streams, and Related Problems

Hossein Jowhari
Simon Fraser University
School of Computing Science
Burnaby, BC, Canada
hjowhari@cs.sfu.ca

Mert Sağlam
Simon Fraser University
School of Computing Science
Burnaby, BC, Canada
mert.saglam@sfu.ca

Gábor Tardos[*]
Rényi Institute of Mathematics
Budapest, Hungary
and
Simon Fraser University
School of Computing Science
Burnaby, BC, Canada
tardos@renyi.hu

ABSTRACT

In this paper, we present near-optimal space bounds for L_p-samplers. Given a stream of updates (additions and subtraction) to the coordinates of an underlying vector $x \in \mathbb{R}^n$, a perfect L_p sampler outputs the i-th coordinate with probability $|x_i|^p / \|x\|_p^p$. In SODA 2010, Monemizadeh and Woodruff showed polylog space upper bounds for approximate L_p-samplers and demonstrated various applications of them. Very recently, Andoni, Krauthgamer and Onak improved the upper bounds and gave a $O(\epsilon^{-p} \log^3 n)$ space ϵ relative error and constant failure rate L_p-sampler for $p \in [1, 2]$. In this work, we give another such algorithm requiring only $O(\epsilon^{-p} \log^2 n)$ space for $p \in (1, 2)$. For $p \in (0, 1)$, our space bound is $O(\epsilon^{-1} \log^2 n)$, while for the $p = 1$ case we have an $O(\log(1/\epsilon)\epsilon^{-1} \log^2 n)$ space algorithm. We also give a $O(\log^2 n)$ bits zero relative error L_0-sampler, improving the $O(\log^3 n)$ bits algorithm due to Frahling, Indyk and Sohler.

As an application of our samplers, we give better upper bounds for the problem of finding duplicates in data streams. In case the length of the stream is longer than the alphabet size, L_1 sampling gives us an $O(\log^2 n)$ space algorithm, thus improving the previous $O(\log^3 n)$ bound due to Gopalan and Radhakrishnan.

In the second part of our work, we prove an $\Omega(\log^2 n)$ lower bound for sampling from 0, ± 1 vectors (in this special case, the parameter p is not relevant for L_p sampling). This matches the space of our sampling algorithms for constant $\epsilon > 0$. We also prove tight space lower bounds for the finding duplicates and heavy hitters problems. We obtain these lower bounds using reductions from the communication complexity problem augmented indexing.

[*]Supported by NSERC grant 329527, OTKA grants T-046234, AT-048826, and NK-62321

Categories and Subject Descriptors

F.2.0 [**Analysis of Algorithms and Problem Complexity**]: General; E.4 [**Coding and Information Theory**]: Formal models of communication; E.m [**Data**]: Miscellaneous

General Terms

Algorithm, Design, Theory

Keywords

Streaming Algorithms, Sampling, Finding Duplicates

1. INTRODUCTION

Sampling has become an indispensable tool in analysing massive data sets, and particularly in processing data streams. In the past decade, several sampling techniques have been proposed and studied for the data stream model [3, 11, 5, 10, 24, 1]. In this work, we study L_p-*samplers*, a new variant of space efficient samplers for data streams that was introduced by Monemizadeh and Woodruff in [24]. Roughly speaking, given a stream of updates (additions and subtraction) to the coordinates of an underlying vector $x \in \mathbb{R}^n$, an L_p-sampler processes the stream and outputs a sample coordinate of x where the i-th coordinate is picked with probability proportional to $|x_i|^p$.

In [24], it was observed that L_p-samplers lead to alternative algorithms for many known streaming problems, including heavy hitters and frequency moment estimation. Here in this paper, we focus on a specific application, namely finding duplicates in long streams; although our L_p samplers work and often give better space performance for all applications listed in [24]. We refer the reader to [24] and [1] for further applications of L_p-samplers.

Observe that we allow both negative and positive updates to the coordinates of the underlying vector. In the case where only positive updates are allowed and $p = 1$, the problem is well understood. For instance the classical reservoir sampling [21] from the 60's (attributed to Alan G. Waterman) gives a simple solution as follows. Given a pair (i, u), indicating an addition of u to the i-th coordinate of the underlying vector x, the sampler having maintained s, the sum of the updates seen so far, replaces the current sample with i with probability u/s, otherwise does nothing and moves to the next update. It is easy to verify that this is a perfect L_1-sampler and the space usage is only $O(1)$ words.

With the presence of negative updates, sampling becomes a non-trivial problem. In this case, it is not clear at all how to maintain samples without keeping track of the updates to the individual coordinates. In fact, the question regarding the mere existence of such samplers was raised few years ago by Cormode, Muthukrishnan, and Rozenbaum in [9]. Last year in SODA 2010, Monemizadeh and Woodruff [24] answered this question affirmatively, however in an approximate sense. Before stating their results we give a formal definition of L_p-samplers.

DEFINITION 1. *Let $x \in \mathbb{R}^n$ be a non-zero vector. For $p > 0$ we call the L_p distribution corresponding to x the distribution on $[n]$ that takes i with probability*

$$\frac{|x_i|^p}{\|x\|_p^p},$$

with $\|x\|_p = (\sum_{i=1}^n |x_i|^p)^{1/p}$. For $p = 0$, the L_0 distribution corresponding to x is the uniform distribution over the non-zero coordinates of x.

We call a streaming algorithm a *perfect L_p-sampler* if it outputs an index according to this distribution and fails only if x is the zero vector. An approximate L_p-sampler may fail but the distribution of its output should be close to the L_p distribution. In particular, we speak of an ϵ relative error L_p-sampler if, conditioned on no failure, it outputs the index i with probability $(1 \pm \epsilon)|x_i|^p/\|x\|_p^p + O(n^{-c})$, where c is an arbitrary constant. For $p = 0$ the corresponding formula is $(1 \pm \epsilon)/k + O(n^{-c})$, where k is the number of non-zero coordinates in x. Unless stated otherwise we assume that the failure probability is at most $1/2$.

In this definition one can consider c to be 2, but all existing constructions of L_p-samplers work for an arbitrary c with just a constant factor increase in the space, so we will not specify c in the following and ignore errors of probability n^{-c}.

Previous work.

A zero relative error L_0-sampler which uses $O(\log^3 n)$ bits was shown in [12]. In [24], the authors gave an ϵ relative error L_p-sampler for $p \in [0, 2]$ which uses poly$(\epsilon^{-1}, \log n)$ space. They also showed a 2-pass $O(\text{polylog } n)$ space zero relative error L_p-sampler for any $p \in [0, 2]$. In addition to these, they demonstrated that L_p-samplers can be used as a blackbox to obtain streaming algorithms for other problems such as L_p estimation (for $p > 2$), heavy hitters, and cascaded norms [15]. Unfortunately, due to the large exponents in their bounds, the L_p-samplers given there do not lead to efficient solutions for the aforementioned applications.

Very recently, Andoni, Krauthgamer and Onak in [1] improved the results of [24] considerably. Through the adaptation of a generic and simple method, named *precision sampling*, they managed to bring down the space upper bounds to $O(\frac{1}{\epsilon^p} \log^3 n)$ bits for ϵ relative error L_p-samplers for $p \in [1, 2]$. Roughly speaking, the idea of precision sampling is to scale the input vector with random coefficients so that the i-th coordinate becomes the maximum with probability roughly proportional to $|x_i|^p$. Moreover the maximum (heavy) coordinate is found through a small-space heavy hitter algorithm. In more detail, the input vector

$(x_1, \ldots, x_n)$ is scaled by random coefficients $(t_1^{-1}, \ldots, t_n^{-1})$, where each t_i is picked uniformly at random from $[0, 1]$. Let $z = (x_1 t_1^{-1}, \ldots, x_n t_n^{-1})$ be the scaled vector. Here the important observation is $\Pr[t_i^{-1} \geq t] = 1/t$ and hence, for instance, by replacing t with $\|x\|_1/|x_i|$, we get $\Pr[|z_i| \geq \|x\|_1] = |x_i|/\|x\|_1$. (In the same manner, one can scale x_i by $t_i^{-1/p}$ instead of t_i^{-1} and get a similar result for general p.) It turns out, we only need to we have a constant approximation to $\|x\|_1$ and look for a coordinate in z that has reached a limit of $\Omega(\|x\|_1)$. On the other hand it is shown that the heaviest coordinate in z has a weight of $\Omega(\log^{-1} n)\|z\|_1$ (with constant probability), and thus a small-space heavy hitter computation can be used to find the maximum. In particular, the L_p-sampler of [1] adapts the popular *count-sketch* scheme [6] for this purpose.

Our contributions.

In this paper, we give L_p-samplers requiring only $O(\epsilon^{-p} \log^2 n)$ space for $p \in (1, 2)$. For $p \in (0, 1)$, our space bound is $O(\epsilon^{-1} \log^2 n)$, while for the $p = 1$ case we have an $O(\log(1/\epsilon) \epsilon^{-1} \log^2 n)$ space algorithm. In essence, our sampler follows the basic structure of the precision sampling method explained above. However compared to [1], we do a sharper analysis of the error terms in the count-sketch, and through additional ideas, we manage to get rid of a log factor and preserve the previous dependence on ϵ. Roughly speaking, we use the fact that the error term in the count-sketch is bounded by the L_2 norm of the tail distribution of z (the heavy coordinates do not contribute). On the other hand, taking the distribution of the random coefficients into account, we bound this by $O(\|x\|_p)$, which enables us to save a log factor. Additionally, to preserve the dependence on ϵ, we have to use a slightly more powerful source of randomness for choosing the scaling factors (in contrast with the pairwise-independence of [1]), and take care of some subtle issues regarding the conditioning on the error terms which are not handled in the previous work (Lemma 3).[1]

As p approaches zero, precision sampling becomes very inefficient, as the random coefficients $t_i^{-1/p}$ tend to infinity. For the $p = 0$ case, we present a zero relative error sampler through a completely different approach. Briefly, our L_0-sampler tries to detect a non-zero coordinate by picking random subsets of $[n]$. The non-zero coordinates are found by an exact sparse recovery procedure and Nisan's PRG [26] is applied to decrease the randomness involved. Our $O(\log^2 n)$ space bound compares favorably to the previous algorithms, which use respectively $O(\log^3 n)$ space [12] and poly$(\log n, \epsilon^{-1})$ space [24] (the latter one gives only ϵ-relative error sampling).

In Section 4, we prove that sampling from $0, \pm 1$ vectors requires $\Omega(\log^2 n)$ space, by a reduction from the communication complexity problem augmented indexing. In this special case p is not relevant for L_p-sampling, hence this shows that our L_0-sampling algorithm uses the optimal space up to constant factors, and our L_p-sampler for $p \in (0, 2)$ has the optimal space (up to constant factors) for $\epsilon > 0$ a constant.

---

[1]Further we note that our algorithm not only produces a sample i from the L_p distribution, but also approximates x_i. Similar approximation is also produced by the L_p sampler of [1], but they claim to give an approximation of $|x_i|^p/\|x\|_p^p$. However, this claim for $p < 2$ cannot hold as it would contradict with the $\Omega(\epsilon^{-2})$ space lower bound for estimating Hamming distance.

Given a stream of length $n + 1$ over the alphabet $[n]$, finding duplicates problem asks to output some $a \in [n]$ that has appeared at least twice in the stream. Observe that by the pigeon-hole principle, such a always exists. Prior to our work, the best upper bound for finding duplicates was due to Gopalan and Radhakrishnan [14], who gave a one-pass $O(\log^3 n)$ bits randomized algorithm with constant failure rate. Here we settle the one-pass complexity of this problem by giving an $O(\log^2 n)$ space algorithm via a direct application of our L_1 sampler, and by giving an $\Omega(\log^2 n)$ lower bound afterwards. Combined with a sparse recovery procedure, our solution also generalizes to a near-optimal $O(\log^2 n + s \log n)$ space algorithm for finding duplicates in streams of length $n - s$, improving on the $O(s \log^3 n)$ result of [14].

Finally, we prove lower bounds for the problem of finding heavy hitters in update streams, which is closely related to the L_p-sampling problem. This lower bound is also obtained by a reduction from the augment indexing and proves that any L_p heavy hitters algorithm (defined in Section 4.4) must use $\Omega(\frac{1}{\phi^p} \log^2 n)$ space, even in the strict turnstile model. Our lower bound essentially matches the known upper bounds [8, 6, 16] which work in the general update model.

Related work.

In [3, 5], the authors have studied sampling from sliding windows, and the recent paper of Cormode et al. [10] generalizes the classical reservoir sampling to distributed streams. These works only consider insertion streams. The basic idea of random scaling used in [1] and in our paper has appeared earlier in the priority sampling technique [11, 7], where the focus is to estimate the weight of certain subsets of a vector, defined by a sequence of positive updates.

Finding duplicates in streams was first considered in the context of detecting fraud in click streams [22]. Muthukrishnan in [25] asked whether this problem can be solved in $O(\text{polylog } n)$ space using a constant number of passes. In [28], Tarui showed that any k-pass deterministic algorithm must use $\Omega(n^{\frac{1}{2k-1}})$ space to find a duplicate.

Heavy hitter algorithms have been studied extensively. The work of Berinde et al. [4] gives tight lower bounds for heavy hitters under insertion only streams. We are not aware of similar works on general update streams, although the recent works of [2, 29], where the authors show lower bounds for respectively approximate sparse recovery, and Johnson-Lindenstrauss transforms (via augmented indexing) is closely related.

Notation.

We write $[n]$ for the set $\{1, \ldots, n\}$. An update stream is a sequence of tuples (i, u), where $i \in [n]$ and $u \in \mathbb{R}$. The stream of updates implicitly define an n-dimensional vector $x \in \mathbb{R}^n$ as follows. Initially, x is the zero vector. An update of the form (i, u) adds u to the coordinate x_i of x (leaving the other coordinates unchanged). In the *strict turnstile model* we are guaranteed that all coordinates of x are non-negative at the end of the stream (although negative updates are still allowed), in the general model such guarantee does not exist. Our algorithms (like most other algorithms in the literature) work by maintaining a linear sketch $L : \mathbb{R}^n \to \mathbb{R}^m$. When computing the space requirement of such a streaming algo-

rithm, we assume all the updates are integers ($u \in \mathbb{Z}$) and the coordinates of the vector x throughout the stream remain bounded by some value $M = \text{poly}(n)$. We make sure that the matrix of L has also polynomially bounded integer entries, this way maintaining $L(x)$ requires updating m integer counters and requires $O(m \log n)$ bits with fast update time (especially since the matrices we consider are sparse). This discretization step is standard and thus we omit most details.

In the standard model for randomized streaming algorithms the random bits used (to generate the random linear map L, for example) are part of the space bound. In contrast, our lower bounds do not make any assumption on the working of the streaming algorithm and allow for the *random oracle model*, where the algorithm is allowed free access to a random string at any time. All lower bounds are proved through reductions from communication problems.

We say an event happens with *low probability* if the probability can be made less than n^{-c}. Here $c > 0$ is an arbitrary constant, for example one can set $c = 2$. The actual value of c has limited effect on the space of our algorithm: it changes only the unspecified constants hidden in the O notation. We will routinely ignore low probability events, sometime even $O(n)$ of them, which is okay as we leave c unspecified. Events complementary to low probability events are referred to as *high probability* events.

For $0 \leq m \leq n$ we call the vector $x \in \mathbb{R}^n$ *m-sparse* if all but at most m coordinates of x are zero. We define $\text{Err}_2^m(x) = \min \|x - \hat{x}\|_2$, where $\hat{x} \in \mathbb{R}^n$ ranges over all the m-sparse vectors.

2. THE L_P SAMPLER

In this section, we present our L_p sampler algorithm. In the following, we assume $p \in (0, 2)$. This particular method does not seem to be applicable for the $p = 2$ case and we know of no $O(\log^2 n)$ space L_2-sampling algorithm. We treat the $p = 0$ case separately later.

We start by stating the properties of the two streaming algorithms we are going to use. Both are based on maintaining $L(x)$ for a well chosen random linear map $L : \mathbb{R}^n \to \mathbb{R}^{n'}$ with $n' < n$.

The *count-sketch* algorithm [6] is so simple we cannot resist the temptation to define it here. For parameter m, the count-sketch algorithm works as follows. It selects independent samples $h_j : [n] \to [6m]$ and $g_j : [n] \to \{1, -1\}$ from pairwise independent uniform hash families for $j \in [l]$ and $l = O(\log n)$. It computes the following linear function of x for $j \in [l]$ and $k \in [6m]$: $y_{k,j} = \sum_{i \in [n], h_j(i)=k} g_j(i) x_i$. Finally it outputs $x^* \in \mathbb{R}^n$ as an approximation of x with $x_i^* = \text{median}(g_j(i) y_{h(i),j} : j \in [l])$ for $i \in [n]$.

The performance guarantee of the count-sketch algorithm is as follows. (For a compact proof see a recent survey by Gilbert and Indyk [13].)

LEMMA 1. [6] *For any $x \in \mathbb{R}^n$ and $m \geq 1$ we have $|x_i - x_i^*| \leq \text{Err}_2^m(x)/m^{1/2}$ for all $i \in [n]$ with high probability, where x^* is the output of the count-sketch algorithm with parameter m. As a consequence we also have*

$$\text{Err}_2^m(x) \leq \|x - \hat{x}\|_2 \leq 10 \text{Err}_2^m(x)$$

with high probability, where $\hat{x}$ is the m-sparse vector best approximating x^* (i.e., $\hat{x}_i = x_i^*$ for the m coordinates i with

$|x_i^*|$ highest and is $\hat{x}_i = 0$ for the remaining $n - m$ coordinates).

We will also need the following result for the estimation of L_p norms.

LEMMA 2. [17] *For any* $p \in (0, 2]$ *there is a streaming algorithm based on a random linear map* $L : \mathbb{R}^n \to \mathbb{R}^l$ *with* $l = O(\log n)$ *that outputs a value* r *computed solely from* $L(x)$ *that satisfies* $\|x\|_p \leq r \leq 2\|x\|_p$ *with high probability.*

Our streaming algorithm on Figure 1 makes use of a single count-sketch and two norm estimate algorithms. The count-sketch is for the randomly scaled version z of the vector x. One of the norm approximation algorithms is for $\|x\|_p$, the other one approximates $\mathrm{Err}_2^m(z)$ through the almost equal value $\|z - \hat{z}\|_2$. A standard L_2 approximation for z works if we modify z by subtracting $\hat{z}$ in the recovery stage. One can get arbitrary good approximations of $\mathrm{Err}_2^m(x)$ this way.

First we estimate the probability that the algorithm aborts because $s > \beta m^{1/2} r$. This depends on the scaling that resulted in z and it will be important for us that the bound holds even after conditioning on any one scaling factor.

LEMMA 3. *Conditioned on an arbitrary fixed value* t *of* t_i *for a single index* $i \in [n]$ *we have* $\Pr[s > \beta m^{1/2} r \mid t_i = t] = O(\epsilon + n^{-c})$.

PROOF. First note that by Lemma 2 we have $r \geq \|x\|_p$ and $s \leq 2\|z - \hat{z}\|_2$ with high probability. By Lemma 1 we have $\|z - \hat{z}\| \leq 10 \, \mathrm{Err}_2^m(z)$ also with high probability. We may therefore assume that all of these inequalities hold, and in particular $r \geq \|x\|_p$ and $s \leq 20 \, \mathrm{Err}_2^m(z)$. It is therefore enough to bound the probability that $20 \, \mathrm{Err}_2^m(z) > \beta m^{1/2} \|x\|_p$.

For simplicity (and without loss of generality) we assume that the fixed scalar is $t_n = t$ and will freely use i for indexes in $[n - 1]$.

Let $T = \beta\|x\|_p$. For each $i \in [n-1]$ we define two variables z_i' and z_i'' determined by z_i as follows. The indicator variable $z_i' = 1$ if $|z_i| > T$ and 0 otherwise. We set $z_i'' = z_i^2(1 - z_i')/T^2 \in [0, 1]$. Let $S' = \sum_{i \in [n-1]} z_i'$ and $S'' = \sum_{i \in [n-1]} z_i''$. Note that $T^2 S'' = \|z - w\|_2^2$, where w is defined by $w_i = z_i z_i'$ for $i \in [n-1]$ and $w_n = z_n$. Here w is $(S' + 1)$-sparse, so we have $\mathrm{Err}_2^m(z) \leq T S''^{1/2}$ unless $S' \geq m$. It is therefore enough to bound the probabilities of the events $S' \geq m$ and $S'' > m\beta^2\|x\|_p^2/(20T)^2 = m/400$, each with $O(\epsilon)$.

We have $\mathbb{E}[z_i'] = |x_i|^p/T^p$, $\mathbb{E}[S'] \leq \beta^{-p} = \epsilon^{1-p}$. By our choice of m and the concentration of S' provided by k-wise independence we have $\Pr[S' \geq m] = O(\epsilon)$ as needed. The calculation for S'' is similar. We have

$$\mathbb{E}[z_i''] < \int_{|x_i|^p/T^p}^{\infty} x_i^2 t^{-2/p} T^{-2} dt = \frac{p}{2-p}|x_i|^p T^{-p}.$$

Thus $\mathbb{E}[S''] \leq \frac{p}{2-p}\|x\|_p^p T^{-p} = O(\beta^{-p}) = O(\epsilon^{1-p})$. Note that the z_i'' are not indicator variables as the z_i', but they are still k-wise independent random variables from $[0, 1]$ and we can bound the probability of large deviation for S'' as we did for S'. This completes the proof of the lemma. $\square$

The fact that our algorithm is an approximate L_p-sampler with both relative error and success probability $\Theta(\epsilon)$ follows from the following lemma. Indeed, if the probabilities were exactly $\epsilon|x_i|^p/r^p$ and if $\|x\|_p \leq r \leq 2\|x\|_p$ would always hold, we would make no relative error and the success probability would be $\mathbb{E}[\epsilon\|x\|_p^p/r^p] \geq \epsilon/2^p$.

LEMMA 4. *The probability that the algorithm of Figure 1 outputs the index* $i \in [n]$ *conditioned on a fixed value for* $r \geq \|x\|_p^p$ *is* $(\epsilon + O(\epsilon^2))|x_i|^p/r^p + O(n^{-c})$. *The relative error of the estimate for* x_i *is at most* ϵ *with high probability.*

PROOF. Optimally, we would output $i \in [n]$ if $|z_i| > \epsilon^{-1/p} r$. This happens if $t_i < \epsilon|x_i|^p/r^p$ and has probability exactly $\epsilon|x_i|^p/r^p$. We have to estimate the probability that something goes wrong and the algorithm outputs i when this simple condition is not met or vice versa.

Three things can go wrong. First, if $s > m^{1/2}\beta r$ the algorithm fails. This is only a problem for our calculation if it should, in fact, output the index i. Lemma 3 bounds the conditional probability of this happening.

Having dealt with the $s > \beta m^{1/2} r$ case we may assume now $s \leq \beta m^{1/2} r$. We also make the assumptions (high probability by Lemma 2) that $\|z - \hat{z}\|_2 \leq s$ and thus $\mathrm{Err}_2^m(z) \leq \|z - \hat{z}\|_2 \leq s \leq \beta m^{1/2} r$. Finally, we also assume $|z_i^* - z_i| \leq \mathrm{Err}_2^m(z)/m^{1/2} \leq \beta r$ for all $i \in [n]$. This is satisfied with high probability by Lemma 1.

A second source of error comes from this βr possible difference between z_i^* and z_i. This can only make a problem if t_i is close to the threshold, namely $(\epsilon^{-1/p} + \beta)^{-p}|x_i|^p/r^p \leq t_i \leq (\epsilon^{-1/p} - \beta)^{-p}|x_i|^p/r^p$. The probability of selecting t_i from this interval is $O(\beta/\epsilon^{1+1/p}|x_i|^p/r^p) = O(\epsilon^2|x_i|^p/r^p)$ as required.

Finally, the third source of error comes from the possibility that i should be output based on $|z_i| > \epsilon^{-1/p} r$, yet we output another index $i' \neq i$ because $z_{i'}^* \geq z_i^*$. In this case we must have $t_{i'} < (\epsilon^{-1/p} - \beta)^{-p}|x_i|^p/r^p$. This has probability $O(\epsilon|x_{i'}|^p/r^p)$. By the union bound the probability that such an index i' exists is $O(\epsilon\|x\|_p^p/r^p) = O(\epsilon)$. Pairwise independence is enough to conclude that the same bound holds after conditioning on $|z_i| > \epsilon^{-1/p} r$. This finishes the proof of the first statement of the lemma.

The algorithm only outputs an index i if $s \leq \beta m^{1/2} r$ and $|z_i^*| \leq \epsilon^{-1/p} r$. The first implies that the absolute approximation error for z_i is at most βr, while the second lower bounds the absolute value of the approximation itself by $\epsilon^{-1/p} r$, thus ensuring a $\beta\epsilon^{1/p} = \epsilon$ relative error approximation. Our approximation for x_i is $z_i t_i^{1/p}$ is $z_i^* t^{1/p}$, so the relative error is the same. Note that the inverse polynomial error probability comes from the various low probability events we neglected. The same is true for the additive error term in the distribution. $\square$

THEOREM 1. *For* $\delta > 0$ *and* $\epsilon > 0$, $0 < p < 2$ *there is an* $O(\epsilon)$ *relative error one pass* L_p-*sampling algorithm with failing probability at most* δ *and having low probability that the relative error of the estimate for the selected coordinate is more than* ϵ. *The algorithm uses* $O_p(\epsilon^{-\max(1,p)} \log^2 n \log(1/\delta))$ *space for* $p \neq 1$ *while for* $p = 1$ *the space is* $O(\epsilon^{-1} \log(1/\epsilon) \log^2 n \log(1/\delta))$.

PROOF. Using Lemma 4 and the fact that $\|x\|_p \leq r \leq 2\|x\|_p$ with high probability one obtains that the failure probability of the algorithm in Figure 1 is at most $1 - \epsilon/2^p + O(n^{-c})$. Conditioning on obtaining an output, returning i has probability $(1 + O(\epsilon))|x_i|^p/\|x\|_p^p + O(n^{-c})$. Clearly, the latter statement remains true for any number of repetitions and the failure probability is raised to power v for v repetitions. Thus using $v = O(\log(1/\delta)/\epsilon)$ repetitions (taking the first non-failing output), the algorithm is an $O(\epsilon)$ relative error δ failure probability L_p-sampling algorithm. Here we

1. For $0 < p < 2$, $p \neq 1$ set $k = 10\lceil 1/|p-1|\rceil$ and $m = O(\epsilon^{-\max(0,p-1)})$ with a large enough constant factor.
2. For $p = 1$ set $k = m = O(\log(1/\epsilon))$ with a large enough constant factor.
3. Set $\beta = \epsilon^{1-1/p}$ and $l = O(\log n)$ with a large enough constant factor.
4. Select k-wise independent uniform scaling factors $t_i \in [0,1]$ for $i \in [n]$.
5. Select the appropriate random linear functions for the execution of the count-sketch algorithm and L and L' for the norm estimations in the processing stage.

Processing Stage:
1. Use count-sketch with parameter m for the scaled vector $z \in \mathbb{R}^n$ with $z_i = x_i/t_i^{1/p}$.
2. Maintain a linear sketch $L(x)$ as needed for the L_p norm approximation of x.
3. Maintain a linear sketch $L'(z)$ as needed for the L_2 norm estimation of z.

Recovery Stage:
1. Compute the output z^* of the count-sketch and its best m-sparse approximation $\hat{z}$.
2. Based on $L(x)$ compute a real r with $\|x\|_p \leq r \leq 2\|x\|_p$.
3. Based on $L'(z - \hat{z})$ compute a real s with $\|z - \hat{z}\|_2 \leq s \leq 2\|z - \hat{z}\|_2$.
4. Find i with $|z_i^*|$ maximal.
5. If $s > \beta m^{1/2} r$ or $|z_i^*| < \epsilon^{-1/p} r$ output FAIL.
6. Output i as the sample and $z_i^* t_i^{1/p}$ as an approximation for x_i.

Figure 1: Our approximate L_p-sampler with both success probability and relative error $\Theta(\epsilon)$

assume $v < n$ as otherwise recording the entire vector x is more efficient.

The low probability of more than ϵ relative error in estimating x_i also follows from Lemma 4. In one round, the algorithm on Figure 1 uses $O(m \log n)$ counters for the count-sketch and this dominates the counters for the norm estimators. Using standard discretization this can be turned into an $O(m \log^2 n)$ bit algorithm. For the discretization we also have to keep our scaling factors polynomial in n. Recall that in the continuous model these factors $t_i^{-1/p}$ were unbounded. But we can safely declare failure if $t_i^{-1} > n^c$ for some $i \in [n]$ as this has low probability n^{1-c}. We have to do the v repetitions of the algorithm in parallel to obtain a single pass streaming algorithm. This increases the space to $O(vm \log^2 n)$ which is the same as the one claimed in the theorem. $\square$

Note that the hidden constant in the space bound of the theorem depends on p, especially that $1/(2-p)$, $1/p$ and $1/|1-p|$ factors come in. The last can always be replaced by a $\log(1/\epsilon)$ factor but the former ones are harder to handle. For $p = 2$ an extra $\log n$ factor seems to be necessary for an algorithm along these lines, see [1].

As we will see in Theorem 7, our space bound is tight for ϵ and δ constants. Note that the lower bound holds also if we only require the overall distribution of the L_p-sampler to be close to the L_p distribution as opposed to the much more strict definition of ϵ relative error sampling.

2.1 The L_0 Sampler

For p near zero, the method of precision sampling becomes intractable. This is because our scaling factors are $t_i^{-1/p}$ which clearly rules out $p = 0$. In the following we present a L_0 using a different approach. First we state the following well-known result on exact recovery of sparse vectors.

LEMMA 5. Let $1 \leq s \leq n$. There is a choice $k = O(s)$ and random linear function $L : \mathbb{R}^n \rightarrow \mathbb{R}^k$ (generated from $O(k \log n)$ random bits) and a recovery procedure that on input $L(x)$ outputs $x' \in \mathbb{R}^n$ or DENSE such that for any s-sparse vector x the output is $x' = x$ with probability 1 and for any vector x that is not s-sparse the output is DENSE with high probability.

THEOREM 2. There exists a zero relative error L_0 sampler which uses $O(\log^2 n \log(1/\delta))$ bits and outputs a coordinate $i \in [n]$ with probability at least $1 - \delta$.

PROOF. We first present our algorithm assuming a random oracle, and then we remove this assumption through the use of the pseudo-random generator of Nisan [26]. Let I_k for $k = 1, \ldots, \lfloor \log n \rfloor$ be subsets of $[n]$ of size 2^k chosen uniformly at random and $I_0 = [n]$. For each k we run the sparse recovery procedure of Lemma 5 on the vector x restricted to the coordinates in I_k with s set to $\lceil 4\log(1/\delta) \rceil$. We return a uniform random non-zero coordinate from the first recovery that gives a non-zero s-sparse vector. The algorithm fails if each recovery algorithm returns zero or DENSE.

Let J be the set of coordinates i with $x_i \neq 0$ (the support of x). Disregarding the low probability error of the procedure in Lemma 5 this procedure returns each index $i \in J$ with equal probability and never returns an index outside J. To bound the failure probability we observe that for $|J| \leq s$ failure is not possible, while for $|J| > s$ one has $k \in [\lfloor \log n \rfloor]$ such that $\mathbb{E}[|I_k \cap J|] = 2^k|J|/n$ is between $s/3$ and $2s/3$. For this k alone $1 \leq |I_k \cap J| \leq s$ is satisfied with probability at least $1 - \delta$ by the Chernoff bound limiting failure probability by δ.

To get rid of the random oracle we use Nisan's generator [26] that produces the random bits for the algorithm (including the ones describing I_k and the ones for the eventual random choice from $I_k \cap J$) from an $O(\log^2 n)$ length seed. It fools every logspace tester including the one that tests for a fixed set $J \subseteq [n]$ and $i \in [n]$ if the algorithm (assuming correct reconstruction) would return i. Thus this version of the algorithm, now using $O(\log^2 n)$ random bits and

$O(\log^2 \log(1/\delta))$ total space, is also a zero relative error L_0-sampler with failure probability bounded by $\delta + O(n^{-c})$. $\square$

As we will see in Theorem 7, this space bound is also tight for δ a constant and better sampling is not possible even if we allow constant relative error or a small overall distance of the output from the L_0 distribution.

3. FINDING DUPLICATES

Recall that, given a data stream of length $n + 1$ over the alphabet $[n]$, finding duplicates problem asks to output some $a \in [n]$ that has appeared at least twice in the stream.

THEOREM 3. *For any $\delta > 0$ there is a $O(\log^2 n \log(1/\delta))$ space one-pass algorithm which, given a stream of length $n + 1$ over the alphabet $[n]$, outputs an $i \in [n]$ or FAIL, such that the probability of outputting FAIL is at most δ and the algorithm outputs a letter $i \in [n]$ that is no duplicate with low probability.*

PROOF. Let x be an n-dimensional vector, initially zero at each coordinate. We run the L_1-sampler of Theorem 1 on x, with both relative error and failure probability set to $1/2$. Before we start processing the stream, we subtract 1 from each coordinate of x; i.e., we feed the updates $(i, -1)$ for $i = 1, \ldots n$ to the L_1 sampling algorithm. When a stream item $i \in [n]$ comes, we increase x_i by 1; i.e., we generate the update $(i, 1)$.

Observe that when the stream is exhausted, we have $x_i \geq 1$ for items i that have at least two occurrences in the stream, $x_i = 0$ for items that appear once, and $x_i = -1$ for items that do not appear. Note that our L_1-sampler, if it does not fail, outputs an index i and an approximation x^* of x_i. If x^* is positive, we output i, if it is negative or the L_1-sampler fails, we output FAIL. We have $\sum_{i=1}^{n} x_i = 1$, hence a perfect L_1 sample from x is positive with more than half probability. Taking into account that our L_1-sampler has $1/2$ relative error and failure probability (and neglecting for a second the chance that x^* has different sign from x_i) we conclude that we output a duplicate with probability at least $1/4$. The event that x^* does not have the same sign as x_i (and thus the relative error is at least 1) has low probability. This low probability can increase the failure probability and/or introduce error when we output non-duplicate items.

Repeating the algorithm $O(\log(1/\delta))$ times in parallel and accepting the first non-failing output reduces the failure rate to δ but keeps the error rate low. $\square$

As we will see in Theorem 6, our space bound is tight for $\delta < 1$ a constant.

It is natural to study the duplicates problem for other ranges of parameters. Assume that we have a stream of length $n - s \leq n$ over the alphabet $[n]$. For this problem, Gopalan et al. [14] gave an $O((s+1)\log^3 n)$ bits algorithm and an $\Omega(s)$ lower bound. Here we give an algorithm which uses $O(s \log n + \log^2 n)$ space.

THEOREM 4. *For any $\delta > 0$ there is an $O(\log^2 n \log 1/\delta + s \log n)$ space one-pass algorithm which, given a stream of length $n - s$ over the alphabet $[n]$, outputs NO-DUPLICATE with probability 1 if the input sequence has no duplicates, otherwise it outputs $i \in [n]$ or reports FAIL. The returned number is a duplicate with high probability while the probability of returning FAIL is at most δ.*

PROOF. Let x be an n-dimensional vector updated according to the description in the proof of Theorem 3; i.e., x_i is one less than the number of times i appears in the stream. In parallel, we run the exact recovery procedure from Lemma 5 with parameter $5s$ and the $1/2$ relative error L_1-sampler of Theorem 1 with failure rate $1/2$, both on the vector x. If the recovery algorithm returns a vector (as opposed to DENSE) we proceed and give the correct output assuming we have learned the entire x. Otherwise we consider the output of the sampling algorithm. If it is (i, x^*) with $x^* > 0$ we report i as a duplicate otherwise (if $x^* \leq 0$ or the sampling algorithm fails) we output FAIL. Define

$$\|x\|_1^+ = \sum_{i:x_i>0} |x_i| \qquad \text{and} \qquad \|x\|_1^- = \sum_{i:x_i<0} |x_i|.$$

Note that $\|x\|_1^+ - \|x\|_1^- = \sum_{i=1}^{n} x_i = -s$. If $\|x\|_1^+ + \|x\|_1^- \leq 5s$, then x is $5s$-sparse, thus the sparse recovery procedure outputs x and the algorithm makes no error. Note that the no repetition case falls into this category. If, however, $\|x\|_1^+ + \|x\|_1^- > 5s$, then the probability that a perfect L_1 sample from x is positive is $\|x\|_1^+/\|x\|_1 > 2/5$. Taking into account the relative error and failing probability (but ignoring the low probability event of the sampler outputting a wrong sign or sparse recovery algorithm reporting a vector), we conclude that with probability at least $1/10$ we get a positive sample and a correct output, otherwise we output FAIL. The failure probability can be decreased to δ by $O(\log(1/\delta))$ independent repetitions of the sampler. Note that the sparse recovery does not have to be repeated as it has low error probability.

The sparse recovery procedure takes $O(s \log n)$ bits by Lemma 5 for $s > 0$ (it takes $O(\log n)$ bits for $s = 0$) and each instance of the L_1-sampler requires $O(\log^2 n)$ bits by Theorem 4, totaling $O(s \log n + \log^2 n \log 1/\delta)$ bits. $\square$

Here we do not have a matching lower bound, but only the $\Omega(\log^2 n + s)$ that follows from the $\Omega(s)$ bound in [14] and our $\Omega(\log^2 n)$ bound on the original version of the duplicates problem.

We remark the last two theorems can be stated in a bit more general form. Instead of considering repetitions in data streams one can consider the problem of finding an index i with $x_i > 0$ for a vector $x \in \mathbb{Z}^n$ given by an update stream. Let $s = -\sum_{i=1}^{n} x_i$. If $s < 0$, then a positive coordinate exists and the algorithm of Theorem 3 finds one using $O(\log^2 n \log(1/\delta))$ space with low error and at most δ failure probability. If $s \geq 0$ a positive coordinate does not necessarily exist, but the algorithm of Theorem 4 finds one, report none exists or fails with the error, failure and space bounds claimed there.

Let us consider finally the version of the duplicates problem, where we have a stream of length $n + s > n$ over the alphabet $[n]$. Our lower and upper bounds are even farther in this case. A duplicate can be found using $O(\min\{\log^2 n, (n/s) \log n\}$ bits of memory in one pass with constant probability as follows. If we sample a random item from the stream, it will appear again unless that was the last appearance of the letter. As there are at most n last appearances in the stream of length $n + s$, the probability for a uniform random sample to repeat later is at least $s/(n + s)$. Therefore, if $n/s < \log n$, we can sample $4\lceil n/s \rceil$ items from the stream uniformly at random and check if one of them appears again to obtain a constant error algorithm for finding duplicates. If on the other hand $n/s \geq \log n$, we use the algorithm in Theorem 3.

Combining our lower bound for the original version of the duplicates problem with the simple lower bound of $\Omega(\log n)$, we conclude that any streaming algorithm that finds a duplicate in length $n+s$ streams must use $\Omega(\log^2(n/s)+\log n)$ bits.

4. LOWER BOUNDS

All our lower bounds follow from the augmented indexing problem. This problem is defined as follows. Let k and m be positive integers. The first player Alice, is given a string $x \in [k]^m$, while the second player Bob is given an integer $i \in [m]$ and x_j for $j < i$. Alice sends a single message to Bob and Bob should output x_i.

LEMMA 6. [23] In any one-way protocol in the joint random source model with success probability at least $1 - \delta > \frac{3}{2k}$, Alice must send a message of size $\Omega((1-\delta)m \log k)$.

We will use this lemma by reducing augmented indexing to other communication or streaming problems.

4.1 Universal Relation

Consider the following two player communication game. Alice gets a string $x \in \{0,1\}^n$, Bob gets $y \in \{0,1\}^n$ with the promise that $x \neq y$. The players exchange messages and the last player to receive a message must output an index $i \in [n]$ such that $x_i \neq y_i$. We call this the *universal relation communication problem* and denote it by UR^n.

This relation has been studied in detail for deterministic communication, as it naturally arises in the context of Karchmer-Wigderson games [20]. We note however that our definition is slightly unusual: in most settings both players must obtain the same index i such that $x_i \neq y_i$, whereas we are satisfied with the last player to receive a message learning such an i. Clearly, the stronger requirement can be met in $\lceil \log n \rceil$ additional bits and one additional round. The additional bits are needed in deterministic case but we are not concerned with $O(\log n)$ terms for our bounds, so the two models are almost equivalent up to the shift of one in the number of rounds.

The best deterministic protocol for UR^n is due to Tardos and Zwick [27]. Improving a previous result by Karchmer [19], they gave a 3 round deterministic protocol using $n + 2$ bits of communication with both players learning the same index i and showed that $n + 1$ bits is necessary for such a protocol. They also gave an $n - \lfloor \log n \rfloor + 2$ bit 2 round deterministic protocol for our weaker version of the problem, which is also tight except for the $+2$ term. They also gave an $n - \lfloor \log n \rfloor + 4$ bit 4 round protocol, where both players find an index where x and y differ—but not necessarily the same index. This shows that finding the same difference is harder.

Let $R_\delta^k(U)$ denote the k-round δ-error communication complexity of the communication problem U. We write $R_\delta(U)$ to denote the δ-error communication complexity when the number of rounds is not bounded. The next proposition follows from similar ideas that were used in Theorem 2.

PROPOSITION 1. *It holds that* $R_\delta^1(UR^n) = O(\log^2 n \log \frac{1}{\delta})$ *and* $R_\delta^2(UR^n) = O(\log n \log \frac{1}{\delta})$.

PROOF (SKETCH). One way to deduce the one round protocol is from Theorem 2. Alice and Bob run a single pass L_0-sampling algorithm on $x - y$. This can be achieved by a single message from Alice to Bob containing the memory after the first set of updates as in the proof of Theorem 8. The sample i Bob finds is an (almost uniform random) index with $x_i \neq y_i$.

A closer look shows that the algorithm of Theorem 2 makes $\lceil \log n \rceil + 1$ guesses for the number of non-zero coordinates of $x - y$ and picks a random subset $I \subseteq [n]$ of proper size for each such guess. If the players are allowed two rounds, the number of bits sent can be reduced to $O(\log n \log \delta^{-1})$ as follows. In the first round, the players estimate the number of non-zero coordinates of $x - y$ up to a factor of 2 via a standard Hamming distance estimation protocol (this takes $O(\log n \log \delta^{-1})$ bits). In the second round, Bob picks a random subset of I of proper size and sends a recovery matrix about I of size $O(\log n \log \delta^{-1})$ to Alice. □

We remark that along similar lines one can find an $\tilde{O}(\log n \log 1/\delta)$ space two-pass zero relative error L_0-sampling algorithm, by estimating L_0 of the vector defined by the stream in the first pass using [18]. Next we will show that the above proposition is best possible up to the $O(\log \delta^{-1})$ terms. We start with an averaging lemma.

LEMMA 7. *Any protocol for* UR^n *can be turned into one that outputs every index* $i \in [n]$ *with* $x_i \neq y_i$ *with the same probability. The new protocol uses a joint random source. The number of bits sent, the number of rounds and the error probability does not change.*

PROOF. Using the joint random source the players take a uniform random permutation π of $[n]$ and use it to permute the digits of x and y. Further they take a uniform random subset $S \subseteq [n]$ and flip the digits with coordinates in S. This requires no communication. Then they run the original protocol on the modified inputs and report $\pi^{-1}(i)$ if the original protocol reports i. All indices where x and y differ are reported with equal probability by symmetry. □

THEOREM 5. *For any* $\delta < 1$ *constant we have* $R_\delta^1(UR^n) = \Omega(\log^2 n)$ *and* $R_\delta = \Omega(\log n)$.

PROOF. The second bound comes from considering a uniform random pair (x, y) with Hamming distance 1. Either player needs to get $\log n$ bits of information to learn the only index where the strings differ.

To prove the first bound suppose Alice and Bob wants to solve the augmented indexing problem with Alice receiving $z \in [2^t]^s$ and Bob getting $i \in [s]$ and z_j for $j < i$.

Let them construct real vectors u and v as follows. Let $e_q \in \mathbb{R}^{2^t}$ be the standard unit vector in the direction of coordinate q. Alice forms the vectors w_j by concatenating 2^{s-j} copies of e_{z_j}, then she forms u by concatenating these vectors w_j for $j \in [s]$. The dimension of u is $n = (2^s - 1)2^t$. Bob obtains v by concatenating the same vectors w_j for $j \in [i-1]$ (these are known to him) and then concatenating enough zeros to reach the same dimension n.

Now Alice and Bob perform the $R_\delta^1(UR^n)$ length δ error one round protocol for UR^n. By Lemma 7 we may assume the protocol returns a uniform random index where u and v differ. Note that each such index reveals one coordinate $z_j \in [2^t]$ to Bob for $j \geq i$. As z_j is revealed by 2^{s-j} such indices more than half the time when the UR^n protocol does not err

Bob learns the correct value of z_i. This yields a $R^1_\delta(\mathrm{UR}^n)$ length one way protocol for augmented indexing with error probability $(1 + \delta)/2$. By Lemma 6 we have $R^1_\delta(\mathrm{UR}^n) = \Omega(st)$. Choosing $s = t$ proves the theorem. $\square$

4.2 Finding Duplicates

THEOREM 6. *Any one-pass streaming algorithm that outputs a duplicate with constant probability uses $\Omega(\log^2 n)$ space. This remains true even if the stream is not allowed to have an element repeated more than twice.*

PROOF. We show our claim by a reduction from the universal relation. Each of Alice and Bob is given a binary string of length n, respectively x and y. Further, the players are guaranteed that $x \neq y$. Alice sends a message to Bob, after which Bob must output an index $i \in [n]$ such that $x_i \neq y_i$. By Theorem 5, to solve this problem with $1/2$ error probability requires $\Omega(\log^2 n)$ bits for one-way communication. Alice constructs the set $S = \{2i - 1 + x_i \mid i \in [n]\} \subseteq [2n]$ and Bob constructs $T = \{2i - y_i \mid i \in [n]\} \subseteq [2n]$. Observe that $|S| = |T| = n$ and $x_i \neq y_i$ if and only if either $2i$ or $2i - 1$ is in both S and T.

Next, using the shared randomness, players pick a random subset P of $[2n]$ of size n. We have

$$\Pr[|S \cap P| + |T \cap P| \geq n + 1] > 1/8.$$

To see this let $i \in S \cap T$ and $j \in [2n] \setminus (S \cap T)$. We have $|P \cap \{i, j\}| = 1$ with probability more than $1/2$. The sets P satisfying this can be partitioned into classes of size four by putting $Q \cup \{i\}$, $Q \cup \{j\}$ and their complements in the same class for any $Q \subseteq [2n] \setminus \{i, j\}$, $|Q| = n - 1$. Clearly, at least one of the four sets P in each class satisfies $|S \cap P| + |T \cap P| > n$.

Given a streaming algorithm A for finding duplicates, Alice feeds the elements of $S \cap P$ to A and sends the memory contents over to Bob, along with the integer $|S \cap P|$. If $|S \cap P| + |T \cap P| < n + 1$, Bob outputs FAIL. Otherwise, feeds arbitrary $n + 1 - |S \cap P|$ elements of $T \cap P$ to A. Note that no element repeats more than twice.

On the other hand $|P| = n$ and we always give $n + 1$ elements of P to the algorithm. Also with constant probability, Bob finds an $a \in S \cap T$, which in turn reveals an i such that $x_i \neq y_i$. Therefore by Theorem 5, any algorithm for finding duplicates must use $\Omega(\log^2 n)$ bits. $\square$

4.3 L_p-sampling

Our algorithm for the duplicates problem (Theorem 3) is based on L_1-sampling, thus the matching lower bound for the duplicates problem implies a similar bound for L_1-sampling. Here we show an $\Omega(\log^2 n)$ lower bound for L_p-sampling for all p. Notice that the L_p distribution corresponding to $0, \pm 1$ vectors are independent of p, so p does not have to be specified for the next theorem.

THEOREM 7. *Any one pass L_p-sampler with an output distribution, whose variation distance from the L_p distribution corresponding to x is at most $1/3$, requires $\Omega(\log^2 n)$ bits of memory. This holds even when all the coodinates of x are guaranteed to be -1, 0 or 1.*

For constants $\delta < 1$ and $\epsilon < 1$ the same lower bound holds for any ϵ relative error L_p-sampler with failure probability δ.

PROOF. Consider the L_1 sampling algorithm that we used to prove Theorem 3. Given a stream of items from $[n]$ we

turned it to an update stream for an n dimensional vector x by first producing an update $(i, -1)$ for all $i \in [n]$ and then for any letter i in the stream producing an update $(i, 1)$. Assuming that no item appears more than twice in the stream all coordinates of the final vector x are -1, 0 or 1. The L_1 distribution for x puts weight more than $1/2$ on the coordinates having value 1. These are the duplicates. Thus if we have another algorithm such that the variation distance of its output is at most $1/3$ from this L_1 distribution, then it returns a coordinate with value 1 with probability at least $1/6$. For an ϵ relative error δ failure probability approximate L_p-sampler the same probability is at least $(1 - \epsilon)(1 - \delta) - n^{1-c}$. Finding a coordinate in x with value 1 is the same as finding a duplicate in the original stream, so we need $\Omega(\log^2 n)$ memory by Theorem 6. $\square$

4.4 Heavy Hitters

The heavy hitters problem in the streaming model is defined as follows. Let x be an n-dimensional integer vector given by an update stream. A heavy hitters algorithm with parameters $p > 0$ and $\phi > 0$ is required to output a set $S \subseteq [n]$ that contains all i with $|x_i| \geq \phi\|x\|_p$ and no i such that $|x_i| \leq \frac{\phi}{2}\|x\|_p$. We call such S a valid heavy hitter set.[2] In this part, we show a tight lower bound for the space complexity of randomized algorithms (assuming constant probability of error) for the heavy hitter problem. First we briefly review the upper bounds.

The count-median algorithm from [8] gives a $O(\phi^{-1}\log^2 n)$ space upper bound for the case of $p = 1$. Here we note the count-sketch [6] in fact gives a $O(\phi^{-p}\log^2 n)$ space upper bound for all $p \in (0, 2]$. The case of $p = 2$ easily follows from Lemma 1. Let $d = \mathrm{Err}_2^m(x)/m^{1/2}$. In general it holds $d \leq \|x\|_p/m^{1/p}$ for any $p \in (0, 2]$. Indeed, let $H \subset [n]$ be the set of indices for which $d^2 = \sum_{i \in H} x_i^2/m$ and let $c = \max_{i \in H} |x_i|$. Then we have $\|x\|_p^p/m = \sum_{i \in [n]} |x_i|^p/m \geq c^p + \sum_{i \in H} |x_i|^p/m \geq c^p + c^{p-2}\sum_{i \in H} x_i^2/m = c^p + c^{p-2}d^2 \geq c^p((1 - p/2) + (p/2)c^{-2}d^2) \geq c^p(c^{-2}d^2)^{p/2} = d^p$. Therefore setting $m = 1/\phi^p$ in the count-sketch scheme gives the desired result.

We remark that a similar upper bound for the heavy hitter problem is shown in [16] (cf. Theorem 1), albeit via different arguments. In the next theorem, we show that the above upper bound is tight for any reasonable range of parameters. Our lower bound holds even in the strict turnstile model and even for very short streams.

THEOREM 8. *Let $p > 0$ and $\phi \in (0, 1)$ be a reals. Any one pass heavy hitter algorithm in the strict turnstile model uses $\Omega(\phi^{-p}\log^2 n)$.*

PROOF. Suppose there is a one pass heavy hitter algorithm for parameters p and ϕ. We allow for a random oracle and assume the updates are polynomially bounded in n and integers. We can also restrict the number of updates to be $O(\phi^{-p}\log n)$ and assume all coordinates of the final vector are positive (strict turnstile model). We turn this streaming algorithm into a protocol for augmented indexing in a similar way as we transformed the protocol for UR^n to a protocol for augmented indexing in the proof of Theorem 5.

---

[2]In general, the parameter $\frac{1}{2}\phi$ can be replaced by any $\epsilon < \phi$. Since here our focus is on lower bounds, we have simplified the definition.

The exponential growth is now achieved not by repetition but by multiplying the coordinates with a growing factor.

Suppose Alice and Bob wants to solve the augmented indexing problem and Alice receives $y \in [2^t]^s$ and Bob gets $i \in [s]$ and y_j for $j < i$. Let them construct real vectors u and v as follows. Let $b = (1 - (2\phi)^p)^{-1/p}$ and let $e_q \in \mathbb{R}^{2^t}$ be the standard unit vector in the direction of coordinate q. Alice obtains u by concatenating the vectors $\lceil b^{s-j} \rceil e_{y_j}$ for $j \in [s]$. The dimension of u is $n' = s2^t$. Bob obtains v by concatenating the same vectors for $j \in [i-1]$ and then concatenating enough zeros, namely $(s - i + 1)2^t$, to reach the same dimension n'. Now Alice and Bob perform the heavy hitter algorithm for the vector $x = u - v$ as follows. Alice generates the necessary updates to increase the initially zero vector $x \in \mathbb{Z}^n$ to reach $x = u$, maintains the memory content throughout these updates and sends the final content to Bob. Now Bob generates the necessary updates to decrease $x = u$ to its final value $x = u - v$ and maintains the memory throughout. Finally Bob learns the heavy hitter set S the streaming algorithm produces and outputs $z \in [2^t]$ if the smallest index in S is $(i - 1)2^t + z$.

We claim that the above protocol errs only if the streaming algorithm makes an error. Notice that all coordinates of x_l of $x = u - v$ are zero except the ones of the form $x_{l_j} = \lceil b^{s-j} \rceil$ for $l_j = (j-1)2^t + y_j$, where $i \leq j \leq s$. Thus x_{l_i} is the first non-zero coordinate. So the claim is true if $x_{l_i} \geq \phi \|x\|_p$. Using $\lceil v \rceil < 2v$ for $v \geq 1$ we get exactly this:

$$
\begin{aligned}
\phi^p \|x\|_p^p &= \phi^p \sum_{j=i}^{s} \lceil b^{s-j} \rceil^p \\
&< (2\phi)^p b^{p(s-i+1)}/(b^p - 1) \\
&= b^{p(s-i)} \qquad \text{(since } b^p = 1/(1 - (2\phi)^p)) \\
&\leq x_{l_i}^p
\end{aligned}
$$

Let us now choose $s = \lceil (2\phi)^{-p} \log n \rceil$ and $t = \lceil \log n/2 \rceil$. For large enough n this gives $n' = s2^t < n$ and all coordinates of x throughout the procedure remain under n. Still if the streaming algorithm works with probability over $1/2$, then by Lemma 6 the message size of the devised protocol is $\Omega(st) = \Omega(\phi^{-p} \log^2 n)$. This proves the theorem as the message size of the protocol is the same as the memory size of the streaming algorithm. $\square$

5. REFERENCES

[1] Alex Andoni, Robert Krauthgamer, and Krzysztof Onak. Streaming algorithms via precision sampling. Manuscript, 2010.

[2] Khanh Do Ba, Piotr Indyk, Eric Price, and David P. Woodruff. Lower bounds for sparse recovery. In *SODA*, pages 1190–1197, 2010.

[3] Brian Babcock, Mayur Datar, and Rajeev Motwani. Sampling from a moving window over streaming data. In *SODA*, pages 633–634, 2002.

[4] Radu Berinde, Graham Cormode, Piotr Indyk, and Martin J. Strauss. Space-optimal heavy hitters with strong error bounds. In *PODS*, pages 157–166, 2009.

[5] Vladimir Braverman, Rafail Ostrovsky, and Carlo Zaniolo. Optimal sampling from sliding windows. In *PODS*, pages 147–156, 2009.

[6] Moses Charikar, Kevin Chen, and Martin Farach-Colton. Finding frequent items in data streams. *Theor. Comput. Sci.*, 312(1):3–15, 2004.

[7] Edith Cohen, Nick G. Duffield, Haim Kaplan, Carsten Lund, and Mikkel Thorup. Stream sampling for variance-optimal estimation of subset sums. In *SODA*, pages 1255–1264, 2009.

[8] Graham Cormode and S. Muthukrishnan. An improved data stream summary: the count-min sketch and its applications. *J. Algorithms*, 55(1):58–75, 2005.

[9] Graham Cormode, S. Muthukrishnan, and Irina Rozenbaum. Summarizing and mining inverse distributions on data streams via dynamic inverse sampling. In *VLDB*, pages 25–36, 2005.

[10] Graham Cormode, S. Muthukrishnan, Ke Yi, and Qin Zhang. Optimal sampling from distributed streams. In *PODS*, pages 77–86, 2010.

[11] Nick G. Duffield, Carsten Lund, and Mikkel Thorup. Priority sampling for estimation of arbitrary subset sums. *J. ACM*, 54(6), 2007.

[12] Gereon Frahling, Piotr Indyk, and Christian Sohler. Sampling in dynamic data streams and applications. In *Proceedings of the twenty-first annual symposium on Computational geometry*, SCG '05, pages 142–149, New York, NY, USA, 2005. ACM.

[13] Anna Gilbert and Piotr Indyk. Sparse recovery using sparse matrices. In *Proceeding of IEEE*, 2010.

[14] Parikshit Gopalan and Jaikumar Radhakrishnan. Finding duplicates in a data stream. In *Proceedings of the twentieth Annual ACM-SIAM Symposium on Discrete Algorithms*, SODA '09, pages 402–411, Philadelphia, PA, USA, 2009. Society for Industrial and Applied Mathematics.

[15] T. S. Jayram and David P. Woodruff. The data stream space complexity of cascaded norms. In *FOCS*, pages 765–774, 2009.

[16] Daniel M. Kane, Jelani Nelson, Ely Porat, and Woodruff David P. Fast moment estimation in data streams in optimal space. Manuscript, 2010.

[17] Daniel M. Kane, Jelani Nelson, and David P. Woodruff. On the exact space complexity of sketching and streaming small norms. In *SODA*, pages 1161–1178, 2010.

[18] Daniel M. Kane, Jelani Nelson, and David P. Woodruff. An optimal algorithm for the distinct elements problem. In *Proceedings of the twenty-ninth ACM SIGMOD-SIGACT-SIGART symposium on Principles of database systems of data*, PODS '10, pages 41–52, New York, NY, USA, 2010. ACM.

[19] Mauricio Karchmer. *A New Approach to Circuit Depth*. PhD thesis, MIT, 1989.

[20] Mauricio Karchmer and Avi Wigderson. Monotone circuits for connectivity require super-logarithmic depth. In *Proceedings of the twentieth annual ACM symposium on Theory of computing*, STOC '88, pages 539–550, New York, NY, USA, 1988. ACM.

[21] Donald E. Knuth. *The Art of Computer Programming, Volume II: Seminumerical Algorithms*. Addison-Wesley, 1969.

[22] Ahmed Metwally, Divyakant Agrawal, and Amr El Abbadi. Duplicate detection in click streams. In *WWW*, pages 12–21, 2005.

[23] Peter Bro Miltersen, Noam Nisan, Shmuel Safra, and Avi Wigderson. On data structures and asymmetric communication complexity. In *Proceedings of the twenty-seventh annual ACM symposium on Theory of computing*, STOC '95, pages 103–111, New York, NY, USA, 1995. ACM.

[24] Morteza Monemizadeh and David P. Woodruff. 1-pass relative-error lp-sampling with applications. In *SODA*, pages 1143–1160, 2010.

[25] S. Muthukrishnan. *Data Streams: Algorithms and Applications*.

[26] N. Nisan. Pseudorandom generators for space-bounded computations. In *Proceedings of the twenty-second annual ACM symposium on Theory of computing*, STOC '90, pages 204–212, New York, NY, USA, 1990. ACM.

[27] Gabor Tardos and Uri Zwick. The communication complexity of the universal relation. In *Proceedings of the 12th Annual IEEE Conference on Computational Complexity*, pages 247–, Washington, DC, USA, 1997. IEEE Computer Society.

[28] Jun Tarui. Finding a duplicate and a missing item in a stream. In Jin-Yi Cai, S. Cooper, and Hong Zhu, editors, *Theory and Applications of Models of Computation*, volume 4484 of *Lecture Notes in Computer Science*, pages 128–135. Springer Berlin / Heidelberg, 2007.

[29] David Woodruff and T. S. Jayram. Optimal bounds for johnson-lindenstrauss transforms and streaming problems with low error. In *SODA*, 2011.

Incomplete Information and Certain Answers in General Data Models

Leonid Libkin
School of Informatics, University of Edinburgh
libkin@inf.ed.ac.uk

ABSTRACT

While incomplete information is ubiquitous in all data models – especially in applications involving data translation or integration – our understanding of it is still not completely satisfactory. For example, even such a basic notion as certain answers for XML queries was only introduced recently, and in a way seemingly rather different from relational certain answers.

The goal of this paper is to introduce a general approach to handling incompleteness, and to test its applicability in known data models such as relations and documents. The approach is based on representing degrees of incompleteness via semantics-based orderings on database objects. We use it to both obtain new results on incompleteness and to explain some previously observed phenomena. Specifically we show that certain answers for relational and XML queries are two instances of the same general concept; we describe structural properties behind the naïve evaluation of queries; answer open questions on the existence of certain answers in the XML setting; and show that previously studied ordering-based approaches were only adequate for SQL's primitive view of nulls. We define a general setting that subsumes relations and documents to help us explain in a uniform way how to compute certain answers, and when good solutions can be found in data exchange. We also look at the complexity of common problems related to incompleteness, and generalize several results from relational and XML contexts.

Categories and Subject Descriptors. H.2.1 [**Database Management**]: Logical Design—*Data Models*; I.7.2 [**Document and Text Processing**]: Document Preparation—*XML*

General Terms. Theory, Languages, Algorithms

Keywords. Incompleteness, naive tables/evaluation, certain answers, XML, orderings, homomorphisms

1. INTRODUCTION

In most database applications, one has to deal with incomplete data – this fact has been recognized almost immediately after the birth of the relational model. And yet for a long time the treatment of incomplete information did not receive the attention that it deserved. The design of SQL, for example, is notorious for its nulls-related features, which, as [14] nicely put it, are "in some ways fundamentally at odds with the way the world behaves" (a well-known example of such an oddity is that the statements $|X| > |Y|$ and $X - Y = \emptyset$ are logically consistent in SQL!). On the theoretical side, foundational research from the 1980s, first by Imielinski and Lipski [25] and then by Abiteboul, Kanellakis, and Grahne [3] provided models of incompleteness appropriate for handling queries in different relational languages, and established the computational costs of the key tasks associated with these models. However, until recently, the topic has seen only sporadic activity.

The situation changed rather dramatically over the past several years though, and handling of incompleteness in databases was brought to the fore of database research. This happened mainly due to a number of new applications such as those dealing with data on the web, integrated data, or data that was moved between different applications. In them, the issue of incompleteness is essential. For example, in data integration and data exchange, null values and associated concepts such as representation systems and certain answers play a central role [1, 6, 18, 28]. Representation and querying of uncertain data has also been an active field of study [5, 32]; another active direction that borders incompleteness is handling of probabilistic data [35].

Most of the classical theory of incompleteness has been developed in the relational context, where the key concepts (such as, e.g., certain answers) are well understood. A number of attempts were made in the 1990s to develop a general theory of incompleteness in databases, applicable to multiple data models [9, 10, 30, 31, 34]. This was done by using techniques from semantics of programming languages [21]. The connection is rather natural: in programming semantics, a program is assigned a meaning in an ordered set, where the order describes how partial, or incomplete, a function is. In databases, we deal with domains of objects, rather than functions, but these are still ordered based on the degree of incompleteness.

Those general theories, while achieving some success with nested relations [29, 30], fell well short of handling incomplete information in more complex data models, notably XML. We shall elaborate on the reasons for it later in the paper. Incompleteness in XML was addressed recently [4, 7, 15], and one issue that required a complete reworking was the concept of certain answers for queries that return XML documents (i.e., the notion of certain information in a family of trees).

Such certain answers were defined in [15] using an approach that, on the surface looked very different from the relational approach. But does it mean that incompleteness in XML is really different from relational incompleteness? And if it is not – as we shall argue – then what is the general theory that encompasses them all and can be applied to other models?

Our main goal is to develop such a general theory of incompleteness in databases, that subsumes in a uniform way existing relational and XML results, is easily extendible to other data models, and is useful in the main applications of incompleteness.

Our theory will again be based on the notion of an information ordering, to represent the degree of an incompleteness of a database object. Unlike investigations from the 1990s, however, we shall use orderings that are closely tied with the semantics of instances that most commonly arise in applications (more precisely, we deal mainly with naïve tables and their analogs). In view of this, we start by examining two different approaches to handling incompleteness: in relational databases, and in XML documents. We reformulate (and in some cases, strengthen) known results to demonstrate the usefulness of information ordering for query answering.

We then present a very general and datamodel-independent framework for handling incompleteness, that allows us to make two conclusions. First, the notions of certainty in relational and XML contexts, while very different on the surface, are really identical, and correspond to computing greatest lower bounds in ordered sets. Second, we find an easily verified criterion for queries that ensures that certain answers can be computed by *naïve evaluation*, i.e., treating nulls as if they were usual attribute values.

After that, we define the most natural ordering for both relational and XML databases: namely, an object x is less informative than an object y if x denotes more complete objects (indeed, no information means that every instance is possible, so the more objects are possible as the denotation of x, the less informative x is). These orderings can be characterized in terms of the existence of homomorphisms between instances. This immediately allows us to adapt techniques from graph theory, where lattices of graphs and their cores with respect

to homomorphism-based orderings have been studied [23] (note, however, that homomorphisms of database instances are not identical to graph homomorphisms, so some work is required in adapting graph-theoretic techniques). We show how to compute greatest lower bounds for finding certain answers, and use this new view of the problem to answer several open problems about the existence of certain answers for XML queries.

To demonstrate that this approach is not limited to relational or XML data, we consider a general setting, reminiscent of data models in [13, 22, 27]. It separates structural and data aspects of a model, which is, essentially, a colored relational structure, where the color of a node determines the length of a tuple of data values attached to it. In relational databases, the underlying structure is just a set; in XML, it is, as expected, a tree.

It turns out that it is often easier to reason about such general models, deriving particular results (say, for XML) as corollaries. For example, the model immediately makes it clear how to compute lower bounds for certain answers – it is the only solution that "type-checks". We also look at upper bounds and explain that they are naturally related to building universal solutions in data exchange.

We conclude by studying computational problems typical in the context of incomplete information. As the underlying structure in our general model conveys some schema information, it gives rise to the consistency problem for incomplete objects. We also look at the membership problem: whether a complete instance represents a possible world for an incomplete one. For this problem, we prove a strong generalization of polynomial-time algorithms for both relational [3] and XML [7] cases under the Codd-interpretation of nulls (when each null occurs at most once). Finally, we look at query answering, and provide broad classes of queries for which upper bounds coincide with those for XML, even for much more general data models.

Organization In Section 2 we review incompleteness in relational and XML models (stating some new results along the way). In Section 3 we present a general model based on orderings. In Section 4 we study homomorphism-based orderings for relations and XML. In Section 5 we present a general data-model that subsumes relations and XML and study incompleteness in it. Section 6 studies common computational problems associated with incompleteness in the general model.

2. INCOMPLETENESS IN RELATIONS AND XML

2.1 Incompleteness in relations

We start with a few standard definitions. We assume two disjoint sets of values: $\mathcal{C}$ of constants, and $\mathcal{N}$ of nulls (which will be denoted by $\perp$, with sub/superscripts). A relational schema is a set of relation names with associated arities. An incomplete relational instance associates with each k-ary relation symbol S a k-ary relation over $\mathcal{C} \cup \mathcal{N}$, i.e., a finite subset of $(\mathcal{C} \cup \mathcal{N})^k$. When the instance is clear from the context we shall write S for the relation itself as well.

Such incomplete relational instances are referred to as *naïve* databases [2, 25]; note that a null $\bot \in \mathcal{N}$ can appear multiple times in such an instance. If each null $\bot \in \mathcal{N}$ appears at most once, we speak of *Codd* databases. If we talk about single relations, it is common to refer to them as naïve tables and Codd tables.

The semantics $[\![D]\!]$ of an incomplete database D is the set of complete databases it can represent. These are defined via *homomorphisms*. We write $\mathcal{C}(D)$ and $\mathcal{N}(D)$ for the sets of constants and nulls, resp., that occur in D. A homomorphism $h : D \to D'$ between two databases of the same schema is a map $h : \mathcal{N}(D) \to \mathcal{C}(D') \cup \mathcal{N}(D')$ such that, for every relation symbol S, if a tuple $\bar{u}$ is in relation S in D, then the tuple $h(\bar{u})$ is in the relation S in D'. As usual, we extend h to constants by letting $h(c) = c$ for every $c \in \mathcal{C}$. The semantics of an incomplete database D, denoted by $[\![D]\!]$ is then defined as the set of complete databases R such that there is a homomorphism $h : D \to R$.

For example, given a naïve table D below, the relation shown next to it is in $[\![D]\!]$, as witnesses by homomorphism $h(\bot_1) = 4$, $h(\bot_2) = 3$, and $h(\bot_3) = 5$:

$D:$

1	2	$\bot_1$
$\bot_2$	$\bot_1$	3
$\bot_3$	5	1

$R:$

1	2	4
3	4	3
5	5	1
3	7	8

Certain answers and naïve evaluation Given an incomplete database D and a query Q, one normally tries to compute *certain answers*:

$$\mathsf{certain}(Q, D) = \bigcap \{Q(R) \mid R \in [\![D]\!]\},$$

that are true regardless of the interpretation of nulls.

Note that when Q is a Boolean (true/false) query, we normally associate true with the set containing the empty tuple, and false with the empty set. Then the above definition says that for a Boolean query, $\mathsf{certain}(Q, D)$ is true iff Q is true in every R from $[\![D]\!]$.

The problem of finding certain answers is undecidable for FO queries (as it becomes finite validity), but for positive relational algebra queries there is a simple polynomial-time algorithm, described below.

Define $Q_{\text{naïve}}(D)$ as follows: first, evaluate Q as if nulls were values (e.g., $\bot_1 = \bot_1$, $\bot_1 \neq \bot_2$, $\bot_1 \neq c$ for every $c \in \mathcal{C}$), and then eliminate tuples with nulls from the result. A classical result from [25] states that if Q is a union of conjunctive queries, then $\mathsf{certain}(Q, D) = Q_{\text{naïve}}(D)$. We can actually show that this is essentially

optimal: one cannot find a larger subclass of FO for which naïve evaluation would compute certain answers.

Proposition 1. *If Q is a Boolean FO query and $\mathsf{certain}(Q, D) = Q_{\text{naïve}}(D)$ for all naïve databases D, then Q is equivalent to a union of conjunctive queries.*

Certain answers via preorders Note that each naïve database D is naturally viewed as a *Boolean conjunctive query (CQ)* Q_D. For example, the naïve database shown earlier is viewed as a CQ

$$\exists x_1, x_2, x_3 \ D(1, 2, x_1) \wedge D(x_2, x_1, 3) \wedge D(x_3, 5, 1),$$

that is, each null $\bot_i$ is replaced by an existentially quantified variable x_i. Likewise, each Boolean CQ Q can be viewed as a naïve database D_Q (its tableau).

By viewing incomplete databases as logical formulae, we can restate the definition of the semantics in terms of satisfaction of formulae: $R \in [\![D]\!]$ iff $R \models Q_D$.

We now relate certain answers to two standard *preorders* (recall that a preorder is a relation that is reflexive and transitive). The first is what we referred to as the *information ordering* in the introduction: a naïve database D_1 is *less informative* than D_2 if it represents more databases, i.e. $D_1 \preceq D_2$ iff $[\![D_2]\!] \subseteq [\![D_1]\!]$. Notice that this is a preorder rather than a partial order: if $[\![D]\!] = [\![D']\!]$, then both $D \preceq D'$ and $D' \preceq D$ hold.

For queries, we have a well-known preorder: containment (denoted, as usual, by $Q_1 \subseteq Q_2$). The following is essentially a restatement of known results:

Proposition 2. *For a Boolean conjunctive query Q and a naïve database D, the following are equivalent:*

1. $\mathsf{certain}(Q, D) = true$;
2. $D_Q \preceq D$;
3. $Q_D \subseteq Q$.

This also immediately implies that $\mathsf{certain}(Q, D)$ is the greatest lower bound of the set $\{Q(D') \mid D \preceq D'\}$, where by $Q(D')$ we mean running a query over an incomplete database as if it were a complete database.

These indicate that information ordering and lower bounds have a close connection with certain answers; this will be made much more precise later in the paper.

2.2 Incompleteness in XML

Although rather elaborate models of incompleteness for XML exist [4, 7], for our purposes we shall present only a fairly simple model, with nulls occurring as attribute values. This will suffice to explain the main concept used for defining certain answers for XML queries.

The data model is unranked trees, with nodes labeled by letters from a finite alphabet Σ. For each letter $a \in \Sigma$, we have an associated arity $ar(a)$ telling us the number of attributes such nodes carry. More precisely, a tree over Σ is defined as $T = \langle V, E, \lambda, \rho \rangle$, where

- $\langle V, E \rangle$ is a rooted directed unranked tree, with nodes V and the child relation E;

- $\lambda : V \to \Sigma$ is a labeling function; if $\lambda(v) = a$ then we refer to v as an a-labeled node;

- the function ρ assigns to each a-labeled node an $ar(a)$-tuple of data values from $\mathcal{C} \cup \mathcal{N}$.

An example is shown below. Here the alphabet is $\{a, b, c\}$, the arity of a is 2, both b and c have arity 1, and data values are shown next to the labels.

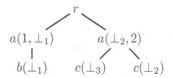

If all the data values in $\rho(v)$ come from $\mathcal{C}$ and the root is labeled by a designated root symbol $r \in \Sigma$, then we refer to a *complete* tree T; otherwise we speak of *incomplete trees*. The semantics of incomplete trees is again defined by means of homomorphisms which act on both tree nodes and data values.

Given a tree T, we use the notation $\mathcal{C}(T)$ for the set of constants in $\mathcal{C}$ that appear as data values in T, and $\mathcal{N}(T)$ for the set of nulls that appear in it. A *homomorphism* $h : T \to T'$ from a tree $T = \langle V, E, \lambda, \rho \rangle$ into a tree $T' = \langle V', E', \lambda', \rho' \rangle$ is a pair of mappings $h_1 : V \to V'$ and $h_2 : \mathcal{N}(T) \to \mathcal{C}(T') \cup \mathcal{N}(T')$ such that:

1. if $(x, y) \in E$ then $(h_1(x), h_1(y)) \in E'$;

2. if x is labeled a in T, then $h_1(x)$ is labeled a in T', i.e., $\lambda'(h_1(x)) = \lambda(x)$; and

3. the data values of $h_1(x)$ are the result of h_2 on the data values of x, i.e., $\rho'(h_1(x)) = h_2(\rho(x))$.

As usual, we extend h_2 to be the identity on constants.

Now the semantics $[\![T]\!]$ of an incomplete tree T is defined as the set of all complete trees T' such that there is a homomorphism $h : T \to T'$.

Certain answers via max-descriptions To define relational certain answers, we used intersection. But how do we define them for trees – what is an analog of intersection then? Most papers addressing incompleteness in XML only looked at queries returning relations, to find a way around this problem.

For proper XML-to-XML queries, the problem was addressed in [15]. If T is an incomplete XML tree, and Q is a query returning XML trees, then certain answers $\mathsf{certain}(Q, T)$ should be the certain information in the set $Q([\![T]\!]) = \{Q(T') \mid T' \in [\![T]\!]\}$. Thus, we need to know how to extract certain information from a collection of XML documents.

For this, it is convenient to use the analogy with naïve tables and CQs, and view trees as both objects and formulae: we say $T \models T'$ iff there is a homomorphism from

T' to T (i.e., T satisfies what is described by an incomplete tree T'; this is the analog of $D \models Q_{D'}$ we used above to describe when D is more informative than D'). In XML, this corresponds to describing incompleteness via tree patterns, as done in, e.g., [4, 7, 8].

Our goal now is to extract the certain information from a set $\mathcal{T}$ of incomplete trees. The proposal of [15] was to view incomplete trees as *both* models and formulas, and reconstruct a classical model/formulas Galois connection (cf. [37]). More precisely, for $\mathcal{T}$ we define:

- its theory $\mathrm{Th}(\mathcal{T}) = \{T' \mid \forall T \in \mathcal{T} : T \models T'\}$;
- its models $\mathrm{Mod}(\mathcal{T}) = \{T' \mid \forall T \in \mathcal{T} : T' \models T\}$.

Under this view, $\mathrm{Th}(\mathcal{T})$ describes the certain knowledge conveyed by $\mathcal{T}$. If we want to capture it by an object, we look for a tree T whose models are the models of the certain knowledge, i.e., $\mathrm{Mod}(T) = \mathrm{Mod}(\mathrm{Th}(\mathcal{T}))$. Such trees T were called *max-description* in [15].

Note that all max-descriptions T, T' are equivalent, i.e., $T \models T'$ and $T' \models T$. The definition of certain answers $\mathsf{certain}(Q, T)$ in [15] was simply to take a max-description of $Q([\![T]\!])$. It was shown that this agrees perfectly with the relational definition when XML documents model relations. It was also shown that every set of complete XML documents has a max-description, and every finite set of complete or incomplete XML documents has a max-description. In the finite case, these are computable in time polynomial in the total size of $\mathcal{T}$, and exponential in the number of trees in $\mathcal{T}$.

It was left open however whether arbitrary sets (in fact, even computable sets) of XML documents have max-descriptions. We shall answer this soon. To do so, we first build a general theory (which will completely demystify max-descriptions, among other things), and then apply it to relations, trees, and beyond.

3. ORDERED SETS AND INCOMPLETE-NESS

The notions of certain answers for relational and XML queries, on the surface, appear to be very different. But in reality, they are not; in fact, they are the same. To see this, we now describe a very general framework for handling incompleteness and certain answers. In this framework, all that we are going to assume is the presence of an information ordering on a set of database objects. Even with this, we can reason about certain answers, max-descriptions, query answering, and naïve evaluation.

First, some very basic definitions. A *preorder* $\preceq$ is a binary relation that is transitive and reflexive. Associated with the preorder we have an equivalence relation $x \sim y$ defined by $(x \preceq y) \wedge (y \preceq x)$, and the quotient of $\preceq$ by $\sim$ is a partial order. We let $\uparrow x = \{y \mid x \preceq y\}$

and $\downarrow x = \{ y \mid y \preceq x \}$. Also $\uparrow X = \bigcup_{x \in X} \uparrow x$ and likewise for $\downarrow X$. A lower bound of a set X is an element y such that $y \preceq x$ for all $x \in X$. A *greatest lower bound (glb)* of X is a lower bound y such that $y' \preceq y$ whenever y' is another lower bound of X. It is denoted by $\bigwedge X$. Note that in a preorder, $\bigwedge X$ is an equivalence class wrt $\sim$, but whenever we do not distinguish between equivalent elements we shall write, slightly abusing notation, $y = \bigwedge X$. Glb's need not exist in general.

By a *database domain* we mean a set $\mathcal{D}$ with a preorder $\preceq$ on it. The interpretation is as follows: $\mathcal{D}$ is a set of database objects (say, incomplete relational databases or incomplete trees over the same schema), and $\preceq$ is the information ordering. That is, we assume that incomplete database objects come with some notion of their semantics $[\![\cdot]\!]$ (what exactly it is, is immaterial to us in this section; this will become important when we look at concrete models), and the interpretation of the preorder is, as before $x \preceq y$ iff $[\![y]\!] \subseteq [\![x]\!]$. The associated equivalence relation $x \sim y$ is simply $[\![x]\!] = [\![y]\!]$.

Next, we need to define *certain information* in a set $X \subseteq \mathcal{D}$ of objects. If this certain information is represented by an object c, then:

1. c is less informative than every object in X, since it defines information common to all objects in X; that is, c is a lower bound of X;

2. if there are two such objects c, c' and $c' \preceq c$, then we prefer c as it has more information.

Thus, we want the most informative object that defines information common to all objects in X, i.e., a maximal element among all lower bounds of X. That is, *the certain information in the set X is $\bigwedge X$, the glb of X*.

If we look at relational databases without nulls (which arise as elements of $Q([\![D]\!])$), then the semantic ordering for them is $\subseteq$. Thus, for any collection $\mathcal{X}$ of complete databases, we have $\bigwedge \mathcal{X} = \bigcap_{D \in \mathcal{X}} D$ (i.e., in the case of relations certain answers are obtained as intersections).

Certain information defined by max-descriptions does not at first seem to be related to greatest lower bounds; nonetheless, we show that this is precisely what it is.

Max-descriptions deconstructed As we did with naïve databases and XML trees, we can view objects as partial descriptions. Then $x \models y$ is just $y \preceq x$: an object x satisfies every description that is less informative than itself. Therefore, $\text{Mod}(x) = \uparrow x$ and $\text{Th}(x) = \downarrow x$; these are extended to sets, as usual, by $\text{Mod}(X) = \bigcap_{x \in X} \text{Mod}(x)$ and similarly for Th.

The definition of certain information in a set X used in [15] (in the XML context) was a max-description of X: an object x such that $\text{Mod}(x) = \text{Mod}(\text{Th}(X))$.

Theorem 1. *Given a subset X of a database domain $\mathcal{D}$, an element x is a max-description of X iff $x = \bigwedge X$. In particular, a max-description of a set exists iff its greatest lower bound exists.*

So max-descriptions are precisely glb's. The XML case was not different after all: for both relations and XML, the certain information in a set of objects is its glb.

Certain answers for queries We can now use the notion of certain information in a set of objects to define certain answers to queries. An abstract view of a query is as follows. For each schema σ, we have a domain $\mathcal{D}_\sigma$ of database objects of that schema, as well as a preorder $\preceq_\sigma$ on it (if clear from the context which relation $\preceq_\sigma$ we refer to, we write just $\preceq$). A *query* is then a mapping $Q : \mathcal{D}_\sigma \to \mathcal{D}_\tau$ between two domains. If we have a set $X \subseteq \mathcal{D}_\sigma$ of objects, then $Q(X) = \{Q(x) \mid x \in X\}$, and certain answers to Q over X are defined as

$$\text{certain}(Q, X) = \bigwedge Q(X).$$

There is a simple recipe for finding certain answers when a query Q is *monotone*, i.e., when $x \preceq_\sigma y$ implies $Q(x) \preceq_\tau Q(y)$.

A *basis* of $X \subseteq \mathcal{D}$ is a set $B \subseteq X$ such that $\uparrow B = \uparrow X$. The following simple observation was already made in some concrete cases (like incompleteness in XML [15]):

Lemma 1. *If Q is monotone and B is a basis of X, then $\text{certain}(Q, X) = \bigwedge Q(B)$.*

Hence, if we can find a finite basis $B = \{b_1, \ldots, b_n\}$ of X, then we can compute certain answers $\text{certain}(Q, X)$ as $Q(b_1) \wedge \ldots \wedge Q(b_n)$. Thus, in such a case it is essential to be able to compute the glb of two (and hence finitely many) elements. The meaning of monotonicity depends on the exact interpretation of the information ordering; this will be addressed in detail in Section 4.

While cases of finite but non-singleton bases do arise in applications [15], most often one computes certain answers over sets X of the form $[\![x]\!]$. In the very general ordered setting, one way of defining the semantics is by $[\![x]\!] = \uparrow x$, i.e., an object represents all objects which are more informative than itself. Then Lemma 1 implies:

Corollary 1. $\text{certain}(Q, \uparrow x) = Q(x)$ *for a monotone Q.*

It says that certain answers can be computed by simply evaluating Q on x. However, in many models the semantics is more refined than just $\bigwedge Q(\uparrow x)$, and is based on *complete* objects that do not have null values. We now study how to incorporate those into our setting.

Complete objects

We extend our setting with the notion of complete objects, i.e., objects without nulls, and explain the properties that lead to naïve evaluation of queries. *Database domains with complete objects* are structures of the form $\langle \mathcal{D}, \preceq, \mathcal{C} \rangle$ where $\preceq$ is a preorder and $\mathcal{C} \subseteq \mathcal{D}$ is a set of objects we view as those having no nulls. To state some basic requirements for these sets, we look at their behavior in the standard models, i.e., in naïve tables.

1. For each object x, the set $\uparrow_{\text{cpl}} x = \uparrow x \cap \mathcal{C}$ of more informative complete objects is not empty (guaranteeing well-defined semantics).

2. For each object x, there is a unique maximal complete object $\pi_{\text{cpl}}(x)$ under x (think of a relation obtained by removing all the rows with nulls from a naïve table). The function π_{cpl} is monotone, and the identity on $\mathcal{C}$. In the standard terminology, this means that $\pi_{\text{cpl}} : \mathcal{D} \to \mathcal{C}$ is a retraction.

3. There are complete objects in $\uparrow_{\text{cpl}} y - \uparrow_{\text{cpl}} x$, unless x is less informative than y. In essence, it says that there are sufficiently many complete objects.

These conditions are satisfied in the standard domains, such as naïve databases or XML documents with nulls. In those domains we define the semantics of x as $\uparrow_{\text{cpl}} x$, the set of complete objects above a given object. It follows immediately from the definition that this notion of the semantics agrees with the ordering.

Lemma 2. *If $\langle \mathcal{D}, \preceq, \mathcal{C} \rangle$ is a database domain with complete objects, then $x \preceq y \Leftrightarrow \uparrow_{\text{cpl}} y \subseteq \uparrow_{\text{cpl}} x$.*

We denote the glb in the restriction $\langle \mathcal{C}, \preceq \rangle$ (when it exists) by $\bigwedge_{\text{cpl}}$. This gives us the notion of certain answers based on complete objects, for a query $Q : \mathcal{D} \to \mathcal{D}'$ that send complete objects to complete objects. It is the glb of the answers to Q over complete objects dominating the input:

$$\text{certain}_{\text{cpl}}(Q, x) = \bigwedge_{\text{cpl}} Q(\uparrow_{\text{cpl}} x).$$

We say that *certain answers are computed by naïve evaluation* if $\text{certain}_{\text{cpl}}(Q, x) = \pi_{\text{cpl}}(Q(x))$: in other words, they are obtained by running Q and then finding the complete approximation of the result.

For relations, these are of course the familiar concepts, as $\text{certain}_{\text{cpl}}(Q, x)$ is exactly $\bigcap \{ Q(R) \mid R \in [\![D]\!] \}$, and $\pi_{\text{cpl}}(Q(D))$ is $Q_{\text{naïve}}(D)$.

To provide a criterion for checking whether certain answers can be computed by naïve evaluation, we say that a function $f : \mathcal{D} \to \mathcal{D}'$ between two database domains with complete objects $\mathcal{C}$ and $\mathcal{C}'$ has the *complete saturation property* if it maps complete objects to complete objects and the following conditions hold:

- if $f(x) \in \mathcal{C}'$ then $f(c) = f(x)$ for some $c \in \uparrow_{\text{cpl}} x$;
- if $f(x) \notin \mathcal{C}'$ and $f(x) \not\preceq c' \in \mathcal{C}'$, then $f(c)$ and c' are incompatible for some $c \in \uparrow_{\text{cpl}} x$.

By incompatibility of two elements we mean that neither of them is less than the other. Intuitively, the conditions say that $\uparrow_{\text{cpl}} x$ has enough complete objects to witness different relationships that involve $f(x)$.

Theorem 2. *For every query that is monotone and has the complete saturation property, certain answers are computed by naïve evaluation.*

Over relational databases, complete saturation is very easy to check for unions of CQs, providing an alternative proof that the naïve evaluation works for them (see Section 4). Note, however, that Theorem 2 is not limited to any language, as it identifies a structural property behind naïve evaluation.

4. HOMOMORPHISM-BASED ORDERING

We now apply the general theory to relational databases with nulls and to incomplete XML trees. In both cases, the ordering was based on the semantics: $D_1 \preceq D_2$ iff $[\![D_2]\!] \subseteq [\![D_1]\!]$ and likewise for trees. There is a simple way to characterize this ordering:

Proposition 3.
- *If D, D' are naïve databases over the same schema, then $D \preceq D'$ iff there is a homomorphism from D to D'.*
- *If T, T' are XML documents over the same alphabet, then $T \preceq T'$ iff there is a homomorphism from T to T'.*

Hence, we deal with a well-established notion, and the ordering corresponds to a concept studied in fields such as graph theory [23] and constraint satisfaction [26]. This raises two questions: how does it relate to orderings previously studied in connection with incompleteness, and what can we get from known results, in particular in graph theory? We now address those.

Information ordering and other orderings As mentioned in the introduction, orderings have been used to provide semantics of incompleteness in the past [9, 10, 30, 31, 34]. A typical ordering (say, for relational model) would be defined as follows. For two tuples over constants and nulls we let $(a_1, \ldots, a_m) \sqsubseteq (b_1, \ldots, b_m)$ if, for each each i, either a_i is a null, or both a_i and b_i are the same constant (i.e., each null is less informative than each constant). This would be lifted to sets by $X \sqsubseteq^\flat Y \Leftrightarrow \forall x \in X \exists y \in Y : x \sqsubseteq y$.

In general, $\sqsubseteq^\flat$ cannot coincide with $\preceq$, as testing the existence of a homomorphism is NP-complete, and $\sqsubseteq^\flat$ is easily testable in quadratic time. But they do coincide for Codd databases (where nulls cannot be reused).

Proposition 4. *If D and D' are Codd databases, then $D \preceq D'$ iff $D \sqsubseteq^\flat D'$.*

Thus, the orderings used back in the 1990s were well suited for the Codd interpretation of nulls, but not the most commonly used naïve interpretation, which arises in applications such as integration and exchange of data.

The lattice of cores Orderings induced by homomorphisms are well known in graph theory. We look at graphs $G = \langle V, E \rangle$, where V is a set of nodes and E is a set of (directed) edges. We write $G \preceq G'$ if there is a homomorphism $h : G \to G'$, i.e., a map $h : V \to V'$ such that $(x, y) \in E$ implies $(h(x), h(y)) \in E'$. We use the same notation $\preceq$ as before, but it will always be clear from the context which homomorphisms we talk about. Clearly $\preceq$ is a preorder, and the associated equivalence relation $G \sim G'$ is given by $\mathrm{core}(G) = \mathrm{core}(G')$. Recall that the core of a graph G is the smallest subgraph G_0 of G such that there is a homomorphism from G to G_0; the core is unique up to isomorphism [23].

When restricted to cores, $\preceq$ defines a lattice with the glb $\wedge$ and the least upper bound $\vee$ given by [23]

- $G \wedge G' = \mathrm{core}(G \times G')$, and
- $G \vee G' = \mathrm{core}(G \bigsqcup G')$ ($\bigsqcup$ is the disjoint union).

In general, $G \times G'$ is an element of the equivalence class defining $G \wedge G'$, and $G \bigsqcup G'$ is an element of the equivalence class defining $G \vee G'$.

There are many facts known about this lattice; many of them stem from the classical result of Erdős [17] that there are graphs of arbitrarily large chromatic number and odd girth (the minimum length of an odd cycle). Since the former is monotone with respect to $\preceq$ and the latter is antimonotone, this lets one construct arbitrary antichains and dense chains inside $\preceq$. In fact, a very deep result [24] says that every countable partial order can be embedded into $\preceq$ over directed graphs.

However, "database homomorphisms" and "graph homomorphisms" are not the same. In naïve databases, homomorphisms are only defined on nulls, but their range is unrestricted. In XML, they are pairs of mappings, one on tree nodes, and the other on nulls. Thus, we cannot use standard graph-theoretic results, but of course we can adapt them.

Lower bounds for naïve databases We have seen that lower bounds are essential for computing certain answers. We now show how to compute the glb of two naïve tables (the construction extends to databases, simply by doing it relation-by-relation). The construction, as suggested by graph-theoretic results, is essentially a product that accounts for the different roles of nulls and constants.

Let R, R' be two naïve tables over the same set of attributes. Take any 1-1 mapping that assigns every pair $(x, y) \in \mathcal{C} \cup \mathcal{N}$ a null $\perp_{xy}$ that does not belong to $\mathcal{N}(R) \cup \mathcal{N}(R')$. As instances R, R' will always be clear from the context, we simply write $\perp_{xy}$ instead of the more formal but cumbersome $\perp_{x,y,R,R'}$. Then, for two tuples $t = (a_1, \ldots, a_m)$ and $t' = (b_1, \ldots, b_m)$, we define

$$t \otimes t' = (c_1, \ldots, c_m): \quad c_i = \begin{cases} a_i & \text{if } a_i = b_i \in \mathcal{C} \\ \perp_{a_i b_i} & \text{otherwise} \end{cases} \quad (1)$$

Proposition 5. *The set $\{t \otimes t' \mid t \in R, \ t' \in R'\}$ is $R \wedge R'$, i.e., a glb of R and R' in the preorder $\preceq$.*

Thus, for every finite collection $\mathcal{X}$ of naïve tables, $\bigwedge \mathcal{X}$ exists. In fact, measuring $\|\mathcal{X}\|$ as the total number of tuples in all relations $R \in \mathcal{X}$, one can easily use the inequality between the arithmetic and geometric means to derive that for $\mathcal{X}$ with n tables, $|\bigwedge \mathcal{X}| \leq (\|\mathcal{X}\|/n)^n$, for $\bigwedge$ constructed in Proposition 5. Results of [15] can also be adapted to show that even $|\mathrm{core}(\bigwedge(\mathcal{X}))|$ is necessarily exponential in the number of relations in $\mathcal{X}$.

What about infinite collections? Recall that in the case of XML, the existence of glb's (called at that time max-descriptions) for arbitrary collections was an open problem. We now show that in general, for arbitrary collections (even recursive ones), glb's need not exist.

Theorem 3. *There is an infinite family $\mathcal{X}$ of naïve tables such that $\bigwedge \mathcal{X}$ does not exist (in fact, there are uncountably many such families). Furthermore, there exist (countably many) recursive families $\mathcal{X}$ of relational databases such that $\bigwedge \mathcal{X}$ does not exist.*

Proof sketch. For the first statement, we use the fact that $\langle \mathbb{Q}, < \rangle$ can be embedded into the lattice of cores. If we look at naïve tables that only contain nulls, we have an embedding of $\langle \mathbb{Q}, < \rangle$ into the ordering $\preceq$. If each set had a glb, the Dedekind-MacNeille completion of $\langle \mathbb{Q}, < \rangle$ would be embeddable into the (countable) set of naïve tables, which is impossible by the cardinality argument.

For the second statement, we show that the family of directed cycles whose length is a power of two does not have a glb. $\square$

Lower bounds for XML First, observe that the notion $T \models T'$ used in [15] to define certain answers is precisely $T \preceq T'$ (the existence of homomorphisms) and thus, by Theorem 1, max-descriptions for XML as defined in [15] are the glb's in the ordering $\preceq$. Now by coding naïve tables as XML documents (for each tuple there is a child of the root, whose attribute values are the values in the tuple), and using Theorem 3, we answer the open question from [15].

Corollary 2. *There are recursive collections $\mathcal{X}$ of XML documents (of depth 2) for which $\bigwedge \mathcal{X}$ does not exist.*

We shall have more to say about glb's for XML documents in the next section. For now, we offer one comment on the interaction between glb's and sibling-ordering in XML documents. Note that all the work on computing certain answers in XML was done for unordered documents. It turns out that if we add sibling-ordering, then glb's do not exist even for finite collections, which justifies restricting to unordered documents for handling certain answers to queries.

Proposition 6. *There are ordered XML trees T, T' such that $T \wedge T'$ does not exist.*

Proof sketch. Both T and T' have a root and two children, labeled a and b, but ordered differently. It is easy to show that $T \wedge T'$ does not exist. $\square$

Naïve evaluation under $\preceq$ Theorem 2 stated two sufficient conditions for queries to admit naïve evaluation: monotonicity and complete saturation property.

We now see what they mean for relational databases wrt to the semantic ordering $D \preceq D' \Leftrightarrow [\![D']\!] \subseteq [\![D]\!]$. Note that monotonicity wrt this ordering is *not* the usual database notion of monotonicity which uses the partial order $\subseteq$: instead, it corresponds to preservation under homomorphisms. The complete saturation property, it turns out, is very easy to check for unions of CQs.

Proposition 7. *Every union of conjunctive queries is monotone and has the complete saturation property with respect to $\preceq$.*

Proof. Monotonicity wrt $\preceq$ (i.e., preservation under homomorphisms) is well known for unions of CQs. To show complete saturation, let Q be a union of UCQs. If $Q(D)$ does not have nulls, then, for h that maps all nulls in D into distinct constants different from those in D, by genericity we get $Q(h(D)) = h(Q(D)) = Q(D)$. For the second property, take a complete $R \not\preceq Q(D)$, assume that $Q(D)$ has nulls, and let h be a 1-1 map that sends nulls to constants not present in D and R. Take the complete database $h(D) \succeq D$. By genericity, $Q(h(D)) = h(Q(D)) \not\subseteq R$. If $R \subseteq Q(h(D))$ then again by genericity $R = h^{-1}(R) \subseteq h^{-1}(Q(h(D))) = Q(D)$, a contradiction which proves complete saturation. $\square$

Together with Theorem 2 this gives an alternative proof of the classical result that certain answers for unions conjunctive queries can be obtained by naïve evaluation. Note that Theorem 2 is a general result that is not restricted to FO queries, as it states a structural condition behind naïve evaluation.

A remark about CWA We worked with the Open World Assumption (OWA) here: the ordering $\preceq$ is defined as the existence of an *into* homomorphism. The Closed World Assumption corresponds to the existence of an *onto* homomorphism $h : D \to D'$; in this case we write $D \preceq_{\text{CWA}} D'$. We now offer one comment on the relationship between this ordering, and orderings corresponding to CWA that were considered in the past. Typically (see [9, 30]), to model CWA, one used the Plotkin ordering [21] for sets, defined as $X \sqsubseteq^\natural Y$ iff $\forall x \in X \exists y \in Y : x \sqsubseteq y$ and $\forall y \in Y \exists x \in X : x \sqsubseteq y$, to lift the ordering on tuples to the ordering on sets. We saw that $\sqsubseteq^\natural$ coincides with $\preceq$ over Codd databases. Will $\preceq_{\text{CWA}}$ coincide with $\sqsubseteq^\natural$ under the same restriction?

It turns out that they do not coincide, but they are very close. Recall that a relation $S \subseteq A \times B$ satisfies Hall's condition iff $|S(U)| \geq |U|$ for every $U \subseteq A$ (this is the requirement for the existence of a perfect matching).

Proposition 8. *Over Codd databases, $D \preceq_{\text{CWA}} D'$ iff $D \sqsubseteq^\natural D'$ and $\sqsubseteq^{-1}$ satisfies Hall's condition.*

5. INCOMPLETENESS IN GENERAL DATA MODELS

To further understand incompleteness in relational, XML, and potentially other models, we need to provide algorithms for computing glb's for certain answers, and to understand the basic computational properties associated with incompleteness (i.e., membership, query answering, consistency). The most general setting provided in Section 3 is too general for reasoning about such concrete tasks, and especially their complexity, and in Section 4 we handled relational and XML cases separately, as they had usually been handled in the literature. But we show now that this artificial separation is not necessary and we can derive many results simultaneously for a variety of data models.

Of course looking for general data models subsuming many others is nothing new in database theory, and several have been proposed (e.g., [13, 22, 27]). What we do here is similar in spirit (and in fact closest to [13]), and the model is well-suited to talk about relations in XML in one common framework.

The basic idea is simple: databases and documents have a structural part (e.g., trees for XML) and data part (tuples of attributes attached to tree nodes). The number of attributes attached to a node is determined by the label of that node. This model also subsumes relations, as the simplest case: the structural part is just a set, as we are about to see.

5.1 Generalized databases and information ordering

We now formalize this as follows. A *generalized schema* $\mathbb{S} = \langle \Sigma, \sigma, ar \rangle$ consists of a finite alphabet Σ, a relational vocabulary σ, and a function $ar : \Sigma \to \mathbb{N}$. To define databases, we assume sets $\mathcal{C}$ of constants and $\mathcal{N}$ of nulls, as before, as well as a set $\mathcal{V}$ of nodes to describe the structural part. A *generalized database* over $\mathbb{S}$ is then $\mathfrak{D} = \langle \mathbf{M}, \lambda, \rho \rangle$ where

- $\mathbf{M}$ is a finite σ-structure over $\mathcal{V}$;
- λ is a labeling of elements of $\mathbf{M}$ in Σ, and
- ρ assigns to each node ν in $\mathbf{M}$ a k-tuple over $\mathcal{C} \cup \mathcal{N}$ where k is the arity of the label of ν, i.e., $ar(\lambda(\nu))$.

Both relational and XML databases are special cases of generalized databases. To code a relational database, let $\sigma = \emptyset$ (i.e., $\mathbf{M}$ is just a set), and let Σ contain relation names, with the same arity as the relations themselves. For example, a relational instance $\{R(1, \perp_1), S(\perp_1, \perp_2, 2)\}$ is represented by a set $\{\nu_1, \nu_2\}$ with $\lambda(\nu_1) = R$ and $\lambda(\nu_2) = S$; the arities of R and S are 2 and 3, and $\rho(\nu_1) = (1, \perp_1)$ and $\rho(\nu_2) = (\perp_1, \perp_2, 2)$. For XML, σ is a vocabulary for unranked trees (there could be several; in the example in Sec. 2 we used only the edge relation, but one can use other axes such as next-sibling), and generalized databases themselves are trees with attribute tuples attached to nodes (again, as shown in the example in Sec. 2).

We shall write $\mathbf{M}_\lambda$ for the colored structure $\langle \mathbf{M}, \lambda \rangle$; technically, it is a structure in the vocabulary σ expanded with unary relations P_a for each $a \in \Sigma$, whose interpretation is the set of nodes labeled a. We also write $\langle \mathbf{M}_\lambda, \rho \rangle$ for a generalized database.

To define the semantics in terms of complete generalized databases (i.e., those not using nulls), we use, as before, homomorphisms between generalized databases. We let $\mathcal{V}(\mathfrak{D})$, $\mathcal{C}(\mathfrak{D})$, and $\mathcal{N}(\mathfrak{D})$ stand for the sets of vertices, constants, and nulls in $\mathfrak{D}$. A *homomorphism* $h : \mathfrak{D} \to \mathfrak{D}'$ between $\mathfrak{D} = \langle \mathbf{M}_\lambda, \rho \rangle$ and $\mathfrak{D}' = \langle \mathbf{M}'_{\lambda'}, \rho' \rangle$ is a pair $h = (h_1, h_2)$ of mappings $h_1 : \mathcal{V}(\mathfrak{D}) \to \mathcal{V}(\mathfrak{D}')$ and $h_2 : \mathcal{N}(\mathfrak{D}) \to \mathcal{C}(\mathfrak{D}') \cup \mathcal{N}(\mathfrak{D}')$ such that:

1. h_1 is a usual homomorphism $\mathbf{M}_\lambda \to \mathbf{M}'_{\lambda'}$;
2. if $\nu \in \mathcal{V}(\mathfrak{D})$ and $\nu' = h_1(\nu)$ then $\rho'(\nu') = h_2(\rho(\nu))$.

As always, we extend h_2 to be the identity on constants. Observe also that in condition 2, ν and ν' have the same label (since h_1 is a homomorphism) and hence tuples $\rho(\nu)$ and $\rho(\nu')$ have the same length. This notion of homomorphism becomes one of the standard notions when we consider relational databases or XML documents.

We now define $[\![\mathfrak{D}]\!]$, the semantics of $\mathfrak{D}$, as the set of all complete generalized databases $\mathfrak{D}'$ such that there is a homomorphism $h : \mathfrak{D} \to \mathfrak{D}'$. As usual, the information ordering is

$$\mathfrak{D} \preceq \mathfrak{D}' \;\Leftrightarrow\; [\![\mathfrak{D}']\!] \subseteq [\![\mathfrak{D}]\!].$$

We have a standard characterization of it:

Proposition 9. $\mathfrak{D} \preceq \mathfrak{D}'$ *iff there is a homomorphism* $h : \mathfrak{D} \to \mathfrak{D}'$.

We now look at constructions of upper and lower bounds wrt the information ordering. The greatest lower bound can be used for computing certain answers, while upper bounds naturally correspond to constructing target instances in data exchange.

5.2 Greatest lower bounds for certain answers

We have already argued that we need greatest lower bounds, or glb's, to compute certain answers to queries. As glb's of arbitrary sets need not exist in general, we want to compute finite bases of databases and calculate glb's over the results of queries on such finite bases. Lemma 1 tells us that this will give us certain answers for queries which are monotone wrt the information ordering.

However, simply calculating glb's as products is not always going to work. For example, the product of two trees is not a tree, so this will not work in the case of XML. In such a case we need glb's in the subclass of generalized databases for which the structural part is a tree. Generally, if we have a class $\mathcal{K}$ of structures $\mathbf{M}_\lambda$, we need a glb $\wedge_\mathcal{K}$ of $\mathcal{K}$-*generalized databases*, i.e., those generalized databases in which the structural part is restricted to be in $\mathcal{K}$ (think, for example, of XML documents: the underlying structures $\mathbf{M}_\lambda$ in this case are not arbitrary but labeled trees).

We now show how to construct such a glb using the minimal possible set of assumptions. In fact, in a way it is easier to do the construction in this general setting, without knowing what the concrete structures in $\mathcal{K}$ are, as the construction is fully guided by the setup: it is the only one that "typechecks". It consists of two steps: first, compute the lower bound for the structural part, and then add data as we did for relations.

Our minimal assumption is that we have a glb $\mathbf{M}_\lambda \sqcap_\mathcal{K} \mathbf{M}'_{\lambda'}$ of structures in class $\mathcal{K}$ (that is, a glb that itself is a member of $\mathcal{K}$). Without knowing anything at all about its structure, we can only conclude that $\mathbf{M}_\lambda \sqcap_\mathcal{K} \mathbf{M}'_{\lambda'} \preceq \mathbf{M}_\lambda \times \mathbf{M}'_{\lambda'}$, since the latter is a glb without the restriction to $\mathcal{K}$. That is, there is a homomorphism $h : \mathbf{M}_\lambda \sqcap_\mathcal{K} \mathbf{M}'_{\lambda'} \to \mathbf{M}_\lambda \times \mathbf{M}'_{\lambda'}$. Composing h with first and second projections from $\mathbf{M}_\lambda \times \mathbf{M}'_{\lambda'}$ to $\mathbf{M}_\lambda$ and $\mathbf{M}'_{\lambda'}$ gives us homomorphisms

$$\iota : \mathbf{M}_\lambda \sqcap_\mathcal{K} \mathbf{M}'_{\lambda'} \to \mathbf{M}_\lambda \;\; \text{and} \;\; \iota' : \mathbf{M}_\lambda \sqcap_\mathcal{K} \mathbf{M}'_{\lambda'} \to \mathbf{M}'_{\lambda'}.$$

This provides the construction of $\mathfrak{D} \wedge_\mathcal{K} \mathfrak{D}'$ of a glb of two $\mathcal{K}$-generalized databases. We let

$$\langle \mathbf{M}_\lambda, \rho \rangle \;\wedge_\mathcal{K}\; \langle \mathbf{M}'_{\lambda'}, \rho' \rangle \;\stackrel{\text{def}}{=}\; \langle \mathbf{M}_\lambda \sqcap_\mathcal{K} \mathbf{M}'_{\lambda'}, \rho \otimes \rho' \rangle \quad (2)$$

where $\rho \otimes \rho'(\nu) = \rho(\iota(\nu)) \otimes \rho'(\iota'(\nu))$.

Here $\otimes$ is the merge operation on tuples (1) we used to define relational glb in Section 4 (technically speaking, it depends on $\mathfrak{D}, \mathfrak{D}'$ as the nulls it generates must be outside $\mathcal{N}(\mathfrak{D}) \cup \mathcal{N}(\mathfrak{D}')$, but the instances are always clear from the context). Since ι and ι' are homomorphisms, the colors of $\iota(\nu)$ and $\iota'(\nu)$ are the same, and hence $\rho(\iota(\nu)) \otimes \rho'(\iota'(\nu))$ is well-defined.

Theorem 4. *For every class $\mathcal{K}$ of labeled σ-structures that admits glbs, $\mathfrak{D} \wedge_\mathcal{K} \mathfrak{D}'$ given by (2) is a glb in the class of $\mathcal{K}$-generalized databases ordered by $\preceq$.*

When $\sigma = \emptyset$, i.e., when we deal with relational databases, this yields precisely the construction for relations in Proposition 5.

When $\mathcal{K}$ is the class of unranked trees (in the vocabulary of the child relations and labels), $\wedge_\mathcal{K}$ is precisely the construction shown for computing certain answers in [15]. The construction of the glb for trees themselves is standard, and is done inductively, level by level, by pairing nodes with the same labels.

5.3 Least upper bounds for data exchange

We now cast the well-studied problem of finding solutions in data exchange [6, 18] in our framework, proving a partial explanation why in some cases finding solutions is easy, and in some it is not. We shall present both relational and XML data exchange uniformly, using our notion of generalized databases.

In data exchange, we have a source schema $\mathbb{S}$, a target schema $\mathbb{S}'$, and a schema mapping $\mathbb{M}$ which consists of the rules of the form $\mathfrak{I} \to \mathfrak{I}'$, where $\mathfrak{I}$ and $\mathfrak{I}'$ are instances over $\mathbb{S}$ and $\mathbb{S}'$, respectively. Given a complete instance $\mathfrak{D}$ over $\mathbb{S}$, an instance $\mathfrak{D}'$ over $\mathbb{S}'$ is called a *solution* for $\mathfrak{D}$ if for every rule $\mathfrak{I} \to \mathfrak{I}'$ in $\mathbb{M}$, and every homomorphism $(h_1, h_2) : \mathfrak{I} \to \mathfrak{D}$, there exists a homomorphism $(g_1, g_2) : \mathfrak{I}' \to \mathfrak{D}'$ such that g_2 coincides with h_2 on nulls common to $\mathfrak{I}$ and $\mathfrak{I}'$. A solution $\mathfrak{D}'$ is called *universal* (or $\mathcal{K}$-universal) if there is exists a homomorphism from $\mathfrak{D}'$ to every other solution (or every other solution whose structural part belongs to the class $\mathcal{K}$).

It is very easy to check that in the cases of relations and XML, this abstract view coincides precisely with the standard definitions of [6, 18] (in the case of XML, we deal of course with $\mathcal{K}$-universal solutions when $\mathcal{K}$ is the class of trees). To give a concrete example, consider a relational rule (these are known as st-tgds)

$$S(x, y, u) \to T(x, z), T(z, y).$$

For a source relational database $\mathfrak{D}_S$ with a ternary relation S over $\mathcal{C}$, a target database $\mathfrak{D}_T$ with a binary relation T over $\mathcal{C}$ and $\mathcal{N}$ is a solution if $\mathfrak{D}_S$ and $\mathfrak{D}_T$ satisfy the sentence $\forall x, y, u\ (S(x, y, u) \to \exists z\ (T(x, z) \wedge T(z, y)))$. We can view the left and right-hand sides of the rule as databases $\mathfrak{I}_S = \{S(x, y, u)\}$ and $\mathfrak{I}_T = \{T(x, z), T(z, y)\}$ over nulls. Then the rule is satisfied iff for each homomorphism $h : \mathfrak{I}_S \to \mathfrak{D}_S$ (i.e., a fact $S(a, b, c)$ in $\mathfrak{D}_S$, where $h(x) = a, h(y) = b, h(u) = c$) we have tuples $T(a, v), T(v, b)$ for some value v: in other words, a homomorphism $g : \mathfrak{I}_T \to \mathfrak{D}_T$ such that $g(z) = v$, and g coincides with h on x and y. Thus, we indeed deal with the standard concepts from data exchange.

We now show that universal solutions are *least upper bounds* (lub's) in the preorder $\preceq$; these will be denoted by $\bigvee$ or $\bigvee_\mathcal{K}$ when restricted to $\mathcal{K}$-generalized databases.

We let $\mathrm{Hom}(\cdot, \cdot)$ denote the set of homomorphisms between two instances. For a source instance $\mathfrak{D}$ and a mapping $\mathbb{M}$, define

$$\mathbb{M}(\mathfrak{D}) = \{h_2(\mathfrak{I}') \mid \mathfrak{I} \to \mathfrak{I}' \in \mathbb{M},\ (h_1, h_2) \in \mathrm{Hom}(\mathfrak{I}, \mathfrak{D})\}.$$

Intuitively, $(h_1, h_2) \in \mathrm{Hom}(\mathfrak{I}, \mathfrak{D})$ provides an instantiation of a rule in the mapping, and then $\mathbb{M}(\mathfrak{D})$ is the set of single-rule applications of rules in $\mathbb{M}$ to the source $\mathfrak{D}$. Computing those is often the first – and easy – step of building a solution in data exchange. Now we can relate $\mathbb{M}(\mathfrak{D})$ to universal solutions.

Theorem 5. *For a mapping $\mathbb{M}$ and a source $\mathfrak{D}$, the $\mathcal{K}$-universal solutions are precisely the elements of the $\sim$-equivalence class $\bigvee_\mathcal{K} \mathbb{M}(\mathfrak{D})$.*

This result partly explains why in some cases computing solutions in data exchange is easy, and in some it is not. Consider, for example, relational databases without putting any restrictions on them. Then lub's exist – as we saw before, they are essentially disjoint unions (technically, disjoint unions after renaming of nulls). Indeed, then $\bigsqcup \mathbb{M}(\mathfrak{D})$ is what is called canonical universal solution in data exchange (without constraints

on the target). Furthermore, the canonical representative of the equivalence class $\bigvee \mathbb{M}(\mathfrak{D})$ in this case is the core solution in data exchange, that is, precisely $\mathrm{core}(\bigsqcup \mathbb{M}(\mathfrak{D}))$.

However, if we move to XML, and let $\mathcal{K}$ be the class of all unranked trees, we immediately encounter the following problem:

Proposition 10. *Least upper bounds do not always exist in the restriction of $\preceq$ to labeled unranked trees.*

Hence, in the case of XML (especially with additional schema information) and relations with extra target constraints, one needs to find not an lub (as it may not exist) but rather *some* upper bound. This loss of canonicity in the choice of a solution leads to the necessarily ad-hoc – and varying – choices for solutions, which we see in data exchange literature outside of restricted cases of nicely behaved mappings.

6. COMPUTATIONAL PROBLEMS

We now address the complexity of the key computational problems associated with incompleteness. We do it in our general model from Section 5, and show that this form of reasoning allows us to get some results for both relational and XML cases in a uniform way.

The standard problems to consider are [2, 3, 4, 7, 25]:

- Consistency: does an incomplete database have a completion satisfying some conditions? This problem is commonly considered in the XML context, where schemas are usually more complex. This problem tends to be NP-complete, and in PTIME with suitable restrictions [7].

- Membership: does an incomplete database represent a complete one? It is NP-complete for naïve databases and XML documents, and in PTIME in both cases under the Codd interpretation (although the proofs of these facts in [3, 7] use very different techniques).

- Query answering. Typically one asks whether a given tuple of values is a certain answer. Complexity tends to range, depending on the language, from undecidable (for sufficiently expressive languages to encode the validity problem) to coNP-complete to PTIME [3, 7].

We now look at these problems in our general setting.

Consistency

Let φ be a condition, given by a logical formula, over the structures $\mathbf{M}_\lambda$. The consistency problem is:

PROBLEM:	CONS(φ)
INPUT:	a generalized database $\langle \mathbf{M}_\lambda, \rho \rangle$
QUESTION:	is there $\langle \mathbf{M}'_{\lambda'}, \rho' \rangle \in [\![\langle \mathbf{M}_\lambda, \rho \rangle]\!]$ such that $\mathbf{M}'_{\lambda'} \models \varphi$?

In general we should avoid undecidable classes of formulae defining structural conditions; indeed, since every generalized database belongs to $[\![\emptyset]\!]$, the consistency problem checks, in particular, satisfiability of sentences. Even though we only deal with data complexity (φ is fixed), we still prefer to avoid problems whose combined complexity is undecidable.

As a sample result on the complexity of the consistency problem, we consider the well-known decidable case of $\exists^*\forall^*$-formulas (i.e., the Bernays-Schönfinkel class, consisting of formulae of the form $\exists x_1, \ldots, x_k \forall y_1, \ldots, y_m \alpha(\bar{x}, \bar{y})$, where α is quantifier-free), and classify the complexity of CONS(φ) based on the exact shape of the quantifier prefix.

Proposition 11.
- *If φ is an $\exists^*\forall^*$ sentence, then* CONS(φ) *is in* NP.

- *There is a $\exists^*\forall$ sentence φ_0 such that* CONS(φ_0) *is* NP-*complete.*

- *If φ is an $\exists^*$ sentence, then* CONS(φ) *is in* PTIME.

Notice that we consider *data* complexity, i.e., the sentence φ is fixed, so there is no contradiction with the known higher complexity for the satisfiability problem for the Bernays-Schönfinkel class.

Membership

The membership question is whether $\mathfrak{D}' \in [\![\mathfrak{D}]\!]$ for a complete database $\mathfrak{D}'$ and an incomplete database $\mathfrak{D}$. More generally, we can ask whether $\mathfrak{D} \preceq \mathfrak{D}'$ (which is the membership problem when $\mathfrak{D}'$ has no nulls).

Since checking whether $\mathfrak{D} \preceq \mathfrak{D}'$ amounts to checking the existence of a homomorphism from $\mathfrak{D}$ to $\mathfrak{D}'$, we deal with the general constraint-satisfaction problem [26]. Such a problem is in NP, and often NP-complete, even for a fixed $\mathfrak{D}'$. One case that is solvable in PTIME in both relational and XML contexts is the case of the Codd interpretation of nulls. The proofs of these results are very different however: for relational Codd tables, [3] reduced the problem to finding matchings in bipartite graphs, and for XML, [7] used an analog of CTL-model-checking algorithms on finite Kripke structures.

Now we provide a uniform explanation. We say that in a generalized database $\langle \mathbf{M}_\lambda, \rho \rangle$, the function ρ has *Codd interpretation* if each null occurs as its value at most once.

Theorem 6. *For each fixed $k > 0$, checking whether $\langle \mathbf{M}_\lambda, \rho \rangle \preceq \langle \mathbf{M}'_{\lambda'}, \rho' \rangle$ can be done in polynomial time if ρ has Codd interpretation, and the treewidth of $\mathbf{M}_\lambda$ is at most k.*

Both relational and XML polynomial-time algorithms for the Codd interpretation of nulls are special cases of Theorem 6 when $k = 1$. This result is not a corollary of the standard results on the tractability of constraint satisfaction problems with bounded treewidth (cf. [19, 26]) due to the presence of data values and special conditions on homomorphisms.

Query answering

To answer questions about the complexity of query answering, we need, of course, a query language for generalized databases. Here we look at a natural analog of FO. For relational databases, we know that query answering is in PTIME for unions of conjunctive queries (i.e., existential positive FO sentences) but undecidable for all of FO [3]. For XML, even for analogs of conjunctive queries on trees [20, 8] the complexity of finding certain answers can be CONP-complete, but this is typically caused by missing structural information or the presence of a schema [7].

Since generalized databases are two-sorted structures, it appears to be natural to consider a two-sorted version of FO. We can however rather easily avoid the cumbersome multi-sorted presentation by considering, for a generalized schema $\mathbb{S} = \langle \Sigma, \sigma, ar \rangle$, the logic FO($\mathbb{S}, \sim$), which is first-order over σ, the labeling predicates, and predicates $=_{ij}(x, y)$ meaning that the ith attribute of x equals the jth attribute of y.

Note that this covers both relational and XML Boolean conjunctive queries (for XML, σ defines the set of axes). So the natural problem we have is the following, where φ is a sentence of FO($\mathbb{S}, \sim$):

PROBLEM:	QA(φ)
INPUT:	a generalized database $\mathfrak{D}$
QUESTION:	is certain($\varphi, \mathfrak{D}$) = true?

We now show that all three cases witnessed for relations and XML – tractability, intractability, and undecidability – are possible.

Theorem 7.
- *If φ is an existential positive sentence of FO($\mathbb{S}, \sim$), then QA(φ) is in DLOGSPACE.*

- *If φ is an existential sentence of FO($\mathbb{S}, \sim$), then QA(φ) is in CONP. Moreover, there exists a generalized schema $\mathbb{S}$ and an existential sentence φ_0 of FO($\mathbb{S}, \sim$) so that QA(φ_0) is CONP-complete.*

- *There exists a generalized schema $\mathbb{S}$ and a sentence φ_1 of FO($\mathbb{S}, \sim$) so that QA(φ_1) is undecidable.*

7. FUTURE WORK

We briefly outline some directions for future work. Many results in this paper are of generic nature, and it would be nice to understand how they work when they are applied for particular classes of structures. For example, Theorem 7 is stated over the class of all generalized databases, and one would like to see how similar results change when we impose restrictions on the structural part (e.g., require it to be a tree).

We have not looked at constraints, but they are known to cause problems in the presence of incompleteness; in particular, they affect complexity and decidability results [12]. We also would like to see if the structural study of constraints imposed on target instances in data exchange will help determine classes for which least upper bounds, and thus universal solutions, exist; to start with, one can attempt to extract such structural conditions from cases when the chase procedure is known to work (e.g. [18, 16]), or from restricted classes of tgds studied in ontological reasoning [11].

The general model we used in Section 5, while inspired by several other graph-based models, is rather close to the model of [13]. The focus of [13] was rather different from ours, but a more detailed study of the connections with that paper may be warranted.

Finally, all the results here (except Proposition 8) are based on the open world assumption. An ordering can naturally be extracted from the closed world semantics as well, and we plan to study it in the future. Going from OWA to CWA is often known to increase the complexity of the main computational tasks though [36].

Acknowledgments I thank Pablo Barceló, Claire David, Egor Kostylev, and Filip Murlak for helpful discussions on incompleteness and certain answers. I am especially grateful to Filip for suggesting a shorter proof of the second part of Theorem 3. Supported by EPSRC grant G049165 and FET-Open Project FoX, grant agreement 233599.

8. References

[1] S. Abiteboul, O. Duschka. Complexity of answering queries using materialized views. In *PODS 1998*, pages 254–263.

[2] S. Abiteboul, R. Hull, and V. Vianu. *Foundations of Databases*. Addison-Wesley, 1995.

[3] S. Abiteboul, P Kanellakis, and G. Grahne. On the representation and querying of sets of possible worlds. *TCS*, 78(1):158–187, 1991.

[4] S. Abiteboul, L. Segoufin, and V. Vianu. Representing and querying XML with incomplete information. *ACM TODS*, 31(1):208–254, 2006.

[5] L. Antova, C. Koch, D. Olteanu. 10^{10^6} worlds and beyond: efficient representation and processing of incomplete information. *VLDB J.* 18(5): 1021-1040 (2009).

[6] M. Arenas, P. Barceló, L. Libkin, F. Murlak. *Relational and XML Data Exchange*. Morgan & Claypool, 2010.

[7] P. Barceló, L. Libkin, A. Poggi, and C. Sirangelo. XML with incomplete information. *J. ACM* 58(1): 1–62 (2010).

[8] H. Björklund, W. Martens, and T. Schwentick. Conjunctive query containment over trees. In *DBPL'07*, pages 66–80.

[9] P. Buneman, A. Jung, A. Ohori. Using powerdomains to generalize relational databases. *TCS* 91 (1991), 23–55.

[10] P. Buneman, S. Davidson, A. Watters. A semantics for complex objects and approximate answers. *JCSS* 43(1991), 170–218.

[11] A. Calì, G. Gottlob, T. Lukasiewicz. Datalog$^{\pm}$: a unified approach to ontologies and integrity constraints. In *ICDT'10*, pages 14–30.

[12] A. Calì, D. Lembo, and R. Rosati. On the decidability and complexity of query answering over inconsistent and incomplete databases. In *PODS'03*, pages 260–271.

[13] S. Cohen and Y. Sagiv. An abstract framework for generating maximal answers to queries. In *ICDT 2005*, pages 129–143.

[14] C. Date and H. Darwin. *A Guide to the SQL Standard*. Addison-Wesley, 1996.

[15] C. David, L. Libkin, F. Murlak. Certain answers for XML queries. In *PODS 2010*, pages 191-202.

[16] A. Deutsch, A. Nash, J. Remmel. The chase revisited. In *PQDS'08*, pages 149–158.

[17] P. Erdős. Graph theory and probability. *Canad. J. Math.* 11 (1959), 34–38.

[18] R. Fagin, Ph. Kolaitis, R. Miller, and L. Popa. Data exchange: semantics and query answering. *TCS*, 336(1):89–124, 2005.

[19] J. Flum and M. Grohe. *Parameterized Complexity Theory*. Springer, 2006.

[20] G. Gottlob, C. Koch, and K. Schulz. Conjunctive queries over trees. *J. ACM* 53(2):238-272, 2006.

[21] C. Gunter. *Semantics of Programming Languages*. The MIT Press, 1992.

[22] M. Gyssens, J. Paredaens, J. Van den Bussche, D. Van Gucht. A graph-oriented object database model *IEEE TKDE* 6(4):572-586, 1994.

[23] P. Hell and J. Nešetřil. *Graphs and Homomorphisms*. Oxford University Press, 2004.

[24] J. Hubička and J. Nešetřil. Finite paths are universal. *Order* 22(1):21–40, 2005.

[25] T. Imieliński and W. Lipski. Incomplete information in relational databases. *J. ACM*, 31(4):761–791, 1984.

[26] P. Kolaitis and M. Vardi. A logical approach to constraint satisfaction. In *Finite Model Theory and Its Applications*, Springer 2007, pages 339–370.

[27] G. Kuper and M. Vardi. The logical data model. *ACM TODS* 18(3):379–413 (1993).

[28] M. Lenzerini. Data integration: a theoretical perspective. In *PODS'02*, pages 233–246.

[29] M. Levene and G. Loizou. Semantics of null extended nested relations. *ACM TODS* 18 (1992), 414-459.

[30] L. Libkin. A semantics-based approach to design of query languages for partial information. In *Semantics in Databases*, LNCS 1358, 1998, pages 170–208.

[31] A. Ohori. Semantics of types for database objects. *Theoretical Computer Science* 76 (1990), 53–91.

[32] D. Olteanu, C. Koch, L. Antova. World-set decompositions: expressiveness and efficient algorithms. *TCS* 403 (2008), 265–284.

[33] B. Rossman. Homomorphism preservation theorems. *J. ACM* 55(3): (2008).

[34] B. Rounds. Situation-theoretic aspects of databases. In *Situation Theory and Appl.*, CSLI vol. 26, 1991, pages 229-256.

[35] D. Suciu. Probabilistic databases. *Encyclopedia of Database Systems*, 2009, pages 2150-2155.

[36] M. Vardi. On the integrity of databases with incomplete information. In *PODS'86*, pages 252–266.

[37] W. Wechler. *Universal Algebra for Computer Scientists*. Springer, 1992.

Determining the Currency of Data

Wenfei Fan
University of Edinburgh &
Harbin Institute of Technology
wenfei@inf.ed.ac.uk

Floris Geerts
School of Informatics
University of Edinburgh
fgeerts@inf.ed.ac.uk

Jef Wijsen
Institut d'Informatique
Université de Mons
jef.wijsen@umons.ac.be

Abstract

Data in real-life databases become obsolete rapidly. One often finds that multiple values of the same entity reside in a database. While all of these values were once correct, most of them may have become stale and inaccurate. Worse still, the values often do not carry reliable timestamps. With this comes the need for studying data currency, to identify the current value of an entity in a database and to answer queries with the current values, in the absence of timestamps.

This paper investigates the currency of data. (1) We propose a model that specifies partial currency orders in terms of simple constraints. The model also allows us to express what values are copied from other data sources, bearing currency orders in those sources, in terms of copy functions defined on correlated attributes. (2) We study fundamental problems for data currency, to determine whether a specification is consistent, whether a value is more current than another, and whether a query answer is certain no matter how partial currency orders are completed. (3) Moreover, we identify several problems associated with copy functions, to decide whether a copy function imports sufficient current data to answer a query, whether such a function copies redundant data, whether a copy function can be extended to import necessary current data for a query while respecting the constraints, and whether it suffices to copy data of a bounded size. (4) We establish upper and lower bounds of these problems, all matching, for combined complexity and data complexity, and for a variety of query languages. We also identify special cases that warrant lower complexity.

Categories and Subject Descriptors: H.2.3 [**Information Systems**]: Database Management – *Languages*; F.4.1 [**Mathematical Logic and Formal Languages**]: Mathematical Logic — *Computational Logic*

General Terms: Languages, Theory, Design.

1. Introduction

The quality of data in a real-life database quickly degenerates over time. Indeed, it is estimated that " 2% of records in a customer file become obsolete in one month" [15]. That

	FN	LN	address	salary	status
s_1:	Mary	Smith	2 Small St	50k	single
s_2:	Mary	Dupont	10 Elm Ave	50k	married
s_3:	Mary	Dupont	6 Main St	80k	married
s_4:	Bob	Luth	8 Cowan St	80k	married
s_5:	Robert	Luth	8 Drum St	55k	married

(a) Relation Emp

	dname	mgrFN	mrgLN	mgrAddr	budget
t_1:	R&D	Mary	Smith	2 Small St	6500k
t_2:	R&D	Mary	Smith	2 Small St	7000k
t_3:	R&D	Mary	Dupont	6 Main St	6000k
t_4:	R&D	Ed	Luth	8 Cowan St	6000k

(b) Relation Dept

Figure 1: A company database

is, in a database of 500 000 customer records, 10 000 records may go stale per month, 120 000 records per year, and within two years about 50% of all the records may be obsolete. In light of this, we often find that multiple values of the same entity reside in a database, which were *once correct, i.e.,* they were true values of the entity at some time. However, most of them have become *obsolete* and *inaccurate*. As an example from daily life, when one moves to a new address, her bank may retain her old address, and worse still, her credit card bills may still be sent to her old address for quite some time (see, *e.g.,* [22] for more examples). Stale data is one of the central problems to data quality. It is known that dirty data costs US businesses 600 billion USD each year [15], and stale data accounts for a large part of the losses.

This highlights the need for studying the *currency of data*, which aims to identify the current values of entities in a database, and to answer queries with the current values.

The question of data currency would be trivial if all data values carried valid timestamps. In practice, however, one often finds that timestamps are unavailable or imprecise [34]. Add to this the complication that data values are often copied or imported from other sources [2, 12, 13], which may not support a uniform scheme of timestamps. These make it challenging to identify the current values.

Not all is lost. One can often deduce currency orders from the semantics of the data. Moreover, data copied from other sources inherit currency orders from those sources. Taken together, these often provide sufficient current values of the data to answer certain queries, as illustrated below.

Example 1.1: Consider two relations of a company shown in Fig. 1. Each Emp tuple is an employee record with name, address, salary and marital status. A Dept tuple specifies the name, manager and budget of a department. Records in these relations may be stale, and do not carry timestamps. By entity identification techniques (see, *e.g.,* [16]), we know that tuples s_1, s_2 and s_3 refer to the same employee Mary, but s_4 and s_5 represent different people distinct from Mary. Consider the following queries posed on these relations.

(1) Query Q_1 is to find Mary's current salary. No timestamps are available for us to tell which of 50k or 80k is more current. However, we may know that the salary of each employee in the company does *not* decrease, as commonly found in real world. This yields currency orders $s_1 \prec_{\mathsf{salary}} s_3$ and $s_2 \prec_{\mathsf{salary}} s_3$, *i.e.*, $s_3[\mathsf{salary}]$ is more current than both $s_1[\mathsf{salary}]$ and $s_2[\mathsf{salary}]$. Hence the answer to Q_1 is 80k.

(2) Query Q_2 is to find Mary's current last name. We can no longer answer Q_2 as above. Nonetheless, we may know the following: (a) marital status can only change from single to married and from married to divorced; but not from married to single; and (b) Emp tuples with the most current marital status also contain the most current last name. Therefore, $s_1 \prec_{\mathsf{LN}} s_2$ and $s_1 \prec_{\mathsf{LN}} s_3$, and the answer to Q_2 is Dupont.

(3) Query Q_3 is to find Mary's current address. We may know that Emp tuples with the most current status or salary contain the most current address. Putting this and (1) above together, we know that the answer to Q_3 is "6 Main St".

(4) Finally, query Q_4 is to find the current budget of department R&D. Again no timestamps are available for us to evaluate the query. However, we may know the following: (a) Dept tuples t_1 and t_2 have copied their mgrAddr values from $s_1[\mathsf{address}]$ in Emp; similarly, t_3 has copied from s_3, and t_4 from s_4; and (b) in Dept, tuples with the most current address also have the most current budget. Taken together, these tell us that $t_1 \prec_{\mathsf{budget}} t_3$ and $t_2 \prec_{\mathsf{budget}} t_3$. Observe that we do not know which budget in t_3 or t_4 is more current. Nevertheless, in either case the most current budget is 6000k, and hence it is the answer to Q_4. □

These suggest that we give a full treatment of data currency, and answer the following questions. How should we specify currency orders on data values in the absence of timestamps but in the presence of copy relationships? When currency orders are only partly available, can we decide whether an attribute value is more up-to-date than another? How can we answer a query with only current data in a database? To answer a query, do we need to import current data from another source, and what to copy? The ability to answer these questions may provide guidance for practitioners to decide, *e.g.,* whether the answer to a query is corrupted by stale data, or what copy functions are needed.

A model for data currency. To answer these questions, we approach data currency based on the following.

(1) For each *attribute* A of a relation D, we assume an (implicit) currency order $\prec_A$ on its tuples such that for tuples t_1 and t_2 in D that represent the same real-world entity, $t_1 \prec_A t_2$ indicates that t_2 is more up-to-date than t_1 in the A attribute value. Here $\prec_A$ is not a total order since in practice, currency information is only partially available. Note that for distinct attributes A and B, we may have $t_1 \prec_A t_2$ and $t_2 \prec_B t_1$, *i.e.,* there may be no single tuple that is most up-to-date in all attribute values.

(2) We express additional currency relationships as denial constraints [3, 7], which are simple universally quantified FO sentences that have been used to improve the consistency of data. We show that the same class of constraints also suffices to express currency semantics commonly found in practice. For instance, all the currency relations we have seen in Example 1.1 can be expressed as denial constraints.

(3) We define a copy relationship from relation D_j to D_k in terms of a partial mapping, referred to as a *copy function*. It specifies what attribute values in D_j have been copied from D_k along with their currency orders in D_k. It also assures that correlated attributes are copied together. As observed in [2, 12, 13], copy functions are common in real world, and can be automatically discovered.

Putting these together, we consider $\mathbf{D} = (D_1, \ldots, D_n)$, a collection of relations such that (a) each D_j has currency orders partially defined on its tuples for each attribute, indicating *available* currency information; (b) each D_j satisfies a set Σ_j of denial constraints, which expresses currency orders derived from the semantics of the data; and (c) for each pair D_j, D_k of relations, there are possibly copy functions defined on them, which import values from one to another.

We study *consistent completions* D_j^c of D_j, which extend $\prec_A$ in D_j to a total order on all tuples pertaining to the same entity, such that D_j^c satisfies Σ_j and constraints imposed by the copy functions. One can construct from D_j^c the *current tuple* for each entity *w.r.t.* $\prec_A$, which contains the entity's most current A value for each attribute A. This yields the *current instance* of D_j^c consisting of only the current tuples of the entities in D_j, from which currency orders are removed. We evaluate a query Q on current instances of relations in $\mathbf{D}$, without worrying about currency orders. We study *certain current answers* to Q in $\mathbf{D}$, *i.e.,* tuples that are the answers to Q in all consistent completions of $\mathbf{D}$.

Reasoning about data currency. We study fundamental problems for data currency. (a) The *consistency problem* is to determine, given denial constraints Σ_j imposed on each D_j and copy functions between these relations, whether there exist consistent completions of every D_j, *i.e.,* whether the specification makes sense. (b) The *certain ordering problem* is to decide whether a currency order is contained in all consistent completions. (c) The *deterministic current instance problem* is to determine whether the current instance of each relation remains unchanged for all consistent completions. The ability to answer these questions allows us to determine whether an attribute value is certainly more current than another, and to identify the current value of an entity. (d) The *certain current query answering problem* is to decide whether a tuple t is a certain current answer to a query Q, *i.e.,* it is certainly computed using current data.

Currency preserving copy functions. It is natural to ask what values should be copied from one data source to another in order to answer a query. To characterize this intuition we introduce a notion of currency preservation. Consider data sources $\mathbf{D} = (D_1, \ldots, D_p)$ and $\mathbf{D}' = (D_1', \ldots, D_q')$, each consisting of a collection of relations with denial constraints imposed on them. Consider copy functions $\bar{\rho}$ from relations in $\mathbf{D}'$ to those in $\mathbf{D}$. For a query Q posed on $\mathbf{D}$, we say that $\bar{\rho}$ is *currency preserving* if no matter how we extend $\bar{\rho}$ by copying from $\mathbf{D}'$ more values of those entities in $\mathbf{D}$, the certain current answers to Q in $\mathbf{D}$ remain unchanged. In other words, $\bar{\rho}$ has already imported data values needed for computing certain current answers to Q.

We identify several problems associated with currency-preserving copy functions. (a) The *currency preservation problem* is to determine, given Q, $\bar{\rho}$, $\mathbf{D}$, $\mathbf{D}'$ and their denial constraints, whether $\bar{\rho}$ is currency preserving for Q. Intuitively, we want to know whether we need to extend $\bar{\rho}$ in order to answer Q. (b) The *minimal copying problem* is to decide whether $\bar{\rho}$ is minimal among all currency-preserving copy functions for Q, *i.e.*, $\bar{\rho}$ copies the least amount of data. This helps us inspect whether $\bar{\rho}$ copies unnecessary data. (c) The *existence problem* is to determine whether $\bar{\rho}$ can be extended to be currency preserving for Q. (d) Moreover, the *bounded copying* problem is to decide whether there exists such an extension that imports additional data of a bounded size. Intuitively, we want to find currency-preserving copy functions that import as few data values as possible.

Complexity results. We provide *combined complexity* and *data complexity* of all the problems stated above. For the combined complexity of the problems that involve queries, we investigate the impact of various query languages, including conjunctive queries (CQ), unions of conjunctive queries (UCQ), positive existential FO ($\exists FO^+$) and FO. We establish upper and lower bounds of these problems, *all matching*, ranging over $O(1)$, NP, coNP, Δ_2^p, Π_2^p, Σ_2^p, Δ_3^p, Π_3^p, Σ_3^p, Σ_4^p and PSPACE. We find that most of the problems are intractable. In light of this, we also identify special practical cases with lower complexity, some in PTIME. We also study the impact of denial constraints. For example, in the absence of denial constraints, the certain current query answering problem is in PTIME for SP queries (CQ queries without "join"), but it becomes intractable when denial constraints are present, even when the constraints are fixed.

This work is a first step towards a systematic study of data currency in the absence of reliable timestamps but in the presence of copy relationships. The results help practitioners specify data currency, analyze query answers and design copy functions. We also provide a complete picture of complexity bounds for important problems associated with data currency and copy functions, which are proved by using a variety of reductions and by providing (PTIME) algorithms.

Related work. There has been a host of work on temporal databases (see, *e.g.*, [8, 30] for surveys). Temporal databases provide support for valid time, transaction time, or both. They assume the availability of timestamps, and refer to "now" by means of current-time variables [9, 14]. Dynamic and temporal integrity constraints allow to restrict the set of legal database evolutions. Our currency model differs from temporal data models in several respects. We do not assume explicit timestamps. Nevertheless, if such timestamps are present, they can be related to currency by means of denial constraints. Unlike temporal databases that timestamp entire tuples, our model allows that different values within the same tuple have distinct currencies. That is, the same tuple can contain an up-to-date value for one attribute, and an outdated value for another attribute.

Since currency orders are different from temporal orders used in temporal databases, our currency (denial) constraints differ from traditional temporal constraints. Currency constraints can sometimes be derived from temporal constraints. For example, when salaries are constrained to be non-decreasing, we can express that the highest salary is the most current one. Also, our copy functions can require certain attributes to be copied together when these attributes cannot change independently, as for example expressed by the dynamic functional dependencies in [33].

Closer to this work are [31, 24, 25, 20] on querying indefinite data. In [31], the evaluation of CQ queries is studied on data that is linearly ordered but only provides a partial order. The problem studied there is similar to (yet different from) certain current query answering. An extension of conditional tables [19, 21] is proposed in [24] to incorporate indefinite temporal information, and in that setting, the complexity bounds for FO query evaluation are provided in [25]. Recently the non-emptiness problem for datalog on linear orders is investigated in [20]. However, none of these considers copying data from external sources, or the analyses of certain ordering and currency-preserving copy functions. In addition, we answer queries using current instances of relations, which are normal relations without (currency) ordering. This semantics is quite different from its counterparts in previous work. We also consider denial constraints and copy functions, which are not expressible in CQ or datalog studied in [31, 20]. In contrast to our work, [24, 25] assume explicit timestamps, while we use denial constraints to specify data currency. To encode denial constraints in extended conditional tables of [24, 25], an exponential blowup is inevitable. Because of these reasons, the results of [31, 24, 25, 20] cannot carry over to our setting, and vice versa.

There has also been a large body of work on the temporal constraint satisfaction problem (TCSP), which is to find a valuation of temporal variables that satisfies a set of temporal constraints (see, *e.g.*, [4, 29]). It differs from our consistency problem in that it considers neither completions of currency orders that satisfy denial constraints, nor copy relationships. Hence the results for TCSP are not directly applicable to our consistency problem, and vice versa.

Copy relationships between data sources have recently been studied in [2, 12, 13]. The previous work has focused on automatic discovery of copying dependencies and functions. Copy relationships are also related to data provenance, which studies propagation of annotations in data transformations and updates (see [5, 6] for recent surveys on data provenance). However, to the best of our knowledge, no previous work has studied currency-preserving copy functions and their associated problems.

Denial constraints have proved useful in detecting data inconsistencies and data repairing (see, *e.g.*, [3, 7]). We adopt the same class of constraints to specify the currency of data, so that data currency and consistency could be treated in a uniform logical framework. Denial constraints can also be automatically discovered, along the same lines as data dependency profiling (see, *e.g.*, [17]).

The study of data currency is also related to research on incomplete information (see [32] for a survey), when missing data concerns data currency. In contrast to that line of work, we investigate how to decide whether a value is more current than another, and study the properties of copy functions. We use denial constraints to specify data currency, which are, as remarked earlier, more succinct than, *e.g.*, C-tables and V-tables for representing incomplete information [19, 21]. In addition, we evaluate queries using current instances, a departure from the study of incomplete information.

Certain query answers have been studied in data integration and exchange. In data integration, for a query Q posed on a global database D_G, it is to find the certain answers to Q over all data sources that are consistent with D_G *w.r.t.* view definitions (see *e.g.*, [27]). In data exchange, it is to find the certain answers to a query over all target databases generated from data sources via schema mapping (see [23]). In contrast, we consider certain answers to a query over all completions of currency orders, which satisfy denial constraints and constraints from copy functions. Certain current query answering is also different from consistent query answering (see, e.g., [3, 7]), which is to find certain answers to a query over all *repairs* of a database and does not distinguish between stale and current data in the repairs. Finally, whereas it may be possible to model our setting as a data exchange scenario with built-in constraints [11], our complexity results do not follow gratuitously and a careful analysis of the chase is required in this setting.

Organization. Section 2 presents the data currency model. Section 3 states its related problems. Section 4 establishes the complexity bounds of those problems. Section 5 introduces the notion of currency preservation and its fundamental problems, followed by their complexity analysis in Section 6. Section 7 summarizes the main results of the paper.

2. Data Currency

We introduce a model for specifying data currency. A specification consists of (a) partial currency orders, (b) denial constraints, and (c) copy functions. We first present these notions, and then study consistent completions of currency orders. Finally, we show how queries are answered on current instances that are derived from these completions.

Data with partial currency orders. A relation schema is specified as $R = (\mathsf{EID}, A_1, \ldots, A_n)$, where EID denotes entity id that identifies tuples pertaining to the same entity, as introduced by Codd [10]. EID values can be obtained using entity identification techniques (*a.k.a.* record linkage, matching and data deduplication; see, e.g., [16]). A finite instance D of R is referred to as a *normal instance of R*.

A *temporal instance* D_t of R is given as $(D, \prec_{A_1}, \ldots, \prec_{A_n})$, where each $\prec_{A_i}$ is a strict partial order on D such that for tuples t_1 and t_2 in D, $t_1 \prec_{A_i} t_2$ implies $t_1[\mathsf{EID}] = t_2[\mathsf{EID}]$. We call $\prec_{A_i}$ the *currency order for attribute A_i*. Recall that a strict partial order is irreflexive and transitive, and therefore asymmetric. Intuitively, if $t_1 \prec_{A_i} t_2$, then t_1 and t_2 refer to *the same entity*, and t_2 contains a *more current* A_i-value for that entity than t_1, i.e., t_2 is more current than t_1 *in attribute A_i*. A currency order $\prec_{A_i}$ is empty when no currency information is known for attribute A_i.

A *completion* of D_t is a temporal instance $D_t^c = (D, \prec_{A_1}^c, \ldots, \prec_{A_n}^c)$ of R, such that for each $i \in [1, n]$, (1) $\prec_{A_i} \subseteq \prec_{A_i}^c$, and (2) for all $t_1, t_2 \in D$, t_1 and t_2 are comparable under $\prec_{A_i}^c$ iff $t_1[\mathsf{EID}] = t_2[\mathsf{EID}]$. The latter condition implies that $\prec_{A_i}^c$ induces a total order on tuples that refer to the same entity, while tuples representing distinct entities are not comparable under $\prec_{A_i}^c$. We call $\prec_{A_i}^c$ a *completed currency order*.

Denial constraints. We use denial constraints [3, 7] to specify additional currency information derived from the semantics of data, which enriches $\prec_{A_i}$. A *denial constraint* φ for R is a universally quantified FO sentence of the form:

$$\forall t_1, \ldots, t_k : R \left(\bigwedge_{j \in [1,k]} (t_1[\mathsf{EID}] = t_j[\mathsf{EID}] \wedge \psi) \rightarrow t_u \prec_{A_i} t_v \right),$$

where $u, v \in [1, k]$, each t_j is a tuple variable denoting a tuple of R, and ψ is a conjunction of predicates of the form (1) $t_j \prec_{A_l} t_h$, i.e., t_h is more current than t_j in attribute A_l; (2) $t_j[A_l] = t_h[A_l]$ (resp. $t_j[A_l] \neq t_h[A_l]$), i.e., $t_j[A_l]$ and

$t_h[A_l]$ are identical (resp. distinct) values; (3) $t_j[A_l] = c$ (resp. $t_j[A_l] \neq c$), where c is a constant; and (4) possibly other built-in predicates defined on particular domains.

The constraint is interpreted over completions D_t^c of temporal instances of R. We say that D_t^c *satisfies* φ, denoted by $D_t^c \models \varphi$, if for all tuples $t_1, \ldots, t_k$ in D that have the same EID value, if these tuples satisfy the predicates in ψ following the standard semantics of FO, then $t_u \prec_{A_i} t_v$. The use of EID in φ enforces that φ is imposed on tuples that refer to *the same entity*. We say that D_t^c satisfies a set Σ of denial constraints, denoted by $D_t^c \models \Sigma$, if $D_t^c \models \varphi$ for all $\varphi \in \Sigma$.

Example 2.1: Recall relations Emp and Dept given in Fig. 1. Denial constraints on these relations include:

$\varphi_1: \forall s, t : \mathsf{Emp}\big((s[\mathsf{EID}] = t[\mathsf{EID}] \wedge s[\mathsf{salary}] > t[\mathsf{salary}]) \rightarrow t \prec_{\mathsf{salary}} s\big)$

$\varphi_2: \forall s, t : \mathsf{Emp}\big((s[\mathsf{EID}] = t[\mathsf{EID}] \wedge s[\mathsf{status}] = \text{``married''} \wedge t[\mathsf{status}] = \text{``single''}) \rightarrow t \prec_{\mathsf{LN}} s\big)$

$\varphi_3: \forall s, t : \mathsf{Emp}\big((s[\mathsf{EID}] = t[\mathsf{EID}] \wedge t \prec_{\mathsf{salary}} s) \rightarrow t \prec_{\mathsf{address}} s\big)$

$\varphi_4: \forall s, t : \mathsf{Dept}\big((s[\mathsf{EID}] = t[\mathsf{EID}] \wedge t \prec_{\mathsf{mgrAddr}} s) \rightarrow t \prec_{\mathsf{budget}} s\big)$

Here φ_1 states that when Emp tuples s and t refer to the same employee, if $s[\mathsf{salary}] > t[\mathsf{salary}]$, then s is more current than t in attribute salary. Note that '<' denotes the built-in predicate "less-than" in the numeric domain of salary, whereas $\prec_{\mathsf{salary}}$ is the currency order for salary. Constraint φ_2 asserts that if $s[\mathsf{status}]$ is married and $t[\mathsf{status}]$ is single, then s is more current than t in LN. Constraint φ_3 states that if s is more current than t in salary, then s is also more current than t in address; similarly for φ_4. □

Copy functions. Consider two temporal instances $D_{(t,1)} = (D_1, \prec_{A_1}, \ldots, \prec_{A_p})$ and $D_{(t,2)} = (D_2, \prec_{B_1}, \ldots, \prec_{B_q})$ of (possibly distinct) relation schemas R_1 and R_2, respectively. A *copy function* ρ of signature $R_1[\vec{A}] \Leftarrow R_2[\vec{B}]$ is a partial mapping from D_1 to D_2, where $\vec{A} = (A_1, \ldots, A_l)$ and $\vec{B} = (B_1, \ldots, B_l)$, denoting attributes in R_1 and R_2, respectively. Here ρ is required to satisfy *the copying condition*: for each tuple t in D_1, if $\rho(t) = s$, then $t[A_i] = s[B_i]$ for all $i \in [1, l]$.

Intuitively, for tuples $t \in D_1$ and $s \in D_2$, $\rho(t) = s$ indicates that the values of the $\vec{A}$ attributes of t have been imported from the $\vec{B}$ attributes of tuple s in D_2. Here $\vec{A}$ specifies a list of *correlated attributes* that should be copied together.

The copy function ρ is called $\prec$-*compatible* (*w.r.t.* the currency orders found in $D_{(t,1)}$ and $D_{(t,2)}$) if for all $t_1, t_2 \in D_1$, for each $i \in [1, l]$, if $\rho(t_1) = s_1$, $\rho(t_2) = s_2$, $t_1[\mathsf{EID}] = t_2[\mathsf{EID}]$ and $s_1[\mathsf{EID}] = s_2[\mathsf{EID}]$, then $s_1 \prec_{B_i} s_2$ implies $t_1 \prec_{A_i} t_2$.

Intuitively, $\prec$-*compatibility* requires that copy functions preserve currency orders. In other words, when attribute values are imported from D_2 to D_1 the currency orders on corresponding tuples defined in $D_{(t,2)}$ are inherited by $D_{(t,1)}$.

Example 2.2: Consider relations Emp and Dept shown in Fig. 1. A copy function ρ of signature $\mathsf{Dept}[\mathsf{mgrAddr}] \Leftarrow \mathsf{Emp}[\mathsf{address}]$, depicted in Fig. 1 by arrows, is given as follows: $\rho(t_1) = s_1$, $\rho(t_2) = s_1$, $\rho(t_3) = s_3$ and $\rho(t_4) = s_4$. That is, the mgrAddr values of t_1 and t_2 have both been imported from $s_1[\mathsf{address}]$, while $t_3[\mathsf{mgrAddr}]$ and $t_4[\mathsf{mgrAddr}]$ are copied from $s_3[\mathsf{address}]$ and $s_4[\mathsf{address}]$, respectively. The function satisfies the copying condition, since $t_1[\mathsf{mgrAddr}] = t_2[\mathsf{mgrAddr}] = s_1[\mathsf{address}]$, $t_3[\mathsf{mgrAddr}] = s_3[\mathsf{address}]$, and $t_4[\mathsf{mgrAddr}] = s_4[\mathsf{address}]$.

Suppose that $\prec_A$ is empty for each attribute A in Emp or Dept. Then copy function ρ is $\prec$-compatible *w.r.t.* these temporal instances of Emp and Dept. In contrast, assume that partial currency orders $s_1 \prec_{\text{address}} s_3$ on Emp and $t_3 \prec_{\text{mgrAddr}} t_1$ are given. Then ρ is not $\prec$-compatible. Indeed, since s_1, s_3 pertain to the same person Mary, and t_1, t_3 to the same department R&D, the relation $s_1 \prec_{\text{address}} s_3$ should carry over into $t_1 \prec_{\text{mgrAddr}} t_3$, as $\rho(t_1) = s_1$ and $\rho(t_3) = s_3$. Clearly, $t_3 \prec_{\text{mgrAddr}} t_1$ and $t_1 \prec_{\text{mgrAddr}} t_3$ are contradictory. □

Consistent completions of temporal orders. A *specification* $\mathbf{S}$ of data currency consists of (1) a collection of temporal instances $D_{(t,i)}$ of schema R_i for $i \in [1, s]$, (2) a set Σ_i of denial constraints imposed on each $D_{(t,i)}$, and (3) a (possibly empty) copy function $\rho_{(i,j)}$ that imports data from $D_{(t,i)}$ to $D_{(t,j)}$ for $i, j \in [1, s]$. It specifies data values and entities (by normal instances embedded in $D_{(t,i)}$), partial currency orders known for each relation (by $D_{(t,i)}$), additional currency information derived from the semantics of the data (Σ_i), and data that has been copied from one source to another ($\rho_{(i,j)}$). These $D_{(t,i)}$'s may denote different data sources, *i.e.*, they may not necessarily be in the same database.

A *consistent completion* $\mathbf{D}^c$ of $\mathbf{S}$ consists of temporal instances $D_{(t,i)}^c$ of R_i such that for all $i, j \in [1, s]$,

1. $D_{(t,i)}^c$ is a completion of $D_{(t,i)}$,

2. $D_{(t,i)}^c \models \Sigma_i$, and

3. $\rho_{(i,j)}$ is compatible *w.r.t.* the completed currency orders found in $D_{(t,i)}^c$ and $D_{(t,j)}^c$.

We use $\mathsf{Mod}(\mathbf{S})$ to denote the set of all consistent completions of $\mathbf{S}$. We say that $\mathbf{S}$ is *consistent* if $\mathsf{Mod}(\mathbf{S}) \neq \emptyset$, *i.e.*, there exists at least one consistent completion of $\mathbf{S}$.

Intuitively, if $D_{(t,i)} = (D_i, \prec_{A_1}, \ldots, \prec_{A_n})$ is part of a specification and $D_{(t,i)}^c = (D_i, \prec_{A_1}^c, \ldots, \prec_{A_n}^c)$ is part of a consistent completion of that specification, then each $\prec_{A_j}^c$ extends $\prec_{A_j}$ to a completed currency order, and the completed orders satisfy the denial constraints Σ_i and the constraints imposed by copy functions. Observe that the copying condition and $\prec$-compatibility impose constraints on consistent completions. This is particularly evident when a data source imports data from multiple sources, and when two data sources copy from each other, directly or indirectly. In addition, these constraints interact with denial constraints.

Example 2.3: Consider a specification $\mathbf{S}_0$ consisting of Emp and Dept of Fig. 1, the denial constraints $\varphi_1 - \varphi_4$ given in Example 2.1, and the copy ρ defined in Example 2.2. Assume that no currency orders are known for Emp and Dept initially. A consistent completion $\mathbf{D}_0^c$ of $\mathbf{S}_0$ defines (1) $s_1 \prec_A s_2 \prec_A s_3$ when A ranges over FN, LN, address, salary and status for Emp tuples, and (2) $t_1 \prec_B t_2 \prec_B t_4 \prec_B t_3$ when B ranges over mgrFN, mgrLN, mgrAddr and budget for Dept tuples (here we assume that dname is the EID attribute of Dept). One can verify that $\mathbf{D}_0^c$ satisfies the denial constraints and the constraints imposed by ρ, and hence, $\mathbf{D}_0^c \in \mathsf{Mod}(\mathbf{S}_0)$. Note that no currency order is defined between any of s_1, s_2, s_3 and any of s_4, s_5, since they represent different entities.

Suppose that Dept also copies from a source D_1 consisting of a single tuple s_1', which is the same as s_1 except that $s_1'[\text{address}] = $ "5 Elm Ave". It uses a copy function ρ_1 that imports $s_1'[\text{address}]$ to $t_1[\text{mrgAddr}]$. Then there exists no consistent completion in this setting since t_1 may not import distinct values $s_1'[\text{address}]$ and $s_1[\text{address}]$ for $t_1[\text{mrgAddr}]$. In other words, the constraints imposed by the copying conditions of ρ and ρ_1 cannot be satisfied at the same time.

D	a normal instance of a relation schema R
D_t	a temporal instance of R with partial currency orders
D_t^c	a completion of partial currency orders in D_t
$\mathbf{S}$	a specification of data currency
$\mathbf{D}^c$	a consistent completion of a specification $\mathbf{S}$
$\mathsf{LST}(\mathbf{D}^c)$	the current instance of $\mathbf{D}^c$
$\bar{\rho}$	a collection of copy functions in $\mathbf{S}$
$\bar{\rho}^e$	an extension of copy functions $\bar{\rho}$
$\mathbf{S}^e$	an extension of specification $\mathbf{S}$ by $\bar{\rho}^e$
$\mathbf{D}^e$	an extension of temporal instances by $\bar{\rho}^e$

Table 1: A summary of notations

As another example, suppose that there is a copy function ρ_2 that imports budget attribute values of t_1 and t_3 from the budget attributes of s_1'' and s_3'' in another source D_2, respectively, where $s_1'' = t_1$ and $s_3'' = t_3$, but in D_2, $s_3'' \prec_{\text{budget}} s_1''$. Then there is no consistent completion in this setting either. Indeed, all completed currency orders of $\prec_{\text{budget}}$ in Dept have to satisfy denial constraints φ_1, φ_3 and φ_4, which enforce $t_1 \prec_{\text{budget}} t_3$, but ρ_2 is not $\prec$-compatible with this currency order. This shows the interaction between denial constraints and currency constraints of copy functions. □

Current instances. In a temporal instance $D_t = (D, \prec_{A_1}, \ldots, \prec_{A_n})$ of R, let $E = \{t[\text{EID}] \mid t \in D\}$, and for each entity $e \in E$, let $I_e = \{t \in D \mid t[\text{EID}] = e\}$. That is, E contains all EID values in D, and I_e is the set of tuples pertaining to the entity whose EID is e.

In a completion D_t^c of D_t, for each attribute A of R, the *current A value* for entity $e \in E$ is the value $t[A]$, where t is the greatest (*i.e.*, most current) tuple in the totally ordered set $(I_e, \prec_A^c)$. The *current tuple* for entity $e \in E$, denoted by $\mathsf{LST}(e, D_t^c)$, is the tuple t_e such that for each attribute A of R, $t_e[A]$ is the current A value for entity e.

We use $\mathsf{LST}(D_t^c)$ to denote $\{\mathsf{LST}(e, D_t^c) \mid e \in E\}$, referred to as the *current instance* of D_t^c. Observe that $\mathsf{LST}(D_t^c)$ is a *normal instance* of R, carrying no currency orders. For any $\mathbf{D}^c \in \mathsf{Mod}(\mathbf{S})$, we define $\mathsf{LST}(\mathbf{D}^c) = \{\mathsf{LST}(D_{(t,i)}^c) \mid D_{(t,i)}^c \in \mathbf{D}^c\}$, the set of all current instances.

Example 2.4: Recall the completion $\mathbf{D}_0^c$ of $\mathbf{S}_0$ from Example 2.3. Then $\mathsf{LST}(\mathbf{D}_0^c) = \{\mathsf{LST}(\text{Emp}), \mathsf{LST}(\text{Dept})\}$, where $\mathsf{LST}(\text{Emp}) = \{s_3, s_4, s_5\}$, and $\mathsf{LST}(\text{Dept}) = \{t_3\}$. Note that $\mathsf{LST}(\text{Emp})$ and $\mathsf{LST}(\text{Dept})$ are normal instances.

As another example, suppose that s_4 and s_5 refer to the same person. Consider an extension of the currency orders given in $\mathbf{D}_0^c$ by adding $s_4 \prec_A s_5$ and $s_5 \prec_B s_4$, where A ranges over FN, LN, address and status while B is salary. Then the current tuple of this person is (Robert, Luth, 8 Drum St, 80k, married), in which the first four attributes are taken from s_5 while its salary attribute is taken from s_4. □

Evaluating queries with current values. Consider a query Q posed on normal instances of $(R_1, \ldots, R_l)$, which does not refer to currency orders, where R_i is in specification $\mathbf{S}$ for $i \in [1, l]$. We say that a tuple t is a *certain current answer* to Q *w.r.t.* $\mathbf{S}$ if t is in

$$\bigcap_{\mathbf{D}^c \in \mathsf{Mod}(\mathbf{S})} Q(\mathsf{LST}(\mathbf{D}^c)).$$

That is, t is warranted to be an answer computed from the current values no matter how the partial currency orders in $\mathbf{S}$ are completed, as long as the denial constraints and constraints imposed by the copy functions of $\mathbf{S}$ are satisfied.

Example 2.5: Recall queries Q_1, Q_2, Q_3 and Q_4 from Example 1.1, and specification $\mathbf{S}_0$ from Example 2.3. One can verify that answers to the queries given in Example 1.1 are certain current answers *w.r.t.* $\mathbf{S}_0$, *i.e.*, the answers remain unchanged in $\mathsf{LST}(\mathbf{D}^c)$ for all $\mathbf{D}^c \in \mathsf{Mod}(\mathbf{S}_0)$. □

We summarize notations in Table 2, including those given in this section and notations to be introduced in Section 5.

3. Decision Problems for Data Currency

We study four problems associated with data currency.

The consistency of specifications. The first problem is to decide whether a given specification $\mathbf{S}$ makes sense, *i.e.*, whether there exists any consistent completion of $\mathbf{S}$. As shown in Example 2.3, there exist specifications $\mathbf{S}$ such that $\mathsf{Mod}(\mathbf{S})$ is empty, because of the interaction between denial constraints and copy functions, among other things.

CPS:	The *consistency problem for specifications*.
INPUT:	A specification $\mathbf{S}$ of data currency.
QUESTION:	Is $\mathsf{Mod}(\mathbf{S})$ nonempty?

Certain currency orders. The next question studies whether a given currency order is contained in all consistent completions of a specification. Given two temporal instances $D_{(t,1)} = (D, \prec_{A_1}, \ldots, \prec_{A_n})$ and $D_{(t,2)} = (D, \prec'_{A_1}, \ldots, \prec'_{A_n})$ of the same schema R, we say that $D_{(t,1)}$ is *contained in* $D_{(t,2)}$, denoted by $D_{(t,1)} \subseteq D_{(t,2)}$, if $\prec_{A_j} \subseteq \prec'_{A_j}$ for all $j \in [1, n]$.

Consider a specification $\mathbf{S}$ in which there is a temporal instance $D_t = (D, \prec_{A_1}, \ldots, \prec_{A_n})$ of schema R. A *currency order* for D_t is a temporal instance $O_t = (D, \prec'_{A_1}, \ldots, \prec'_{A_n})$ of R. Observe that O_t does not necessarily contain D_t.

COP:	The *certain ordering problem*.
INPUT:	A specification $\mathbf{S}$ in which D_t is a temporal instance, and a currency order O_t for D_t.
QUESTION:	Is for all $\mathbf{D}^c \in \mathsf{Mod}(\mathbf{S})$, $O_t \subseteq D_t^c$? Here D_t^c is the completion of D_t in $\mathbf{D}^c$.

Example 3.1: Consider specification $\mathbf{S}_0$ of Example 2.3. We want to know whether $s_1 \prec_{\mathsf{salary}} s_3$ is assured by every completion $\mathbf{D}^c \in \mathsf{Mod}(\mathbf{S}_0)$. To this end we construct a currency order $O_t = (\mathsf{Emp}, \prec_{\mathsf{FN}}, \prec_{\mathsf{LN}}, \prec_{\mathsf{address}}, \prec_{\mathsf{salary}}, \prec_{\mathsf{status}})$, in which $s_1 \prec_{\mathsf{salary}} s_3$ is in $\prec_{\mathsf{salary}}$, but the partial orders for all other attributes are empty. One can verify that O_t is indeed a certain currency order, as assured by denial constraint φ_1.

Similarly, one can define a currency order O'_t to check whether $t_3 \prec_{\mathsf{mgrFN}} t_4$ is entailed by all $\mathbf{D}^c \in \mathsf{Mod}(\mathbf{S}_0)$. One can readily verify that it is not the case. Indeed, there exists $\mathbf{D}_1^c \in \mathsf{Mod}(\mathbf{S}_0)$, such that $t_4 \prec_{\mathsf{mgrFN}} t_3$ is given in $\mathbf{D}_1^c$. □

Certain current instances. Given a specification $\mathbf{S}$ of data currency, one naturally wants to know whether every consistent completion of $\mathbf{S}$ yields the same current instances. We say that a specification $\mathbf{S}$ of data currency is *deterministic for current instances* if for all consistent completions $\mathbf{D}_1^c, \mathbf{D}_2^c \in \mathsf{Mod}(\mathbf{S})$, $\mathsf{LST}(\mathbf{D}_1^c) = \mathsf{LST}(\mathbf{D}_2^c)$. This definition naturally carries over to a particular relation schema R: specification $\mathbf{S}$ is said to be *deterministic for current R instances* if for all consistent completions $\mathbf{D}_1^c, \mathbf{D}_2^c \in \mathsf{Mod}(\mathbf{S})$, the instance of R in $\mathsf{LST}(\mathbf{D}_1^c)$ is equal to the instance of R in $\mathsf{LST}(\mathbf{D}_2^c)$.

DCIP:	The *deterministic current instance problem*
INPUT:	A specification $\mathbf{S}$.
QUESTION:	Is $\mathbf{S}$ deterministic for current instances?

Example 3.2: The specification $\mathbf{S}_0$ of Example 2.3 is deterministic for current Emp instances. Indeed, for all

$\mathbf{D}^c \in \mathsf{Mod}(\mathbf{S}_0)$, if D_{Emp}^c is the completion of the Emp instance in $\mathbf{D}^c$, then $\mathsf{LST}(D_{\mathsf{Emp}}^c) = \{s_3, s_4, s_5\}$. □

Query answering. Given a query Q, we want to know whether a tuple t is in $Q(\mathsf{LST}(\mathbf{D}^c))$ for all $\mathbf{D}^c \in \mathsf{Mod}(\mathbf{S})$.

$\mathsf{CCQA}(\mathcal{L}_Q)$:	The *certain current query answering* problem.
INPUT:	A specification $\mathbf{S}$, a tuple t and a query $Q \in \mathcal{L}_Q$.
QUESTION:	Is t a certain current answer to Q *w.r.t.* $\mathbf{S}$?

We study $\mathsf{CCQA}(\mathcal{L}_Q)$ when $\mathcal{L}_Q$ ranges over the following query languages (see, *e.g.*, [1] for the details):

- CQ, the class of conjunctive queries built up from relation atoms and equality ($=$), by closing under conjunction $\wedge$ and existential quantification $\exists$;

- UCQ, unions of conjunctive queries of the form $Q_1 \cup \cdots \cup Q_k$, where for each $i \in [1, k]$, Q_i is in CQ;

- $\exists\mathsf{FO}^+$, first-order logic (FO) queries built from atomic formulas, by closing under $\wedge$, *disjunction* $\vee$ and $\exists$; and

- FO queries built from atomic formulas using $\wedge$, $\vee$, *negation* $\neg$, $\exists$ and universal quantification $\forall$.

While different query languages have no impact on the data complexity of $\mathsf{CCQA}(\mathcal{L}_Q)$, as will be seen soon, they do make a difference when the combined complexity is concerned.

4. Reasoning about the Currency of Data

In this section we focus on CPS, COP, DCIP and CCQA. We establish the data complexity and combined complexity of these problems. For the data complexity, we fix denial constraints and queries (for CCQA), and study the complexity in terms of varying size of data sources and copy functions. For the combined complexity we also allow denial constraints and queries to vary (see, *e.g.*, [1] for a detailed discussion of data and combined complexity).

The consistency of specifications. We start with CPS, which is to decide, given a specification $\mathbf{S}$ consisting of partial currency orders, denial constraints and copy functions, whether there exists any consistent completion in $\mathsf{Mod}(\mathbf{S})$.

The result below tells us the following. (1) The problem is nontrivial: it is Σ_2^p-complete. It remains intractable when denial constraints are fixed (data complexity). (2) Denial constraints are a major factor that makes the problem hard. Indeed, the complexity bounds are not affected even when no copy functions are defined in $\mathbf{S}$.

Theorem 4.1: For CPS, (1) the combined complexity is Σ_2^p-complete, and (2) the data complexity is NP-complete. The upper bounds and lower bounds remain unchanged even in the absence of copy functions. □

Proof sketch: (1) *Lower bounds.* For the combined complexity, we show that CPS is Σ_2^p-hard by reduction from the $\exists^*\forall^*3\mathsf{SAT}$ problem, which is Σ_2^p-complete (cf. [28]). Given a sentence $\phi = \exists X \forall Y \psi(X, Y)$, we construct a specification $\mathbf{S}$ consisting of a single temporal instance D_t of a binary relation schema and a set Γ of denial constraints, such that ϕ is true iff $\mathsf{Mod}(\mathbf{S}) \neq \emptyset$. We use D_t to encode truth assignments μ_X for X, and Γ to assure that μ_X satisfies $\forall Y \psi(X, Y)$ if there exists a consistent completion of D_t. Here $\forall Y \psi(X, Y)$ is encoded by leveraging the property $\forall Y(\bigwedge_{i \in [1,r]} C_i(X, Y)) = \bigwedge_{i \in [1,r]} \forall Y C_i(X, Y)$, for $\psi(X, Y) = \bigwedge_{i \in [1,r]} C_i(X, Y)$.

For the data complexity, we show that CPS is NP-hard by reduction from the Betweenness problem, which is NP-complete (cf. [18]). Given two sets E and $F = \{(e_i, e_j, e_k) \mid e_i, e_j, e_k \in E\}$, the Betweenness problem is to decide whether there is a bijection $\pi : E \rightarrow \{1, \dots, |E|\}$ such that for each $(e_i, e_j, e_k) \in E$, either $\pi(e_i) < \pi(e_j) < \pi(e_k)$ or $\pi(e_k) < \pi(e_j) < \pi(e_i)$. Given E and F, we define a specification $\mathbf{S}$ with a temporal instance D_t of a 4-ary schema, and a set of *fixed* denial constraints. We show that there exists a solution to the Betweenness problem iff $\mathsf{Mod}(\mathbf{S})$ is nonempty.

(2) *Upper bounds.* We provide an algorithm that, given a specification $\mathbf{S}$, guesses a completion $\mathbf{D}^c$ of total orders in $\mathbf{S}$, and then checks whether $\mathbf{D}^c \in \mathsf{Mod}(\mathbf{S})$. The checking involves (a) denial constraints and (b) the copying condition and $\prec$-compatibility of copy functions in $\mathbf{S}$. Step (b) is in PTIME. Step (a) is in PTIME if the denial constraints are fixed, and it uses an NP-oracle otherwise. Hence CPS is in NP for data complexity and in Σ_2^p for combined complexity.

In the proofs for the lower bounds, no copy functions are defined, and the relation schemas are fixed. □

The certainty of currency orders. We next study COP and DCIP. The certain currency ordering problem COP is to determine, given a specification $\mathbf{S}$ and a currency order O_t, whether each $t \prec_A s$ in O_t is entailed by the partial currency orders, denial constraints and copy functions in $\mathbf{S}$. The deterministic current instance problem DCIP is to decide, given $\mathbf{S}$, whether the current instance of each temporal instance of $\mathbf{S}$ is unchanged for all consistent completions of $\mathbf{S}$. These problems are, unfortunately, also beyond reach in practice.

Corollary 4.2: For both COP and DCIP, (1) the combined complexity is Π_2^p-complete, and (2) the data complexity is coNP-complete. The complexity bounds remain unchanged when no copy functions are present. □

Proof sketch: (1) *Lower bounds.* For both COP and DCIP, the lower bounds are verified by reduction from the complement of CPS, for data complexity and combined complexity.
(2) *Upper bounds.* A non-deterministic algorithm is developed for each of COP and DCIP, which is in coNP (data complexity) and Π_2^p (combined complexity). □

Query answering. The certain currency query answering problem $\mathsf{CCQA}(\mathcal{L}_Q)$ is to determine, given a tuple t, a specification $\mathbf{S}$ and a query $Q \in \mathcal{L}_Q$, whether $t \in Q(\mathsf{LST}(\mathbf{D}^c))$ for all $\mathbf{D}^c \in \mathsf{Mod}(\mathbf{S})$. The result below provides the data complexity of the problem, as well as its combined complexity when $\mathcal{L}_Q$ ranges over CQ, UCQ, $\exists \mathsf{FO}^+$ and FO. It tells us the following. (1) Disjunctions in UCQ and $\exists \mathsf{FO}^+$ do not incur extra complexity to CCQA. Indeed, CCQA has the same complexity for CQ as for UCQ and $\exists \mathsf{FO}^+$. (2) In contrast, the presence of negation in FO complicates the analysis. (3) Copy functions have no impact on the complexity bounds.

Theorem 4.3: The combined complexity of $\mathsf{CCQA}(\mathcal{L}_Q)$ is
- Π_2^p-complete when $\mathcal{L}_Q$ is CQ, UCQ or $\exists \mathsf{FO}^+$, and
- PSPACE-complete when $\mathcal{L}_Q$ is FO.

The data complexity is coNP-complete when $\mathcal{L}_Q \in \{$CQ, UCQ, $\exists \mathsf{FO}^+$, FO$\}$. These complexity bounds are unchanged in the absence of copy functions. □

Proof sketch: *Lower bounds.* For the combined complexity, we show the following: (a) CCQA is already Π_2^p-hard for CQ, and (b) it is PSPACE-hard for FO.

(a) For CQ, we verify it by reduction from the $\forall^* \exists^* 3\mathsf{SAT}$ problem, which is Π_2^p-complete (cf. [28]). Given a sentence $\phi = \forall X \exists Y \psi(X, Y)$, we define a CQ query Q, a fixed tuple t, and a specification $\mathbf{S}$ consisting of five temporal instances of fixed schemas. We use these temporal instances to encode (i) disjunction and negation, which are not expressible in CQ, (ii) truth assignments μ_X for X, with an instance D_X, and (iii) relations for inspecting whether t is an answer to Q. Query Q encodes $\exists Y \psi(X, Y)$ w.r.t. μ_X, such that ϕ is true iff t is an answer to Q for each consistent completion of D_X, i.e., when μ_X ranges over all truth assignments for X.

(b) For FO, we show that CCQA is PSPACE-hard by reduction from Q3SAT, which is PSPACE-complete (cf. [28]). Given an instance ϕ of Q3SAT, we define an FO query Q, a fixed tuple t and a specification $\mathbf{S}$ with a single temporal instance. Query Q encodes ϕ, and the relation encodes Boolean values for which there is a single completion $\mathbf{D}_0^c$ in $\mathsf{Mod}(\mathbf{S})$. We show that ϕ is true iff t is in $Q(\mathbf{D}_0^c)$.

For the data complexity, we show that CCQA is coNP-hard even for CQ, by reduction from the complement of 3SAT. Given a propositional formula ψ, we define a *fixed* CQ query Q, a fixed tuple t and a specification $\mathbf{S}$ consisting of two temporal instances D_ψ and $D_{\neg \psi}$ of fixed relation schemas. We use D_ψ to encode (i) truth assignments μ_X for variables X in ψ, and (ii) literals in ψ. We encode the negations of clauses in ψ using $D_{\neg \psi}$, for which there is a unique consistent completion. For each consistent completion of D_ψ, i.e., each μ_X for X, query Q returns t iff ψ is not satisfied by μ_X.

In the lower bound proofs, neither denial constraints nor copy functions are defined, and all the schemas are fixed.

Upper bounds. We develop an algorithm that, given a query Q, a tuple t and a specification $\mathbf{S}$, returns "no" if there exists $\mathbf{D}^c \in \mathsf{Mod}(\mathbf{S})$ such that $t \notin Q(\mathsf{LST}(\mathbf{D}^c))$. The algorithm first guesses $\mathbf{D}^c$, and then checks whether (a) $\mathbf{D}^c \in \mathsf{Mod}(\mathbf{S})$ and (b) $t \notin Q(\mathsf{LST}(\mathbf{D}^c))$. Step (b) is in coNP when Q is in $\exists \mathsf{FO}^+$, and is in PSPACE if Q is in FO. When Q is fixed, step (b) is in PTIME no matter whether Q is in CQ or FO. Putting these together with Theorem 4.1 (for step (a)), we conclude that the data complexity of CCQA is in coNP, and its combined complexity is in Π_2^p for $\exists \mathsf{FO}^+$ and in PSPACE for FO. □

Special cases. The results above tell us that it is nontrivial to reason about data currency. In light of this, we look into special cases of these problems with lower complexity. As shown by Theorem 4.1 and Corollary 4.2, denial constraints make the analyses of CPS, COP and DCIP intricate. Indeed, these problems are intractable even when denial constraints are fixed. Hence we consider specifications with no denial constraints, but containing partial currency orders and copy functions. The result below shows that the absence of denial constraints indeed simplifies the analyses.

Theorem 4.4: In the absence of denial constraints, CPS, COP and DCIP are in PTIME. □

Proof sketch: For CPS, we develop an algorithm that, given a specification $\mathbf{S}$ with no denial constraints defined, checks whether $\mathsf{Mod}(\mathbf{S}) \neq \emptyset$. Let $\bar{\rho}$ denote the collection of copy functions in $\mathbf{S}$. One can verify that in the absence of denial constraints, $\mathbf{S}$ is consistent iff there exists no violation of the copying condition or $\prec$-compatibility of $\bar{\rho}$ in any temporal instance of $\mathbf{S}$. Hence it suffices to detect violations in the instances of $\mathbf{S}$, rather than in their completions.

As shown in Example 2.2, it is not straightforward to check $\prec$-compatibility, especially when tuples are imported indirectly from other sources. Nonetheless, we show that this can be done in $O(|\mathbf{S}|^2)$ time, where $|\mathbf{S}|$ is the size of $\mathbf{S}$.

For COP, we show that given a specification $\mathbf{S}$ without denial constraints, to decide whether a currency order is contained in all completions of $\mathbf{S}$, it suffices to check temporal instances of $\mathbf{S}$. This can be decided by a variation of the algorithm for CPS, also in PTIME; similarly for DCIP. $\square$

In contrast, the absence of denial constraints does not make our lives easier when it comes to CCQA. Indeed, in the proof of Theorem 4.3, the lower bounds of CCQA are verified using neither denial constraints nor copy functions.

Corollary 4.5: In the absence of denial constraints, $\mathsf{CCQA}(\mathcal{L}_Q)$ remains coNP-hard (data complexity) and

- Π_2^p-hard (combined complexity) even for CQ, and
- PSPACE-hard (combined complexity) for FO. $\square$

Theorem 4.3 tells us that the complexity of CCQA for CQ is rather robust: adding disjunctions does not increase the complexity. We next investigate the impact of removing Cartesian product from CQ on the complexity of CCQA. We consider SP queries, which are CQ queries of the form

$$Q(\vec{x}) = \exists e\,\vec{y}\,\big(R(e,\vec{x},\vec{y}) \wedge \psi\big),$$

where ψ is a conjunction of equality atoms and $\vec{x}$ and $\vec{y}$ are disjoint sequences of variables in which no variable appears twice. SP queries support projection and selection only. For instance, $Q_1 - Q_4$ of Example 1.1 are SP queries. SP queries in which ψ is a tautology are referred to as *identity queries*.

We show that for SP queries, denial constraints make a difference. Without denial constraints, CCQA is in PTIME for SP queries. In contrast, when denial constraints are imposed, CCQA is no easier for identity queries than for $\exists \mathsf{FO}^+$.

Corollary 4.6: For SP queries, CCQA(SP) is

- in PTIME in the absence of denial constraints, and
- coNP-complete (data complexity) and Π_2^p-complete (combined complexity) in the presence of denial constraints, even for identity queries. $\square$

Proof sketch: (1) In the absence of denial constraints, one can verify that for any specification $\mathbf{S}$ and each SP query Q, $\bigcap_{\mathbf{D}^c \in \mathsf{Mod}(\mathbf{S})} Q(\mathsf{LST}(\mathbf{D}^c))$ can be obtained from (1) evaluating Q on a representation $\mathsf{repr}(\mathbf{S})$ of $\{\mathsf{LST}(\mathbf{D}^c) \mid \mathbf{D}^c \in \mathsf{Mod}(\mathbf{S})\}$, where $\mathsf{repr}(\mathbf{S})$ compactly represents all possible latest values by special symbols; and (2) by removing all tuples in $Q(\mathsf{repr}(\mathbf{S}))$ that contain such special symbols. Capitalizing on this property, we develop an algorithm that takes as input an SP query Q, a tuple t and a specification $\mathbf{S}$ without denial constraints. It checks whether t is a certain current answer to Q w.r.t. $\mathbf{S}$ as follows: (a) check whether $\mathbf{S}$ is consistent, and return "no" if not; (b) compute the representation $\mathsf{repr}(\mathbf{S})$; (c) check whether t is in the "stripped" version of $Q(\mathsf{repr}(\mathbf{S}))$; and (d) return "yes" if so, and "no" otherwise. Step (c) is PTIME for SP queries. By Theorem 4.4 and by leveraging the certain order computed by the algorithm for CPS, steps (a) and (b) are also in PTIME. Therefore, CCQA is in PTIME in this setting, for both combined complexity (when queries are not fixed) and data complexity.

(2) In the presence of denial constraints, we show that CCQA

is coNP-hard (data complexity) and Π_2^p-hard (combined complexity) by reduction from the complement of CPS, for which the complexity is established in Theorem 4.1. Given a specification $\mathbf{S}$, we construct a specification $\mathbf{S}'$, a tuple t and an identity query Q, such that $\mathsf{Mod}(\mathbf{S})$ is *empty* iff t is in $Q(\mathsf{LST}(\mathbf{D}^c))$ for each $\mathbf{D}^c \in \mathsf{Mod}(\mathbf{S}')$. The upper bounds of CCQA is this setting follow from Theorem 4.3. $\square$

5. Currency Preservation in Data Copying

As we have seen earlier, copy functions tell us what data values in a relation have been imported from other data sources. Naturally we want to leverage the imported values to improve query answers. This gives rise to the following questions: do the copy functions import sufficient current data values for answering a query Q? If not, how do we extend the copy functions such that Q can be answered with more up-to-date data values? To answer these questions we introduce a notion of currency-preserving copy functions.

We consider a specification $\mathbf{S}$ of data currency consisting of two collections of temporal instances (data sources) $\mathbf{D} = (D_1, \ldots, D_p)$ and $\mathbf{D}' = (D_1', \ldots, D_q')$, with (1) a set Σ_i (resp. Σ_j') of denial constraints on D_i for each $i \in [1, p]$ (resp. D_j' for $j \in [1, q]$), and (2) a collection $\bar{\rho}$ of copy functions $\rho_{(j,i)}$ that imports tuples from D_j' to D_i, for $i \in [1, p]$ and $j \in [1, q]$, *i.e.*, all the functions of $\bar{\rho}$ import data from $\mathbf{D}'$ to $\mathbf{D}$.

Extensions. To formalize currency preservation, we first present the following notions. Assume that $D_i = (D, \prec_{A_1}, \ldots, \prec_{A_n})$ and $D_j' = (D', \prec_{B_1}, \ldots, \prec_{B_m})$ are temporal instances of relation schemas $R_i = (\mathsf{EID}, A_1, \ldots, A_n)$ and $R_j' = (\mathsf{EID}, B_1, \ldots, B_m)$, respectively. Assume that $n \leq m$.

An *extension* of D_i is a temporal instance $D_i^e = (D^e, \prec_{A_1}^e, \ldots, \prec_{A_n}^e)$ of R_i such that (1) $D \subseteq D^e$, (2) $\prec_{A_h} \subseteq \prec_{A_h}^e$ for all $h \in [1, n]$, and (3) $\pi_{\mathsf{EID}}(D^e) = \pi_{\mathsf{EID}}(D)$. Intuitively, D_i^e extends D_i by adding new tuples for those entities that are already in D_i. It does not introduce new entities.

Consider two copy functions: $\rho_{(j,i)}$ imports tuples from D_j' to D_i, and $\rho_{(j,i)}^e$ from D_j' to D_i^e, both of signature $R_i[\vec{A}] \Leftarrow R_j'[\vec{B}]$, where $\vec{A} = (A_1, \ldots, A_n)$ and $\vec{B}$ is a sequence of n attributes in R_j'. We say that $\rho_{(j,i)}^e$ *extends* $\rho_{(j,i)}$ if

1. D_i^e is an extension of D_i;
2. for each tuple t in D_i, if $\rho_{(j,i)}(t)$ is defined, then so is $\rho_{(j,i)}^e(t)$ and moreover, $\rho_{(j,i)}^e(t) = \rho_{(j,i)}(t)$;
3. for each tuple t in $D_i^e \setminus D_i$, there exists a tuple s in D_j' such that $\rho_{(j,i)}^e(t) = s$.

We refer to D_i^e as the *extension of D_i by $\rho_{(j,i)}^e$*.

Observe that D_i^e is not allowed to expand arbitrarily. (a) Each new tuple t in D_i^e is copied from a tuple s in D_j'. (b) No new entity is introduced. Note that only copy functions that cover all attributes but EID of R_i can be extended. This assures that all the attributes of a new tuple are in place.

An *extension* $\bar{\rho}^e$ of $\bar{\rho}$ is a collection of copy functions $\rho_{(j,i)}^e$ such that $\bar{\rho}^e \neq \bar{\rho}$ and moreover, for all $i \in [1, p]$ and $j \in [1, q]$, either $\rho_{(j,i)}^e$ is an extension of $\rho_{(j,i)}$, or $\rho_{(j,i)}^e = \rho_{(j,i)}$.

We denote the set of all extensions of $\bar{\rho}$ as $\mathsf{Ext}(\bar{\rho})$.

For each $\bar{\rho}^e$ in $\mathsf{Ext}(\bar{\rho})$, we denote as $\mathbf{S}^e$ the *extension of $\mathbf{S}$ by $\bar{\rho}^e$*, which consists of the same $\mathbf{D}'$ and denial constraints as in $\mathbf{S}$, but has copy functions $\bar{\rho}^e$ and $\mathbf{D}^e = (D_1^e, \ldots, D_p^e)$, where D_i^e is an extension of D_i by $\rho_{(j,i)}^e$ for all $j \in [1, q]$.

Currency preservation. We are now ready to define currency preservation. Consider a collection $\bar{\rho}$ of copy functions

	FN	LN	address	salary	status	phone
s_1':	Mary	Dupont	6 Main St	60k	married	6671975
s_2':	Mary	Dupont	6 Main St	80k	married	6671975
s_3':	Mary	Smith	2 Small St	80k	divorced	2902845

Figure 2: Relation Mgr

in a specification **S**. We say that $\bar{\rho}$ is *currency preserving* for a query Q *w.r.t.* **S** if (a) $\mathsf{Mod}(\mathbf{S}) \neq \emptyset$, and moreover, (b) for all $\bar{\rho}^e \in \mathsf{Ext}(\bar{\rho})$ such that $\mathsf{Mod}(\mathbf{S}^e) \neq \emptyset$, we have that

$$\bigcap_{\mathbf{D}^c \in \mathsf{Mod}(\mathbf{S})} Q(\mathsf{LST}(\mathbf{D}^c)) = \bigcap_{\mathbf{D}_e^c \in \mathsf{Mod}(\mathbf{S}^e)} Q(\mathsf{LST}(\mathbf{D}_e^c)).$$

Intuitively, $\bar{\rho}$ is currency preserving if (1) $\bar{\rho}$ is meaningful; and (2) for each extension $\bar{\rho}^e$ of $\bar{\rho}$ that makes sense, the certain current answers to Q are not improved by $\bar{\rho}^e$, *i.e.*, no matter what additional tuples are imported for those entities in **D**, the certain current answers to Q remain unchanged.

Example 5.1: As shown in Fig. 2, relation Mgr collects manager records. Consider a specification $\mathbf{S}_1$ consisting of the following: (a) temporal instances Mgr of Fig. 2 and Emp of Fig. 1, in which partial currency orders are $\emptyset$ for all attributes; (b) denial constraints $\varphi_1 - \varphi_3$ of Example 2.1 and

$$\varphi_5 : \forall s,t : \mathsf{Mgr}\ ((s[\mathsf{EID}] = t[\mathsf{EID}]\ \wedge\ s[\mathsf{status}] = \text{``divorced''}\ \wedge$$
$$t[\mathsf{status}] = \text{``married''})\ \rightarrow\ t \prec_{\mathsf{LN}} s),$$

i.e., if $s[\mathsf{status}]$ is divorced and $t[\mathsf{status}]$ is married, then s is more current than t in LN; and (c) a copy function ρ with signature $\mathsf{Emp}[\vec{A}] \Leftarrow \mathsf{Mgr}[\vec{A}]$, where $\vec{A}$ is (FN, LN, address, salary, status), such that $\rho(s_3) = s_2'$, *i.e.*, s_3 of Emp is copied from s_2' of Mgr. Obviously $\mathbf{S}_1$ is consistent.

Recall query Q_2 of Example 1.1, which is to find Mary's current last name. For Q_2, ρ is not currency preserving. Indeed, there is an extension ρ_1 of ρ by copying s_3' to Emp. In all consistent completions of the extension Emp_1 of Emp by ρ_1, the answer to Q_2 is Smith. However, the answer to Q_2 in all consistent completions of Emp is Dupont (see Examples 1.1 and 2.5). In contrast, ρ_1 is currency preserving for Q_2. Indeed, copying more tuples from Mgr (*i.e.*, tuple s_1') to Emp does not change the answer to Q_2 in Emp_1. $\square$

Deciding currency preservation. There are several decision problems associated with currency-preserving copy functions, which we shall investigate in the rest of the paper. The first problem is to decide whether given copy functions have imported necessary current data for answering a query.

CPP($\mathcal{L}_Q$):	The *currency preservation problem.*
INPUT:	A query Q in $\mathcal{L}_Q$, and a specification **S** of data currency with copy functions $\bar{\rho}$.
QUESTION:	Is $\bar{\rho}$ currency preserving for Q?

Minimal copying. Moreover, we want to know whether a currency preserving $\bar{\rho}$ does not copy unnecessary or redundant data. To this end, we use $|\bar{\rho}|$ to denote the sum of the sizes of data values copied by $\bar{\rho}$. We say that $\bar{\rho}$ is *minimal* for Q if there exists no collection $\bar{\rho}'$ of copy functions such that (1) $\bar{\rho} \in \mathsf{Ext}(\bar{\rho}')$, (2) $|\bar{\rho}'| < |\bar{\rho}|$, and (3) $\bar{\rho}'$ is currency preserving for Q. That is, there exists no currency-preserving $\bar{\rho}'$ that imports less data from $\mathbf{D}'$ to $\mathbf{D}$ than $\bar{\rho}$.

MCP($\mathcal{L}_Q$):	The *minimal copying problem.*
INPUT:	**S** and Q as in CPP, with a collection $\bar{\rho}$ of currency-preserving copy functions in **S**.
QUESTION:	Is $\bar{\rho}$ minimal for Q?

Extending copy functions. Consider a consistent specification **S** in which $\bar{\rho}$ is not currency preserving for a query

Q. The next problem is to decide whether $\bar{\rho}$ in **S** can be extended to be currency preserving for Q.

ECP($\mathcal{L}_Q$):	The *existence problem.*
INPUT:	A query Q in $\mathcal{L}_Q$, and a consistent specification **S** with non-currency-preserving $\bar{\rho}$
QUESTION:	Does there exist $\bar{\rho}^e$ in $\mathsf{Ext}(\bar{\rho})$ that is currency preserving for Q?

Bounded extension. We also want to know whether it suffices to extend $\bar{\rho}$ by copying additional data of a bounded size, and make it currency preserving.

BCP($\mathcal{L}_Q$):	The *bounded copying problem.*
INPUT:	**S**, $\bar{\rho}$ and Q as in ECP, and a positive number k.
QUESTION:	Does there exist $\bar{\rho}^e \in \mathsf{Ext}(\bar{\rho})$ such that $\bar{\rho}^e$ is currency preserving for Q and $|\bar{\rho}^e| \leq k + |\bar{\rho}|$?

6. Deciding Currency Preservation

We next study the decision problems in connection with currency-preserving copy functions, namely, CPP($\mathcal{L}_Q$), MCP($\mathcal{L}_Q$), ECP($\mathcal{L}_Q$) and BCP($\mathcal{L}_Q$) when $\mathcal{L}_Q$ is CQ, UCQ, $\exists$FO$^+$ or FO. We provide their combined complexity and data complexity, and identify special cases with lower complexity.

Checking currency preservation. We first investigate CPP($\mathcal{L}_Q$), the problem of deciding whether a collection of copy functions in a given specification is currency preserving for a query Q. We show that CPP is nontrivial. Indeed, its combined complexity is already Π_3^p-hard when Q is in CQ, and it is PSPACE-complete when Q is in FO.

One might be tempted to think that fixing denial constraints would make our lives easier. Indeed, in practice denial constraints are often predefined and fixed, and only data, copy functions and query vary. Moreover, as shown in Theorem 4.1 for the consistency problem, fixing denial constraints indeed helps there. Unfortunately, it does not simplify the analysis of the combined complexity when it comes to CPP. Even when both query and denial constraints are fixed, the problem is Π_2^p-complete (data complexity).

Theorem 6.1: For CPP($\mathcal{L}_Q$), the combined complexity is

- Π_3^p-complete when $\mathcal{L}_Q$ is CQ, UCQ or $\exists$FO$^+$, and
- PSPACE-complete when $\mathcal{L}_Q$ is FO.
- Its data complexity is Π_2^p-complete when $\mathcal{L}_Q \in \{$CQ, UCQ, $\exists$FO$^+$,FO$\}$.

The combined complexity bounds remain unchanged when denial constraints and copy functions are fixed. $\square$

Proof sketch: (1) *Lower bounds.* For the combined complexity, it suffices to show that CPP is already Π_3^p-hard for CQ, while for FO, it is PSPACE-hard. For the data complexity, we show that CPP is Π_2^p-hard with CQ queries.

The Π_3^p lower bound is verified by reduction from the $\forall^* \exists^* \forall^*$3SAT problem, which is Π_3^p-complete (cf. [28]). Given a sentence $\phi = \forall X \exists Y \forall Z \psi(X, Y, Z)$, we construct a query Q in CQ, and a specification **S** with (i) two data sources **D** and $\mathbf{D}'$, (ii) a single copy function ρ and (iii) a set of denial constraints. Source **D** consists of four relations encoding Boolean values, disjunction, conjunction and negation, as well as a relation D_b for testing certain current query answers. Source $\mathbf{D}'$ has a single relation D_b' from which some tuples are copied to D_b by ρ. Query Q encodes ϕ by leveraging the relations in **D** for Boolean operations, and the property of $\forall Z \psi(X,Y,Z)$ explored in the proof of Theorem 4.1. We show that ϕ is true iff ρ is currency preserving for Q.

When it comes to FO, we show that CPP is PSPACE-hard by a straightforward reduction from Q3SAT.

In these proofs, both denial constraints and copy functions are fixed, independent of $\forall^*\exists^*\forall^*$3SAT or Q3SAT instances.

For the data complexity, we verify the Π_2^p lower bound for CQ by reduction from the $\forall^*\exists^*$3SAT problem. Given a sentence $\phi = \forall X \exists Y \psi(X,Y)$, we define a query Q in CQ and a specification **S** such that ϕ is true iff ρ is currency preserving for Q w.r.t. **S**. Here Q is fixed, *i.e.*, it is independent of ϕ.

(2) *Upper bounds.* We give an algorithm that takes a query Q and a specification **S** as input, and checks whether the copy functions $\bar{\rho}$ in **S** are currency preserving for Q. It invokes oracles to check whether **S** is consistent and whether some guessed tuples are certain current answers to Q in $\mathbf{D}^c \in \mathrm{Mod}(\mathbf{S})$ but are not answers to Q in some $\mathbf{D}_e^c \in \mathrm{Mod}(\mathbf{S}^e)$, where $\mathbf{S}^e$ is an extension of **S** by extending copy functions. The oracles are in Π_2^p or Σ_2^p when Q is in $\exists\mathrm{FO}^+$, and in PSPACE when Q is in FO. When Q is fixed, the oracles are in NP or coNP. From these the upper bounds follow. □

Minimal copying. We next study $\mathrm{MCP}(\mathcal{L}_Q)$, which is to decide whether currency-preserving copy functions import any data that is unnecessary or redundant for a query Q. This problem is even harder than CPP: for CQ queries, its combined complexity is Δ_4^p-complete ($P^{\Sigma_3^p}$) even if denial constraints are fixed, and its data complexity is Δ_3^p-complete. For FO queries, it is still PSPACE-complete.

Theorem 6.2: For $\mathrm{MCP}(\mathcal{L}_Q)$, the combined complexity is
- Δ_4^p-complete when $\mathcal{L}_Q$ is CQ, UCQ or $\exists\mathrm{FO}^+$, and
- PSPACE-complete when $\mathcal{L}_Q$ is FO.
- Its data complexity is Δ_3^p-complete when $\mathcal{L}_Q \in \{\mathrm{CQ}, \mathrm{UCQ}, \exists\mathrm{FO}^+, \mathrm{FO}\}$.

The combined complexity bounds remain unchanged when denial constraints and copy functions are fixed. □

Proof sketch: (1) *Lower bounds.* For FO, the proofs are similar to their counterparts of CPS. For CQ queries, we show that MCP is Δ_4^p-hard (combined complexity) by reduction from the $\mathrm{MSA}(\exists^*\forall^*\exists^*$3SAT) problem, which is Δ_4^p-complete [26]. The latter problem is to determine, given a satisfiable sentence $\phi = \exists X \forall Y \exists Z \psi(X,Y,Z)$, whether in the lexicographically maximum truth assignment μ_X for variables in X such that $\forall Y \exists Z \psi(\mu_X(x_1), \ldots, \mu_X(x_n), Y, Z)$ evaluates to true, the last variable $x_n \in X$ has value 1, *i.e.*, whether $\mu_X(x_n) = 1$. For the data complexity, we verify that it is Δ_3^p-hard for CQ by reduction from $\mathrm{MSA}(\exists^*\forall^*$3SAT)-problem. These reductions need to encode the lexicographical successor function for variables in X, and are more involved than those given in the proof of Theorem 6.1.

(2) *Upper bounds.* We provide an algorithm that takes as input a query Q and a specification **S** with currency preserving copy functions $\bar{\rho}$. For each tuple t copied by $\bar{\rho}$, it checks whether removing t makes the copy functions not currency preserving, by using the algorithm for CPP in the proof of Theorem 6.1 as an oracle. Hence MCP is in Δ_4^p ($P^{\Sigma_3^p}$, combined complexity) and in Δ_3^p (data complexity). □

The feasibility of currency preservation. We now consider $\mathrm{ECP}(\mathcal{L}_Q)$. It is to decide, given a query Q and a spec-

ification **S** in which copy functions $\bar{\rho}$ are not currency preserving for Q, whether we can extend $\bar{\rho}$ to preserve currency. The good news is that the answer to this question is affirmative: we can always extend $\bar{\rho}$ and make them currency preserving for Q. Hence the decision problem ECP is in $O(1)$ time, although it may take much longer time to explicitly construct a currency preserving extension of $\bar{\rho}$.

Proposition 6.3: $\mathrm{ECP}(\mathcal{L}_Q)$ is decidable in $O(1)$ time for both the combined complexity and data complexity, when $\mathcal{L}_Q$ is CQ, UCQ, $\exists\mathrm{FO}^+$ or FO. □

Proof sketch: To show the existence of currency preserving extensions of ρ, we give an algorithm to construct one. Let $\mathbf{D}'$ be the data source in **S** from which tuples can be copied. For all copy function ρ in $\bar{\rho}$, if ρ can be extended, the algorithm expands ρ by copying tuples one by one from $\mathbf{D}'$, starting from the most current ones, as long as the extended instances satisfy the denial constraints in **S** and the constraints of the copy functions. It proceeds until no more tuples from $\mathbf{D}'$ can be copied while satisfying the constraints, and yields a currency-preserving extension of $\bar{\rho}$. □

Bounded extensions. In contrast to ECP, when it comes to deciding whether $\bar{\rho}$ can be made currency-preserving by copying data within a bounded size, the analysis becomes far more intricate. Indeed, the result below tells us that even for CQ, BCP is Σ_4^p-hard, and fixing denial constraints and copy functions does not help. When both queries and denial constraints are fixed, BCP is Σ_3^p-complete.

Theorem 6.4: For $\mathrm{BCP}(\mathcal{L}_Q)$, the combined complexity is
- Σ_4^p-complete when $\mathcal{L}_Q$ is CQ, UCQ or $\exists\mathrm{FO}^+$, and
- PSPACE-complete when $\mathcal{L}_Q$ is FO.
- Its data complexity is Σ_3^p-complete when $\mathcal{L}_Q \in \{\mathrm{CQ}, \mathrm{UCQ}, \exists\mathrm{FO}^+, \mathrm{FO}\}$.

The combined complexity bounds remain unchanged when denial constraints and copy functions are fixed. □

Proof sketch: (1) *Lower bounds.* For FO, we show that BCP is PSPACE-hard by a simple reduction from Q3SAT.

For CQ, we show that BCP is Σ_4^p-hard by reduction from the $\exists^*\forall^*\exists^*\forall^*$3SAT problem, which is Σ_4^p-complete (cf. [28]). Given a sentence $\phi = \exists W \forall X \exists Y \forall Z \psi(W,X,Y,Z)$, we define a CQ query Q, a positive number k and a specification **S** with two copy functions $\bar{\rho}$. We show that ϕ is true iff there exists an extension $\bar{\rho}^e$ of $\bar{\rho}$ such that $|\bar{\rho}^e| \leq |\bar{\rho}| + k$ and $\bar{\rho}^e$ is currency preserving for Q. We use temporal instances in **S** to encode disjunction and negation, which Q leverages to express ϕ. We also define a data source in **S** whose current instance ranges over all truth assignments for W, and use the data source to inspect possible extensions of $\bar{\rho}$.

For the data complexity, we verify the Σ_3^p lower bound for CQ by reduction from the $\exists^*\forall^*\exists^*$3SAT problem. This reduction is more involved than the one developed for the combined complexity. Given an $\exists^*\forall^*\exists^*$ sentence ϕ, we define a query Q in CQ that is independent of ϕ but nonetheless, is able to encode the negations of the clauses in ϕ, by making use of temporal instances in a specification constructed.

In all these proofs, denial constraints and copy functions are independent of input sentences, *i.e.*, they are fixed.

(2) *Upper bounds.* We develop an algorithm for BCP, which first guesses an extension $\bar{\rho}^e$ of $\bar{\rho}$ that copies more data of a

bounded size, and then checks whether $\bar{\rho}^e$ is currency preserving, by invoking the algorithm for CPP. From Theorem 6.1 the upper bounds for BCP follow immediately. □

Special cases. Theorem 6.1, 6.2 and 6.4 motivate us to explore special cases that simplify the analyses. In contrast to Theorem 4.1 and Corollary 4.2, we have seen that fixing denial constraints does not make our lives easier when it comes to CPP, MCP or BCP. However, when denial constraints are absent, these problems become tractable for SP queries. This is consistent with Corollary 4.6.

Theorem 6.5: When denial constraints are absent, for SP queries both the combined complexity and the data complexity are in PTIME for CPP, MCP and BCP (when the bound k on the size of additional data copied is fixed). □

Proof sketch: (1) CPP. We develop a PTIME algorithm $\mathcal{A}$ that takes as input a specification $\mathbf{S}$ and an SP query Q defined on instances of a relation schema R. It checks whether the copy functions $\bar{\rho}$ in $\mathbf{S}$ are currency preserving for Q. The main idea behind $\mathcal{A}$ is as follows. Let E be the set of all entities in D_t, where D_t is the temporal instance of R in $\mathbf{S}$. Let C be the set of certain current answers to Q. By Corollary 4.6, C can be computed in PTIME. For each $e \in E$, $\mathcal{A}$ inspects tuples t in $\mathbf{D}'$ one by one, to find whether it would "spoil" some answer $s \in C$ produced by the current tuple of e if t were imported, *i.e.*, adding t would make $\mathsf{LST}(e, \mathbf{D}^c)$ either empty or a distinct tuple that does not produce s via Q. Here $\mathbf{D}'$ is the data source in $\mathbf{S}$ from which tuples are copied. When denial constraints are absent and Q is in SP, this can be done in PTIME. The algorithm then checks spoilers for all $c \in E$, to find whether there exists $s \in C$ spoiled by importing tuples for all entities that yield s, or whether some spoilers introduce a new certain current answer. This can be done in PTIME since the entities in E are independent of each other. The algorithm returns "yes" iff no such spoilers exist. It is in PTIME as argued above.

(2) MCP. Given $\mathcal{A}$, an algorithm for MCP is immediate: for each "reduced" $\bar{\rho}_c$ that removes one imported tuple from $\bar{\rho}$, it checks whether $\bar{\rho}_c$ is currency preserving for Q by using $\mathcal{A}$. The algorithm is obviously in PTIME.

(3) BCP. When the bound k is fixed, there are polynomially many extensions $\bar{\rho}^e$ of $\bar{\rho}$ such that $|\bar{\rho}^e| \le |\bar{\rho}| + k$. For each such $\bar{\rho}^e$ we check whether $\bar{\rho}^e$ is currency preserving for Q by invoking $\mathcal{A}$. This can be done in PTIME. □

For $\mathsf{BCP}(\mathcal{L}_Q)$, when the bound k is predefined and fixed, the analysis also becomes simpler when $\mathcal{L}_Q$ is CQ, UCQ or $\exists\mathsf{FO}^+$. For FO, however, BCP remains PSPACE-complete.

Corollary 6.6: When k is fixed, $\mathsf{BCP}(\mathcal{L}_Q)$ is
- Δ_4^p-complete (combined) for CQ, UCQ and $\exists\mathsf{FO}^+$,
- Δ_3^p-complete (data) for CQ, UCQ and $\exists\mathsf{FO}^+$, but is
- PSPACE-complete for FO (combined complexity). □

Proof sketch: (1) *Upper bounds.* As remarked earlier, when k is fixed there are polynomially many extensions $\bar{\rho}^e$ of $\bar{\rho}$ such that $|\bar{\rho}^e| \le |\bar{\rho}| + k$. For each such $\bar{\rho}^e$ we check whether $\bar{\rho}^e$ is currency preserving, by invoking the algorithm for checking CPP given in the proof of Theorem 6.1. Therefore, BCP is in $P^{\Sigma_3^p} = \Delta_4^p$ for $\exists\mathsf{FO}^+$(combined complexity). Moreover, when queries and denial constraints are fixed, it is in $P^{\Sigma_2^p} = \Delta_3^p$ (data complexity). For FO, the CPP checking is in PSPACE, and hence so is the upper bound for BCP.

(2) *Lower bounds.* We show that when k is fixed, BCP is already Δ_4^p-hard (combined complexity) for CQ queries, by reduction from the MSA($\exists^*\forall^*\exists^*3\mathrm{SAT}$) problem. In addition, we verify that it is Δ_3^p-hard (data complexity) for CQ queries by reduction from the MSA($\exists^*\forall^*3\mathrm{SAT}$) problem. For FO queries, we show that it remains PSPACE-hard (combined complexity) by reduction from Q3SAT. □

7. Conclusions

We have proposed a model to specify the currency of data in the absence of reliable timestamps but in the presence of copy relationships. We have also introduced a notion of currency preservation to assess copy functions for query answering. We have identified eight fundamental problems associated with data currency and currency preservation (CPS, COP, DCIP, CCQA($\mathcal{L}_Q$), CPP($\mathcal{L}_Q$), MCP($\mathcal{L}_Q$), ECP($\mathcal{L}_Q$) and BCP($\mathcal{L}_Q$)). We have provided a complete picture of the lower and upper bounds of these problems, all matching, for their data complexity as well as combined complexity when $\mathcal{L}_Q$ ranges over a variety of query languages. These results are not only of theoretical interest in their own right, but may also help practitioners distinguish current values from stale data, answer queries with current data, and design proper copy functions to import data from external sources.

The main complexity results are summarized in Tables 2 and 3, annotated with their corresponding theorems.

The study of data currency is still preliminary. An open issue concerns generalizations of copy functions. To simplify the presentation we assume a single copy function from one relation to another. Nonetheless we believe that all the results remain intact when multiple such functions coexist. For currency-preserving copy functions, we assume that the signatures "cover" all attributes (except EID) of the importing relation. It is nontrivial to relax this requirement, however, since otherwise unknown values need to be introduced for attributes whose value is not provided by the extended copy functions. A second issue is about practical use of the study. As shown in Tables 2 and 3, most of the problems are intractable. To this end we expect to (a) identify practical PTIME cases in various applications, (b) develop efficient heuristic algorithms with certain performance guarantees, and (c) conduct incremental analysis when data or copy functions are updated, which is expected to result in a lower complexity than its batch counterpart when the area affected by the updates is small, as commonly found in practice. A third issue concerns the interaction between data consistency and data currency. There is an intimate connection between these two central issues of data quality. Indeed, identifying the current value of an entity helps resolve data inconsistencies, and conversely, repairing data helps remove obsolete data. While these processes should logically be unified, we are not aware of any previous work on this topic. Finally, it is interesting to develop syntactic characterizations of currency-preserving copy functions.

Acknowledgments. Fan and Geerts are supported in part by an IBM scalable data analytics for a smarter planet innovation award, and the RSE-NSFC Joint Project Scheme.

8. References

[1] S. Abiteboul, R. Hull, and V. Vianu. *Foundations of Databases*. Addison-Wesley, 1995.

	CPS	COP	DCIP
Data complexity	NP-complete (Th 4.1)	coNP-complete (Cor 4.2)	coNP-complete (Cor 4.2)
Combined complexity	Σ_2^p-complete (Th 4.1)	Π_2^p-complete (Cor 4.2)	Π_2^p-complete (Cor 4.2)
Special case	In the absence of denial constraints		
Combined and data complexity	PTIME (Th 4.4)	PTIME (Th 4.4)	PTIME (Th 4.4)

Table 2: Complexity of problems for reasoning about data currency (CPS, COP, DCIP)

Complexity	CCQA($\mathcal{L}_Q$)	CPP($\mathcal{L}_Q$)	MCP($\mathcal{L}_Q$)	ECP($\mathcal{L}_Q$)	BCP($\mathcal{L}_Q$)
Data	coNP-complete (Th 4.3)	Π_2^p-complete (Th 6.1)	Δ_2^p-complete (Th 6.2)	$O(1)$ (Prop 6.3)	Σ_3^p-complete (Th 6.4)
Combined ($\mathcal{L}_Q$)					
CQ, UCQ, $\exists$FO$^+$	Π_2^p-complete (Th 4.3)	Π_3^p-complete (Th 6.1)	Δ_3^p-complete (Th 6.2)	$O(1)$ (Prop 6.3)	Σ_4^p-complete (Th 6.4)
FO	PSPACE-complete (Th 4.3)	PSPACE-complete (Th 6.1)	PSPACE-complete (Th 6.2)	$O(1)$ (Prop 6.3)	PSPACE-complete (Th 6.4)
Special case	SP queries in the absence of denial constraints				
Combined & data	PTIME (Cor 4.6)	PTIME (Th 6.5)	PTIME (Th 6.5)	$O(1)$ (Prop 6.3)	PTIME (Th 6.5)

Table 3: Complexity of problems for query answering and for determining currency preservation

[2] L. Berti-Equille, A. D. Sarma, X. Dong, A. Marian, and D. Srivastava. Sailing the information ocean with awareness of currents: Discovery and application of source dependence. In *CIDR*, 2009.

[3] L. Bertossi. Consistent query answering in databases. *SIGMOD Rec.*, 35(2), 2006.

[4] M. Bodirsky and J. Kára. The complexity of temporal constraint satisfaction problems. *JACM*, 57(2), 2010.

[5] P. Buneman, J. Cheney, W. Tan, and S. Vansummeren. Curated databases. In *PODS*, 2008.

[6] J. Cheney, L. Chiticariu, and W. C. Tan. Provenance in databases: Why, how, and where. *Foundations and Trends in Databases*, 1(4):379–474, 2009.

[7] J. Chomicki. Consistent query answering: Five easy pieces. In *ICDT*, 2007.

[8] J. Chomicki and D. Toman. Time in database systems. In M. Fisher, D. Gabbay, and L. Vila, editors, *Handbook of Temporal Reasoning in Artificial Intelligence*. Elsevier, 2005.

[9] J. Clifford, C. E. Dyreson, T. Isakowitz, C. S. Jensen, and R. T. Snodgrass. On the semantics of "now" in databases. *TODS*, 22(2):171–214, 1997.

[10] E. F. Codd. Extending the database relational model to capture more meaning. *TODS*, 4(4):397–434, 1979.

[11] A. Deutsch, A. Nash, and J. B. Remmel. The chase revisited. In *PODS*, 2008.

[12] X. Dong, L. Berti-Equille, Y. Hu, and D. Srivastava. Global detection of complex copying relationships between sources. In *VLDB*, 2010.

[13] X. Dong, L. Berti-Equille, and D. Srivastava. Truth discovery and copying detection in a dynamic world. In *VLDB*, 2009.

[14] C. E. Dyreson, C. S. Jensen, and R. T. Snodgrass. Now in temporal databases. In L. Liu and M. T. Özsu, editors, *Encyclopedia of Database Systems*. Springer, 2009.

[15] W. W. Eckerson. Data quality and the bottom line: Achieving business success through a commitment to high quality data. Data Warehousing Institute, 2002.

[16] A. K. Elmagarmid, P. G. Ipeirotis, and V. S. Verykios. Duplicate record detection: A survey. *TKDE*, 19(1):1–16, 2007.

[17] W. Fan, F. Geerts, J. Li, and M. Xiong. Discovering conditional functional dependencies. *TKDE*, 23(4):683–698, 2011.

[18] M. Garey and D. Johnson. *Computers and Intractability: A Guide to the Theory of NP-Completeness*. W. H. Freeman and Company, 1979.

[19] G. Grahne. *The Problem of Incomplete Information in Relational Databases*. Springer, 1991.

[20] M. Grohe and G. Schwandtner. The complexity of datalog on linear orders. *Logical Methods in Computer Science*, 5(1), 2009.

[21] T. Imieliński and W. Lipski, Jr. Incomplete information in relational databases. *JACM*, 31(4), 1984.

[22] Knowledge Integrity. Two sides to data decay. DM Review, 2003.

[23] P. G. Kolaitis. Schema mappings, data exchange, and metadata management. In *PODS*, 2005.

[24] M. Koubarakis. Database models for infinite and indefinite temporal information. *Inf. Syst.*, 19(2):141–173, 1994.

[25] M. Koubarakis. The complexity of query evaluation in indefinite temporal constraint databases. *TCS*, 171(1-2):25–60, 1997.

[26] M. W. Krentel. Generalizations of Opt P to the polynomial hierarchy. *TCS*, 97(2):183–198, 1992.

[27] M. Lenzerini. Data integration: A theoretical perspective. In *PODS*, 2002.

[28] C. H. Papadimitriou. *Computational Complexity*. Addison-Wesley, 1994.

[29] E. Schwalb and L. Vila. Temporal constraints: A survey. *Constraints*, 3(2-3):129–149, 1998.

[30] R. T. Snodgrass. *Developing Time-Oriented Database Applications in SQL*. Morgan Kaufmann, 1999.

[31] R. van der Meyden. The complexity of querying indefinite data about linearly ordered domains. *JCSS*, 54(1), 1997.

[32] R. van der Meyden. Logical approaches to incomplete information: A survey. In J. Chomicki and G. Saake, editors, *Logics for Databases and Information Systems*. Kluwer, 1998.

[33] V. Vianu. Dynamic functional dependencies and database aging. *J. ACM*, 34(1):28–59, 1987.

[34] H. Zhang, Y. Diao, and N. Immerman. Recognizing patterns in streams with imprecise timestamps. In *VLDB*, 2010.

Data Exchange beyond Complete Data

Marcelo Arenas
Department of Computer Science
PUC Chile
marenas@ing.puc.cl

Jorge Pérez
Department of Computer Science
Universidad de Chile
jperez@dcc.uchile.cl

Juan Reutter
School of Informatics
University of Edinburgh
juan.reutter@ed.ad.uk

ABSTRACT

In the traditional data exchange setting, source instances are restricted to be *complete* in the sense that every fact is either true or false in these instances. Although natural for a typical database translation scenario, this restriction is gradually becoming an impediment to the development of a wide range of applications that need to exchange objects that admit several interpretations. In particular, we are motivated by two specific applications that go beyond the usual data exchange scenario: exchanging *incomplete information* and exchanging *knowledge bases*.

In this paper, we propose a general framework for data exchange that can deal with these two applications. More specifically, we address the problem of exchanging information given by *representation systems*, which are essentially finite descriptions of (possibly infinite) sets of complete instances. We make use of the classical semantics of mappings specified by sets of logical sentences to give a meaningful semantics to the notion of exchanging representatives, from which the standard notions of solution, space of solutions, and universal solution naturally arise. We also introduce the notion of *strong representation system for a class of mappings*, that resembles the concept of strong representation system for a query language. We show the robustness of our proposal by applying it to the two applications mentioned above: exchanging incomplete information and exchanging knowledge bases, which are both instantiations of the exchanging problem for representation systems. We study these two applications in detail, presenting results regarding expressiveness, query answering and complexity of computing solutions, and also algorithms to materialize solutions.

Categories and Subject Descriptors

H.2.5 [**Heterogeneous Databases**]: Data translation

General Terms

Algorithms, Theory

Keywords

Data exchange, knowledge exchange, data integration, representation system, metadata management, schema mapping

1. INTRODUCTION

In the typical data exchange setting, one is given a source schema and a target schema, a schema mapping $\mathcal{M}$ that specifies the relationship between the source and the target, and an instance I of the source schema. The basic problem then is how to materialize an instance of the target schema that reflects the source data as accurately as possible [13]. In data exchange terms, the problem is how to materialize the *best solution* for I under $\mathcal{M}$.

In this traditional setting, source instances are restricted to be *complete*: every fact in them is either true or false. While natural in many scenarios, this restriction cannot capture a wide range of applications dealing with objects that admit several interpretations. We are motivated by two such applications: exchanging *incomplete information* and exchanging *knowledge bases*.

Exchanging Incomplete Information. Universal solutions have been proposed as the preferred solutions for data exchange. Given a source instance I and a schema mapping $\mathcal{M}$, a universal solution J is a target instance that represents, in a precise sense, all the possible solutions for I [13]. Even in the scenario in which mappings are specified by source-to-target tuple-generating dependencies (st-tgds), it has been noted that universal solutions need *null* values to correctly reflect the data in the source [13]. Thus, the preferred solutions in this scenario are *incomplete databases* [20]. But what if one needs to exchange data from these instances with null values? What is the semantics of data exchange in this case? This issue has been raised before by Afrati et al. in the context of query answering [2] and also by Fagin et al. in the context of metadata management [16]. But the problem is much wider, as it is not even clear what a *good translation* is for a source instance with null values, even in the most simplest data exchange settings. Just as an example of the questions that need to be answered, given a source instance with null values, is a target instance with null values enough to correctly represent the source information?

Exchanging Knowledge Bases. Nowadays several applications use knowledge bases to represent their data. A prototypical example is the Semantic Web, where repositories store information in the form of RDFS graphs [19] or OWL specifications [24]. In both cases, we have not only data but also *rules* that allow one to infer new data. Thus, in a data exchange application over the Semantic Web, one would naturally have as input a schema mapping and a source specification consisting of data together with some rules, and then one would like to create a target specification materializing data and creating new rules to correctly represent the knowledge in the source. But what does it mean for a target knowledge base to be a valid translation of a source knowledge base? Or, in data exchange terms, when does a target knowledge base can be considered a solution for a source knowledge base under a schema mapping? And more importantly, what constitutes a *good* solution for a source knowledge base? These questions motivate the development of a general *knowledge exchange* framework.

In this paper, we propose a general framework for data exchange that can deal with the above two applications. More specifically, we address the problem of exchanging information given by *represen-*

tation systems, which are essentially finite descriptions of (possibly infinite) sets of complete instances. We make use of the classical semantics of mappings specified by sets of logical sentences to give a meaningful semantics to the notion of exchanging representatives, thus not altering the usual semantics of schema mappings. From this, the standard notions of solution, space of solutions, and universal solution naturally arise. We also introduce the notion of *strong representation system for a class of mappings*, which resembles the concept of strong representation system for a query language [20, 17]. A strong representation system for a class $\mathcal{C}$ of mapping is, intuitively, a *closed system* in the sense that for every representative $\mathcal{I}$ in the system and mapping $\mathcal{M}$ in $\mathcal{C}$, the space of solutions of $\mathcal{I}$ under $\mathcal{M}$ can be represented in the same system.

As our first application, we study the exchange of incomplete information. One of the main issues when managing incomplete information is that most of its associated tasks, in particular query answering, are considerably harder than in the classical setting of complete data [20, 17]. Thus, it is challenging to find representation systems that are expressive enough to deserve investigation, while admitting efficient procedures for practical data exchange purposes.

In this paper, we study the representation system given by *positive conditional tables*, which are essentially conditional tables [20] that do not use negation. For positive conditional tables we show that, given a mapping specified by st-tgds, it is possible to materialize universal solutions and compute certain answers to unions of conjunctive queries in polynomial time, thus matching the complexity bounds of traditional data exchange. But more importantly, we show that positive conditional tables are expressive enough to form a strong representation system for the class of mappings specified by st-tgds. We prove that this result is optimal in the sense that the main features of positive conditional tables are needed to obtain a strong representation system for this class of mappings. Moreover, we prove that instances with null values, that have been widely used as a representation system in data exchange [13, 21, 2, 22, 16], do not form a strong representation system for the class of mappings specified by st-tgds, and thus, cannot correctly represent the space of solutions of a source instance with null values. Finally, we show that positive conditional instances can be used in schema mapping management to solve some fundamental and problematic issues that arise when combining the *composition* and *inverse* operators [7, 8].

We then apply our framework to knowledge bases. A knowledge base is composed of explicit data, in our context a relational database, plus implicit data given in the form of a set of logical sentences Σ. This set Σ states how to infer new data from the explicit data. The semantics of a knowledge base is given by its set of *models*, which are all the instances that contain the explicit data and satisfy Σ. In this sense, a knowledge base is also a representation system and, thus, can be studied in our general framework. In fact, by applying this framework we introduce the notion of *knowledge exchange*, which is the problem of materializing a target knowledge base that correctly represents the source information. We then study several issues including the complexity of recognizing knowledge-base solutions, the problem of characterizing when a knowledge base can be considered a *good* solution, and the problem of computing such knowledge-base solutions for mappings specified by full st-tgds (which are st-tgds that do not use existential quantification). Our results are a first step towards the development of a general framework for exchanging specifications that are more expressive than the usual database instances. In particular, this framework can be used in the exchange of RDFS graphs and OWL specifications, a problem becoming more and more important in Semantic Web applications.

We have structured the paper into three parts. We present some terminology and our general exchange framework for representation systems in Sections 2 and 3. In Sections 4, 5 and 6, we present our results regarding the exchange of incomplete information. Finally, in Sections 7 and 8, we introduce and study the problem of exchanging knowledge bases.

2. PRELIMINARIES

A *schema* $\mathbf{S}$ is a finite set $\{R_1, \ldots, R_k\}$ of relation symbols, with each R_i having a fixed arity $n_i \geq 0$. Let $\mathbf{D}$ be a countably infinite domain. An instance I of $\mathbf{S}$ assigns to each relation symbol R_i of $\mathbf{S}$ a finite relation $R_i^I \subseteq \mathbf{D}^{n_i}$. INST($\mathbf{S}$) denotes the set of all instances of $\mathbf{S}$. We denote by $\mathrm{dom}(I)$ the set of all elements that occur in any of the relations R_i^I. We say that $R_i(t)$ is a fact of I if $t \in R_i^I$. We sometimes denote an instance by its set of facts.

Given schemas $\mathbf{S}_1$ and $\mathbf{S}_2$, a *schema mapping* (or just *mapping*) from $\mathbf{S}_1$ to $\mathbf{S}_2$ is a subset of INST($\mathbf{S}_1$) × INST($\mathbf{S}_2$). We say that J is a *solution for I under $\mathcal{M}$* whenever $(I, J) \in \mathcal{M}$. The set of all solutions for I under $\mathcal{M}$ is denoted by $\mathrm{SOL}_{\mathcal{M}}(I)$. Let $\mathbf{S}_1$ and $\mathbf{S}_2$ be schemas with no relation symbols in common and Σ a set of first-order logic (FO) sentences over $\mathbf{S}_1 \cup \mathbf{S}_2$. A mapping $\mathcal{M}$ from $\mathbf{S}_1$ to $\mathbf{S}_2$ is *specified* by Σ, denoted by $\mathcal{M} = (\mathbf{S}_1, \mathbf{S}_2, \Sigma)$, if for every $(I, J) \in \mathrm{INST}(\mathbf{S}_1) \times \mathrm{INST}(\mathbf{S}_2)$, we have that $(I, J) \in \mathcal{M}$ if and only if (I, J) satisfies Σ. Notice that mappings are binary relations, and thus we can define the composition of mappings as for the composition of binary relations. Let $\mathcal{M}_{12}$ be a mapping from schema $\mathbf{S}_1$ to schema $\mathbf{S}_2$ and $\mathcal{M}_{23}$ a mapping from $\mathbf{S}_2$ to schema $\mathbf{S}_3$. Then $\mathcal{M}_{12} \circ \mathcal{M}_{23}$ is a mapping from $\mathbf{S}_1$ to $\mathbf{S}_3$ given by the set $\{(I, J) \in \mathrm{INST}(\mathbf{S}_1) \times \mathrm{INST}(\mathbf{S}_3) \mid$ there exists K such that $(I, K) \in \mathcal{M}_{12}$ and $(K, J) \in \mathcal{M}_{23}\}$ [14].

Dependencies: A relational atom over $\mathbf{S}$ is a formula of the form $R(\bar{x})$ with $R \in \mathbf{S}$ and $\bar{x}$ a tuple of (not necessarily distinct) variables. A tuple-generating dependency (tgd) over a schema $\mathbf{S}$ is a sentence of the form $\forall \bar{x} \forall \bar{y} (\varphi(\bar{x}, \bar{y}) \rightarrow \exists \bar{z}\, \psi(\bar{x}, \bar{z}))$, where $\varphi(\bar{x}, \bar{y})$ and $\psi(\bar{x}, \bar{z})$ are conjunctions of relational atoms over $\mathbf{S}$. The left-hand side of the implication in a tgd is called the premise, and the right-hand side the conclusion. A *full tgd* is a tgd with no existentially quantified variables in its conclusion. We usually omit the universal quantifier when writing tgds.

Given disjoint schemas $\mathbf{S}_1$ and $\mathbf{S}_2$, a *source-to-target tgd* (st-tgd) from $\mathbf{S}_1$ to $\mathbf{S}_2$ is a tgd in which the premise is a formula over $\mathbf{S}_1$ and the conclusion is a formula over $\mathbf{S}_2$. As for the case of full tgds, a full st-tgd is an st-tgd with no existentially quantified variables in its conclusion. In this paper, we assume that all sets of dependencies are finite.

Queries and certain answers: A k-ary query Q over a schema $\mathbf{S}$, with $k \geq 0$, is a function that maps every instance $I \in \mathrm{INST}(\mathbf{S})$ into a k-relation $Q(I) \subseteq \mathrm{dom}(I)^k$. In this paper, CQ is the class of conjunctive queries and UCQ is the class of unions of conjunctive queries. If we extend these classes by allowing equalities or inequalities, then we use superscripts $=$ and $\neq$, respectively. Thus, for example, $\mathrm{UCQ}^{\neq}$ is the class of union of conjunctive queries with inequalities. Let $\mathcal{M}$ be a mapping from a schema $\mathbf{S}_1$ to a schema $\mathbf{S}_2$, I an instance of $\mathbf{S}_1$ and Q a query over $\mathbf{S}_2$. Then $\mathrm{certain}_{\mathcal{M}}(Q, I)$ denotes the set of *certain answers* of Q over I under $\mathcal{M}$, that is, $\mathrm{certain}_{\mathcal{M}}(Q, I) = \bigcap_{J \in \mathrm{SOL}_{\mathcal{M}}(I)} Q(J)$.

3. SCHEMA MAPPINGS AND REPRESENTATION SYSTEMS

A (usual) database instance I is said to contain complete information as every fact $R(t)$ is either true or false in I. In that sense, there is a single possible interpretation of the information in I. On the other hand, in a database instance with incomplete information some values are unknown (which are usually represented by null values) and, hence, one is not certain about its content. In that sense, one has several possible interpretations for the information in such instances. In the same spirit, a knowledge base usually has several models, which represent different ways to interpret the rules or axioms in the knowledge base. In this section, we present the notion of *representation system* [20, 3], which is a general way to deal with objects that admit different interpretations, and then we show how to extend a schema mapping to deal with representation systems. This extension is fundamental for our study as it allows us to extend, in a simple and natural way, the data exchange framework proposed by Fagin et al. [13] to the case of database instances with incomplete information as well as to the case of knowledge bases.

3.1 Exchanging information given by representation systems

A *representation system* is composed of a set $\mathbf{W}$ of *representatives* and a function rep that assigns a set of instances to every element in $\mathbf{W}$. We assume that every representation system $(\mathbf{W}, \text{rep})$ is uniform in the sense that for every $\mathcal{W} \in \mathbf{W}$, there exists a relational schema $\mathbf{S}$, that is called the type of $\mathcal{W}$, such that $\text{rep}(\mathcal{W}) \subseteq \text{INST}(\mathbf{S})$ [20]. Representation systems are used to describe sets of possible interpretations in a succinct way. Typical examples of representation systems are Codd tables, naive tables, conditional tables [20], and world-set decompositions [3].

Assume that $\mathcal{M}$ is a mapping from a schema $\mathbf{S}_1$ to a schema $\mathbf{S}_2$. Given a set $\mathcal{X}$ of instances of $\mathbf{S}_1$, define $\text{SOL}_{\mathcal{M}}(\mathcal{X})$ as $\bigcup_{I \in \mathcal{X}} \text{SOL}_{\mathcal{M}}(I)$. That is, $\text{SOL}_{\mathcal{M}}(\mathcal{X})$ is the set of possible solutions for the instances in $\mathcal{X}$. In the following definition, we use $\text{SOL}_{\mathcal{M}}(\cdot)$ to extend the notion of solution to the case of representation systems.

Definition 3.1 *Let* $\mathcal{R} = (\mathbf{W}, \text{rep})$ *be a representation system,* $\mathcal{M}$ *a mapping from a schema* $\mathbf{S}_1$ *to a schema* $\mathbf{S}_2$ *and* $\mathcal{V}, \mathcal{W}$ *elements of* $\mathbf{W}$ *of types* $\mathbf{S}_1$ *and* $\mathbf{S}_2$*, respectively. Then* $\mathcal{W}$ *is an* $\mathcal{R}$-solution *for* $\mathcal{V}$ *under* $\mathcal{M}$ *if* $\text{rep}(\mathcal{W}) \subseteq \text{SOL}_{\mathcal{M}}(\text{rep}(\mathcal{V}))$.

In other words, given a representation system $\mathcal{R} = (\mathbf{W}, \text{rep})$ and $\mathcal{V}, \mathcal{W} \in \mathbf{W}$, it holds that $\mathcal{W}$ is an $\mathcal{R}$-solution for $\mathcal{V}$ under a mapping $\mathcal{M}$ if for every $J \in \text{rep}(\mathcal{W})$, there exists $I \in \text{rep}(\mathcal{V})$ such that $(I, J) \in \mathcal{M}$.

Assume given a representation system $\mathcal{R} = (\mathbf{W}, \text{rep})$ and a mapping $\mathcal{M}$. An element of $\mathbf{W}$ can have a large number of $\mathcal{R}$-solutions under $\mathcal{M}$, even an infinite number in some cases, and, thus, it is natural to ask what is a *good* solution for this element under $\mathcal{M}$. Next we introduce the notion of universal $\mathcal{R}$-solution, which is a simple extension of the concept of $\mathcal{R}$-solution introduced in Definition 3.1.

Definition 3.2 *Let* $\mathcal{R} = (\mathbf{W}, \text{rep})$ *be a representation system,* $\mathcal{M}$ *a mapping from a schema* $\mathbf{S}_1$ *to a schema* $\mathbf{S}_2$ *and* $\mathcal{V}, \mathcal{W}$ *elements of* $\mathbf{W}$ *of types* $\mathbf{S}_1$ *and* $\mathbf{S}_2$*, respectively. Then* $\mathcal{W}$ *is a* universal $\mathcal{R}$-solution *for* $\mathcal{V}$ *under* $\mathcal{M}$ *if* $\text{rep}(\mathcal{W}) = \text{SOL}_{\mathcal{M}}(\text{rep}(\mathcal{V}))$.

This new notion captures the intuition of exactly representing the space of possible solutions of the interpretations of an element of a representation system.

3.2 Strong representation systems for a class of mappings

The classical work on incomplete databases [20] defines the notion of *strong representation system* for a class of queries. In fact, the classical result in [20] about these systems states that conditional tables are a strong representation system for relational al-

gebra. In our context, we are interested in defining the notion of strong representation system for a class of mappings.

Definition 3.3 *Let* $\mathcal{C}$ *be a class of mappings and* $(\mathbf{W}, \text{rep})$ *a representation system. Then* $(\mathbf{W}, \text{rep})$ *is a* strong representation system *for* $\mathcal{C}$ *if for every mapping* $\mathcal{M} \in \mathcal{C}$ *from a schema* $\mathbf{S}_1$ *to a schema* $\mathbf{S}_2$*, and for every* $\mathcal{U} \in \mathbf{W}$ *of type* $\mathbf{S}_1$*, there exists* $\mathcal{W} \in \mathbf{W}$ *of type* $\mathbf{S}_2$ *such that* $\text{rep}(\mathcal{W}) = \text{SOL}_{\mathcal{M}}(\text{rep}(\mathcal{U}))$.

In other words, a representation system $\mathcal{R} = (\mathbf{W}, \text{rep})$ is a strong representation system for a class of mappings $\mathcal{C}$ if for every mapping $\mathcal{M} \in \mathcal{C}$ from a schema $\mathbf{S}_1$ to a schema $\mathbf{S}_2$, and for every $\mathcal{U} \in \mathbf{W}$ of type $\mathbf{S}_1$, a universal $\mathcal{R}$-solution for $\mathcal{U}$ under $\mathcal{M}$ can be represented in the same system (it is an element of $\mathbf{W}$). Notice that if $\mathcal{C}$ allows for mappings in which no solution exist for some of their instances, then any strong representation system for $\mathcal{C}$ must be able to represent the *empty* set of instances.

4. STRONG REPRESENTATION SYSTEMS FOR ST-TGDS

As pointed out before, one of the goals of this paper is to study the problem of exchanging databases with incomplete information. To this end, we first borrowed from [20, 3] the notion of representation system, which gives us a way to represent databases with incomplete information, and then we introduced the notion of strong representation system for a class of mappings, which essentially tell us that a particular way of representing databases with incomplete information is appropriate for a class of mappings. In this section, we apply these concepts to the widely used class of mappings specified by st-tgds and, in particular, we answer the question of what is a good representation system for this class. Notice that our mappings only contain instances with complete information. Thus, as opposed to previous work [13, 21, 16], we make a clear distinction between instances participating in a mapping and incomplete instances that are used as representatives for spaces of solutions.

The starting points for our study are naive tables, which are widely used in the data exchange context [13, 21, 16], and conditional tables, which are known to be an expressive way to represent databases with incomplete information [20]. In Section 4.1, we define the representation systems based on these two types of tables, together with a representation system based on *positive* conditional tables, a fragment of conditional tables proposed in this paper. In Section 4.2, we show that both conditional tables and positive conditional tables form strong representation systems for the class of mappings given by st-tgds, and we also show that naive tables are not expressive enough to form such a system. Finally, in Section 4.3, we give strong evidence that positive conditional tables are the right representation system for the class of mappings specified by st-tgds, by proving that the main features in these instances are needed to obtain a strong representation system for this class.

4.1 Naive and conditional instances

Our database instances are constructed by using elements of a countably infinite set $\mathbf{D}$. To represent incomplete information we assume the existence of a countably infinite set $\mathbf{N}$ of *labeled nulls*, disjoint with $\mathbf{D}$. To differentiate from nulls we call *constant values* the elements in $\mathbf{D}$. Fix a relational schema $\mathbf{S}$ for this section. Then a *naive instance* $\mathcal{I}$ of $\mathbf{S}$ assigns to each relation symbol $R \in \mathbf{S}$ of arity k, a finite k-ary relation $R^{\mathcal{I}} \subseteq (\mathbf{D} \cup \mathbf{N})^k$, that is, a k-ary relation including constants and null values. A *conditional instance* extends the notion of naive instance with a *local* condition attached to each fact. More precisely, an *element-condition* is a positive Boolean combination (only connectives $\wedge$ and $\vee$ are allowed) of formulas of the form $x = y$ and $x \neq y$, with $x \in \mathbf{N}$ and $y \in (\mathbf{D} \cup$

N). Then a conditional instance $\mathcal{I}$ of $\mathbf{S}$ assigns to each relation symbol R of arity k, a pair $(R^{\mathcal{I}}, \rho_R^{\mathcal{I}})$, where $R^{\mathcal{I}} \subseteq (\mathbf{D} \cup \mathbf{N})^k$ and $\rho_R^{\mathcal{I}}$ is a function that associates to each tuple $t \in R^{\mathcal{I}}$ an element-condition $\rho_R^{\mathcal{I}}(t)$ (the local condition of the fact $R(t)$ [20]).

To define the sets of interpretations associated to naive and conditional instances, we need to introduce some terminology. Given a naive or conditional instance $\mathcal{I}$, define nulls($\mathcal{I}$) as the set of nulls mentioned in $\mathcal{I}$ (if $\mathcal{I}$ is a conditional instance, nulls($\mathcal{I}$) also includes the nulls mentioned in the local conditions of $\mathcal{I}$). Moreover, given a null substitution $\nu : \text{nulls}(\mathcal{I}) \to \mathbf{D}$, define $\nu(R^{\mathcal{I}}) = \{\nu(t) \mid t \in R^{\mathcal{I}}\}$, where $\nu(t)$ is obtained by replacing every null n in t by its image $\nu(n)$. Then for every naive instance $\mathcal{I}$, and slightly abusing notation, define the set of representatives of $\mathcal{I}$, denoted by $\text{rep}_{\text{naive}}(\mathcal{I})$, as:

$$\{I \in \text{INST}(\mathbf{S}) \mid \text{there exists } \nu : \text{nulls}(\mathcal{I}) \to \mathbf{D}$$
$$\text{such that for every } R \in \mathbf{S}, \text{ it holds that } \nu(R^{\mathcal{I}}) \subseteq R^I\}$$

Moreover, for every conditional instance $\mathcal{I}$, define the set of representatives of $\mathcal{I}$, denoted by $\text{rep}_{\text{cond}}(\mathcal{I})$, as follows. Given an element-condition φ and a null substitution $\nu : V \to \mathbf{D}$, where V is a set of nulls that contains every null value mentioned in φ, notation $\nu \models \varphi$ is used to indicate that ν satisfies φ in the usual sense. Moreover, given a null substitution $\nu : \text{nulls}(\mathcal{I}) \to \mathbf{D}$ and $R \in \mathbf{S}$, define $\nu(R^{\mathcal{I}}, \rho_R^{\mathcal{I}})$ as $\{\nu(t) \mid t \in R^{\mathcal{I}} \text{ and } \nu \models \rho_R^{\mathcal{I}}(t)\}$. Then $\text{rep}_{\text{cond}}(\mathcal{I})$ is the following set of instances:

$$\{I \in \text{INST}(\mathbf{S}) \mid \text{there exists } \nu : \text{nulls}(\mathcal{I}) \to \mathbf{D}$$
$$\text{such that for every } R \in \mathbf{S}, \text{ it holds that } \nu(R^{\mathcal{I}}, \rho_R^{\mathcal{I}}) \subseteq R^I\}.$$

We use $\text{rep}_{\text{naive}}$ and rep_{cond} to define two fundamental representation systems. Assume that $\mathbf{W}_{\text{naive}}$ and $\mathbf{W}_{\text{cond}}$ are the set of all possible naive instances and conditional instances (over all possible relational schemas), respectively. Then $\mathcal{R}_{\text{naive}} = (\mathbf{W}_{\text{naive}}, \text{rep}_{\text{naive}})$ and $\mathcal{R}_{\text{cond}} = (\mathbf{W}_{\text{cond}}, \text{rep}_{\text{cond}})$ are representation systems.

We conclude this section by introducing a fragment of the class of conditional instances that will be extensively used in this paper. We say that an element-condition is *positive* if it does not mention any formula of the form $x \neq y$. Then a conditional instance $\mathcal{I}$ of $\mathbf{S}$ is said to be positive if for every $R \in \mathbf{S}$ and $t \in R^{\mathcal{I}}$, it holds that $\rho_R^{\mathcal{I}}(t)$ is a positive element-condition. We denote by $\mathbf{W}_{\text{pos}}$ the set of all positive conditional instances, by rep_{pos} the restriction of function rep_{cond} to the class of positive conditional instances, and by $\mathcal{R}_{\text{pos}}$ the representation system $(\mathbf{W}_{\text{pos}}, \text{rep}_{\text{pos}})$. When it is clear from the context, we just use rep instead of $\text{rep}_{\text{naive}}$, rep_{cond} or rep_{pos}.

4.2 Building a strong representation system for st-tgds

Fagin et al. showed in [13] that for the class of mappings specified by st-tgds, naive instances are enough to represent the space of solutions of any complete database. More precisely, assuming that $\mathcal{M} = (\mathbf{S}_1, \mathbf{S}_2, \Sigma_{12})$, where Σ_{12} is a set of st-tgds, we have that for every instance I_1 of $\mathbf{S}_1$, there exists a naive instance $\mathcal{I}_2$ of $\mathbf{S}_2$ such that $\text{rep}(\mathcal{I}_2) = \text{SOL}_{\mathcal{M}}(I_1)$. Thus, given that the target data generated by a mapping can be used as the source data in other mappings, it is natural to ask whether the same result holds when naive instances are considered as source instances. That is, it is natural to ask whether for every mapping $\mathcal{M}$ specified by a set of st-tgds and for every source naive instance $\mathcal{I}_1$, there exists a target naive instance $\mathcal{I}_2$ such that $\text{rep}(\mathcal{I}_2) = \text{SOL}_{\mathcal{M}}(\text{rep}(\mathcal{I}_1))$. Unfortunately, the following example shows that it is not the case.

Example 4.1. Let $\mathbf{S}_1 = \{P(\cdot, \cdot)\}$, $\mathbf{S}_2 = \{T(\cdot), R(\cdot, \cdot)\}$ and Σ_{12} a

set consisting of the following st-tgds:

$$P(x, y) \rightarrow R(x, y),$$
$$P(x, x) \rightarrow T(x).$$

Moreover, let $\mathcal{I}$ be a naive instance of $\mathbf{S}_1$ such that $P^{\mathcal{I}} = \{(n, a)\}$, where n is a null value and a is a constant. It is not difficult to prove that if $\mathcal{J}$ is a naive instance of $\mathbf{S}_2$, then $\text{rep}(\mathcal{J}) \neq \text{SOL}_{\mathcal{M}}(\text{rep}(\mathcal{I}))$. The reason for this is that a naive instance cannot represent the fact that if n is given value a in some representative of $\mathcal{I}$, then $T(a)$ holds in every solution for that representative. $\square$

From the previous example, we conclude that:

Proposition 4.2 *Naive instances do not form a strong representation system for the class of mappings specified by st-tgds.*

What should be added to naive instances to obtain a strong representation system for the class of mapping given by st-tgds? A natural candidate are the local conditions presented in Section 4.1, as shown in the following example. In this example, and in the rest of the paper, we assume that $\top$ is an arbitrary element-condition that always holds (for example, $n = n$ with $n \in \mathbf{N}$).

Example 4.3. Let $\mathcal{M}$ and $\mathcal{I}$ be as in Example 4.1, and $\mathcal{J}$ be a conditional instance that contains the following facts and conditions in the relations R and T:

$$R(n, a) \quad \top$$
$$T(n) \quad n = a$$

Then it can be proved that $\text{rep}(\mathcal{J}) = \text{SOL}_{\mathcal{M}}(\text{rep}(\mathcal{I}))$. $\square$

In the previous example, we use only positive element-conditions to represent the space of solutions of the source naive instance. Thus, it is natural to ask whether this is a general phenomenon, or whether one needs to consider non-positive element-conditions of the form $x \neq y$ to find a strong representation system for the class of mappings specified by st-tgds. In the following theorem, we prove that positive conditions are indeed enough.

Theorem 4.4 *Positive conditional instances form a strong representation system for the class of mappings specified by st-tgds.*

We conclude this section by showing that conditional instances also form a strong representation system for the class of mappings specified by st-tgds, thus giving us an alternative system to deal with incomplete information in schema mappings.

Theorem 4.5 *Conditional instances form a strong representation system for the class of mappings specified by st-tgds.*

4.3 Positive conditional instances are the needed fragment

In the previous section, we show that both conditional instances and positive conditional instances form strong representation systems for the class of mappings specified by st-tgds. Given these alternatives, it is natural to ask whether there exist other possible strong representation systems for this class of mappings and which one could be considered as the *right* system for this class. In this section, we give strong evidence that positive conditional instances are the right representation system for mappings specified by st-tgds, by proving that the main features in these instances are needed to obtain a strong representation system for this class of mappings.

In a positive conditional instance, a local condition is attached to each fact. The distinctive features of these local conditions are the use of disjunction, equalities of the form $n_1 = n_2$, with $n_1, n_2 \in \mathbf{N}$, and equalities of the form $n = c$, with $n \in \mathbf{N}$ and $c \in \mathbf{D}$. In this section, we show that if one removes any of these features and keeps the other two, then the resulting representation system does not form a strong representation system for the class of mappings specified by st-tgds. More precisely, given a positive conditional instance $\mathcal{I}$ of a relational schema $\mathbf{S}$, we say that $\mathcal{I}$ is null-comparison free if no local condition in $\mathcal{I}$ mentions a formula of the form $n_1 = n_2$ with $n_1, n_2 \in \mathbf{N}$, and we say that $\mathcal{I}$ is null-constant-comparison free if no local condition in $\mathcal{I}$ mentions a formula of the form $n = c$ with $n \in \mathbf{N}$ and $c \in \mathbf{D}$. Moreover, we say that $\mathcal{I}$ is disjunction free if for every $R \in \mathbf{S}$ and $t \in R^{\mathcal{I}}$, it holds that $\rho_R^{\mathcal{I}}(t)$ does not mention Boolean connective $\vee$.

Theorem 4.6 *None of the following form a strong representation system for the class of mappings specified by st-tgds: (1) null-comparison free positive conditional instances, (2) null-constant-comparison free positive conditional instances and (3) disjunction free positive conditional instances.*

5. DATA EXCHANGE WITH POSITIVE CONDITIONAL INSTANCES

In the data exchange setting, one is given a mapping $\mathcal{M}$ from a source schema to a target schema and a source instance I, and the goal is to materialize a solution J for I under $\mathcal{M}$. This setting has been widely studied in the literature, where many important problems have been addressed in order to develop data exchange tools. In this section, we focus on three of the most important tasks in data exchange: materializing solutions, computing certain answers to target queries, and checking whether a target instance is a solution for a source instance under a mapping [13], and show how these tasks are performed in the presence of positive conditional instances. In particular, we prove that the fundamental problems of materializing solutions and computing certain answers to target queries can be solved efficiently in this extended data exchange scenario, thus showing that positive conditional instances not only allow a uniform way of dealing with the exchange of incomplete information, but also that they can be used in practice.

5.1 Materializing solutions

The most important problem in data exchange is the problem of materializing a *good* solution for a given source instance. For mappings specified with st-tgds, these are the *universal solutions*. Polynomial-time algorithms have been developed to compute these solutions [13], which have allowed the construction of practical data exchange tools. In the context of a representation system $\mathcal{R}$, universal $\mathcal{R}$-solutions are the preferred option as they are able to exactly represent the spaces of solutions of the source data. Thus, to show that positive conditional instances can be used in practice, one needs to develop an efficient algorithm for computing universal $\mathcal{R}_{\text{pos}}$-solutions. In the following theorem, we show that such an algorithms exists.

Theorem 5.1 *Let $\mathcal{M} = (\mathbf{S}_1, \mathbf{S}_2, \Sigma_{12})$, where Σ_{12} is a set of st-tgds. Then there exists a polynomial-time algorithm that, given a positive conditional instance $\mathcal{I}$ of $\mathbf{S}_1$, computes a universal $\mathcal{R}_{pos}$-solution for $\mathcal{I}$ under $\mathcal{M}$.*

It is important to notice that in the previous result the set of st-tgds defining a schema mapping is assumed to be fixed. This is the usual assumption when studying the complexity of materializing solutions in data exchange [13].

The algorithm in Theorem 5.1 is based on the *chase* procedure, as usual in data exchange [13]. In particular, our procedure is based on the chase algorithms presented in [17], and is similar to the one recently proposed in [18]. Notice that, as shown in Section 4.2, the straightforward application of the chase may not deliver the expected result, as naive instances do not form a strong representation

system for the class of mappings specified by st-tgds. Thus, one needs to modify the chase procedure to take into consideration the element-conditions in positive conditional instances. In particular, one has to consider that some relationships between null values can fire the application of a dependency, and one has to make explicit these relationships in the generated tuples by using new element-conditions. Due to the lack of space, we do not present this chase procedure in detail but show the basic ideas behind our algorithm in the following example.

Example 5.2. Let $\mathbf{S}_1 = \{P(\cdot, \cdot), R(\cdot, \cdot)\}$, $\mathbf{S}_2 = \{S(\cdot, \cdot), T(\cdot)\}$ and Σ_{12} a set consisting of the following st-tgds:

$$
\begin{aligned}
P(x, y) &\rightarrow S(x, y), \\
R(x, x) &\rightarrow T(x).
\end{aligned}
$$

Moreover, let $\mathcal{I}$ be a positive conditional instance given by:

$$
\begin{array}{ll}
P(n_1, n_2) & \top \\
R(n_1, n_2) & (n_1 = a),
\end{array}
$$

where n_1 and n_2 are null values and a is a constant. To create a universal $\mathcal{R}_{\text{pos}}$-solution $\mathcal{J}$, the procedure works as follows. For the first dependency, it works as the classical chase, that is, it adds tuple (n_1, n_2) to $S^{\mathcal{J}}$ with $\top$ as local condition. For the second dependency, the procedure considers that this dependency should be fired when condition $n_1 = n_2$ holds. In this case, the procedure also needs to carry along the element-condition $n_1 = a$. Thus, it adds the tuple (n_1) to $T^{\mathcal{J}}$, but this time the local condition consists of the conjunction of $(n_1 = a)$ with $(n_1 = n_2)$. Summing up, the following instance is constructed:

$$
\begin{array}{ll}
S(n_1, n_2) & \top \\
T(n_1) & (n_1 = a) \wedge (n_1 = n_2)
\end{array}
$$

It can be shown that this instance is a universal $\mathcal{R}_{\text{pos}}$-solution for $\mathcal{I}$ under $\mathcal{M}$. $\square$

5.2 Computing certain answers

A second fundamental problem in data exchange is the task of computing certain answers to target queries. In our context, this problem is defined as follows. Given a positive conditional instance $\mathcal{I}$ of a schema $\mathbf{S}$ and a query Q over $\mathbf{S}$, define $Q(\mathcal{I})$ as $\bigcap_{I \in \text{rep}(\mathcal{I})} Q(I)$. Moreover, given a mapping $\mathcal{M}$ from a schema $\mathbf{S}_1$ to a schema $\mathbf{S}_2$, a positive conditional instance $\mathcal{I}$ of $\mathbf{S}_1$ and a query Q over $\mathbf{S}_2$, the set of certain answers of Q over $\mathcal{I}$ under $\mathcal{M}$, denoted by $\text{certain}_{\mathcal{M}}(Q, \mathcal{I})$, is defined as:

$$
\bigcap_{\mathcal{J} \, : \, \mathcal{J} \text{ is an } \mathcal{R}_{\text{pos}}\text{-solution for } \mathcal{I} \text{ under } \mathcal{M}} Q(\mathcal{J}).
$$

It should be noticed that this definition of certain answers, in the presence of an incomplete source instance $\mathcal{I}$, coincides with the definition in [2] for the case of naive instances (which is the representation system used in [2]).

Given a data exchange setting $\mathcal{M}$ from a schema $\mathbf{S}_1$ to a schema $\mathbf{S}_2$, and a k-ary query Q over $\mathbf{S}_2$, we consider in this section the following decision problem:

Problem:	CERTAINANSWERS($\mathcal{M}, Q$)
Input:	A positive conditional instance $\mathcal{I}$ of $\mathbf{S}_1$ and a k-tuple t of elements from $\mathbf{D}$.
Question:	Does t belong to $\text{certain}_{\mathcal{M}}(Q, \mathcal{I})$?

In the previous problem, we assume that the data exchange setting $\mathcal{M}$ and the query Q are fixed. Thus, we are interested in the data complexity of the problem of computing certain answers.

It was proved in [13] that for the class of mappings specified by st-tgds, each universal solution of an instance I can be directly used to compute the certain answers of any unions of conjunctive queries. In the following proposition, we show that this result can be extended to any query if one considers universal $\mathcal{R}_{pos}$-solutions.

Proposition 5.3 *Let* $\mathcal{M} = (\mathbf{S}_1, \mathbf{S}_2, \Sigma_{12})$, *where* Σ_{12} *is a set of st-tgds,* $\mathcal{I}$ *a positive conditional instance of* $\mathbf{S}_1$ *and* Q *an arbitrary query over* $\mathbf{S}_2$. *Then for every universal* $\mathcal{R}_{pos}$-*solution* $\mathcal{J}$ *for* $\mathcal{I}$ *under* $\mathcal{M}$, *it holds that* $\text{certain}_{\mathcal{M}}(Q, \mathcal{I}) = Q(\mathcal{J})$.

In Theorem 5.1, we showed that if a mapping $\mathcal{M}$ is specified by a set of st-tgds, then there exists a polynomial time algorithm that, given a source instance $\mathcal{I}$, computes a universal $\mathcal{R}_{pos}$-solution $\mathcal{J}$ for $\mathcal{I}$ under $\mathcal{M}$. Moreover, from the results in [17], it is possible to conclude that for every unions of conjunctive queries Q, there exists a polynomial time algorithm that, given a positive conditional instance $\mathcal{I}$, computes $Q(\mathcal{I})$. From these results, we conclude that:

Theorem 5.4 *Let* $\mathcal{M} = (\mathbf{S}_1, \mathbf{S}_2, \Sigma_{12})$, *where* Σ_{12} *is a set of st-tgds, and* Q *be a union of conjunctive queries over* $\mathbf{S}_2$. *Then* $\text{CERTAINANSWERS}(\mathcal{M}, Q)$ *can be solved in polynomial time.*

This result matches the upper bound in [13] for the problem of computing certain answers to a union of conjunctive queries in a usual data exchange setting, thus giving more evidence that positive conditional instances can be used in practical data exchange tools.

We conclude this section by pointing out that Fagin et al. also showed in [13] that the above polynomial-time upper bound holds if one considers unions of conjunctive queries with at most one inequality per disjunct. Here we show the corresponding result for our framework, which is proved by a nontrivial extension of the techniques in [13] for the case of positive conditional instances.

Theorem 5.5 *Let* $\mathcal{M} = (\mathbf{S}_1, \mathbf{S}_2, \Sigma_{12})$, *where* Σ_{12} *is a set of st-tgds, and* Q *be a union of conjunctive queries over* $\mathbf{S}_2$ *with at most one inequality per disjunct. Then* $\text{CERTAINANSWERS}(\mathcal{M}, Q)$ *can be solved in polynomial time.*

5.3 Complexity of recognizing solutions

Let $\mathcal{M}$ be a mapping from $\mathbf{S}_1$ to $\mathbf{S}_2$, and $\mathcal{R} = (\mathbf{W}, \text{rep})$ a representation system. In this section, we study the complexity of verifying, given a pair $(\mathcal{U}, \mathcal{W})$ of representatives, whether $\mathcal{W}$ is an $\mathcal{R}$-solution of $\mathcal{U}$ under a mapping $\mathcal{M}$. That is, we consider the following decision problem:

Problem:	$\text{CHECKSOLUTION}(\mathcal{M}, \mathcal{R})$
Input:	A pair of representatives $\mathcal{U}, \mathcal{W} \in \mathbf{W}$ of types $\mathbf{S}_1$ and $\mathbf{S}_2$, respectively.
Question:	Is $\mathcal{W}$ an $\mathcal{R}$-solution for $\mathcal{U}$ under $\mathcal{M}$?

In a traditional data exchange setting, deciding whether an instance J is a solution for I under a fixed mapping $\mathcal{M} = (\mathbf{S}_1, \mathbf{S}_2, \Sigma_{12})$ can be solved by checking if $(I, J) \models \Sigma_{12}$, which gives a straightforward polynomial-time procedure when Σ_{12} is a set of FO sentences. For the case of naive, positive conditional and conditional instances, this problem becomes more interesting. Our first result shows that the complexity for positive conditional instances is no more than for naive instances, in both cases NP.

Theorem 5.6 *Let* $\mathcal{M} = (\mathbf{S}_1, \mathbf{S}_2, \Sigma_{12})$, *where* Σ_{12} *is a set of st-tgds. Then* $\text{CHECKSOLUTION}(\mathcal{M}, \mathcal{R}_{naive})$ *and* $\text{CHECKSOLUTION}(\mathcal{M}, \mathcal{R}_{pos})$ *are both NP-complete.*

The following theorem shows that the complexity of the problem is higher for conditional instances. This gives evidence in favor of using positive conditional instances instead of conditional instances as a representation system for st-tgds.

Theorem 5.7 *Let* $\mathcal{M} = (\mathbf{S}_1, \mathbf{S}_2, \Sigma_{12})$, *where* Σ_{12} *is a set of st-tgds. Then* $\text{CHECKSOLUTION}(\mathcal{M}, \mathcal{R}_{cond})$ *is* Π_2^P-*complete.*

It should be noticed that this result cannot be directly obtained from [1], since in that paper conditional instances allow *global conditions* that we do not consider in this paper.

6. METADATA MANAGEMENT WITH POSITIVE CONDITIONAL INSTANCES

In the previous sections, we have presented a number of results that give evidence that positive conditional instances are appropriate for data exchange purposes. In this section, we give a step forward in this direction, and show that they are also appropriate for metadata management purposes.

In the data exchange setting proposed by Fagin et al in [13] two types of schemas are considered: source and target schemas. In the former, only the usual instances with complete information are allowed, while in the latter naive instances are also considered. This setting has played a key role in the study and development of schema mapping operators, which are of fundamental importance in metadata management [7, 8].

Two of the most fundamental operations in metadata management are the *composition* and *inversion* of schema mappings. The problem of composing schema mappings was solved in [14] for the class of mappings specified by st-tgds. More precisely, Fagin et al. proposed in [14] the language of SO tgds (see Section 6.1 for a formal definition of this language), and showed that it is the *minimal* class of mappings capable of expressing the composition of mappings specified by st-tgds [14]. On the other hand, the definition of an inverse operator has turned out to be a very difficult problem, and even the definition of a *good* semantics for this operator has been the main topic of several papers in the area [12, 15, 6, 16, 5]. Furthermore, people have also realized that the composition and inverse operators have to be used together in many metadata management tasks, such as schema evolution [8]. This has brought more complexity into the picture, as the combined use of the composition and inverse operators requires that the target data generated by a mapping could be used by other mappings as the source data. This was recognized by Fagin et al. in [16], where the notion of inversion proposed in [6] was extended to deal with source naive instances. Nevertheless, even though the language of SO tgds has proved to be the right language for composing mappings specified by st-tgds, none of the proposed inverse operators has been properly assembled with the language of SO tgds. Indeed, SO tgds do not always admit an inverse under the notions of inversion defined in [12, 15, 6, 5], and it is not clear whether the notion of inversion introduced in [16] is appropriate for the language of SO tgds.

Why does the problem of combining the composition and inverse operators seem to be so difficult? We give strong evidence here that the reason is that naive instances are not expressive enough to deal with the spaces of solutions of SO tgds. But, most significantly, we show here that positive conditional instances can be used to overcome this limitation, as we prove that they form a strong representation system for the class of mappings given by SO tgds, and that SO tgds admit an inverse under the notion proposed in [6], if positive conditional instances are allowed in source and target schemas. It remains an open problem to show whether this inverse can always be specified with an SO tgd or not.

6.1 Positive conditional instances form a strong representation system for SO-tgds

A fundamental tool in the study of the composition of schema mappings is the language of second-order st-tgds (SO tgds [14]), that we define next. Given schemas $\mathbf{S}_1$ and $\mathbf{S}_2$, an SO tgd from $\mathbf{S}_1$ to $\mathbf{S}_2$ is a second-order formula of the form:

$$\exists f_1 \cdots \exists f_\ell \left(\forall \bar{x}_1(\varphi_1 \to \psi_1) \wedge \cdots \wedge \forall \bar{x}_n(\varphi_n \to \psi_n) \right),$$

where (1) each f_i is a function symbol, (2) each φ_i is a conjunction of relational atomic formulas of $\mathbf{S}_1$ and equality atoms of the form $t = t'$, where t and t' are terms built from $\bar{x}_i$ and $f_1, \ldots, f_\ell$, (3) each ψ_i is a conjunction of relational atomic formulas of $\mathbf{S}_2$ mentioning terms built from $\bar{x}_i$ and $f_1, \ldots, f_\ell$, and (4) each variable in $\bar{x}_i$ appears in some relational atomic formula of φ_i. For example, the following is an SO tgd:

$$\exists f \left(\forall x \left(E(x) \to R(x, f(x)) \right) \wedge \right.$$
$$\left. \forall x \left(E(x) \wedge x = f(x) \to T(x) \right) \right). \quad (1)$$

A mapping $\mathcal{M}$ from a schema $\mathbf{S}_1$ to a schema $\mathbf{S}_2$ is said to be specified by an SO tgd σ_{12} from $\mathbf{S}_1$ to $\mathbf{S}_2$ *, denoted by $\mathcal{M} = (\mathbf{S}_1, \mathbf{S}_2, \sigma_{12})$, if for every pair of instances I_1, I_2 of $\mathbf{S}_1$ and $\mathbf{S}_2$, respectively, it holds that $(I_1, I_2) \in \mathcal{M}$ if and only if (I_1, I_2) satisfies σ_{12} in the usual second-order logic sense (see [14] for a precise definition of the semantics of SO tgds).

As our first result, we show that one can efficiently materialize positive conditional instances for a mapping given by an SO tgd.

Theorem 6.1 *Let* $\mathcal{M} = (\mathbf{S}_1, \mathbf{S}_2, \sigma_{12})$, *where* σ_{12} *is an SO tgd. Then there exists a polynomial-time algorithm, that given a positive conditional instance* $\mathcal{I}$ *of* $\mathbf{S}_1$, *computes a universal* $\mathcal{R}_{pos}$-*solution for* $\mathcal{I}$ *under* $\mathcal{M}$.

As a corollary, we obtain that positive conditional instances are appropriate for representing the spaces of solutions of SO tgds.

Corollary 6.2 *Positive conditional instances form a strong representation system for the class of mappings specified by SO tgds.*

An important remark about the previous results is that they follow directly from the fact that positive conditional instances form a strong representation system for the class of mappings specified by st-tgds (see Theorems 4.4 and 5.1), and the fact that for every mapping $\mathcal{M} = (\mathbf{S}_1, \mathbf{S}_2, \sigma_{12})$, where σ_{12} is an SO tgd, there exists a finite sequence of mappings $\mathcal{M}_1, \ldots, \mathcal{M}_k$, each specified by a set of st-tgds, such that $\mathcal{M} = \mathcal{M}_1 \circ \cdots \circ \mathcal{M}_k$ [14]. Indeed, in order to obtain a universal $\mathcal{R}_{pos}$-solution for a positive conditional instance $\mathcal{I}$ under $\mathcal{M}$, one can use the techniques described in Section 5 to construct a sequence $\mathcal{I}_1, \ldots, \mathcal{I}_k$ of positive conditional instances such that: (1) $\mathcal{I}_1$ is a universal $\mathcal{R}_{pos}$-solution for $\mathcal{I}$ under $\mathcal{M}_1$ and (2) $\mathcal{I}_i$ is a universal $\mathcal{R}_{pos}$-solution for $\mathcal{I}_{i-1}$ under $\mathcal{M}_i$, for every $i \in \{2, \ldots, k\}$. In this case one concludes that $\mathcal{I}_k$ is a universal $\mathcal{R}_{pos}$-solution for $\mathcal{I}$ under $\mathcal{M}$ since $\mathcal{M} = \mathcal{M}_1 \circ \cdots \circ \mathcal{M}_k$. Notice that this approach cannot be used to prove similar results within the data exchange setting proposed by Fagin et al. [13], as naive instances do not form a strong representation system for the class of mappings specified by st-tgds.

6.2 Positive conditional instances as first class citizens

In the next sections, we study the composition and inversion of schema mappings in the presence of positive conditional instances. But for doing this, we have to show first how positive conditional instances are included as first class citizens in schema mappings.

We have defined mappings as sets of pairs of instances with complete information. Here we do not deviate from this definition and,

thus, we introduce a new terminology to refer to mappings that also contain positive conditional instances. In general, a *positive conditional* mapping, or just PC-mapping, from a schema $\mathbf{S}_1$ to a schema $\mathbf{S}_2$ is a set of pairs $(\mathcal{I}_1, \mathcal{I}_2)$, where $\mathcal{I}_1$ is a positive conditional instance of $\mathbf{S}_1$ and $\mathcal{I}_2$ is a positive conditional instance of $\mathbf{S}_2$. In this section, we will be mostly dealing with PC-mappings that are generated from a usual mapping by using the notion of solution for positive conditional instances. More precisely, given a (usual) mapping $\mathcal{M}$ from a schema $\mathbf{S}_1$ to a schema $\mathbf{S}_2$, define the PC-mapping *generated* from $\mathcal{M}$, denoted by $\text{PC}(\mathcal{M})$, as:

$$\{(\mathcal{I}_1, \mathcal{I}_2) \mid \mathcal{I}_1, \ \mathcal{I}_2 \text{ are positive conditional}$$
$$\text{instances of } \mathbf{S}_1 \text{ and } \mathbf{S}_2, \text{ respectively, and}$$
$$\mathcal{I}_2 \text{ is an } \mathcal{R}_{pos}\text{-solution for } \mathcal{I}_1 \text{ under } \mathcal{M}\}.$$

That is, $\text{PC}(\mathcal{M})$ is obtained from $\mathcal{M}$ by including the pairs $(\mathcal{I}_1, \mathcal{I}_2)$ of positive conditional instances such that $\mathcal{I}_2$ is a solution for $\mathcal{I}_1$ under $\mathcal{M}$, according to the notion of solution for instances with incomplete information introduced in this paper.

Given a mapping $\mathcal{M}$, $\text{PC}(\mathcal{M})$ only includes positive conditional instances in the source and target schemas. We have decided to exclude the usual instances with complete information from $\text{PC}(\mathcal{M})$, as if $\mathcal{M}$ is specified by a set of st-tgds (and, more generally, by an SO tgd), then the relationship between the usual instances according to $\mathcal{M}$ is captured by $\text{PC}(\mathcal{M})$. More precisely, an instance I of a schema $\mathbf{S}$ can be considered as a positive conditional instance without null values and with the element-condition $\top$ associated to every fact. Then it is possible to prove the following.

Proposition 6.3 *Let* $\mathcal{M}$ *be a mapping from a schema* $\mathbf{S}_1$ *to a schema* $\mathbf{S}_2$ *that is closed-down on the left and closed-up on the right. Then for every pair of instances* I_1, I_2 *of* $\mathbf{S}_1$ *and* $\mathbf{S}_2$, *respectively, it holds that* $(I_1, I_2) \in \mathcal{M}$ *iff* $(I_1, I_2) \in \text{PC}(\mathcal{M})$.

In this proposition, a mapping $\mathcal{M}$ is said to be closed-down on the left if for every $(I, J) \in \mathcal{M}$ and instance I' such that $I' \subseteq I$, it holds that $(I', J) \in \mathcal{M}$, and it is said to be closed-up on the right if for every $(I, J) \in \mathcal{M}$ and instance J' such that $J \subseteq J'$, it holds that $(I, J') \in \mathcal{M}$. For example, every mapping specified by a set of st-tgds satisfies these conditions, as well as every mapping specified by an SO tgd.

6.3 Composition in the presence of positive conditional instances

In [14], SO tgds were introduced to deal with the problem of composing schema mappings. In fact, it was proved in [14] that (1) the composition of a finite number of mappings specified by st-tgds can always be specified by an SO tgd, (2) that SO tgds are closed under composition, and (3) that every SO tgd specifies the composition of a finite number of mappings specified by st-tgds. Thus, SO tgds are a natural candidate to study the composition of schema mappings including positive conditional instances. We confirm this intuition by showing that SO tgds satisfy the conditions (1), (2) and (3) for the case of PC-mappings. Notice that for mappings $\mathcal{M}_{12}$ and $\mathcal{M}_{23}$, $\text{PC}(\mathcal{M}_{12})$ and $\text{PC}(\mathcal{M}_{23})$ are binary relations and, thus, the composition $\text{PC}(\mathcal{M}_{12}) \circ \text{PC}(\mathcal{M}_{23})$ is defined as the usual composition of binary relations. More precisely, $\text{PC}(\mathcal{M}_{12}) \circ \text{PC}(\mathcal{M}_{23})$ is the set of all pairs of positive conditional instances $(\mathcal{I}_1, \mathcal{I}_3)$ for which there exists a positive conditional instance $\mathcal{I}_2$ such that $(\mathcal{I}_1, \mathcal{I}_2) \in \text{PC}(\mathcal{M}_{12})$ and $(\mathcal{I}_2, \mathcal{I}_3) \in \text{PC}(\mathcal{M}_{23})$. In this study, the following lemma is the key ingredient.

Lemma 6.4 *Let* $\mathcal{M}_{12} = (\mathbf{S}_1, \mathbf{S}_2, \sigma_{12})$ *and* $\mathcal{M}_{23} = (\mathbf{S}_2, \mathbf{S}_3, \sigma_{23})$, *where* σ_{12} *and* σ_{23} *are SO tgds. Then* $\text{PC}(\mathcal{M}_{12} \circ \mathcal{M}_{23}) = \text{PC}(\mathcal{M}_{12}) \circ \text{PC}(\mathcal{M}_{23})$.

---

*We consider a single SO tgd in this definition as this class of dependencies is closed under conjunction (thus, a finite set of SO tgds is equivalent to a single SO tgd).

From the results in [14] and Lemma 6.4, it is straightforward to prove the desired results.

Corollary 6.5

(1) For every $i \in \{1,\ldots,k-1\}$, let $\mathcal{M}_{i\,i+1} = (\mathbf{S}_i, \mathbf{S}_{i+1}, \Sigma_{i\,i+1})$ with $\Sigma_{i\,i+1}$ a set of st-tgds. Then there exists a mapping $\mathcal{M}_{1k} = (\mathbf{S}_1, \mathbf{S}_k, \sigma_{1k})$, where σ_{1k} is an SO tgd, such that $\text{PC}(\mathcal{M}_{12}) \circ \cdots \circ \text{PC}(\mathcal{M}_{k-1\,k}) = \text{PC}(\mathcal{M}_{1k})$.

(2) Let $\mathcal{M}_{12} = (\mathbf{S}_1, \mathbf{S}_2, \sigma_{12})$ and $\mathcal{M}_{23} = (\mathbf{S}_2, \mathbf{S}_3, \sigma_{23})$, where σ_{12} and σ_{23} are SO tgds. Then there exists a mapping $\mathcal{M}_{13} = (\mathbf{S}_1, \mathbf{S}_3, \sigma_{13})$, where σ_{13} is an SO tgd, such that $\text{PC}(\mathcal{M}_{12}) \circ \text{PC}(\mathcal{M}_{23}) = \text{PC}(\mathcal{M}_{13})$.

(3) Let $\mathcal{M} = (\mathbf{S}_1, \mathbf{S}_2, \sigma_{12})$, where σ_{12} is an SO tgd. Then there exists a sequence $\mathcal{M}_1$, $\mathcal{M}_2$, ..., $\mathcal{M}_k$ of mappings, each specified by a set of st-tgds, such that $\text{PC}(\mathcal{M}) = \text{PC}(\mathcal{M}_1) \circ \text{PC}(\mathcal{M}_2) \circ \cdots \circ \text{PC}(\mathcal{M}_k)$.

We have shown that SO tgds are the right language to deal with the composition of schema mappings including positive conditional instances. Interestingly, we show in the following section that the inclusion of this type of instances also allow mappings specified with SO tgds to become *invertible*.

6.4 Inversion in the presence of positive conditional instances

We consider in this section the notion of mapping inversion introduced in [6]. In that paper, the authors give a formal definition for what it means for a mapping $\mathcal{M}'$ to recover *sound information* with respect to a mapping $\mathcal{M}$. Such a mapping $\mathcal{M}'$ is called a *recovery* of $\mathcal{M}$ in [6]. Given that, in general, there may exist many possible recoveries for a given mapping, an order relation on recoveries is introduced in [6] that naturally gives rise to the notion of maximum recovery, which is a mapping that brings back the maximum amount of sound information.

Let $\mathbf{S}_1$, $\mathbf{S}_2$ be relational schemas, $\mathcal{P}_{12}$ a PC-mapping from $\mathbf{S}_1$ to $\mathbf{S}_2$ and $\mathcal{P}_{21}$ a PC-mapping from $\mathbf{S}_2$ to $\mathbf{S}_1$. Then $\mathcal{P}_{21}$ is said to be a *recovery* of $\mathcal{P}_{12}$ if for every positive conditional instance $\mathcal{I}_1$ of $\mathbf{S}_1$, it holds that $(\mathcal{I}_1, \mathcal{I}_1) \in \mathcal{P}_{12} \circ \mathcal{P}_{21}$. Moreover, $\mathcal{P}_{21}$ is said to be a *maximum recovery* of $\mathcal{P}_{12}$ if $\mathcal{P}_{21}$ is a recovery of $\mathcal{P}_{12}$ and for every PC-mapping $\mathcal{P}'_{21}$ that is a recovery of $\mathcal{P}_{12}$, it holds that $\mathcal{P}_{12} \circ \mathcal{P}_{21} \subseteq \mathcal{P}_{12} \circ \mathcal{P}'_{21}$. That is, the smaller the space of solutions generated by $\mathcal{P}_{12} \circ \mathcal{P}_{21}$, the more informative $\mathcal{P}_{21}$ is about the initial source instances.

It was shown in [5] that there exist mappings specified by SO tgds that admit neither a Fagin-inverse [12] nor a quasi-inverse [15] nor a maximum recovery [6]. The same has been shown for the notion of CQ-maximum recovery studied in [5], and it is not clear whether the notion of inversion introduced in [16] is appropriate for the language of SO tgds. Thus, up to this point, no inverse notion has shown to be appropriate for the fundamental language of SO tgds. As our most important result regarding metadata management, we show that the situation is completely different if positive conditional instances are allowed in source and target schemas.

Theorem 6.6 *Let $\mathcal{M} = (\mathbf{S}_1, \mathbf{S}_2, \sigma_{12})$, where σ_{12} is an SO tgd. Then $\text{PC}(\mathcal{M})$ admits a maximum recovery.*

7. KNOWLEDGE BASES

In this section, we apply our framework for representation systems to *knowledge bases*. In particular, we introduce the novel notion of *exchanging implicit knowledge* via a schema mapping. A knowledge base is composed of *explicit data*, in our context given by a database instance, and *implicit data* usually given by a set of *rules* specified in some logical formalism. Examples of knowledge bases are Datalog programs (where the explicit data is called *extensional database* and the implicit data *intentional database*), and Description Logics specifications (where the explicit data is called *ABox* and the implicit data *TBox*). Let us motivate this section with a simple example.

Example 7.1. Consider a schema $\mathbf{S}_1$ consisting of relations $F(\cdot,\cdot)$, $M(\cdot,\cdot)$, $P(\cdot,\cdot)$ and $GP(\cdot,\cdot)$, which are used to store genealogical data (F stands for *father*, M for *mother*, P for *parent*, and GP for *grandparent*). Consider the following set Σ_1 of rules that states some natural implicit knowledge over $\mathbf{S}_1$:

$$
\begin{aligned}
F(x,y) &\rightarrow P(x,y) \\
M(x,y) &\rightarrow P(x,y) \\
P(x,y) \wedge P(y,z) &\rightarrow GP(x,z)
\end{aligned}
$$

Thus, if $I = \{F(a,b), M(c,b), F(b,d)\}$, then from I and Σ_1 one can *infer* that a and c are *parents* of b, and that a and c are *grandparents* of d. That is, one can infer the atoms $P(a,b)$, $P(c,b)$, $GP(a,d)$, and $GP(c,d)$. Now assume that one needs to exchange data from $\mathbf{S}_1$ to a new schema $\mathbf{S}_2 = \{F'(\cdot,\cdot), GP'(\cdot,\cdot)\}$ by using the following set Σ_{12} of st-tgds:

$$
\begin{aligned}
F(x,y) &\rightarrow F'(x,y), \\
GP(x,y) &\rightarrow GP'(x,y)
\end{aligned}
$$

In this case, one would like to create a knowledge base over $\mathbf{S}_2$ that represents both the explicit data in I and the implicit data given by Σ_1. Thus, one could try first to represent Σ_1 over $\mathbf{S}_2$ according to the relationship established by Σ_{12}. Given that one is copying F and GP through Σ_{12}, the following rule over $\mathbf{S}_2$ is a natural way of representing the implicit knowledge in Σ_1 that is transferred to $\mathbf{S}_2$ through Σ_{12}:

$$
F'(x,y) \wedge F'(y,z) \rightarrow GP'(x,z),
$$

This dependency states that if in schema $\mathbf{S}_2$ we have that x is the father of y and that y is the father of of z, then x should be a grand parent of z. Let Σ_2 be consisting of the above rule. If one considers Σ_2 as the implicit knowledge over $\mathbf{S}_2$, then one can materialize the instance $J = \{F'(a,b), F'(b,d), GP'(c,d)\}$ to obtain a natural knowledge base over $\mathbf{S}_2$ that represents the initial knowledge base given by I and Σ_1. Notice that the fact $GP'(c,d)$ needs to be explicitly included in J, since it comes from an atom that is inferred from predicate M in $\mathbf{S}_1$, and one does not have any information about M in $\mathbf{S}_2$. On the other hand, one does not need to include in J the fact $GP'(a,d)$, as it can be inferred from J and Σ_2. $\square$

This example shows that for the case of knowledge bases, one might be interested in exchanging not only explicit data but also the implicit information in the source knowledge base. As we will see, in general one would have many possibilities when deciding what to make explicit and what to keep implicit when exchanging knowledge bases.

Next we formalize the notion of knowledge base used in this paper, and introduce the notion of knowledge-base solution for a mapping. A *knowledge base* over a schema $\mathbf{S}$ is a pair (I, Σ), where $I \in \text{INST}(\mathbf{S})$ and Σ is a set of logical sentences over $\mathbf{S}$. Given a knowledge base (I, Σ), we denote by $\text{MOD}(I, \Sigma)$ the set of possible *models* of this base, which are all the instances that contain the explicit data in I and satisfy Σ:

$$
\text{MOD}(I, \Sigma) = \{K \in \text{INST}(\mathbf{S}) \mid I \subseteq K \text{ and } K \models \Sigma\}.
$$

Let $\mathbf{K}$ be the class of all knowledge bases (over all possible relational schemas). Then the pair $\mathcal{K} = (\mathbf{K}, \text{MOD})$ is a representation system, and thus, we can apply Definition 3.1 to obtain a notion of solution for knowledge bases. More precisely, given a mapping $\mathcal{M}$ from $\mathbf{S}_1$ to $\mathbf{S}_2$ and knowledge bases (I, Σ_1), (J, Σ_2) over $\mathbf{S}_1$ and $\mathbf{S}_2$, respectively, we have that (J, Σ_2) is a $\mathcal{K}$-solution for (I, Σ_1) under $\mathcal{M}$ if for every $L \in \text{MOD}(J, \Sigma_2)$ there exists an instance $K \in \text{MOD}(I, \Sigma_1)$ such that $(K, L) \in \mathcal{M}$, or equivalently $\text{MOD}(J, \Sigma_2) \subseteq \text{SOL}_{\mathcal{M}}(\text{MOD}(I, \Sigma_1))$. In this case, we also call call (J, Σ_2) a *knowledge-base solution* of (I, Σ_1) under $\mathcal{M}$.

Example 7.2. Let (I, Σ_1), (J, Σ_2) and $\mathcal{M} = (\mathbf{S}_1, \mathbf{S}_2, \Sigma_{12})$ be defined as in Example 7.1. Then it can be shown that (J, Σ_2) is a knowledge-base solution of (I, Σ_1) under the mapping $\mathcal{M}$. □

Many algorithmic problems arise in the context of knowledge bases and schema mappings. In Section 7.1, we study the fundamental problem of checking, given a schema mapping $\mathcal{M}$ and knowledge bases K_1 and K_2, whether K_2 is a knowledge-base solution for K_1 under $\mathcal{M}$. In Section 8, we study the novel notion of *exchanging knowledge*, that is, the problem of materializing (good) target knowledge bases. But before considering these problems, we introduce some notation that will be extensively used in the rest of the paper. We use the standard notion of *chase* of an instance with a set of full tgds (see [23] for a formalization of the chase). Let $\mathbf{S}_1$ and $\mathbf{S}_2$ be disjoint schemas, and let I be an instance of $\mathbf{S}_1$. For a set of full tgds Σ_1 over a schema $\mathbf{S}_1$, we denote by $\text{chase}_{\Sigma_1}(I)$ the result of chasing I with Σ_1. Moreover, let Σ_{12} be a set of full st-tgds from $\mathbf{S}_1$ to $\mathbf{S}_2$, and $J_\emptyset$ the empty instance of $\mathbf{S}_2$. Notice that the result of chasing $(I, J_\emptyset)$ with Σ_{12} is an instance $(I, J^\star)$ of $\mathbf{S}_1 \cup \mathbf{S}_2$. We denote by $\text{chase}_{\Sigma_{12}}(I)$ the resulting instance $J^\star$ (which is the standard notation in the data exchange context [13]). Thus, $\text{chase}_{\Sigma_1}(I)$ is an instance of $\mathbf{S}_1$, while $\text{chase}_{\Sigma_{12}}(I)$ is an instance of $\mathbf{S}_2$.

7.1 Complexity of recognizing solutions

Given a mapping $\mathcal{M}$ from $\mathbf{S}_1$ to $\mathbf{S}_2$, and a representation system $\mathcal{R} = (\mathbf{W}, \text{rep})$, the problem CHECKSOLUTION$(\mathcal{M}, \mathcal{R})$ was defined in Section 5.3 as the problem of verifying, given $\mathcal{U} \in \mathbf{W}$ of type $\mathbf{S}_1$ and $\mathcal{V} \in \mathbf{W}$ of type $\mathbf{S}_2$, whether $\mathcal{V}$ is an $\mathcal{R}$-solution of $\mathcal{U}$ under $\mathcal{M}$. In this section, we study the complexity of this problem for the class of mappings specified by st-tgds and for the representation system $\mathcal{K}$ of knowledge bases.

Two representation systems that are of particular interest in our study are the systems of *tgds knowledge bases* and *full-tgds knowledge bases*, denoted by $\mathcal{K}_{\text{tgd}} = (\mathbf{K}_{\text{tgd}}, \text{MOD})$, and $\mathcal{K}_{\text{full-tgd}} = (\mathbf{K}_{\text{full-tgd}}, \text{MOD})$, respectively. More specifically, $\mathcal{K}_{\text{tgd}}$ is the system obtained by restricting $\mathcal{K}$ to the class of all knowledge bases (I, Σ) with Σ a set of tgds, and $\mathcal{K}_{\text{full-tgd}}$ the representation system obtained by restricting $\mathcal{K}$ to the class of knowledge bases (I, Σ) with Σ a set of full tgds.

Our first theorem is an undecidability result for knowledge bases that are specified by general tgds. The undecidability result holds even for a fixed schema mapping $\mathcal{M}$ specified by full st-tgds.

Theorem 7.3 *There exists a mapping $\mathcal{M} = (\mathbf{S}_1, \mathbf{S}_2, \Sigma_{12})$, with Σ_{12} a set of full st-tgds, for which* CHECKSOLUTION$(\mathcal{M}, \mathcal{K}_{\text{tgd}})$ *is undecidable.*

Theorem 7.3 tells us that to obtain decidability results, we have to focus on some fragments of $\mathcal{K}_{\text{tgd}}$. In what follows, we study the complexity of the problem for the class of knowledge bases given by full tgds. We start by stating the complexity of CHECKSOLUTION$(\mathcal{M}, \mathcal{K}_{\text{full-tgd}})$ when the source implicit knowledge or the target implicit knowledge is assumed to be fixed. In the former case, we assume that we are given a fixed set Σ_1 of full tgds over the source schema and the problem is to check, given a source instance I and a target knowledge base (J, Σ_2), whether (J, Σ_2) is

a knowledge-base solution for (I, Σ_1) under $\mathcal{M}$. The latter case is defined analogously.

Theorem 7.4 *Let $\mathcal{M} = (\mathbf{S}_1, \mathbf{S}_2, \Sigma_{12})$, where Σ_{12} is a set of st-tgds. Then the problem* CHECKSOLUTION$(\mathcal{M}, \mathcal{K}_{\text{full-tgd}})$ *is: (1) in PTIME if both source implicit knowledge and target implicit knowledge are fixed, (2) NP-complete if source implicit knowledge is fixed, (3) coNP-complete if target implicit knowledge is fixed.*

In the general case, where the implicit knowledge is not assumed to be fixed, we obtain that the problem is complete for $\Delta_2^P[O(\log n)]$, which is the class of all problems that can be decided in polynomial time by a deterministic Turing machine that is allowed to make a logarithmic number of calls to an NP oracle [25].

Theorem 7.5 *Let $\mathcal{M} = (\mathbf{S}_1, \mathbf{S}_2, \Sigma_{12})$, where Σ_{12} is a set of st-tgds. Then* CHECKSOLUTION$(\mathcal{M}, \mathcal{K}_{\text{full-tgd}})$ *is $\Delta_2^P[O(\log n)]$-complete. The problem is $\Delta_2^P[O(\log n)]$-hard even if $\mathcal{M}$ is specified by a set of full st-tgds.*

There are only a few natural problems that are complete for $\Delta_2^P[O(\log n)]$. It is interesting that a complete problem for this class arises in the simple framework of data exchange. Some other problems in the context of databases and logic programming that are complete for this class can be found in [11, 9].

A natural question at this point is whether one can obtain decidability for a representation system that is in between $\mathcal{K}_{\text{full-tgd}}$ and $\mathcal{K}_{\text{tgd}}$. An obvious candidate would be the class of knowledge bases defined by *weakly acyclic sets of tgds* [10, 13]. We leave for future research the study of the complexity in this case.

8. KNOWLEDGE EXCHANGE

The most important problem in data exchange is the problem of materializing a target solution for a given source instance. In the previous section, we have extended the notion of solution for knowledge bases and, thus, it is natural to consider the problem of *knowledge exchange*, that is, the problem of materializing a target knowledge base that correctly represents a source knowledge base according to a given mapping. To this end, the first question to answer is what is a *good* knowledge base to materialize. In Section 8.1, we consider the notion of *universal $\mathcal{K}$-solution* that is obtained by applying Definition 3.2 to the representation system $\mathcal{K}$ of knowledge bases. In Section 8.2, we show that there are other natural $\mathcal{K}$-solutions that extend universal $\mathcal{K}$-solutions and that can also be considered good alternatives to materialize. We present algorithms for computing such solutions in Section 8.3.

Given the undecidability results about knowledge bases specified by (non-full) tgds, proved in Section 7.1, we focus our investigation on full tgds. It is important to notice that this case includes some of the motivating scenarios for our investigation, such as RDFS graphs [19].

8.1 Universal $\mathcal{K}$-solutions

Let $\mathcal{K} = (\mathbf{K}, \text{MOD})$ be the representation system of knowledge bases. We can directly apply the notion of universal $\mathcal{K}$-solution to define a class of good solutions. More precisely, we obtain from Definition 3.2 that (J, Σ_2) is a universal $\mathcal{K}$-solution of (I, Σ_1) under a mapping $\mathcal{M}$ if

$$\text{MOD}(J, \Sigma_2) = \text{SOL}_{\mathcal{M}}(\text{MOD}(I, \Sigma_1)). \qquad (2)$$

It is easy to show that for $\mathcal{M} = (\mathbf{S}_1, \mathbf{S}_2, \Sigma_{12})$, where Σ_{12} is a set of full st-tgds, and for every set Σ_1 of full tgds over $\mathbf{S}_1$, the knowledge base $(\text{chase}_{\Sigma_{12}}(\text{chase}_{\Sigma_1}(I)), \Sigma_2)$ with $\Sigma_2 = \emptyset$, is always a universal $\mathcal{K}$-solution of (I, Σ_1). Notice that this induces a straightforward procedure to compute a good solution: we just chase I with Σ_1 and then with Σ_{12}. Thus we obtain the following result.

Proposition 8.1 *Let $\mathcal{M} = (\mathbf{S}_1, \mathbf{S}_2, \Sigma_{12})$, with Σ_{12} a set of full st-tgds. There exists an exponential-time algorithm that, given a knowledge base (I, Σ_1) over $\mathbf{S}_1$, with Σ_1 a set of full tgds, produces a polynomial-size universal $\mathcal{K}$-solution of (I, Σ_1) under $\mathcal{M}$.*

Moreover, it immediately follows from equation (2) that universal $\mathcal{K}$-solutions can be used to compute the certain answers of an arbitrary query Q over (I, Σ_1) under a mapping $\mathcal{M}$.

8.2 Minimal knowledge-base solutions

The universal $\mathcal{K}$-solutions generated in the previous section use the empty set as the implicit knowledge in the target. We argue in this section that there could be other natural $\mathcal{K}$-solutions that may not be universal but still desirable to materialize, mostly because they make good use of the implicit knowledge in the target schema.

Example 8.2. In Example 7.1, we give a $\mathcal{K}$-solution (J, Σ_2) that can be considered as a good solution. However, we have that $\mathrm{MOD}(J, \Sigma_2) \subsetneq \mathrm{SOL}_{\mathcal{M}}(\mathrm{MOD}(I, \Sigma_1))$ and, thus, (J, Σ_2) is not a universal $\mathcal{K}$-solution for (I, Σ_1). The reason is that mapping $\mathcal{M}$ is *closed-up on the right* and, hence, if $K \in \mathrm{SOL}_{\mathcal{M}}(\mathrm{MOD}(I, \Sigma_1))$ and $K \subseteq K'$, then $K' \in \mathrm{SOL}_{\mathcal{M}}(\mathrm{MOD}(I, \Sigma_1))$. On the other hand, $\mathrm{MOD}(J, \Sigma_2)$ does not satisfy this property. To see why this is the case, consider the instance $K = J \cup \{GP'(a, d)\}$. It is easy to see that $K \in \mathrm{MOD}(J, \Sigma_2)$. But if we now consider the instance $K' = K \cup \{F'(b, e)\}$, then we have that $K \subseteq K'$ but $K' \notin \mathrm{MOD}(J, \Sigma_2)$ since K' does not satisfy rule $F'(x, y) \wedge F'(y, z) \rightarrow GP'(x, z)$ (given that $F'(a, b), F'(b, e) \in K'$ but $GP'(a, e) \notin K'$). $\square$

In what follows, we introduce a new class of good $\mathcal{K}$-solutions that captures the intuition in Example 7.1. But before we need to introduce some terminology. Let $\mathcal{X}$ be a set of instances over a schema $\mathbf{S}$. We say that $\mathcal{X}$ is *closed-up* if whenever $K \in \mathcal{X}$ and K' is an instance of $\mathbf{S}$ such that $K \subseteq K'$, we have that $K' \in \mathcal{X}$. Moreover, we define the set of *minimal instances* of $\mathcal{X}$ as:

$$\mathrm{Min}(\mathcal{X}) = \{K \in \mathcal{X} \mid \text{ there is no } K' \in \mathcal{X} \text{ such that } K' \subsetneq K\}.$$

A closed-up set of instances is characterized by its set of minimal instances, as if $\mathcal{X}$ and $\mathcal{Y}$ are closed-up, then $\mathcal{X} = \mathcal{Y}$ if and only if $\mathrm{Min}(\mathcal{X}) = \mathrm{Min}(\mathcal{Y})$.

For every mapping $\mathcal{M}$ specified by a set of st-tgds, and more generally for every mapping that is closed-up on the right, and for every knowledge base (I, Σ_1), it holds that $\mathrm{SOL}_{\mathcal{M}}(\mathrm{MOD}(I, \Sigma_1))$ is a closed-up set. Thus, since $\mathrm{SOL}_{\mathcal{M}}(\mathrm{MOD}(I, \Sigma_1))$ is essentially characterized by its minimal instances, we can naturally relax equation (2) by not requiring that $\mathrm{MOD}(J, \Sigma_2)$ is equal to $\mathrm{SOL}_{\mathcal{M}}(\mathrm{MOD}(I, \Sigma_1))$, but instead that both sets coincide in their sets of minimal instances. Notice that by doing this we retain the same query answering properties as universal $\mathcal{K}$-solutions when considering monotone queries. All the above discussion suggests the following definition of *minimal knowledge-base solution*. In the definition, we use $\mathcal{X} \equiv_{\mathrm{Min}} \mathcal{Y}$ to denote that $\mathrm{Min}(\mathcal{X}) = \mathrm{Min}(\mathcal{Y})$.

Definition 8.3 *Let $\mathcal{M}$ be a mapping from a schema $\mathbf{S}_1$ to a schema $\mathbf{S}_2$, and (I, Σ_1), (J, Σ_2) knowledge bases over $\mathbf{S}_1$ and $\mathbf{S}_2$, respectively. Then (J, Σ_2) is a* minimal knowledge-base solution *for (I, Σ_1) under $\mathcal{M}$ if:*

$$\mathrm{MOD}(J, \Sigma_2) \quad \equiv_{\mathrm{Min}} \quad \mathrm{SOL}_{\mathcal{M}}(\mathrm{MOD}(I, \Sigma_1)).$$

The following result is a simple yet useful characterization of minimal knowledge-base solutions for the case of full tgds. It also gives evidence of the naturalness of our definition of good solution.

Proposition 8.4 *Let $\mathcal{M} = (\mathbf{S}_1, \mathbf{S}_2, \Sigma_{12})$, and (I, Σ_1), (J, Σ_2) be knowledge bases over $\mathbf{S}_1$ and $\mathbf{S}_2$, respectively. If Σ_{12}, Σ_1 and Σ_2 are sets of full tgds, then the following are equivalent:*

(1) (J, Σ_2) is a minimal knowledge-base solution of (I, Σ_1).

(2) $\mathrm{chase}_{\Sigma_{12}}(\mathrm{chase}_{\Sigma_1}(I)) = \mathrm{chase}_{\Sigma_2}(J)$.

Notice that every universal $\mathcal{K}$-solution is a minimal knowledge-base solution, but, as the following example shows, the opposite does not hold in general.

Example 8.5. Let $\mathcal{M} = (\mathbf{S}_1, \mathbf{S}_2, \Sigma_{12})$, (I, Σ_1), and (J, Σ_2) be as in Example 7.1. We have that $\mathrm{chase}_{\Sigma_1}(I)$ is the instance:

$$\begin{aligned} I' = \{ \quad & F(a, b), M(c, b), F(b, d), P(a, b), \\ & P(c, b), P(b, d), GP(a, d), GP(c, d) \quad \}. \end{aligned}$$

If we compute $\mathrm{chase}_{\Sigma_{12}}(I')$, we obtain the instance $\{F'(a, b), F'(b, d), GP'(a, d), GP'(c, d)\}$. If we now compute $\mathrm{chase}_{\Sigma_2}(J)$, we obtain the instance $\{F'(a, b), F'(b, d), GP'(a, d), GP'(c, d)\}$. Thus, given that $\mathrm{chase}_{\Sigma_{12}}(\mathrm{chase}_{\Sigma_1}(I)) = \mathrm{chase}_{\Sigma_2}(J)$, we conclude from Proposition 8.4 that (J, Σ_2) is a minimal knowledge-base solution for (I, Σ_1). $\square$

8.3 Computing minimal knowledge-base solutions

As we pointed out in the previous section, when doing knowledge exchange, it is desirable to materialize target knowledge bases with *as much implicit knowledge as possible*. Yet there is another requirement that one would like to impose to this process. Consider a mapping $\mathcal{M}$ and a source knowledge base (I, Σ_1). In the computation of a solution (J, Σ_2) for (I, Σ_1), it would be desirable that the resulting set Σ_2 depends only on Σ_1 and $\mathcal{M}$, that is, one would like that the implicit knowledge in the target depends only on the mapping and the implicit knowledge in the source. This motivates the following definition of a *safe* set of dependencies.

Definition 8.6 *Let $\mathcal{M} = (\mathbf{S}_1, \mathbf{S}_2, \Sigma_{12})$, where Σ_{12} is a set of full st-tgds, and Σ_1 be a set of full tgds over $\mathbf{S}_1$. Then a set Σ_2 of dependencies over $\mathbf{S}_2$ is* safe *for Σ_1 and $\mathcal{M}$ if for every instance I of $\mathbf{S}_1$, there exists an instance J of $\mathbf{S}_2$ such that (J, Σ_2) is a minimal knowledge-base solution of (I, Σ_1) under $\mathcal{M}$.*

There are many safe sets. In particular, $\Sigma_2 = \emptyset$ is safe for every Σ_1 and $\mathcal{M}$, but it is obviously useless as implicit knowledge. In general, one would like to materialize a safe set Σ_2 that is as informative as possible. In this section, we show how to compute such safe sets and how to use them to materialize knowledge-base solutions. More specifically, we show in Section 8.3.1 that there exists an algorithm that computes *optimal* safe sets; with input Σ_1 and $\mathcal{M}$, the algorithm computes a set Σ_2 such that Σ_2 is safe for Σ_1 and $\mathcal{M}$, and for every other safe set Σ_2' for Σ_1 and $\mathcal{M}$, it holds that Σ_2 logically implies Σ_2'. The output of the algorithm is a set of second-order logic sentences, which motivate us to consider in Section 8.3.1 the problem of generating nontrivial safe sets that, although not optimal, can be expressed in a much simpler language. Finally, we propose in Section 8.3.2 a strategy that uses safe sets to compute minimal knowledge-base solutions.

8.3.1 Computing safe implicit knowledge

Let $\mathcal{M}$ be a mapping from $\mathbf{S}_1$ to $\mathbf{S}_2$, Σ_1 a set of full tgds over $\mathbf{S}_1$ and Σ_2 an arbitrary set of dependencies over $\mathbf{S}_2$. From now on, we say that Σ_2 is optimal-safe for Σ_1 and $\mathcal{M}$ if: (1) Σ_2 is safe for Σ_1 and $\mathcal{M}$, and (2) for every Σ_2' that is safe for Σ_1 and $\mathcal{M}$, it holds that Σ_2 implies Σ_2'. In our first result, we show that there exists an algorithm for computing optimal-safe sets.

Theorem 8.7 *There exists a polynomial-time algorithm OPTI-MALSAFE that, given $\mathcal{M} = (\mathbf{S}_1, \mathbf{S}_2, \Sigma_{12})$, where Σ_{12} is a set of full st-tgds, and a set Σ_1 of full tgds over $\mathbf{S}_1$, computes a set Σ_2 of second-order logic sentences that is optimal-safe for Σ_1 and $\mathcal{M}$.*

A natural question at this point is whether one could modify OPTIMALSAFE to return a set of FO-sentences. Unfortunately, the following theorem gives a negative answer to this question.

Theorem 8.8 *There exist $\mathcal{M} = (\mathbf{S}_1, \mathbf{S}_2, \Sigma_{12})$, where Σ_{12} is a set of full st-tgds, and a set Σ_1 of full tgds over $\mathbf{S}_1$ such that there is no set Σ_2 of FO-sentences that is optimal-safe for Σ_1 and $\mathcal{M}$.*

Theorem 8.8 shows that FO is not enough, in general, to specify an optimal-safe set of dependencies. Nevertheless, in practice one might be more interested in generating nontrivial safe sets that, although not optimal, can be expressed in a simple language. The ideal would be to have nontrivial safe sets specified by full tgds or a mild extension of full tgds. In what follows, we present an algorithm that, given a mapping $\mathcal{M}$ specified by a set of full st-tgds and an *acyclic* set Σ_1 of full tgds over the source schema, generates a set Σ_2 that is safe for Σ_1 and $\mathcal{M}$, and which is specified by a set of full tgds with inequalities in their premises.

A set Σ of full tgds is acyclic if there exists a function that assigns a natural number to each predicate symbol in Σ in such a way that for every $\sigma \in \Sigma$, if P is a relation symbol in the premise of σ and R is the relation symbol in the conclusion of σ, then $f(P) < f(R)$. A well-know property of an acyclic set Σ of full tgds is that it has a *finite unfolding*; for every relational atom $R(\bar{x})$ in the conclusion of a dependency of Σ, there exists a formula $\alpha(\bar{x})$ in $UCQ^=$ such that for every instance I, it holds that $R(\bar{a})$ is in $\text{chase}_\Sigma(I)$ if and only if $\alpha(\bar{a})$ holds in I. The *unfolding* of Σ, that we denote by Σ^+, is constructed by first computing $\alpha(\bar{x})$ for every $R(\bar{x})$ in the conclusion of a tgd in Σ, then adding $\beta(\bar{x}) \to R(\bar{x})$ to Σ^+ for every $\beta(\bar{x})$ in $CQ^=$ that is a disjunct in $\alpha(\bar{x})$, and then eliminating equalities by using variable substitutions.

To present our algorithm, we need to introduce some terminology. Given a mapping $\mathcal{M} = (\mathbf{S}_1, \mathbf{S}_2, \Sigma_{12})$ and a query Q over $\mathbf{S}_1$, we say that Q is *target rewritable* under $\mathcal{M}$ if there exists a query Q' over $\mathbf{S}_2$ such that for every instance I of $\mathbf{S}_1$, it holds that $Q(I) = \text{certain}_\mathcal{M}(Q', I)$. It is implicit in [4] that if Σ_{12} is a set of full tgds and Q is a conjunctive query, then it is decidable in coN-EXPTIME whether Q is target rewritable (see Theorems 4.1 and 4.3 in [4]). Moreover, from the results in [4], we know that there exists a procedure $\text{TREW}(\mathcal{M}, Q)$ that computes a query in $UCQ^{=,\neq}$ that is a target rewriting of Q under $\mathcal{M}$ (if such a rewriting exists). Besides, we also need a procedure to compose full st-tgds. In [14], the authors show that there exists a procedure COMPOSEFULL that given sets Σ_{12} and Σ_{23} of full st-tgds from a schema $\mathbf{S}_1$ to a schema $\mathbf{S}_2$ and from $\mathbf{S}_2$ to a schema $\mathbf{S}_3$, respectively, computes a set Σ_{13} of full st-tgds from $\mathbf{S}_1$ to $\mathbf{S}_3$ such that $(I, J) \models \Sigma_{13}$ if and only if there exists K such that $(I, K) \models \Sigma_{12}$ and $(K, J) \models \Sigma_{23}$. It can be easily shown that if Σ_{12} is a set of full st-tgds with inequalities in the premises, then COMPOSEFULL returns a set of full st-tgds with inequalities in the premises that defines the composition of Σ_{12} and Σ_{23}. With procedures TREW and COMPOSEFULL, we have all the necessary ingredients for our algorithm.

Algorithm: FULLSAFE$(\mathcal{M}, \Sigma_1)$

Input:	$\mathcal{M} = (\mathbf{S}_1, \mathbf{S}_2, \Sigma_{12})$, where Σ_{12} is a set of full st-tgds, and an acyclic set Σ_1 of full tgds over $\mathbf{S}_1$.
Output:	A set Σ_2 of full tgds with inequalities over $\mathbf{S}_2$ that is safe for Σ_1 and $\mathcal{M}$.

1. Construct a set of formulas Σ_1^+ by unfolding Σ_1.
2. Construct a set Σ' of full st-tgds with inequalities from $\mathbf{S}_2$ to $\mathbf{S}_1$ as

follows. Begin with $\Sigma' = \emptyset$. For every tgd $\alpha(\bar{x}) \to R(\bar{x})$ in Σ_1^+ do the following:

  2.1. If $\alpha(\bar{x})$ is target rewritable under $\mathcal{M}$, then let $\beta(\bar{x})$ be the query in $UCQ^{=,\neq}$ over $\mathbf{S}_2$ that is the output of $\text{TREW}(\mathcal{M}, \alpha(\bar{x}))$. For every disjunct $\gamma(\bar{x})$ in $\beta(\bar{x})$ add to Σ' the dependency $\gamma(\bar{x}) \to R(\bar{x})$ (and eliminate equalities by using variable substitutions).

3. Let $\hat{\mathbf{S}}_2$ be a copy of $\mathbf{S}_2$, and Σ'_{12} the set of full st-tgds from $\mathbf{S}_1$ to $\hat{\mathbf{S}}_2$ obtained from Σ_{12} by replacing every $R \in \mathbf{S}_2$ by $\hat{R}$.
4. Let Σ'' be the set of full st-tgds with inequalities from $\mathbf{S}_2$ to $\hat{\mathbf{S}}_2$ that is obtained as the output of COMPOSEFULL(Σ', Σ'_{12}).
5. Let Σ_2 be the set of formulas over $\mathbf{S}_2$ obtained from Σ'' by replacing every $\hat{R} \in \hat{\mathbf{S}}_2$ by R. Return Σ_2. $\qquad\square$

Theorem 8.9 FULLSAFE$(\mathcal{M}, \Sigma_1)$ *computes a set Σ_2 of full tgds with inequalities in the premises which is safe for Σ_1 and $\mathcal{M}$.*

Example 8.10. Let $\mathcal{M} = (\mathbf{S}_1, \mathbf{S}_2, \Sigma_{12})$ and Σ_1 be as defined in Example 7.1. It is not difficult to see that dependency σ given by

$$\exists y (F(x, y) \wedge F(y, z)) \quad \to \quad GP(x, z)$$

is in Σ_1^+. Now the query given by $\exists y (F(x, y) \wedge F(y, z))$ is target rewritable under $\mathcal{M}$, and its rewriting is $\exists y (F'(x, y) \wedge F'(y, z))$. Thus, in Step 2 of FULLSAFE, we add dependency:

$$\exists y (F'(x, y) \wedge F'(y, z)) \quad \to \quad GP(x, z)$$

to Σ'. In the set Σ'_{12} created in Step 3, we have the dependency:

$$GP(x, z) \quad \to \quad \widehat{GP'}(x, z).$$

Thus, the output of COMPOSEFULL(Σ', Σ'_{12}) contains the dependency $\exists y (F'(x, y) \wedge F'(y, z)) \to \widehat{GP'}(x, z)$, which implies that:

$$\exists y (F'(x, y) \wedge F'(y, z)) \quad \to \quad GP'(x, z) \tag{3}$$

is in the output of FULLSAFE$(\mathcal{M}, \Sigma_1)$. In fact, it can be proved that the set Σ_2 returned by FULLSAFE$(\mathcal{M}, \Sigma_1)$ is logically equivalent to the set consisting of dependency (3). $\qquad\square$

8.3.2 Using safe implicit knowledge to compute minimal knowledge-base solutions

For a mapping $\mathcal{M}$ and a source knowledge base (I, Σ_1), a minimal knowledge-base solution of (I, Σ_1) consists of an instance J and a set Σ_2 of dependencies. Up to this point, we have described two alternative algorithms that compute the set Σ_2 from Σ_1 and $\mathcal{M}$. In this section, we propose a strategy to compute instance J.

Let $\mathcal{M} = (\mathbf{S}_1, \mathbf{S}_2, \Sigma_{12})$, where Σ_{12} is a set of full st-tgds, and (I, Σ_1) a knowledge base over $\mathbf{S}_1$, where Σ_1 is a set of full tgds. As we pointed out before, $J = \text{chase}_{\Sigma_{12}}(\text{chase}_{\Sigma_1}(I))$ can always be used as the explicit data in a minimal knowledge-base solution of (I, Σ_1). However, such an instance does not need to make use of any implicit knowledge and, thus, it does not take advantage of any of the algorithms proposed in the previous section for computing safe sets. In fact, given these algorithms, one would expect that some parts of the instance $\text{chase}_{\Sigma_1}(I)$ are not necessary given the target implicit knowledge. In what follows, we propose an approach that given (I, Σ_1), $\mathcal{M}$ and a safe set Σ_2 for Σ_1 and $\mathcal{M}$, computes an instance J that makes use of the implicit knowledge in Σ_2. More precisely, the approach first constructs a minimal set Σ'_1 of full tgds such that for every instance I_1 of $\mathbf{S}_1$, it holds that:

(C1) $\text{chase}_{\Sigma'_1}(I_1)$ is contained in $\text{chase}_{\Sigma_1}(I_1)$, and

(C2) $(\text{chase}_{\Sigma_{12}}(\text{chase}_{\Sigma'_1}(I_1)), \Sigma_2)$ is a minimal knowledge-base solution of (I_1, Σ_1).

Then for the input knowledge base (I, Σ_1), it materializes knowledge base $(\text{chase}_{\Sigma_{12}}(\text{chase}_{\Sigma'_1}(I)), \Sigma_2)$. Notice that in the previous approach, the minimal set Σ'_1 can be used for any source knowledge base (I, Σ_1). This is an important feature of our proposal, as the computation of Σ_1' only depends on Σ_1, $\mathcal{M}$ and Σ_2, which are usually much smaller than the source explicit data. Besides, this is the most typical scenario in practice [19, 24], where for a specific domain the rules in a knowledge base remains unchanged, while the explicit data changes from one repository to another.

We now present the algorithm that given $\mathcal{M}$, Σ_1 and Σ_2 as above, returns a set Σ_1' of full tgds satisfying conditions (C1) and (C2). In the algorithm, we assume that Σ_1 is an acyclic set of full tgds, as in this case the problem of verifying whether conditions (C1) and (C2) hold for every instance I_1 of $\mathbf{S}_1$ is decidable in exponential time.

Algorithm: MINIMIZE$(\mathcal{M}, \Sigma_1, \Sigma_2)$

Input: $\mathcal{M} = (\mathbf{S}_1, \mathbf{S}_2, \Sigma_{12})$, where Σ_{12} is a set of full st-tgds, an acyclic set Σ_1 of full tgds, and a set Σ_2 of full tgds with inequalities that is safe for Σ_1 and $\mathcal{M}$.

Output: A minimal set Σ_1' that satisfies conditions (C1) and (C2) for every instance I_1 of $\mathbf{S}_1$.

1. Let Σ_1^+ be the set obtained by unfolding Σ_1, and $\Gamma = \Sigma_1^+$.
2. If there exists $\sigma \in \Gamma$ such that the set $\Sigma_1' = \Gamma \smallsetminus \{\sigma\}$ satisfies conditions (C1) and (C2) for every instance I_1 of $\mathbf{S}_1$, then remove σ from Γ and repeat Step 2.
3. Let $\Sigma_1' = \Gamma$, and return Σ_1'. $\qquad\qquad\qquad\qquad$ $\square$

Notice that algorithm MINIMIZE can compute different outputs depending on the order in which the dependencies in Γ are chosen in Step 2. Also notice that we are searching for a minimal set in order to minimize the explicit data materialized in the target. Putting together procedures FULLSAFE and MINIMIZE, we can give a complete strategy to compute minimal knowledge-base solutions.

Theorem 8.11 *Let* $\mathcal{M} = (\mathbf{S}_1, \mathbf{S}_2, \Sigma_{12})$, *where* Σ_{12} *is a set of full st-tgds, and* Σ_1 *an acyclic set of full tgds over* $\mathbf{S}_1$. *Moreover, let* Σ_2 *be the output of* FULLSAFE$(\mathcal{M}, \Sigma_1)$, *and* Σ_1' *the output of* MINIMIZE$(\mathcal{M}, \Sigma_1, \Sigma_2)$. *Then for every instance* I *of* $\mathbf{S}_1$ *it holds that* $\big(\mathrm{chase}_{\Sigma_{12}}(\mathrm{chase}_{\Sigma_1'}(I)), \Sigma_2\big)$ *is a minimal knowledge-base solution of* (I, Σ_1) *under* $\mathcal{M}$.

Example 8.12. Let $\mathcal{M} = (\mathbf{S}_1, \mathbf{S}_2, \Sigma_{12})$ and Σ_1 be as in Example 7.1. From Example 8.10, we know that the output of FULLSAFE$(\mathcal{M}, \Sigma_1)$ is the set Σ_2 consisting of dependency $F'(x, y) \wedge F'(y, z) \rightarrow GP'(x, z)$. It can be proved that there exists an order over the dependencies in Σ_1^+ such that the output of MINIMIZE$(\mathcal{M}, \Sigma_1, \Sigma_2)$ is the following set Σ_1' of dependencies:

$$
\begin{aligned}
M(x, y) &\rightarrow P(x, y) \\
P(x, y) \wedge P(y, z) &\rightarrow GP(x, z) \\
F(x, y) \wedge P(y, z) &\rightarrow GP(x, z) \\
P(x, y) \wedge F(y, z) &\rightarrow GP(x, z)
\end{aligned}
$$

Consider now the source instance I of Example 7.1, that is, $I = \{F(a, b), M(c, b), F(b, d)\}$. If we chase I with Σ_1', we obtain instance $I' = \{F(a, b), M(c, b), F(b, d), P(c, b), GP(c, d)\}$. If we now chase I' with Σ_{12}, we obtain the instance $J = \{F'(a, b), F'(b, d), GP'(c, d)\}$. Thus, we conclude from Theorem 8.11 that (J, Σ_2) is a minimal knowledge-base solution for (I, Σ_1) under $\mathcal{M}$. Notice that this is exactly the solution that we considered as a good solution in Example 7.1. $\quad\square$

9. CONCLUDING REMARKS

We have presented a framework to exchange data beyond the usual setting in which instances are considered to have complete information. We showed the robustness of our proposal by applying it to the problems of exchanging incomplete information and exchanging knowledge bases. In the former case, we proved several results regarding expressiveness, query answering and complexity

of materializing solutions. In particular, we made the case that positive conditional instances are the right representation system to deal with the inherent incompleteness that emerges when exchanging data by using st-tgds. We also applied our framework to define the novel notion of knowledge exchange. This can be considered as a starting point for formalizing and studying the exchange of data in the Semantic Web, in particular, the exchange of RDFS graphs and OWL specifications. Many problems remain open. In particular, we would like to study knowledge exchange under mappings defined by non full st-tgds, which will probably require combining the results for knowledge bases and positive conditional instances.

Acknowledgments: We thank the anonymous referees for many helpful comments. Arenas was supported by Fondecyt grant 1090565, and Reutter by EPSRC grant G049165 and FET-Open project FoX.

10. REFERENCES

[1] S. Abiteboul, P. C. Kanellakis, and G. Grahne. On the representation and querying of sets of possible worlds. *TCS*, 78(1):158–187, 1991.

[2] F. Afrati, C. Li, and V. Pavlaki. Data exchange: Query answering for incomplete data sources. In *InfoScale*, 2008.

[3] L. Antova, C. Koch, and D. Olteanu. 10^{10^6} worlds and beyond: Efficient representation and processing of incomplete information. In *ICDE*, pages 606–615, 2007.

[4] M. Arenas, J. Pérez, J. L. Reutter, and C. Riveros. Foundations of schema mapping management. In *PODS*, pages 227–238, 2010.

[5] M. Arenas, J. Pérez, J. L. Reutter, and C. Riveros. Inverting schema mappings: Bridging the gap between theory and practice. *PVLDB*, 2(1):1018–1029, 2009.

[6] M. Arenas, J. Pérez, and C. Riveros. The recovery of a schema mapping: Bringing exchanged data back. *TODS*, 34(4), 2009.

[7] P. Bernstein. Applying model management to classical meta data problems. In *CIDR*, 2003.

[8] P. Bernstein and S. Melnik. Model management 2.0: manipulating richer mappings. In *SIGMOD*, pages 1–12, 2007.

[9] G. Brewka and T. Eiter. Preferred answer sets for extended logic programs. *Artif. Intell.*, 109(1-2):297–356, 1999.

[10] A. Deutsch and V. Tannen. Reformulation of XML queries and constraints. In *ICDT*, pages 225–241, 2003.

[11] T. Eiter and G. Gottlob. On the complexity of propositional knowledge base revision, updates, and counterfactuals. In *PODS*, pages 261–273, 1992.

[12] R. Fagin. Inverting schema mappings. *TODS*, 32(4), 2007.

[13] R. Fagin, P. G. Kolaitis, R. J. Miller, and L. Popa. Data exchange: semantics and query answering. *TCS*, 336(1):89–124, 2005.

[14] R. Fagin, P. G. Kolaitis, L. Popa, and W.-C. Tan. Composing schema mappings: Second-order dependencies to the rescue. *TODS*, 30(4):994–1055, 2005.

[15] R. Fagin, P. G. Kolaitis, L. Popa, and W.-C. Tan. Quasi-inverses of schema mappings. In *PODS*, pages 123–132, 2007.

[16] R. Fagin, P. G. Kolaitis, L. Popa, and W.-C. Tan. Reverse data exchange: coping with nulls. In *PODS*, pages 23–32, 2009.

[17] G. Grahne. *The Problem of Incomplete Information in Relational Databases*. Springer, 1991.

[18] G. Grahne, A. Onet. Closed World Chasing. In *LID* 2011.

[19] P. Hayes. RDF Semantics, W3C Recommendation. February 2004.

[20] T. Imielinski and W. Lipski. Incomplete information in relational databases. *Journal of the ACM*, 31(4):761–791, 1984.

[21] L. Libkin. Data exchange and incomplete information. In *PODS*, pages 60–69, 2006.

[22] L. Libkin and C. Sirangelo. Data exchange and schema mappings in open and closed worlds. In *PODS*, pages 139–148, 2008.

[23] D. Maier, A. Mendelzon, and Y. Sagiv. Testing implications of data dependencies. *TODS*, 4(4):455–469, 1979.

[24] P. F. Patel-Schneider, P. Hayes, and I. Horrocks. OWL Web Ontology Language, W3C Recommendation. February 2004.

[25] K. W. Wagner. More complicated questions about maxima and minima, and some closures of NP. *TCS*, 51:53–80, 1987.

Space-efficient Substring Occurrence Estimation

Alessio Orlandi
Dipartimento di Informatica
University of Pisa, Italy
aorlandi@di.unipi.it

Rossano Venturini
ISTI-CNR
Pisa, Italy
venturini@isti.cnr.it

ABSTRACT

We study the problem of estimating the number of occurrences of substrings in textual data: A text T on some alphabet Σ of size σ is preprocessed and an index $\mathcal{I}$ is built. The index is used in lieu of the text to answer queries of the form $\mathsf{Count}{\approx}(P)$, returning an approximated number of the occurrences of an arbitrary pattern P as a substring of T. The problem has its main application in selectivity estimation related to the *LIKE* predicate in textual databases [15, 14, 5]. Our focus is on obtaining an algorithmic solution with guaranteed error rates and small footprint. To achieve that, we first enrich previous work in the area of compressed text-indexing [8, 11, 6, 17] providing an optimal data structure that requires $\Theta(\frac{|T| \log \sigma}{l})$ bits where $l \geq 1$ is the additive error on any answer. We also approach the issue of guaranteeing exact answers for sufficiently frequent patterns, providing a data structure whose size scales with the amount of such patterns. Our theoretical findings are sustained by experiments showing the practical impact of our data structures.

Categories and Subject Descriptors

E.1 [**Data Structures**]: Arrays, Tables; E.4 [**Coding and Information Theory**]: Data compaction and compression; E.5 [**Files**]: Sorting/searching; F.2.2 [**Analysis of Algorithms and Problem Complexity**]: Nonnumerical algorithms and Problems—*Pattern matching*; H.3 [**Information Storage and Retrieval**]: Content Analysis and Indexing, Information Storage, Information Search and Retrieval.

General Terms

Algorithms, Design, Theory.

Keywords

Compressed Full-Text indexes, Pattern Matching, Full-text Indexing, Data structures

1. INTRODUCTION

A large fraction of the data we process every day consists of a sequence of symbols from an alphabet, i.e., a text. Unformatted natural language documents, XML structured data, HTML collections, textual columns in relational databases, biological sequences, are just few examples. With nowadays growth of data it is not uncommon to have massive data sets at hand, on which operations must be performed. Thinking about text, the basic class of operations are simple pattern matching queries (or variations, e.g. regular expressions). The challenge, especially on massive data sets, is to obtain low time complexities and little space requirements. On one hand, one would like to achieve the maximum speed in solving matching queries on the text, and thus indexing the data is mandatory. On the other hand, when massive data sets are involved, the cost for extra index data may be non-negligible, and thus compressing the data is mandatory too. It is not surprising that the last decade has seen a trending growth of *compressed text indexes* [8, 11, 6, 17, 10]. Their main role is to match both requirements at the same time, allowing textual data to be stored in compressed format while being able to efficiently perform pattern matching queries on the indexed text itself.

Nonetheless, there exists a bound on the compression ratio they can achieve. Such a limit can be surpassed by allowing pattern matching operations to have approximated results. This is a realistic scenario, as with massive amounts of data and answers that provide millions of strings, a small absolute error is clearly tolerable in many situations. In this paper we follow such idea by studying the problem called **Substring Occurrence Estimation**:

Given a text $T[1, n]$ drawn from an alphabet Σ of size σ and fixed any error parameter l, we would like to design an index that, without the need of accessing/storing the original text, is able to count the number of occurrences of any pattern $P[1, p]$ in T. The index is allowed to err by at most l: precisely, the reported number of occurrences of P is in the range $[\mathsf{Count}(P), \mathsf{Count}(P) + l - 1]$ where $\mathsf{Count}(P)$ is the actual number of occurrences of P in T. In the following we will refer this operation, which we say has *uniform error range* with $\mathsf{Count}{\approx}_l(P)$. We also consider a stronger version of the problem denoted $\mathsf{Count}{\geq}_l(P)$, namely having *lower-sided error range*, where $\mathsf{Count}{\geq}_l(P) = \mathsf{Count}(P)$ whenever $\mathsf{Count}(P) \geq l$, and $\mathsf{Count}{\geq}_l(P) \in [0, l-1]$ otherwise.

A relative of additive error is multiplicative error, i.e. when the estimation lays in $[\mathsf{Count}(P), (1 + \varepsilon)\mathsf{Count}(P)]$ for some fixed $\varepsilon > 0$. In theory, such an error could provide better estimates for low frequency patterns. Solving the multiplicative error problem would imply an index able to discover for sure whether a pattern P appears in T or not (set $\mathsf{Count}(P) = 0$ in the above formulas). This turns out to be the hard part of estimation. In fact, we are able to prove (Theorem 4) that an index with multiplicative error would require as much as T to be represented. Hence, the forthcoming discussion will focus solely on additive error.

Occurrence estimation finds its main application in *Substring Selectivity Estimation*: given a textual column of a database, create a limited space index that finds (approximately) the percentage of rows satisfying the predicate *LIKE '%P%'* for any pattern P. Provided with a data structure for substring occurrence estimation with lower-sided error, solutions in literature [15, 14, 5] try to reduce the error when the data structure is not able to guarantee a correct answer, i.e., $\mathsf{Count}(P) < l$. This phase, called *error reduction*, usually involves splitting P into pieces appearing in the data structure and using a probabilistic model to harness such information to generate a selectivity estimate for the whole pattern. Apart from providing an effective model, solutions for substring selectivity incur in a space/error trade-off: the more space-efficient is the underlying data structure, the more information can be stored, hence yielding a more accurate estimate. To date, most data structures used in selectivity estimation are simple and waste space; therefore, we can indirectly boost selectivity accuracy by studying space-efficient substring occurrence estimation.

In the forthcoming discuss, we will focus on occurrence estimation on whole texts only. Nonetheless, the techniques immediately apply to collections of strings (i.e., rows in a db column): given the content of strings $R_1, R_2, \ldots R_n$ we introduce a new special symbol $\triangleright$ and create the text $T(R) = \triangleright R_1 \triangleright R_2 \triangleright \cdots \triangleright R_n \triangleright$. A substring query is then performed directly on $T(R)$.

The main data structure for occurrence estimation, and the one used in [15, 14], is the *pruned suffix tree* $\mathcal{PST}_l(T)$. Here, we briefly review it and defer a full explanation of related work to Section 7. For a fixed error $l \geq 1$, the $\mathcal{PST}_l(T)$ is obtained from the suffix tree [12] of T by pruning away all nodes of suffixes that appear less than l times in T. It is immediate to see that the resulting data structure has, indeed, lower-sided error. However, the space occupancy of $\mathcal{PST}_l$ is a serious issue, both in theory and practice: it requires a total of $O(m \log n + g \log \sigma)$ bits where m is the number of nodes surviving the pruning phase and g is the amount of symbols that label the edges of such nodes. The number of nodes in the pruned tree could raise to $O(n - l)$ and could slowly decrease as the error l increases: observe that we require to increase the error up to $n/2$ just to halve the number of nodes in the tree. Consider the text $T = a^n$. The shape of its suffix tree is a long chain of $n - 1$ nodes with two children each. Therefore, for any value of l, the space required to store its pruned suffix tree is at least $O((n - l) \log n)$ bits. This quantity further increases due to the need of storing explicitly edges' labels. We point out that the number of these symbols is at least equal to the number of nodes but can significantly increase whenever the suffixes represented in the tree share long common prefixes. It goes without saying that the number of symbols we need to store can exceed the length of the text itself. One could resort to techniques like blind search over compacted tries [7] to remove the need of storing full labels for the edges. However, it would incur in

an uncontrollable error when the pattern is not in the $\mathcal{PST}_l$, since solutions based on compacted tries require the original text to perform membership queries. Thus, the space occupancy of the pruned suffix tree may be not sublinear w.r.t. the text. Moreover, the lower bound of Theorem 3 formally proves that the space complexity for an index with threshold l is $\Omega(n \log(\sigma)/l)$ bits, hence stating that a pruned suffix tree is highly non-optimal.

To provide solutions with smaller footprint, one can resort to compressed full-text indexes [8, 11, 6, 17], which are well known in the field of succinct data structures. They deliver a framework to keep a copy of text T compressed together with auxiliary information for efficient (i.e., without decompressing the whole T) substring search. Such solutions however work on the entire text and are not designed to allow errors or pruning of portions of the string, yet they provide a good baseline for our work. Our objective is to heavily reduce the space of compressed text indexes as l increases.

We provide two different solutions: one in the uniform error model and one in the lower-sided error model. Section 4 illustrates the former and shows how to build an index (called $\mathcal{APX}_l$) that requires $O(n \log(\sigma l)/l)$ bits of space. This is the first index that has both guaranteed space, sublinear with respect to the size of the indexed text, and provable error bounds. It turns out (Theorem 3) that such index is space-optimal up to constant factors for sufficiently small l (namely, $\log l = O(\log \sigma)$).

We also provide a data structure ($\mathcal{CPST}_l$) for the lower-sided error problem (Section 5) that presents a space bound of $O(m \log(\sigma l))$ where m is the number of nodes in the $\mathcal{PST}_l(T)$. Hence, our $\mathcal{CPST}_l$ does not require to store the labels (the $g \log \sigma$ factor), which account for most of the space in practice. Such data structure outperforms our previous solution only when $m = O(n/l)$; surprisingly, many real data sets exhibit the latter property[1]. Both the $\mathcal{APX}_l$ and $\mathcal{CPST}_l$ data structures heavily rely on the Burrows-Wheeler Transform (BWT), which proves to be an effective tool to tackle the problem. As part of our contribution, we prove how the pruning of Suffix Trees

In Section 6 we support our claims with tests on real data sets. We show the improvement in space occupancy of both $\mathcal{APX}_l$ and $\mathcal{CPST}_l$, both ranging from 5 to 60 w.r.t. to $\mathcal{PST}_l$, and we show our sharp advantage over compressed text indexing solutions. As an example, for an english text of about 512 MB, it suffices to set $l = 256$ to obtain an index of 5.1 MB (roughly, 1%). We also confirm that m and n/l are close most of the times. In such sense we also note that the main component in $\mathcal{PST}_l$'s space is given by the labels, hence guaranteeing to our $\mathcal{CPST}_l$ a clear advantage over $\mathcal{PST}_l$.

Concerning the selectivity estimation problem, we illustrate the gain in estimation quality given by employing our indexes as underlying data structure. For such purposes we employ the MOL algorithm (see [14]). Given two thresholds yielding similar space occupancies between $\mathcal{PST}_l$ and $\mathcal{CPST}_l$, we exhibit an improvement factor ranging from 5 to 790. Combining MOL and our CPST with reasonably small l, it is possible to solve the selectivity estimation problem with an average additive error of 1 by occupying (on average) around $1/7$ of the original text size.

---

[1] Recall that the condition on m is not enough to obtain a small $\mathcal{PST}_l$ due to the edge labels.

2. NOTATION

Let $T[1, n]$ be a string drawn from the alphabet Σ of size σ.[2] For each $c \in \Sigma$, we let n_c be the number of occurrences of c in T. The zero-th order *empirical* entropy of T is defined as: $H_0(T) = (1/n) \sum_{c \in \Sigma} n_c \log(n/n_c)$.

Note that $|T|H_0(T)$ provides an information-theoretic lower bound to the output size of any compressor that encodes each symbol of T with a fixed code [19]. For any string w of length k, we denote by w_T the string of single symbols following the occurrences of w in T, taken from left to right. For example, if $T = $ abracadabra and $w = $ br, we have $w_T = $ aa since the two occurrences of br in T are followed by the symbol a. The k-th order *empirical* entropy of T is defined as: $H_k(T) = (1/n) \sum_{w \in \Sigma^k} |w_T| H_0(w_T)$.

We have $H_k(T) \geq H_{k+1}(T)$ for any $k \geq 0$. As usual in data compression [16], we will adopt $nH_k(T)$ as an information-theoretic lower bound to the output size of any compressor that encodes each symbol of T with a code that depends on the symbol itself and on the k immediately preceding symbols.

Both our solutions rely on basic data structures that can answer rank and select queries. In the binary version, let B be a bit vector of length u, having m bits set to 1. Here, $\mathrm{rank}_b(B, x)$ for $b \in \{0, 1\}$ counts the number of occurrences of bit b in the prefix $B[0..x-1]$. $\mathrm{select}_b(B, x)$ for $b \in \{0, 1\}$ returns the position of the xth occurrence of bit b in B, or -1. Among all available solutions, we employ Elias Fano sequences (also known as SDarrays) ([18, Section 6]):

THEOREM 1. *There exists a data structure encoding a bit-vector B of length u with m bits set to 1 in $m \log(u/m) + O(m)$ bits, supporting select_1 in $O(1)$ time and select_0, rank_1 and rank_0 in $O(\log(\min\{u/m, m\}))$ time.*

The idea of rank and select can be extended from binary to arbitrary alphabets in the natural way. The best solutions to date have been presented in [1, 2, 9]:

THEOREM 2. *Given a text $T[1, n]$ drawn from an alphabet of size σ there exists data structures storing T and supporting rank and select over it with the following trade-offs:*

Ref.	space (bits)	rank/ select (time)	σ
[9]	$nH_0(T) + o(n)$	$O(1)$	$\log^{O(1)} n$
[9]	$nH_0(T) + o(n) \cdot \log \sigma$	$O(1 + \frac{\log \sigma}{\log \log n})$	$o(n)$
[2]	$nH_0(T) + n \cdot o(\log \sigma)$	$O(\log \log \sigma) / O(1)$	$O(n)$
[1]	$(n + o(n))H_0(T) + o(n)$	$O(\log \log \sigma) / O(1)$	$O(n)$

3. LOWER BOUNDS

The following lower bound proves the minimum amount of space needed to solve the substring occurrence estimation problem for both error ranges, uniform and lower-sided.

THEOREM 3. *For a fixed additive error $l \geq 1$, an index built on a text $T[1, n]$ drawn from an alphabet Σ of size σ that approximates the number of occurrences of any pattern P in T within l must use $\Omega(n \log(\sigma)/l)$ bits of space.*

PROOF. Assume that there exists an index answering any approximate counting query within an additive error l by requiring $o(n \log(\sigma)/l)$ bits of space. Given any text $T[1, n]$, we derive a new text $T'[1, (l+1)(n+1)]$ that is formed by repeating the string $T\$$ for $l+1$ times, where $\$$ is a symbol

---

[2] In the following we will adopt the common assumption that $\sigma = O(n)$.

	F	L
abracadabra$	$ abracadabr	a
bracadabra$a	a $abracadab	r
racadabra$ab	a bra$abraca	d
acadabra$abr	a bracadabra	$
cadabra$abra	a cadabra$ab	r
adabra$abrac $\Longrightarrow$	a dabra$abra	c
dabra$abraca	b ra$abracad	a
abra$abracad	b racadabra$	a
bra$abracada	c adabra$abr	a
ra$abracadab	d abra$abrac	a
a$abracadabr	r a$abracada	b
$abracadabra	r acadabra$a	b

Figure 1: Example of Burrows-Wheeler transform for the string $T = $ abracadabra$. The matrix on the right has the rows sorted in lexicographic order. The output of the BWT is the column $L = $ ard$rcaaaabb.

that does not belong to Σ. Then, we build the index on T' that requires $o((l+1)(n+1) \log(\sigma+1)/l) = o(n \log \sigma)$ bits. We observe that we can recover the original text T by means of this index: we search all possible strings of length n drawn from Σ followed by a $\$$, the only one for which the index answers with a value greater than l is T. A random text has entropy $\log(\sigma^n) - O(1) = n \log \sigma - O(1)$ bits. Hence, the index would represent a random text using too few bits, a contradiction. $\square$

Using the same argument we can prove the following Theorem, which justifies the need of focusing on additive errors.

THEOREM 4. *For a fixed multiplicative error $(1 + \varepsilon) > 1$, an index built on a text $T[1, n]$ drawn from an alphabet Σ of size σ that approximates the number of occurrences of any pattern P in T within $(1 + \epsilon)$ must use $\Omega(n \log \sigma)$ bits of space.*

By similar arguments we are able to prove that even when restricting to pattern of fixed, sufficiently large length, i.e. $\geq 2 \log n$, the problem remains within the same space complexity. On the other hand, for sufficiently shorter lengths, the problem becomes trivial. Details are deferred to the final version.

4. OPTIMAL ERROR/SPACE SOLUTION

In this section we describe our first solution which is able to report the number of occurrences of any pattern within an additive error at most l. Its error/space trade-off is provably optimal whenever the error l is such that $\log l = O(\log \sigma)$. In this section we will prove the following Theorem:

THEOREM 5. *Given $T[1, n]$ drawn from an alphabet Σ of size σ and fixed an error threshold l, there exists an index that answers $\mathsf{Count}_{\approx l}(P[1, p])$ in $O(p \times f(n, \sigma))$ time by using $O((n \log(\sigma l))/l + \sigma \log n)$ bits of space, where $f(n, \sigma)$ depends on the chosen rank and select data structure (see Theorem 2).*

In order to understand this solution we require some background related to compressed full-text indexes [17, 6]. We start by presenting the Burrows-Wheeler Transform [4] which

Algorithm Count($P[1,p]$)

1. $i = p$, $c = P[p]$, First$_p = C[c] + 1$, Last$_p = C[c+1]$;

2. **while** ((First$_i \leq$ Last$_i$) **and** ($i \geq 2$)) **do**

3. $c = P[i-1]$;

4. First$_{i-1} = C[c] + \text{rank}_c(L, \text{First}_i - 1) + 1$;

5. Last$_{i-1} = C[c] + \text{rank}_c(L, \text{Last}_i)$;

6. $i = i - 1$;

7. **if** (Last$_i <$ First$_i$) **then return** "no rows prefixed by P" **else return** [First$_i$, Last$_i$].

Figure 2: The algorithm to find the range [First$_1$, Last$_1$] of rows of $\mathcal{M}(T)$ prefixed by $P[1,p]$ (if any).

is a tool originally designed for data compression that recently turned out to be fundamental for most of known compressed full-text indexes. Then, we present Backward Search [8] that efficiently supports searching operations by exploiting properties of the Burrows-Wheeler Transform.

4.1 Burrows-Wheeler Transform

Burrows and Wheeler [4] introduced a new compression algorithm based on a reversible transformation, now called the *Burrows-Wheeler Transform* (BWT from now on). The BWT transforms the input string T into a new string that is easier to compress. The BWT of T, hereafter denoted by Bwt(T), consists of three basic steps (see Figure 1): (1) append at the end of T a special symbol \$ smaller than any other symbol of Σ; (2) form a *conceptual* matrix $\mathcal{M}(T)$ whose rows are the cyclic rotations of string $T\$$ in lexicographic order; (3) construct string L by taking the last column of the sorted matrix $\mathcal{M}(T)$. It is Bwt(T) = L.

Every column of $\mathcal{M}(T)$, hence also the transformed string L, is a permutation of $T\$$. In particular the first column of $\mathcal{M}(T)$, call it F, is obtained by lexicographically sorting the symbols of $T\$$ (or, equally, the symbols of L). Note that when we sort the rows of $\mathcal{M}(T)$ we are essentially sorting the suffixes of T because of the presence of the special symbol \$. For our purposes, we hereafter concentrate on compressed indexes [17, 6]. They efficiently support the search of any pattern $P[1,p]$ as a substring of the indexed string $T[1,n]$ by requiring a space which is close to the one of best compressors. Two properties are crucial for their design [4]: (a) Given the cyclic rotation of rows in $\mathcal{M}(T)$, $L[i]$ *precedes* $F[i]$ in the original string T; (b) For any $c \in \Sigma$, the ℓ-th occurrence of c in F and the ℓ-th occurrence of c in L correspond to the *same* symbol of string T.

In order to map symbols in L to their corresponding symbols in F, [8] introduced the following function:

$$\text{LF}(i) = C[L[i]] + \text{rank}_{L[i]}(L, i)$$

where $C[c]$ counts the number of symbols smaller than c in the whole string L. Given Property (b) and the alphabetic ordering of F, it is not difficult to see that symbol $L[i]$ corresponds to symbol $F[\text{LF}(i)]$.

4.2 Backward search

The *backward search* [8] is a surprisingly simple algorithm that, given a pattern $P[1,p]$, is able to identify the range of rows in $\mathcal{M}(T)$ prefixed by P in $O(p)$ steps. In particular, the authors proved that data structures for support-

ing **rank** queries on the string L are enough to search for an arbitrary pattern $P[1,p]$ as a substring of the indexed text T. The resulting search procedure is illustrated in Figure 2. It works in p phases. In each phase it is guaranteed that the following invariant is kept: *At the end of the i-th phase, [First$_i$, Last$_i$] is the range of contiguous rows in $\mathcal{M}(T)$ which are prefixed by $P[i,p]$.* Count starts with $i = p$ so that First$_p$ and Last$_p$ are determined via the array C (step 1). At any other phase, the algorithm (see pseudo-code in Figure 2) has inductively computed First$_{i+1}$ and Last$_{i+1}$ and thus it can derive the next interval of suffixes prefixed by $P[i,p]$ by setting First$_i = C[P[i]] + \text{rank}_{P[i]}(L, \text{First}_{i+1} - 1) + 1$ and Last$_i = C[P[i]] + \text{rank}_{P[i]}(L, \text{Last}_{i+1})$. These two computations are actually mapping (via LF) the first and last occurrences (if any) of symbol $P[i]$ in the substring $L[\text{First}_{i+1}, \text{Last}_{i+1}]$ to their corresponding occurrences in F. As a result, the backward-search algorithm requires to solve $2p$ rank queries on $L = $ Bwt(T) in order to find out the (possibly empty) range [First$_1$, Last$_1$] of text suffixes prefixed by P. The number of occurrences of P in T is, thus, $occ(P) = $ Last$_1 - $ First$_1 + 1$.

The data structures to support **rank** and **select** queries of Theorem 2 achieve better space bounds when they are built on strings which are the result of the Burrows-Wheeler transform (i.e., $L = $ Bwt(T)). In this cases the achieved upper bounds are in terms of the k-th order entropy of the original text for sufficiently small values of k. It follows:

THEOREM 6. *Given a text $T[1,n]$ drawn from an alphabet Σ of size σ, there exists a compressed index that takes $p \times t_{\text{rank}}$ time to support* Count($P[1,p]$) *where t_{rank} is the time required to perform a* **rank** *query. The following are the best space/time complexities depending on σ.*

Ref.	space (bits)	t_{rank}	σ
[9]	$nH_k(T) + o(n)$	$O(1)$	$\log^{O(1)} n$
[9]	$nH_k(T) + o(n) \cdot \log \sigma$	$O(1 + \frac{\log \sigma}{\log \log n})$	$o(n)$
[2]	$nH_k(T) + n \cdot o(\log \sigma)$	$O(\log \log \sigma)$	$O(n)$

The space bounds hold for any $k \leq \alpha \log_\sigma n$ and $0 < \alpha < 1$.

Notice that compressed indexes support also other operations, like locate and display of pattern occurrences, which are slower than Count in that they require polylog(n) time per occurrence (See [17, 6]). We do not enter into details since these kind of operations are out of our scope.

4.3 Our solution

The idea behind our solution is that of sparsifying the string $L = $ Bwt(T) by removing most of its symbols (namely, for each symbol we just keep track of one every $l/2$ of its occurrences). Similarly to backward search, our algorithm searches a pattern $P[1,p]$ by performing p phases. In each of them, it computes two indexes of rows of $\mathcal{M}(T)$ (First$_{\approx i}$ and Last$_{\approx i}$) which are obtained by performing rank queries on the sampled BWT and then by applying a correction mechanism. Corrections are required to guarantee that both indexes are within a distance $l/2$ from the actual indexes First$_i$ and Last$_i$ (i.e., the indexes that the backward search would compute for P in phase i). More formally, in each phase it is guaranteed that First$_{\approx i} \in [\text{First}_i - (l/2)) - 1), \text{First}_i]$ and Last$_{\approx i} \in [\text{Last}_i, \text{Last}_i + (l/2) - 1]$. Clearly, also the last step obeys to the invariant, hence all rows in [First$_{\approx 1}$, Last$_{\approx 1}$] contain suffixes prefixed by P, with the possible exception of the first and last $l/2$ ones. Hence, the maximum error such algorithm can commit is l.

Algorithm Count$\approx_l(P[1,p])$

1. $i = p$, $c = P[p]$, First$\approx_p = C[c] + 1$, Last$\approx_p = C[c+1]$;
2. **while** ((First$\approx_i \leq$ Last$\approx_i$) **and** ($i \geq 2$)) **do**
3. $c = P[i-1]$;
4.   DiscrFirst$_i = $ Succ(First$\approx_i$, D$_c$)
5. $RL = \min($DiscrFirst$_i -$ First$\approx_i, l/2 - 1)$
6.   First$\approx_{i-1} = $ LF(DiscrFirst$_i) - RL$;
7.   DiscrLast$_i = $ Pred(Last$\approx_i$, D$_c$)
8. $RR = \min($Last$\approx_i -$ DiscrLast$_i, l/2 - 1)$
9.   Last$\approx_{i-1} = $ LF(DiscrLast$_i) + RR$;
10. $i = i - 1$;
11. **if** (Last$\approx_i <$ First$\approx_i$) **then return** "no occurrences of P" **else return** [First$\approx_i$, Last$\approx_i$].

Figure 3: Our algorithm to find the approximate range [First$_1$, Last$_1$] of rows of $\mathcal{M}(T)$ prefixed by $P[1,p]$ (if any).

For each symbol c, the sampling of $L = $ Bwt(T) keeps track of a set D$_c$ of positions, called *discriminant positions* (for symbol c), containing:

- the position of the first occurrence of c in L;
- the positions x of the ith occurrence of c in L where $i \bmod l/2 \equiv 0$;
- the position of the last occurrence of c in L.

Algorithm 3 searches a pattern $P[1,p]$ by performing predecessor and successor queries on sets Ds.[3] The crucial steps are lines $4 - 9$ where the algorithm computes the values of First$\approx_{i-1}$ and Last$\approx_{i-1}$ using the values computed in the previous phase. To understand the intuition behind these steps, let us focus on the computation of First$\approx_{i-1}$ and assume that we know the value of First$_i$. The original backward search would compute the number of occurrences, say v, of symbol c in the prefix $L[1 :$ First$_i - 1]$. Since our algorithm does not have the whole L, the best it can do is to identify the rank, say r, of the position in D$_c$ closest (but larger) to First$_i$. Clearly, $r \cdot l/2 - l/2 < v \leq r \cdot l/2$. Thus, setting First$\approx_{i-1} = C[c] + r \cdot l/2 - l/2 - 1$ would suffice to guarantee that First$\approx_{i-1} \in [$First$_{i-1} - (l/2 - 1)$, First$_{i-1}]$. Notice that we are using the crucial assumption that the algorithm knows First$_i$. If we replace First$_i$ with its approximation First$\approx_i$, this simple argumentation cannot be applied since the error would grow phase by phase. Surprisingly, it is enough to use the simple correction computed at line 5 to fix this problem. The following Lemma provides a formal proof of our claims.

LEMMA 1. *For any fixed $l \geq 0$ and any phase i, both* First$\approx_i \in [$First$_i - (l/2-1)$, First$_i]$ *and* Last$\approx_i \in [$Last$_i$, Last$_i + l/2 - 1]$ *hold.*

PROOF. We prove only that First$\approx_i \in [$First$_i - (l/2 - 1)$, First$_i]$ (a similar reasoning applies for Last$\approx_i$). The proof is by induction. For the first step p, we have that First$\approx_p = $

[3]A predecessor query Pred(x,A) returns the predecessor of x in a set A i.e., $\max\{y \mid y \leq x \ \wedge \ y \in A\}$. A successor query is similar but finds the minimum of $y \geq x$.

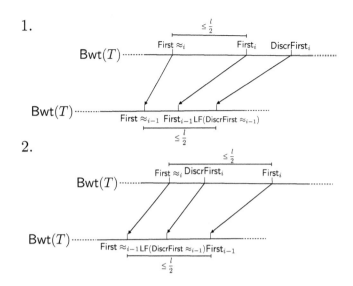

Figure 4: How First$\approx_i$, DiscrFirst$_i$ and First$_i$ interact.

First$_p$, thus the thesis immediately follows. Otherwise, we assume that First$\approx_i \in [$First$_i - (l/2 - 1)$, First$_i]$ is true and prove that First$\approx_{i-1} \in [$First$_{i-1} - (l/2 - 1)$, First$_{i-1}]$. Recall that First$_{i-1}$ is computed as $C[c] + \text{rank}_c(L, $First$_i - 1) + 1$. We distinguish two cases: (1) First$_i \leq $ DiscrFirst$_i$ and (2) First$_i >$ DiscrFirst$_i$, both of which are illustrated also in Figure 4.

Case 1) Let z be the number of occurrences of symbol c in the substring $L[$First$_i$, DiscrFirst$_i - 1]$, so that First$_{i-1} = $ LF(DiscrFirst$_i) - z$ [4]. Then, the difference First$_{i-1} -$ First$\approx_{i-1}$ equals to LF(DiscrFirst$_i) - z - $LF(DiscrFirst$_i) + \min($DiscrFirst$_i - $First$\approx_i, l/2 - 1) = \min($DiscrFirst$_i - $First$\approx_i, l/2 - 1) - z \leq l/2$. Since (by inductive hypothesis) $0 \leq $ First$_i - $First$\approx_i \leq l/2$ and DiscrFirst$_i$ is the closest discriminant position for c larger than First$\approx_i$, we have that $z \leq \min($DiscrFirst$_i - $First$\approx_i, l/2 - 1)$. Thus, the difference is also always non negative.

Case 2) Let $k = |$First$\approx_i - $DiscrFirst$_i|$ and z be the number of occurrences of c in $L[$DiscrFirst$_i$, First$_i - 1]$. Start by noting that $z < l/2$ since $L[$DiscrFirst$_i$, First$_i - 1]$ contains at most $l/2$ symbols. Since (by inductive hypothesis) First$_i - $First$\approx_i < l/2$, we have that $k + z < l/2$; moreover, First$_{i-1}$ can be rewritten as LF(DiscrFirst$_i) + z + 1$. Thus, First$_{i-1} - $First$\approx_{i-1} = $ LF(DiscrFirst$_i) + z + 1 - $LF(DiscrFirst$_i) + k = z + k + 1 \leq l/2$. Finally, since k and z are non negative, First$_{i-1} - $First$\approx_{i-1}$ is non negative. $\square$

By combining Lemma 1 with the proof of correctness of Backward Search (Lemma 3.1 in [8]) we easily obtain the following Theorem.

THEOREM 7. *For any pattern $P[1,p]$ that occurs* Count(P) *times in T Algorithm 3 returns in $O(p)$ steps as result a value* Count$\approx_l(P) \in [$Count(P), Count$(P) + l - 1]$.

Notice that, if [First, Last] is the range of indexes corresponding to the consecutive suffixes that are prefixed by

[4]Observe that $L[$DiscrFirst$_i] = c$ by definition of discriminant position for c.

P, then the algorithm identifies a range [First≈, Last≈] such that First − $l/2$ < First≈ ≤ First and Last ≤ Last≈ < Last + $l/2$.

It remains to show how to represent the sets of discriminant positions D_c to support predecessor and successor queries on them. We represent each of these sets by means of two different objects. We conceptually divide the string $L = \mathsf{Bwt}(T)$ into $\lceil 2n/l \rceil$ blocks of equal length and for each of them we create the characteristic set B_i, such that B_i contains c iff there exists a position in D_c belonging to block i. Considering sets B_i as strings (with arbitrary order), we compute the string $B = B_0 \# B_1 \# \ldots B_{2n/l} \#$ where $\#$ is a symbol outside Σ and augment it with rank and select data structures (see Theorem 2). Let r be the total number of discriminant positions. We also create an array V of r cells, designed as follows. Let x be a discriminant position and assume that it appears as the jth one in B, then $V[j] = x \bmod l/2$. The following Lemma states that a constant number rank and select queries on B and V suffice for computing $\mathsf{Pred}(x, D_c)$ and $\mathsf{Succ}(x, D_c)$.

LEMMA 2. $\mathsf{Pred}(x, D_c)$ and $\mathsf{Succ}(x, D_c)$ can be computed with a constant number of rank and select queries on B and V.

PROOF. We show only how to support $\mathsf{Pred}(x, D_c)$ since $\mathsf{Succ}(x, D_c)$ is similar. Let $p = \mathsf{rank}_c(B, \mathsf{select}_\#(B, \lfloor x/l \rfloor))$, denoting the number of blocks containing a discriminant position of c before the one addressed by $\lfloor x/l \rfloor$. Let $q = \mathsf{select}_c(B, p) - \lfloor x/l \rfloor$ be the index of the discriminant position preceding x (the subtraction removes the $\#$ spurious symbols). Then, $\mathsf{rank}_\#(B, \mathsf{select}_c(B, p))$ finds the block preceding (or including) $\lfloor x/l \rfloor$ that has a discriminant position for c. And, $V[q]$ contains the offset, within that block, of the discriminant position. Such position can be either in a block preceding $\lfloor x/l \rfloor$ or in the same block. In the latter case we have an additional step to make, as we have so far retrieved a position that just belongs to the same block but could be greater than x. In such case, we decrease p by 1 and repeat all the calculations. Note that since the first occurrence of c is also a discriminant than this procedure can never fail. □

Once we have computed the correct discriminant positions, Algorithms 3 requires to compute an LF-step from them (lines 7 and 9). The following Lemma states that this task is simple.

FACT 1. For any symbol c, given any discriminant position d in D_c but the largest one, we have that $\mathsf{LF}(d) = C[c] + (i-1) \cdot l/2 + 1$ where i is such that D_c's ith element in left-to-right position is d. For the largest discriminant position d in D_c we have $\mathsf{LF}(d) = C[c+1]$.

It follows immediately that while performing the calculations of Lemma 2 we can also compute the LF mapping of the discriminant position retrieved.

PROOF OF THEOREM 5. Correctness has been proved. The time complexity is easily seen to be $O(|P|)$ instances of Lemma 2, hence the claim. The space complexity is given by three elements. The array C, containing counters for each symbol, requires $O(\sigma \log n)$ bits. The number of discriminant positions is easily seen to be at most $2n/l$ in total,

hence the array V requires at most $O(n/l)$ cells of $O(\log l)$ bits each. Finally, the string B requires one symbol per block plus one symbol per discriminant positions, accounting for $O(n \log(\sigma)/l)$ bits in total. The theorem follows. □

5. COMPACT PRUNED SUFFIX TREE

Let $\mathcal{PST}_l(T)$ be the pruned suffix tree as discussed in the introduction, and let m be the number of its nodes. Recall that $\mathcal{PST}_l(T)$ is obtained from the suffix tree of T by removing all the nodes with less than l leaves in their subtrees, and hence constitutes a good solution to our lower-sided error problem: when $\mathsf{Count}(P) \geq l$, the answer is correct, otherwise an arbitrary number below l can be returned. Compared with the solution of Section 4 it has the great advantage of being perfectly correct if the pattern appears frequently enough, but is extremely space inefficient. Our objective in this section is that explaining a compact version of the $\mathcal{PST}_l(T)$, by means of proving the following:

THEOREM 8. Given $T[1, n]$ drawn from an alphabet Σ of size σ and given an error threshold l, there exists a representation of $\mathcal{PST}_l(T)$ using $O(m \log(\sigma l) + \sigma \log n)$ bits that can answer to $\mathsf{Count}_{\geq l}(P)$ in $O(|P| \times f(n, \sigma))$ time where m is the number of nodes of $\mathcal{PST}_l(T)$ and $f(n, \sigma)$ is the chosen rank and select time complexity summed up (see Theorem 2).

To appreciate Theorem 8, as also observed in the introduction, consider that the original $\mathcal{PST}_l(T)$ representation requires, apart from node pointers, labels together with their length for a total of $O(m \log n + g \log \sigma)$. The predominant space complexity is given by the edge labels, since it can reach $n \log \sigma$ bits even when m is small. Therefore, our objective is to build an alternative search algorithm that does not require all the labels to be written.

5.1 Suffix trees

We now review the suffix tree[12] in greater detail, introducing useful notation and some of its properties. The *suffix tree* [12] of a text T is the compacted trie, i.e., a trie in which all unary nodes omitted, denoted as $\mathcal{ST}(T)$ or simply $\mathcal{ST}$, built on all the n suffixes of T. We ensure that no suffix is a proper prefix of another suffix by simply assuming that a special symbol, say $\$$, terminates the text T. The symbol $\$$ does not appear anywhere else in T and is assumed to be lexicographically smaller than any other symbol in Σ. This constraint immediately implies that each suffix of T has its own unique leaf in the suffix tree, since any two suffixes of T will eventually follow separate branches in the tree. For a given edge, the *edge label* is simply the substring in T corresponding to the edge. For edge between nodes u and v in $\mathcal{ST}$, the edge label (denoted $\mathsf{label}(u, v)$) is always a non-empty substring of T. For a given node u in the suffix tree, its *path label* (denoted $\mathsf{pathlabel}(u)$) is defined as the concatenation of edge labels on the path from the root to u. The *string depth* of node u is simply $|\mathsf{pathlabel}(u)|$. In order to allow a linear space representation of the tree, each edge label is usually represented by a pair of integers denoting, respectively, the starting position in T of the substring describing the edge label and its length. In this way, the suffix tree can be stored in $\Theta(n \log n)$ bits of space. It is very well-known that to search a pattern $P[1, p]$ in T we have to identify, if any, the highest node u in $\mathcal{ST}$ such that P prefixes $\mathsf{pathlabel}(u)$. To do this, we start from the root of $\mathcal{ST}$ and follow the path matching symbols of P, until a mismatch occurs or P is completely matched. In the former case P does not occur in T. In the latter case, each leaf in the subtree below the matching position gives an occurrence of P. The number of these occurrences can be obtained in constant time by simply storing in any node u the number $C(u)$ of leaves in its subtree. Therefore, this algorithm counts the occurrences of any pattern $P[1, p]$ in time $O(p \log \sigma)$. This time complexity can be reduced up to $O(p)$ by placing a (minimal) perfect hashing function [13] in each node to speed up percolation. This will increase the space just by a constant factor.

5.2 Computing counts

As a crucial part of our explanation, we will refer to nodes using their preorder traversal times, with an extra requirement. Recall the branching symbol in a set of children of node u is the first symbol of children edge labels. During the visit we are careful to descend into children in ascending lexicographical order over their branching symbols. Therefore, $u < v$ iff u is either an ancestor of v or their corresponding path labels have the first mismatching symbols, say in position k, such that $\mathsf{pathlabel}(u)[k] < \mathsf{pathlabel}(v)[k]$.

We begin by explaining how to store and access the basic information that our algorithm must recover: Given a node $u \in \mathcal{PST}_l(T)$ we would like to compute $C(u)$, the number of occurrences of $\mathsf{pathlabel}(u)$ as a substring in T [5]. A straightforward storage of such data would require $m \log n$ bits for a tree of m nodes. We prove we can obtain better bounds and still compute $C(u)$ in $O(1)$ time, based on the following simple observation:

OBSERVATION 1. *Let u be a node in $\mathcal{PST}_l(T)$ and let $v_1, v_2, \ldots, v_k$ be children of u in $\mathcal{PST}_l(T)$ that have been pruned away. Denote by $g(u)$ the sum $C(v_1) + C(v_2) + \cdots + C(v_k)$. Then $g(u) < \sigma l$.*

PROOF. Each of the v_is represents a suffix that has been pruned away, hence, for any i, $C(v_i) < l$ in T by definition. Since each node can have at most σ children, the observation follows. $\square$

Note that Observation 1 applies in a stronger form to leaves, where for a leaf x, $C(x) = g(x)$. We refer to the $g(\cdot)$ values as *correction factors* (albeit for leaves they are actual counts). For an example refer to Figure 5. It is easy to see that to obtain $C(v)$ it suffices to sum all correction factors of all descendants of v in $\mathcal{PST}_l(T)$. Precisely, it suffices to build the binary string $G = 0^{g(0)} 1 0^{g(1)} 1 \cdots 0^{g(m-1)} 1$ together with support for binary $\mathtt{select}$ queries.

LEMMA 3. *Let $v \in \mathcal{PST}_l(T)$ and let z be the identifier of its rightmost leaf, Define $\mathsf{CNT}(u, z) = \mathtt{select}_1(G, z) - z - \mathtt{select}_1(G, u) + u$. Then $C(u) = \mathsf{CNT}(u, z)$.*

PROOF. By our numbering scheme, $[u, z]$ contains all values in G for nodes in the subtree of u. $\mathtt{select}_1(G, x) - x$ is equivalent to $\mathtt{rank}_0(G, \mathtt{select}_1(G, x))$, i.e. it sums up all correction factors in nodes before x in the numbering scheme. Computing the two prefix sums and subtracting is sufficient. $\square$

LEMMA 4. *Let m be the number of nodes in $\mathcal{PST}_l(T)$, then G can be stored using at most $m \log(\sigma l) + O(m)$ bits and each call $\mathsf{CNT}(u, z)$ requires $O(1)$ time.*

PROOF. Each correction factor has size σl at most, hence the number of $\mathbf{0}$s in G is at most $m \sigma l$. The number of $\mathbf{1}$s in G is m. The thesis follows by storing G with the structure of Lemma 1. $\square$

5.3 Finding the correct node

In our solution we will resort to the concepts of suffix links and inverse suffix links in a suffix tree. For each node u of $\mathcal{PST}_l(T)$, the *suffix link* $\mathsf{SL}(u)$ is v iff we obtain $\mathsf{pathlabel}(v)$ from $\mathsf{pathlabel}(u)$ by removing its first symbol. The *inverse suffix link* of v for some symbol c, denoted $\mathsf{ISL}(v, c)$, is u iff $u = SL(v)$ and the *link symbol* is c. We say that v possesses an inverse suffix link for c if $\mathsf{ISL}(v, c)$ is defined. We also refer to the lowest common ancestor of two nodes u and v as $\mathsf{LCA}(u, v)$. An inverse suffix link $\mathsf{ISL}(u, c) = v$ exists only if $\mathsf{pathlabel}(v) = c \cdot \mathsf{pathlabel}(u)$, however many search algorithms require also *virtual* inverse suffix links to be available. We say a node w has a virtual inverse suffix link for symbol c (denoted $\mathsf{VISL}(w, c)$) if and only if at least one of its descendant (including w) has an inverse suffix link for c. The value of $\mathsf{VISL}(w, c)$ is equal to $\mathsf{ISL}(u, c)$ where u is the highest descendant of w having an inverse suffix link for c [6]. As we will see in Lemma 7, it is guaranteed that this highest descendant is unique and, thus, this definition is always well formed. The intuitive meaning of virtual suffix links is the following: $\mathsf{VISL}(w, c)$ links node w to the highest node w' in the tree whose pathlabel is prefixed by $c \cdot \mathsf{pathlabel}(w)$.

Our interest in virtual inverse suffix links is motivated by an alternative interpretation of the classic backward search. When the backward search is performed, the algorithm virtually starts at the root of the suffix tree, and then traverses (*virtual*) inverse suffix links using the pattern to induce the linking symbols, prefixing a symbol at the time to the suffix found so far. The use of virtual inverse suffix links is necessary to accommodate situations in which the pattern P exists but only an extension $P \cdot \alpha$ of it appears as a node in the suffix tree. Note that the algorithm can run directly on the suffix tree if one has access to virtual inverse suffix links, and such property can be directly extended to pruned suffix trees. Storing virtual inverse suffix links explicitly is prohibitive since there can be up to σ of them outgoing from a single node, therefore we plan to store real inverse suffix links and provide a fast search procedure to evaluate the VISL function.

In the remaining part of this section we will show properties of (virtual) suffix links that allow us to store/access them efficiently and to derive a proof of correctness of the searching algorithm sketched above.

The following two Lemmas state that inverse suffix links preserve the relative order between nodes.

LEMMA 5. *Let w, z be nodes in $\mathcal{PST}_l(T)$ such that $\mathsf{ISL}(w, c) = w'$ and $\mathsf{ISL}(z, c) = z'$. Let $u = \mathsf{LCA}(w, z)$ and $u' = \mathsf{LCA}(w', z')$. Then, $\mathsf{ISL}(u, c) = u'$.*

PROOF. If w is a descendant of z or viceversa, the lemma is proved. Hence, we assume $u \neq w$ and $u \neq z$. Let $\alpha = \mathsf{pathlabel}(u)$. Since u is a common ancestor of w and z, it holds $\mathsf{pathlabel}(w) = \alpha \cdot \beta$ and $\mathsf{pathlabel}(z) = \alpha \cdot \zeta$ for some non-empty strings β and ζ. By definition of inverse suffix link, we have that $\mathsf{pathlabel}(w') = c \cdot \alpha \cdot \beta$ and $\mathsf{pathlabel}(z) =$

---

[5] Here, $C(u)$ is the number of leaves in the subtree of u in the *original* suffix tree.

[6] Notice that w and u are the same node whenever w has an inverse suffix link for c.

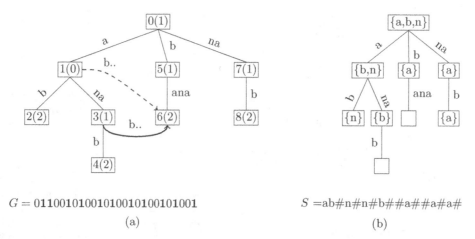

$G = 0110010100101010010100101001$

(a)

$S = \text{ab\#n\#n\#b\#\#a\#\#a\#a\#}$

(b)

Figure 5: The pruned suffix tree of banabananab with threshold 2. Each node contains its preorder traversal id and in brackets, its correction factor. Arrow denotes an inverse suffix link for b; dashed arrow a virtual one. (b) The same PST of (a), with information associated to Theorem 9. Each node is given the set of symbols for which a virtual inverse suffix link is defined. The binary string G contains corrections factor in unary format (separators are in bold for clarity). The string S contains the separated encoding, in preorder traversal, of suffix links chosen by our procedure.

$c \cdot \alpha \cdot \zeta$. Since w and z do not share the same path below u, the first symbols of β and ζ must differ. This implies the existence of a node v whose path label is $\mathsf{pathlabel}(v) = c \cdot \alpha$ which is the lowest common ancestor between w' and z'. Again by definition of inverse suffix link, it follows that $\mathsf{ISL}(u, c) = u' = v$. □

LEMMA 6. *Given any pair of nodes u and v with $u < v$ such that both have an inverse suffix link for symbol c, it holds $\mathsf{ISL}(u, c) < \mathsf{ISL}(v, c)$.*

PROOF. Since $u < v$, we have that $\mathsf{pathlabel}(u)$ is lexicographically smaller than $\mathsf{pathlabel}(v)$. Thus, obviously $c \cdot \mathsf{pathlabel}(u)$ is lexicographically smaller than $c \cdot \mathsf{pathlabel}(v)$. Since $c \cdot \mathsf{pathlabel}(u)$ is the path label of $u' = \mathsf{ISL}(u, c)$ and $c \cdot \mathsf{pathlabel}(v)$ is is the path label of $v' = \mathsf{ISL}(v, c)$, u' precedes v' in the preorder traversal of $\mathcal{PST}_l(T)$. □

Computing the virtual inverse suffix link of node u for symbol c requires to identify the highest descendant of u (including u) having an inverse suffix link for c. If such a node does not exist we conclude that the virtual inverse suffix link is undefined. The following Lemma states that such node, say v, must be unique meaning that if there exists an other descendant of u having an inverse suffix link for c, then this node must be also descendant of v.

LEMMA 7. *For any node u in the $\mathcal{PST}_l(T)$, if exists, the highest descendant of u (including u) having an inverse suffix link for a symbol c is unique.*

PROOF. Pick any pair of nodes that descend from u having an inverse suffix link for the symbol c. By Lemma 5 their common ancestor must also have an inverse suffix link for c. Thus, there must exist an unique node which is common ancestor of all of these nodes. □

In our solution we conceptually associate each node u in $\mathcal{PST}_l(T)$ with the set of symbols $\mathcal{D}_u$ for which u has an inverse suffix link. We represent each set with a string $\mathrm{Enc}(\mathcal{D}_u)$ built by concatenating the symbols in $\mathcal{D}_u$ in any order and ending with a special symbol $\#$ not in Σ. We

then build a string S as $\mathrm{Enc}(\mathcal{D}_0)\mathrm{Enc}(\mathcal{D}_1) \cdots \mathrm{Enc}(\mathcal{D}_{m-1})$ so that the encodings follow the preorder traversal of the tree. We also define the array $C[1, \sigma]$ whose entry $C[c]$ stores the number of nodes of $\mathcal{PST}_l(T)$ whose path label starts with a symbol lexicographically smaller than c. The next Theorem proves that string S together with $\mathbf{rank}$ and $\mathbf{select}$ capabilities is sufficient to compute VISL. This is crucial to prove that our data structure works, proving virtual inverse suffix links can be induced from real ones.

THEOREM 9. *Let $u \in \mathcal{PST}_l(T)$ and let z be the rightmost leaf descending from u. For any character c, let $c_u = \mathbf{rank}_c(S, \mathbf{select}_{\#}(S, u))$ and, similarly, let $c_z = \mathbf{rank}_c(S, \mathbf{select}_{\#}(S, z))$. Then (a) if $c_z = c_u$, $\mathsf{VISL}(u, c)$ is undefined. Otherwise, (b) $C[c] + c_u + 1 = \mathsf{VISL}(u, c)$ and (c) $C[c] + c_z$ is the rightmost leaf descending from $\mathsf{VISL}(u, c)$.*

PROOF. Let $\mathcal{A}$ be the set of nodes of $\mathcal{PST}_l(T)$ whose pathlabel is lexicographically smaller than the pathlabel of u and let $\mathcal{B}$ be the set of nodes in the subtree of u. Let $S(\mathcal{A})$ and $S(\mathcal{B})$ be the concatenations of, respectively, $\mathrm{Enc}(\mathcal{D}_w)$ for $w \in \mathcal{A}$ and $\mathrm{Enc}(\mathcal{D}_w)$ for $w \in \mathcal{B}$. Due to the preorder numbering of nodes, we know that $\mathcal{A} = [0, u-1]$ and $\mathcal{B} = [u, z]$. Thus, $S(\mathcal{A})$ is a prefix of S that ends where $S(\mathcal{B})$ begins. Notice that the operations $\mathbf{select}_{\#}(S, u)$ and $\mathbf{select}_{\#}(S, z)$ return respectively the ending positions of $S(\mathcal{A})$ and $S(\mathcal{B})$ in S. Thus, c_u counts the number of inverse suffix links of nodes in $\mathcal{A}$ while c_z includes also the number of inverse suffix links of nodes in $\mathcal{B}$. Hence, if $c_u = c_z$ no node of $\mathcal{B}$ has an inverse suffix link and, thus, proposition (a) is proved.

By Lemma 6 we know that inverse suffix links map nodes by preserving their relative order. Thus, the first node in $\mathcal{B}$ that has an inverse suffix link for c is mapped to node $C[c] + c_u + 1$. By the numbering of node, this first node is obviously also the highest one. Thus, proposition (b) is proved.

Proposition (c) is proven by resorting to similar considerations. □

Figure 5 illustrates the whole situation: from a pruned suffix tree, we illustrate the resulting string containing correction factors and the data to rebuild inverse suffix links.

Algorithm Count$_{\geq l}(P[1,p])$

1. $i = p$, $c = P[p]$, $u_p = C[c] + 1$, $z_p = C[c+1]$;
2. **while** $((u_i \neq z_i)$ **and** $(i \geq 2))$ **do**
3. $\quad c = P[i-1]$;
4. $\quad u_{i-1} = \textsf{VISL}(u_i, c) = C[c] + \texttt{rank}_c(S, \texttt{select}_\#(S, u_i)) + 1$;
5. $\quad z_{i-1} = \textsf{VISL}(z_i, c) = C[c] + \texttt{rank}_c(S, \texttt{select}_\#(S, z_i))$;
6. $\quad i = i - 1$;
7. **if** $(u_i = z_i)$ **then return** "no occurrences of P" **else return** $\textsf{CNT}(u_1, z_1)$

Figure 6: Our algorithm to report the number of occurrences of a pattern $P[1,p]$ in our Compact Pruned Suffix Tree.

Exploiting $\textsf{VISL}$, Algorithm 6 searches a pattern $P[1,p]$ backward. The algorithm starts by setting u_p to be $C[P[p]]+1$. At the ith step, we inductively assume that u_{i+1} is known, and its pathlabel to be prefixed by $P[i+1,p]$. Similarly, we keep z_{i+1}, the address of the rightmost leaf in u's subtree. Using u_{i+1} and z_{i+1} we can evaluate if $\textsf{VISL}(u_{i+1}, P[i])$ and, in such case, follow it. In the end, we have to access the number of suffixes of T descending from u_1. The next Theorem formally proves the whole algorithm correctness:

THEOREM 10. *Given any pattern $P[1,p]$, Algorithm 6 retrieves $C(u)$, where u is the highest node of $\mathcal{PST}_l(T)$ such that $\mathsf{pathlabel}(u)$ is prefixed by P. If such node does not exist, it terminates reporting -1.*

PROOF. We start by proving that such node u, if any, is found, by induction. It is easy to observe that $C[P[p]] + 1$ is the highest node whose path label is prefixed by the single symbol $P[p]$.

By hypothesis, we assume that u_{i+1} is the highest node in $\mathcal{PST}_l(T)$ whose path label is prefixed by $P[i+1,p]$, and we want to prove the same for $u_i = \textsf{VISL}(u_{i+1}, P[p-i])$. The fact that $\mathsf{pathlabel}(u_i)$ is prefixed by $P[p-i,p]$ easily follows by definition of inverse suffix link. We want to prove that u_i is the highest one with this characteristic: by contradiction assume there exists an other node w' higher that $u_i = \textsf{VISL}(u_{i+1}, P[i])$. This implies that there exists a node $w = \textsf{SL}(w')$, prefixed by $P[i+1,p]$. Also, the virtual inverse suffix link of u_{i+1} is associated with a proper one whose starting node is $z = \textsf{SL}(u_{i+1})$, which by definition of $\textsf{VISL}$ is also the highest one in u's subtree. Thus, by Lemma 7 w is a descendant of z. Hence, $w > z$ but $\textsf{ISL}(w', c) < \textsf{ISL}(z, c)$, contradicting Lemma 6.

Finally, if at some point of the procedure a node u_{i+1} does not have a virtual inverse suffix link, then it is straightforward the claimed node u does not exist (i.e. P occurs in T less than l times). Once u is found, also z is present, hence we resort to Lemma 3 to obtain $C(u) = \textsf{CNT}(u, z)$. $\square$

By combining this Theorem with the discussion of the previous section, we derive the proof of our main Theorem.

PROOF OF THEOREM 8. We need to store: the C array, holding the count of nodes in $\mathcal{PST}_l(T)$ whose pathlabel prefixed by each of the σ characters; the G string, together with binary $\texttt{select}$ capabilities and the S string, together with arbitrary alphabet $\texttt{rank}$ and $\texttt{select}$ capabilities. Let

m be the number of nodes in $\mathcal{PST}_l(T)$. We know C occupies at most $\sigma \log n$ bits. By Lemma 4 G occupies at most $m \log(\sigma l) + O(m)$ bits. String S can be represented in different ways, related to σ, picking a choice from Theorem 2, but the space is always limited by $m \log \sigma + o(m \log \sigma)$. Hence the total space is $\sigma \log n + m \log(\sigma l) + O(m) + O(m \log(\sigma)) = O(m \log(\sigma l) + \sigma \log n)$, as claimed. For the time complexity, at each of the p steps, we perform four $\texttt{rank}$ and $\texttt{select}$ queries on arbitrary alphabets which we account as $f(\sigma)$. The final step on G takes $O(1)$ time, hence the bound. $\square$

6. EXPERIMENTS

In this section we show an experimental comparison among the known solutions and our solutions. We use four different datasets downloaded from `Pizza&Chili` corpus [6] that correspond to four different types of texts: DNA sequences, structured text (XML), natural language and source codes. Text and alphabet size for the texts in the collection are reported in the first column of Figure 7.

We compare the following solutions:

- `FM-index`. This is an implementation of a compressed full-text index available at the `Pizza&Chili` site [6]. Since it is the compressed full-text index that achieves the best compression ratio, it is useful to establish which is the minimum space required by known solutions to answer to counting queries without errors.

- `APPROX` − l. This is the implementation of our solution presented in Section 4.

- `PST` − l. This is an implementation of the Pruned Suffix Tree as described in [15].

- `CPST` − l. This is the implementation of our Compact Pruned Suffix Tree described in Section 5.

Recall that `APPROX` − l reports results affected by an error of at most l while `PST` − l and `CPST` − l are always correct whenever the pattern occurs at least l times in the indexed text. Due to the lack of space we leave details regarding the various implementations to the final version.

The plots in Figure 8 show the space occupancies of the four indexes depending on the chosen threshold l. We do not plot space occupancies worse than `FM-index`, since in those cases `FM-index` is clearly the index to choose.

As anticipated in the previous sections, it turns out that in all texts of our collection the number of nodes in the pruned suffix tree is small (even smaller than n/l) (these statistics are reported in Figure 7). This is the reason why our `CPST` is slightly more space efficient than `APPROX`. In practice, the former should be indubitably preferred with respect to the latter: it requires less space and it is always correct for patterns that occur at least l times. Even though, the latter remains interesting due to its better theoretical guarantees. In both solutions by halving the error threshold, we obtain indexes that are between 1.75 and 1.95 times smaller. Thus, we can obtain very small indexes by setting relatively small values of l. As an example, `CPST` with $l = 256$ on text `english` requires 5.1 Mbytes of space which is roughly 100 times smaller than the original text. We observe that both `CPST` and `APPROX` are in general significantly smaller than `FM-index` and remain competitive even for small value of l. As an example, `FM-index` requires 232.5 Mbytes on `english` which is roughly 45 times larger than `CPST`−256.

Dataset	Size	σ	$l=8$			$l=64$			$l=256$		
			$\lvert T \rvert/l$	$\lvert \mathcal{PST}_l \rvert$	$\sum_i \lvert \text{edge}(i) \rvert$	$\lvert T \rvert/l$	$\lvert \mathcal{PST}_l \rvert$	$\sum_i \lvert \text{edge}(i) \rvert$	$\lvert T \rvert/l$	$\lvert \mathcal{PST}_l \rvert$	$\sum_i \lvert \text{edge}(i) \rvert$
dblp	275	96	36064	28017	1034016	4508	3705	103383	1127	941	20200
dna	292	15	38399	42361	814993	4799	5491	102127	1199	1317	19194
english	501	225	65764	53600	660957	8220	6491	64500	2055	1616	14316
sources	194	229	25475	25474	11376730	3184	3264	9430627	796	982	8703817

Figure 7: Statistics on the datasets. The second column denotes the original text in MBytes. Each subsequent group of three columns describe $\mathcal{PST}_l$ information for a choice of ℓ: expected amount of nodes, $\lvert T \rvert/l$; real amount of nodes in $\mathcal{PST}_l(T)$; sum of length of labels in $\mathcal{PST}_l(T)$. All numbers are expressed in thousands.

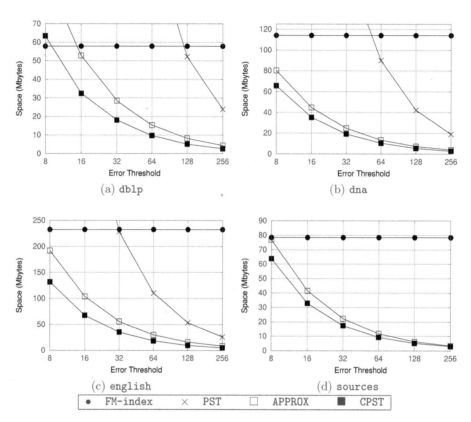

Figure 8: Space occupancies of indexes as a function of the error threshold l.

As far as PST is concerned, it is always much worse than CPST and APPROX. As expected, its space inefficiencies are due to the need of storing edge labels since their amount grows rapidly as l decreases (see Figure 7). Moreover, this quantity strictly depends on the indexed text while the number of nodes is more stable. Thus, the performances of PST are erratic: worse than CPST by a factor 6 on english that becomes 60 on sources. It is remarkable that on sources we have to increase PST's error threshold up to 11,000 to achieve a space occupancy close to our CPST with $l=8$.

For what concerns applications, we use our best index, i.e. CPST together with one estimation algorithm: MOL. The reader can find a lightweight explanation of the algorithm in Section 7.2; the algorithm is oblivious of the underlying data structure as long as a lower-sided error one is used. We performed (details omitted) a comparison between MO, MOL and KVI [15, 14] and found out that MOL delivered the best estimates. We also considered MOC and MOLC, but for some of our data sets the creation of the constraint network was prohibitive in term of running memory. Finally, we tried to compare with CRT [5]; however, we lacked the original implementation and a significative training set for our data sets. Hence, we discarded the algorithm from our comparison.

Figure 9 shows the average error of the estimates obtained with MOL on our collection by using either CPST or PST as base data structure. For each text, we searched 4 Millions patterns of different lengths that we randomly extracted from the text. For each set we identified two pairs of thresholds such that our CPST and PST have roughly the same space occupancy. Thus, this table gives the idea of the significant boost in accuracy that one can achieve by replacing PST with our solution. As an example, consider the case of sources where the threshold of PST is considerably high due to its uncontrollable space occupancy. In this case the factor of improvement that derives by using our solution is more than 790. The improvements for the other texts are less impressive but still considerable.

Dataset	Indices	$|P| = 6$	$|P| = 8$	$|P| = 10$	$|P| = 12$	Avg improvement
dblp	PST-256	10.06 ± 32.372	12.43 ± 34.172	14.20 ± 35.210	15.57 ± 36.044	$19.03\times$
	CPST-16	0.68 ± 1.456	0.86 ± 1.714	1.00 ± 1.884	1.14 ± 2.009	
dna	PST-256	0.47 ± 1.048	0.49 ± 2.433	4.26 ± 15.732	11.09 ± 19.835	$5.51\times$
	CPST-32	0.47 ± 0.499	0.43 ± 0.497	0.52 ± 0.904	1.77 ± 2.976	
english	PST-256	7.03 ± 27.757	12.45 ± 31.712	13.81 ± 28.897	11.43 ± 23.630	$9.68\times$
	CPST-32	0.80 ± 2.391	1.40 ± 3.394	2.07 ± 3.803	2.45 ± 3.623	
sources	PST-11000	816.06 ± 1646.57	564.94 ± 1418.53	400.62 ± 1229.35	313.68 ± 1120.94	$792.52\times$
	CPST-8	0.70 ± 1.028	0.93 ± 1.255	1.13 ± 1.367	1.28 ± 1.394	

Figure 9: Comparison of error (difference between number of occurrences and estimate) for MOL estimates over different pattern lengths. PST and CPST parameters chosen as to obtain close index sizes. Tests performed on $1M$ random patterns appearing in the text. The last column shows the average factor of improvement obtained by using our CPST instead of PST.

7. RELATED WORK

In this section we introduce known solutions (or unpublished simple solutions that use known techniques) for the Substring Occurrence Estimation problem. We also review the literature about our main application, Substring Selectivity Estimation. Unfortunately, they suffer from two important drawbacks: 1) they are not space optimal since they require $\Theta(n \log(n)/l)$ bits of space; 2) they actually solve a relaxed version of our problem in which we do not care on the results whenever the patterns occur less than l times (in these cases, the result may be arbitrarily far from $\mathsf{Count}(P)$, i.e., ignoring the rules of lower-sided and uniform error).

7.1 Occurrence estimation

$\mathcal{PST}_l$ has been already explored in previous sections, hence we skip it and move to other solutions. An alternative pruning strategy consists in building a pruned Patricia Trie $\mathcal{PT}_{l/2}(T)$ that stores just a suffix every $l/2$ suffixes of T sorted lexicographically and resort to Blind Search. A plain Patricia Trie $\mathcal{PT}(T)$ [12] coincides with $\mathcal{ST}(T)$ in which we replace each substring labeling an edge by its first symbol only, called *branching symbol*. More formally, let $T_1, T_2, \ldots, T_n$ denote the n suffixes of T sorted lexicographically, $\mathcal{PT}_{l/2}(T)$ is the patricia trie of the set of $O(n/l)$ strings $\mathcal{S} = \{T_i \mid i \equiv 1 \pmod{l/2}\}$. The pruned patricia trie $\mathcal{PT}_{l/2}(T)$ can be stored in $O(n/l \cdot (\log \sigma + \log n)) = O(n \log n/l)$ bits. We use the blind search described in [7] to search a pattern $P[1, p]$ in time $O(p)$. Such algorithm returns a node u that either corresponds to P, if P is a prefix of some string in $\mathcal{S}$ or another node otherwise (whereas there is a connection between such node and P, without the original text it is not possible to exploit it). Once we identify the node u, we return the number of leaves descending from that node multiplied by l. If P occurs at least $l/2$ times in T, it is easy to see that the number of reported occurrences is a correct approximation of its occurrences in T. Instead, if P occurs less than $l/2$ times in T, the blind search returns a different node. Thus, in such cases the algorithm may fail reporting as result a number of occurrences that may be arbitrarily far from the correct one.

A similar solution resorts to a recent data structure presented by Belazzougui *et al.* [3]. Their solution solves via hashing functions a problem somehow related to ours, called *weak prefix search*. The problem is as follows: We have a set $\mathcal{V}$ of v strings and want to build an index on them. Given a pattern P, the index outputs the ranks (in lexicographic order) of the strings that have P as prefix, if such strings do

not exist the output of the index is arbitrary. Their main solution needs just $O(|P| \log \sigma/w + log|P| + \log \log \sigma)$ time and $O(v \log(L \log \sigma))$ bits of space where L is the average length of the strings in the set and w is the machine word size. We can use their data structure to index the set of suffixes $\mathcal{S}$, so that we can search $P[1, p]$ and report its number of occurrences multiplied by l. Since in our case $L = \Theta(n)$, the index requires $O(n \log(n \log \sigma)/l) = O(n \log n/l)$ bits of space. As in the case of pruned patricia tries, the answer is arbitrary when P is not prefix of any suffix in $\mathcal{S}$ (i.e., it occurs less that l times). Hence, this solution improves the time complexity but has the same drawback of the previous one.

7.2 Selectivity estimation

In this section we present in more detail the three main algorithms for substring selectivity estimation: KVI [15], the class of MO-based estimators [14] and CRT [5], in chronological order. For a given threshold l, the work of KVI starts by assuming to have a data structure answering correctly to queries $\mathsf{Count}(P)$ when $\mathsf{Count}(P) \geq l$ and strives to obtain a one-sided error estimate for infrequent ($< l$) strings. It also assume the data structure can detect if $\mathsf{Count}(P) < l$. Their main observation is as follows: let $P = \alpha\beta$ where $\mathsf{Count}(P) < l$ and assume $\mathsf{Count}(\alpha) \geq l$ and $\mathsf{Count}(\beta) \geq l$, then one can estimate $\mathsf{Count}(P)$ from $\mathsf{Count}(\alpha)$ and $\mathsf{Count}(\beta)$ in a probabilistic way, using a model in which the probability of β appearing in the text given that α appears is roughly the same of β appearing by itself. Generalizing this concept, KVI starts from P and retrieves the longest prefix of P, say P', such that $\mathsf{Count}(P') > l$, and then reiterates on the remaining suffix.

Requiring the same kind of data structure beneath, the MO class starts by observing that instead of splitting the pattern P into known fragments of information, one can rely on the concept of maximum overlap: given two strings α and β, the maximum overlap $\alpha \oslash \beta$ is the longest prefix of β that is also a suffix of α. Hence, instead of estimating $\mathsf{Count}(P)$ from $\mathsf{Count}(\alpha)$ and $\mathsf{Count}(\beta)$ alone, it also computes and exploits the quantity $\mathsf{Count}(\alpha \oslash \beta)$. In probabilistic terms, this is equivalent to introducing a light form of conditioning between pieces of the string, hence yielding better estimates. The change is justified by an empirically proved Markovian property that makes maximum overlap estimates very significant. MO is also presented in different variants: MOC, introducing constraint network from the strings to avoid overestimation, MOL, performing a more thorough search of substrings of the pattern, and `MOLC`, combining the two previous strategies.

In particular, `MOL` relies on the *lattice* $\mathcal{L}_P$ of the pattern P. For a string $P = a \cdot \alpha \cdot b$ ($|\alpha| \geq 0$), the *l-parent* of P is the string $\alpha \cdot b$ and the *r-parent* of P is $a \cdot \alpha$. The lattice $\mathcal{L}_P$ is described recursively: P is in the lattice and for any string ζ in the lattice, also its l-parent and r-parent are in the lattice. Two nodes β and ζ of the lattice are connected if β is an l-parent or an r-parent of ζ or viceversa. To estimate $\mathsf{Count}(P)$, the algorithm starts by identifying all nodes in the lattice for which $\mathsf{Count}(\alpha)$ can be found in the underlying data structure and retrieve it, so that $Pr(\alpha) = \mathsf{Count}(\alpha)/N$, where N is a normalization factor. For all other nodes, it computes $Pr(a \cdot \alpha \cdot b) = Pr(a \cdot \alpha) \times Pr(\alpha \cdot b)/Pr(a \cdot \alpha \oslash \alpha \cdot b)$ recursively. In the end, it obtains $Pr(P)$, i.e. the normalized ratio of occurrences of P in T.

The `CRT` method was presented to circumvent underestimation, a problem that may afflict estimators with limited probabilistic knowledge as those above. The first step is to build an a-priori knowledge of which substrings are highly distinctive in the database: in that, they rely on the idea that most patterns exhibit a short substring that is usually sufficient to identify the pattern itself. Given a pattern to search, they retrieve all distinctive substrings of the pattern and use a machine learning approach to combine their value. At construction time, they train a regression tree over the distinctive substrings by using a given query log; the tree is then exploited at query time to obtain a final estimate.

8. FUTURE WORK

We presented two different solutions to the problem of substring occurrence estimation. Our first solution is a space-optimal data structure when the index is allowed to have a uniform error on the reported number of occurrences. Our second solution can be seen as a very succinct version of the classical Pruned Suffix Tree for the harder problem of having one-sided errors. It guarantees better space complexities with respect to the pruned suffix tree both in theory and in practice. It is not clear if the latter solution is space-optimal or not, thus, proving a lower bound for the latter problem would provide greater insight into the problem.

As a second open problem, we note that the entire article is forced to deal with additive errors due to lower bounds. A natural question is: is there a way to relax the model, in order to circumvent the multiplicative lower bound (Theorem 4)? For example, what if we allow non-existing substrings to have an arbitrary estimation error, forcing all others with a multiplicative bound?

Acknowledgments

The authors would like to thank Roberto Grossi for fruitful discussions on the topic of this paper.

This work was partially supported by the EU-PSP-BPN-250527 (ASSETS), the POR-FESR 2007-2013 No 63748 (VIS-ITO Tuscany) projects, the MIUR of Italy under project AlgoDEEP prot. 2008TFBWL4, and the PRIN MadWeb 2008.

9. REFERENCES

[1] J. Barbay, T. Gagie, G. Navarro, and Y. Nekrich. Alphabet partitioning for compressed rank/select and applications. In *ISAAC (2)*, pages 315–326, 2010.

[2] J. Barbay, M. He, J.I. Munro, and S. Srinivasa Rao. Succinct indexes for string, binary relations and multi-labeled trees. In *Proc. ACM-SIAM Symposium on Discrete Algorithms (SODA)*, pages 680–689, 2007.

[3] D. Belazzougui, P. Boldi, R. Pagh, and S. Vigna. Fast prefix search in little space, with applications. In *ESA (1)*, pages 427–438, 2010.

[4] M. Burrows and D. Wheeler. A block sorting lossless data compression algorithm. Technical Report 124, Digital Equipment Corporation, 1994.

[5] S. Chaudhuri, V. Ganti, and L. Gravano. Selectivity estimation for string predicates: Overcoming the underestimation problem. In *Proceedings of the 20th International Conference on Data Engineering*, ICDE '04, pages 227–, 2004.

[6] P. Ferragina, R. González, G. Navarro, and R. Venturini. Compressed text indexes: From theory to practice. *ACM Journal of Experimental Algorithmics*, 13, 2008.

[7] P. Ferragina and R. Grossi. The string b-tree: a new data structure for string search in external memory and its applications. *J. ACM*, 46:236–280, March 1999.

[8] P. Ferragina and G. Manzini. Indexing compressed text. *Journal of the ACM*, 52(4):552–581, 2005.

[9] P. Ferragina, G. Manzini, V. Mäkinen, and G. Navarro. Compressed representations of sequences and full-text indexes. *ACM Transactions on Algorithms*, 3(2), 2007.

[10] P. Ferragina and R. Venturini. Compressed permuterm index. In *SIGIR*, pages 535–542, 2007.

[11] R. Grossi and J. S. Vitter. Compressed suffix arrays and suffix trees with applications to text indexing and string matching. *SIAM Journal on Computing*, 35(2):378–407, 2005.

[12] D. Gusfield. *Algorithms on Strings, Trees, and Sequences: Computer Science and Computational Biology*. Cambridge University Press, 1997.

[13] T. Hagerup and T. Tholey. Efficient minimal perfect hashing in nearly minimal space. In *Proceedings of the 18th Annual Symposium on Theoretical Aspects of Computer Science(STACS)*, pages 317–326, 2001.

[14] H.V. Jagadish, R. T. Ng, and D. Srivastava. Substring selectivity estimation. In *Proceedings of the eighteenth ACM SIGMOD-SIGACT-SIGART symposium on Principles of database systems*, PODS '99, pages 249–260, 1999.

[15] P. Krishnan, J. S. Vitter, and B. R. Iyer. Estimating alphanumeric selectivity in the presence of wildcards. In *SIGMOD Conference*, pages 282–293, 1996.

[16] G. Manzini. An analysis of the Burrows-Wheeler transform. *Journal of the ACM*, 48(3):407–430, 2001.

[17] G. Navarro and V. Mäkinen. Compressed full text indexes. *ACM Computing Surveys*, 39(1), 2007.

[18] D. Okanohara and K. Sadakane. Practical entropy-compressed rank/select dictionary. In *ALENEX*, 2007.

[19] I. H. Witten, A. Moffat, and T. C. Bell. *Managing Gigabytes: Compressing and Indexing Documents and Images*. Morgan Kaufmann Publishers, 1999.

On Finding Skylines in External Memory

Cheng Sheng
CUHK
Hong Kong
csheng@cse.cuhk.edu.hk

Yufei Tao
CUHK
Hong Kong
taoyf@cse.cuhk.edu.hk

ABSTRACT

We consider the *skyline problem* (a.k.a. the *maxima problem*), which has been extensively studied in the database community. The input is a set P of d-dimensional points. A point *dominates* another if the former has a lower coordinate than the latter on every dimension. The goal is to find the *skyline*, which is the set of points $p \in P$ such that p is not dominated by any other data point. In the external-memory model, the 2-d version of the problem is known to be solvable in $O((N/B) \log_{M/B}(N/B))$ I/Os, where N is the cardinality of P, B the size of a disk block, and M the capacity of main memory. For fixed $d \geq 3$, we present an algorithm with I/O-complexity $O((N/B) \log_{M/B}^{d-2}(N/B))$. Previously, the best solution was adapted from an in-memory algorithm, and requires $O((N/B) \log_2^{d-2}(N/M))$ I/Os.

Categories and Subject Descriptors

F2.2 [**Analysis of algorithms and problem complexity**]: Nonnumerical algorithms and problems—geometric problems and computations

General Terms

Algorithms, theory

Keywords

Skyline, admission point, pareto set, maxima set

1. INTRODUCTION

This paper studies the *skyline problem*. The input is a set P of d-dimensional points in *general position*, i.e., no two points of P share the same coordinate on any dimension. Given a point $p \in \mathbb{R}^d$, denote its i-th ($1 \leq i \leq d$) coordinate as $p[i]$. A point p_1 is said to *dominate* another point p_2,

represented as $p_1 \prec p_2$, if p_1 has a smaller coordinate on all d dimensions, namely:

$$\forall i = 1, ..., d, \ p_1[i] < p_2[i].$$

The goal is to compute the *skyline* of P, denoted as $SKY(P)$, which includes all the points in P that are not dominated by any other point, namely:

$$SKY(P) = \{p \in P \mid \nexists p' \in P \text{ s.t. } p' \prec p\}. \quad (1)$$

The skyline is also known under other names such as the *pareto set*, the set of *admission points*, and the set of *maximal vectors* (see [24]).

Figure 1: The skyline is $\{1, 5, 7\}$

Ever since its debut in the database literature a decade ago [7], skyline computation has generated considerable interests in the database area (see [24] for a brief survey). This is, at least in part, due to the relevance of skylines to *multi-criteria optimization*. Consider, for example, a hotel recommendation scenario, where each hotel has two attributes `price` and `rating` (a smaller rating means better quality). Figure 1 illustrates an example with 8 hotels, of which the skyline is $\{1, 5, 7\}$. Every hotel *not* in the skyline is worse than at least one hotel in the skyline on both dimensions, i.e., more expensive and rated worse at the same time. In general, for any scoring function that is monotone on all dimensions, the skyline always contains the *best* (top-1) point that minimizes the function. This property is useful when it is difficult, if not impossible, for a user to specify a suitable scoring function that accurately reflects her/his preferences on the relative importance of various dimensions. In Figure 1, for instance, $\{1, 5, 7\}$ definitely includes the best hotel, no matter the user emphasizes more, and how much more, on price or rating.

1.1 Computation model

Our complexity analysis is under the standard *external memory (EM)* model [2], which has been successful in capturing the characteristics of algorithms dealing with massive data that do not fit in memory (see [27] for a broad summary of results in this model). Specifically, in this model, a computer has a main memory that is able to accommodate M words, and a disk of unbounded size. The disk is formatted into disjoint *blocks*, each of which contains B consecutive words. The memory should have at least two blocks, i.e., $M \geq 2B$. An *I/O operation* reads a block of data from the disk into memory, or conversely, writes a block of memory information into the disk. The time complexity is measured in the number of I/Os performed by an algorithm. CPU calculation is free.

In EM, *linear* cost should be interpreted as $O(N/B)$ for a dataset of size N, as opposed to $O(N)$ in a memory-resident model such as RAM. In this paper, *poly-logarithmic* should be understood as $O(\text{polylog}_{M/B}(N/B))$, instead of $O(\text{polylog } N)$, namely, it is important to achieve base M/B. In this paper, a function is said to be *near-linear* if it is in $O((N/B)\,\text{polylog}_{M/B}(N/B))$ but not in $O(N/B)$.

1.2 Previous results

In internal memory, Matousek [21] showed how to find the skyline in $O(N^{2.688})$ time when the dimensionality d of the dataset P is as high as the number N of points in P. In 2-d space, Kung et al. [19] proposed an $O(N \log N)$-time algorithm. For any fixed dimensionality $d \geq 3$, they also gave an algorithm with time complexity $O(N \log^{d-2} N)$. Bentley [4] developed an alternative algorithm achieving the same bounds as those of [19]. Kirkpatrick and Seidel [16] presented algorithms whose running time is sensitive to the result size, and has the same complexity as the algorithms in [4, 19] when the skyline has $\Omega(N)$ points. It can be shown that any algorithm in the *comparison class*[1] must incur $\Omega(N \log N)$ time, implying that the solutions of [4, 19] are already optimal in this class for $d = 2$ and 3 (see also some recent results on instance optimality due to Afshani et al. [1]). For $d \geq 4$, Gabow et al. [11] discovered an algorithm terminating in $O(N \log^{d-3} N \log \log N)$ time, which still remains the best result up to this day. Note, however, that the solution of [11] does not belong to the comparison class, due to its reliance on the van Emde Boas structure [26] that uses features of the RAM model. Faster algorithms have been developed in some special circumstances where, for example, the data follow special distributions [5, 6, 10], or each dimension has a small domain [22].

All the RAM algorithms can be applied in the EM model directly by treating the disk as virtual memory. Such a brute-force approach, however, can be expensive in practice because it fails to take into account the effects of blocking, which do not exist in RAM but are inherent in external memory. For example, running the solution of [11] in EM naively

would entail $O(N \log^{d-3} N \log \log N)$ I/Os, which amounts to reading the entire dataset $O(B \log^{d-3} N \log \log N)$ times (B is at the order of thousands in practice). Hence, there is a genuine need to design I/O-oriented algorithms. For $d = 2$, such an algorithm can be easily found, as Kung et al. [19] showed that the problem can be settled by sorting the data followed by a single scan (we will come back to this in Section 2), which takes $O((N/B) \log_{M/B}(N/B))$ I/Os in total. To our knowledge, for general d, the RAM algorithm that can be most efficiently adapted to EM is the one by Bentley [4], which performs $O((N/B) \log_2^{d-2}(N/M))$ I/Os – note that the base of the log is 2, instead of M/B. We are not aware of any algorithm that can achieve near-linear (or better) running time.

For $d \geq 3$, the skyline of a dataset P can be trivially obtained by computing the cartesian product $P \times P$ (i.e., by comparing all pairs of points in P) which, in turn, can be produced by a *blocked nested loop (BNL)* in $\Theta(N^2/(MB))$ I/Os. It has been observed [7] that such a quadratic complexity is too slow in practice for large N. In the past decade, several algorithms, as we survey below, have been designed to alleviate the deficiency, typically by leveraging the *transitivity* of the dominance relation (i.e., $p_1 \prec p_2$ and $p_2 \prec p_3$ imply $p_1 \prec p_3$). Although empirical evaluation has confirmed their effectiveness on selected datasets, *none* of those algorithms has been proved to be asymptotically faster than *BNL* in the worst case. We say that they are captured by the *quadratic trap*.

Borzsonyi et al. [7] presented a *divide and conquer (DC)* method that partitions P into disjoint groups $P_1, ..., P_s$ where the number s of groups is large enough so that each P_i ($i \leq s$) fits in memory. *DC* proceeds by invoking an in-memory algorithm to find the skyline $SKY(P_i)$ of each P_i, and then, deleting those points of $SKY(P_i)$ dominated by some point in the skyline of another group. Although divide and conquer is a promising paradigm for attacking the skyline problem (it is also employed in our solutions), its application in *DC* is heuristic and does not lead to any interesting performance bound.

The *sort first skyline (SFS)* algorithm by Chomicki et al. [9] works by sorting the points $p \in P$ in ascending order of $score(p)$, where $score$ can be any function $\mathbb{R}^d \to \mathbb{R}$ that is monotonically increasing on all dimensions. The monotonicity ensures that, $p_1 \prec p_2$ implies $score(p_1) < score(p_2)$ (but the opposite is *not* true). As a result, a point $p \in P$ cannot be dominated by any point that ranks *behind* it in the ordering. Following this rationale, *SFS* scans P in its sorted order, and maintains the skyline Σ of the points already seen so far (note that $\Sigma \subseteq SKY(P)$ at any time). As expected, the choice of $score$ is crucial to the efficiency of the algorithm. No choice, unfortunately, is known to be able to escape the quadratic trap in the worst case.

In *SFS*, sorting is carried out with the standard external sort. Intuitively, if mutual comparisons are carried out among the data that ever co-exist in memory (during the external sort), many points may get discarded right away once confirmed to be dominated, at no extra I/O cost at all. Based on this idea, Godfrey et al. [12] developed the *linear elimination sort for skyline (LESS)* algorithm. *LESS* has the property that, it terminates in linear expected I/Os under the *independent-and-uniform* assumption (i.e., all di-

---

[1] A skyline algorithm is *comparison-based* if it can infer the dominance relation by only comparing pairs of points. The comparison class includes all such algorithms.

method	I/O complexity	remark
Kung et al. [19]	$O(N \log^{d-2} N)$	
Gabow et al. [11]	$O(N \log^{d-3} N \log \log N)$	not in the comparison class.
Bentley [4]	$O((N/B) \log_2^{d-2}(N/M))$	adapted from Bentley's $O(N \log^{d-2} N)$ algorithm in RAM
BNL	$\Theta(N^2/(MB))$	also applies to the BNL variant of Borzsonyi et al. [7]
DC [7]	$\Omega(N^2/(MB))$	
SFS [9]	$O(N^2/(MB))$	
LESS [12]	$O(N^2/(MB))$	
RAND [24]	$O(\mu N/(MB))$ expected	μ is the number of points in the skyline, which can be $\Omega(N)$.
this paper	$O((N/B) \log_{M/B}^{d-2}(N/B))$	optimal for $d = 3$ in the comparison class

Table 1: Comparison of skyline algorithms for fixed $d \geq 3$

mensions are independent, and the points of P distribute uniformly in the data space), provided that the memory size M is not too small [12]. When the assumption does not hold, however, it remains unknown whether the cost of LESS is $o(N^2/(MB))$.

Sarma et al. [24] described an output-sensitive randomized algorithm RAND, which continuously shrinks P with repetitive iterations, each of which performs a three-time scan on the current P as follows. The first scan takes a random sample set $S \subseteq P$ with size $\Theta(M)$. The second pass replaces (if possible) some samples in S with other points that have stronger pruning power. All samples at the end of this scan are guaranteed to be in the skyline, and thus removed from P. The last scan further reduces $|P|$, by eliminating all the points that are dominated by some sample. At this point, another iteration sets off as long as $P \neq \emptyset$. RAND is efficient when the result has a small size. Specifically, if the skyline has μ points, RAND entails $O(\mu N/(MB))$ I/Os in expectation. When $\mu = \Omega(N)$, however, the time complexity falls back in the quadratic trap.

There is another line of research that concerns preprocessing a dataset P into a structure that supports fast retrieval of the skyline, as well as insertions and deletions on P (see [14, 15, 18, 20, 23] and the references therein). In our context, such pre-computation-based methods do not have a notable advantage over the algorithms mentioned earlier.

1.3 Our results

Our main result is:

THEOREM 1.1. *The skyline of N points in $\mathbb{R}^d$ can be computed in $O((N/B) \log_{M/B}^{d-2}(N/B))$ I/Os for any fixed $d \geq 3$.*

The theorem concerns only $d \geq 3$ because, as mentioned before, the skyline problem is known to be solvable in $O((N/B) \log_{M/B}(N/B))$ I/Os in 2-d space. Unlike the result of Godfrey et al. [12], we make no assumption on the data distribution. Our algorithm is the first one that beats the quadratic trap and, at the same time, achieves near-linear running time. In 3-d space, our I/O complexity $O((N/B) \log_{M/B}(N/B))$ is asymptotically optimal in the class of comparison-based algorithms. For any fixed d, Theorem 1.1 shows that the skyline problem can be settled in $O(N/B)$ I/Os, when $N/B = (M/B)^c$ for some constant c (a situation that is likely to happen in practice). No previous

algorithm is known to have such a property. See Table 1 for a comparison of our and existing results.

The core of our technique is a *distribution-sweep*[2] algorithm for solving the *skyline merge* problem, where we are given s skylines $\Sigma_1, ..., \Sigma_s$ that are separated by $s-1$ hyperplanes orthogonal to a dimension; and the goal is to return the skyline of the union of all the skylines, namely, $SKY(\Sigma_1 \cup ... \cup \Sigma_s)$. It is not hard to imagine that this problem lies at the heart of computing the skyline using a divide-and-conquer approach. Indeed, the lack of a fast solution to skyline merging has been the obstacle in breaking the curse of quadratic trap, as can be seen from the divide-and-conquer attempt of Borzsonyi et al. [7]. We overcome the obstacle by lowering the dimensionality to 3 gradually, and then settling the resulting 3-d problem in linear I/Os. Our solution can also be regarded as the counterpart of Bentley's algorithm [4] in external memory.

Remark. We have defined our problem by assuming that P is in general position. The skyline $SKY(P)$ is still well defined without this assumption. Specifically, let P be a set of points in $\mathbb{R}^d$ (implying that P has no duplicates). Given two points p, p' in P, we have $p \prec p'$ if $p[i] \leq p'[i]$ for all $1 \leq i \leq d$. Note that since $p \neq p'$, the equality does not hold for at least one i. Then, $SKY(P)$ is still given by Equation 1. Our algorithms can be extended to solve this version of the skyline problem, retaining the same performance guarantee as in Theorem 1.1. Details can be found in Section 3.3.

2. PRELIMINARIES

In this section, we review some skyline algorithms designed for memory-resident data. The purposes of the review are three fold. First, we will show that the 2-d solution of Kung et al. [19] can be easily adapted to work in the EM model. Second, our discussion of their algorithm and Bentley's algorithm [4] for $d \geq 3$ not only clarifies some characteristics of the underlying problems, but also sheds light on some obstacles preventing a direct extension to achieve near-linear time complexity in external memory. Finally, we briefly explain the cost lower bound established in [19] and why a similar bound also holds in the I/O context.

Let us first agree on some terminologies. We refer to the

---

[2] An algorithm paradigm proposed by Goodrich et al. [13] that can be regarded as the counterpart of plane-sweep in external memory.

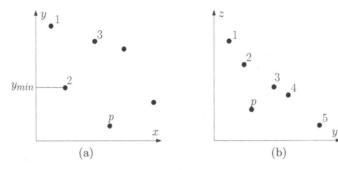

Figure 2: Illustration of algorithms by Kung et al. [19]: (a) 2-d, (b) 3-d

first, second, and third coordinate of a point as its x-, y-, and z-coordinate, respectively. Sometimes, it will be convenient to extend the definition of dominance to subspaces in a natural manner. For example, in case p_1 has smaller x- and y-coordinates than p_2, we say that p_1 dominates p_2 in the x-y plane. No ambiguity can arise as long as the subspace concerning the dominance is always mentioned.

2-d. The skyline $SKY(P)$ of a set P of 2-d points can be extracted by a single scan, provided that the points of P have been sorted in ascending order of their x-coordinates. To understand the rationale, consider any point $p \in P$; and let P' be the set of points of P that rank before p in the sorted order. Apparently, p cannot be dominated by any point that ranks *after* p, because p has a smaller x-coordinate than any of those points. On the other hand, p is dominated by *some* point in P' if and only if the y-coordinate of p is greater than y_{min}, where y_{min} is the smallest y-coordinate of all the points in P'. See Figure 2a where P' includes points 1, 2, 3; and that no point in P' dominates p can be inferred from the fact that p has a lower y-coordinate than y_{min}. Therefore, to find $SKY(P)$, it suffices to read P in its sorted order, and at any time, keep the smallest y-coordinate y_{min} of all the points already seen. The next point p scanned is added to $SKY(P)$ if its y-coordinate is below y_{min}, in which case y_{min} is updated accordingly. In the EM model, this algorithm performs $O((N/B) \log_{M/B}(N/B))$ I/Os, which is the time complexity of sorting N elements in external memory.

3-d. Suppose that we have sorted P in ascending order of their x-coordinates. Similar to the 2-d case, consider any point $p \in P$, with P' being the set of points before p. It is clear that p cannot be dominated by any point that ranks after p. Judging whether p is dominated by a point of P', however, is more complex than the 2-d scenario. The general observation is that, since all points of P' have smaller x-coordinates than p, we only have to check whether p is dominated by some point of P' in the y-z plane. Imagine that we project all the points of P' onto the y-z plane, which yields a 2-d point set P''. Let Σ be the (2d) skyline of P''. It is sufficient to decide whether a point in Σ dominates p in the y-z plane.

It turns out that such a dominance check can be done efficiently. In general, a 2-d skyline is a "staircase". In the y-z plane, if we walk along the skyline in the direction of growing y-coordinates, the points encountered must have descending z-coordinates. Figure 2b illustrates this with a Σ that consists of points 1, ..., 5. To find out whether p

is dominated by any point of Σ in the y-z plane, we only need to find the predecessor o of p along the y-dimension among the points of Σ, and give a "yes" answer if and only if o has a lower z-coordinate than p. In Figure 2b, the answer is "no" because the predecessor of p, i.e., point 2, actually has a greater z-coordinate than p. Returning to the earlier context with P', a "no" indicates that p is not dominated by any point in P', and therefore, p belongs to the skyline $SKY(P)$.

Based on the above reasoning, the algorithm of [19] maintains Σ while scanning P in its sorted order. To find predecessors quickly, the points of Σ are indexed by a binary tree T on their y-coordinates. The next point p is added to $SKY(P)$ upon a "no" answer as explained before, which takes $O(\log N)$ time with the aid of T. Furthermore, a "no" also necessitates the deletion from Σ of all the points that are dominated by p in the y-z plane (e.g., points 3, 4 in Figure 2b). Using T, this requires only $O(\log N)$ time per point removed. As each point of P is deleted at most once, the entire algorithm finishes in $O(N \log N)$ time.

A straightforward attempt of externalizing the algorithm is to implement T as a B-tree. This will result in the total execution time of $\Theta(N \log_B N)$, which is higher than the cost $O((N/B) \log_{M/B}(N/B))$ of our solution by a factor of $\Omega(B \log_B M)$. The deficiency is due to the fact (see [13]) that plane sweep, which is the methodology behind the above algorithm, is ill-fitted in external memory, because it issues a large number of queries (often $\Omega(N)$), rendering it difficult to control the overall cost to be at the order of N/B.

Following a different rationale, Bentley [4] gave another algorithm of $O(N \log N)$ time. We will not elaborate his solution here because our algorithm in the next section degenerates into Bentley's, when M and B are set to constants satisfying $M/B = 2$.

Dimensionalities at least 4. Kung et al. [19] and Bentley [4] deal with a general d-dimensional ($d \geq 4$) dataset P by divide-and-conquer. More specifically, their algorithms divide P into P_1 and P_2 of roughly the same size by a hyperplane perpendicular to dimension 1. Assume that the points of P_1 have smaller coordinates on dimension 1 than those of P_2. Let Σ_1 be the skyline $SKY(P_1)$ of P_1, and similarly, $\Sigma_2 = SKY(P_2)$. All points of Σ_1 immediately belong to $SKY(P)$, but a point $p \in \Sigma_2$ is in $SKY(P)$ if and only if no point in Σ_1 dominates p. Hence, after obtaining Σ_1 and Σ_2 from recursion, a skyline merge is carried out to evict such points as p.

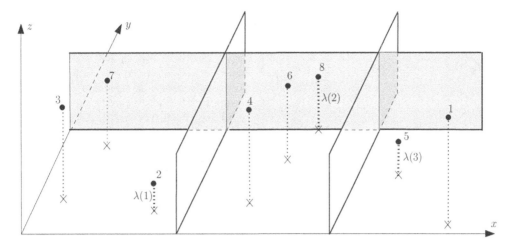

Figure 3: Illustration of 3-d skyline merge. The value of s is 3. Only the points already encountered are shown. Points are labeled in ascending order of their y-coordinates (which is also the order they are fetched). Point 8 is the last one seen. Each cross is the projection of a point in the x-y plane. $\Sigma(1)$ contains points 2, 3, 7, $\Sigma(2)$ includes 4, 6, 8, and $\Sigma(3)$ has 5, 1. $\lambda(1), \lambda(2), \lambda(3)$ equal the z-coordinate of point 2, 8, 5, respectively. Point 8 does not belong to $SKY(P)$ because its z-coordinate is larger than $\lambda(1)$ (i.e., it violates Inequality 2 on $j = 1$).

Externalization of the algorithms of Kung et al. [19] and Bentley [4] is made difficult by a common obstacle. That is, the partitioning in the divide-and-conquer is binary, causing a recursion depth of $\Omega(\text{polylog}(N/M))$. To obtain the performance claimed in Theorem 1.1, we must limit the depth to $O(\text{polylog}_{M/B}(N/B))$. This cannot be achieved by simply dividing P into a greater number $s > 2$ of partitions $P_1, ..., P_s$, because doing so may compromise the efficiency of merging skylines. To illustrate, let $\Sigma_i = SKY(P_i)$ for each $1 \le i \le s$. A point $p \in S_i$ must be compared to $SKY(P_j)$ for all $j < i$. Applying the skyline merge strategy of [4] or [19] would blow up the cost by a factor of $\Omega(s^2)$, which would offset all the gains of a large s. Remedying the drawback calls for a new skyline merge algorithm, which we give in the next section.

Cost lower bound. Kung et al. [19] proved that any 2-d skyline algorithm in the comparison class must incur $\Omega(N \log N)$ execution time. To describe the core of their argument, let us define the *rank permutation* of a sequence S of distinct numbers $(x_1, ..., x_N)$, as the sequence $(r_1, ..., r_N)$ where r_i $(1 \le i \le N)$ is the number of values of S that are at most x_i. For example, the rank permutation of $(9, 20, 3)$ is $(2, 3, 1)$. Kung et al. [19] identified a series of hard datasets, where each dataset P has N points $p_1, ..., p_N$ whose x-coordinates can be any integers. They showed that, any algorithm that correctly finds the skyline of P must have determined the rank permutation of the sequence formed by the x-coordinates of $p_1, ..., p_N$. In the EM model, it is known [2] that deciding the rank permutation of a set of N integers demands $\Omega((N/B) \log_{M/B}(N/B))$ I/Os in the worst case for any comparison-based algorithm. It thus follows that this is also a lower bound for computing 2-d skylines in external memory. Note that the same bound also holds in higher-dimensional space where the problem is no easier than in the 2-d space.

It is worth mentioning that the I/O lower bound $\Omega((N/B) \log_{M/B}(N/B))$ is also a direct corollary of a result due to Arge et al. [3].

3. OUR SKYLINE ALGORITHM

We will present the proposed solution in a step-by-step manner. Section 3.1 first explains the overall divide-and-conquer framework underpinning the algorithm by clarifying how it works in 3-d space. To tackle higher dimensionalities d, there is another layer of divide-and-conquer inside the framework, as elaborated in Section 3.2 for $d = 4$. The 4-d description of our algorithm can then be easily extended to general d, which is the topic of Section 3.3.

3.1 3-d

Our algorithm accepts as input a dataset P whose points are sorted in ascending order of x-coordinates. If the size N of P is at most M (i.e., the memory capacity), we simply find the skyline of P using a memory-resident algorithm. The I/O cost incurred is $O(N/B)$.

In case $N > M$, we divide P into $s = \Theta(M/B)$ partitions $P(1), ..., P(s)$ with roughly the same size, such that each point in $P(i)$ has a smaller x-coordinate than all points in $P(j)$ for any $1 \le i < j \le s$. As P is already sorted on the x-dimension, the partitioning can be done in linear cost, while leaving the points of each $P(i)$ sorted in the same way.

The next step is to obtain the skyline $\Sigma(i)$ of each $P(i)$, i.e., $\Sigma(i) = SKY(P(i))$. Since this is identical to solving the original problem (only on a smaller dataset), we recursively invoke our algorithm on $P(i)$. Now consider the moment when all $\Sigma(i)$ have been returned from recursion. Our algorithm proceeds by performing a *skyline merge*, which finds the skyline of the union of all $\Sigma(i)$, that is, $SKY(\Sigma(1) \cup ... \cup \Sigma(s))$, which is exactly $SKY(P)$. We enforce an invariant that, $SKY(P)$ be returned in a disk file where the points are sorted in ascending order of y-coordinates (to be used by the upper level of recursion, if any). Due to recursion, the invariant implies that, the same ordering has been applied to all the $\Sigma(i)$ at hand.

We now elaborate the details of the skyline merge. $SKY(P)$ is empty in the outset. $\Sigma(1), ..., \Sigma(s)$ are scanned synchronously in ascending order of y-coordinates. In other words, the next point fetched is guaranteed to have the lowest y-coordinate among the points of all $\Sigma(i)$ that have not been encountered yet. As $s = \Theta(M/B)$, the synchronization can be achieved by assigning a block of memory as the input buffer to each $\Sigma(i)$. We maintain a value $\lambda(i)$, which equals the minimum z-coordinate of all the points that have already been seen from $\Sigma(i)$. If no point from $\Sigma(i)$ has been read, $\lambda(i) = \infty$.

We decide whether to include a point p in $SKY(P)$ when p is fetched by the synchronous scan. Suppose that p is from $\Sigma(i)$ for some i. We add p to $SKY(P)$ if

$$p[3] < \lambda(j), \forall j < i \tag{2}$$

where $p[3]$ denotes the z-coordinate of p. See Figure 3 for an illustration. The lemma below shows the correctness of this rule.

LEMMA 3.1. $p \in SKY(P)$ if and only if Inequality 2 holds.

PROOF. Clearly, p cannot be dominated by any point in $\Sigma(i+1), ..., \Sigma(s)$ because p has a smaller x-coordinate than all those points. Let S be the set of points in $\Sigma(j)$ already scanned before p, for any $j < i$. No point $p' \in \Sigma(j) \setminus S$ can possibly dominate p, as p has a lower y-coordinate than p'. On the other hand, all points in S dominate p in the x-y plane. Thus, *some* point in S dominates p in $\mathbb{R}^3$ if and only if Inequality 2 holds. $\square$

We complete the algorithm description with a note that a single memory block can be used as an output buffer, so that the points of $SKY(P)$ can be written to the disk in linear I/Os, by the same order they entered $SKY(P)$, namely, in ascending order of their y-coordinates. Overall, the skyline merge finishes in $O(N/B)$ I/Os.

Running time. Denote by $F(N)$ the I/O cost of our algorithm on a dataset with cardinality N. It is clear from the above discussion that

$$F(N) = \begin{cases} O(N/B) & \text{if } N \leq M \\ s \cdot F(N/s) + G(N) & \text{otherwise} \end{cases} \tag{3}$$

where $G(N) = O(N/B)$ is the cost of a skyline merge. Solving the recurrence gives $F(N) = O((N/B) \log_{M/B}(N/B))$.

3.2 4-d

To find the skyline of a 4-d dataset P, we proceed as in the 3-d algorithm by using a possibly smaller $s = \Theta(\min\{\sqrt{M}, M/B\})$. The only difference lies in the way that a skyline merge is performed. Formally, the problem we face in a skyline merge can be described as follows. Consider a partition $P(1), ..., P(s)$ of P such that each point in $P(i)$ has a smaller coordinate on dimension

1 than all points in $P(j)$, for any $1 \leq i < j \leq s$. Equivalently, the data space is divided into s *slabs* $\sigma_1(1), ..., \sigma_1(s)$ by $s - 1$ hyper-planes orthogonal to dimension 1 such that $P(i) = P \cap \sigma_1(i)$ for all $1 \leq i \leq s$. We are given the skyline $\Sigma_1(i)$ of each $P(i)$, where the points of $\Sigma_1(i)$ are sorted in ascending order of their 2nd coordinates. The goal is to compute $SKY(\Sigma_1(1) \cup ... \cup \Sigma_1(s))$, which is equivalent to $SKY(P)$. Further, the output order is important (for backtracking to the upper level of recursion): we want the points of $SKY(P)$ to be returned in ascending order of their 2nd coordinates.

The previous subsection solved the problem in 3-d space with $O(N/B)$ I/Os where $N = |P|$. In 4-d space, our objective is to pay only an extra factor of $O(\log_{M/B}(N/B))$ in the cost. We fulfill the purpose with an algorithm called `preMerge-4d`, the input of which includes

- slabs $\sigma_1(1), ..., \sigma_1(s)$

- a set Π of points sorted in ascending order of their 2nd coordinates. Π has the property that, if two points $p_1, p_2 \in \Pi$ fall in the same slab, they do not dominate each other.

`preMerge-4d` returns the points of $SKY(\Pi)$ in ascending order of their *3rd* coordinates.

Although stated somewhat differently, the problem settled by `preMerge-4d` is (almost) the same as skyline merge. Notice that Π can be obtained by merging $\Sigma_1(1), ..., \Sigma_1(s)$ in $O(N/B)$ I/Os. Moreover, we can sort the points of $SKY(\Pi)$ (output by `preMerge-4d`) ascendingly on dimension 2 to fulfill the order requirement of skyline merge, which demands another $O((N/B) \log_{M/B}(N/B))$ I/Os.

Algorithm preMerge-4d. In case Π has at most M points, `preMerge-4d` solves the problem in memory. Otherwise, in $O(|\Pi|/B)$ I/Os the algorithm divides Π into s partitions $\Pi(1), ..., \Pi(s)$ of roughly the same size, with the points of $\Pi(i)$ having smaller 2nd coordinates than those of $\Pi(j)$ for any $1 \leq i < j \leq s$. We then invoke `preMerge-4d` recursively on each $\Pi(i)$, feeding the same $\{\sigma_1(1), ..., \sigma_1(s)\}$, to calculate $\Sigma_2(i) = SKY(\Pi(i))$. Apparently, $SKY(\Pi)$ is equivalent to the skyline of the union of all $\Sigma_2(i)$, namely, $SKY(\Pi) = SKY(\Sigma_2(1) \cup ... \cup \Sigma_2(s))$. It may appear that we are back to where we started — this is another skyline merge! The crucial difference, however, is that only two dimensions remain "unprocessed" (i.e., dimensions 3 and 4). In this case, the problem can be solved directly in linear I/Os, by a synchronous scan similar to the one in Section 3.1.

By recursion, the points of each $\Sigma_2(i)$ have been sorted ascendingly on dimension 3. This allows us to enumerate the points of $\Sigma_2(1) \cup ... \cup \Sigma_2(s)$ in ascending order of their 3rd coordinates, by synchronously reading the $\Sigma_2(i)$ of all $i \in [1, s]$. In the meantime, we keep track of s^2 values $\lambda(i_1, i_2)$ for every pair of $i_1, i_2 \in [1, s]$. Specifically, $\lambda(i_1, i_2)$ equals the lowest 4th coordinate of all the points in $\sigma_1(i_1) \cap \Sigma_2(i_2)$ that have been scanned so far; or $\lambda(i_1, i_2) = \infty$ if no such point exists. Note that the choice of s makes it possible to maintain all $\lambda(i_1, i_2)$ in memory, and meanwhile, allocate an input buffer to each $\Sigma_2(i)$ so that the synchronous scan can be completed in linear I/Os.

$SKY(\Pi)$ is empty at the beginning of the synchronous scan. Let p be the next point fetched. Suppose that p falls in $\sigma_1(i_1)$, and is from $\Sigma_2(i_2)$, for some i_1, i_2. We insert p in $SKY(\Pi)$ if

$$p[4] < \lambda(j_1, j_2), \forall j_1 < i_1, j_2 < i_2 \qquad (4)$$

where $p[4]$ is the coordinate of p on dimension 4. An argument similar to the proof of Lemma 3.1 shows that $p \in SKY(\Pi)$ if and only if the above inequality holds. Note that checking the inequality happens in memory, and incurs no I/O cost. Finally, as the points of $SKY(\Pi)$ enter $SKY(\Pi)$ in ascending order of their 3rd coordinates, they can be written to the disk in the same order.

Running time. Let $H(K)$ be the I/O cost of `preMerge-4d` when Π has K points. We have

$$H(K) = \begin{cases} O(K/B) & \text{if } K \le M \\ s \cdot H(K/s) + O(K/B) & \text{otherwise} \end{cases}$$

where $s = \Omega(\sqrt{M/B})$. This recurrence gives $H(K) = O((K/B) \log_{M/B}(K/B))$.

Following the notations in Section 3.1, denote by $G(N)$ the cost of a skyline merge when the dataset P has size N, and by $F(N)$ the cost of our 4-d skyline algorithm. $G(N)$ equals $H(N)$ plus the overhead of sorting $SKY(P)$. Hence:

$$G(N) = O((N/B) \log_{M/B}(N/B)).$$

With the above, we solve the recurrence in Equation 3 as $F(N) = O((N/B) \log^2_{M/B}(N/B))$.

3.3 Higher dimensionalities

We are now ready to extend our technique to dimensionality $d \ge 5$, the core of which is to attack the following problem (that generalizes the skyline merges encountered in the preceding subsections). The input includes:

- A parameter h satisfying $0 \le h \le d - 2$.

- A set of $s = \Theta(\min\{M^{1/(d-2)}, M/B\})$ slabs $\sigma_i(1), ..., \sigma_i(s)$ for each dimension $i \in [1, h]$ (there are h sets in total), if $h > 0$. No slab needs to be given for $h = 0$. Each set of $\sigma_i(1), ..., \sigma_i(s)$ is obtained by cutting the data space $\mathbb{R}^d$ with $s - 1$ hyper-planes perpendicular to dimension i. We follow the convention that all points in $\sigma_i(j_1)$ have smaller coordinates on dimension i than those in $\sigma_i(j_2)$ for any $1 \le j_1 < j_2 \le s$.

- A set Π of points which are sorted in ascending order of their coordinates on dimension $h + 1$. These points have the property that, for any $p_1, p_2 \in \Pi$, they do not dominate each other if they are covered by the same slab, namely, both p_1 and p_2 fall in a $\sigma_i(j)$ for some $i \in [1, h]$ and $j \in [1, s]$.

The objective is to output $SKY(\Pi)$ in ascending order of their coordinates on dimension $h + 1$. We refer to the problem as (h, d)-merge.

Let $K = |\Pi|$. Our earlier analysis essentially has shown that $(1, 3)$- and $(2, 4)$-merges can both be settled in linear I/Os, while $(1, 4)$-merge in $O((K/B) \log_{M/B}(K/B))$ I/Os. Next, we will establish a general result:

LEMMA 3.2. *The (h, d)-merge problem can be solved in $O((K/B) \log^{d-h-2}_{M/B}(K/B))$ I/Os.*

The subsequent discussion proves the lemma by handling $h = d - 2$ and $h < d - 2$ separately.

$h = d - 2$. Our algorithm in this case performs a single scan of Π. At any time, we maintain s^h memory-resident values $\lambda(i_1, ..., i_h)$, where $1 \le i_j \le s$ for each $j \in [1, h]$. Specifically, $\lambda(i_1, ..., i_h)$ equals the lowest coordinate on dimension d of all the points already scanned that fall in $\sigma_1(i_1) \cap ... \cap \sigma_h(i_h)$; or $\lambda(i_1, ..., i_h) = \infty$ if no such point has been encountered yet. By remembering in memory the description of all slabs, we can update the corresponding $\lambda(i_1, ..., i_h)$ (if necessary) right after a point is read, without any extra I/O.

$SKY(\Pi)$ is empty at the beginning of the algorithm. Let p be the next point of Π found by the scan. Assume, without loss of generality, that p falls in $\sigma_1(i_1) \cap ... \cap \sigma_h(i_h)$ for some $i_1, ..., i_h$. We add p to $SKY(\Pi)$ if

$$p[d] < \lambda(j_1, ..., j_h), \forall j_1 < i_1, ..., j_h < i_h \qquad (5)$$

where $p[d]$ is the d-th coordinate of p. With the experience from Equations 2 and 4, it is not hard to see that $p \in SKY(\Pi)$ if and only if Inequality 5 holds. Obviously, $SKY(\Pi)$ can be easily output in ascending order of the coordinates of dimension $h + 1$ as this is the order by which points enter $SKY(\Pi)$.

The above process requires $O(s^h)$ memory to store the slab description and all the $\lambda(i_1, ..., i_h)$, plus an extra block as the input buffer of Π and output buffer of $SKY(\Pi)$, respectively. This is not a problem because $s^h = O(M)$. The algorithm terminates in $O(K/B)$ I/Os.

$h < d - 2$. We deal with this scenario by converting the problem to $(h + 1, d)$-merge, using a divide-and-conquer approach similar to transforming $(1, 4)$-merge into $(2, 4)$-merge in Section 3.2. Our approach is to generalize the algorithm `preMerge-4d` in Section 3.2. The resulting algorithm, named `preMerge`, solves the same problem as (h, d)-merge except that it outputs the points of $SKY(\Pi)$ in ascending order of their coordinates on dimension $h + 2$. This is minor because $SKY(\Pi)$ can then be sorted again in $O((K/B) \log_{M/B}(K/B))$ I/Os to meet the order requirement of (h, d)-merge.

If $K \le M$, `preMerge` trivially computes $SKY(\Pi)$ in memory. Otherwise, in linear I/Os the algorithm divides Π into $\Pi(1), ..., \Pi(s)$ of roughly the same size, such that points of $\Pi(i)$ have lower coordinates on dimension $h + 1$ than those of $\Pi(j)$, for any $1 \le i < j \le s$. Naturally, each $\Pi(i)$ corresponds to a slab $\sigma_{h+1}(i)$, such that $\sigma_{h+1}(1), ..., \sigma_{h+1}(s)$ are separated by $s - 1$ hyper-planes perpendicular to dimension $h + 1$.

We then invoke `preMerge` recursively on $\Pi(i)$, feeding the same h sets of slabs $\{\sigma_i(1), ..., \sigma_i(s)\}$ of all $i \in [1, h]$. On return, we have obtained $\Sigma(i) = SKY(\Pi(i))$, with the points therein sorted ascendingly on dimension $h + 2$. In $O(K/B)$ I/Os, $\Sigma(1), ..., \Sigma(s)$ can be merged into a single list Σ' where all points remain in ascending order of dimension $h + 2$. At this point, we are facing a $(h + 1, d)$-merge problem on Σ' and

```
merge(h, Π)
/* perform a (h, d)-merge on Π */
1.  if h = d − 2 then
2.      compute SKY(Π) in O(|Π|/B) I/Os
        /* SKY(Π) now sorted by dimension h + 1 */
3.  else
4.      SKY(Π) ← preMerge(h, Π)
5.      sort the points of SKY(Π) by dimension h + 1
6.  return SKY(Π)
```

```
preMerge(h, Π)
1.  if Π fits in memory then
2.      compute SKY(Π) in O(|Π|/B) I/Os
        /* sort the points of SKY(Π) in memory by
           dimension h + 2 */
3.  else
4.      divide Π into Π(1), ..., Π(s) on dimension h + 1
5.      for i ← 1 to s do
6.          Σ(i) ← preMerge(h, Π(i))
7.      merge Σ(1), ..., Σ(s) into Σ′
        /* Σ′ now sorted by dimension h + 2 */
8.      SKY(Π) ← merge(h + 1, Σ′)
        /* SKY(Π) now sorted by dimension h + 2 */
9.  return SKY(Π)
```

Figure 4: High-level description of the algorithms for performing a (h, d)-merge

$h + 1$ sets of slabs $\{\sigma_i(1), ..., \sigma_i(s)\}$ of all $i \in [1, h + 1]$. The converted problem is solved recursively as described above.

Running time of (h, d)-merge. The pseudocode of Figure 4 summarizes the main ideas of (h, d)-merge and pre-Merge. Let $H(h, K)$ be the cost of preMerge(h, Π) on a dataset Π of size K, and $G(h, K)$ the cost of a (h, d)-merge on Π. From the earlier discussion, we have:

$$G(h, K) = \begin{cases} O(K/B) & \text{if } h = d - 2 \\ H(h, K) + O\left(\left(\frac{K}{B}\right)\log_{M/B}\left(\frac{K}{B}\right)\right) & \text{otherwise} \end{cases} \quad (6)$$

and, for $h \le d - 3$:

$$H(h, K) = \begin{cases} O(K/B) & \text{if } K < M \\ s \cdot H\left(h, \frac{K}{s}\right) + O\left(\frac{K}{B}\right) + G(h+1, K) & \text{otherwise} \end{cases} \quad (7)$$

where $s = \Omega((M/B)^{1/(d-2)})$. To solve the above recurrences, first notice that

$$H(d - 3, K) = O((K/B)\log_{M/B}(K/B)) \quad (8)$$

which, together with Equation 6, implies that, for $h \le d - 3$:

$$G(h, K) = O(H(h, K)) \quad (9)$$

Hence, for $h \le d - 4$:

$$H(h, K) = \begin{cases} O(K/B) & \text{if } K < M \\ s \cdot H\left(h, \frac{K}{s}\right) + O(H(h+1, K)) & \text{otherwise} \end{cases}$$

From the above and Equation 8, we obtain $H(h, K) = O((K/B)\log_{M/B}^{d-h-2}(K/B))$ for all $h \le d - 3$. This, together with Equation 9 and the first case of Equation 6, completes the proof of Lemma 3.2.

Computing the skyline. Let P be a dataset that has been sorted in ascending order along dimension 1.

We find $SKY(P)$ by simply performing a (0, d)-merge on P. By Lemma 3.2, the overall I/O complexity is $O((N/B)\log_{M/B}^{d-2}(N/B))$, which concludes the proof of Theorem 1.1.

Eliminating the general-position assumption. As mentioned by the remark in Section 1.3, the skyline problem is still well defined on a set P of points that are not in general position, namely, two points may have identical coordinates on some (but not all) dimensions. Next, we explain how to extend our algorithm to support such P.

The only part that needs to be clarified is how to deal with ties in sorting. Recall that, in several places of our algorithm, we need to sort a set $\Pi \subseteq P$ of points in ascending order of their coordinates on dimension i, where $1 \le i \le d$. The goal of tie-breaking is to ensure that if a point p_1 ranks *after* another point p_2, then p_1 cannot dominate p_2. This purpose can be achieved as follows. If p_1 and p_2 have the same i-th coordinate, we rank them lexicographically. Specifically, we first find the smallest j such that p_1 and p_2 have different coordinates on dimension j. Note that j must exist because P is a set, and hence, does not have duplicate points. If the j-th coordinate of p_1 is smaller than that of p_2, we rank p_1 earlier; otherwise, p_2 is ranked earlier.

4. CONCLUDING REMARKS

We have shown that, in the EM model, the skyline problem of any fixed dimensionality $d \ge 3$ can be settled in $O((N/B)\log_{M/B}^{d-2}(N/B))$ I/Os, where N is the dataset size, B is the size of a disk block, and M is the capacity of main memory.

Chan et al. [8] proposed the concept of *k-dominant skyline*, where k is a positive integer at most d. Intuitively, the dominance relation accompanying the new concept requires a point p_1 to be better than another p_2 only on k dimensions, instead of all dimensions. Specifically, p_1 is said to *k-dominate* p_2, denoted as $p_1 \prec_k p_2$, if:

$$\exists \text{ at least } k \text{ dimensions } i_1, ..., i_k \text{ s.t.}$$
$$p_1[i_j] < p_2[i_j] \text{ for each } j = 1, ..., k.$$

The *k-dominant skyline* of P is the set of points in P that are not k-dominated by any other point in P. This problem can be trivially solved by BNL in $O(N^2/(MB))$ I/Os. The existing k-dominant-skyline algorithms [8, 17, 25] are heuristic, and have the same complexity as BNL in the worst case.

For a fixed d, our technique can be utilized to settle this problem in $O((N/B) \log_{M/B}^{k-2}(N/B))$ I/Os for any $k \geq 3$. Let a k-subspace be the space $\mathbb{S}$ defined by k dimensions of $\mathbb{R}^d$. We say that a point $p \in P$ is in the skyline under $\mathbb{S}$, if p is a skyline point of the k-dimensional dataset obtained by projecting P onto $\mathbb{S}$. Clearly, there are $\binom{d}{k} = O(1)$ k-subspaces. It is easy to verify that p belongs to k-dominant skyline of P if and only if p is in the skyline under *all* k-subspaces. The proposed skyline algorithm allows us to find the skyline under each of the k-subspaces in totally $O((N/B) \log_{M/B}^{k-2}(N/B))$ I/Os, after which it is easy to extract the k-dominant skyline in $O((N/B) \log_{M/B}(N/B))$ I/Os. Finally, note that the 2-dominant skyline can be found in $O((N/B) \log_{M/B}(N/B))$ I/Os using similar ideas, whereas the 1-dominant skyline can be retrieved in $O(N/B)$ I/Os by scanning the dataset once (to get the minimum coordinate of the points in P on every dimension).

5. ACKNOWLEDGEMENTS

This work was supported by grants GRF 4173/08, GRF 4169/09, and GRF 4166/10 from HKRGC.

6. REFERENCES

[1] P. Afshani, J. Barbay, and T. M. Chan. Instance-optimal geometric algorithms. In *Proceedings of Annual IEEE Symposium on Foundations of Computer Science (FOCS)*, pages 129–138, 2009.

[2] A. Aggarwal and J. S. Vitter. The input/output complexity of sorting and related problems. *Communications of the ACM (CACM)*, 31(9):1116–1127, 1988.

[3] L. Arge, M. Knudsen, and K. Larsen. A general lower bound on the I/O-complexity of comparison-based algorithms. In *Algorithms and Data Structures Workshop (WADS)*, pages 83–94, 1993.

[4] J. L. Bentley. Multidimensional divide-and-conquer. *Communications of the ACM (CACM)*, 23(4):214–229, 1980.

[5] J. L. Bentley, K. L. Clarkson, and D. B. Levine. Fast linear expected-time algorithms for computing maxima and convex hulls. *Algorithmica*, 9(2):168–183, 1993.

[6] J. L. Bentley, H. T. Kung, M. Schkolnick, and C. D. Thompson. On the average number of maxima in a set of vectors and applications. *Journal of the ACM (JACM)*, 25(4):536–543, 1978.

[7] S. Borzsonyi, D. Kossmann, and K. Stocker. The skyline operator. In *Proceedings of International Conference on Data Engineering (ICDE)*, pages 421–430, 2001.

[8] C. Y. Chan, H. V. Jagadish, K.-L. Tan, A. K. H. Tung, and Z. Zhang. Finding k-dominant skylines in high dimensional space. In *Proceedings of ACM*

[9] J. Chomicki, P. Godfrey, J. Gryz, and D. Liang. Skyline with presorting. In *Proceedings of International Conference on Data Engineering (ICDE)*, pages 717–816, 2003.

Management of Data (SIGMOD), pages 503–514, 2006.

[10] H. K. Dai and X.-W. Zhang. Improved linear expected-time algorithms for computing maxima. In *Latin American Theoretical Informatics*, pages 181–192, 2004.

[11] H. N. Gabow, J. L. Bentley, and R. E. Tarjan. Scaling and related techniques for geometry problems. In *Proceedings of ACM Symposium on Theory of Computing (STOC)*, pages 135–143, 1984.

[12] P. Godfrey, R. Shipley, and J. Gryz. Algorithms and analyses for maximal vector computation. *The VLDB Journal*, 16(1):5–28, 2007.

[13] M. T. Goodrich, J.-J. Tsay, D. E. Vengroff, and J. S. Vitter. External-memory computational geometry. In *Proceedings of Annual IEEE Symposium on Foundations of Computer Science (FOCS)*, pages 714–723, 1993.

[14] R. Janardan. On the dynamic maintenance of maximal points in the plane. *Information Processing Letters (IPL)*, 40(2):59–64, 1991.

[15] S. Kapoor. Dynamic maintenance of maxima of 2-d point sets. *SIAM Journal of Computing*, 29(6):1858–1877, 2000.

[16] D. G. Kirkpatrick and R. Seidel. Output-size sensitive algorithms for finding maximal vectors. In *Symposium on Computational Geometry (SoCG)*, pages 89–96, 1985.

[17] M. Kontaki, A. N. Papadopoulos, and Y. Manolopoulos. Continuous k-dominant skyline computation on multidimensional data streams. In *Proceedings of ACM Symposium on Applied Computing (SAC)*, pages 956–960, 2008.

[18] D. Kossmann, F. Ramsak, and S. Rost. Shooting stars in the sky: An online algorithm for skyline queries. In *Proceedings of Very Large Data Bases (VLDB)*, pages 275–286, 2002.

[19] H. T. Kung, F. Luccio, and F. P. Preparata. On finding the maxima of a set of vectors. *Journal of the ACM (JACM)*, 22(4):469–476, 1975.

[20] X. Lin, Y. Yuan, W. Wang, and H. Lu. Stabbing the sky: Efficient skyline computation over sliding windows. In *Proceedings of International Conference on Data Engineering (ICDE)*, pages 502–513, 2005.

[21] J. Matousek. Computing dominances in E^n. *Information Processing Letters (IPL)*, 38(5):277–278, 1991.

[22] M. D. Morse, J. M. Patel, and H. V. Jagadish.

Efficient skyline computation over low-cardinality domains. In *Proceedings of Very Large Data Bases (VLDB)*, pages 267–278, 2007.

[23] D. Papadias, Y. Tao, G. Fu, and B. Seeger. Progressive skyline computation in database systems. *ACM Transactions on Database Systems (TODS)*, 30(1):41–82, 2005.

[24] A. D. Sarma, A. Lall, D. Nanongkai, and J. Xu. Randomized multi-pass streaming skyline algorithms. *Proceedings of the VLDB Endowment (PVLDB)*, 2(1):85–96, 2009.

[25] M. A. Siddique and Y. Morimoto. K-dominant skyline computation by using sort-filtering method. In *Proceedings of Pacific-Asia Conference on Knowledge Discovery and Data Mining (PAKDD)*, pages 839–848, 2009.

[26] P. van Emde Boas. Preserving order in a forest in less than logarithmic time and linear space. *Information Processing Letters (IPL)*, 6(3):80–82, 1977.

[27] J. S. Vitter. Algorithms and data structures for external memory. *Foundation and Trends in Theoretical Computer Science*, 2(4):305–474, 2006.

Beyond Simple Aggregates:
Indexing for Summary Queries

Zhewei Wei   Ke Yi
Hong Kong University of Science and Technology
Clear Water Bay, Hong Kong, China
{wzxac, yike}@cse.ust.hk

ABSTRACT

Database queries can be broadly classified into two categories: reporting queries and aggregation queries. The former retrieves a collection of records from the database that match the query's conditions, while the latter returns an aggregate, such as count, sum, average, or max (min), of a particular attribute of these records. Aggregation queries are especially useful in business intelligence and data analysis applications where users are interested not in the actual records, but some statistics of them. They can also be executed much more efficiently than reporting queries, by embedding properly precomputed aggregates into an index.

However, reporting and aggregation queries provide only two extremes for exploring the data. Data analysts often need more insight into the data distribution than what those simple aggregates provide, and yet certainly do not want the sheer volume of data returned by reporting queries. In this paper, we design indexing techniques that allow for extracting a statistical summary of all the records in the query. The summaries we support include frequent items, quantiles, various sketches, and wavelets, all of which are of central importance in massive data analysis. Our indexes require linear space and extract a summary with the optimal or near-optimal query cost.

Categories and Subject Descriptors

E.1 [**Data**]: Data structures; F.2.2 [**Analysis of algorithms and problem complexity**]: Nonnumerical algorithms and problems

General Terms

Algorithms, theory

Keywords

Indexing, summary queries

1. INTRODUCTION

A database system's primary function is to answer users' queries. These queries can be broadly classified into two categories: reporting queries and aggregation queries. The former retrieves a collection of records from the database that match the query's conditions, while the latter only produces an aggregate, such as count, sum, average or max (min), of a particular attribute of these records. With reporting queries, the database is simply used as a data storage-retrieval tool. Many modern business intelligence applications, however, require ad hoc analytical queries with a rapid execution time. Users issuing these analytical queries are interested not in the actual records, but some statistics of them. This has therefore led to extensive research on how to perform aggregation queries efficiently. By augmenting a database index (very often a B-tree) with properly precomputed aggregates, aggregation queries can be answered efficiently at query time without going through the actual data records.

However, reporting and aggregation queries provide only two extremes for analyzing the data, by returning either all the records matching the query condition or one (or a few) single-valued aggregates. These simple aggregates are not expressive enough, and data analysts often need more insight into the data distribution. Consider the following queries:

(Q1) In a company's database: What is the distribution of salaries of all employees aged between 30 and 40?

(Q2) In a search engine's query logs: What are the most frequently queried keywords between May 1 and July 1, 2010?

The analyst issuing the query is perhaps not interested in listing all the records in the query range one by one, while probably not happy with a simple aggregate such as average or max, either. What would be nice is some summary on the data, which is more complex than the simple aggregates, yet still much smaller than the raw query results. Some useful summaries include the frequent items, the ϕ-quantiles for, say, $\phi = 0.1, 0.2, \ldots, 0.9$, a sketch (e.g., the Count-Min sketch [8] or the AMS sketch [4]), or some compressed data representations like wavelets. All these summaries are of central importance in massive data analysis, and have been extensively studied for offline and streaming data. Yet, to use the existing algorithms, one still has to first issue a reporting query to retrieve all query results, and then construct the desired summary afterward. This is clearly time-consuming and wasteful.

In this paper, we propose to add a native support for *summary queries* in a database index, such that a summary can be returned in time proportional to the size of the summary itself, not the size of the raw query results. The problem we consider can be defined more precisely as follows. Let $\mathcal{D}$ be a database containing N records. Each record $p \in \mathcal{D}$ is associated with a *query attribute* $A_q(p)$ and a *summary attribute* $A_s(p)$, drawing values possibly from different domains. A *summary query* specifies a range constraint $[q_1, q_2]$ on A_q and the database returns a summary on the A_s attribute of all records whose A_q attribute is within the range. For example, in the query (Q1) above, A_q is "age" and A_s is "salary". Note that A_s and A_q could be the same attribute, but it is more useful when they are different, as the analyst is exploring the relationship between two attributes. Our goal is to build an index on $\mathcal{D}$ so that a summary query can be answered efficiently. As with any indexing problem, the primary measures are the query time and the space the index uses. The index should also work in external memory, where it is stored in blocks of size B, and the query cost is measured in terms of the number of blocks accessed (I/Os). Finally, we also would like the index to support updates, i.e., insertion and deletion of records.

1.1 Related work on indexing for aggregation queries

In one dimension, most aggregates can be supported easily using a binary tree (a B-tree in external memory). At each internal node of the binary tree, we simply store the aggregate of all the records below the node. This way an aggregation query can be answered in $O(\log N)$ time ($O(\log_B N)$ I/Os in external memory).

In higher dimensions, the problem becomes more difficult and has been extensively studied in both the computational geometry and the database communities. Solutions are typically based on space-partitioning hierarchies, like partition trees, quadtrees and R-trees, where an internal node stores the aggregate for its subtree. There is a large body of work on spatial data structures; please refer to the survey by Agarwal and Erickson [2] and the book by Samet [26]. When the data space forms an array, the data cube [13] is an efficient structure for answering aggregation queries.

However, all the past research, whether in computational geometry or databases, has only considered queries that return simple aggregates like count, sum, max (min), and very recently top-k [1] and median [7, 18]. The problem of returning complex summaries has not been addressed.

1.2 Related work on (non-indexed) summaries

There is also a vast literature on various summaries in both the database and algorithms communities, motivated by the fact that simple aggregates cannot well capture the data distribution. These summaries, depending on the context and community, are also called *synopses*, *sketches*, or *compressed representations*. However, all past research has focused on how to construct a summary, either offline or in a streaming fashion, on the *entire* data set. No one has considered the indexing problem where the focus is to intelligently compute and store auxiliary information in the index at pre-computation time, so that a summary on a *requested subset* of the records in the database can be built quickly at query time. Since we cannot afford to look at all the requested records to build the summary at query time, this poses new challenges that past research cannot address: All existing construction algorithms need to at least read

the data records once. The problem of how to maintain a summary as the underlying data changes, namely under insertions and deletions of records, has also been extensively studied. But this should not be confused with our dynamic index problem. The former maintains a single summary for the entire dynamic data set, while the latter aims at maintaining a dynamic structure from which a summary for any queried subset can be extracted, which is more general than the former. Of course for the former there often exist small-space solutions, while for the indexing problem, we cannot hope for sublinear space, as a query range may be small enough so that the summary degenerates to the raw query results.

Below we review some of the most fundamental and most studied summaries in the literature. Let D be a bag of items, and let $f_D(x)$ be the frequency of x in D.

Heavy hitters. A heavy hitters summary allows one to extract all frequent items approximately, i.e., for a user-specified $0 < \phi < 1$, it returns all items x with $f_D(x) > \phi |D|$ and no items with $f_D(x) < (\phi - \varepsilon)|D|$, while an item x with $(\phi - \varepsilon)|D| \leq f_D(x) \leq \phi |D|$ may or may not be returned. A heavy hitters summary of size $O(1/\varepsilon)$ can be constructed in one pass over D, using the MG algorithm [23] or the Space-Saving algorithm [22].

Sketches. Various sketches have been developed as a useful tool for summarizing massive data. In this paper, we consider the two most widely used ones: the *Count-Min sketch* [8] and the *AMS sketch* [4]. They summarize important information about D and can be used for a variety of purposes. Most notably, they can be used to estimate the join size of two data sets, with self-join size being a special case. Given the Count-Min sketches (resp. AMS sketches) of two data sets D_1 and D_2, we can estimate $|D_1 \bowtie D_2|$ within an additive error of $\varepsilon F_1(D_1) F_1(D_2)$ (resp. $\varepsilon \sqrt{F_2(D_1) F_2(D_2)}$) with probability at least $1 - \delta$ [3, 8], where F_k is the k-th frequency moment of D: $F_k(D) = \sum_x f_D^k(x)$. Note that $\sqrt{F_2(D)} \leq F_1(D)$, so the error of the AMS sketch is no larger. However, its size is $O((1/\varepsilon^2) \log(1/\delta))$, which is larger than the Count-Min sketch's size $O((1/\varepsilon) \log(1/\delta))$, so they are not strictly comparable. Which one is better will depend on the skewness of the data sets. In particular, since $F_1(D) = |D|$, the error of the Count-Min sketch does not depend on the skewness of the data, but $F_2(D)$ could range from $|D|$ for uniform data to $|D|^2$ for highly skewed data.

Quantiles. The quantiles (a.k.a. the *order statistics*), which generalize the median, are important statistics about the data distribution. Recall that the ϕ-*quantile*, for $0 < \phi < 1$, of a set D of items from a totally ordered universe is the one ranked at $\phi |D|$ in D (for convenience, for the quantile problem it is usually assumed that there are no duplicates in D). A *quantile summary* contains enough information so that for any $0 < \phi < 1$, an ε-approximate ϕ-quantile can be extracted, i.e., the summary returns a ϕ'-quantile where $\phi - \varepsilon \leq \phi' \leq \phi + \varepsilon$. A quantile summary has size $O(1/\varepsilon)$, and can be easily computed by sorting D, and then taking the items ranked at $\varepsilon |D|, 2\varepsilon |D|, 3\varepsilon |D|, \ldots, |D|$.

Wavelets. *Wavelet representations* (or just *wavelets* for short) take a different approach to approximating the data distribution by borrowing ideas from signal processing. Suppose the records in D are drawn from an ordered universe

$[u] = \{1, \ldots, u\}$ and let $\mathbf{f}_D = (f_D(1), \ldots, f_D(u))$ be the frequency vector of D. Briefly speaking, in wavelet transformation we take u inner products $s_i = \langle \mathbf{f}_D, \mathbf{w}_i \rangle$ where $\mathbf{w}_i, i = 1, \ldots, u$ are the *wavelet basis vectors* (please refer to [12, 20] for details on wavelet basis vectors). The s_i's are called the *wavelet coefficients* of $\mathbf{f}_D$. If we kept all u wavelet coefficients, we would be able to reconstruct $\mathbf{f}_D$ exactly, but this would not be a "summary". The observation is that, for most real-world distributions, $\mathbf{f}_D$ yields few wavelet coefficients with large absolute values. Thus for a parameter k, even if we keep the k coefficients with the largest absolute values, and assume all the other coefficients are zero, we can still reconstruct $\mathbf{f}_D$ reasonably well. In fact, it is well known that among all the choices, retaining the k largest (in absolute value) coefficients minimizes the ℓ_2 error between the original $\mathbf{f}_D$ and the reconstructed one. Matias et al. [20] were the first to apply wavelet transformation to approximating data distributions. After that, wavelets have been extensively studied [9, 11, 12, 15, 21, 29], and have been shown to be highly effective at summarizing many real-world data distributions.

All the aforementioned work studies how to construct or maintain the summary on the given D. In our case, D is the A_s attributes of all records whose A_q attributes are within the query range. Our goal is to design an index so that the desired summary on D can be constructed efficiently without actually going through the elements of D.

1.3 Other related work

A few other lines of work also head to the general direction of addressing the gap between reporting all query results and returning some simple aggregates. Lin et al. [19] and Tao et al. [27] propose returning only a subset of the query results, called "representatives". But the "representatives" do not summarize the data as we do. They also only consider skyline queries. The line of work on *online aggregation* [16, 17] aims at producing a random sample of the query results at early stages of long-running queries, in particular, joins. A random sample indeed gives a rough approximation of the data distribution, but it is much less accurate than the summaries we consider: For heavy hitters and quantiles, a random sample of size $\Theta(1/\varepsilon^2)$ is needed [28] to achieve the same accuracy as the $O(1/\varepsilon)$-sized summaries we mentioned earlier; for estimating join sizes, a random sample of size $\Omega(\sqrt{N})$ is required to achieve a constant approximation, which is much worse than using the sketches [3]. Furthermore, the key difference is that they focus on query processing techniques for joins rather than indexing issues. Correlated aggregates [10] aim at exploring the relationship between two attributes. They are computed on one attribute subject to a certain condition on the other. However, this condition has to be specified in advance and the goal is to compute the aggregate in the streaming setting, thus the problem is fundamentally different from ours.

1.4 Our results

To take a unified approach we classify all the summaries mentioned in Section 1.2 into F_1-based ones and F_2-based ones. The former includes heavy hitters, the Count-Min sketch, and quantiles, all of which provide an error guarantee of the form $\varepsilon F_1(D)$ (note that an ε-approximate quantile is a value with a rank that is off by $\varepsilon F_1(D)$ from the correct rank). The latter includes the AMS sketch and wavelets, both of which provide an error guarantee related to $F_2(D)$.

In Section 2 we first design a baseline solution that works for all *decomposable* summaries. A summary is *decomposable* if given the summaries for t data sets (bags of elements) $D_1, \ldots, D_t$ with error parameter ε, we can combine them together into a summary on $D_1 \uplus \cdots \uplus D_t$ with error parameter $O(\varepsilon)$, where $\uplus$ denotes multiset addition. All the F_1 and F_2 based summaries have this property and thus can be plugged into this solution. Assuming that we can combine the summaries with cost linear to their total size, the resulting index has linear size and answers a summary query in $O(s_\varepsilon \log N)$ time, where s_ε is the size of the summary returned. It also works in external memory, with the query cost being $O(\frac{s_\varepsilon}{B} \log N)$ I/Os if $s_\varepsilon \geq B$ and $O(\log N / \log(B/s_\varepsilon))$ I/Os if $s_\varepsilon < B$. Note that this decomposable property has been exploited in many other works on maintaining summaries in the streaming context [5, 6, 8].

In Section 3 we improve upon this baseline solution by identifying another, stronger decomposable property of the F_1 based summaries, which we call *exponentially decomposable*. The size of the index remains linear, while its query cost improves to $O(\log N + s_\varepsilon)$. In external memory, the query cost is $O(\log_B N + s_\varepsilon/B)$ I/Os. This resembles the classical B-tree query cost, which includes an $O(\log_B N)$ search cost and an "output" cost of $O(s_\varepsilon/B)$, whereas the output in our case is a summary of size s_ε. This is clearly optimal (in the comparison model). For not-too-large summaries $s_\varepsilon = O(B)$, the query cost becomes just $O(\log_B N)$, the same as that for a simple aggregation query or a lookup on a B-tree.

In Section 4, we demonstrate how various summaries have the desired decomposable or exponentially decomposable property and thus can be plugged into our indexes. Finally we show how to support updates in Section 5.

2. A BASELINE SOLUTION

In this and the next section, we will describe our structures without instantiating with any particular summary. Instead we just use "ε-summary" as a placeholder for any summary with error parameter ε. Let $\mathcal{S}(\varepsilon, D)$ denote an ε-summary on data set D. We use s_ε to denote the size of an ε-summary[1].

Internal memory structure. Based on the decomposable property of a summary, a baseline solution can be designed using standard techniques. We first describe the internal memory structure. Sort all the N data records in the database on the A_q attribute and partition them into N/s_ε groups, each of size s_ε. Then we build a binary tree $\mathcal{T}$ on top of these groups, where each leaf (called a *fat leaf*) stores a group of s_ε records. For each internal node u of $\mathcal{T}$, let $\mathcal{T}_u$ denote the subtree of $\mathcal{T}$ rooted at u. We attach to u an ε-summary on the A_s attribute of all records stored in the subtree below u. Since each ε-summary has size s_ε and the number of internal nodes is $O(N/s_\varepsilon)$, the total size of the structure is $O(N)$. To answer a query $[q_1, q_2]$, we do a search on $\mathcal{T}$. It is well known that any range $[q_1, q_2]$ can be decomposed into $O(\log(N/s_\varepsilon))$ disjoint *canonical* subtrees $\mathcal{T}_u$, plus at most two fat leaves that may partially overlap. We retrieve the ε-summaries attached to the roots of these

---

[1]Strictly speaking we should write $s_{\varepsilon,D}$. But as most ε-summaries have sizes independent of D, we drop the subscript D for brevity.

subtrees. For each of the fat leaves, we simply read all the s_ε records stored there. Then we combine all of them into an $O(\varepsilon)$-summary for the entire query using the decomposable property. We can adjust ε by a constant factor in the construction to ensure that the output is an ε-summary. The total query time is thus the time required to combine the $O(\log(N/s_\varepsilon))$ summaries. For the Count-Min sketch and AMS sketch, the combining time is linear in the total size of the summaries, so the query time is $O(s_\varepsilon \log N)$. For the quantile summary and heavy hitters summary the query time becomes $O(s_\varepsilon \log N \log \log N)^2$ as we need to merge $O(\log(N/s_\varepsilon))$ sorted lists (Details in Section 4).

External memory index. The baseline solution easily extends to external memory. If $s_\varepsilon \geq B$, then each internal node and fat leaf occupies $\Theta(s_\varepsilon/B)$ blocks, so we can simply store each of them separately. The space is still linear and we load $O(\log N)$ nodes on each query. The query cost becomes $O(\frac{s_\varepsilon}{B} \log N)$ I/Os for the Count-Min and AMS sketch and $O(\frac{s_\varepsilon}{B} \log N \log_{M/B} \log N)$ I/Os for the quantile and heavy hitters summary.

For $s_\varepsilon < B$, each node occupies a fraction of a block, and we can pack multiple nodes in one block. We use a standard B-tree blocking of the tree $\mathcal{T}$ where each block contains $\Theta(B/s_\varepsilon)$ nodes, except possibly the root block. Thus each block stores a subtree of height $\Theta(\log(B/s_\varepsilon))$ of $\mathcal{T}$. Then standard analysis shows that the nodes we need to access are stored in $O(\log N/\log(B/s_\varepsilon))$ blocks. This implies a query cost of $O(\log_{B/s_\varepsilon} N)$ I/Os for the Count-Min and AMS sketch and $O(\log_{B/s_\varepsilon} N \log_{M/B}(\log_{B/s_\varepsilon} N))$ I/Os for the quantile and heavy hitters summary.

3. OPTIMAL INDEXING FOR F_1 BASED SUMMARIES

The baseline solution of the previous section is not that impressive: Its "output" term has an extra $O(\log N)$ factor; in external memory, we are missing the ideal $O(\log_B N)$ term which is the main benefit of block accesses.

The main bottleneck in the baseline solution is not the search cost, but the fact that we need to assemble $O(\log N)$ summaries, each of size s_ε. In the absence of additional properties of the summary, it is impossible to make further improvement. Fortunately, we observe that many of the F_1 based summaries have what we call the *exponentially decomposable* property, which allows us to assemble summaries of exponentially decreasing sizes. This turns out to be the key to optimality for indexing these summaries.

DEFINITION 1 (EXPONENTIALLY DECOMPOSABLE). *For $0 < \alpha < 1$, a summary $\mathcal{S}$ is α-exponentially decomposable if there exists a constant $c > 1$, such that for any t multisets $D_1, \ldots, D_t$ with their sizes satisfying $F_1(D_i) \leq \alpha^{i-1} F_1(D_1)$ for $i = 1, \ldots, t$, given $\mathcal{S}(\varepsilon, D_1), \mathcal{S}(c\varepsilon, D_2) \ldots, \mathcal{S}(c^{t-1}\varepsilon, D_t)$, (1) we can construct an $O(\varepsilon)$-summary for $D_1 \uplus \cdots \uplus D_t$; (2) the total size of $\mathcal{S}(\varepsilon, D_1), \ldots, \mathcal{S}(c^{t-1}\varepsilon, D_t)$ is $O(s_\varepsilon)$ and they can be combined in $O(s_\varepsilon)$ time; and (3) for any multiset D, the total size of $\mathcal{S}(\varepsilon, D), \ldots, \mathcal{S}(c^{t-1}\varepsilon, D)$ is $O(s_\varepsilon)$.*

Intuitively, since an F_1 based summary $\mathcal{S}(\varepsilon, D)$ provides an error bound of $\varepsilon|D|$, the total error from $\mathcal{S}(\varepsilon, D_1), \mathcal{S}(c\varepsilon, D_2)$,

---

$\ldots, \mathcal{S}(c^{t-1}\varepsilon, D_t)$ is

$$\varepsilon|D_1| + c\varepsilon|D_2| + \cdots + c^{t-1}\varepsilon|D_t|$$
$$\leq \quad \varepsilon|D_1| + (c\alpha)\varepsilon|D_1| + \cdots + (c\alpha)^{t-1}\varepsilon|D_1|.$$

If we choose c such that $c\alpha < 1$, then the error is bounded by $O(\varepsilon|D_1|)$, satisfying (1). Meanwhile, the F_1 based summaries usually have size $s_\varepsilon = \Theta(1/\varepsilon)$, so (2) and (3) can be satisfied, too. In Section 4 we will formally prove the α-exponentially decomposable property for all the F_1 based summaries mentioned in Section 1.2.

3.1 Optimal internal memory structure

Let $\mathcal{T}$ be the binary tree built on the A_q attribute as in the previous section. Without loss of generality we assume $\mathcal{T}$ is a complete balanced binary tree; otherwise we can always add at most N dummy records to make N/s_ε a power of 2 so that $\mathcal{T}$ is complete.

We first define some notation on $\mathcal{T}$. We use $\mathcal{S}(\varepsilon, u)$ to denote the ε-summary on the A_s attribute of all records stored in u's subtree. Fix an internal node u and a descendant v of u, let $\mathcal{P}(u, v)$ to be the set of nodes on the path from u to v, excluding u. Define the *left sibling set* of $\mathcal{P}(u, v)$ to be $\mathcal{L}(u, v) = \{w \mid w$ is a left child and has a right sibling $\in \mathcal{P}(u, v)\}$ and similarly the *right sibling set* of $\mathcal{P}(u, v)$ to be $\mathcal{R}(u, v) = \{w \mid w$ is a right child and has a left sibling $\in \mathcal{P}(u, v)\}$. To answer a query $[q_1, q_2]$, we first locate the two fat leaves a and b in $\mathcal{T}$ that contain q_1 and q_2, respectively. Let u be the lowest common ancestor of a and b. We call $\mathcal{P}(u, a)$ and $\mathcal{P}(u, b)$ the left and respectively the right query path. We observe that the subtrees rooted at the nodes in $\mathcal{R}(u, a) \cup \mathcal{L}(u, b)$ make up the canonical set for the query range $[q_1, q_2]$.

Focusing on $\mathcal{R}(u, a)$, let $w_1, \ldots, w_t$ be the nodes of $\mathcal{R}(u, a)$ and let $d_1 < \ldots < d_t$ denote their depths in $\mathcal{T}$ (the root of $\mathcal{T}$ is said to be at depth 0). Since $\mathcal{T}$ is a balanced binary tree, we have $F_1(w_i) \leq (1/2)^{d_i - d_1} F_1(w_1)$ for $i = 1, \ldots, t$. Here we use $F_1(w)$ to denote the first frequency moment (i.e., size) of the point set rooted at node w. Thus, if the summary is $(1/2)$-exponentially decomposable, and we have $\mathcal{S}(c^{d_i - d_1}\varepsilon, w_i)$ for $i = 1, \ldots, t$ at our disposal, we can combine them and form an $O(\varepsilon)$-summary for all the data covered by $w_1, \ldots, w_t$. We do the same for $\mathcal{L}(u, b)$. Finally, the two fat leaves can always supply the exact data (it is a summary with no error) of size $O(s_\varepsilon)$ in the query range. Plus the initial $O(\log N)$ search cost for locating $\mathcal{R}(u, a)$ and $\mathcal{L}(u, b)$, the query time now improves to the optimal $O(\log N + s_\varepsilon)$.

It only remains to show how to supply $\mathcal{S}(c^{d_i - d_1}\varepsilon, w_i)$ for each of the w_i's. In fact, we can afford to attach to each node $u \in \mathcal{T}$ all the summaries: $\mathcal{S}(\varepsilon, u), \mathcal{S}(c\varepsilon, u), \ldots \mathcal{S}(c^q\varepsilon, u)$ where q is an integer such that $s_{c^q \varepsilon} = O(1)$. Nicely, these summaries still have total size $O(s_\varepsilon)$ by the exponentially decomposable property, thus the space required by each node is still $O(s_\varepsilon)$ as in the previous section, and the total space remains linear. A schematic illustration of the overall structure is shown in Figure 1.

THEOREM 1. *For any $(1/2)$-exponentially decomposable summary, a database $\mathcal{D}$ of N records can be stored in an internal memory structure of linear size so that a summary query can be answered in $O(\log N + s_\varepsilon)$ time.*

---

[2]In fact, an alternative solution achieves query time $O(s_\varepsilon \log N / \log \log N)$ by issuing s_ε range-quantile queries to the data structure in [7], but this solution does not work in external memory.

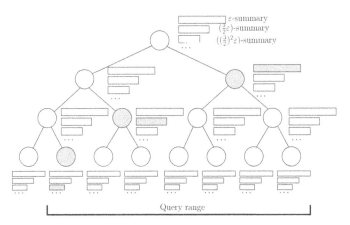

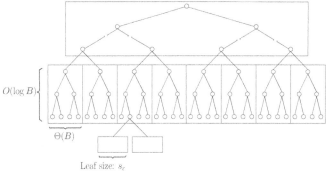

Figure 2: The standard B-tree blocking of a binary tree.

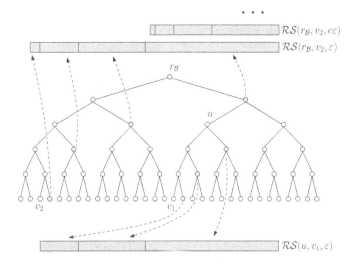

Figure 3: The summaries we store for an internal block $\mathcal{B}$.

Figure 1: A schematic illustration of our internal memory structure. The grayed nodes form the canonical decomposition of the query range, and the grayed summaries are those we combine into the final summary for the queried data. In this example we use $c = \frac{3}{2}$.

3.2 Optimal external memory indexing

In this section we show how to achieve the $O(\log_B N + s_\varepsilon/B)$-I/O query cost in external memory still with linear space. Here, the difficulty that we need to assemble $O(\log N)$ summaries lingers. In internal memory, we managed to get around it by the exponentially decomposable property so that the total size of these summaries is $O(s_\varepsilon)$. However, they still reside in $O(\log N)$ separate nodes. If we still use a standard B-tree blocking, for $s_\varepsilon \geq B$ we need to access $\Omega(\log N)$ blocks; for $s_\varepsilon < B$, we need to access $\Omega(\log N/\log(B/s_\varepsilon))$ blocks, neither of which is optimal. Below we first show how to achieve the optimal query cost by increasing the space to super-linear, then propose a packed structure to reduce the space back to linear.

Consider an internal node u and one of its descendants v. Let the sibling sets $\mathcal{R}(u, v)$ and $\mathcal{L}(u, v)$ be as previously defined. In the following we only describe how to handle the $\mathcal{R}(u, v)$'s; we will do the same for the $\mathcal{L}(u, v)$'s. Suppose $\mathcal{R}(u, v)$ contains nodes $w_1, \ldots, w_t$ at depths $d_1, \ldots, d_t$. We define the *summary set* for $\mathcal{R}(u, v)$ with error parameter ε to be

$$\mathcal{RS}(u, v, \varepsilon) = \{\mathcal{S}(\varepsilon, w_1), \mathcal{S}(c^{d_2 - d_1}\varepsilon, w_2), \ldots, \mathcal{S}(c^{d_t - d_1}\varepsilon, w_t)\}.$$

The following two facts easily follow from the exponentially decomposable property.

FACT 1. *The total size of the summaries in $\mathcal{RS}(u, v, \varepsilon)$ is $O(s_\varepsilon)$;*

FACT 2. *The total size of all the summary sets $\mathcal{RS}(u, v, \varepsilon)$, $\mathcal{RS}(u, v, c\varepsilon), \ldots, \mathcal{RS}(u, v, c^t\varepsilon)$ is $O(s_\varepsilon)$.*

The indexing structure. We first build the binary tree $\mathcal{T}$ as before with a fat leaf size of s_ε. Before attaching any summaries, we block $\mathcal{T}$ in a standard B-tree fashion so that each block stores a subtree of $\mathcal{T}$ of size $\Theta(B)$, except possibly the root block which may contain 2 to B nodes of $\mathcal{T}$. The resulting blocked tree is essentially a B-tree where each leaf occupies $O(s_\varepsilon/B)$ blocks and each internal node occupies 1

block. Please see Figure 2 for an example of the standard B-tree blocking.

Consider an internal block $\mathcal{B}$ in the B-tree. Below we describe the additional structures we attach to $\mathcal{B}$. Let $\mathcal{T}_\mathcal{B}$ be the binary subtree of $\mathcal{T}$ stored in $\mathcal{B}$ and let $r_\mathcal{B}$ be the root of $\mathcal{T}_\mathcal{B}$. To achieve the optimal query cost, the summaries attached to the nodes of $\mathcal{T}_\mathcal{B}$ that we need to retrieve for answering any query must be stored consecutively, or in at most $O(1)$ consecutive chunks. Therefore, the idea is to store all the summaries for a query path in $\mathcal{T}_\mathcal{B}$ together, which is the reason we introduced the summary set $\mathcal{RS}(u, v, \varepsilon)$. The detailed structures that we attach to $\mathcal{B}$ are as follows:

1. For each internal node $u \in \mathcal{T}_\mathcal{B}$ and each leaf v in u's subtree in $\mathcal{T}_\mathcal{B}$, we store all summaries in $\mathcal{RS}(u, v, \varepsilon)$ sequentially.

2. For each leaf v, we store the summaries in $\mathcal{RS}(r_\mathcal{B}, v, c^j\varepsilon)$ sequentially, for all $j = 0, \ldots, q$. Recall that q is an integer such that $s_{c^q\varepsilon} = O(1)$.

3. For the root $r_\mathcal{B}$, we store $\mathcal{S}(c^j\varepsilon, r_\mathcal{B})$ for $j = 0, \ldots, q$.

An illustration of the first and the second type of structures is shown in Figure 3. The size of the structure can be determined as follow:

1. For each leaf $v \in \mathcal{T}_{\mathcal{B}}$, there are at most $O(\log B)$ ancestors of v, so there are in total $O(B \log B)$ such pairs (u, v). For each pair we use $O(s_\varepsilon)$ space, so the space usage is $O(s_\varepsilon B \log B)$.

2. For each leaf $v \in \mathcal{T}_{\mathcal{B}}$ we use $O(s_\varepsilon)$ space, so the space usage is $O(s_\varepsilon B)$.

3. For the root $r_{\mathcal{B}}$, the space usage is $O(s_\varepsilon)$.

Summing up the above cases, the space for storing the summaries of any internal block $\mathcal{B}$ is $O(s_\varepsilon B \log B)$. Note that each internal block has fanout $\Theta(B)$, and each leaf has size $\Theta(s_\varepsilon)$, so there are in total at most $O(N/(Bs_\varepsilon))$ internal blocks, and thus the total space usage is $O(N \log B)$. Next we show that this structure can indeed be used to answer queries in the optimal $O(\log_B N + s_\varepsilon/B)$ I/Os.

Query procedure. Given a query range $[q_1, q_2]$, let a and b be the two leaves containing q_1 and q_2, respectively. We focus on how to retrieve the necessary summaries for the right sibling set $\mathcal{R}(u, a)$, where u is the lowest common ancestor of a and b; the left sibling set $\mathcal{L}(u, b)$ can be handled symmetrically. By the previous analysis, we need exactly the summaries in $\mathcal{RS}(u, a, \varepsilon)$. Recall that $\mathcal{R}(u, a)$ are the right siblings of the left query path $\mathcal{P}(u, a)$. Let $\mathcal{B}_0, \ldots, \mathcal{B}_l$ be the blocks that $\mathcal{P}(u, a)$ intersects from u to a. The path $\mathcal{P}(u, a)$ is partitioned into $l + 1$ segments by these $l + 1$ blocks. Let $\mathcal{P}(u, v_0), \mathcal{P}(r_1, v_1), \ldots, \mathcal{P}(r_l, v_l = a)$ be the $l + 1$ segments, with r_i being the root of the binary tree $\mathcal{T}_{\mathcal{B}_i}$ in block $\mathcal{B}_i$ and v_i being a leaf of $\mathcal{T}_{\mathcal{B}_i}$, $i = 0, \ldots, l$. Let $w_1, \ldots, w_t$ be the nodes in $\mathcal{R}(u, a)$, at depths $d_1, \ldots, d_t$ of $\mathcal{T}$. We claim that w_i is either a node of $\mathcal{T}_{\mathcal{B}_k}$ for some $k \in \{0, \ldots, l\}$, or a right sibling of r_k for some $k \in \{0, \ldots, l\}$, which makes w_i a root of some other block. This is because by the definition of $\mathcal{R}(u, a)$, we know that w_i is a right child whose left sibling is in some $\mathcal{B}_k$. If w_i is not in $\mathcal{B}_k$, it must be the root of some other block. Recall that we need to retrieve $\mathcal{S}(c^{d_i - d_1}\varepsilon, w_i)$ for $i = 1, \ldots, t$. Below we show how this can be done efficiently using our structure.

For the w_i's in the first block $\mathcal{B}_0$, since we have stored all summaries in $\mathcal{RS}(u, v_0, \varepsilon)$ sequentially for $\mathcal{B}_0$ (case 1.), they can be retrieved in $O(1 + s_\varepsilon/B)$ I/Os.

For any w_i being the root of some other block $\mathcal{B}'$ not on the path $\mathcal{B}_0, \ldots, \mathcal{B}_l$, since we have stored the summaries $\mathcal{S}(c^j\varepsilon, w_i)$ for $j = 0, \ldots, q$ for every block (case 3.), the required summary $\mathcal{S}(c^{d_i - d_1}\varepsilon, w_i)$ can be retrieved in $O(1 + s_{c^{d_i - d_1}\varepsilon}/B)$ I/Os. Note that the number of such w_i's is bounded by $O(\log_B N)$, so the total cost for retrieving summaries for these nodes is at most $O(\log_B N + s_\varepsilon/B)$ I/Os.

The rest of the w_i's are in $\mathcal{B}_1, \ldots, \mathcal{B}_l$. Consider each $\mathcal{B}_k, k = 1, \ldots, l$. Recall that the segment of the path $\mathcal{P}(u, a)$ in $\mathcal{B}_k$ is $\mathcal{P}(r_k, v_k)$, and the w_i's in $\mathcal{B}_k$ are exactly $\mathcal{R}(r_k, v_k)$. We have stored $\mathcal{RS}(r_k, v_k, c^j\varepsilon)$ for $\mathcal{B}_k$ for all j (case 2.), so no matter at which relative depths $d_i - d_1$ the nodes in $\mathcal{R}(r_k, v_k)$ start and end, we can always find the required summary set. Retrieving the desired summary set takes $O\left(1 + s_{c^{d'-d_1}\varepsilon}/B\right)$ I/Os, where d' is the depth of the highest node in $\mathcal{R}(r_k, v_k)$. Summing over all blocks $\mathcal{B}_1, \ldots, \mathcal{B}_l$, the total cost is $O(\log_B N + s_\varepsilon/B)$ I/Os.

Reducing the size to linear. The structure above has a super-linear size $O(N \log B)$. Next we show how to reduce its size back to $O(N)$ while not affecting the optimal query cost.

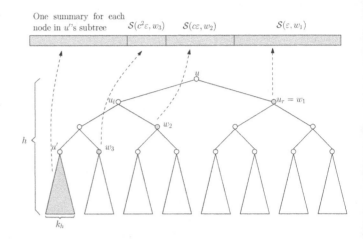

Figure 4: A schematic illustration of our packed structure.

Observe that the $\log B$ factor comes from case 1., where we store $\mathcal{RS}(u, v, \varepsilon)$ for each internal node u and each leaf v in u's subtree in u's block $\mathcal{B}$. Focus on $\mathcal{B}$ and the binary tree $\mathcal{T}_{\mathcal{B}}$ stored in it. Abusing notation, we use $\mathcal{T}_u$ to denote the subtree rooted at u in $\mathcal{T}_{\mathcal{B}}$. Assume $\mathcal{T}_u$ has height h (in $\mathcal{T}_{\mathcal{B}}$). Our idea is to pack the $\mathcal{RS}(u, v, \varepsilon)$'s for some leaves $v \in \mathcal{T}_u$ to reduce the space usage. Let u_l and u_r be the left and right child of u, respectively. The first observation is that we only need to store $\mathcal{RS}(u, v, \varepsilon)$ for each leaf v in u_l's subtree. This is because for any leaf v in u_r's subtree, the sibling set $\mathcal{R}(u, v)$ is the same as $\mathcal{R}(u_r, v)$, so $\mathcal{RS}(u, v, \varepsilon) = \mathcal{RS}(u_r, v, \varepsilon)$, which will be stored when considering u_r in place of u. For any leaf v in u_l's subtree, observe that the highest node in $\mathcal{R}(u, v)$ is u_r. This means for a node $w \in \mathcal{R}(u, v)$ with height i in tree $\mathcal{T}_u$, the summary for w in $\mathcal{RS}(u, v, \varepsilon)$ is $\mathcal{S}(c^{h-i-1}\varepsilon, w)$. Let u' be an internal node in u_l's subtree, and suppose u' has k_h leaves below it. We will decide later the value of k_h and, thus, the height $\log k_h$ at which u' is chosen (the leaves are defined to be at height 0). We do the following for each u' at height $\log k_h$ in u_l's subtree. Instead of storing the summary set $\mathcal{RS}(u, v, \varepsilon)$ for each leaf v in u''s subtree, we store $\mathcal{RS}(u, u', \varepsilon)$, which is the common prefix of all the $\mathcal{RS}(u, v, \varepsilon)$'s, together with a summary for each of the nodes in u''s subtree. More precisely, for each node w in u''s subtree, if its height is i, we store a summary $\mathcal{S}(c^{h-i-1}\varepsilon, w)$. All these summaries below u' are stored sequentially. A schematic illustration of our packed structure is shown in Figure 4.

Recall that all the summary sets we store in case 1. are used to cover the top portion of the query path $\mathcal{P}(u, v_0)$ in block $\mathcal{B}_0$, i.e., $\mathcal{RS}(u, v_0, \varepsilon)$. Clearly the packed structure still serves this purpose: We first find the u' which has v_0 as one of its descendants. Then we load $\mathcal{RS}(u, u', \varepsilon)$, followed by the summaries $\mathcal{S}(c^{h-i-1}, w)$ required in $\mathcal{RS}(u, v_0, \varepsilon)$. Loading $\mathcal{RS}(u, u', \varepsilon)$ still takes $O(1 + s_\varepsilon/B)$ I/Os, but loading the remaining individual summaries may incur many I/Os since they may not be stored sequentially. Nevertheless, if we ensure that all the individual summaries below u' have total size $O(s_\varepsilon)$, then loading any subset of them does not take more than $O(1 + s_\varepsilon/B)$ I/Os. Note that there are $k_h/2^i$ nodes at height i in u''s subtree, the total size of all summaries below u' is

$$\sum_{i=0}^{\log k_h} \frac{k_h}{2^i} s_{c^{h-i-1}\varepsilon}. \tag{1}$$

Thus it is sufficient to choose k_h such that (1) is $\Theta(s_\varepsilon)$. Note that such a k_h always exists[3]: When $k_h = 1$, (1) is $s_{c^{h-1}\varepsilon} = O(s_\varepsilon)$; when k_h takes the maximum possible value $k_h = 2^{h-1}$, the last term (when $i = h$) in the summation of (1) is s_ε, so (1) is at least $\Omega(s_\varepsilon)$; every time k_h doubles, (1) increases by at most $O(s_\varepsilon)$.

It only remains to show that by employing the packed structure, the space usage for a block is indeed $O(Bs_\varepsilon)$. For a node u at height h in $\mathcal{T}_B$, the number of u''s at height $\log k_h$ under u is $2^h/k_h$. For each such u', storing $\mathcal{RS}(u, u', \varepsilon)$, as well as all the individual summaries below u', takes $O(s_\varepsilon)$ space. So the space required for node u is $O(2^h s_\varepsilon/k_h)$. There are $O(B/2^h)$ nodes u at height h. Thus the total space required is

$$O\left(\sum_{h=1}^{\log B} 2^h s_\varepsilon/k_h \cdot B/2^h\right) = O\left(\sum_{h=1}^{\log B} Bs_\varepsilon/k_h\right).$$

Note that the choice of k_h implies that

$$s_\varepsilon/k_h = O\left(\sum_{i=0}^{\log k_h} \frac{1}{2^i} s_{c^{h-i-1}\varepsilon}\right) = O\left(\sum_{i=0}^{h-1} \frac{1}{2^i} s_{c^{h-i-1}\varepsilon}\right),$$

so the total size of the packed structures in $\mathcal{B}$ is bounded by

$$
\begin{aligned}
\sum_{h=1}^{\log B} Bs_\varepsilon/k_h &\leq B\sum_{h=0}^{\log B}\sum_{i=0}^{h-1} \frac{1}{2^i} s_{c^{h-i-1}\varepsilon} \\
&= B\sum_{h=0}^{\log B}\sum_{i=0}^{h-1} \frac{1}{2^{h-i-1}} s_{c^i\varepsilon} \\
&\leq B\sum_{i=0}^{\log B} s_{c^i\varepsilon} \sum_{h=i}^{\log B} \frac{1}{2^{h-i-1}} \\
&\leq 2B\sum_{i=0}^{\log B} s_{c^i\varepsilon} \\
&= O(Bs_\varepsilon).
\end{aligned}
$$

THEOREM 2. *For any $(1/2)$-exponentially decomposable summary, a database $\mathcal{D}$ of N records can be stored in an external memory index of linear size so that a summary query can be answered in $O(\log_B N + s_\varepsilon/B)$ I/Os.*

Remark. One technical subtlety is that the $O(s_\varepsilon)$ combining time in internal memory does not guarantee that we can combine the $O(\log N)$ summaries in $O(s_\varepsilon/B)$ I/Os in external memory. However if the merging algorithm only makes linear scans on the summaries, then this is not a problem, as we shall see in Section 4.

4. SUMMARIES

In this section we demonstrate the decomposable or exponentially decomposable properties for the summaries mentioned in Section 1.2. Thus, they can be used in our indexes in Section 2 and 3.

---

[3]We define k_h in this implicit way for its generality. When instantiating into specific summaries, there are often closed forms for k_h. For example when $s_\varepsilon = \Theta(1/\varepsilon)$ and $1 < c < 2$, $k_h = \Theta(c^h)$.

4.1 Heavy hitters

Given a multiset D, let $f_D(x)$ be the frequency of x in D. The MG summary [23] with error parameter ε consists of $s_\varepsilon = 1/\varepsilon$ items and their associated counters. For any item x in the counter set, the MG summary maintains an estimated count $\hat{f}_D(x)$ such that $f_D(x) - \varepsilon F_1(D) \leq \hat{f}_D(x) \leq f_D(x)$; for any item x not in the counter set, it is guaranteed that $f_D(x) \leq \varepsilon F_1(D)$. Thus in either case, the MG summary provides an additive $\varepsilon F_1(D)$ error: $f_D(x) - \varepsilon F_1(D) \leq \hat{f}_D(x) \leq f_D(x)$ for any x. The SpaceSaving summary is very similar to the MG summary except that the SpaceSaving summary provides an $\hat{f}_D(x)$ overestimating $f_D(x)$: $f_D(x) \leq \hat{f}_D(x) < f_D(x) + \varepsilon F_1(D)$. Thus they clearly solve the heavy hitters problem.

The MG summary is clearly decomposable. Below we show that it is also α-exponentially decomposable for any $0 < \alpha < 1$. The same proof also works for the SpaceSaving summary.

Consider t multisets $D_1, \ldots, D_t$ with $F_1(D_i) \leq \alpha^{i-1}F_1(D_1)$ for $i = 1, \ldots, t$. We set $c = 1/\sqrt{\alpha} > 1$. Given a series of MG summaries $\mathcal{S}(\varepsilon, D_1)$, $\mathcal{S}(c\varepsilon, D_2)$, $\ldots$, $\mathcal{S}(c^{t-1}\varepsilon, D_t)$, we combine them by adding up the counters for the same item. Note that the total size of these summaries is bounded by

$$\sum_{j=0}^{t-1} s_{c^j\varepsilon} = \sum_{j=0}^{t-1} \frac{1}{c^j\varepsilon} = O(1/\varepsilon) = O(s_\varepsilon).$$

In order to analyze the error in the combined summary, let $f_j(x)$ denote the true frequency of item x in D_j and $\hat{f}_j(x)$ be the estimator of $f_j(x)$ in $\mathcal{S}(c^{j-1}\varepsilon, D_j)$. The combined summary uses $\sum_{j=1}^t \hat{f}_j(x)$ to estimate the true frequency of x, which is $\sum_{j=1}^t f_j(x)$. Note that

$$f_j(x) \geq \hat{f}_j(x) \geq f_j(x) - c^{j-1}\varepsilon F_1(D_j)$$

for $j = 1, \ldots, t$. Summing up the first inequality over all j yields $\sum_{j=1}^t f_j(x) \geq \sum_{j=1}^t \hat{f}_j(x)$. For the second inequality, we have

$$
\begin{aligned}
\sum_{j=1}^t \hat{f}_j(x) &\geq \sum_{j=1}^t f_j(x) - \sum_{j=1}^t c^{j-1}\varepsilon F_1(D_j) \\
&\geq \sum_{j=1}^t f_j(x) - \sum_{j=1}^t \left(\frac{\alpha}{\sqrt{\alpha}}\right)^{j-1}\varepsilon F_1(D_1) \\
&\geq \sum_{j=1}^t f_j(x) - \varepsilon F_1(D_1)\sum_{j=1}^t (\sqrt{\alpha})^{j-1} \\
&= \sum_{j=1}^t f_j(x) - O(\varepsilon F_1(D_1)).
\end{aligned}
$$

Therefore the error bound is $O(\varepsilon F_1(D_1)) = O(\varepsilon(F_1(D_1 \uplus \cdots \uplus D_t)))$.

To combine the summaries we require that each summary maintains its (item, counter) pairs in the increasing order of items (we impose an arbitrary ordering if the items are from an unordered domain). In this case each summary can be viewed as a sorted list and we can merge the t sorted lists into a single list, where the counters for the same item are added up. Note that if each summary is of size s_ε, then we need to employ a t-way merging algorithm and it takes $O(s_\varepsilon t \log t)$ time in internal memory and $O(\frac{s_\varepsilon t}{B} \log_{M/B} t)$ I/Os in external memory. However, when the sizes of the t summaries form a geometrically decreasing sequence, we can repeatedly perform two-way merges in a bottom-up fashion with linear total cost. The merging algorithm starts with an empty list, at step i, it merges the current list with the summary $\mathcal{S}(\varepsilon_{t+1-i}, D_{t+1-i})$. Note that in this process every counter of $\mathcal{S}(\varepsilon_j, D_j)$ is merged j times, but since the size of $\mathcal{S}(\varepsilon_j, D_j)$ is $\frac{1}{c^{j-1}\varepsilon}$, the total running time is bounded by

$$\sum_{j=1}^{t} \frac{j}{c^{j-1}\varepsilon} = O\left(\frac{1}{\varepsilon}\right) = O(s_\varepsilon).$$

In external memory we can perform the same trick and achieve the $O(s_\varepsilon/B)$ I/O bound if the smallest summary $\mathcal{S}(c^{t-1}\varepsilon, D_t)$ has size $\frac{1}{c^{t-1}\varepsilon} > B$; otherwise we can take the smallest k summaries, where k is the maximum number such that the smallest k summaries can fit in one block, and merge them in the main memory. In either case, we can merge the t summaries in s_ε/B I/Os.

4.2 Quantiles

Recall that in the ε-approximate quantile problem, we are given a set D of N items from a totally ordered universe, and the goal is to have a summary $\mathcal{S}(\varepsilon, D)$ from which for any $0 < \phi < 1$, a record with rank in $[(\phi - \varepsilon)N, (\phi + \varepsilon)N]$ can be extracted. It is easy to obtain a quantile summary of size $O(1/\varepsilon)$: We simply sort D and take an item every εN consecutive items. Given any rank $r = \phi N$, there is always an element within rank $[r - \varepsilon N, r + \varepsilon N]$.

Below we show that quantile summaries are α-exponentially decomposable. Suppose we are given a series of such quantile summaries $\mathcal{S}(\varepsilon_1, D_1), \mathcal{S}(\varepsilon_2, D_2), \ldots, \mathcal{S}(\varepsilon_t, D_t)$, for data sets $D_1, \ldots, D_t$. We combine them by sorting all the items in these summaries. We claim this forms an approximate quantile summary for $D = D_1 \cup \cdots \cup D_t$ with error at most $\sum_{j=1}^{t} \varepsilon_j F_1(D_j)$, that is, given a rank r, we can find an item in the combined summary whose rank is in $[r - \sum_{j=1}^{t} \varepsilon_j F_1(D_j), r + \sum_{j=1}^{t} \varepsilon_j F_1(D_j)]$ in D. For an element x in the combined summary, let y_j and z_j be the two consecutive elements in $\mathcal{S}(\varepsilon_j, D_j)$ such that $y_j \leq x \leq z_j$. We define $r_j^{\min}(x)$ to be the rank of y_j in D_j and $r_j^{\max}(x)$ to be rank of z_j in D_j. In other words, $r_j^{\min}(x)$ (resp. $r_j^{\max}(x)$) is the minimum (resp. maximum) possible rank of x in D_j. We state the following lemma that describes the properties of $r_j^{\min}(x)$ and $r_j^{\max}(x)$:

LEMMA 1. *(1) For an element x in the combined summary,*

$$\sum_{j=1}^{t} r_j^{\max}(x) - \sum_{j=1}^{t} r_j^{\min}(x) \leq \sum_{j=1}^{t} \varepsilon_j F_1(D_j).$$

(2) For two consecutive elements $x_1 \leq x_2$ in the combined summary,

$$\sum_{j=1}^{t} r_j^{\min}(x_2) - \sum_{j=1}^{t} r_j^{\min}(x_1) \leq \sum_{j=1}^{t} \varepsilon_j F_1(D_j).$$

PROOF. Since $r_j^{\max}(x)$ and $r_j^{\min}(x)$ are the local ranks of two consecutive elements in $\mathcal{S}(\varepsilon_j, D_j)$, we have $r_j^{\max}(x) - r_j^{\min}(x) \leq \varepsilon_j F_1(D_j)$. Taking summation over all j, part (1) of the lemma follows. We also note that if x_1 and x_2 are consecutive in the combined summary, $r_j^{\min}(x_1)$ and $r_j^{\min}(x_2)$ are local ranks of either the same element or two

consecutive elements of $\mathcal{S}(\varepsilon_j, D_j)$. In either case we have $r_j^{\min}(x_2) - r_j^{\min}(x_1) \leq \varepsilon_j F_1(D_j)$. Summing over all j proves part (2) of the lemma. $\square$

Now for each element x in the combined summary, we compute the global minimum rank $r^{\min}(x) = \sum_{j=1}^{t} r_j^{\min}(x)$. Note that all these global ranks can be computed by scanning the combined summary in sorted order. Given a query rank r, we find the smallest element x with $r^{\min}(x) \geq r - \sum_{j=1}^{t} \varepsilon_j F_1(D_j)$. We claim that the actual rank of x in D is in the range $[r - \sum_{j=1}^{t} \varepsilon_j F_1(D_j), r + \sum_{j=1}^{t} \varepsilon_j F_1(D_j)]$. Indeed, we observe that the actual rank of x in set D is in the range $[\sum_{j=1}^{t} r_j^{\min}(x), \sum_{j=1}^{t} r_j^{\max}(x)]$ so we only need to prove that this range is contained by $[r - \sum_{j=1}^{t} \varepsilon_j F_1(D_j), r + \sum_{j=1}^{t} \varepsilon_j F_1(D_j)]$. The left side trivially follows from the choice of x. For the right side, let x' be the largest element in the new summary such that $x' \leq x$. By the choice of x, we have $\sum_{j=1}^{t} r_j^{\min}(x') < r - \sum_{j=1}^{t} \varepsilon_j F_1(D_j)$. By Lemma 1 we have $\sum_{j=1}^{t} r_j^{\min}(x) - \sum_{j=1}^{t} r_j^{\min}(x') \leq \sum_{j=1}^{t} \varepsilon_j F_1(D_j)$ and $\sum_{j=1}^{t} r_j^{\max}(x) - \sum_{j=1}^{t} r_j^{\min}(x) \leq \sum_{j=1}^{t} \varepsilon_j F_1(P_j)$. Summing up these three inequalities yields $\sum_{j=1}^{t} r_j^{\max}(x) \leq r + \sum_{j=1}^{t} \varepsilon_j F_1(D_j)$, so the claim follows.

For α-exponentially decomposability, the t data sets have $F_1(D_i) \leq \alpha^{i-1} F_1(D_1)$ for $i = 1, \ldots, t$. We choose $c = 1/\sqrt{\alpha} > 1$. The summaries $\mathcal{S}(\varepsilon_1, D_1), \mathcal{S}(\varepsilon_2, D_2), \ldots, \mathcal{S}(\varepsilon_t, D_t)$ have $\varepsilon_i = c^{i-1}\varepsilon$. Therefore we can combine them with error

$$
\begin{aligned}
\sum_{j=1}^{t} c^{j-1}\varepsilon F_1(D_j) & \leq \sum_{j=1}^{t} \left(\frac{\alpha}{\sqrt{\alpha}}\right)^{j-1} \varepsilon F_1(D_1) \\
& = \varepsilon F_1(D_1) \sum_{j=1}^{t} \left(\sqrt{\alpha}\right)^{j-1} \\
& = O(\varepsilon F_1(D_1)) \\
& = O(\varepsilon F_1(D_1 \cup \cdots \cup D_t)).
\end{aligned}
$$

To combine the t summaries, we notice that we are essentially merging k sorted lists with geometrically decreasing sizes, so we can adapt the algorithm in Section 4.1. The cost of merging the t summaries is therefore $O(s_\varepsilon)$ in internal memory and $O(s_\varepsilon/B)$ I/Os in external memory. The size of combined summary is

$$\sum_{j=1}^{t} \frac{1}{c^{j-1}\varepsilon} = O\left(\frac{1}{\varepsilon}\right) = O(s_\varepsilon).$$

4.3 The Count-Min sketch

Given a multiset D where the items are drawn from a universe $[u] = \{1, \ldots, u\}$. Let $f_D(x)$ be the frequency of x in D. The Count-Min sketch makes use of a 2-universal hash function $h : [u] \to [1/\varepsilon]$ and a collection of $1/\varepsilon$ counters $C[1], \ldots, C[1/\varepsilon]$. Then it computes $C[j] = \sum_{h(x)=j} f_D(x)$ for $j = 1, \ldots, 1/\varepsilon$. A single collection of $1/\varepsilon$ counters achieve a constant success probability for a variety of estimation purposes, and the probability can be boosted to $1 - \delta$ by using $O(\log(1/\delta))$ copies with independent hash functions. Here we only show the decomposability of a single copy; the same result also holds for $O(\log(1/\delta))$ copies.

Given multiple Count-Min sketches with the same h (hence the same number of counters), they can be easily combined by adding up the corresponding counters. So the Count-Min sketch is decomposable. However, for exponentially decomposability we are dealing with t Count-Min sketches with exponentially increasing ε's, hence different hash functions, so they cannot be easily combined. Thus we simply put them together without combining any counters. Although the resulting summary is not a true Count-Min sketch, we argue that it can be used to serve all the purposes a Count-Min is supposed to serve.

More precisely, for t data sets $D_1, \ldots, D_t$ with $F_1(D_i) \leq \alpha^{i-1} F_1(D_1)$, we have t Count-Min sketches $\mathcal{S}(\varepsilon, D_1)$, $\ldots$, $\mathcal{S}(c^{t-1}\varepsilon, D_t)$. The i-th sketch $\mathcal{S}(c^{j-1}\varepsilon, D_t)$ uses a hash function $h_i : [u] \to [1/c^{j-1}\varepsilon]$. Again we set $c = 1/\sqrt{\alpha}$. Note that the total size of all the sketches is $O(1/\varepsilon + 1/c\varepsilon + 1/c^2\varepsilon + \cdots) = O(1/\varepsilon) = O(s_\varepsilon)$, so we only need to show that the error is the same as what a Count-Min sketch $\mathcal{S}(\varepsilon, D_1 \uplus \cdots \uplus D_t)$ would provide. Below we consider the problem of estimating inner products (join sizes), which has other applications, such as point queries and self-join sizes, as special cases.

Let $\mathbf{f}_i$ denote the frequency vector of D_i, and let $\mathbf{f} = \sum_{i=1}^{t} \mathbf{f}_i$ be the frequency vector of $D = D_1 \uplus \ldots \uplus D_t$. The goal is to estimate inner product $\langle \mathbf{f}, \mathbf{g} \rangle$ where $\mathbf{g}$ is the frequency vector of some other data set. Note that when $\mathbf{g}$ is a standard basic vector (i.e., containing only one "1"), $\langle \mathbf{f}, \mathbf{g} \rangle$ becomes a point query; when $\mathbf{g} = \mathbf{f}$, $\langle \mathbf{f}, \mathbf{g} \rangle$ is the self-join size of $\mathbf{f}$. We distinguish between two cases: (1) $\mathbf{g}$ is given explicitly; and (2) $\mathbf{g}$ is also represented by a summary returned by our index, i.e., a collection of t Count-Min sketches $\mathcal{S}(\varepsilon, G_1), \ldots, \mathcal{S}(c^{t-1}\varepsilon, G_t)$, where $\mathbf{g} = \sum_{i=1}^{t} \mathbf{g}_i$ and $\mathbf{g}_i$ is the frequency vector of G_i. Recall that the Count-Min sketch estimates $\langle \mathbf{f}, \mathbf{g} \rangle$ with an additive error of $\varepsilon F_1(\mathbf{f})F_1(\mathbf{g})$, and we will show that we can do the same when $\mathbf{f}$ is represented by the collection of t Count-Min sketches.

Inner product with an explicit vector. For a $\mathbf{g}$ given explicitly, we can construct a Count-Min sketch $\mathcal{S}(c^{i-1}\varepsilon, \mathbf{g})$ for $\mathbf{g}$ with hash function h_i, for $i = 1, \ldots, t$. We observe that $\langle \mathbf{f}, \mathbf{g} \rangle$ can be expressed as $\sum_{i=1}^{t} \langle \mathbf{f}_i, \mathbf{g} \rangle$, and $\langle \mathbf{f}_i, \mathbf{g} \rangle$ can be estimated using $\mathcal{S}(c^{i-1}\varepsilon, D_i)$ and $\mathcal{S}(c^{i-1}\varepsilon, \mathbf{g})$ as described in [8] since they use the same hash function. The error is $c^{i-1}\varepsilon ||\mathbf{f}_i||_1 ||\mathbf{g}||_1 \leq (c\alpha)^{i-1}\varepsilon ||\mathbf{f}_1||_1 ||\mathbf{g}||_1$. For $c = 1/\sqrt{\alpha}$, the total error is bounded by

$$\sum_{i=1}^{t} \alpha^{(i-1)/2}\varepsilon ||\mathbf{f}_1||_1 ||\mathbf{g}||_1 = O(\varepsilon ||\mathbf{f}_1||_1 ||\mathbf{g}||_1) = O(\varepsilon F_1(\mathbf{f})F_1(\mathbf{g})),$$

as desired.

Inner product with a vector returned by a summary query. Next we consider the case where $\mathbf{g}$ is also represented by a series[4] of t Count-Min sketches $\mathcal{S}(\varepsilon, G_1), \ldots, \mathcal{S}(c^{t-1}\varepsilon, G_t)$ with $F_1(G_i) \geq \alpha^{i-1} F_1(G_1)$. We will show how to estimate $\langle \mathbf{f}, \mathbf{g} \rangle$ using the two series of sketches. This will allow the user to estimate the join size between the results of two queries. Note that this includes the special case of estimating the self-join size of $\mathbf{f}$.

In this case we will inevitably face the problem of pairing two sketches of different sizes. To do so we need more insight into the hash functions used. Suppose $1/\varepsilon$ is a power of 2.

---

[4]More precisely, $\mathbf{g}$ is represented by two such series: one from the left query path and one from the right query path, and so is $\mathbf{f}$. But we can decompose $\langle \mathbf{f}, \mathbf{g} \rangle$ into 4 subproblems by considering the cross product of these series, where each subproblem involves only a single series of sketches for either $\mathbf{f}$ or $\mathbf{g}$.

Let p be a prime within the range $[u, 2u]$ and a, b be random numbers uniformly chosen from $\{0, \ldots, p-1\}$. If we use the following 2-universal hash functions:

$$h_i(x) = ((ax + b) \bmod p)) \bmod \frac{1}{2^{i-1}\varepsilon}, i = 1, \ldots, \log(1/\varepsilon),$$

then we observe that each bucket of h_{i+1} is partitioned into two buckets of h_i. This means that given a Count-Min sketch $\mathcal{S}(2^{i-1}\varepsilon, D)$ constructed with h_i, one can convert it to a Count-Min sketch $\mathcal{S}(2^{j-1}\varepsilon, D)$ constructed with h_j for any $j \geq i$. Thus two sketches of different sizes can still be used together by reducing the size of the larger one to match that of the smaller one. Of course we will only get the error guarantee of the smaller sketch, but this will not be a problem as we show later.

Now, set $c = 2$ and we have the sketches $\mathcal{S}(2^{i-1}\varepsilon, D_i)$ and $\mathcal{S}(2^{i-1}\varepsilon, G_i)$ with hash function h_i, for $i = 1, \ldots, \log(1/\varepsilon)$. We express $\langle \mathbf{f}, \mathbf{g} \rangle$ as

$$\langle \mathbf{f}, \mathbf{g} \rangle = \left\langle \sum_{i=1}^{t} \mathbf{f}_i, \sum_{i=1}^{t} \mathbf{g}_i \right\rangle = \sum_{i=1}^{t} \langle \mathbf{f}_i, \mathbf{g}_i \rangle + \sum_{i<j} \langle \mathbf{f}_i, \mathbf{g}_j \rangle + \sum_{i<j} \langle \mathbf{g}_i, \mathbf{f}_j \rangle.$$

First, $\langle \mathbf{f}_i, \mathbf{g}_i \rangle$ can be estimated using $\mathcal{S}(2^{i-1}\varepsilon, D_i)$ and $\mathcal{S}(2^{i-1}\varepsilon, G_i)$. The error is at most $2^{i-1}\varepsilon F_1(D_i)F_1(G_i) \leq (2\alpha^2)^{i-1}\varepsilon F_1(D_1)F_1(G_1)$. It follows that $\sum_{i=1}^{t} \langle \mathbf{f}_i, \mathbf{g}_i \rangle$ can be estimated with error $\sum_{i=1}^{t} (2\alpha^2)^{i-1}\varepsilon F_1(D_1)F_1(G_1)$. For $\alpha < 1/\sqrt{2}$, this error is bounded by $O(\varepsilon F_1(D_1)F_1(G_1))$.

For $\langle \mathbf{f}_i, \mathbf{g}_j \rangle$ with $i < j$, we first convert $\mathcal{S}(2^{i-1}\varepsilon, D_i)$ to $\mathcal{S}(2^{j-1}\varepsilon, D_i)$, and do the estimation with $\mathcal{S}(2^{j-1}\varepsilon, G_i)$, which gives us an error of $2^{j-1}\varepsilon F_1(D_i)F_1(G_i)$. Therefore the error of estimating $\sum_{i<j} \langle \mathbf{f}_i, \mathbf{g}_j \rangle$ can be bounded by

$$\sum_{i<j} 2^{j-1}\varepsilon ||\mathbf{f}_i||_1 ||\mathbf{g}_j||_1 = \sum_{i=1}^{t-1} \varepsilon ||\mathbf{f}_i||_1 \sum_{j=i+1}^{t} 2^{j-1} ||\mathbf{g}_j||_1$$

$$\leq \sum_{i=1}^{t-1} 2^i \varepsilon ||\mathbf{f}_i||_1 \sum_{j=i+1}^{t} (2\alpha)^{j-i-1} ||\mathbf{g}_1||_1$$

$$= \sum_{i=1}^{t-1} 2^i \varepsilon ||\mathbf{f}_i||_1 ||\mathbf{g}_1||_1 \sum_{j=i+1}^{t} (2\alpha)^{j-i-1}.$$

For constant $\alpha < 1/2$, we have $\sum_{j=i+1}^{t} (2\alpha)^{j-i-1} = O(1)$, so the error of estimating $\sum_{i<j} \langle \mathbf{f}_i, \mathbf{g}_j \rangle$ is at most

$$O\left(\sum_{i=1}^{t-1} 2^{i-1}\varepsilon ||\mathbf{f}_i||_1 ||\mathbf{g}_1||_1\right) \leq O\left(\sum_{i=1}^{t-1} (2\alpha^2)^{i-1}\varepsilon ||\mathbf{f}_1||_1 ||\mathbf{g}_1||_1\right)$$

$$= O(\varepsilon ||\mathbf{f}_1||_1 ||\mathbf{g}_1||_1).$$

We can similarly bound $\sum_{i<j} \langle \mathbf{g}_i, \mathbf{f}_j \rangle = O(\varepsilon ||\mathbf{f}_1||_1 ||\mathbf{g}_1||_1)$.

This proves that Count-Min sketch is α-exponentially decomposable for any constant $0 < \alpha < 1/2$. One technicality is that our data structures only support $1/2$-exponentially decomposable summaries as described in Section 3. This is caused by the use of a binary tree $\mathcal{T}$. To get around the problem, we replace the binary tree $\mathcal{T}$ with a ternary tree, so that subtree sizes decrease by a factor of 3 from a level to the one below. Now the left query path may have two nodes on each level in the canonical decomposition of the query range, and so does the right query path. This results in 4 series of sketches for representing $\mathbf{f}$ and $\mathbf{g}$. But this does not affect our analysis by more than a constant factor as argued earlier.

Remark. One technical subtlety is that, since we are now making $O(\log^2 N)$ estimations, in order to be able to add up the errors, we need all the estimations to succeed, i.e., stay within the claimed error bounds. To achieve a $1 - \delta$ overall success probability, each individual estimation should succeed with probability $1 - \delta/\log^2 N$, by the union bound. Thus each Count-Min sketch $\mathcal{S}(c^{i-1}\varepsilon, D_i)$ we use should have size $O((1/c^{i-1}\varepsilon)\log(\frac{\log N}{\delta}))$.

4.4 The AMS sketch and wavelets

Given a multiset D in which the frequency of x is $f_D(x)$, the AMS sketch computes $O((1/\varepsilon^2)\log(1/\delta))$ counters $Y_i = \sum_x h_i(x)f_D(x)$, where each $h_i : [u] \to \{+1, -1\}$ is a uniform 4-wise independent hash function (Dobra and Rusu [25] show that some 3-wise independent hash functions also suffice). The AMS sketch is clearly decomposable. But since it provides an error guarantee depending on $F_2(D)$, it is not exponentially decomposable. Intuitively, the size of a data set could drop by a constant factor without reducing its F_2 significantly. More precisely, for two data sets D_1 and D_2 with $F_1(D_2) \leq \alpha F_1(D_1)$ for a constant $\alpha < 1$, $F_2(D_1) - F_2(D_2)$ may be $o(F_2(D_1))$. Thus the AMS sketch can only be used in the baseline solution of Section 2.

Gilbert et al. [12] have shown that an AMS sketch of an appropriate size also incorporates enough information from which we can build a wavelet representation of the underlying data set. Thus, the baseline index of Section 2 can also be used to return a wavelet representation for the data records in the query range.

5. HANDLING UPDATES

If the summary itself supports updates, our indexes also support updates. In particular, the MG summary [23], the GK summary for quantiles [14] support insertions, while the Count-Min sketch and the AMS sketch support both insertions and deletions. The corresponding summary indexes then also support insertions or both insertions and deletions. In this section we briefly describe how we handle updates for the two internal memory structures in Section 2 and 3. The techniques are quite standard [24], so we just sketch the high-level ideas. The external memory indexes also support updates; the details will appear in the full version of the paper.

The baseline structure. We first assume that the structure of the binary tree $\mathcal{T}$ remains unchanged during updates, then we show how to maintain its balance dynamically. We will show how to handle insertions; deletions can be handled similarly, provided that the summary itself supports deletions.

To do an insertion, we first search down the tree $\mathcal{T}$ using the new record's A_q attribute and locate the fat leaf v where the new record should reside. Then we insert it into v. This new insertion affects all the summaries attached to the $O(\log N)$ nodes on the path from the root of $\mathcal{T}$ to v. For each such node u, a summary on all the items stored below u is attached, so we need to insert the new record to the summary as well. Assuming the update cost for a single summary is $O(\mu)$, the total cost of this insertion is $O(\mu \log N)$.

We can maintain the structure of $\mathcal{T}$ using a *weight-balanced* tree and *partial rebuildings* [24]. For any node $u \in \mathcal{T}$, the *weight* of u is defined to be the number of records stored below u. Then we restrict the weight of a node u at height i to vary on the order of $\Theta(2^i s_\varepsilon)$. The fanout of each node of $\mathcal{T}$ may not be 2 any more, but the weight constraint ensures that it is still a constant. After inserting a new record into a leaf v, the weight constraints at the ancestors of v might be violated. Then we find the highest node u where this happens, and simply rebuild the whole subtree rooted at the parent of u. Suppose the parent of u is at height i. We rebuild the subtree level by level. At level j, there are 2^{i-j} summaries we need to build, each on a data set of size $O(s_\varepsilon 2^j)$. So building each summary by simply inserting the records into an initially empty summary takes $O(\mu s_\varepsilon 2^j)$ time. This is $O(\mu s_\varepsilon 2^i)$ in total for level j. Summing over all i levels, the total cost of the rebuilding is $O(\mu s_\varepsilon 2^i \cdot i) = O(\mu s_\varepsilon 2^i \log N)$. After the rebuilding, the weight of u decreases by $\Theta(2^i s_\varepsilon)$, so the cost of the rebuilding can be charged to this weight decrease. Since every insertion increases the weights of $O(\log N)$ nodes by one, the cost of all the rebuildings converts to an $O(\mu s_\varepsilon 2^i \log N / 2^i s_\varepsilon \cdot \log N) = O(\mu \log^2 N)$ cost per insertion amortized.

THEOREM 3. *If the summary can be updated in $O(\mu)$ time, the baseline internal memory structure can be updated in $O(\mu \log^2 N)$ time amortized.*

Remark. In the above rebuilding algorithm, we do not assume any properties of the summary. In fact, for all the summaries considered in this paper, they do not have to be built from scratch for every level. Instead, the summaries at all levels can be constructed more efficiently in $O(\mu s_\varepsilon 2^i)$ time. This will reduce the amortized update cost to $O(\mu \log N)$. Details will appear in the full version of the paper.

The optimal internal memory structure for F_1 based summaries. The update procedure for the optimal internal memory structure of Theorem 1 is almost the same as the baseline solution, except that at each node, we now have $O(\log s_\varepsilon)$ summaries with exponentially decreasing sizes. This adds an $O(\log s_\varepsilon)$ factor to the cost of updating all affected summaries upon each insertion, as well as the partial rebuilding cost. Thus we have:

THEOREM 4. *If the summary can be updated in $O(\mu)$ time, the optimal internal memory structure of Theorem 1 can be updated in $O(\mu \log^2 N \log s_\varepsilon)$ time amortized.*

Remark. The above theorem does not assume any special properties of the summary. Again for all the summaries considered in this paper, the update time can be improved to $O(\mu \log N \log s_\varepsilon)$. Details will appear in the full version of the paper.

6. FUTURE DIRECTIONS

In this paper, we presented some initial positive results on supporting summary queries natively in a database system, that many useful summaries can be extracted with almost the same cost as computing simple aggregates. There are many interesting directions to explore:

1. Our index for the F_2 based summaries does not have the optimal query cost. Can we improve it to optimal? In fact, we can partition the data in terms of F_2 so that the F_2 based summaries are also exponentially decomposable, but we meet some technical difficulties since the resulting tree $\mathcal{T}$ is not balanced.

2. We have only considered the case where there is only one query attribute. In general there could be more than one query attribute and the query range could be any spatial constraint. For example, one could ask the following queries:

(Q3) Return a summary on the salaries of all employees aged between 20 and 30 with ranks below VP.

(Q4) Return a summary on the household income distribution for the area within 50 miles from Washington, DC.

In the most general and challenging case, one could consider any SELECT-FROM-WHERE aggregate SQL query and replace the aggregate operator with a summary operator.

3. Likewise, the summary could also involve more than one attribute. When the user is interested in the joint distribution of two or more attributes, or the spatial distribution of the query results, a multi-dimensional summary would be very useful. An example is

(Q5) What is the geographical distribution of households with annual income below $50,000?

Note how this query serves the complementing purpose of (Q4). To summarize multi-dimensional data, one could consider the multi-dimensional extensions of quantiles and wavelets, as well as geometric summaries such as ε-approximations and various clusterings. The former is useful for multiple relational attributes, while the latter is more suitable for summarizing geometric distributions as in (Q5).

7. REFERENCES

[1] P. Afshani, G. S. Brodal, and N. Zeh. Ordered and unordered top-k range reporting in large data sets. In *Proc. ACM-SIAM Symposium on Discrete Algorithms*, 2011.

[2] P. K. Agarwal and J. Erickson. Geometric range searching and its relatives. In *Advances in Discrete and Computational Geometry*, pages 1–56. American Mathematical Society, 1999.

[3] N. Alon, P. B. Gibbons, Y. Matias, and M. Szegedy. Tracking join and self-join sizes in limited storage. *Journal of Computer and System Sciences*, 64(3):719–747, 2002.

[4] N. Alon, Y. Matias, and M. Szegedy. The space complexity of approximating the frequency moments. *Journal of Computer and System Sciences*, 58(1):137–147, 1999.

[5] A. Arasu and G. Manku. Approximate counts and quantiles over sliding windows. In *Proc. ACM Symposium on Principles of Database Systems*, 2004.

[6] K. Beyer, P. J. Haas, B. Reinwald, Y. Sismanis, and R. Gemulla. On synopses for distinct-value estimation under multiset operations. In *Proc. ACM SIGMOD International Conference on Management of Data*, 2007.

[7] G. S. Brodal, B. Gfeller, A. G. Jørgensen, and P. Sanders. Towards optimal range medians. *Theoretical Computer Science*, to appear.

[8] G. Cormode and S. Muthukrishnan. An improved data stream summary: The count-min sketch and its applications. *Journal of Algorithms*, 55(1):58–75, 2005.

[9] M. Garofalakis and A. Kumar. Wavelet synopses for general error metrics. *ACM Transactions on Database Systems*, 30(4):888–928, 2005.

[10] J. Gehrke, F. Korn, and D. Srivastava. On computing correlated aggregates over continual data streams. In *Proc. ACM SIGMOD International Conference on Management of Data*, 2001.

[11] A. C. Gilbert, S. Guha, P. Indyk, Y. Kotidis, S. Muthukrishnan, and M. J. Strauss. Fast, small-space algorithms for approximate histogram maintenance. In *Proc. ACM Symposium on Theory of Computing*, 2002.

[12] A. C. Gilbert, Y. Kotidis, S. Muthukrishnan, and M. Strauss. Surfing wavelets on streams: One-pass summaries for approximate aggregate queries. In *Proc. International Conference on Very Large Data Bases*, 2001.

[13] J. Gray, S. Chaudhuri, A. Bosworth, A. Layman, D. Reichart, M. Venkatrao, F. Pellow, and H. Pirahesh. Data cube: A relational aggregation operator generalizing group-by, cross-tab, and sub-totals. *Data Mining and Knowledge Discovery*, 1(1):29–53, 1997.

[14] M. Greenwald and S. Khanna. Space-efficient online computation of quantile summaries. In *Proc. ACM SIGMOD International Conference on Management of Data*, 2001.

[15] S. Guha, C. Kim, and K. Shim. XWAVE: Optimal and approximate extended wavelets for streaming data. In *Proc. International Conference on Very Large Data Bases*, 2004.

[16] J. Hellerstein, P. Haas, and H. Wang. Online aggregation. In *Proc. ACM SIGMOD International Conference on Management of Data*, 1997.

[17] C. Jermaine, S. Arumugam, A. Pol, and A. Dobra. Scalable approximate query processing with the dbo engine. *ACM Transactions on Database Systems*, 33(4), Article 23, 2008.

[18] A. Jørgensen and K. Larsen. Range selection and median: Tight cell probe lower bounds and adaptive data structures. In *Proc. ACM-SIAM Symposium on Discrete Algorithms*, 2011.

[19] X. Lin, Y. Yuan, Q. Zhang, and Y. Zhang. Selecting stars: The k most representative skyline operator. In *Proc. IEEE International Conference on Data Engineering*, 2007.

[20] Y. Matias, J. S. Vitter, and M. Wang. Wavelet-based histograms for selectivity estimation. In *Proc. ACM SIGMOD International Conference on Management of Data*, 1998.

[21] Y. Matias, J. S. Vitter, and M. Wang. Dynamic maintenance of wavelet-based histograms. In *Proc. International Conference on Very Large Data Bases*, 2000.

[22] A. Metwally, D. Agrawal, and A. Abbadi. An integrated efficient solution for computing frequent and top-k elements in data streams. *ACM Transactions on Database Systems*, 31(3):1095–1133, 2006.

[23] J. Misra and D. Gries. Finding repeated elements. *Science of Computer Programming*, 2:143–152, 1982.

[24] M. H. Overmars. *The Design of Dynamic Data Structures*. Springer-Verlag, LNCS 156, 1983.

[25] F. Rusu and A. Dobra. Pseudo-random number generation for sketch-based estimations. *ACM Transactions on Database Systems*, 32(2), Article 11, 2007.

[26] H. Samet. *Foundations of Multidimensional and Metric Data Structures*. Morgan Kaufmann, 2006.

[27] Y. Tao, L. Ding, X. Lin, and J. Pei. Distance-based representative skyline. In *Proc. IEEE International Conference on Data Engineering*, 2009.

[28] V. N. Vapnik and A. Y. Chervonenkis. On the uniform convergence of relative frequencies of events to their probabilities. *Theory of Probability and its Applications*, 16:264–280, 1971.

[29] J. S. Vitter and M. Wang. Approximate computation of multidimensional aggregates of sparse data using wavelets. In *Proc. SIGMOD International Conference on Management of Data*, 1999.

New Results on Two-dimensional Orthogonal Range Aggregation in External Memory

Cheng Sheng
CUHK
Hong Kong
csheng@cse.cuhk.edu.hk

Yufei Tao
CUHK
Hong Kong
taoyf@cse.cuhk.edu.hk

ABSTRACT

We consider the *orthogonal range aggregation* problem. The dataset S consists of N axis-parallel rectangles in $\mathbb{R}^2$, each of which is associated with an integer *weight*. Given an axis-parallel rectangle Q and an aggregate function F, a query reports the aggregated result of the weights of the rectangles in S intersecting Q. The goal is to preprocess S into a structure such that all queries can be answered efficiently. We present indexing schemes to solve the problem in external memory when $F = max$ (hence, *min*) and $F = sum$ (hence, *count* and *average*), respectively. Our schemes have linear or near-linear space, and answer a query in $O(\log_B N)$ or $O(\log_B^2 N)$ I/Os, where B is the disk block size.

Categories and Subject Descriptors

F2.2 [**Analysis of algorithms and problem complexity**]: Nonnumerical algorithms and problems—*geometric problems and computations*; H3.1 [**Information storage and retrieval**]: Content analysis and indexing—*indexing methods*

General Terms

Algorithms, theory

Keywords

Indexing, range searching

1. INTRODUCTION

Orthogonal range aggregation is a classic topic in computational geometry and the database area. In this paper, we consider that the aggregate function F is *max* or *sum*, with a particular focus on *max*.

In the *rectangle-intersection-max* problem, the dataset S consists of N rectangles[1] r in $\mathbb{R}^2$, each of which is associated with a *weight $w(r) \in \mathbb{N}$*. Given a rectangle Q, a query reports the maximum weight of all the rectangles in S intersecting Q, namely:

$$\max\{w(r) \mid r \in S \wedge r \cap Q \neq \emptyset\}.$$

Several special instances of the problem have been studied separately:

- *Window-max*, where each rectangle $r \in S$ degenerates to a point. Of special interest to this paper is *3-sided window-max*, which is a restricted version of window-max where Q has the form $[x_1, x_2] \times (-\infty, y]$.

- *Stabbing-max*, where Q degenerates to a point.

- *Segment-intersection-max*, where r (Q) degenerates to a horizontal (vertical) segment.

See Figure 1 for some illustrations.

In a straightforward manner, the above definitions can be adapted to $F = sum$, where the goal becomes finding the total weight of the rectangles in S intersecting Q. The ability of handling *max* and *sum* implies the ability of supporting *min* (which is symmetric to *max*), *count* (a special case of *sum* where all rectangles have a unit weight), and *average* (which can be derived from *count* and *sum*).

1.1 Applications

This subsection gives several applications of orthogonal range aggregation, which sheds some light on its importance in practice. We discuss first $F = max$ and *min*, before extending to other aggregate functions.

In a *spatial database*, each object in S can be the location of a hotel, with the object's weight set to the hotel's rate. A window-min query is *"retrieve the cheapest rate of the hotels in Manhattan"*, where Q is a rectangle describing the area of Manhattan. Sometimes, a data region can be so complex that it needs to be represented as the union of simple geometric shapes like rectangles. An example can be found in the *hurricane inquiry system*, where an object is the region struck by a hurricane. In this case, S consists of the rectangles used to approximate those regions, whereas

---

[1] All rectangles in this paper are orthogonal.

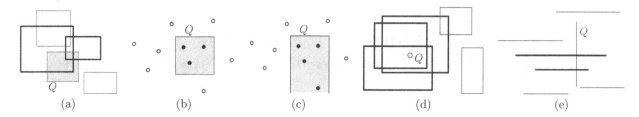

Figure 1: Variants of orthogonal range max search: (a) rectangle-intersection-max, (b) window-max, (c) 3-sided window-max, (d) stabbing max, (e) segment-intersection-max. In each example, the maximum weight of the bold objects is reported.

the weight of a rectangle $r \in S$ is set to the scale of the hurricane hitting the region represented by r. A rectangle-intersection-max query is *"find the most severe scale of all the hurricanes that struck Florida before"*. The query becomes a stabbing-max query if Q is given as a location in Florida.

Segment-intersection-max is useful in *temporal databases*, which manage the historical versions of a dataset evolving with time. Consider a database that stores the balances of bank accounts. Each record has the form $([t_s, t_e], k)$, indicating that a balance started to be k at time t_s and remained so until time t_e. This record can be regarded as a horizontal segment in a 2-d space, where the x- (y-) dimension is time (balance). Let S be a set of such segments, each associated with a weight equal to the monthly premium of medical insurance paid by the account owner. A meaningful query is *"return the highest monthly premium paid by the owners of those accounts whose balances were within [\$10k, \$20k] on Dec 1, 2010"*. The query is a vertical segment in the time-balance space.

Rectangle-intersection-max has also been studied in *bi-temporal databases* [17], *OLAP* [15, 16], and *meteorology systems* [21], whereas stabbing-max has been identified as a core operation in *packet classification* [14].

An extensive list of applications for $F = count$, sum, and *average* can be obtained by combining the applications in [15, 16, 18, 20]. In fact, all the queries given earlier in italic are still meaningful if they are modified to retrieve the average (e.g., the query in our first application becomes *"retrieve the average rate of the hotels in the Manhattan district"*), whereas computation of the average can be achieved by solving the corresponding *count* and *sum* problems.

1.2 Computation model

Our complexity analysis is under the *external memory* (*EM*) model [5], which has been successful in capturing the I/O characteristics of database algorithms (see a survey in [19]). In this model, the (main) memory has a capacity of M words, whereas the disk has an unbounded size, and is formatted into *blocks* with B words each. We require $B \geq 9$ in our analysis. An I/O transfers a block of data between the disk and memory. Space complexity measures the number of disk blocks occupied, whereas time complexity gauges the number of I/Os performed. *Linear cost* is interpreted as $O(N/B)$ for a dataset cardinality N. In this paper, *poly-logarithmic cost* should be understood as $O(\log_B^c N)$ for some constant c.

We assume that each word has at least $\log_2 N$ bits, and that each weight fits in $O(1)$ words. These assumptions also exist in the previous work [3, 4, 6, 11, 13, 18] on aggregation problems. We also make the *tall-cache assumption* [3, 8] that $M \geq B^2$. A typical value of B in reality is 1024 (words), in which case the assumption essentially says that the memory should have at least 1 mega words. This is not a demanding requirement for today's machines. In any case, the assumption is needed only to simplify the construction of the proposed structures, while all our space and query bounds hold for any $M \geq 2B$.

1.3 Previous results

There is a rich literature on orthogonal range aggregation in the EM model. When the aggregate function F is *max*, the existing results can be summaized as:

- For window-max, the CRB-tree of Govindarajan et al. [13] answers a query in $O(\log_B^2 N)$ I/Os, and consumes $O(\frac{N}{B} \log_B N)$ space (according to [3]). This has been improved by Agarwal et al. [3], whose structure has linear space, and retains the same query complexity as the CRB-tree. It is unclear whether the two structures can be improved for 3-sided window-max, which can be settled by a modified persistent B-tree of [18, 20] in $O(\log_B N)$ I/Os per query, occupying $O(\frac{N}{B} \log_B N)$ space.

- For stabbing-max, the best linear-space structure is also due to Agarwal et al. [3] and solves a query in $O(\log_B^4 N)$ I/Os. In [4], Agarwal et al. developed an alternative index that has a better query complexity $O(\log_B^2 N)$ but uses $O(\frac{N}{B} \log_B N)$ space.

- For segment-intersection-max, the modified persistent B-tree of [18, 20] can be deployed to process a query in $O(\log_B N)$ I/Os, but its space consumption is $O(\frac{N}{B} \log_B N)$. No linear-space structure is known to have poly-logarithmic query time for this problem.

- Using a reduction explained later, the rectangle-intersection-max problem can be solved in $O(\log_B^2 N)$ I/Os using an indexing scheme with $O(\frac{N}{B} \log_B N)$ space. Again, there is no linear-space structure with poly-logarithmic query cost.

When $F = count$ and sum, the counterparts of the above problems are equivalent to each other [12]. Thus, it suffices to discuss only rectangle-intersection-count and rectangle-intersection-sum. The CRB-tree [13] settles the former in

	previous	ours	remarks
3-sided window-max	$(N/B, \log_B^2 N)$ [3] $(\frac{N}{B}\log_B N, \log_B N)$ [18, 20]	$(N/B, \log_B N)$	the result of [3] holds for general window-max.
stabbing-max	$(N/B, \log_B^4 N)$ [3] $(\frac{N}{B}\log_B N, \log_B^2 N)$ [4]	$(N/B, \log_B^2 N)$	
segment-intersection-max	$(\frac{N}{B}\log_B N, \log_B N)$ [18, 20]		
rectangle-intersection-max	$(\frac{N}{B}\log_B N, \log_B^2 N)$ [3, 4, 18, 20]		
rectangle-intersection-count	$(N/B, \log_B N)$ [13]	$\left(\frac{N}{B}\max\{1, \log_B \frac{W}{N}\}, \log_B N\right)$	$W=\sum_{r\in S} w(r)$. Hence, $W=N$ for rectangle-intersection-count, for which our space is $O(N/B)$.
rectangle-intersection-sum	$(\frac{N}{B}\log_B \frac{W\log_2 W}{N}, \log_B N)$ [13]		

Table 1: **Comparison of the existing and our results. Each result is in the format of (space, query). All complexities are in big-O and worst case.**

linear space and logarithmic query cost. For $F = sum$, Govindarajan et al. [13] gave an alternative version of the CRB-tree that has the same query complexity, but requires $O(\frac{N}{B}\log_B \frac{W\log_2 W}{N})$ space, where W is the total weight of all the objects, namely, $W = \sum_{r\in S} w(r)$.

Observe that there is a gap between the space cost of the two CRB-trees. When each data rectangle has a unit weight (i.e., $W = N$), the *sum* CRB-tree has space $O(\frac{N}{B}\log_B \log_2 N)$, which is worse than the linear space of the *count* CRB-tree. This suggests that the space complexity of the sum CRB-tree may be unnecessarily large for small W. It remains open how to close the gap.

Various heuristic access methods [15, 16, 21] are available for orthogonal range aggregation, and have been empirically shown to work well for selected data and query distributions. However, they are not known to carry any interesting performance guarantee in the worst case.

1.4 Our results

Our main results can be summarized in three theorems:

THEOREM 1.1. *For 3-sided window-max, there is a linear-space structure that answers a query in $O(\log_B N)$ I/Os. The structure can be built in $O(\frac{N}{B}\log_B N)$ I/Os.*

THEOREM 1.2. *For rectangle-intersection-max, there is a linear-space structure that answers a query in $O(\log_B^2 N)$ I/Os. The structure can be built in $O(\frac{N}{B}\log_B N)$ I/Os.*

THEOREM 1.3. *For rectangle-intersection-sum, there is a structure that answers a query in $O(\log_B N)$ I/Os, and occupies $O(\frac{N}{B}\max\{1,\log_B \frac{W}{N}\})$ space, where W is the total weight of all the objects. The structure can be built in $O(\frac{N}{B}\log_B N)$ I/Os.*

Table 1 presents a detailed comparison of our and previous results.

Our techniques, except for several technical constructs, revolve around a compressed structure which we call the *bundled compressed B-tree (BCB-tree)*, and is designed for the so-called *bundled predecessor problem*. While its precise definition will appear in Section 3, informally speaking, in this problem we are given $b = O(B)$ sets of integers: $P_1, ..., P_b$.

The goal is to preprocess them so that, given an integer q, we can efficiently find the predecessor of q in every P_i ($i \le b$) at the same time, i.e., b predecessors need to be reported. Let $K = \sum_i |P_i|$. We observe that if every data integer falls in a domain of size $K \cdot B^{O(1)}$, our structure (i.e., the BCB-tree) only needs to consume space *sub-linear* in K, while guaranteeing logarithmic query cost. Another observation made in this paper is that the BCB-tree presents itself as a powerful weapon in approaching several aggregation problems. Note, however, that the idea of solving a single query in multiple datasets simultaneously is not new; see, for example, [1, 2].

Remark 1. In our problem definitions, the weight of each data object is an integer. This is not necessary for $F = max$, and Theorems 1.1 and 1.2 still hold for real-valued weights as well. All that needs to be done is to map each real-valued weight to an integer, and use a B-tree to index the resulting integers so that we can convert each of them back to its real-valued counterpart in $O(\log_B N)$ I/Os. The same trick, however, does not apply to $F = sum$, for which our methods work for integer weights only (this is also true for the CRB-trees of [13]).

Remark 2. As a corollary of Theorem 1.1, we obtain a linear-space structure with logarithmic query time for the following *segment dragging* problem defined in [10]. The dataset S is a set of N points in $\mathbb{R}^2$. The goal is to build an index on S such that, given a horizontal segment s, we can quickly report the first point hit if we move s downwards. This can be converted to the 3-sided window-max problem, where each point in S is associated with a weight equal to its y-coordinate, and each query is replaced by a 3-sided rectangle whose upper boundary is s, and its lower boundary is open.

Remark 3. Theorem 1.2 is clearly applicable to all the special instances of the rectangle-intersection-max problem. Hence, we improve the stabbing-max structure of [3], which incurs $O(\log_B^4 N)$ query cost.

Remark 4. Theorem 1.3 improves the CRB-tree in a small but interesting way. For rectangle-intersection-count (where $W = N$), the space complexity of our structure automatically reduces to $O(N/B)$. We thus close the space gap left by the CRB-tree. Furthermore, the theorem indicates that, if $W = N \cdot B^{O(1)}$, rectangle-intersection-sum is solvable in logarithmic query time by a linear-space index. This feature is absent in the CRB-tree.

2. PRELIMINARIES

We denote by $[x]$ the set of integers $\{1, ..., x\}$. Recall that, in our problems, each data object can be a point, segment, or rectangle. In any case, by standard tie-breaking techniques, we can assume that all the x- (y-) coordinates of the data objects are distinct. Similarly, we assume that their weights are also distinct. The rest of the section gives some basic facts relevant to our discussion.

Reduction for rectangle-intersection-max. For any intersecting rectangles r and Q, at least one of the following occurs: (i) Q contains a corner of r, (ii) r contains a corner of Q, and (iii) an edge of r intersects an edge of Q. Based on the observation, rectangle-intersection-max can be reduced to a collection of window-max, stabbing-max, and segment-intersection-max problems as follows. From the original dataset S, we create a set S_1 of points, and a set S_2 (S_3) of horizontal (vertical) segments by adding, for each rectangle $r \in S$, its four corners to S_1 and horizontal (vertical) edges to S_2 (S_3). Given a rectangle-intersection-max query with rectangle Q, we execute:

- a window-max query on S_1 using Q itself as the search region;

- four stabbing-max queries on S using the corners of Q as the query points;

- two segment-intersection-max queries on S_2 (S_3), using the vertical (horizontal) edges of Q as the query segments.

The final answer is the maximum of all the weights retrieved.

Integer encoding. Our structures require an encoding scheme that compresses a positive integer x into $O(\log x)$ bits, and meanwhile, permits lossless decompression when given a bit-stream that encodes a list of integers. One such scheme, for instance, is the *gamma Elias code*, which converts x into a binary string of $\lfloor \log_2 x \rfloor$ zeros followed by the binary form of x (e.g., 7 is represented as 00111). In other words, the compressed form of x has no more than $1 + 2 \log_2 x$ bits. To decompress a bit string σ, we first count the number z of preceding zeros in σ, and then, take the next $z + 1$ bits as a decompressed value. If σ has not been exhausted, the process is repeated to decompress the next value. The above description does not capture $x = 0$, but this can be easily handled by adding another bit.

KL-divergence inequality. We need the following mathematical fact in our analysis:

LEMMA 2.1 (KL-DIVERGENCE INEQUALITY). *Let* $\{x_1, ..., x_b\}$ *and* $\{y_1, ..., y_b\}$ *be two sets of positive values, and* $X = \sum_i x_i$, $Y = \sum_i y_i$. *It holds that:*

$$\sum_i \left(x_i \log_2 \frac{y_i}{x_i} \right) \leq X \log_2 \frac{Y}{X}.$$

PROOF. For each $i \in [b]$, introduce $\alpha_i = x_i/X$ and $\beta_i = y_i/Y$. Then:

$$\begin{aligned}
\sum_i \left(x_i \log_2 \frac{y_i}{x_i} \right) &= X \sum_i \left(\alpha_i \log_2 \left(\frac{\beta_i}{\alpha_i} \frac{Y}{X} \right) \right) \\
&= X \sum_i \left(\alpha_i \log_2 \frac{\beta_i}{\alpha_i} \right) + \left(X \log_2 \frac{Y}{X} \right)
\end{aligned}$$

We will prove the lemma by showing that $\sum_i (\alpha_i \log_2 \frac{\beta_i}{\alpha_i})$ is always non-positive. Regard $(\alpha_1, ..., \alpha_b)$ as the pdf of a (discrete) random variable α, and $(\beta_1, ..., \beta_b)$ as the pdf of random variable β. Observe that:

$$\begin{aligned}
\sum_i \left(\alpha_i \log_2 \frac{\beta_i}{\alpha_i} \right) &= -\sum_i \left(\alpha_i \log_2 \frac{\alpha_i}{\beta_i} \right) \\
&= D_{KL}(\alpha \| \beta)
\end{aligned}$$

where $D_{KL}(\alpha \| \beta)$ is the KL-divergence from α to β, and (as a well-known fact) is always non-negative. This completes the proof. $\square$

COROLLARY 2.2. *Let* $x_1, ..., x_b$ *be* b *positive values, and* $X = \sum_i x_i$. *For any* $C > 0$, *it holds that:*

$$\sum_i \left(x_i \log_2 \frac{C}{x_i} \right) \leq X \log_2 \frac{Cb}{X}.$$

3. BUNDLED COMPRESSED B-TREE

This section discusses the following *bundled predecessor* problem. Let $P_1, ..., P_b$ be $b \leq B$ sets of integer *keys* in $[D]$ where $D = N^{O(1)}$. Each key $k \in P_i$ ($i \in [b]$) is associated with a *label* $\ell(k, i) \in [L]$, where $L = N^{O(1)}$. These labels have a *monotonicity property*: for any keys $k < k'$ in the same P_i, it always holds that $\ell(k, i) \leq \ell(k', i)$. Given a value $q \in [D]$, a bundled-predecessor query reports, for every $i \in [b]$, the label associated with the largest key in P_i that is no greater than q (if such a key exists). We refer to $\{P_1, ..., P_b\}$ as a *bundle*, each P_i as a *category*, and D as the *domain size* of the bundle.

Next we describe a structure named *bundled compressed B-tree* (BCB-tree) to solve the above problem. For each key $k \in P_i$ ($i \in [b]$), define $\delta(k, i) = \ell(k, i) - \ell(k', i)$, where k' is the integer in P_i preceding k. If k' does not exist, $\delta(k, i) = \ell(k, i)$. Set $K = \sum_i |P_i|$, and let P be the multiset that unions all of $P_1, ..., P_b$ (i.e., a key appears in P as many times as the number of categories containing it). Let $k_1, ..., k_K$ be the keys of P in non-descending order. Define $\hat{\delta}(1) = k_1$, and $\hat{\delta}(j) = k_j - k_{j-1}$ for $j > 1$. We create a list Δ of length K as follows. The j-th entry of Δ is a triple $(\hat{\delta}(j), i, \delta(k_j, i))$, where i is such that $k_j \in P_i$. Since there are totally b categories, i can be represented with $\lceil \log_2 b \rceil$ bits. We store $\hat{\delta}(j)$ and $\delta(k_j, i)$ using the gamma Elias code (see Section 2).

Δ precisely captures $P_1, ..., P_b$, but we must scan it from the beginning to restore any key/label of any P_i. To remedy the drawback, we materialize Δ in a blocked manner. Let us define a *fat block* to be 4 consecutive blocks (i.e., $4B$ words). Recall that each triple in Δ corresponds to a key in P, so the tuples can be grouped by their corresponding keys. We make sure that each group (which has at most b tuples) resides in a fat block as follows: adjacent groups are always placed in the same fat block, as long as it still has enough space; otherwise, we put the succeeding group in a new fat block. Since each group occupies at most $3b \leq 3B$ words, at least B words are used in every fat block, except possibly the last one. Denote by $\mathcal{I}(v)$ the minimal interval enclosing all the keys in a fat block v. Clearly all the $\mathcal{I}(v)$ are disjoint.

Each fat block v is associated with a *relay set*, denoted as $\texttt{relay}(v)$, which contains $b + 1$ values. To explain, assume $\mathcal{I}(v) = [\alpha, \beta]$. The i-th ($i \leq b$) value in $\texttt{relay}(v)$ equals $\ell(k, i)$, where k is the greatest integer in P_i smaller than α (if k does not exist, store 0 instead). Refer to $\ell(k, i)$ as the *relay-label* of P_i. The last value in $\texttt{relay}(v)$ is α. Note that the relay set allows us to convert each triple $(\hat{\delta}(j), i, \delta(k_j, i))$ in v to $(k_j, i, \ell(k_j, i))$ accurately. As $b \leq B$, $\texttt{relay}(v)$ can be stored in $O(1)$ blocks. The first address of these blocks is kept in v, so that we can load $\texttt{relay}(v)$ after having accessed v. Finally, we create a B-tree[2] on the $\mathcal{I}(v)$ of all fat blocks v. The B-tree, the fat blocks and their relay sets constitute the BCB-tree.

To answer a bundled-predecessor query q, first descend to the fat block v whose $\mathcal{I}(v) = [\alpha, \beta]$ covers q. Then, we load $\texttt{relay}(v)$, and set $l[i]$ to the relay-label of P_i ($i \in [b]$) in $\texttt{relay}(v)$. Next we scan all the triples in v that correspond to keys at most q. For each triple $(\hat{\delta}(j), i, \delta(k_j, i))$ scanned, increase $l[i]$ by $\delta(k_j, i)$. Finally, $l[1], ..., l[b]$ are returned as the answers.

LEMMA 3.1. *For $b \leq B$, the BCB-tree consumes*

$$O\left(\frac{K}{B \log N}\left(1 + \log \frac{\max\{L, D, K\}}{K} + \log b\right)\right)$$

space, and answers a bundled-predecessor query in $O(\log_B K)$ I/Os. If all the keys have been sorted, the tree can be built in $O(K/B)$ I/Os.

PROOF. It suffices to consider $L \geq K$ and $D \geq K$. Let us first bound the number of bits in Δ. Recall that each triple in Δ has the form $(\hat{\delta}(j), i, \delta(k_j, i))$. Apparently, $O(K \log_2 b)$ bits are required to encode the i-fields of all the triples. In the sequel, we focus on the other fields.

Consider any P_i for some $i \in [b]$; and set $n_i = |P_i|$. Let $k_1' < ... < k_{n_i}'$ be the keys in P_i. Hence, $\delta(k_1', i) = \ell(k_1', i)$, and $\delta(k_j', i) = \ell(k_j', i) - \ell(k_{j-1}', i)$ for $j > 1$. The number of bits required to store the $\delta(k_j', i)$ of all $j \in [n_i]$ equals $O(n_i + \sum_j \log_2 \delta(k_j', i))$. We have

$$\sum_j \log_2 \delta(k_j', i) = \log_2 \prod_j \delta(k_j', i)$$
$$\leq \log_2(L/n_i)^{n_i} = n_i \log_2(L/n_i)$$

where the inequality used the fact that $\sum_j \delta(k_j', i) = \ell(k_{n_i}', i) \leq L$.

Hence, the number of bits to encode the $\delta(k_j', i)$ of all j, i is bounded by $O(\sum_i(n_i + n_i \log_2(L/n_i)))$. As $\sum_i n_i = K$, a direct application of Corollary 2.2 gives:

$$\sum_i(n_i + n_i \log_2(L/n_i)) = O(K(1 + \log(Lb/K))).$$

An analogous argument shows that $O(K(1 + \log(D/K)))$ bits are sufficient to encode the $\hat{\delta}(j)$ of all j. As each fat block (except possibly the last one) packs at least $B \log N$ bits of Δ, the total number of blocks is

$$O\left(\frac{K}{B \log N}\left(1 + \log \frac{\max\{L, D\}}{K} + \log b\right)\right).$$

The relay sets, as well as the B-tree, increase the space by only a constant factor.

As both L and D are $N^{O(1)}$, the height of the BCB-tree is bounded by

$$O\left(\log_B\left(\frac{K}{B \log N}\log(LDb/K)\right)\right) = O(\log_B K).$$

This is also the query cost. Finally, it is straightforward to build the structure bottom-up in $O(K/B)$ I/Os. $\square$

Remark 1. When $L = B^{O(1)}K$ and $D = B^{O(1)}K$, the space complexity is bounded by $O(\frac{K}{B \log_B N})$.

Remark 2. In the above discussion, we assumed that each key of a category is associated with a single label. Sometimes, it may be useful to associate $k \in P_i$ with a constant number c of labels $\ell_1(k, i), ..., \ell_c(k, i)$, where $\ell_j(k, i) \in [L_j]$ for each $j \in [c]$, and $L_j = N^{O(1)}$. In this case, given an integer $q \in [D]$, a bundled-predecessor query reports, for each $i \in [b]$, all the c labels associated with the largest integer in each P_i that is no greater than q. The BCB-tree can be easily extended to support such queries. Lemma 3.1 still holds, except that L should be set to $\max_{i=1}^c L_i$.

4. THREE-SIDED WINDOW-MAX

This section tackles the 3-sided window-max problem. Let S be a set of N points in $\mathbb{R}^2$. Each point $p \in S$ is associated with a weight $w(p) \in \mathbb{N}$. Given a 3-sided rectangle Q : $[x_1, x_2] \times (-\infty, y]$, the goal is to report the maximum $w(p)$ of all points $p \in S \cap Q$.

4.1 The first structure

This subsection describes a structure with query overhead $O(\log_B^2 N)$, which will be improved in Section 4.2.

Structure. The base tree is a B-tree $\mathcal{T}$ on the x-coordinates of the points in S. Let $root(\mathcal{T})$ be the root of $\mathcal{T}$. Given a node u of $\mathcal{T}$, denote by $\rho(u)$ the parent node of u (if

---

[2] All B-trees in this paper have a leaf capacity of B. Unless otherwise stated, the internal fanout is also B.

$u = root(\mathcal{T})$, $\rho(u) = \emptyset$). Let S_u be the set of data points in the subtree of u. Set $K_u = |S_u|$.

Given the weight w of a point in S_u, we define the *u-rank* of w as λ, if w is the λ-th smallest (among the weights of the points) in S_u. For a point set X and a point p, let $Y(X, p)$ be the set of points in X whose y-coordinates are at most that of p. Also, we may refer to the largest weight of all the points in X simply as *the maximum weight in X*.

Each internal node u is associated with two BCB-trees Γ_u and Λ_u, except for $root(\mathcal{T})$, where only $\Gamma_{root(\mathcal{T})}$ is needed. Γ_u is employed to find the maximum weight, say w, of the points in $S_u \cap Q$. The retrieved value of w, however, is its u-rank. The usage of Λ_u is to convert the u-rank of w to its $\rho(u)$-rank.

Let $u_1, ..., u_B$ be the child nodes of u. Γ_u is built on a bundle $\{P_1(u), ..., P_B(u)\}$ that has domain size K_u. Consider any value $k \in [K_u]$. Let p be the point in S_u satisfying $|Y(S_u, p)| = k$, i.e., p has the k-th smallest y-coordinate in S_u. Assume that p is in the subtree of u_i for some $i \in [B]$. We assign k to category $P_i(u)$. Meanwhile, k is associated with two labels $\ell_{\text{rank}}(k, i)$ and $\ell_y(k, i)$. Specifically, $\ell_{\text{rank}}(k, i)$ is the u-rank of the maximum weight in $Y(S_{u_i}, p)$, while $\ell_y(k, i)$ is set to $|Y(S_{u_i}, p)|$. In the sequel, when referring to a label, we will omit the category if it can be inferred from the context. For example, $\ell_{\text{rank}}(k, i)$ and $\ell_y(k, i)$ will be abbreviated as $\ell_{\text{rank}}(k)$ and $\ell_y(k)$, respectively.

Λ_u is created on a special bundle that has only a single category with domain size K_u. Each $k \in [K_u]$ has a label $\ell_{\text{p-rank}}(k)$ that equals the $\rho(u)$-rank of w, where w is the k-th smallest weight in S_u. Finally, for each point $p \in S$ in a leaf node z of $\mathcal{T}$, we store the $\rho(z)$-rank of $w(p)$ along with p.

Query. To answer a query $Q : [x_1, x_2] \times (-\infty, y]$, our algorithm first executes a *downward* step, followed by an *upward* step. In the downward step, we traverse (at most) two root-to-leaf paths, and compute a candidate weight at each node accessed. The upward step then ascends the same paths to merge those candidate weights into the final result.

The downward phase maintains an invariant:

> Prior to accessing a node u, we should have obtained the number $C(u)$ of points in S_u whose y-coordinates are no greater than y.

At the beginning, $C(root(\mathcal{T}))$ is the total number of points in S with y-coordinates at most y, and can be determined in $O(\log_B N)$ I/Os using a B-tree. In general, let u be an internal node being accessed. Naturally, u corresponds to an interval $\mathcal{I}(u) \subseteq \mathbb{R}$, which encloses all the real values that may reside in the subtree of u. Let $u_1, ..., u_B$ be the child nodes of u. Assume that x_1 and x_2 are covered by $\mathcal{I}(u_\alpha)$ and $\mathcal{I}(u_\beta)$, respectively (we assume that both α and β exist; otherwise, the algorithm can be modified in a straightforward manner). Perform a bundled-predecessor query with search key $C(u)$ on Γ_u, which returns a pair of labels $(l_{\text{rank}}[i], l_y[i])$ for each category $P_i(u)$ ($i \in [B]$). Set $\gamma(u) = \max_{\alpha < i < \beta} l_{\text{rank}}[i]$. In case $\beta <= \alpha + 1$, $\gamma(u) = 0$. Note that $\gamma(u)$ is the u-rank of the maximum weight of the points in $(S_{u_{\alpha+1}} \cup ... \cup S_{u_{\beta-1}}) \cap Q$. Setting $C(u_\alpha) = l_y[\alpha]$ and $C(u_\beta) = l_y[\beta]$, we descend to u_α

and u_β, respectively. The downward step terminates when the leaf level is reached.

The upward step also keeps an invariant:

> Prior to backtracking from u to $\rho(u)$, $\gamma(u)$ must be equal to the $\rho(u)$-rank of the maximum weight in $S_u \cap Q$.

This step starts from the (at most) two leaf nodes where the downward phase ended. For each such leaf node z, simply check all the points in $S_z \cap Q$, and set $\gamma(z)$ to the $\rho(z)$-rank of the maximum weight of those points (recall that the $\rho(z)$-rank is explicitly stored in z). In general, consider that the upward step has backtracked to an internal node u from two child nodes u_α and u_β. We update $\gamma(u) = \max\{\gamma(u), \gamma(u_\alpha), \gamma(u_\beta)\}$. Note that $\gamma(u)$ now equals the u-rank of the maximum weight w in $S_u \cap Q$. So if $u = root(\mathcal{T})$, $\gamma(u)$ can be used to restore w in $O(\log_B N)$ I/Os with a B-tree. Otherwise, $\gamma(u)$ needs to be converted to the $\rho(u)$-rank of w. For this purpose, we query Λ_u using $\gamma(u)$ as the search key, and set $\gamma(u)$ to the label retrieved from Λ_u. The algorithm then backtracks to $\rho(u)$.

As $O(\log_B N)$ I/Os are performed to search the BCB-trees at each level of $\mathcal{T}$, the query complexity is $O(\log_B^2 N)$.

4.2 The improved structure

To obtain logarithmic query cost, we aim at spending only constant I/Os at each level of $\mathcal{T}$. Naturally, we resort to fractional cascading, whose application, however, results in super-linear space. To keep the space linear, we must squeeze $\omega(B)$ pointers in a block. Fortunately, this can be achieved this by utilizing BCB-trees for pointer compression.

Structure. We now clarify the necessary modification on the structure of the previous subsection. Let u be an internal node $\mathcal{T}$ with child nodes $u_1, ..., u_B$. Recall that, in the BCB-tree Γ_u, each $k \in [K_u]$ has been associated with labels $\ell_{\text{rank}}(k)$ and $\ell_y(k)$. We give it two more labels $\ell_{\text{c-addr}}(k)$ and $\ell_{\text{addr}}(k)$ defined as below. Assume that the point $p \in S_u$ with $|Y(S_u, p)| = k$ is in the subtree of u_i for some $i \in [B]$. If u_i is a leaf node, $\ell_{\text{c-addr}}(k)$ equals the address of u_i. Otherwise, $\ell_{\text{c-addr}}(k)$ is the address of the (unique) fat block v in Γ_{u_i} such that $\mathcal{I}(v)$ covers $\ell_y(k)$ (recall that $\mathcal{I}(v)$ is the minimal interval enclosing all the keys in v). As for $\ell_{\text{addr}}(k)$, it is the address of the fat block v in Λ_u whose $\mathcal{I}(v)$ covers $\ell_{\text{rank}}(k)$. Specially, if $u = root(\mathcal{T})$, label $\ell_{\text{addr}}(k)$ is unnecessary.

We also need to slightly augment Λ_u if $\rho(u) \neq root(\mathcal{T})$. In Λ_u, each $k \in [K_u]$ currently has only a label $\ell_{\text{p-rank}}(k)$. We associate it with another label $\ell_{\text{p-addr}}(k)$, which equals the address of the fat block v in $\Lambda_{\rho(u)}$ whose $\mathcal{I}(v)$ covers $\ell_{\text{p-rank}}(k)$.

Finally, for each leaf node z of $\mathcal{T}$, we augment each point p in z with the address of the fat block v in $\Lambda_{\rho(z)}$ whose $\mathcal{I}(v)$ covers the $\rho(z)$-rank of $w(p)$.

Query. We continue to elaborate the changes to the query algorithm. The downward step now maintains an extra invariant:

Prior to accessing an internal node u, we should know the address of the fat block v in Γ_u whose $\mathcal{I}(v)$ covers $C(u)$. Denote that address as $A_\Gamma(u)$.

At $root(\mathcal{T})$, we find $A_\Gamma(root(\mathcal{T}))$ by simply searching Γ_u with $C(root(\mathcal{T}))$ in $O(\log_B N)$ I/Os. In general, given $A_\Gamma(u)$, we proceed as follows at an internal node u with child nodes $u_1, ..., u_B$. First, we retrieve, in $O(1)$ I/Os (by accessing the fat block of Γ_u at address $A_\Gamma(u)$ and its relay set), directly the result of the bundled-predecessor query on Γ_u with search key $C(u)$. The result contains four labels $l_{\mathrm{rank}}[i], l_y[i], l_{\text{c-addr}}[i], l_{\mathrm{addr}}[i]$ for each $P_i(u)$ ($i \in [B]$). As before, set $\gamma(u) = \max_{\alpha < i < \beta} l_{\mathrm{rank}}[i]$ (see Section 4.1 for the meanings of α and β). We also need to remember an address $A_\Lambda(u) = l_{\mathrm{addr}}[i^*]$, where $i^* = \arg\max_{\alpha < i < \beta} l_{\mathrm{rank}}[i]$ (in case $\beta \le \alpha + 1$, $A_\Lambda(u) = \emptyset$). Note that $A_\Lambda(u)$ references the fat block v in Λ_u whose $\mathcal{I}(v)$ covers $\gamma(u)$. At this moment, we are ready to descend to u_α and u_β, setting $A_\Gamma(u_\alpha) = l_{\text{c-addr}}[\alpha]$ and $A_\Gamma(u_\beta) = l_{\text{c-addr}}[\beta]$, respectively.

The upward step also keeps one more invariant:

Prior to backtracking from u to $\rho(u) \ne root(\mathcal{T})$, $A_\Lambda(u)$ must have been set to the address of the fat block v in $\Lambda_{\rho(u)}$ whose $\mathcal{I}(v)$ covers $\gamma(u)$ (review Section 4.1 for the meaning of $\gamma(u)$ at this stage).

This can be trivially done if z is a leaf node, where the required address is explicitly stored. In general, suppose we have backtracked to u from child nodes u_α and u_β. If u is the root of $\mathcal{T}$, the algorithm continues in the way as described in Section 4.1. Otherwise, as before, set $\gamma(u) = \max\{\gamma(u), \gamma(u_\alpha), \gamma(u_\beta)\}$; in case now $\gamma(u)$ equals $\gamma(u_\alpha)$ (or $\gamma(u_\beta)$), we reset $A_\Lambda(u)$ to $A_\Lambda(u_\alpha)$ (or $A_\Lambda(u_\beta)$). Then, we retrieve, using $O(1)$ I/Os directly the result of the bundled-predecessor query on Λ_u with search key $\gamma(u)$, i.e., a pair of labels $(l_{\text{p-rank}}, l_{\text{p-addr}})$. After setting $\gamma(u) = l_{\text{p-rank}}$ and $A_\Lambda(u) = l_{\text{p-addr}}$, we backtrack to $\rho(u)$.

Analysis. The query cost is $O(\log_B N)$ because $O(1)$ I/Os are spent at each level, except for $root(\mathcal{T})$ where $O(\log_B N)$ I/Os are performed. As for the space, $\mathcal{T}$ itself obviously has linear size. The subsequent discussion will show that the BCB-trees of all nodes at the same level of $\mathcal{T}$ occupy $O(\frac{N}{B \log_B N})$ space in total, which implies that all the secondary structures require only linear space.

Consider an internal node u with child nodes $u_1, ..., u_B$. It suffices to prove that (i) Γ_u, and (ii) $\Lambda_{u_1}, ..., \Lambda_{u_B}$ together consume $O(\frac{K_u}{B \log_B N})$ space. Let us first observe a trivial space bound of $O(K_u/B)$ for both (i) and (ii).

In Γ_u, each $k \in [K_u]$ is associated with labels: $\ell_{\mathrm{rank}}(k)$, $\ell_y(k), \ell_{\text{c-addr}}(k)$, and $\ell_{\mathrm{addr}}(k)$. It is easy to see that $\ell_{\mathrm{rank}}(k) \in [K_u]$, and $\ell_{\mathrm{addr}}(k)$ belongs to a domain of size $O(K_u/B)$. As the space of $\Gamma_{u_1}, ..., \Gamma_{u_B}$ is bounded by $O(K_{u_1}/B), ..., O(K_{u_B}/B)$ respectively, $\ell_{\text{c-addr}}(k)$ falls in a domain of size $\sum_i O(K_{u_i}/B) = O(K_u/B)$. Similarly, $\ell_y(k)$ is in a domain of size $\max_i O(K_{u_i}) = O(K_u)$. Therefore, by Lemma 3.1, the space of Γ_u is bounded by $O(\frac{K_u}{B \log_B N})$.

In Λ_{u_i} ($i \in [B]$), each $k \in [K_{u_i}]$ is associated with two labels: $\ell_{\text{p-rank}}(k)$ and $\ell_{\text{p-addr}}(k)$. Clearly, $\ell_{\text{p-rank}}(k) \in [K_u]$

and $\ell_{\text{p-addr}}(k)$ belongs to a domain of size $O(K_u/B)$. Hence, by Lemma 3.1, the space of all $\Lambda_{u_1}, ..., \Lambda_{u_B}$ is at most

$$O\left(\sum_i \frac{K_{u_i}}{B \log N} \left(\log \frac{K_u}{K_{u_i}}\right)\right)$$

which, by Corollary 2.2, is bounded by $O(\frac{K_u}{B \log_B N})$.

Construction. We will complete the proof of Theorem 1.1 by explaining how to build our structure in $O(\frac{N}{B} \log_B N)$ I/Os, using B blocks of memory. The construction of $\mathcal{T}$ is straightforward. Hence, we focus on the BCB-trees Γ_u and Λ_u of the internal nodes u of $\mathcal{T}$. Let $u_1, ..., u_B$ be the child nodes of u.

To create Λ_u, we arrange S_u into a list J_u such that (i) the points in J_u are sorted in ascending order of their weights, and (ii) if $u \ne root(\mathcal{T})$, each point $p \in J_u$ has a label equal to the $\rho(u)$-rank of $w(p)$. At $root(\mathcal{T})$, $J_{root(\mathcal{T})}$ is obtained by sorting in $O(\frac{N}{B} \log_B N)$ I/Os. In general, after J_u is ready, we can produce $J_{u_1}, ..., J_{u_B}$ by partitioning J_u in $O(K_u/B)$ I/Os. $\Lambda_{u_1}, ..., \Lambda_{u_B}$ can then be built in $O(K_u/B)$ I/Os by a synchronous scan of $J_{u_1}, ..., J_{u_B}$ and, if $u \ne root(\mathcal{T})$, also Λ_u. Totally, $O(N/B)$ I/Os are performed at each non-root level of $\mathcal{T}$.

Γ_u is constructed in two phases. The first one arranges S_u into a list J'_u where points are sorted in ascending order of their y-coordinates. Each $p \in J'_u$ is associated with:

- a label $\sigma_u(p)$ that equals the u-rank of the maximum weight in $Y(J'_u, p)$;

- if $u \ne root(\mathcal{T})$, another label $\hat{\sigma}_u(p)$ that equals the $\rho(u)$-rank of the maximum weight in $Y(J'_u, p)$.

$J'_{root(\mathcal{T})}$ can be computed in $O(\frac{N}{B} \log_B N)$ I/Os. First, sort the points of S_u by their weights, to obtain the u-rank of $w(p)$ for every $p \in S_u$. Then, sort S_u another time but in ascending order of y-coordinates. Finally, scan S_u in the new sorted order. As we go, monitor the greatest u-rank λ of all the points already seen, and assign λ to the $\sigma_u(p)$ of the last point p scanned.

In general, after J'_u is available, $J'_{u_1}, ..., J'_{u_B}$ can be generated in $O(K_u/B)$ I/Os as follows:

1. Create an array MAP_u of size K_u. For each $j \in [K_u]$, $MAP_u[j]$ equals the u_i-rank of $w(p)$, where p is the point having the j-th smallest weight in S_u, and u_i is the child node that contains p in its subtree. This array can be obtained in $O(K_u/B)$ I/Os by a scan of J_u (which was produced in building Λ_u).

2. Divide J'_u into $J'_{u_1}, ..., J'_{u_B}$ with $O(K_u/B)$ I/Os. Points of each J'_{u_i} are now in ascending order of y-coordinates, but their σ_u and $\hat{\sigma}_u$ labels are not ready yet.

3. Scan each J'_{u_i} (in its order) separately to decide the $\hat{\sigma}_{u_i}(p)$ of each $p \in J'_{u_i}$. Specifically, during the scan, we monitor the largest u-rank of the points already encountered (the u-ranks were inherited from J'_u), and assign it to the $\hat{\sigma}_{u_i}(p)$ of the last point p seen.

135

4. Go through $J'_{u_1}, ..., J'_{u_B}$ and MAP_u once to determine all $\sigma_{u_i}(p)$, where $p \in J'_{u_i}$ and $i \in [B]$. For each J'_{u_j}, monitor the maximum $\hat{\sigma}_{u_i}(p')$ of all the points $p' \in J'_{u_i}$ already seen. Use λ_i to represent that maximum. For the last point $p \in J'_{u_i}$ scanned, set $\sigma_{u_i}(p) = MAP_u[\lambda_i]$. Synchronize the accesses to $J'_{u_1}, ..., J'_{u_B}$ and MAP_u appropriately so that the entire process finishes in $O(K_u/B)$ I/Os.

Thus, the first phase performs $O(N/B)$ I/Os for each level of $\mathcal{T}$, entailing $O(\frac{N}{B} \log_B N)$ I/Os overall.

The second phase constructs Γ_u bottom-up. If $u_1, ..., u_B$ are leaf nodes, Γ_u can be built by one scan of the leaf level of Λ_u, while keeping $u_1, ..., u_B$ in memory. Otherwise, we create Γ_u in $O(K_u/B)$ I/O by synchronously scanning $\Gamma_{u_1}, ..., \Gamma_{u_B}, J'_{u_1}, ..., J'_{u_B}$, and Λ_u (ignore Λ_u if $u = root(\mathcal{T})$). The cost in either case is $O(K_u/B)$ I/Os. Therefore, the second step performs $O(N/B)$ I/Os at each level of $\mathcal{T}$, and thus, $O(\frac{N}{B} \log_B N)$ I/Os in total.

5. SEGMENT-INTERSECTION-MAX

Let S be a set of N horizontal segments in $\mathbb{R}^2$. Each segment $s \in S$ carries a weight $w(s) \in \mathbb{N}$. Given a vertical segment $Q : x \times [y_1, y_2]$, the goal is to report the maximum weight of the segments in S intersecting Q.

Bundled 1-d window-max. Let $V_1, ..., V_b$ be b sets of 1-d points in $\mathbb{R}$. Set $K = \sum_i |V_i|$. Each point $p \in V_i$ is associated with an integer weight $w(p)$. Given an interval $[x_1, x_2] \subseteq \mathbb{R}$, a *bundled window-max* query reports, for each $i \in [b]$, the maximum weight of the points of $V_i \cap [x_1, x_2]$.

LEMMA 5.1. *For $b = B^{1-\epsilon}$ (where ϵ is a constant satisfying $0 < \epsilon < 1$), there is a linear-space structure that answers a bundled 1-d window-max query in $O(\log_B K)$ I/Os. The structure can be constructed in $O(K/B)$ I/Os if all the points in $V_1 \cup ... \cup V_b$ have been sorted.*

PROOF. Let $V = V_1 \cup ... \cup V_b$. Build a B-tree $\mathcal{T}$ with fanout $f = B^{\epsilon/2}$ on V. Each node u of $\mathcal{T}$ naturally corresponds to an interval $\mathcal{I}(u) \subseteq \mathbb{R}$ (defined in the same way as in Section 4.1). At the leaf level, keep with each point p the i such that $p \in V_i$. Consider u as an internal node of $\mathcal{T}$ with child nodes $u_1, ..., u_f$. Let set S_u include the points of V in the subtree of u, and $S_u(i,j) = S_{u_i} \cup ... \cup S_{u_j}$ where $1 \leq i \leq j \leq f$. For each such i, j, store an array $A[i,j]$ of size b, where the k-th ($k \in [b]$) entry $A[i,j,k]$ equals the maximum weight of the points in $S_u(i,j) \cap V_k$. These arrays have no more than $f^2 b = B$ values in total and hence can be stored in 1 block.

Given a query interval $[x_1, x_2]$, first initiate in memory a size-b array γ with $\gamma[k] = -\infty$ for all $k \in [b]$. Then, visit two root-to-leaf paths of $\mathcal{T}$ to reach the leaf nodes z_1, z_2 such that $x_1 \in \mathcal{I}(z_1)$ and $x_2 \in \mathcal{I}(z_2)$. Let u be an internal node accessed. Assume $x_1 \in \mathcal{I}(u_\alpha)$ and $x_2 \in \mathcal{I}(u_\beta)$ for some $\alpha, \beta \in [f]$. In case α (β) does not exist, set it to 0 ($f + 1$). If $\beta \geq \alpha + 2$, retrieve array $A[\alpha + 1, \beta - 1]$, and set $\gamma[k] = \max\{\gamma[k], A[\alpha + 1, \beta - 1, k]\}$ for each $k \in [b]$. At z_1 (the case of z_2 is similar), if a point $p \in V_k$ (for some $k \in [b]$) has weight greater than $\gamma[k]$, set $\gamma[k] = w(p)$. The final $\gamma[1], ..., \gamma[b]$ are returned.

The total space is linear because each internal node of $\mathcal{T}$ is associated with only one extra block. The height of $\mathcal{T}$ is $O(\log_B K)$. A query performs $O(1)$ I/Os at each level, resulting in $O(\log_B K)$ I/Os overall. If V has been sorted, $\mathcal{T}$ (as well as the arrays of the internal nodes) can be constructed bottom-up in $O(K/B)$ I/Os. $\square$

Segment-intersection-max. Our structure is similar to the *external interval tree* of [9], but with two main differences. First, the base structure $\mathcal{T}$ has an (internal) fanout $f = B^{1/4}$. Second, the secondary structures of the nodes in $\mathcal{T}$ are the indexes developed earlier in this paper.

Specifically, $\mathcal{T}$ is a B-tree on the x-coordinates of the endpoints of the segments in S. Associate each endpoint with the segment it belongs to. As before, each node u of $\mathcal{T}$ naturally corresponds to an interval $\mathcal{I}(u)$, which in the context here represents a vertical *slab* $\mathcal{I}(u)$ in $\mathbb{R}^2$. Assign each segment $s \in S$ to the lowest node u whose $\mathcal{I}(u)$ covers s. Denote by G_u the set of segments assigned to u.

Let $u_1, ..., u_f$ be the child nodes of u. Define a *multi-slab* $\mathcal{I}(u[i,j]) = \mathcal{I}(u_i) \cup ... \cup \mathcal{I}(u_j)$ for i, j satisfying $1 \leq i \leq j \leq f$. Process each segment $s \in G_u$ as follows. Let α, β be such that $\mathcal{I}(u_\alpha)$ and $\mathcal{I}(u_\beta)$ contain the left and right endpoints of s, respectively. Then:

- If $\beta \geq \alpha + 2$, add the y-coordinate of s to a set $G_u(\alpha + 1, \beta - 1)$, after associating the coordinate with $w(s)$.

- Insert the left and right endpoints of s to sets $G_u^{\sqsupset}(\alpha)$ and $G_u^{\sqsubset}(\beta)$ respectively, after associating both endpoints with $w(s)$.

There are less than $f^2 = \sqrt{B}$ sets $G_u(i,j)$ ($1 \leq i \leq j \leq f$), on which we create a structure $\mathcal{M}_u$ of Lemma 5.1. For each $i \in [f]$, build a structure $\mathcal{L}_u(i)$ of Theorem 1.1 on $G_u^{\sqsupset}(i)$ to support 3-sided window-max queries whose search regions have the form $(-\infty, x] \times [y_1, y_2]$. Symmetrically, construct another structure $\mathcal{R}_u(i)$ on $G_u^{\sqsubset}(i)$ to support queries of the form $[x, \infty) \times [y_1, y_2]$.

Each segment $s \in S$ generates $O(1)$ information in at most 3 secondary structures. Since each secondary structure has linear size, the overall space is linear. To construct the structure, we first build $\mathcal{T}$, and then create the G_u of each node u top-down in $O(\frac{N}{B} \log_B N)$ I/Os. After this, the secondary structures are constructed in $O(\frac{N}{B} \log_B N)$ I/Os (see Theorem 1.1 and Lemma 5.1).

To answer a query $Q : x \times [y_1, y_2]$, our algorithm initiates a value $\gamma = -\infty$, and then follows a root-to-leaf path of $\mathcal{T}$ to the leaf node z whose $\mathcal{I}(z)$ covers x. Let u be an internal node on the path. Let $\alpha \in [f]$ be such that $\mathcal{I}(u_\alpha)$ covers x. Perform a bundled window-max query $[y_1, y_2]$ on $\mathcal{M}_u$, which reports a weight from each $G_u(i,j)$ of all $1 \leq i \leq j \leq f$. Let w_1 be the maximum of the weights from the $G_u(i,j)$ satisfying $i \leq \alpha \leq j$. Next, perform a 3-sided window-max query $(-\infty, x] \times [y_1, y_2]$ on $\mathcal{L}_u(\alpha)$, and a query $[x, \infty) \times [y_1, y_2]$ on $\mathcal{R}_u(\alpha)$. Let w_2 and w_3 be their results, respectively. Set $\gamma = \max\{\gamma, w_1, w_2, w_3\}$. Finally, at z, simply check all the segments in z, and identify the maximum weight w of those segments intersecting Q. Return $\max\{w, \gamma\}$ as the final result. By Theorem 1.1 and Lemma 5.1, $O(\log_B N)$ I/Os are performed at each level of $\mathcal{T}$, resulting in $O(\log_B^2 N)$ I/Os overall.

LEMMA 5.2. *There is a linear-space structure that answers a segment-intersection-max query in $O(\log_B^2 N)$ I/Os. The structure can be constructed in $O(\frac{N}{B} \log_B N)$ I/Os.*

6. STABBING-MAX

Let S be a set of N rectangles in $\mathbb{R}^2$. Each rectangle $r \in S$ is associated with a weight $w(r) \in \mathbb{N}$. Given a query point $Q : (x, y)$, the goal is to report the maximum $w(r)$ of the rectangles $r \in S$ that cover Q.

6.1 Ray-segment-max

We first tackle the following *ray-segment-max* problem that is a special instance of segment-intersection-max, and lies at the heart of stabbing-max. Let H be a set of horizontal segments in $\mathbb{R}^2$. Each segment $s \in H$ is associated with a weight $w(s) \in \mathbb{R}$. Given a vertical ray $Q : x \times (-\infty, y]$, a query reports the maximum $w(s)$ of the segments $s \in H$ intersecting Q. We will solve the problem with a linear-space structure that guarantees logarithmic query cost.

Structure. Our index combines the external segment tree [7] with techniques developed in Sections 3 and 4. The base tree $\mathcal{T}$ is a B-tree with fanout $f = \sqrt{B}$ on the x-coordinates of the endpoints of the segments in H. Each node u of $\mathcal{T}$ corresponds to a vertical slab $\mathcal{I}(u)$ in $\mathbb{R}^2$. We associate u with a set H_u of segments s such that s has at least an endpoint in $\mathcal{I}(u)$. Observe that s appears in the H_u of at most two u at each level of $\mathcal{T}$. If w is the λ-th smallest weight (of the segments) in H_u, we say that the u-*rank* of w is λ. At a leaf node z of $\mathcal{T}$, associate each endpoint in z with the segment s the endpoint belongs to, as well as the $\rho(z)$-rank of $w(s)$, where $\rho(z)$ is the parent of z.

Given a segment-set X and a segment s (all horizontal), let $Y(X, s)$ be the set of segments in X whose y-coordinates are at most that of s. Now consider u as an internal node with $u_1, ..., u_f$ as its child nodes. Define a multi-slab $\mathcal{I}(u[i, j]) = \mathcal{I}(u_i) \cup ... \cup \mathcal{I}(u_j)$ for i, j satisfying $1 \le i \le j \le f$. Let $H_u(i, j)$ be the set of segments s in H_u such that $\mathcal{I}(u[i, j])$ is the maximal multi-slab spanned by s.

We build two BCB-trees Γ_u and Λ_u (only Γ_u if u is the root of $\mathcal{T}$). Γ_u indexes a bundle of domain size $K_u = |H_u|$ with $f(f+1)/2 + f \le B$ categories (recall $B \ge 9$). Precisely, there is a category $P_u^{\mathtt{multi}}(i, j)$ for each multi-slab $\mathcal{I}(u[i, j])$, and a category $P_u^{\mathtt{slab}}(i)$ for each slab $\mathcal{I}(u_i)$. Λ_u indexes a bundle of domain size K_u with a single category.

Next, we clarify the labels in the BCB-trees, starting with Γ_u. Consider a key $k \in [K_u]$, and the segment s having the k-th smallest y-coordinate in H_u. We decide the categories and labels of k as follows:

- If the left endpoint of s falls in the $\mathcal{I}(u_\alpha)$ of some α, assign k to $P_u^{\mathtt{slab}}(\alpha)$ with two labels. The first one $\ell_{\mathtt{y}}(k)$ equals $|Y(H_{u_\alpha}, s)|$. The second $\ell_{\mathtt{c-addr}}(k)$ references the fat block v in Γ_{u_i} whose $\mathcal{I}(v)$ covers $\ell_{\mathtt{y}}(k)$. Repeat the same with respect to the right endpoint of s.

- If $s \in H_u(\alpha, \beta)$ for some α and β, assign k to $P_u^{\mathtt{multi}}(\alpha, \beta)$ also with two labels. The first one $\ell_{\mathtt{rank}}(k)$

equals the u-rank of the maximum weight of the points in $Y(H_u(\alpha, \beta), s)$. The second $\ell_{\mathtt{addr}}(k)$ references the fat block v in Λ_u whose $\mathcal{I}(v)$ encloses $\ell_{\mathtt{rank}}(k)$.

Finally, in Λ_u, every $k \in [K_u]$ has two labels:

- $\ell_{\mathtt{p-rank}}(k)$, which equals the $\rho(u)$-rank of the k-th smallest weight in H_u;

- $\ell_{\mathtt{p-addr}}(k)$, which references the fat block v in $\Lambda_{\rho(u)}$ whose $\mathcal{I}(v)$ contains $\ell_{\mathtt{p-rank}}(k)$. If $\rho(u)$ is the root, $\ell_{\mathtt{p-addr}}(k)$ is undefined.

Query. The query algorithm involves a downward step and an upward step. Given a ray $Q : x \times (-\infty, y]$, the downward step searches a root-to-leaf path Π to reach the leaf node z such that $x \in \mathcal{I}(z)$. Let u be an internal node on Π, u_α ($\alpha \in [f]$) the child node of u on Π, and $C(u)$ the number of segments in H_u whose y-coordinates are at most y. Perform a bundled-predecessor query on Γ_u with $C(u)$. Let $P_u^{\mathtt{multi}}(i^*, j^*)$ be the category whose $\ell_{\mathtt{rank}}$-label retrieved by the query is the largest among all categories $P_u^{\mathtt{multi}}(i, j)$ satisfying $i \le \alpha \le j$. Set $\gamma(u)$ to that label, and $A_\Lambda(u)$ to the retrieved $\ell_{\mathtt{addr}}$-label of $P_u^{\mathtt{multi}}(i^*, j^*)$. Before descending to u_α, set $C(u_\alpha)$ and $A_\Gamma(u_\alpha)$ to the $\ell_{\mathtt{y}}$- and $\ell_{\mathtt{c-addr}}$-labels fetched from category $P_u^{\mathtt{slab}}(\alpha)$, respectively. With $C(u_\alpha)$ and $A_\Gamma(u_\alpha)$, the bundled-predecessor query on Γ_{u_α} can be answered in $O(1)$ I/Os. In other words, only $\Gamma_{root(\mathcal{T})}$ is searched completely.

The upward step starts from z, and follows the same path back to the root. Along the way, we make use of the $\gamma(u)$, $A_\Lambda(u)$, and Λ_u of each internal node $u \in \Pi$ to determine the answer in the way explained in Section 4.2.

Analysis. The key to proving the linear size of our structure is to show that all the BCB-trees require linear space in total. We focus on Γ_u (where u is a node of $\mathcal{T}$) because the analysis of Λ_u is the same as in Theorem 1.1. It suffices to argue that Γ_u occupies $O(\frac{K_u}{B \log_B N})$ space. Let $u_1, ..., u_f$ ($f \le \sqrt{B}$) be the child nodes of u. Each key $k \in [K_u]$ indexed by Γ_u is assigned to constant categories. Hence, the total number of keys of all categories is $O(K_u)$. Γ_u has four types of labels: $\ell_{\mathtt{rank}}(k)$, $\ell_{\mathtt{y}}(k)$, $\ell_{\mathtt{c-addr}}(k)$, and $\ell_{\mathtt{addr}}(k)$. We know:

- $\ell_{\mathtt{rank}}(k) \in [K_u]$;

- the domain of $\ell_{\mathtt{y}}(k)$ has size $\sum_i K_{u_i} = O(K_u)$;

- the domain of $\ell_{\mathtt{c-addr}}(k)$ has size $\sum_i O(K_{u_i}/B) = O(K_u/B)$;

- the domain of $\ell_{\mathtt{addr}}(k)$ has size $O(K_u/B)$.

By Lemma 3.1, Γ_u occupies $O(\frac{K_u \log f}{B \log N}) = O(\frac{K_u}{B \log_B N})$ space.

A query performs $O(\log_B N)$ I/Os at the root of $\mathcal{T}$, and $O(1)$ I/Os at every other level. The construction algorithm in Theorem 1.1 can be adapted to build the structure in $O(\frac{N}{B} \log_B N)$ I/Os. Omitting the tedious details, we conclude:

LEMMA 6.1. *There is a linear-space structure that answers a ray-segment-max query in $O(\log_B N)$ I/Os. The structure can be built in $O(\frac{N}{B} \log_B N)$ I/Os.*

6.2 Stabbing-max

Assume that the ray-segment-max problem can be settled by a linear-space structure that has query cost $T_Q(N, B)$, and can be built in $T_{build}(N, B)$ I/Os. Agarwal et al. [3] showed how to obtain a linear-space structure that answers a stabbing-max query in $O(T_{query}(N, B) \log_B N + \log_B^2 N)$ I/Os, and takes $O(T_{build}(N, B) + \frac{N}{B} \log_B N)$ I/Os to construct. Combining their technique with Lemma 6.1 gives:

LEMMA 6.2. *There is a linear-space structure that answers a stabbing-max query in $O(\log_B^2 N)$ I/Os. The structure can be built in $O(\frac{N}{B} \log_B N)$ I/Os.*

Theorem 1.2 can now be established from the reduction in Section 2, the window-max result of [3], and Lemmas 5.2 and 6.2.

7. RECTANGLE-INTERSECTION-SUM

Let S be a set of N points in $\mathbb{R}^2$. Each point $p \in S$ is associated with a weight $w(p) \in \mathbb{N}$. Given a 2-sided rectangle $Q : (-\infty, x] \times (-\infty, y]$, the goal is to find the sum of the weights of all the points covered by Q. Once the above *2-sided window-sum* problem is settled, rectangle-intersection-sum can be solved with asymptotically the same space, query, and preprocessing cost (see [12]).

Structure. The base tree of our structure is still a B-tree $\mathcal{T}$ on the x-coordinates of the points in S. Define $root(\mathcal{T})$, $Y(X, p)$, K_u, S_u and $\mathcal{I}(u)$ (where u is a node in $\mathcal{T}$) as in Section 4. Consider an internal node u with child nodes $u_1, ..., u_B$. We associate u with a BCB-tree Γ_u indexing a bundle $\{P_1(u), ..., P_B(u)\}$ with domain size K_u. Key $k \in [K_u]$ is assigned to category $P_i(u)$ if the point p, which has the k-th smallest y-coordinate in S_u, is in the subtree of u_i for some $i \in [B]$. We assign to k three labels $\ell_{\text{sum}}(k)$, $\ell_{\text{y}}(k)$, and $\ell_{\text{c-addr}}(k)$, where $\ell_{\text{sum}}(k)$ is the sum of the weights in $Y(S_{u_i}, p)$, and both $\ell_{\text{y}}(k)$ and $\ell_{\text{c-addr}}(k)$ are as defined in Section 4.

Query. We answer a query with $Q : (-\infty, x] \times (-\infty, y]$ by accessing a root-to-leaf path of $\mathcal{T}$. The algorithm keeps an invariant that, prior to visiting a node u, we know (i) the number $C(u)$ of points in S_u whose y-coordinates are at most y, and (ii) the address $A(u)$ of the fat block v in Γ_u whose $\mathcal{I}(v)$ covers $C(u)$. $C(root(\mathcal{T}))$ and $A(root(\mathcal{T}))$ can be obtained in $O(\log_B N)$ I/Os as in Section 4.

The algorithm maintains at any moment the current result γ, which equals 0 at the beginning. Assume, in general, that we are visiting a node u. If u is a leaf node, simply add to γ the total weight of all the points in u that fall in Q. The final γ is then returned. For an internal u, let $u_1, ..., u_B$ be the child nodes of u, and α an integer such that $x \in \mathcal{I}(u_\alpha)$. In a constant number of I/Os, we (utilizing $A(u)$) answer the bundled-predecessor query on Γ_u with search key $C(u)$. The result contains a label-set $(l_{\text{sum}}[i], l_{\text{y}}[i], l_{\text{c-addr}}[i])$, retrieved from category $P_i(u)$, for each $i \in [B]$. We increase γ by $\sum_{i=1}^{\alpha-1} l_{\text{sum}}[i]$. After setting $C(u_\alpha)$ to $l_{\text{y}}[\alpha]$ and $A(u_\alpha)$ to $l_{\text{c-addr}}[\alpha]$, the algorithm descends to u_α.

Analysis. It is easy to see that the query cost is $O(\log_B N)$. As for space consumption, we focus on bounding the size of

BCB-trees. Our analysis below utilizes the fact that W, which is the total weight of all the objects in S, is $N^{O(1)}$, as each weight fits in a constant number of words.

Consider an internal node u with child nodes $u_1, ..., u_B$. Γ_u has three types of labels $\ell_{\text{sum}}(k)$, $\ell_{\text{y}}(k)$, and $\ell_{\text{c-addr}}(k)$. Let W_u be the sum of the weights of all the points in S_u. Each $\ell_{\text{sum}}(k)$ is in a domain with size $\sum_i W_{u_i} = W_u$. The sizes of the domains for $\ell_{\text{y}}(k)$ and $\ell_{\text{c-addr}}(k)$ are as explained in Section 4.2. By Lemma 3.1, Γ_u occupies $O(\frac{K_u}{B \log N}(\log \frac{W_u}{K_u} + \log B))$ space.

Consider any particular level of $\mathcal{T}$, and denote by X the set of all nodes at this level. The space of the BCB-trees associated with the nodes in X is

$$O\left(\sum_{u \in X} \frac{K_u}{B \log N}\left(\log \frac{W_u}{K_u} + \log B\right)\right)$$
$$= O\left(\frac{1}{B \log N}\left(\sum_{u \in X}\left(K_u \log \frac{W_u}{K_u}\right) + \log B \sum_{u \in X} K_u\right)\right).$$

As $\sum_{u \in X} K_u = N$ and $\sum_{u \in X} W_u = W$, Lemma 2.1 shows that the above equation is bounded by

$$O\left(\frac{1}{B \log N}\left(N \log \frac{W}{N} + N \log B\right)\right)$$
$$= O\left(\frac{N \max\{1, \log_B \frac{W}{N}\}}{B \log_B N}\right).$$

Hence, the BCB-trees at all $O(\log_B N)$ levels of $\mathcal{T}$ consume totally $O(\frac{N}{B} \max\{1, \log_B \frac{W}{N}\})$ space. Our structure can be easily constructed bottom-up in $O(\frac{N}{B} \log_B N)$ I/Os. This proves Theorem 1.3.

8. ACKNOWLEDGEMENTS

This work was supported by grants GRF 4173/08, GRF 4169/09, and GRF 4166/10 from HKRGC.

9. REFERENCES

[1] P. Afshani, L. Arge, and K. D. Larsen. Orthogonal range reporting in three and higher dimensions. In *Proceedings of Annual IEEE Symposium on Foundations of Computer Science (FOCS)*, pages 149–158, 2009.

[2] P. Afshani, L. Arge, and K. D. Larsen. Orthogonal range reporting: query lower bounds, optimal structures in 3-d, and higher-dimensional improvements. In *Symposium on Computational Geometry (SoCG)*, pages 240–246, 2010.

[3] P. K. Agarwal, L. Arge, J. Yang, and K. Yi. I/O-efficient structures for orthogonal range-max and stabbing-max queries. In *Proceedings of European Symposium on Algorithms (ESA)*, pages 7–18, 2003.

[4] P. K. Agarwal, L. Arge, and K. Yi. An optimal dynamic interval stabbing-max data structure? In

Proceedings of the Annual ACM-SIAM Symposium on Discrete Algorithms (SODA), pages 803–812, 2005.

[5] A. Aggarwal and J. S. Vitter. The input/output complexity of sorting and related problems. *Communications of the ACM (CACM)*, 31(9):1116–1127, 1988.

[6] S. Alstrup, G. S. Brodal, and T. Rauhe. New data structures for orthogonal range searching. In *Proceedings of Annual IEEE Symposium on Foundations of Computer Science (FOCS)*, pages 198–207, 2000.

[7] L. Arge. The buffer tree: A technique for designing batched external data structures. *Algorithmica*, 37(1):1–24, 2003.

[8] L. Arge and J. Vahrenhold. I/O-efficient dynamic planar point location. *Computational Geometry*, 29(2):147–162, 2004.

[9] L. Arge and J. S. Vitter. Optimal dynamic interval management in external memory. In *Proceedings of Annual IEEE Symposium on Foundations of Computer Science (FOCS)*, pages 560–569, 1996.

[10] B. Chazelle. An algorithm for segment-dragging and its implementation. *Algorithmica*, 3:205–221, 1988.

[11] B. Chazelle. A functional approach to data structures and its use in multidimensional searching. *SIAM Journal of Computing*, 17(3):427–462, 1988.

[12] H. Edelsbrunner and M. H. Overmars. On the equivalence of some rectangle problems. *Information Processing Letters (IPL)*, 14(3):124–127, 1982.

[13] S. Govindarajan, P. K. Agarwal, and L. Arge. CRB-tree: An efficient indexing scheme for range-aggregate queries. In *Proceedings of International Conference on Database Theory (ICDT)*, pages 143 157, 2003.

[14] H. Kaplan, E. Molad, and R. E. Tarjan. Dynamic rectangular intersection with priorities. In *Proceedings of ACM Symposium on Theory of Computing (STOC)*, pages 639–648, 2003.

[15] I. Lazaridis and S. Mehrotra. Progressive approximate aggregate queries with a multi-resolution tree structure. In *Proceedings of ACM Management of Data (SIGMOD)*, pages 401–412, 2001.

[16] D. Papadias, P. Kalnis, J. Zhang, and Y. Tao. Efficient OLAP operations in spatial data warehouses. In *Proceedings of Symposium on Advances in Spatial and Temporal Databases (SSTD)*, pages 443–459, 2001.

[17] B. Salzberg and V. J. Tsotras. Comparison of access methods for time-evolving data. *ACM Computing Surveys*, 31(2):158–221, 1999.

[18] Y. Tao and D. Papadias. Range aggregate processing in spatial databases. *IEEE Transactions on Knowledge and Data Engineering (TKDE)*, 16(12):1555–1570, 2004.

[19] J. S. Vitter. Algorithms and data structures for external memory. *Foundation and Trends in Theoretical Computer Science*, 2(4):305–474, 2006.

[20] D. Zhang, A. Markowetz, V. J. Tsotras, D. Gunopulos, and B. Seeger. On computing temporal aggregates with range predicates. *ACM Transactions on Database Systems (TODS)*, 33(2), 2008.

[21] D. Zhang and V. J. Tsotras. Optimizing spatial min/max aggregations. *The VLDB Journal*, 14(2):170–181, 2005.

On Provenance Minimization *

Yael Amsterdamer
Tel Aviv University
and University of Pennsylvania
yaelamst@post.tau.ac.il

Daniel Deutch
Ben Gurion University
and University of Pennsylvania
deutchd@cs.bgu.ac.il

Tova Milo
Tel Aviv University
milo@post.tau.ac.il

Val Tannen
University of Pennsylvania
val@cis.upenn.edu

ABSTRACT

Provenance information has been proved to be very effective in capturing the computational process performed by queries, and has been used extensively as the input to many advanced data management tools (e.g. view maintenance, trust assessment, or query answering in probabilistic databases). We study here the *core* of provenance information, namely the part of provenance that appears in the computation of every query equivalent to the given one. This provenance core is informative as it describes the part of the computational process that is inherent to the query. It is also useful as a compact input to the above mentioned data management tools. We study algorithms that, given a query, compute an equivalent query that realizes the core provenance for all tuples in its result. We study these algorithms for queries of varying expressive power. Finally, we observe that, in general, one would not want to require database systems to evaluate a specific query that realizes the core provenance, but instead to be able to find, possibly off-line, the core provenance of a given tuple in the output (computed by an arbitrary equivalent query), without rewriting the query. We provide algorithms for such direct computation of the core provenance.

Categories and Subject Descriptors

H.2.1 [**Database Management**]: [Data Models]

General Terms

Algorithms, Theory

---

*This work has been partially funded by the NSF grant IIS-0629846, the NSF grant IIS-0803524, by the Israel Science Foundation, by the US-Israel Binational Science Foundation, by the EU grant MANCOOSI and by the ERC grant Webdam under agreement 226513.

1. INTRODUCTION

Recording *provenance* information for query results, that explains the computational process leading to their generation, is now a common technique. In particular, the work of [19] suggested capturing provenance information via *polynomials*. The idea is to associate every tuple in the input database with an annotation, and to extend the operations of relational algebra so that they will work on these annotated tuples. The resulting annotation of every output tuple is a polynomial over the original annotations, that reflects the operations performed on the original tuples to obtain the output tuple. Provenance polynomials were shown to be very useful, serving as input to many advanced data management tools, such as view maintenance, trust assessment, or query answering in probabilistic databases (See e.g. [18, 25, 30]). We note that provenance polynomials give a *trace* of the computational process associated with every tuple in the query result. For example, if the provenance annotation p of an output tuple is $x \cdot y \cdot y + z + z$ $(= x \cdot y^2 + 2z)$ where x, y, z are annotations that uniquely identify three input tuples (e.g., tuple ids) then p indicates that there are three different ways (derivations) to compute the output tuple, one uses x once and y twice while the other two use only z, once.

Consequently, the evaluation of two equivalent queries (in the standard sense of [9]), on a given input database instance, may lead to different provenance polynomials for the same output tuples. While this is sometimes useful, there are many cases in which what is of interest is not the computational process induced by the query chosen among equivalent queries (which is affected by optimizers and may change over time), but rather the "core" computational process, whose use of input tuples must be "included" in the query evaluation *for every equivalent query*. We are therefore led to a notion of *core provenance* capturing the core computation. We will define this notion formally, for provenance that is defined in a very general way (namely, using the $N[X]$ semiring [19]) and then see that the core provenance is not only informative in exposing the core of the execution, but is also *compact*. We propose using this compact representation to alleviate practical challenges that arise in data management tools due to the size of provenance information [10, 27].

Following the above observations, the present paper addresses two main challenges: defining the core provenance, and then realizing it. Towards the definition, we introduce an *order relation* $p \le p'$ on provenance polynomials. Intuitively, this order relation captures the "terseness" in the use of tuples. For example, in this order using a tuple once is terser than using it twice, within the alternative ways of computing the same answer. In a more complex example, $x \cdot y^2 + 2z \le x \cdot y^2 + x \cdot z + y \cdot z$ but the opposite is not true. The ordering of polynomials lifts naturally to queries. Given two equivalent queries Q, Q' (denoted $Q \equiv Q'$), we say that Q is "terser" w.r.t. provenance than Q', and we write $Q \subseteq_P Q'$ if for any input database D and any tuple t in the output, where the annotation of t in $Q(D)$ is p and that of t in $Q'(D)$ is p', we have $p \le p'$. Now, given a class of queries $\mathcal{C}$, we can formally define core provenance for a query $Q \in \mathcal{C}$: it is the provenance yielded by a query $Q' \in \mathcal{C}$ such that $Q' \equiv Q$ and for any other $Q'' \in \mathcal{C}$ equivalent to Q, we have $Q' \subseteq_P Q''$. In that case, we say that Q' is a provenance-minimal (p-minimal) query in $\mathcal{C}$ equivalent to Q.

We then study the realization of this core provenance, first via queries and then by direct computation, as follows.

Realization via Queries. Given a query Q and a class of queries $\mathcal{C}$ we aim at finding a p-minimal query in $\mathcal{C}$ equivalent to Q. Since the identification of the p-minimal query (and thus the core provenance) depend on a "context" class of alternative query plans $\mathcal{C}$, the choices for this class become important. In this paper we study the p-minimization in query classes of increasing expressivity, for which there exist solid foundations of provenance management using polynomials: conjunctive queries (CQ), conjunctive queries with disequalities ($CQ^{\ne}$) and unions of conjunctive queries with disequalities ($UCQ^{\ne}$). When considering disequalities, we further distinguish the classes of *complete* queries, i.e. queries that disequate all of their distinct arguments. The classes of complete conjunctive queries and unions thereof are denoted $cCQ^{\ne}$ and $cUCQ^{\ne}$, respectively.

We note that query minimization in terms of the query length (or number of joins [9], referred to hereinafter as "standard minimization") has been extensively studied for these classes of queries. Interestingly, in general the queries that realize the core provenance may be very different than the minimal ones in the sense of [9]. In particular, there are conjunctive queries for which an equivalent query in $UCQ^{\ne}$ yields a "terser" provenance, as the latter query allows only a subset of the original derivations for each output tuple.

Table 1 summarizes the results on finding p-minimal queries, contrasted with results on standard minimization. Following the above discussion we distinguish between finding the p-minimal equivalent query among all queries in $UCQ^{\ne}$, or in a further restricted class $\mathcal{C}$. For instance, when given as input a query in $CQ^{\ne}$, there are cases where not only that terser provenance can be obtained by resorting to $UCQ^{\ne}$, but furthermore no equivalent query that realizes its core provenance in $CQ^{\ne}$ exists. I.e., for some sets of equivalent queries in $CQ^{\ne}$, each query leads to strictly more provenance than some other query in the set, for some output tuple. If the input query is in CQ, then we can use standard minimization to obtain an equivalent CQ query which is p-minimal among all those in CQ, but an equivalent query entailing terser provenance may be still found in $UCQ^{\ne}$.

The complexity of our p-minimization algorithms is in general exponential in the query size (with the exception of $cCQ^{\ne}$ for which we suggest a PTIME algorithm). This is unavoidable as the corresponding decision problem (described in the sequel) is DP-complete [16].

Query Class	"Standard" Minimal in Class/Overall	P-minimal in Class	P-minimal Overall
$CQ^{\ne}$	In $CQ^{\ne}$	No p-minimal query exists	In $UCQ^{\ne}$, EXPTIME
CQ	In CQ	same as "standard" minimization	In $UCQ^{\ne}$, EXPTIME
$cCQ^{\ne}$	In $cCQ^{\ne}$	same as "standard" minimization	In $cCQ^{\ne}$, PTIME
$UCQ^{\ne}$	In $UCQ^{\ne}$	different than "standard" minimization	In $UCQ^{\ne}$, EXPTIME

Table 1: Summary of Results

Realization by Direct Computation. Core provenance is also useful in improving the efficiency of provenance-based analysis tools, in the sense that they may be fed with smaller provenance polynomials. While so, we would not want database systems to be obligated to evaluate a specific query that realizes the core provenance, but would rather allow optimizers to evaluate the most efficient query. We would thus like to be able to evaluate any equivalent query, but then (possibly off-line) find the core provenance of given tuples in the result, *without re-evaluating the query.* We show that this is possible by manipulations on the provenance polynomials of the individual tuples in the query result. Moreover, we show that this can be done *even in absence of the original query* (e.g. if it is not available due to confidentiality or to its loss, etc.), assuming that we know the input database and the set of constants used in the query (if any are used).

Paper Organization. The rest of this paper is organized as follows. In Section 2 we provide the main definitions used throughout the paper. In Section 3 we study provenance-wise minimization of conjunctive queries, and in Section 4 we study it for union of conjunctive queries. In section 5 we study minimization applied directly on provenance polynomials. In Section 7 we provide an overview of related work, and we conclude in Section 8.

2. PRELIMINARIES

We provide in this section the formal definitions used throughout the paper. The definitions of these notions will be accompanied by simple examples, which nevertheless will be valuable in explaining the more complicated constructions in the sections that follow.

2.1 Classes of Queries

We start by briefly recalling the basic definitions for conjunctive queries and union thereof from [1]. We use the standard notions of relational databases and schema, without repeating their definitions in [1].

We assume in the sequel the existence of a domain $\mathcal{V}$ of variables and a domain $\mathcal{C}$ of constants. Conjunctive queries are then defined as follows:

DEFINITION 2.1. *A rule based conjunctive query Q with disequalities, over a database schema S, is an expression of the form:*

$$ans(u_0) := R_1(u_1), ..., R_n(u_n), E_1, ..., E_m \text{ where:}$$

- $R_1, ..., R_n$ *are relation names in S, ans is a relation name not in S.*

- Each u_i is a vector $(l_1, ..., l_k)$, where $\forall j \in \{1, .., k\}$ $l_j \in \mathcal{V} \cup \mathcal{C}$.

- Each E_i is an expression of the form $l_j \neq l_k$ where $l_j \in \mathcal{V}$ and $l_k \in \mathcal{V} \cup \mathcal{C}$.

$R_1(u_1), ..., R_n(u_n)$ are called the relational atoms of Q, and $E_1, ..., E_m$ are the disequality atoms. We require that every variable that appears in a disequality E_i appears also in a relational atom u_j of the query. $ans(u_0)$ is called the rule head, and is denoted $head(Q)$, while $R_1(u_1), ..., R_n(u_n)$, $E_1, ..., E_m$ is the rule body, denoted $body(Q)$. The variables and constants in the body of Q are called the arguments of Q, and are denoted $Var(Q)$ and $Const(Q)$ respectively. The variables appearing in $head(Q)$ are called the distinguished variables of Q, and each of them must also appear in $body(Q)$. Finally, if $head(Q)$ is of arity 0, we say that Q is boolean.

We use $CQ^{\neq}$ to denote the set of all conjunctive queries with disequalities; the subset of queries in which no disequality expression appears is denoted by CQ.

We say that a conjunctive query is *complete* (following [21]) if it explicitly specifies all disequalities between pairs of distinct variables (or a variable and a constant) occurring in it. More formally:

DEFINITION 2.2. *A query $Q \in CQ^{\neq}$ is* complete *if (1) for every pair of distinct variables $x, y \in Var(Q)$, the query contains the disequality $x \neq y$ (or $y \neq x$), (2) for every $x \in Var(Q)$ and $c \in Const(Q)$, it contains $x \neq c$.*

We use $cCQ^{\neq}$ to denote the class of all *complete* conjunctive queries with disequalities.

EXAMPLE 2.3. *In the following example, x, y are variables and c is a constant. Q, Q' are both in $CQ^{\neq}$ but only Q' is complete (i.e. $Q' \in cCQ^{\neq}$):*

Q: $ans(x,y) := R(x,y), S(y,c), x \neq y, y \neq c$
Q': $ans(x,y) := R(x,y), S(y,c), x \neq y, y \neq c, x \neq c$

We next also recall the definition of union of conjunctive queries, as follows:

DEFINITION 2.4. *A* union of conjunctive queries with disequalities *is an expression of the form $Q = Q_1 \cup Q_2 \cup ... \cup Q_m$ where for each $i \in \{1, ..., m\}$, $Q_i \in CQ^{\neq}$, and for each $i, j \in \{1, ..., m\}$ $head(Q_i)$ and $head(Q_j)$ are of the same relation. We say that each Q_i is an* adjunct *of the query Q. The set of adjuncts of Q is denoted by $Adj(Q)$.*

We use UCQ to denote the class of union of conjunctive queries with no disequalities, use $UCQ^{\neq}$ where the adjuncts may include disequalities, and $cUCQ^{\neq}$ where each adjunct is complete.

We further intuitively extend the definitions of Var and $Const$ for unions of conjunctive queries, such that $Var(Q) = \bigcup_{Q_i \in Adj(Q)} Var(Q_i)$ and $Const(Q) = \bigcup_{Q_i \in Adj(Q)} Const(Q_i)$.

EXAMPLE 2.5. *Figure 1 depicts the query Q_{union}, which is in $cUCQ^{\neq}$. Intuitively, its first adjunct Q_1 looks for pairs of different tuples (since it requires $x \neq y$) where the value of the first (second) attribute in the first tuple equals the value of the second (first) attribute in the second tuple, while the second adjunct Q_2 seeks for a single tuples, where the values in the two attributes are equal. For both adjuncts, the head relation is a tuple which contains a single variable x.*

$\mathbf{Q_1}$:	$ans(x) :=$	$R(x,y), R(y,x), x \neq y$
$\mathbf{Q_2}$:	$uns(x) :=$	$R(x,x)$
$\mathbf{Q_{union}}$:	$Q_1 \cup Q_2$	
$\mathbf{Q_{conj}}$:	$ans(x) :=$	$R(x,y), R(y,x)$

Figure 1: Example Queries

Assignments and Query Results. We formally define the notion of *assignments* of database tuples to query relational atoms, and use it to define query results, as follows:

DEFINITION 2.6. *An assignment α of a query $Q \in CQ^{\neq}$ to a database instance D is a mapping of the relational atoms of Q to tuples in D that respects relation names and induces a mapping over arguments, i.e. if a relational atom $R(l_0, ..., l_n)$ is mapped to a tuple $R(a_0, ..., a_n)$ then we say that l_i is mapped to a_i (denoted $\alpha(l_i) = a_i$) and we require that a variable l_i will not be mapped to multiple distinct values, and a constant l_i will be mapped to itself. We also require the induced mapping over arguments to respect disequalities appearing in Q.*

Given such an assignment α, we define $\alpha(head(Q))$ as the tuple obtained from $head(Q)$ by replacing each occurrence of a variable l_i by $\alpha(l_i)$, and a constant l_i by its value.

The set of all such assignments for a database instance D is denoted $A(Q, D)$, and the result of evaluating a query $Q \in CQ^{\neq}$, denoted $Q(D)$, is then defined as $\bigcup_{\alpha \in A(Q,D)} \alpha(head(Q))$. For $Q = Q_1 \cup Q_2 \cup ... \cup Q_n$, we further denote $Q(D) = \bigcup_{i=1,...,n} Q_i(D)$, and $A(Q, D) = \bigcup_{i=1,...,n} A(Q_i, D)$ Finally, we define $A(t, Q, D) = \{\alpha \in A(Q, D) \mid t = \alpha(head(Q))\}$ as the set of all assignments yielding t.

A	B	Provenance
a	a	s_1
a	b	s_2
b	a	s_3
b	b	s_4

Table 2: Relation R

A	Provenance
a	$s_2 \cdot s_3 + s_1$
b	$s_3 \cdot s_2 + s_4$

Table 3: Relation ans

EXAMPLE 2.7. *Consider the query Q_{union} depicted in Figure 1, and the database D whose single relation R is depicted in Table 2 (ignore for now the Provenance column). There are two possible assignments for the first adjunct Q_1, the first(second) maps the atom $R(x,y)$ to the tuple (a,b) (the tuple (b,a)), the atom $R(y,x)$ to the tuple (b,a) (the tuple (a,b)), and the head to the tuple (a) (the tuple (b)); there are two possible assignments for Q_2, mapping its single atom either to (a,a) or (b,b), and its head to (a) or (b) respectively. $A((a), Q_{union}, D)$, for instance, contains exactly the first assignment of Q_1 and the first of Q_2, since these are the only assignments that map the head to (a).*

2.2 Query Containment and Homomorphisms

We next recall the definitions of query containment and equivalence, as well as the definition of homomorphism between queries.

DEFINITION 2.8. *Given queries Q and Q' over a database schema R, we say that Q is contained in a query Q' (denoted*

$Q \subseteq Q'$) if for every database instance D of the schema R, $Q(D) \subseteq Q'(D)$. We say that Q, Q' are equivalent (denoted $Q \equiv Q'$) if $Q \subseteq Q'$ and $Q' \subseteq Q$.

EXAMPLE 2.9. Consider the queries Q_2 and Q_{conj} in Fig. 1. It is easy to verify that $Q_2 \subseteq Q_{conj}$.

Homomorphisms between Queries. We next define homomorphism between conjunctive queries, as follows:

DEFINITION 2.10. Let $Q, Q' \in CQ^{\neq}$; a homomorphism $h : Q \to Q'$ is a mapping from the atoms of Q to those of Q', inducing a mapping on the instances of arguments occurring in these atoms, such that:

1. If an atom a uses a relation R (resp. is a disequality) so does (is) $h(\mathsf{a})$.

2. The head of Q is mapped to the head of Q'.

3. If one instance of a variable $x \in Var(Q)$ is mapped to an instance of $y \in Var(Q')$ then all instances of x are mapped to instances of y.

4. Each occurrence of a constant $c \in Const(Q)$ must be mapped to an occurrence of c.

EXAMPLE 2.11. Reconsider Q_2, Q_{conj} from figure 1. There exists a homomorphism from Q_{conj} to Q_2 mapping the two atoms of Q_{conj} to the single atom of Q_2. The induced homomorphism over variables maps both x, y to x. Note that there is no homomorphism from Q_2 to Q_{conj} because x will necessarily be mapped to both x and y.

2.3 Provenance of Query Results

We use here provenance annotations that are elements from the *provenance semiring* [19], as these annotations allow to capture the computational process inflicted by a given query evaluation. A semiring is an algebraic structure with two operations: addition and multiplication [23]; the provenance semiring is defined as $(\mathbb{N}[X], +, \cdot, 0, 1)$, where $\mathbb{N}[X]$ is the set of all polynomials with natural numbers as coefficients, over some pre-defined set of variables X. Each multiplicative term in a polynomial is called a monomial. For instance, the monomials of $x + x \cdot y \cdot z$ are x and $x \cdot y \cdot z$.

An $\mathbb{N}[X]$-relation P maps each tuple t to a provenance annotation $P(t)$. We consider here input $\mathbb{N}[X]$-relations that are *abstractly-tagged* [19], meaning that $\forall t \; P(t) \in X$, and $\forall t \neq t' \; P(t) \neq P(t')$ (the case of non-abstractly-tagged input relations is discussed in Section 6). For instance, reconsider the relation depicted in Table 2: the provenance annotations are depicted in the last column; all annotations are distinct and the relation is abstractly-tagged.

In the sequel we will use the notations s (or s_i for some index i) for provenance annotations, p (or p_i) for polynomials, and m (or m_i) for monomials.

Given a database instance D and a query $Q \in UCQ^{\neq}$, we adopt the definition of [20] for the provenance of each tuple in the query result[1]:

DEFINITION 2.12. Given a query $Q \in CQ^{\neq}$, a database instance D of $\mathbb{N}[X]$-relations, a tuple $t \in Q(D)$, we define the provenance of t w.r.t. Q and D, denoted by $P(t, Q, D)$, as follows: $P(t, Q, D) = \sum_{\alpha \in A(t,Q,D)} \prod_{R_i \in body(Q)} P(\alpha(R_i))$, where $A(t, Q, D)$ is the set of all assignments yielding t as a

---

[1] The definition in [20] for UCQ is an adaptation of the original definition in [19] for SPJU queries.

result (See Definition 2.6). If $Q = Q_1 \cup Q_2 \cup ... \cup Q_n$ then $P(t, Q, D) = \sum_{i=1,...,n} P(t, Q_i, D)$.

In the case of boolean queries, where the only possible tuple in the result is the empty tuple, we may use the notation $P(Q, D)$ for the provenance of this single tuple, and call it the provenance of Q for D.

EXAMPLE 2.13. Reconsider the relation R depicted in Table 2, this time along with the provenance annotation of its tuples, and reconsider the query Q_{union} from Figure 1.

The output relation ans along with the provenance annotations assigned to its tuples is depicted in Table 3. Consider for example the output tuple (a); it is computed from Q_1 as the result of an assignment that maps the first (second) atom to the tuples annotated by s_2 (s_3 resp.), and from Q_2 as the result of an assignment that maps its single atom to s_1. Consequently its provenance is computed as $s_2 \cdot s_3 + s_1$. Similarly, (b) is obtained due to the assignment for Q_1 that assigns s_3 to the first atom and s_2 to the second one, and the assignment that assigns the single atom of Q_2 to s_4.

We note that different queries which are equivalent with respect to containment may yield different provenance polynomials for the same database and result tuple.

EXAMPLE 2.14. Reconsider Q_{conj} as well as Q_{union} from Figure 1. These two queries are equivalent. However, consider the provenance of the output tuple (a) for Q_{conj} and the relation R depicted in Table 2. This output tuple is yielded by an assignment that maps the first atom of Q_{conj} to s_2 and the second atom to s_3, and by an assignment that maps both atoms to s_1. Thus, the provenance of (a) for Q_{conj} is $s_2 \cdot s_3 + s_1 \cdot s_1$. The provenance of tuple (b) would be $s_3 \cdot s_2 + s_4 \cdot s_4$. In both cases, the provenance polynomial is different than the polynomial yielded by query Q_{union}.

Note. The above definition of provenance polynomials indicates the existence of an *isomorphism* between the assignments and the monomials of the polynomial, when the monomials are written in a form where all coefficients and exponents equal 1 (This isomorphism simply maps each assignment to the monomial it yields). For ease of presentation and to have the isomorphism between assignments and monomials clearly visible, we will assume that the polynomial is indeed written in this form. When this complicates the reading, we will also give (in brackets) the "compact" expression with coefficients and exponents. For instance, in Example 2.14 above we wrote $s_2 \cdot s_3$ (rather than $s_3 \cdot s_2$) as one of the monomials in the provenance of the tuple (a) to reflect the fact that the corresponding assignment mapped the first atom of Q_{conj} to a tuple annotated with s_2, and the second to a tuple annotated with s_3. Similarly, we wrote the other monomial as $s_1 \cdot s_1$ to reflect that the corresponding assignment mapped both the first and second atoms to s_1.

So far we have repeated existing definitions for general concepts. The following subsection presents definitions which are specific to the context of core provenance.

2.4 An Order Relation

We next define an order relation over the provenance polynomials, that will allow comparing different provenance polynomials yielded by equivalent queries. The order relation we define below reflects relative "terseness" of a provenance of a given tuple in the query result, and will be used in the sequel for defining minimal provenance. Intuitively, we will say that $p \leq p'$ if there is an injective mapping of the monomials in p to the monomials in p', such that each monomial is mapped to a monomial in which it is contained. Recall the correlation between the polynomials and assignments of atoms to tuples, where each monomial corresponded to such an assignment; consequently, if a query Q (Q') generates a tuple t with provenance p (p'), then $p \leq p'$ means that each assignment of Q is contained within an assignment of Q', thus the provenance of Q is more "terse". Formally,

DEFINITION 2.15. *Given two monomials $m = s_1 \cdot \ldots \cdot s_k$ and $m' = s'_1 \cdot \ldots \cdot s'_{k'}$ we say that $m \leq m'$ if there exists an injective mapping $I_m : \{1, ..., k\} \to \{1, ..., k'\}$ such that $s_i = s'_{I_m(i)}$ for every $1 \leq i \leq k$.*

Given two polynomials $p = \sum_{i=1,...,n} m_i$ and $p' = \sum_{i=1,...,n'} m'_i$, we say that $p \leq p'$ if there exists an injective mapping I_p from monomials in p to monomials in p' such that $m_i \leq I_p(m_i)$ for every $1 \leq i \leq n$.

We say that $p = p'$ if it holds that $p \leq p'$ and $p' \leq p$. Finally, we say that $p < p'$ if $p \leq p'$ but not $p = p'$.

EXAMPLE 2.16. *Let $p_1 = s_1 \cdot s_2 + s_3 + s_3$ and $p_2 = s_1 \cdot s_2 \cdot s_2 + s_2 \cdot s_3 + s_3 \cdot s_4 + s_5$, then $p_1 < p_2$. To see that this holds, observe that we can map the monomial $s_1 \cdot s_2$ to $s_1 \cdot s_2 \cdot s_2$, map the first occurrence of s_3 to $s_2 \cdot s_3$, and the second occurrence of s_3 to $s_3 \cdot s_4$; but in the other direction we cannot e.g. map the monomial $s_3 \cdot s_4$ of p_2 to any monomial of p_1.*

We then utilize the order relation over provenance polynomials to define an order relation over *queries* which are equivalent in the "standard" sense.

DEFINITION 2.17. *For two equivalent queries Q, Q' we say that $Q \subseteq_P Q'$ if for every abstractly-tagged database instance D, and for every tuple t in the result of evaluating Q (Q') over D, $P(t, Q, D) \leq P(t, Q', D)$. We say that $Q \equiv_P Q'$ if $Q \subseteq_P Q'$ and $Q' \subseteq_P Q$; we say that $Q \subset_P Q'$ if $Q \subseteq_P Q'$ but not $Q \equiv_P Q'$.*

EXAMPLE 2.18. *Reconsider the queries Q_{conj}, Q_{union} from Figure 1. As observed above, Q_{union} and Q_{conj} are equivalent. We will show in the sequel (Theorem 3.11) that $Q_{union} \subset_P Q_{conj}$. But already now we can observe that in some cases Q_{conj} entails more provenance (and thus that the queries are not equivalent in terms of provenance): in examples 2.13 and 2.14 we have shown that for the output tuple (a) the provenance of Q_{union} was $s_2 \cdot s_3 + s_1$ while the provenance of Q_{conj} was $s_2 \cdot s_3 + s_1 \cdot s_1$, which is strictly larger.*

We now define the notion of minimal query in terms of provenance, as follows:

DEFINITION 2.19 (MINIMAL PROVENANCE). *We say that a query Q is provenance-minimal (p-minimal) in a class of queries $\mathcal{C}$ [2] if $\forall Q' \in \mathcal{C}$ $Q' \equiv Q \Rightarrow Q \subseteq_P Q'$.*

The provenance yielded by a p-minimal query is called *core provenance*.

We then define the PROVENANCE-MINIMIZATION problem, with respect to a given class $\mathcal{C}$ of queries, as follows: given a query $Q \in \mathcal{C}$, find, if exists, a query $Q' \in \mathcal{C}$ such that $Q' \equiv Q$ and Q' is p-minimal. We study in the sequel PROVENANCE-MINIMIZATION for the query classes $CQ, CQ^{\neq}, cCQ^{\neq}, UCQ^{\neq}$.

---

[2] $\mathcal{C}$ may e.g. be CQ, $CQ^{\neq}$, etc.

Note. We note that "standard" query minimization ([9, 22, 26]) aims at minimizing the query *length*, i.e. the number of relational atoms in the query (equivalently, minimizing the number of joins [22]). We show in the sequel that such minimization does not necessarily minimize the provenance. Another important note is that (unlike for comparison based on length) it can be the case that two equivalent queries will be incomparable with respect to our order relation, and we will show such an example in the sequel (See Theorem 3.5).

3. MINIMIZING CONJUNCTIVE QUERIES

In this section we focus on solving PROVENANCE-MINIMIZATION for conjunctive queries. We start by presenting a homomorphism theorem that will be of use in all of our p-minimization algorithms. We then consider first p-minimization within the most general class, $CQ^{\neq}$. Then we turn to analyze subclasses of $CQ^{\neq}$ which are of interest, namely CQ and $cCQ^{\neq}$.

3.1 Homomorphisms and Provenance

In the work on "standard" minimization, where one aims at minimizing the number of joins in a given query, homomorphism mappings between queries play an important role. Evidently, this is also the case for provenance minimization, albeit in a different manner. We first recall the homomorphism theorems from [9, 21]:

THEOREM 3.1 ([9, 21]). *Given two queries $Q \in CQ$ $(Q \in cCQ^{\neq})$ and $Q' \in CQ$ $(Q' \in CQ^{\neq})$, there exists a homomorphism from Q' to Q if and only if $Q \subseteq Q'$.*

We note that the requirement on Q with disequalities to be complete is essential; otherwise, homomorphism implies inclusion but the converse fails in general, as indicated by the following example:

EXAMPLE 3.2 (ADAPTED FROM [22]). *Consider the following queries:*

$Q : ans() := R(x, y), R(y, z), x \neq z$
$Q' : ans() := R(x, y), x \neq y$

Q is included in Q': if there exists x, y, z such that $R(x, y)$, $R(y, z)$ and $x \neq z$, then either $x \neq y$ or $y \neq z$, in both cases there exists a tuple $R(w, t)$ with $w \neq t$ which thus matches Q'. But there is no homomorphism from Q' to Q as if we can either map $R(x, y)$ occurring in Q' to $R(x, y)$ or $R(y, z)$ occurring in Q; but in both cases the disequality $x \neq y$ could not be mapped to $x \neq z$.

We shall see below that the property exemplified in Example 3.2 will have interesting implications on the (in)existence of p-minimal queries equivalent to a given query in $CQ^{\neq}$.

We next present a counterpart theorem that will form the basis for our provenance minimization algorithms.

THEOREM 3.3. *Given two equivalent queries $Q, Q' \in CQ^{\neq}$, if there exists a homomorphism h from Q' to Q that is surjective on relational atoms, then $Q \subseteq_P Q'$.*

PROOF SKETCH. Let D be an input database, and let $t \in Q(D)$ (thus $t \in Q'(D)$). Let $p = \sum_i m_i$ $(p' = \sum_i m'_i)$ be the provenance of t with respect to Q (Q') and D. We claim that $p \leq p'$. For that we need to show an injective mapping I mapping each monomial m_i in p and some monomial $m'_{i'}$ in p', such that $m_i \leq m'_{i'}$.

We define I as follows: for m_i, there exists an assignment α to Q that yielded it. Given the surjective mapping $h : Q' \to Q$, define β as the assignment which assigns each relational atom a' of Q', $\alpha(h(a'))$. It is straightforward to show that β is indeed a satisfying assignment for Q' (proof omitted). Since h is surjective on relational atoms, every tuple t' assigned to k different atoms by α is assigned to at least k atoms by β. Finally, let $I(m_i)$ be $m_{i'}'$, the monomial yielded by the assignment of β to Q'. Then each variable $P(t')$ which appears k times in m_i appears at least k times in $m_{i'}'$, and by definition of the order relation, $m_i \leq m_{i'}'$.

We still have to show that the mapping I between the monomials is injective. For that, consider m_i, m_j s.t. $i \neq j$. Let α_i (resp. β_i), α_j (resp. β_j) be the assignments that yielded these monomials, respectively, in the evaluation of Q (resp. Q'). Different monomials in our presentation (See note at the end of Section 2.4) are always yielded by different assignments; thus α_i and α_j must be distinct assignments; that is only possible if they assign some relational atom a in Q different tuples, let us call them t_i and t_j respectively. Then there exists some relational atom a' in Q' such that $h(a') = a$ (by the surjectiveness of h). By the construction of β_i and β_j, β_i (β_j) assigns a' the tuple $\alpha_i(h(a')) = t_i$ ($\alpha_j(h(a')) = t_j$), and thus they are distinct assignments, which yield different monomials. That means m_i and m_j are always mapped by I to different monomials in p', i.e. I is injective. $\square$

We note that unlike the case of queries inclusion (Theorem 3.1), Theorem 3.3 requires the homomorphism to be surjective. The following example shows that a non-surjective mapping does not guarantee an order on the provenance.

EXAMPLE 3.4. *Consider the following two simple boolean queries Q, Q':*

Q: ans() := R(x),R(y)
Q': ans() := R(x)

There exists a (trivial) homomorphism from Q' to Q, but no surjective one (since Q' has less atoms). For the simple unary relation R bearing a single tuple $R(a)$ with provenance s, the provenance of the (boolean) result of evaluating Q over R is $s \cdot s$, while for Q' the provenance is $s < s \cdot s$.

In contrast, mapping both atoms of Q to the one of Q' is a surjective homomorphism from Q to Q'. It is easy to see that the provenance of Q' is smaller.

In the sequel we consider different subclasses of $CQ^{\neq}$, and, where possible, utilize the above results for minimizing the provenance of a given query within the sub-class.

3.2 General Conjunctive Queries

We start with general queries in $CQ^{\neq}$. Note that [22] has shown that for standard minimization, for each query $Q \in CQ^{\neq}$ there exists a minimal equivalent query in $CQ^{\neq}$. Interestingly, this is not the case for p-minimal queries, as the following theorem holds:

THEOREM 3.5. *There exists a query $Q \in CQ^{\neq}$ such that Q has no p-minimal equivalent query in $CQ^{\neq}$.*

PROOF SKETCH. Consider the queries Q_{noPmin} and Q_{alt} from Figure 2. We can show that Q_{noPmin} is equivalent to Q_{alt}. But none of these queries is p-minimal, as the following Lemma holds:

A	B	Provenance
a	b	s_1
b	a	s_2
a	a	s_3

Table 4: Relation R in Database D

A	B	Provenance
a	b	s_1'
b	c	s_2'
c	a	s_3'
a	a	s_4'

Table 5: Relation R in Database D'

$\mathbf{Q_{noPmin}}:$ $ans() := R(x_1, x_2), R(x_2, x_3), R(x_3, x_4),$
$R(x_4, x_5), R(x_5, x_1), S(x_1), x_1 \neq x_2$

$\mathbf{Q_{alt}}:$ $ans() := R(x_1, x_2), R(x_2, x_3), R(x_3, x_4),$
$R(x_4, x_5), R(x_5, x_1), S(x_1), x_1 \neq x_3$

$\mathbf{Q_{alt2}}:$ $ans() := R(x_1, x_2), R(x_2, x_3), R(x_3, x_4),$
$R(x_4, x_5), R(x_5, x_1), S(x_1), x_1 \neq x_4$

$\mathbf{Q_{alt3}}:$ $ans() := R(x_1, x_2), R(x_2, x_3), R(x_3, x_4),$
$R(x_4, x_5), R(x_5, x_1), S(x_1), x_1 \neq x_5$

Figure 2: Queries in $CQ^{\neq}$

LEMMA 3.6. *It neither holds that $Q_{noPmin} \subseteq_P Q_{alt}$, nor that $Q_{alt} \subseteq_P Q_{noPmin}$.*

PROOF. Consider a database D with the Relation R depicted in Table 4, and the relation S consisting of a single tuple (a) annotated with s_0. The provenance expression for Q_{noPmin} is

$s_1 \cdot s_2 \cdot s_1 \cdot s_2 \cdot s_3 \cdot s_0 + s_1 \cdot s_2 \cdot s_3 \cdot s_1 \cdot s_2 \cdot s_0 + s_1 \cdot s_2 \cdot s_3 \cdot s_3 \cdot s_3 \cdot s_0$
$\left(= 2 \cdot (s_1)^2 \cdot (s_2)^2 \cdot s_3 \cdot s_0 + s_1 \cdot s_2 \cdot (s_3)^3 \cdot s_0. \right)$

For Q_{alt}, the provenance expression is

$s_3 \cdot s_1 \cdot s_2 \cdot s_1 \cdot s_2 \cdot s_0 + s_3 \cdot s_1 \cdot s_2 \cdot s_3 \cdot s_3 \cdot s_0$
$\left(= (s_1)^2 \cdot (s_2)^2 \cdot s_3 \cdot s_0 + s_1 \cdot s_2 \cdot (s_3)^3 \cdot s_0. \right)$

which is strictly smaller. In contrast, for a database D' with Relation R as depicted in Table 5, and relation S as before, the provenance obtained for Q_{noPmin} is

$s_1' \cdot s_2' \cdot s_3' \cdot s_4' \cdot s_4' \cdot s_0$

and for Q_{alt} it is

$s_1' \cdot s_2' \cdot s_3' \cdot s_4' \cdot s_4' \cdot s_0 + s_4' \cdot s_1' \cdot s_2' \cdot s_3' \cdot s_4' \cdot s_0$

which is strictly greater. $\square$

The following lemma concludes the proof by showing that no other equivalent query in $CQ^{\neq}$ has a minimal provenance:

LEMMA 3.7. *There exist database instances D, D' for which there is no query $Q \in CQ^{\neq}$ equivalent to Q_{noPmin} (and to Q_{alt}) such that both $P(Q, D) \leq P(Q_{noPmin}, D)$ and $P(Q, D') \leq P(Q_{alt}, D')$ hold.*

PROOF SKETCH. The databases D, D' are as in the proof of Lemma 3.6 above. Assume by contradiction the existence of such Q. It must contain exactly 5 atoms in which R occur and exactly one atom in which S occur (otherwise if it contains less it will not be equivalent and if it contains more it will have greater provenance for one of the Databases). Since all the variables of Q_{noPmin} can be different, there

146

must be at least 5 different variables in Q; it follows that Q must be of the form

$$Q : ans() := R(z_1, z_2), R(z_2, z_3), R(z_3, z_4),$$
$$R(z_4, z_5), R(z_5, z_1), S(z1), E$$

Where E is some conjunction of disequalities between $z_1, ..., z_5$. However, for most choices of E there exists a database instance for which the query result is not equivalent to Q_{noPmin}. There are only two other queries equivalent to Q_{noPmin} of the form of Q, depicted in figure 2: Q_{alt2}, whose provenance is equivalent to that of Q_{alt} on D, D'; and Q_{alt3}, whose provenance is equivalent to that of Q_{noPmin} on D, D'. Thus, neither of them could be Q, implying that such Q does not exist. $\square$

This concludes the proof of Theorem 3.5. $\square$

The construction that we have used in the proof is inspired by [17]. Interestingly, note that in the above proof we constructed two equivalent queries, both minimal in the standard sense (but not isomorphic). This settles an open problem posed in [22], indicating the correctness of the following Lemma:

LEMMA 3.8. *There exists a query $Q \in CQ^{\neq}$ such that Q has no minimal equivalent query which is* unique *up to isomorphism in $CQ^{\neq}$.*

While there are queries for which no p-minimal equivalent query in $CQ^{\neq}$ exists, we will see in Section 4 that there always exists an equivalent p-minimal query in $UCQ^{\neq}$. But before that, let us consider other restricted classes in which the p-minimal query can be found. The conclusions for these restricted classes will gradually lead us towards the general solution for the overall p-minimal query in $UCQ^{\neq}$.

3.3 Conjunctive Queries without Disequalities

We consider CQ, i.e. the class of conjunctive queries with no disequalities. The following theorem shows that in CQ, the "standard" minimal query is also p-minimal. As a result, a standard minimization algorithm (such as in [9]) can be used here to obtain the p-minimal query.

THEOREM 3.9. *Let $Q \in CQ$. Then Q is a minimal query (in the standard sense) iff Q is p-minimal in CQ.*

PROOF SKETCH. Assume that Q is minimal, and consider some query $Q' \in CQ$ equivalent to Q. By the equivalence between Q and Q', and from theorem 3.1 there is a homomorphism $h : Q' \to Q$. We can show that this homomorphism is surjective on relational atoms, and thus from theorem 3.3, $Q \subseteq_P Q'$. $\square$

Following the lines of [16] (for standard query minimization), we define the decision problem corresponding to p-minimization in CQ as follows: *given two queries $Q, Q' \in CQ$, where Q' is a sub-query of Q, decide if Q' is the p-minimal equivalent of Q.* Note that *verifying* p-minimality of a query Q is a restricted case. The following is a corollary of Theorem 3.9, resulting from the known hardness of conjunctive query minimization [16]:

COROLLARY 3.10. *The decision problem corresponding to* PROVENANCE-MINIMIZATION *in CQ is DP-Complete [3].*

---

[3]DP is the class of decision problems that can be expressed as the intersection of an NP and a co-NP problem [16].

In the context of "standard" minimization, the obtained minimal query is minimal also among all equivalent queries in $UCQ^{\neq}$ [9]. Interestingly, this is not the case for provenance minimization, as the following theorem holds.

THEOREM 3.11. *There exists a query $Q \in CQ$ such that Q is p-minimal in CQ but there exists an equivalent query $Q' \in UCQ^{\neq}$, such that $Q' \subset_P Q$.*

PROOF. Consider again the queries Q_{conj} and Q_{union} from Figure 1. It is easy to see that there is no surjective homomorphism from Q_{conj} to any of its sub-queries, and thus (following theorem 3.9) Q_{conj} is p-minimal within CQ. To show that $Q_{union} \subseteq_P Q_{conj}$, observe that every assignment to Q_{union} that yields every output tuple t is either an assignment to its first adjunct, Q_1, or its second argument Q_2. In the former case the same assignment to Q_{conj} will also yield the output tuple t, and in the latter case this assignment will have a counterpart assignment to Q_{conj} that maps two atoms to the same tuple. In both cases the provenance monomials yielded by Q_{conj} are greater or equal, and thus the provenance polynomial of each tuple for Q_{conj} is greater or equal, i.e. $Q_{union} \subseteq_P Q_{conj}$.

Last, $Q_{union} \subset_P Q_{conj}$ because there exists a database instance and output tuple for which Q_{union} yields strictly less provenance (See Example 2.18). $\square$

The above theorem shows that even for queries which are p-minimal in CQ, there may be equivalent queries in $UCQ^{\neq}$ with smaller provenance. In the next section we show that equivalent p-minimal queries in $UCQ^{\neq}$ always exist, and explain how to compute them.

3.4 Complete Conjunctive Queries with Disequalities

The last sub-class of $CQ^{\neq}$ that we study here, and will be very useful when we consider $UCQ^{\neq}$ in the next section, is $cCQ^{\neq}$, the class of *complete* conjunctive queries with disequalities. Recall that completeness means here that for every pair of distinct variable x and argument l occurring in the query, $x \neq l$ appears in the query. In this case, we will show that like in CQ, p-minimization within the $cCQ^{\neq}$ class is equivalent to standard minimization. However, we will further show that in contrast to Theorem 3.11 the p-minimal in $cCQ^{\neq}$ is also the *overall p-minimal in $UCQ^{\neq}$*. Another difference from CQ is the complexity of (p-)minimization in $cCQ^{\neq}$, which we prove to be polynomial.

The following theorem holds:

THEOREM 3.12. *Given a query $Q \in cCQ^{\neq}$, Q is minimal in the standard sense iff Q is p-minimal in $cCQ^{\neq}$, and that is iff Q is p-minimal in $UCQ^{\neq}$. The (p-)minimal equivalent of any $Q \in cCQ^{\neq}$ can be computed in time polynomial in the size of Q.*

PROOF SKETCH. Recall the proof sketch of theorem 3.9, showing that in CQ minimality and p-minimality are the same. Note that this proof was based only on theorems 3.1 and 3.3. Since those theorems also hold for $cCQ^{\neq}$, it can be proved in a similar manner that p-minimality and minimality in $cCQ^{\neq}$ are the same. Thus, if we minimize Q we will get Q', the equivalent of Q which is p-minimal in $cCQ^{\neq}$. The p-minimality of Q' in $UCQ^{\neq}$ (thus making it the general p-minimal equivalent of Q) is a corollary of Theorem 4.6 shown in the sequel.

To show that Q' can be computed efficiently, we use the following Lemma:

LEMMA 3.13. *A query $Q \in cCQ^{\neq}$ is (p-)minimal if and only if Q does not contain duplicated relational atoms (i.e. two atoms of the same relation with the same arguments).*

Thus, a simple minimization algorithm for $cCQ^{\neq}$ will compare every two relational atoms and remove the duplicates. This can be done in PTIME. □

4. MINIMIZING UNIONS

We next consider minimizing the provenance for $UCQ^{\neq}$, union of conjunctive queries with disequalities. As observed above, resorting to $UCQ^{\neq}$ in search of a query with minimal provenance may be necessary even if the input query is guaranteed to be a conjunctive query. Our study of minimization of queries in this class is done in two steps, as follows. We start by introducing the *canonical rewriting* of a query, which is essentially its rewriting as a union of *complete* queries; we then introduce a minimization algorithm, based on canonical rewritings, and we show that its result is a p-minimal equivalent of the original query.

4.1 Canonical Rewritings

Recall the queries in Example 2.18: the queries Q_{conj}, Q_{union} are equivalent, but Q_{union} has less provenance. Intuitively, this is because Q_{union} employs a by-case reasoning: each combination of equalities and disequalities among each pair of variables is dealt with separately, using distinct conjunctive queries. Intuitively, such a by-case reasoning is implemented by the canonical rewriting of a query. We next first define a *possible completion* of a query, which corresponds to a particular "case", and then the canonical rewriting, which encapsulates all the possible "cases".

DEFINITION 4.1. *Let $Q \in CQ^{\neq}$. A possible completion of Q is a query in $cCQ^{\neq}$ obtained by splitting the arguments $Var(Q) \cup Const(Q)$ into m disjoint subsets, $V_1, ..., V_m$, such that (1) each set contains at most one constant, and (2) if Q contains the disequality $l_i \neq l_j$, then l_i and l_j are not in the same subset. Then, for each subset V_i that contains a constant c, every occurrence of an argument from this subset is replaced in the relational atoms of Q by c; for each subset V_i without a constant, all the occurrences of arguments within it are replaced in Q by some new variable v_i; and finally all the disequalities in Q are removed, and instead a disequality $v_i \neq v_j$ for each two new variables v_i, v_j and a disequality $v_i \neq c$ for each new variable v_i and $c \in Const(Q)$ are added.*

A canonical rewriting of Q, denoted by $Can(Q)$, is then a query in $cUCQ^{\neq}$ where each possible completion of Q is isomorphic to exactly one adjunct in Q, and vice versa.

Finally, an extended canonical rewriting with respect to a set of constants C which is a superset of $Const(Q)$, is defined in a similar manner, except that every possible completion is obtained by splitting $Var(Q) \cup C$ into disjoint sets as before. We denote it $Can(Q, C)$. In particular, $Can(Q) = Can(Q, Const(Q))$.

EXAMPLE 4.2. *Consider for example the query*

$Q : ans(x, y) := R(x, y), x \neq a, x \neq y$

Its canonical rewriting with respect to $C = \{a, b\}$ (which contains $Const(Q)$) is

$Can(Q, C) := Q_1 \cup Q_2 \cup Q_3 \cup Q_4 \cup Q_5$

$\begin{aligned}
Q_1 : \quad & ans(v_1, a) := && R(v_1, a), v_1 \neq a, v_1 \neq b \\
Q_2 : \quad & ans(v_1, b) := && R(v_1, b), v_1 \neq a, v_1 \neq b \\
Q_3 : \quad & ans(v_1, v_2) := && R(v_1, v_2), v_1 \neq a, v_1 \neq v_2, v_2 \neq a, \\
& && v_1 \neq b, v_2 \neq b \\
Q_4 : \quad & ans(b, a) := && R(b, a) \\
Q_5 : \quad & ans(b, v_2) := && R(b, v_2), v_2 \neq a, v_2 \neq b
\end{aligned}$

We next study some basic properties of the (extended) canonical rewriting. First, it is easy to show that it preserves the query results:

THEOREM 4.3. *For any query $Q \in CQ^{\neq}$, and any superset C of the constants in Q, $Q \equiv Can(Q, C)$.*

Furthermore, we show that the output tuples of the canonical representation bear the same provenance as those of the original query:

THEOREM 4.4. *For every query $Q \in CQ^{\neq}$ and any superset C of the constants in Q, $Q \equiv_P Can(Q, C)$.*

PROOF SKETCH. We use the following lemma:

LEMMA 4.5. *For every query $Q \in CQ^{\neq}$, and two different adjuncts Q_1, Q_2 in $Can(Q)$, if α is an assignment for Q_1, then it is not valid for Q_2.*

Now, let D be an input database and t a tuple in the query result. It follows from the lemma that each assignment to $Can(Q)$ satisfies exactly one of its adjuncts, and thus has the same provenance as its corresponding assignment for Q, i.e. $P(t, Can(Q), D) \leq P(t, Q, D)$. Conversely an assignment to Q decides (in)equalities between variables (and constants), consequently corresponds to an assignment to exactly one adjunct of $Can(Q)$, thus $P(t, Q, D) \leq P(t, Can(Q), D)$; since this holds for every tuple t in the result set, it follows that $Can(Q) \equiv_P Q$. □

4.2 Provenance Minimization Algorithm

We are now ready to present an algorithm for finding a p-minimal equivalent of a query in $UCQ^{\neq}$. By doing so, we will prove the following theorem:

THEOREM 4.6. *Given a query $Q \in UCQ^{\neq}$, there exists a p-minimal equivalent query $Q' \in UCQ^{\neq}$; Q' may be found in time exponential in the size of Q.*

We next give the algorithm, analyze it and then show that its exponential complexity is inevitable.

Algorithm. The minimization method $MinProv$ is depicted in Algorithm 1 and operates in 3 steps. First (step I), it replaces each adjunct of the input query Q by its canonical rewriting with respect to the full set of constants in Q, obtaining a query Q_I as a result. Then, in step II, each of the adjuncts is minimized separately, using any efficient algorithm for minimization of $cCQ^{\neq}$ queries (such as the simple algorithm depicted in the proof of theorem 3.12), obtaining Q_{II} as the union of minimized queries. Finally, in step III the algorithm checks every pair of adjuncts in Q_{II} for query containment: recall that since Q_{II} is a canonical rewriting,

Algorithm 1: MinProv

Input: Query Q
Output: An equivalent p-minimal query

// Step I
1   $Q_I \leftarrow \phi$;
2   $C \leftarrow Const(Q)$;
3   **foreach** $Q_i \in Adj(Q)$ **do**
4   **foreach** $Q_{i,j}$ adjunct in $Can(Q_i, C)$ **do**
5   Add $Q_{i,j}$ to Q_I;
6   **end**
7   **end**
// Step II
8   $Q_{II} \leftarrow \phi$;
9   **foreach** $Q_i \in Adj(Q_I)$ **do**
10   Minimize Q_i and add to Q_{II}
11   **end**
// Step III
12   $Q_{III} \leftarrow Q_{II}$;
13   **foreach** $Q_i \in Adj(Q_{III})$ **do**
14   **foreach** $Q_j \in Adj(Q_{III})$ other than Q_i **do**
15   **if** $Q_j \subseteq Q_i$ **then**
16   Remove Q_j from Q_{III}
17   **end**
18   **end**
19   **end**
20   **return** Q_{III} ;

$\hat{Q}$: $ans() := R(x,y), R(y,z), R(z,x)$

$\hat{Q}_I$: $\hat{Q}_1 \cup \hat{Q}_2 \cup \hat{Q}_3 \cup \hat{Q}_4 \cup \hat{Q}_5$

$\hat{Q}_1$: $ans() := R(v_1, v_1), R(v_1, v_1), R(v_1, v_1)$
$\hat{Q}_2$: $ans() := R(v_1, v_2), R(v_2, v_1), R(v_1, v_1), v_1 \neq v_2$
$\hat{Q}_3$: $ans() := R(v_1, v_2), R(v_2, v_2), R(v_2, v_1), v_1 \neq v_2$
$\hat{Q}_4$: $ans() := R(v_1, v_1), R(v_1, v_2), R(v_2, v_1), v_1 \neq v_2$
$\hat{Q}_5$: $ans() := R(v_1, v_2), R(v_2, v_3), R(v_3, v_1), v_1 \neq v_2,$
      $v_2 \neq v_3, v_1 \neq v_3$

$\hat{Q}_{II}$: $\hat{Q}_{min1} \cup \hat{Q}_2 \cup \hat{Q}_3 \cup \hat{Q}_4 \cup \hat{Q}_5$

$\hat{Q}_{min1}$: $ans() := R(v_1, v_1)$

$\hat{Q}_{III}$: $\hat{Q}_{min1} \cup \hat{Q}_5$

Figure 3: Example for $MinProv$, Step by Step

LEMMA 4.9. *Let $Q \in cCQ^{\neq}, Q' \in UCQ^{\neq}$, such that Q is complete with respect to the constants in Q', $Q \subseteq Q'$ iff there exists an adjunct $Q'_i \in Adj(Q')$ s.t. $Q \subseteq Q'_i$.*

Now, let $C = Const(MinProv(Q)) \cup Const(Q')$. We next show that $Can(MinProv(Q), C) \subseteq_P Q'$; since $Can(MinProv(Q), C) \equiv_P MinProv(Q)$, this will prove proposition 4.8. Let Q_i be one of the adjuncts in $Can(MinProv(Q), C)$. Since we removed contained adjuncts in step III of the algorithm, and thus every two adjuncts must differ in some equality/disequality, every monomial contributed to the provenance by Q_i must be unique. Since $Can(MinProv(Q), C) \subseteq Can(Q', C)$, it holds that $Q_i \subseteq Can(Q', C)$. Thus, by lemma 4.9 (Q_i is complete on all the constants in Q') there exists some adjunct Q'_j in $Can(Q', C)$ s.t. $Q_i \subseteq Q'_j$. The containment and completeness on the other direction also holds, thus there exists some adjunct Q_k in $Can(MinProv(Q), C)$ s.t. $Q'_j \subseteq Q_k$. We get that $Q_i \subseteq Q'_j \subseteq Q_k$, and since we removed all containments from $MinProv(Q)$, $Q_i \equiv Q_k$, thus $Q_i \subseteq Q'_j \subseteq Q_i$, i.e. $Q_i \equiv Q'_j$.

Since at step II we minimized each adjunct, Q_i is p-minimal. In particular, $Q_i \subseteq_P Q'_j$. Thus, for every input database D and $t \in Q(D)$, Q_i contributes at most the provenance that Q'_j does. This is true for every such adjunct Q_i in $Can(MinProv(Q), C)$, thus $P(t, Can(MinProv(Q), C), D) \leq P(t, Can(Q', C), D)$. Since it is true for every t and D, $Can(MinProv(Q), C) \subseteq_P Can(Q', C)$. $\square$

Complexity Upper Bound. The complexity of $MinProv$ is EXPTIME in the size of its input query: step I of the algorithm replaces each adjunct of the original query Q with its canonical rewriting, which is of exponential size. Then we may have an exponential number of adjuncts, but each of them is of *polynomial size* (by definition of the canonical rewriting). Then the overall complexity of steps II and III is (respectively) polynomial and exponential in the maximal size (number of relational atoms) of an adjunct in their input query.

This concludes the proof of Theorem 4.6 above.

Complexity Lower bound. The EXPTIME complexity of $MinProv$ is inevitable as the following theorem holds:

THEOREM 4.10. *For every $n \in \mathbb{N}$ there exists a query Q_n of size $\Theta(n)$ such that any p-minimal equivalent of Q_n is of size $2^{\Omega(n)}$.*

each adjunct in it is complete, therefore Theorem 3.1 holds and checking for containment amounts to checking for the existence of a homomorphism. Whenever a contained query is found, it is omitted by the algorithm. Q_{III} (and the algorithm output) is then Q_{II} without the contained adjuncts.

EXAMPLE 4.7. *Consider the queries depicted in figure 3. We apply the MinProv algorithm on $\hat{Q}$, showing the obtained intermediate queries. Step I of the algorithm computes the canonical rewriting of (the single adjunct of) $\hat{Q}$, resulting in $\hat{Q}_I$ Then, in step II, each of the adjuncts of $\hat{Q}_I$ are (p-)minimized. Recall (Lemma 3.13) that a complete conjunctive query is p-minimal if and only if it has no duplicated relational atoms; the only adjunct which is not p-minimal is $\hat{Q}_1$. We remove the duplicated atoms to obtain its p-minimal equivalent, $\hat{Q}_{min1}$. Consequently the result of step II of the algorithm is $\hat{Q}_{II}$. Finally, in step III of the algorithm we eliminate contained adjuncts. In this case we can easily verify that $\hat{Q}_2, \hat{Q}_3$ and $\hat{Q}_4$ are contained in $\hat{Q}_{min1}$. There are no other containments between adjuncts; thus the result of step III (and the algorithm output), $\hat{Q}_{III}$, is the union of the remaining adjuncts, $\hat{Q}_{min1}$ and $\hat{Q}_5$.*

Correctness. First, it is easy to see that $Q \equiv MinProv(Q)$. We next show that the query that is computed is indeed the minimal one.

PROPOSITION 4.8. *For every two equivalent queries, $Q, Q' \in UCQ^{\neq}$, $MinProv(Q) \subseteq_P Q'$, i.e. $MinProv$ returns a p-minimal query equivalent to Q.*

PROOF. We say in the sequel that a query Q is complete w.r.t. a set of constants C if it is complete and additionally contains a disequality $v \neq c$ for every $v \in Var(Q), c \in C$. The following lemma is an adaptation of a Theorem in [26], adapted to consider queries with disequalities.

A	B	Provenance
a	a	s_1
a	b	s_2
b	a	s_3
b	c	s_4
c	a	s_5

Table 6: Relation R in $\hat{D}$

The proof is based on constructing a query Q_n which is of the form

$ans() := R_1(x_1, y_1), R_1(y_1, x_1), ..., R_n(x_n, y_n), R_n(y_n, x_n)$. We can show that a p-minimal equivalent of Q_n must consider exponentially many "cases" of (dis)equalities, hence is of exponential size.

It is interesting to compare this result to "standard" minimization, where the output is at most of the same size of the input (albeit minimization still requires EXPTIME).

5. DIRECT PROVENANCE MINIMIZATION

In the previous sections we have discussed the computation of a p-minimal query equivalent to a given query. As explained above, this p-minimal query realizes the core provenance for the query and every database instance. However, in some real-life scenarios we may wish not to change the query that is evaluated, since it is determined by optimizers and governed by evaluation time considerations. In such cases it is preferable to compute the core provenance directly from the provenance of tuples in the query result. This section shows how such a direct computation can be done. We present the next theorem.

THEOREM 5.1. *Let $Q \in UCQ^{\neq}$ be a query, D be some input database, t a tuple in $Q(D)$ and let $p = P(t, Q, D)$. Let p' be the provenance of t as computed by Q', a p-minimal query equivalent to Q.*

- *Given p, (and without any other information on Q, Q', D or t), p' can be computed in time polynomial in the size of p, up to the number of occurrences of equal monomials (corresponding to its coefficient).*

- *Given p, D, t and $Const(Q)$, and without any other information on Q or Q', p' can be exactly computed (including the correct number of occurrences of equal monomials) in time exponential in the size of p.*

The rest of the section is dedicated to proving Theorem 5.1. Our proof technique is to (i) closely examine the three steps of Algorithm $MinProv$ (given in Section 4), (ii) study the effect that each step has on the provenance polynomials, and (iii) prove that we can simulate this effect by directly working on the polynomials.

Several notations will be used in the sequel: given a query $Q \in UCQ^{\neq}$, an input instance D and a tuple t in $Q(D)$, we use $Q_I, Q_{II}, Q_{III} \in cUCQ^{\neq}$ to denote the queries obtained after step I,II,III respectively of applying $MinProv$ on Q; and the corresponding provenance polynomials $p_I = P(t, Q_I, D)$, $p_{II} = P(t, Q_{II}, D)$, $p_{III} = P(t, Q_{III}, D)$.

5.1 Step I of MinProv

Recall that the first step of $MinProv$ replaces each adjunct with its canonical rewriting. By theorem 4.4, this does not affect the provenance. We exemplify this next.

EXAMPLE 5.2. *Recall the query $\hat{Q}$ from Example 4.7 (depicted in Figure 3). Let $\hat{D}$ be a database with R relation as in table 6. The provenance of the boolean result of $\hat{Q}$ (and thus also $\hat{Q}_I$) when evaluated on $\hat{D}$ is given next (each row contains the monomials yielded by one adjunct of $\hat{Q}_I$):*

$s_1 \cdot s_1 \cdot s_1 +$
$s_2 \cdot s_3 \cdot s_1 +$
$s_3 \cdot s_1 \cdot s_2 +$
$s_1 \cdot s_2 \cdot s_3 +$
$s_2 \cdot s_4 \cdot s_5 + s_4 \cdot s_5 \cdot s_2 + s_5 \cdot s_2 \cdot s_4$

5.2 Step II of MinProv

We next consider the impact of step II on the provenance polynomial. The following Lemma holds:

LEMMA 5.3. *For each monomial m_i in p_I there is a monomial m_j in p_{II} which contains every variable s of m_i exactly once.*

EXAMPLE 5.4. *Consider again $\hat{Q}_I$ from Example 4.7 and recall that only the first adjunct $\hat{Q}_1$ was further minimized. Accordingly, only the monomial contributed by the first adjunct is changed (compare to the provenance in Example 5.2), and we get the following provenance (for database $\hat{D}$).*

$s_1 +$
$s_2 \cdot s_3 \cdot s_1 +$
$s_3 \cdot s_1 \cdot s_2 +$
$s_1 \cdot s_2 \cdot s_3 +$
$s_2 \cdot s_4 \cdot s_5 + s_4 \cdot s_5 \cdot s_2 + s_5 \cdot s_2 \cdot s_4$

5.3 Step III of MinProv

Step III of Algorithm $MinProv$ eliminates adjuncts which are contained in other adjuncts. It turns out that removing *contained* adjuncts from the query, causes the elimination of *containing* monomials from the provenance polynomial. We first show this, then study the effect of step III on the number of occurrences of the remaining monomials.

LEMMA 5.5. *For every monomial m_i of p_{III}, it holds that $m_i \in p_{II}$ and there is no $m_j \in p_{II}$ such that $m_j < m_i$*

PROOF SKETCH. It is easy to see that each monomial in p_{III} is also in p_{II} (since at step III the algorithm only removes adjuncts). Assume by contradiction the existence of such m_i, m_j. Let α_i and α_j be the assignments corresponding to m_i and m_j respectively, and Q_i, Q_j the adjuncts on which α_i and α_j are applied, respectively. By definition of the order relation, there exists an injective mapping $I : m_j \to m_i$ from each multiplicand of m_j to an identical multiplicand in m_i. We define $h : Q_j \to Q_i$ s.t. every atom R_k^j in Q_j is mapped by h to R_l^i in Q_i, where $I(P(\alpha_j(R_k^j))) = P(\alpha_i(R_l^i))$. That means every atom in Q_j is mapped to an atom in Q_i which is assigned the same tuple. We can show that h is a homomorphism, thus $Q_i \subseteq Q_j$. Then, we can further show that there exists no homomorphism from Q_i to Q_j, thus $Q_i \subset Q_j$ and Q_i would have been eliminated in step III of $MinProv$. $\square$

Our analysis so far leads to the following corollary:

COROLLARY 5.6. *Up to number of equal monomial occurrences, p_{III} may be obtained from p by removing all the multiple occurrences of the same variable in each monomial, and omitting every monomial m_i in p that includes some monomial m_j in p.*

This transformation can easily be done in PTIME, proving part (1) of theorem 5.1. We next prove part (2).

Computing the number of monomial occurrences. We first characterize the number of occurrences of each remaining monomial. The following Lemma holds:

LEMMA 5.7. *Let m_i be a monomial of p_{II} that was yielded by an adjunct of Q, that has k automorphisms. If m_i appears in p_{III} then k monomials equal to m_i appear in p_{III}.*

PROOF SKETCH. Let α_i be the assignment corresponding to m_i. Then we define k different assignments as follows. For every automorphism τ we define the assignment $\alpha_\tau = \alpha_i \circ \tau$. We can show that: (i) $\alpha_\tau \in A(t, Q, D)$, i.e. it is an assignment for Q that yields t; (ii) for $\tau \neq \tau'$, $\alpha_\tau \neq \alpha_{\tau'}$, and (iii) an assignment contributes a monomial equal to m_i to the provenance of t iff it is in $\{\alpha_\tau | \tau$ is an automorphism of $Q\}$. $\square$

EXAMPLE 5.8. *Recall that according to Example 4.7, the second, third and forth adjuncts of the result of step II, $\hat{Q}_{II}$, are eliminated, since they were contained in the first adjunct, $\hat{Q}_{min1}$. Consider again the provenance polynomial corresponding to $\hat{Q}_{II}$, which appears in Example 5.4. Observe that the monomials yielded by the eliminated adjuncts strictly contain the monomial yielded by the first adjunct. For instance, $s_1 < s_2 \cdot s_3 \cdot s_1$. The three equivalent monomials yielded by the last adjunct remain intact. Indeed, the last adjunct has exactly 3 automorphisms.*

$s_1 +$
$s_2 \cdot s_4 \cdot s_5 + s_4 \cdot s_5 \cdot s_2 + s_5 \cdot s_2 \cdot s_4$

Computing the number of automorphisms for the adjunct corresponding to a monomial m (denoted $Aut(m)$) is straightforward to do (in EXPTIME) if we have the corresponding query adjunct in hand. But interestingly, we can do it without seeing the query, if we are given the input database and the set of *constants* used by the query (if any are used). This will conclude the proof of Theorem 5.1. Formally,

LEMMA 5.9. *Given a monomial m in polynomial $P(t, Q, D)$ on database D and the output tuple t, and given $Const(Q)$, where Q is a p-minimal query, $Aut(m)$ can be computed in time exponential in m.*

6. GENERAL ANNOTATIONS

So far we have limited our discussion to abstractly-tagged databases, i.e. databases in which every tuple has a distinct annotation. However, we note that in some cases, input relations are not abstractly-tagged, for instance if they are the result of some previous computation. We can show that since our core provenance captures the essence of the computation in terms of the participating tuples and regardless of their annotations, the p-minimal query remains the same. Intuitively, the proof is by replacing all annotations in the database with unique new annotations, and then show that the order between provenance polynomials in the result of query evaluation remains intact after these replacements.

THEOREM 6.1. *Let Q be a p-minimal query (w.r.t abstractly tagged databases), within the class $\mathcal{C}$. Then for every equivalent query $Q' \in \mathcal{C}$, a non-abstractly-tagged database D and a tuple $t \in Q(D)$, $P(t, Q, D) \leq P(t, Q', D)$.*

In contrast, our results for direct provenance computation (Section 5) do not go through to non-abstractly-tagged database. We can show that such direct computation is impossible *without knowing the query*. Intuitively, this is because two occurrences of the same annotation can either come from the same tuple or different tuples.

THEOREM 6.2. *There exist a database D and a tuple t, for which there exist two non-equivalent queries Q, Q', such that $Const(Q) = Const(Q')$, $t \in Q(D) \cap Q'(D)$ and $P(t, Q, D) = P(t, Q', D)$, but $P(t, MinProv(Q), D) \neq P(t, MinProv(Q'), D)$.*

PROOF. Let D have a single relation R, with the tuples (a) and (b), both annotated with s and let t be (a). Consider the following queries:

$Q : ans(x) := R(x), R(y), x \neq y$
$Q' : ans(x) := R(x), R(x)$

The provenance of both queries is $P(t, Q, D) = P(t, Q', D) = s \cdot s$. It is easy to see that Q is p-minimal in $UCQ^{\neq}$ w.r.t. abstractly-tagged databases, thus by the above theorem, $P(t, Q, D) = P(t, MinProv(Q), D) = s \cdot s$. However, the p-minimal equivalent of Q', $MinProv(Q')$, is $ans(x) := R(x)$ (obtained by removing the duplicated atom) and thus $P(t, MinProv(Q'), D) = s \neq s \cdot s$. $\square$

7. RELATED WORK

Management of provenance information has been extensively studied in the database literature, in multiple branches. In [6, 12, 7, 4, 5] and other works, the authors define different provenance management techniques (e.g. Why Provenance [7], Trio Provenance [4]). In [19] the authors suggest the use of a *provenance semiring*, where provenance expressions are represented as polynomials detailing the computation of the different output tuples. [20] has shown that Trio provenance can be represented as polynomials with no exponents, while Why provenance is a set of sets and can be captured as a polynomial with no exponents or coefficients. Since the current paper focuses on the core computational processes, we found the model of provenance semirings best suited to our needs. We mention in this context that [5] studies problem of identifying "maximal" provenance, namely the (possibly infinite) union of all provenance expressions obtained for equivalent queries; in contrast we study here the "minimal" provenance, for provenance polynomials. Defining and studying "maximal" provenance for provenance polynomials is an interesting future research. Our analysis of "direct" identification of the core provenance (Section 5) also sheds light on the provenance polynomials obtained, and shows that there are some "core coefficients" in the polynomials, appearing in the provenance of tuples for every equivalent query. The core provenance is more minimal than Trio provenance: containing monomials are not omitted in Trio; core provenance also gives more details on the core *computation* than both Trio and Why Provenance, due to the coefficients reflecting this core computation (in Why provenance there are no coefficients, in Trio provenance the coefficients may be different among equivalent queries). As mentioned in the Introduction, provenance information is extensively used as input to various data management tools (e.g. trust assessment, update propagation [18, 25, 30, 29]). A particular challenge here arises from the size of provenance, both in terms of storage and efficiency of the operation of the tools [10, 27].

We believe that the identification of core provenance can be the basis of optimization techniques that reduce the size of the input given to these tools, helping to alleviate these challenges.

Query minimization in a "classic" sense, that aims at minimizing the number of joins has been well investigated for the different classes discussed here. Minimization of conjunctive queries was first suggested in [9], and was extended to union of conjunctive queries in [26]. Minimization of conjunctive queries with inequalities was studied in [22]. We have compared and contrasted our results with classic minimization for all of these classes, except that we restricted the discussion to queries with disequalities ($\neq$) instead of general inequalities ($<, \leq, ...$). Query inclusion and minimization were further studied for queries of various classes, for instance, aggregation, bag semantics and arithmetic comparisons [13, 14, 2, 8]; identifying the core provenance for queries of these classes, and for queries with general inequalities ($<, \leq, ...$), is an interesting future work. Practically efficient heuristics (e.g. [28, 11]) are known for "standard" minimization of queries. For CQ queries, such algorithms will also serve as heuristics for p-minimization; for other classes their adaptation to p-minimization is an intriguing challenge.

Last, we note that our reference to the minimal provenance as "core provenance" was inspired by the notion of core of universal solutions in Data Exchange [16, 3, 15, 24], with the intuition that the core provenance be a part of the computational process, for every "solution". Studying the connection between the core in data exchange and the core provenance is an interesting future research.

8. CONCLUSIONS

We have studied in this paper the core of provenance information, namely the part of provenance that appears in the result of evaluating every query equivalent to the query in hand. We have considered query classes of varying expressive power, and studied the problem of computing an equivalent query that realizes the provenance core for the query in hand, and for every input database instance. We have analyzed the existence of such a query in the different classes, and have given algorithms for computing it where it exists. We have further presented algorithms that compute the core provenance directly from the provenance information of tuples in the query result, and showed its applicability even for cases when the input query is absent.

In the previous section we have mentioned several intriguing research directions such as exploiting the compact size of the core provenance for practical applications, and studying the nature of core provenance in the presence of additional query constructs. Due to the importance of provenance in general, and of provenance polynomials in particular, we believe them to be promising subjects for future work. Additionally, we have restricted our study to Conjunctive Queries with disequalities, and unions thereof. Considering provenance minimization for more expressive query languages, e.g. Datalog, is an additional further research challenge. Last, we note that different *physical query plans* for the same query may result in different provenance, and finding the p-minimal among those is an intriguing research challenge.

Acknowledgements. We are grateful to Georg Gottlob for providing us with a counter-example for non-unique minimal query for $CQ^{\neq}$, which helped us to prove the non-existence of a p-minimal query for this class (Theorem 3.5 and Lemma 3.8). We are also grateful to the anonymous reviewers of PODS for their comments that have helped to improve the final version of this paper.

9. REFERENCES

[1] S. Abiteboul, R. Hull, and V. Vianu. *Foundations of Databases.* Addison-Wesley, 1995.

[2] F. N. Afrati, C. Li, and P. Mitra. On containment of conjunctive queries with arithmetic comparisons. In *EDBT*, 2004.

[3] M. Arenas, P. Barceló, L. Libkin, and F. Murlak. *Relational and XML Data Exchange.* Synthesis Lectures on Data Management. Morgan & Claypool Publishers, 2010.

[4] O. Benjelloun, A.D. Sarma, A.Y. Halevy, M. Theobald, and J. Widom. Databases with uncertainty and lineage. *VLDB J.*, 17:243–264, 2008.

[5] Deepavali Bhagwat, Laura Chiticariu, Wang-Chiew Tan, and Gaurav Vijayvargiya. An annotation management system for relational databases. In *VLDB*, 2004.

[6] P. Buneman, J. Cheney, and S. Vansummeren. On the expressiveness of implicit provenance in query and update languages. *ACM Trans. Database Syst.*, 33(4), 2008.

[7] P. Buneman, S. Khanna, and W.C. Tan. Why and where: A characterization of data provenance. In *ICDT*, 2001.

[8] D. Calvanese, G. De Giacomo, and M. Lenzerini. On the decidability of query containment under constraints. In *PODS*, 1998.

[9] A. K. Chandra and P. M. Merlin. Optimal implementation of conjunctive queries in relational data bases. In *STOC*, 1977.

[10] A. Chapman, H. V. Jagadish, and P. Ramanan. Efficient provenance storage. In *SIGMOD Conference*, 2008.

[11] C. Chekuri and A. Rajaraman. Conjunctive query containment revisited. In *ICDT*, 1997.

[12] J. Cheney, S. Chong, N. Foster, M. I. Seltzer, and S. Vansummeren. Provenance: a future history. In *Proc. of OOPSLA*, 2009.

[13] S. Cohen. Equivalence of queries combining set and bag-set semantics. In *PODS*, pages 70–79, 2006.

[14] S. Cohen, W. Nutt, and Y. Sagiv. Rewriting queries with arbitrary aggregation functions using views. *ACM Trans. Database Syst.*, 31(2):672–715, 2006.

[15] G. De Giacomo, D. Lembo, M. Lenzerini, and R. Rosati. On reconciling data exchange, data integration, and peer data management. In *PODS*, 2007.

[16] R. Fagin, P.G. Kolaitis, and L. Popa. Data exchange: getting to the core. *ACM Trans. Database Syst.*, 30:174–210, 2005.

[17] G. Gottlob, 2010. private communication.

[18] T. J. Green, G. Karvounarakis, Z. Ives, and V. Tannen. Update exchange with mappings and provenance. In *VLDB*, 2007.

[19] T. J. Green, G. Karvounarakis, and V. Tannen. Provenance semirings. In *Proc. of PODS*, 2007.

[20] T.J. Green. Containment of conjunctive queries on annotated relations. In *ICDT*, 2009.

[21] G. Karvounarakis and V. Tannen. Conjunctive queries and mappings with unequalities. Technical report, 2008.

[22] A. Klug. On conjunctive queries containing inequalities. *J. ACM*, 35(1), 1988.

[23] W. Kuich. Semirings and formal power series. In *Handbook of Formal Languages*, 1997.

[24] L. Libkin and C. Sirangelo. Open and closed world assumptions in data exchange. In *Description Logics*, 2009.

[25] A. Meliou, W. Gatterbauer, K. F. Moore, and D. Suciu. The complexity of causality and responsibility for query answers and non-answers. *PVLDB*, 4(1), 2010.

[26] Y. Sagiv and M. Yannakakis. Equivalences among relational expressions with the union and difference operators. *J. ACM*, 27(4):633–655, 1980.

[27] Y. L. Simmhan, B. Plale, and D. Gannon. A survey of data provenance in e-science. *SIGMOD Rec.*, 34, September 2005.

[28] I. Tatarinov and A. Halevy. Efficient query reformulation in peer data management systems. In *SIGMOD*, 2004.

[29] S. Vansummeren and J. Cheney. Recording provenance for sql queries and updates. *IEEE Data Eng. Bull.*, 30(4):29–37, 2007.

[30] W. Zhou, M. Sherr, T. Tao, X. Li, B. T. Loo, and Y. Mao. Efficient querying and maintenance of network provenance at internet-scale. In *SIGMOD Conference*, 2010.

Provenance for Aggregate Queries *

Yael Amsterdamer
Tel Aviv University
and University of Pennsylvania
yaelamst@post.tau.ac.il

Daniel Deutch
Ben Gurion University
and University of Pennsylvania
deutchd@cs.bgu.ac.il

Val Tannen
University of Pennsylvania
val@cis.upenn.edu

ABSTRACT

We study in this paper provenance information for queries with *aggregation*. Provenance information was studied in the context of various query languages that do not allow for aggregation, and recent work has suggested to capture provenance by annotating the different database tuples with elements of a *commutative semiring* and propagating the annotations through query evaluation. We show that aggregate queries pose novel challenges rendering this approach inapplicable. Consequently, we propose a new approach, where we annotate with provenance information not just tuples but also the *individual values* within tuples, using provenance to describe the values computation. We realize this approach in a concrete construction, first for "simple" queries where the aggregation operator is the last one applied, and then for arbitrary (positive) relational algebra queries with aggregation; the latter queries are shown to be more challenging in this context. Finally, we use aggregation to encode queries with *difference*, and study the semantics obtained for such queries on provenance annotated databases.

Categories and Subject Descriptors

H.2.1 [**Database Management**]: [Data Models]

General Terms

Algorithms, Theory

1. INTRODUCTION

The annotation of the results of database transformations with provenance information has quite a few applications [17, 4, 36, 9, 10, 38, 35, 23, 25, 39, 27, 2]. Recent work [22, 15, 19] has proposed a framework of *semiring annotations* that allows us to state formally what is expected of such provenance information. These papers have developed the framework for the positive fragment of the relational algebra (as well as for Datalog, the positive Nested Relational Calculus, and some query languages on trees/XML). The main goal of this paper is to extend the framework to *aggregate operations*.

R

EmpId	*Dept*	*Sal*	
1	d_1	20	p_1
2	d_1	10	p_2
3	d_1	15	p_3
4	d_2	10	r_1
5	d_2	15	r_2

(*a*)

Dept	
d_1	$p_1 + p_2 + p_3$
d_2	$r_1 + r_2$

(*b*)

Figure 1: Projection on annotated relations

In the perspective promoted by these papers, *provenance* is a general form of annotation information that can be specialized for different purposes, such as multiplicity, trust, cost, security, or identification of "possible worlds" which in turn applies to incomplete databases, deletion propagation, and probabilistic databases. In fact, the introduction of the framework in [22] was motivated by the need to track trust and deletion propagation in the Orchestra system [21]. What makes such a diversity of applications possible is that each is captured by a different semiring, while provenance is represented by elements of a semiring of *polynomials*. One then relies on the property that any semiring-annotation semantics *factors* through the provenance polynomials semantics. This means that storing provenance polynomials allows for many other practical applications. For example, to capture access control, where the access to different tuples require different security credentials, we can simply evaluate the polynomials in the *security semiring*, and propagate the security annotations through query evaluation (see Section 2.1), assigning security levels to query results.

Let us briefly illustrate *deletion propagation* as an application of provenance. Consider a simple example of an employee/department/salary relation R shown in Figure 1(a).

The variables p_1, p_2, p_3, r_1, r_2 can be thought of as tuple identifiers and in the framework of *provenance polynomials* [22] they are the "provenance tokens" or "indeterminates" out of which provenance is built. We denote by $\mathbb{N}[X]$ the set of provenance polynomials (here $X = \{p_1, p_2, p_3, r_1, r_2\}$). R can be seen as an $\mathbb{N}[X]$-annotated relation; as defined in [22] the evaluation of query, for example $\Pi_{Dept}R$, produces another $\mathbb{N}[X]$-annotated relation, in this example the one shown in Figure 1(b). Intuitively, in this simple example,

*This work has been partially funded by the NSF grant IIS-0629846, the NSF grant IIS-0803524, and by the ERC grant Webdam under agreement 226513.

PODS'11, June 13–15, 2011, Athens, Greece.

Dept	SalMass	
d_1	45	$p_1 p_2 p_3$
d_1	30	$p_1 p_2 \widehat{p_3}$
d_1	35	$p_1 \widehat{p_2} p_3$
d_1	25	$\widehat{p_1} p_2 p_3$
d_1	20	$p_1 \widehat{p_2} \widehat{p_3}$
d_1	10	$\widehat{p_1} p_2 \widehat{p_3}$
d_1	15	$\widehat{p_1} \widehat{p_2} p_3$
...	...	...

(a)

Dept	SalMass	
d_1	30	$p_1 p_2$
d_1	20	$p_1 \widehat{p_2}$
d_1	10	$\widehat{p_1} p_2$
...	...	...

(b)

Figure 2: A naive approach to aggregation

the summation in the annotation of every result tuple is over the identifiers of its alternative origins [1].

Now, the result of propagating the deletions of tuples with *EmpId* 3 and 5 in R is obtained by simply setting $p_3 = r_2 = 0$ in the answer. We get the same two tuples in the query answer but their provenances change to $p_1 + p_2$ and r_1, respectively. If the tuple with *EmpId* 4 is also deleted from R then we also set $r_1 = 0$, and the second tuple in the answer is deleted because its provenance has now become 0. This algebraic treatment of deletions is related to the counting algorithm for view maintenance [24], but is more general as it incrementally maintains not just the data but also the provenance.

An intuitive way of understanding what happens is that provenance-aware evaluation of queries conveniently "commutes" with deletions. In fact, in [22, 15] this intuition is captured formally by theorems that state that query evaluation commutes with semiring homomorphisms. The factorization through provenance relies on this and on the fact that the polynomial provenance semiring is "freely generated". All applications of provenance polynomials we have listed, for trust, security, etc., are based on these theorems.

Thus, commutation with homomorphisms is an essential criterion for our proposed framework extension to aggregate operations. However, in Section 3.1 we prove that the framework of semiring-annotated relations introduced in [22] cannot be extended to handle aggregation while both satisfying commutation with homomorphisms and working as usual on set or bag relations.

If the semiring operations are not enough then perhaps we can add others? This is a natural idea so we illustrate it on the same R in Figure 1(a) and we use again the necessity to support deletion propagation to guide the approach. Consider the query that groups by *Dept* and sums *Sal*. The result of the summation depends on which tuples participate in it. To provide enough information to obtain all the possible summation results for all possible sets of deletions, we could use the representation in Figure 2(a) where we add to the semiring operations an unary operation $\widehat{}$ with the property that $\widehat{p} = 1$ whenever $p = 0$. This will indeed satisfy the deletion criterion. For example when the tuple with *Id* 3 is deleted we get the relation in Figure 2(b). In fact, there exist semirings with the additional structure needed to define $\widehat{}$. For example in the semiring of polynomials with *integer* coefficients, $\mathbb{Z}[X]$, we can take $\widehat{p} = 1 - p$ while in the semiring of boolean expressions with variables from X, BoolExp(X), we can take $\widehat{p} = \neg p$. The latter is essentially the approach taken in [32]. However, whether we use $\mathbb{Z}[X]$

or BoolExp(X), we still have, in the worst case, *exponentially many different results* to account for, at least in the case of summation (a lower bound recognized also in [32]). It follows that summation in particular (and therefore any uniform approach to aggregation) cannot be represented with a feasible amount of annotation as long as the annotation stays at the tuple level.

Instead, we will present a provenance representation for aggregation results that leads only to a *poly-size increase* with respect to the size of the input database, one that we believe is tractably implementable using methods similar to the ones used in Orchestra [21]. We achieve this via a more radical approach: we annotate with provenance information not just the tuples of the answer but also *the manner in which the values in those tuples are computed*.

We can gain intuition towards our representation from the particular case of bags, which are in fact $\mathbb{N}$-relations, i.e., relations whose tuples are annotated with elements of the semiring $(\mathbb{N}, +, \cdot, 0, 1)$. Assume that R in Figure 1(a) is such a relation, i.e., $p_1, \ldots, r_2 \in \mathbb{N}$ are tuple multiplicities. Then, after sum-aggregation the value of the attribute *SalMass* in the tuple with *Dept* d_1 is computed by $p_1 \times 20 + p_2 \times 10 + p_3 \times 15$. Now, if the multiplicities are, for example $p_1 = 2, p_2 = 3, p_3 = 1$ then the aggregate value is 85. But what if R is a relation annotated with provenance polynomials rather than multiplicities? Then, the aggregate value does not correspond to any number.

We will make $p_1 \times 20$ into an *abstract* construction, $p_1 \otimes 20$ and the aggregate value will be the formal expression $p_1 \otimes 20 + p_2 \otimes 10 + p_3 \otimes 15$.

Intuitively, we are embedding the domain of sum-aggregates, i.e., the reals $\mathbb{R}$, into a larger domain of formal expressions that capture how the sum-aggregates are computed from values annotated with provenance. We do the same for other kinds of aggregation, for instance min-aggregation gives $p_1 \otimes 20 \min p_2 \otimes 10 \min p_3 \otimes 15$. We call these *annotated aggregate* expressions.

In this paper we consider only aggregations defined by commutative-associative operations [2]. Specifically, our framework can accommodate aggregation based on any *commutative monoid*. For example the commutative monoid for summation is $(\mathbb{R}, +, 0)$ while the one for min is $(\mathbb{R}^\infty, \min, \infty)$ [3].

To combine an aggregation monoid M with an annotation semiring K, in a way capturing aggregates over K-relations, we propose the use of the algebraic structure of K-*semimodules* (see Section 2.2). Semimodules are a way of generalizing (a lot!) the operations considered in linear algebra. Its "vectors" form only a commutative monoid (rather than an abelian group) and its "scalars" are the elements of K which is only a commutative semiring (rather than a field).

In general, a commutative monoid M does not have an obvious structure of K-semimodule. To make it such we may need to add new elements corresponding to the scalar multiplication of elements of M with elements from K, thus ending up with the formal expressions that represent aggregate computations, motivated above, as elements of a *tensor product* construction $K \otimes M$. We show that the use of tensor product expressions as a formal representation of aggrega-

---

[1] We explain how the annotations of query results are computed in Section 2.1

[2] As shown in [33], for list collections it also makes sense to consider non-commutative aggregations.

[3] K-annotated relations with *union* (see Section 2.1) also form such a structure.

tion result is effective in managing the provenance of "simple aggregate" queries, namely queries where the aggregation operators are the last ones applied.

We show that certain semirings are "compatible" with certain monoids, in the sense that the results of computation done in $K \otimes M$ may be mapped to M, faithfully representing the aggregation results. Interestingly, compatibility is aligned with common wisdom: it is known that some (idempotent) aggregation functions such as MIN and MAX work well for set relations, while SUM and PROD require the treatment of relations as bags. We show that non-idempotent monoids are compatible only with "bag" semirings, from which there exists an homomorphism to $\mathbb{N}$.

In general, aggregation results may be used by the query as the input to further operators, such as value-based joins or selections. Here the formal representation of values leads to a difficulty: the truth values of comparison operators on such formal expressions is undetermined! Consequently, we extend our framework and construct semirings in which formal comparison expressions between elements of the corresponding semimodule are elements of the semiring. This means that an expression like $[p_1 \otimes 20 = p_2 \otimes 10 + p_3 \otimes 15]$ may be used as part of the provenance of a tuples in the join result. This expression is simply treated as a new provenance token (with constraints), until p_1, p_2, p_3 are assigned e.g. values from $\mathbb{B}$ or $\mathbb{N}$, in which case we can interpret both sides of the equality as elements of the monoid and determine the truth value of the equality (see Section 4). We show in Section 4 that this construction allows us to manage provenance information for arbitrary queries with aggregation, while *keeping the representation size polynomial in the size of the input database*.

We note in this context that provenance expressions are inherently large and it may be difficult for humans to read and understand them. In this paper we will present simple examples that are human-readable, to ease the understanding of the introduced concepts. However, in general, the provenance expressions that we will introduce are mainly intended for automated processing. Presenting it to human users is the role of a provenance query language that takes these expressions as input, such as in [28].

The main result of this paper is providing, for the first time, a semantics for aggregation (including group by) on semiring-annotated relations that:

- Coincides with the usual semantics on set/bag relations for min/max/sum/prod.

- Commutes with homomorphisms of semirings

- Is representable with only poly-size overhead with respect to the database size.

A second result of this paper is a new semantics for *difference* on relations annotated with elements from *any* commutative semiring. This is done via an encoding of relational difference using nested aggregation. The fact that such an encoding can be done is known (see e.g. [29, 8]), but combined with our provenance framework, the encoding gives a semantics for "provenance-aware" difference. Our new semantics for $R - S$ is a hybrid of bag-style and set-style semantics, in the sense that tuples of R that appear in S do not appear in $R - S$ (i.e. a boolean negative condition is used), while those that do not appear in S appear in $R - S$ with the same annotation (multiplicity, if $K = \mathbb{N}$ is used) that they had in R.

This makes the semantics different from the bag-monus semantics and its generalization to "monus-semirings" in [17] as well as from the "negative multiplicities" semantics in [20] (more discussion in Section 6). We examine the equational laws entailed by this new semantics, in contrast to those of previously proposed semantics for difference. In our opinion, this semantics is probably not the last word on difference of annotated relations, but we hope that it will help inform and calibrate future work on the topic.

Paper Organization. The rest of the paper is organized as follows. Section 2 describes and exemplifies the main mathematical ingredients used throughout the paper. Section 3 describes our proposed framework for "simple" aggregation queries, and this framework is extended in Section 4 to nested aggregation queries. We consider difference queries in Section 5. Related Work is discussed in Section 6, and we conclude in Section 7.

2. PRELIMINARIES

We provide in this section the algebraic foundations that will be used throughout the paper. We start by recalling the notion of semiring and its use in [22] to capture provenance for the SPJU algebra queries. We then consider aggregates, and show the new algebraic construction that is required to accurately support it.

2.1 Semirings and SPJU

We briefly review the basic framework introduced in [22]. A *commutative monoid* is an algebraic structure $(M, +_M, 0_M)$ where $+_M$ is an associative and commutative binary operation and 0_M is an identity for $+_M$. A monoid homomorphism is a mapping $h : M \to M'$ where M, M' are monoids, and $h(0_M) = 0_{M'}, h(a + b) = h(a) + h(b)$. We will consider database operations on relations whose tuples are annotated with elements from *commutative semirings*. These are structures $(K, +_K, \cdot_K, 0_K, 1_K)$ where $(K, +_K, 0_K)$ and $(K, \cdot_K, 1_K)$ are commutative monoids, $\cdot_K$ is distributive over $+_K$, and $a \cdot_K 0_K = 0 \cdot_K a = 0_K$. A semiring homomorphism is a mapping $h : K \to K'$ where K, K' are semirings, and $h(0_K) = 0_{K'}, h(1_K) = 1_{K'}, h(a + b) = h(a) + h(b), h(a \cdot b) = h(a) \cdot h(b)$. Examples of commutative semirings are any commutative ring (of course) but also any distributive lattice, hence any boolean algebra. Examples of particular interest to us include the boolean semiring $(\mathbb{B}, \vee, \wedge, \bot, \top)$ (for usual set semantics), the natural numbers semiring $(\mathbb{N}, +, \cdot, 0, 1)$ (its elements are multiplicities, i.e., annotations that give bag semantics), and the *security* semiring $(\mathbb{S}, \min, \max, 0_S, 1_S)$ where $\mathbb{S}$ is the ordered set, $1_S < C < S < T < 0_S$ whose elements have the following meaning when used as annotations: 1_S : public ("always available"), C : confidential, S : secret, T : top secret, and 0_S means "never available".

Certain semirings play an essential role in capturing provenance information. Given a set X of *provenance tokens* which correspond to "atomic" provenance information, e.g., tuple identifiers, the semiring of *polynomials* $(\mathbb{N}[X], +, \cdot, 0, 1)$ was shown in [22] to adequately, and most generally, capture provenance for positive relational queries. The *provenance interpretation* of the semiring structure is the following. The $+$ operation on annotations corresponds to *alternative use* of data, the $\cdot$ operation to *joint use* of data, 1 annotates data that is always and unrestrictedly available, and 0 annotates absent data. The definition of the K-relational algebra (see bellow for union, projection and join) fits indeed this interpretation. Algebraically, $\mathbb{N}[X]$ is the commutative semiring freely generated by X, i.e., for any other commutative semiring K, any valuation of the provenance tokens $X \to K$ extends uniquely to a semiring homomorphism $\mathbb{N}[X] \to K$ (an evaluation in K of the polynomials). We say that any semiring annotation semantics *factors* through the provenance polynomials semantics, which means that for practical purposes storing provenance information suffices for many other applications too. Other semirings can also be used to capture certain forms of provenance, albeit less generally than $\mathbb{N}[X]$ [22, 19]. For example, boolean expressions capture enough provenance to serve in the intensional semantics of queries on incomplete [26] and probabilistic data [16, 40].

To define annotated relations we use here the named perspective of the relational model [1]. Fix a countably infinite *domain* $\mathbb{D}$ of values (constants). For any finite set U of attributes a tuple is a function $t : U \to \mathbb{D}$ and we denote the set of all such possible tuples by $\mathbb{D}^U$. Given a commutative semiring K, a K-*relation* (with schema U) is a function $R : \mathbb{D}^U \to K$ whose *support*, $\mathrm{supp}(R) = \{t \mid R(t) \neq 0_K\}$ is *finite*. For a fixed set of attributes U we denote by K-Rel (when U is clear from the context) the set of K-relations with schema U. We also define a K-*set* to be a function $S : \mathbb{D} \to K$ again of finite support. We then define:

Union If $R_i : \mathbb{D}^U \to K$, $i = 1, 2$ then $R_1 \cup_K R_2 : \mathbb{D}^U \to K$ is defined by $(R_1 \cup_K R_2)(t) = R_1(t) +_K R_2(t)$. The definition of union of K-sets follows similarly.

We also define the *empty* K-relation (K-set) by $\emptyset_K(t) = 0_K$. It is easy to see that $(K\text{-Rel}, \cup_K, \emptyset_K)$ is a commutative monoid [4]. Similarly, we get the commutative monoid of K-sets $(K\text{-Set}, \cup_K, \emptyset_K)$.

Given a named relational schema, K-databases are defined from K-relations just as relational databases are defined from usual relations, and in fact the usual (set semantics) databases correspond to the particular case $K = \mathbb{B}$. The (positive) K-*relational algebra* defined in [22] corresponds to a semantics on K-databases for the usual operations of the relational algebra. We have already defined the semantics of union above and we give here just two other cases referring the reader to [22] for the rest (for a tuple t and an attributes set U', $t|_{U'}$ is the restriction of t to U'):

Projection If $R : \mathbb{D}^U \to K$ and $U' \subseteq U$ then $\Pi_{U'} R : \mathbb{D}^{U'} \to K$ is defined by $(\Pi_{U'} R)(t) = \sum_K R(t')$ where the $+_K$ sum is over all $t' \in \mathrm{supp}(R)$ such that $t'|_{U'} = t$.

Natural Join If $R_i : \mathbb{D}^{U_i} \to K$, $i = 1, 2$ then $R_1 \bowtie R2 : \mathbb{D}^{U_1 \cup U_2} \to K$ is defined by $(R_1 \bowtie R_2)(t) = R_1(t_1) \cdot_K R_2(t_2)$ where $t_i = t|_{U_i}$, $i = 1, 2$.

2.2 Semimodules and aggregates

We will consider aggregates defined by commutative monoids. Some examples are SUM $= (\mathbb{R}, +, 0)$ for summation [5], MIN $= (\mathbb{R}^{\pm\infty}, \min, +\infty)$ for min, MAX $= (\mathbb{R}^{\pm\infty}, \max, -\infty)$ for max, and PROD $= (\mathbb{R}, \times, 1)$ for product.

In dealing with aggregates we have to extend the operation of a commutative monoid to operations on relations

---

[4]In fact, it also has a semiring structure.
[5]COUNT is particular case of summation and AVG is obtained from summation and COUNT.

annotated with elements of semirings. This interaction will be captured by *semimodules*.

DEFINITION 2.1. *Given a commutative semiring K, a structure $(W, +_W, 0_W, *_W)$ is a K-semimodule if $(W, +_W, 0_W)$ is a commutative monoid and $*_W$ is a binary operation $K \times W \to W$ such that (for all $k, k_1, k_2 \in K$ and $w, w_1, w_2 \in W$):*

$$k *_W (w_1 +_W w_2) = k *_W w_1 +_W k *_W w_2 \quad (1)$$
$$k *_W 0_W = 0_W \quad (2)$$
$$(k_1 +_K k_2) *_W w = k_1 *_W w +_W k_2 *_W w \quad (3)$$
$$0_K *_W w = 0_W \quad (4)$$
$$(k_1 \cdot_K k_2) *_W w = k_1 *_W (k_2 *_W w) \quad (5)$$
$$1_K *_W w = w \quad (6)$$

In any (commutative) monoid $(M, +_M, 0_M)$ define for any $n \in \mathbb{N}$ and $x \in M$

$$nx = x +_M \cdots +_M x \quad (n \text{ times})$$

in particular $0x = 0_M$. Thus M has a canonical structure of $\mathbb{N}$-semimodule. Moreover, it is easy to check that a commutative monoid M is a $\mathbb{B}$-semimodule if and only if its operation is *idempotent*: $x +_M x = x$. The K-relations themselves form a K-semimodule $(K\text{-Rel}, \cup_K, \emptyset_K, *_K)$ where $(k *_K R)(t) = k \cdot_K R(t)$ [6].

We now show, for any K-semimodule W, how to define W-*aggregation* of a K-set of elements from W. We assume that $W \subseteq \mathbb{D}$ and that we have just one attribute, whose values are all from W. Consider the K-set S such that $\mathrm{supp}(S) = \{w_1, \ldots, w_n\}$ and $S(w_i) = k_i \in K, i = 1, \ldots, n$ (i.e., each w_i is annotated with k_i). Then, the result of W-aggregating S is defined as

$$\mathrm{SetAgg}_W(S) = k_1 *_W w_1 +_W \cdots +_W k_n *_W w_n \in W$$

For the empty K-set we define $\mathrm{SetAgg}_W(\emptyset_K) = 0_W$. Clearly, SetAgg_W is a *semimodule homomorphism* [7]. Since all commutative monoids are $\mathbb{N}$-semimodules this gives the usual sum, prod, min, and max aggregations on bags. Since MIN and MAX are $\mathbb{B}$-semimodules this gives the usual min and max aggregation on sets [8].

Note that SetAgg is an operation on sets, not an operation on relations. In the sequel we show how to extend it to one.

2.3 A tensor product construction

More generally, we want to investigate M-aggregation on K-relations where M is a commutative monoid and K is some commutative semiring. Since M may not have enough elements to represent K-annotated aggregations we construct a K-semimodule in which M can be embedded, by transferring to semimodules the basic idea behind a standard algebraic construction, as follows.

Let K be any commutative semiring and M be any commutative monoid. We start with $K \times M$, denote its elements $k \otimes m$ instead of $\langle k, m \rangle$ and call them "simple tensors". Next we consider (finite) bags of such simple tensors, which, with

---

[6]In fact, it is the K semimodule freely generated by $\mathbb{D}^U$.
[7]In fact, it is the free homomorphism determined by the identity function on W.
[8]The fact that the right algebraic structure to use for aggregates is that of *semimodules* can be justified in the same way in which using semirings was justified in [22]: by showing how the laws of semimodules follow from desired equivalences between aggregation queries.

bag union and the empty bag, form a commutative monoid. It will be convenient to denote bag union by $+_{K \otimes M}$, the empty bag by $0_{K \otimes M}$ and to abuse notation denoting singleton bags by the unique element they contain. Then, every non-empty bag of simple tensors can be written (repeating summands by multiplicity) $k_1 \otimes m_1 +_{K \otimes M} \cdots +_{K \otimes M} k_n \otimes m_n$. Now we define

$$k *_{K \otimes M} \sum k_i \otimes m_i = \sum (k \cdot_K k_i) \otimes m_i$$

Let $\sim$ be the smallest congruence w.r.t. $+_{K \otimes M}$ and $*_{K \otimes M}$ that satisfies (for all k, k', m, m'):

$$
\begin{aligned}
(k +_K k') \otimes m &\sim k \otimes m +_{K \otimes M} k' \otimes m \\
0_K \otimes m &\sim 0_{K \otimes M} \\
k \otimes (m +_M m') &\sim k \otimes m +_{K \otimes M} k \otimes m' \\
k \otimes 0_M &\sim 0_{K \otimes M}
\end{aligned}
$$

We denote by $K \otimes M$ the set of *tensors* i.e., equivalence classes of bags of simple tensors modulo $\sim$. We can show that $K \otimes M$ forms a K-semimodule.

Lifting homomorphisms. Given a homomorphism of semirings $h : K \to K'$, and some commutative monoid M, we can "lift" h to a homomorphism of monoids in a natural way. The lifted homomorphism is denoted $h^M : K \otimes M \to K' \otimes M$ and defined by:

$$h^M(\sum k_i \otimes m_i) = \sum h(k_i) \otimes m_i$$

3. SIMPLE AGGREGATION QUERIES

In this section we begin our study of the "provenance-aware" evaluation of aggregate queries, focusing on "simple" such queries, that is, queries in which aggregations are done last; for example, un-nested SELECT FROM WHERE GROUP BY queries. This avoids the need to compare values which are the result of annotated aggregations and simplifies the treatment. The restriction is relaxed in the more general framework presented in Section 4.

The section is organized as follows. We list the desired features of a provenance-aware semantics for aggregation, and first try to design a semantics with these features, *without* using the tensor product construction, i.e. by simply working with K-relations as done in [22]. We show that this is impossible. Consequently, we turn to semantics that are based on combining aggregation with values via the tensor product construction. We propose such semantics that do satisfy the desired features, first for relational algebra with an additional AGG operator on relations (that allows aggregation of all values in a chosen attributes, but no grouping); and then for GROUP BY queries.

3.1 Semantic desiderata and first attempts

We next explain the desired features of a provenance-aware semantics for aggregation. To illustrate the difficulties and the need for a more complex construction, we will first attempt to define a semantics on K-relations, without using the tensor product construction of Section 2.3.

We consider a commutative semiring K (e.g., $\mathbb{B}, \mathbb{N}, \mathbb{N}[X], \mathbb{S}$, etc.) for tuple annotations and a commutative monoid M (e.g., $\text{SUM} = (\mathbb{R}, +, 0), \text{PROD} = (\mathbb{R}, \times, 1), \text{MAX} = (\mathbb{R}^{-\infty}, \max, -\infty), \text{MIN} = (\mathbb{R}^{\infty}, \min, \infty)$ etc.) for aggregation. We will assume that the elements of M already belong to the database domain, $M \subseteq \mathbb{D}$.

We have recalled the semantics of SPJU queries in Section 2.1. Now we wish to add an M-aggregation operation AGG on relations. We then denote by SPJU-A the restricted class of queries consisting of any SPJU-expression followed possibly by just one application of AGG. This corresponds to SELECT AGG(*) FROM WHERE queries (no grouping).

For the moment, we do not give a concrete semantics to $\text{AGG}_M(R)$, allowing any possible semantics where the result of $\text{AGG}_M(R)$ is a K-relation. We note that $\text{AGG}_M(R)$ should be defined iff R is a K-relation with one attribute whose values are in M.

What properties do we expect of a reasonable semantics for SPJU-A (including, of course, a semantics for $\text{AGG}_M(R)$)? A basic sanity check is

Set/Bag Compatibility The semantics coincides with the usual one when $K = \mathbb{B}$ (sets) and $M = \text{MAX}$ or MIN, and when $K = \mathbb{N}$ (bags) and $M = \text{SUM}$ or PROD.

Note that we associate min and max with sets and sum and product with bags. Min and max work fine with bags too, but we get the same result if we convert a bag to a set (eliminate duplicates) and then apply them. Sum and product (in the context of other operations such as projection) require us to use bags semantics in order to work properly. This is well-known, but our general approach sheds further light on the issue by discussing such "compatibility" for arbitrary semirings and monoids in Section 3.4.

As discussed in the introduction, a fundamental desideratum with many applications is *commutation with homomorphisms*. Note that a semiring homomorphism $h : K \to K'$ naturally extends to a mapping $h_{Rel} : K\text{-Rel} \to K'\text{-Rel}$ via $h_{Rel}(R) = h \circ R$ (i.e. the homomorphism is applied on the annotation of every tuple), which then further extends to K-databases. With this, the second desired property is

Commutation with Homomorphisms Given any two commutative semirings K, K' and any homomorphism $h : K \to K'$, for any query Q, its semantics on K-databases and on K'-databases satisfy $h_{Rel}(Q(D)) = Q(h_{Rel}(D))$ for any K-database D.

It turns out that this property determines quite precisely the way in which tuple annotations are defined. We say that the semantics of an operation Ω on K-databases is *algebraically uniform* with respect to the class of commutative semirings if the annotations of the output $\Omega(D)$ are defined by the same (for all K) $\{+_K, \cdot_K, 0_K, 1_K\}$-expressions, where the elements in the expressions are the annotations of the input D. One can see that the definition of the SPJU-algebra is indeed algebraically uniform and was shown in [22, 15] to commute with homomorphisms. The connection between the two properties is general:

PROPOSITION 3.1. *A semantics commutes with homomorphisms iff it is algebraically uniform.*

After stating two of the desired properties, namely set/bag compatibility and commutation with homomorphisms we can already show that it is not possible to give a satisfactory semantics to the SPJU-A algebra within the framework used in [22] for the SPJU-algebra.

PROPOSITION 3.2. *There is no K-relation semantics for MAX-(or MIN-)aggregation that is both set-compatible and* *commutes with homomorphisms. Similarly, there is no K-relation semantics for SUM-aggregation that is both bag-compatible and commutes with homomorphisms.*

Alternatively, one may consider going beyond semirings, to algebraic structures with additional operations. We have briefly explored the use of "negative" information in the introduction. As we show there, one could use the ring structure on $\mathbb{Z}[X]$ (the additional subtraction operation) or the boolean algebra structure on $\text{BoolExp}(X)$ (the additional complement operation) but the use of negative operation does not avoid the need to enumerate in separate tuples of the answer all the possible aggregation results given by subsets of the input. In the case of summation, at least, there are exponentially many such tuples. We reject such an approach and we state as an additional desideratum:

Poly-Size Overhead For any query Q and database D, the size of $Q(D)$, including annotations, should be only polynomial in the size of the databse D.

We shall next show a semantics to the SPJU-A -algebra that satisfies all three properties we have listed.

3.2 Annotations ⊗ values and SPJU-A

Let us fix a commutative monoid M (for aggregation) and a commutative semiring K (for annotation). The *inputs* of our queries are, as before, K-databases whose domain $\mathbb{D}$ includes the values M over which we aggregate. However, the outputs are more complicated. The basic idea for the semantics of aggregation was already shown in Section 2.2 where it is assumed that the domain of aggregation has a K-semimodule structure. As we have shown in Section 2.3, we can give a tensor product construction that embeds M in the K-semimodule $K \otimes M$ (note that this embedding is not always *faithful*, as discussed in Section 3.4).

For the output relations of our algebra queries, we thus need results of aggregation (i.e., the elements of $K \otimes M$) to also be part of the domain out of which the tuples are constructed. Thus, for the output domain we will assume that $K \otimes M \subseteq \mathbb{D}$, i.e. the result "combines annotations with values". The elements of M (e.g., real numbers for sum or max aggregation) are still present, but only via the embedding $\iota : M \to K \otimes M$ defined by $\iota(m) = 1_K \otimes m$.

Having annotations from K appear in the values will change the way in which we apply homomorphisms to query results, so to emphasize the change we will call (M, K)-*relations* the K-annotated relations over data domain $\mathbb{D}$ that includes $K \otimes M$. To summarize, the semantics of the SPJU-A -algebra will map databases of K-relations (with $M \subseteq \mathbb{D}$) to (M, K)-relations (with $K \otimes M \subseteq \mathbb{D}$).

As we define the semantics of the SPJU-A -algebra, we first note that for selection, projection, join and union the definition is the same as for the SPJU-algebra on K-databases. The last step of the query is aggregation, denoted $\text{AGG}_M(R)$, and is well-defined iff R is a K-relation with one attribute whose values are in the M subset of $\mathbb{D}$. To apply the definition that uses the semimodule structure (shown in Section 2.2), we convert R to an (M, K)-relation $\iota(R)$ by replacing each $m \in M$ with $\iota(m) = 1_K \otimes m \in K \otimes M$. Then, if $\text{supp}(R) = \{m_1, \ldots, m_{\tilde{n}}\}$ and $R(m_i) = k_i \in K, i = 1, \ldots, n$ (i.e., each m_i is annotated with k_i) we define $\text{AGG}_M(R)$ as a one-attribute relation, with one tuple, annotated with 1_K

whose content is $\text{SetAgg}_{K \otimes M}(\iota(R))$; the latter is equal to

$$k_1 *_{K \otimes M} \iota(m_1) +_{K \otimes M} \cdots +_{K \otimes M} k_n *_{K \otimes M} \iota(m_n)$$
$$= k_1 \otimes m_1 +_{K \otimes M} \cdots +_{K \otimes M} k_n \otimes m_n$$

We define the annotation of the only tuple in the output of AGG_M to be 1_K, since this tuple is always available. However, the *content* of this tuple does depend on R. For example, even when R is empty the output is not empty: by the semimodule laws, its content is $0_{K \otimes M} = \iota(0_M)$.

Commutation with Homomorphisms. We have explained in Section 2.3 how to lift a homomorphism $h : K \to K'$ to a homomorphism $h^M : K \otimes M \to K' \otimes M$. This allows us to lift h to a homomorphism h_{Rel} on (M, K)-*relations*, as follows. Let R be such a relation and recall that some values in R are elements of $K \otimes M$, and the annotations of these tuples are elements of K. Then $h_{Rel}(R)$ denotes the relation obtained from R by replacing every $k \in K$ with $h(k)$, and additionally replacing every $k \otimes M \in K \otimes M$ with $h^M(k \otimes m)$. All other values in R stay intact. Applying h_{Rel} on a (M, K)-database D amounts to applying h_{Rel} on each (M, K)-relation in D.

We can now state the main result for our SPJU-A -algebra:

THEOREM 3.3. *Let K, K' be semirings, $h : K \to K'$, Q an SPJU-A query and let M be a commutative monoid. For every (M, K)-database D, $Q(h_{Rel}(D)) = h_{Rel}(Q(D))$ if and only if h is a semiring homomorphism.*

The proof is by induction on the query structure, and is straightforward given that for the constructs of SPJU queries homomorphism commutation was shown in [22], while commutation for the new AGG_M construct follows directly from the definition.

EXAMPLE 3.4. *Consider the following $\mathbb{N}[X]$-relation R:*

Sal	
20	r_1
10	r_2
30	r_3

Let M be some commutative monoid, then $AGG_M(R)$ consist of a single tuple with value $r_1 \otimes 20 +_{K \otimes M} r_2 \otimes 10 +_{K \otimes M} r_3 \otimes 30$. The intuition is that this value captures multiple possible aggregation values, each of which may be obtained by mapping the r_i annotations to $\mathbb{N}$, standing for the multiplicity of the corresponding tuple. The commutation with homomorphism allows us to first evaluate the query and only then map the r_i's, changing directly the expression in the query result. For example, if $M = SUM$ and we map r_1 to $1, r_2$ to $0, r_3$ to 2, we obtain $1 \otimes 20 +_{K \otimes M} 2 \otimes 30 = 1 \otimes 20 +_{K \otimes M} 1 \otimes 30 +_{K \otimes M} 1 \otimes 30 = 1 \otimes 80$ (which corresponds to the M element 80). As another example, the commutation with homomorphisms allows us to propagate the deletion of the first tuple in R, by simply setting in the aggregation result $r_1 = 0$ (keeping the other annotations intact) and obtaining $2 \otimes 30 = (1 + 1) \otimes 30 = 1 \otimes 30 + 1 \otimes 30 = 1 \otimes (30 + 30) = 1 \otimes 60$.

We further demonstrate an application for *security*.

EXAMPLE 3.5. *Consider the following relation R, annotated by elements from the security semiring $\mathbb{S}$.*

Sal	
20	S
10	1_s
30	S

Recall (from Section 2.1) the order relation $1_s < C < S < T < 0_s$; a user with credentials cred *can only view tuples annotated with security level equal or less than* cred*. Now let $M = MAX$ and we obtain: $AGG_{MAX}(R) = S \otimes 20 +_{K \otimes M} 1_s \otimes 10 +_{K \otimes M} S \otimes 30 = S \otimes (20 +_{MAX} 30) + 1_s \otimes 10$ and we get $S \otimes 30 + 1_s \otimes 10$.*

Assume now that we wish to compute the query results as viewed by a user with security credentials cred*. A naive computation would delete from R all tuples that require higher credentials, and re-evaluate the query (which in general may be complex). But observe that the deletion of tuples is equivalent to applying to R a homomorphism that maps every annotation $t > $ cred to 0, and $t \leq $ cred to 1. Using homomorphism commutation we can do better by applying this homomorphism only on the result representation (namely $S \otimes 30 + 1_s \otimes 10$). For example, for a user with credentials C, we map S to 0 and 1_s to 1, and obtain $0 \otimes 30 + 1 \otimes 10 = 1 \otimes 10$; similarly for a user with credentials S we get $1 \otimes 30 + 1 \otimes 10 = 1 \otimes (30 +_{MAX} 10) = 1 \otimes 30$.*

We can show that the defined semantics fulfills the poly-size overhead property.

3.3 Group By

So far we have considered aggregation in a limited context, where the input relation contains a single attribute. In common cases, however, aggregation is used on arbitrary relations and in conjunction with grouping, so we next extend the algebra to handle such an operation. The idea behind the construction is quite simple: we separately group the tuples according to the values of their "group-by" attributes, and the aggregated values for each such group are computed similarly to the computation for the *AGG* operator. When considering the *annotation* of the aggregated tuple, we encounter a technical difficulty: we want this annotation to be equal 1_K if the input relation includes at least one tuple in the corresponding group, and 0_K otherwise (for intuition, consider the case of bag relations, in which the aggregated result can have at most multiplicity 1); we consequently enrich our structure to include an additional construct δ that will capture that, as follows:

DEFINITION 3.6. *A (commutative) δ-semiring is an algebraic structure $(K, +_K, \cdot_K, 0_K, 1_K, \delta_K)$ where $(K, +_K, \cdot_K, 0_K, 1_K)$ is a commutative semiring and $\delta_K : K \to K$ is a unary operation satisfying the "δ-laws" $\delta_K(0_K) = 0_K$ and $\delta_K(n1_K) = 1_K$ for all $n \geq 1$. If K and K' are δ-semirings then a homomorphism between them is a semiring homomorphism $h : K \to K'$, for which we have in addition $h(\delta_K(k)) = \delta_{K'}(h(k))$.*

The δ-laws completely determine $\delta_\mathbb{B}$ and $\delta_\mathbb{N}$. But they leave a lot of freedom for the definition of δ_K in other semirings; in particular for the security semiring, a reasonable choice for $\delta_\mathbb{S}$ is the identity function.

As with any equational axiomatization, we can construct the commutative δ-semiring *freely generated* by a set X, denoted $\mathbb{N}[X, \delta]$, by taking the quotient of the set of

$\{+, \cdot, 0, 1, \delta\}$-algebraic expressions by the congruence generated by the equational laws of commutative semirings and the δ-laws. For example, if e and e' are elements of $\mathbb{N}[X, \delta]$ (i.e., congruence classes of expressions given by some representatives) then $e +_{\mathbb{N}[X, \delta]} e'$ is the congruence class of the expression $e + e'$. The elements of $\mathbb{N}[X, \delta]$ are not standard polynomials but certain subexpressions can be put in polynomial form, for example $\delta(2 + 3xy^2)$ or $3 + 2\delta(x^2 + 2y)z^2$.

We are now ready to define the group by (denoted GB) operation; subsequently we exemplify its use, including in particular the role of δ:

DEFINITION 3.7. *Let R be a K-relation on set of attributes U, let $U' \subseteq U$ be a subset of attributes that will be grouped and $U'' \in U$ be the subset of attributes with values in M (to be aggregated). We assume that $U' \cap U'' = \emptyset$. For a tuple t, we define $T = \{t' \in supp(R) \mid \forall u \in U' \ t'(u) = t(u)\}$.*

We then define the aggregation result $R' = GB_{U', U''}(R)$ as follows:

$$R'(t) = \begin{cases} \delta_K \left(\Sigma_{t' \in T} R(t') \right) & T \neq \phi, \text{ and} \\ & \forall u \in U'' \ t(u) = \Sigma_{t' \in T} R(t') \otimes t'(u) \\ 0 & \text{Otherwise.} \end{cases}$$

EXAMPLE 3.8. *Consider the relation R:*

Dept	Sal	
d_1	20	r_1
d_1	10	r_2
d_2	10	r_3

and a query $GB_{\{Dept\}, Sal}R$, where the monoid used is SUM. The result (denoted R') is:

Dept	Sal	
d_1	$r_1 \otimes 20 +_{K \otimes SUM} r_2 \otimes 10$	$\delta_K(r_1 +_K r_2)$
d_2	$r_3 \otimes 10$	$\delta_K(r_3)$

Each aggregated value (for each department) is computed very similarly to the computation in Example 3.4. Consider the provenance annotation of the first tuple: intuitively, we expect it to be 1_K if at least one of the first two tuples of R exists, i.e. if at least one out of r_1 or r_2 is non-zero. Indeed the expression is $\delta(r_1 +_K r_2)$ and if we map r_1, r_2 to e.g. 2 and 1 respectively, we obtain $\delta_\mathbb{N}(3) = 1$.

We use SPJU-AGB as the name for relational algebra with the two new operators AGG and GB. We note that the poly-size overhead property (w.r.t. data complexity) is still fulfilled for queries in SPJU-AGB; commutation with homomorphism also extends to SPJU-AGB.

Recall that an additional desideratum from the semantics was bag / set compatibility. Recall that sets and bags are modeled by $K = \mathbb{N}$ and $K = \mathbb{B}$ respectively. We next study compatibility in a more general way, for arbitrary K and M.

3.4 Annotation-aggregation compatibility

The first desideratum we listed was an obvious sanity check: whatever semantics we define, when specialized to the familiar aggregates of max, min and summation, it should produce familiar results. Since we had to take an excursion through the tensor product $K \otimes M$, this familiarity is not immediate. However, the following proposition holds (its correctness will follow from theorems 3.12 and 3.13).

PROPOSITION 3.9. *In the following constructions:* $\mathbb{B} \otimes$
MAX, $\mathbb{B} \otimes MIN$, *and* $\mathbb{N} \otimes SUM$, $\iota : M \to K \otimes M$ *where*
$\iota(m) = 1_K \otimes m$ *is a monoid isomorphism.*

and this means our semantics satisfies the set/bag compatibility property because in these cases computing in $K \otimes M$ exactly mirrors computing in M.

But of course, we are also interested in working with other semirings, in particular the provenance semiring, for which $\mathbb{N}[X] \otimes M$ and M are in general not isomorphic (in particular, ι is not surjective and thus not an isomorphism). In fact, the whole point of working in $\mathbb{N}[X] \otimes$ MAX, for example, is to add annotated aggregate computations to the domain of values. Most of these do not correspond to actual real numbers as e.g. $\iota($MAX$)$ is a strict subset of $\mathbb{N}[X] \otimes$ MAX (and similarly $\iota($SUM$)$ is a strict subset of $\mathbb{N}[X] \otimes$ SUM etc.). However, when provenance tokens are valuated to obtain set (or bag) instances, we can go back into $\iota($MAX$)$ (or $\iota($SUM$)$ etc.), and then we should obtain familiar results by "stripping off" the ι. It turns out that this works correctly with $\mathbb{N}[X]$ but not necessarily with arbitrary commutative semirings K. this is because ι in general may be *unfaithful* (not injective). Indeed $\iota :$ SUM $\to \mathbb{B} \otimes$ SUM is not injective:

$$\iota(4) = \iota(2+2) = \iota(2) +_{K \otimes M} \iota(2) = \top \otimes 2 +_{K \otimes M} \top \otimes 2 =$$

$$= (\top \vee \top) \otimes 2 = \top \otimes 2 = \iota(2)$$

This is not surprising, as it is related to the well-known difficulty of making summation work properly with set semantics. In general, we thus define compatibility as follows:

DEFINITION 3.10. *We say that a commutative semiring K and a commutative monoid M are* compatible *if ι is injective.*

The point of the definition is that when there is compatibility, we can work in $K \otimes M$ and whenever the results belong to $\iota(M)$, we can *safely* read them as familiar answers from M. We give three theorems that capture some general conditions for compatibility.

First, we note that if we work with a semiring in which $+_K$ is idempotent, such as $\mathbb{B}$ or $\mathbb{S}$, a compatible monoid must also be idempotent (e.g. MIN or MAX but not SUM):

PROPOSITION 3.11. *Let K be some commutative semiring such that $+_K$ is idempotent, and let M be some commutative monoid. If M is compatible with K, then $+_M$ is idempotent.*

PROOF. $\iota(m) = 1_K \otimes m = (1_K +_K 1_K) \otimes m = 1_K \otimes m +_{K \otimes M}$
$1_K \otimes m = 1_K \otimes (m +_M m) = \iota(m +_M m)$ $\square$

Nicely enough, idempotent aggregations are compatible with *every* annotation semiring K that is *positive with respect to* $+_K$. K is said to be positive with respect to $+_K$ if $k +_K k' = 0_K \Rightarrow k = k' = 0_K$. For instance, $\mathbb{B}$, $\mathbb{N}$, $\mathbb{S}$ and $\mathbb{N}[X]$ are such semirings (but not $(\mathbb{Z}, +, \cdot, 0, 1)$). The following theorem holds:

THEOREM 3.12. *If M is a commutative monoid such that $+_M$ is idempotent, then M is compatible with any commutative semiring K which is positive with respect to $+_K$.*

PROOF SKETCH. We define $h : K \otimes M \to M$ as
$h(\sum_{i \in I} k_i \otimes m_i) = \sum_{j \in J} m_j$ where $J = \{j \in I | k_j \neq 0\}$. We can show that h is well-defined; since $\forall m \in M$ $h \circ \iota(m) = m$, ι is injective and thus K and M are compatible. $\square$

For general (and in particular non-idempotent) monoids (e.g. SUM) we identify a sufficient condition on K (which in particular holds for $\mathbb{N}[X]$), that allows for compatibility:

THEOREM 3.13. *Let K be a commutative semiring. If there exists a semiring homomorphism from K to $\mathbb{N}$ then K is compatible with all commutative monoids.*

PROOF SKETCH. Let h' be a homomorphism from K to $\mathbb{N}$, and M be an arbitrary commutative monoid. We define a mapping $h : K \otimes M \to M$ by $h(\Sigma k_i \otimes m_i) = \Sigma h'(k_i) m_i$. We can show that h is well-defined and that $h \circ \iota$ is the identity function hence ι is injective. $\square$

COROLLARY 3.14. *The semiring of provenance polynomials $\mathbb{N}[X]$ is compatible with all commutative monoids.*

Now consider the security semiring $\mathbb{S}$. It is idempotent, and therefore not compatible with non-idempotent monoids such as SUM. Still, we want to be able to use $\mathbb{S}$ and other non-idempotent semirings, while allowing the evaluation of aggregation queries with non-idempotent aggregates. This would work if we could construct annotations that would allow us to use Theorem 3.13, in other words, if we could *combine* annotations from $\mathbb{S}$, with multiplicity annotations (i.e. annotations from $\mathbb{N}$). We explain next the construction of such a semiring $\mathbb{SN}$ (for security-bag), and its compatibility with any commutative monoid M will follow from the existence of a homomorphism $h : \mathbb{SN} \to \mathbb{N}$.

Constructing a compatible semiring. We start with the semiring of polynomials $\mathbb{N}[\mathbb{S}]$, i.e. polynomials where instead of indeterminates(variables) we have members of $\mathbb{S}$, and the coefficients are natural numbers. Already $\mathbb{N}[\mathbb{S}]$ is compatible with any commutative monoid M, as there exists a homomorphism $h : \mathbb{N}[\mathbb{S}] \to \mathbb{N}$; but if we work with $\mathbb{N}[\mathbb{S}]$ we lose the ability to use the identities that hold in $\mathbb{S}$ and to thus reduce the size of annotations in query results. We can do better by taking the quotient of $\mathbb{N}[\mathbb{S}]$ by the smallest congruence containing the following identities:

- $\forall s_1, s_2 \in \mathbb{S}$ $s_1 \geq s_2 \Longrightarrow s_1 \cdot_{\mathbb{N}[\mathbb{S}]} s_2 = s_1$.
- $\forall c \in \mathbb{N}, s \in \mathbb{S}$ $0 \cdot_{\mathbb{N}[\mathbb{S}]} s = c \cdot_{\mathbb{N}[\mathbb{S}]} 0_\mathbb{S} = 0$.
- $\forall c \in \mathbb{N}$ $c \cdot_{\mathbb{N}[\mathbb{S}]} 1_\mathbb{S} = c$.

We will denote the resulting quotient semiring by $\mathbb{SN}$. It is easy to check that the faithfulness of the embeddings of $\mathbb{N}$ and $\mathbb{S}$ in $\mathbb{N}[\mathbb{S}]$ is preserved by taking the quotient. Most importantly, $\mathbb{SN}$ is still homomorphic to $\mathbb{N}$. Thus,

COROLLARY 3.15. *$\mathbb{SN}$ is compatible with any commutative monoid M.*

EXAMPLE 3.16. *Consider the SUM monoid. Let R, S be the following $\mathbb{SN}$-relations:*

A	
30	S
10	S

R

A	
30	T

S

Consider the query: $AGG(R \cup \Pi_{S.A}(S \bowtie R))$. *Ignoring the annotations, the expected result (under bag semantics) is 70. Working within the (compatible) semantics defined by*

$\mathbb{SN} \otimes SUM$, the query result contains an aggregated value of $(\mathsf{T} \cdot_{\mathsf{SN}} \mathsf{S} +_{\mathsf{SN}} \mathsf{S}) \otimes 30 +_{\mathsf{S}} \otimes 10$. We can further simplify this to $\mathsf{T} \otimes 30 + \mathsf{S} \otimes 30 + \mathsf{S} \otimes 10 - \mathsf{T} \otimes 30 + \mathsf{S} \otimes 40$. This means that e.g. for a user with credentials T the query result is $1_{\mathsf{SN}} \otimes 70$, and we can use the inverse of ι to map it to $\mathbb{N}$ and obtain 70. Similarly, for a user with credentials S, the query result is mapped to 40. These are indeed the expected results.

Note that if we would have used in the above example $\mathbb{S}$ instead of $\mathbb{SN}$ we would have $(\mathsf{T} +_{\mathsf{S}} \mathsf{S}) = \mathsf{S}$ so $(\mathsf{T} +_{\mathsf{S}} \mathsf{S}) \otimes 30$ would be the same as $\mathsf{S} \otimes 30$. For a user with credentials T we could either use this, leading to the result of $1_{\mathsf{S}} \otimes 40$, or use the same computation done in the example, to obtain $1_{\mathsf{S}} \otimes 70$. Indeed, in $\mathbb{S} \otimes SUM$, we have $1_{\mathsf{S}} \otimes 40 = 1_{\mathsf{S}} \otimes 70$. This is the same phenomenon demonstrated in the beginning of this subsection for $\mathbb{B}$, where ι is not injective, preventing us from stripping it away.

Note also that if we would have used $\mathbb{N}[\mathbb{S}]$ instead of $\mathbb{SN}$ then we could not have done the illustrated simplifications.

4. NESTED AGGREGATION QUERIES

So far we have studied only queries where the aggregation operator is the last one performed. In this section we extend the discussion to queries that involve comparisons on aggregate values.

Note. For simplicity, all results and examples are presented for queries in which the comparison operator is equality (=). However the results can easily be extended to arbitrary comparison predicates, that can be decided for elements of M.

4.1 Difficulties

We start by exemplifying where the algebra proposed for restricted aggregation queries, fails here:

EXAMPLE 4.1. *Reconsider the relation (denoted R') which is the result of aggregation query, depicted in Example 3.8. Further consider a query Q_{select} that selects from R' all tuples for which the aggregated salary equals 20. The crux is that deciding the truth value of the selection condition involves interpreting the comparison operator on symbolic representation of values in R'; so far, we have no way of interpreting the obtained comparison expression, for instance $r_1 \otimes 20 + r_2 \otimes 10$ "equals" 20, and thus we cannot decide the existence of tuples in the selection result.*

Note that in this example, the comparison truth value (and consequently the tuples in the query result) depends in a *non-monotonic way* on existence of tuples in the input relation R: if we map r_1 to 1 and r_2 to 0 then the tuple with dept. d_1 appears in the query result, but not if we map both to 1. We can show that the challenge that this non-monotonicity poses is fundamental, and encountered by any algebra on (M, K)-relations. A more intricate construction is thus required for nested aggregation queries.

4.2 An Extended Structure

We start with an example of our treatment of nested aggregation queries, then give the formal construction.

EXAMPLE 4.2. *Reconsider example 4.1, and recall that the challenge in query evaluation lies in comparing elements of $K \otimes M$ with elements of M (or $K \otimes M$, e.g. in case of joins). Our solution is to introduce to the semiring K new*

elements, of the form $[x = y]$ where $x, y \in K \otimes M$ *(if we need to compare with $m \in M$, we use $\iota(m)$ instead). The result of evaluating the query in example 4.1 (using $M = SUM$) will then be captured by:*

Dept	Sal	
d_1	$r_1 \otimes 20$	$\delta(r_1 +_K r_2)_K$
	$+_{K \otimes M} r_2 \otimes 10$	$[r_1 \otimes 20 +_{K \otimes M} r_2 \otimes 10 = 1_K \otimes 20]$
d_2	$r_3 \otimes 10$	$\delta(r_3) \cdot_K [r_3 \otimes 10 = 1_K \otimes 20]$

Intuitively, since we do not know which tuples will satisfy the selection criterion, we keep both tuples and multiply the provenance annotation of each of them by a symbolic equality expression. These equality expressions are kept as symbols until we can embed the values in $M = SUM$ and decide the equality (e.g. if $K = \mathbb{N}$), in which case we "replace" it by 1_K if it holds or 0_K otherwise. For example, given a homomorphism $h : \mathbb{N}[X] \to \mathbb{N}$, $h(r_1) = h(r_2) = 1$, then $h^M(r_1 \otimes 20 +_{K \otimes M} r_2 \otimes 10) = h(r_1) \otimes 20 +_{K \otimes M} h(r_2) \otimes 10 = 1 \otimes 30 \neq 1 \otimes 20$, thus the equality expression is replaced with (i.e. mapped by the homomorphism to) 0_K.

We next define the construction formally; the idea underlying the construction is to define a semiring whose elements are polynomials, in which equation elements are additional indeterminates. To achieve that, we introduce for any semiring K and any commutative monoid M, the "domain" equation $\widehat{K} = \mathbb{N}[K \cup \{[c_1 = c_2] \mid c_1, c_2 \in \widehat{K} \otimes M\}]$. The right-hand-side is a monotone, in fact continuous w.r.t. the usual set inclusion operator, hence this equation has a set-theoretic least solution (no need for order-theoretic domain theory). The solution also has an obvious commutative semiring structure. The solution semiring is denoted $\widehat{K} = (X, +_{\widehat{K}}, \cdot_{\widehat{K}}, 0_{\widehat{K}}, 1_{\widehat{K}})$, and we continue by taking the quotient on $\widehat{K}$ defined by the following axioms.

For all $k_1, k_2 \in K, c_1, c_2, c_3, c_4 \in \widehat{K} \otimes M$:

$$
\begin{aligned}
0_{\widehat{K}} &\sim 0_K \\
1_{\widehat{K}} &\sim 1_K \\
k_1 +_{\widehat{K}} k_2 &\sim k_1 +_K k_2 \\
k_1 \cdot_{\widehat{K}} k_2 &\sim k_1 +_K k_2 \\
[c_1 = c_3] &\sim [c_2 = c_4] \; (\text{if } c_1 =_{\widehat{K} \otimes M} c_2, \, c_3 =_{\widehat{K} \otimes M} c_4)
\end{aligned}
$$

and if K and M are such that ι defined by $\iota(m) = 1_K \otimes m$ is an isomorphism (and let h be its inverse), we further take the quotient defined by: for all $a, b \in K \otimes M$,

$$
\begin{aligned}
(*) \; [a = b] &\sim 1_K \, (\text{if } h(a) =_M h(b)) \\
[a = b] &\sim 0_K \, (\text{if } h(a) \neq_M h(b))
\end{aligned}
$$

We use K^M to denote the semiring obtained by applying the above construction on a semiring K and a commutative monoid M. A key property is that, when we are able to interpret the equalities in M, K^M collapses to K. Formally,

PROPOSITION 4.3. *If K and M are such that $K \otimes M$ and M are isomorphic via ι then $K^M = K$.*

The proof is by induction on the structure of elements in K^M, showing that at each step we can "solve" an equality sub-expression, and replace it with 0_K or 1_K.

Lifting homomorphisms. To conclude the description of the construction we explain how to lift a semiring homomorphism from $h : K \to K'$ to $h^M : K^M \to K'^M$, for any commutative monoid M and semirings K, K'. h^M is defined recursively on the structure of $a \in K^M$: if $a \in K$ we define $h^M(a) = h(a)$, otherwise $a = [b \otimes m_1 = c \otimes m_2]$ for some $b, c \in K^M$ and $m_1, m_2 \in M$ and we define $h^M(a) = [h^M(b) \otimes m_1 = h^M(c) \otimes m_2]$. Note that the application of a homomorphism h^M maps equality expressions to equality expressions (in which elements in K' appear instead of elements of K appeared before). If K' and M are such that their corresponding $\iota : M \to K \otimes M$ defined by $\iota(m) = 1_K \otimes M$ is injective, then we may "resolve the equalities", otherwise the (new) equality expression remains.

4.3 The Extended Semantics

The extended semiring construction allows us to design a semantics for general aggregation queries.

In the sequel we assume, to simplify the definition, that the query aggregates and compares only values of $K^M \otimes M$ (a value $m \in M$ is first replaced by $\iota(m) = 1_K \otimes m$). In what follows, let $R(R_1, R_2)$ be (M, K^M)-relations on an attributes set U. Recall that for a tuple t, $t(u)$ (where $u \in U$) is the value of attribute u in t; also for $U' \subseteq U$, recall that we use $t|_{U'}$ for the restriction of t to the attributes in U'. Last, we use $(K^M \otimes M)^U$ to denote the set of all tuples on U, with values from $K^M \otimes M$. The semantics follows:

1. *empty relation:* $\forall t \quad \phi(t) = 0_K$.

2. *union:* $(R_1 \cup R_2)(t) =$

$$\begin{cases} \sum_{t' \in supp(R_1)} R_1(t') \cdot_K \prod_{u \in U} [t'(u) = t(u)] & \text{if } t \in supp(R_1) \\ + \sum_{t' \in supp(R_2)} R_2(t') \cdot_K \prod_{u \in U} [t'(u) = t(u)] & \cup supp(R_2) \\ 0_K & \text{Otherwise.} \end{cases}$$

3. *projection:* Let $U' \subseteq U$, and let $T = \{t|_{U'} \mid t \in supp(R)\}$. Then $\Pi_{U'}(t) =$

$$\begin{cases} \sum_{t' \in Supp(R)} R(t') \cdot_K \prod_{u \in U'} [t(u) = t'(u)] & \text{if } t \in T \\ 0_K & \text{Otherwise.} \end{cases}$$

4. *selection:* If P is an equality predicate involving the equation of some attribute $u \in U$ and a value $m \in M$ then $(\sigma_P(R))(t) = R(t) \cdot_K [t(u) = \iota(m)]$.

5. *value based join:* We assume for simplicity that R_1 and R_2 have disjoint sets of attributes, U_1 and U_2 resp., and that the join is based on comparing a single attribute of each relation. Let $u'_1 \in U_1$ and $u'_2 \in U_2$ be the attributes to join on. For every $t \in (K^M \otimes M)^{U_1 \cup U_2}$:
$(R_1 \bowtie_{R_1.u_1 = R_2.u_2} R_2)(t) =$
$R_1(t|_{U_1}) \cdot_K R_2(t|_{U_2}) \cdot_K [t(u_1) = t(u_2)].$

6. *Aggregation:* For relations with a single attribute u
$AGG_M(R)(t) =$

$$\begin{cases} 1 & t(u) = \sum_{t' \in supp(R)} R(t') *_{K \otimes M} t'(u) \\ 0 & \text{otherwise} \end{cases}$$

7. *Group By:* Let $U' \subseteq U$ be a subset of attributes that will be grouped and $u \in U \setminus U'$ be the aggregated attribute. Then for every $t \in (K^M \otimes M)^{U' \cup \{u\}}$:

$GB_{U',u}R(t) =$

$$\begin{cases} \delta((\Pi_{U'} R)(t|_{U'})) & t(u) = \sum_{t' \in supp(R)} (R(t') \cdot_K \\ & \prod_{u \in U'} [t'(u) = t(u)]) *_{K \otimes M} t'(u) \\ 0 & \text{otherwise} \end{cases}$$

We can show that the algebra satisfies set/bag compatibility, poly-size overhead, and homomorphism coomutation.

EXAMPLE 4.4. *Reconsider the relation in Example 4.2, and let us perform another sum aggregation on Sal. The value in the result now contains equation expressions:*

$$\delta(r_1 +_K r_2) \cdot_K [r_1 \otimes 20 +_{K \otimes M} r_2 \otimes 10 = 1_K \otimes 20]$$
$$*_{K \otimes M} (r_1 \otimes 20 +_{K \otimes M} r_2 \otimes 10)$$
$$+_{K \otimes M} \delta(r_3) \cdot_K [r_3 \otimes 10 = 1_K \otimes 20] *_{K \otimes M} r_3 \otimes 10$$

Given a homomorphism $h : \mathbb{N}[X] \to \mathbb{N}$ we can "solve" the equations, e.g. if $h(r_1) = 1$, $h(r_2) = 0$ and $h(r_3) = 2$, we obtain an aggregated value of $1 \otimes 40$. Note that the aggregation value is not monotone in r_1, r_2, r_3: map r_2 to 1 (and keep r_1, r_3 as before), to obtain $1 \otimes 20$.

5. DIFFERENCE

We next show that via our semantics for aggregation, we can obtain for the first time a semantics for arbitrary queries with difference on K-relations. We describe the obtained semantics and study some of its properties.

5.1 Semantics for Difference

We first note that difference queries may be encoded as queries with aggregation, using the monoid $\hat{\mathbb{B}} = (\{\bot, \top\}, \lor, \bot)$ (the following encoding was inspired by [29, 8]):

$$R - S = \Pi_{a_1 \dots a_n} \{ (GB_{\{a_1, \dots a_n\}, b}(R \times \bot_b \cup S \times \top_b)) \\ \bowtie_{a_1 \dots a_n} (R \times \bot_b) \}.$$

$\bot_b$ and $\top_b$ are relations on a single attribute b, containing a single tuple $(\bot)$ and $(\top)$ respectively, with provenance 1_K. Using the semantics of Section 4, we obtain a semantics for the difference operation.

Interestingly, we next show that the obtained semantics can be captured by a simple and intuitive expression. First, we note that since $\hat{\mathbb{B}}$ is idempotent, every semiring K positive with respect to $+_K$ is compatible with $\hat{\mathbb{B}}$ (see Theorem 3.12). The following proposition then holds for every K, K' and every two $(\hat{\mathbb{B}}, K)$-relations R, S:

PROPOSITION 5.1. *For every tuple t, semirings K, K' such that $K'^{\hat{\mathbb{B}}} \otimes \hat{\mathbb{B}}$ is isomorphic to $\hat{\mathbb{B}}$ via $\iota(m) = 1_K \otimes m$, if $h : K \to K'$ is a semiring homomorphism then:*
$h^{\hat{\mathbb{B}}}([(R - S)(t)]) = h^{\hat{\mathbb{B}}}([S(t) \otimes \top = 0] \cdot_K R(t)).$

The obtained provenance expression is thus "equivalent" (in the precise sense of Proposition 5.1) to $[S(t) \otimes \top = 0] \cdot R(t)$. The following lemma helps us to understand the meaning of the obtained equality expression:

LEMMA 5.2. *For every semiring K positive w.r.t. $+_K$ and $h : K \to \mathbb{B}$, $h^M([S(t) \otimes \top = 0]) = \top$ iff $h(S(t)) = \bot$.*

Intuitive Interpretation. It follows from our definition that a tuple t appears in $R - S$ if it appears in R, but does not appear in S. When the tuple appears in the result of $R - S$, it carries its original annotation from R. I.e. the existence of t in S is used as a boolean condition. This means that in particular, for $\mathbb{B}$, or semantics is equivalent to set semantics. But for $\mathbb{N}$ it is a hybrid of set and bag semantics: tuples that appear in R but not in S, appear in $R - S$ with their original multiplicity that they had in R.

EXAMPLE 5.3. *Let R, S be the following relations, where R contains employees and their departments and S containing departments that are designated to be closed:*

ID	Dep	
1	d$_1$	t_1
2	d$_1$	t_2
2	d$_2$	t_3

R

Dep	
d$_1$	t_4

S

To obtain a relation with all departments that remains active, we can use the query $(\Pi_{Dep} R) - S$, resulting in:

Dep	
d$_1$	$[t_4 \otimes \top = 0] \cdot (t_1 + t_2)$
d$_2$	$[0 = 0] \cdot t_3 \quad (= t_3)$

Now consider some homomorphism $h : \mathbb{N}[X] \to \mathbb{N}$ (multiplicity e.g. stands for number of employees in the department). Note that if $h(t_4) > 0$ then the department d$_1$ is closed and indeed d$_1$ is omitted from the support of the difference query result, otherwise it retains each original annotation that it had in R. Assume now that we decide to revoke the decision of closing the department d$_1$. This corresponds to mapping t_4 to 0; we can easily propagate this deletion to the query results; the equality appearing in the annotation of the first tuple is now $[0 = 0] = 1_K$ and we obtain as expected:

Dep	
d$_1$	$t_1 + t_2$
d$_2$	t_3

In particular, we obtain a semantics for the entire Relational Algebra, including difference. It is interesting to study the specialization of the obtained semantics for particular semirings: $\mathbb{B}, \mathbb{N}, \mathbb{Z}$, and to compare it to previously studied semantics for difference.

5.2 Comparison with other semantics

For a semiring K and a commutative monoid M we say that two queries Q, Q' are equivalent if for every input (M, K)-database D, the results (including annotations) $Q(D)$ and $Q'(D)$ are congruent (namely the corresponding values and annotations are congruent) according to the axioms of $K^M \otimes M$ and K^M. In the sequel we fix $M = \widehat{B}$ and consider different instances of K, exemplifying different equivalence axioms for queries with difference while comparing them with previously suggested semantics. We use $Q \equiv_K Q'$ to denote the equivalence of Q, Q' with respect to K and $\widehat{B}$.

$\mathbb{B}$-*relations.* For $K = \mathbb{B}$, our semantics is the same as set-semantics, thus the following proposition holds:

PROPOSITION 5.4. *For $Q, Q' \in RA$ it holds that $Q \equiv_{\mathbb{B}} Q'$ if and only if $Q \equiv Q'$ under set semantics.*

$\mathbb{N}$-*relations.* For $K = \mathbb{N}$, we compare our semantics to bag equivalence and observe that they are different (for queries with difference, even without aggregation). Intuitively, this is because in our semantics, the righthand side of the difference is treated as a boolean condition, rather than having the effect of decreasing the multiplicity. Formally,

PROPOSITION 5.5. *$Q \equiv_{\mathbb{N}} Q'$ does not imply that $Q \equiv Q'$ under bag semantics, and vice versa.*

PROOF. Observe that $A - (B \cup B) \equiv_{\mathbb{N}} A - B$; but this does not hold for bag semantics. In contrast, under bag semantics $(A \cup B) - B \equiv A$, but not for our semantics. $\square$

$\mathbb{Z}$-*relations.* Finally, in [20] the authors have presented $\mathbb{Z}$ semantics for difference. Intuitively, their semantics entails that an element appears in $R - S$ with multiplicity that is the substraction of its multiplicity in S from its multiplicity in S; the resulting multiplicity may be negative. Consequently, the semantics also entails equivalence axioms that are different from those that we have here for $\mathbb{Z}$-relations:

PROPOSITION 5.6. *$Q \equiv_{\mathbb{Z}} Q'$ does not imply $Q \equiv Q'$ under $\mathbb{Z}$ semantics [9], and vice versa.*

PROOF. Under $\mathbb{Z}$ semantics it was shown in [20] that $(A - (B - C)) \equiv (A \cup C) - B$. This does not hold for our semantics. In contrast $A - (B \cup B) \equiv_{\mathbb{Z}} A - B$, but this equivalence does not hold under $\mathbb{Z}$ semantics. $\square$

Deciding Query Equivalence. We conclude with a note on the decidability of equivalence of queries using our semantics. It turns out that for semirings such as $\mathbb{B}, \mathbb{N}$ for which we can interpret the results in $\widehat{\mathbb{B}}$ (in the sense of proposition 5.1 above), query equivalence is undecidable.

PROPOSITION 5.7. *Let K be such that $K^{\widehat{\mathbb{B}}} \otimes \widehat{\mathbb{B}}$ is isomorphic to $\widehat{\mathbb{B}}$. Equivalence of Relational Algebra queries on K-relations is undecidable.*

6. RELATED WORK

Provenance information has been extensively studied in the database literature. Different provenance management techniques are introduced in [13, 6, 7, 4, 31, 5], etc., and it was shown in [22, 19] that these approaches can be compared in the semiring framework. The usefulness of using the general framework of provenance semirings rather than e.g. simple logging of query evaluation has been demonstrated in this paper via applications such as deletion propagation. To our knowledge, this work is the first to study aggregate queries in the context of provenance semirings. Provenance information has a variety of applications (see introduction) and we believe that our novel framework for aggregate queries will benefit all of these. Specifically, workflow provenance has been so far managed mainly in a coarse-grained manner (i.e. at a flow level rather than individual data items level). Since aggregate queries play a key role in workflows, we believe that the framework presented here can be an important step towards fine-grained provenance management for workflows.

---

[9] As defined in [20].

Aggregate queries have been extensively studied in e.g. [11, 12] for bag and set semantics. As explained in [11], such queries are fundamental in many applications: OLAP queries, mobile computing, the analysis of streaming data, etc. We note that Monoids are used to capture general aggregation operators in [12], but our paper seems to be the first to study their interaction with provenance.

Several semantics of *difference* on relations with annotations have been proposed, starting with the *c*-tables of [26]. The semirings with monus of [17] generalize this as well as bag-semantics. Difference on relations with annotations from $\mathbb{Z}$ are considered in [20] and from $\mathbb{Z}[X]$ in [18].

There are interesting connections between provenance management and query evaluation on uncertain (and probabilistic) databases (e.g. [30, 14, 4, 3]), as observed in [22]. Evaluation of aggregate queries on probabilistic databases has been studied in e.g. [37, 34]. Optimizing aggregate query evaluation on probabilistic databases via provenance management is an intriguing research challenge.

7. CONCLUSION

We have studied in this paper provenance information for queries with *aggregation* in the semiring framework. We have identified three desiderata for the assessment of candidate approaches: compatibility with the usual set/bag semantics, commutation with semiring homomorphisms and poly-size overhead with respect to the database size, and have suggested a semantics that satisfies all three desiderata.

We have exemplified in the paper the application of our approach for deletion propagation and security annotations, and have mentioned other areas in which provenance is useful. A practical, compact representation of the obtained provenance expressions is key to their applicability to these areas. Such compact representation of provenance was realized for the positive relational algebra via the notion of provenance graphs, and their applicability was proven in the context of Orchestra [28]. Finding similar compact representation for the provenance expressions obtained for aggregates, and applying the construction in the context of practical systems, is an intriguing future research.

Acknowledgements. Val Tannen is grateful to Christoph Koch for discussions on the relationship between aggregates and difference and to Vittorio Perduca for discussions on the tensor product constructions.

8. REFERENCES

[1] S. Abiteboul, R. Hull, and V. Vianu. *Foundations of Databases.* Addison-Wesley, 1995.

[2] F. N. Afrati and A. Vasilakopoulos. Managing lineage and uncertainty under a data exchange setting. In *SUM*, 2010.

[3] L. Antova, C. Koch, and D. Olteanu. $10^{(10^6)}$ worlds and beyond: efficient representation and processing of incomplete information. *VLDB J.*, 18(5), 2009.

[4] O. Benjelloun, A.D. Sarma, A.Y. Halevy, M. Theobald, and J. Widom. Databases with uncertainty and lineage. *VLDB J.*, 17, 2008.

[5] P. Buneman, J. Cheney, and S. Vansummeren. On the expressiveness of implicit provenance in query and update languages. In *ICDT*, 2007.

[6] P. Buneman, J. Cheney, and S. Vansummeren. On the expressiveness of implicit provenance in query and update languages. *ACM Trans. Database Syst.*, 33(4), 2008.

[7] P. Buneman, S. Khanna, and W.C. Tan. Why and where: A characterization of data provenance. In *ICDT*, 2001.

[8] P. Buneman, S. Naqvi, V. Tannen, and L. Wong. Principles of programming with complex objects and collection types. *TCS*, 149(1), 1995.

[9] J. Cheney, L. Chiticariu, and W. C. Tan. Provenance in databases: Why, how, and where. *Foundations and Trends in Databases*, 1(4), 2009.

[10] J. Cheney, S. Chong, N. Foster, M. I. Seltzer, and S. Vansummeren. Provenance: a future history. In *OOPSLA Companion*, 2009.

[11] S. Cohen. Containment of aggregate queries. *SIGMOD Record*, 34(1), 2005.

[12] S. Cohen, W. Nutt, and Y. Sagiv. Rewriting queries with arbitrary aggregation functions using views. *ACM Trans. Database Syst.*, 31(2), 2006.

[13] Y. Cui, J. Widom, and J.L. Wiener. Tracing the lineage of view data in a warehousing environment. *ACM Transactions on Database Systems*, 25(2), 2000.

[14] N. N. Dalvi, C. Ré, and D. Suciu. Probabilistic databases: diamonds in the dirt. *Commun. ACM*, 52(7), 2009.

[15] J.N. Foster, T.J. Green, and V. Tannen. Annotated XML: queries and provenance. In *PODS*, 2008.

[16] N. Fuhr and T. Rölleke. A probabilistic relational algebra for the integration of information retrieval and database systems. *ACM Trans. Inf. Syst.*, 15(1), 1997.

[17] F. Geerts and A. Poggi. On database query languages for k-relations. *J. Applied Logic*, 8(2), 2010.

[18] T.J. Green. *Collaborative data sharing with mappings and provenance.* PhD thesis, University of Pennsylvania, 2009.

[19] T.J. Green. Containment of conjunctive queries on annotated relations. In *ICDT*, 2009.

[20] T.J. Green, Z. Ives, and V. Tannen. Reconcilable differences. In *ICDT*, 2009.

[21] T.J. Green, G. Karvounarakis, Z. Ives, and V. Tannen. Update exchange with mappings and provenance. In *VLDB*, 2007.

[22] T.J. Green, G. Karvounarakis, and V. Tannen. Provenance semirings. In *PODS*, 2007.

[23] T.J. Green, G. Karvounarakis, N. E. Taylor, O. Biton, Z. Ives, and V. Tannen. Orchestra: facilitating collaborative data sharing. In *Proc. of SIGMOD*, 2007.

[24] A. Gupta, I.S. Mumick, and V.S. Subrahmanian. Maintaining views incrementally. In *SIGMOD*, 1993.

[25] J. Huang, T. Chen, A. Doan, and J. F. Naughton. On the provenance of non-answers to queries over extracted data. *Proc. VLDB*, 1, 2008.

[26] T. Imielinski and W. Lipski. Incomplete information in relational databases. *J. ACM*, 31(4), 1984.

[27] S. Issam, F. Adrian, and S. Vladimiro. A formal model of provenance in distributed systems. In *First workshop on on Theory and practice of provenance*, 2009.

[28] G. Karvounarakis, Z. G. Ives, and V. Tannen. Querying data provenance. In *SIGMOD Conference*, 2010.

[29] C. Koch. Incremental query evaluation in a ring of databases. In *PODS*, 2010.

[30] C. Koch and D. Olteanu. Conditioning probabilistic databases. *PVLDB*, 1(1), 2008.

[31] N. Kwasnikowska and J. Van den Bussche. Mapping the nrc dataflow model to the open provenance model. In *IPAW*, pages 3–16, 2008.

[32] J. Lechtenbörger, H. Shu, and G. Vossen. Aggregate queries over conditional tables. *J. Intell. Inf. Syst.*, 19(3), 2002.

[33] S.K. Lellahi and V. Tannen. A calculus for collections and aggregates. In *Cat. Theory and Comp. Science*, 1997.

[34] J. Li, B. Saha, and A. Deshpande. A unified approach to ranking in probabilistic databases. *Proc. VLDB*, 2, 2009.

[35] B. Liu, L. Chiticariu, V. Chu, H.V. Jagadish, and F. Reiss. Refining information extraction rules using data provenance. *IEEE Data Eng. Bull.*, 33(3), 2010.

[36] A. Meliou, W. Gatterbauer, K. F. Moore, and D. Suciu. The complexity of causality and responsibility for query answers and non-answers. *PVLDB*, 4(1), 2010.

[37] C. Ré and D. Suciu. Efficient evaluation of having queries on a probabilistic database. In *DBPL*, 2007.

[38] S. Vansummeren and J. Cheney. Recording provenance for sql queries and updates. *IEEE Data Eng. Bull.*, 30(4), 2007.

[39] W. Zhou, M. Sherr, T. Tao, X. Li, B. T. Loo, and Y. Mao. Efficient querying and maintenance of network provenance at internet-scale. In *SIGMOD*, 2010.

[40] E. Zimányi. Query evaluation in probabilistic relational databases. *Theor. Comput. Sci.*, 171(1-2), 1997.

On the Complexity of Privacy-Preserving Complex Event Processing

Yeye He
University of
Wisconsin-Madison
heyeye@cs.wisc.edu

Siddharth Barman
University of
Wisconsin-Madison
sid@cs.wisc.edu

Di Wang
Worcester Polytechnic Institute
diwang@cs.wpi.edu

Jeffrey F. Naughton
University of
Wisconsin-Madison
naughton@cs.wisc.edu

ABSTRACT

Complex Event Processing (CEP) Systems are stream processing systems that monitor incoming event streams in search of user-specified event patterns. While CEP systems have been adopted in a variety of applications, the privacy implications of event pattern reporting mechanisms have yet to be studied — a stark contrast to the significant amount of attention that has been devoted to privacy for relational systems. In this paper we present a privacy problem that arises when the system must support desired patterns (those that should be reported if detected) and private patterns (those that should not be revealed). We formalize this problem, which we term privacy-preserving, utility maximizing CEP (PP-CEP), and analyze its complexity under various assumptions. Our results show that this is a rich problem to study and shed some light on the difficulty of developing algorithms that preserve utility without compromising privacy.

Categories and Subject Descriptors: F.2 Analysis of Algorithms and Problem Complexity

General Terms: Algorithms, Theory

Keywords: CEP Stream Processing, Privacy, Complexity

1. INTRODUCTION

Complex Event Processing (CEP) is a stream event processing paradigm that has received increasing attention from the data management research community [4, 5, 7, 17, 21, 22] and also from industry [1, 2, 3]. In the CEP model, the data is a stream of events, which is monitored and queried in search of some user-defined event patterns. When a pattern of interest is detected, it is reported by the CEP system. Such CEP systems have demonstrated utility in a variety of applications including financial trading, credit-card fraud detection, and security monitoring. However, to our knowledge the problem of privacy in such systems has not yet been addressed.

In a nutshell, the problem we consider is this: consider two kinds

of patterns, those that should be detected and reported (which we term "public" patterns), and those that should be eliminated and not reported (which we term "private" patterns). The decision of what is public and what is private is made by a user or administrator and is input to the system. Then the task is to "destroy" any private patterns that occur by deleting some events from the stream; however, we wish to do so in such a way that maximizes the number of public patterns that remain to be detected. The challenge of the problem arises from the number of options as to what should be retained or deleted.

We begin with a motivating example inspired by a health care monitoring system, HyReminder [20]. HyReminder, currently being deployed in the University of Massachusetts Memorial Hospital, is a hospital infection control system powered by CEP technologies that aims to track, monitor and remind health-care workers with respect to hygiene compliance. In this hospital setting, each health care worker wears an RFID tag that can be read by sensors installed throughout the hospital. As the worker walks around the hospital, the RFID tags they wear are detected by the sensors, generating "event" data, which is transfered to a monitoring central CEP engine. As an example of such a pattern, a doctor who exits a patient room (represented by an "exit" event), cleanses his hands (indicated by a "sanitize" event), and finally enters an ICU (an "enter" event), generates an event pattern SEQ(exit, sanitize, enter), showing an instance of hygiene regulations compliance. Conversely, an instance of hygiene violation in which the doctor exits the patient room, does *not* cleanse his hands before entering an ICU, would correspond to an event sequence SEQ(exit, !sanitize, enter) where "!sanitize" indicates the absence of the "sanitize" event. Both the hygiene compliance and violation instances should be captured and reported by the CEP system.

While the benefit of such CEP systems is apparent, the implications of this CEP querying model for privacy are somewhat subtle. Intuitively, while it is clear that a CEP system may reveal useful event patterns, it may also reveal patterns that the individuals being monitored would prefer to keep hidden. Using the hospital example again, a doctor who visits a patient then immediately enters a psychiatrist's office might serve as an indication that this patient is experiencing psychiatric problems. While a system like HyReminder will not directly monitor and report such private event patterns, the occurrences of hygiene violations it does report may be used by an adversary to infer such private patterns.

In this paper we study an abstract problem inspired by privacy-preserving, utility maximizing CEP. We classify patterns of interest into two categories: the *query patterns*, which should be detected and reported; and the *private patterns*, which should be suppressed. The goal of privacy-preserving CEP is to maximize the reporting of query patterns without disclosing any private patterns. To be more concrete, in this paper we explore filtering or dropping events to eliminate the occurrence of private patterns; the "trick" is to do so intelligently, so as to avoid dropping events as much as possible while eliminating the occurrence of query patterns.

This abstract problem has many interesting variants. We begin by studying two of the most straightforward variants: the *windowed* variant, in which, when deciding which events to drop, we consider the events that arrived in a specified window preceding the current event; and the *oblivious* variant, where prior events are not taken into consideration. Both variants are interesting to study: while the *windowed* variant can potentially better preserve utility, it is also intuitively more computationally expensive.

To our knowledge, no previous studies — practical or theoretical — have investigated PP-CEP. We observe that the problem has a simple but rich structure, and point out an interesting array of complexity results. Specifically, the general problem of PP-CEP is NP-hard and hard to approximate (namely, it is $|\Sigma|^{1-\epsilon}$-inapproximable for utility gain by constructing a reduction from independent set, where $|\Sigma|$ is the size of the events, and $\ln(|\mathcal{P}|)$-inapproximable for utility loss by constructing a reduction from set cover, where $|\mathcal{P}|$ is the number of private patterns). However, we explore various combinations of the input parameters and show that there are a variety of scenarios in which the complexity can be reduced. For instance, the oblivious PP-CEP problem can be formulated as an integer program that is polynomially solvable when the sum of the number of private patterns and query patterns is some fixed constant, or when the sum of the number of the event types and query patterns is some fixed constant. In addition, exploiting the submodularity of the utility loss function we prove that the oblivious PP-CEP problem is l_p-approximable where l_p is the maximum length of the private patterns. We also show that in the special case where the window size is some fixed constant the windowed PP-CEP is also l_p-approximable.

These complexity results shed some light on the difficulty of developing PP-CEP solutions in practice, but more importantly also leave open many more possible avenues for future research. We hope that our first step towards understanding the PP-CEP problem will serve as a springboard for future work tackling the theoretic and practical issues that arise from the problem of PP-CEP.

2. A SEQUENCE-BASED CEP MODEL

2.1 The data/query model

We adopt the following event sequence-based model to represent continuously arriving events. Let the domain of possible event types be the alphabet $\Sigma = \{e_i\}$, where e_i represents a type of event. We model a stream of events as follows.

DEFINITION 1. *A **time-stamped event sequence** is a sequence $S = (c_1, c_2, ...c_n)$, where each event c_j is associated with a particular event type $e_i \in \Sigma$, and has a unique time stamp t_j. The sequence S is temporally ordered, that is $t_j < t_k$ for all $j < k$.*

While logically we consider only one temporally ordered event sequence, in practice events can come from multiple data sources. A common complication that can arise is that events from multiple sources may arrive out of order. In this work we make the simplifying assumption that events in the sequence are in strictly increasing time order, and there are no out-of-order events in the sequence. This assumption helps us to better focus our discussions on the pri-

vacy aspect of CEP systems, and is consistent with the state-of-the-art CEP literature [4, 5, 17, 22]. In practice, existing work that use buffer-based techniques for out-of-order event streams processing [7, 16] can be similarly applied to handle out-of-order events in our problem.

We further define *subsequence* which is an ordered subpart of a given sequence.

DEFINITION 2. *A **subsequence** S' of the event sequence $S = (c_1, c_2, ...c_n)$ is a sequence $(c_{i_1}, c_{i_2}, ...c_{i_m})$ such that $1 \leq i_1 \leq i_2... \leq i_m \leq n$, where $m \leq n$.*

Note that subsequence preserves the temporal order of the original sequence. Also observe that unlike substrings, a subsequence does not have to be a consecutive subcomponent of the sequence. As a result, there are a total of 2^n possible subsequences.

We next define queries over event sequences. Unlike relational data processing, where the queries are typically ad-hoc and dynamically composed at query time, queries in the CEP model are standing queries, which are submitted ahead of time and are static. Let the set of queries be $\mathcal{Q} = \{Q_i\}$, where each query Q_i is a sequence query defined as follows.

DEFINITION 3. *A **sequence query pattern** Q_i is of the form $Q_i = (q_1^i, q_2^i, ...q_n^i)$, with $q_k^i \in \Sigma$ being event types. In addition, for each query Q_i there is a specified window of size $T(Q_i) \in \mathbb{R}^+$ over which Q_i will be evaluated.*

A sequence query looks for the conjunction of the occurrences of events of certain types in specified order within a given time window. This sequence query is essentially the "SEQ" query construct in the CEP query language used by most existing systems [10, 17, 22]. While negation of an event can also be included in "SEQ" queries to indicate the absence of event occurrences, we in this work only consider positive event occurrences and leave negation of events as future work.

DEFINITION 4. *A sequence query pattern $Q_i = (q_1^i, q_2^i, ...q_n^i)$ with window size $T(Q_i)$ produces an instance of **query pattern match** over an event sequence S, if there exists a subsequence $S' = (c_{j_1}, c_{j_2}, ... c_{j_n})$ of S, such that c_{j_l} is of type q_l^i for all $l \in [1, n]$, and $t_{j_n} - t_{j_1} \leq T(Q_i)$. We say the sequence of events S' is an instance of match of Q_i. We denote $M(Q_i, S)$ as the set of all instances of matches produced for query Q_i over S.*

We use the following example to illustrate event sequences and query matches in our CEP model.

EXAMPLE 1. *Suppose there are five event types denoted by the five characters $\Sigma = \{A, B, C, D, E\}$. Each character represents a certain type of event (for example, A could stand for doctors entering the ICU, B denotes doctors washing hands at the sanitization desks, and so forth).*

Let the stream of arriving events be $S = (A_1, B_2, A_3, C_4, D_5, D_6, C_7, A_8, D_9, E_{10})$ where each character is an instance of a particular type of event arriving at time stamp t_i given subscript i. Assume in this example that events arrive at fixed intervals t for simplicity. In other words, A_1 arrives at $t_1 = t$, B_2 arrives at $t_2 = 2t$, so on and so forth.

Suppose there are two query patterns: $Q_1 = (A, B)$ with the associated window size $T(Q_1) = t$, and $Q_2 = (C, D)$ with $T(Q_2) = 2t$. To give some interpretation for the queries, if A stands for doctors entering the ICU, B for doctors washing hands, then Q_1 is looking for such patterns where doctors wash hands immediately after entering the ICU, and the time interval between the two events is within the window size $T(Q_1) = t$.

Over the event sequence S, there is only one subsequence (A_1, B_2) that matches Q_1. Note that the subsequence (B_2, A_3) does not match Q_1, because by definition a subsequence that matches for Q_1 has to maintain that an event of type A arrives before an event of type B.

There are three matches of Q_2, namely (C_4, D_5), (C_4, D_6), and (C_7, D_9). Observe that the subsequence (C_4, D_9) does not match Q_2 because the time interval between C_4 and D_9 is $9t - 4t = 5t$, which is larger than $T(Q_2) = 2t$.

DEFINITION 5. *A **CEP** system is a function that takes as input an event sequence S, a set of query patterns $\mathcal{Q} = \{Q_i\}$, and outputs a set $\mathcal{M} = \bigcup_{Q_i \in \mathcal{Q}} M(Q_i, S)$, where $M(Q_i, S)$ is the set of all query matches of Q_i over S.*

In this work we focus on the CEP that only accept sequence query patterns. While in practice CEP systems may also include support for query language extensions like negation [10] and Kleene closure [10], among other features, we in this work limit the query language to allow only conjunctions of positive event occurrences and study the complexity of different variants based on this core language subset. Investigating the privacy implication of CEP on this restricted language subset already presents us with a rich problem to study. Expanding the query language to a more expressive one and exploring its impact on complexity is an interesting direction for future work.

2.2 Private patterns

We now turn to introduce the notion of private patterns. Intuitively, private patterns are just like query patterns. The fundamental difference, however, is that as many query patterns as possible should be detected, whereas there is a strict requirement that no private patterns should be reported.

There are multiple ways in which an adversary could compromise privacy in search of private patterns. The most intrusive way is to break into the CEP system and monitor the arriving event streams. Preventing this type of adversary involves addressing security aspects of the CEP system and is out of the scope of our work. Accordlingly, we assume the CEP system is secure and focus on adversaries who observe the reported matches for the query patterns, and only infer the occurrences of the private patterns from the *externally observable event sequence*, which is a "union" of all the events reported in the query results. We first define externally observable event sequences.

DEFINITION 6. *Let S be a time-stamped event sequence. Let $M = \{M_i\}$ be the set of matches in S produced by a CEP system with respect to the query set $\mathcal{Q}$, that is, $\forall i, M_i$ is a match of some query in $\mathcal{Q}$. The sequence of events obtained by unioning the events in M is called the **externally observable event sequence**. We denote the externally observable event sequence of the original sequence S with respect to the query set $\mathcal{Q}$ as $\overline{S} = O(S, \mathcal{Q})$.*

The semantics for matches of private patterns $\mathcal{P}$ over a given event sequence S are similar to matches of query patterns $\mathcal{Q}$, but they are defined over the external observable event sequence $\overline{S} = O(S, \mathcal{Q})$, instead of the original event sequence S. Specifically, let the set of private patterns be $\mathcal{P} = \{P_i\}, 1 \leq i \leq |\mathcal{P}|$. Each private pattern is defined as follows.

DEFINITION 7. *A **sequence private pattern** P_i is of the form $(p_1^i, p_2^i, ... p_n^i)$, with $p_k^i \in \Sigma$ being event types in the alphabet.*

Let $T(P_i) \in \mathbb{R}^+$ be the window size for each query P_i. There is an instance of **private pattern match** of P_i over a given event sequence S, if there exists a sequence $\overline{S}' = (c_{j_1}, c_{j_2}, ... c_{j_n})$, that is the subsequence of the externally observable event sequence $\overline{S} = O(S, \mathcal{Q})$, such that $c_{j_l} = p_l^i$ for all $l \in [1, n]$, and $t_{j_n} - t_{j_1} \leq T(P_i)$. We say the sequence $\overline{S}'$ is an instance of match of P_i.

Clearly any match of private pattern over the externally observable event sequence constitutes a breach of privacy and should be disallowed. We use the following example to illustrate matches of private patterns.

EXAMPLE 2. *Given the event sequence S and the query patterns Q_1 and Q_2 in Example 1, suppose there are also two private patterns $P_1 = (B, C)$ with $T(P_1) = 2t$, $P_2 = (D, E)$ with $T(P_2) = t$.*

Recall that in Example 1, four instances of the query matches are reported, namely (A_1, B_2), (C_4, D_5), (C_4, D_6) and (C_7, D_9). Using the time-stamps associated with each event, an adversary observing the set of query results will be able to reconstruct the externally observable event sequence in temporal order $\overline{S} = (A_1, B_2, C_4, D_5, D_6, C_7, D_9)$, which is a subsequence of the original event sequence $S = (A_1, B_2, A_3, C_4, D_5, D_6, C_7, A_8, D_9, E_{10})$.

In this example, one instance of matches for P_1 can be produced over $\overline{S}$, namely (B_2, C_4), which results in a breach of privacy. However, there is no match for $P_2 = (D, E)$ with $T(P_2) = t$ over $\overline{S}$, even though in the real event stream S that passes through the CEP engine there is an instance of match (D_9, E_{10}) for P_2. Because we assume that the adversary is only able to observe the reported query results to construct $\overline{S}$, and has no direct knowledge of S, or more specifically the existence of E_{10}, no matches for P_2 can be produced by the adversary.

Since we restrict queries to be simple conjunction of event occurrences, certain events that participate in private patterns have to be suppressed in order to ensure that no private patterns are disclosed. While alternative strategies are possible with an extended query language (inserting fake events, for instance, may be used to prevent private patterns when the private pattern includes negation), in this work we only consider the strategy in which events are suppressed.

DEFINITION 8. *For fixed query and private sets, $\mathcal{Q}$ and $\mathcal{P}$ respectively, a **PP-CEP** system is a function which, for any event sequence S, produces a subsequence S' of S such that no matches of private pattern in $\mathcal{P}$ can be produced over the externally observable sequence $\overline{S} = O(S', \mathcal{Q})$*

Apparently there are various kinds of PP-CEP in which different events can be suppressed to ensure privacy. For instance, in Example 1, given that there is a match of private patterns $P_1 = (B, C)$, the intuitive way to suppress such match is to drop either of the events B or C. In order to measure the relative merits of different strategies and to ultimately determine a preferable strategy, we define a utility function.

2.3 The utility function

We quantify utility based on the number of instances of query matches reported. In addition, because each query pattern may have different real-world importance, we differentiate between queries using a weight function $w(Q_i)$, which measures the importance of reporting an instance of matching Q_i. We define the query utility as follows.

DEFINITION 9. *Let $\mathcal{C}(Q_i, S)$ be the number of distinct matches for query Q_i in S. The **utility** generated for query pattern Q_i is*

$$U(Q_i, S) = w(Q_i) \cdot \mathcal{C}(Q_i, S) \qquad (1)$$

The sum of the utility generated over $\mathcal{Q} = \{Q_i\}$ is

$$U(\mathcal{Q}, S) = \sum_{Q_i \in \mathcal{Q}} U(Q_i, S). \qquad (2)$$

As we have discussed, there are multiple ways in which events can be suppressed to prevent private pattern matches. The utility metric can be used to choose the strategy that preserves the most utility. We will illustrate the concept of utility in Example 3.

EXAMPLE 3. *We continue to use the event stream and query/private patterns of the Example 2. To measure utility, assume for simplicity that the weight associated with query Q_1 and Q_2 is one. Given that there is one instance of match for Q_1 and three matches for Q_2, the total utility gain over $S = (A_1, B_2, A_3, C_4, D_5, D_6, C_7, A_8, D_9, E_{10})$ without privacy consideration is thus $1 + 1 \times 3 = 4$.*

As we have mentioned, in order to suppress the one match produced for $P_1 = (B, C)$ over $\overline{S} = (A_1, B_2, C_4, D_5, D_6, C_7, D_9)$ (namely, (B_2, C_4)), there are two possible event dropping strategies: we could either drop B_2, or drop event C_4. If B_2 is dropped, we will derive $\overline{S}_1 = (A_1, C_4, D_5, D_6, C_7, D_9)$. With that suppression there are a total of three matches for Q_2 left (the match (A_1, B_2) for Q_1 is dropped due to the suppression of B_2), yielding a utility of 3.

Alternatively, the event C_4 can be dropped. This gives us $\overline{S}_2 = (A_1, B_2, D_5, D_6, C_7, D_9)$. With this suppression strategy there is one match of Q_1 ((A_1, B_2)) and one match of Q_2 ((C_7, D_9)) retained, thus the utility for this strategy is $1 + 1 = 2$.

Apparently, while both strategie suppress matches for private patterns, dropping B_2 is the better strategy as measured by the amount of utility it preserves.

Ultimately, the choice of dropping event B or C in the previous example depends on the characteristics of the arriving events in general, or alternatively the distribution of the event types. Intuitively, if C arrives much more frequently than B, and is more likely to produce query match for $Q_2 = (C, D)$, then it may be a good idea to drop B instead of C, as the utility preserved for Q_2 can outweigh the loss of Q_1.

In order to quantify the "expected" query matches to estimate expected utility, we need statistical information about the arriving events. In this work we make the simplifying assumption that the arrival of each type of event is an independent Poisson process, which is typical statistical assumption and is used to model event arrival in performance modeling literature [14]. Furthermore, we assume that the arrival rate λ_i of each Poisson process is known to us. In practice, such an arrival rate can be estimated by sampling the arriving events.

Further, let $|\Sigma|$ be the number of event types, $|\mathcal{Q}|$ and $|\mathcal{P}|$ number of query patterns and private patterns, respectively. Denote by l_q and l_p the maximum length of query patterns and private patterns, respectively, and finally d_q and d_p the maximum number of query patterns/private patterns in which any type of event $e_i \in \Sigma$ participates. We summarize the symbols used in this paper in Table 1.

The end goal of PP-CEP is to find an event suppression strategy such that utility can be maintained as much as possible without compromising privacy. In the following we will discuss in detail two variants that arise from the general formulation.

Σ	The set of all possible event types
e_i	Event of type i
λ_i	The arrival rate of e_i
$\mathcal{Q}$	The set of query patterns
Q_i	Query pattern i
$T(Q_i)$	The time window associated with Q_i
$w(Q_i)$	The utility weight associated with Q_i
q_k^i	The k-th participating event in query pattern Q_i
$\mathcal{P}$	The set of private patterns
P_i	Private pattern i
$T(P_i)$	The time window associated with P_i
$w(P_i)$	The utility weight associated with P_i
p_k^i	The k-th participating event in private pattern P_i
l_q	The maximum length of any query patterns
l_p	The maximum length of any private patterns
d_q	The maximum number of query patterns that any event participates
d_p	The maximum number of private patterns that any event participates

Table 1: Summary of the symbols used

3. THE OBLIVIOUS PP-CEP

The first variant of privacy-preserving CEP we discuss is the *oblivious* PP-CEP.

DEFINITION 10. *Let $\mathcal{P} = \{P_i\}$ be the set of private patterns, with $P_i = (p_1^i, p_2^i, ...p_n^i)$. An **oblivious PP-CEP** is a PP-CEP that suppresses all events of type $e_i \in D$, $D \subseteq \Sigma$, while preserving events in $K = \Sigma \setminus D$, such that for all private pattern P_i, at least one participating event p_j^i is suppressed, or $p_j^i \in D$.*

An oblivious suppression decision drops at least one participating event type from the private patterns. This is a sufficient condition for privacy — if all instances of some event type that participates the private pattern are dropped, no matches for that private pattern can be produced. Oblivious suppression is a global approach that preserves privacy irrespective of the event sequence that may occur, that is, regardless of what has just arrived and what may arrive in the future. The notion of obliviousness is in contrast to the *windowed* PP-CEP that we will discuss in the next section, which also takes into consideration the events that have just arrived in the local window to devise an event suppression strategy. We first use the following example to demonstrate the concept of oblivious PP-CEP.

EXAMPLE 4. *Continuing with Example 3, we illustrate oblivious PP-CEP using the private pattern $P_1 = (B, C)$. Recall that an oblivious PP-CEP decision suppresses at least one participating event type in each private pattern. In this case it could either drop event type B or C.*

Specifically, given the sequence $\overline{S} = (A_1, B_2, C_4, D_5, D_6, C_7, D_9)$, one could either drop all events of type B, or drop all events of type C. Observe that either oblivious decision is sufficient for privacy — if all instances of B (similarly, C) are dropped, the private pattern $P_1 = (B, C)$ will not be disclosed. However oblivious event suppression is not necessary for privacy. In particular, if we decide to drop events of type C, C_7 does not have to be dropped from $\overline{S} = (A_1, B_2, C_4, D_5, D_6, C_7, D_9)$, because based on the events that have arrived at time-stamp t_7 it is clear that preserving C_7 will not compromise privacy (this is because there is no event of type B that arrives between t_5 to t_7, or $T(P_1) = 2t$ prior to C_7).

As a matter of fact, not dropping C_7 allows us to produce one more query match (C_7, D_9) and improves utility.

This example illustrates the key idea of oblivious suppression. Oblivious PP-CEP devise an event suppression strategy that is sufficient, but not always necessary, to preserve privacy. Precisely due to the simplicity in its obliviousness, in practice we expect it to have lower added computation overhead to an existing CEP system than a more sophisticated PP-CEP system (for example, the windowed PP-CEP that we will discuss in Section 4). This property may be especially desired for the CEP model, which typically requires real-time query processing and low computational overhead [5, 10, 17, 22]. However, as we will show, even this oblivious PP-CEP problem is very difficult in terms of computational complexity. This problem of utility-maximizing oblivious PP-CEP is formally defined as follows.

DEFINITION 11. *Let $\Sigma = \{e_i\}$ be the domain of event types where each type of event e_i arrives following an independent Poisson process with arrival rate λ_i. Let the set of query patterns and private patterns be $\mathcal{Q} = \{Q_j\}$ and $\mathcal{P} = \{P_k\}$, respectively. The utility of an oblivious PP-CEP that preserves events $K \subseteq \Sigma$ is denoted as $\mathcal{G}(\mathcal{Q}, K, S) = U(\mathcal{Q}, \Pi_K(S))$, where S is the given event sequence, and $\Pi_K(S)$ is the projection of S which only preserves events in K and none other. The problem of **utility gain maximizing oblivious PP-CEP** given an event sequence S is to find the oblivious PP-CEP with the maximum utility $\mathcal{G}(\mathcal{Q}, K, S)$. Similarly we can define **utility loss minimizing oblivious PP-CEP** as the one that minimizes the utility loss $\mathcal{L}(\mathcal{Q}, K, S) = U(\mathcal{Q}, S) - U(\mathcal{Q}, \Pi_K(S))$.*

Given an event sequence S we can choose over the space of all possible oblivious suppression decisions to find the optimal one with respect to utility. Observe that in Definition 11 we deliberately introduce two utility metrics to optimize, the utility gain metric $\mathcal{G}$ and the utility loss metric $\mathcal{L}$. While they are essentially equivalent to each other and reach the optimal point at the same time, their approximability results are different as we will discuss in detail. We will see that it is easier to approximate the utility loss function than to approximate the utility gain function.

It is worth noting that the event sequence S we consider is the most likely sequence constructed based on the event arrival rate λ_i, and we optimize the utility only based on the expected count of query matches over this most likely event sequence rather than the analysis of the space of all possible event sequence. This technique of using expected counts of random variables to produce simple estimates is used in [12], although more sophisticated and complex techniques like *stochastic programming* [12] can be used to account for the random variables more accurately.

Our reason for using expected counts over stochastic programming is twofold. First, since the arrival rate is already an estimate produced by sampling, over-complicating the problem formulation by using stochastic programming for extra accuracy seems to be overkill. Furthermore, recall that our goal is to explore the difficulty of the PP-CEP problem rather than to produce an accurate utility estimate. And as we will see, using the simple expected count to estimate utility for each query already renders the problem hard in general.

In the following we will first analyze the complexity of the general oblivious PP-CEP and show inapproximability results in Section 3.1. We will then descend into a number of special cases with assumptions on various parameters, and show that for each case how the complexity of the problem can be reduced.

3.1 A general complexity analysis

We study in this section the complexity of the general version of the oblivious PP-CEP problem. Again, rather than considering the stochastic event sequence, we in this work only investigate the complexity of the PP-CEP problem over the expected event sequence that may arise given the arrival rates. As we will see in the following, even with this simplification we can already obtain a number of negative complexity results for the general version of the problem.

THEOREM 1. *The problem of utility gain maximizing oblivious PP-CEP is NP-hard.*

Proof Sketch. We use a reduction from the independent set problem to prove the hardness result. Recall that a set of vertices $V' \subseteq V$ in a graph $G = (V, E)$ is said to be an independent set if no two vertices in V' are adjacent in the graph G (or $\forall u, v \in V', (u, v) \notin E$). The maximum independent set is the independent set with the largest size.

Given an instance of the independent set problem over a graph $G = (V, E)$, we construct an instance of oblivious PP-CEP as follows. We set the symbol set Σ to be the vertex set V, that is we place a symbol corresponding to each vertex in the graph. In addition we set the event sequence S as a list of all symbols in the alphabet in any order, to correspond to all the vertices in the graph. For each edge (u, v) in E we add a private pattern $P_i = (u, v)$ (and (v, u)) into the set of private patterns $\mathcal{P}$. Finally let all vertices $v \in V$ be a query pattern $Q_j = (v)$ in the set of query patterns $\mathcal{Q}$. Let all query patterns $Q_j \in \mathcal{Q}$ have the unit utility weight, $w(Q_j) = 1$ for all j, so that each instance of query match will produce unit utility 1.

Say a solution with utility k or more for the constructed oblivious PP-CEP involves dropping events $D \subseteq \Sigma$ while keeping events $K = \Sigma \setminus D$. Note that the feasibility of D ensures that no private pattern is disclosed. Then the vertex set V_K that corresponds to the set of events K must be an independent set of size k (recall that there is a one-to-one mapping between the event types in the PP-CEP problem we construct and the vertices in the graph).

Overall if dropping D, equivalently reporting all of K, preserves privacy, then no private pattern is a subsequence of K. If this is not the case then there is a pair of vertices $u, v \in V_K$ such that $(u, v) \in E$, which means that both the events corresponding to u and v are kept in the event set K. Since $P = (u, v)$ is a private pattern, this would have violated the privacy constraints, contradicting the fact that keeping K is privacy preserving. Since the solution achieves a utility of k or more, this implies $|K|$ is at least k. This follows from the fact that each alphabet is a query pattern with unit utility. In the other direction if the original graph has an independent set I of size k the we can drop the symbols of the alphabet corresponding to vertices in $V \setminus I$ to obtain a privacy preserving solution of utility k.

Hence the constructed oblivious PP-CEP instance has a solution achieving utility of k or more if and only if the original graph has an independent set of size k or more. This shows that the oblivious PP-CEP is NP-hard. $\square$

Note that although in our proof, oblivious PP-CEP algorithms consider the whole expected event sequence as input, they are not really off-line algorithms, which only produce solutions when the whole input event sequence is seen. Instead, the input event sequence from which suppression strategies are derived is the expected input that can be known a prior based on event arrival rate. Oblivious PP-CEP algorithms simply operate based on the strategies so produced independent of the real input seen in a particular random experiment, and are thus on-line algorithms. This is consistent with the real-time event processing requirement essential to CEP.

We further show some inapproximability results for both the utility gain maximization problem and the utility loss minimization problem of oblivious PP-CEP.

THEOREM 2. *There is a fixed constant $\epsilon \geq 0$ such that if there is a $|\Sigma|^{1-\epsilon}$ factor approximation algorithm for utility gain maximizing oblivious PP-CEP problem, then $P = NP$.*

Proof Sketch. We note that the reduction in Theorem 1 is approximation preserving. In particular, the reduction from an independent set problem over graph G of n vertices produces an instance with $|\Sigma| = n$. Also, the value of optimal solution of the PP-CEP instance is no less than the size of the maximum independent set of G and a privacy preserving solution with utility of k implies an independent set of size at least k. This proves that PP-CEP is as hard as independent set, as an α factor approximation algorithm for PP-CEP gives an α factor approximation for independent set. Using the inapproximability of independent set [19] we get the desired result. $\square$

In addition to the $|\Sigma|^{1-\epsilon}$-inapproximability, we have an alternative inapproximability result based on the parameters l_q, d_p and d_q.

THEOREM 3. *There is a fixed constant $\epsilon \geq 0$ such that if there is a $(1-\epsilon)(l_q d_q d_p - 2)$ factor approximation algorithm for utility gain maximizing oblivious PP-CEP problem, then $P = NP$.*

Proof Sketch. This second inapproximability result is based on l_q (the maximum length of the query patterns), d_q and d_p (the maximum number of query/private patterns that any event participates). This result follows from the inapproximability result shown in [19], which states that for independent set, the approximation factor cannot be better than $(d-2)$, where d is the edge degree of the graph. We show the inapproximability of $(1-\epsilon)(l_q d_q d_p - 2)$ by contradiction. If there is an algorithm that has approximation factor of $(1-\epsilon)(l_q d_q d_p - 2)$, using the approximation preserving reduction from independent set the corresponding independent set problem instance would also have an approximation factor of $(1-\epsilon)(l_q d_q d_p - 2)$. Given that $d_q = 1$, $l_q = 1$, and d_p being the degree of the graph in our reduction construction, we would have an approximation factor better than $d-2$. This contradicts [19]. We cannot approximate beyond the factor of $(l_q d_q d_p - 2)$ as a result. $\square$

THEOREM 4. *For any constant $\delta > 0$, if there is a $(1-\delta) \times \ln(|\mathcal{P}|)$ factor approximation algorithm for utility loss minimizing oblivious PP-CEP problem then $NP \subseteq DTIME(n^{O(\log \log n)})$.*

Proof Sketch. We provide an approximation preserving reduction from set cover. The claim then follows from the inapproximability of set cover [8].

Given a universe U of n elements and a collection of m subsets of U, $\mathcal{C} = \{S_i\}_{i=1}^{m}$, the cardinality set cover problem is to determine if $\mathcal{C}$ contains k or fewer subsets such that their union covers all the elements. The reduction to utility loss minimizing oblivious PP-CEP is as follows: we construct an alphabet set Σ of size m, with an alphabet symbol e_i for each set S_i in the collection. A private pattern P_j corresponding to each element $j \in U$ is introduced. Say element j is contained in p distinct sets: $S_{i_1}, S_{i_2}, \ldots, S_{i_p}$ with $i_1 < i_2 < \ldots < i_p$, we set private pattern P_j to be $(e_{i_1}, e_{i_2}, \ldots e_{i_p})$ with unbounded time window. The

query patterns are simply the m alphabets of Σ with unit utility and unbounded time window. Finally the sequence S is set to be $(e_1, e_2, \ldots, e_m)$.

First note that if the set cover instance has a solution of size k' or less then we can achieve a solution for the PP-CEP problem with utility loss of k'. In particular, say $\mathcal{K} \subseteq \mathcal{C}$ is a collection of subsets covering U. Then we can drop the symbols of the alphabet corresponding to sets in $\mathcal{K}$ to achieve a privacy preserving solution with utility loss of $|\mathcal{K}|$. This follows from the fact that if we drop $|\mathcal{K}| = k'$ alphabet symbols then the loss in utility is exactly k', as each query pattern is an alphabet symbol with utility of one. Each element j is covered by at least one subset in $\mathcal{K}$, say S_a, which implies that dropping alphabet symbol e_a would preserve the privacy of pattern P_j. This overall implies that the generated solution is privacy preserving.

In the other direction, a privacy preserving solution for the PP-CEP instance with a utility loss of k' implies a set cover of size k'. Say we drop all the alphabet symbols in D. Then the utility loss is exactly $|D|$. The relevant observation is that the sets corresponding to alphabet symbols in D form a cover of U. For any private pattern P_j, there is an alphabet symbol, say e_a, which is in D (else D would not be privacy preserving). This implies that set S_a contains element j, thereby proving that the collection of subsets corresponding to subsets in D forms a cover and the size of this cover is exactly $|D|$.

The above approximation preserving reduction shows that utility loss minimizing oblivious PP-CEP problem is at least as hard as set cover, thereby proving the stated claim. $\square$

While the problem of oblivious PP-CEP is in general NP-hard, there are scenarios where certain parameters are small constants, in which cases the complexity of the problem can be different. In the following sections we carve out two special cases and show complexity results under alternative problem formulations.

3.2 A polynomially solvable special case

In this section we formulate the problem as an integer programming problem as follows. Let $x_i \in \{0, 1\}$ be the decision variables to keep/drop events of type $e_i \in \Sigma$ in order to ensure privacy, with $x_i = 1$ being the decision of keeping event e_i, and $x_i = 0$ dropping event e_i. Further let $y_j \in \{0, 1\}$ to be the variable to denote whether query Q_j can be reported. The set of queries that can be reported depends on decision variables, in other words y_js are completely dependent on x_is.

We determine the expected utility produced by query patterns using arrival rates of event types. Recall that λ_i is the arrival rate of event type e_i. Given a query Q_j and its associated time window $T(Q_j)$, we can first compute for each event type in Q_j the expected number of event occurrences in the time window $T(Q_j)$ using the event arrival rate. Then using the expected count of each event that participates Q_j we can compute the expected number of query matches for Q_j in the time window $T(Q_j)$. In this section we will just use $F(Q_j, \vec{\lambda})$ to denote the expected query matches for Q_j so computed, with $\vec{\lambda} \in \mathbb{R}_+^{|\Sigma|}$ being the vector with arrival rate λ_i as components. For details of the computation of $F(Q_j, \vec{\lambda})$ please see the explanation in Appendix A.

Using $F(Q_j, \vec{\lambda})$, the expected utility produced by query pattern Q_j over its associated time window $T(Q_j)$ can be written as

$$E(Q_j) = w(Q_j) \times F(Q_j, \vec{\lambda}) \qquad (3)$$

The expected utility gain per unit time of Q_j, $\overline{E}(Q_j)$, can be obtained by normalizing $E(Q_j)$

$$\overline{E}(Q_j) = \frac{E(Q_j)}{T(Q_j)} \qquad (4)$$

Hence expected total utility gain per unit time, denoted as $G(X)$, where $X = \{x_i\}$ being the vector of event dropping decisions, can be expressed as

$$G(X) = \sum_{Q_j \in \mathcal{Q}} \overline{E}(Q_j) \cdot y_j \qquad (5)$$

Similarly the utility loss function $L(X)$ can be defined as

$$L(X) = \sum_{Q_j \in \mathcal{Q}} \overline{E}(Q_j) \cdot (1 - y_j) \qquad (6)$$

As we mentioned, here we use the expected value of query matches to quantify the utility for each query $E(Q_i)$. Using this simple technique to estimate utility allows us to explore the intrinsic difficulty in the structure of the problem unencumbered.

The oblivious PP-CEP can then be viewed as the problem of maximizing $G(X)$ (or, equivalently, minimizing $L(X)$) under the constraint that no private patterns are disclosed, which means that for each private pattern, at least one of the events that participate the private pattern should be dropped to ensure that no matches for the private patterns will ever be produced. Formally, for each $P_i \in \mathcal{P}$, the privacy-preserving constraints can be written as:

$$\sum_{p_j^i \in P_i} x_j < |P_i| \qquad (7)$$

Furthermore, whether or not query pattern Q_i can be reported (y_i variables) can be expressed using the variables denoting whether events have been dropped (as represented by x_i) using the following linear constraints. For all $Q_i \in \mathcal{Q}$

$$y_i \leq \frac{1}{|Q_i|} \sum_{q_j^i \in Q_i} x_i \qquad (8)$$

Intuitively, this is to say that Q_i can be reported ($y_i = 1$) if and only if all participating events are not dropped.

The problem of utility maximization $G(X)$ is then a integer linear programming problem subject to the constraints in Equation (7) and Equation (8). With this formulation, using Lenstra's algorithm [15], we have the following theorem:

THEOREM 5. *The oblivious PP-CEP problem is polynomially solvable if the total size of the alphabet and query patterns, $|\Sigma| + |\mathcal{Q}|$, or the total number of query and private patterns, $|\mathcal{P}| + |\mathcal{Q}|$ is some fixed constant.*

The proof of this Theorem follows directly from Lenstra's algorithm [15], which shows that the ILP problem is polynomially solvable if the number of variables, or the number of constraints is no more than a small constant. In our ILP formulation, we have a total of $|\Sigma|$ x variables, and $|\mathcal{Q}|$ y variables, with a total of $|\mathcal{P}| + |\mathcal{Q}|$ constraints. Given Lenstra's algorithm, the optimal utility gain (and similarly utility loss) is solvable if either of these two is no greater than a small constant, thus the Theorem 5.

3.3 An approximable special case

Alternatively, we could formulate the oblivious PP-CEP problem as as follows. Let $\overline{x}_i \in \{0, 1\}$ be the reverse of the decision variable x_i defined before. In other words, it is the decision variables to drop/keep events of type $e_i \in \Sigma$, with $\overline{x}_i = 1$ being the decision of dropping event e_i, and $\overline{x}_i = 0$ keeping event e_i (the reverse of

the meaning of x_i). Instead of introducing variables y_i, we express the expected overall utility using $\overline{x}_i$ directly. Specifically, given the expected utility $\overline{E}(Q_i)$ produced for each query pattern Q_i per unit time in Equation 5, the expected total utility gain per unit of time can be expressed as

$$G'(X) = \sum_{Q_i \in \mathcal{Q}} \overline{E}(Q_i) \cdot r(Q_i) \qquad (9)$$

where $r(Q_i)$ denotes whether Q_i can be reported based on the decisions of dropping events x_i: query Q_i can be reported only if no participating events are dropped.

$$r(Q_i) = \prod_{q_j^i \in Q_i} (1 - \overline{x}_i) \qquad (10)$$

Similarly the utility loss function $L'(X)$ can be defined using $\overline{x}_i$ as

$$L'(X) = \sum_{Q_i \in \mathcal{Q}} \overline{E}(Q_i) \cdot (1 - r(Q_i)) \qquad (11)$$

Like the previous ILP formulation, the privacy constraint in this formulation is that for each private pattern, at least one of the events that participate the private pattern should be dropped. For each $P_i \in \mathcal{P}$, we need to have:

$$\sum_{p_j^i \in P_i} \overline{x}_j \geq 1 \qquad (12)$$

Note that instead of the packing constraints as specified in Equation (7) and Equation (8) for the ILP formulation, here with the use of variables $\overline{x}_i$ we instead get a set of covering constraints.

Now we have a new optimization problem with (non-linear) objective function in Equation (9) and Equation (11), and the linear constraints in Equation (12). While we cannot leverage the results established for ILPs, we observe that the new objective function have the nice property of being *sub-modular*.

Submodularity [9] is an important function property that has been studied in the theoretical computer science for its use in optimization algorithms. It can be formally defined as follows.

DEFINITION 12. *[9] Let V be a set of cardinality n. A real-valued functions f over subsets of X, $f : 2^V \to \mathbb{R}$ is submodular if it satisfies*

$$f(X + e) - f(X) \geq f(Y + e) - f(Y), \text{for all } X \subset Y \subseteq V$$

The intuitive interpretation of submodularity is that as the input set grows, the incremental gain in f will decrease for the same addition in input (the e). This property is sometimes also known as *diminishing returns*.

LEMMA 1. *The utility loss function $L'(X)$ in Equation (11) is a submodular function.*

We can intuitively see why $L'(X)$ is submodular. The utility for a given query pattern Q_i will be lost the first time a constituent event gets dropped. Any additional events being dropped for the same query Q_i will not yield any increase in the utility loss $L'(X)$. In other words, the decisions of dropping one additional event given a larger set of events have been dropped will produce less increment in utility loss than that of case when the additional event is dropped given a smaller set of events have been dropped, a classical definition of diminishing returns.

Based on the submodular property, we can show a good approximation ratio for $L'(X)$ in the problem of oblivious PP-CEP processing in Theorem 6.

THEOREM 6. *Let l_p be the maximum length of any private pattern that is no greater than some small constant. The utility loss function $L'(X)$ in oblivious PP-CEP processing is l_p-approximable.*

The proof of Theorem 6 is built on the results in [11]. Specifically, observe that the integer program we have is l_p row sparse, with covering constraints (in Equation (12)), and a submodular objective function (Lemma 1). It has been shown in [11] that such an integer program is l_p approximable, thus our result in Theorem 6.

This approximability result for $L'(X)$, however, does not extend in a similar manner to the utility gain function $G'(X)$. Specifically, while the approximation ratio for $L'(X)$, l_p, is essentially the column sparsity of the coefficient matrix of the constraints, we cannot obtain a similar row sparsity approximation ratio for the utility gain function $G'(X)$. The reason is because for utility gain it becomes a *supermodular* function maximization with packing constraints, which is known to be hard to approximate. We in the following construct an algorithm and show that utility gain is $l_q d_q d_p$ approximable. This is almost tight as it is also $(l_q d_q d_p - 2)(1 - \epsilon)$-inapproximable as described in Theorem 3.

THEOREM 7. *The maximization of the utility gain function $G'(X)$ in the oblivious PP-CEP is $l_q d_q d_p$-approximable.*

Proof Sketch. We show the $l_q d_q d_p$-approximation factor by constructing an algorithm that has no less than $\frac{1}{l_q d_q d_p}$ utility gain of the optimal utility gain. The algorithm works as follows. First we pre-process the query set by removing queries that can never be satisfied due to the presence of the private patterns (for example, those queries that are subsequences of some private pattern). We then sort all remaining feasible queries Q_i in $\mathcal{Q}$ by utility weight $W(Q_i)$. We pick in $\mathcal{Q}$ the query Q_{s_1} that has the largest weight. Let the set of events that participate Q_{s_1} be E_{s_1}. For each event $e_i \in E_{s_1}$, denote the set of private patterns that contain e_i as $\mathcal{P}_{e_i}$. Randomly select an event e_i^j in each pattern $P^j \in \mathcal{P}_{e_i}$ and suppress it. This would affect all queries that contain event e_i^j, denoted as $Q_{e_i^j}$, because these queries would never be reported due to the suppression of e_i^j. Removes all such affected queries $Q_{e_i^j}$ from $\mathcal{Q}$. In the remaining queries that are not affected, again find the Q_{s_2} with the highest utility weight and proceed as above. The claim is that this algorithm is $l_q d_q d_p$-approximate.

We get $l_q d_q d_p$ approximation ratio because each query Q_{s_k} we pick has at most l_q events. For each such event e_i there are no more than d_p private patterns that contain it. Since we suppress one event for each such private pattern, the total number of suppressed events cannot be more than $l_q d_p$. In addition, each suppressed event participates no more than d_q query patterns, that will affect at most $d_p d_q l_q$ queries. That means in each iteration, keeping the query with the highest weight entails removing at most $d_p d_q l_q$ queries, all of which with less utility weight than the one we keep. As a result, we can keep at least $\frac{1}{d_p d_q l_q}$ utility out of maximum possible utility (the utility sum of all queries), which has to be no less than the optimal oblivious PP-CEP utility, thus the approximation ratio in Theorem 7. □

3.4 A robustness analysis

The approximation analysis conducted in Section 3.2 and Section 3.3 are based on the assumption that events arrive exactly as expected as specified by the arrival rate λ_i of the Poisson process. In reality the actual arrival process can deviate from the expectations. In this section we give a robustness analysis to show the utility bound in such cases.

Recall that the overall utility gain is defined in Equation (2) as $\sum_{Q_i \in \mathcal{Q}} w(Q_i) \cdot \mathcal{C}(Q_i, S)$, where $\mathcal{C}(Q_i, S)$ denotes the number of matches for Q_i over the event sequence S. In our analysis we use the arrival rates λ_i for each type of event to compute the expected count of matches $\mathcal{C}_E(Q_i, S)$. Suppose the actual count of matches $\mathcal{C}_A(Q_i, S)$ deviates from the expected value by a ratio of l, or alternatively

$$\frac{1}{l} \leq \frac{\mathcal{C}_E(Q_i, S)}{\mathcal{C}_A(Q_i, S)} \leq l \qquad (13)$$

Since we estimate the arrival rate λ_i by sampling of the arriving events which may not perfectly predict the arriving events in the future, we quantify the robustness of the approximation ratio given the inaccurate statistics in the following proposition.

PROPOSITION 1. *If algorithm $\mathcal{A}$ is a k-approximate algorithm for utility gain maximization (or utility loss minimization) PP-CEP, for any real event sequence whose true count of query matches deviates from the expected count by no more than a ratio of l, the approximation ratio of $\mathcal{A}$ must be better than $l^2 k$.*

This robust approximation ratio applies to previous results in Theorem 6 and Theorem 7. We show the approximation ratio $l^2 k$ for utility maximization problem and the ratio for utility loss minimization are similar. Let U_A be the actual utility using algorithm $\mathcal{A}$, and U_E be the expected utility using $\mathcal{A}$. Given the deviation ratio of at most l, we know that $U_A \cdot l \geq U_E$. We know that $\mathcal{A}$ has approximation ratio k, so the expected utility $U_E \cdot k \geq U_E^{OPT}$. Furthermore the actual optimal utility cannot be off from the expected optimal by a ratio of l or $U_E^{OPT} \cdot l \geq U_A^{OPT}$. Summarizing the three inequalities we obtain $U_A \cdot l^2 k \geq U_A^{OPT}$, meaning the utility of using $\mathcal{A}$ on the actual event sequence is at most off by $l^2 k$ from the optimal utility on the actual event sequence.

4. THE WINDOWED PP-CEP

In this section we explore a different variant of the problem, which we term the *windowed* version of PP-CEP. While the oblivious PP-CEP suppresses events in a global manner independent of events just arrived, the windowed version takes into account the events that have just arrived in the window Δ of size $|\Delta|$ to devise suppression decisions. Here Δ is a window over the event sequence, $|\Delta|$ is the number of events present in the window, and $T(\Delta)$ is its length in time.

DEFINITION 13. *A **windowed PP-CEP** is a PP-CEP, that suppresses events based on a suppression function $R : (\Sigma \cup \Phi)^{|\Delta|} \times \Sigma \to \{0, 1\}$, where the first input, $(\Sigma \cup \Phi)^{|\Delta|}$ represents the events that have arrived in the window Δ immediately prior to the current arriving event, and the second input, Σ, stands for the current arriving event e. A suppression decision has to be made for e, with 1 representing suppressing the current event e and 0 keeping it. Here Φ represents the absence of an event when there is less than $|\Delta|$ events in the window.*

In order to ensure privacy of the CEP system, the size of the window $|\Delta|$ has to be sufficiently large to accommodates all possible events that may arrive in $\max_{P_i \in \mathcal{P}}(T(P_i))$, for otherwise the suppression decisions devised may not be aware of the events that previously arrived and are outside of the window Δ. Such events coupled with the presence of certain events in the current window, can produce matches of private patterns and compromise privacy.

We use the following example to illustrate the windowed PP-CEP.

EXAMPLE 5. *We continue with Example 4, and consider the private pattern $P_1 = (B, C)$. Let the window size $|\Delta| = 2$.*

*Informally, use the shorthand notation $\star$ to denote zero or more occurrences of any event. Among the space of all possible windowed PP-CEP, we consider two strategies, $R_B(*, B) = 1$ or intuitively the one that suppresses B; and $R_C(*B*, C) = 1$ or the one that suppresses C.*

Given R_B, and the original event sequence $S = (A_1, B_2, A_3, C_4, D_5, D_6, C_7, A_8, D_9, E_{10})$, at time t_2, B_2 will be suppressed to produce $S_B = (A_1, A_3, C_4, D_5, D_6, C_7, A_8, D_9, E_{10})$, over which the query set will be executed. Note that this particular strategy, $R_B(*, B) = 1$, suppresses B irrespective of the window Δ, and is equivalent to the oblivious PP-CEP that suppresses B obliviously. In this example it produces the same suppression result as the one in Example 4.

Now we consider the R_C suppression function. At t_4 the event C_4 will be suppressed because at that point, window Δ has the sequence (B_2, A_3), which leads to the suppression of C_4 as specified by R_C. In contrast, at t_7, given the window $\Delta = (D_5, D_6)$, C_7 will be preserved as R_C outputs 0. This is possible because at t_7, given the window Δ, it is clear that revealing C_7 will not compromise privacy due to the absence of B in Δ. This produces the suppressed event sequence $S_C = (A_1, B_2, A_3, D_5, D_6, C_7, A_8, D_9, E_{10})$. Note that this is different from the oblivious PP-CEP in Example 4 that suppresses all events of type C, which includes C_7 that does not have to be suppressed.

While it is apparent that it is necessary that any arriving event that can produce an match for some private pattern needs to be suppressed to ensure privacy, a utility maximizing suppression function R does not necessarily suppress the arriving event only when the arriving event can cause some private patterns to be matched (or equivalently, only suppressing the last event of each private pattern). As an intuitive example if there is one private pattern $P = (A, B, C)$, in which the event B rarely happens and has little contribution to the expected utility, while C arrives much more frequently and contributes to many query patterns, it may be a better choice to suppress B whenever it is seen and with A in the window Δ, instead of waiting until the last moment to suppress C. In general the whole space of all windowed PP-CEP suppression functions have to be considered.

The hardness results in Section 3.1 obtained for the oblivious PP-CEP, including the NP-hardness and the inapproximability results (Theorem 2, Theorem 3 and Theorem 4) still hold in the windowed PP-CEP. To see this, the set cover problem and the independence set problem can be reduced to the windowed PP-CEP in the same fashion as previously shown if the time windows of private patterns are set to infinite.

We consider the special case where the window size $|\Delta|$ is no more than some fixed constant (or the window Δ of size $|\Delta|$ can always accommodate all events that arrive within the time window $\max_{P_i \in \mathcal{P}}(T(P_i))$). This can in some sense be viewed as the special case where among the input parameters listed in Table 1, both $T(P_i)$ and λ_i are small. Essentially, this allows us to consider all possible subsequences that may appear in the window. In this special scenario we show an approximability result for utility loss minimization as follows.

THEOREM 8. *Let l_p, the maximum length of any private pattern, and $|\Delta|$, the window size, be fixed constant. Then there exists a polynomial time approximation algorithm that achieves a l_p-approximation factor for utility loss function in windowed PP-CEP processing.*

Proof Sketch. We sketch the proof of this theorem, which is similar to that of Theorem 6. First we enumerate all possible event combinations in the window of size $|\Delta|$. This is possible given that $|\Delta|$ is some fixed constant. Let p_i be the probability variable of each possible window Γ_i, and x_i^j be suppression variables given Γ_i and the arriving event of type e_j (which is essentially the suppression function $x_i^j = R(\Gamma_i, e_j)$). We can build a system of equations that represents the transition of the probabilities between possible windows Γ_i, using the suppression variables x_i^j and event arrival rate λ_k. That is, we set up a system of equations with x_i^j and p_i as unknowns for all windows Γ_i and event types e_j. Solving this system of equations allows us to represent the probabilities of seeing each window Γ_i using x_i^j and event arrival rate λ_k. Given the probabilities of each window as a function of x_i^j and λ_k, and the suppression variables x_i^j, we can write the expected utility loss $L(X)$ as a function of λ_k and x_i^j.

Similar to the argument made in Lemma 1, the utility loss function $L(X)$ in the windowed PP-CEP is also submodular due to the "diminishing gain" in utility loss when additional events of some window are suppressed.

The privacy constraints can also be expressed using a covering constrains of l_p row-sparsity. Specifically, for each query $P_i = (p_1^i, p_2^i, \ldots, p_n^i)$, let the event types of p_k^i be $e_{m_k}^i \in \Sigma$, privacy will be breached if the sequence, with m_n events of types $e_{m_k}^i$, for all such k in $[1, n]$, has none of the m_n events dropped. This can be expressed as a constraint, which is the sum of $R(\Gamma_{w_j}, e_j)$ can be no less than 1, where Γ_{w_j} is any possible window immediately prior to event of type e_j, or $\sum_{e_j \in P_i} R(\Gamma_{w_j}, e_j) \geq 1$, which is a covering constraint. Also observe that $R(\Gamma_{w_j}, e_j)$ are just the x variables used in the utility function. While there are many possible windows $((|\Sigma| + 1)^\Delta)$ prior to each event e_j, and consequently many such constraints, in each constraint the total number of variables are at most n, the length of the private patterns. Given that n is no more than l_p, the row sparsity of the constrain matrix cannot be greater than l_p.

It is thus a submodular minimization problem with covering constraints. Using the framework of Iwata et al. [11] we can obtain a factor l_p approximation for minimizing utility loss. □

5. CONCLUSIONS AND FUTURE WORK

There are a number of interesting ways in which this work can be further extended. First, in this work we restrict the CEP query language to be simple conjunctions of occurrences of events. Extending the complexity analysis to more expressive query languages is of practical and theoretical interest. Furthermore, in addition to the oblivious and the windowed PP-CEP, alternative strategies, like delaying the decision of dropping events for a delay window instead of making real-time decision, may offer opportunities to further enhance utility. Understanding the complexity of such a quasi-real-time approach and the utility/responsiveness trade-offs would be interesting. In addition, in this work the event arrival process is assumed to be an independent Poisson process. Modeling the dependence of the arriving events using models like Markov chains is also an interesting direction for future research.

6. REFERENCES

[1] Coral8: www.coral8.com.
[2] Streambase: www.streambase.com.
[3] Streaminsight:
    http://www.microsoft.com/sqlserver/2008/en/us/r2-complex-event.aspx.

[4] J. Agrawal, Y. Diao, D. Gyllstrom, and N. Immerman. Efficient pattern matching over event streams. In *SIGMOD*, 2008.

[5] M. H. Ali and C. G. et al. Microsoft cep server and online behavioral targeting. In *VLDB*, 2009.

[6] N. Bansal, N. Korula, V. Nagarajan, and A. Srinivasan. On *k*-column sparse packing programs. *CoRR*, 0908.2256, 2009.

[7] R. S. Barga, J. Goldstein, M. Ali, and M. Hong. Consistent streaming through time: A vision for event stream processing. 2007.

[8] U. Feige. A threshold of ln n for approximating set cover. *Journal of the ACM*, 45 (4), 1998.

[9] S. Fujishige. *Submodular functions and optimization*. 2005.

[10] D. Gyllstrom, E. Wu, H.-J. Chae, Y. Diao, P. Stahlberg, and G. Anderson. SASE: Complex event processing over streams. In *CIDR*, 2007.

[11] S. Iwata and K. Nagano. Submodular function minimization under covering constraints. In *FOCS*, 2009.

[12] P. Kall and S. W. Wallace. *Stochastic Programming*. Wiley, 1994.

[13] C. Koufogiannakis and N. E. Young. Greedy Δ-approximation algorithm for covering with arbitrary constraints and submodular cost. In *Proceedings of the 36th International Colloquium on Automata, Languages and Programming: Part I*, pages 634–652, Berlin, Heidelberg, 2009. Springer-Verlag.

[14] E. D. Lazowska, J. Zahorjan, G. S. Graham, and K. C. Sevcik. *Quantitative System Performance*. Prentice Hall, 1984.

[15] H. W. Lenstra. Integer programming with a fixed number of variables. *Mathematics of Operation Research*, 1983.

[16] M. Liu, M. Li, D. Golovnya, E. A. Rundensteiner, and K. Claypool. Sequence pattern query processing over out-of-order event streams. In *ICDE*, 2009.

[17] Y. Mei and S. Madden. Zstream: A cost-based query processor for adaptively detecting composite events. In *SIGMOD*, 2009.

[18] D. Pritchard and D. Chakrabarty. Approximability of sparse integer programs. *CoRR*, 0904.0859, 2009.

[19] L. Trevisan. Inapproximability of combinatorial optimization problems. Technical report, University of California Berkeley, 2004.

[20] D. Wang, E. Rundensteiner, and R. Ellison. Active complex event processing for realtime health care. In *VLDB*, 2010.

[21] W. White, M. Riedewald, J. Gehrke, and A. Demers. What is "next" in event processing? In *PODS*, 2007.

[22] E. Wu, Y. Diao, and S. Rizvi. High-performance complex event processing over streams. In *SIGMOD*, 2006.

APPENDIX

A. EXPECTED QUERY UTILITY

In this section we describe how the expected query matches for Q_j over the time window $T(Q_j)$, denoted as $F(Q_j, \vec{\lambda})$, can be estimated using arrival rates of event types, where λ_i is the arrival rate of event type e_i.

We first compute for each event type in Q_j the expected number of event occurrences in the time window $T(Q_j)$. Specifically, for each event type e_i, the expected number of e_i occurrences in $T(Q_j)$, denoted as l_i, can be computed as $l_i = \lambda_i T(Q_j)$. Further denote $\sigma(Q_j)$ as the set of the types of the events that are part of Q_j, $|Q_j|$ as the total number of events in Q_j, and let $n(e_i)$ be the number of occurrences of event type e_i in Q_j (for example, a query $Q = (A, A, B)$ would have $\sigma(Q) = \{A, B\}$, $n(A) = 2$, $n(B) = 1$, and $|Q| = 3$). Denote $L = \sum_{e_i \in \sigma(Q_j)} l_i$ be the total number of occurrences of events relevant to Q_j in time window $T(Q_j)$.

We can then estimate the expected number of query matches for Q_j in $T(Q_j)$ as

$$F(Q_j, \lambda) = \binom{L}{|Q_j|} \frac{\prod_{e_i \in \sigma(Q_j)} \prod_{k=0}^{n(e_i)} (l_i - k)}{\prod_{r=0}^{|Q_j|} (L - r)} \qquad (14)$$

The reasoning of $F(Q_j, \lambda)$ works as follows. Given a total of L event occurrences in $T(Q_j)$, we only pick a total $|Q_j|$ events to form a query match. Let us pick the first $|Q_j|$ events to form random permutations and compute the probability that the first $|Q_j|$ events produces a match. Let the first position of Q_j be an event of type e_{p_1}. The probability of actually seeing the event that type is $\frac{l_{e_{p_1}}}{L}$. For the second event in Q_j, if it is also of type e_{p_1}, the probability of seeing that event that type is $\frac{l_{e_{p_1}} - 1}{L - 1}$, otherwise it is $\frac{l_{e_{p_1}}}{L-1}$, so on and so forth. In the end this gives us the term $\frac{\prod_{e_i \in \sigma(Q_j)} \prod_{k=0}^{n(e_i)} (l_i - k)}{\prod_{r=0}^{|Q_j|} (L-r)}$. Given that there are a total of $\binom{L}{|Q_j|}$ such possible positions out of L event occurrences and each of which is symmetric, the expected count of query matches can be expressed as the product of the two, thus the Equation (14).

Provenance Views for Module Privacy

Susan B. Davidson
University of Pennsylvania
Philadelphia, PA, USA
susan@cis.upenn.edu

Sanjeev Khanna
University of Pennsylvania
Philadelphia, PA, USA
sanjeev@cis.upenn.edu

Tova Milo
Tel Aviv University
Tel Aviv, Israel
milo@cs.tau.ac.il

Debmalya Panigrahi
CSAIL, MIT
Massachusetts, MA, USA
debmalya@mit.edu

Sudeepa Roy
University of Pennsylvania
Philadelphia, PA, USA
sudeepa@cis.upenn.edu

ABSTRACT

Scientific workflow systems increasingly store provenance information about the module executions used to produce a data item, as well as the parameter settings and intermediate data items passed between module executions. However, authors/owners of workflows may wish to keep some of this information confidential. In particular, a *module* may be proprietary, and users should not be able to infer its behavior by seeing mappings between all data inputs and outputs.

The problem we address in this paper is the following: Given a workflow, abstractly modeled by a relation R, a privacy requirement Γ and costs associated with data. The *owner* of the workflow decides which data (attributes) to hide, and provides the *user* with a view R' which is the projection of R over attributes which have *not* been hidden. *The goal is to minimize the cost of hidden data while guaranteeing that individual modules are Γ-private.* We call this the Secure-View problem. We formally define the problem, study its complexity, and offer algorithmic solutions.

Categories and Subject Descriptors

H.2.0 [**Database Management**]: General—*Security, integrity, and protection*; H.2.8 [**Database Management**]: Database applications—*Scientific databases*

General Terms

Algorithms, Theory

Keywords

workflows, provenance, privacy, approximation

1. INTRODUCTION

The importance of data provenance has been widely recognized. In the context of scientific workflows, systems such as myGrid/Taverna [19], Kepler [4], and VisTrails [10] now

capture and store provenance information, and a standard for provenance representation called the Open Provenance Model (OPM) [17] has been designed. By maintaining information about the module executions (processing steps) used to produce a data item, as well as the parameter settings and intermediate data items passed between module executions, the validity and reliability of data can be better understood and results be made reproducible.

However, authors/owners of workflows may wish to keep some of this provenance information private. For example, intermediate *data* within an execution may contain sensitive information, such as the social security number, a medical record, or financial information about an individual. Although users with the appropriate level of access may be allowed to see such confidential data, making it available to all users is an unacceptable breach of privacy. Beyond data privacy, a *module* itself may be proprietary, and hiding its description may not be enough: users without the appropriate level of access should not be able to infer its functionality by observing all inputs and outputs of the module. Finally, details of how certain modules in the workflow are connected may be proprietary, and therefore showing how data is passed between modules may reveal too much of the *structure* of the workflow. *There is thus an inherent trade-off between the utility of provenance information and the privacy guarantees that authors/owners desire.*

While data privacy was studied in the context of statistical databases and ideas related to structural privacy were dealt with in the context of workflow views, module privacy has not been addressed yet. Given the importance of the issue [7], this paper therefore focuses on the problem of preserving the privacy of *module functionality*, i.e. the mapping between input and output values produced by the module (rather than the actual *algorithm* that implements it).

Abstracting the workflow models in [19, 4, 10], we consider a module to be a finite relation which takes a set I of input data (attributes), produces a set O of output data (attributes), and satisfies the functional dependency $I \longrightarrow O$. A row in this relation represents one execution of the module. In a *workflow*, n such data processing modules are connected in a directed acyclic multigraph (network), and jointly produce a set of final outputs from a set of initial inputs. Each module receives input data from one or more modules, or from the initial external input, and sends output data to one or more modules, or produces the final output. Thus a workflow can be thought of as a relation which is the input-output join of the constituent module relations. Each row in this relation represents a workflow execution, and captures the provenance of data that is produced during that execution. We call this the *provenance relation*.

To ensure the privacy of module functionality, we extend the notion of ℓ-diversity [15] to our network setting[1]: A module with functionality m in a workflow is said to be Γ-private if for every input x, the actual value of the output $m(x)$ is indistinguishable from $\Gamma - 1$ other possible values w.r.t. the visible data values in the provenance relation. This is achieved by carefully selecting a subset of data items and hiding those values in *all* executions of the workflow – i.e. by showing the user a *view* of the provenance relation for the workflow in which the selected data items (attributes) are hidden. Γ-privacy of a module ensures that even with arbitrary computational power and access to the view for all possible executions of workflow, an adversary can not guess the correct value of $m(x)$ with probability $> \frac{1}{\Gamma}$.

Identical privacy guarantees can be achieved by hiding different subsets of data. To reflect the fact that some data may be more valuable to the user than other data, we assign a *cost* to each data item in the workflow, which indicates the utility lost to the user when the data value is hidden. It is important to note that, due to *data sharing* (i.e. computed data items that are passed as input to more than one module in the workflow), hiding some data can be used to guarantee privacy for more than one module in the network.

The problem we address in this paper is the following: We are given a workflow, abstractly modeled by a relation R, a privacy requirement Γ and costs associated with data. An instance of R represents the set of workflow executions that have been run. The *owner* of the workflow decides which attributes to hide, and provides the *user* with a view R' which is the projection of R over the visible attributes. *The goal is to minimize the cost of hidden data while guaranteeing that individual modules are Γ-private.* We call this the secure-view problem. We formally define the problem, study its complexity, and offer algorithmic solutions.

Contributions. Our first contribution is to formalize the notion of Γ-privacy of a private module when it is a standalone entity (*standalone privacy*) as well as when it is a component of a workflow interacting with other modules (*workflow privacy*). For standalone modules, we then analyze the computational and communication complexity of obtaining a minimal cost set of input/output data items to hide such that the remaining, visible attributes guarantee Γ-privacy (a *safe subset*). We call this the *standalone secure-view* problem.

Our second set of contributions is to study workflows in which all modules are *private*, i.e. modules for which the user has no a priori knowledge and whose behavior must be hidden. For such *all-private workflows*, we analyze the complexity of finding a minimum cost set of data items in the workflow, as a whole, to hide such that the remaining visible attributes guarantee Γ-privacy for all modules. We call this the *workflow secure-view* problem. Although the privacy of a module within a workflow is inherently linked to the workflow topology and functionality of other modules, we are able to show that guaranteeing workflow secure-views in this setting essentially reduces to implementing the stan-

dalone privacy requirements for each module. We then study two variants of the workflow secure-view problem, one in which module privacy is specified in terms of attribute sets (*set constraints*) and one in which module privacy is specified in terms of input/output cardinalities (*cardinality constraints*). Both variants are easily shown to be NP-hard, and we give poly-time approximation algorithms for these problems. While the cardinality constraints version has an linear-programming-based $O(\log n)$-approximation algorithm, the set constraints version is much harder to approximate. However, both variants becomes more tractable when the workflow has *bounded data sharing*, i.e. when a data item acts as input to a small number of modules. In this case a constant factor approximation is possible, although the problem remains NP-hard even without any data sharing

Our third set of contributions is in *general workflows*, i.e workflows which contain private modules as well as modules whose behavior is known (*public* modules). Here we show that ensuring standalone privacy of private modules no longer guarantees their workflow privacy. However, by making some of the public modules private (*privatization*) we can attain workflow privacy of all private modules in the workflow. Since privatization has a cost, the optimization problem, becomes much harder: Even without data sharing the problem is $\Omega(\log n)$-hard to approximate. However, for both all-private and general workflows, there is an LP-based $\ell_{\max}$-approximation algorithm, where $\ell_{\max}$ is the length of longest requirement list for any module.

Related Work. *Workflow privacy* has been considered in [6, 12, 11]. In [6], the authors discuss a framework to output a *partial* view of a workflow that conforms to a given set of access permissions on the connections between modules and data on input/output ports. The problem of ensuring the *lawful use* of data according to specified privacy policies has been considered in [12, 11]. The focus of the work is a policy language for specifying relationships among data and module sets, and their properties relevant to privacy. Although all these papers address workflow privacy, the privacy notions are somewhat informal and no guarantees on the quality of the solution are provided in terms of privacy and utility. Furthermore, our work is the first, to our knowledge, to address module privacy rather than data privacy.

Secure provenance for workflows has been studied in [14, 5, 13]. The goal is to ensure that provenance information has not been forged or corrupted, and a variety of cryptographic and trusted computing techniques are proposed. In contrast, we assume that provenance information has not been corrupted, and focus on ensuring module privacy.

In [16], the authors study information disclosure in data exchange, where given a set of public views, the goal is to decide if they reveal any information about a private view. This does not directly apply to our problem, where the private elements are the $(\mathbf{x}, m(\mathbf{x}))$ relations. For example, if all $\mathbf{x}$ values are shown without showing any of the $m(\mathbf{x})$ values for a module m, then information is revealed in their setting but not in our setting.[2]

Privacy-preserving data mining has received considerable attention (see surveys [2, 22]). The goal is to hide individual data attributes while retaining the suitability of data for mining patterns. For example, the technique of *anonymiz-*

---

[1] In the Related Work, we discuss why a stronger notion of privacy, like differential privacy, is not suitable here.

[2] In contrast, it can be shown that showing all $m(\mathbf{x})$ values while hiding the $\mathbf{x}$'s, may reveal information in our setting.

ing data makes each record indistinguishable from a large enough set of other records in certain identifying attributes [21, 15]. Privacy preserving approaches were studied for *social networks* [3, 20] *auditing queries* [18] and in other contexts. Our notion of *standalone* module privacy is close to that of *ℓ-diversity* [15], in which the values of *non-sensitive attributes* are generalized so that, for every such generalization, there are at least *ℓ* different values of *sensitive attributes*. We extend this work in two ways: First, we place modules (relations) in a network of modules, which significantly complicates the problem, Second, we analyze the complexity of attaining standalone as well as workflow privacy of modules.

Another widely used technique is that of *data perturbation* where some noise (usually random) is added to the the output of a query or to the underlying database. This technique is often used in *statistical databases*, where a query computes some aggregate function over the dataset [8] and the goal is to preserve the privacy of data elements. In contrast, in our setting the private elements are $(\mathbf{x}, m(\mathbf{x}))$ pairs for a private module m and the queries are select-project-join style queries over the provenance relation rather than aggregate queries.

Privacy in *statistical databases* is typically quantified using *differential privacy*, which requires that the output distribution is *almost* invariant to the inclusion of any particular record (see survey [9] and the references therein). Although this is an extremely strong notion of privacy, *no deterministic algorithm can guarantee differential privacy*. Since provenance is used to ensure reproducibility of experiments (and therefore data values must be accurate), adding random noise to provenance information may render it useless. Thus standard mechanisms for differential privacy are unsuitable for our purpose. Our approach of outputting a safe view allows the user to know the name of all data items and the exact values of data that is visible. The user also does not lose any utility in terms of *connections* in the workflow, and can infer exactly which module produced which visible data item or whether two visible data items depend on each other.

Organization. Section 2 defines our workflow model and formalizes the notions of Γ-privacy of a module, both when it is standalone and when it appears in a workflow. The secure-view problem for standalone module privacy is studied in Section 3. Section 4 then studies the problem for workflows consisting only of private modules, whereas Section 5 generalizes the results to general workflows consisting of both public and private modules. Finally we conclude and discuss directions for future work in Section 6.

2. PRELIMINARIES

We start by introducing some notation and formalizing our notion of privacy. We first consider the privacy of a single module, which we call *standalone module privacy*. Then we consider privacy when modules are connected in a workflow, which we call *workflow module privacy*.

2.1 Modules and Relations

We model a module m with a set I of input variables and a set O of (computed) output variables as a relation R over a set of attributes $A = I \cup O$ that satisfies the functional dependency $I \to O$. In other words, I serves as a (not necessarily minimal) key for R. We assume that $I \cap O = \emptyset$

and will refer to I as the *input attributes* of R and to O as its *output attributes*.

We assume that the values of each attribute $a \in A$ come from a finite but arbitrarily large domain Δ_a, and let $\mathtt{Dom} = \prod_{a \in I} \Delta_a$ and $\mathtt{Range} = \prod_{a \in O} \Delta_a$ denote the *domain* and *range* of the module m respectively. The relation R thus represents the (possibly partial) function $m : \mathtt{Dom} \to \mathtt{Range}$ and tuples in R describe executions of m, namely for every $t \in R$, $\pi_O(\mathbf{t}) = m(\pi_I(\mathbf{t}))$. We overload the standard notation for projection, $\pi_A(R)$, and use it for a tuple $\mathbf{t} \in R$. Thus $\pi_A(\mathbf{t})$, for a set A of attributes, denotes the projection of $\mathbf{t}$ to the attributes in A.

EXAMPLE 1. *Figure 1 shows a simple workflow involving three modules m_1, m_2, m_3 with boolean input and output attributes; we will return to it shortly and focus for now on the top module m_1. Module m_1 takes as input two data items, a_1 and a_2, and computes $a_3 = a_1 \vee a_2$, $a_4 = \neg(a_1 \wedge a_2)$ and $a_5 = \neg(a_1 \oplus a_2)$. (The symbol $\oplus$ denotes XOR). The relational representation (functionality) of module m_1 is shown in Figure 1a as relation R_1, with the functional dependency $a_1 a_2 \longrightarrow a_3 a_4 a_5$. For clarity, we have added I (input) and O (output) above the attribute names to indicate their role.*

I		O		
a_1	a_2	a_3	a_4	a_5
0	0	0	1	1
0	1	1	1	0
1	0	1	1	0
1	1	1	0	1

(a) R_1: Functionality of m_1

a_1	a_2	a_3	a_4	a_5	a_6	a_7
0	0	0	1	1	1	0
0	1	1	1	0	0	1
1	0	1	1	0	0	1
1	1	1	0	1	1	1

(b) R: Workflow executions

$I \cap V$	$O \cap V$	
a_1	a_3	a_5
0	0	1
0	1	0
1	1	0
1	1	1

(c) $R_V = \pi_V(R_1)$

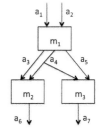

Figure 1: Module and workflow executions as relations

2.2 Standalone Module Privacy

Our approach to ensuring standalone module privacy, for a module represented by the relation R, will be to hide a carefully chosen subset of R's attributes. In other words, we will project R on a restricted subset V of attributes (called the *visible attributes* of R), allowing users access only to the view $R_V = \pi_V(R)$. The remaining, non visible, attributes of R are called *hidden attributes*.

We distinguish below two types of modules. (1) *Public modules* whose behavior is fully known to users when the name of the module is revealed. Here users have a priori knowledge about the full content of R and, even if given only the view R_V, they are able to fully (and exactly) reconstruct R. Examples include reformatting or sorting modules. (2) *Private modules* where such a priori knowledge does not exist, even if the name of the module is revealed. Here, the only information available to users, on the module's behavior, is the one given by R_V. Examples include proprietary software, e.g. a genetic disorder susceptibility module[3].

Given a view (projected relation) R_V of a private module m, the *possible worlds* of m are all the possible full relations (over the same schema as R) that are consistent with R_V w.r.t the visible attributes. Formally,

DEFINITION 1. *Let m be a private module with a corresponding relation R, having input and output attributes I and O, resp., and let $V \subseteq I \cup O$. The set of possible worlds for R w.r.t. V, denoted $\mathtt{Worlds}(R, V)$, consist of all relations R' over the same schema as R that satisfy the functional dependency $I \to O$ and where $\pi_V(R') = \pi_V(R)$.*

EXAMPLE 2. *Returning to module m_1, suppose the visible attributes are $V = \{a_1, a_3, a_5\}$ resulting in the view R_V in Figure 1c. For clarity, we have added $I \cap V$ (visible input) and $O \cap V$ (visible output) above the attribute names to indicate their role. Naturally, $R_1 \in \mathtt{Worlds}(R_1, V)$. Figure 2 shows four additional sample relations $R_1^1, R_1^2, R_1^3, R_1^4$ in $\mathtt{Worlds}(R_1, V)$, such that $\forall i \in [1, 4], \pi_V(R_1^i) = \pi_V(R_1) = R_V$. (Overall there are sixty four relations in $\mathtt{Worlds}(R_1, V)$).*

a_1	a_2	a_3	a_4	a_5
0	0	0	0	1
0	1	1	0	0
1	0	1	0	0
1	1	1	0	1

(a) R_1^1

a_1	a_2	a_3	a_4	a_5
0	0	0	1	1
0	1	1	1	0
1	0	1	0	0
1	1	1	0	1

(b) R_1^2

a_1	a_2	a_3	a_4	a_5
0	0	1	0	0
0	1	0	0	1
1	0	1	0	0
1	1	1	0	1

(c) R_1^3

a_1	a_2	a_3	a_4	a_5
0	0	1	1	0
0	1	0	1	1
1	0	1	0	0
1	1	1	0	1

(d) R_1^4

Figure 2: $R_1^i \in \mathtt{Worlds}(R_1, V)$, $i \in [1, 4]$

To guarantee privacy of a module m, the view R_V should ensure some level of uncertainly w.r.t the value of the output $m(\pi_I(\mathbf{t}))$, for tuples $t \in R$. To define this, we introduce the notion of Γ-standalone-privacy, for a given parameter $\Gamma \geq 1$. Informally, R_V is Γ-standalone-private if for every $t \in R$, the possible worlds $\mathtt{Worlds}(R, V)$ contain at least Γ distinct output values that could be the result of $m(\pi_I(\mathbf{t}))$.

DEFINITION 2. *Let m be a private module with a corresponding relation R having input and output attributes I and O resp. Then m is Γ-standalone-private w.r.t a set of visible attributes V, if for every tuple $\mathbf{x} \in \pi_I(R)$, $|\mathrm{OUT}_{\mathbf{x},m}| \geq \Gamma$, where $\mathrm{OUT}_{\mathbf{x},m} = \{\mathbf{y} \mid \exists R' \in \mathtt{Worlds}(R, V),\ \exists \mathbf{t}' \in R'\ s.t\ \mathbf{x} = \pi_I(\mathbf{t}') \wedge \mathbf{y} = \pi_O(\mathbf{t}')\}$.*

If m is Γ-standalone-private w.r.t. V, then we will call V a safe subset for m and Γ.

Γ-standalone-privacy implies that for *any* input the adversary cannot guess m's output with probability $> \frac{1}{\Gamma}$, even if the module is executed an arbitrary number of times.

---

[3]We discuss in Section 6 how partial prior knowledge can be handled by our approach.

EXAMPLE 3. *It can be verified that, if $V = \{a_1, a_3, a_5\}$ then for all $\mathbf{x} \in \pi_I(R_1)$, $|\mathrm{OUT}_{\mathbf{x}}| \geq 4$, so $\{a_1, a_3, a_5\}$ is safe for m_1 and $\Gamma = 4$. As an example, from Figure 2, when $\mathbf{x} = (0, 0)$, $\mathrm{OUT}_{\mathbf{x},m} \supseteq \{(0, \underline{0}, 1), (0, \underline{1}, 1), (1, \underline{0}, 0), (1, \underline{1}, 0)\}$ (hidden attributes are underlined). Also, hiding any two output attributes from $O = \{a_3, a_4, a_5\}$ ensures standalone privacy for $\Gamma = 4$, e.g., if $V = \{a_1, a_2, a_3\}$ (i.e. $\{a_4, a_5\}$ are hidden), then the input $(0, 0)$ can be mapped to one of $(0, \underline{0}, \underline{0}), (0, \underline{0}, \underline{1}), (0, \underline{1}, \underline{0})$ and $(0, \underline{1}, \underline{1})$; this holds for other assignments of input attributes as well. But, $V = \{a_3, a_4, a_5\}$ (i.e. when only input attributes are hidden) is not safe for $\Gamma = 4$: for any input $\mathbf{x}$, $\mathrm{OUT}_{\mathbf{x},m} = \{(0, 1, 1), (1, 1, 0), (1, 0, 1)\}$, containing only three possible output tuples.*

There may be several safe subsets V for a given module m and parameter Γ. Some of the corresponding R_V views may be preferable to others, e.g. they provide users with more useful information, allow to answer more common/critical user queries, etc. Let $\overline{V} = (I \cup O) \setminus V$ denote the attributes of R that do not belong to the view. If $\mathsf{c}(\overline{V})$ denotes the penalty of hiding the attributes in $\overline{V}$, a natural goal is to choose a safe subset V that minimizes $\mathsf{c}(\overline{V})$. To understand the difficulty of this problem, we study a version of the problem where the cost function is additive: each attribute a has some penalty value $\mathsf{c}(a)$ and the penalty of hiding $\overline{V}$ is $\mathsf{c}(\overline{V}) = \Sigma_{a \in \overline{V}} \mathsf{c}(a)$. We call this optimization problem the *standalone* Secure-View *problem* and discuss it in Section 3.

2.3 Workflows and Relations

A workflow W consists of a set of modules $m_1, \cdots, m_n$, connected as a DAG (see, for instance, the workflow in Figure 1). Each module m_i has a set I_i of input attributes and a set O_i of output attributes. We assume that (1) for each module, its input and output attributes are disjoint, i.e. $I_i \cap O_i = \emptyset$, (2) the output attributes of distinct modules are disjoint, namely $O_i \cap O_j = \emptyset$, for $i \neq j$ (since each data item is produced by a unique module), and (3) whenever an output of a module m_i is fed as input to a module m_j the corresponding output and input attributes of m_i and m_j are the same. The DAG shape of the workflow guarantees that these requirements are not contradictory.

We model executions of W as a relation R over the set of attributes $A = \cup_{i=1}^{n}(I_i \cup O_i)$, satisfying the set of functional dependencies $F = \{I_i \to O_i : i \in [1, n]\}$. Each tuple in R describes an execution of the workflow W. In particular, for every $t \in R$, and every $i \in [1, n]$, $\pi_{O_i}(\mathbf{t}) = m_i(\pi_{I_i}(\mathbf{t}))$.

EXAMPLE 4. *Returning to the sample workflow in Figure 1, the input and output attributes of modules m_1, m_2, m_3 respectively are (i) $I_1 = \{a_1, a_2\}$, $O_1 = \{a_3, a_4, a_5\}$, (ii) $I_2 = \{a_3, a_4\}$, $O_2 = \{a_6\}$ and (iii) $I_3 = \{a_4, a_5\}$, $O_3 = \{a_7\}$. The underlying functional dependencies in the relation R in Figure 1b reflect the keys of the constituent modules, e.g. from m_1 we have $a_1 a_2 \longrightarrow a_3 a_4 a_5$, from m_2 we have $a_3 a_4 \longrightarrow a_6$, and from m_3 we have $a_4 a_5 \longrightarrow a_7$.*

Note that the output of a module may be input to several modules. It is therefore possible that $I_i \cap I_j \neq \emptyset$ for $i \neq j$. We call this *data sharing* and define the degree of data sharing in a workflow as follows:

DEFINITION 3. *A workflow W is said to have γ-bounded data sharing if every attribute in W can appear in the left hand side of at most γ functional dependencies $I_i \to O_i$.*

In the workflow of our running example, $\gamma = 2$. Intuitively, if a workflow has γ-bounded data sharing then a data item can be fed as input to at most γ different modules. In the following sections we will see the implication of such a bound on the complexity of the problems studied.

2.4 Workflow Module Privacy

To define privacy in the context of a workflow, we first extend our notion of *possible worlds* to a workflow view. Consider the view $R_V = \pi_V(R)$ of a workflow relation R. Since the workflow may contain private as well as public modules, a possible world for R_V is a full relation that not only agrees with R_V on the content of the visible attributes, but is also consistent w.r.t the expected behavior of the public modules. In the following definitions, $m_1, \cdots, m_n$ denote the modules in the workflow W and F denotes the set of functional dependencies $I_i \to O_i$, $i \in [1, n]$ in the relation R.

DEFINITION 4. *The set of* possible worlds *for the workflow relation R w.r.t. V, denoted also* Worlds(R, V), *consists of all the relations R' over the same attributes as R that satisfy the functional dependencies in F and where (1) $\pi_V(R') = \pi_V(R)$, and (2) for every public module m_i in W and every tuple $\mathbf{t}' \in R'$, $\pi_{O_i}(\mathbf{t}') = m_i(\pi_{I_i}(\mathbf{t}'))$.*

Note that when a workflow consists only of private modules, the second constraint does not need to be enforced. We call these *all-private workflows* and study them in Section 4. We then show in Section 5 that attaining privacy when public modules are also used is fundamentally harder.

We are now ready to define the notion of Γ-workflow-privacy, for a given parameter $\Gamma \geq 1$. Informally, a view R_V is Γ-workflow-private if for every tuple $t \in R$, and every private module m_i in the workflow, the possible worlds Worlds(R, V) contain at least Γ distinct output values that could be the result of $m_i(\pi_{I_i}(\mathbf{t}))$.

DEFINITION 5. *A private module m_i in W is Γ-workflow-private w.r.t a set of visible attributes V, if for every tuple $\mathbf{x} \in \pi_{I_i}(R)$, $|\text{OUT}_{\mathbf{x}, W}| \geq \Gamma$, where $\text{OUT}_{\mathbf{x}, W} = \{\mathbf{y} \mid \exists R' \in \text{Worlds}(R, V), s.t., \forall \mathbf{t}' \in R' \ \mathbf{x} = \pi_{I_i}(\mathbf{t}') \Rightarrow \mathbf{y} = \pi_{O_i}(\mathbf{t}')\}$.*

W is called Γ-private if every private module m_i in W is Γ-workflow-private. If W (resp. m_i) is Γ-private (Γ-workflow-private) w.r.t. V, then we call V a safe subset for Γ-privacy of W (Γ-workflow-privacy of m_i).

For simplicity, in the above definition we assumed that the privacy requirement of every module m_i is the same Γ. The results and proofs in this paper remain unchanged when different modules m_i have different privacy requirements Γ_i.

In the rest of the paper, for a set of visible attributes $V \subseteq A$, $\overline{V} = A \setminus V$ will denote the hidden attributes in the workflow. The following proposition is easy to verify, which will be useful later:

PROPOSITION 1. *If V is a safe subset for Γ-workflow-privacy of a module m_i in W, then any V' such that $V' \subseteq V$ (or, $\overline{V'} \supseteq \overline{V}$) also guarantees Γ-workflow-privacy of m_i.*

As we illustrate later, given a workflow W and a parameter Γ there may be several incomparable (in terms of set inclusion) safe subsets V for Γ-privacy of W. Our goal is to choose one that minimizes the penalty $\mathsf{c}(\overline{V}) = \Sigma_{a \in \overline{V}} \mathsf{c}(a)$ of the hidden attributes $\overline{V}$. This we call the *workflow* Secure-View *problem*, or simply the Secure-View problem. The candidates are naturally the maximal, in terms of set inclusion, safe sets V (and correspondingly the minimal $\overline{V}$s).

2.5 Complexity Classes and Approximation

In the following sections we will study the Secure-View problem: minimize cost of the hidden attributes that ensures that a workflow is Γ-private. We will prove that this problem is NP-hard even in very restricted cases and study polynomial time *approximation algorithms* as well as the *hardness of approximations* for different versions of the problem. We will use the following standard notions of approximation: an algorithm is said to be a *$\mu(n)$-approximation algorithm* for a given optimization problem, for some non-decreasing function $\mu(n) : \mathbb{N}^+ \to \mathbb{R}^+$, if for every input of size n it outputs a solution of value at most a multiplicative factor of $\mu(n)$ away from the optimum. An optimization problem is said to be *$\mu(n)$-hard to approximate* if a poly-time $\mu(n)$-approximation algorithm for the problem does not exist under standard complexity assumptions. In this paper we will use standard complexity assumptions of the form $NP \nsubseteq DTIME(n^{f(n)})$, where $f(n)$ is a poly-logarithmic or sub-logarithmic function of n and $DTIME$ represents deterministic time. For example, the hardness result in Theorem 5 says that there cannot be an $O(\log n)$-approximation algorithm unless all problems in NP have $O(n^{\log \log n})$-time deterministic exact algorithms. Finally, a problem is said to be *APX-hard* if there exists a constant $\epsilon > 0$ such that a $(1 + \epsilon)$-approximation in polynomial time would imply $P = NP$. If a problem is APX-hard, then the problem cannot have a *PTAS*, i.e, a $(1 + \epsilon)$-approximation algorithm which runs in poly-time for all constant $\epsilon > 0$, unless $P = NP$.

3. STANDALONE MODULE PRIVACY

We start our study of workflow privacy by considering the privacy of a standalone module, which is the simplest special case of a workflow. Hence understanding it is a first step towards understanding the general case. We will also see that standalone-privacy guarantees of individual modules may be used as building blocks for attaining workflow privacy.

We analyze below the time complexity of obtaining (minimal cost) guarantees for standalone module privacy. Though the notion of Γ-standalone-privacy is similar to the well-known notion of ℓ-diversity [15], to the best of our knowledge the time complexity of this problem has not been studied.

Optimization problems and parameters. Consider a standalone module m with input attributes I, output attributes O, and a relation R. Recall that a visible subset of attributes V is called a *safe subset* for module m and privacy requirement Γ, if m is Γ-standalone-private w.r.t. V (see Definition 2). If each attribute $a \in I \cup O$ has cost $\mathsf{c}(a)$, *the standalone* Secure-View *problem* aims to find a safe subset V s.t. the cost of the hidden attributes, $\mathsf{c}(\overline{V}) = \sum_{a \in \overline{V}} \mathsf{c}(a)$, is minimized. The corresponding decision version will take a cost limit C as an additional input, and decide whether there exists a safe subset V such that $\mathsf{c}(\overline{V}) \leq C$.

One natural way of solving the optimization version of the standalone Secure-View problem is to consider all possible subsets $V \subseteq I \cup O$, check if V is safe, and return the safe subset V s.t. $\mathsf{c}(\overline{V})$ is minimized. This motivates us to define and study the simpler Safe-View *problem*, which takes a subset V as input and decides whether V is a safe subset.

To understand how much of the complexity of the standalone Secure-View problem comes from the need to consider different subsets of attributes, and what is due to the need to determine the safety of subsets, we study the time complexity of standalone Secure-View, with and without access to *an oracle for the Safe-View problem*, henceforth called a Safe-View *oracle*. A Safe-View oracle takes a subset $V \subseteq I \cup O$ as input and answers whether V is safe. In the presence of a Safe-View oracle, the time complexity of the Safe-View problem is mainly due to the number of oracle calls, and hence we study the *communication complexity*. Without access to such an oracle, we also study the *computational complexity* of this problem.

In our discussion below, $k = |I| + |O|$ denotes the total number of attributes in the relation R, and N denotes the number of rows in R (i.e. the number of executions). Then $N \leq \prod_{a \in I} |\Delta_a| \leq \delta^{|I|} \leq \delta^k$ where Δ_a is the domain of attribute a and δ is the maximum domain size of attributes.

3.1 Lower Bounds

We start with lower bounds for the Safe-View problem. Observe that this also gives lower bounds for the standalone Secure-View problem without a Safe-View oracle. To see this, consider a set V of attributes and assume that each attribute in V has cost > 0 whereas all other attributes have cost zero. Then Safe-View has a positive answer for V iff the standalone Secure-View problem has a solution with cost $= 0$ (i.e. the one that only hides the attributes $\overline{V}$).

Communication complexity of Safe-View . Given a visible subset $V \subseteq I \cup O$, we show that deciding whether V is safe needs $\Omega(N)$ time. Note that just to read the table as input takes $\Omega(N)$ time. So the lower bound of $\Omega(N)$ does not make sense unless we assume the presence of a *data supplier* (we avoid using the term "oracle" to distinguish it from Safe-View oracle) which supplies the tuples of R on demand: Given an assignment $\mathbf{x}$ of the input attributes I, the data supplier outputs the value $\mathbf{y} = m(\mathbf{x})$ of the output attributes O. The following theorem shows the $\Omega(N)$ communication complexity lower bound in terms of the number of calls to the data supplier; namely, that (up to a constant factor) one indeed needs to view the full relation.

THEOREM 1. *(Safe-View Communication Complexity) Given a module m, a subset $V \subseteq I \cup O$, and a privacy requirement Γ, deciding whether V is safe for m and Γ requires $\Omega(N)$ calls to the data supplier, where N is the number of tuples in the relation R of m.*

PROOF SKETCH. This theorem is proved by a reduction from the *set-disjointness problem*, where Alice and Bob hold two subsets A and B of a universe U and the goal is decide whether $A \cap B \neq \emptyset$. This problem is known to have $\Omega(N)$ communication complexity where N is the number of elements in the universe. $\square$

Computational Complexity of Safe-View : The above $\Omega(N)$ computation complexity of Safe-View holds when the relation R is given explicitly tuple by tuple. The following theorem shows that even when R is described implicitly in a succinct manner, there cannot be a poly-time (in the number of attributes) algorithm to decide whether a given subset V is safe unless $P = NP$.

THEOREM 2. *(Safe-View Computational Complexity) Given a module m with a poly-size (in $k = |I| + |O|$) description of functionality, a subset $V \subseteq I \cup O$, and a privacy requirement Γ, deciding whether V is safe w.r.t. m and Γ is co-NP-hard in k.*

PROOF SKETCH. The proof of this theorem works by a reduction from the UNSAT problem, where given a boolean CNF formula g on variables $x_1, \cdots, x_\ell$, the goal is to decide whether, for *all* assignments of the variables, g is not satisfied. Here given any assignment of the variables $x_1, \cdots, x_\ell$, $g(x_1, \cdots, x_\ell)$ can be evaluated in polynomial time, which simulates the function of the data supplier. $\square$

Lower Bound of Standalone Secure-View with a Safe-View Oracle: Now suppose we have access to a Safe-View oracle, which takes care of the "hardness" of the Safe-View problem given in Theorems 1 and 2, in constant time. The oracle takes a visible subset $V \subseteq I \cup O$ as input, and answers whether V is safe for module m and privacy requirement Γ. The following theorem shows that the decision version of standalone Secure-View remains hard (i.e. not solvable in poly-time in the number of attributes):

THEOREM 3. *(Standalone Secure-View Communication Complexity, with Safe-View oracle) Given a Safe-View oracle and a cost limit C, deciding whether there exists a safe subset $V \subseteq I \cup O$ with cost bounded by C requires $2^{\Omega(k)}$ oracle calls, where $k = |I| + |O|$.*

PROOF SKETCH. The proof of this theorem involves a novel construction of two functions, m_1 and m_2, on ℓ input attributes and a single output attribute, such that for m_1 the minimum cost of a safe subset is $\frac{3\ell}{4}$ whereas for m_2 it is $\frac{\ell}{2}$ ($C = \frac{\ell}{2}$). In particular, for both m_1 and m_2, all subsets of size $< \frac{\ell}{4}$ are safe and all other subsets are unsafe, except that for m_2, there is exactly one special subset of size $\frac{\ell}{2}$ such that this subset and all subsets thereof are safe.

We show that for an algorithm using $2^{o(k)}$ calls, there always remains at least one special subset of size $\frac{\ell}{2}$ that is consistent with all previous answers to queries. Hence after $2^{o(k)}$ calls, if the algorithm decides that there is a safe subset with cost $\leq C$, we choose m to be m_1; on the other hand, if it says that there is no such subset, we set $m = m_2$. In both the cases the answer of the algorithm is wrong which shows that there cannot be such an algorithm distinguishing these two cases with $2^{o(k)}$ calls. $\square$

3.2 Upper Bounds

The lower bound results given above show that solving the standalone Secure-View problem is unlikely in time sub-exponential in k or sub-linear in N. We now present simple algorithms for solving the Secure-View and Safe-View problems, in time exponential in k and polynomial in N.

First note that, with access to a Safe-View oracle, the standalone Secure-View problem can be easily solved in $O(2^k)$ time, by calling the oracle for all 2^k possible subsets and outputting the safe subset with minimum cost.

Without access to a Safe-View oracle, we first "read" relation R using N data supplier calls. Once R is available, the simple algorithm sketched below implements the Safe-View oracle (i.e. tests if a set V of attributes is safe) and works in time $O(2^k N^2)$: For a visible subset V, we look at all possible assignments to the attributes in $I \setminus V$. For each input value we then check if it leads to at least $\frac{\Gamma}{\prod_{a \in O \setminus V} |\Delta_a|}$ different values of the visible output attributes in $O \cap V$ (Δ_a is the domain of attribute a). This is a necessary and sufficient condition for guaranteeing Γ privacy: by all possible $\prod_{a \in O \setminus V} |\Delta_a|$ extensions of the output attributes, for each input, there will be Γ different possible output values.

We mention here also that essentially the same algorithms (with same upper bounds) can be used to output *all* safe attribute sets of a standalone module, rather than just one with minimum cost. Such exhaustive enumeration will be useful in the following sections.

Remarks. These results indicate that, in the worse case, finding a minimal-cost safe attribute set for a module may take time that is exponential in the number of attributes. Note, however, that the number of attributes of a single module is typically not large (often less than 10, see [1]), so the computation is still feasible. Expert knowledge of module designers, about the module's behavior and safe attribute sets may also be exploited to speed up the computation. Furthermore, a given module is often used in many workflows. For example, sequence comparison modules, like BLAST or FASTA, are used in many different biological workflows. We will see that safe subsets for individual modules can be used as building blocks for attaining privacy for the full workflow. The effort invested in deriving safe subsets for a module is thus amortized over all uses.

4. ALL-PRIVATE WORKFLOWS

We are now ready to consider workflows that consist of several modules. We first consider in this section workflows where all modules are *private* (called *all-private workflows*). Workflows with a mixture of private and public modules are then considered in Section 5.

As in Section 3, we want to find a safe visible subset V with minimum cost s.t. all the modules in the workflow are Γ-workflow-private w.r.t. V (see Definition 5). One option is to devise algorithms similar to those described for standalone modules in the previous section. However, the time complexity of those algorithms is now exponential in the *total number of attributes of all modules in the workflow* which can be as large as $\Omega(nk)$, n being the number of modules in the workflow and k the maximum number of attributes of a single module. To avoid the exponential dependency on n, the number of modules in the workflow, which may be large [1], and to exploit the safe attribute subsets for standalone modules, which may have been already computed, we attempt in this section to assemble workflow privacy guarantees out of standalone module guarantees. We first prove, in Section 4.1, that this is indeed possible. Then, in the rest of this section, we study the optimization problem of obtaining a safe view with minimum cost.

Let W be a workflow consisting of modules $m_1, \cdots, m_n$, where I_i, O_i denote the input and output attributes of m_i, $i \in [1,n]$, respectively. We use below R_i to denote the relation for the *standalone* module m_i. The relations $R = R_1 \bowtie R_2 \bowtie \cdots \bowtie R_n$, with attributes $A = \bigcup_{i=1}^n (I_i \cup O_i)$, then describes the possible executions of W. Note that the projection $\pi_{I_i \cup O_i}(R)$ of R on $I_i \cup O_i$ is a subset of (but not necessarily equal to) the standalone module relation R_i.

In this section (and throughout the rest of the paper), for a set of visible attributes $V \subseteq A$, $\overline{V} = A \setminus V$ will denote the hidden attributes. Further, $V_i = (I_i \cup O_i) \cap V$ will denote the visible attributes for module m_i, whereas $\overline{V_i} = (I_i \cup O_i) \setminus V_i$ will denote the hidden attributes for m_i, for $i \in [1,n]$.

4.1 Standalone-Privacy vs. Workflow-Privacy

We show that if a set of visible attributes guarantees Γ-standalone-privacy for a module, then if the module is placed in a workflow where only a subset of those attributes is made visible, then Γ-workflow-privacy is guaranteed for the module in this workflow. In other words, in an all-private workflow, hiding the union of the corresponding hidden attributes of the individual modules guarantees Γ-workflow-privacy for all of them[4]. We formalize this next.

THEOREM 4. *Let W be an all-private workflow with modules $m_1, \cdots, m_n$. Given a parameter $\Gamma \geq 1$, let $V_i \subseteq (I_i \cup O_i)$ be a set of visible attributes w.r.t which m_i, $i \in [1,n]$, is Γ-standalone-private. Then the workflow W is Γ-private w.r.t the set of visible attributes V s.t. $\overline{V} = \bigcup_{i=1}^n \overline{V_i}$.*

Before we prove the theorem, recall that Γ-standalone-privacy of a module m_i requires that for every input $\mathbf{x}$ to the module, there are at least Γ *potential outputs* of $\mathbf{x}$ in the possible worlds $\texttt{Worlds}(R_i, V_i)$ of the standalone module relation R_i w.r.t. V_i; similarly, Γ-workflow-privacy of m_i requires at least Γ potential outputs of $\mathbf{x}$ in the possible worlds $\texttt{Worlds}(R, V)$ of the workflow relation R w.r.t. V. Since $R = R_1 \bowtie \cdots \bowtie R_n$, a possible approach to prove Theorem 4 may be to show that, whenever the hidden attributes for m_i are also hidden in the workflow W, any relation $R_i' \in \texttt{Worlds}(R_i, V_i)$ has a corresponding relation $R' \in \texttt{Worlds}(R, V)$ s.t. $R_i' = \pi_{I_i \cup O_i}(R')$. If this would hold, then for $\overline{V} = \bigcup_{i=1}^n \overline{V_i}$, the set of possible outputs, for any input tuple $\mathbf{x}$ to a module m_i, will remain unchanged.

Unfortunately, Proposition 2 below shows that the above approach fails. Indeed, $|\texttt{Worlds}(R, V)|$ can be significantly smaller than $|\texttt{Worlds}(R_i, V_i)|$ even for very simple workflows.

PROPOSITION 2. *There exist a workflow W with relation R, a module m_1 in W with (standalone) relation R_1, and a set of visible attributes V_1 that guarantees both Γ-standalone-privacy and Γ-workflow-privacy of m_1, such that the ratio of $|\texttt{Worlds}(R_1, V_1)|$ and $|\texttt{Worlds}(R, V_1)|$ is doubly exponential in the number of attributes of W.*

PROOF SKETCH. To prove the proposition, we construct a simple workflow with two modules m_1, m_2 connected as a chain. Both m_1, m_2 are one-one functions with k boolean inputs and k boolean outputs (e.g., assume that m_1 is an identity function, whereas m_2 complements each of its k inputs). The module m_1 gets initial input attributes I_1, produces $O_1 = I_2$ which is fed to m_2 as input, and m_2 produces final attribute set O_2. Let V_1 be an arbitrary subset of O_1 such that $|\overline{V_1}| = \log \Gamma$ (assume that Γ is a power of 2). It can be verified that, m_1 as a standalone module is Γ-standalone-private w.r.t. visible attributes V_1 and both m_1, m_2, being one-one modules, are Γ-workflow-private w.r.t. V_1.

We show that the one-one nature of m_1 and m_2 restricts the size of $\texttt{Worlds}(R, V_1)$ compared to that of $\texttt{Worlds}(R_1, V_1)$. Since both m_1 and m_2 are one-one functions, the workflow W also computes a one-one function. Hence any relation S in $\texttt{Worlds}(R, V_1)$ has to compute a one-one function as well. But when m_1 was standalone, any function consistent with V_1 could be in $\texttt{Worlds}(R_1, V_1)$. By a careful computation, the ratio can be shown to be doubly exponential in k. □

Nevertheless, we show below that for every input $\mathbf{x}$ of the module, the set of its possible outputs, in these worlds, is exactly the same as that in the original (much larger number of) module worlds. Hence privacy is indeed preserved.

---

[4]By Proposition 1, this also means that hiding any superset of this union would also be safe for the same Γ.

Recall that $\text{OUT}_{\mathbf{x},m_i}$ and $\text{OUT}_{\mathbf{x},W}$ denote the possible output for an input $\mathbf{x}$ to module m_i w.r.t. a set of visible attributes when m_i is standalone and in a workflow W respectively (see Definition 2 and Definition 5). The following lemma will be useful in proving Theorem 4.

LEMMA 1. *Let $\dot{m}_i$ be a standalone module with relation R_i, let $\mathbf{x}$ be an input to m_i, and let $V_i \subseteq (I_i \cup O_i)$ be a subset of visible attributes. If $\mathbf{y} \in \text{OUT}_{\mathbf{x},m_i}$ then there exists an input $\mathbf{x}' \in \pi_{I_i}(R_i)$ to m_i with output $\mathbf{y}' = m_i(\mathbf{x}')$ such that $\pi_{V_i \cap I_i}(\mathbf{x}) = \pi_{V_i \cap I_i}(\mathbf{x}')$ and $\pi_{V_i \cap O_i}(\mathbf{y}) = \pi_{V_i \cap O_i}(\mathbf{y}')$.*

The proof of Lemma 1 is simple and is in the full version; instead we illustrate the statement of the lemma with the module m_1 whose relation R_1 appears Figure 1a. Its visible portion (for visible attributes $V = \{a_1, a_3, a_5\}$) is given in Figure 1c. Consider the input $\mathbf{x} = (0, \underline{0})$ to m_1 and a candidate output $\mathbf{y} = (1, \underline{0}, 0)$ (hidden attributes are underlined). From Figure 2c, $\mathbf{y} \in \text{OUT}_{\mathbf{x},m_1}$. This is because there exists $\mathbf{x}' = (0, \underline{1})$, s.t. $\mathbf{y}' = m_1(\mathbf{x}') = (1, \underline{1}, 0)$, and, $\mathbf{x}, \mathbf{x}'$ and $\mathbf{y}, \mathbf{y}'$ have the same values of the visible (non-underlined) attributes. Note that $\mathbf{y}$ does not need to be the actual output $m_1(\mathbf{x})$ on $\mathbf{x}$ or even share the same values of the visible attributes (indeed, $m_1(\mathbf{x}) = (0, \underline{1}, 1)$).

However, in proving Theorem 4, our main technical tool is Lemma 2, which states that given a set of visible attributes V_i of a standalone module m_i, the set of possible outputs for *every* input $\mathbf{x}$ to m_i remains unchanged when m_i is placed in an all-private workflow, provided the corresponding hidden attributes $\overline{V_i}$ remains hidden in the workflow.

LEMMA 2. *Consider any module m_i and any input $\mathbf{x} \in \pi_{I_i}(R)$. If $\mathbf{y} \in \text{OUT}_{\mathbf{x},m_i}$ w.r.t. a set of visible attributes $V_i \subseteq (I_i \cup O_i)$, then $\mathbf{y} \in \text{OUT}_{\mathbf{x},W}$ w.r.t. $V_i \cup (A \setminus (I_i \cup O_i))$.*

We fix a module m_i, an input $\mathbf{x}$ to m_i and a candidate output $\mathbf{y} \in \text{OUT}_{\mathbf{x},m_i}$ for $\mathbf{x}$ w.r.t. visible attributes V_i. For $V = V_i \cup (A \setminus (I_i \cup O_i))$, $\overline{V} = A \setminus V = (I_i \cup O_i) \setminus V_i = \overline{V_i}$ (since, $V_i \subseteq I_i \cup O_i \subseteq A$). We will show that $\mathbf{y} \in \text{OUT}_{\mathbf{x},W}$ w.r.t. visible attributes V by showing the existence of a possible world $R' \in \text{Worlds}(R, V)$, for $\overline{V} = \overline{V_i}$, s.t. if $\pi_{I_i}(\mathbf{t}) = \mathbf{x}$ for some $\mathbf{t} \in R'$, then $\pi_{O_i}(\mathbf{t}) = \mathbf{y}$.

Two key tools used in the proof of Lemma 2 are *tuple flipping* and *function flipping*. Given a tuple $\mathbf{w}$ on a subset of attributes $P \subseteq A$, and two tuples $\mathbf{p}, \mathbf{q}$ on a subset of attributes $Q \subseteq A$, flipping $\mathbf{w}$ w.r.t. $\mathbf{p}, \mathbf{q}$ produces a tuple $\mathbf{z} = \text{FLIP}_{\mathbf{p},\mathbf{q}}(\mathbf{w})$ on P as follows: if $\mathbf{w}$ shares the same attribute as well as the same attribute value with $\mathbf{p}$ (resp. $\mathbf{q}$), replace the attribute value by that of $\mathbf{q}$ (resp. $\mathbf{p}$), otherwise copy the attribute value of $\mathbf{w}$ to $\mathbf{z}$. Flipping function m w.r.t tuples $\mathbf{p}, \mathbf{q}$ produces a function g with the same domain and range that of m, denoted by $\text{FLIP}_{m,\mathbf{p},\mathbf{q}}$, where for all input $\mathbf{w}$ to g, $g(\mathbf{w}) = \text{FLIP}_{\mathbf{p},\mathbf{q}}(m(\text{FLIP}_{\mathbf{p},\mathbf{q}}(\mathbf{w})))$ (flip the input, apply the original function m, again flip the output). Next we give a proof sketch of the lemma.

PROOF SKETCH OF LEMMA 2. Consider $\mathbf{x}, \mathbf{y}$ as given in the statement of Lemma 2. By Lemma 1, there are two tuples $\mathbf{x}', \mathbf{y}'$ such that $\pi_{V_i \cap I_i}(\mathbf{x}) = \pi_{V_i \cap I_i}(\mathbf{x}')$ and $\pi_{V_i \cap O_i}(\mathbf{y}) = \pi_{V_i \cap O_i}(\mathbf{y}')$. We replace the module sequence $\langle m_1, \cdots, m_n \rangle$ by $\langle g_1, \cdots, g_n \rangle$ by defining $g_j = \text{FLIP}_{m_j,\mathbf{p},\mathbf{q}}$, for all $j \in [1, n]$, where $\mathbf{p}$ (resp. $\mathbf{q}$) is formed by concatenating $\mathbf{x}, \mathbf{y}$ (resp. $\mathbf{x}', \mathbf{y}'$); in this process some modules may remain unchanged. We show that the relation R' produced by the join of the standalone relations of $\langle g_1, \cdots, g_n \rangle$ satisfies the properties:

(1) $g_i(\mathbf{x}) = \mathbf{y}$, in other words, for all tuples $\mathbf{t} \in R'$ where $\pi_{I_i}(\mathbf{t}) = \mathbf{x}$, $\pi_{O_i}(\mathbf{t}) = \mathbf{y}$; and (2) $\pi_V(R) = \pi_V(R')$, i.e. the projections of R and R' on the visible attribute set are the same. Since every g_j is a function having domain and range the same as that of m_j, R' satisfies all functional dependencies $I_i \to O_i$, and therefore $R' \in \text{Worlds}(R, V)$. Together, these two properties show that $\mathbf{y} \in \text{OUT}_{\mathbf{x},W}$. $\square$

It is important to note that the assumption of all-private workflow is crucial in proving Lemma 2 – if some of the modules m_j are public, we can not redefine them to g_j (the projection to the public modules should be unchanged - see Definition 5) and we may not get a member of $\text{Worlds}(R, V)$. We will return to this point in Section 5 when we consider workflows with a mixture of private and public modules.

Finally we complete the proof of Theorem 4 using Lemma 2:

PROOF OF THEOREM 4. We are given that each module m_i is Γ-standalone-private w.r.t. V_i, i.e., $|\text{OUT}_{\mathbf{x},m_i}| \geq \Gamma$ for all input $\mathbf{x}$ to m_i, for all modules m_i, $i \in [1, n]$ (see Definition 2). From Lemma 2, this implies that for all input $\mathbf{x}$ to all modules m_i, $|\text{OUT}_{\mathbf{x},W}| \geq \Gamma$ w.r.t $V' = V_i \cup (A \setminus (I_i \cup O_i))$. We already argued that, for this choice of V', $\overline{V'} = A \setminus V' = (I_i \cup O_i) \setminus V_i = \overline{V_i}$. Now, using Proposition 1, when the visible attributes set V is such that $\overline{V} = \bigcup_{i=1}^{n} \overline{V_i} \supseteq \overline{V_i} = \overline{V'}$, every module m_i is Γ-workflow-private. $\square$

4.2 The Secure-View Problem

We have seen above that one can assemble workflow privacy guarantees out of the standalone module guarantees. Recall however that each individual module may have several possible safe attributes sets (see, e.g., Example 3). Assembling different sets naturally lead to solutions with different cost. The following example shows that assembling optimal (cheapest) safe attributes of the individual modules may not lead to an optimal safe attributes set for the full workflow. The key observation is that, due to data sharing, it may be more cost effective to hide expensive shared attributes rather than cheap non-shared ones (though later we show that the problem remains NP-hard even without data sharing).

EXAMPLE 5. *Consider a workflow with $n + 2$ modules, $m, m_1, \cdots, m_n, m'$. The module m gets an input data item a_1, with cost 1, and sends as output the same data item, a_2, with cost $1 + \epsilon$, $\epsilon > 0$, to all the m_i-s. Each m_i then sends a data item b_i to m' with cost 1. Assume that standalone privacy is preserved for module m if either its incoming or outgoing data is hidden and for m' if any of its incoming data is hidden. Also assume that standalone privacy is preserved for each m_i module if either its incoming or its outgoing data is hidden. As standalone modules, m will choose to hide a_1, each m_i will choose to hide the outgoing data item b_i, and m' will choose to hide any of the b_i-s. The union of the optimal solutions for the standalone modules has cost $n + 1$. However, a lowest cost solution for preserving workflow privacy is to hide a_2 and any one of the b_i-s. This assembly of (non optimal) solutions for the individual modules has cost $2 + \epsilon$. In this case, the ratio of the costs of the union of standalone optimal solutions and the workflow optimal solution is $\Omega(n)$.*

This motivates us to define the combinatorial optimization problem Secure-View (for workflow secure view), which generalizes the Secure-View problem studied in Section 3. The goal of the Secure-View problem is to choose, for each module, a safe set of attributes (among its possible sets of safe attributes) s.t. together the selected sets yield a minimal cost safe solution for the workflow. We define this formally below. In particular, we consider the following two variants of the problem, trading-off expressibility and succinctness.

Set constraints. The possible safe solutions for a given module can be given in the form of a list of hidden attribute sets. Specifically, we assume that we are given, for each module m_i, $i \in [1, n]$, a list of pairs $L_i = \langle (\overline{I_i^1}, \overline{O_i^1}), (\overline{I_i^2}, \overline{O_i^2}) \ldots (\overline{I_i^{l_i}}, \overline{O_i^{l_i}}) \rangle$. Each pair $(\overline{I_i^j}, \overline{O_i^j})$ in the list describes one possible safe (hidden) solution for m_i: $\overline{I_i^j} \subseteq I_i$ (resp. $\overline{O_i^j} \subseteq O_i$) is the set of input (output) attributes of m_i to be hidden in this solution. l_i (the length of the list) is the number of solutions for m_i that are given in the list, and we use below $\ell_{\max}$ to denote the length of the longest list, i.e. $\ell_{\max} = \max_{i=1}^n \ell_i$.

When the input to the Secure-View problem is given in the above form (with the candidate attribute sets listed explicitly) we call it *the Secure-View problem with set constraints*.

Cardinality constraints. Some modules may have many possible candidate safe attribute sets. Indeed, their number may be exponential in the number of attributes of the module. This is illustrate by the following two simple examples.

EXAMPLE 6. *First observe that in any one-one function with k boolean inputs and k boolean outputs, hiding any k incoming or any k outgoing attributes guarantees 2^k-privacy. Thus listing all such subsets requires a list of length $\Omega(\binom{2k}{k}) = \Omega(2^k)$. Another example is majority function which takes $2k$ boolean inputs and produces 1 if and only if the number of one-s in the input tuple is $\geq k$. Hiding either $k + 1$ input bits or the unique output bit guarantee 2-privacy for majority function, but explicitly listing all possible subsets again leads to exponential length lists.*

Note that, in both examples, the actual identity of the hidden input (resp. output) attributes is not important, as long as sufficiently many are hidden. Thus rather than explicitly listing all possible safe sets we could simply say what combinations of numbers of hidden input and output attributes are safe. This motivates the following variant of the Secure-View problem, called *the Secure-View problem with cardinality constraints*: Here for every module m_i we are given a list of pairs of numbers $L_i = \langle (\alpha_i^1, \beta_i^1) \ldots (\alpha_i^{l_i}, \beta_i^{l_i}) \rangle$, s.t. for each pair (α_i^j, β_i^j) in the list, $\alpha_i^j \leq |I_i|$ and $\beta_i^j \leq |O_i|$. The interpretation is that hiding any attribute set of m_i that consists of at least α_i^j input attributes and at least β_i^j output attributes, for some $j \in [1, \ell_i]$, makes m_i safe w.r.t the remaining visible attributes.

To continue with the above example, the list for the first module may consists of $(k, 0)$ and $(0, k)$, whereas the list for the second module consists of $(k + 1, 0)$ and $(0, 1)$.

It is easy to see that, for cardinality constraints, the lists are of size at most quadratic in the number of attributes of the given module (unlike the case of set constraints where the lists could be of exponential length)[5]. In turn, cardinality constraints are less expressive than set constraints that can specify arbitrary attribute sets. This will affect the complexity of the corresponding Secure-View problems.

---

[5]In fact, if one assumes that there is no redundancy in the list, the lists become of at most linear size.

Problem Statement. Given an input in one of the two forms, a *feasible* safe subset V for the workflow, for the version with set constraints (resp. cardinality constraints), is such that for each module m_i $i \in [1, n]$, $\overline{V} \supseteq (\overline{I_i^j} \cup \overline{O_i^j})$ (resp. $|\overline{V} \cap I_i| \geq \alpha_i^j$ and $|\overline{V} \cap O_i| \geq \beta_i^j$) for some $j \in [1, \ell_i]$. The goal of the Secure-View problem is to find a safe set V where $c(\overline{V})$ is minimized.

4.3 Complexity results

We present below theorems which give approximation algorithms and matching hardness of approximation results of different versions of the Secure-View problem. The hardness results show that the problem of testing whether the Secure-View problem (in both variants) has a solution with cost smaller than a given bound is NP-hard even in the most restricted case. But we show that certain approximations of the optimal solution are possible. Theorem 5 and 6 summarize the results for the cardinality and set constraints versions, respectively. For space constraints we only sketch the proofs, details appear in the full version of the paper.

THEOREM 5. *(Cardinality Constraints)* There is an $O(\log n)$-approximation of the Secure-View problem with cardinality constraints. Further, this problem is $\Omega(\log n)$-hard to approximate unless $NP \subseteq DTIME(n^{O(\log \log n)})$, even if the maximum list size $\ell_{\max} = 1$, each data has unit cost, and the values of α_i^j, β_i^j-s are 0 or 1.

PROOF SKETCH. The proof of the hardness result in the above theorem is by a reduction from the set cover problem. The approximation is obtained by randomized rounding a carefully written linear program (LP) relaxation of this problem. A sketch is given below.

Our algorithm is based on rounding the fractional relaxation (called the LP relaxation) of the integer linear program (IP) for this problem presented in Figure 3.

$$\text{Minimize } \sum_{b \in A} c_b x_b \quad \text{subject to}$$

$$\sum_{j=1}^{\ell_i} r_{ij} \geq 1 \quad \forall i \in [1, n] \tag{1}$$

$$\sum_{b \in I_i} y_{bij} \geq r_{ij} \alpha_i^j \quad \forall i \in [1, n], \forall j \in [1, \ell_i] \tag{2}$$

$$\sum_{b \in O_i} z_{bij} \geq r_{ij} \beta_i^j \quad \forall i \in [1, n], \forall j \in [1, \ell_i] \tag{3}$$

$$\sum_{j=1}^{\ell_i} y_{bij} \leq x_b \quad \forall i \in [1, n], \forall b \in I_i \tag{4}$$

$$\sum_{j=1}^{\ell_i} z_{bij} \leq x_b \quad \forall i \in [1, n], \forall b \in O_i \tag{5}$$

$$y_{bij} \leq r_{ij} \quad \forall i \in [1, n], \forall j \in [1, \ell_i], \forall b \in I_i \tag{6}$$

$$z_{bij} \leq r_{ij} \quad \forall i \in [1, n], \forall j \in [1, \ell_i], \forall b \in O_i \tag{7}$$

$$x_b, r_{ij}, y_{bij}, z_{bij} \in \{0, 1\} \tag{8}$$

Figure 3: IP for Secure-View with cardinality constraints

Recall that each module m_i has a list $L_i = \{(\alpha_i^j, \beta_i^j) : j \in [1, \ell_i]\}$, a feasible solution must ensure that for each $i \in [1, n]$, there exists a $j \in [1, \ell_i]$ such that at least α_i^j input data and β_i^j output data of m_i are hidden.

In this IP, $x_b = 1$ if data b is hidden, and $r_{ij} = 1$ if at least α_i^j input data and β_i^j output data of module m_i are hidden. Then, $y_{bij} = 1$ (resp., $z_{bij} = 1$) if both $r_{ij} = 1$ and $x_b = 1$, i.e. if data b contributes to satisfying the input requirement α_i^j (resp., output requirement β_i^j) of module m_i. Let us first verify that the IP indeed solves the **Secure-View** problem with cardinality constraints. For each module m_i, constraint (1) ensures that for some $j \in [1, \ell_i]$, $r_{ij} = 1$. In conjunction with constraints (2) and (3), this ensures that for some $j \in [1, \ell_i]$, (i) at least α_i^j input data of m_i have $y_{bij} = 1$ and (ii) at least β_i^j output data of m_i have $z_{bij} = 1$. But, constraint (4) (resp., constraint (5)) requires that whenever $y_{bij} = 1$ (resp., $z_{bij} = 1$), data b be hidden, i.e. $x_b = 1$, and a cost of c_b be added to the objective. Thus the set of hidden data satisfy the privacy requirement of each module m_i and the value of the objective is the cost of the hidden data. Note that constraints (6) and (7) are also satisfied since y_{bij} and z_{bij} are 0 whenever $r_{ij} = 0$. Thus, the IP represents the **Secure-View** problem with cardinality constraints. It can be shown that simpler LP relaxations of this problem without some of the above constraints lead to unbounded and $\Omega(n)$ integrality gaps showing that an $O(\log n)$-approximation cannot be obtained from those LP relaxations (details are in the full version).

We round the fractional solution to the LP relaxation using Algorithm 1. For each $j \in [1, \ell_i]$, let I_{ij}^{min} and O_{ij}^{min} be the α_i^j input and β_i^j output data of m_i with minimum cost. Then, B_i^{min} represents $I_{ij}^{min} \cup O_{ij}^{min}$ of minimum cost.

Algorithm 1 Rounding algorithm of LP relaxation of the IP given in Figure 3,
Input: An optimal fractional solution $\{x_b | b \in A\}$,
Output: A safe subset V for Γ-privacy of W.

1: Initialize $B = \phi$.
2: For each attribute $b \in A$ (A is the set of all attributes in W), include b in B with probability $\min\{1, 16x_b \log n\}$.
3: For each module m_i whose privacy requirement is not satisfied by B, add B_i^{min} to B.
4: Return $V = A \setminus B$ as the safe visible attribute.

The following lemma shows that step 2 satisfies the privacy requirement of each module with high probability:

LEMMA 3. *Let m_i be any module in workflow W. Then with probability at least $1 - 2/n^2$, there exists a $j \in [1, \ell_i]$ such that $|I_i^h| \geq \alpha_i^j$ and $|O_i^h| \geq \beta_i^j$.*

PROOF SKETCH. The LP solution returns a probability distribution on r_{ij}, and therefore on the pairs in list L_i. Let p be the index of the median of this distribution when list L_i is ordered by both α_i^j and β_i^j values, as described above. Our proof consists of showing that with probability $\geq 1 - 2/n^2$, $|I_i^h| \geq \alpha_{ip}$ and $|O_i^h| \geq \beta_{ip}$.

Note that since p is the median, the sum of y_{bij} over all incoming data of module v_i in the LP solution must be at least $\alpha_{ip}/2$ (from constraint (2)). Further, constraint (6) ensures that this sum is contributed to by at least $\alpha_{ip}/2$ different input data, and constraint (4) ensures that x_b for any input data b must be at least its contribution to this sum, i.e. $\sum_j y_{bij}$. Thus, at least $\alpha_{ip}/2$ different input data have a large enough value of x_b, and randomized rounding produces a good solution. An identical argument works for the output data of m_i. □

Since the above lemma holds for every module, by standard arguments, the $O(\log n)$-approximation follows.

We next show that the richer expressiveness of set constraints increases the complexity of the problem.

THEOREM 6. *(Set Constraints)* The **Secure-View** problem with set constraints cannot be approximated to within a factor of $\ell_{\max}^\epsilon$ for some constant $\epsilon > 0$ (also within a factor of $\Omega(2^{\log^{1-\gamma} n})$ for all constant $\gamma > 0$) unless $NP \subseteq DTIME(n^{\text{polylog } n})$. The hardness result holds even when the maximum list size $\ell_{\max}$ is a (sufficiently large) constant, each data has unit cost, and the subsets $\overline{I}_i^j, \overline{O}_i^j$-s have cardinality at most 2. Finally, it is possible to get a factor $\ell_{\max}$-approximation in polynomial time.*

PROOF SKETCH. When we are allowed to specify arbitrary subsets for individual modules, we can encode a hard problem like *label-cover* which is known to have no polylogarithmic approximation given standard complexity assumptions. The corresponding approximation is obtained by an LP rounding algorithm which shows that a good approximation is still possible when the number of specified subsets for individual modules is not too large. □

The hardness proofs in the above two theorems use extensively data sharing, namely the fact that an output attribute of a given module may be fed as input to several other modules. Recall that a workflow is said to have γ-bounded data sharing if the maximum number of modules which takes a particular data item as input is bounded by γ. In real life workflows, the number of modules where a data item is sent is not very large. The following theorem shows that a better approximation is possible when this number is bounded.

THEOREM 7. *(Bounded Data Sharing)* There is a $(\gamma + 1)$-approximation algorithm for the **Secure-View** problem (with both cardinality and set constraints) when the workflow has γ-bounded data sharing. On the other hand, the cardinality constraint version (and consequently also the set constraint version) of the problem remain APX-hard even when there is no data sharing (i.e. $\gamma = 1$), each data has unit cost, the maximum list size $\ell_{\max}$ is 2, and the values of α_i^j, β_i^j-s are bounded by 3.

PROOF SKETCH. The APX-hardness in the above theorem is obtained by a reduction from vertex-cover in cubic graphs. This reduction also shows that the NP-completeness of this problem does not originate from data-sharing, and the problem is unlikely to have an exact solution even without any data sharing. The $\gamma + 1$-approximation is obtained by a greedy algorithm, which chooses the least cost attribute subsets for individual modules, and outputs the union of all of them. Since any attribute is produced by a unique module and is fed to at most γ modules, in any optimal solution, a single attribute can be used to satisfy the requirement of at most $\gamma + 1$ modules. This gives a $\gamma + 1$-approximation. Observe that when data sharing is not bounded, γ can be $\Omega(n)$ and this greedy algorithm will not give a good approximation to this problem. □

5. PUBLIC MODULES

In the previous section we restricted our attention to workflows where all modules are private. In practice, typical workflows use also public modules. Not surprisingly, this makes privacy harder to accomplish. In particular, we will see below that it becomes harder to assemble privacy guarantees for the full workflow out of those that suffice for component modules. Nevertheless a refined variant of Theorem 4 can still be employed.

5.1 Standalone vs. Workflow Privacy (Revisited)

We have shown in Section 4.1 (Theorem 4) that when a set of hidden attributes guarantees Γ-standalone-privacy for a private module, then the same set of attributes can be used to guarantee Γ-workflow-privacy *in an all-private network*. Interestingly, this is no longer the case for workflows with public modules. To see why, consider the following example.

EXAMPLE 7. *Consider a private module m implementing a one-one function with k boolean inputs and k boolean outputs. Hiding any $\log \Gamma$ input attributes guarantees Γ-standalone-privacy for m even if all output attributes of m are visible. However, if m gets all its inputs from a public module m' that computes some constant function (i.e. $\forall \mathbf{x}, m'(\mathbf{x}) = \mathbf{a}$, for some constant $\mathbf{a}$), then hiding $\log \Gamma$ input attributes no longer guarantees Γ-workflow-privacy of m – this is because it suffices to look at the (visible) output attributes of m to know the value $m(\mathbf{x})$ for $x = \mathbf{a}$.*

In an analogous manner, hiding any $\log \Gamma$ output attributes of m, leaving all its input attributes visible, also guarantees Γ-standalone-privacy of m. But if m sends all its outputs to another public module m'' that implements a one-one invertible function, and whose output attributes happen to be visible, then for any input $\mathbf{x}$ to m, $m(\mathbf{x})$ can be immediately inferred using the inverse function of m''.

Modules that compute a constant function (or even one-one invertible function) may not be common in practice. However, this simple example illustrates where, more generally, the proof of Theorem 4 (or Lemma 2) fails in the presence of public modules: when searching for a possible world that is consistent with the visible attributes, one needs to ensure that the functions defined by the public modules remain unchanged. So we no longer have the freedom of freely changing the values of the hidden input (resp. output) attributes, if those are supplied by (to) a public module.

One way to overcome this problem is to "privatize" such problematic public modules, in the sense that the name of the public module is not revealed to users (either in the workflow specification or in its execution logs). Here we assume that once we rename a module the user loses all knowledge about it (we discuss other possible approaches in the conclusion). We refer to the public modules whose identity is hidden (resp. revealed) as *hidden* (*visible*) public modules. Observe that now, since the identity of the hidden modules is no longer known to the adversary, condition (2) in Definition 4 no longer needs to be enforced for them, and a larger set of possible words can be considered. Formally,

DEFINITION 6. *(Definition 4 revisited) Let P be a subset of the public modules, and, as before, let V be a set of the visible attributes. Then, the set of* possible worlds *for the relation R w.r.t. V and P, denoted* Worlds(R, V, P), *consists of all relations R' over the same attributes as R that satisfy the functional dependencies in F and where (1) $\pi_V(R') = \pi_V(R)$, and (2) for every public module $m_i \in P$ and every tuple $\mathbf{t'} \in R'$, $\pi_{O_i}(\mathbf{t'}) = m_i(\pi_{I_i}(\mathbf{t'}))$.*

The notion of Γ-privacy for a workflow W, with both private and public modules (w.r.t a set V of visible attributes and a set P of visible public modules) is now defined as before (Definition 5), except that the set of possible worlds that is considered is the refined one from Definition 6 above. Similarly, if W is Γ-*private* w.r.t. V and P, then we will call the pair (V, P) a *safe subset* for Γ-privacy of W.

We can now show that, by making visible only public modules whose input and output attribute values need not be masked, one can obtain a result analogous to Theorem 4. Namely, assemble the privacy guarantees of the individual modules to form privacy guarantees for the full workflow. Wlog., we will assume that $m_1, m_2, \cdots, m_K$ are the private modules and $m_{K+1}, \cdots, m_n$ are the public modules in W.

THEOREM 8. *Given a parameter $\Gamma \geq 1$, let $V_i \subseteq (I_i \cup O_i)$, $i \in [1, K]$, be a set of visible attributes w.r.t which the private module m_i is Γ-standalone-private. Then the workflow W is Γ-private w.r.t the set of visible attributes V and any set of visible public modules $P \subseteq \{m_{K+1}, \cdots, m_n\}$, s.t. $\overline{V} = \bigcup_{i=1}^{K} \overline{V_i}$ and all the input and output attributes of modules in P are visible and belong to V.*

PROOF SKETCH. The proof is similar to that of Thm. 4. Here analogous to Lemma 2, we can show that, if a public module $m_j, j \in [K+1, n]$ is redefined to g_j, then m_j is hidden. In other words, the visible public modules in P are never redefined and therefore condition (2) in Definition 6 holds. □

EXAMPLE 8. *Consider a chain workflow with three modules $m' \rightarrow m \rightarrow m''$, where m' is a public module computing a constant function, m is a private module computing a one-one function and m'' is another public module computing an invertible one-one function. If we hide only a subset of the input attributes of m, m' should be hidden, thus $P = \{m''\}$. Similarly, if we hide only a subset of the output attributes of m, m'' should be hidden. Finally, if we hide a combination of input and output attributes, both m', m'' should be hidden and in that case $P = \phi$.*

5.2 The Secure-View Problem (Revisited)

The Secure-View optimization problem in general workflows is similar to the case of all-private workflows, with an additional cost due to hiding (privatization) of public modules: when a public module m_j is hidden, the solution incurs a cost $c(m_j)$. Following the notation of visible and hidden attributes, V and $\overline{V}$, we will denote the set of hidden public modules by $\overline{P}$. The total cost due to hidden public modules is $c(\overline{P}) = \sum_{m_j \in \overline{P}} c(m_j)$, and the total cost of a safe solution (V, P) is $c(\overline{V}) + c(\overline{P})$. The definition of the Secure-View problem, with cardinality and set constraints, naturally extends to this refined cost function and the goal is to find a safe solution with minimum cost. This generalizes the Secure-View problem for all-private workflows where $\overline{P} = \phi$ (and hence $c(\overline{P}) = 0$).

Complexity Results In Section 4.3 we showed that the Secure-View problem has an $O(\log n)$-approximation in an all-private workflow even when the lists specifying cardinality requirements are $\Omega(n)$-long and when the workflow has arbitrary data sharing. But by a reduction from the label-cover problem, it can be shown that the cardinality constraints version in general workflows is $\Omega(2^{\log^{1-\gamma} n})$-hard to approximate (for all constant $\gamma > 0$), and thus unlikely to have any polylogarithmic-approximation. In contrast, the approximation factor for the set constraints version remains the same and Theorem 6 still holds for general workflows by a simple modification to the proof. However, γ-bounded data sharing no longer give a constant factor approximation any more for a constant value of γ. By a reduction from the set-cover problem, it can be shown that the problem is $\Omega(\log n)$-hard to approximate even when the workflow has no data sharing, and when the maximum size of the requirement lists and the individual cardinality requirements in them are bounded by 1. Details of these results are deferred to the full version of the paper.

6. CONCLUSIONS

This paper proposes the use of provenance views for preserving the privacy of module functionality in a workflow. Our model motivates a natural optimization problem, **Secure-View** , which seeks to identify the smallest amount of data that needs to be hidden so that the functionality of every module is kept private. We give algorithms and hardness results that characterize the complexity of the problem.

In our analysis, we assume that users have two sources of knowledge about module functionality: the module name (identity) and the visible part of the workflow relation. Module names are informative for public modules, but the information is lost once the module name is hidden/renamed. Names of private modules are non-informative, and users know only what is given in the workflow view. However, if users have some additional prior knowledge about the behavior of a private module, we may hide their identity by renaming them, and then run our algorithms.

Our work suggests several promising directions for future research. First, a finer privacy analysis may be possible if one knows what *kind* of prior knowledge the user has on a private module, e.g. the distribution of output values for a specific input value, or knowledge about the types and names of input/output attributes (certain integers may be illegal social security numbers, certain character sequences are more likely to represent gene sequences than others, etc). Our definitions and algorithms currently assume that all data values in an attribute domain are equally possible, so the effect of knowledge of a possibly non-uniform prior distribution on input/output values should be explored. Second, some additional sources of user knowledge on functionality of public modules (e.g. types of attributes and connection with other modules) may prohibit hiding their functionality using privatization (renaming), and we would like to explore alternatives to privatization to handle public modules. A third direction to explore is an alternative model of privacy. As previously mentioned, standard mechanisms to guarantee differential privacy (e.g. adding random noise to data values) do not seem to work for ensuring module privacy w.r.t. provenance queries, and new mechanisms suitable to our application have to be developed. Other natural directions for future research include considering *non-additive cost functions*, in which some attribute subsets are more useful than others, efficiently handling *infinite or very large domains* of attributes, and exploring alternate objective functions, such as *maximizing utility* of visible data instead of minimizing the cost of hidden data.

Acknowledgements. S. B. Davidson, S. Khanna and S. Roy were supported in part by NSF-IIS Award 0803524; T. Milo was supported in part by NSF-IIS Award 1039376, the Israel Science Foundation, the US-Israel Binational Science Foundation and the EU grant MANCOOSI; and D. Panigrahi was supported in part by NSF-STC Award 0939370.

7. REFERENCES

[1] *www.myexperiment.org.*

[2] C. C. Aggarwal and P. S. Yu. *Privacy-Preserving Data Mining: Models and Algorithms.* Springer, 2008.

[3] L. Backstrom, C. Dwork, and J. M. Kleinberg. Wherefore art thou r3579x?: anonymized social networks, hidden patterns, and structural steganography. In *WWW*, pages 181–190, 2007.

[4] S. Bowers and B. Ludäscher. Actor-oriented design of scientific workflows. In *Int. Conf. on Concept. Modeling*, pages 369–384, 2005.

[5] U. Braun, A. Shinnar, and M. Seltzer. Securing provenance. In *USENIX HotSec*, pages 1–5, 2008.

[6] A. Chebotko, S. Chang, S. Lu, F. Fotouhi, and P. Yang. Scientific workflow provenance querying with security views. In *WAIM*, pages 349–356, 2008.

[7] S. B. Davidson, S. Khanna, S. Roy, J. Stoyanovich, V. Tannen, Y. Chen, and T. Milo. Enabling privacy in provenance-aware workflow systems. In *CIDR*, 2011.

[8] I. Dinur and K. Nissim. Revealing information while preserving privacy. In *PODS*, pages 202–210, 2003.

[9] C. Dwork. Differential privacy: A survey of results. In *TAMC*, pages 1–19, 2008.

[10] J. Freire, C. T. Silva, S. P. Callahan, E. Santos, C. E. Scheidegger, and H. T. Vo. Managing rapidly-evolving scientific workflows. In *IPAW*, pages 10–18, 2006.

[11] Y. Gil, W. K. Cheung, V. Ratnakar, and K. kin Chan. Privacy enforcement in data analysis workflows. In *PEAS*, 2007.

[12] Y. Gil and C. Fritz. Reasoning about the appropriate use of private data through computational workflows. In *Intelligent Information Privacy Management*, pages 69–74, 2010.

[13] R. Hasan, R. Sion, and M. Winslett. Introducing secure provenance: problems and challenges. In *StorageSS*, pages 13–18, 2007.

[14] J. Lyle and A. Martin. Trusted computing and provenance: better together. In *TAPP*, page 1, 2010.

[15] A. Machanavajjhala, J. Gehrke, D. Kifer, and M. Venkitasubramaniam. ℓ-diversity: Privacy beyond k-anonymity. In *ICDE*, page 24, 2006.

[16] G. Miklau and D. Suciu. A formal analysis of information disclosure in data exchange. In *SIGMOD*, pages 575–586, 2004.

[17] L. Moreau, J. Freire, J. Futrelle, R. E. McGrath, J. Myers, and P. Paulson. The open provenance model: An overview. In *IPAW*, pages 323–326, 2008.

[18] R. Motwani, S. U. Nabar, and D. Thomas. Auditing sql queries. In *ICDE*, pages 287–296, 2008.

[19] T. 'Oinn *et al.* Taverna: a tool for the composition and enactment of bioinformatics workflows. *Bioinformatics*, 20(1):3045–3054, 2003.

[20] V. Rastogi, M. Hay, G. Miklau, and D. Suciu. Relationship privacy: output perturbation for queries with joins. In *PODS*, pages 107–116, 2009.

[21] L. Sweeney. k-anonymity: a model for protecting privacy. *Int. J. Uncertain. Fuzziness Knowl.-Based Syst.*, 10(5):557–570, 2002.

[22] V. S. Verykios, E. Bertino, I. N. Fovino, L. P. Provenza, Y. Saygin, and Y. Theodoridis. State-of-the-art in privacy preserving data mining. *SIGMOD Rec.*, 33(1):50–57, 2004.

Maximizing Conjunctive Views in Deletion Propagation

Benny Kimelfeld   Jan Vondrák   Ryan Williams

IBM Research–Almaden
San Jose, CA 95120, USA
{kimelfeld, jvondrak, ryanwill}@us.ibm.com

ABSTRACT

In deletion propagation, tuples from the database are deleted in order to reflect the deletion of a tuple from the view. Such an operation may result in the (often necessary) deletion of additional tuples from the view, besides the intentionally deleted one. The complexity of deletion propagation is studied, where the view is defined by a conjunctive query (CQ), and the goal is to maximize the number of tuples that remain in the view. Buneman et al. showed that for some simple CQs, this problem can be solved by a trivial algorithm. This paper identifies additional cases of CQs where the trivial algorithm succeeds, and in contrast, it proves that for some other CQs the problem is NP-hard to approximate better than some constant ratio. In fact, this paper shows that among the CQs without self joins, the hard CQs are *exactly* the ones that the trivial algorithm fails on. In other words, for every CQ without self joins, deletion propagation is either APX-hard or solvable by the trivial algorithm.

The paper then presents approximation algorithms for certain CQs where deletion propagation is APX-hard. Specifically, two constant-ratio (and polynomial-time) approximation algorithms are given for the class of star CQs without self joins. The first algorithm is a greedy algorithm, and the second is based on randomized rounding of a linear program. While the first algorithm is more efficient, the second one has a better approximation ratio. Furthermore, the second algorithm can be extended to a significant generalization of star CQs. Finally, the paper shows that self joins can have a major negative effect on the approximability of the problem.

Categories and Subject Descriptors: H.2 [Database Management]: Systems, Database Administration

General Terms: Algorithms, Theory

Keywords: Deletion propagation, dichotomy, approximation

1. INTRODUCTION

Classical in database management is the *view update problem* [2, 8, 9, 11, 15, 20]: translate an update operation on the view to an update of the source database, so that the update on the view is properly reflected. A special case of this problem is that of *deletion propagation* in relational databases: given an *undesired* tuple in the view (defined by some monotonic query), delete some tuples from the base relations (where such tuples are referred to as *facts*), so that the undesired tuple disappears from the view, but the other tuples in the view remain. The database resulting from this deletion of tuples is said to be *side-effect free* [4], where the "side effect" is the set of deleted view tuples that are different from the undesired one. Very often, a solution that is side-effect free does not exist, and hence, the task is relaxed to that of *minimizing* the side effect [4,8]. That is, the problem is to delete tuples from the source relations so that the undesired tuple disappears from the view, and the maximum possible number of other tuples remain in the view.

Though view update is a classical database problem, recent applications provide a renewed motivation for it. Specifically, view update naturally arises when debugging *Information Extraction* (IE) programs, which can be highly complicated [23]. As a concrete example, the MIDAS system [1] extracts basic relations from multiple (publicly available) financial data sources, some of which are semistructured or just text, and integrates them into composite *entities*, *events* and *relationships*. Naturally, this task is error prone, and due to the magnitude and complexity of MIDAS, it is practically impossible to reach complete precision. An erroneous conclusion, though, can be observed by a user viewing the final output of MIDAS, and such a conclusion is likely to be the result of errors or ambiguity in the base relations. When the integration query is taken as the view definition, deletion propagation becomes the task of suggesting tuples to be deleted from the base relations for eliminating the erroneous conclusion, while minimizing the effect on the remaining conclusions. Furthermore, eliminating tuples from the base relations may itself entail deletion propagation, since these tuples are typically extracted by consulting external (possibly unclean) data sources [23, 25].

Another motivation arises in *business reorganization*, and the specific application is that of eliminating undesired links, such as between a specific employee and a specific customer. This problem is nicely illustrated by the following simple example by Cui and Widom [10] (also referenced and used by Buneman et al. [4]). Let GroupUser(group, user) and GroupFile(group, file) be two relations representing memberships of users in groups and access permissions of groups to files. A user u can access the file f if u belongs to a group that can access f; that is, there is some g, such that GroupUser(g, u) and GroupFile(g, f). Suppose that we want to restrict the access of a specific user to a specific file, by eliminating some user-group or group-file pairings. Furthermore, we would like to do so in a way that a maximum number of user-file access permissions remain. This is exactly the deletion-propagation problem, where the view is defined by the following conjunctive query (CQ):

$$\text{Access}(y_1, y_2) :- \text{GroupUser}(x, y_1), \text{GroupFile}(x, y_2) \quad (1)$$

A formal definition of a CQ is given in Section 2. For some of the above applications of deletion propagation (e.g., IE), the involved queries can be much more complicated than CQs. Nevertheless, we believe that understanding deletion propagation for the basic class of CQs is an essential step towards practical algorithms for these applications. Hence, the focus of this paper is on the complexity of deletion propagation, where the view is defined by a CQ.

Formally, for a CQ Q (the view definition), the input for the deletion-propagation problem consists of a database instance I and a tuple $\mathbf{a} \in Q(I)$. A *solution* is an subinstance J of I (i.e., J is obtained from I by deleting facts) such that $\mathbf{a} \notin Q(J)$, and an *optimal solution* maximizes the number of tuples in $Q(J)$. The *side effect* is $(Q(I) \setminus \{\mathbf{a}\}) \setminus Q(J)$. Buneman et al. [4] identify some classes of CQs (e.g., projection-free CQs) for which a straightforward algorithm produces an optimal solution in polynomial time; we recall this algorithm in Section 3 and call it *the trivial algorithm*. But those tractable classes are highly restricted, as Buneman et al. show that even for a CQ as simple as the above Access(y_1, y_2), testing whether there is a solution that is side-effect free is NP-complete. Therefore, finding an *optimal solution* minimizing the side effect is NP-hard for Access(y_1, y_2). Of course, one can often settle for a solution that is just *approximately* optimal, such as a solution that has a side effect that is at most twice as large as the minimum. Nevertheless, as noted by Buneman et al. [4], approximating the minimum side effect is still hard, since such an approximation can be used to test for the existence of a side-effect free solution (because an approximately optimal solution must be side-effect free when a side-effect-free solution exists).

In spite of the above hardness in deletion propagation, we still want to design algorithms (at least for important classes of CQs) with provable guarantees on the quality of a solution. We achieve that by slightly tweaking the optimization measure: instead of trying to minimize the side effect (i.e., the cardinality of $(Q(I) \setminus \{a\}) \setminus Q(J)$), our goal is to maximize the number of remaining tuples (i.e., the cardinality of $Q(J)$). We denote this problem by $\text{MAXDP}\langle Q \rangle$. Of course, for finding an optimal solution, this maximization problem is *the same* as the original minimization problem. But in terms of approximation, the picture drastically changes. For example, we show that for *every* CQ Q without self joins, $\text{MAXDP}\langle Q \rangle$ is approximable by a constant factor that depends only on Q. More specifically, for every CQ Q without self joins there is a constant $\alpha_Q \in (0, 1)$ (lower bounded by the reciprocal of the arity of Q), such that the solution J produced by the trivial algorithm satisfies $|Q(J)| \geq \alpha_Q |Q(J')|$ for all solutions J'.

In Section 4, we formulate the *head-domination* property

of CQs. We prove that when a CQ Q without self joins has this property, $\text{MAXDP}\langle Q \rangle$ is solved optimally (and in polynomial time) by the trivial algorithm. Unfortunately, for many other CQs there is a limit to the extent to which $\text{MAXDP}\langle Q \rangle$ can be approximated. Particularly, we consider the self-join-free CQs, and show a remarkable phenomenon (Theorem 4.8): for those CQs that do not have the head domination property, not only is the trivial algorithm suboptimal for $\text{MAXDP}\langle Q \rangle$, this problem is hard to solve optimally, and even hard to approximate better than some constant ratio. More precisely, we show the following dichotomy. For every CQ Q without self joins, one of the following holds:

- Q has the head-domination property (thus, the trivial algorithm *optimally* solves $\text{MAXDP}\langle Q \rangle$ in polynomial time).

- There is a constant $\alpha_Q \in (0, 1)$, such that $\text{MAXDP}\langle Q \rangle$ is NP-hard to α_Q-approximate.

The proof of this dichotomy is nontrivial. Regarding the constant α_Q, we show that it is necessary to have it dependent on Q, since there is no global constant $\alpha \in (0, 1)$ that works for all the CQs Q (without self joins); however, we show that such a global constant exists for a large class of CQs (that contains the *acyclic* CQs [3, 12]). The above dichotomy also holds for the aforementioned problems of Buneman et al. [4]. That is, for the problem of determining whether there is a side-effect-free solution, and for the problem of finding an optimal solution, the following holds when there are no self joins: if the CQ has the head-domination property, then the problems are solvable by the trivial algorithm; otherwise, these problems are NP-hard.

So far, the only algorithm we have considered for deletion propagation is the trivial one. Recall that for every CQ Q without self joins, the trivial algorithm is a constant-factor approximation (with a constant depending on Q). In Section 5, we devise approximation algorithms with much better ratios, for the important class of star CQs without self joins[1] (which generalize the queries that are processed by the *Fagin algorithm* [13] and the *threshold algorithm* [14]). We first give an algorithm that provides a $\frac{1}{2}$-approximation for $\text{MAXDP}\langle Q \rangle$, where Q is a star CQ without self joins. This algorithm, which we call *the greedy algorithm*, is based on purely combinatorial arguments. This algorithm is very simple and has a highly desirable complexity: its running time is polynomial not just under the standard *data complexity*, but also under *query-and-data* complexity (which means that the worst-case cost of this algorithm is significantly smaller than that of evaluating the CQ over the database instance).

We then present an approximation for $\text{MAXDP}\langle Q \rangle$ that is based on randomized rounding of a linear program (LP). This randomized algorithm[2] is more complicated than the greedy algorithm. We formulate the problem as an integer linear program, which is relaxed to an ordinary linear program by means of randomized rounding that translates the resulting LP solution into a probabilistic choice of tuples to delete. The LP-based algorithm terminates in polynomial time, but unlike the greedy algorithm, the polynomial is only under data complexity (as it essentially requires the

---

[1]See Section 5 for the exact definition of a star CQ.

[2]A discussion on randomness in optimization is given in Section 5.

evaluation of the CQ). However, the LP-based algorithm has important two advantages over the greedy one.

The first advantage of the LP-based algorithm is that its approximation ratio is higher: $1 - \frac{1}{e}$ (roughly, 0.632) rather than $\frac{1}{2}$ (which is shown to be tight for the greedy algorithm). The second advantage is that the LP-based algorithm can be extended to a significant generalization of star CQs. Roughly speaking, in this generalization (which we formally define in Section 5) the star restriction is limited just to the existential variables. As we demonstrate, the greedy algorithm inherently fails on CQs of this generalization. The LP-based approach alone is not enough for this generalization, but interestingly, the trivial algorithm handles the cases where the LP fails. Hence, our generalized algorithm takes the best solution from those returned by the LP-based algorithm and the trivial algorithm.

Finally, in Section 6 we show that self joins in CQs introduce inherent hardness. Recall that for every CQ Q without self joins, $\mathrm{MaxDP}\langle Q\rangle$ can be efficiently α_Q-approximated by the trivial algorithm, where α_Q is bounded by the reciprocal of the arity of Q. We show that this result does not extend to CQs with self joins. Specifically, the trivial algorithm fails to give the desired approximation, and furthermore, we show an infinite set of CQs Q, such that the achievable approximation ratio for $\mathrm{MaxDP}\langle Q\rangle$ is exponentially smaller than the reciprocal of the arity of Q. In addition, we show a CQ Q with self joins, such that Q has the head-domination property and yet the trivial algorithm is sub-optimal; furthermore, $\mathrm{MaxDP}\langle Q\rangle$ is hard to approximate better than some constant ratio.

Note that the work reported here considers a basic and restricted case of the view update problem: deletion propagation for conjunctive views, with the goal of preserving as many tuples of the view as possible. We found that even in this basic case, approximation is a nontrivial topic. We believe that the insights and techniques drawn from this work will be helpful in the exploration of additional aspects of view update, and deletion propagation in particular, like those studied in the literature. For example, deletion propagation has been explored under the goal of minimizing the *source side effect* [4,8], namely, finding a solution with a minimal number of missing facts. Cong et al. [8] also studied the complexity of deletion propagation (with the goal of finding an optimal solution) in the presence of *key constraints*. Naturally, update operations other than deletion (e.g., insertion and replacement) have also been investigated [2], and especially in the presence of functional dependencies [9,11,20]. The work of Cosmadakis and Papadimitriou [9] is distinguished by their requirement for a view to keep intact a *complement view* (which has also been explored more recently by Lechtenbörger and Vossen [22]) that, intuitively, contains the information ignored by the view.

Due to a lack of space, some of the proofs are presented in the extended version of this paper [21].

2. PRELIMINARIES

2.1 Schemas, Instances, and CQs

We fix an infinite set Const of *constants*. We usually denote constants by lowercase letters from the beginning of the Latin alphabet (e.g., a, b and c). A *schema* is a finite sequence $\mathbf{R} = \langle R_1, \ldots, R_m\rangle$ of distinct relation symbols, where each R_i has an arity $r_i > 0$. An *instance* I (over

$\mathbf{R}$) is a sequence $\langle R_1^I, \ldots, R_m^I\rangle$, such that each R_i^I is a finite relation of arity r_i over Const (i.e., R_i^I is a finite subset of Const^{r_i}). We may abuse this notation and use R_i to denote both the relation symbol and the relation R_i^I that interprets it. If $\mathbf{c} \in \mathsf{Const}^{r_i}$, then $R_i(\mathbf{c})$ is called a *fact*, and it is a fact *of* the instance I if $\mathbf{c} \in R_i^I$. Notationally, we view an instance as the set of its facts (hence, we may write $R(\mathbf{c}) \in I$ to say that $R(\mathbf{c})$ is a fact of I).

If I and J are two instances over $\mathbf{R} = \langle R_1, \ldots, R_m\rangle$, then J is a *sub-instance* of I, denoted $J \subseteq I$, if $R_i^J \subseteq R_i^I$ for all $i = 1, \ldots, m$.

We fix an infinite set Var of *variables*, and assume that Const and Var are disjoint sets. We usually denote variables by lowercase letters from the end of the Latin alphabet (e.g., x, y and z). We use the Datalog style for denoting a conjunctive query (abbrev. CQ): a CQ over a schema $\mathbf{R}$ is an expression of the form

$$Q(\mathbf{y}) :\!- \varphi(\mathbf{x}, \mathbf{y}, \mathbf{c})$$

where $\mathbf{x}$ and $\mathbf{y}$ are tuples of variables (from Var), $\mathbf{c}$ is a tuple of constants (from Const), and $\varphi(\mathbf{x}, \mathbf{y}, \mathbf{c})$ is a conjunction of atomic formulas $R_i(\mathbf{x}, \mathbf{y}, \mathbf{c})$ over $\mathbf{R}$; an atomic formula is also called an *atom*. We may write just $Q(\mathbf{y})$ or Q if $\varphi(\mathbf{x}, \mathbf{y}, \mathbf{c})$ is irrelevant. We denote by atoms(Q) the set of atoms of Q. We usually write $\varphi(\mathbf{x}, \mathbf{y}, \mathbf{c})$ by simply listing atoms(Q). We make the requirement that each variable occurs at most once in $\mathbf{x}$ and $\mathbf{y}$, and no variable occurs in both $\mathbf{x}$ and $\mathbf{y}$. Furthermore, we require every variable of $\mathbf{y}$ to occur (at least once) in $\varphi(\mathbf{x}, \mathbf{y}, \mathbf{c})$.

When we mention a CQ Q, we usually avoid specifying the underlying schema $\mathbf{R}$, and rather assume that this schema is the one that consists of the relation symbols (with the proper arities) that appear in Q. When we want to refer to that schema, we denote it by schema(Q). Multiple occurrences of the same relation symbol in Q form a *self join*; hence, when we say that Q *has no self joins* we mean that every relation symbol appears at most once in $\varphi(\mathbf{x}, \mathbf{y}, \mathbf{c})$.

Let $Q(\mathbf{y}) :\!- \varphi(\mathbf{x}, \mathbf{y}, \mathbf{c})$ be a CQ. A variable of $\mathbf{x}$ is called an *existential* variable of Q, and a variable of $\mathbf{y}$ is called a *head* variable of Q. We use $\mathsf{Var}_\exists(Q)$ and $\mathsf{Var}_\mathsf{h}(Q)$ to denote the sets of existential variables and head variables of Q, respectively. Similarly, if ϕ is an atom of Q, then $\mathsf{Var}_\exists(\phi)$ and $\mathsf{Var}_\mathsf{h}(\phi)$ denote the set of existential variables and head variables, respectively, that occur in ϕ. We denote by $\mathsf{Var}(Q)$ and $\mathsf{Var}(\phi)$ the unions $\mathsf{Var}_\exists(Q) \cup \mathsf{Var}_\mathsf{h}(Q)$ and $\mathsf{Var}_\exists(\phi) \cup \mathsf{Var}_\mathsf{h}(\phi)$, respectively. A *join variable* of Q is a variable that occurs in two or more atoms of Q (note that a join variable can be an existential variable or a head variable). Finally, the *arity of Q*, denoted arity(Q), is the length of the tuple $\mathbf{y}$.

EXAMPLE 2.1. An important CQ in this work is the CQ $Q_2^\star$, which is the same as the CQ $\mathrm{Access}(y_1, y_2)$ defined in (1) (and discussed in the introduction), up to renaming of relation symbols.

$$Q_2^\star(y_1, y_2) :\!- R_1(x, y_1), R_2(x, y_2) \qquad (2)$$

Here and later, in our examples R_i and R_j are assumed to be different symbols when $i \neq j$. The atoms of $Q_2^\star$ are $\phi_1 = R_1(x, y_1)$ and $\phi_2 = R_2(x, y_2)$. Note that $Q_2^\star$ has no self joins (but it would have a self join if we replaced the symbol R_2 with R_1). There is only one existential variable in $Q_2^\star$, namely x, and the two head variables are y_1 and y_2.

Hence $\mathsf{Var}_\exists(Q) = \{x\}$ and $\mathsf{Var}_\mathsf{h}(Q) = \{y_1, y_2\}$. Furthermore, $\mathsf{Var}_\exists(\phi_1) = \{x\}$ and $\mathsf{Var}_\mathsf{h}(\phi_1) = \{y_1\}$. Finally, note that x is the single join variable of $Q_2^\star$.

We generalize the notation $Q_2^\star$ to $Q_k^\star$, for all positive integers k, where the CQ $Q_k^\star$ is defined as follows.

$$Q_k^\star(y_1, \ldots, y_k) :\!- R_1(x, y_1), \ldots, R_k(x, y_k) \qquad (3)$$

Note that $\mathrm{schema}(Q_k^\star)$ consists of the k (distinct) binary relations $R_1, \ldots, R_k$. $\square$

Observe that the CQ $Q_k^\star$ from Example 2.1 does not contain any constants. An example of a query with the constant Emma is the following.

$$Q(y_1, y_2) :\!- R_1(x, y_1), R_2(x, y_2, \mathsf{Emma})$$

Consider the CQ $Q(\mathbf{y})$, and let I be an instance over $\mathrm{schema}(Q)$. An *assignment* for Q is a mapping $\mu : \mathsf{Var}(Q) \to \mathsf{Const}$. For an assignment μ for Q, the tuple $\mu(\mathbf{y})$ is the one obtained from $\mathbf{y}$ by replacing every head variable y with the constant $\mu(y)$. Similarly, for an atom $\phi \in \mathrm{atoms}(Q)$, the fact $\mu(\phi)$ is the one obtained from ϕ by replacing every variable z with the constant $\mu(z)$. A *match for Q in I* is an assignment μ for Q, such that $\mu(\phi)$ is a fact of I for all atoms $\phi \in \mathrm{atoms}(Q)$. If μ is a match for Q in I, then $\mu(\mathbf{y})$ is called an *answer* (for Q in I). The *result* of evaluating Q over I, denoted $Q(I)$, is the set of all the answers for Q in I.

2.2 Deletion Propagation

Let Q be a CQ. The problem of maximizing the view in deletion propagation, with Q as the view definition, is denoted by $\mathrm{MaxDP}\langle Q \rangle$ and is defined as follows. The input consists of an instance I over $\mathrm{schema}(Q)$, and a tuple $\mathbf{a} \in Q(I)$. A *solution* (for I and $\mathbf{a}$) is an instance $J \subseteq I$, such that $\mathbf{a} \notin Q(J)$. The goal is to find an *optimal* solution, which is a solution J that maximizes $|Q(J)|$; that is, J is such that $|Q(J)| \geq |Q(K)|$ for all solutions K.

As we discuss later, finding an optimal solution for the problem $\mathrm{MaxDP}\langle Q \rangle$ may be intractable. Often, though, we can settle for *approximations*, which we naturally define as follows. For a number $\alpha \in [0, 1]$, a solution J is *α-optimal* if $|Q(J)| \geq \alpha \cdot |Q(K)|$ for all solutions K. An *α-approximation* for $\mathrm{MaxDP}\langle Q \rangle$ is an algorithm that, given I and $\mathbf{a}$, always returns an α-optimal solution.

3. THE TRIVIAL ALGORITHM

In this section, we recall a straightforward algorithm of Buneman et al. [4], which they gave for proving the tractability of finding a solution J with a minimum-size side effect (recall that the *side effect* is the set $(Q(I) \setminus \{\mathbf{a}\}) \setminus Q(J)$), in the case where there is no projection (i.e., Q has no existential variables); here, we trivially extend that algorithm to general CQs.

Consider a CQ $Q(\mathbf{y})$, and suppose that I and $\mathbf{a}$ are input for $\mathrm{MaxDP}\langle Q \rangle$. Let ϕ be an atom of Q. A *ϕ-fact* of I is a fact $f \in I$ that is equal to $\mu(\phi)$ for some assignment μ for Q (note that μ is not necessarily a match for Q in I); furthermore, if there is such μ that satisfies $\mu(\mathbf{y}) = \mathbf{a}$ (in addition to $\mu(\phi) = f$), then we say that f is *consistent with* $\mathbf{a}$. The *trivial algorithm* for generating a solution for I and $\mathbf{a}$ is as follows. For each $\phi \in \mathrm{atoms}(Q)$, we obtain from I the sub-instance J_ϕ by removing all of the ϕ-facts that are consistent with $\mathbf{a}$. Then, we return the J_ϕ that maximizes $|Q(J_\phi)|$. Pseudo-code for $\mathsf{Trivial}\langle Q \rangle$ is shown in Figure 1.

Algorithm $\mathsf{Trivial}\langle Q \rangle(I, \mathbf{a})$

1: $J \leftarrow \emptyset$
2: **for all** $\phi \in \mathrm{atoms}(Q)$ **do**
3:      $J_\phi \leftarrow I$
4:      remove from J_ϕ all ϕ-facts consistent with $\mathbf{a}$
5:      **if** $|Q(J_\phi)| > |Q(J)|$ **then**
6:          $J \leftarrow J_\phi$
7: **return** J

Figure 1: The trivial algorithm

EXAMPLE 3.1. Consider the following CQ $Q_3^\star$, which is a special case of (3).

$$Q_3^\star(y_1, y_2, y_3) :\!- R_1(x, y_1), R_2(x, y_2), R_3(x, y_3).$$

Figure 2 shows an instance I_3 over $\mathrm{schema}(Q_3^\star)$, and let $\mathbf{a}$ be the tuple $(\diamond, \diamond, \diamond)$. Let us show how the trivial algorithm operates on I_3 and $\mathbf{a}$. For $i \in \{1, 2, 3\}$, let ϕ_i be the atom $R_i(x, y_i)$. Then $\mathrm{atoms}(Q_3^\star) = \{\phi_1, \phi_2, \phi_3\}$. For $i \in \{1, 2, 3\}$, the ϕ_i-facts are those that belong to the relation R_i, and the ones that are consistent with $\mathbf{a}$ are those of the form $R_i(j, \diamond)$; the solution J_{ϕ_i} is therefore obtained from I_3 by removing from R_i all the facts except for $R_i(i, \square)$. Thus, we have $Q_3^\star(J_{\phi_1}) = \{(\square, \diamond, \diamond)\}$, $Q_3^\star(J_{\phi_2}) = \{(\diamond, \square, \diamond)\}$, and $Q_3^\star(J_{\phi_3}) = \{(\diamond, \diamond, \square)\}$. It follows that $|Q_3^\star(J_{\phi_i})| = 1$ for all $i \in \{1, 2, 3\}$, and therefore, the trivial algorithm can return any J_{ϕ_i} (depending on the traversal order over the atoms). $\square$

The following (straightforward) proposition states the correctness and efficiency of the trivial algorithm. Unless stated otherwise, in this paper we use *data complexity* [26] for analyzing the complexity of deletion propagation and algorithms thereof; this means that the CQ Q is held fixed, and the input consists of the instance I and the tuple $\mathbf{a}$.

PROPOSITION 3.2. $\mathsf{Trivial}\langle Q \rangle$ *returns a solution, and terminates in polynomial time.*

Next, we show that in the case where Q has no self joins, the trivial algorithm approximates $\mathrm{MaxDP}\langle Q \rangle$ within a constant ratio that depends only on Q. (A discussion on CQs with self joins is in Section 6.)

3.1 Approximation

The following proposition shows that, if Q is a CQ without self joins, then the trivial algorithm is a constant-factor approximation for $\mathrm{MaxDP}\langle Q \rangle$ (where the constant depends on Q). The proof is fairly straightforward.

PROPOSITION 3.3. *If Q is a CQ without self joins, then* $\mathsf{Trivial}\langle Q \rangle$ *is a $\frac{1}{k}$-approximation for* $\mathrm{MaxDP}\langle Q \rangle$, *where* $k = \min\{\mathrm{arity}(Q), |\mathrm{atoms}(Q)|\}$.

Next, we will show that $\frac{1}{k}$ is also a tight lower bound on the approximation ratio of the trivial algorithm, for some queries without self joins. More precisely, we will show that for all natural numbers k, the CQ $Q_k^\star$ (Example 2.1), which satisfies $\mathrm{arity}(Q_k^\star) = |\mathrm{atoms}(Q)| = k$, is such that the trivial

Figure 2: Instance I_3 over schema($Q_3^\star$)

Figure 3: The graphs $\mathcal{G}_\exists(Q)$ and $\mathcal{G}_\exists(Q')$ for the CQs Q and Q' of Example 4.2

algorithm returns no better than a $\frac{1}{k}$-approximation. So, let k be a natural number. We will construct an instance I_k and a tuple $\mathbf{a} \in Q_k^\star(I_k)$ that realize the $\frac{1}{k}$ ratio. Each of the k relations R_i contains the k tuples $(1, \diamond), \ldots, (k, \diamond)$; in addition, each relation R_i contains the tuple $(i, \square)$. As an example, Figure 2 shows I_3. The tuple $\mathbf{a}$ is $\diamond^k$ (i.e., a tuple that consists of k diamonds).

To see that I_k and $\mathbf{a}$ are as desired, let J be the sub-instance of I_k that is obtained by removing $(i, \diamond)$ from each relation R_i. Then $Q_k^\star(J)$ contains k tuples $\mathbf{b}_1, \ldots, \mathbf{b}_k$, where each $\mathbf{b}_i$ is the tuple that comprises only $\diamond$s, except for the ith element that is $\square$. Note that J is optimal, since $Q_k^\star(I_k) = Q_k^\star(J) \cup \{\mathbf{a}\}$. Nevertheless, the trivial algorithm will remove from one of the relations, say R_i, all the tuples of the form $(x, \diamond)$, as described for $k = 3$ in Example 3.1. By doing so, the trivial algorithm produces a sub-instance J', such that $Q_k^\star(J')$ contains exactly one tuple, thus no better than a $\frac{1}{k}$-approximation.

In the next section we will characterize the CQs, among those without self joins, for which the trivial algorithm is optimal. Furthermore, we will show that (in the absence of self joins) the trivial algorithm is optimal for $\textsc{MaxDP}\langle Q \rangle$ *precisely* for those CQs Q with a tractable $\textsc{MaxDP}\langle Q \rangle$; for the remaining CQs Q, $\textsc{MaxDP}\langle Q \rangle$ is hard, and even hard to approximate better than some constant ratio.

4. DICHOTOMY

In this section, we define the *head-domination* property of a CQ, and show that if a CQ Q without self joins has this property, then the trivial algorithm (optimally) solves $\textsc{MaxDP}\langle Q \rangle$. Furthermore, we show that this property *exactly* captures the tractability of $\textsc{MaxDP}\langle Q \rangle$, in the sense that in the absence of this property, $\textsc{MaxDP}\langle Q \rangle$ is not only intractable, but actually cannot be approximated better than some constant ratio (it is APX-hard).

4.1 Head Domination

Let Q be a CQ. The *existential-connectivity graph* of Q, denoted $\mathcal{G}_\exists(Q)$, is the undirected graph that has atoms(Q) as the set of nodes, and that has an edge $\{\phi_1, \phi_2\}$ whenever ϕ_1 and ϕ_2 have at least one existential variable in common (that is, $\mathsf{Var}_\exists(\phi_1) \cap \mathsf{Var}_\exists(\phi_2) \neq \emptyset$). Let ϕ be an atom of Q, and let P be a set of atoms of Q. We say that P is *head-dominated* by ϕ if ϕ contains all the head variables that occur in P (i.e., $\mathsf{Var}_\mathsf{h}(\phi') \subseteq \mathsf{Var}_\mathsf{h}(\phi)$ for all $\phi' \in P$).

DEFINITION 4.1. (**Head Domination**) A CQ Q has the *head-domination* property if for every connected component P of $\mathcal{G}_\exists(Q)$ there is an atom $\phi \in \mathsf{atoms}(Q)$, such that P is head-dominated by ϕ. $\square$

As an example, for the CQ $Q_k^\star$ defined in (3), the graph $\mathcal{G}_\exists(Q_k^\star)$ is a clique over atoms($Q_k^\star$), and so it has only one

connected component. For $k > 1$, none of the atoms of $Q_k^\star$ contains all the head variables y_i, and hence, $Q_k^\star$ does not have the head-domination property. (Note that $Q_1^\star$ has the head-domination property, as does every CQ with only one atom or only one head variable.) Another example follows.

EXAMPLE 4.2. Consider the CQ Q defined by

$$Q(y_1, y_2, y_3) :- R(y_1, x_1), S(x_1, x_2), T(x_2, y_2, x_3),$$
$$U(y_2, y_3, x_4).$$

The left side of Figure 3 shows the graph $\mathcal{G}_\exists(Q)$. Note that $\mathcal{G}_\exists(Q)$ has two connected components: the first component is $\{R(y_1, x_1), S(x_1, x_2), T(x_2, y_2, x_3)\}$ and the second is $\{U(y_2, y_3, x_4)\}$. The CQ Q does not have the head-domination property, since the first connected component is not head-dominated by any atom of Q (since no atom contains both y_1 and y_2). Now, consider the following CQ Q', which is obtained from Q by adding an atom $V(y_1, y_2)$.

$$Q'(y_1, y_2, y_3) :- R(y_1, x_1), S(x_1, x_2), T(x_2, y_2, x_3),$$
$$U(y_2, y_3, x_4), V(y_1, y_2)$$

The graph $\mathcal{G}_\exists(Q')$ is shown on the right of Figure 3. Note that the atom $V(y_1, y_2)$ head-dominates the connected component $\{R(y_1, x_1), S(x_1, x_2), T(x_2, y_2, x_3)\}$; hence, Q' has the head-domination property. $\square$

4.2 Optimality of the Trivial Algorithm

The following theorem states that if a CQ Q without self joins has the head-domination property, then the trivial algorithm is optimal for $\textsc{MaxDP}\langle Q \rangle$.

THEOREM 4.3. *Let Q be a CQ without self joins. If Q has the head-domination property, then $\mathsf{Trivial}\langle Q \rangle$ optimally solves $\textsc{MaxDP}\langle Q \rangle$.*

PROOF. Let Q be a CQ without self joins, such that Q has the head-domination property. Consider the input I and $\mathbf{a}$ for $\textsc{MaxDP}\langle Q \rangle$. Let J be any solution (e.g., an optimal solution). Let f be a fact in $I \setminus J$. Note that such a fact f must exist, since $\mathbf{a} \in Q(I)$ and $\mathbf{a} \notin Q(J)$. Assume, w.l.o.g., that $\mathbf{a} \in Q(J \cup \{f\})$; otherwise, f can be added to J without losing any tuple from $Q(J)$, and then we can choose another f, and so on. Let ϕ be the atom of Q, such that f is a ϕ-fact. Let P_f be the connected component of ϕ in $\mathcal{G}_\exists(Q)$, and let γ be an atom of Q such that γ dominates P_f. Such an atom γ exists, since Q has the head-domination property.

Consider the solution J_γ that the trivial algorithm constructs (by removing from I all the γ-facts that are consistent with $\mathbf{a}$). We will prove the theorem by showing that $Q(J) \subseteq Q(J_\gamma)$ (and hence, $|Q(J)| \leq |Q(J_\gamma)|$). If $J \subseteq J_\gamma$, then the claim is obvious (since Q is a monotonic query). Otherwise, let g be a fact in $J \setminus J_\gamma$. Then g is a γ-fact that is consistent with $\mathbf{a}$, since $g \notin J_\gamma$. We will prove that there is no match μ for Q in J, such that $\mu(\gamma) = g$. Since Q has no self joins, this would mean that g is actually useless for producing $Q(J)$. As a result, by repeating this argument for all $g \in J \setminus J_\gamma$ we will get that for $J' = J \cap J_\gamma$ it holds that $Q(J) = Q(J')$; and since $Q(J') \subseteq Q(J_\gamma)$ (as $J' \subseteq J_\gamma$ and Q is monotonic), it holds that $Q(J) \subseteq Q(J_\gamma)$.

Suppose, by way of contradiction, that μ_g is a match for Q in J, such that $\mu_g(\gamma) = g$. We will show that $\mathbf{a} \in Q(J)$, and thereby obtain a contradiction to the fact that J is a solution. Let $\mathbf{y}$ be the tuple of head variables of Q. Recall that $\mathbf{a} \in Q(J \cup \{f\})$, and let μ_f be a match for Q in $J \cup \{f\}$ with $\mu_f(\mathbf{y}) = \mathbf{a}$. Note that $\mu_f(\phi) = f$. (Remember that Q has no self joins.)

Observe that μ_f and μ_g agree on all the head variables of P_ϕ, due to the fact that γ contains all these variables, and due to the fact that g is consistent with $\mathbf{a}$. Also note that no existential variable occurs both in P_ϕ and outside P_ϕ, since P_ϕ is a connected component. It thus follows that μ_f and μ_g agree on *all* the variables that occur both inside P_ϕ and outside P_ϕ.

We now construct a match μ for Q in J, as follows: for each $z \in \mathsf{Var}(Q)$ we define $\mu(z) = \mu_g(z)$ if z appears in P_ϕ, and otherwise $\mu(z) = \mu_f(z)$. Recall that ϕ is in P_ϕ, and hence, $\mu(\phi) = \mu_g(\phi)$; thus, $\mu(\phi)$ belongs to J (and in particular, $\mu(\phi) \neq f$). It follows that μ is indeed a match for Q in J. To complete the proof, we will show that $\mu(\mathbf{y}) = \mathbf{a}$. Suppose that $\mathbf{y} = (y_1, \ldots, y_k)$ and $\mathbf{a} = (a_1, \ldots, a_k)$. Let i be an index in $\{1, \ldots, k\}$. If y_i appears in P_ϕ, then $\mu(y_i) = a_i$, since $\mu(y_i) = \mu_g(y_i)$, $\mu_g(\gamma) = g$, and g is consistent with $\mathbf{a}$. If y_i does not appear in P_ϕ, then $\mu(y_i) = a_i$ again, since $\mu(y_i) = \mu_f(y_i)$ and $\mu_f(\mathbf{y}) = \mathbf{a}$. We conclude that $\mu(\mathbf{y}) = \mathbf{a}$, and hence, $\mathbf{a} \in Q(J)$, as claimed. $\quad\square$

As a simple consequence of Theorem 4.3, if Q is a CQ without self joins, and every join variable of Q is a head variable, then the trivial algorithm optimally solves $\textsc{MaxDP}\langle Q \rangle$ (since then $\mathcal{G}_\exists(Q)$ has no edges). Actually, we can show that if every head variable is a join variable, then this statement is true even without requiring lack of self joins. However, in Section 6 we show that Theorem 4.3 is not correct for all the CQs that have self joins. Specifically, we show an example of a CQ Q with self joins, such that Q has the head-domination property, and yet the trivial algorithm does not optimally solve $\textsc{MaxDP}\langle Q \rangle$; even more, for that Q we show that $\textsc{MaxDP}\langle Q \rangle$ is hard to approximate better than some constant ratio.

4.3 Hardness

The following theorem[3] states that if a CQ Q without self joins does not have the head-domination property, then in contrast to Theorem 4.3, $\textsc{MaxDP}\langle Q \rangle$ is hard, and even hard to approximate better than some constant ratio. In Section 4.3.1 we discuss the proof.

THEOREM 4.4. *Assume $P \neq NP$, and let Q be a CQ without self joins. If Q does not have the head-domination property, then there is a constant $\alpha_Q \in (0,1)$, such that $\textsc{MaxDP}\langle Q \rangle$ cannot be α_Q-approximated in polynomial time.*

One may wonder whether, in Theorem 4.4, it is necessary to have α_Q depending on Q. In other words, does Theorem 4.4 hold for a global α that is applicable to all the CQs without self joins? The following theorem shows that the answer is positive if we are restricted to the class of *acyclic* CQs [3, 12] and the class of CQs over binary[4] relation symbols. The proof is, essentially, through insights on the reductions used for proving Theorem 4.4 (see Section 4.3.1) in these special cases.

THEOREM 4.5. *There is a constant $\alpha \in (0,1)$, such the following holds for every CQ Q without self joins, provided that Q is acyclic or schema(Q) consists of binary relation symbols. If Q does not have the head-domination property, then it is NP-hard to α-approximate $\textsc{MaxDP}\langle Q \rangle$.*

However, in contrast to Theorem 4.5, the following proposition shows that no such global α exists for the class of all the CQs without self joins.

PROPOSITION 4.6. *For all natural numbers $k > 1$, there exists a CQ Q_k with the following properties.*

1. *Q_k has no self joins.*

2. *Q_k does not have the head-domination property.*

3. *$\mathsf{Trivial}\langle Q_k \rangle$ is a $(1 - \frac{1}{k})$-approximation for $\textsc{MaxDP}\langle Q_k \rangle$.*

PROOF. We define Q_k as follows. The schema of Q_k has k relation symbols $R_1, \ldots, R_k$, where each R_i is k-ary. Define

$$Q_k(y_1, \ldots, y_k) :\text{-} \phi_1, \phi_2, \ldots, \phi_k$$

where, for $i = 1, \ldots, k$, the atom ϕ_i is given by

$$\phi_i = R_i(x, y_1, \ldots, y_{i-1}, y_{i+1}, \ldots, y_k).$$

Note that ϕ_i contains all the variables of Q, except for y_i. Clearly, Q satisfies Properties 1 and 2 (i.e., Q has no self joins and it violates the head-domination property). It is left to prove Property 3. Let I and $\mathbf{a}$ be input for $\textsc{MaxDP}\langle Q_k \rangle$. Let i and j be such that $1 \leq i < j \leq k$, and let f_i and f_j be a ϕ_i-fact and a ϕ_j-fact, respectively, that are consistent with $\mathbf{a}$ (where consistency is defined in Section 3). The only answer of $Q(I)$ that agrees with both f_i and f_j on the head variables is $\mathbf{a}$. Therefore, among the answers in $Q(I) \setminus \{\mathbf{a}\}$, those that require f_i are disjoint from those that require f_j. Hence, if we take the best J_ϕ constructed by $\mathsf{Trivial}\langle Q_k \rangle$ (Figure 1), it must be the case that $Q(J_\phi)$ misses at most $\frac{1}{k}$ of the tuples in $Q(I) \setminus \{\mathbf{a}\}$. In particular, the best J_ϕ is a $(1 - \frac{1}{k})$-approximation, as claimed. $\quad\square$

Next, we discuss the proof of Theorem 4.4.

4.3.1 Proving Theorem 4.4

The full proof of Theorem 4.4 is in the extended version of this paper [21]. Here, we give a brief overview of the proof.

Our first step is to show hardness of $Q_2^\star$ (defined in (2)), which is a special case of a CQ that does not have the head-domination property. Buneman et al. [4] showed that deciding whether there is a solution that is side-effect free is NP-complete for $Q_2^\star$. To show that, they described a reduction from *non-mixed 3-satisfiability*, which is the problem of deciding on the satisfiability of a formula in 3-CNF,

[3]This result was found after the submission of the reviewed version of this paper, and was added (with the consent of the program committee) after the paper was accepted for publication. In the reviewed version, a similar result was shown for a more restricted class of CQs without self joins.

[4]This theorem further extends to the class of CQs where each atom has at most two influential variables, where an *influential variable* is either a join or a head variable

where no clause contains both negated and non-negated variables (that is, each clause is the disjunction of three literals, where the three are either all negative or all positive). Guruswami [17] showed a constant-factor bound on the approximability of non-mixed 3-satisfiability. However, we cannot simply combine the reduction of Buneman et al. and the result of Guruswami, since that reduction does not preserve approximation (or PTAS). Nevertheless, we prove inapproximability by combining that reduction with a more recent result of Guruswami and Khot [18] showing constant-factor inapproximability for non-mixed 3-satisfiability in the case where each variable occurs in at most five clauses. Thus, we get the following.

LEMMA 4.7. *There is a constant $\alpha \in (0,1)$, such that $\mathrm{MaxDP}\langle Q_2^\star \rangle$ is NP-hard to α-approximate.*

Next, we fix a CQ Q, such that Q has neither self joins nor the head-domination property. Our goal is to prove that $\mathrm{MaxDP}\langle Q \rangle$ is hard to approximate within some factor α_Q. We fix a component P of $\mathcal{G}_\exists(Q)$, such that P is head-dominated by none of the atoms of Q. We call two variables y and y' *atomic neighbors* if Q has an atom that contains both y and y'. An important idea in the proof is to distinguish between two cases. The first case is where two of the head variables of P are *not* atomic neighbors. The second case is the complement: every two head variables of P are atomic neighbors.

In the first case, suppose that y_1' and y_2' are head variables of P that are not atomic neighbors. We show a (fairly simple) reduction from $\mathrm{MaxDP}\langle Q_2^\star \rangle$ to $\mathrm{MaxDP}\langle Q \rangle$ where, roughly speaking, the variable y_i' ($i = 1, 2$) of Q simulates the variable y_i of $Q_2^\star$.

In the second case, we again show a reduction from the problem $\mathrm{MaxDP}\langle Q_2^\star \rangle$ to $\mathrm{MaxDP}\langle Q \rangle$, and we again find y_1' and y_2' in Q that can simulate y_1 and y_2, respectively, in $Q_2^\star$; but here this task is much more subtle. In essence, for the proof to work we need to be able to assume that in a solution, it is not worth to remove any ϕ-fact if ϕ contains both y_1' and y_2'. To do that, we choose y_1' and y_2' carefully, and we handle differently those ϕ that are *inside P* and those that are *outside P*. By *handling* ϕ we essentially augment the constructed instance I (over schema(Q)) with additional tuples; this is also subtle, since we need to make sure that not too many answers are added to $Q(I)$, or else we can easily lose the (rough) preservation of the approximation ratio in the reduction. Needed for facing the last problem is the fact that every two head variables in P are atomic neighbors.

4.4 Dichotomy

We summarize this section with the following dichotomy[3] that is obtained by combining Theorem 4.3 and 4.4.

THEOREM 4.8 (DICHOTOMY). *For a CQ Q without self joins, one of the following holds.*

1. *The trivial algorithm optimally solves $\mathrm{MaxDP}\langle Q \rangle$ in polynomial time.*

2. *There is a constant $\alpha_Q \in (0,1)$, such that it is NP-hard to α_Q-approximate $\mathrm{MaxDP}\langle Q \rangle$.*

Moreover, 1 holds if and only if Q has the head-domination property.

A proof similar to (actually, simpler than) that of Theorem 4.8 gives a similar dichotomy for the problem of testing whether there is a solution that is side-effect free (i.e., a solution J such that $Q(J) = Q(I) \setminus \{\mathbf{a}\}$), which has been studied by Buneman et al. [4]. Specifically, for a CQ Q without self joins, testing whether there is a side-effect-free solution is in polynomial time when Q has the head-domination property (due to Theorem 4.3), and is NP-complete otherwise.

5. APPROXIMATIONS FOR STAR CQS

A CQ is a *star CQ* if every join variable occurs in every atom; in other words, a CQ Q is a star CQ if there is a set $Z \subseteq \mathrm{Var}(Q)$, such that $Z = \mathrm{Var}(\phi_1) \cap \mathrm{Var}(\phi_2)$ whenever $\phi_1, \phi_2 \in Q$ and $\phi_1 \neq \phi_2$ (note that Z can be empty). As an example, every $Q_k^\star$ (defined in (3)) is a star CQ (with $Z = \{x\}$). Furthermore, every CQ with two or fewer atoms is a star CQ. An additional example is the following.

$$Q_1(y_1, y_2, y_3) :\!\!- R(x_1, y_1), S(y_1, x_1, y_2), T(x_3, y_1, x_1, x_1)$$

Note that in Q_1, the join variables are x_1 and y_1, and they indeed occur in each of the three atoms.

In this section, we present approximation algorithms for the problems $\mathrm{MaxDP}\langle Q \rangle$, where Q is a star CQ without self joins. The following corollary of Theorem 4.5 (for the case of acyclic CQs) shows that star CQs are intractable to approximate within some factor α, except for trivial cases.

COROLLARY 5.1. *There is a number $\alpha \in (0,1)$, such that the following holds for all star CQs Q without self joins. If every join variable is a head variable, or one of the atoms contains all the head variables, then $\mathrm{Trivial}\langle Q \rangle$ optimally solves $\mathrm{MaxDP}\langle Q \rangle$; otherwise, α-approximating $\mathrm{MaxDP}\langle Q \rangle$ is NP-hard.*

The constant factor α that we found for the hardness part Theorem 5.1 is fairly close to 1 (it is larger than 0.9), so this result does not preclude good approximations (though it does preclude PTAS algorithms). Recall from Proposition 3.3 that for every CQ Q without self joins, $\mathrm{MaxDP}\langle Q \rangle$ is $\frac{1}{k}$-approximated using the trivial algorithm, where $k = \min\{\mathrm{arity}(Q), |\mathrm{atoms}(Q)|\}$. In this section, we give constant-factor approximation algorithms for $\mathrm{MaxDP}\langle Q \rangle$, where the factor does not depend on Q, assuming that Q is a star CQ without self joins. Towards the end of this section, we will show how to extend one of the approximations to a significant generalization of star CQs.

5.1 A Greedy Algorithm

We now present a $\frac{1}{2}$-approximation for $\mathrm{MaxDP}\langle Q \rangle$, for the case where Q is a star CQ without self joins. We first consider the special case where Q is the CQ $Q_k^\star$ (for some $k > 0$). Later on, we will discuss the extension of the algorithm to the general case.

Fix a natural number $k > 0$. The goal is to approximate $\mathrm{MaxDP}\langle Q_k^\star \rangle$. We call the approximation algorithm we present here the *greedy approximation*, and denote it by $\mathsf{Greedy}\langle k \rangle$. Figure 4 shows pseudo-code for the algorithm. The input includes an instance I and a tuple $\mathbf{a} = (a_1, \ldots, a_k)$, and the algorithm returns a solution J.

We use the following notation. For a tuple $\mathbf{d} = (d_1, \ldots, d_k)$, we call a constant $b \in \mathrm{Const}$ a $\mathbf{d}$-*joining constant* if $R_i(b, d_i)$ is a fact of I for all $i = 1, \ldots, k$ (i.e., there is a match μ for $Q_k^\star$ in I, such that $\mu(\mathbf{y}) = \mathbf{d}$ and $\mu(x) = b$).

Algorithm Greedy$\langle k \rangle (I, \mathbf{a})$

1: let $\mathbf{a} = (a_1, \ldots, a_k)$
2: $J \leftarrow I$
3: **for all a**-joining constants b **do**
4:    **if** exists j where $R_j(b, c) \in I$ for some $c \neq a_j$ **then**
5:       $i \leftarrow$ a minimal j with $R_j(b, c) \in I$ for some $c \neq a_j$
6:    **else**
7:       $i \leftarrow$ an arbitrary number in $\{1, \ldots, k\}$
8:    delete $R_i(b, a_i)$ from J
9: **return** J

Figure 4: Greedy approximation for MaxDP$\langle Q_k^\star \rangle$

The algorithm Greedy$\langle k \rangle$ starts with $J = I$. It traverses over all the **a**-joining constants b. For each b, the fact $R_i(b, a_i)$ is deleted from J, where i is chosen to be the minimal j such that I contains a fact $R_j(b, c)$ for some $c \neq a_j$; if no such j exists, then i is chosen arbitrarily among $\{1, \ldots, k\}$.

The following lemma states that the algorithm returns a solution. The proof is immediate from the fact that for each **a**-joining constant b, the returned instance J misses $R_i(b, a_i)$ for some (actually, for exactly one) $i \in \{1, \ldots, k\}$.

LEMMA 5.2. Greedy$\langle k \rangle (I, \mathbf{a})$ *returns a solution.*

Next, we show that Greedy$\langle k \rangle$ is a 2-approximation for MaxDP$\langle Q_k^\star \rangle$. Fix the input I for the algorithm, and let J be the returned sub-instance of I. We will show that $|Q_k^\star(J)| \geq |Q_k^\star(I) \setminus \{\mathbf{a}\}|/2$. This implies that Greedy$\langle k \rangle$ is a $\frac{1}{2}$-approximation regardless of the performance of an optimal algorithm, since $|Q_k^\star(J')| \leq |Q_k^\star(I) \setminus \{\mathbf{a}\}|$ holds for every solution J'. Moreover, this implies that there is always a solution that retains at least half of the original (non-**a**) tuples of $Q_k^\star(I)$.

To show that $|Q_k^\star(J)| \geq |Q_k^\star(I) \setminus \{\mathbf{a}\}|/2$, we use the following counting argument. We map the surviving answers to deleted answers in a way that each deleted answer is the image of some surviving answer. Since no surviving answer has two images, this will imply that the number of surviving answers is at least as large as the number of deleted answers. The intuitive reason for the existence of such a mapping is that we try to delete only facts $R_i(b, a_i)$ where there is an alternative fact $R_i(b, c)$ for the same joining constant b; the fact $R_i(b, c)$ will preserve some answers to account for those that have been deleted.

Formally, we define a function $\Psi : Q_k^\star(J) \to \text{Const}^k$, and show that Ψ is onto $(Q_k^\star(I) \setminus \{\mathbf{a}\}) \setminus Q_k^\star(J)$. The function Ψ is defined as follows. For a tuple $\mathbf{c} \in Q_k^\star(J)$, where $\mathbf{c} = (c_1, \ldots, c_k)$, the tuple $\Psi(\mathbf{c})$ is obtained from $\mathbf{c}$ by choosing the minimal i with $c_i \neq a_i$, and replacing that occurrence of c_i with a_i. For example, for $k = 4$ and $\mathbf{a} = (\diamond, \diamond, \diamond, \diamond)$, the tuple $\Psi(\diamond, \heartsuit, \square, \diamond)$ is $(\diamond, \diamond, \square, \diamond)$.

LEMMA 5.3. Ψ *is onto* $(Q_k^\star(I) \setminus \{\mathbf{a}\}) \setminus Q_k^\star(J)$.

PROOF. Let $\mathbf{d} = (d_1, \ldots, d_k)$ be a tuple of $Q_k^\star(I)$, such that $\mathbf{d}$ is neither **a** nor in $Q_k^\star(J)$. We need to show that there is some $\mathbf{c} \in Q_k^\star(J)$, such that $\Psi(\mathbf{c}) = \mathbf{d}$. Let b be a

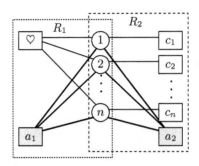

Figure 5: An instance I **where Greedy**$\langle k \rangle (I, \mathbf{a})$ **pro-vides a** $(\frac{1}{2} + \frac{1}{2n})$**-approximation**

d-joining constant (b exists since $\mathbf{d} \in Q_k^\star(I)$). The fact that $\mathbf{d} \notin Q_k^\star(J)$ implies that b is an **a**-joining constant, and that when b was visited we deleted one of the $R_i(b, d_i)$. Consider such an index i, and note that $d_i = a_i$ follows from the definition of the algorithm. Now, $\mathbf{d} \neq \mathbf{a}$ implies that, in the iteration of b, the condition of Line 4 is true, and hence, the deleted fact $R_i(b, d_i)$ satisfies that i is the minimal j where $R_i(b, c) \in I$ for some $c \neq a_i$. Hence, we must have $d_j = a_j$ for all $j < i$ (and recall that we also have $d_i = a_i$). Let $c \neq a_i$ be a constant such that $R_i(b, c) \in I$, and let $\mathbf{c}$ be obtained from $\mathbf{d}$ by replacing the ith element, d_i, with c. We have that $\mathbf{c} \in Q_k^\star(J)$ and, moreover, $\Psi(\mathbf{c}) = \mathbf{d}$, as required. $\square$

From Lemmas 5.2 and 5.3 we get the following theorem.

THEOREM 5.4. Greedy$\langle k \rangle$ *is a* $\frac{1}{2}$*-approximation for the problem* MaxDP$\langle Q_k^\star \rangle$.

Next, we show that in the worst case, Greedy$\langle k \rangle$ indeed gives just $\frac{1}{2}$-approximation. Our example is for $k = 2$, and it is depicted in Figure 5. The relation R_1 contains the tuples (i, a_1) and $(i, \heartsuit)$, for all $i \in \{1, \ldots, n\}$. Note that the visual position of nodes on the edges that correspond to R_1 is in opposition to the order of the values in R_1 (i.e., the edge from $\heartsuit$ to 2 corresponds to the fact $R_1(2, \heartsuit)$). The relation R_2 contains the tuples (i, a_2) and (i, c_i) for all $i \in \{1, \ldots, n\}$. The greedy algorithm will remove all the facts $R_1(i, a_1)$, generating a sub-instance J with $|Q_2^\star(J)| = n + 1$. On the other hand, one could remove all the facts $R_2(i, a_2)$, and then get a solution J', such that $|Q_2^\star(J')| = 2n$. Hence, the approximation ratio is at most $\frac{1}{2} + \frac{1}{2n}$.

Finally, we discuss the generalization of the greedy algorithm to general star CQs without self joins. Let Q be a star CQ without self joins. Suppose that Q has k atoms. We reduce MaxDP$\langle Q \rangle$ to MaxDP$\langle Q_k^\star \rangle$ in an approximation-preserving manner. Specifically, given the input I and **a** for MaxDP$\langle Q \rangle$, we generate an instance I' over schema$(Q_k^\star)$ and a tuple $\mathbf{a}'$, and apply Greedy$\langle k \rangle (I', \mathbf{a}')$ to get a solution J' for I' and $\mathbf{a}'$. Finally, we transform J' into a solution J for I and **a**. This reduction is fairly straightforward, and the details are in the extended version of this paper [21]. In conclusion, we get the following theorem.

THEOREM 5.5. *Let* Q *be a star CQ without self joins. There is a* $\frac{1}{2}$*-approximation for* MaxDP$\langle Q \rangle$*, where the running time is polynomial under query-and-data complexity.*

Recall that *query-and-data complexity* means that the running time is measured as if the query Q is given as part of the input (in addition to I and $\mathbf{a}$), and is not fixed. The polynomial running time under query-and-data complexity is due to the fact that both $\mathsf{Greedy}\langle k\rangle$ and the reduction from $\mathrm{MAXDP}\langle Q\rangle$ to $\mathrm{MAXDP}\langle Q_k^\star\rangle$ take polynomial time under query-and-data complexity. In contrast, recall that the trivial algorithm is polynomial time only under data complexity (since it requires the evaluation of Q over the J_ϕ).

5.2 A Randomized-Rounding Algorithm

In this section, we describe a *randomized-rounding* algorithm for approximating $\mathrm{MAXDP}\langle Q\rangle$ when Q is a star CQ without self joins. We will show that this algorithm gives an approximation ratio that is higher than $\mathsf{Greedy}\langle k\rangle$, namely, $1-\frac{1}{e}$ (which is, roughly, 0.632) instead of $\frac{1}{2}$; the running time is still polynomial, but it is not as fast as $\mathsf{Greedy}\langle k\rangle$. In particular, the algorithm we describe here will terminate in polynomial time under (the usual) data complexity, but not under query-and-data complexity. At the end of this section, we will show that this algorithm can be used to approximate CQs from a class that significantly generalizes the star CQs without self joins.

More precisely, the algorithm we present is a randomized $(1-\frac{1}{e})$-approximation, where a *randomized α-approximation* for $\mathrm{MAXDP}\langle Q\rangle$ is a randomized algorithm that, given I and $\mathbf{a}$, returns a solution J such that the expected $|Q(J)|$ is at least $\alpha \cdot |Q(K)|$ for all solutions K. Put differently, if J_{opt} is an optimal solution, then $\mathbb{E}[|Q(J)|] \geq \alpha \cdot |Q(J_{\mathrm{opt}})|$. This is a standard notion of randomized optimization (e.g., [16, 19]). Such a randomized algorithm can be easily transformed into a randomized algorithm that returns an α-approximation, where α is arbitrarily close to $(1-\frac{1}{e})$, and the error probability is arbitrarily small. We further note that the algorithm we present here can be derandomized into a deterministic (i.e., ordinary) $(1-\frac{1}{e})$-approximation, using the *pipage-rounding* technique of Calinescu et al. [5]; however, that derandomization is beyond the scope of this paper.

Our algorithm uses ideas from the framework of *submodular maximization subject to a matroid constraint* [5,6]. In fact, our problem can be formally reduced to the problem of maximizing a monotone submodular function subject to a matroid constraint, for which a $(1-\frac{1}{e})$-approximation has been developed recently [6]. However, it is simpler (and

Algorithm RRLP$\langle k\rangle(I)$

1: let $\mathbf{a} = (a_1, \ldots, a_k)$
2: $J \leftarrow I$
3: solve $\mathrm{LP}(I, \mathbf{a})$
4: **for all a**-joining constants b **do**
5:     independently pick a random $i \in [k]$ with probability X_j^b for j
6:     delete $R_i(b, a_i)$ from J
7: **return** J

Figure 7: Randomized rounding for MaxDP$\langle Q_k^\star\rangle$

more instructive) to give a self-contained description, which is what we do in the remainder of this section.

As we did in the previous section, we will first describe the algorithm for the special CQs $Q_k^\star$ (defined in (3)), and consider general star CQs later. We fix the input I and $\mathbf{a} = (a_1, \ldots, a_k)$. Recall that for a tuple $\mathbf{d} = (d_1, \ldots, d_k)$, a $\mathbf{d}$-joining constant is a constant $b \in \mathsf{Const}$ such that $R_i(b, d_i) \in I$ for all $i = 1, \ldots, k$. We make the assumption that for each fact $R_i(b, d)$ of I, the constant b is an $\mathbf{a}$-joining constant. There is no loss of generality in making this assumption, since there is no reason to delete a fact $R_i(b', d)$ if b' is not an $\mathbf{a}$-joining constant; hence, the existence of such $R_i(b', d)$ can only increase the approximation ratio that we achieve by the algorithm. For a tuple $\mathbf{d} \in Q_k^\star(I)$, we denote by $JC(\mathbf{d})$ the set of all the $\mathbf{d}$-joining constants. Note that our assumption above implies that $JC(\mathbf{d}) \subseteq JC(\mathbf{a})$ for all $\mathbf{d} \in Q_k^\star(I)$.

Let us first formulate $\mathrm{MAXDP}\langle Q_k^\star\rangle$ as an integer linear program (LP). For every $\mathbf{a}$-joining constant b and index $i \in \{1, \ldots, k\}$, we have the variable X_i^b that gets values in $\{0, 1\}$. We interpret $X_i^b = 1$ as saying that the fact $R_i(b, a_i)$ should be removed. So, we will have the following constraints which ensure that the resulting sub-instance is a solution. Note that $[k]$ is a shorthand notation for $\{1, \ldots, k\}$.

$$\forall b \in JC(\mathbf{a}) \quad \sum_{i=1}^{k} X_i^b = 1$$

$$\forall b \in JC(\mathbf{a}), i \in [k] \quad X_i^b \in \{0, 1\}$$

Next, we construct the objective function. Suppose that $\mathbf{d} = (d_1, \ldots, d_k)$ is a tuple in $Q_k^\star(I)$. We define the variable $Y_{\mathbf{d}}$ that gets the value 1 if $\mathbf{d}$ *survives* (i.e., belongs to $Q_k^\star(J)$), and 0 otherwise. For that, we denote by $\mathbf{d} \sqcap \mathbf{a}$ the set of indices $i \in [k]$, such that $d_i = a_i$. For example, if $\mathbf{a} = (\diamond, \diamond, \diamond, \diamond)$ and $d = (\diamond, \heartsuit, \square, \diamond)$, then $\mathbf{d} \sqcap \mathbf{a} = \{1, 4\}$. So, we have the following constraint:

$$\forall \mathbf{d} \in Q_k^\star(I) \quad Y_{\mathbf{d}} = \min\left(1, \sum_{b \in JC(\mathbf{d})} \sum_{i \in [k] \setminus (\mathbf{d} \sqcap \mathbf{a})} X_i^b\right)$$

Note that $\sum_{i \in [k] \setminus (\mathbf{d} \sqcap \mathbf{a})} X_i^b \geq 1$ means that the fact $R_i(b, a_i)$ that we delete is such that $a_i \neq d_i$, and hence, none of the $R_j(b, d_j)$ is deleted (and then $\mathbf{d}$ survives).

Finally, the goal is to maximize the sum of the $Y_{\mathbf{d}}$. Figure 6 shows the program $\mathrm{LP}(I, \mathbf{a})$, which is the LP relaxation of the integer LP.

$$\text{maximize} \sum_{\mathbf{d} \in Q_k^\star(I)} Y_{\mathbf{d}}$$

$$\text{subject to}$$

$$\forall \mathbf{d} \in Q_k^\star(I) \quad Y_{\mathbf{d}} \leq \sum_{b \in JC(\mathbf{d})} \sum_{i \in [k] \setminus (\mathbf{d} \sqcap \mathbf{a})} X_i^b$$

$$\forall b \in JC(\mathbf{a}) \quad \sum_{i=1}^{k} X_i^b = 1$$

$$\forall b \in JC(\mathbf{a}), i \in [k] \quad 0 \leq X_i^b \leq 1$$

$$\forall \mathbf{d} \in Q_k^\star(I) \quad 0 \leq Y_{\mathbf{d}} \leq 1$$

Figure 6: The program $\mathrm{LP}(I, \mathbf{a})$

The algorithm for $\textsc{MaxDP}\langle Q_k^\star\rangle$, called $\mathsf{RRLP}\langle k\rangle(I, \mathbf{a})$, is described by the pseudo-code of Figure 7. The algorithm first solves $\mathsf{LP}(I, \mathbf{a})$, and as a result, gets an optimal (fractional) assignment for each X_i^b and $Y_\mathbf{d}$. Like $\mathsf{Greedy}\langle k\rangle(I, \mathbf{a})$, this algorithm constructs a sub-instance J of I and returns J in the last line. Still similarly to $\mathsf{Greedy}\langle k\rangle(I, \mathbf{a})$, for each $\mathbf{a}$-joining constant b, the algorithm selects an index $i \in [k]$ and deletes from J the fact $R_i(i, a_i)$. The difference between the algorithms is in the way i is chosen. Here, we apply the standard action in randomized rounding, namely, i is picked randomly and independently from $[k]$, where the probability of the index j is X_j^b. Note that the constraints of $\mathsf{LP}(I, \mathbf{a})$ ensure that, for a specific b, the X_i^b constitute a probability distribution over $[k]$.

Next, we prove the correctness of $\mathsf{RRLP}\langle k\rangle(I, \mathbf{a})$. The following lemma shows that the algorithm returns a solution, and that its running time is polynomial. The proof is straightforward. In particular, as noted before Lemma 5.2 about $\mathsf{Greedy}\langle k\rangle$, for each $\mathbf{a}$-joining constant b the returned instance J misses $R_i(b, a_i)$ for some (actually, for exactly one) $i \in [k]$.

LEMMA 5.6. $\mathsf{RRLP}\langle k\rangle(I, \mathbf{a})$ *returns a solution, and terminates in polynomial time.*

Next, we show that $\mathsf{RRLP}\langle k\rangle(I)$ is a randomized $(1 - \frac{1}{e})$-approximation. The proof is based on the following lemma, which states that a tuple $\mathbf{d} \in Q(I)$ survives with a probability of at least $(1 - \frac{1}{e})Y_\mathbf{d}$.

LEMMA 5.7. *Consider an execution of* $\mathsf{RRLP}\langle k\rangle(I, \mathbf{a})$ *that results in a random solution J, and let $\mathbf{d} \in Q_k^\star(I)$.*

$$\Pr(\mathbf{d} \in Q_k^\star(J)) \geq (1 - \frac{1}{e})Y_\mathbf{d}.$$

Based on Lemma 5.7, we next prove that $\mathsf{RRLP}\langle k\rangle(I)$ is indeed a randomized $(1 - \frac{1}{e})$-approximation.

THEOREM 5.8. *Consider an execution of* $\mathsf{RRLP}\langle k\rangle(I, \mathbf{a})$ *that results in a random solution J, and let J_{opt} be an optimal solution. Then* $\mathbb{E}[|Q_k^\star(J)|] \geq (1 - \frac{1}{e})|Q_k^\star(J_{\mathrm{opt}})|$.

PROOF. Consider the execution of $\mathsf{LP}(I, \mathbf{a})$ in Line 3 of $\mathsf{RRLP}\langle k\rangle(I, \mathbf{a})$. Let M be the sum $\sum_{\mathbf{d} \in Q_k^\star(I)} Y_\mathbf{d}$. W.l.o.g., we can assume that in J_{opt} it holds that for all $\mathbf{a}$-joining constants b, exactly one $R_i(b, a_i)$ is missing. Then J_{opt} defines a solution for $\mathsf{LP}(I, \mathbf{a})$, and therefore, $M \geq |Q_k^\star(J_{\mathrm{opt}})|$. On the other hand, from Lemma 5.7 and the linearity of expectation we have that

$$\mathbb{E}[|Q_k^\star(J)|] = \sum_{\mathbf{d} \in Q_k^\star(I)} \Pr(\mathbf{d} \in Q_k^\star(J))$$
$$\geq (1 - \frac{1}{e}) \sum_{\mathbf{d} \in Q_k^\star(I)} Y_\mathbf{d} = (1 - \frac{1}{e})M$$

Therefore, $\mathbb{E}[|Q_k^\star(J)|] \geq (1 - \frac{1}{e})|Q_k^\star(J_{\mathrm{opt}})|$, as claimed. $\square$

We now consider general star CQs without self joins. As we noted before Theorem 5.5, there is a simple approximation-preserving (and polynomial-time) reduction from the problem $\textsc{MaxDP}\langle Q\rangle$, where Q is a star CQ without self joins, to $\textsc{MaxDP}\langle Q_k^\star\rangle$, where $k = |\mathrm{atoms}(Q)|$. Hence, Theorem 5.8 immediately implies the following result.

THEOREM 5.9. *Let Q be a star CQ without self joins. There is a randomized $(1 - \frac{1}{e})$-approximation for $\textsc{MaxDP}\langle Q\rangle$, with a polynomial running time.*

5.3 Beyond Star CQs

In this section, we extend Theorem 5.9 to the class of *existentially star* CQs, which generalizes the class of star CQs without self joins. Intuitively, in an existentially star CQ the "star requirement" is restricted to the existential variables of the query.

More formally, let Q be a CQ. We denote by $\mathsf{Var}_\exists^{\bowtie}(Q)$ the set of existential join variables of Q. We say that Q is *existentially star* if for every atom ϕ of Q, either every variable of $\mathsf{Var}_\exists^{\bowtie}(Q)$ occurs in Q, or none of them does.

EXAMPLE 5.10. Consider the following CQ:

$$Q(y_1, y_2, y_3, y_4) :\text{--} R(x_1, y_1, y_2), S(x_1, y_2, y_3), T(y_3, y_1, x_2)$$

The CQ Q is existentially star, since $\mathsf{Var}_\exists^{\bowtie}(Q) = \{x_1\}$, and every atom either contains x_1 or not. Actually, by the same argument, every CQ that has at most one existential join variable is existentially star. $\square$

Next, we give a short overview of how we handle existentially star CQs without self joins. We denote by $Q_{|\exists}$ the CQ that comprises all the atoms ϕ of Q having $\mathsf{Var}_\exists^{\bowtie}(Q) \subseteq \mathsf{Var}(\phi)$. Note that if Q is existentially star, then $Q_{|\exists}$ is also existentially star. Also observe that the arity of Q can be strictly larger than that of $Q_{|\exists}$. As an example, for the CQ Q of Example 5.10, the CQ $Q_{|\exists}$ is:

$$Q_{|\exists}(y_1, y_2, y_3) :\text{--} R(x_1, y_1, y_2), S(x_1, y_2, y_3)$$

Note that the arity of Q is 4, while that of $Q_{|\exists}$ is 3.

Let Q be an existentially-star CQ Q without self joins. Our general approach to approximating $\textsc{MaxDP}\langle Q\rangle$ is as follows. Instead of approximating $\textsc{MaxDP}\langle Q\rangle$, we approximate $\textsc{MaxDP}\langle Q_{|\exists}\rangle$; furthermore, instead of using the input tuple $\mathbf{a}$ of $\textsc{MaxDP}\langle Q\rangle$, for $\textsc{MaxDP}\langle Q_{|\exists}\rangle$ we use the restriction of $\mathbf{a}$ to the head variables of $Q_{|\exists}$. Finally, we view every occurrence of a head join variable as a distinct head variable, and thus assume that every join variable is existential. Hence, we treat $Q_{|\exists}$ as if it is a star CQ, and then we apply Theorem 5.9, to get a solution J.

There are two main problems with the above approach. First, by restricting to $Q_{|\exists}$ and ignoring the fact that head variables can be join variables, when solving $\textsc{MaxDP}\langle Q_{|\exists}\rangle$ we may end up saving tuples of $Q_{|\exists}(J)$ that do not give rise to *any* tuple of $Q(J)$, while eliminating tuples of $Q_{|\exists}(I)$ that give rise to *multiple* tuples of $Q(I)$. To handle that, we consider again the program $\mathsf{LP}(I, \mathbf{a})$ of Figure 6, and observe that we can assign a *weight* $w(\mathbf{d})$ to each variable $Y_\mathbf{d}$. That is, the objective function can be as follows.

$$\text{maximize} \sum_{\mathbf{d} \in Q_k^\star(I)} w(\mathbf{d}) \cdot Y_\mathbf{d}$$

Indeed, we are able to handle the first problem by using proper weights $w(\mathbf{d})$. Let us call the final algorithm that reduces $\textsc{MaxDP}\langle Q\rangle$ to $\textsc{MaxDP}\langle Q_k^\star\rangle$ and uses weights as described above the *extended* $\mathsf{RRLP}\langle k\rangle$.

Unfortunately, the extended $\mathsf{RRLP}\langle k\rangle$ does not guarantee a proper approximation, due to a second problem, which is the following. By restricting to $Q_{|\exists}$ instead of Q, we ignore the ϕ-facts of I for $\phi \in \mathrm{atoms}(Q) \setminus \mathrm{atoms}(Q_{|\exists})$. But it may still be the case that deleting facts among those ϕ-facts is necessary to obtain a proper approximate solution. As an example, consider the following existentially-star CQ.

$$Q(y_1, y_2, y_3) :\text{--} R_1(x, y_1), R_2(x, y_2), R_3(y_2, y_3)$$

Let $\mathbf{a}$ be the tuple $(\diamond, \diamond, \diamond)$, and let I be the instance that consists of the facts $R_1(1, \diamond)$, $R_2(1, \diamond)$, $R_3(\diamond, \diamond)$, and $R_3(\diamond, \heartsuit)$. Note that $Q_{|\exists}$ is Q_2^*. By removing the fact $R_3(\diamond, \diamond)$, the answer $(\diamond, \diamond, \heartsuit)$ survives. However, when trying to solve $\text{MaxDP}\langle Q_{|\exists}\rangle$ first, as described above, we necessarily lose every tuple of $Q(I)$ (and hence do not get any constant-factor approximation).

The above problem can be solved by running the trivial algorithm in addition to the extended $\text{RRLP}\langle k\rangle$, and taking the maximum. More precisely, at least one of the following must hold for given input I and $\mathbf{a}$.

1. The trivial algorithm returns an optimal solution for I and $\mathbf{a}$.

2. The generalized $\text{RRLP}\langle k\rangle$ returns a $(1 - \frac{1}{e})$-optimal solution, in expectation, for I and $\mathbf{a}$.

Thus, we get the following result.

THEOREM 5.11. *Let Q be an existentially-star CQ without self joins. There is a randomized $(1 - \frac{1}{e})$-approximation for $\text{MaxDP}\langle Q\rangle$, with a polynomial running time.*

6. ABOUT SELF JOINS

In this section, we give a brief discussion on CQs with self joins. In particular, we show that results from Section 3 and 4 do not extend to (all the) CQs with self joins.

We first show that in Theorem 4.3, the requirement for lack of self joins is necessary. For that, we will show a CQ Q that has the head-domination property, and input I and $\mathbf{a}$ for $\text{MaxDP}\langle Q\rangle$, such that the trivial algorithm returns a solution that is not optimal. The CQ Q is the following.

$$Q(y) :- R(x, y, x_1), R(x, x_2, y) \qquad (4)$$

Let I be the instance that consists of the facts $R(\diamond, 0, 1)$, $R(\diamond, 6, 0)$, $R(\diamond, 1, 8)$, $R(\square, 0, 7)$, $R(\square, 2, 0)$, and $R(\square, 9, 2)$. Let $\mathbf{a}$ be the tuple (0). The trivial algorithm will take the best out of two: the solution J_1 that is obtained by deleting $R(\diamond, 0, 1)$ and $R(\square, 0, 7)$, and the solution J_2 that is obtained by deleting and $R(\diamond, 6, 0)$ and $R(\square, 2, 0)$. It is easy to show that $Q(J_1) = \{(2)\}$ and $Q(J_2) = \{(1)\}$. Hence, the solution J returned by the trivial algorithm is such that $|Q(J)| = 1$. Now, the solution J' that is obtained by deleting $R(\diamond, 6, 0)$ and $R(\square, 0, 7)$ satisfies $Q(J') = \{(1), (2)\}$, and thus $|Q(J')| > |Q(J)|$. Hence, the trivial algorithm is not optimal for $\text{MaxDP}\langle Q\rangle$, as claimed. In fact, the following theorem states that for this CQ, $\text{MaxDP}\langle Q\rangle$ is hard to approximate better than some constant ratio α. The proof is by a reduction from maximum 3-satisfiability.

THEOREM 6.1. *For $Q(y) :- R(x, y, x_1), R(x, x_2, y)$, there is a constant $\alpha \in (0, 1)$, such that no polynomial-time algorithm α-approximates $\text{MaxDP}\langle Q\rangle$, unless $P = NP$.*

Recall from Proposition 3.3 that for every CQ without self joins, there is a $\frac{1}{k}$-approximation for $\text{MaxDP}\langle Q\rangle$, where $k = \min\{\text{arity}(Q), |\text{atoms}(Q)|\}$. Next, we show that this result does not extend to all CQs with self joins, as for some of these CQs an exponential bound (in k) applies. Formally, we show the following.

THEOREM 6.2. *Assume $P \neq NP$. For some constant $\alpha \in (0, 1)$, the following holds. For all $k > 0$ there exists a CQ Q_k, such that $\text{arity}(Q_k) = k$, $|\text{atoms}(Q_k)| = 2k$, and no polynomial-time algorithm α^k-approximates $\text{MaxDP}\langle Q_k\rangle$.*

Next, we give a simple proof for Theorem 6.2. We first set some basic notation. Let $\mathbf{a}$ be a tuple, let Q be a CQ, and let k be a natural number. By $\mathbf{a}^k$ we denote the tuple that is obtained from $\mathbf{a}$ by concatenating it k times. By Q^k we denote the CQ that is obtained by concatenating k copies of Q, where in each copy the variables are renamed into a set of distinct fresh variables. For example, for the CQ Q of (4), the CQ Q^2 is the following.

$$Q^2(y, y') :- R(x, y, x_1), R(x, x_2, y)$$
$$R(x', y', x_1'), R(x', x_2', y')$$

More formally, for $Q(\mathbf{y}) :- \varphi(\mathbf{x}, \mathbf{y}, \mathbf{c})$, the CQ Q^k is

$$Q(\mathbf{y}_1, \ldots, \mathbf{y}_k) :- \varphi(\mathbf{x}_1, \mathbf{y}_1, \mathbf{c}), \ldots, \varphi(\mathbf{x}_k, \mathbf{y}_k, \mathbf{c}),$$

where each $\mathbf{x}_i$ is of the arity of $\mathbf{x}$, each $\mathbf{y}_i$ is of the arity of $\mathbf{y}$, and $\mathbf{x}_1, \ldots, \mathbf{x}_k, \mathbf{y}_1, \ldots, \mathbf{y}_k$ are pairwise-disjoint vectors of variables.

Let k be a natural number, let Q be a CQ, and let $\mathbf{a}$ be a tuple in $\text{Const}^{\text{arity}(Q)}$. Moreover, let I be an instance, and let J be a sub-instance of I. The proof is based on the following (straightforward) observations.

1. $\mathbf{a} \in Q(I)$ if and only if $\mathbf{a}^k \in Q^k(I)$.

2. J is a solution (w.r.t. Q) for I and $\mathbf{a}$ if and only if J is a solution (w.r.t. Q^k) for I and $\mathbf{a}^k$.

3. $|Q^k(I)| = |Q(I)|^k$.

We now prove Theorem 6.2. Fix a natural number k. We choose as Q_k the CQ Q^k, where Q is the CQ of (4) and α is the one of Theorem 6.1. Clearly, Q_k satisfies $\text{arity}(Q_k) = k$ and $|\text{atoms}(Q_k)| = 2k$. Now, suppose that an algorithm A is an α^k-approximation for $\text{MaxDP}\langle Q_k\rangle$. So, given the input I and $\mathbf{a}$ for $\text{MaxDP}\langle Q\rangle$, we feed A with the input I and $\mathbf{a}^k$. Let J be the output of A. Then J is a solution for I and $\mathbf{a}$ (by Property 2 above). Let J_{opt} be an optimal solution for I and $\mathbf{a}$. From Properties 1–3 above it easily follows that J_{opt} is also optimal for I and $\mathbf{a}^k$. We obtain the following.

$$|Q(J)| = |Q_k(J)|^{\frac{1}{k}} \geq (\alpha^k |Q_k(J_{\text{opt}})|)^{\frac{1}{k}} = \alpha |Q(J_{\text{opt}})|$$

Thus, using A we get an α-approximation for $\text{MaxDP}\langle Q\rangle$, and then Theorem 6.2 follows immediately from Theorem 6.1. This concludes the proof.

7. CONCLUSIONS

We studied the complexity of $\text{MaxDP}\langle Q\rangle$ for CQs Q, and established several results for CQs without self joins. Among these results, we showed that for every Q, the problem $\text{MaxDP}\langle Q\rangle$ is α-approximable (in polynomial time) for some constant α that is inversely proportional to the size of Q, and that $\text{MaxDP}\langle Q\rangle$ is solved optimally by the trivial algorithm if Q has the head-domination property. We also showed a strong dichotomy: inapproximability when head domination does not hold. We gave approximation algorithms for star CQs, and for the more general existentially star CQs. Finally, we considered CQs with self joins, and showed an example of such a CQ Q, such that Q has the head-domination property, and yet, $\text{MaxDP}\langle Q\rangle$ is inapproximable beyond some constant ratio; we also showed a family of CQs with self joins, where the approximability of $\text{MaxDP}\langle Q\rangle$ deteriorates exponentially with the size of Q.

Many related open problems and practically important challenges remain, and are left for future work. Among the open problems, perhaps most basic are the following.

1. Does a dichotomy in the spirit of Theorem 4.8 hold for the class of all CQs with self joins?

2. Is there a fixed ratio $\alpha \in (0,1)$, independent of Q, such that $\text{MAXDP}\langle Q \rangle$ is α-approximable in polynomial time for *every* CQ Q without self joins?[5]

3. For the class of (existentially) star CQs, can we do better than Theorem 5.11? That is, is there a polynomial-time α-approximation for some $\alpha > 1 - \frac{1}{e}$?

Practically important remaining challenges include complexity analyses, and algorithmic solutions in particular, for deletion propagation within the following generalizations.

- **Deleting multiple tuples.** Instead of one answer **a**, in this generalization we are required to delete from the view a *set* of answers (and the goal is, as usual, to maximize $|Q(J)|$).

- **Incorporating database constraints.** In this generalization, database constraints are enforced. In the presence of constraints, deletion of tuples may incur following the deletion of others (e.g., in the case of *inclusion dependencies* [7] like foreign keys); thus, constraints are significant for deletion propagation [8].

- **Maximizing a different view.** In this generalization, when deleting the answer $\mathbf{a} \in Q(I)$, the goal is to maximize $|Q'(J)|$ for a CQ Q' that is different from Q, or even for multiple CQs Q' simultaneously.

- **Forbidden source deletions.** In our problem setting, every fact of the instance I is a possible candidate for deletion. But in some cases, we may want to forbid the deletion of certain facts. For example, in IE it makes sense to forbid deletion from some clean relations like the English or country-name dictionary.[6]

As part of future work, we intend to explore whether and how the techniques we presented here for approximating $\text{MAXDP}\langle Q \rangle$ can help in developing algorithmic solutions within more general settings like the ones above.

Acknowledgments

We are grateful to Laura Chiticariu, Ronald Fagin, Rajasekar Krishnamurthy and Wang Chiew Tan for fruitful discussions. We are also grateful to members of the PODS 2011 Program Committee for providing valuable comments and suggestions.

8. REFERENCES

[1] S. Balakrishnan, V. Chu, M. A. Hernández, H. Ho, R. Krishnamurthy, S. Liu, J. Pieper, J. S. Pierce, L. Popa, C. Robson, L. Shi, I. R. Stanoi, E. L. Ting, S. Vaithyanathan, and H. Yang. Midas: integrating public financial data. In *SIGMOD Conference*, pages 1187–1190. ACM, 2010.

[2] F. Bancilhon and N. Spyratos. Update semantics of relational views. *ACM Trans. Database Syst.*, 6(4):557–575, 1981.

[3] C. Beeri, R. Fagin, D. Maier, and M. Yannakakis. On the desirability of acyclic database schemes. *J. ACM*, 30(3):479–513, 1983.

[4] P. Buneman, S. Khanna, and W.-C. Tan. On propagation of deletions and annotations through views. In *PODS*, pages 150–158. ACM, 2002.

[5] G. Calinescu, C. Chekuri, M. Pál, and J. Vondrák. Maximizing a submodular set function subject to a matroid constraint (extended abstract). In *IPCO*, volume 4513 of *Lecture Notes in Computer Science*, pages 182–196. Springer, 2007.

[6] G. Calinescu, C. Chekuri, M. Pál, and J. Vondrák. Maximizing a submodular set function subject to a matroid constraint. *SIAM Journal on Computing*, special issue on ACM STOC 2008, to appear.

[7] M. A. Casanova, R. Fagin, and C. H. Papadimitriou. Inclusion dependencies and their interaction with functional dependencies. In *PODS*, pages 171–176. ACM, 1982.

[8] G. Cong, W. Fan, and F. Geerts. Annotation propagation revisited for key preserving views. In *CIKM*, pages 632–641. ACM, 2006.

[9] S. S. Cosmadakis and C. H. Papadimitriou. Updates of relational views. *J. ACM*, 31(4):742–760, 1984.

[10] Y. Cui and J. Widom. Run-time translation of view tuple deletions using data lineage. Technical report, Stanford University, 2001. http://dbpubs.stanford.edu:8090/pub/2001-24.

[11] U. Dayal and P. A. Bernstein. On the correct translation of update operations on relational views. *ACM Trans. Database Syst.*, 7(3):381–416, 1982.

[12] R. Fagin. Degrees of acyclicity for hypergraphs and relational database schemes. *J. ACM*, 30(3):514–550, 1983.

[13] R. Fagin. Combining fuzzy information from multiple systems. *J. Comput. Syst. Sci.*, 58(1):83–99, 1999.

[14] R. Fagin, A. Lotem, and M. Naor. Optimal aggregation algorithms for middleware. *J. Comput. Syst. Sci.*, 66(4):614–656, 2003.

[15] R. Fagin, J. D. Ullman, and M. Y. Vardi. On the semantics of updates in databases. In *PODS*, pages 352–365. ACM, 1983.

[16] M. X. Goemans and D. P. Williamson. Improved approximation algorithms for maximum cut and satisfiability problems using semidefinite programming. *J. ACM*, 42(6):1115–1145, 1995.

[17] V. Guruswami. Inapproximability results for set splitting and satisfiability problems with no mixed clauses. *Algorithmica*, 38(3):451–469, 2003.

[18] V. Guruswami and S. Khot. Hardness of max 3SAT with no mixed clauses. In *IEEE Conference on Computational Complexity*, pages 154–162. IEEE Computer Society, 2005.

[19] H. J. Karloff and U. Zwick. A 7/8-approximation algorithm for max 3sat? In *FOCS*, pages 406–415, 1997.

[20] A. M. Keller. Algorithms for translating view updates to database updates for views involving selections, projections, and joins. In *PODS*, pages 154–163. ACM, 1985.

[21] B. Kimelfeld, J. Vondrák, and R. Williams. Maximizing conjunctive views in deletion propagation (extended version). Accessible at the first author's home page, 2011.

[22] J. Lechtenbörger and G. Vossen. On the computation of relational view complements. *ACM Trans. Database Syst.*, 28(2):175–208, 2003.

[23] B. Liu, L. Chiticariu, V. Chu, H. V. Jagadish, and F. Reiss. Automatic rule refinement for information extraction. *PVLDB*, 3(1):588–597, 2010.

[24] A. Meliou, W. Gatterbauer, K. F. Moore, and D. Suciu. The complexity of causality and responsibility for query answers and non-answers. *PVLDB*, 4(1):34–45, 2011.

[25] E. Riloff and R. Jones. Learning dictionaries for information extraction by multi-level bootstrapping. In *AAAI/IAAI*, pages 474–479, 1999.

[26] M. Y. Vardi. The complexity of relational query languages (extended abstract). In *Proceedings of the Fourteenth Annual ACM Symposium on Theory of Computing*, pages 137–146. ACM, 1982.

---

[5] Recall that the approximation ratio of Proposition 3.3 depends on Q, and that Theorem 6.2 implies that no such α exists if self joins are allowed (unless $P = NP$).

[6] This distinction between forbidden facts and other facts is in the spirit of the distinction between *exogenous* and *endogenous* tuples in "causality" for query answers [24].

Querying Graph Patterns

Pablo Barcelo
Department of Computer
Science, Universidad de Chile
pbarcelo@dcc.uchile.cl

Leonid Libkin
School of Informatics,
University of Edinburgh
libkin@inf.ed.ac.uk

Juan Reutter
School of Informatics,
University of Edinburgh
juan.reutter@ed.ac.uk

ABSTRACT

Graph data appears in a variety of application domains, and many uses of it, such as querying, matching, and transforming data, naturally result in incompletely specified graph data, i.e., graph patterns. While queries need to be posed against such data, techniques for querying patterns are generally lacking, and properties of such queries are not well understood.

Our goal is to study the basics of querying graph patterns. We first identify key features of patterns, such as node and label variables and edges specified by regular expressions, and define a classification of patterns based on them. We then study standard graph queries on graph patterns, and give precise characterizations of both data and combined complexity for each class of patterns. If complexity is high, we do further analysis of features that lead to intractability, as well as lower-complexity restrictions. We introduce a new automata model for query answering with two modes of acceptance: one captures queries returning nodes, and the other queries returning paths. We study properties of such automata, and the key computational tasks associated with them. Finally, we provide additional restrictions for tractability, and show that some intractable cases can be naturally cast as instances of constraint satisfaction problem.

Categories and Subject Descriptors. H.2.1 [**Logical Design**]: *Data Models*; F.1.1 [**Models of Computation**]: *Automata*

General Terms. Theory, Languages, Algorithms

Keywords. Graph databases, graph patterns, query languages, complexity, automata, constraint satisfaction.

1. INTRODUCTION

Querying and mining graph-structured data has received much attention lately, due to numerous applications in areas such as biological networks [32, 33, 35], social networks [37, 38], and the semantic Web [25, 36]. In such applications, the underlying data is naturally modeled as graphs, in which nodes are objects, and edge labels define relationships between those objects [2].

A standard way of querying graph data is to look for reachability patterns. Such patterns specify that paths satisfying certain conditions should exist between nodes. Initially proposed in a simple form in [15, 14], pattern languages have been developed over time and used in a variety of applications, such as biology, studying network traffic, crime detection, modeling object-oriented data, querying and searching RDF data, etc. [20, 21, 25, 26, 32, 33, 34, 36, 37, 38, 39, 40]; see also the survey [2]. In their simplest form, patterns are just graphs, whose occurrences in large graphs are of interest. Already in this simple form, they are very important in biological applications, where search for network motifs [33] is a common task. But for applications such as, for example, crime detection or RDF data, more complex patterns are needed, as one can look for connections between elements in a network that involve complex paths via some intermediaries.

The notions of finding matches for complex patterns also evolved with time, from traditional NP-complete subgraph isomorphism (used, nonetheless, in practical applications, e.g., in [12, 39]) to notions based on graph homeomorphisms (i.e., mapping edges to paths) and simulation relations between patterns and graphs [20, 21]. Outputs of matching queries are patterns themselves: their nodes are those that are involved in the simulation relation, and relationships between them are those specified in the pattern. For example, in a crime detection scenario, a query may output a set of individuals who might be involved in a crime network, together with descriptions of paths specifying their relationships. Similar scenarios arise in querying semistructured data as well, where it is sometimes natural to output incomplete query results [29]. When such matching and query results require extracting additional information

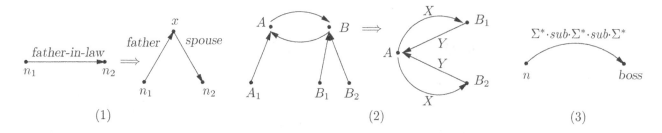

Figure 1: **Examples of (1) node variables, (2) label variables, and (3) regular expressions**

from them, one ends up querying patterns rather than graphs.

There are other scenarios where the need for querying patterns naturally arises. A pattern represents partial information about graph-structured data. Querying partial information is commonly present in integrating and exchanging (or translating) data [3, 19, 31]. In such applications, one queries the result of applying some schema mapping rules to source data, which yields a partially specified database. Partial databases – whether relational or XML – are typically viewed as patterns [27, 4, 6]. For graph data, the study of schema mappings and transformations for data exchange an integration has started recently [11, 38], but techniques for querying resulting partially specified graphs are currently lacking.

Motivated by these considerations, we would like to study querying partially defined graph data, i.e., graph patterns. As for other data models [3, 4, 19, 27, 31], one is looking for answers that are independent of the way in which the missing parts of patterns are interpreted, i.e., certain answers.

Based on the examples arising in querying and transforming graph data, we now analyze types of features that need to be addressed in the study of querying graph patterns. Recall that in the relational case, one deals with variables in place of missing data values [27]. In the case of XML, one may also have missing structural information [4]. For graph databases, partiality of specifications mainly arises in the following three ways.

Node variables Similarly to values missing in relational or XML data, identities of some nodes can be missing in graph data. For example, in transforming a social network that has different types of relationship edges, we can split an edge *(Name1, father-in-law, Name2)* into two edges *(Name1, father, x)* and *(x, spouse, Name2)*, with an unknown identity x. Variables can also be used to model blank nodes in RDF [36].

Label variables We may also miss the precise relationships between nodes. But even if we do not know them, we may still know that some of the relationships are the same. Taking an example from social networks, consider transforming a network where we have two 'celebrities' A and B who have 'followers' $A_1, \ldots, A_n$

and $B_1, \ldots, B_m$ (like on the Twitter network). Suppose we know the relationship between A and B (e.g., they like, or dislike each other). We may wish to record this as a relationship between their followers: for instance, if A hates B and A_i follows A, we may deduce something about how A_i relates to B. At the time of transforming a network we may not know the exact nature of such a relationship, but we know there exists one, and it should be the same for all the followers of A. Likewise, all the followers of B will be in some relationship with A (but not necessarily the same as the followers of A with B). So we add edges

$$(A_1, X, B), \ldots, (A_n, X, B), \ (B_1, Y, A), \ldots, (B_m, Y, A)$$

where X and Y are edge labels: we do not yet know what the relationship will be, but want to record that it is the same among all the followers.

Regular expressions Returning to the example with crime detection in a network of people, the result of a matching may contain facts like "there is a path between x and the boss that goes via at least two intermediaries", which will be expressed by a regular expression $\Sigma^* \cdot sub \cdot \Sigma^* \cdot sub \cdot \Sigma^*$, where *sub* indicates subordinacy in the hierarchy, and Σ is the set of all labels. In general, the situation where only regular paths between nodes can be deduced from a matching is very common [22]. Thus, when we do not have an exact path between two nodes, we attempt to replace it by an edge (A, e, B), where e is a regular expression.

These three examples are illustrated in Fig. 1. Once we have these features added to patterns, we need to define a query language for them. Most commonly used query languages for graph databases specify the existence of paths between nodes, with the restriction that the labels of such path belong to regular languages [1, 15, 14, 26, 10]. The simplest such queries are known as *regular path queries*, or RPQs [15]; those select nodes connected by a path that belongs to a regular language. *Conjunctive* RPQs, or CRPQs, extend them by allowing intermediate nodes in paths. Dealing with incomplete data, we often have *duality* between data and queries. For example, relational naive tables are tableaux of conjunctive queries, and in XML, typical query languages are based on tree patterns, i.e., incomplete descriptions of documents. We shall see that queries such as RPQs and CRPQs arise as special cases of graph patterns, continuing the analogy with the well studied cases.

To sum up, our *main goal* is to define classes of graph patterns, study their properties, and query answering over them. Our main contributions are as follows.

1. We define classes of graph patterns that have the key features listed above – node variables, label variables, and edges labeled with regular expressions – and provide a complete classification of their expressiveness.

2. We study the complexity of query answering (i.e., the problem of finding certain answers to queries over graph patterns). We fully analyze it for CRPQs, both for data complexity (which ranges from NLOGSPACE to CONP) and for combined complexity (which ranges from NP to EXPSPACE). For classes of high complexity, we do an in-depth analysis, showing which features lead to intractability. We also show that upper bounds for CRPQs extend to more expressive queries.

3. We provide an automaton model for query answering. Specifically, we define a class of automata, called *incomplete automata*, that naturally give rise to two acceptance notions that precisely capture certain answers: one of them corresponds to queries that return nodes, and the other to queries that return paths. In the latter case, answers to queries are represented by NFAs. We analyze the complexity of incomplete automata, and prove lower bounds on the sizes of NFAs representing query answers.

4. Returning to the intractable cases for query answering, we look at two ways of reducing complexity: by imposing structural restrictions, and by reducing to problems for which many efficient heuristics are known. Along these lines, we prove that for several classes of graph patterns, the bounded treewidth restriction guarantees tractability. We also show how to cast finding certain answers as a constraint satisfaction problem, which allows us to use algorithmic techniques from that field.

Organization In Section 2 we define graph databases and queries over them. In Section 3 we define graph patterns and in Section 4 we study their classifications and structural properties. In Section 5 we analyze both data and combined complexity of query answering. In Section 6 we deal with incomplete automata, and relate them to answering queries over graph patterns. In Section 7 we look at tractability restrictions and reduction to constraint satisfaction.

2. GRAPH DATABASES, RPQS AND CRPQS

A *graph database* [2, 10, 15] is just a finite edge-labeled graph. Let Σ be a finite alphabet, and $\mathcal{N}$ a countably infinite set of node ids. Then a graph database over Σ is a pair $G = (N, E)$, where N is the set of nodes (a finite subset of $\mathcal{N}$), and E is the set of edges, i.e., $E \subseteq N \times \Sigma \times N$. That is, we view each edge as a triple (n, a, n'), whose interpretation, of course, is an a-labeled edge from n to n'. When Σ is clear from the context, we shall simply speak of a graph database.

A *path* ρ from n_0 to n_m in G is a sequence (n_0, a_0, n_1), $(n_1, a_1, n_2), \cdots, (n_{m-1}, a_{m-1}, n_m)$, for some $m \geq 0$, where each (n_i, a_i, n_{i+1}), for $i < m$, is an edge in E. In particular, all the n_i's are nodes in N and all the a_j's are letters in Σ. The *label* of ρ, denoted by $\lambda(\rho)$, is the word $a_0 \cdots a_{m-1} \in \Sigma^*$. We also define the empty path as (n, ϵ, n) for each $n \in N$; the label of such path is the empty word ϵ.

The basic querying mechanism for graph databases is provided by means of *regular path queries*, or *RPQs* [1, 15, 10]. They retrieve pairs of nodes in a graph database connected by a path whose label belongs to a given regular language. Formally, an RPQ Q is an expression of the form (x, L, y) where $L \subseteq \Sigma^*$ is a regular language. We shall assume that syntactically L is given as a regular expression. Given a graph database $G = (N, E)$ and an RPQ Q, both over Σ, the answer $Q(G)$, is the set of all pairs $(n, n') \in N$ such that there is path ρ between them whose label $\lambda(\rho)$ is in L.

It has been argued (see, e.g., [1, 15, 14, 7]) that analogs of conjunctive queries whose atoms are RPQs are much more useful in practice than simple RPQs. In such queries, multiple RPQs can be combined, and some variables can be existentially quantified. Formally, a *conjunctive regular path query*, or *CRPQ* Q over a finite alphabet Σ is an expression of the form:

$$Ans(\bar{z}) \leftarrow \bigwedge_{1 \leq i \leq m} (x_i, L_i, y_i), \qquad (1)$$

such that $m > 0$, each (x_i, L_i, y_i) is an RPQ, and $\bar{z}$ is a tuple of variables among $\bar{x}$ and $\bar{y}$. A query with the head $Ans()$ (i.e., no variables in the output) is called a *Boolean* query.

Intuitively, such a query Q selects tuples $\bar{z}$ for which there exist values of the remaining node variables from $\bar{x}$ and $\bar{y}$ such that each RPQ in the body is satisfied. Formally, given Q of the form (1) and a graph $G = (N, E)$, a valuation is a map $\sigma : \bigcup_{1 \leq i \leq m} \{x_i, y_i\} \to N$. We write $(G, \sigma) \models Q$ if $(\sigma(x_i), \sigma(y_i))$ is in the answer to RPQ $(x_i.L_i, y_i)$ in G, i.e., if there is a path ρ_i in G from $\sigma(x_i)$ to $\sigma(y_i)$ with $\lambda(\rho_i) \in L_i$. Then $Q(G)$ is the set of all tuples $\sigma(\bar{z})$ such that $(G, \sigma) \models Q$. If Q is Boolean, we let $Q(G)$ be `true` if $(G, \sigma) \models Q$ for some σ (that is, as usual, the singleton set with the empty tuple models `true`, and the empty set models `false`).

We also allow existentially quantified variables in path queries. That is, RPQs will be of the form $Ans(\bar{z}) \leftarrow (x, L, y)$, where $\bar{z}$ contains variables from $\{x, y\}$. For example, $Ans() \leftarrow (x, L, y)$ is a Boolean RPQ checking whether there is a path whose label is in L.

3. GRAPH PATTERNS

As explained in the introduction, the key new features of graph patterns are the ability to use the following (in addition to nodes and edge labels of graph databases):

- node variables, i.e., marked nulls for graph nodes;

- label variables, i.e., marked nulls for edge labels;

- regular expressions as labels for edges.

Thus, we shall define graph patterns as graph databases over constant nodes and node variables, whose edges will be labeled with regular expressions that may use label variables. To do this, we shall use the following (countably infinite) sets:

- $\mathcal{V}_{\text{node}}$ of *node variables* (normally denoted by lower-case letters), and

- $\mathcal{V}_{\text{lab}}$ of *label variables* (normally denoted by upper-case letters).

If Γ is an arbitrary (finite or infinite) set of symbols, we write $\text{REG}(\Gamma)$ to denote the set of nonempty regular languages over Γ (if Γ is infinite, then each $L \in \text{REG}(\Gamma)$ only uses finitely many symbols from Γ). Recall that a graph database over a labeling alphabet Σ was defined as a labeled graph, (N, E), where $N \subseteq \mathcal{N}$ is the set of nodes and $E \subseteq N \times \Sigma \times N$ is the set of labeled edges. We are now in a position to define graph patterns formally.

Definition 1. *A graph pattern over finite alphabet Σ is a pair $\pi = (N, E)$ where*

- $N \subseteq \mathcal{N} \cup \mathcal{V}_{\text{node}}$ *is the finite set of nodes, and*

- $E \subseteq N \times \text{REG}(\Sigma \cup \mathcal{V}_{\text{lab}}) \times N$ *is the set of edges.*

Semantics In complete analogy with relational naive tables or incomplete XML documents, the semantics is defined via homomorphisms. To define those, we need extensions of partial functions $f : \Gamma \to \Gamma$ to languages $L \in \text{REG}(\Gamma)$ defined as $f(L) = \{f(w) \mid w \in L\}$, where $f(w)$ is obtained by replacing each symbol a of a word w on which f is defined by $f(a)$, and leaving symbols b on which f is not defined intact.

Since variables can occur at the level of both nodes and edge labels, homomorphisms will be in fact *pairs* of mappings. Given a graph database $G = (N, E)$ and a pattern $\pi = (N', E')$, a *homomorphism* $h : \pi \to G$ is a pair $h = (h_1, h_2)$ of mappings $h_1 : N' \to N$ and h_2 that maps label variables used in π to labels used in G such that:

1. $h_1(n) = n$ for every node id $n \in \mathcal{N}$; and

2. for every edge $(p, L, p') \in E'$, there is path between $h_1(p)$ and $h_1(p')$ in G whose label is in $h_2(L)$.

We now write $G \models \pi$ if there is a homomorphism $h : \pi \to G$. The semantics is defined with respect to a labeling alphabet Σ:

$$[\![\pi]\!]_\Sigma \;=\; \{G \text{ over } \Sigma \mid G \models \pi\}.$$

Most often Σ is clear from the context and we write simply $[\![\pi]\!]$ then.

Example 1. An illustration is given in Fig. 2: a homomorphism is defined by letting label variable X be b, and by mapping both node variables x and y into n_3. The edge $(n_1, (a|b)(a|b), x)$ is then mapped into the *path* $(n_1, a, n_4), (n_4, b, n_3)$ with label ab. The edge $(n_1, (ab)^*, y)$ is mapped into the same path, since ab belongs to regular languages denoted by both $(a|b)(a|b)$ and $(ab)^*$. The edge (y, a^*X, n_2) is mapped into (n_3, b, n_2), since b is in the language denoted by a^*b.

Certain answers Consider queries Q that take graph databases as input and return sets of tuples of their nodes. For example, RPQs and CRPQs are such queries. For them, we can define their certain answers on graph patterns in the standard way:

$$\text{certain}_\Sigma(Q, \pi) \;=\; \bigcap\{Q(G) \mid G \in [\![\pi]\!]_\Sigma\}.$$

Again, if Σ is clear from the context, we write simply $\text{certain}(Q, \pi)$.

Example 2. The labeling alphabet can make a difference in finding certain answers. Consider a pattern with edges $(n_1, a, n_2), (n_2, X, n_3), (n_3, b, n_4)$, where X is a label variable. Let Q be the Boolean RPQ $Ans() \leftarrow (x, ab, y)$. Then $\text{certain}_{\{a,b\}}(Q, \pi) = \text{true}$: whether X is a or b, there is a path labeled ab. However, $\text{certain}_{\{a,b,c\}}(Q, \pi) = \text{false}$ (by setting $X = c$). □

Graph patterns as queries Graph patterns can naturally be viewed as queries – again in complete analogy with relational databases (where naive tables are a natural representation of conjunctive queries, i.e., tableaux) and XML documents (where tree patterns form the basis of tree conjunctive queries [6, 24]). This view has also been explored in [13].

We adopt the convention that patterns used in queries are denoted by ξ, and patterns used as data are denoted by π. A *graph query* is a pair $Q = (\xi, \bar{x})$, where $\xi = (N, E)$ is a graph pattern, and $\bar{x}$ is a tuple of elements from N. For example, a CRPQ $Ans(\bar{z}) \leftarrow \bigwedge_{i \le m}(x_i, L_i, y_i)$, can be viewed as a graph query $(\xi, \bar{z})$, where ξ simply contains the edges (x_i, L_i, y_i) for $i \le m$.

We now define the semantics of a graph query on graph databases (later, we shall extend it to graph patterns). Given a graph database $G = (N, E)$ with $N \subset \mathcal{N}$, and a graph query $Q = (\xi, \bar{x})$ with $|\bar{x}| = k$, the answer to Q on G is $Q(G) = \{\bar{v} \in N^k \mid G \models \xi[\bar{v}/\bar{x}]\}$. Here $\xi[\bar{v}/\bar{x}]$ is the result of substituting $\bar{v}$ for $\bar{x}$ in the pattern ξ.

It is easy to see that when Q is a CRPQ viewed as a graph query, the result $Q(G)$ coincides with the standard semantics of CRPQs.

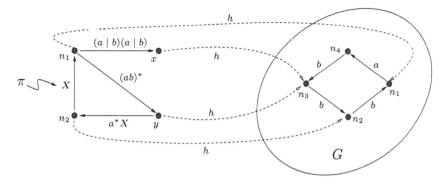

Figure 2: A homomorphism $h : \pi \to G$

Example 3. Consider again the example in Fig. 2 and the homomorphism described in Example 1. Let ξ be the pattern obtained from π by changing X to b, and replacing n_1 and n_2 with variables z_1 and z_2. The resulting pattern can be viewed as a CRPQ (ξ, x, y):

$$Ans(x, y) \leftarrow (z_1, (a|b)(a|b), x), (z_1, (ab)^*, y),$$
$$(y, a^*b, z_2), (z_2, b, z_1)$$

If it is evaluated in graph G shown in Fig. 2, one tuple in the output will be (n_3, n_3), since $G \models \xi[n_3/x, n_3/y]$, as witnessed by homomorphism h. □

4. CLASSIFICATION AND BASIC PROPERTIES

The three key features of graph patterns – node variables, label variables, and regular expressions – provide a natural classification of patterns. We shall refer to classes of patterns as $\mathcal{P}^\sigma$, where σ enumerates the present features. We use 'nv' for node variables, 'lv' for label variables, and 're' for regular expressions. This gives us 8 classes, from $\mathcal{P}$ (none of the features is present) to $\mathcal{P}^{\mathrm{nv,lv,re}}$ (all are present).

Of course $\mathcal{P}$ is the class of graph databases (N, E) with $N \subseteq \mathcal{N}$ and $E \subseteq N \times \Sigma \times N$, and $\mathcal{P}^{\mathrm{nv,lv,re}}$ is the class of all graph patterns as in Definition 1 with $N \subseteq \mathcal{N} \cup \mathcal{V}_{\mathrm{node}}$ and $E \subseteq N \times \mathrm{REG}(\Sigma \cup \mathcal{V}_{\mathrm{lab}}) \times N$. We now examine some others.

$\mathcal{P}^{\mathrm{nv}}$ is the class of graphs where nodes could be either constants, or node variables; all edges are labeled with alphabet letters, i.e. $N \subseteq \mathcal{N} \cup \mathcal{V}_{\mathrm{node}}$ and $E \subseteq N \times \Sigma \times N$. These patterns can be represented by relational naive tables.

$\mathcal{P}^{\mathrm{nv,re}}$ is the class of patterns where nodes could be either constants or node variables, and edges are labeled with regular expressions over Σ. That is, $N \subseteq \mathcal{N} \cup \mathcal{V}_{\mathrm{node}}$ and $E \subseteq N \times \mathrm{REG}(\Sigma) \times N$.

These are essentially CRPQs, which are graph queries $(\xi, \bar{x})$ where ξ is from $\mathcal{P}^{\mathrm{nv,re}}$ and uses only node variables (without this restriction we have the class of CRPQs that can mention constants).

$\mathcal{P}^{\mathrm{nv,lv}}$ is the class of patterns where nodes could be either constants or node variables, and edges are labeled with letters or variables. That is, $N \subseteq \mathcal{N} \cup \mathcal{V}_{\mathrm{node}}$ and $E \subseteq N \times (\Sigma \cup \mathcal{V}_{\mathrm{lab}}) \times N$. The class $\mathcal{P}^{\mathrm{lv}}$ is its restriction when $N \subseteq \mathcal{N}$.

Given multiple features of graph patterns, it is natural to ask whether all are necessary, or some are expressible with others. We now show that all three are essential.

Classes of patterns are of the form $\mathcal{P}^\sigma$, where σ is a subset of $\{\mathrm{nv, lv, re}\}$. We write $\mathcal{P}^\sigma \preceq \mathcal{P}^{\sigma'}$ if $\mathcal{P}^{\sigma'}$ is at least as expressive as $\mathcal{P}^\sigma$: for every pattern $\pi \in \mathcal{P}^\sigma$, there is a pattern $\pi' \in \mathcal{P}^{\sigma'}$ so that $[\![\pi]\!] = [\![\pi']\!]$ (i.e., $[\![\pi]\!]_\Sigma = [\![\pi']\!]_\Sigma$ for each Σ containing the labels used in π). We write $\mathcal{P}^\sigma \sim \mathcal{P}^{\sigma'}$ if $\mathcal{P}^\sigma$ and $\mathcal{P}^{\sigma'}$ are equally expressive (i.e., $\mathcal{P}^\sigma \preceq \mathcal{P}^{\sigma'}$ and $\mathcal{P}^{\sigma'} \preceq \mathcal{P}^\sigma$). Finally, $\mathcal{P}^\sigma \prec \mathcal{P}^{\sigma'}$ means that $\mathcal{P}^{\sigma'}$ is strictly more expressive than $\mathcal{P}^\sigma$: that is, $\mathcal{P}^\sigma \preceq \mathcal{P}^{\sigma'}$, but they are not equally expressive.

Theorem 1. *Adding each new feature to graph patterns strictly increases their expressiveness: in other words, $\mathcal{P}^\sigma \prec \mathcal{P}^{\sigma'}$ iff $\sigma \subsetneq \sigma'$, and $\mathcal{P}^\sigma \sim \mathcal{P}^{\sigma'}$ iff $\sigma = \sigma'$.*

These relationships are visualized in the figure below.

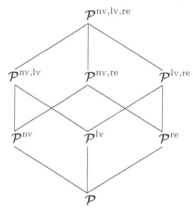

In both relational and XML patterns it is common to consider a restriction in which variables cannot be repeated. In relations, these are Codd tables [27] that model SQL's nulls. We say that a graph pattern is a *Codd pattern* if every variable – node or label – occurs at most once in it. In other words, Codd patterns do not allow us to express equality between unknown entities.

If σ contains nv or lv, we shall write $\mathcal{P}^\sigma_{\text{Codd}}$ for the Codd patterns in $\mathcal{P}^\sigma$. We next show that Codd patterns are strictly weaker than the usual ones, and describe classes of patterns for which adding variables under Codd interpretation increases expressiveness.

Proposition 1.
- *Codd patterns are strictly less expressive:* $\mathcal{P}^\sigma_{\text{Codd}} \prec \mathcal{P}^\sigma$ *when σ contains* nv *or* lv.
- *Adding variables under Codd interpretation makes patterns more expressive except adding label variables to regular expressions. That is, if $\sigma' \subsetneq \sigma$ and $\sigma - \sigma'$ contains either* nv *or* lv*, then $\mathcal{P}^{\sigma'} \prec \mathcal{P}^\sigma_{\text{Codd}}$ except one case: $\mathcal{P}^{\text{re}} \sim \mathcal{P}^{\text{lv,re}}_{\text{Codd}}$.*

5. QUERY ANSWERING

The goal of this section is to study the complexity – both data and combined – of query answering over graph patterns. Recall that for queries Q returning tuples of nodes, we want to find certain answers defined as $\text{certain}(Q, \pi) = \bigcap \{Q(G) \mid G \in [\![\pi]\!]\}$. More precisely, one needs to find $\text{certain}_\Sigma(Q, \pi)$, with G ranging over graph databases with edges labeled in Σ; it will be clear from the proofs, however, that the complexity of query answering does not depend on the labeling alphabet.

Since each class of patterns gives rise to a class of graph queries $Q = (\xi, \bar{x})$, one could potentially ask for the exact bounds on combined and data complexity for all these classes of queries on all the classes of patterns. Of course we are not going to consider all the resulting 128 cases. Instead, we do the following.

As our benchmark language we use CRPQs, and provide exact complexity bounds for CRPQs over all classes of patterns. Recall that CRPQs can be viewed as graph queries $(\xi, \bar{x})$ with $\xi \in \mathcal{P}^{\text{nv,re}}$. We then show that the upper bounds for CRPQs extend to the most expressive patterns from $\mathcal{P}^{\text{nv,lv,re}}$. After that, we delve further into intractable cases, and analyze what really causes intractability. In such cases, we consider restricted classes of queries based on simpler graph patterns. We shall discuss lower bounds for more expressive patterns in the full version of the paper.

Certain answers as pattern implication It is a standard and yet useful observation that the problem of computing certain answers can be cast as the problem of *implication of patterns*. Recall that pattern implication is defined as follows: if π_1 and π_2 are two patterns, then we say that π_1 *implies* π_2, and write $\pi_1 \models \pi_2$ if $[\![\pi_1]\!] \subseteq [\![\pi_2]\!]$. In other words, $\pi_1 \models \pi_2$ if $G \models \pi$ entails $G \models \pi_2$ for every graph database G. The following is now immediate from the definitions.

Lemma 1. *Given a graph pattern $\pi = (N, E)$ and a graph query $Q = (\xi, \bar{x})$ with $|\bar{x}| = k$,*

$$\text{certain}(Q, \pi) = \{\bar{v} \in N^k \mid \pi \models \xi[\bar{v}/\bar{x}]\}.$$

For Boolean graph queries $Q = (\xi, ())$ with the empty tuple of output variables (i.e., true/false queries), Lemma 1 states that $\text{certain}(Q, \pi) = \text{true}$ iff $\pi \models \xi$. This simple connection with the implication problem will let us use known results on containment of CRPQs [7] to obtain some of the bounds for the combined complexity of query answering.

Remark: using naive evaluation Some classes of patterns can be represented as naive tables, perhaps with constraints. For example, patterns from $\mathcal{P}^{\text{nv}}$ can be stored as naive tables, and patterns without regular expressions (from $\mathcal{P}^{\text{nv,lv}}$) are represented as relational naive tables with an additional constraint that the interpretation for label variables must come from the labeling alphabet Σ. This can easily be coded as an inclusion constraint.

Since CRPQs can be expressed in datalog, such a representation gives us good tractable bounds for data complexity for $\mathcal{P}^{\text{nv}}$ patterns. But for combined complexity, and for data complexity for other classes, we cannot use known results to get tight bounds. For example, even evaluating conjunctive queries over naive tables with inclusion constraints is known to be PSPACE-hard [28], and we shall see better bounds obtained for CRPQs over $\mathcal{P}^{\text{nv,lv}}$ patterns.

5.1 Combined complexity

The problem we are dealing with is as follows:

INPUT:	a pattern $\pi = (N, E)$, a graph query $Q = (\xi, \bar{x})$ with $|\bar{x}| = k$, a tuple $\bar{v} \in N^k$.
QUESTION:	Is $\bar{v} \in \text{certain}(Q, \pi)$?

Checking $\bar{v} \in \text{certain}(Q, \pi)$ amounts to checking $\pi \models \xi[\bar{v}/\bar{x}]$, and the problem is known to be EXPSPACE-complete when both π and ξ are in $\mathcal{P}^{\text{nv,re}}$ [7]. We now provide a complete analysis of the complexity.

Theorem 2. *The combined complexity of answering CRPQs over classes of graph patterns is as shown in Figure 3.*

The abbreviation '-c.' in the figure means, of course, complete for the class. The combined complexity of CRPQs on usual graph databases is the same as the combined complexity of conjunctive queries over the usual relational database, i.e., NP-complete. Thus, adding node variables comes with no cost, while adding both node and label variables carries a small cost in terms of combined complexity (jumping up one level in the polynomial hierarchy). Adding regular expressions comes at a significant cost (jumping up an exponential).

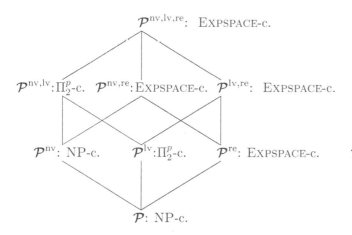

$\mathcal{P}^{nv,lv,re}$: EXPSPACE-c.

$\mathcal{P}^{nv,lv}$:Π_2^p-c. $\mathcal{P}^{nv,re}$:EXPSPACE-c. $\mathcal{P}^{lv,re}$: EXPSPACE-c.

$\mathcal{P}^{nv}$: NP-c. $\mathcal{P}^{lv}$:Π_2^p-c. $\mathcal{P}^{re}$: EXPSPACE-c.

$\mathcal{P}$: NP-c.

Figure 3: Combined complexity for CRPQs over graph patterns

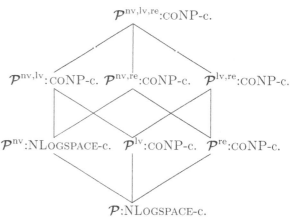

$\mathcal{P}^{nv,lv,re}$:coNP-c.

$\mathcal{P}^{nv,lv}$:coNP-c. $\mathcal{P}^{nv,re}$:coNP-c. $\mathcal{P}^{lv,re}$:coNP-c.

$\mathcal{P}^{nv}$:NLOGSPACE-c. $\mathcal{P}^{lv}$:coNP-c. $\mathcal{P}^{re}$:coNP-c.

$\mathcal{P}$:NLOGSPACE-c.

Figure 4: Data complexity for CRPQs over graph patterns

Using essentially the same techniques as in [7], we can prove that the previous upper bound extends beyond CRPQs.

Proposition 2. *The combined complexity of arbitrary graph queries on arbitrary patterns is in* EXPSPACE.

The next question is whether we can lower the EXPSPACE bound for patterns in $\mathcal{P}^{re}$. There are two natural ways of looking for better behaved subclasses: by restricting queries, or restricting patterns. Restrictions on queries by means of simplifying regular languages were studied in [17]. For example, it showed that for regular languages built with concatenation and the Kleene star, the combined complexity drops to Π_2^p-complete. Another possibility is to restrict to RPQs; then, using techniques similar to [7], we can prove a PSPACE bound, matching the combined complexity of relational calculus. It also follows from [7] that restricting the class of patterns does not help lower the combined complexity.

Proposition 3.   • *The combined complexity of answering CRPQs on patterns* $\pi \in \mathcal{P}^{re}$ *is* EXPSPACE-*hard even for patterns* π *that contain a single edge.*

   • *The combined complexity of answering RPQs on graph patterns from* $\mathcal{P}^{nv,lv,re}$ *is* PSPACE-*complete. The problem remains* PSPACE-*hard even for answering RPQs on patterns* $\pi \in \mathcal{P}^{re}$ *that contain a single edge.*

5.2 Data complexity

We now turn to data complexity, i.e. the complexity of query answering when the query is fixed. In what follows, Q refers to a graph query $(\xi, \bar{x})$ with $|\bar{x}| = k$.

PROBLEM: DATA COMPLEXITY(Q)
INPUT: a pattern $\pi = (N, E)$, a tuple $\bar{v} \in N^k$.
QUESTION: Is $\bar{v} \in$ certain(Q, π) ?

This too can be viewed as a pattern-implication problem $\pi \models \xi[\bar{v}/\bar{x}]$ but for a *fixed* pattern ξ.

As already mentioned, some cases are simple: for example, patterns in $\mathcal{P}$ are graphs, and thus due to the monotonicity of CRPQs, computing certain answers is the same as evaluating CRPQs on graphs, i.e., NLOGSPACE-complete. Similarly, since $\mathcal{P}^{nv}$ patterns can be represented as a naive table, and since CRPQ queries can be translated into datalog, we retain an NLOGSPACE bound. For other cases, as it turns out, the complexity is intractable.

Theorem 3. *The data complexity of answering CRPQs over classes of graph patterns is as shown in Figure 4.*

Proof sketch. The coNP upper bound follows from a more general result presented in Proposition 4.

We have already explained how to obtain the NLOGSPACE upper bounds, thus we only need to show coNP-hardness for $\mathcal{P}^{re}$ and $\mathcal{P}^{lv}$. We now present a simple hardness proof for $\mathcal{P}^{re}$. It will be tightened significantly (and extended to $\mathcal{P}^{lv}$) in the remainder of the section.

For $\mathcal{P}^{re}$, we use reduction to non-3-colorability. Assume we have an arbitrary undirected graph G; we represent it as a labeled graph where between two nodes n_1 and n_2 connected by an edge we have two edges labeled a, i.e., (n_1, a, n_2) and (n_2, a, n_1). Now we turn it into a $\mathcal{P}^{re}$ pattern π_G over the alphabet $\{a, r, g, b\}$ by adding edges $(n, rr|gg|bb, n)$ for each node n. That is, in every graph represented by this pattern, associated with each node n there is another node n' and edges $(n, \ell, n'), (n', \ell, n)$ where ℓ is one of r, g, b. It is now easy to see that the certain answer to the Boolean RPQ $Ans() \leftarrow (x, rar|gag|bab, y)$ over π_G is true iff G is not 3-colorable.   □

The upper bound again extends to arbitrary queries. In order to prove this, we apply similar techniques to those used in [8] to show that the data complexity of the problem of answering RPQs using views is in coNP.

Proposition 4. *Data complexity of arbitrary graph queries over arbitrary graph patterns is in* coNP.

Looking at Figure 4, we see that there are two features that cause coNP-hardness: label variables, and regular expressions. We now analyze their role in causing the high complexity of query answering. In both cases, we need to investigate two ways of lowering the complexity: by restricting queries, and by restricting their inputs.

The role of label variables For restrictions on queries, we shall look at simple RPQs. To define restrictions on inputs, we use the notion of the *underlying graph* G_π of a pattern $\pi = (N, E)$: this is simply the graph obtained by erasing labels on edges, i.e. $G_\pi = (N, \{(v_1, v_2) \mid (v_1, L, v_2) \in E\})$.

We now show that the coNP-hardness result is very robust. Recall that $\mathcal{P}^\sigma_{\mathrm{Codd}}$ stands for class of Codd patterns in $\mathcal{P}^\sigma$, i.e., patterns that use each variable once.

Theorem 4.
- *There is a Boolean RPQ Q such that* DATA COMPLEXITY*(Q) is* coNP-*hard even over input patterns in* $\mathcal{P}^{\mathrm{lv}}$ *whose underlying graph is a path. Moreover, the regular language in Q is built using only concatenation and the Kleene star.*

- *There is a Boolean RPQ Q of the form Ans()* $\leftarrow$ *(x, w, y), where w is a word in* $\{0, 1\}^*$, *such that* DATA COMPLEXITY*(Q) is* coNP-*hard even over* $\mathcal{P}^{\mathrm{lv}}_{\mathrm{Codd}}$ *patterns whose underlying graph is a DAG.*

The only possibility for a polynomial-time query answering algorithm left open by this result appears to be Codd patterns in $\mathcal{P}^{\mathrm{lv}}$ with very nice underlying graphs. We shall see in Section 7, when we study tractable restrictions, that there is indeed a tractable class obtained along these lines.

The role of regular expressions In the case of patterns from $\mathcal{P}^{\mathrm{re}}$ we have an additional parameter to vary: the regular expressions used in patterns. Nevertheless, we shall see that coNP-hardness is already witnessed by very simple regular expressions.

Theorem 5.
- *There exists a Boolean RPQ Q of the form Ans()* $\leftarrow$ *(x, w, y), where w is a single word over* $\Sigma = \{0, 1\}$, *such that* DATA COMPLEXITY*(Q) is* coNP-*hard even over input patterns in* $\mathcal{P}^{\mathrm{re}}$ *over* Σ *whose underlying graph is a DAG. It remains* coNP-*hard even if each regular expression used in input patterns is* 0|1.

- *There exists a Boolean RPQ Q such that* DATA COMPLEXITY*(Q) is* coNP-*hard even over input patterns in* $\mathcal{P}^{\mathrm{re}}$ *that only use regular expressions of the form a, for* $a \in \Sigma$, *or* $a_1^* \ldots a_n^*$, *where the* a_i*'s are distinct letters in* Σ.

Like the case of patterns with label variables, this leaves open the possibility that more restrictive underlying graphs may lead to tractability. Indeed, we shall prove such results in Section 7.

6. INCOMPLETE AUTOMATA FOR QUERYING PATTERNS

Notice that graph databases can be viewed as finite automata. Graph patterns in turn can be viewed as *incomplete automata*. We now define those, and show that they naturally generate two notions of acceptance. These notions correspond to certain answers: one for certain answers as we defined them, and the other for certain answers for queries that can output paths.

Extensions of CRPQs outputting paths have been defined in [5]. We shall present this notion for RPQs (for CRPQs, it includes the concept of synchronizing paths, which will complicate the presentation). An *RPQ with a path output* is a query of the form

$$Ans(\bar{z}, \rho) \leftarrow (x, \rho : L, y)$$

where, on top of the usual RPQ $Ans(\bar{z}) \leftarrow (x, L, y)$, one is allowed to name the path ρ witnessing the query, and to output its label. Of course the number of L-paths between two nodes could be infinite, but one easily observes that for every nodes n_1, n_2 in a graph database, the set of labels of L-paths between them is regular, and thus can be represented by a finite automaton.

Assume we have an RPQ Q with a path variable, as above, and a graph pattern π. Let n_1, n_2 be two nodes from $\mathcal{N}$ that occur in π. We say that a word $\rho \in \Sigma^*$ is a *certain path between n_1 and n_2 with respect to Q* if for every $G \in [\![\pi]\!]$, there is an L-path between n_1 and n_2 with label ρ. The set of such certain paths will be denoted by certain$^{\mathrm{path}}(Q; \pi, n_1, n_2)$. We shall write certain$^{\mathrm{path}}_\Sigma$ when Σ is not clear from the context.

The following example illustrates this concept.

Example 4. For $m > 0$, consider the pattern π_m over $\Sigma = \{0, 1\}$ shown in the figure below.

Notice that each $G \in [\![\pi_m]\!]$ will contain a path from node n_0 to node n_m. In particular, (n_0, n_m) is a certain answer to the RPQ Q given by $(x, \rho : (0|1)^*, y)$.
However, one can see that every word in certain$^{\mathrm{path}}_\Sigma(Q; \pi, n_0, n_m)$ must contain, as subwords, all the 2^m words of length m over $\{0, 1\}$ since the X_is can be instantiated arbitrarily. Due to the presence of the loops, the converse also holds, and certain$^{\mathrm{path}}_\Sigma(Q; \pi, n_0, n_m)$ consists precisely of the words that contain all the 2^m subwords of length m. In particular, the smallest certain paths are precisely the non-circular De Bruijn sequences of order m, and thus

have length $2^m + m - 1$. One can also easily show that any NFA accepting $\text{certain}_\Sigma^{\text{path}}(Q; \pi, n_0, n_m)$ will have exponentially many states (in m). $\qquad\square$

This example suggests that the problem of computing the certain paths is inherently different from the problem of computing certain answers for graph patterns, and thus we need to develop new tools for solving this problem. This is what we do next.

6.1 Incomplete automata and certain answers

For convenience, we shall assume that NFAs can have edges labeled by words. That is, NFAs will be of the form $\mathcal{A} = (Q, \Sigma, q_0, F, \delta)$, where Q is the set of states, Σ is the alphabet, q_0 is the initial state, F is the set of final states, and the transition relation δ is a finite subset of $Q \times \Sigma^* \times Q$. The notion of acceptance extends to such an automaton in the standard way: if there is a transition (q, w, q'), the automaton is in state q, then, if w is a subword that starts in the current position, the automaton skips it and moves to the state q'. When all the w's used in transitions are single letters, this is the standard notion of NFAs; in that case we shall refer to them as *standard NFAs*.

The language accepted by an NFA is denoted by $L(\mathcal{A})$. Note that for each NFA, one can construct, in polynomial time, a standard NFA $\mathcal{A}'$ such that $L(\mathcal{A}) = L(\mathcal{A}')$. This is done by converting each word in a transition into a DFA (in polynomial time) and plugging it in place of the transition. Hence, using extended transitions is indeed just a matter of convenience.

Definition 2. *An incomplete automaton $\mathcal{A}$ is a tuple $\mathcal{A} = (Q, \Sigma, \mathcal{W}, q_0, F, \delta)$, where $\mathcal{W}$ is a finite set of label variables from $\mathcal{V}_{\text{lab}}$, and $\delta \subseteq Q \times \text{REG}(\Sigma \cup \mathcal{W}) \times Q$.*

Thus, an incomplete automaton is really just a graph pattern from $\mathcal{P}^{\text{nv,lv,re}}$ with a distinguished node corresponding to the initial state, and a set of nodes corresponding to the final states.

To define acceptance by these automata, we need the notion of *valuation*. For an incomplete automaton $\mathcal{A} = (Q, \Sigma, \mathcal{W}, q_0, F, \delta)$, a valuation is a pair $\nu = (\eta, \theta)$, where $\eta : \mathcal{W} \to \Sigma$ maps label variables in $\mathcal{W}$ to Σ, and $\theta : (Q \times \text{REG}(\Sigma \cup \mathcal{W}) \times Q) \to (Q \times \Sigma^* \times Q)$ assigns to each transition $(q, L, q') \in \delta$ a transition (q, w, q'), where w is a word that belongs to $\eta(L)$. Thus, a valuation $\nu = (\eta, \theta)$ for an incomplete automaton $\mathcal{A}$ defines an NFA $\nu(\mathcal{A}) = (Q, \Sigma, q_0, F, \theta(\delta))$.

We now consider two notions of acceptance. *Weak acceptance* refers to the consistency of a *language* with the automaton, regardless of the interpretation of variables, and *strong acceptance* refers to the consistency of a *word* and an automaton.

Definition 3. • *A regular language $L \subseteq \Sigma^*$ is weakly accepted by an incomplete automaton $\mathcal{A}$ if $L \cap L(\nu(\mathcal{A})) \neq \emptyset$ for every valuation ν.*

• *A word $w \in \Sigma^*$ is strongly accepted by an incomplete automaton $\mathcal{A}$ if $w \in L(\nu(\mathcal{A}))$ for every valuation ν.*

We write $\mathcal{L}_w(\mathcal{A})$ for the set of languages weakly accepted by $\mathcal{A}$, and $L_s(\mathcal{A})$ for the set of words strongly accepted by $\mathcal{A}$. Note that $\mathcal{L}_w(\mathcal{A}) \subseteq 2^{\Sigma^*}$ while $L_s(\mathcal{A}) \subseteq \Sigma^*$.

While not immediately obvious from the definition, we can show the following.

Proposition 5. *For an incomplete automaton $\mathcal{A}$, the language $L_s(\mathcal{A})$ of words strongly accepted by $\mathcal{A}$ is regular. An NFA accepting $L_s(\mathcal{A})$ can be constructed in doubly exponential time.*

We shall see later (Theorem 8) that the bound is tight.

Given a graph pattern $\pi = (N, E) \in \mathcal{P}^{\text{nv,lv,re}}$ over Σ that uses label variables $\mathcal{W}$, and two nodes n_1, n_2 from $\mathcal{N} \cap N$ (i.e., nodes which are not variables), we let $\mathcal{A}_\pi(n_1, n_2)$ be the incomplete automaton $(N, \Sigma, \mathcal{W}, n_1, \{n_2\}, E)$.

Theorem 6. *Let $Ans(x, y, \rho) \leftarrow (x, \rho : L, y)$ be an RPQ, $\pi = (N, E)$ a graph pattern, and n_1, n_2 two of its nodes from $\mathcal{N}$. Then*

1. *$(n_1, n_2) \in \text{certain}(Q, \pi)$ iff L is weakly accepted by $\mathcal{A}_\pi(n_1, n_2)$.*

2. *$w \in \text{certain}^{\text{path}}(Q; \pi, n_1, n_2)$ iff $w \in L$ and w is strongly accepted by $\mathcal{A}_\pi(n_1, n_2)$.*

Thus, the query evaluation problem, for both nodes and paths, can be stated in purely automata-theoretic terms. In particular, the set $\text{certain}^{\text{path}}(Q; \pi, n_1, n_2)$ is regular for every RPQ. Thus, our next goal is to study properties of incomplete automata.

6.2 Computational problems for incomplete automata

Theorem 6 suggests studying computational problems for incomplete automata related to query evaluation. Results for weak acceptance have, in essence, been established earlier, so we are interested in strong acceptance, which accounts for having paths in the output.

For weak acceptance, *membership* (i.e., given incomplete automaton $\mathcal{A}$ and a regular language L, presented as a regular expression or as an NFA, does L belong to $\mathcal{L}_w(\mathcal{A})$?) is the problem of finding certain answers to RPQs. Hence, we have

Corollary 1. *The membership problem for incomplete automata under weak acceptance is PSPACE-complete, and coNP-complete if the language L is fixed.*

It can also be easily seen that the emptiness problem under weak acceptance, i.e., whether $\mathcal{L}_w(\mathcal{A}) \neq \emptyset$, is solvable in polynomial time.

Now we address the case of strong acceptance, which, by Theorem 6, gives us complexity bounds for computing paths that are returned with certainty. There are three versions of the problem we consider:

- Checking whether the query output is not empty. In automata-theoretic terms, this is the *emptiness problem under strong acceptance*: given an incomplete autoimaton $\mathcal{A}$, check whether $L_s(\mathcal{A}) \neq \emptyset$.

- Checking whether a specific path belongs to the output, i.e., whether $w \in \text{certain}^{\text{path}}(Q; \pi, n_1, n_2)$. In automata-theoretic terms, we are interested in the *membership problem under strong acceptance*, i.e., given an incomplete automaton $\mathcal{A}$ and a word w, check whether $w \in L_s(\mathcal{A})$.

- Computing $\text{certain}^{\text{path}}(Q; \pi, n_1, n_2)$. As this set is regular, in automata-theoretic terms, we study the following problem: For an incomplete automaton $\mathcal{A}$, construct an NFA $\mathcal{A}'$ so that $L(\mathcal{A}') = L_s(\mathcal{A})$.

As we analyze these problems, we shall see that hardness results will be witnessed by an especially simple kind of incomplete automata: namely, *wildcard automata*, in which all regular languages used in transitions are single letters (alphabet letters or variables). Formally, a wildcard automaton $\mathcal{A}$ is $(Q, \Sigma, \mathcal{W}, q_0, F, \delta)$, where $\delta \subseteq Q \times (\Sigma \cup \mathcal{W}) \times Q$.

We now show that problems related to computing certain paths are computationally hard as long as regular expressions or label variables are present in the edges. The following does not appear to follow from known EXPSPACE-completeness results for graph databases [7, 5], and requires a new and quite involved proof.

Theorem 7. *The emptiness problem under strong acceptance is* EXPSPACE*-complete. It remains* EXPSPACE*-hard for wildcard automata, as well as for incomplete automata that do not use any label variables.*

We now consider problems related to query answering. The first is finding certain paths, or, in automata-theoretic terms, the membership problem under strong acceptance.

Proposition 6. *The membership problem under strong acceptance for incomplete automata is* CONP*-complete. It remains* CONP*-hard for wildcard automata and for incomplete automata that do not use any label variables.*

The next question is about the size of automata defining $L_s(\mathcal{A})$. Normally large size bounds are easy to obtain for deterministic automata, while NFAs could be exponentially smaller. Here we use techniques from [23] to show that even the smallest NFAs capturing certain paths in the answer to an RPQ could be doubly exponential, matching the upper bound of Proposition 5.

Theorem 8. *There exists a polynomial p and a family $\{\mathcal{A}_n\}_{n \in \mathbb{N}}$ of wildcard automata such each $\mathcal{A}_n$ is of size at most $p(n)$ and uses n wildcards, and every NFA $\mathcal{A}'_n$ satisfying $L(\mathcal{A}'_n) = L_s(\mathcal{A}_n)$ has $2^{2^{\Omega(n)}}$ states.*

There also exists a family of incomplete automata without label variables with the same property.

This gives a lower bound on the size of automata for representing certain paths in answers to RPQs.

Corollary 2. *There exists a polynomial p, a family $\{\pi_n\}_{n \in \mathbb{N}}$ of $\mathcal{P}^{\text{lv}}$ graph patterns, each with two distinguished nodes n_1 and n_2, and an RPQ Q such that the size of π_n is at most $p(n)$, and every NFA defining $\text{certain}^{\text{path}}(Q; \pi_n, n_1, n_2)$ has $2^{2^{\Omega(n)}}$ states. The same holds for $\mathcal{P}^{\text{re}}$ patterns.*

Note there is an exponential gap between the complexity of the membership problem and the size of a representation of all words strongly accepted by an incomplete automaton. There is no contradiction, of course, between Theorem 8 and Proposition 6 as smallest NFAs accepting even finite languages L can be of size exponential in the maximum length of a word in L.

Remark: Theorems 7 and 8, Proposition 6, and Corollary 2 remain true even for the Codd interpretation of patterns and wildcard automata (i.e., each label variable is used in at most one transition).

7. TRACTABILITY RESTRICTIONS AND HEURISTICS

While many results of Sections 5 and 6 point to a rather high complexity of query answering, they still leave a few routes for finding tractable classes, or providing heuristics that – at least based on the experience of other areas – may be useful.

If we look at data complexity, results of Subsection 5.2 show that one possibility of getting tractable cases is to impose further restrictions on underlying graphs of patterns. Being DAGs, as we saw, is not enough, which suggests trees. We shall in fact get a more general result, replacing trees with graphs of bounded treewidth.

Combined complexity results in Subsection 5.1 point to $\mathcal{P}^{\text{nv,lv}}$ as the largest class with acceptable combined complexity (i.e., not exceeding that of FO; in fact staying in the 2nd level of the polynomial hierarchy). The data complexity for the class, although intractable, drops to the 1st level of the polynomial hierarchy. This suggests using techniques from a field that has achieved great success in solving problems of this complexity, namely constraint satisfaction [16, 30]. The field has identified many tractable restrictions and, what is equally important, provided many practical heuristics that help solve intractable problems. The connection between RPQs on graph databases and constraint satisfaction was already established in [9]. As the second contribution of this section, we show how to cast the query answering problem for RPQs over graph patterns as a constraint satisfaction problem, with a particularly simple translation for several classes.

7.1 Tractability restrictions

Recall the standard definition of tree decompositions and treewidth of a graph $G = (N, E)$, with $E \subseteq N \times N$ (see, e.g., [18]). A tree decomposition is a pair (T, f) where T is a tree and $f : T \to 2^N$ assigns to each node t in T a set of nodes $f(t)$ of G such that every edge of G is contained in one of the sets $f(t)$, and each set $\{t \mid n \in f(t)\}$ is a connected subset of T for all $n \in N$. The width of such a decomposition is $\max_t |f(t)| - 1$. The *treewidth* of G is the minimum width of a tree decomposition of G. The treewidth of a connected graph G equals 1 iff G is a tree.

A class of graph patterns is of *bounded treewidth* if there is a fixed $k \in \mathbb{N}$ so that for every pattern π in the class, the treewidth of its underlying graph G_π is at most k.

We saw that label variables and regular expressions lead to intractable data complexity of query answering. We now show that bounded treewidth guarantees tractability for large classes of patterns with these features.

Theorem 9. *The data complexity of finding certain answers to CRPQs over classes of graph patterns of bounded treewidth in $\mathcal{P}^{\mathrm{nv,re}}$ and $\mathcal{P}^{\mathrm{nv,lv}}_{\mathrm{Codd}}$ is in* PTIME.

The Codd interpretation of label variables is essential, since without it the problem is already CONP-hard for treewidth 1 (see Theorem 4). For $\mathcal{P}^{\mathrm{re}}$ patterns, CONP-hardness results of Theorem 5 used classes of DAGs of unbounded treewidth.

7.2 Certain answers via constraint satisfaction

We now demonstrate the potential of using techniques from constraint satisfaction for answering queries over graph patterns, in the spirit of [9]. We shall consider patterns in $\mathcal{P}^{\mathrm{nv,lv}}$, for which data complexity is in CONP. Of course pure complexity-theoretic argument tells us that (the complement of) query answering can be cast as a constraint satisfaction problem; what we show here is that the translation for RPQs is very transparent, opening up the possibility of bringing the huge arsenal of tools from constraint satisfaction [16].

We adopt the standard view of the constraint satisfaction problem (CSP) as checking for the existence of a homomorphism from a relational structure $\mathcal{M}_1$ to another structure $\mathcal{M}_2$ of the same vocabulary [30], referring to this problem as $\mathrm{CSP}(\mathcal{M}_1, \mathcal{M}_2)$. Often this problem is considered with $\mathcal{M}_2$ fixed, in which case one refers to non-uniform CSP.

Consider a pattern $\pi = (N, E)$ in $\mathcal{P}^{\mathrm{nv,lv}}$, i.e., $E \subseteq N \times (\Sigma \cup \mathcal{W}) \times N$ for a finite set $\mathcal{W}$ of label variables. Let Q be an RPQ given by $Ans(x, y) \leftarrow (x, L, y)$, where $L \subseteq \Sigma^*$ is a regular language. We now define logical structures $\mathcal{M}_\pi(n, n')$ and $\mathcal{M}_Q$ over vocabulary

$$(Nodes, Expr, (Lab_a)_{a \in \Sigma}, Src, Sink, Edge),$$

where $Edge$ is a ternary relation and other relations are unary. Here n and n' are two node ids of π.

Structure $\mathcal{M}_\pi(n, n')$ The domain is the disjoint union of N, Σ, and $\mathcal{W}$, the set of label variables used in π. The interpretation of the predicates is as follows:

$$
\begin{aligned}
Nodes &:= N & Edge &:= E \\
Lab_a &:= \{a\} & Src &:= \{n\} \\
Expr &:= \mathcal{W} & Sink &:= \{n'\}
\end{aligned}
$$

Structure $\mathcal{M}_Q$ Assume that L is recognized by an NFA $(S, \Sigma, q_0, F, \delta)$ with $\delta : S \times \Sigma \to 2^S$ (extended, as usual, to a transition function on sets $\delta(S', a) = \bigcup_{s \in S'} \delta(s, a)$). The domain of $\mathcal{M}_Q$ is the disjoint union of 2^S and Σ. The interpretation of the predicates is:

$$
\begin{aligned}
Nodes &:= 2^S & Edge &:= \{(S', a, S'') \in 2^S \times \Sigma \times 2^S \mid \\
& & & \quad \delta(S', a) \subseteq S''\} \\
Lab_a &:= \{a\} & Src &:= \{S' \in 2^S \mid q_0 \in S'\} \\
Expr &:= \Sigma & Sink &:= 2^{S-F}
\end{aligned}
$$

Theorem 10. *For patterns $\pi \in \mathcal{P}^{\mathrm{nv,lv}}$, under the above translations, $(n, n') \in \mathrm{certain}(Q, \pi)$ iff there is no solution to $\mathrm{CSP}(\mathcal{M}_\pi(n, n'), \mathcal{M}_Q)$.*

Many algorithmic techniques for constraint satisfaction for $\mathrm{CSP}(\mathcal{M}_1, \mathcal{M}_2)$ are based on exploiting properties of the structure $\mathcal{M}_1$, so the extremely simple construction of $\mathcal{M}_\pi(n, n')$ indeed opens up the possibility of using a large body of heuristics developed in that area.

The case of data complexity corresponds to the non-uniform version of CSP, with $\mathcal{M}_Q$ fixed. In that case one can immediately conclude (using known results on CSP [16, 30]) that if we have a class of patterns $\pi \in \mathcal{P}^{\mathrm{nv,lv}}$ which, when viewed as ternary relations E, has bounded treewidth, then the data complexity of RPQs over such a class is in PTIME (note that this is incompatible with Theorem 9 which gives a PTIME result for a larger class of queries, but under the restriction of the Codd interpretation of label variables).

An analog of Theorem 10 for patterns in $\mathcal{P}^{\mathrm{nv,re}}$ was shown in [9]. Combining both techniques we can extend the result to all patterns in $\mathcal{P}^{\mathrm{nv,lv,re}}$, but at the cost of much more complex definitions of the structures $\mathcal{M}_\pi(n, n')$ and $\mathcal{M}_Q$ compared to those we used here. We shall discuss this in the full version of the paper.

8. CONCLUSIONS

We studied structural properties and querying of graph patters. We looked at three main features of patterns: node variables, label variables, and regular expressions specifying paths. We showed that each of these features strictly increases the expressiveness of patters. We looked at data and combined complexity of answering CRPQs and other queries (both extensions and restrictions of CRPQs). We developed a model of automata that capture query answering, both for returning nodes and paths, and studied their properties. Finally, we identified tractable restrictions, as well as classes of reasonable combined complexity for which query answering is naturally viewed as a constraint satisfaction property.

The main conclusion is that, without carefully chosen restrictions, querying graph patterns is computationally harder than querying relational or XML patterns. In particular, this has implications for ongoing work on defining schema mappings as well as integration and exchange techniques for graph-structured data. However, we can identify rather robust classes with either tractable query answering, or for which one can hope to find good heuristics by using techniques from other fields. Developing such techniques is a natural continuation of this work. Another line for further work is to study tractable restrictions for integrating and exchanging graph data.

Acknowledgments We thank Wenfei Fan and Peter Wood for their comments. Partial support provided by Fondecyt grant 1110171, EPSRC grant G049165 and FET-Open Project FoX, grant agreement 233599. Part of this work was done when the first author visited Edinburgh, and the second and the third author visited Santiago.

9. References

[1] S. Abiteboul, P. Buneman, D. Suciu. *Data on the Web: From Relations to Semistructured Data and XML*. Morgan Kauffman, 1999.

[2] R. Angles, C. Gutiérrez. Survey of graph database models. *ACM Comput. Surv.* 40(1): (2008).

[3] M. Arenas, P. Barceló, L. Libkin, F. Murlak. *Relational and XML Data Exchange*. Morgan & Claypool, 2010.

[4] P. Barceló, L. Libkin, A. Poggi, C. Sirangelo. XML with incomplete information. *J. ACM* 58(1): 1–62 (2010).

[5] P. Barceló, C. Hurtado, L. Libkin, P. Wood. Expressive languages for path queries over graph-structured data. In *PODS*, pages 3-14, 2010.

[6] H. Björklund, W. Martens, and T. Schwentick. Conjunctive query containment over trees. In *DBPL'07*, pages 66–80.

[7] D. Calvanese, G. de Giacomo, M. Lenzerini, M. Y. Vardi. Containment of conjunctive regular path queries with inverse. In *KR'00*, pages 176–185.

[8] D. Calvanese, G. de Giacomo, M. Lenzerini, M. Y. Vardi. Answering regular path queries using views. In *ICDE*, pages 389-398, 2000.

[9] D. Calvanese, G. de Giacomo, M. Lenzerini, M. Y. Vardi. View-based query processing and constraint satisfaction. In *LICS*, pages 361-371, 2000.

[10] D. Calvanese, G. de Giacomo, M. Lenzerini, M. Y. Vardi. Rewriting of regular expressions and regular path queries. *JCSS*, 64(3):443–465, 2002.

[11] D. Calvanese, G. de Giacomo, M. Lenzerini, M. Y. Vardi. Simplifying schema mappings. In *ICDT 2011*, to appear.

[12] J. Cheng, J. X. Yu, B. Ding, P. S. Yu, and H. Wang. Fast graph pattern matching. In *ICDE 2008*, pages 913–922.

[13] S. Cohen and Y. Sagiv. An abstract framework for generating maximal answers to queries. In *ICDT 2005*, pages 129–143.

[14] M. P. Consens, A. O. Mendelzon. GraphLog: a visual formalism for real life recursion. In *PODS'90*, pages 404–416.

[15] I. Cruz, A. Mendelzon, P. Wood. A graphical query language supporting recursion. In *SIGMOD'87*, pages 323-330.

[16] R. Dechter. *Constraint Processing*. Morgan Kaufmann, 2003.

[17] A. Deutsch, V. Tannen. Optimization properties for classes of conjunctive regular path queries. *DBPL'01*, pages 21–39.

[18] R. Diestel. *Graph Theory*. Springer, 2005.

[19] R. Fagin, Ph. Kolaitis, R. Miller, and L. Popa. Data exchange: semantics and query answering. *TCS*, 336(1):89–124, 2005.

[20] W. Fan, J. Li, S. Ma, H. Wang, Y. Wu. Homomorphism revisited for graph matching. *PVLDB* 3(1): 1161-1172 (2010).

[21] W. Fan, J. Li, S. Ma, N. Tang, Y. Wu. Graph pattern matching: from intractable to polynomial time. *PVLDB* 3(1): 264-275 (2010).

[22] W. Fan, J. Li, S. Ma, N. Tang, Y. Wu. Adding regular expressions to graph reachability and pattern queries. In *ICDE 2011*, to appear.

[23] I. Glaister, J. Shallit. A lower bound technique for the size of nondeterministic finite automata. *IPL* 59:75-77, 1996.

[24] G. Gottlob, C. Koch, K. Schulz. Conjunctive queries over trees. *J. ACM* 53(2) (2006), 238-272.

[25] C. Gutierrez, C. Hurtado, A. Mendelzon. Foundations of semantic web databases. In *PODS 2004*, pages 95–106.

[26] M. Gyssens, J. Paredaens, J. Van den Bussche, D. Van Gucht. A graph-oriented object database model. *IEEE TKDE* 6(4) (1994), 572–586.

[27] T. Imielinski, W. Lipski. Incomplete information in relational databases. *J. ACM* 31 (1984), 761–791.

[28] D. Johnson, A. Klug. Testing containment of conjunctive queries under functional and inclusion dependencies. *JCSS*, 28(1) (1984), pages 167-189.

[29] Y. Kanza, W. Nutt, Y. Sagiv. Querying incomplete information in semistructured data. *JCSS* 64 (3) (2002), 655–693.

[30] P. Kolaitis and M. Vardi. A logical approach to constraint satisfaction. In *Finite Model Theory and Its Applications*, Springer 2007, pages 339–370.

[31] M. Lenzerini. Data integration: a theoretical perspective. In *PODS'02*, pages 233–246.

[32] U. Leser. A query language for biological networks. *Bioinformatics* 21 (suppl 2) (2005), ii33–ii39.

[33] R. Milo, S. Shen-Orr, S. Itzkovitz, N. Kashtan, D. Chklovskii, U. Alon. Network motifs: simple building blocks of complex networks. *Science* 298(5594) (2002), 824–827.

[34] M. Natarajan. Understanding the structure of a drug trafficking organization: a conversational analysis. *Crime Prevention Studies* 11 (2000), 273–298.

[35] F. Olken. Graph data management for molecular biology. *OMICS* 7(1): 75-78 (2003).

[36] J. Pérez, M. Arenas, C. Gutierrez. Semantics and complexity of SPARQL. *ACM TODS* 34(3): 2009.

[37] R. Ronen and O. Shmueli. SoQL: a language for querying and creating data in social networks. In *ICDE 2009*.

[38] M. San Martín, C. Gutierrez. Representing, querying and transforming social networks with RDF/SPARQL. In *ESWC 2009*, pages 293–307.

[39] H. Tong, C. Faloutsos, B. Gallagher, and T. Eliassi-Rad. Fast best-effort pattern matching in large attributed graphs. In *KDD 2007*.

[40] G. Weikum, G. Kasneci, M. Ramanath, F. Suchanek. Database and information-retrieval methods for knowledge discovery. *CACM* 52(4):56-64 (2009).

Determining Relevance of Accesses at Runtime

Michael Benedikt
Computing Laboratory
Oxford University
Oxford OX1 3QD, UK
michael.benedikt@comlab.ox.ac.uk

Georg Gottlob
Computing Laboratory
& Oxford Man Institute
Oxford University
georg.gottlob@comlab.ox.ac.uk

Pierre Senellart
Institut Télécom; Télécom ParisTech
CNRS LTCI, 46 rue Barrault
75634 Paris, France
pierre.senellart@telecom-paristech.fr

ABSTRACT

Consider the situation where a query is to be answered using Web sources that restrict the accesses that can be made on backend relational data by requiring some attributes to be given as input of the service. The accesses provide lookups on the collection of attributes values that match the binding. They can differ in whether or not they require arguments to be generated from prior accesses. Prior work has focused on the question of whether a query can be answered using a set of data sources, and in developing static access plans (e.g., Datalog programs) that implement query answering. We are interested in dynamic aspects of the query answering problem: given partial information about the data, which accesses could provide relevant data for answering a given query? We consider immediate and long-term notions of "relevant accesses", and ascertain the complexity of query relevance, for both conjunctive queries and arbitrary positive queries. In the process, we relate dynamic relevance of an access to query containment under access limitations and characterize the complexity of this problem; we produce several complexity results about containment that are of interest by themselves.

Categories and Subject Descriptors

H.2.3 [**Database Management**]: Logical Design, Languages—*data models, query languages*; F.2.0 [**Analysis of Algorithms and Problem Complexity**]: General

General Terms

Algorithms, Theory

Keywords

Access patterns, binding patterns, deep Web, relevance

1. INTRODUCTION

Relevance under access limitations. A large part of the information on the World Wide Web is not available through

the *surface Web*, the set of Web pages reachable by following hyperlinks, but lies in the *deep Web* (or *hidden Web*), that provides entry points to databases accessible via HTML forms or Web services. Hundreds of thousands of such deep-Web sources exist [16]. Even when the information is available on the surface Web, it can be more effective to access it through a (possibly elaborate) Web form query. Each source of the deep Web has one or several interfaces that limit the kind of accesses that can be performed, e.g., some fields of the forms have to be filled in before submission.

A number of works, e.g. [25, 13], have dealt with the problems of answering queries using views in the presence of such access restrictions but the focus is usually on obtaining a static query plan (e.g., a rewriting of an original conjunctive query, or a Datalog program). We consider a dynamic approach to query answering and study the following problem: given some existing knowledge about the data, knowledge that is bound to evolve as we access sources, is making this particular access relevant to a query? In other words, can this particular access give, immediately or after some other accesses, some knowledge that will yield an answer to the query?

Let us consider the following example. A user wishes to get information about the loan capabilities of a large bank. A relation schema for this can be visualized as:

```
Employee(EmpId, Title, LastName, FirstName, OffId)
Office(OffId, StreetAddress, State, Phone)
Approval(State, Offering)
Manager(EmpId, EmpId)
```

`Employee` stores information about employees, including their title and office. `Office` stores information about offices, including the state in which they are located. `Approval` tells which kinds of loans a bank is approved to make in each state, while `Manager` stores which employee manages which other employee.

Data from a number of distinct Web data sources (or distinct query interfaces from the same source) can be used to answer the query:

- a form `EmpOffAcc` where an `EmpId` can be entered, which returns office records for that employee;
- a form `EmpManAcc` where an `EmpId` can be entered, and the identifiers of their managers are returned;
- a form `OfficeInfoAcc` that allows one to enter an `OffId`, and returns all the office information;
- a form `StateApprAcc` that allows one to enter a state, and returns the approval information for that state.

A user wishes to know if there is some loan officer for their bank located in Illinois, and also whether the company is authorized to perform 30-year mortgages in Illinois. This can be phrased as a Boolean query Q, expressible in SQL as follows:

```
SELECT DISTINCT 1
FROM Employee E, Office O, Approval A
WHERE E.Title='loan officer' AND E.OffId=O.OffId
   AND O.State='Illinois'    AND A.State='Illinois'
   AND A.Offering='30yr'
```

A federated query engine that tries to answer this query will require querying the distinct interfaces with concrete values. At a certain stage the query engine may know about a particular set of employee names, and also know certain facts – either via querying or via an additional knowledge base. Which interfaces should it use to answer the query? In particular: Is an access to the EmpManAcc form with EmpId "12345" useful for answering Q? There are actually a number of subtleties in this question, that we discuss now.

The relevance of an access depends on the existing knowledge base. At the beginning of the process, when no other information is known about the data, the access might be useful to get some other EmpId which may in turn be used in the EmpOffAcc interface to find an Illinoisan loan officer. But if we already know that the company has a loan officer located in Illinois, then clearly such an access is unnecessary. We call this existing knowledge base the *configuration* in which the access is made.

The relevance depends on how closely linked the Web forms are. Clearly the interface is irrelevant to the query if the query engine is free to enter EmpId values "at random" into the EmpOffAcc interface. But if such values are widely dispersed and there is no way to guess them, an efficient tactic might be to take EmpId's that we know about, query for their managers using the EmpManAcc interface, and then use the resulting offices in the OfficeInfoAcc interface. In this work we will thus distinguish between accesses that require a value that is already in the knowledge base of the engine (*dependent* accesses), from those that allow a "free guess". Note that in the case of *static* query answering plans, the notion of a "free access" trivializes the questions.

The relevance depends on whether one is interested in immediate or long-term impact. Without any initial knowledge, there is no way an access to EmpOffAcc may directly provide a witness for the query. On the other hand, as discussed above, the result to an access may be used in some cases to gain some information that will ultimately satisfy the query. In this work, we consider both *immediate relevance* and *long-term relevance* of a particular access.

Main questions studied. In this article, we are interested in the following problems:

(i) How to define a model for querying under access restrictions that takes into account the history of accesses?

(ii) What is the complexity of relevance?

(iii) Calì and Martinenghi have studied in [5] the complexity of *containment under access constraints*, motivated by query optimization. How does relevance relate to containment? Are these notions at all related, and if so, can the respective decision problems be transformed into one another?

(iv) What is the complexity of containment under access constraints?

(v) If problems are hard, can we identify the source of this complexity?

One particular reason why these problems are challenging is that they do not deal with a concrete database, but a virtual database of which we have a partial view, a view that evolves as we access it. The notion of relevance of accesses has not been investigated in the literature; the closest work, on containment under access constraints [5], only provides an upper bound of coNEXPTIME, for a restricted query language (conjunctive queries, with only limited use of constants). Determining a lower bound for containment was left as an open problem. Hardness results are difficult to obtain, because the access model that we present is quite simple and does not offer obvious clues of how to encode known hard problems to get lower bounds.

Results. We emphasize the following contributions of our work.

We provide the first formal definition of dynamic relevance of accesses for a query Q, using a simple and powerful model, answering thus item (i).

We give a combined complexity characterization of the relevance problem in all combinations of cases (immediate or long-term relevance, independent or dependent accesses, conjunctive or positive queries), inside the polynomial and exponential hierarchy of complexity classes; for long-term relevance, we mostly focus on accesses without any input, extension to arbitrary accesses is left for future work. This gives a satisfactory answer to question (ii). For several of our hardness results, we invented sophisticated coding techniques to enforce database accesses to produce grids that would then allow us to encode tiling problems. One particular hurdle to overcome was the limited "coding power" of conjunctive queries. We therefore had to use and extend techniques for encoding disjunctions into a conjunctive query.

We exhibit reductions in both directions between dynamic relevance and containment under access constraints. By these results, we succeed in elucidating the relationship between containment and long term relevance, thus providing an exhaustive answer to item (iii).

We generalize the coNEXPTIME upper bound to a stronger notion of containment, and provide a matching lower bound, solving thus item (iv). This coNEXPTIME upper bound for containment, and the associated NEXPTIME upper bound for relevance are rather surprising and not at all obvious. In fact, the more immediate upper bounds, that we show for positive queries, are co2NEXPTIME and 2NEXPTIME, respectively.

We highlight specific cases of interest where the complexity of relevance is lower, e.g., conjunctive queries with a single occurrence of a relation, or conjunctive queries with small arity. We also show that all problems are polynomial-time in data complexity (for the independent case, AC^0), suggesting the feasibility of the relevance analysis. These two points together bring a first answer to item (v).

A summary of complexity results is shown in Table 1.

Organization. We start with formal definitions of the problem and the various degrees of relevance of a query to an access in Section 2. We next establish (Section 3) the connection between relevance and the topic of containment that was studied in [5]. In Section 4, we study the case of independent accesses (accesses that do not require the input

Table 1: Summary of combined complexity results

	Immediate relevance	Long-term relevance (Boolean access)	Containment
Independent accesses (CQs)	DP-complete	Σ_2^P-complete	Π_2^P-complete
Independent accesses (PQs)	DP-complete	Σ_2^P-complete	Π_2^P-complete
Dependent accesses (CQs)	DP-complete	NEXPTIME-complete	coNEXPTIME-complete
Dependent accesses (PQs)	DP-complete	2NEXPTIME-complete	co2NEXPTIME-complete

value having been generated by a previous access). Here the access patterns play quite a small role, but relevance is still a non-trivial notion – the issues revolve around reasoning about a very restricted form of query containment. In Section 5 we turn to dependent accesses, where the notion of containment is of primary interest. We extend techniques of [5] to isolate the complexity of containment under access patterns for both conjunctive queries and positive queries; in the process we give the complexity of relevance for both these classes. Related work is discussed in Section 6. Due to space constraints, many proofs are omitted; they can be found in the full paper [3], together with the study of the specific case of relations of small arity, where the complexity of relevance is lower.

2. PRELIMINARIES

We use bold face (e.g., $\mathbf{a}$) to denote sets of attributes or tuples of constants.

Modeling data sources. We have a schema Sch consisting of a set of relations Tables(Sch) = $\{S_1 \ldots S_n\}$, each S_i having a set of attributes ATT(S_i). Following [19, 5], we assume each attribute a_{ij} of relation S_i has an *abstract domain* Dom(a_{ij}) chosen in some countable set of abstract domains. Two attributes may share the same domain and different domains may overlap. In the dependent case, domains are used to constrain some input values to come from constants of the appropriate type.

Given a source instance I for Sch, a *configuration for* I, (with respect to Sch, when not understood from context) is a subset Conf of I, that is, for each S_i, a subset Conf(S_i) of the tuples in I(S_i) (the content of relation S_i in I). By a *configuration* we mean any Conf that is a configuration for some instance I. We then say that a configuration Conf is *consistent* with I if Conf $\subseteq$ I. Note that a configuration will generally be consistent with many instances (in particular, the empty configuration is consistent with all instances).

We have a set of *access methods* ACS = { $\text{AcM}_1 \ldots \text{AcM}_m$ } with each AcM_i consisting of a source relation Rel(AcM_i) and a set InputAtt(AcM_i) of input attributes from the set of attributes of Rel(AcM_i); implicitly, each access method allows one to put in a tuple of values for InputAtt(AcM_i) and get as a result a set of matching tuples. If a relation does not have any access methods, no new facts can be learned about this relation: its content is fixed as that of the initial configuration.

Access methods are of two different varieties, based on the values that can be entered into them An access method may be either *dependent* or *independent*. In a dependent access, one can only use as an input bindings values that have appeared in the configuration in the appropriate domain. An independent access can make use of any value.

A combination of an access method and a binding to the input places of the accessed relation will be referred to as an *access*. We will often write an access by adding "?" to the non-input places, omitting the exact method: e.g. $R(3, ?)$ is an access (via some method) to R with the first place bound to 3. If R does not have any output attributes, we say that it is a *Boolean* access, and we write for instance $R(3)$? for an access that checks whether $3 \in R$. If R does not have any input attributes, we say that it is a *free* access. We do not assume access methods to be *exact*, i.e., to return all tuples that are compatible with the binding. They are only assumed to be *sound*, i.e., they can return any sound subset of the data, and possibly a different subset on each use.

Given a set of attributes $\mathbf{a}$ of a relation S_i, a database instance I, and a binding Bind of each attribute in $\mathbf{a}$ to a value from Dom($\mathbf{a}$), we let I(Bind, S_i) to be the set of tuples in I whose projection onto $\mathbf{a}$ agrees with Bind. For a configuration Conf, its *active domain* Adom(Conf) = $\{ (c, \mathcal{C}) \}$ is the set of constants that appear in a Conf(S_i) for some i, together with their abstract domains: for instance, if $(c, d) \in \text{Conf}(S)$ and Dom(ATT(S)) = $(\mathcal{C}, \mathcal{D})$, both $(c, \mathcal{C})$ and $(d, \mathcal{D})$ belong to Adom(Conf).

Given a configuration Conf, a *well-formed access* consists of an access method AcM and an assignment Bind of values to the attributes of InputAtt(AcM) such that either a) AcM is independent; or b) AcM is dependent and all values in Bind, together with corresponding domains of the input attributes, are in Adom(Conf). A well-formed access (AcM, Bind) at configuration Conf on instance I leads, possibly non-deterministically, to any new configuration Conf' in which:

(i) Conf(Rel(AcM)) $\subseteq$ Conf'(Rel(AcM));
(ii) Conf'(Rel(AcM) $\subseteq$ Conf(Rel(AcM)) $\cup$ I(Bind, Rel(AcM));
(iii) Conf(S_i) = Conf'(S_i) for all $S_i \neq$ Rel(AcM).

That is, the tuples seen in S_i = Rel(AcM) can increase by adding some tuples consistent with the access, the access (AcM, Bind) is now completed and every other access stays the same in terms of completion. Note that the new configuration is still consistent with the instance.

In general, there can be many successor configurations. We sometimes write Conf + (AcM, Bind, Resp) to denote an arbitrary such "response configuration".

A configuration Conf' is *reachable* from another configuration Conf (w.r.t. an instance) if there is some sequence of well-formed accesses that can lead from Conf to Conf'.

Queries. We will consider conjunctive queries (CQs), i.e., conjunctions of atomic facts, and positive existential queries, or just positive queries (PQs) for short, i.e., first-order formulas without universal quantifiers or negation. PQs have the inconvenient of being *unsafe* [2] query languages; however, as discussed at the end of this section, we focus on Boolean queries in this work, for which the problem does not occur. We recall some basic facts about the complexity of these languages: query evaluation over CQs or PQs is NP-complete in combined complexity (membership in NP holds for any existentially quantified first-order query, NP-hardness is a classical result [8]), while the data complexity of evaluating an arbitrary first-order query is AC^0 [2]. On the other hand, the query containment problem is NP-complete for CQs [8], but it is Π_2^p-complete for PQs [26]. We require that variables shared across subgoals of a query are consistent with domain restrictions: if the same variables x occur in attribute a of R and attribute a' of R' then $\mathsf{Dom}(a) = \mathsf{Dom}(a')$. The *output domain* of a query Q is the tuple of domains of the output variables of the query. We also assume that all constants appearing in the query are present in the configuration; in this way, constants from the query can be used in dependent accesses.

The fundamental question we ask in this work is: given a configuration Conf, which well-formed accesses for that configuration can contribute to answering the query Q?

Immediate relevance. We begin with analyzing whether a given access can have immediate impact on a query – whether the result of the access can impact the information we have about a query output.

We recall the notion of certain answers, which capture the notion of "information" precisely. Given a configuration Conf and a tuple $\mathbf{t}$ of constants from Conf with the same domain as the output domain of a query Q, we say that $\mathbf{t}$ is a *certain answer for Q at Conf* if for every instance I consistent with Conf we have $\mathbf{t} \in Q(\mathsf{I})$. If the query Q is Boolean (i.e., with no free variables), we say that it is certain (or simply true) in a configuration Conf if for every instance I consistent with Conf, $Q(\mathsf{I})$ is true.

We now consider the impact of a new well-formed access $(\mathsf{AcM}, \mathsf{Bind})$ on source S in a configuration Conf. The result of this is some new set of tuples Resp for S.

Let $\mathsf{Conf} + (\mathsf{AcM}, \mathsf{Bind}, \mathsf{Resp})$ be a response configuration for the access $(\mathsf{AcM}, \mathsf{Bind})$. We say the configuration (or even the response Resp, seen as a collection of tuples) is an *increasing response* for Q to $(\mathsf{AcM}, \mathsf{Bind})$ in Conf if there exists a tuple $\mathbf{t}$ such that $\mathbf{t}$ is not a certain answer for Q at Conf while $\mathbf{t}$ is a certain answer for Q at $\mathsf{Conf} + (\mathsf{AcM}, \mathsf{Bind}, \mathsf{Resp})$.

An access $(\mathsf{AcM}, \mathsf{Bind})$ is *immediately relevant* for the query Q (IR in short) in a configuration Conf if there is some increasing response to the access.

Long-term impact. We formalize the notion of an access that can *eventually* yield information.

Given an access $(\mathsf{AcM}, \mathsf{Bind})$, a *path* from $(\mathsf{AcM}, \mathsf{Bind})$ starting from configuration Conf on database instance I is a sequence of configurations and accesses

$$\mathsf{Conf}_1, (\mathsf{AcM}_1, \mathsf{Bind}_1), \dots, (\mathsf{AcM}_{n-1}, \mathsf{Bind}_{n-1}), \mathsf{Conf}_n$$

where $\mathsf{Conf}_1 = \mathsf{Conf}$, $(\mathsf{AcM}_1, \mathsf{Bind}_1) = (\mathsf{AcM}, \mathsf{Bind})$, and Conf_{i+1} is a successor configuration for access $(\mathsf{AcM}_i, \mathsf{Bind}_i)$ on Conf_i.

By "the certain answers to Q after p" we mean the certain answers to Q on Conf_n, where p terminates in configuration Conf_n.

Given a path p, the *truncated path* of p is the maximal subpath

$$\mathsf{Conf}_1, (\mathsf{AcM}_2, \mathsf{Bind}_2), \mathsf{Conf}_2', \dots, (\mathsf{AcM}_i, \mathsf{Bind}_i), \mathsf{Conf}_i'$$

such that each $(\mathsf{AcM}_j, \mathsf{Bind}_j) : 2 \leqslant j \leqslant i$ is a well-formed access at Conf_{j-1}' (with $\mathsf{Conf}_1' = \mathsf{Conf}_1$). That is, we eliminate the initial access in p, and then find the longest subpath of p that did not depend on this initial access.

We say that an access $(\mathsf{AcM}, \mathsf{Bind})$ is *long-term relevant* (LTR) *for Q at configuration Conf* if for some instance I consistent with Conf, for some path p beginning with $(\mathsf{AcM}, \mathsf{Bind})$ the certain answers to Q at p are different from those at the truncated path of p.

EXAMPLE 2.1. Suppose that we have a schema with relations S, T, and a query $Q = S \bowtie T$. Suppose we have a configuration Conf in which S and T have not yet been accessed, and there is a dependent access method on T. Now consider an access $(\mathsf{AcM}, \mathsf{Bind})$ on S. It is long-term relevant for Q, since it is possible that $(\mathsf{AcM}, \mathsf{Bind})$ returns some new values, and using these values to access T could yield some new tuples for Q. $\square$

When we speak about the problem of "determining whether an access is relevant", we mean either of the problems IR or LTR.

The complexity of relevance. We make a few general observations about the complexity of determining if an access is relevant for a query.

First, we observe that there is a tight relation between the general question of relevance and the special case of Boolean queries. For a number k, let $\mathsf{IR}(k)$ be the problem of determining whether an access in a given configuration is immediately relevant for a query with output arity k, relative to a schema, and similarly for LTR. Let $\mathbf{c}_k$ be a tuple of k new constant symbols. For any fixed k we can solve $\mathsf{IR}(k)$ by considering every tuple of items that come either from the configuration or from $\mathbf{c}_k$ substituting them in for the head of the query and then determining whether the access is IR on the configuration for the Boolean query thus created. This shows:

PROPOSITION 2.2. *Let k be any number. There is a polynomial time reduction from $\mathsf{IR}(k)$ to $\mathsf{IR}(0)$, and from $\mathsf{LTR}(k)$ to $\mathsf{LTR}(0)$.*

We will thus focus on the Boolean case $k = 0$ in this work.

Second, note that checking that an access is relevant, for any of the notion of relevance we have defined, requires that we know that the query is not already satisfied in the configuration, which is coNP-hard.

3. RELEVANCE AND CONTAINMENT

In this section, we introduce the notion of *containment of queries under access limitations* and show how it is strongly related to long-term relevance. We will use this connection to ascertain the complexity of relevance in some cases.

Containment under access limitations. Query containment under access limitations was shown to be decidable by Li and Chang [20], and further investigated by Calì and Martinenghi in [5]. We adapt here the definition to our setting, and show further in Proposition 3.6 that the definition of [5] is essentially a special case of ours. We give the definition for queries of arbitrary arity, but as we explained we will focus on the Boolean case further on.

DEFINITION 3.1. Let Sch be a schema and ACS a set of access methods over Sch. Let Q_1 and Q_2 be two queries defined over ACS and Conf a configuration over Sch. We assume Q_1 and Q_2 have the same arity. We say that Q_1 is contained in Q_2 under ACS starting from Conf, denoted $Q_1 \sqsubseteq_{\mathsf{ACS},\mathsf{Conf}} Q_2$, if for every configuration Conf' reachable from Conf, $Q_1(\mathsf{Conf'}) \subseteq Q_2(\mathsf{Conf'})$. We simply say that Q_1 is contained in Q_2 under ACS and note $Q_1 \sqsubseteq_{\mathsf{ACS}} Q_2$ if Conf is the empty configuration. □

As noted in [5], in the presence of dependent accesses, the notion of query containment under access limitations is strictly weaker than the usual notion of query containment:

EXAMPLE 3.2. Let R and S be two unary relations with the same domain, each one with a single dependent access method: Boolean for R, and free for S. Consider queries $Q_1 = \exists x\, R(x)$ and $Q_2 = \exists x\, S(x)$. Starting from the empty configuration, the only well-formed access paths that make Q_1 true, i.e., produce an $R(x)$ atom, must first access S and produce $S(x)$. This means that $Q_1 \sqsubseteq_{\mathsf{ACS}} Q_2$ while, obviously, $Q_1 \not\sqsubseteq Q_2$. □

More generally, many classical results that hold for the classical notion of query containment are not true any more in the presence of access constraints: for instance, query containment of conjunctive queries cannot be tested by the existence of a homomorphism, and query containment of unions of conjunctive queries does not mean that all disjuncts of the first query are contained in some disjunct of the second query, as is true without access constraints [26].

Relating containment to relevance. Query containment under access limitations is of interest in its own right, but also for the connection to long-term relevance. We begin by showing that containment under access limitations can be reduced to the complement of long-term relevance.

PROPOSITION 3.3. *There is a polynomial-time many-one reduction from the problem of query containment of Boolean CQs (resp., PQs) under access limitations, starting from a given configuration, to determining whether an access is* not *long-term relevant to a Boolean CQ (resp., PQ), in another configuration. If the query is a PQ, the configuration can be chosen to be the same.*

PROOF. We give an overview of the main idea, details are in [3]. For positive queries, the proof works by "coding two queries as one disjunction" – we create a query $\tau(Q, Q')$ and access such that if the access returns successfully, then the query is equivalent to Q, and otherwise to Q'. Disjunction can be eliminated by the idea of "coding Boolean operations in relations", which will be used often in this paper. □

We can thus prove lower bounds for relevance using lower bounds for containment. As an example, query containment under access limitations obviously covers the classical notion of query containment (just make all access methods free). This immediately entails that long-term relevance is coNP-hard for CQs and Σ_2^{P}-hard for PQs, even if all variables are from the same abstract domain. Conjunctive query containment in the presence of datatype restrictions and fixed relations is Π_2^{P}-hard (this follows from [26]) and hence containment under access in our setting is Π_2^{P}-hard. We will show that this latter lower bound actually already holds for conjunctive queries even in very restricted settings (cf. Proposition 4.5).

In the other direction, from relevance to containment, we also have a polynomial-time many-one reduction, but only for positive queries and only for Boolean accesses.

PROPOSITION 3.4. *There is a polynomial-time many-one reduction from the problem of long-term relevance of a Boolean access for a Boolean positive query in a given configuration, to the* complement *of query containment of Boolean positive queries under access limitations, starting from another configuration.*

PROOF. We assume given a schema Sch and a set of access methods ACS. Let Conf and Q be, respectively, a configuration and a positive query over Sch. We consider an access $(\mathsf{AcM}, \mathsf{Bind})$ with $\mathsf{AcM} \in \mathsf{ACS}$. Let $R = \mathsf{Rel}(\mathsf{AcM})$. To simplify the presentation we assume that input attributes of AcM come before output attributes.

We add to Sch a relation $IsBind$ with same arity k and domain as Bind, without any access. We add to Conf the single fact $IsBind(\mathsf{Bind})$ and let Conf' denote the new configuration. We rewrite Q as Q' by replacing every occurrence of $R(i_1 \ldots i_k, o_1 \ldots o_p)$ with

$$R(i_1 \ldots i_k, o_1 \ldots o_p) \vee IsBind(i_1 \ldots i_k).$$

Then $(\mathsf{AcM}, \mathsf{Bind})$ is LTR for Q in Conf if and only if $Q' \not\sqsubseteq_{\mathsf{ACS},\mathsf{Conf'}} Q$.

Assume $(\mathsf{AcM}, \mathsf{Bind})$ is LTR for Q in Conf. There is a well-formed path p starting with the access, with truncated path p', such that Q is true in $\mathsf{Conf} + p$ and false in $\mathsf{Conf} + p'$ (and, since $IsBind$ does not occur in Q, also false in $\mathsf{Conf'} + p'$). For every subgoal $R(i_1 \ldots i_k, o_1 \ldots o_p)$ of Q that is witnessed by the first access of p, $IsBind(i_1 \ldots i_k)$ is true in Conf' and thus a witness that Q is true in $\mathsf{Conf} + p$ yields a witness that Q' is true in $\mathsf{Conf'} + p'$.

Conversely, assume there is a path p' such that Q' is true and Q is false in $\mathsf{Conf'} + p'$. For every $R(i_1 \ldots i_k, o_1 \ldots o_p)$ that is false in Q while the corresponding disjunction is true in Q', we construct a ground fact $R(\mathsf{Bind}, c_1 \ldots c_p)$ where $(c_1 \ldots c_p)$ are the constants that $(o_1 \ldots o_p)$ are mapped to in a witness of Q'. Then we build a new path p by prepending to p' all these ground facts, returned by $(\mathsf{AcM}, \mathsf{Bind})$. The path p witnesses that $(\mathsf{AcM}, \mathsf{Bind})$ is LTR for Q in Conf. □

Finally, for conjunctive queries, we prove similarly a different form of reduction, a Turing reduction in nondeterministic polynomial time:

PROPOSITION 3.5. *Long-term relevance of a Boolean access for a CQ can be decided with a nondeterministic polynomial-time algorithm with access to an oracle for query containment of CQs under access limitations.*

Both reductions will be used to show that upper bound results can be lifted from containment to relevance. Even though the latter reduction seems weak, it will be enough for our purpose (see Section 5).

Containment and containment. Our notion of query containment under access limitations starting from a given configuration differs in some ways from the notion introduced by Calì and Martinenghi in [5]. In this part of the paper, to emphasize the distinction, we refer to the former as *config-containment* and to the latter as *CM-containment*. The differences are as follows: (i) In CM-containment, there is always exactly one access method per regular relation, whereas in config-containment there may be zero or several access methods per relations; (ii) CM-containment is defined with respect to a set of existing constants (of the various abstract domains) that can be used in access paths, while config-containment, as its name implies, uses a more general notion of pre-existing configuration, with constants as well as ground facts; (iii) Access methods in CM-containment are always exact, they return the complete collection of facts compatible with the binding that are present in the database instance; we do not make such an assumption for config-containment and merely assume accesses are sound; (iv) In addition to regular relations, CM-containment also supports *artificial relations* which are unary (monadic) relations "whose content is accessible and amounts only to" some constant value. To the best of our understanding, they correspond in our setting to relations without any access methods, except that config-containment allows them to have arbitrary arity. It would be interesting to see if the result of this paper (and of [5]) can be extended to the case where all relations have an access method.

Among these four, the significant difference is the forbidding of multiple accesses per relation, which means CM-containment is a special case of config-containment:

PROPOSITION 3.6. *There are polynomial-time reductions in both directions between CM-containment and the special case of config-containment when relations have at most one access method and relations without an access method have arity bounded by a constant K. The query language (CQs, PQs) is preserved by the reductions.*

PROOF. The argument from CM-containment to config-containment is simple, since config-containment allows a richer initial condition.

The reduction the other way requires us to code the configuration in the contained query. □

As can be verified, all hardness proofs for containment that we present in this paper make use of no relation with multiple access methods, and the arity the relations with no accesses is bounded by 3. This means all lower bounds for config-containment obtained in this paper yield identical lower bounds for CM-containment.

Calì and Martinenghi give in [5] a proof that the CM-containment problem is decidable in coNEXPTIME for conjunctive queries, without any lower bound. We give in Section 5 the same upper bound of coNEXPTIME for config-containment, as well as a matching lower bound.

By having the possibility of several access methods per relation, and of some fixed base knowledge given by relations without accesses, we allow modeling of a more realistic setting, where multiple sources of the deep Web may share the same schema, and where we want to ask queries over these sources as well as over some fully accessible local knowledge.

4. INDEPENDENT ACCESSES

We establish in this section complexity bounds for the problem of determining whether an access is relevant to a query, when all access methods are *independent*. Our upper bounds will be fairly immediate – the main work involved is in the lower bounds.

In the case of independent accesses, we have some immediate facts: (i) An access to a relation that is not mentioned in the query can not be relevant in either of our senses. (ii) A path witnessing the fact that an access is long-term relevant can always be pruned to include only subgoals of the query, with each subgoal occurring at most once. This gives a bound of Σ_2^P in combined complexity for checking long-term relevance, since checking that the truncation of the path does not satisfy the query is in coNP for the considered query languages. (iii) Since constants can be guessed at will, abstract domain constraints do not have any impact on relevance for independent accesses and we can assume all attributes to share the same domain.

We study the complexity of whether an access is relevant, for immediate and long-term relevance.

Immediate relevance. The following result characterizes the combined and data complexity of IR for independent access methods.

PROPOSITION 4.1. *We assume all access methods to be independent. Given a Boolean positive query Q, configuration Conf, and access (AcM, Bind), determining whether (AcM, Bind) is immediately relevant for the query Q in Conf is a DP-complete problem. If we know the query is not certain in Conf, then the problem is NP-complete. Lower bounds hold even if the query is conjunctive.*

If the query is fixed, the problem is in AC^0.

PROOF. Membership in DP works via guessing a witness configuration and verifying it. One can show that the witness need not be large, and verifying it requires checking a conjunctive query and a negation of a conjunctive query.

Hardness uses a coding of satisfiable/unsatisfiable pairs of queries. □

Long-term relevance. We now move to LTR for independent methods.

EXAMPLE 4.2. Consider $Q = R(x, 5) \land S(5, z)$, a configuration in which only $R(3, 5)$ holds, and an access method to R on the second component. Clearly, an access $R(?, 5)$ is not long-term relevant, since any witness x discovered in the response to this access could be replaced by 3. On the other hand, if the configuration had $R(3, 6)$ then an access $R(?, 5)$ would be long-term relevant. □

Let us first consider a simple case: that of conjunctive queries where the accessed relation only occurs once. In this particular case, it is possible to decide LTR by checking whether the subgoal containing the accessed relation is not in a connected component of the query that is already certain.

More formally, let $R = \text{Rel}(\text{AcM})$. Let h be the (necessarily unique) partial mapping substituting the binding for the corresponding elements of the subgoal of the conjunctive query Q containing R, and Q_h be the query obtained by applying h to the variables of Q. If no such h exists (since the subgoal conflicts with the binding), then clearly the access is not LTR. Otherwise, let $G(Q_h)$ be the graph whose vertices are the subgoals of Q_h with an edge between subgoals if and only if they share a variable in Q_h. Let $Q_h - Sat(\text{Conf})$ be the query obtained from Q_h by removing any subgoal that lies in a component of $G(Q_h)$ that is satisfied in Conf. If $Q_h - Sat(\text{Conf})$ contains the R subgoal, we return true, otherwise we return false.

If this algorithm returns true, then let g be the subgoal containing R, h the homomorphism, and C be the component of g in $G(Q_h)$. If C contains only g, then clearly the access is long-term relevant, since we can consider any path that begins with the access and then continues through every subgoal. If C contains other subgoals, then there is some variable shared between g and other subgoals; again we take a path beginning at R, accessing each additional subgoal in turn (in an arbitrary order) and using new elements as inputs while returning elements not in Conf for all variables in the subgoals. Note that we do not have to access the other subgoals using the shared variables – we use an arbitrary access method for other relations (we know at least one exists), and choose a response such that the results match the subgoals. This witnesses that the access is LTR. Conversely, suppose R does not occur in $Q_h - Sat(\text{Conf})$ and that we have a path p witnessing that the access is long-term relevant. Let h' be a homomorphism from Q into the Conf $+ p$, and let h'' be formed from h' by replacing all elements in C by witnesses in Conf. The existence of h'' proves that the path is not a witness of the fact the access is LTR.

We have thus the following complexity result in this particular case of conjunctive queries with only one occurrence of the accessed relation (hardness is again shown via a coding argument).

PROPOSITION 4.3. *We assume all access methods to be independent. Given a Boolean conjunctive query Q, a configuration* Conf, *and an access* (AcM, Bind), *such that* Rel(AcM) *only occurs once in Q, determining whether* (AcM, Bind) *is long-term relevant for the query Q in* Conf *is a coNP-complete problem.*

In the case where a relation is repeated, however, simply looking at satisfied components is not sufficient.

EXAMPLE 4.4. Consider $Q = R(x, y) \wedge R(x, 5)$, an empty configuration, and an access to R with second component 3 (i.e., $R(?, 3)$). Clearly this access is not long-term relevant in the empty configuration, since in fact Q is equivalent to the existential closure of $R(x, 5)$, and the access can reveal nothing about such a query. But no subgoals are realized in the configuration. □

In the general case (repeated relations, positive queries), we can fall back on the Σ_2^P algorithm described at the beginning of the section. Surprisingly, this is the best we can do even in very limited situations:

PROPOSITION 4.5. *We assume all access methods to be independent. Given a Boolean positive query Q, a configuration* Conf, *and an access* (AcM, Bind), *determining whether* (AcM, Bind) *is long-term relevant for the query Q in* Conf *is Σ_2^P-complete. The lower bound holds even if Q is conjunctive and known not to be certain in* Conf, *and even if all relations are freely accessible and all variables have the same infinite datatype.*

If the query is fixed, the problem is AC^0.

PROOF. The lower bound follows from results of Miklau and Suciu [21]; we explain the connection to their notion of *criticality*, which is closely related to relevance. For a query Q on a single relation R and a finite domain D (i.e., a finite set of constants), a tuple $\mathbf{t}$ (with same arity as R) is *critical* for Q if there exists an instance I of R with values in D such that deleting $\mathbf{t}$ from I changes the value of Q.

THEOREM 4.6 (4.10 OF [21]). *The problem of deciding, for conjunctive query Q and set D whether a tuple $\mathbf{t}$ is not critical is Π_2^P-hard, even for fixed D and $\mathbf{t}$.*

It is easy to see that $\mathbf{t}$ is critical iff the Boolean access $R(\mathbf{t})$ is LTR in the empty configuration (or, more precisely,

in a configuration that only contains constants of the queries but no facts for R): this holds since LTR is easily seen to be equivalent to the existence of some instance of size at most $|Q|$ where adding the tuple given by the access changes the truth value of Q to true. Hence the theorem above shows that LTR is Σ_2^P-hard even for a fixed configuration.

The combined complexity upper bound has already been discussed. We now discuss data complexity. We can assume without loss of generality Q is in disjunctive normal form (i.e., a union of conjunctive queries). Let us present the Σ_2^P algorithm slightly differently. We make a guess for each subgoal G of Q of the following nondeterministic choices:

1. G is not witnessed;
2. G is witnessed by the configuration;
3. G is witnessed by the first access;
4. G is witnessed by a further access.

For such a guess h, we write $\mathcal{G}_1^h, \mathcal{G}_2^h, \mathcal{G}_3^h, \mathcal{G}_4^h$ the corresponding partition of the set of subgoals. We restrict valid guesses to those where (i) at least one of the disjuncts of Q has all its subgoals witnessed (i.e., in $\mathcal{G}_2^h \cup \mathcal{G}_3^h \cup \mathcal{G}_4^h$); (ii) all subgoals in $\mathcal{G}_3^h$ are compatible with (AcM, Bind) (if we want the access to also be part of the input, we can easily encode this condition into the constructed formula).

Let $\mathcal{H}$ be the set of all valid guesses (there is a fixed number of them once the query is fixed). For a given $h \in \mathcal{H}$, we rewrite Q into two queries Q'_h and Q''_h. Q'_h is obtained from Q by replacing every variable mapped to an input attribute of subgoals in $\mathcal{G}_h^3$ with the binding, by replacing every subgoal of $\mathcal{G}_4^h$ with *true*, and by dropping every disjunct of $\mathcal{H}$ that has a subgoal in $\mathcal{G}_1^h$. Q''_h is obtained from Q'_h by replacing every subgoal in $\mathcal{G}_3^h$ with *true*. Then (AcM, Bind) is LTR for Q in Conf if and only if the following first-order query evaluates to *true* on Conf: $\bigvee_{h \in \mathcal{H}} Q''_h \wedge \neg Q'_h$. This query is exponential in the size of Q. □

As shown, long-term relevance, even in the independent case and for the relatively simple language of conjunctive queries, is already at the second level of the polynomial hierarchy in combined complexity. Introducing dependent accesses will move the problem into the exponential hierarchy.

5. DEPENDENT ACCESSES

We now turn to the case when some of the accesses are dependent. The results for IR are clearly the same as in the independent case, since this only considers the impact of a single access. We thus only discuss long-term relevance.

In this abstract, we deal *only with long-term relevance for boolean accesses*. We strongly rely for establishing the upper bound results of this section on the connection between relevance and containment that was established in Section 3. Lower bound arguments will be based on constraining paths to be exponentially or doubly exponentially long, using reductions from tiling.

The upper bounds will make use of methods due to Calì and Martinenghi, which are related to those of Chaudhuri and Vardi [9, 10] for Datalog containment. In [5], Calì and Martinenghi show that we can assume that counterexamples to containment of Q in Q' (or witnesses to long-term relevance) are *tree-like*. In the containment setting, this means that every element outside the initial configuration and the image of Q under a homomorphism occurs in at most two accesses, one as an output and possibly one as an input. Each element outside of the configuration can be associated with an atom – the atom that generated that element as output. For elements n_1, n_2 neither in Conf or $h(Q)$, say that $n_1 \prec n_2$ if n_2 is generated by an access to n_1, and let $\prec^*$ be the transitive closure of $\prec$. Then the tree-like requirement corresponds to the fact that $\prec^*$ is a tree. This is exactly what Calì and Martinenghi refer to as a *crayfish* chase database, and in [5] they give the "unfolding" construction that shows that such counterexample models always exist – we use this often throughout this section. By exploiting the limited structure of a tree-like database further we will be able to extend the upper bounds of [5], taking into account configuration constants and multiple accesses.

In contrast with what happens for the independent case, results are radically different for conjunctive and positive queries. We thus study the complexity of long-term relevance and query containment in turn for both query languages.

5.1 Conjunctive Queries

For conjunctive queries, we show we have coNEXPTIME-completeness of containment and NEXPTIME-completeness of the LTR problem. We first establish the hardness through a reduction of a tiling problem of an exponential-size corridor that yields an exponential-size path. Recall that the lower bound for query containment directly implies the lower bound for relevance, thanks to Proposition 3.3.

THEOREM 5.1. *Boolean conjunctive query containment under access limitations is* coNEXPTIME-*hard. Consequently, long-term relevance of an access for a conjunctive query is* NEXPTIME-*hard.*

PROOF. We show a reduction from the NEXPTIME-complete problem consisting in tiling a $2^n \times 2^n$ corridor, where n is given in unary, under horizontal and vertical constraints (see Section 3.2 of [17]). A tile will be represented by an access atom $Tile(t, \mathbf{b}, \mathbf{c}, x, y)$, where $\mathbf{b}$ is the vertical position (i.e., the row), $\mathbf{c}$ the horizontal position (i.e., the column), t the tile type, and x, y are values that link one tile to the next generated tile in the witness path, as will become clear later. The n bit binary representation of the decimal number d is denoted by $[d]$.

For a given tiling problem with tile types $t_1, \ldots, t_k$, horizontal relation H, vertical relation V, and initial tiles of respective type $t_{i_0}, \ldots t_{i_{m-1}}$, we construct the following containment problem. The schema has the following relations with their respective arities as superscripts: $Bool^1$, $TileType^1$, $SameTile^3$, $Horiz^3$, $Vert^3$, And^3, Or^3, Eq^3, all of them having no access methods, and $Tile^{2n+3}$, with a single access method whose input arguments are all but the last. We generate the following configuration Conf:

> $Bool(0), Bool(1);$
> $TileType(t_1), \ldots, TileType(t_k);$
> $SameTile(t_i, t_i, 1)$ for $1 \leqslant i \leqslant m,$
> $SameTile(t_i, t_j, 0)$ for $i \neq j, 1 \leqslant i, j \leqslant m;$
> $Horiz(t_i, t_j, 1)$ for all $\langle t_i, t_j \rangle \in H,$
> $Horiz(t_i, t_j, 0)$ for all $\langle t_i, t_j \rangle \notin H;$
> $Vert(t_i, t_j, 1)$ for all $\langle t_i, t_j \rangle \in V,$
> $Vert(t_i, t_j, 0)$ for all $\langle t_i, t_j \rangle \notin V;$
> $And(0, 0, 0), And(1, 0, 0), And(0, 1, 0), And(1, 1, 1);$
> $Or(0, 0, 0), Or(0, 1, 1), Or(1, 0, 1), Or(1, 1, 1);$
> $Eq(0, 0, 1), Eq(1, 0, 0), Eq(0, 1, 0), Eq(1, 1, 1);$
> $Tile(t_{i_0}, [0], [0], c_0, c_1), Tile(t_{i_1}, [0], [1], c_1, c_2).$

We use three domains: $\mathcal{B}$ (used for Booleans), $\mathcal{T}$ (used for tile types), $\mathcal{C}$ (used for chaining up tiles). They are assigned

as follows: $Bool$, And, Or, Eq have all their argument in $\mathcal{B}$; the argument of $TileType$ has domain $\mathcal{T}$; $SameTile$, $Horiz$, and $Vert$ have their first two arguments of domain $\mathcal{T}$ and the third of domain $\mathcal{B}$; finally, the first argument of $Tile$ has domain $\mathcal{T}$ and the remaining ones domain $\mathcal{B}$, except for the last two, that are in $\mathcal{C}$.

We reduce to the complement of query containment of Q_1 into Q_2 where Q_1 is the atom $Tile(u, [2^n - 1], [2^n - 1], x, y)$ and Q_2 consists of the following conjunction of atoms:

$$Tile(u, \mathbf{b}, \mathbf{c}, x, y) \wedge Tile(v, \mathbf{d}, \mathbf{e}, y, z) \wedge Tile(w, \mathbf{f}, \mathbf{g}, y', z')$$
$$\wedge\, Tile(q, \mathbf{v}, \mathbf{h}, y', z") \wedge BOOLCONS,$$

where u, v, w, q are variables intended for tile types, each of $\mathbf{b}, \mathbf{c}, \mathbf{d}, \mathbf{e}, \mathbf{f}, \mathbf{g}, \mathbf{h}, \mathbf{v}$ is a tuple of n variables intended for Booleans, and $x, y, y', z, z', z"$ are variables intended for linking elements, and where $BOOLCONS$ consists of a conjunction of And, Or, and Eq atoms imposing a number of Boolean constraints on the bit-vectors $\mathbf{b}, \mathbf{c}, \mathbf{d}, \mathbf{e}, \mathbf{f}, \mathbf{g}, \mathbf{h}, \mathbf{v}$. Since we want $BOOLCONS$ to remain conjunctive, its construction is a bit intricate, but in essence it states that there is "something wrong" with the tiling. More precisely, it consists of a conjunction of the following subformulas:

1. A subformula $SUB_1(i_1)$ such that $SUB_1(0)$ holds true iff the functional dependency from the next-to-last argument of the $Tile$ relation to the $2n$ bit-valued attributes in the same relation is violated for some tuple. To express this, we use the last two of the four $Tile$ atoms in the above formula, because they have both the same variable y' in their next-to-last position. We require that some f_i differs from the corresponding v_i or some g_j differs from its corresponding h_j. We can assert this as: $Eq(f_1, v_1, a_1) \wedge Eq(f_2, v_2, a_i) \wedge \ldots \wedge Eq(f_n, v_n, a_n) \wedge Eq(g_1, h_1, a_{n+1}) \wedge Eq(g_2, h_2, a_{n+i}) \wedge \ldots \wedge Eq(g_n, h_n, a_{2n}) \wedge And(a_1, a_2, r_1) \wedge And(r_1, a_3, r_2) \wedge \ldots \wedge And(r_{2n-2}, a_{2n}, i_1)$.

2. A subformula $SUB_2(i_2)$ such that $SUB_2(0)$ holds true iff two accesses A_1 and A_2 on the $Tile$ relation, where the output value of A_1 is equal to the value of the penultimate argument of A_2 are such that their bit-vectors are in a wrong relationship. The latter just means that the concatenated two bit-vectors of A_1 are *not* a predecessor of the concatenated two bit-vectors of A_2. To express this, we use the first two atoms of Q_2. Indeed, they are already linked via variable y. It is now just necessary to express that their bit-vectors are wrong. To do this, we design a conjunction of atoms $SUCC(\mathbf{b}, \mathbf{c}, \mathbf{d}, \mathbf{e}, s)$ for which $s = 1$ iff vector $\langle \mathbf{b}, \mathbf{c} \rangle$ is a numeric predecessor of $\langle \mathbf{d}, \mathbf{e} \rangle$, and $s = 0$ otherwise. Then, let $SUB_2(i_2) = SUCC(\mathbf{b}, \mathbf{c}, \mathbf{d}, \mathbf{e}, i_2)$. The $SUCC(\mathbf{b}, \mathbf{c}, \mathbf{d}, \mathbf{e}, s)$ subformula can be easily constructed by using purely Boolean atoms only. Briefly, we first define a $SUCC_i(\mathbf{b}, \mathbf{c}, \mathbf{d}, \mathbf{e}, s_i)$ formula for $1 \leqslant i \leqslant 2n$ such that $s_i = 1$ iff the leading $i - 1$ bits of both vectors coincide. The ith bit of $\langle \mathbf{b}, \mathbf{c} \rangle$ is 0, while the ith bit of $\langle \mathbf{d}, \mathbf{e} \rangle$ is 1, and all bits in positions above i are 1 in $\langle \mathbf{b}, \mathbf{c} \rangle$ and 0 in $\langle \mathbf{d}, \mathbf{e} \rangle$. All this is easily done with And and Eq atoms. Finally, $SUCC$ is constructed by taking all $SUCC_i$ and or-ing their s_i-values: $Or(s_1, s_2, k_1) \wedge Or(k_1, s_3, k_2) \wedge \ldots \wedge Or(k_{2n-2}, s_{2n}, s)$. Note that we only need a polynomial number of atoms.

3. A subformula $SUB_3(i_3)$ such that $SUB_3(0)$ holds true iff some vertical or horizontal constraints are violated or if the initial m tiles are of wrong tile type. Informally, we thus need to assert in this subformula that there exist two tiles, such that some tiling constraint is violated. Here we can, for example, use the second and third atoms of Q_2.

For the horizontal constraints, we define in the obvious way subformulas that check that $\mathbf{d}$ is the predecessor of $\mathbf{f}$, that $\mathbf{e}$ and $\mathbf{g}$ are equal, and $Horiz(v, w, 0)$. The resulting truth value is or-red with a violation of the vertical constraints which is encoded in a similar way. To all this, we also connect disjunctively (conjoining Or atoms) all possible violations of the correct tile-type of the m initial tiles. We can use the third atom of Q_2 for this. Such a violation arises if in $Tile(w, \mathbf{f}, \mathbf{g}, y', z')$ $\mathbf{f} = [0]$, $\mathbf{g} = [i] < [m]$, and w is any tile type but the correct one. This can be easily expressed using the $SameTile$ predicate and Boolean operators.

4. Finally, we add to the conjunction so far $SUB_1(i_1) \wedge SUB_2(i_2) \wedge SUB_3(i_3)$ a subformula SUB_4 expressing that at least one of the bits i_1, i_2, i_3 must be zero: $SUB_4 = And(i_1, i_2, j) \wedge And(j, i_3, 0)$. This concludes the construction of Q_2.

We claim that the grid is tiled iff there is an access path p based on conf Conf that falsifies Q_2 and satisfies Q_1 (see [3] for the proof of this fact). □

We now deal with upper bounds. Chang and Li noted that for every conjunctive query (or UCQ) Q, and any set of access patterns, one can write a Monadic Datalog query Q_{acc} that represents the answers to Q that can be obtained according to the access patterns – the intentional predicates represent the accessible elements of each datatype, which can be axiomatized via recursive rules corresponding to each access method. One can thus show that containment of Q in Q' under access patterns is reduced to containment of the Monadic Datalog query Q_{acc} in Q'. Although containment between Datalog queries is undecidable, containment of Monadic Datalog queries is decidable (in 2EXPTIME [11]) and containment of Datalog queries in UCQs is decidable (in 3EXPTIME [10]), this does not give tight bounds for our problem. Chaudhuri and Vardi [10] have shown that containment of Monadic Datalog queries in *connected* UCQs is in coNEXPTIME. The queries considered there have a head predicate with one free variable, and the connectedness requirement is that the graph connecting atoms when they share a variable is connected – thus the head atom is connected to every other variable. Connectedness is a strong condition – it implies that in a tree-like model one need only look for homomorphisms that lie close to the root.

We now show a coNEXPTIME upper bound, matching our lower bound and extending the prior results above. From the nondeterministic polynomial-time Turing reduction from containment to relevance (Proposition 3.3), we deduce NEXPTIME membership for long-term relevance of Boolean accesses.

THEOREM 5.2. *Boolean conjunctive query containment under access limitations is in* coNEXPTIME. *Long-term relevance of a Boolean access for a conjunctive query is in* NEXPTIME.

We now outline the proof of coNEXPTIME-membership for containment under access patterns. Consider queries Q, Q', and configuration Conf.

An element n in an instance I is *fresh* if it is not in the initial configuration Conf. Call a homomorphism h of a subquery Q'' of Q' into an instance *freshly-connected* if the following graph G'' is connected: The vertices of G'' are the atoms of Q'' and there is an edge between two such atoms if they overlap in a variable mapped to the same fresh value by

h. Given an element n, a homomorphism of query $Q'(x)$ is *rooted at* n if it maps the distinguished variable x to n and includes only one atom containing x.

In this proof, we assume for convenience that all values of enumerated types mentioned in the queries are in the initial configuration – and thus fresh values are always of a non-enumerated type. This hypothesis can be removed, since the part of any witness to non-containment that involves enumerated types can always be guessed, staying within the required bounds.

In order to get an exponential-sized witness to non-containment, we would like to abstract an element of an instance by *all* subqueries of Q' that it satisfies, or even all the freshly-connected homomorphisms. However, this would require looking at many queries, giving a doubly exponential bound (as in Theorem 5.6).

The following key lemma states that it suffices to look at just one freshly-connected homomorphism.

CLAIM 5.3. *For each tree-like instance* I *and element* n *in* I, *and for each query atom* A *that maps into an* I-*atom containing* n, *there is a unique maximal freshly-connected partial homomorphism rooted in* n *that includes atom* A *in its domain.*

PROOF. Consider a function h mapping variables of the atom A into I such that $h(x) = n$. We claim that there is only one way to extend h to a freshly connected homomorphism including other atoms. Clearly, to satisfy the freshness requirement, any other atom A' must include at least one other variable in common with A, say y, mapped to n_2 by h. To satisfy rootedness, this variable must not contain x. But in a tree-like model there can be only one other fact F in I that contains y, and hence for every position p of A' we can only map a variable in that position to the corresponding argument of F. □

For elements n_1 and n_2 and atom A, let h_1^A and h_2^A be the maximal freshly-connected partial homomorphisms given by the claim above for n_1 and n_2, respectively. We say two elements n_1 and n_2 in I are *maxfresh-equivalent* if for every A in Q' there is an isomorphism r of I that preserves the initial configuration, and such that $h_1^A \circ r = h_2^A$.

We say that fresh elements n_1 and n_2 are *similar* if they are maxfresh-equivalent, and if n_1 occurs as input variable i in atom A, then the same is true for n_2 – recall that fresh elements in tree-like insances occur as the inputs to at most one atom.

We now show that the maxfresh-equivalence classes of subtrees can be determined compositionally.

LEMMA 5.4. *Suppose* A *is an atom satisfied by fresh elements* $n_0, n_1 \ldots n_k$ *along with configuration elements* $\mathbf{c}$ *in a tree-like instance* I, *with each* n_i *in the subtree of* n_0. *Suppose that the same is true for fresh* $n_0', n_1' \ldots n_k'$ *and* $\mathbf{c}$, *with* $\mathbf{c}$ *in the same arguments of* A. *If each* n_i *is maxfresh-equivalent to* n_i', *then* n_0 *is maxfresh-equivalent to* n_0'.

PROOF. We show that the subtrees of n_0 and n_0' satisfy the same subqueries of Q'. Suppose a freshly-connected subquery Q'' were to hold in n_0 with h a witness. Let $Q'(x)$ be the query where x is made free, and let h_i be the restriction of h to the variables that are connected to x and map within subtrees of the n_i. This is a freshly-connected homomorphism, so must also be realized in the subtree of n_i' in I. But then we can extend the homomorphism to the subtree of n_0' by mapping A according to the fact holding in common within n_0' and n_0. $\square$

We now show that one representative of each similarlity class suffices for a counterexample model.

LEMMA 5.5. *If Q is not contained in Q' under access patterns, then there is a witness instance I in which no two elements are similar.*

Proof: Consider an arbitrary tree-like instance I satisfying the access patterns, such that I satisfies Q and not Q'. Given distinct n_1 and n_2 that are similar. we show that they can be identified, possibly shrinking the model. By Lemma 5.4 this identification preserves the similarity type, so assuming we have proven this, we can get a single representative by induction.

Consider the case where n_1 is an ancestor of n_2 (the case where the two are incomparable is similar). Consider the model I' obtained by identifying n_1 and n_2, removing all items that lie below n_1 and which do not lie below n_2 in the dependency graph. Let n' denote the image of n_1 under the identification in I'. I' is still generated by a well-formed access path, while Q is still satisfied, since the homomorphic image of Q was not modified. If Q' were satisfied in I', let h' be a homomorphism witnessing this. Clearly the image of h' must include n'. Let $h_{n'}$ be the maximal connected subquery of Q' that maps to a contiguous subtree rooted at n'. Then up to isomorphism $h_{n'}$ is the same as the maximal fresh homomorphism rooted at n_2; and since n_1 and n_2 are max-fresh equivalent, this means that $h_{n'}$ is (modulo composition with an isomorphism) the same as h_{n_1} the maximal fresh homomorphism rooted at n_1.

Let IM be the image of h'. We define a mapping f taking elements of IM to I as follows: nodes in the image of $h_{n'}$ go to their isomorphic image in the image of h_{n_1}; other nodes lying in both IM and the subtree of n' go to their isomorphic image in the subtree of n_2, while nodes lying outside the subtree of n' are mapped to the identity. We argue that the composition of h' with f gives a homomorphism of Q' into I. Atoms all of whose elements are in the domain of $h_{n'}$ are preserved since n' and n_1 are max-fresh equivalent. The properties of maximal equivalence classes guarantee that for all other atoms of Q' either: a) all variables that are mapped by h' to fresh elements are mapped to elements in the subtree of n' outside of $h_{n'}$; hence such atoms are preserved by f; or b) all variables that are mapped by h' to fresh elements are mapped to elements either in $h_{n'}$ or above it; such atoms are preserved, since f is an isomorphism on these elements. Thus Q' holds in I, a contradiction.

From Lemma 5.5 we see that whenever there is a counterexample to containment, there is a DAG-shaped model of size the number of similarity classes – since this is exponential in the input, an access path that generates it can be guessed by a NEXPTIME algorithm, and the verification that it is a well-formed access path and witnesses $Q \wedge \neg Q'$ can be done in polynomial time in the size of the path (albeit in D^P in the size of the queries).

5.2 Positive Queries

We now turn to the case where queries can use nesting of $\vee$ and $\wedge$, but no negation. Here we will see that the complexity of the problems becomes exponentially harder. The upper bounds will be via a type-abstraction mechanism; the lower bounds will again go via tiling problems, although of a more involved sort.

THEOREM 5.6. *The problem of determining whether query Q is contained in Q' under access constraints is complete for co2NEXPTIME, while determining whether a Boolean access is LTR for a positive query Q is complete for 2NEXPTIME.*

PROOF. Again, results about relevance are derived by the reductions of Section 3.

The upper bound holds by showing that if there is a counterexample to containment then there is one of doubly-exponential size – this is in turn shown by seeing that we can identify two elements if they satisfy the same queries of size at most the maximum of $|Q|, |Q'|$.

Hardness follows from reducing to the problem of tiling a corridor of width and height doubly-exponential in n. By choosing Q' appropriately, we can force the model to consist of a sequence of linked elements each of which lies at the root of a tree of polynomial size. Such a tree can spell out a string of exponentially many bits, and we can further ensure that successive occurrences trees encode a description of a doubly-exponential sized tiling. $\square$

We note that in terms of data complexity, we still have tractability, even in this very general case:

PROPOSITION 5.7. *When the queries are fixed, the complexity of containment is in polynomial time. Similarly, the complexity of LTR is in polynomial time once the query is fixed.*

PROOF. Again we give the argument only for containment and use Proposition 3.3 to conclude for relevance (note the remark in Proposition 3.3 about configurations being the same). In the co2NEXPTIME membership argument for containment in Theorem 5.6 we have shown a witness instance in which the elements consist of $k(Q, Q')$ elements of each type, where the number of types is $l(Q, Q')$, hence with a constant number of elements outside the configuration once Q and Q' are fixed. The number of possible access sequences is thus polynomial in the configuration, and verifying that a sequence is well-formed and satisfies $Q \wedge \neg Q'$ can be done in polynomial time since Q and Q' are fixed. $\square$

6. RELATED WORK

We overview the existing literature on answering queries in the presence of limited access patterns, highlighting the differentiators of our approach using the vocabulary of Section 2. The problem of querying under access restrictions was originally motivated by access to built-in-predicates with infinitely many tuples (such as $<$) – which is only reasonable if all variables are bound – and by the desire to access relations only on their indexed attributes (see [27], chapter 12). More recently, the rise of data-integration systems with sources whose content are accessible through interfaces with limited capabilities [25] has been the main driver of interest in the subject; the most well-known example is the querying of deep Web sources [16] accessible through Web forms. Research efforts on deep Web exploration [16] and on the use of Web services to complement extensional knowledge bases [24] are practical settings where the notion of dynamic relevance of a Web source is fundamental.

With a few exceptions that will be noted, most of the existing work focuses on static analysis for dependent accesses. By static we mean that they seek a means to answer the query *ab initio* that does not consider the configuration or adapt to it. By dependent we mean, as in the second part of this paper, that it is impossible to guess a constant to be used in a bound access. Typically accesses are also supposed to be exact and not merely sound. This last limitation is unrealistic in the case of deep Web sources, where a given source will often have only partial knowledge over some data collection In contrast, our results give new bounds on static problems, but also consider dynamic relevance. We allow a collection of sound accesses that can be dependent or independent. Queries considered in the literature are usually conjunctive, but work on query answerability and rewriting has also considered richer query languages, such as unions of conjunctive queries (UCQs) [18], UCQs with negations [23, 12], or even first-order logic [22]. In a few cases [25, 13, 12], existing work assumes that both queries and sources are expressed as *views* over a global schema, and the limited access problem is combined to that of answering queries using views [15]. In the other cases, the query is supposed to be directly expressed in terms of the source relations, as we have done in this work.

Static analysis. The first study of query answering when sources have limited patterns is by Rajamaran, Sagiv, and Ullman [25]. Given a conjunctive query over a global schema and a set of views over the same schema, with exact dependent access patterns, they show that determining whether there exists a conjunctive query plan over the views that is equivalent to the original query and respects the access patterns is NP-complete. This is based on the observation that the size of a query plan can be bounded by the size of the query: one can just keep in the plan subgoals that either are mapped to one of the subgoal of the query, or provide an initial binding for one of the variables of the queries.

Duschka, Genesereth, and Levy study in [13] the general problem of answering queries using views. They solve this by constructing a Datalog query plan formed of *inverse rules* obtained from the source descriptions, a plan computing the maximally contained answer to a query. Although this approach was geared towards data integration without limitations, the same work extends it to incorporate limited access patterns on sources in a straightforward manner.

Li and Chang [19] propose a static query planning framework based on Datalog for getting the maximally contained answer to a query with exact dependent access pattern; the query language considered is a proper subset of UCQs, with only natural joins allowed. In the follow-up work [18], the query language is lifted to UCQs, and Li shows that testing the existence of an exact query rewriting is NP-complete, which can be seen as an extension of the result from [25], from CQs to UCQs (though views are not considered in [18]). That article also proposes a dynamic approach when an exact query rewriting does not exist, which we discuss further.

Nash and Ludäscher [23] extend the results of [18] to the case of UCQs with negations. The complexity of the exact rewriting problem is reduced to standard query containment and thus becomes in this case Π_2^p-complete. Other query languages are also considered in [22], up to first-order-logic, for which the rewriting problem becomes undecidable. Deutsch, Ludäscher, and Nash add in [12] views and constraints (in the form of weakly acyclic tuple-generating dependencies) to the setting of dependent exact patterns. Using the chase procedure, they show that the exact rewriting problem remains Π_2^p-complete in the presence of a large class of integrity constraints, and they provide algorithms for obtaining maximally contained answer and minimally containing static plan.

Finally, still in the case of dependent exact accesses and for conjunctive queries, Calì and Martinenghi [6] build on the query planning framework of [19] and show how to obtain a query plan for maximally contained answer that is minimal in terms of the number of accesses made to the sources.

Dynamic computation of maximal answers. Some works referenced in the previous paragraphs also consider dynamic, runtime, aspects of the problem, i.e., taking into account the current configuration. Thus, [18] provides an algorithm that finds the complete answer to a query under dependent exact accesses whenever possible, even if an exact query rewriting plan cannot be obtained. This is based on a recursive, exhaustive, enumeration of all constants that can be retrieved from sources, using the techniques of the inverse rule algorithm [13]. The algorithm has no optimality guarantee, since no check is made for the relevance of an access to the query, for any notion of relevance. An extension to UCQs with negation is proposed in [23], with a very similar approach.

Dynamic relevance. To our knowledge, the only work to consider the dynamic relevance of a set of accesses with binding patterns is by Calì, Calvanese, and Martinenghi [4]. They define an access with a binding as *dynamically relevant* under a set of constraints (functional dependencies and a very restricted version of inclusion dependencies) for a given configuration if this access can produce new tuples. They show dynamic relevance can be decided in polynomial time. The fact that a source has limited access patterns does not play any role here since one only considers a given binding and disregards all other accesses, and there is no query involved.

Related work on query containment. We want to conclude this section by mentioning a few other works that are not dealing with answering queries under binding patterns *per se* but are still pertinent to the problem studied in this paper. We have already compared in detail in Section 3 our work with the complexity analysis [5] of query containment under access limitations – in brief, our results generalize the upper bounds to a richer model, provide matching lower bounds, and give bounds for larger collections of queries. However the arguments used in proofs of our upper bound results of this paper rely heavily on the crayfish chase procedure described in this work.

Chaudhuri and Vardi [9, 10] consider the problem of containment of Datalog queries in unions of conjunctive queries – it is easily seen (e.g. from the Datalog-based approaches to limited access patterns mentioned earlier) that this problem subsumes containment under access patterns. Indeed, containment under access patterns is subsumed by containment of Monadic Datalog in UCQs, a problem shown by [9] to be in coNEXPTIME in special cases (e.g. connected queries without constants): the upper-bounds rely on the ability to make models tree-like, as ours do. In the case of binary accesses, containment under access limitations can be reduced to containment of a *path query* in a conjunctive query. This problem is studied in [14, 7] which together give an PSPACE-bound for containment of path queries – as our results show, these results give neither tight bounds for the binary case or the best lower bound for the general case.

Other related work. Finally, Abiteboul, Bourhis, and Marinoiu [1] consider dynamic relevance of a service call to a query in the framework of ActiveXML (XML documents with service calls). A service call is dynamically relevant if it can produce new parts of the tree that will eventually change the query result. They show in particular that non-relevance is in Σ_2^P (an unpublished extension of their work shows Σ_2^P-hardness also by reduction from the critical tuple problem [21]). Though the framework is different, their notion of relevance is close in spirit to our notion of long-term relevance.

7. CONCLUSION

We investigated here the problems of analyzing the access paths that can originate from a particular data access. When accesses are not tightly coupled, the problem is closely-related to reasoning whether a tuple is "critical" to a given query result. Here we have fairly tight complexity bounds, although admittedly no algorithms that are promising from a practical perspective as yet.

In the setting where accesses are dependent on one another, we have shown a tight connection between relevance problems and containment under access limitations for Boolean accesses. We have shown new bounds for both the relevance and containment problems for conjunctive and positive queries. However, there are still many open issues regarding complexity. For low arity (see [3]) we do not have tight bounds on LTR. For arbitrary arity we have tight bounds for CQs and for positive queries, but we do not know if our lower bounds for positive queries also hold for positive queries of restricted forms (e.g., UCQs). We believe that all of our results for containment can be extended to relevance of non-Boolean accesses, using the same proofs, but we leave this for future work.

8. ACKNOWLEDGMENTS

M. Benedikt is supported in part by EP/G004021/1 and EP/H017690/1 of the Engineering and Physical Sciences Research Council UK and in part by EC FP7-ICT-233599. G. Gottlob's and P. Senellart's research leading to these results has received funding from the European Research Council under the European Community's Seventh Framework Programme (FP7/2007-2013) / ERC grant agreements 246858 *DIADEM* and 226513 *Webdam*, respectively. We thank Pierre Bourhis for great assistance with an earlier draft of the paper.

9. REFERENCES

[1] S. Abiteboul, P. Bourhis, and B. Marinoiu. Satisfiability and relevance for queries over active documents. In *PODS*, 2009.

[2] S. Abiteboul, R. Hull, and V. Vianu. *Foundations of Databases*. Addison-Wesley, 1995.

[3] M. Benedikt, G. Gottlob, and P. Senellart. Determining relevance of accesses at runtime (extended version). *CoRR*, 2011.

[4] A. Calì, D. Calvanese, and D. Martinenghi. Dynamic query optimization under access limitations and dependencies. *J. UCS*, 15(1):33–62, 2009.

[5] A. Calì and D. Martinenghi. Conjunctive query containment under access limitations. In *ER*, 2008.

[6] A. Calì and D. Martinenghi. Querying data under access limitations. In *ICDE*, 2008.

[7] D. Calvanese, G. D. Giacomo, M. Lenzerini, and M. Y. Vardi. Containment of conjunctive regular path queries with inverse. In *KR*, 2000.

[8] A. K. Chandra and P. M. Merlin. Optimal implementation of conjunctive queries in relational data bases. In *STOC*, Boulder, USA, 1977.

[9] S. Chaudhuri and M. Y. Vardi. On the complexity of equivalence between recursive and nonrecursive Datalog programs. In *PODS*, 1994.

[10] S. Chaudhuri and M. Y. Vardi. On the equivalence of recursive and nonrecursive Datalog programs. *JCSS*, 54(1):61–78, 1997.

[11] S. S. Cosmadakis, H. Gaifman, P. C. Kanellakis, and M. Y. Vardi. Decidable optimization problems for database logic programs. In *STOC*, 1988.

[12] A. Deutsch, B. Ludäscher, and A. Nash. Rewriting queries using views with access patterns under integrity constraints. *Theor. Comput. Sci.*, 371(3):200–226, 2007.

[13] O. M. Duschka and A. Y. Levy. Recursive plans for information gathering. In *IJCAI*, 1997.

[14] D. Florescu, A. Levy, and D. Suciu. Query containment for conjunctive queries with regular expressions. In *PODS*, 1998.

[15] A. Y. Halevy. Answering queries using views: A survey. *VLDB Journal*, 10:270–294, 2001.

[16] B. He, M. Patel, Z. Zhang, and K. C.-C. Chang. Accessing the deep Web: A survey. *Communications of the ACM*, 50(2):94–101, 2007.

[17] D. S. Johnson. A catalog of complexity classes. In *Handbook of Theoretical Computer Science*. MIT Press, 1990.

[18] C. Li. Computing complete answers to queries in the presence of limited access patterns. *VLDB J.*, 12(3):211–227, 2003.

[19] C. Li and E. Y. Chang. Answering queries with useful bindings. *ACM Trans. Database Syst.*, 26(3):313–343, 2001.

[20] C. Li and E. Y. Chang. On answering queries in the presence of limited access patterns. In *ICDT*, 2001.

[21] G. Miklau and D. Suciu. A formal analysis of information disclosure in data exchange. *JCSS*, 73(3):507–534, 2007.

[22] A. Nash and B. Ludäscher. Processing first-order queries under limited access patterns. In *PODS*, 2004.

[23] A. Nash and B. Ludäscher. Processing union of conjunctive queries with negation under limited access patterns. In *EDBT*, 2004.

[24] N. Preda, G. Kasneci, F. M. Suchanek, T. Neumann, W. Yuan, and G. Weikum. Active knowledge: dynamically enriching RDF knowledge bases by Web services. In *SIGMOD*, 2010.

[25] A. Rajaraman, Y. Sagiv, and J. D. Ullman. Answering queries using templates with binding patterns. In *PODS*, 1995.

[26] Y. Sagiv and M. Yannakakis. Equivalences among relational expressions with the union and difference operators. *J. ACM*, 27(4):633–655, 1980.

[27] J. D. Ullman. *Principles of Database and Knowledge-Base Systems*, volume 2. Computer Science Press, 1989.

Parallel Evaluation of Conjunctive Queries[*]

Paraschos Koutris
University of Washington
Seattle, WA
pkoutris@cs.washington.edu

Dan Suciu
University of Washington
Seattle, WA
suciu@cs.washington.edu

ABSTRACT

The availability of large data centers with tens of thousands of servers has led to the popular adoption of massive parallelism for data analysis on large datasets. Several query languages exist for running queries on massively parallel architectures, some based on the MapReduce infrastructure, others using proprietary implementations. Motivated by this trend, this paper analyzes the parallel complexity of conjunctive queries. We propose a very simple model of parallel computation that captures these architectures, in which the complexity parameter is the number of parallel steps requiring synchronization of all servers. We study the complexity of conjunctive queries and give a complete characterization of the queries which can be computed in one parallel step. These form a strict subset of hierarchical queries, and include *flat* queries like $R(x,y), S(x,z), T(x,v), U(x,w)$, *tall* queries like $R(x), S(x,y), T(x,y,z), U(x,y,z,w)$, and combinations thereof, which we call *tall-flat* queries. We describe an algorithm for computing in parallel any tall-flat query, and prove that any query that is not tall-flat cannot be computed in one step in this model. Finally, we present extensions of our results to queries that are not tall-flat.

Categories and Subject Descriptors

H.2.4 [**Systems**]: Distributed Databases

General Terms

Algorithms, Theory

Keywords

Database Theory, Distributed Databases, Parallel Computation

1. INTRODUCTION

In this paper we study the parallel complexity of conjunctive queries. Our motivation comes from the recent increase in the use of massive parallelism for performing data analysis on very large datasets. In addition to traditional parallel database systems, such as Teradata or Greenplum, new query languages and implementations have been introduced recently for the purpose of massively parallel data analytics: the MapReduce architecture for parallelism [8], SCOPE [4], DryadLINQ [25], Pig [10], Hive [22], Dremel [17]. Most of the effort and the engineering work in these systems has been focused on fault-tolerance, resource allocation, and scheduling, and restricted to basic operations like filtering, group-by, aggregation, and join. As these systems evolve towards general-purpose data analytics languages, they need to optimize and execute in parallel general conjunctive queries.

The parallel complexity of conjunctive queries on today's parallel architectures is not well understood. The data complexity of every relational query is in AC^0 [16], and it is generally acknowledged that SQL is "embarrassingly parallel". Immerman [13] analyzed the parallel complexity of First Order Logic on CRCW PRAM (Concurrent Read, Concurrent Write Parallel Random Access Machine) [21] and showed that the parallel time is equivalent to the number of times one needs to iterate a First Order sentence; an immediate corollary is that *every* relational query takes $O(1)$ parallel time in this model. But circuits and PRAMs are not accurate models of parallel systems. Even in the 80's and 90's researchers have proposed alternative models to capture parallelism. Valiant introduced the BSP model [23] and Culler et al. further refined it into the LogP model [6]. Both view the parallel computation as a sequence of relatively short parallel computation steps, each followed by a global synchronization barrier. The length of a parallel step is called periodicity parameter, L, and most of the analysis of parallel algorithms in these models consists of theoretical guarantees that servers finish their tasks within the periodicity parameter (or else, the next step needs to be dedicated to the unfinished step). Therefore, the models focus on the details of the communication protocol, and trace meticulously the network's latency, overhead, and gap (in the LogP model). These models no longer capture today's parallel architectures well.

Nowadays, massive parallelism is achieved on commodity hardware interconnected by a high speed network. The communication cost is less dependent on the low level protocol, but is dominated by the amount of data being exchanged. In addition, the granularity of a parallel step has increased, since each server needs to process a large amount of data before synchronization, making each synchronization step even more expensive.

The main bottleneck in today's massively parallel computations is the global synchronization steps of a computation [12]. Two factors make a global synchronization step

---

[*]This work was partially supported by NSF IIS-0627585 and IIS-0713576.

expensive: data skew and stragglers. Data skew refers to the fact that some servers end up processing much more data than others. Theoretically, one addresses data skew by requiring that each server is allocated only $O(n/P)$ of the total data, where n is the number of data items and P the number of servers. This guarantees that no server gets an excessive load[1]. Stragglers are a new phenomenon, not encountered in older parallel systems. A straggler is a server that takes significantly longer time to execute its share of the computation than the others. This can be caused by a faulty disk, the server being overloaded with other tasks, by server failure, or by the algorithm itself. Stragglers occur in today's systems because the large number of servers (tens of thousands) and the long processing times (often several hours) dramatically increase the probability that some servers will straggle. All systems to date, starting with the original MapReduce [8], pay special attention to stragglers. They monitor slow responders, and, once a straggler is identified, its work is redistributed to other servers. Despite these measures, stragglers add a significant cost to each synchronization step, and the way to mitigate that cost in a theoretical model is to reduce the number of global synchronization steps.

We propose a simple parallel model of computation, called the *Massively Parallel*, or MP model, to enable us to analyze the parallel complexity of conjunctive queries. In MP, computation proceeds in a sequence of parallel steps, each followed by global synchronization of all servers. We do not impose any restriction on the time of a parallel step. Instead, we impose the restriction that the load at each server is no more than $O(n/P)$ data items during the entire computation, where n is the total size of the input and the output, and P is the number of servers. Each parallel step consists of a broadcast phase (where a limited amount of data is shared among servers, typically in order to detect skewed elements), followed by a communication phase, followed by a computation phase. The cost of an algorithm in the MP model is given by the *number of parallel steps*: we ignore the time of the computation phase and also, in this paper, we ignore the total amount of data transferred during communication. However, notice that the amount of data transferred is always $O(n)$, because the P processors can receive at most $P \cdot O(n/P)$ data items during each communication step; this is in contrast to Afrati and Ullman [1], who allow a total amount of $O(n \sqrt[k]{P^{k-1}})$ data exchanged in one step (see Section 7). Thus, we only count the number of synchronization steps. For example, if Algorithm A computes a query in two parallel steps, each taking time T, and Algorithm B computes the same query in a single parallel step of time $T' = 2T$, then both algorithms take time $2T$, and would be considered equivalent in a traditional model. But, under MP, Algorithm B is better, since it uses one parallel step instead of two.

In this paper we study the evaluation of conjunctive queries in the MP model. We restrict our discussion to *full conjunctive queries* (without projections). Our main result is a complete characterization of queries computable in one MP step; the most significant aspect of this result is that not all queries are easily parallelizable, as older models of parallelism suggest. The queries computable in one MP step are the *tall-flat* queries. A flat query is one where every two atoms share the same sets of variables, for example $q(x,y,z,u) = R(x,y), S(x,z), T(x,u)$ is flat because

any two atoms share $\{x\}$; in other words, a flat query is a star join where all join conditions are on the same variable(s). A tall query is one where the set of variables in the atoms forms a linear chain, for example $q(x,y,z,u) = R(x), S(x,y), T(x,y,z), U(x,y,z,u)$; tall queries occur in data warehouse schemas, e.g `Country(`co`, ...)`, `City(`co`,`ci`,...)`, `Store(`co`,`ci`,`st`,...)`. A tall-flat query consists of a tall part followed by a flat part (formal definition in Section 3), and we prove that a query can be evaluated in one MP step iff it is tall-flat. For the "if" part of the proof, we give a concrete algorithm that computes any tall-flat query in one parallel step, while guaranteeing perfect load balance (which is a requirement in the MP model), even if the data is skewed. We give the algorithm in two stages: we describe the algorithm separately for tall, and for flat queries in Section 4, then combine them into a general algorithm in Section 5. The simple case of a 2-way join $q(x,y,z) = R(x,y), S(y,z)$ can be computed by an alogorithm similar in spirit to the *skew join* in Pig [10]; k-way flat queries with $k \geq 3$ and tall queries require non-trivial extensions. For the "only if" part of the proof, we show in Section 6 that for any non tall-flat query, any one-step parallel algorithm will be skewed, thus violating the MP model.

Our results depend critically on the load balance requirement, which strictly limits the amount of data per processor to $O(n/P)$, and, hence, limits the communication cost to $O(n)$. Afrati and Ullman [1] describe a simple algorithm for computing the query $RST(x,y) = R(x), S(x,y), T(y)$ (which is not tall-flat) in one parallel step, by allowing each server to store $O(n/\sqrt{P})$ amount of data, and, thus, with communication cost $O(n\sqrt{P})$. In general, any conjunctive query with k variables can be computed in one parallel step if one allows the load per processor to increase to $O(n/\sqrt[k]{P})$ (and the communication cost to $O(n\sqrt[k]{P^{k-1}})$).

Organization. We first discuss in Section 2 about related work in parallel and distributed database models. Then, we describe the model and the main algorithmic techniques in Section 3, and the main algorithms in Section 4. We prove the main result in Section 5 and Section 6. Finally, we discuss some extensions in Section 7 and conclude in Section 8.

2. RELATED WORK

The recent success of the MapReduce framework [8] in efficiently parallelizing computations has inspired theoretical research on new models of parallel computation, which capture the characteristics and limitations of the new architecture, while also considering the capabilities of modern hardware and infrastructure.

Afrati and Ullman [1] describe a model of computation where every query is executed in one parallel step and the primary measure of complexity is communication. Our model always restricts the communication to $O(n)$, but needs multiple communication steps, hence this is our main complexity metric. By contrast, in their work they allow a larger amount of communication, typically $O(n\sqrt[k]{P^{k-1}})$, and therefore the main complexity metric is the total amount of communication.

Another theoretical approach to analyzing MapReduce is presented in [14]. In this paper, the authors allow only a limited amount of storage in each processor, and add randomization, in the sense of allowing false computations as well. Their main measure of complexity is similar to ours: the number of MapReduce steps; however, they do not examine queries, but general algorithms, comparing their model to the PRAM model.

---

[1]We assume that each of the n items takes about the same time to process. This assumption may fail for jobs with user defined functions.

Measuring parallel complexity in terms of the the number of communication steps was also proposed by Hellerstein [12], who introduced the notion of *Coordination Complexity*. The author argues that both communication and computation are cheap using today's infrastructure; the bottleneck in parallelizing queries lies in the coordination of global barriers during computation.

Apart from recent approaches to modeling the MapReduce framework, various parallel models have been extensively studied, for example the widely used *bulk-synchronous parallel* model [23] and the LogP model [6]. However, both models do not seem to adequately capture the concerns of today's massively parallel computations.

The idea that we handle skewed elements in a special way during computation is not a new one; in [24], the authors develop and implement an algorithm similar to ours that handles skewed join computation in shared-nothing architectures. Nevertheless, they assume that they have knowledge of the skewed elements and do not provide any theoretical guarantees on their algorithm.

Grohe et al. [11] introduced the *Finite Cursor Machines* model of computation, in which queries are evaluated in a sequence of "streaming" steps: each relation can be sorted at the beginning of the step, but afterwards can be read a constant number of times using a constant amount of memory, in a streaming fashion. They do not restrict to full queries, but they do restrict to conjunctive queries in the *semi-join algebra* in order to ensure that the output is linear in the size of the input (this rules out cartesian product queries like $q(x,y) = R(x), S(y)$). For example, a query like $q(x) = R(x,y), S(x,z), T(x,u)$ can be computed in one step, by first sorting the relations on x, then merge-joining the three streams. The authors prove that the query $q(x,y) = R(x), S(x,y), T(y)$ cannot be computed in one streaming step in this model. A conjunctive query is called *hierarchical* if, denoting $at(x)$ the set of atoms that contain the variable x, the family of sets $\{at(x) \mid x \in Var(Q)\}$ form a hierarchy (formal definition in Subsection 3.1). Although the authors [11] do not state this explicitly, it follows immediately from their result that a conjunctive query in the semi-join algebra can be evaluated in one step iff it is hierarchical. Dalvi et al.[7] show that, over tuple-independent probabilistic databases, queries that can be evaluated efficiently are precisely the hierarchical queries [2]. Thus, both in the streaming and probabilistic data model, the tractable queries have the property of being hierarchical. In our work we consider full conjunctive queries, but do not restrict to the semi-join algebra. Thus, we allow cartesian product queries, and show that the queries computable in one pass are the tall-flat queries: for example the cartesian product query $q(x,y) = R(x), S(y)$ is flat, and therefore computable in one MP step. Yet, not every hierarchical query is tall-flat, for example $q(x,y) = R(x), S(x), T(y)$, and these cannot be computed in one MP step (Section 6). When restricting to queries that are both full *and* in the semi-join algebra of [11], we prove that hierarchical queries coincide with tall queries and tall-flat queries collapse to tall queries [15]. Thus, for the intersection of the language considered in [11] and the one in this paper, the class of "easy" queries coincides.

3. THE MODEL AND THE MAIN RESULT

We define here the *Massively Parallel* (MP) model of query evaluation. We fix throughout this paper a domain, U,

called *universe*. A relational database instance D contains constants from U, and has a relational schema $\mathbf{R} = R, S, T, \ldots$ We consider in this paper only *full conjunctive queries*, i.e. where all variables are head variables. Denote the *problem size* to be the size of the input database plus the size of the query's answer, $n = size(D) + size(Q)$.

Let P be the number of parallel servers. Each server stores two kinds of data: *generic data* (values from U) and *numerical data* (integers). The data is stored in arrays, on disks or in main memory. Generic values can be manipulated only in three ways: they can be copied, they can be tested for equality $a = b$, and they can be subjected to a hash function, from a fixed set of hash functions $\bar{h}$. Each hash function has type $h : U^k \to [P]$, where k is its arity. For example, an algorithm may use three hash functions, $\bar{h} = (h_1, h_2, h_3)$, where $h_1, h_2 : U \to [P]$ and $h_3 : U^3 \to [P]$. Each hash function is randomized at the beginning of the algorithm, i.e. chosen randomly from a finite set[3] $\mathcal{H}$ of a family of hash functions [4].

Initially, all relations are already uniformly distributed over the servers (so no additional communication is necessary), and their sizes are known by all servers.

An algorithm in the MP model runs as follows. The *input* is the database instance D. Each relation R is partitioned into P fragments $R_1, R_2, \ldots, R_P$ of equal size, and distributed over the P servers; server s holds the fragments $R_s, S_s, T_s, \ldots$ The initial load of each server is $size(D)/P$. The algorithm proceeds in a number of *parallel computation steps*, each consisting of three phases:

Broadcast Phase: The P servers exchange some data globally. This data is shared among all servers, and we call it *broadcast data*, B. At the end of this phase each server has a copy of B. We require the total amount of communication in this phase to be $O(n^\varepsilon)$, for some $0 < \varepsilon < 1$; in particular, $size(B) = O(n^\varepsilon/P)$.

Communication Phase: Each server sends data to other servers. There is no restriction imposed on how a server distributes the data to the other servers; it could send its entire data to a single server, distribute it uniformly among servers, or broadcast its entire data to all servers (but see the skew-free requirement below).

Computation Phase: Each server performs some local computation on its data. There is no restriction imposed on the time taken for the computation. At the end of this phase the algorithm may stop and leave the result in the local memory of the P servers, or may continue with the next parallel step.

We allow local computation to be performed during all three phases; in our model local computation is free. A *parallel algorithm* is a sequence of parallel computation steps, and its *cost* is the number of parallel steps. Let n_s denote the total number of tuples stored at sever s during the entire execution of the algorithm. The algorithm is called *load balanced*, or *skew free*, if, for sufficiently large n, $\mathbb{E}[\max_s n_s] = O(n/P)$, where the expectation is taken over the random choices of the hash functions $\bar{h} \in \mathcal{H}$. Formally:

---

[2]This result applies only to conjunctive queries without self-joins.

[3]Strictly speaking, we need a separate family for each hash function used: $h_1 \in \mathcal{H}_1$, $h_2 \in \mathcal{H}_2$, etc. To simplify things, we use a single family and write $\bar{h} \in \mathcal{H}$ with some abuse.

[4]Although in this paper we allow randomization only in the choice of hash functions (with the exception of Subsection 4.1), all the hardness results (apart from Proposition 4.3, which we defer to the full version) easily extend to arbitrary use of randomization.

DEFINITION 3.1. *An algorithm is* load balanced *if there exists a constant factor $c > 0$ s.t. for all number of servers P there exists an integer n_0 such that $size(D) = n \geq n_0$, implies $\mathbb{E}_{\bar{h} \in \mathcal{H}}[\max_{s=1,P} n_s] \leq c \cdot n/P$.*

We require every algorithm to be load balanced. This requirement is a key element of the MP model. Without it, any query could be computed in one step, because all servers could send their data to server number 1, which computes the query locally. It has two consequences. First, it ensures linear speedup [9] (by doubling the number of servers P, the load per server will be cut in half[5]) and constant scaleup (by doubling both the size of the data n and the number of processors P, the running time remains unchanged). Second, it implies that the total amount of data exchanged during each communication step is $O(n)$ in expectation. Indeed, let n_s be the number of tuples received by server $s = 1, P$: since $\mathbb{E}[n_s] = O(n/P)$, the total amount of data exchanged is $\mathbb{E}[\sum_s n_s] = O(n)$.

Thus, the amount of communication is guaranteed to be $O(n)$. In most algorithms, this is also a lower bound, but in some cases one can design algorithms with strictly less communication. For example, consider the intersection query $q(x) = R(x), S(x)$; *partitioned hash join* has communication cost $n = |R| + |S|$ (Proposition 3.3). But if we know that $|R| \ll |S|$, then we can use *broadcast join*: broadcast R to all servers, then each server intersects R with its local fragment of S. The communication cost is $P \cdot |R|$, which may be much less than n. In this paper, we do not distinguish between these two algorithms, since both require one parallel step.

The MP model is related to, but not identical to a Map Reduce (MR) job [8]. MR corresponds to one MP step: there is no broadcast phase, the communication phase is the *map job* followed by data reshuffling, and the computation phase is the *reduce job*. However, to implement an MP algorithm over MR one has to implement the broadcast phase either as a separate, lightweight MR job, or by sampling the data before it is partitioned into servers at the beginning of the map job. As we show in Proposition 3.5, the broadcast phase is necessary to ensure load balance even for the simplest of the join algorithms, and this is why we include it in the model. Using sampling in order to improve load balance is a popular technique in practice, for example it is used in *skew join* in Pig [10].

Finally, note that in Definition 3.1, n_0 is allowed to depend on P. In other words, once P is fixed, load balance is expected only for n "large enough". In some of our algorithms we require $P = O(n^\varepsilon)$, for some $0 < \varepsilon < 1$.

3.1 Main Result

The main result in this paper is a complete characterization of queries that are computable in one MP step by a load balanced algorithm. To describe this result we first need some definitions.

Given a conjunctive query Q and a variable x, denote by $at(x)$ the set of atoms that contain x. A query is called *hierarchical* if for any two variables x, y, one of the following holds: $at(x) \subseteq at(y)$ or $at(x) \supseteq at(y)$ or $at(x) \cap at(y) = \emptyset$.

A conjunctive query is called *tall-flat* if one can order its variables $x_1, \ldots, x_k, y_1, \ldots, y_\ell$ such that: (1) $at(x_1) \supseteq at(x_2) \supseteq \ldots \supseteq at(x_k)$, (2) $at(x_k) \supseteq at(y_i)$ for $i = 1, \ldots, \ell$, and (3) $|at(y_i)| = 1$. Clearly, every tall-flat query is hierarchical. Furthermore, if $l = 0$ then we call it a tall query, and

---

[5] And, thus, the time of the computation phase will also be halved, assuming that the computation time is linear in the size of the data.

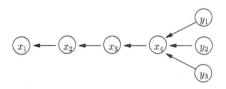

Figure 1: The tall-flat query L. An arrow $u \to v$ denotes that $at(u) \subseteq at(v)$.

if $k = 1$ then we call it a flat query. For example the query

$$L(x_1, x_2, x_3, x_4, y_1, y_2, y_3) : -$$
$$R_1(x_1), R_2(x_1, x_2), R_3(x_1, x_2, x_3),$$
$$R_4(x_1, x_2, x_3, x_4), S_1(x_1, x_2, x_3, x_4, y_1),$$
$$S_2(x_1, x_2, x_3, x_4, y_2), S_3(x_1, x_2, x_3, x_4, y_3)$$

is a tall-flat query (Figure 1). The main result we prove is:

THEOREM 3.2. *Every tall-flat conjunctive query can be evaluated in one MP step by a load balanced algorithm. Conversely, if a query is not tall-flat, then every algorithm consisting of one MP step is not load balanced.*

3.2 Datalog Notation for MP Algorithms

Throughout the paper, we express algorithms using a simple extension to non-recursive datalog, which allows us to specify the location where data is stored. For this purpose we adopt the syntax from [2]. If $R(x, y)$ is a relation (binary in this case), then the notation $\text{R}(@s, x, y)$ denotes the *fragment* of the relation R which is stored at server s. Using this notation, we can define computations and communication in the following way:

- Local computation: $\text{R}(@s, x, y) :- \text{S}(@s, x, y), \text{T}(@s, x)$
- Broadcast: $\text{R}(@*, x) :- \text{S}(@s, x), \text{T}(@s, x)$
- Point-to-point communication: $\text{R}(@h(x), x, y) :- \text{S}(@s, x, y)$

3.3 Examples

We illustrate our model by giving two simple algorithms, for computing the intersection of two sets, and a semijoin.

The first query computes the intersection of two sets R, S, $Q(x) : -R(x), S(x)$. This query is both tall and flat, and can be computed by the distributed hash-join Algorithm 1.

Algorithm 1: INTERSECTION($R(x), S(x)$)

```
/* Communication Phase */
R2(@h(x), x) :- R(@s, x)
S2(@h(x), x) :- S(@s, x)

/* Computation Phase */
Q(@s, x) :- R2(@s, x), S2(@s, x)
```

In this algorithm, h is a hash function $h : U \to [P]$. Each server s applies the hash function h to each tuple $R(a)$ and sends it to the destination server $h(a)$; similarly for tuples $S(b)$. In the computation phase, the tuples placed in the same server are joined. Clearly, this algorithm is correct, and runs in one parallel step, having no broadcast phase. We will prove next that it is load balanced.

No fixed hash function h can guarantee load balance, because there exists a worst case data instance such that all its data values collude under h. Instead, we follow here the standard approach, and assume that h is a *uniform family*[6] of hash functions [18]. Thus, in general, any MP algorithm starts by choosing randomly its hash functions from $\mathcal{H}$: once these choices $\bar{h} \in \mathcal{H}$ are made, we call the execution of the algorithm a *run*. The load balance requirement can be rephrased as follows: $\mathbb{E}_{\bar{h} \in \mathcal{H}}[\max_s n_s] = O(n/P)$, where the expectation is taken over all runs.

PROPOSITION 3.3. *Assuming $n = \Omega(P \log P)$, Algorithm 1 is load balanced, i.e. the expected maximum server load is $\mathbb{E}[\max_s n_s] = O(n/P)$.*

PROOF. Consider the classical *balls in bins* problem: n balls are randomly thrown into P bins. If $n = \Omega(P \log P)$, the expected maximum load of a bin is $\Theta(n/P)$ [19]. This immediately proves the claim: each of the n tuples in R and S is a ball, and h places each tuple independently in one of the P servers (= bins), because h is chosen from a uniform family of hash functions, hence $\mathbb{E}[\max_s n_s] = \Theta(n/P)$. □

Our second example illustrates the broadcast phase. Consider the query $Q(x,y) : -R(x), S(x,y)$: this is a semijoin, and it is a tall query. A naive extension of the previous algorithm would partition both $R(x)$ and $S(x,y)$ according to a hash function $h(x)$, but this may result in data skew: for example, if all tuples $S(x,y)$ have the same value $x = a$, then they will be hashed to the same server $h(a)$, whose load increases to $O(n)$. Here it is necessary to obtain some information about the distribution of tuples in S, using the broadcast phase. Algorithm 2 performs a load balanced computation of the semijoin query.

Algorithm 2: SEMI-JOIN$(R(x), S(x,y))$

```
/* Broadcast Phase */
/* Compute skewed elements; τ = |S|/(P log P) */
G(@s, x, count(*)) :- S(@s,x,y)
H(@s, x)  :- G(@s,x,f), f > τ/P
B(@*, x)  :- H(@s, x)      /* Broadcast */
/* Communication Phase */
R2(@h(x), x) :- R(@s, x), not B(@s, x)
S(@h(x), x, y) :- S(@s, x, y), not B(@s, x)
R2(@*, x) :- R(@s, x), B(@s, x)
S(@h2(x,y), x) :- S(@s, x, y), B(@s, x)
/* Computation Phase */
Q(@s, x, y) :- R2(@s, x), S2(@s, x, y)
```

In general, for any relation $S(x, \ldots)$ and attribute x of S, define the *frequency* $f_{S,x}(a)$ of a constant a to be the number of elements in S that have a on the x position. Let $\tau > 0$ be a value called a *threshold*. A value a is called (S, x, τ)-skewed, or simply *skewed*, or *frequent*, if $f_{S,x}(a) \geq \tau$; we denote $F_{S,x,\tau}(x)$ the set of skewed elements. Notice that $|F_{S,x,\tau}| \leq |S|/\tau$.

The semi-join Algorithm 2 starts by computing all τ-skewed elements, for $\tau = |S|/(P \log P)$. This set cannot be efficiently computed exactly, because S is distributed; instead we compute a superset B. Each server s computes all elements x whose local frequency is $\geq \tau/P$; the count(*) notation is from [5]. There are $\leq (|S|/P)/(\tau/P) = |S|/\tau$ locally skewed elements. These sets are broadcast, and each server computes their union, B. The set B contains $F_{S,x,\tau}$,

---

[6]The family $\mathcal{H}$ is called *uniform* on a set $S = \{x_1, \ldots, x_k\}$ if $h \in \mathcal{H}$ maps S to k values that are uniformly random and independent. Uniformity is strictly stronger than *universality* [3]. In all our algorithms, $|S| = O(n)$.

and $|B| \leq P \cdot |S|/\tau$; thus the communication cost of the broadcast phase is $\leq P^2 \cdot |S|/\tau = P^3 \log P = O(n^\varepsilon)$ (we show in Subsection 4.1 how to further improve this). Next, the semi-join algorithm proceeds as follows. For all non-skewed elements x, both $R(x)$ and $S(x,y)$ are sent to the server $h(x)$; for the skewed elements, $S(x,y)$ is distributed using a second hash function $h2(x,y)$, while $R(x)$ is broadcast to all servers. This is similar to *skew join* in Pig [10], but computes the skewed elements differently.

PROPOSITION 3.4. *Assuming $n = \Omega(P^3 \log P)$, Algorithm 2 is load balanced.*

The proof follows as a corollary of Theorem 4.4, which we prove in the next section.

We now prove that, without a broadcast phase, no load-balanced algorithm can compute the semi-join in one step. This justifies including a broadcast phase in the MP model.

PROPOSITION 3.5. *If an algorithm for computing the semi-join $Q(x,y) : -R(x), S(x,y)$ has one single parallel step and no broadcast phase, then it is skewed.*

PROOF. We start by revisiting how the data is partitioned. In the MP model the input data is partitioned *jointly*: each sever holds a fragment from each relation. But in impossibility proofs we will assume that the database is partitioned *separately*: each server holds a fragment from only one relation: $P \cdot |R|/(|R| + |S|)$ severs hold fragments of R, and $P \cdot |S|/(|R| + |S|)$ servers hold fragments of S. Any impossibility result for the separate partition implies an impossibility result for the joint partition, because any load balanced algorithm A over the separate partition can be simulated by a balanced algorithm A' over the joint partition as follows. Given a separately partitioned instance R, S, extend it to a joint partitioned instance R', S', by inserting new R-tuples in the servers holding S, and inserting new S-tuples in the servers holding R, such that $|R'| = |S'| = |R| + |S|$. The new tuples are chosen s.t. they do not join with any other tuples. Run A' on R', S': the result is $S' \ltimes R' = S \ltimes R$. Thus, w.l.o.g., we will assume a separate partition in all impossibility proofs.

Assume A is a load balanced algorithm computing the query Q. Let c be the constant in Definition 3.1, let $P \geq 64c^2$, and let $n = n_0$, where n_0 is given by Definition 3.1 (it may depend on P). We will show that A does not compute correctly Q on an instance of size $2n$ using P processors. To simplify the notations we assume that A uses a single hash function h, of arity k: the extension to multiple hash functions is straightforward. Fix two n-vectors $X = (x_1, \ldots, x_n)$ and $Y = (y_1, \ldots, y_n) \in U^n$ of distinct elements. For each $m = 1, n$, denote $D^{(m)} = (R, S^{(m)})$ the instance $R = \{x_1, \ldots, x_n\}$, and $S^{(m)} = \{(x_m, y_1), \ldots, (x_m, y_n)\}$. For any run $h \in \mathcal{H}$, let $K_h(R(x_i))$ and $K_h(S(x_i, y_j)) \subseteq [P]$ be the set of servers that receive $R(x_i)$ or $S(x_i, y_j)$ respectively.

LEMMA 3.6. *If A is load balanced, then for any $X, Y \in U^n$, there exists an instance $D^{(m)}$ (constructed from X, Y, m as explained above), a run $h \in \mathcal{H}$, and an element $y_i \in Y$, such that $K_h(R(x_m)) \cap K_h(S(x_m, y_i)) = \emptyset$.*

PROOF. Let $n_s(D^{(m)}, h)$ be the load at server s for the instance $D^{(m)}$ and the run h. Since $size(D^{(m)}) = 2n$, by Definition 3.1, $\mathbb{E}_{h \in \mathcal{H}}(\max_s n_s(D^{(m)}, h)) \leq 2 \cdot c \cdot n/P$. Let $d = 4 \cdot c$. We say that h is *balanced for $D^{(m)}$* if $\max_s(n_s(D^{(m)}, h)) \leq 2 \cdot d \cdot n/P$, and we say that h is *balanced* if it is balanced for some $D^{(m)}$. Denote by $\mathcal{H}^{(m)}$ the set of runs balanced for $D^{(m)}$, and $\mathcal{H}^{(*)} = \bigcup_m \mathcal{H}^{(m)}$. By Markov's inequality, $|\mathcal{H}^{(m)}|/|\mathcal{H}| \geq 1 - c/d = 3/4$, and also $|\mathcal{H}^{(*)}|/|\mathcal{H}| \geq 3/4$: thus, most runs are balanced.

Call an element x_i *good* for run h if, on some input $D^{(m)}$, $|K_h(R(x_i))| < P/(2 \cdot d)$: "goodness" does not depend on $D^{(m)}$, because the input is partitioned separately, and all instances $D^{(m)}$ have the same R. We claim that there exists m such that x_m is good for some $h \in \mathcal{H}^{(m)}$. The claim proves the lemma: indeed, consider the run h on the instance $D^{(m)}$. Each server in $K_h(R(x_m))$ stores at most $2 \cdot d \cdot n/P$ tuples (since h is balanced for $D^{(m)}$); hence, together they hold $< P/(2 \cdot d) \times 2 \cdot d \cdot n/P = n$ tuples. This implies that at least one of the n tuples $S(x_m, y_i)$, $i = 1, n$ is not sent to any server in $K_h(R(x_m))$.

To prove the claim, denote for each $h \in \mathcal{H}^{(*)}$:

$$B_h = \{x_i \mid |K_h(R(x_i))| \geq P/(2 \cdot d)\} \quad (bad \text{ elements})$$
$$G_h = \{x_i \mid |K_h(R(x_i))| < P/(2 \cdot d)\} \quad (good \text{ elements})$$

Clearly, $B_h \cup G_h = \{x_1, \ldots, x_n\}$. Since h is balanced for some $D^{(m)}$ we have $|B_h| \cdot P/(2 \cdot d) \leq 2 \cdot d \cdot n$. Therefore:

$$|G_h| \geq (1 - \frac{4d^2}{P}) \times n \geq 3/4 \cdot n \qquad \forall h \in \mathcal{H}^{(*)} \quad (1)$$

The last inequality holds because $P \geq 64c^2 = 16d^2$. We now prove that there exists a set $\mathcal{H}' \subseteq \mathcal{H}^{(*)}$ such that:

$$\bigcap_{h \in \mathcal{H}'} G_h \neq \emptyset \quad \text{and} \quad |\mathcal{H}'| \geq 3/4 \cdot |\mathcal{H}^{(*)}| \geq 9/16 \cdot |\mathcal{H}| \quad (2)$$

For that, consider the $\{0,1\}$-matrix $E = (e_{ih})$ of dimensions $n \times |\mathcal{H}^{(*)}|$, where $e_{ih} = 1$ iff $x_i \in G_h$. By Equation 1, every column h has at least $3/4$ of entries equal to 1; thus, at least $3/4$ of entries in the entire matrix are 1; thus, there exists a row m with at least $3/4$ of the entries 1. Then, $\mathcal{H}' = \{h \mid e_{mh} = 1\}$ satisfies Equation 2.

To prove the claim, we show that $\mathcal{H}^{(m)} \cap \mathcal{H}' \neq \emptyset$. This follows from $|\mathcal{H}^{(m)}| + |\mathcal{H}'| \geq 3/4 \cdot |\mathcal{H}| + 9/16 \cdot |\mathcal{H}| = 21/16 \cdot |\mathcal{H}|$: the two sets combined have more elements than $\mathcal{H}$ and therefore have a non-empty intersection. $\square$

Fix $D = D^{(m)} = (R, S^{(m)})$, and the run h given by the lemma. We will show that the algorithm is incorrect on the run h, by showing that it fails to output the tuple (x_m, y_i). Servers $\notin K_h(S(x_m, y_i))$ cannot output this tuple, since they don't receive y_i and cannot fabricate a generic value in U. Servers $\in K_h(S(x_m, y_i))$ don't receive $R(x_m)$. To show that they cannot output this tuple either, consider the execution of the algorithm on a second instance $D' = (R', S^{(m)})$ where R' is obtained from R by replacing the single tuple $R(x_m)$ with $R(x_m')$, where $x_m' \neq x_m$: (x_m', y_i) is no longer an answer to Q on D'. Servers holding input fragments of S will send their data to the same destinations, since S is unchanged; in particular, $S(x_m, y_i)$ is sent to the same set $K_h(S(x_m, y_i))$. We claim that, during the two execution of the algorithm, on D and D' respectively, the server holding $R(x_m)$ (in D) or $R(x_m')$ (in D') will obtain exactly the same hash values; in particular, it will send its elements to exactly the same destinations, hence $K_h(R(x_m')) \cap K_h(S(x_m, y_i)) = \emptyset$. Thus, the servers in $K_h(S(x_m, y_i))$ receive exactly the same elements during the two executions, and will not be able to distinguish between D and D', thus cannot determine whether to output the tuple (x_m, y_i).

It remains to prove the claim. For $X \in U^n$ denote $\mathcal{H}(X)$ the array consisting of all hash functions $h \in \mathcal{H}$ applied to all values in X. One can view $\mathcal{H}$ as assigning a color to each point in U^n. The number of colors is finite, c: for example, if all hash functions in $\mathcal{H}$ have type $h : U^k \to [P]$, then $c = [P]^{|\mathcal{H}| \cdot n^k}$. Call a set $\bar{V} = V_1 \times \cdots \times V_n \subseteq U^n$ a *p-space* if

$|V_i| \geq p$, for $i = 1, n$. A p-space is *unicolored* if all its points have the same color. We prove that there exists a unicolored 2-space $\{x_1, x_1'\} \times \cdots \times \{x_n, x_n'\}$. This implies Corollary 3.8, which proves the claim.

LEMMA 3.7. *Suppose all points in U^n are colored with c colors. Then, for every $p > 0$ there exists $M > 0$ such that every M-space has a unicolored p-subspace. In particular, if U is infinite, then U^n has a unicolored 2-subspace.*

PROOF. We set $M = f_n(p)$, where $f_1(p) = (p-1) \cdot c + 1$, $f_{n+1}(p) = f_n^{(f_1(p))}(p)$ (where $f_n^{(k)}(p) = f_n(\cdots f_n(p) \cdots)$, k times). The proof is by induction on n. For $n = 1$, consider a set V_1 with $f_1(p)$ points: at least p have the same color. Assuming the lemma is true for n, we prove it for $n+1$. Let $M = f_{n+1}(p)$ and consider an $(n + 1)$-dimensional M-space $\bar{V}^0 \times V_{n+1}$, where $\bar{V}^0 = V_1 \times \cdots \times V_n$. Let $k = (p-1) \cdot c + 1$. Fix k distinct elements $x_1, \ldots, x_k \in V_{n+1}$ (this is possible since $|V_{n+1}| \geq M = f_{n+1}(p) \geq f_1(p) = k$). Denote $p_k = p$, $p_{i-1} = f_n(p_i)$ for $i = k, \ldots, 1$; thus, $M = p_0$. For every $i = 1, k$ there exists an n-dimensional p_i-space $\bar{V}^i$ such that $\bar{V}^i \times \{x_i\}$ is unicolored, and $\bar{V}^i \subseteq \bar{V}^{i-1}$: indeed, $\bar{V}^0 \times \{x_1\}$ is an n-dimensional space, hence by induction on n has a unicolored subspace $\bar{V}^1 \times \{x_1\}$; suppose $\bar{V}^{i-1} \times \{x_{i-1}\}$ is unicolored: since $\bar{V}^{i-1} \times \{x_i\}$ is an n-dimensional p_{i-1}-space, it has a unicolored p_i-subspace $\bar{V}^i \times \{x_i\}$. Thus, we obtain k unicolored spaces, $\bar{V}^1 \times \{x_1\}, \ldots, \bar{V}^k \times \{x_k\}$, and at least p of them have the same color: $\bar{V}^{i_1} \times \{x_{i_1}\}, \ldots, \bar{V}^{i_p} \times \{x_{i_p}\}$. Then $\bar{V}^{i_p} \times \{x_{i_1}, \ldots, x_{i_p}\}$ is a unicolored p-space. $\square$

COROLLARY 3.8. *There exist vectors $X = (x_1, \ldots, x_n)$ and $Y = (x_1', \ldots, x_n')$ such that for any m, the vectors X and $X' = (x_1, \ldots, x_m', \ldots, x_n)$ collude.*

4. THREE BUILDING BLOCKS

In this section, we describe the building blocks for the algorithm computing any tall-flat query in one MP step: we give an algorithm for computing the frequent elements of a relation, an algorithm for computing any flat query, and an algorithm for computing any tall query. In Section 5 we combine them to give a general algorithm for any tall-flat query.

4.1 Computing High Frequency Elements

The *distributed frequent elements problem* is the following: given a distributed relation $R(x, \ldots)$ of size $r = |R|$, and a threshold τ, compute a set F containing all skewed elements $F_{R,x,\tau}$, and distribute F to all servers. We consider algorithms that proceed in two steps: (a) compute and broadcast a set B to all servers, and (b) compute a subset F of B at each server s.t. F is a superset of $F_{R,x,\tau}$. We define two costs: the *amortized communication cost*, $|B|$, and the *excess cost*, $|F|$. Our goal is to keep the amortized cost $O(n^\varepsilon/P)$, becuase the total communication cost is $P \cdot |B|$. The excess is at least r/τ, because, in the worst case, there are r/τ frequent elements $F_{R,x,\tau}$: our goal is to prevent it from being much larger. We present here three algorithms for the distributed frequent element problem.

The *naive algorithm* consists of the top three rules in Algorithm 2. Here $F = B$, hence both amortized cost and excess are $\leq P \cdot r/\tau$.

The *Deterministic Frequency*, Algorithm 3, has essentially the same amortized cost, but a smaller excess. It starts by computing all elements whose local frequency is $\geq \tau/(2P)$, and retains their local frequencies, then broadcasts these elements: thus, the amortized communication cost is $|B| \leq$

Algorithm 3: DETERMINISTIC FREQUENCY(R, τ)

```
HS(@s,x,count(*)):- R(@s,x,...)
G(@s,x,f) :- HS(@s,x,f), f > τ/(2P)
B(@*,x,f,s) :- G(@s,x,f) /* Broadcast */
H(@s,x,sum(*)) :- B(@s,x,f,-)
F(@s,x) :- H(@s, x, f), f ≥ τ/2
```

$2 \cdot P \cdot r / \tau$, twice that of the naive algorithm. Then, it retains in F only those elements x whose total frequency exceeds $\tau/2$; therefore, the excess is $|F| \leq 2 \cdot r/\tau$, a factor of $P/2$ smaller than the naive algorithm.

Algorithm 4: FREQUENCY SAMPLING(R, τ)

```
T = c · r · log r/τ /* c is a constant */
t_s ~ B(r,T/(P·r)) /* binomial sample */
H(@s, x, ...) :- sampling(@s, R, t_s)
G(@s, x, count(*)) :- H(@s, x, ...)
B(@*, x, s) :- H(@s, x, ...) /* Broadcast */
K(@s, x, count(*)) :- B(@s, x, -)
F(@s, x) :- K(@s, x, f), f ≥ c·τ·T/r
```

The *Frequency Sampling*, Algorithm 4, has both a smaller amortized communication, and a smaller excess cost over the naive algorithm. Denote $T = c \cdot r \cdot \log r/\tau$, where $c > 0$ is some constant. The algorithm starts by computing a "coin-flip" sample B of R, where each element of R is sampled independently, without replacement, with probability T/r. Thus, $\mathbb{E}[|B|] = T$, and the amortized communication cost is $c \cdot r \cdot \log r/\tau$ in expectation, which is significantly lower than $P \cdot r/\tau$ when $\log r \ll P$. To compute B distributively, each server s generates a random number t_s drawn from a binomial distribution $B(r, T/(P \cdot r))$ (thus, $\mathbb{E}[t_s] = T/P$), then samples t_s elements without replacement from its local fragment R_s, using the primitive function $\mathtt{sampling}(@s, R, t_s)$. Once B has been computed and broadcast, we retain in F only those elements whose total frequency is $\geq c \cdot \tau \cdot \frac{T}{r}$. We prove in the appendix (Proposition A.1) that, with high probability, the frequency of all elements in F is $\Omega(\tau)$, hence the excess is, in expectation, $O(r/\tau)$.

4.2 Flat Queries

We start with Algorithm 5, which computes the full join $Q(x, y, z) : -R(x, y), S(x, z)$. Similarly to the semijoin algorithm, during the broadcast phase we compute the high frequency elements in R and in S. We set frequency threshold for R to $\tau_R = \sqrt{r/(P \log P)}$ and for S to $\tau_S = \sqrt{s/(P \log P)}$. Using one of the distributed high frequency algorithms in Subsection 4.1, we compute a set RF containing all frequent elements F_{R, x, τ_R} and a set SF containing all frequent elements F_{S, x, τ_S}. Then we proceed similarly to the semijoin algorithm: if x is frequent in R then we duplicate the $S(x, z)$ elements; otherwise, if it is frequent in S then we duplicate the $R(x, y)$ elements; otherwise we don't duplicate, but hash on x.

THEOREM 4.1. *Assuming* $|R|/\log^2 |R| = \Omega(P^3 \log P)$, *and similarly for* S, *the* JOIN *algorithm is load balanced and has one MP step.*

PROOF. We will analyze each of the three cases of the Algorithm 5 separately. For any value a, let[7] $N(a) = f_R(a) + f_S(a) + f_Q(a)$ be the number of tuples from R, S and Q that

---

[7]We abbreviate $f_{R,x}$ with f_R, etc.

Algorithm 5: JOIN$(R(x, y), S(y, z))$

```
/* Broadcast Phase: compute RF, SF */
/* Communication Phase*/
/* CASE 1: R hashed, S duplicated */
 HR(@h1(x,y),x,y) :- R(@s,x,y), RF(x)
 DS(@*,x,z)       :- S(@s,x,z), RF(x)

/* CASE 2: S hashed, R duplicated */
 HS(@h2(x,z),x,z):- S(@s,x,z), SF(x), not RF(x)
 DR(@*,x,y)       :- R(@s,x,y), SF(x), not RF(x)

/* CASE 3: both R, S hashed */
 TR(@h3(x),x,y):- R(@s,x,y), not SF(x), not RF(x)
 TS(@h3(x),x,z):- S(@s,x,z), not SF(x), not RF(x)

/* Computation Phase */
 Q(@s,x,y,z)  :- HR(@s,x,y), DS(@s,x,z)
 Q(@s,x,y,z)  :- DR(@s,x,y), HS(@s,x,z)
 Q(@s,x,y,z)  :- TR(@s,x,y), TS(@s,x,z)
```

contain the element a. Moreover, let $N_s(a)$ the number of these tuples sent to server s. We extend these notations for a set of elements V, that is, $N_s(V) = \sum_{a \in V} N_s(a)$.

First, consider a frequent value $a \in RF$. Then, $N(a) = f_R(a) \cdot f_S(a) + f_R(a) + f_S(a)$. Since the hashing we use is uniform, using the balls in bins argument, the expected maximum number of tuples from R containing a in any server is bounded by $2f_R(a)/P$ (as long as $f_R(a) \geq P \log P$, which holds when $r = \Omega(P^3 \log^3 P)$). In the case that $f_S(a) = 0$, we have $N(a) = f_R(a)$ and thus $\mathbb{E}[\max_s N_s(a)] \leq 2f_R(a)/P$. Otherwise, $f_S(a) \geq 1$ and

$$\mathbb{E}[\max_s N_s(a)] \leq f_S(a) + 2 \cdot \frac{f_R(a)}{P}(f_S(a) + 1) \leq 8 \cdot \frac{f_R(a)f_S(a)}{P}$$

The last inequality holds since $1 \leq f_S(a)$ and $f_R(a)/P > 1$. By combining the two cases for $f_S(a)$, we have that for some constant c:

$$\mathbb{E}[\max_s N_s(a)] \leq \frac{c}{P} \cdot [f_R(a)f_S(a) + f_R(a)]$$

Similarly for a frequent value $a \in SF \setminus RF$, it holds that

$$\mathbb{E}[\max_s N_s(a)] \leq \frac{c}{P} \cdot [f_R(a)f_S(a) + f_S(a)]$$

Last, we consider the case of the non-frequent values $Y_f = \{a : \neg RF(a), \neg SF(a)\}$. We can bound the load $N(a)$ of a value $a \in Y_f$ by observing that $N(a) \leq \tau_R + \tau_S + \tau_R \cdot \tau_S \leq 4\tau_R \cdot \tau_S = 4 \cdot \sqrt{r \cdot s}/(P \log P) \leq 2 \cdot (r+s)/(P \log P)$. In this case, all tuples which contain a are sent to the same server. Thus, we can associate each value a with a ball of size $N(a)$ which is thrown u.a.r. to a server. We showed that the maximum size of such a ball is $w_{max} = 2 \cdot (r+s)/(P \log P)$. Let W be the total size of the balls, i.e. $W = N(Y_f) \leq |Q|$.

Now, we apply the lemma from [20]: the expected maximum load when we throw balls with maximum size w_{max} and total size W into P bins is maximized when we consider $B = W/w_{max}$ balls of size w_{max}. If $B \leq P \log P$, then the expected maximum number of balls on a server will be $\Theta(\log P)$; then, $\mathbb{E}[\max_s N_s(Y_f)] = \Theta(\log P) \cdot w_{max} = \Theta((r + s)/P)$. In the case that $B \geq P \log P$, it follows from the balls in bins that $\mathbb{E}[\max_s N_s(Y_f)] \leq \left(\frac{2}{P} \cdot \frac{W}{w_{max}}\right) \cdot w_{max} = \frac{2W}{P}$.

Finally, we sum for all the cases and all values a.

$$\mathbb{E}[\max_s n_s] \leq \sum_{a \in RF} \mathbb{E}[\max_s N_s(a)] +$$

$$\sum_{a \in SF \setminus RF} \mathbb{E}[\max_s N_s(a)] + \mathbb{E}[\max_s N_s(Y_f)]$$

By substituting the bounds we have computed and summing, we conclude that the load is indeed balanced among the servers, that is, $\mathbb{E}[\max_s n_s] = O\left(\frac{|R|+|S|+|Q|}{P}\right)$. $\square$

Generalizing to k-way joins for $k > 2$ is non-trivial. We illustrate the algorithm for $k = 3$, on the query $Q(x,y,z,w) = R(x,y), S(x,z), T(x,w)$. To see the difficulty, recall that, for a single join, $R(x,y), S(x,z)$, if $x \in RF$ then all tuples $S(x,z)$ are replicated to all servers: the cost of replication is justified by the size of the answer. But in the three-way join, they may not be in the answer, namely when x does not occur in $T(x,w)$. Thus, we need a second round of broadcast to compute the intersection of RF, SF, TF with the x-values occurring in R, S, T. We sketch the main parts of the algorithm.

Set the frequency threshold for R to $\tau_R = \sqrt[3]{r/P \log P}$; similarly for S, T. The broadcast phase has two rounds:

Broadcast 1: Compute and broadcast the sets RF, SF, TF, which contain all frequent elements in R, S, T respectively (using any of the algorithms in Subsection 4.1).

Broadcast 2: Compute and broadcast the intersections. We show this only for R (it works similarly for S, T):

```
RH^S(@s, x)  :-  RF(@s, x), S(@s,x,y)
RH^T(@s, x)  :-  RF(@s, x), T(@s,x,z)
RG^S(@*, x)  :-  RF^S(@s,x)    /* Broadcast */
RG^T(@*, x)  :-  RF^T(@s,x)    /* Broadcast */
RF'(@s,x)    :-  RG^S(@s, x), RG^T(@s, x)
```

Informally, each server s computes $RH_s^S = RF \cap S_s$ and $RF_s^T = RF \cap T_s$; it then broadcasts these values. Last, each server computes the final set $RF' = \left(\bigcup_s RF_s^S\right) \cap \left(\bigcup_s RF_s^T\right)$.

The communication phase is a straightforward generalization of Algorithm 5. There are four cases: (1) $x \in RF'$, (2) $x \in SF' \setminus RF'$, (3) $x \in TF' \setminus (RF' \cup SF')$ and (4) $x \notin (RF' \cup SF' \cup TF')$. We give the formal description of only the first case.

```
/* Case 1: R hashed, S, T replicated
HR(@h(x,y),x,y) :- R(@s,x,y), RF'(x)
HS(@*,x,z)      :- S(@s,x,z), RF'(x)
HT(@*,x,w)      :- T(@s,x,w), RF'(x)
...
Q(@s,x,y,z,w)   :- HR(@s,x,y), HS(x,z), HT(x,w)
```

PROPOSITION 4.2. *The algorithm computing the 3-JOIN is load balanced and runs in one MP step.*

We give the proof in the appendix, using essentially the same techniques as in the case of the single join. This algorithm generalizes straightforwardly to arbitrary flat queries: note that the algorithm continues to use only two rounds in the broadcast phase.

We end this subsection by proving that two rounds are necessary in the broadcast phase. The proof is included in the appendix.

PROPOSITION 4.3. *Any MP algorithm that computes the query $Q'(x,y,z) :- R(x,y), S(x,z), T(x)$ using at most one broadcast round is skewed.*

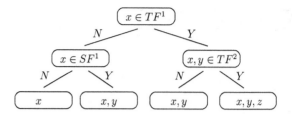

Figure 2: The decision tree for the tall query Q.

4.3 Tall Queries

We describe here the algorithm for the tall query $Q(x,y,z) :- R(x), S(x,y), T(x,y,z)$. The generalization to arbitrary tall queries is straightforward and omitted.

For the broadcast phase, we first set the thresholds $\tau_S = s/P \log P$ and $\tau_T = t/P \log P$. Using any algorithm in Subsection 4.1, we compute the following sets:

- $SF^1 \supseteq \{x \mid f_S(x) \geq \tau_S\}$
- $TF^1 \supseteq \{x \mid f_T(x) \geq \tau_T\}$
- $TF^2 \supseteq \{x,y \mid f_T(x,y) \geq \tau_T\}$

Next, each server constructs the decision tree of Figure 2. Consider a server s and any tuple t belonging to one of its fragments R_s, S_s, T_s. Depending on which of the relations t belongs to, a subset of the variables x, y, z is bound. That is, if $t \in R$ then it binds x; if $t \in S$ then it binds x, y; and if $t \in T$ then it binds x, y, z. Starting from the root, we follow the decision tree until one of two things happens:

- We reach a node asking for a variable not bound by t, e.g. if $t \in R$ and we reach a node asking for x, y. In this case, we broadcast t to all the servers.
- We reach a leaf of the tree. Then, we hash t according to the hash function with parameters the variables of the leaf node, that is, we send t either to $h1(x)$ or to $h2(x,y)$ or to $h3(x,y,z)$.

For example, consider a tuple $S(a,b)$, such that a is frequent in T and a,b is not frequent in T. Then, this tuple will be sent to server $h2(a,b)$. After distributing the tuples, each server locally computes the join.

THEOREM 4.4. *For $|S|, |T|$ large enough: $|S|/\log|S| = \Omega(P^2 \log P)$ (similarly for T), the algorithm for computing the tall query Q is load balanced and has one MP step.*

PROOF. First, consider all the tuples that are broadcast by the algorithm. R may broadcast at most $P \log P$ tuples for frequent values in S and T. Moreover, S may broadcast a tuple for a frequent value in T, which are at most $P \log P$. Hence, each server receives at most $3 \cdot P \log P = O(n/P)$ such tuples, since $n = \Omega(P^2 \log P)$.

Thus, it suffices to measure the load caused by the tuples which are hashed. We partition the tuples into equivalence classes (*balls*), according to the values they are hashed on (notice that it suffices to consider only input tuples, since the output size is at most the input size). For example, ball $B(a)$ contains all tuples from R, S, T which are hashed only to $h1(a)$. Notice also that if $a \in TF^1$, then $B(a)$ is empty. The following properties hold for any ball:

1. Every tuple of a ball is sent to the same server.
2. Every ball is sent to a u.a.r. chosen server.
3. The maximum size w_{max} of a ball is $(s+t)/(P \log P)$.
4. The total size of the balls is $W \leq |R| + |S| + |T|$.

We only prove property (3), since the others are straight-forward. Consider the case for a ball $B(a)$. Any tuple from S belonging to $B(a)$ is hashed only on the x variable; hence, by the structure of the decision tree, $a \in SF^1$, which implies that $f_S(a) < \tau_S$; hence, there exist at most τ_S such tuples. Similarly, we have at most τ_T tuples from T in $B(a)$. Thus, $|B(a)| < 1 + \tau_S + \tau_T$. For a $B(a,b)$ ball, we have that $|B(a,b)| < 2 + \tau_T$ (and for $B(a,b,c)$ the size is constant).

Following from these properties, the expected maximum load is maximized in the case of W/w_{max} balls with size w_{max}. Using the same argument as in the proof of Theorem 4.1, we obtain that $\mathbb{E}[\max_s n_s] = \Theta(\frac{|R|+|S|+|T|}{P})$. □

5. THE MAIN ALGORITHM

In this section, we show how the techniques presented in the previous sections can be combined to build a load balanced algorithm for any tall-flat query.

For ease of exposition, let us denote by $x_{1:k}$ the sequence of variables or values $x_1, x_2, \ldots, x_k$. We will also assume w.l.o.g. the following form for tall-flat queries: $Q(x_{1:k}, y_{1:\ell}) = R_1(x_1), \ldots, R_k(x_{1:k}), S_1(x_{1:k}, y_1), \ldots, S_\ell(x_{1:k}, y_\ell)$. For simplicity, we will also refer to $S_1, \ldots, S_\ell$ as $R_{k+1}, \ldots, R_{k+\ell}$.

For the algorithm, we will assume that R_i, S_i are large enough: in particular, we will need that $|R_i|/\log|R_i| = \Omega(P^2 \log P)$ and that $|S_i|/\log^\ell |S_i| = \Omega(P^{l+1} \log P)$. We also define the frequency thresholds $\tau_{R_i} = |R_i|/P \log P$ and $\tau_{S_i} = \sqrt[\ell]{|S_i|/P \log P}$.

In order to distribute the tuples in a load balanced way, the algorithm considers two cases: (1) values which cause a large load to the query result Q and (2) the rest of the values. Intuitively, we use flat-query techniques to deal with the first case and tall-query techniques for the second case.

BROADCAST PHASE

Broadcast 1: Using any of the algorithms in Subsection 4.1, compute the sets
$$RF_i^j \supseteq \{x_{1:j} \mid f_{R_i}(x_{1:j}) \geq \tau_{R_i}\} \quad (i = 1, k; \ j = 1, i)$$
$$SF_i^j \supseteq \{x_{1:j} \mid f_{S_i}(x_{1:j}) \geq \tau_{S_i}\} \quad (i = 1, \ell; \ j = 1, k)$$
In particular, using *Frequency Sampling*, we can compute these sets by sampling only once. One can easily check that the communication is $O(n^\varepsilon)$.

Broadcast 2: For every relation $V \neq S_i$, server s computes $SF_i(V, s) = SF_i^k \cap V_s$, i.e. intersects SF_i^k with its local copy of V. These sets are then broadcast. Finally, each server computes the sets $SF_i = \bigcap_{V \neq S_i} \left(\bigcup_s SF_i(V, s) \right)$.

COMMUNICATION PHASE

1. For $i = 1, \ldots, \ell$: for every $x_{1:k} \in SF_i \setminus \bigcup_{j<i} SF_j$, send every tuple of S_i containing $x_{1:k}$ to the server $h(x_{1:k}, y_i)$. Broadcast every tuple $t \in S_j, j \neq i$ containing $x_{1:k}$.

2. Consider a tuple $x_{1:q}, q \leq k$, which does not belong to case (1). For any S_i, all tuples with the same value $x_{1:k}$ are hashed to the same server. In order to decide where to hash (or broadcast) the tuple, we construct a decision tree, which generalizes the one in Figure 2. Initially, let $i = k+\ell$ and $j = 1$ (*root*). At each step, we check whether $x_{1:j} \in RF_i^j$: if this holds, we increment j (*right child*), else we decrement i (*left child*). The algorithm stops when either $j > q$, in which case we broadcast $x_{1:q}$, or when $i = 0$ (a *leaf* is reached) and the tuple is hashed to $h(x_{1:j})$.

COMPUTATION PHASE

The query is locally computed at each server.

THEOREM 5.1. *The algorithm computes any tall-flat query in a load balanced way and has one MP step.*

PROOF. We first analyze the load for the tuples that fall into the first case of the communication phase. Let us consider the case of the FOR loop where $i = 1$ (the same argument can be applied for every i). Consider a value $x_{1:k} \in SF_1$. The total load attributed to this value is $N(x_{1:k}) = \prod_{i=1}^\ell f_{S_i}(x_{1:k}) + \sum_{i=1,\ell} f_{S_i}(x_{1:k})$. Since any tuple from S_1 containing $x_{1:k}$ is hashed on $(x_{1:k}, y_1)$, using the balls in bins argument, we have $\mathbb{E}[\max_s N_s(x_{1:k})] \leq \sum_{i>1} f_{S_i}(x_{1:k}) + (2f_{S_1}(x_{1:k})/P) \cdot (1 + \prod_{i=2}^\ell f_{S_i}(x_{1:k}))$. Moreover, notice that $f_{S_i}(x_{1:k}) \geq 1$ is guaranteed from the second step of the broadcast phase and also $f_{S_1}(x_{1:k}) \geq P$. Thus,

$$\mathbb{E}[\max_s N_s(x_{1:k})] \leq \frac{2k}{P} \cdot \prod_{i=1}^\ell f_{S_i}(x_{1:k})$$

We next consider the values of the second case. In order to compute the load from the tuples that are broadcast to all servers, notice that we have $O(P \log P)$ frequent values for each $x_{1:j}$ in relation R_i, hence a total load of $O(k^2 P \log P)$ for each server. As for relations S_i, we have $|S_i|/\tau_{S_i}$ frequent values for each $x_{1:j}$ in S_i. Thus, each relation causes a load of $O(k \cdot |S_i|/\tau_{S_i})$ to each server from broadcasting tuples. As long as $|S_i| \geq P^{\ell+1} \log P$, this load is bounded by $O(|S_i|/P)$.

Finally, let us measure the load caused by the tuples which are hashed. We partition the tuples into equivalence classes (*balls*), according to the values they are hashed with. Notice that every ball has the following properties: (1) every tuple of a ball is sent to exactly one server, and (2) every ball is sent to a u.a.r. chosen server.

Now, consider a ball $B(x_{1:q}), q \leq k$. We define the size of the ball to include the size of the output. Consider any tuple t from a relation R_i belonging to $B(x_{1:q})$. Clearly, for $i \leq q$, each relation R_i sends at most one tuple to this ball. For $R_i, i > q$, by the structure of the decision tree, $f_{R_i}(x_{1:q}) < \tau_{R_i}$ and thus there exist at most τ_{R_i} such tuples. The same holds for any S_i. Thus,

$$|B(x_{1:q})| \leq q + \sum_{i=q+1}^k \tau_{R_i} + \sum_{i=1}^\ell \tau_{S_i} + |Q_{B(x_{1:q})}|$$

where $Q_{B(x_1)}$ denotes the tuples of Q produced by the tuples in $B(x_{1:q})$. Next, notice that

$$|Q_{B(x_{1:q})}| = \sum_{x_{q+1:k} \in B(x_{1:q})} \prod_{i=1}^\ell f_{S_i}(x_{1:q}, x_{q+1:k})$$

Since every tuple is hashed only on $x_{1:q}$, it must hold that $\sum_{x_{q+1:k} \in B(x_{1:q})} f_{S_i}(x_{1:q}, x_{q+1:k}) \leq \tau_{S_i}$. This implies that $|Q_{B(x_{1:q})}|$ is maximized when there exists a value $x'_{q+1:k}$ such that for every S_i, $f_{S_i}(x_{1:q}, x'_{q+1:k}) = \tau_{S_i}$ (and zero for all the other values). Then, using the Arithmetic-Geometric means inequality, we obtain that

$$|Q_{B(x_{1:q})}| \leq \prod_{i=1}^\ell \tau_{S_i} = \frac{\prod_{i=1}^\ell s_i^{1/\ell}}{P \log P} \leq \frac{1}{\ell} \cdot \frac{\sum_{i=1}^\ell s_i}{P \log P}$$

This implies that $|B(x_{1:q})| \leq c \cdot \frac{size(D)}{P \log P}$, ($c$ is some constant); hence $w_{max} = c \cdot \frac{size(D)}{P \log P}$.

Let W be the total load of the balls. The expected maximum load is maximized when we have just W/w_{max} balls with size w_{max}. Using the same argument as in the proof of Theorem 4.1, we obtain that the expected maximum weight attributed to the hashed values is $\Theta(W/P)$. Summing over all cases, we conclude that the algorithm is indeed load balanced. □

231

6. IMPOSSIBILITY RESULTS

In this section we prove that any query that is not tall-flat cannot be computed in one MP step. First, we show this result for two specific queries, $RST(x,y) : -R(x), S(x,y), T(y)$ and $J(x,y) : -R(x), S(x), T(y)$. Using these results, we prove the claim for any query that is not tall-flat.

THEOREM 6.1. *Any algorithm that computes the query* $RST(x,y) : -R(x), S(x,y), T(y)$ *in one MP step is skewed.*

PROOF. Let A be a one step, load balanced algorithm for RST. Recall from the proof of Proposition 3.5 that we assume that R, S, T are partitioned separately. Using Corollary 3.8, we construct vectors $X = (x_1, \ldots, x_n)$ and $Y = (y_1, \ldots, y_n)$, such that we can substitute each value x_i (y_i) with a value x_i' (y_i') and obtain a colluding set. Now, let us consider an instance D of the database where $R = X$, $T = Y$ and $S = \{(x_i, y_i) \mid i = 1, \ldots, n\}$. Fix also a run $h \in \mathcal{H}$ such that the computation for this instance is load balanced.

Let us first consider the broadcast phase. Since R, T contain disjoint elements and the information exchanged may be only generic (i.e. obtained by generic computations on the instance), the only way for the servers to gain any information about the other relations is to exchange tuples $R(x_i)$, or $T(y_i)$, or $S(x_i, y_i)$: we say that the values $x_i \in X$ or $y_i \in Y$ or both have been *broadcast*. The total amount of communication is bounded by $O(n^\varepsilon)$, hence at most $O(n^\varepsilon)$ values from X and from Y are broadcast. Let X' and Y' be the other values, that are not broadcast: hence $|X'| = n - O(n^\varepsilon)$ and similarly for $|Y'|$. Let $S' = \{(x_i, y_i) \mid x_i \in X', y_i \in Y'\}$; it follows that $|S'| = n - O(n^\varepsilon)$.

Claim: Suppose that we replace S by S_π such that $S_\pi = \{(x_i, y_i) \mid (x_i, y_i) \notin S'\} \cup \{(x_i, y_{\pi(i)}) \mid (x_i, y_i) \in S'\}$, where π is any permutation on the indices of S'. Let us call this instance D_π. Using the argument in Corollary 3.8, we can prove that every server containing R, T tuples will receive exactly the same information under D or D_π.

Thus, the tuples of R, T will be distributed as before, that is, in a load balanced way. Denote $R' = X'$ and $T' = Y'$.

We say that a pair $(R'(x_i), T'(y_j))$ meets when both tuples are placed in the same server. We next compute the total number of pairs which meet for an instance D_π. Since each server holds $O(n/P)$ tuples from R', T', it contains at most $O(n^2/P^2)$ pairs that meet, which gives us a total of $O(n^2/P)$ pairs. However, drawing values from R', T', there are $O(n^2)$ possible pairs. By the pigeonhole principle, there exists a pair such that $R(x_i), T(y_j)$ are not placed in the same server. Then, we fix a permutation π such that the tuple $S(x_i, y_j)$ appears in S_π.

Finally, let us examine the instance $D_\pi : R, T, S_\pi$. For this instance, the tuple (x_i, y_j) is included in the final result. However, the server s where $S(x_i, y_j)$ is sent can not contain both $R(x_i), T(y_j)$. Let us assume w.l.o.g. that it does not contain $R(x_i)$. Then, consider the instance D_π' where we substitute the tuple $R(x_i)$ with $R(x_i')$.

Following from the collusion property, and since x_i' or x_i are not communicated during the broadcast phase, the computation will be identical. This time, however, the tuple (x_i, y_j) does not belong in the output. Nevertheless, the server s that decides upon whether to output the tuple or not does not contain x_i'; due to the genericity of the computation, s must again output the tuple (x_i, y_j), which leads to a contradiction. $\square$

THEOREM 6.2. *Any algorithm that computes the query* $J(x,y) : -R(x), S(x), T(y)$ *in one MP step is skewed.*

PROOF. Let A be an algorithm computing J. First, we fix the instance of $T = \{y_1, \ldots, y_n\}$. Applying Corollary 3.8, we can then find a vector $X = (x_1, \ldots, x_n)$ with distinct elements, such that for each element $x_i \in X$, there exists a vector X_i' where x_i is replaced by $x_i' \neq x_i$ and X, X_i' collude.

Now, let us consider an instance D of the database where $R = X$ and $S = \{x_i' \mid x_i \in X\}$. Following our construction, R and S are disjoint. This means that J is empty and thus the total load is $\sum_s n_s = O(n)$. Since A is load balanced, there exists a run $h \in H$ such that the computation is load balanced.

Notice that, since the elements are disjoint within each relation and we allow only generic computation during the broadcast phase, the only way to gain information is by sending tuples. However, the amount of tuples we can send is limited to $O(n^\varepsilon)$. This means that from each relation, at most $O(n^\varepsilon)$ tuples can be sent to other servers. From this point, we consider only the tuples $t \in R$, such that t, t' are not communicated (call these set R'). Clearly, $|R'| = n - O(n^\varepsilon)$. We similarly define S'.

We say that a pair of elements (x_i, y_j) meets when $T(y_j)$ is placed in the same server with either $R'(x_i)$ or $S'(x_i')$. Since each server receives at most $O(n/P)$ values from each relation, each server holds $O(n^2/P^2)$ pairs that meet; in total, $O(n^2/P)$ pairs. However, the total number of possible pairs is $O(n^2)$. This implies that, by the pigeonhole principle, we can find a pair (x_i, y_j) such that the tuple $T(y_j)$ does not occur in the same server with either $R(x_i)$ or $S(x_i')$.

For the last step of the proof, consider an instance D' where we replace in R the value x_i with x_i'. The servers will receive exactly the same information, since x_i or x_i' are not communicated during the broadcast phase. Thus, due to the collusion property, the behavior of the algorithm will be identical and, for the new instance, $T(y_j)$ will not be placed in the same server as $R(x_i'), S(x_i')$. Consequently, A will not include the tuple (x_i', y_j) in the query output, which is a contradiction, sine (x_i', y_j) now belongs in the final result. $\square$

Based on Theorem 6.1 and Theorem 6.2, we can now prove the following characterization.

THEOREM 6.3. *Let Q be any query that is not tall-flat. Any algorithm that computes Q in one MP step is skewed.*

PROOF. We first show that the queries computable in one MP step are a subset of hierarchical queries. Indeed, consider a query Q which is not hierarchical. Then, there exists a pair of variables x, y such that $at(x) \cap at(y) \neq \emptyset$ and none of $at(x), at(y)$ is a subset of the other. This means that w.l.o.g. we can find atoms R, S, T such that $at(x) \setminus at(y) = \{R\}$, $at(y) \setminus at(x) = \{T\}$ and $at(x) \cap at(y) = \{S\}$. Fix any variable $\neq x, y$ to obtain the same constant value in any relation. Then, Q reduces to computing the query $RST(x,y) : -R(x), S(x,y), T(y)$, which by Theorem 6.1 cannot be computed in one MP step.

We also have the following property: if $|at(x)| > 1$ for a variable x, then for every variable y we have that $at(x) \cap at(y) \neq \emptyset$. Indeed, if that was not true, then by fixing all other variables $\neq x, y$ to obtain the same constant value, we reduce Q to $J(x,y) : -R(x), S(x), T(y)$, which cannot be computed in one MP step by Theorem 6.2. Thus, if x appears in more than one relation, then for every variable $y \neq x$ it holds that either $at(x) \subseteq at(y)$ or $at(y) \subseteq at(x)$.

Let us now order the m variables in decreasing order of $|at(x)|$: $x_1, x_2, \ldots, x_m$. Consider the smallest index k such that for every $i > k$, $|at(x_i)| = 1$. Using the above property, for the first k variables we have that $at(x_1) \supseteq at(x_2) \ldots \supseteq at(x_k)$. Finally, consider a variable $x_j, j > k$; by construction $|at(x_j)| = 1$. We use again the property to see that for any $i \leq k$, $at(x_j) \subseteq at(x_i)$, since $at(x_j)$ is a singleton set. Thus, Q satisfies all three properties of a tall-flat query. □

7. DISCUSSION

Star queries. Consider the following question: given a query Q, what is the smallest number of MP steps necessary to compute Q ? We answer this question for *star queries*, and leave it open for arbitrary conjunctive queries. W.l.o.g. we assume that the star query is of the form $Q(x_1, \ldots, x_k) : -R(x_1, \ldots, x_k), S_1(x_1), \ldots, S_k(x_k)$. Since Q is not tall-flat, we need at least two MP steps to compute it. We show here that two steps are indeed optimal.

PROPOSITION 7.1. *A star query can be computed in two MP steps.*

PROOF. The load balanced algorithm for any star query works as follows. In the first step, compute all subqueries $Q_i(x_1, \ldots, x_k) : -R(x_1, \ldots, x_k), S_i(x_i)$ in parallel, in one MP step (each is a semijoin query). In the second step, compute the intersection $Q(\bar{x}) : -Q_1(\bar{x}), Q_2(\bar{x}), \ldots, Q_k(\bar{x})$ (this MP step does not need a broadcast phase). □

General queries. If Q is a general conjunctive query, it seems difficult to determine the minimum number of parallel steps required to compute Q, because the intermediate results may be much larger than the output. For example, the output may be empty, but in any query plan, some subplan may return an intermediate result whose size is quadratic in the size of the input. One possibility is to adjust the definition of load balance to include in n the size of any intermediate computations.

An algorithm for this case would work as follows. Let us assume a query Q and a query plan P for Q. First, reduce the nodes of P by combining consecutive query computations which correspond to a tall-flat query in one MP step. For example, if the plan operator computes $P_1(x) : -R(x), S(x)$ and its parent computes $P_2(x) : -P_1(x), T(x)$, then we compress the computation in one step: $P_2(x) : -R(x), S(x), T(x)$, since it is a flat query. Each plan P can be thus converted into a minimal plan P'; let d be its depth. It is easy to observe that one can compute P' in d MP steps.

EXAMPLE 7.2. *Let us consider the following chain query: $C(x, y, z, w, v) : -R(x, y), S(y, z), T(z, w), U(w, v)$. A naive query plan would sequentially compute the 3 joins to get the final result: this requires 3 MP steps. However, we can do better if we consider the following query plan:*

$$(R(x, y) \bowtie S(y, z)) \bowtie (T(z, w) \bowtie U(w, v))$$

This plan corresponds to a query tree of depth 2; notice that $R \bowtie S$ and $T \bowtie U$ can be computed in parallel in the same MP step. Hence, we can compute the query in just two MP steps, which is also optimal (since it is not tall-flat).

This example generalizes to any chain query: a chain query with k atoms can be computed in $\log k$ MP steps.

Using Data Statistics. So far, our discussion has focused on the worst case scenario, and both our algorithms and our impossibility results assumed that the sizes of the input relations are independent. In practice, one often knows the sizes of the relations, and can determine that one is much larger than the other. Afrati and Ullman [1] have shown how to compute any conjunctive query in one parallel step. We illustrate their algorithm on the k-way star

query Q at the beginning of this section. Assume that the P processors are organized in a k-dimensional grid. Thus, each server is indexed by a k-tuple of integers $(s_1, \ldots, s_k)$, where $s_i \in [\sqrt[k]{P}]$, for $i = 1, k$. For each $i = 1, k$, let $h_i : U \to [\sqrt[k]{P}]$ be a hash function. Then, during the communication phase the algorithm sends $R(x_1, \ldots, x_k)$ to the server $(h_1(x_1), \ldots, h_k(x_k))$ and replicates $S_i(x_i)$ to all servers of the form $(*, *, \ldots, h_i(x_i), \ldots, *)$; in other words, $S_i(x_i)$ is replicated $\sqrt[k]{P^{k-1}}$ times. In the computation phase, each server computes the join locally. Thus, the algorithm takes a single communication step. In our framework, the algorithm is skewed, because it replicates the relations S_i. However, suppose that it holds $|R| = n$, $|S_1| = \ldots = |S_k| = m$, and $m \sqrt[k]{P^{k-1}} = O(n)$; then the algorithm is load balanced, and computes the star query in one step. This discussion shows that better MP algorithms can be designed by taking into account statistics on the input relations.

8. CONCLUSIONS

In this work, we propose a new theoretical model which captures massive parallelism in today's systems. In this model, the measure of complexity consists of the number of parallel steps necessary to compute a query. Under this context, we study the complexity of conjunctive queries and we give a complete characterization of the queries computable in one parallel step. Future work may include several directions: for any given conjunctive query, can we find the most efficient query plan in terms of steps of the MP model; what is the parallel complexity for more general sets of queries (e.g. queries with unions); and, finally, how can we implement and make the algorithms presented here practical.

Acknowledgments. We would like to thank Foto Afrati, Magda Balazinska, Bill Howe, YongChul Kwon and Jeffrey Ullman for the useful discussions and suggestions.

9. REFERENCES

[1] F. N. Afrati and J. D. Ullman. Optimizing joins in a map-reduce environment. In *EDBT*, pages 99–110, 2010.

[2] P. Alvaro, W. Marczak, N. Conway, J. M. Hellerstein, D. Maier, and R. C. Sears. Dedalus: Datalog in time and space. Technical Report UCB/EECS-2009-173, EECS Department, University of California, Berkeley, Dec 2009.

[3] L. Carter and M. N. Wegman. Universal classes of hash functions. *J. Comput. Syst. Sci.*, 18(2):143–154, 1979.

[4] R. Chaiken, B. Jenkins, P.-A. Larson, B. Ramsey, D. Shakib, S. Weaver, and J. Zhou. Scope: easy and efficient parallel processing of massive data sets. *Proc. VLDB Endow.*, 1:1265–1276, August 2008.

[5] S. Cohen. Containment of aggregate queries. *SIGMOD Record*, 34(1):77–85, 2005.

[6] D. E. Culler, R. M. Karp, D. A. Patterson, A. Sahay, K. E. Schauser, E. E. Santos, R. Subramonian, and T. von Eicken. Logp: Towards a realistic model of parallel computation. In *PPOPP*, pages 1–12, 1993.

[7] N. N. Dalvi and D. Suciu. Efficient query evaluation on probabilistic databases. *VLDB J.*, 16(4):523–544, 2007.

[8] J. Dean and S. Ghemawat. Mapreduce: Simplified data processing on large clusters. In *OSDI*, pages 137–150, 2004.

[9] D. J. DeWitt and J. Gray. Parallel database systems: The future of high performance database systems. *Commun. ACM*, 35(6):85–98, 1992.

[10] A. Gates, O. Natkovich, S. Chopra, P. Kamath, S. Narayanam, C. Olston, B. Reed, S. Srinivasan, and U. Srivastava. Building a highlevel dataflow system on top of mapreduce: The pig experience. *PVLDB*, 2(2):1414–1425, 2009.

[11] M. Grohe, Y. Gurevich, D. Leinders, N. Schweikardt, J. Tyszkiewicz, and J. V. den Bussche. Database query processing using finite cursor machines. *Theory Comput. Syst.*, 44(4):533–560, 2009.

[12] J. M. Hellerstein. The declarative imperative: experiences and conjectures in distributed logic. *SIGMOD Rec.*, 39:5–19, September 2010.

[13] N. Immerman. Expressibility and parallel complexity. *SIAM J. Comput.*, 18(3):625–638, 1989.

[14] H. J. Karloff, S. Suri, and S. Vassilvitskii. A model of computation for mapreduce. In *SODA*, pages 938–948, 2010.

[15] P. Koutris and D. Suciu. Parallel evaluation of conjunctive queries. Research Report UW-CSE-11-03-01, University of Washington, 2011.

[16] L. Libkin. *Elements of Finite Model Theory*. Springer, 2004.

[17] S. Melnik, A. Gubarev, J. J. Long, G. Romer, S. Shivakumar, M. Tolton, and T. Vassilakis. Dremel: Interactive analysis of web-scale datasets. *PVLDB*, 3(1):330–339, 2010.

[18] A. Pagh and R. Pagh. Uniform hashing in constant time and optimal space. *SIAM J. Comput.*, 38(1):85–96, 2008.

[19] M. Raab and A. Steger. "balls into bins" - a simple and tight analysis. In *RANDOM*, pages 159–170, 1998.

[20] P. Sanders. On the competitive analysis of randomized static load balancing. In *Proceedings of the first Workshop on Randomized Parallel Algorithms, RANDOM*, 1996.

[21] L. J. Stockmeyer and U. Vishkin. Simulation of parallel random access machines by circuits. *SIAM J. Comput.*, 13(2):409–422, 1984.

[22] A. Thusoo, J. S. Sarma, N. Jain, Z. Shao, P. Chakka, S. Anthony, H. Liu, P. Wyckoff, and R. Murthy. Hive - a warehousing solution over a map-reduce framework. *PVLDB*, 2(2):1626–1629, 2009.

[23] L. G. Valiant. A bridging model for parallel computation. *Commun. ACM*, 33(8):103–111, 1990.

[24] Y. Xu, P. Kostamaa, X. Zhou, and L. Chen. Handling data skew in parallel joins in shared-nothing systems. In *SIGMOD '08: Proceedings of the 2008 ACM SIGMOD international conference on Management of data*, pages 1043–1052, New York, NY, USA, 2008. ACM.

[25] Y. Yu, M. Isard, D. Fetterly, M. Budiu, Ú. Erlingsson, P. K. Gunda, and J. Currey. Dryadlinq: A system for general-purpose distributed data-parallel computing using a high-level language. In *OSDI*, pages 1–14, 2008.

APPENDIX

PROPOSITION A.1. FREQUENCY SAMPLING *(Subsection 4.1) includes in F every value x with $f_R(x) \geq \tau$ with high probability. Moreover, for some constant b, F contains no value x' with $f_R(x') < b \cdot \tau$ w.h.p.*

PROOF. The proof is based on a standard application of Chernoff bounds. For the first part, we compute the probability that a frequent value a is not included in F. The probability that we sample a tuple with this value is $f_R(a)/r \geq \tau/r$ and the probability that $a \notin F$ equals the probability that tuples with a are sampled less than $c \cdot \tau \cdot T/r$ times. If $K(a,v)$, we denote v by $f'(a)$, i.e. $f'(a)$ gives the *estimation* for the frequency of a. Then, $Pr[a \notin F] = Pr[f'(a) < c \cdot \tau \cdot T/r]$.

Notice that each sample is an independent random choice and a is chosen with probability $\geq \tau/r$. Moreover, $\mathbb{E}[f'(a)] = \sum_{j=1,T} f_R(a)/r \geq \tau \cdot T/r$. We can thus apply the Chernoff bound with $\delta = (c-1)/c$, which gives us that $Pr[f'(a) < \frac{c \cdot \tau \cdot T}{r}] \leq Pr[f'(a) < (1-\delta) \cdot \mathbb{E}[f'(a)]] < e^{-\mathbb{E}[f'(a)]\delta^2/2}$. Since there are $\leq r/\tau$ frequent values, we can apply a union bound: $Pr[\exists a \notin F] \leq \sum_{a:f_R(a) \geq \tau} Pr[a \notin F] < (r/\tau)e^{-\mathbb{E}[f'(x)]\delta^2/2} = (r/\tau)e^{-C \cdot \tau \cdot T/r}$, where $C = (c-1)^2/2c^2$. For $T = d_1 \cdot \frac{r \log r}{\tau}$, where d_1 is a constant, the probability of failure becomes arbitrarily small.

For the second part, consider a value a such that $f_R(a) < b \cdot \tau$ for some constant $b < 1$. Using similar arguments as above, we can show that $\mathbb{E}[f'(a)] < b \cdot \tau \cdot T/r$. We apply again the Chernoff bound (for a suitable choice of δ): $Pr[a \in F] = Pr[f'(a) \geq \frac{c \cdot \tau \cdot T}{r}] = Pr[f'(a) > (1+\delta) \cdot \mathbb{E}[f'(a)]] < 2^{-(1+\delta) \cdot \mathbb{E}[f'(a)]} = 2^{-C \cdot \tau \cdot T/r}$, where C is some constant depending on b, c. We use again a union bound to get that $Pr[\exists a \in F] \leq \sum_{a:f_R(a) < b \cdot \tau} Pr[a \in F] \leq r \cdot 2^{-\frac{C \cdot \tau \cdot T}{r}}$. For $T = d_2 \cdot \frac{r \log r}{\tau}$, where d_2 is an appropriate constant, the probability of failure becomes arbitrarily small ($O(1/r)$).

By choosing $d = \max\{d_1, d_2\}$, for $T = d \cdot \frac{r \log r}{\tau}$, both parts of the proposition are satisfied w.h.p. □

PROOF. (Of Proposition 4.3) Recall that we assume separate partitioning of the input relations. Let A be a load balanced algorithm computing Q with one broadcast round.

Moreover, let us denote by $\mathcal{H}$ the set of hash families from where A randomly picks a hash family. Applying Corollary 3.8, we can find a vector $X = (x_1, \ldots, x_n)$ such that for each $x_i \in X$, there exists a vector X'_i where x_i is substituted by a value $x'_i \neq x_i$ and X, X'_i collude.

Now, consider any instance where $T = X$. During the broadcast step, the servers containing T decide, independently of the relations R, S, to communicate $O(n^\varepsilon)$ tuples of X. Denote by X' the set containing the rest of the tuples, $|X'| = n - O(n^\varepsilon)$. Next, pick a value $x_i \in X'$ and consider the instance where $R = \{(x_i, y_1), \ldots, (x_i, y_n)\}$, $S = \{(x_i, z_1), \ldots, (x_i, z_n)\}$ and $T = \{x_1, \ldots, x'_i, \ldots, x_n\}$.

Since the computation is load balanced, and the output empty, there exists a run $h \in \mathcal{H}$ such that the maximum load of any server is $O(n/P)$. We say that a pair (y_j, z_k) meets when both tuples $R(x_i, y_j), S(x_i, z_k)$ are placed in the same server. There are $O(n^2)$ possible pairs; however, each server cannot hold more than $O(n^2/P^2)$ pairs that meet. Thus, in total the servers hold $O(n^2/P)$ pairs, which implies that there exists at least one pair (y_j, z_k) such that $R(x_i, y_j), S(x_i, z_k)$ are never placed in the same server.

Finally, let us examine the case where we substitute the tuple $T(x'_i)$ with $T(x_i)$. Since the two vectors collude, T, R, S will send exactly the same information during the broadcast phase. Moreover, since the replaced tuple will not be communicated, servers containing R, S will distribute their tuples in exactly the same way, hence $R(x_i, y_j), S(x_i, z_k)$ will never meet. Following from the genericity of the computation, the tuple (x_i, y_j, z_k) can not belong in the output; however, since $x_i \in T$, this is a contradiction. □

PROOF. (Of Proposition 4.2) Notice that each value of x falls into exactly one of the four cases. Let us first consider the first case and a value $a \in RF'$.

We have that $N(a) = f_R(a)f_S(a)f_T(a) + f_R(a) + f_S(a) + f_T(a)$. The second step of the broadcast phase guarantees that $f_S(a), f_T(a) \geq 1$. Hence $\mathbb{E}[\max_s N_s(a)] \leq f_S(a) + f_T(a) + \frac{2f_R(a)}{P} \cdot (f_S(a)f_T(a) + 1) \leq \frac{c}{P} \cdot f_R(a)f_S(a)f_T(a)$ for some constant c. We can obtain a similar bound for values of x which fall into the cases 2,3. It remains to consider the last case, where a is not frequent in any of the relations. Let X_f be the set of these values. For any value $a \in X_f$, we have that $N(a) \leq \tau_R \tau_S \tau_T + \tau_R + \tau_S + \tau_T \leq 4\tau_R \tau_S \tau_T$. Applying the Arithmetic-Geometric means inequality, we get that $\tau_R \tau_S \tau_T = \frac{\sqrt[3]{rst}}{P \log P} \leq \frac{r+s+t}{3P \log P}$. Hence, $N(a) \leq c' \cdot \frac{r+s+t}{P \log P}$ for some constant c'.

Using the balls in bins framework, we are throwing balls u.a.r. into servers and $w_{max} = c' \cdot \frac{r+s+t}{P \log P}$. Following again the argument of the proof for Theorem 4.1, we derive that $\mathbb{E}[\max_s N_s(X_f)] = \Theta(W/P)$, where W denotes the total load attributed to the set X_f.

Summing over the values of x for all cases, we obtain that the computation is indeed load-balanced. □

234

Finding a Minimal Tree Pattern
Under Neighborhood Constraints

Benny Kimelfeld
IBM Research–Almaden
San Jose, CA 95120, USA
kimelfeld@us.ibm.com

Yehoshua Sagiv*
Dept. of Computer Science
The Hebrew University
Jerusalem 91094, Israel
sagiv@cs.huji.ac.il

ABSTRACT

Tools that automatically generate queries are useful when schemas are hard to understand due to size or complexity. Usually, these tools find minimal tree patterns that contain a given set (or bag) of labels. The labels could be, for example, XML tags or relation names. The only restriction is that, in a tree pattern, adjacent labels must be among some specified pairs. A more expressive framework is developed here, where a schema is a mapping of each label to a collection of bags of labels. A tree pattern conforms to the schema if for all nodes v, the bag comprising the labels of the neighbors is contained in one of the bags to which the label of v is mapped. The problem at hand is to find a minimal tree pattern that conforms to the schema and contains a given bag of labels. This problem is NP-hard even when using the simplest conceivable language for describing schemas. In practice, however, the set of labels is small, so efficiency is realized by means of an algorithm that is fixed-parameter tractable (FPT). Two languages for specifying schemas are discussed. In the first, one expresses pairwise mutual exclusions between labels. Though W[1]-hardness (hence, unlikeliness of an FPT algorithm) is shown, an FPT algorithm is described for the case where the mutual exclusions form a circular-arc graph (e.g., disjoint cliques). The second language is that of regular expressions, and for that another FPT algorithm is described.

Categories and Subject Descriptors: H.3.3 [Information Storage and Retrieval]: Information Search and Retrieval—*query formulation, search process*; H.2[Database Management]: Heterogeneous Databases, Miscellaneous

General Terms: Algorithms, Theory

Keywords: Query extraction, minimal tree pattern, graph search

1. INTRODUCTION

Without a close familiarity with the schema of a given database, manual query formulation can be prohibitively laborious and time consuming. In the case of schemas that are very large and complex (for example, SAP schemas that may have ten thousand or more relations [12]), it may become practically impossible. Various paradigms tackle this problem, such as tools for schema exploration and semi-automatic query formulation [15], schema-free (or flexible) queries [5, 16], and keyword search over structured data [3, 11, 13, 22]. A standard module in the realization of these paradigms is an algorithm that finds small tree patterns that connect a given set of items (where an item can be the name of a relation, the value of an attribute, an XML tag, an XML CDATA value, and so on). However, none of the existing implementations of this module take into account even very simple constraints on the patterns, such as: a person has one gender, the identifier of a person is not shared by others, and so on. More complex constraints are imposed by XML schemas, where regular expressions qualify the possible sets of sub-elements. When ignoring these constraints in practical schemas, a huge number of patterns either make no sense to the end user, or do not lead to actual results in the overall application.

As an example, we discuss keyword search over structured data (e.g. relational databases, RDF triples, XML documents, etc.). The typical approach to this problem considers abstractly a *data graph*, where nodes represent objects (e.g., tuples or XML elements), and edges represent pairwise associations between the objects (e.g., foreign keys or element nesting). The keywords phrased by the user match some of the objects, and search results are subtrees of the data graph that cover all those keywords. A dominant factor in the quality of a result is its size (or weight), since smaller subtrees represent closer associations between the keywords. The computational goal is to find these small subtrees. For that, there are two main approaches. The *graph* approach (e.g., [3, 8, 13]) extracts the subtrees directly from the data, while ignoring the schema and the particular patterns of those subtrees. The *pattern* approach [11, 17, 22, 25], which is investigated in this paper, deploys two steps. In the first step, a set of candidate patterns is generated; in the second step, search results are obtained by evaluating the patterns as queries over the data graph (e.g., finding subtrees that are isomorphic to those patterns).

The pattern approach has several important advantages. The obvious one is the ability to use existing systems (e.g., RDBMS) that already have highly optimized query engines. Thus, the pattern approach can be implemented rather easily over such systems. Furthermore, as enunciated in [19], keyword search over data graphs is carried out across two dimensions. In one dimension, the user explores the different semantic connections (where each one is represented by a tree pattern). In the second dimension, the user looks for specific answers for each tree pattern that is of interest. The pattern approach facilitates the search across those two dimensions as follows. First, it can display early on results of diversified seman-

*Work supported by The German-Israeli Foundation for Scientific Research & Development (Grant 973–150.6/2007).

tic connections (i.e., patterns), rather than inundate the user with many answers of just one tree pattern. Second, with the proper interface, it is fairly easy for a user to refine her query by phrasing conditions on the patterns that have already been displayed to her (e.g., filtering out some labels, adding selections, etc.) [1, 15].

Efficiency in producing a set of candidate patterns is crucial, since in all of the above applications, the patterns are generated in real time in response to a user query. The effectiveness of existing algorithms has been exhibited on tiny schemas (usually designed just for experiments). We believe that those algorithms are not likely to scale up to the sizes of real-world schemas. Specifically, most of the algorithms (e.g., [17, 18, 21, 25]) follow DISCOVER [11] by essentially producing all the possible *partial patterns* (i.e., trees that do not necessarily include the keywords) up to some size, or until sufficiently many *complete patterns* are produced. The complete patterns include all of the keywords (of the query), and they are evaluated against the database. This generation of the complete patterns is grossly inefficient, because the incremental construction can exponentially blowup the number of partial patterns. Moreover, many of the generated complete patterns may make no sense (and in particular produce empty results), simply because they violate basic constraints imposed on (or just happened to be satisfied by) the database.

To the best of our knowledge, the only algorithm that generates patterns with guaranteed efficiency is that of Talukdar et al. [22]. To illustrate this approach, consider Figure 1. The left side of the figure shows a *schema graph*. That graph has a node for each label (i.e., entity type). There is an edge between two labels if entities of those types could be connected by an edge in the underlying data graph. Given a query (which is a set of labels), the patterns generated by Talukdar et al. [22] are non-redundant subtrees (of the schema graph) that contain the labels of the query.[1] Now, suppose that we want to find patterns that connect `female` and `male` (given the schema graph of Figure 1). Intuitively, we would like to get the pattern in the bottom row at the right side of the figure. That pattern connects two persons, such that one is a male and the other is a female who is the wife of the male. But this pattern is not a subtree of the schema graph, because the label `person` is repeated. The only non-redundant subtree (of the schema graph) that contains the labels `female` and `male` is the one in the top row, namely, a person that is both a male and a female. Clearly, this pattern is useless; that is, it will never match actual results. Useful patterns necessarily include more than one person (i.e., a male and a female). But the algorithm of Talukdar et al. cannot find them, because it cannot generate patterns with repeated labels. Conceivably, this problem could be fixed by introducing repetitions in the schema graph (e.g., `person1`, `person2`, and so on). But then, we would get new useless patterns. For example, the pattern in the middle row refers to a male that is the *wife* of a female.

It should be noted that Talukdar et al. [22] employ the algorithm of Kimelfeld and Sagiv [13] for finding the k minimal non-redundant subtrees. In fact, the algorithm of [13] was designed for the aforementioned graph approach. As shown by the above example, using the algorithm of [13] for the pattern approach may provide an unsatisfactory solution. The algorithms we present in this paper are substantially different from those of [13].

To summarize thus far, we need an algorithm that can efficiently generate the patterns that will actually be evaluated against the database (in particular, we should not waste time on constructing partial patterns that are not even going to be evaluated). In addition, the algorithm should be able to generate patterns with repeated

---

[1]A subtree is *non-redundant* if it has no proper subtree that also contains all the labels of the query.

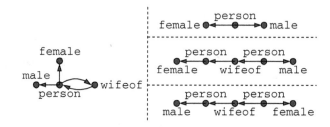

Figure 1: Possible relationships (left), and three patterns connecting `female` and `male` (right)

labels (or else we may miss important answers). And finally, it should avoid creating useless patterns that violate basic constraints that hold in the database.

Designing an algorithm that avoids useless patterns is not an easy task and it depends on the type of constraints that are used. In this paper, we do it for *neighborhood* constraints. As an example, such a constraint can state that a node labeled with `person` can have either a `male` neighbor or a `female` neighbor, but not both; furthermore, an incoming `wifeof` neighbor is allowed only if an outgoing `female` neighbor exists. Formally, a constraint[2] maps a label to a (possibly infinite) set comprising finite bags (i.e., multisets) of labels. A schema S is a collection of constraints $S(\sigma)$— one for each label σ, and it also specifies weights on the nodes and edges. For a node v of a pattern, where v is labeled with σ, the neighboring labels of v (including their multiplicities) must form a subbag of a bag in $S(\sigma)$. Given a bag Λ of labels derived from a user's query, the problem is to find a minimal Λ-*pattern*, which is a tree t such that the labels of t form a superbag of Λ, and every node of t satisfies the constraint for its label. In this paper, we give algorithms for finding minimal Λ-patterns. In practice, we would like to find the top-k Λ-patterns (rather than just the minimal one). We defer to future work the development of an algorithm for the task of finding the top-k Λ-patterns. However, we discuss this task in Section 6, and in particular show that even the definition of the top-k Λ-patterns is not obvious.

In practice, neighborhood constraints can be derived in several ways. A schema of some sort (if available) is an obvious source. Additionally, an analysis of the data itself may provide some constraints; for example, the data may show that a wife is always a female. Finally, in keyword search, the schema is typically augmented with keywords given by the user [11]. The connections between the keywords and the schema's entities may indicate some neighborhood constraints. For example, the keywords `IBM` and `SAP` are always connected to `company` (at most once), and no `company` is connected by edges to both `IBM` and `SAP`.

Naturally, the complexity of our problem depends on the language used for expressing the neighborhood constraints. However, this problem is NP-hard even in the case of the simplest conceivable languages (e.g., each $S(\sigma)$ is a finite set that is specified explicitly). But that hardness builds on the assumption that the given bag Λ of labels is large, whereas in practice the size of Λ is similar to that of the user's query; a user's query is typically very small, and in particular, significantly smaller than the schema. Hence, we focus on *parameterized complexity* [6, 9] with the size of Λ as the parameter. A problem is deemed tractable if it is *Fixed-Parameter Tractable (FPT)*, which means that the running time is polynomial, except that the parameter can have an arbitrarily large effect on the constant of the polynomial (but not on the degree).

---

[2]As stated, this constraint is undirected, but there are also directed ones.

236

In Section 3, we present a generic algorithm that reduces the problem of finding a minimal Λ-pattern to a generalization of minimal set cover (which is defined in that section). The algorithm is generic in the sense that it does not depend on any particular language for specifying constraints. An immediate result of the algorithm is that if the size of Λ is fixed, then we can find a minimal Λ-pattern in polynomial time under a reasonable assumption about the constraint language (i.e., one can efficiently test whether a fixed-size bag is contained in some element of $S(\sigma)$, which is specified by the language). But this result means that $|\Lambda|$ affects the degree of the polynomial, rather than just the constant. More importantly, Section 4 shows that this reduction leads to FPT algorithms for two practical constraint languages.

In the first language, constraints are specified in terms of pairwise mutual exclusions between labels, such as "if male then not female and vice-versa." The formal specification of these constraints is by means of an undirected *mux* graph, where edges represent mutual exclusions. Though extremely simple, our problem is unlikely to be FPT under this language—we show that it is $W[1]$-hard [6, 9]. Nonetheless, we give an FPT algorithm for the important case where the mux graph consists of pairwise-disjoint cliques. We then generalize this FPT algorithm to interval graphs, and even to circular-arc graphs with multiplicity bounds (e.g., at most one male neighbor and at most two parent neighbors). Based on our algorithm for mux graphs, we present an FPT algorithm for the second language, namely, regular expressions. This language is essentially the core of DTDs,[3] where the content of an element having a specified tag (label) is determined by a regular expression over the possible sub-elements.

In summary, algorithms and systems that find minimal or even top-k patterns are abundant, but to the best of our knowledge, none of them has both nontrivial efficiency guarantees and support for nontrivial (and practical) constraints. This paper presents the first step towards top-k algorithms with these qualities by showing how to efficiently find a minimal pattern under practical neighborhood constraints. Interestingly, it is nontrivial to even define the meaning of *top-k patterns*, and we discuss this issue in Section 6. The problem of actually finding the top-k patterns is left for future work. We believe that our algorithms are going to be a primary building block when developing a solution to the top-k problem.

For clarity of presentation, we start with a model (Section 2) and algorithms (Sections 3 and 4) for undirected Λ-patterns. The directed case (e.g., Figure 1) is more involved, and is considered in Section 5. Finally, in Section 6, we discuss how to define the problem of finding the top-k Λ-patterns.

2. FORMAL SETTING

In this section, we describe our framework and the problem we study. We start with some preliminary definitions.

2.1 Bags, Labels, and Regular Expressions

Recall that a *bag* (or *multiset*) is a pair $b = (X, \mu_b)$, where X is a set and $\mu_b : X \to \mathbb{N}$ is a *multiplicity function* that maps every element $x \in X$ to its multiplicity $\mu_b(x)$ (which is a positive integer). Throughout the paper, we implicitly assume that the multiplicity function of a bag b is μ_b. By a slight abuse of notation, we may assume that μ_b is also defined on an element $z \notin X$, and then $\mu_b(z) = 0$. To distinguish a bag from a set, we use double braces instead of braces; for example, $\{0, 1, 1\}$ is a set of size 2 (and is equal to $\{0, 1\}$), whereas $b = \{\!\{0, 1, 1\}\!\}$ is a bag of size 3 with

$\mu_b(0) = 1$ and $\mu_b(1) = 2$. The operator $\uplus$ denotes bag union. Recall that containment has a special meaning when applied to bags; specifically, given two bags $b = (X, \mu_b)$ and $b' = (X', \mu_{b'})$, we say that b is a *subbag* of b', denoted by $b \subseteq b'$, if $X \subseteq X'$ and $\mu_b(x) \le \mu_{b'}(x)$ for all $x \in X$.

We assume an infinite set Σ of *labels*. The main players in this work are bags of labels. By $\mathcal{F}_\Sigma$ we denote the set of all the finite bags of labels. For a subset B of $\mathcal{F}_\Sigma$, we define the *containment closure* of B, denoted by $[\![B]\!]$, as the set:

$$[\![B]\!] \stackrel{\text{def}}{=} \bigcup_{b \in B} \{b' \in \mathcal{F}_\Sigma \mid b' \subseteq b\}.$$

That is, $[\![B]\!]$ is the set consisting of all the bags of B, and all the subbags of the bags of B.

We use regular expressions over Σ. Specifically, regular expressions are defined by the language

$$e := \sigma \mid \epsilon \mid e* \mid e? \mid e\,e \mid e|e$$

where $\sigma \in \Sigma$, and ϵ is the empty string. A regular expression e defines a language $\mathcal{L}(e)$, namely, the set of strings over Σ that match the expression e. We define the *bag language* $\mathcal{L}^{\text{b}}(e)$ of e in the standard way (e.g., as in [2]), namely, $\mathcal{L}^{\text{b}}(e)$ contains all the bags $b \in \mathcal{F}_\Sigma$, such that there exists a string $x \in \mathcal{L}(e)$ where every label has the same multiplicity in x and b (that is, $b \in \mathcal{L}^{\text{b}}(e)$ if b can be ordered to formulate a word in $\mathcal{L}(e)$).

2.2 Graphs, Schemas and Patterns

In this paper, we consider finite graphs with labeled nodes. To simplify the presentation, we focus on undirected graphs up to Section 5, where we extend our results to directed graphs. The set of nodes of the graph g is denoted by $\mathsf{V}(g)$, and the set of edges of g is denoted by $\mathsf{E}(g)$. Note that an edge of $\mathsf{E}(g)$ is a set $\{u, v\} \subseteq \mathsf{V}(g)$. For a node $v \in \mathsf{V}(g)$, the label of v is denoted by $\lambda^g(v)$. If U is a subset of $\mathsf{V}(g)$, then $\lambda^g(U)$ denotes the bag that is obtained from U by replacing each node u with its label $\lambda^g(u)$ (that is, the multiplicity of each label σ is $|\{u \in U \mid \lambda^g(u) = \sigma\}|$). Note that $\lambda^g(v) \in \Sigma$ and $\lambda^g(U) \in \mathcal{F}_\Sigma$. If all the labels of the nodes of g belong to a subset L of Σ, then we say that g is a graph *over* L. For a node v of g, the set of neighbors of v is denoted by $\mathsf{nbr}^g(v)$. Usually, the graph g is clear form the context, and then we may write just $\lambda(v)$, $\lambda(U)$ and $\mathsf{nbr}(v)$ instead of $\lambda^g(v)$, $\lambda^g(U)$ and $\mathsf{nbr}^g(v)$, respectively. Also, a node labeled with σ is called a σ-*node*. A *tree* is a connected and acyclic graph.

A *graph schema* (or just *schema* for short) identifies a set of valid graphs by imposing restrictions thereon. In this paper, we consider restrictions that are applied to neighborhoods of nodes having a specified label; that is, a schema qualifies, for each label σ, the bags of labels that a σ-node can have for its neighbors. A more formal definition is the following. An *lb-constraint* (where "lb" stands for "label bags") is a nonempty[4] (and possibly infinite) subset of $\mathcal{F}_\Sigma$. A schema S is associated with a finite set of labels, denoted by $dom(S)$, and it maps every label $\sigma \in dom(S)$ to an lb-constraint $S(\sigma)$. A graph g *conforms to* S, denoted by $g \models S$, if for all nodes $v \in \mathsf{V}(g)$ it holds that $\lambda(v) \in dom(S)$ and $\lambda(\mathsf{nbr}(v)) \in S(\lambda(v))$.

For a schema S, we denote by $[\![S]\!]$ the schema that is obtained from S by replacing every $S(\sigma)$ (where $\sigma \in dom(S)$) with its containment closure $[\![S(\sigma)]\!]$.

DEFINITION 2.1. *Let S be a schema, and let Λ be a bag in $\mathcal{F}_\Sigma$. A Λ-pattern (under S) is a tree t, such that $\Lambda \subseteq \lambda(\mathsf{V}(t))$ and $t \models [\![S]\!]$.* $\square$

---

[3]Actually, in DTDs, regular expressions are restricted to be one-unambiguous, but we do not require that.

[4]An lb-constraint may comprise just the empty bag.

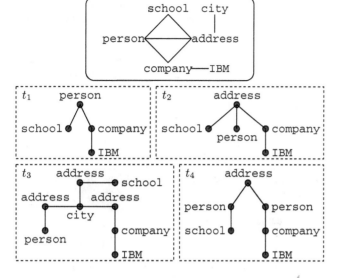

Figure 2: A neighboring relationship (top) and four trees

Note that for a Λ-pattern to exist, it is necessary (yet not sufficient) that every label in Λ belongs to $dom(S)$. Also note that in a Λ-pattern, each label σ of Λ occurs at least $\mu_\Lambda(\sigma)$ times.

EXAMPLE 2.2. Let S_1 be the schema such that $dom(S_1)$ consists of the six labels that appear at the top of Figure 2 (i.e., school, person, IBM and so on). In addition, for every label σ, the set $S_1(\sigma)$ comprises all the bags that have only neighbors of σ (in the graph at the top of Figure 2). For example, $S_1(\text{person})$ comprises all the bags that contain school, company, and address, each with some multiplicity.

Let Λ be the bag $\{\!\!\{\,\text{IBM}, \text{person}, \text{school}\,\}\!\!\}$. The four patterns t_1, t_2, t_3 and t_4 in Figure 2 are all Λ-patterns. The pattern t_1 corresponds to a person that is associated with both a school and a company (and that company is "IBM"). It may very well be the case that in the underlying data, a person that attends a school does not work in a company, and vice versa. Hence, the Λ-pattern t_1 has no occurrences in the data (that is, if t_1 is viewed as a query, then it has no results). As another example, the pattern t_2 has the same address for a school, a person, and a company; in most conceivable databases, there are no occurrences of t_2. In order to avoid such invalid patterns, we would like our schema to be more expressive. Hence, we define the schema S_2 to have the same domain as S_1, but now $S_2(\sigma)$ is $\mathcal{L}^b(e_\sigma)$, where:

$$e_{\text{person}} = (\text{school}? \mid \text{company}*)\ \text{address}$$
$$e_{\text{school}} = \text{person}*\ \text{address}$$
$$e_{\text{company}} = \text{person}*\ \text{address}\ \text{IBM}?$$
$$e_{\text{address}} = (\text{school}? \mid \text{person}* \mid \text{company}?)\ \text{city}$$
$$e_{\text{city}} = \text{address}*$$
$$e_{\text{IBM}} = \text{company}$$

Neither t_1 nor t_2 conforms to $[\![S_2]\!]$; hence, they are not Λ-patterns under S_2. To see that $t_1 \not\models [\![S_2]\!]$, note that $\lambda(\text{nbr}(v_p))$, where v_p is the person-node of t_1, does not belong to $[\![\mathcal{L}^b(e_{\text{person}})]\!]$. Similarly, $t_2 \not\models [\![S_2]\!]$ since the labels of the neighbors of its address-node do not form a bag in the set $[\![\mathcal{L}^b(e_{\text{address}})]\!]$.

It is easy to verify that both t_3 and t_4 are Λ-patterns under S_2, since both contain Λ and both conform to $[\![S_2]\!]$. Let Λ' be the same as Λ, except that person has multiplicity 2; that is, $\Lambda' =$

$\{\!\!\{\,\text{IBM}, \text{person}, \text{person}, \text{school}\,\}\!\!\}$. Then t_4 is a Λ'-pattern, and t_3 is not, since t_4 has (at least) two person-nodes, and t_3 has only one person-node. $\square$

2.3 Weighted Schemas and Minimal Patterns

When extracting patterns from schemas, some labels may be preferred over others, and some relationships could be viewed as stronger than others. For example, the label city may be deemed more important than road. Similarly, the person-address relationship could be viewed as more significant than person-company. To support such preferences, we augment a schema with weights for labels and edges. Formally, a *weight function* for a schema S is a mapping $W : dom(S) \cup (dom(S) \times dom(S)) \to [0, \infty)$ that is symmetric over $dom(S) \times dom(S)$ (which means that $W(\sigma, \tau) = W(\tau, \sigma)$ for all σ and τ in $dom(S)$).

A weight function W for S is naturally extended to any graph g over $dom(S)$ by defining $W(g)$ as follows.

$$W(g) \overset{\text{def}}{=} \sum_{v \in \mathsf{V}(g)} W(\lambda(v)) + \sum_{\{u,v\} \in \mathsf{E}(g)} W(\lambda(u), \lambda(v)) \quad (1)$$

A *weighted schema* comprises a schema S and a weight function W for S, and is denoted by S^W.

We follow the convention that a lower weight means a higher preference. Thus, the goal is to find a minimal-weight pattern. Formally, we investigate the MINPATTERN problem, where the input consists of a weighted schema S^W and a bag Λ of labels, and the goal is to find a Λ-pattern t, such that $W(t) \le W(t')$ for all Λ-patterns t'.

EXAMPLE 2.3. Consider S_2^W that is obtained from the schema S_2 of Example 2.2, and the weight function W, such that for all labels σ and τ it holds that $W(\sigma) = 1$ and $W(\sigma, \tau) = 0$ (hence, for a graph g we have $W(g) = |\mathsf{V}(g)|$). As in Example 2.2, let Λ be the bag $\{\!\!\{\,\text{IBM}, \text{person}, \text{school}\,\}\!\!\}$. Recall from Example 2.2 that, among the four trees of Figure 2, only t_3 and t_4 are Λ-patterns under S_2^W (since the other two do not conform to $[\![S_2]\!]$). Since $W(t_3) = 8$ and $W(t_4) = 6$, we get that t_3 is not a minimal pattern. It can be shown that t_4 is actually a minimal Λ-pattern under S_2^W.

Now, let W' be the weight function that is similar to W, except that $W'(\text{person}, \text{address}) = 5$. Then, we have that $W'(t_3) = 13$ and $W'(t_4) = 16$, and hence, t_4 is not a minimal Λ-pattern under $S_2^{W'}$. $\square$

2.4 Complexity Basics

Recall that a schema S maps every label of $dom(S)$ to an lb-constraint (i.e., a nonempty and possibly infinite set of finite bags of labels). As expected, the complexity of MINPATTERN depends on how the lb-constraints are specified. An *lb-specification* is a finite object (e.g., a formal expression, a graph, etc.) that compactly represents an lb-constraint. Given an lb-specification s, we use $\mathcal{F}_\Sigma(s)$ to denote the subset of $\mathcal{F}_\Sigma$ that is represented by s.

In Section 4, we study two types of lb-specifications; one allows to express *mutual exclusions* among labels, and the other employs regular expressions. For now, consider an extremely restricted type, where an lb-specification is simply a bag $s \in \mathcal{F}_\Sigma$ with $\mathcal{F}_\Sigma(s) = \{s\}$. One can easily show (e.g., by a reduction from minimal set cover) that even for this restricted type of lb-specifications, the problem MINPATTERN is already NP-hard (moreover, approximation within any constant factor is also NP-hard).

However, in practical scenarios, the input bag Λ corresponds to a user query, and so, is typically very small. Thus, our main yardstick for efficiency is *fixed-parameter tractability* [6, 9], where $|\Lambda|$ is the parameter. Formally, an algorithm for solving MINPATTERN is

Fixed-Parameter Tractable (abbr. FPT) if its running time is bounded by a function of the form $f(|\Lambda|) \cdot p(|S^W|)$, where $f(k)$ is a computable function (e.g., 2^k), $p(m)$ is a polynomial, and $|S^W|$ is the size of the representation of S^W. (We usually do not formally define $|S^W|$, but rather assume a simple encoding.) A weaker yardstick for efficiency, in the spirit of *data complexity* [24], is *polynomial time* under the assumption that $|\Lambda|$ is *fixed*.

Later, we will show that MINPATTERN is FPT for types of lb-specifications that are far more expressive than the restricted one mentioned earlier. Our first step is to present a generic algorithm that is independent of the language used for lb-specifications.

3. A GENERIC ALGORITHM

We now describe a generic algorithm for solving MINPATTERN. The running time depends on the language for lb-specifications that is employed, but the algorithm itself does not use any specific details of that language. This algorithm reduces MINPATTERN to a generalization of the set-cover problem, which is defined next.

3.1 Labeled Bag Cover

Minimum labeled bag cover is a generalization of the minimum (weighted) set-cover problem. The former differs from the latter in three ways. First, labeled bags are used instead of sets. Second, a labeled bag can be used more than once in a cover. Third, the bag of labels of a cover has to be contained in some bag of a given lb-constraint. Next, we give the formal definition.

Let $b_1 = (X_1, \mu_1)$ and $b_2 = (X_2, \mu_2)$ be two bags. Recall that $b_1 \uplus b_2$ is the *multiset sum* (or bag union) of b_1 and b_2. That is, $b_1 \uplus b_2$ is the bag $b = (X, \mu)$, such that $X = X_1 \cup X_2$ and $\mu(x) = \mu_1(x) + \mu_2(x)$ for each $x \in X$ (recall that $\mu_i(x) = 0$ if $x \notin X_i$).

The minimum labeled bag-cover problem, which we denote by MINLBCOVER, is the following. The input consists of a bag Γ, an lb-constraint $\mathcal{B}$, and a set $\mathcal{C}$ of triples $\Delta = (b, \tau, w)$, where b is a bag, $\tau \in \Sigma$ is the *label* of Δ, and $w \in [0, \infty)$ is the *weight* of Δ. A *legal cover* (of Γ by $\mathcal{C}$) is a bag $\{\!\{\Delta_1, \ldots, \Delta_n\}\!\}$, where each Δ_i is a triple (b_i, τ_i, w_i) in $\mathcal{C}$, such that $\Gamma \subseteq \uplus_{i=1}^n b_i$ and $\{\!\{\tau_1, \ldots, \tau_n\}\!\} \in [\![\mathcal{B}]\!]$; the *weight* of the legal cover is the sum $\sum_{i=1}^n w_i$. As in the ordinary set-cover problem, the goal is to find a legal cover that has a minimal weight.

3.2 The Algorithm

Our algorithm, called FindMinPattern, reduces MINPATTERN to MINLBCOVER. It operates in the spirit of existing algorithms for finding Steiner trees [7, 14]. We first describe some notation and data structures.

The algorithm FindMinPattern gets as input a weighted schema S^W and a bag Λ of labels, and returns a Λ-pattern that has a minimal weight. In the remainder of this section, we fix the input S^W and Λ.

We use the following notation. Let $\mathcal{B}$ be an lb-constraint, and let $\varsigma \in \Sigma$ be a label. By $\mathcal{B}_{-\varsigma}$ we denote the set that comprises all the bags $b \in \mathcal{F}_\Sigma$, such that $b \uplus \{\!\{\varsigma\}\!\} \in \mathcal{B}$. We use a special label $\star$, such that $\star \notin dom(S)$ and $\star \notin \Lambda$. The label $\star$ has the following special role. For all lb-constraints $\mathcal{B}$, it holds that $\mathcal{B}_{-\star}$ is equal to $\mathcal{B}$. We say that $\mathcal{B}$ *mentions* ς if ς belongs to some bag of $\mathcal{B}$. Note that $\mathcal{B}_{-\varsigma}$ is nonempty (hence, an lb-constraint) if and only if $\varsigma = \star$ or $\mathcal{B}$ mentions ς. Also note that $[\![\mathcal{B}_{-\varsigma}]\!] \subseteq [\![\mathcal{B}]\!]$.

EXAMPLE 3.1. Consider the lb-constraint $\mathcal{B} = \mathcal{L}^b(e_{\text{person}})$ of Example 2.2. If ς is the label `company`, then $\mathcal{B}_{-\varsigma}$ is the lb-constraint $\mathcal{L}^b(\text{company}^* \text{address})$. If ς is the label `school`, then $\mathcal{B}_{-\varsigma}$ contains a single bag: $\{\!\{\text{address}\}\!\}$. $\square$

The algorithm uses two data structures. One is an array $\mathcal{T}$. An index of $\mathcal{T}$ is a triple $\langle \sigma, b, \varsigma \rangle$, such that $\sigma \in dom(S)$, b is a subbag of Λ, and ς is either $\star$ or a label mentioned by $S(\sigma)$. Throughout the execution, $\mathcal{T}[\langle \sigma, b, \varsigma \rangle]$ is either $\bot$ (null), or a b-pattern t that has a node v, such that $\lambda(v) = \sigma$ and $\lambda(\text{nbr}(v)) \in [\![S(\sigma)_{-\varsigma}]\!]$. In other words, node v of t has the following properties. First, v is a σ-node. Second, if $\varsigma = \star$, then v satisfies the lb-constraint $[\![S(\sigma)]\!]$ (i.e., $\lambda(\text{nbr}(v)) \in [\![S(\sigma)]\!]$); otherwise (i.e., $\varsigma \neq \star$), v will continue to satisfy $[\![S(\sigma)]\!]$ even if we add a new ς-node as a neighbor of v.

The b-patterns that are stored in $\mathcal{T}$ are created by increasing weight (more precisely, a tree is created from smaller ones). For that we use the priority queue $\mathcal{Q}$ that stores the indexes of $\mathcal{T}$, namely, triples of the form $\langle \sigma, b, \varsigma \rangle$ as described above. The priority of $\langle \sigma, b, \varsigma \rangle$ in $\mathcal{Q}$ is determined by the weight of the b-pattern stored in $\mathcal{T}[\langle \sigma, b, \varsigma \rangle]$ (i.e., $W(\mathcal{T}[\langle \sigma, b, \varsigma \rangle])$). A higher weight means a lower priority. We define $W(\bot) = \infty$, so a triple $\langle \sigma, b, \varsigma \rangle$ has the lowest priority if $\mathcal{T}[\langle \sigma, b, \varsigma \rangle] = \bot$.

During the execution, when $\langle \sigma, b, \varsigma \rangle$ is removed from the top of $\mathcal{Q}$, it is the case that $\mathcal{T}[\langle \sigma, b, \varsigma \rangle]$ has a minimal weight among all the b-patterns having a node v with the above property (i.e., $\lambda(v) = \sigma$ and $\lambda(\text{nbr}(v)) \in [\![S(\sigma)_{-\varsigma}]\!]$), unless no such b-patterns exist and then $\mathcal{T}[\langle \sigma, b, \varsigma \rangle] = \bot$.

The pseudo code of the algorithm FindMinPattern is given in Figure 3. The main procedure is shown at the top, and there are also three subroutines. We first describe the subroutine Initialize() that is called in line 1 of the main procedure. In that subroutine, line 1 initializes $\mathcal{Q}$ to the empty priority queue. The loop of line 2 iterates over all triples $\langle \sigma, b, \varsigma \rangle$ that could be indexes of $\mathcal{T}$. Line 3 checks that the triple $\langle \sigma, b, \varsigma \rangle$ is indeed a valid index, as defined earlier. In lines 4–6, $\mathcal{T}[\langle \sigma, b, \varsigma \rangle]$ is initialized to $\bot$, unless b is the singleton $\{\!\{\sigma\}\!\}$ and then $\mathcal{T}[\langle \sigma, b, \varsigma \rangle]$ is set to a tree that consists of a single node labeled with σ. Line 7 inserts into $\mathcal{Q}$ the triple $\langle \sigma, b, \varsigma \rangle$ with the priority $W(\mathcal{T}[\langle \sigma, b, \varsigma \rangle])$.

After initialization, the main procedure executes the loop of line 2. Line 3 removes the top triple $\langle \sigma', b, \sigma \rangle$ from $\mathcal{Q}$. Next, three cases are considered. First, in lines 4–5, the algorithm terminates in failure if $\mathcal{T}[\langle \sigma', b, \sigma \rangle] = \bot$. Namely, a Λ-pattern does not exist in this case. The second case is when $b = \Lambda$ and $\mathcal{T}[\langle \sigma', b, \sigma \rangle] \neq \bot$. The former is the test of line 6 and the latter must hold if that line is reached. In this case, line 7 returns $\mathcal{T}[\langle \sigma', b, \sigma \rangle]$ and the algorithm terminates. The third case is when line 8 is reached (which happens only if $\mathcal{T}[\langle \sigma', b, \sigma \rangle] \neq \bot$ and $b \neq \Lambda$) and the test of that line is true (i.e., $\sigma \neq \star$). In this case, we need to update all the entries of $\mathcal{T}$ that could potentially incorporate $\mathcal{T}[\langle \sigma', b, \sigma \rangle]$ as a subtree. This is done in lines 9–10 by calling the subroutine Update(σ, ς) for every label ς, such that for some $\hat{b}$ the triple $\langle \sigma, \hat{b}, \varsigma \rangle$ is an index of $\mathcal{T}$.

For every subbag b of Λ, the subroutine Update(σ, ς) tries to find a new (and better) b-pattern t for $\mathcal{T}[\langle \sigma, b, \varsigma \rangle]$. The main idea is to create a new σ-node v and connect it to some existing trees $t_1, \ldots, t_m$ as follows. Each tree t_i should have a τ_i-node u_i, such that $\lambda(\text{nbr}^{t_i}(u_i)) \in [\![S(\tau_i)_{-\sigma}]\!]$. Thus, we can connect v to every u_i without causing the u_i to violate conformity to the schema S. Of course, we also need to verify that, in the new tree t, node v satisfies $\lambda(\text{nbr}^t(v)) \in [\![S(\sigma)_{-\varsigma}]\!]$ and $b \subseteq \lambda(V(t))$.

The search for t is done by a reduction to the following instance I of MINLBCOVER. The set $\mathcal{C}$ consists of all triples (b', τ, w), such that $S(\sigma)$ mentions τ, $\mathcal{T}[\langle \tau, b', \sigma \rangle] \neq \bot$ (in particular, $S(\tau)$ should mention σ so that the index $\langle \tau, b', \sigma \rangle$ is well defined), and $w = W(\mathcal{T}[\langle \tau, b', \sigma \rangle])$. The lb-constraint (of the instance I) is $S(\sigma)_{-\varsigma}$ and the bag of labels is b. The triples of a legal cover correspond to entries of $\mathcal{T}$ that form the trees $t_1, \ldots, t_m$ mentioned earlier.

Lines 1–5 of Update(σ, ς) construct the set $\mathcal{C}$. Line 6 simultaneously solves the MINLBCOVER problem for all subbags b of Λ.

Algorithm FindMinPattern(S^W, Λ)

1: Initialize()
2: **while** $\mathcal{Q} \neq \emptyset$ **do**
3:     $\langle \sigma', b, \sigma \rangle \leftarrow \mathcal{Q}.\text{pop}()$
4:     **if** $\mathcal{T}[\langle \sigma', b, \sigma \rangle] = \bot$ **then**
5:         **fail** (no Λ-pattern exists)
6:     **if** $b = \Lambda$ **then**
7:         **return** $\mathcal{T}[\langle \sigma', b, \sigma \rangle]$
8:     **if** $\sigma \neq \star$ **then**
9:         **for all** $\varsigma \in dom(S) \cup \{\star\}$ s.t. $S(\sigma)_{-\varsigma} \neq \emptyset$ **do**
10:             Update(σ, ς)

Subroutine Initialize()

1: $\mathcal{Q} \leftarrow$ empty priority queue
2: **for all** $\sigma \in dom(S), \varsigma \in dom(S) \cup \{\star\}$, and $b \subseteq \Lambda$ **do**
3:     **if** $S(\sigma)_{-\varsigma} \neq \emptyset$ **then**
4:         $\mathcal{T}[\langle \sigma, b, \varsigma \rangle] \leftarrow \bot$
5:         **if** $b = \{\!\{\sigma\}\!\}$ **then**
6:             $\mathcal{T}[\langle \sigma, b, \varsigma \rangle] \leftarrow$ a tree having a single σ-node
7:             $\mathcal{Q}.\text{insert}(\langle \sigma, b, \varsigma \rangle, W(\mathcal{T}[\langle \sigma, b, \varsigma \rangle]))$

Subroutine Update(σ, ς)

1: $\mathcal{C} \leftarrow \emptyset$
2: **for all** labels τ mentioned by $S(\sigma)$ **do**
3:     **for all** subbags $b' \subseteq \Lambda$ **do**
4:         **if** $S(\tau)$ mentions σ and $\mathcal{T}[\langle \tau, b', \sigma \rangle] \neq \bot$ **then**
5:             $\mathcal{C} \leftarrow \mathcal{C} \cup \{(b', \tau, W(\mathcal{T}[\langle \tau, b', \sigma \rangle]))\}$
6:     $MinCovers \leftarrow$ FindMinCovers$(\Lambda, S(\sigma)_{-\varsigma}, \mathcal{C})$
7:     **for all** subbags $b \subseteq \Lambda$ **do**
8:         **if** $MinCovers[b - \{\!\{\sigma\}\!\}] \neq \bot$ **then**
9:             $\mathcal{T}[\langle \sigma, b, \varsigma \rangle] \leftarrow$ Assemble$(\sigma, MinCovers[b - \{\!\{\sigma\}\!\}])$
10:            $\mathcal{Q}.\text{update}(\langle \sigma, b, \varsigma \rangle, W(\mathcal{T}[\langle \sigma, b, \varsigma \rangle]))$

Subroutine Assemble$(\sigma, \mathcal{C}')$

1: $t \leftarrow$ a tree with a single σ-node v
2: **for all** $(b', \tau, w) \in \mathcal{C}'$ **do**
3:     $t_{b'} \leftarrow \mathcal{T}[\langle \tau, b', \sigma \rangle]$
4:     let u be a τ-node of $t_{b'}$ s.t. nbr$(u) \in [\![S(\tau)]\!]_{-\sigma}$
5:     $t \leftarrow t \cup t_{b'} \cup \{v, u\}$

Figure 3: Finding a minimal Λ-pattern

Hence, Λ (rather than some b) is the first argument of the call to FindMinCovers in line 6. That call returns the array $MinCovers$ that has an index b for every subbag b of Λ. $MinCovers[b]$ is a minimal legal cover of b (if there is no cover, then $MinCovers[b] = \bot$). From each $MinCovers[b]$, we need to construct a b-pattern t and assign it to $\mathcal{T}[\langle \sigma, b, \varsigma \rangle]$. Line 7 iterates over all subbags b of Λ. Line 8 tests that[5] $b - \{\!\{\sigma\}\!\}$ has a cover. If so, line 9 calls Assemble$(\sigma, \mathcal{C}')$, where $\mathcal{C}'$ is $MinCovers[b - \{\!\{\sigma\}\!\}]$, in order to construct t, as described earlier. Note that we need a cover of

---

[5]Note that this is bag difference, that is, if $\sigma \in b$ then $b - \{\!\{\sigma\}\!\}$ is obtained from b by decrementing the multiplicity of σ by 1, and otherwise, $b - \{\!\{\sigma\}\!\}$ is just b.

$b - \{\!\{\sigma\}\!\}$, because the label σ of v could be in b. Line 10 updates the priority of $\langle \sigma, b, \varsigma \rangle$ in $\mathcal{Q}$ with the weight of the new t.

Observe that in the subroutine Assemble$(\sigma, \mathcal{C}')$, each execution of line 3 uses a new variable for $t_{b'}$. Thus, this subroutine constructs a tree even if the same triple appears more than once in $\mathcal{C}'$.

3.3 Correctness and Complexity

The description in the previous section shows that the subroutine Assemble constructs b-patterns that are valid entries of $\mathcal{T}$, as defined earlier. The crux of showing correctness of FindMinPattern is the following lemma. The proof is similar to the one given in [14] for an algorithm that finds minimal Steiner trees.

LEMMA 3.2. *In an execution of* FindMinPattern(S^W, Λ), *the triples* $\langle \sigma', b, \sigma \rangle$ *are removed from* $\mathcal{Q}$ *in an order of increasing* $W(\mathcal{T}[\langle \sigma', b, \sigma \rangle])$. *Furthermore, whenever* $\langle \sigma', b, \sigma \rangle$ *is removed from* $\mathcal{Q}$ *in line 3:*

1. *If* $\sigma \neq \star$, *then* $\mathcal{T}[\langle \sigma', b, \sigma \rangle]$ *is a minimal b-pattern having a σ'-node v with* $\lambda(\text{nbr}(v)) \in [\![S(\sigma)_{-\varsigma}]\!]$. *(And* $\mathcal{T}[\langle \sigma', b, \sigma \rangle] = \bot$ *if no such b-pattern exists.)*

2. *If* $\sigma = \star$, *then* $\mathcal{T}[\langle \sigma', b, \sigma \rangle]$ *is a minimal b-pattern having a σ'-node. (And* $\mathcal{T}[\langle \sigma', b, \sigma \rangle] = \bot$ *if no such b-pattern exists.)*

As a result of Lemma 3.2, we get the following theorem, which states the correctness of the algorithm. This theorem also states a dependency of the running time on the input, and on the running time of FindMinCovers (which we consider in the next section).

THEOREM 3.3. FindMinPattern(S^W, Λ) *returns a minimal Λ-pattern, or fails if none exists. The number of operations and function calls is polynomial in* $2^{|\Lambda|} \cdot |dom(S)|$.

Recall that MINLBCOVER gets as input a bag Γ, an lb-constraint $\mathcal{B}$, and a set $\mathcal{C}$ of triples. When we consider the parameterized complexity of MINLBCOVER, the parameter is $|\Gamma|$. Theorem 3.3 implies the following corollary that relates the parameterized complexity of MINPATTERN to that of MINLBCOVER under a language of lb-specifications.

COROLLARY 3.4. *Under a language of lb-specifications, the following holds. If* MINLBCOVER *is FPT, then* MINPATTERN *is FPT.*

Let k be a natural number. The definition of the problem k-*bounded* MINPATTERN is the same as MINPATTERN, except that we make the assumption that $|\Lambda| \leq k$ (but the size of the schema S can be unbounded). For a language of lb-specifications, *containment checking* is the problem of testing whether $b \in [\![\mathcal{B}]\!]$, when given a bag $b \in \mathcal{F}_\Sigma$ and an lb-constraint $\mathcal{B}$ represented by an lb-specification. A procedure for containment checking is sufficient for solving MINLBCOVER (but not necessarily most efficiently). The problem k-*bounded* containment checking is the same as containment checking, except that $|b| \leq k$ is assumed. The following corollary of Theorem 3.3 relates k-bounded MINPATTERN to k-bounded containment checking.

COROLLARY 3.5. *Let k be a fixed natural number. For a language of lb-specifications, if k-bounded containment checking is in polynomial time then so is k-bounded* MINPATTERN.

Regarding Corollaries 3.4 and 3.5, it may seem that to guarantee the running times, the language of lb-specifications should support an efficient construction of $\mathcal{B}_{-\varsigma}$ when $\mathcal{B}$ and ς are given. However, this is not really necessary, because we can use $S(\sigma)$ instead of $S(\sigma)_{-\varsigma}$ in the call to FindMinCovers by incorporating the following changes. We add to $\mathcal{C}$ the triple $(\{\rho\}, \varsigma, 1)$, where ρ is a fresh new label, and compute covers that contain ρ.

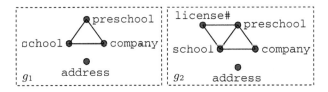

Figure 4: Mux graphs g_1 and g_2

4. LB-SPECIFICATIONS

We now consider languages for lb-specifications, and study the complexity of MINLBCOVER under them. We note that there are many (practically motivated) such languages, and this section by no means covers all of them; rather, our goal is to study the complexity of MINPATTERN for a few basic languages. We start with a language that allows one to specify mutual exclusions between pairs of labels.

4.1 Mutual-Exclusion Graphs

Recall that an lb-constraint is a nonempty subset $\mathcal{B}$ of $\mathcal{F}_{\Sigma}$. A *mutual-exclusion graph* (abbr. *mux graph*) defines an lb-constraint by specifying the set of allowed labels, along with pairwise mutual exclusions among them. Our goal in studying the class of mux-graph specifications is threefold. First, this class captures the basic constraint of mutual exclusion, which is practically useful. Second, as we will show, this class enables us to exhibit the fact that fine details may make the difference between tractability (FPT) and intractability. Third, the algorithm we devise here will be used in the next section for handling regular expressions.

Formally, a mux graph g has nodes that are uniquely labeled (i.e., for all nodes u and v of g, if $u \neq v$ then $\lambda(u) \neq \lambda(v)$).[6] The lb-constraint $\mathcal{F}_{\Sigma}(g)$ that is defined by the mux graph g comprises all the bags $b \in \mathcal{F}_{\Sigma}$, such that all the labels of b belong to $\lambda(g)$, and for all edges $\{u, v\}$ of g, at most one of $\lambda(u)$ and $\lambda(v)$ is in b. In other words, $b \in \mathcal{F}_{\Sigma}(g)$ if the set of labels that occur in b corresponds to an independent set of g. Note that $\mathcal{F}_{\Sigma}(g)$ is closed under containment, which means that $[\![\mathcal{F}_{\Sigma}(g)]\!] = \mathcal{F}_{\Sigma}(g)$. Later we will generalize mux graphs by allowing some restrictions on the multiplicity of labels.

EXAMPLE 4.1. The two mux graphs g_1 and g_2 shown in Figure 4 could be used for specifying $S(\texttt{person})$. The lb-constraint $\mathcal{F}_{\Sigma}(g_1)$ consists of all the bags that include `address` and one of `school`, `preschool` and `company`, with any multiplicity (including 0). The lb-constraint $\mathcal{F}_{\Sigma}(g_2)$ is the same as $\mathcal{F}_{\Sigma}(g_1)$, except that the label `#license` can be included provided that both `school` and `preschool` are absent (i.e., students in schools are not permitted to drive). $\square$

For a mux graph g and a bag b, containment checking (i.e., testing whether $b \in [\![\mathcal{F}_{\Sigma}(g)]\!]$) is trivial. Hence, Corollary 3.5 implies that MINPATTERN is solvable in polynomial time if lb-specifications are given by mux graphs and $|\Lambda|$ is fixed. Next, we develop FPT algorithms for MINPATTERN that apply to some classes of mux graphs. Recall from Corollary 3.4 that it is enough to find FPT algorithms for MINLBCOVER.

4.1.1 Disjoint Cliques

We first present an FPT algorithm for MINLBCOVER in the special case of mux graphs consisting of *disjoint cliques*, that is, graphs

---

6 A mux graph could be defined as a graph over labels; we use the given definition for uniformity of presentation.

Algorithm MuxMinCovers$(\Gamma, g, \mathcal{C})$

1: let $v_1, \ldots, v_n$ be a friendly order of $\mathsf{V}(g)$
2: **for all** subbags $b \subseteq \Gamma$ **do**
3:    $\mathcal{M}_0[b] \leftarrow \bot$
4:    **for** $i = 1$ to n **do**
5:       $\mathcal{N}_i[b] \leftarrow \bot$
6: $\mathcal{M}_0[\emptyset] \leftarrow \emptyset$
7: **for** $i = 1$ to n **do**
8:    **for all** subbags $b \subseteq \Gamma$ by increasing $|b|$ **do**
9:       **for all** $\Delta = (b_\Delta, \tau, w) \in \mathcal{C}$ where $\tau = \lambda(v_i)$ **do**
10:          **for all** subbags $b' \subseteq b$ such that $b \subseteq b' \uplus b_\Delta$ **do**
11:             let $j < i$ be the maximal s.t. $\{v_j, v_i\} \notin \mathsf{E}(g)$, or 0 if $\{v_{j'}, v_i\} \in \mathsf{E}(g)$ for all $1 \leq j' < i$
12:             let $\mathcal{C}_i = \mathcal{N}_i[b] \uplus \{\!\{\Delta\}\!\}$ and $\mathcal{C}_j = \mathcal{M}_j[b'] \uplus \{\!\{\Delta\}\!\}$
13:             $\mathcal{N}_i[b] \leftarrow \min(\mathcal{N}_i[b], \mathcal{C}_i, \mathcal{C}_j)$
14:       $\mathcal{M}_i[b] \leftarrow \min(\mathcal{M}_{i-1}[b], \mathcal{N}_i[b])$
15: **return** $\mathcal{M}_n$

Figure 5: Algorithm MuxMinCovers for finding minimal covers

such that every connected component is a clique. In Figure 4, for example, g_1 comprises two disjoint cliques, but g_2 is not a disjoint-clique graph. Later, we will show that the algorithm we present here can be applied to a much broader class of mux graphs (that includes g_2).

The pseudo code of the algorithm, called MuxMinCovers, is given in Figure 5. The input consists of a bag Γ, a disjoint-clique mux graph g, and a set $\mathcal{C}$ of triples $\Delta = (b, \tau, w)$ (where b is a bag, τ is a label, and w is a weight).

Since g consists of disjoint cliques, there is a *friendly order* $v_1, \ldots, v_n$ of its nodes, which means that every clique constitutes a consecutive subsequence (i.e., substring) of $v_1, \ldots, v_n$.

For each i in $\{1, \ldots, n\}$, the algorithm maintains an array $\mathcal{M}_i$ and an array $\mathcal{N}_i$. In addition, there is another array $\mathcal{M}_0$. For each of those arrays, an index is a subbag b of Γ. So, if $\Gamma = (X, \mu_\Gamma)$, then the size of each array is $\prod_{\sigma \in X}(\mu_\Gamma(\sigma) + 1)$.

Before we proceed, we need some notation. For a number $i \in \{0, \ldots, n\}$ and a subbag b of Γ, a legal cover $\mathcal{C}'$ of b is called an *i-cover* of b if for every triple (b_Δ, τ, w) in $\mathcal{C}'$, the label τ is one of $\lambda(v_1), \ldots, \lambda(v_i)$. In particular, note that only the empty bag has a 0-cover (and this cover is the empty bag). Also note that every legal cover is an n-cover, and every i-cover is a j-cover for $j \geq i$. For $i \in \{1, \ldots, n\}$, the bag $\mathcal{C}'$ is called a *strict i-cover* of b if $\mathcal{C}'$ is an i-cover of b and contains one or more occurrences of $\lambda(v_i)$ (i.e., $\mathcal{C}'$ contains a triple (b_Δ, τ, w) such that $\tau = \lambda(v_i)$). In other words, an i-cover is strict if it is not an $(i-1)$-cover.

When the algorithm terminates, each $\mathcal{M}_i[b]$ contains a minimal i-cover of b, and each $\mathcal{N}_i[b]$ contains a minimal strict i-cover of b. In line 15, the algorithm returns the array $\mathcal{M}_n$. Lines 2–6 initialize all the $\mathcal{M}_i[b]$ and $\mathcal{N}_i[b]$ to $\bot$, except for $\mathcal{M}_o[\emptyset]$ which is initialized to $\emptyset$. Note that the weight of $\emptyset$ is 0, and $\bot$ has an infinite weight.

The main part of the algorithm is the dynamic programming in lines 7–14. The loop of line 7 iterates over all $i \in \{1, \ldots, n\}$ in increasing order. In the ith iteration, lines 8–14 set the arrays $\mathcal{M}_i$ and $\mathcal{N}_i$ to their final values as follows. Line 8 iterates over all subbags b of Γ by increasing size. Lines 9–13 set the value of $\mathcal{N}_i[b]$, and line 14 sets the value of $\mathcal{M}_i[b]$. Lines 11–13 are executed for all triples $\Delta = (b_\Delta, \tau, w)$ of $\mathcal{C}$ with $\tau = \lambda(v_i)$, and all the subbags b' of b, such that $b \subseteq b' \uplus b_\Delta$; these lines attempt to improve the

241

strict i-cover of b found so far, by adding Δ to an i-cover $\mathcal{C}'$ of b'. The algorithm considers two such $\mathcal{C}'$ where the addition of Δ does not violate the lb-constraint specified by g. The first (denoted $\mathcal{C}_i$ in the algorithm) is a strict i-cover of b', and then $\triangle$ can be added $\mathcal{C}'$ because $\mathcal{C}'$ already has a triple labeled with $\tau = \lambda(v_i)$. The second (denoted $\mathcal{C}_j$ in the algorithm) is a j-cover of b', where j is the maximal index (subject to $j < i$) such that either $j = 0$ or v_j and v_i are in different cliques (here we use the fact that $v_1 \ldots, v_n$ is a friendly order). Line 11 finds j, and line 13 sets $\mathcal{N}_i[b]$ to the strict i-cover that has the minimum weight among the current $\mathcal{N}_i[b]$ and the two $\mathcal{C}' \uplus \{\!\{ \triangle \}\!\}$ mentioned earlier. Note that $\perp \uplus \Delta = \perp$. Finally, line 14 sets $\mathcal{M}_i[b]$ to the cover that has the minimum weight among $\mathcal{M}_{i-1}[b]$ and $\mathcal{N}_i[b]$.

Correctness of the algorithm follows from the next lemma. The proof is by a rather straightforward (double) induction on i and $|b|$.

LEMMA 4.2. *Let b be a subbag of Γ. At the end of the ith iteration of the loop of line 7 of* MuxMinCovers$(\Gamma, g, \mathcal{C})$,

1. $\mathcal{N}_i[b]$ *is a minimal strict i-cover of b (or $\perp$ if none exist).*

2. $\mathcal{M}_i[b]$ *is a minimal i-cover of b (or $\perp$ if none exist).*

The following theorem states the correctness and running time of the algorithm. Correctness is an immediate corollary of Lemma 4.2, and the running-time analysis is straightforwardly obtained from the pseudo code of Figure 5.

THEOREM 4.3. *Let g be a disjoint-clique graph, and $\mathcal{M}$ be the array returned by* MuxMinCovers$(\Gamma, g, \mathcal{C},)$. *For all $b \subseteq \Gamma$, the entry $\mathcal{M}[b]$ is a minimal cover of b (or $\perp$ if none exist). The running time is polynomial in the input size and 2^{Γ}.*

4.1.2 Beyond Disjoint Cliques

We now extend, beyond disjoint cliques, the class of mux graphs that MuxMinCovers can handle. First, we generalize the notion of a *friendly order* over the nodes of a graph.

DEFINITION 4.4. *Let g be a graph. A friendly order of g is a total (linear) order $\prec$ on $\mathsf{V}(g)$, such that for all nodes $w \in \mathsf{V}(g)$, the preceding neighbors of w succeed the preceding non-neighbors of w; that is, for all $u, v, w \in \mathsf{V}(g)$:*

$$u \prec v \prec w \land \{u, w\} \in \mathsf{E}(g) \;\Rightarrow\; \{v, w\} \in \mathsf{E}(g). \qquad \square$$

Put differently, $v_1, \ldots, v_n$ is a friendly order of g if for all i, node v_i and all its preceding neighbors form a suffix of $v_1, \ldots, v_i$. We use the term "friendly" because every node is placed right after its (already placed) neighbors.

As an example, the following is a friendly order of the graph g_2 of Figure 4 (nodes are represented by their labels).

#license, school, preschool, company, address

As other examples, observe that a graph g has a friendly order if g is a clique, a star, or a path. Of course, these cases do not cover all the graphs with a friendly order (as observed in Figure 4). Note that g has a friendly order if (and only if) every connected component of g has a friendly order. Finally, not every graph has a friendly order; for instance, it can easily be shown that a cycle of four or more nodes does not have any friendly order.

Obviously, the algorithm MuxMinCovers is correct whenever we have a friendly order (according to Definition 4.4), and not just in the case of disjoint cliques. We would like to identify when a mux graph has a friendly order. Interestingly, friendly orders are tightly related to *interval graphs*. We say that g is an interval graph if there is a function I that maps every node $v \in \mathsf{V}(g)$

to a closed interval $I(v)$ on the real line, such that for every two nodes $v, w \in \mathsf{V}(g)$ it holds that $\{v, w\} \in \mathsf{E}(g)$ if and only if $I(v) \cap I(w) \neq \emptyset$. If g is an interval graph, then I is called a *realizer*. Examples of interval graphs are cliques and *caterpillar trees* (which generalize paths and stars). Booth and Lueker [4] showed that determining whether g is an interval graph, and finding a realizer if so, are in polynomial time, and a more recent algorithm by Habib et al. [10] performs these tasks in linear time in g. This is important, because finding a realizer is *the same problem* as finding a friendly order.

PROPOSITION 4.5. *A graph g has a friendly order if and only if it is an interval graph. Furthermore, a friendly order can be obtained in polynomial time from a realizer.*

We conclude that if interval mux graphs are used for expressing lb-specifications, then both MINPATTERN and MINLBCOVER are tractable. Next, we further push this tractability to the class of *circular-arc* graphs.

We say that a graph g is a circular-arc graph if every node v of g can be mapped to an arc $a(v)$ on a circle, such that two arcs $a(u)$ and $a(v)$ intersect if and only if u and v are adjacent (in other words, it is the same definition as that of an interval graph, except that now arcs are used instead of intervals). Observe that circular-arc graphs are a proper generalization of interval graphs. For example, every cycle is a circular-arc graph, but most of the cycles are not interval graphs. Tucker [23] showed that recognition of circular-arc graphs is in polynomial time, and more recently McConnell [20] gave a linear-time recognition algorithm.

Now, consider the problem MINLBCOVER with an lb-constraint that is specified by a circular-arc mux graph. We can efficiently reduce this problem to MINLBCOVER with an interval mux graph. Therefore, it follows that both MINPATTERN and MINLBCOVER are FPT if lb-specifications are given by circular-arc mux graphs.

Next, we consider another (tractable) extension. Mux graphs lack the ability to express constraints on the multiplicity of nodes having a given label. As a simple example, the mux graph g_2 in Figure 4 allows any multiplicity of #license. As another example, the *Mondial* schema[7] does not allow a border element to have more than two country children. We extend mux graphs so that they can specify an upper bound on the number of occurrences of a label, as follows. A *multiplicity-bounded* mux graph, denoted as $\overline{\text{mux}}$ graph, is a pair (g, β), where g is a mux graph and $\beta : \mathsf{V}(g) \to \mathbb{N} \cup \{\infty\}$ is a function. The lb-constraint $\mathcal{F}_\Sigma((g, \beta))$ comprises all the bags $b \in \mathcal{F}_\Sigma(g)$, such that for each node v of g it holds that $\mu_b(\lambda(v)) \leq \beta(v)$.

The algorithm MuxMinCovers (Figure 5) can be easily extended to (efficiently) support multiplicity bounds. In a nutshell, instead of the arrays $\mathcal{M}_i$ and $\mathcal{N}_i$, we compute the arrays $\mathcal{M}_i^j$ and $\mathcal{N}_i^j$, respectively, for $j \leq \beta(v_i)$. Upon termination, each $\mathcal{M}_i^j[b]$ (resp., $\mathcal{N}_i^j$) contains a minimal i-cover (resp., minimal strict i-cover) of b with at most j occurrences of $\lambda(v_i)$. An observation needed here is that $\beta(v_i) \leq |\Lambda|$ can be assumed. The above is also applicable when circular-arc graphs are used.

We conclude this section with the following theorem, which states the tractability of the problems MINLBCOVER and MINPATTERN when lb-specifications belong to the class of circular-arc $\overline{\text{mux}}$ graphs.

THEOREM 4.6. *If lb-specifications are circular-arc $\overline{\text{mux}}$ graphs, then both* MINLBCOVER *and* MINPATTERN *are FPT.*

---

[7]http://www.dbis.informatik.uni-goettingen.de/Mondial/

Next, we address the question of whether Theorem 4.6 can be extended to the whole class of mux graphs (even regardless of multiplicity bounds). Next, we give a negative answer to this question (under standard complexity assumptions). Specifically, the following theorem shows that when general mux graphs are allowed, both MinPattern and MinLBCover are hard for the complexity class $W[1]$, which is believed not to be contained in FPT [6, 9]. The proof is by a reduction from the problem of determining whether a graph has an independent set of size k, with k being the parameter.

THEOREM 4.7. *Suppose that lb-constraints are specified by mux graphs. The following decision problems are $W[1]$-hard with the parameters $|\Lambda|$ and $|\Gamma|$, respectively.*

1. *Given a schema S and a bag Λ of labels, is there a Λ-pattern with $2|\Lambda| + 1$ or fewer nodes?*

2. *Given an input $(\Gamma, g, \mathcal{C})$ for MinLBCover, is there any legal cover of Γ?*

Thus, under standard complexity assumptions, Theorem 4.6 does not extend to general mux graphs (i.e., without the restriction to circular-arc graphs).

4.2 Regular Expressions

In this section, we consider lb-specifications that are given as regular expressions, similarly to Example 2.2. As in that example, we define $\mathcal{F}_{\Sigma}(e)$ to be the set $\mathcal{L}^{b}(e)$. The following theorem states the tractability of MinLBCover and MinPattern when regular expressions are used for specifying lb-constraints.

THEOREM 4.8. *If lb-specifications are regular expressions, then both MinLBCover and MinPattern are FPT.*

Next, we prove Theorem 4.8 by presenting an FPT algorithm for MinLBCover (recall Corollary 3.4).

4.2.1 The Algorithm

The input of our algorithm is $(\Gamma, e, \mathcal{C})$, where Γ is a bag, e is a regular expression specifying the lb-constraint $[\![\mathcal{L}^{b}(e)]\!]$, and $\mathcal{C}$ is a set of triples. The algorithm applies a recursion on the structure of e. In each recursive step, we consider a sub-expression e' of e, and construct an array $\mathcal{M}$, which is similar to the arrays $\mathcal{M}_i$ built in MuxMinCovers. That is, an index of $\mathcal{M}$ is a subbag b of Γ, and when the step terminates, each $\mathcal{M}[b]$ is a minimal legal cover with respect to $(b, e', \mathcal{C})$. The construction of $\mathcal{M}$ is by a reduction to MinLBCover under $\overline{\text{mux}}$-graph specifications with multiplicity bounds, where each $\overline{\text{mux}}$ graph is an extremely simple interval graph. Actually, we could give a more direct algorithm that does not use a reduction to $\overline{\text{mux}}$ graphs; however, using this reduction shortens the presentation (by avoiding the repetition of arguments from the previous section).

We now describe the algorithm in detail. Recall that a regular expression is defined by the following language.

$$e := \sigma \mid \epsilon \mid e* \mid e? \mid ee \mid e|e$$

So, we consider the six options of composing regular expressions. The case where $e = \sigma$ or $e = \epsilon$ is straightforward. For $e = e_1?$, we simply ignore the question mark and solve the problem for e_1. So, three cases remain.

Case 1: $e = e_1*$. Suppose that $\mathcal{M}_1$ is the result of the algorithm for e_1. Let σ_1 be a label, let g be the mux graph consisting of a single σ_1-node, and let $\mathcal{C}'$ be the set of triples $\Delta_b = (b, \sigma_1, \text{weight}(\mathcal{M}_1[b]))$ for all bags $b \subseteq \Gamma$. The next step is to execute MuxMinCovers$(\Gamma, g, \mathcal{C}')$. Let $\mathcal{M}'$ be the result. The array $\mathcal{M}$ that we return is the following. For each $b' \subseteq \Gamma$, we set $\mathcal{M}[b']$ to $\biguplus_{\Delta_b \in \mathcal{M}'[b']} \mathcal{M}_1[b]$.

Case 2: $e = e_1 e_2$. Suppose that $\mathcal{M}_1$ and $\mathcal{M}_2$ are the results of the algorithm for e_1 and e_2, respectively. Let (g, β) be a $\overline{\text{mux}}$ graph, such that g has exactly two nodes v_1 and v_2 labeled with σ_1 and σ_2, respectively, and $\beta(v_1) = \beta(v_2) = 1$. There are no edges in g. Let $\mathcal{C}'$ be the set of triples $\Delta_b = (b, \sigma_i, \text{weight}(\mathcal{M}_i[b]))$ for all bags $b \subseteq \Gamma$ and $i \in \{1, 2\}$. We execute MuxMinCovers$(\Gamma, (g, \beta), \mathcal{C}')$, and suppose that $\mathcal{M}_0$ is the result. Due to β, the cover $\mathcal{M}_0[b]$ is either a singleton or a pair (except for $b = \emptyset$ where $\mathcal{M}_0[b]$ can be empty). We define $\mathcal{M}[b]$, where $b \subseteq \Gamma$, as follows. If $\mathcal{M}_0[b]$ is a singleton $\Delta_b = (b, \sigma_i, \text{weight}(\mathcal{M}_i[b]))$, then we set $\mathcal{M}[b]$ to $\mathcal{M}_i[b]$. Otherwise, $\mathcal{M}_0(b)$ contains two triples Δ_{b_1} and Δ_{b_2} with the labels σ_1 and σ_2, respectively, such that $b = b_1 \uplus b_2$. Then we set $\mathcal{M}[b]$ to $\mathcal{M}_1[b_1] \uplus \mathcal{M}_2[b_2]$.

Case 3: $e = e_1 \mid e_2$. This case is handled exactly like the previous case, except for the following change. In the $\overline{\text{mux}}$ graph (g, β), an edge connects the two nodes of g. Note that in this case, $\mathcal{M}_0[b]$ is always a singleton (or the empty set).

This completes the description of the algorithm, and by that, the proof of Theorem 4.8.

5. DIRECTED PATTERNS

Often, direction of edges are important, and even crucial. As an example, in the tree t_3 of Figure 7, only directions can determine whether the top company sells to the bottom one or vice-versa. Directions are also needed for handling format restrictions. For example, in an XML document, each node (except the root) has one parent. To distinguish between a parent and a child, directions are needed. In this section, we extend our framework and complexity results to a directed model.

5.1 Problem Definition

We first modify the basic definitions. Recall that an lb-constraint was defined as a nonempty subset of $\mathcal{F}_{\Sigma}$. A *directed lb-constraint* is a nonempty subset of $\mathcal{F}_{\Sigma} \times \mathcal{F}_{\Sigma}$. The *containment closure* of a directed lb-constraint $\mathcal{B}$, denoted by $[\![\mathcal{B}]\!]$, is the set of all the pairs $(b'_{\text{in}}, b'_{\text{out}})$, such that there is some $(b_{\text{in}}, b_{\text{out}}) \in \mathcal{B}$ that satisfies $b'_{\text{in}} \subseteq b_{\text{in}}$ and $b'_{\text{out}} \subseteq b_{\text{out}}$.

A *directed schema* S maps each label $\sigma \in dom(S)$ to a directed lb-constraint $S(\sigma)$. Given a σ-node v, the directed lb-constraint $S(\sigma)$ imposes constraints on the labels of $\text{nbr}_{\text{in}}^g(v)$ and $\text{nbr}_{\text{out}}^g(v)$, which are the sets of incoming and outgoing neighbors of v, respectively. Formally, a directed graph g *conforms to* S, denoted by $g \models S$, if for all nodes $v \in V(g)$ it holds that $\lambda(v) \in dom(S)$ and $(\lambda(\text{nbr}_{\text{in}}^g(v)), \lambda(\text{nbr}_{\text{out}}^g(v)) \in S(\lambda(v))$. As earlier, $[\![S]\!]$ denotes the directed schema that is obtained from S by replacing every $S(\sigma)$ with its closure $[\![S(\sigma)]\!]$. We say that t is a *directed tree* if t is a tree when directions are ignored. (Towards the end of this section, we consider another popular notion of directed trees.) For a directed schema S and a bag $\Lambda \in \mathcal{F}_{\Sigma}$, a *directed Λ-pattern* (*under S*) is defined similarly to a Λ-pattern. Namely, it is a directed tree t, such that $\Lambda \subseteq \lambda(V(t))$ and $t \models [\![S]\!]$.

EXAMPLE 5.1. We define three directed schemas S_1, S_2 and S_3, each having the domain consisting of all the labels that appear in Figure 6. Let $\Lambda = \{\text{company}, \text{coke}, \text{pizza}\}$ and $\Lambda' = \{\text{company}, \text{company}, \text{company}\}$.

The schema S_1 is defined by the graph g of Figure 6 as follows. For a label $\sigma \in dom(S_1)$, the directed lb-constraint $S_1(\sigma)$ is the pair $\mathcal{B}_{\text{in}} \times \mathcal{B}_{\text{out}}$, such that $(b_{\text{in}}, b_{\text{out}}) \in \mathcal{B}_{\text{in}} \times \mathcal{B}_{\text{out}}$ if for all labels

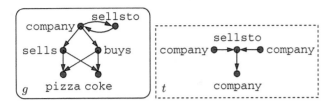

Figure 6: A graph g defining S_1 and a directed Λ'-pattern t for $\Lambda' = \{\!\{\texttt{company}, \texttt{company}, \texttt{company}\}\!\}$

τ_{in} and τ_{out} in b_{in} and b_{out}, respectively, the (directed) edges $(\tau_{\text{in}}, \sigma)$ and $(\sigma, \tau_{\text{out}})$ are in g. As an example, a $\texttt{sells}$-node can have any number of incoming $\texttt{company}$-nodes, and any number of outgoing $\texttt{pizza}$-nodes and $\texttt{coke}$-nodes. Under S_1, each of the three trees of Figure 7 is a directed Λ-pattern. In addition, the tree t of Figure 6 is a directed Λ'-pattern.

The schema S_2 is defined by regular expressions as follows. The meaning of the subscripts in and out is explained below.

$$e_{\texttt{company}} = \texttt{sellsto}_{\text{out}}\text{*}\ \texttt{sellsto}_{\text{in}}\text{*}\ \texttt{sells}_{\text{out}}?\ \texttt{buys}_{\text{out}}?$$

$$e_{\texttt{sellsto}} = \texttt{company}_{\text{in}}\ \texttt{company}_{\text{out}}$$

$$e_{\texttt{sells}} = e_{\texttt{buys}} = \texttt{company}_{\text{in}}\ (\texttt{pizza}_{\text{out}}\ |\ \texttt{coke}_{\text{out}})? \quad (2)$$

$$e_{\texttt{pizza}} = e_{\texttt{coke}} = \texttt{buys}_{\text{in}}\text{*}\ \texttt{sells}_{\text{in}}\text{*}$$

Each e_σ specifies a directed lb-constraint $S_2(\sigma)$ as follows. For every bag b matching e_σ, construct a pair $(b_{\text{in}}, b_{\text{out}}) \in S_2(\sigma)$ such that b_x, where $x \in \{\text{in}, \text{out}\}$, is obtained by selecting all elements of b with the subscript x and then removing x. For example, the tree t of Figure 6 is not a directed Λ'-pattern under S_2, since $e_{\texttt{sellsto}}$ says that a $\texttt{sellsto}$-node cannot have more than one incoming $\texttt{company}$-node. As another example, the tree t_1 of Figure 7 is also not a directed Λ-pattern (under S_2), because $e_{\texttt{sells}}$ states that a $\texttt{sells}$-node cannot have both $\texttt{pizza}$ and $\texttt{coke}$ outgoing nodes. However, both t_2 and t_3 are directed Λ-patterns under S_2.

The schema S_3 is similar to S_2, except that a company cannot be both a buyer and a seller. Hence, $e_{\texttt{company}}$ is:

$$(\texttt{sellsto}_{\text{out}}\text{*}\ \texttt{sells}_{\text{out}}?)\ |\ (\texttt{sellsto}_{\text{in}}\text{*}\ \texttt{buys}_{\text{out}}?) \quad (3)$$

Note that S_3 is more restrictive than S_2, and hence, t is not a directed Λ'-pattern and t_1 is not a directed Λ-pattern. Also, now t_2 is not a directed Λ-pattern, since the $\texttt{company}$-node has outgoing edges to both a $\texttt{sells}$-node and a $\texttt{buys}$-node. But t_3 is a directed Λ-pattern. In particular, note that the top $\texttt{company}$-node has outgoing edges to a $\texttt{sells}$-node and a $\texttt{sellsto}$-node, and the bottom $\texttt{company}$ has an outgoing $\texttt{buys}$-node and an incoming $\texttt{sellsto}$-node. $\square$

A *weight function* W for a directed schema S is defined similarly

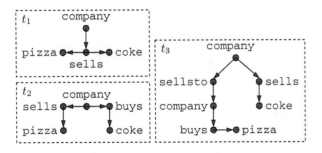

Figure 7: Three directed Λ-patterns t_1, t_2 and t_3, for $\Lambda = \{\!\{\texttt{company}, \texttt{coke}, \texttt{pizza}\}\!\}$

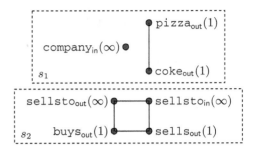

Figure 8: $\overline{\texttt{mux}}$ graphs over $L_{\text{in}} \cup L_{\text{out}}$

to the undirected case (Section 2.3), except that W does not have to be symmetric over $dom(S) \times dom(S)$. Given a weighted directed schema S^W and a directed graph g, the weight $W(g)$ of g is defined as in (1).

EXAMPLE 5.2. Consider the schemas S_1, S_2 and S_3 of Example 5.1, and the directed Λ-patterns t_1, t_2 and t_3 of Figure 7, where $\Lambda = \{\!\{\texttt{company}, \texttt{coke}, \texttt{pizza}\}\!\}$. Let W assign weight 1 to all nodes and edges. It can be verified that under S_1, the tree t_1 is a minimal directed Λ-pattern. Similarly, t_2 is minimal under S_2, and t_3 is minimal under S_3. $\square$

Next, we consider the problem MINDIPATTERN, which is the directed version of MINPATTERN and is naturally defined as follows. The input consists of a weighted directed schema S^W and a bag Λ of labels, and the goal is to find a directed Λ-pattern t that has the minimum weight. Again, for this problem to be well defined, we need to describe languages for lb-specifications.

5.2 Directed lb-Specifications

For directed lb-specifications, we combine the undirected ones (e.g., those of Section 4) with the following transformation, which is essentially how S_2 and S_3 are specified in Example 5.1. We generate two disjoint sets of labels L_{in} and L_{out} by replacing every $\sigma \in dom(S)$ with the new labels σ_{in} and σ_{out}, respectively. At first, we define an lb-constraint $\mathcal{B}$ over $L_{\text{in}} \cup L_{\text{out}}$ by means of some undirected lb-specification. Then, $\mathcal{B}$ is conceptually translated into a directed lb-constraint by splitting each bag $b \in \mathcal{B}$ into a pair $(b_{\text{in}}, b_{\text{out}})$: the bag b_x, where $x \in \{\text{in}, \text{out}\}$, is obtained by selecting all the elements of b with the subscript x and then removing x.

We can now define two types of directed lb-specifications. The first consists of the $\overline{\texttt{mux}}$ graphs (g, β), such that $\lambda(V(g))$ (i.e., the set of labels that appear in g) is a subset of $L_{\text{in}} \cup L_{\text{out}}$. The second type uses regular expressions over $L_{\text{in}} \cup L_{\text{out}}$.

Example 5.1 uses directed lb-specifications of the second type. The $\overline{\texttt{mux}}$ graphs $s_1 = (g_1, \beta_1)$ and $s_2 = (g_2, \beta_2)$ of Figure 8 are directed lb-specifications of the second type. Note that $\beta(v)$ is written in parentheses on the right of $\lambda(v)$. The (undirected) lb-constraints $\mathcal{F}_\Sigma(s_1)$ and $\mathcal{F}_\Sigma(s_2)$ are equal to $\mathcal{L}^{\text{b}}(e_{\texttt{sells}})$ and $\mathcal{L}^{\text{b}}(e_{\texttt{company}})$ of Equations (2) and (3), respectively. Also, note that s_1 is an interval (hence, circular-arc) $\overline{\texttt{mux}}$ graph, whereas s_2 is a circular-arc, but not interval $\overline{\texttt{mux}}$ graph.

5.3 Tractability

In order to extend our results to directed lb-specifications, we need only to adapt the generic algorithm FindMinPattern of Figure 3, which is fairly straightforward. Thus, we get the next theorem that extends Corollary 3.5 and Theorems 4.6 and 4.8.

Note that k-bounded MINDIPATTERN is defined similarly to k-bounded MINPATTERN (i.e., $|\Lambda| \leq k$ is assumed). Containment

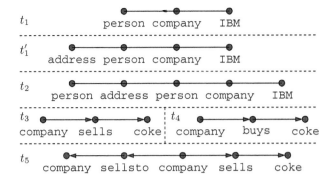

t_1 person company IBM

t_1' address person company IBM

t_2 person address person company IBM

t_3 company sells coke t_4 company buys coke

t_5 company sellsto company sells coke

Figure 9: Redundant and (weakly) non-redundant patterns

checking for directed lb-constraints is the problem of testing whether $(b_{in}, b_{out}) \in [\![\mathcal{B}]\!]$, when given a pair $(b_{in}, b_{out}) \in \mathcal{F}_\Sigma \times \mathcal{F}_\Sigma$ and a directed lb-constraint $\mathcal{B}$ (represented by a directed lb-specification). In the k-bounded version, $|b_{in}| \leq k$ and $|b_{out}| \leq k$ are assumed.

THEOREM 5.3. *The following hold.*

1. *Let k be a fixed natural number. Under a language of directed lb-specifications, if k-bounded containment checking is in polynomial time, then so is k-bounded MINDIPATTERN.*

2. *If lb-specifications are given as circular-arc $\overline{mux}$ graphs or as regular expressions, then MINDIPATTERN is FPT.*

Sometimes a stronger definition of a Λ-pattern t is used, whereby t is required to be *rooted*, that is, have a node r such that every other node of t is reachable from r via a directed path in t. We can adapt FindMinPattern also to this stronger definition, and hence the above theorem remains valid in this case as well. Details are omitted due to a lack of space.

6. DEFINING THE TOP-K PATTERNS

In this section, we discuss how to define the problem of finding k-*minimal* (or *top-k*) patterns. When dealing with non-minimal patterns, we need a suitable notion of non-redundancy. We describe such a notion and use it to formally define the top-k Λ-patterns. Intuitively, the top-k Λ-patterns are required to be non-redundant and have the k-minimal weights (among all the non-redundant Λ-patterns). Developing an algorithm for finding the top-k Λ-patterns is left for future work.

Suppose that S is a schema or a directed schema, and consider a bag $\Lambda \in \mathcal{F}_\Sigma$. By Definition 2.1, a Λ-pattern is a tree t, such that $\Lambda \subseteq \lambda(V(t))$ and $t \models [\![S]\!]$. For instance, under the schema S_2 of Example 2.2 and for $\Lambda = \{\!\{person, IBM\}\!\}$, each of the trees t_1, t_1' and t_2 of Figure 9 is a Λ-pattern. Recall that Λ-patterns are automatically generated queries, as in the schema-free [16] or flexible [5] paradigms. In that sense, t_1' is useless, because it does not convey any information about the relationship between a person and IBM, beyond what is already known from t_1. This is a severe problem when top-k patterns are desired, because many patterns among those with the k-minimal weights could be likewise useless. For example, the patterns for $\{\!\{person, IBM\}\!\}$ with the k-minimal weights might be t_1 and another $k-1$ patterns obtained from t_1 by adding irrelevant nodes (like the address-node of t_1').

The common approach to excluding useless patterns is by requiring non-redundancy [3, 5, 11, 13]. Formally, a Λ-pattern t is *redundant* if t has a proper subtree $t' \neq t$, such that t' is also a Λ-pattern;

otherwise, t is *non-redundant*. Put differently, a Λ-pattern t is non-redundant if the removal of any leaf[8] from t violates $\Lambda \subseteq \lambda(V(t))$. As an example, consider again Figure 9. For S_2 of Example 2.2 and $\Lambda = \{\!\{person, IBM\}\!\}$, the tree t_1 is non-redundant, but the tree t_1' is redundant because even if the address leaf is removed, the result is still a Λ-pattern.

The above definition of non-redundancy has been applied when the goal is to find actual answers (i.e., subtrees of the underlying data graph), rather than patterns that are queries extracted from the schema. In that context, non-redundancy is relative to a set of nodes, rather than a bag of labels, of the tree. This subtle difference renders non-redundancy overly restrictive. As an example, the tree t_2 of Figure 9 represents a meaningful relationship, namely, some person and an IBM employee live in the same address. Although that relationship is not obtained from any subtree of t_2, the above definition deems t_2 a redundant Λ-pattern (when $\Lambda = \{\!\{person, IBM\}\!\}$), because t_1 is (isomorphic to) a proper subtree of t_2. So next, we propose a relaxation of non-redundancy.

We view t_2 as a meaningful Λ-pattern, because we can use the leftmost and rightmost nodes of t_2 as the output corresponding to $\Lambda = \{\!\{person, IBM\}\!\}$. The middle person-node serves only as part of the connection between the output nodes, and it just happens to have a label from Λ. Building on this intuition, we define *weak non-redundancy* as follows. We fix a label $\star \in \Sigma$, and assume that $\star$ is never used in either a schema or Λ. An *output designation* of a Λ-pattern t is a tree t' that is obtained as follows. We choose $|\Lambda|$ nodes of t whose labels form the same bag as Λ and *designate* them as the *output*; we then replace the label of every non-output node with $\star$. Now, consider a (directed) schema S and a bag $\Lambda \in \mathcal{F}_\Sigma$. A (directed) Λ-pattern t is *weakly non-redundant* if there is an output designation t' of t, such that t' is non-redundant (i.e., removing any leaf from t' causes a violation of $\Lambda \subseteq \lambda(V(t'))$).

An easy observation is that a Λ-pattern t is weakly non-redundant if and only if no label has a higher multiplicity among the leaves of t than in Λ; that is, $b \subseteq \Lambda$, where b is the bag comprising the labels of the leaves. For example, given $\Lambda = \{\!\{person, IBM\}\!\}$, the tree t_2 of Figure 9 is weakly non-redundant, but t_1' is not (because address is not in Λ). For $\Lambda = \{\!\{company, coke\}\!\}$, the tree t_5 of Figure 9 is weakly non-redundant. Finally, if Λ is the bag $\{\!\{company, company, company\}\!\}$, then the tree t of Figure 6 is weakly non-redundant. But that tree is weakly redundant for either $\{\!\{company\}\!\}$ or $\{\!\{company, company\}\!\}$, because company occurs three times among the leaves of t.

Observe that a minimal-weight Λ-pattern can be easily made non-redundant by repeatedly removing redundant leaves. So, the algorithms of the previous sections actually find Λ-patterns that are both minimal and (weakly) non-redundant.

COMMENT 6.1. Interestingly, some natural types of constraints require a suitable notion of non-redundancy even when looking just for a minimal Λ-pattern. One such case is that of *through* constraints. As an intuitive example, consider the schema of Figure 2, and let $\Lambda = \{\!\{person, school, city\}\!\}$. Suppose that we are interested in a Λ-pattern, such that the connection between person and city is through school. Then we impose a through constraint on school, which means that school should be on the path connecting person and city (and in particular cannot be a leaf). Such a Λ-pattern conveys, for example, the information that the person attends the school which is located in the city, as opposed to a Λ-pattern stating that both the person and the school are in the same city. The requirement that a Λ-pattern satisfies some through constraints is defined using the notion of weak non-

---

[8]A *leaf* is a node with exactly one incident edge.

redundancy, as follows. Suppose that $\Lambda = \Lambda_1 \uplus \Lambda_2$, where a through constraint is imposed on each label of Λ_2 but on none of Λ_1. A Λ-pattern satisfies the through constraints if it is weakly non-redundant with respect to Λ_1 (i.e., we ignore the labels of Λ_2 in the definition of weak non-redundancy). $\square$

Next, we define top-k patterns. Consider a (directed) weighted schema S^W and a bag $\Lambda \in \mathcal{F}_\Sigma$. Let k be a natural number. We say that T is a *top-k set* of (directed) Λ-patterns if $|T| = k$ and all of the following hold.

1. All the Λ-patterns of T are weakly non-redundant.

2. No two distinct members of T are isomorphic.

3. For all (directed) Λ-patterns t', if t' is weakly non-redundant, then either t' is isomorphic to some $t \in T$, or no $t \in T$ has a weight greater than $W(t')$.

If there are only $k' < k$ weakly non-redundant and pairwise non-isomorphic Λ-patterns, then a top-k set is a top-k' set.

As an example, consider the trees of Figure 9, and suppose that all nodes and edges have weight 1. For the schema S_2 of Example 2.2 and $\Lambda = \{\!\{\texttt{person}, \texttt{IBM}\}\!\}$, a top-2 set is $T = \{t_1, t_2\}$. For the schema S_2 of Example 5.1 and $\Lambda = \{\!\{\texttt{company}, \texttt{coke}\}\!\}$, a top-3 set is $T = \{t_3, t_4, t_5\}$.

As mentioned in the beginning of this section, the development of algorithms for finding a top-k set of (directed) Λ-patterns (where the input consists of a weighted schema S^W, a bag $\Lambda \in \mathcal{F}_\Sigma$, and a number k) is a challenge that we defer to future work.

7. CONCLUSIONS

We gave a generic reduction of MINPATTERN to MINLBCOVER, which is independent of a particular language for expressing lb-specifications. As a corollary, k-bounded MINPATTERN is in polynomial time under the (reasonable) assumption that so is k-bounded containment. More importantly, we developed FPT algorithms for MINLBCOVER under the language of circular-arc $\overline{\text{mux}}$ graphs (recall that for general mux graphs the problem is $W[1]$-hard), and under the language of regular expressions. We also extended these results to the directed model. We believe that the results presented here are the basis for algorithms that find top-k Λ-patterns. But actually designing those algorithms is left for future work.

The formal setting we have used has labeled nodes, but no labeled edges. This is suitable for XML, but not for RDF. It is easy to model labeled edges by introducing a node in the "middle" of each edge. We call such a node a *connector*. For example, the label wifeof in Figure 1 is actually a connector (because it represents a relationship rather than an entity). If a connector appears in a Λ-pattern, then it should not be a leaf (or else we would not know which is the second entity in that relationship). Finding a minimal Λ-pattern under this restriction can be reduced to the problem of finding a minimal Λ-pattern under through constraints. It is fairly easy to adapt our generic algorithm to the latter (the details will be given in the full version).

The language of regular expressions captures the constraints imposed by DTDs. To model *XML Schemas* and *RDF Schemas* (and thereby exploit their expressiveness to the maximal extent), additional types of constraints are needed. Furthermore, an ontology should be taken into account in the case of RDF. Dealing with these extensions is an important task for future work.

We believe that the languages we proposed are sufficiently expressive to be useful in practice; in particular, these algorithms can substantially enhance the practicality of the pattern approach in keyword search on data graphs. We emphasize that in practice, lb-specifications can be derived either from DTDs or other schemas, or by an offline analysis of the underlying database.

Acknowledgments

We thank C. Seshadhri for fruitful discussions, and are grateful to Virginia Vassilevska Williams and Ryan Williams for observing Proposition 4.5.

8. REFERENCES

[1] H. Achiezra, K. Golenberg, B. Kimelfeld, and Y. Sagiv. Exploratory keyword search on data graphs. In *SIGMOD Conference*, pages 1163–1166. ACM, 2010.

[2] C. Beeri and T. Milo. Schemas for integration and translation of structured and semi-structured data. In *ICDT*, pages 296–313. Springer, 1999.

[3] G. Bhalotia, A. Hulgeri, C. Nakhe, S. Chakrabarti, and S. Sudarshan. Keyword searching and browsing in databases using BANKS. In *ICDE*, pages 431–440, 2002.

[4] K. S. Booth and G. S. Lueker. Testing for the consecutive ones property, interval graphs, and graph planarity using PQ-tree algorithms. *J. Comput. Syst. Sci.*, 13(3):335–379, 1976.

[5] S. Cohen, Y. Kanza, B. Kimelfeld, and Y. Sagiv. Interconnection semantics for keyword search in XML. In *CIKM*, pages 389–396. ACM, 2005.

[6] R. G. Downey and M. R. Fellows. *Parameterized Complexity*. Monographs in Computer Science. Springer, 1999.

[7] S. Dreyfus and R. Wagner. The Steiner problem in graphs. *Networks*, 1:195–207, 1972.

[8] K. Golenberg, B. Kimelfeld, and Y. Sagiv. Keyword proximity search in complex data graphs. In *SIGMOD Conference*, pages 927–940. ACM, 2008.

[9] M. Grohe and J. Flum. *Parameterized Complexity Theory*. Theoretical Computer Science. Springer, 2006.

[10] M. Habib, R. M. McConnell, C. Paul, and L. Viennot. Lex-BFS and partition refinement, with applications to transitive orientation, interval graph recognition and consecutive ones testing. *Theor. Comput. Sci.*, 234(1-2):59–84, 2000.

[11] V. Hristidis and Y. Papakonstantinou. DISCOVER: Keyword search in relational databases. In *VLDB*, pages 670–681. Morgan Kaufmann, 2002.

[12] A. Kemper, D. Kossmann, and B. Zeller. Performance tuning for SAP R/3. *IEEE Data Eng. Bull.*, 22(2):32–39, 1999.

[13] B. Kimelfeld and Y. Sagiv. Finding and approximating top-k answers in keyword proximity search. In *PODS*, pages 173–182. ACM, 2006.

[14] B. Kimelfeld and Y. Sagiv. New algorithms for computing Steiner trees for a fixed number of terminals. Accessible from the first author's home page (http://www.cs.huji.ac.il/~bennyk), 2006.

[15] B. Kimelfeld, Y. Sagiv, and G. Weber. ExQueX: exploring and querying XML documents. In *SIGMOD Conference*, pages 1103–1106. ACM, 2009.

[16] Y. Li, C. Yu, and H. V. Jagadish. Schema-free XQuery. In *VLDB*, pages 72–83. Morgan Kaufmann, 2004.

[17] Y. Luo, W. Wang, and X. Lin. SPARK: A keyword search engine on relational databases. In *ICDE*, pages 1552–1555. IEEE, 2008.

[18] A. Markowetz, Y. Yang, and D. Papadias. Keyword search over relational tables and streams. *ACM Trans. Database Syst.*, 34(3), 2009.

[19] Y. Mass, M. Ramanath, Y. Sagiv, and G. Weikum. IQ: The case for iterative querying for knowledge. In *CIDR 2011, Fifth Biennial Conference on Innovative Data Systems Research, Asilomar, CA, USA, January 9-12, 2011, Online Proceedings*, pages 38–44. www.crdrdb.org, 2011.

[20] McConnell. Linear-time recognition of circular-arc graphs. *Algorithmica*, 37(2):93–147, 2003.

[21] L. Qin, J. X. Yu, and L. Chang. Keyword search in databases: the power of RDBMS. In *SIGMOD Conference*, pages 681–694. ACM, 2009.

[22] P. P. Talukdar, M. Jacob, M. S. Mehmood, K. Crammer, Z. G. Ives, F. Pereira, and S. Guha. Learning to create data-integrating queries. *PVLDB*, 1(1):785–796, 2008.

[23] Tucker. An efficient test for circular-arc graphs. *SIAM J. Comput.*, 9(1):1–24, 1980.

[24] M. Y. Vardi. The complexity of relational query languages (extended abstract). In *Proceedings of the Fourteenth Annual ACM Symposium on Theory of Computing*, pages 137–146. ACM, 1982.

[25] G. Zenz, X. Zhou, E. Minack, W. Siberski, and W. Nejdl. From keywords to semantic queries - incremental query construction on the semantic Web. *J. Web Sem.*, 7(3):166–176, 2009.

The Complexity of Text-Preserving XML Transformations[*]

Timos Antonopoulos
Hasselt University and
Transnational University of
Limburg
timos.antonopoulos@uhasselt.be

Wim Martens[†]
TU Dortmund
wim.martens@udo.edu

Frank Neven
Hasselt University and
Transnational University of
Limburg
frank.neven@uhasselt.be

ABSTRACT

While XML is nowadays adopted as the de facto standard for data exchange, historically, its predecessor SGML was invented for describing electronic documents, i.e., marked-up text. Actually, today there are still large volumes of such XML texts. We consider simple transformations which can change the internal structure of documents, that is, the mark-up, and can filter out parts of the text but do not disrupt the ordering of the words. Specifically, we focus on XML transformations where the transformed document is a subsequence of the input document when ignoring mark-up. We call the latter *text-preserving* XML transformations. We characterize such transformations as copy- and rearrange-free transductions. Furthermore, we study the problem of deciding whether a given XML transducer is text-preserving over a given tree language. We consider top-down transducers as well as the abstraction of XSLT called DTL. We show that deciding whether a transformation is text-preserving over an unranked regular tree language is in PTIME for top-down transducers, EXPTIME-complete for DTL with XPath, and decidable for DTL with MSO patterns. Finally, we obtain that for every transducer in one of the above mentioned classes, the maximal subset of the input schema can be computed on which the transformation is text-preserving.

Categories and Subject Descriptors

H.2.3 [**Database Management**]: Languages—*Data manipulation languages (DML)*; F.4.3 [**Mathematical Logic and Formal Languages**]: Formal Languages; D.2.4 [**Software Engineering**]: Software/Program Verification

[*]We acknowledge the financial support of the Future and Emerging Technologies (FET) programme within the Seventh Framework Programme for Research of the European Commission, under the FET-Open grant agreement FOX, number FP7-ICT-233599.
[†]Supported by a grant of the North-Rhine Westfalian Academy of Sciences and Arts, and the Stiftung Mercator Essen.

General Terms

Algorithms, Theory, Verification

1. INTRODUCTION

While XML is embraced by the industry as the de facto standard for data exchange on the Web, XML can also be used to describe marked-up text. Actually, XML's predecessor, SGML, was exactly intended for this purpose. We refer to such documents as text-centric. Examples are poems, books, legislative text, e-governments text, and so on. A characteristic of such documents is that data values are words and sentences, and that their ordering matters. In this paper, we are interested in simple transformations which can change the internal structure of the document, that is, the mark-up, and can filter out parts of the text but do not disrupt the ordering of the words. In this way, the transformations can preserve the meaning of the filtered text. Specifically, we focus on XML transformations where the transformed document is a subsequence of the input document when ignoring mark-up. We call such transformations *text-preserving*. The central problem we consider in this paper, is to decide whether a given transformation is text-preserving for a given class of XML documents. Classes of XML documents will be defined by unranked regular tree languages and transformations by various kinds of transducers. We will show that, modulo some technical restrictions on transductions, transductions are text-preserving if and only if they are not copying and not rearranging.

We will not consider arbitrary transductions but will focus on XSLT-like transformations and use the abstraction of XSLT called DTL, introduced in [11], extended for dealing with data values. DTL is a rule-based language and is parameterized by a pattern language which is used for navigating in the tree and for deciding which rules can be executed. We consider three kinds of settings. The first is a top-down setting where navigation is restricted to children and rule patterns are restricted to label tests. Actually, to ease presentation, we define the top-down fragment of DTL separately as it corresponds to the formalism of top-down uniform tree transducers. In the two other settings, we consider XPath and MSO for both navigational and rule patterns. We refer to these fragments as DTL^{XPath} and DTL^{MSO}, respectively. We show that testing whether a transduction is text-preserving is in PTIME, in EXPTIME and decidable, respectively, for top-down transducers, DTL^{XPath} and DTL^{MSO} over the class of regular tree languages represented by non-deterministic tree automata.

The high-level proof idea underlying all three results is

the same, but the details differ greatly, leading to the different complexities. We essentially show that the set of trees for which the given transduction is not text-preserving is a regular tree language. We refer to the latter as the language of counter-examples. The result then follows by testing emptiness of the intersection of that language with the tree automaton representing the input schema. Of course, the language of counter-examples depends on the transducers. We represent it in the three respective settings by non-deterministic top-down tree automata, alternating tree-walking automata, and non-deterministic tree-jumping automata with MSO-transitions. Of independent interest, we observe that non-deterministic tree-jumping automata with MSO-transitions define only regular tree languages. As regular languages are closed under complement, it readily follows that a regular tree language can be constructed which represents the largest subset of the input schema on which a given transducer is text-preserving.

Outline. In Section 2, we introduce the necessary definitions. In Section 3, we characterize text-preserving transductions. In Section 4 and Section 5, we consider top-down uniform tree transducers and DTL, respectively. In Section 6, we discuss related work and we conclude in Section 7.

2. DEFINITIONS

For any $n, m \in \mathbb{N}$ with $m \geq n$, $[n, m]$ denotes the set of integers $\{n, n+1, \ldots, m-1, m\}$. In this paper we consider finite and infinite alphabets, but Σ always denotes a finite alphabet. We denote symbols from Σ by σ, σ_1, and so on. We assume that special symbols such as "(", ")", etc. are not in Σ.

Strings. A *symbol* is an element of a (finite or infinite) alphabet Δ and a *string* w is a finite sequence of symbols $\sigma_1 \cdots \sigma_n$ for some $n \in \mathbb{N}$. We define the *length* of a string $w = \sigma_1 \cdots \sigma_n$, denoted by $|w|$, to be n and we also refer to $|w|$ as the *size* of w. The empty string is denoted by ε. We assume that readers are familiar with standard operations on strings and sets of strings such as concatenation.

Automata. A *nondeterministic finite string automaton (NFA)* A over an alphabet Σ is a tuple $(Q, \Sigma, \delta, q_0, F)$, such that Q is a finite set of states, $q_0 \in Q$ is the initial state, $F \subseteq Q$ is the set of final states and $\delta : Q \times \Sigma \to 2^Q$ is the transition function. A *run* of the automaton A on a string $w = a_1 \cdots a_n$ is a sequence of states $q_0 q_1 \cdots q_n$ such that, for each $i \in [1, n]$, $q_i \in \delta(q_{i-1}, a_i)$. A run on w is *accepting* if $q_n \in F$, and a string w is *accepted* by A, if there exists an accepting run of A on w. The *size* $|A|$ of an NFA A is its total number of states and transitions. By $\mathcal{L}(A)$ we denote the set of strings accepted by A. A string language L over Σ is *regular* if there is an NFA A such that $\mathcal{L}(A) = L$. We denote the set of regular languages over alphabet Σ by $\mathsf{REG}(\Sigma)$.

Hedges and trees. The set of *unranked trees* over alphabet Σ, denoted by Trees_Σ, is the smallest set S of strings over Σ and the parenthesis symbols "(" and ")" such that, $\varepsilon \in S$ and for each $\sigma \in \Sigma$ and $w \in S^*$, we have that $\sigma(w)$ is in S. For readability, we denote the tree $\sigma()$ by σ. A *tree language* over Σ is a subset of Trees_Σ. The set of *unranked hedges* over alphabet Σ, denoted by Hedges_Σ, is defined as $\mathsf{Hedges}_\Sigma = \mathsf{Trees}_\Sigma^*$. In particular, each tree is also a hedge.

When we write a tree t as $t = \sigma(t_1 \cdots t_n)$ or a hedge h as $h = t_1 \cdots t_n$, we implicitly assume that all t_i are trees.

The *set of nodes* of a tree t and of a hedge h, denoted by Nodes^t and Nodes^h, respectively, are sets of strings in $\mathbb{N}^*$ and are inductively defined as follows. If $h = \sigma_1 \cdots \sigma_n$, then $\mathsf{Nodes}^h = \{1, \ldots, n\}$. Here, for each $i \in [1, n]$, the node i is labelled by σ_i, which we denote by $\mathsf{lab}^h(i) = \sigma_i$. If $t = \sigma(h)$, then $\mathsf{Nodes}^t = \{1\} \cup \{1u \mid u \in \mathsf{Nodes}^h\}$. Here, the root node is 1 and the other nodes are nodes of the subhedge h, prefixed by a 1. The root is labeled σ, i.e., $\mathsf{lab}^t(1) = \sigma$ and, for every node $1u \in \mathsf{Nodes}^t$ we define $\mathsf{lab}^t(1u) = \mathsf{lab}^h(u)$. Finally, if $h = t_1 \cdots t_n$, then $\mathsf{Nodes}^h = \cup_{i=1}^n \{iu \mid 1u \in \mathsf{Nodes}^{t_i}\}$. Here, the labels from the t_i carry over to h, that is, for each $i \in [1, n]$ and each node $iu \in \mathsf{Nodes}^h$, we have $\mathsf{lab}^h(iu) = \mathsf{lab}^{t_i}(1u)$. The *depth* of a node $u \in \mathbb{N}^*$ is $|u|$. Hence, the depth of the root of a tree is one.

From the definition of nodes we can see that the lexicographic order $<_{\mathsf{lex}}$ on Nodes^h corresponds to the order generated by the depth-first (left-to-right) traversal of the hedge h. More specifically, for two nodes iu and $jv \in \mathsf{Nodes}^h$ with $i, j \in \mathbb{N}$, we have $iu <_{\mathsf{lex}} jv$ if $i < j$ or if $i = j$ and $u <_{\mathsf{lex}} v$. The *children* of a node v in h are all nodes $v' \in \mathsf{Nodes}^h$ such that $v' = v \cdot i$ for $i \in \mathbb{N}$. A node $v \in \mathsf{Nodes}^h$ is a *leaf* if it has no children.

The *size* of a hedge h, denoted by $|h|$, is its number of nodes. For a tree t and a node $u \in \mathsf{Nodes}^t$, we denote by $\mathsf{anc\text{-}str}^t(u)$ the *ancestor string of u in t*, i.e., the string formed by the labels on the path in the tree t from the root to u, including the label of u. The *lowest common ancestor* of two nodes v_1 and v_2 in Nodes^t is the node corresponding to the longest common prefix of v_1 and v_2.

The *subtree of hedge h at a node u* is the tree induced by the set of nodes with prefix u and is denoted by $\mathsf{subtree}^h(u)$. For any hedge h, node u, and for any hedge h', $h[u \leftarrow h']$, denotes the hedge obtained from h by replacing $\mathsf{subtree}^h(u)$ with h' and by redefining the set of nodes and the label function accordingly. For any two alphabets Σ and Γ, $\mathsf{Trees}_\Sigma(\Gamma)$ is the set of trees over the alphabet $\Sigma \cup \Gamma$, where only leaves are allowed to be labelled with symbols from Γ. Similarly, $\mathsf{Hedges}_\Sigma(\Gamma)$ is $(\mathsf{Trees}_\Sigma(\Gamma))^*$. Finally, the *frontier*[1] of a hedge h, denoted by $\mathsf{frontier}(h)$, is the largest sequence $\mathsf{lab}^h(v_1) \cdots \mathsf{lab}^h(v_n)$, where, for every $i \in [1, n]$, v_i is a leaf of h, and for every $i \in [1, n-1]$, $v_i <_{\mathsf{lex}} v_{i+1}$.

In the following, we will often write Nodes, lab, etc. without index whenever the tree or hedge is clear from the context.

Text trees. Let Text be an infinite set, disjoint from any finite alphabet we consider here, such as Σ. A *text tree* t over Σ is a tree in $\mathsf{Trees}_\Sigma(\mathsf{Text})$ or, in other words, a tree over the alphabet $\Sigma \cup \mathsf{Text}$ where symbols from Text can only appear at the leaves. We refer to these nodes as *text nodes* and denote the set of text nodes of a tree t by $\mathsf{text\text{-}nodes}^t$. A text tree language is a subset of $\mathsf{Trees}_\Sigma(\mathsf{Text})$. In the following, unless otherwise stated, whenever we say *tree* we always mean *text tree*. In particular, we also simply say *tree language* instead of *text tree language*.

A tree language L is *closed under Text-substitutions* if, for any tree $t \in L$ and any text node u of t, the tree obtained from t by changing u's label to another value in Text is also in the language L. Formally, a Text-*substitution* ρ is a function from $\mathsf{Trees}_\Sigma(\mathsf{Text})$ to $\mathsf{Trees}_\Sigma(\mathsf{Text})$, such that

---

[1] A frontier is sometimes also called a *yield*.

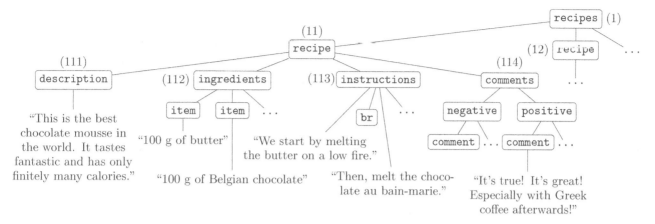

Figure 1: A text tree representing an XML document for recipes.

for each $t \in \text{Trees}_\Sigma(\text{Text})$, $\text{Nodes}^t = \text{Nodes}^{\rho(t)}$, for each node $v \notin \text{text-nodes}^t$, $\text{lab}^t(v) = \text{lab}^{\rho(t)}(v)$ and for each node $v \in \text{text-nodes}^t$, $\text{lab}^{\rho(t)}(v) \in \text{Text}$. In other words, a Text-substitution relabels zero or more leaf nodes labelled with a label in Text, to some other label in Text.

In the sequel we only consider tree languages that are closed under Text-substitutions primarily because we want to consider Text as an abstract set. Furthermore, when ignoring integrity constraints, XML schema languages are rather restricted in enforcing constraints on actual text values. Therefore, it makes sense to simply consider one infinite set of possible values so that replacing a certain text value with another does not change validity of the document with respect to the schema.

The *text-content* of a tree t, denoted by $\text{text-content}(t)$, is the string over alphabet Text obtained by concatenating the text values of all text nodes in document order, which is the lexicographic order induced by $\mathbb{N}^*$. Notice that, for any tree t, $\text{text-content}(t)$ is the substring of $\text{frontier}(t)$ containing exactly the labels from Text.

EXAMPLE 2.1. Figure 1 depicts a tree representation of an XML document underlying a web site with recipes. Each recipe has a description, a list of ingredients, instructions, and a list of comments by users. The text nodes of the tree are the ones that contain text in quotation marks. The ancestor path of the node labeled **positive** is **recipes recipe comments positive**. The text-content of the tree is the concatenation of all the text between the quotation marks, from left to right. For clarity, we annotate some nodes with their name in braces.

A *tree transduction* T is a mapping $T : L_1 \to L_2$ for tree languages L_1 and L_2. We say that a string $s_1 = \sigma_1 \cdots \sigma_n$ over alphabet Δ is a *subsequence* of s_2, denoted $s_1 \prec s_2$, if s_2 is of the form $w_0 \sigma_1 w_1 \cdots w_{n-1} \sigma_n w_n$ for some $w_0, \ldots, w_n \in \Delta^*$. We are now ready to define the notion central to this paper.

DEFINITION 2.2. A tree transduction T is *text preserving* over a tree language L if, for all trees $t \in L$,

$$\text{text-content}(T(t)) \prec \text{text-content}(t).$$

Schema languages. We abstract the schema languages *Document Type Definition (DTD)* and Relax NG by ex-

tended context-free grammars and by unranked tree automata, respectively.

A *Document Type Definition (DTD)* over some finite alphabet Σ is a tuple $D = (\Sigma \uplus \{\text{text}\}, C, d, S_d)$ where C is a set of regular string languages over $\Sigma \uplus \{\text{text}\}$, d is a function that maps symbols in Σ to languages in C, and $S_d \subseteq \Sigma$ is a set of start symbols. We refer to the languages in C as the *content models* of the DTD. A tree t is *valid with respect to* a DTD D or *satisfies* D, if its root is labelled by an element of S_d and, for every node labelled with some $\sigma \in \Sigma$, the sequence $\sigma_1 \cdots \sigma_n$ of labels of its children, where any element in Text is replaced by the symbol text, is in the language $d(\sigma)$. So, text serves as a placeholder for text nodes. In the remainder of this paper, we assume that the regular languages in C are represented by regular expressions or NFAs.

The set of trees that are valid with respect to a DTD D is denoted by $\mathcal{L}(D)$. A DTD D is *reduced* if, for every $\sigma \in \Sigma$ for which $d(\sigma)$ is defined, there exists a tree $t \in \mathcal{L}(D)$ such that the label σ occurs somewhere in t. Any DTD can be transformed to an equivalent reduced DTD in polynomial time [1, 16]. However, reducing a DTD is PTIME-complete.[2] In the following, we assume that all DTDs are reduced.

EXAMPLE 2.3. The tree in Figure 1 is valid w.r.t. the DTD $(\Sigma \uplus \{\text{text}\}, C, d, S_d)$, where Σ is the set of labels used in the boxed nodes of the tree, i.e., **recipes**, **recipe**, ... We represent the regular languages in C by regular expressions. Then, $S_d = \{\text{recipes}\}$ and d is defined as:

recipes	$\mapsto$	recipe*
recipe	$\mapsto$	description · ingredients
		·instructions · comments
ingredients	$\mapsto$	item*
instructions	$\mapsto$	(br + text)*
br	$\mapsto$	ε
comments	$\mapsto$	negative · positive
positive	$\mapsto$	comment*
negative	$\mapsto$	comment*
description	$\mapsto$	text
item	$\mapsto$	text
...		

Notice that the children of **instructions** can come from Σ

---

[2]More accurately, *deciding* whether a DTD is reduced is PTIME-complete.

and from Text. For every Σ-symbol σ for which we did not yet define d, we define $d(\sigma) = \texttt{text}$.

Relax NG schemas are abstracted by *nondeterministic un-ranked tree automata (NTA)*. An NTA N over some finite alphabet Σ, is a tuple $(Q, \Sigma \uplus \{\texttt{text}\}, \delta, q_0, F)$ where Q is a finite set of states, $q_0 \in Q$ is the initial state, F is the set of final states, and $\delta : Q \times (\Sigma \uplus \{\texttt{text}\}) \to \mathrm{REG}(Q)$ is the transition function. A *run* of N over some tree t is a function $\rho : \mathsf{Nodes}^t \to Q$ such that $\rho(1) = q_0$, i.e., the root of t is assigned q_0 and, for any node v labeled with $\sigma \in \Sigma$ with n children, it holds that $\rho(v1) \cdots \rho(vn)$ is in the language $\delta(\rho(v), \sigma)$. A run ρ of N on some tree t is *accepting* if $\varepsilon \in \delta(\rho(v), \mathsf{lab}(v))$ for every leaf v of t if $\mathsf{lab}(v) \in \Sigma$, and $\delta(\rho(v), \texttt{text}) = \{\varepsilon\}$ if $\mathsf{lab}(v) \in \mathsf{Text}$. So, also here $\texttt{text}$ serves as a placeholder for Text-values. We define F to be the set of states q such that $\varepsilon \in \delta(q, a)$ for some $a \in \Sigma \uplus \{\texttt{text}\}$. A tree t is *accepted* by N if there exists an accepting run of N on t. By $\mathcal{L}(N)$ we denote the set of trees accepted by N. A tree language L is *regular*, if there is an NTA N such that $L = \mathcal{L}(N)$. It is well-known that regular tree languages are closed under union, intersection, and complementation.

Unless otherwise mentioned, we assume that the regular languages $\delta(q, \sigma)$ in NTAs are represented by NFAs. The *size* $|N|$ of an NTA $N = (Q, \Sigma, \delta, q_0, F)$ is equal to $|Q| + |\delta|$, where $|\delta| = \sum_{q \in Q, a \in \Sigma} |\delta(q, a)|$.

Central problem. In the rest of this paper, we consider the following decision problem. Let $\mathcal{T}$ be a class of tree transductions and let $\mathcal{L}$ be a class of tree languages. We then study the question:

Given a language $L \in \mathcal{L}$ and a transduction $T \in \mathcal{T}$, is T text-preserving over L?

Recall that, in this paper, the languages $\mathcal{L}$ are always closed under Text-substitutions. In the conclusions we discuss how our technique also allows to solve more complex decision problems.

3. A CHARACTERIZATION OF TEXT-PRE-SERVING TRANSDUCTIONS

We provide a characterization of when a transduction is text-preserving in terms of its copying and rearranging behavior. First, we need some terminology. We say that a tree is *value-unique* when all its Text-values occurring at leaves are different. Notice that, since we only consider tree languages that are closed under Text-substitutions, all the tree languages we consider contain at least one tree which is value-unique.

DEFINITION 3.1. A transduction T is *copying over a tree language L* if there is a value-unique $t \in L$ such that $T(t)$ contains multiple occurrences of the same Text-value. A transduction T is *rearranging over a tree language L* if there is a value-unique $t \in L$ such that, for some γ_1 and $\gamma_2 \in \mathsf{Text}$, $\gamma_1 \gamma_2 \prec \mathsf{text\text{-}content}(t)$ and $\gamma_2 \gamma_1 \prec \mathsf{text\text{-}content}(T(t))$.

Up to now, transductions are general mappings from trees to trees. We will next put some restrictions on them. Let $\maltese \notin \mathsf{Text}$. For $\gamma \in \mathsf{Text} \cup \{\maltese\}$, let ρ_γ be the Text-substitution that for every tree t, relabels every text node with γ. A transduction T is *Text-independent* if for every tree t and every Text-substitution ρ on t,

$$\rho_\maltese(T(\rho(t))) = \rho_\maltese(T(t)).$$

Informally, this ensures that the structure of the transduced tree $T(t)$ does not depend on the Text-values occurring in t. Only the concrete Text-values in $T(t)$ and $T(\rho(t))$ can differ. The final notion we need is that of a Text-functional transduction. A transduction T is Text-*functional* if, for every tree t, there exists a function f from the set of text nodes of $T(t)$ to the set of text nodes of t, such that for every Text-substitution ρ on t, $\mathsf{lab}^{T(\rho(t))}(v) = \mathsf{lab}^{\rho(t)}(f(v))$ for every node $v \in \mathsf{text\text{-}nodes}^{T(\rho(t))}$. Intuitively, this means that Text-values in the output tree are determined by the Text-value at the corresponding node, determined by f, in the input tree. Note that a Text-functional transduction can never introduce Text-values that do not appear in the input tree.

DEFINITION 3.2. A transduction is *admissible* if it is Text-independent and Text-functional.

We will show in the sequel that all transductions we consider in this paper are admissible. We are now ready to prove the characterization of text-preserving transductions.

THEOREM 3.3. *An admissible transduction T is text-preserving over a language L if and only if it is not copying and not rearranging over L.*

PROOF. When T is copying or rearranging over L then T is obviously not text-preserving over L.

When T is not text-preserving, there exists a tree $t \in L$ such that $\mathsf{text\text{-}content}(T(t)) \not\prec \mathsf{text\text{-}content}(t)$. Let ρ be a Text-substitution such that $\rho(t)$ is value-unique. First, we argue that $\mathsf{text\text{-}content}(T(\rho(t))) \not\prec \mathsf{text\text{-}content}(\rho(t))$. Assume for the sake of contradiction that $\mathsf{text\text{-}content}(T(\rho(t))) \prec \mathsf{text\text{-}content}(\rho(t))$ and let g be a function from $\mathsf{text\text{-}nodes}^{T(\rho(t))}$ to $\mathsf{text\text{-}nodes}^{\rho(t)}$ that witnesses this subsequence relation. In other words, since $\rho(t)$ is value-unique, g maps every text node in $T(\rho(t))$ to the unique text node in $\rho(t)$ with the same text value. In particular, g is unique.

Since T is Text-functional by assumption, there exists a function $f : \mathsf{text\text{-}nodes}^{T(t)} \to \mathsf{text\text{-}nodes}^t$ such that, for every Text-substitution ρ' and every node $v \in \mathsf{text\text{-}nodes}^{T(\rho'(t))}$, $\mathsf{lab}^{T(\rho'(t))}(v) = \mathsf{lab}^{\rho'(t)}(f(v))$. Since this condition holds for every substitution ρ', it holds for ρ in particular. Therefore it is also the case that, for every node $v \in \mathsf{text\text{-}nodes}^{T(\rho(t))}$, $\mathsf{lab}^{T(\rho(t))}(v) = \mathsf{lab}^{\rho(t)}(f(v))$. Since $\rho(t)$ is value unique and T is Text-independent, it follows that f maps every text node in $T(\rho(t))$ to the unique text node in $\rho(t)$ with the same text value.

Since $\mathsf{text\text{-}nodes}^t = \mathsf{text\text{-}nodes}^{\rho(t)}$ and $\mathsf{text\text{-}nodes}^{T(t)} = \mathsf{text\text{-}nodes}^{T(\rho(t))}$ because T is Text-independent, it follows that f and g are the same function. By definition of f, for every node $v \in \mathsf{text\text{-}nodes}^{T(t)}$, $\mathsf{lab}^{T(t)}(v) = \mathsf{lab}^t(f(v))$ and therefore, f is a witness function to $\mathsf{text\text{-}content}(T(t)) \prec \mathsf{text\text{-}content}(t)$, which contradicts our assumption that T is not text-preserving on t.

It remains to show that T is either copying or rearranging on t. Consider the function f, and notice that since $\mathsf{text\text{-}content}(T(t)) \not\prec \mathsf{text\text{-}content}(t)$, f is either not injective or does not preserve the order $<_{\mathrm{lex}}$ in trees. In the first case, T is copying and in the second case T is rearranging. $\square$

4. TOP-DOWN TRANSDUCERS

We start with the simple uniform top-down tree transducers considered in [13, 14, 15] in the context of type checking.

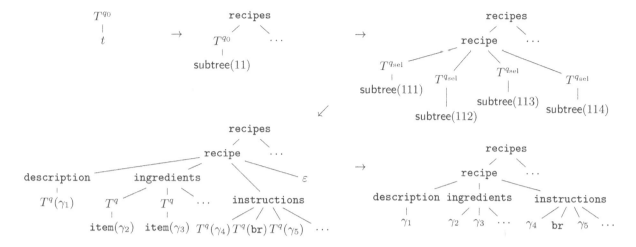

Figure 2: A uniform transducer selecting all descriptions, ingredients, and instructions from the tree of Fig. 1.

These correspond to a simple top-down fragment of XSLT and are equivalent to DTL, defined in the next section, instantiated with only downward navigation.

4.1 Definition

DEFINITION 4.1. A *top-down uniform tree transducer* is a tuple $T = (Q, \Sigma \cup \{\texttt{text}\}, q^0, R)$, where Q is a finite set of states, Σ is a finite alphabet, $q^0 \in Q$ is the initial state, and R is a finite set of rules of the form $(q, a) \to h$, where $q \in Q$ and

(a) if $a \in \Sigma$ then $h \in \mathsf{Hedges}_\Sigma(Q)$ and

(b) if $a = \texttt{text}$ then h is $\texttt{text}$.

When $q = q^0$, then h is restricted to $\mathsf{Trees}_\Sigma(Q)$ and should contain at least one Σ-label. This restriction of h ensures that the output of T is always a tree. For each state $q \in Q$ and symbol $a \in \Sigma$ there is at most one hedge $h \in \mathsf{Hedges}_\Sigma(Q)$ such that $(q, a) \to h$ is a rule in R.

The translation defined by T on a tree t in state q, denoted by $T^q(t)$, is defined inductively as follows:

(i) $T^q(\varepsilon) = \varepsilon$;

(ii) for each $\gamma \in \mathsf{Text}$, if there is a rule $(q, \texttt{text}) \to \texttt{text}$ then $T^q(\gamma) = \gamma$, if there is no such rule, then $T^q(\gamma) = \varepsilon$;

(iii) if $t = a(t_1 \cdots t_n)$ for some $a \in \Sigma$ and there is a rule $(q, a) \to h$, then $T^q(t)$ is obtained from h by replacing every node u in h labelled with $p \in Q$, by the hedge $T^p(t_1) \cdots T^p(t_n)$. If there is no such rule, then $T^q(t) = \varepsilon$.

The transformation of t by T, denoted by $T(t)$, is defined as $T^{q^0}(t)$. To make use of our characterization in Theorem 3.3, we need to be able to reason about the function that is defined by T. To this end, we say that the *transduction defined by T* or *transduction of T* is the function mapping every tree t onto $T(t)$. For any rule $(q, a) \to h$ in R, we denote the hedge h on its right hand side by $\mathsf{rhs}(q, a)$. The *size* of T, denoted by $|T|$, is equal to $|Q| + |R|$, where $|R| = \sum_{q \in Q, a \in \Sigma} |\mathsf{rhs}(q, a)|$. In the remainder of this section, we simply say transducer rather than top-down uniform tree transducer.

EXAMPLE 4.2. The uniform transducer defined by the rules

$$
\begin{aligned}
(q_0, \texttt{recipes}) &\to \texttt{recipes}(q_0) \\
(q_0, \texttt{recipe}) &\to \texttt{recipe}(q_{\mathrm{sel}}) \\
(q_{\mathrm{sel}}, \sigma) &\to \sigma(q) \quad (\sigma \in \{\texttt{description}, \texttt{ingredients}, \texttt{instructions}\}) \\
(q, \texttt{item}) &\to q \\
(q, \texttt{br}) &\to \texttt{br}(q) \\
(q, \texttt{text}) &\to \texttt{text}
\end{aligned}
$$

Selects, from the tree of Figure 1, all recipes, their descriptions, ingredients lists, and instructions; and deletes the comments. Furthermore, it keeps the markup (i.e., the $\texttt{br}$ nodes) in the instructions, but deletes the $\texttt{item}$ nodes. The transformation on the tree in Figure 1 is illustrated in Figure 2. For readability in the figure, we sometimes write a function call of the form $T^q(t)$ as a (sub)tree where t is a child of a node labelled T^q.

We call a state q of T *reachable* if there is a sequence of pairs $(q_1, a_1) \cdots (q_n, a_n)$ for some $n \in \mathbb{N}$, such that $q_1 = q^0$, $q_n = q$ and, for all $i \in [1, n-1]$, we have that q_{i+1} occurs as the label of a leaf in the hedge $\mathsf{rhs}(q_i, a_i)$. Notice that, if a transducer has a rule of the form $(q, a) \to \varepsilon$, we can remove this rule and the resulting transducer is equivalent (due to rule (iii) in the definition of $T^q(t)$). We therefore say that a rule of the form $(q, a) \to \varepsilon$ is *useless*. A transducer is *reduced*, if all its states are reachable and it contains no useless rules. In the following, we assume that transducers are always reduced.

Notice that rules in transducers do not contain any values from Text. This ensures that transducers can not introduce a Text-value not present in the input tree. We note that the transducers in this section are admissible, in the sense of Definition 3.2.

LEMMA 4.3. *Top-down uniform tree transducers are admissible.*

4.2 Copying and rearranging transducers

In this section, we provide equivalent formalizations for the notions of copying and rearranging introduced in Section 3. In Section 4.3, we then show that it is decidable in PTIME whether a transducer is copying or rearranging thereby obtaining PTIME-decidability for testing whether a transducer is text-preserving.

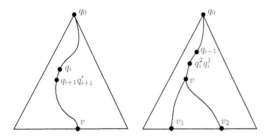

Figure 3: Illustration of copying (left) and rearranging (right) for top-down uniform tree transducers.

First we formally define copying and rearranging for a transducer.

DEFINITION 4.4. *Let L be a tree language. A transducer T is copying over L if the transduction defined by T is copying over L. It is rearranging over L if the transduction defined by T is rearranging over L.*

In the following lemma, we provide an operational condition that is equivalent to the general notion of copying defined above. First, we introduce the following definitions. A *text path* is a sequence in $\Sigma^* \cdot \mathsf{Text}$. A *path run* of T on a text path $a_1 \cdots a_n \gamma$ is a sequence $q_1, \ldots, q_n, q_{n+1}$ such that $q_1 = q^0$, and for all $i \in [1, n]$, q_{i+1} occurs at a leaf of $\mathsf{rhs}(q_i, a_i)$ and $(q_{n+1}, \mathtt{text}) \to \mathtt{text}$. Intuitively, a path run is a set of states that T assumes when processing the text path. Note that there can be several path runs for the same text path as the transducer can use rules containing multiple states in a right-hand side.

LEMMA 4.5. *A transducer $T = (Q, \Sigma \cup \{\mathtt{text}\}, q^0, R)$ is copying over a tree language L if and only if there exists a tree $t \in L$ and a leaf node v in t such that $\mathsf{anc\text{-}str}(v) = a_1 \cdots a_n \cdot \gamma$ is a text path on which either*
(1) T has two different path runs, or
(2) T has a path run $q_1, \ldots, q_n, q_{n+1}$, where for some $i \in [1, n]$, $q_{i+1} \cdot q_{i+1} \prec \mathsf{frontier}(\mathsf{rhs}(q_i, a_i))$.

Recall that $\prec$ denotes the subsequence relation. Condition (2) therefore states that q_{i+1} occurs on two different leaves of $\mathsf{rhs}(q_i, a_i)$. The condition in Lemma 4.5 is illustrated in Figure 3. In the figure, if $q_{i+1} \neq q'_{i+1}$, there are two path runs and if $q_{i+1} = q'_{i+1}$, then $q_{i+1} \cdot q_{i+1} \prec \mathsf{frontier}(\mathsf{rhs}(q_i, a_i))$.

Next, we characterize when a transducer rearranges two Text-values in a tree t. Similarly as for copying, we provide an operational condition for rearranging. Intuitively, a transducer rearranges when there are two leaves v_1 and v_2 in t and $T(t)$ swaps the Text-values corresponding to v_1 and v_2. In terms of a top-down uniform tree transducer, this means that, on the path from the root to the lowest common ancestor of v_1 and v_2, a swap operation takes place.

LEMMA 4.6. *A transducer $T = (Q, \Sigma \cup \{\mathtt{text}\}, q^0, R)$ is rearranging over a tree language L if and only if there exists a tree $t \in L$, two leaf nodes v_1, v_2 of t with $v_1 <_{lex} v_2$ with text paths $\mathsf{anc\text{-}str}(v_1) = a_1^1 \cdots a_n^1 \cdot \gamma^1$ and $\mathsf{anc\text{-}str}(v_2) = a_1^2 \cdots a_m^2 \cdot \gamma^2$ on which which T has path runs $q_1^1, \ldots, q_n^1, q_{n+1}^1$ and $q_1^2, \ldots, q_m^2, q_{m+1}^2$, such that the following holds. If the lowest common ancestor v of v_1 and v_2 has depth k, then there exists an $i \leq k$ such that*
(1) for all $j < i$, we have $(q_j^1, a_j^1) = (q_j^2, a_j^2)$ and
(2) $q_i^2 \cdot q_i^1 \prec \mathsf{frontier}(\mathsf{rhs}(q_{i-1}^1, a_{i-1}^1))$.

The condition in Lemma 4.6 for rearranging is illustrated in Figure 3. From Lemmas 4.5 and 4.6 and from Theorem 3.3 we now obtain the following characterization for text-preserving top-down uniform transducers:

THEOREM 4.7. *A uniform top-down transducer T is not text-preserving over a tree language L if and only if the condition in Lemma 4.5 or the condition in Lemma 4.6 holds.*

4.3 PTIME Result

This section is devoted to the proof of Theorem 4.11 which states that it is decidable in PTIME whether a top-down tree transducer is text-preserving over an unranked regular tree language represented by an NTA.

For a tree language L, we denote by $L_{\mathtt{text}}$ the language over alphabet $\Sigma \uplus \{\mathtt{text}\}$ obtained from L by replacing, in each tree, each label $\gamma \in \mathsf{Text}$ by the label $\mathtt{text}$. The *path language* of a regular tree language L is the language of all root-to-leaf paths in trees of $L_{\mathtt{text}}$ that end with $\mathtt{text}$. More formally, the text path language of L is $\{w \mid t \in L_{\mathtt{text}}, \mathsf{lab}^t(u) = \mathtt{text}, \text{ and } w = \mathsf{anc\text{-}str}^t(u)\}$. We say that an NFA A_L is a *path automaton for regular tree language* L if A_L accepts the path language of L. For a tree transducer T, we say that an NFA A_T is a *transducer path automaton for* T if it accepts exactly the text paths on which T has a path run. Notice that A_L and A_T accept only strings that end with $\mathtt{text}$. We show that they can be constructed in PTIME.

LEMMA 4.8. *(1) Given an NTA N, we can construct a path automaton A_N for $\mathcal{L}(N)$ in polynomial time.*
(2) Given a uniform tree transducer T, we can construct a transducer path automaton A_T for T in polynomial time.

From now on, we refer to A_T as *the* transducer path automaton of T and to A_N as *the* path automaton of N. As our next step, we use the two types of path automata to test for copying or rearranging. First, we treat copying.

LEMMA 4.9. *Given a uniform tree transducer T and an NTA N, it is decidable in PTIME whether T is copying over $\mathcal{L}(N)$.*

PROOF SKETCH. We define an NFA M that accepts text paths satisfying condition (1) or condition (2) of Lemma 4.5. So, M is non-empty iff T is copying over $\mathcal{L}(N)$. As M can be constructed in PTIME and testing non-emptiness of NFAs is in PTIME as well, the result follows. Basically, M simulates both A_N (as the text path should come from a tree accepted by N) and two copies of A_T (as there should be a path run of T) while checking for the existence of two different path runs or while trying to reach a rule in T which copies. $\square$

LEMMA 4.10. *Given a uniform tree transducer T and an NTA N, it is decidable in PTIME whether T is rearranging over $\mathcal{L}(N)$.*

PROOF SKETCH. We will construct in PTIME an NTA M accepting the set of trees on which T is rearranging. Therefore, the intersection of M and N is non-empty if and only if T is rearranging over $\mathcal{L}(N)$. As the latter can be done in PTIME, the result follows. Intuitively, M directly searches for nodes satisfying the properties mentioned in Lemma 4.6. We describe M as if operating in a top-down fashion. Starting from the root of an input tree t, M guesses a path, simulating A_T. At a certain non-deterministically chosen point, M decides it has found state $q_{i-1}^1 = q_{i-1}^2$ and non-deterministically picks q_i^1 and q_i^2 (cf. Lemma 4.6). From then on, M continues until it (non-deterministically) arrives at the lowest common ancestor of v_1 and v_2. On this path, M will simulate two copies of A_T; one copy continuing from state q_i^1 and one copy continuing from state q_i^2. At the lowest common ancestor of v_1 and v_2, the simulation of these two copies of M will split again. Towards v_1, M simulates the copy that started from q_i^1, and towards v_2, M simulates the copy that started from q_i^2. Finally, M accepts when the copy for q_i^1 leads to acceptance of A_T at node v_1 and the copy of q_i^2 leads to acceptance of A_T at node v_2. Recall that the acceptance condition of A_T means that the text value of the last node is copied to the output of T. $\square$

By the previous lemmas the main complexity result of this section readily follows:

THEOREM 4.11. *Given a uniform tree transducer T and an NTA N, it is decidable in* PTIME *whether T is* Text-*preserving over* $\mathcal{L}(N)$.

5. DTL

5.1 General DTL Transducers

In this section, we consider the abstraction of XSLT called DTL, which was introduced in [11]. DTL programs can navigate in a tree through the use of *binary patterns*. While XSLT employs XPath, we leave the concrete pattern language implicit for now and introduce the following terminology. A *unary pattern* over Σ is a subset of $\bigcup_{t \in \mathsf{Trees}_\Sigma}(\{t\} \times \mathsf{Nodes}^t)$ and a *binary pattern* over Σ is a subset of $\bigcup_{t \in \mathsf{Trees}_\Sigma}(\{t\} \times \mathsf{Nodes}^t \times \mathsf{Nodes}^t)$. We refer to the set of unary and binary patterns over Σ as $\mathcal{UP}(\Sigma)$ and $\mathcal{BP}(\Sigma)$, respectively. We will denote unary patterns by φ, ψ and binary patterns by α, β. To emphasize that unary and binary patterns will be specified by pattern languages, we will also write $(t, u) \in \varphi$ as $t \models \varphi(u)$ and $(t, u, v) \in \alpha$ as $t \models \alpha(u, v)$.

Our definition of DTL differs slightly from the one in [11]. To simplify presentation, we disregard construction functions (cf. Section 6 for a discussion). On the other hand, we do extend DTL to deal with text values.

DEFINITION 5.1. A DTL *transducer* is a tuple $T = (\Sigma, \Delta, Q, q_0, R_\Sigma, R_{\mathsf{Text}})$, where

- Σ is the finite alphabet of input symbols,
- Δ is the finite alphabet of output symbols,
- Q is the finite set of states,
- $q_0 \in Q$ is the initial state,
- R_Σ is a finite set of rules of the form $(q, \varphi) \to h$, where $q \in Q$, $\varphi \in \mathcal{UP}(\Sigma)$, and h is in $\mathsf{Hedges}_\Delta(Q \times \mathcal{BP}(\Sigma))$. If $q = q_0$, h is required to be a tree such that $\mathsf{lab}^h(1) \notin Q \times \mathcal{BP}(\Sigma)$.[3]
- R_{Text} is a finite set of rules of the form $(q, \mathtt{text}) \to \mathtt{text}$, with $q \in Q$.

To ensure determinism, we require that when $(q, \varphi) \to h$ and $(q, \varphi') \to h'$ are rules in R_Σ, then there exists no tree t such

that $t \models \varphi(v)$ and $t \models \varphi'(v)$ for any node v in t.[4] Notice in the above definition that there are no restrictions on the allowed patterns. Later, we will use concrete pattern languages like monadic second-order logic and XPath to define patterns.

We are now ready to define the transformation induced by T on a tree t. Intuitively, T starts in state q_0 at the root of t (note that the root of a tree is always 1). The latter is encoded by the initial configuration $(q_0, 1)$. Formally, a *configuration* is a pair in $Q \times \mathsf{Nodes}^t$. During computation T will rewrite the initial configuration into a partial output tree $\xi \in \mathsf{Trees}_\Delta(Q \times \mathsf{Nodes}^t)$. That is, a Δ-tree where some leaves will be labeled with configurations. The transducer then proceeds by rewriting these configurations extending ξ until all configurations are gone and the transduction stops. Basically, rewriting of a configuration (q, v) can be done by a rule $(q, \varphi) \to h$ when $t \models \varphi(v)$. The output tree is then appended with the hedge h where the leaves carrying binary patterns result in new configurations.

We next formally define the transduction relation. Thereto, given a tree t, the transformation relation induced by T on t, denoted by $\Rightarrow_{T,t}$, is the binary relation on $\mathsf{Trees}_\Delta(Q \times \mathsf{Nodes}^t)$ defined as follows. For $\xi, \xi' \in \mathsf{Trees}_\Delta(Q \times \mathsf{Nodes}^t)$, $\xi \Rightarrow_{T,t} \xi'$, if there is a leaf node $u \in \mathsf{Nodes}^\xi$ such that

1. $\mathsf{lab}^\xi(u) = (q, v)$ with $q \in Q$ and $v \in \mathsf{Nodes}^t$,

2. if $\mathsf{lab}^t(v) \in \mathsf{Text}$ then $\xi' = \xi[u \leftarrow \mathsf{lab}^t(v)]$ if there is a rule $(q, \mathtt{text}) \to \mathtt{text}$ and $\xi' = \xi[u \leftarrow \varepsilon]$ otherwise.[5]

3. if $\mathsf{lab}^t(v) \in \Sigma$,

   - if there is a rule $r = ((q, \varphi) \to h) \in R_\Sigma$ such that $t \models \varphi(v)$, then $\xi' = \xi[u \leftarrow h\Theta]$, where Θ denotes the substitution of replacing every pair (q', α) by the hedge $(q', v_1) \cdots (q', v_m)$, where
     - $\{v_1, \ldots, v_m\} = \{u \mid t \models \alpha(v, u)\}$, and
     - $v_1 <_{\mathrm{lex}} \cdots <_{\mathrm{lex}} v_m$,
   - if there is no rule $r = ((q, \varphi) \to h) \in R_\Sigma$ s.t. $t \models \varphi(v)$, then $\xi' = \xi[u \leftarrow \varepsilon]$.

For any tree t and DTL transducer T, $T(t)$ is defined to be the tree $t' \in \mathsf{Trees}_\Delta$, such that $(q_0, 1) \Rightarrow^*_{T,t} t'$, when such a tree exists and is undefined otherwise.[6] As configurations for which no rule applies are rewritten into the empty hedge, $T(t)$ can only be undefined when T does not stop. Furthermore, when $T(t)$ is defined, it is unique because of the determinism restriction on unary patterns.

Example 5.15 contains a DTL transducer which selects all recipes with their description, ingredients, and instructions if they have at least three positive comments. The unary and binary patterns in the example are given in an XPath syntax, formally defined in Section 5.4.

Notice that each top-down tree transducer T as introduced in the previous section can be defined by a DTL program T'. Indeed, for each rule $(q, a) \to h$ of T, T' has a rule $(q, \varphi) \to h'$ where $t \models \varphi(v) \Leftrightarrow \mathsf{lab}^t(v) = a$; and h' is obtained from h by replacing each q that appears as a leaf with the pair $(q, \mathtt{children})$ where $\mathtt{children}$ is the pattern selecting all children of the node at hand.

---

[3]This is just a technical restriction which forces the transducer to output trees.

[4]Note that for the tree patterns we consider, testing determinism is decidable.

[5]Recall that ε is the empty hedge.

[6]Here, R^* denotes the reflexive transitive closure of the binary relation R.

LEMMA 5.2. DTL *transducers are admissible.*

5.2 Copying and Rearranging

Next, we will give an operational characterization of text-preserving DTL transducers in terms of copying and rearranging. Copying and rearranging for DTL transducers is defined analogously as before.

DEFINITION 5.3. For any DTL transducer T and tree language L, T is *copying over* L if the transduction defined by T is copying over L. It is *rearranging over* L, if the transduction defined by T is rearranging over L.

For characterizing these notions, we need some terminology. For the remainder of the discussion, fix a tree t. We next define when a configuration (q', v') can *follow* a configuration (q, v) in the transduction of t. Formally, we define $(q, v) \rightsquigarrow (q', v')$ to hold whenever there are $\xi, \xi' \in \mathsf{Trees}_\Delta(Q \times \mathsf{Nodes}^t)$ with $(q_0, 1) \Rightarrow^*_{T,t} \xi \Rightarrow_{T,t} \xi'$ such that $\mathsf{frontier}(\xi) = \theta_1(q, v)\theta_2$, $\mathsf{frontier}(\xi') = \theta_1\theta\theta_2$, and $(q', v') \prec \theta$ for $\theta_1, \theta_2, \theta \in (\Delta \cup (Q \times \mathsf{Nodes}^t))^*$. Basically, this says that (q, v) is rewritten into a tree containing the configuration (q', v') at its frontier.

A *path run of* T *over* t is a sequence $(q_0, v_0) \cdots (q_n, v_n)$, where $v_0 = 1$ (the root of t), and, for all $i \in [1, n]$, (q_i, v_i) follows (q_{i-1}, v_{i-1}). A *text path run* is a path run such that $\mathsf{lab}^t(v_n) \in \mathsf{Text}$ and $(q_n, \mathsf{text}) \to \mathsf{text} \in R_{\mathsf{Text}}$. We say that the path run ends in node v_n. Intuitively, a text path run is part of a run (which incidentally is a path) of T on t which outputs a text value. The next definition determines when a transducer copies, that is, outputs the Text-value carried by the same leaf node v, either using two different text path runs (ending in v), or by using one text path run (ending in v) which actually occurs twice in the transduction.

We need one additional notion. Let $(q, v) \rightsquigarrow (q', v')$. Then, we say that (q', v') *doubles at* (q, v) if there is a rule $(q, \varphi) \to h$ and binary patterns $\alpha_1, \alpha_2 \in \mathcal{BP}(\Sigma)$, such that $t \models \varphi(v)$, $t \models \alpha_1(v, v')$, $t \models \alpha_2(v, v')$ and $(q', \alpha_1) \cdot (q', \alpha_2) \prec \mathsf{frontier}(h)$. That is, rewriting (q, v) introduces two occurrences of the configuration (q', v').

The following lemma gives our operational characterization of copying for DTL transducers.

LEMMA 5.4. *A DTL transducer T is copying over a tree language L, if and only if there exists a tree $t \in L$, such that there are two different text path runs over t ending in the same node, or one text path run $(q_0, v_0) \cdots (q_n, v_n)$ such that (q_i, v_i) doubles at (q_{i-1}, v_{i-1}) for some $i \in [1, n]$.*

Next, we characterize when a transducer rearranges two Text-values in a tree. Recall that this happens when there are two leaves v and u in t both carrying a Text-value and where $v <_{\mathrm{lex}} u$, but $T(t)$ swaps the order of the Text-values corresponding to v and u. We will show that the latter happens only when during the transduction a rule with rhs h is used such that

- $(q_u, \alpha_1) \cdot (q_v, \alpha_2) \prec \mathsf{frontier}(h)$, and the configurations (q_u, α_1) and (q_v, α_2) proceed to output the text value at u and v, respectively; or,

- when $(q', \alpha') \prec \mathsf{frontier}(h)$ and α' selects u_1, v_1 with $u_1 <_{\mathrm{lex}} v_1$ where (q', u_1) and (q', v_1) proceed to output the Text-value at u and v, respectively.

We are now ready to prove a characterization for when a DTL transducer is rearranging.

LEMMA 5.5. *A DTL transducer T is rearranging over a tree language L, if and only if there exists a tree $t \in L$, two text path runs $\theta(q, v)(q_1, v_1) \cdots (q_n, v_n)$ and $\theta(q, v)(p_1, u_1) \cdots (p_m, u_m)$ with $v_n <_{\mathrm{lex}} u_m$, a rule $(q, \varphi) \to h$, and binary patterns α_1, α_2, such that $t \models \varphi(v)$, $t \models \alpha_1(v, v_1)$, $t \models \alpha_2(v, u_1)$ and either*

(1) $(p_1, \alpha_2) \cdot (q_1, \alpha_1) \prec \mathsf{frontier}(h)$, or

(2) $(q_1, \alpha_1) = (p_1, \alpha_2)$, $(q_1, \alpha_1) \prec \mathsf{frontier}(h)$ and $u_1 <_{\mathrm{lex}} v_1$.

From Lemmas 5.2, 5.4, and 5.5 and from Theorem 3.3 we now obtain a characterization of text-preserving DTL transducers that can be syntactically tested.

THEOREM 5.6. *A DTL transducer T is not text-preserving over a tree language L if and only if the condition in Lemma 5.4 or the condition in Lemma 5.5 holds.*

5.3 Transducers with MSO Transitions

In the present section, we consider the instantiation of DTL with MSO-definable patterns, called DTL^{MSO}. The main result of this section is a proof that testing whether a DTL^{MSO} transduction is text-preserving with respect to a regular tree language, is decidable.

We first define trees over the alphabet Σ as relational structures over the vocabulary E, $<$ and $(\mathsf{lab}_\sigma)_{\sigma \in \Sigma}$. The domain of a tree then is its set of nodes. Furthermore, for two nodes v_1, v_2 of a tree t, $E(v_1, v_2)$ if v_2 is a child of v_1, and $v_1 < v_2$ if v_1 and v_2 share the same parent v, and $v_1 <_{\mathrm{lex}} v_2$. Finally, for each $\sigma \in \Sigma$, lab_σ is the set of nodes labelled with σ. *Monadic Second-order Logic* (MSO) then is the extension of First-order Logic (FO) that allows the use of set variables ranging over subsets of the domain, in addition to the individual variables ranging over elements of the domain, as provided by first-order logic. We assume standard practice. We denote by $\phi(x_1, \ldots, x_k)$ that ϕ is a k-ary formula with k free first-order variables. Furthermore, for a tree t, and nodes $v_1, \ldots, v_k$, we denote by $t \models \phi(v_1, \ldots, v_k)$ that ϕ holds when the free variables of ϕ are instantiated by $v_1, \ldots, v_k$. We refer the reader to, e.g., [8] for more background.

Unary and binary patterns will now be defined by unary and binary MSO formulas, respectively. For instance, the formula $\varphi(x)$ defines the pattern $\bigcup_{t \in \mathsf{Trees}_\Sigma} \{t\} \times \{u \mid t \models \varphi(u)\}$. Then, DTL^{MSO} is the instantiation of DTL with MSO-definable patterns. In the definition of DTL^{MSO} transducers, we will simply specify the formulas rather than the patterns they define.

To prove the main result of this section, we need a number of different automata which we define next: tree-jumping automata with MSO transitions, and tree-walking automata with and without MSO tests.

DEFINITION 5.7. A nondeterministic *tree-jumping automaton with* MSO *transitions* over an alphabet Σ, denoted by TJA^{MSO}, is a tuple $B = (Q, \Sigma, \delta, q_0, F, M_u, M_b)$ where Q is a finite set of states, $q_0 \in Q$ is the initial state, $F \subseteq Q$ is a set of final states, M_u is a finite set of unary MSO formulas, M_b is a finite set of binary MSO formulas, and $\delta : Q \times M_u \times M_b \to 2^Q$ is the transition function. A *run* of B on a tree t that starts at a node v_0 of t and ends at a node v_n of t, is a sequence $(q_0, v_0, \varphi_0, \alpha_0) \cdots (q_n, v_n, \varphi_n, \alpha_n)$, where for each $i \in [0, n-1]$, $t \models \varphi_i(v_i)$, $t \models \alpha_i(v_i, v_{i+1})$, and $q_{i+1} \in \delta(q_i, \varphi_i, \alpha_i)$. A run is *accepting* if $q_n \in F$.

The tree language accepted by B, denoted $\mathcal{L}(B)$, consists of those trees t for which there exists an accepting run starting at the root of t. If there exists a run of B that starts at a node v_1 in state q_1 and ends at node v_2 in state q_2, we sometimes also say that, when started in state q_1 in v_1, B ends in state q_2 in v_2.

We define two restrictions of tree-jumping automata. A nondeterministic *tree-walking automaton with* MSO *tests*, denoted by TWA^{MSO}, is a TJA^{MSO} where M_b contains only the predicates first-child(x, y), next-sibling(x, y), parent(x, y), previous-sibling(x, y) and equality. Here, the just mentioned predicates have the obvious semantics. For instance, first-child(x, y) holds when y is the first-child of x, and so on. Note that these are easily MSO-definable.

We show that TJA^{MSO} coincides with the class of unranked regular tree languages strongly bearing on a result by Bloem and Engelfriet [4].

LEMMA 5.8. *(1) For each* MSO *formula $\alpha(x, y)$, there exists a* TWA^{MSO} $A_\alpha = (Q, \Sigma, \delta, q_0, f, M_u)$, *such that for any tree t and nodes $v, u \in \text{Nodes}^t$, $t \models \alpha(v, u)$ if and only if there exists a run of A_α on t starting at node v at state q_0 and ending at node u at state f. The converse statement also holds.*

(2) For each TJA^{MSO} $B = (Q, \Sigma, \delta, q_0, F, M_u, M_b)$ *there exists a* TWA^{MSO} A, *such that $\mathcal{L}(B) = \mathcal{L}(A)$.*

PROOF SKETCH. (1) Bloem and Engelfriet [4] have shown the exact same statement for ranked trees. As the first-child next-sibling encoding between ranked and unranked trees is MSO-definable, the result follows for unranked trees as well.

(2) Essentially, the TWA^{MSO} A simulates the TJA^{MSO} B by invoking the automaton A_α for every transition α of B. $\square$

We note that the constructions in Lemma 5.8 are effective. Furthermore, note that Lemma 5.8(1) together with the fact that MSO-definable unranked tree languages are regular, implies that TWA^{MSO} define the unranked regular tree languages. Therefore, we have the following corollary:

COROLLARY 5.9. TJA^{MSO} *define precisely the unranked regular tree languages.*

The above implies that emptiness of TJA^{MSO} is decidable. In the remainder of this section we will reduce testing whether a DTL^{MSO} transducer is text-preserving to the emptiness test for TJA^{MSO}. More specifically, for a transducer T, we will create a TJA^{MSO} A_T^{copy} and $A_T^{\text{rearrange}}$ such that A_T^{copy} and $A_T^{\text{rearrange}}$ are empty iff T is not copying and not rearranging, respectively. By Theorem 3.3, T then is text-preserving.

We need to introduce a number of automata. We fix a transducer $T = (Q, \Sigma, \Delta, q_0, R_\Sigma, R_{\text{Text}})$. For states $q, q' \in Q$, let $A_T^{q,q'}$ be the TJA^{MSO} which when started in state q on node v of a tree t ends in state q' at node v' iff $(q, v) \rightsquigarrow^* (q', v')$. That is, when T reaches configuration (q, v) when processing t, T can reach configuration (q', v'). By $A_{T,\sigma,\sigma'}^{q,q'}$, we denote the automaton $A_T^{q,q'}$ which additionally checks that the start position is labelled with σ and the end position is labelled with σ'.

We start with $A_T^{\text{rearrange}}$. The automaton will accept a tree t when T is rearranging over $\{t\}$. Intuitively, by Lemma 5.5,

the automaton needs to look for the following kind of configurations (ignore the bullets for now):

$$(q_0, 1) \quad \rightsquigarrow^* \quad (\overset{\bullet}{q, v}) \quad \begin{matrix} \overset{\sim^*}{} & (q_1, v_1) & \rightsquigarrow^* & (q_n, v_n) \\ & \bullet_1 & & \circ_1 \\ \overset{\sim^*}{} & \bullet_2 & & \circ_2 \\ & (p_1, u_1) & \rightsquigarrow^* & (p_m, u_m) \end{matrix} \qquad (\dagger)$$

which satisfy some additional criteria. In particular, we will make sure later that v_n and u_m are text nodes and that $(q, v) \rightsquigarrow (q_1, v_1)$ and $(q, v) \rightsquigarrow (p_1, u_1)$, i.e., we can make these transitions in one step.

The automaton makes use of an extended alphabet. Let $\Sigma_{\text{mark}} = (\Sigma \cup \{\text{text}\}) \times 2^{\{\circ, \circ_1, \circ_2, \bullet, \bullet_1, \bullet_2\}}$. Intuitively, the alphabet allows us to mark a node with a set of markers. Then, for a marker $c \in \{\circ, \circ_1, \circ_2, \bullet, \bullet_1, \bullet_2\}$, we slightly abuse notation and say simply that a node is labelled with c, when actually there is a $C \subseteq \{\circ, \circ_1, \circ_2, \bullet, \bullet_1, \bullet_2\}$ with $c \in C$ and a $\sigma \in \Sigma$ such that it is labelled with (σ, C). To check $(\dagger)$, we assume v is labelled with $\bullet$, v_1 is labelled with $\bullet_1$, u_1 is labelled with $\bullet_2$, v_n is labelled with $\circ_1$, u_m is labelled with $\circ_2$. Then, the configurations in $(\dagger)$ occur in a tree t if and only if there is a marking t' of t such that

$$t' \in A_{T,\text{root},\bullet}^{q_0,q} \cap A_{T,\bullet,\bullet_1}^{q,q_1} \cap A_{T,\bullet,\bullet_2}^{q,p_1} \cap A_{T,\bullet_1,\circ_1}^{q_1,q_n} \cap A_{T,\bullet_2,\circ_2}^{p_1,p_m}.$$

Here, the automaton $A_{T,\text{root},\bullet}^{q_0,q}$ tests whether the state q is reachable from q_0 in T. By $A_{(\dagger)}^{q,q_1,p_1}$ we refer to this automaton that tests whether there are states q_n, p_m such that condition $(\dagger)$ holds for given states q, q_1, p_1.

We need some additional regular languages over Σ_{mark}. They can for instance easily be defined in MSO. We assume that they are represented by NTAs:

(i) A_{mark} : for all $c \in \{\bullet, \bullet_1, \bullet_2, \circ_1, \circ_2\}$, there is exactly one node labelled with c. Furthermore, the node labelled with $\circ_1$ (resp., $\circ_2$), is a leaf labelled with (text, C) and $\circ_1 \in C$(resp., $\circ_2 \in C$). We will abuse notation and refer to the nodes labelled with c simply as c.

(ii) $A_{<,\bullet}$: $\bullet_2 <_{\text{lex}} \bullet_1$;

(iii) $A_{<,\circ}$: $\circ_1 <_{\text{lex}} \circ_2$;

(iv) $A_\bullet^\varphi$: $t \models \varphi(\bullet)$;

(v) $A_{\bullet_1}^\alpha$: $t \models \alpha(\bullet, \bullet_1)$; and,

(vi) $A_{\bullet_2}^\beta$: $t \models \beta(\bullet, \bullet_2)$.

We define two automata $A_1^{\text{rearrange}}$ and $A_2^{\text{rearrange}}$ corresponding to the two conditions of Lemma 5.5. To state the conditions, we assume as before that the nodes are marked as in condition $(\dagger)$.

In the first condition, we need to test, in addition to $(\dagger)$, whether $\circ_1 <_{\text{lex}} \circ_2$ and there is a rule $(q, \varphi) \rightarrow h$ in T with $(p_1, \beta) \cdot (q_1, \alpha) \prec \text{frontier}(h)$ such that $t \models \varphi(\bullet)$, $t \models \alpha(\bullet, \bullet_1)$, and $t \models \beta(\bullet, \bullet_2)$. In order to formally capture this condition, we define a relation G that contains precisely the tuples $(q, \varphi, p_1, \beta, q_1, \alpha)$ such that there exists a rule $(q, \varphi) \rightarrow h$ in T with $(p_1, \beta) \cdot (q_1, \alpha) \prec \text{frontier}(h)$. We are now ready to define $A_1^{\text{rearrange}}$:

$$A_1^{\text{rearrange}} := A_{\text{mark}} \cap A_{<,\circ} \cap \left(\bigcup_{(q,\varphi,p_1,\beta,q_1,\alpha) \in G} (A_{(\dagger)}^{q,q_1,p_1} \cap A_\bullet^\varphi \cap A_{\bullet_1}^\alpha \cap A_{\bullet_2}^\beta) \right)$$

In the second condition of Lemma 5.5, we need to test, in addition to $(\dagger)$, whether $\circ_1 <_{\text{lex}} \circ_2$ and there is a rule $(q, \varphi) \rightarrow h$ in T with $(q_1, \alpha) \prec \text{frontier}(h)$ such that $(q_1, \alpha) = (p_1, \beta)$, $\bullet_2 <_{\text{lex}} \bullet_1$, $t \models \varphi(\bullet)$, $t \models \alpha(\bullet, \bullet_1)$, and $t \models \alpha(\bullet, \bullet_2)$.

In order to formally capture this condition, we define a relation H that contains precisely the tuples $(q, \varphi, q_1, \alpha)$ such that there exists a rule $(q, \varphi) \rightarrow h$ in T with $(q_1, \alpha) \prec$ frontier(h). We are now ready to define $A_2^{\mathrm{rearrange}}$:

$$A_2^{\mathrm{rearrange}} := A_{\mathrm{mark}} \cap A_{<,\circ} \cap A_{<,\bullet}$$
$$\left(\bigcup_{(q,\varphi,q_1,\alpha) \in H} (A_{(\dagger)}^{q,q_1,q_1} \cap A_\bullet^\varphi \cap A_{\bullet_1}^\alpha \cap A_{\bullet_2}^\alpha) \right)$$

LEMMA 5.10. *Given a* DTL^{MSO} *transducer* T, *the language defined by the* TJA^{MSO} $A_1^{\mathrm{rearrange}} \cup A_2^{\mathrm{rearrange}}$ *is nonempty if and only if* T *is rearranging over* Trees$_\Sigma$.

The overall procedure for A_T^{copy} is similar. The automaton will accept a tree t when T is copying over $\{t\}$. Intuitively, by Lemma 5.4, the automaton needs to look for the following kind of configurations

$$
\begin{array}{c}
\\
(q_0, 1) \;\rightsquigarrow^* \; (q, u)
\end{array}
\begin{array}{c}
(q_1, u_1) \;\rightsquigarrow^* \; (q_n, v) \\
\bullet_1 \qquad\qquad \circ \\
\rightsquigarrow^* \\
\bullet_2 \qquad\qquad \circ \\
(p_1, u_2) \;\rightsquigarrow^* \; (p_m, v)
\end{array}
\quad (\ddagger)
$$

which satisfy some additional criteria. The node v should be a text node and the transitions from (q, u) to (q_1, u_1) and to (p_1, u_2) should be possible in one step. Note that both paths in the picture lead to the same node v.

As before the automaton makes use of the extended alphabet Σ_{mark}. With the same conventions as before, to check $(\ddagger)$, we assume u is labelled with $\bullet$, u_1 is labelled with $\bullet_1$, u_2 is labelled with $\bullet_2$, and v is labelled with $\circ$. Then, the configurations in $(\ddagger)$ occur in a tree t if and only if there is a marking t' of t such that

$$t' \in A_{T,\mathrm{root},\bullet}^{q_0,q} \cap A_{T,\bullet,\bullet_1}^{q,q_1} \cap A_{T,\bullet,\bullet_2}^{q,p_1} \cap A_{T,\bullet_1,\circ}^{q_1,q_n} \cap A_{T,\bullet_2,\circ}^{p_1,p_m}.$$

Analogously as before, the automaton $A_{T,\mathrm{root},\bullet}^{q_0,q}$ tests whether the state q is reachable from q_0 in T. By $A_{(\ddagger)}^{q,q_1,p_1}$ we refer to this automaton that tests whether there are states q_n, p_m such that condition $(\ddagger)$ holds for given states q, q_1, p_1.

In addition to the NTAs for the regular languages (i)–(vi) above, we need

(vii) A'_{mark}: for any $c \in \{\bullet, \bullet_1, \bullet_2, \circ\}$, there is exactly one node labelled with c and the node labelled $\circ$ is a text node in t,

$(viii)$ $A_{\bullet_1 \neq \bullet_2}$: $\bullet_1 \neq \bullet_2$.

(ix) $A_{\bullet_1 = \bullet_2}$: $\bullet_1 = \bullet_2$.

We define two automata A_1^{copy} and A_2^{copy} corresponding to the two conditions of Lemma 5.4. To state the conditions, we assume as before that the nodes are marked as in condition $(\ddagger)$. We also assume that the nodes labelled with $\bullet, \bullet_1, \bullet_2, \circ$ are unique.

In the first condition, we need to test, in addition to $(\ddagger)$, if there are two different text path runs over t ending in the same node v. Since the path from $(q_0, 1)$ to (q, u) can have arbitrary length, we can assume w.l.o.g. that the last configuration in which these two text path runs are the same is (q, u). This means that there exists a rule $(q, \varphi) \rightarrow h$ in T with $(q_1, \alpha) \prec$ frontier(h) and $(p_1, \beta) \prec$ frontier(h) such that $t \models \varphi(\bullet)$, $t \models \alpha(\bullet, \bullet_1)$, and $t \models \beta(\bullet, \bullet_2)$. Furthermore, since (q, u) is the last configuration for which the text path runs are the same, we either have that (a) $q_1 \neq p_1$ or (b) $\bullet_1 \neq \bullet_2$. In order to formalize this condition, let I be the set that contains all tuples $(q, \varphi, q_1, \alpha, p_1, \beta)$ such that $(q, \varphi) \rightarrow h$ is a

rule in T with $(q_1, \alpha) \prec$ frontier(h) and $(p_1, \beta) \prec$ frontier(h). Then, we can define A_{1a}^{copy} and A_{1b}^{copy}:

$$A_{1a}^{\mathrm{copy}} := A'_{\mathrm{mark}} \cap$$
$$\left(\bigcup_{(q,\varphi,p_1,\beta,q_1,\alpha) \in I \wedge p_1 \neq q_1} (A_{(\ddagger)}^{q,q_1,p_1} \cap A_\bullet^\varphi \cap A_{\bullet_1}^\alpha \cap A_{\bullet_2}^\beta) \right)$$

$$A_{1b}^{\mathrm{copy}} := A'_{\mathrm{mark}} \cap A_{\bullet_1 \neq \bullet_2} \cap$$
$$\left(\bigcup_{(q,\varphi,p_1,\beta,q_1,\alpha) \in I} (A_{(\ddagger)}^{q,q_1,p_1} \cap A_\bullet^\varphi \cap A_{\bullet_1}^\alpha \cap A_{\bullet_2}^\beta) \right)$$

In the second condition of Lemma 5.4 we need to test whether there exists a text path run with two consecutive configurations such that the second one doubles at the first one. W.l.o.g., we can assume that (q_1, u_1) doubles at (q, u). This means that there exists a rule $(q, \varphi) \rightarrow h$ in T with $(q_1, \alpha) \cdot (q_1, \beta) \prec$ frontier(h), such that $t \models \varphi(\bullet)$, $t \models \alpha(\bullet, \bullet_1)$, $t \models \beta(\bullet, \bullet_2)$, and $u_1 = u_2$, i.e., the node u_1 is labelled by $\bullet_1$ and $\bullet_2$. In order to formalize this condition, let J be the set that contains all tuples $(q, \varphi, q_1, \alpha, \beta)$ such that $(q, \varphi) \rightarrow h$ is a rule in T with $(q_1, \alpha) \cdot (q_1, \beta) \prec$ frontier(h). Then, we can define A_2^{copy}:

$$A_2^{\mathrm{copy}} := A'_{\mathrm{mark}} \cap A_{\bullet_1 = \bullet_2} \cap$$
$$\left(\bigcup_{(q,\varphi,q_1,\alpha,\beta) \in J} (A_{(\ddagger)}^{q,q_1,q_1} \cap A_\bullet^\varphi \cap A_{\bullet_1}^\alpha \cap A_{\bullet_2}^\beta) \right)$$

LEMMA 5.11. *Given a* DTL^{MSO} *transducer* T, *the language defined by the* TJA^{MSO} $A_{1a}^{\mathrm{copy}} \cup A_{1b}^{\mathrm{copy}} \cup A_2^{\mathrm{copy}}$ *is nonempty if and only if* T *is copying over* Trees$_\Sigma$.

To test whether a DTL^{MSO} transducer T is text-preserving over a regular tree language $\mathcal{L}$, it follows from Theorem 3.3 that it is sufficient to test the conditions in Lemmas 5.10 and 5.11. We therefore obtain the following theorem.

THEOREM 5.12. *Given a* DTL^{MSO} *transducer* T *and a regular language* $\mathcal{L}$, *it is decidable whether* T *is text-preserving.*

As satisfiability of MSO is non-elementary over trees, testing whether a DTL^{MSO} transducer is text-preserving is non-elementary as well. Indeed, consider a transducer which outputs two copies of the input tree when an MSO-sentence is satisfied at the root. Then this transduction is text-preserving if and only if the formula is not satisfiable.

5.4 Transducers with XPath Transitions

We recall the definition of Core XPath. Since we do not use other fragments of XPath, we will use the term XPath to refer to Core XPath. We use the definition from [24]. We denote XPath node expressions by $\varphi, \psi, \ldots$ and path expressions by $\alpha, \beta, \ldots$

DEFINITION 5.13. XPath node expressions and path expressions are defined by simultaneous induction, as follows:
Path expressions: $\alpha ::= R \mid R^* \mid \cdot \mid \alpha/\beta \mid \alpha \cup \beta \mid \alpha[\varphi]$
Node expressions: $\varphi ::= \sigma \mid \langle \alpha \rangle \mid \top \mid \neg \varphi \mid \varphi \wedge \psi$

Here, $\sigma \in \Sigma$ is a label test and R is one of the relations child, parent, next-sibling, or previous-sibling. We denote these relations by $\downarrow, \uparrow, \rightarrow$, and $\leftarrow$, respectively.

$$
\begin{aligned}
[\![R]\!]_{\mathsf{PExpr}} &= \text{the pairs in relation } R \\
[\![R^*]\!]_{\mathsf{PExpr}} &= \text{reflexive and transitive closure of } [\![R]\!]_{\mathsf{PExpr}} \\
[\![\cdot]\!]_{\mathsf{PExpr}} &= \{(u,u) \mid u \in \mathsf{Nodes}^t\} \\
[\![\alpha/\beta]\!]_{\mathsf{PExpr}} &= \{(u,w) \mid \exists v.(u,v) \in [\![\alpha]\!]_{\mathsf{PExpr}} \text{ and} \\
&\qquad\qquad\qquad (v,w) \in [\![\beta]\!]_{\mathsf{PExpr}}\} \\
[\![\alpha \cup \beta]\!]_{\mathsf{PExpr}} &= [\![\alpha]\!]_{\mathsf{PExpr}} \cup [\![\beta]\!]_{\mathsf{PExpr}} \\
[\![\alpha[\varphi]]\!]_{\mathsf{PExpr}} &= \{(u,v) \in [\![\alpha]\!]_{\mathsf{PExpr}} \mid v \in [\![\varphi]\!]_{\mathsf{NExpr}}\} \\[6pt]
[\![\sigma]\!]_{\mathsf{NExpr}} &= \{u \in \mathsf{Nodes}^t \mid \mathsf{lab}^t(u) = \sigma\} \\
[\![\langle\alpha\rangle]\!]_{\mathsf{NExpr}} &= \{u \in \mathsf{Nodes}^t \mid \exists v \in \mathsf{Nodes}^t.(u,v) \in [\![\alpha]\!]_{\mathsf{PExpr}}\} \\
[\![\top]\!]_{\mathsf{NExpr}} &= \mathsf{Nodes}^t \\
[\![\neg\varphi]\!]_{\mathsf{NExpr}} &= \mathsf{Nodes}^t \setminus [\![\varphi]\!]_{\mathsf{NExpr}} \\
[\![\varphi \wedge \psi]\!]_{\mathsf{NExpr}} &= [\![\varphi]\!]_{\mathsf{NExpr}} \cap [\![\psi]\!]_{\mathsf{NExpr}}
\end{aligned}
$$

Table 1: Semantics of XPath.

The semantics of XPath expressions relative to a tree t is given by the functions $[\![\ ]\!]^t_{\mathsf{PExpr}}$ and $[\![\ ]\!]^t_{\mathsf{NExpr}}$. These functions are defined in Table 1. We omit the tree t if it is clear from the context. In the remainder of this section, we denote by $\varphi(u)$ and $\alpha(u,v)$ that $u \in [\![\varphi]\!]_{\mathsf{NExpr}}$ and $(u,v) \in [\![\alpha]\!]_{\mathsf{PExpr}}$, respectively.

DEFINITION 5.14. A DTL^{XPath} transducer is a DTL transducer in which all unary and binary patterns are XPath node and XPath path expressions, respectively.

EXAMPLE 5.15. The following DTL transducer selects the descriptions, ingredients, and instructions from all recipes that have at least three positive comments in our running example.

$$
\begin{aligned}
(q_0, \mathtt{recipes}) &\rightarrow \mathtt{recipes}((q,\downarrow)) \\
(q, \varphi) &\rightarrow \mathtt{recipe}((q,\downarrow)) \\
(q, \sigma) &\rightarrow \sigma((q,\downarrow)) \quad (\sigma \in \{\mathtt{description}, \mathtt{ingre\text{-}} \\
&\qquad\qquad\qquad\qquad \mathtt{dients}, \mathtt{br}, \mathtt{instructions}\}) \\
(q, \mathtt{item}) &\rightarrow (q,\downarrow) \\
(q, \mathtt{text}) &\rightarrow \mathtt{text}
\end{aligned}
$$

where

$$
\begin{aligned}
\varphi = \mathtt{recipe} \wedge \langle &\downarrow [\mathtt{comments}]/\downarrow[\mathtt{positive}] \\
&/\downarrow[\mathtt{comment}]/\rightarrow[\mathtt{comment}]/\rightarrow[\mathtt{comment}]\rangle.
\end{aligned}
$$

As in Section 5.3, we will reduce testing whether a DTL^{XPath} transducer is text-preserving to the emptiness test of an automaton. The beginning of our construction is similar to the one in Section 5.3. We will simulate partial computations of a DTL^{XPath} transducer by a *tree-jumping automaton with XPath transitions* (TJA^{XPath}). A TJA^{XPath} is a TJA^{MSO} in which all unary and binary formulas are XPath node and XPath path expressions, respectively.

Fix a DTL^{XPath} transducer $T = (Q, \Sigma, \Delta, q_0, R_\Sigma, R_{\mathsf{Text}})$. For states $q, q' \in Q$ and $\sigma, \sigma' \in \Sigma$, we denote by $A^{q,q'}_{T,\sigma,\sigma'}$ the TJA^{XPath} which, when started in state q on some node v in a tree t ends in state q' at node v' if and only if $(q,v) \rightsquigarrow^* (q',v')$ in T. Furthermore, it checks whether v is labelled by σ and v' is labelled by σ'. Furthermore, each of these automata can be constructed from T in linear time.

It remains to show that we can perform a similar construction as in Section 5.3. However, in this section, we also have to mind the complexity bounds. In order to avoid a large blow-up when performing unions and intersections of

automata, we will translate TJA^{XPath} to two-way alternating tree walking automata using techniques from [3].

LEMMA 5.16. *For each TJA^{XPath}, we can construct an equivalent 2ATWA in polynomial time.*

Two-way alternating tree walking automata have the interesting property that their intersections and unions can be constructed very efficiently. More precisely, for 2ATWAs $A_1, \ldots, A_n$, we can construct a 2ATWA for $\mathcal{L}(A_1) \cup \cdots \cup \mathcal{L}(A_n)$ and a 2ATWA for $\mathcal{L}(A_1) \cap \cdots \cap \mathcal{L}(A_n)$ in time linear in $|A_1| + \cdots + |A_n|$. This implies that we can perform the constructions from Section 5.3 on the 2ATWAs in polynomial time.

LEMMA 5.17. *Given a DTL^{XPath} transducer T and an NTA N, we can construct, in polynomial time, a 2ATWA A such that T is text-preserving over $\mathcal{L}(N)$ if and only if $\mathcal{L}(A) = \emptyset$.*

Since testing emptiness of a 2ATWA is in EXPTIME [5], we now know that testing whether a DTL^{XPath} transducer is text-preserving is in EXPTIME as well. Furthermore, since XPath satisfiability w.r.t. a DTD is EXPTIME-complete [17, 21], testing whether a DTL^{XPath} transducer is text-preserving is also EXPTIME-hard.

THEOREM 5.18. *Given a DTL^{XPath} transducer T and an NTA N, deciding whether T is text-preserving over $\mathcal{L}(N)$ is EXPTIME-complete.*

Actually, EXPTIME-hardness can also be obtained through a reduction from emptiness of deterministic tree-walking automata known to be EXPTIME-complete [20, 23].

6. RELATED WORK

The advent of XML induced a renewed interest in tree transducers. Milo, Suciu, and Vianu used k-pebble transducers in their seminal paper [18] as a general model for XML transformations, encompassing a variety of languages like XML-QL, XQuery, and XSLT. Engelfriet and Maneth showed that these form a subclass of the macro tree transducers [7].

In the present paper, we focus on XSLT-like transformations. The simplest of these are the top-down uniform transducers introduced in [13]. A more accurate formalization capturing the navigational power of XSLT as well, is given by DTL as introduced by Maneth and Neven [11]. We extend DTL to deal with text values, albeit in a modest way in accordance with our focus on simple transformations: when encountering Text-values, they can only be immediately output or discarded. Transducer models for XSLT equipped to employ text- or data values during computation have been considered in [2, 19]. To simplify presentation, we disregarded the construction functions employed in [11]. Intuitively, the difference is as follows. DTL as defined here associates one state with every binary pattern, while through the use of construction functions, the selection mechanism is generalized, by associating several states to every binary pattern. As this level of expressiveness is not present in XSLT, we decided to neglect it.

The most deeply studied problem concerning XML and transducers is undoubtedly the XML typechecking problem [18, 13, 14, 15, 9, 12, 22, 10], where it is asked whether $T(t) \in S_{\mathrm{out}}$ for all $t \in S_{\mathrm{in}}$ for given input and output schema S_{in} and S_{out} and transducer T. The typechecking problem is quite different from the problem considered in this paper, both in statement as in computational difficulty. For instance, typechecking top-down uniform tree transducers against unranked tree automata is already EXPTIME-complete while testing whether one is text-preserving is in PTIME for the corresponding setting.

Finally, we note that our Text-trees are different from the data trees in, e.g., [6], where each node carries a label from Σ and a label from Text. Moreover, unlike the logics and automata described in [6], the presented transducer model can not perform equality tests on Text-values.

7. CONCLUSION

Text-preserving transformations can be seen as a well-defined simple class of transformations for text-centric XML documents. In this paper, we showed that for XSLT-style transformations this property is decidable and even tractable for the top-down case.

From the employed proof technique it follows that for every transducer in one of the above mentioned classes, the maximal subset of the input schema can be computed on which the transformation is text-preserving. Indeed, we have actually shown that the class of trees on which a transducer is not text-preserving is a regular tree language. It would be interesting to pinpoint the exact size of a representation of that maximal subclass.

Another interesting question for future research is whether there is a normal form for text-preserving transformations in the considered formalisms.

Finally, although we think that mappings which restrict the output to be a subsequence of the input are relevant, there might be other notions that could be interesting in the context of text-centric mappings. It would therefore be interesting to develop more general notions of which text-preserving is a special case.

Actually, our employed proof technique already allows to test stronger properties than just text-preserving. For instance, we can specify a set of tree types (for example, a set of node labels) under which text values in the subtree can not be deleted. In our running example, we could require, e.g., that the transformation is text-preserving and that it does not delete any text values under a node labelled **instructions**. These more flexible tests do not influence the complexity of the problem.

Acknowledgment

We thank Maarten Marx for bringing the notion of text-preserving mappings and its relevance for text-centric documents to our attention.

8. REFERENCES

[1] J. Albert, D. Giammerresi, D. Wood. Normal form algorithms for extended context free grammars. *Theor. Comp. Sc.*, 267(1–2):35–47, 2001.

[2] G. J. Bex, S. Maneth, F. Neven. A formal model for an expressive fragment of XSLT. *Inf. Syst.*, 27(1):21–39, 2002.

[3] H. Björklund, W. Gelade, W. Martens. Incremental XPath evaluation. *ACM Trans. Database Syst.*, 35(4), 2011.

[4] R. Bloem, J. Engelfriet. A comparison of tree transductions defined by monadic second order logic and by attribute grammars. *J. Comput. Syst. Sci.*, 61(1):1–50, 2000.

[5] M. Bojanczyk. Tree-walking automata. In *LATA*, pages 1–2, 2008.

[6] M. Bojanczyk, A. Muscholl, T. Schwentick, L. Segoufin. Two-variable logic on data trees and XML reasoning. *Journal of the ACM*, 56(3), 2009.

[7] J. Engelfriet, S. Maneth. A comparison of pebble tree transducers with macro tree transducers. *Acta Inf.*, 39(9):613–698, 2003.

[8] L. Libkin. *Elements Of Finite Model Theory*. Springer Verlag, 2004.

[9] S. Maneth, A. Berlea, T. Perst, H. Seidl. XML type checking with macro tree transducers. In *PODS*, pages 283–294, 2005.

[10] S. Maneth, S. Friese, H. Seidl. Type checking of tree walking transducers. In *Modern Applications of Automata Theory*. World Scientific Publishing, 2011.

[11] S. Maneth, F. Neven. Structured document transformations based on XSL. In *DBPL*, pages 80–98, 1999.

[12] S. Maneth, T. Perst, H. Seidl. Exact XML type checking in polynomial time. In *ICDT*, pages 254–268, 2007.

[13] W. Martens, F. Neven. On the complexity of typechecking top-down XML transformations. *Theor. Comp. Sc.*, 336(1):153–180, 2005.

[14] W. Martens, F. Neven. Frontiers of tractability for typechecking simple XML transformations. *J. Comput. Syst. Sci.*, 73(3):362–390, 2007.

[15] W. Martens, F. Neven, M. Gyssens. Typechecking top-down XML transformations: Fixed input or output schemas. *Inf. and Comput.*, 206(7):806–827, 2008.

[16] W. Martens, F. Neven, T. Schwentick. Complexity of decision problems for XML schemas and chain regular expressions. *SIAM J. Comput.*, 39(4):1486–1530, 2009.

[17] M. Marx. XPath with conditional axis relations. In *EDBT*, pages 477–494, 2004.

[18] T. Milo, D. Suciu, V. Vianu. Typechecking for XML transformers. *J. Comput. Syst. Sci.*, 66(1):66–97, 2003.

[19] F. Neven. On the power of walking for querying tree-structured data. In *PODS*, pages 77–84, 2002.

[20] F. Neven. Attribute grammars for unranked trees as a query language for structured documents. *J. Comput. Syst. Sci.*, 70(2):221–257, 2005.

[21] F. Neven, T. Schwentick. On the complexity of XPath containment in the presence of disjunction, DTDs, and variables. *Log. Meth. in Comp. Sc.*, 2(3), 2006.

[22] T. Perst and H. Seidl. Macro forest transducers. *Inf. Process. Lett.*, 89(3):141–149, 2004.

[23] M. Samuelides and L. Segoufin. Complexity of pebble tree-walking automata. In *FCT*, pages 458–469, 2007.

[24] B. ten Cate and C. Lutz. The complexity of query containment in expressive fragments of XPath 2.0. *Journal of the ACM*, 56(6), 2009.

Efficient Evaluation for a Temporal Logic on Changing XML Documents[*]

Mikołaj Bojańczyk
University of Warsaw
bojan@mimuw.edu.pl

Diego Figueira
University of Warsaw
University of Edinburgh
df gueir@inf.ed.ac.uk

ABSTRACT

We consider a sequence $t_1, \ldots, t_k$ of XML documents that is produced by a sequence of local edit operations. To describe properties of such a sequence, we use a temporal logic. The logic can navigate both in time and in the document, e.g. a formula can say that every node with label a eventually gets a descendant with label b. For every fixed formula, we provide an evaluation algorithm that works in time $O(k \cdot \log(n))$, where k is the number of edit operations and n is the maximal size of document that is produced. In the algorithm, we represent formulas of the logic by a kind of automaton, which works on sequences of documents. The algorithm works on XML documents of bounded depth.

Categories and Subject Descriptors

F.4.1 [**Mathematical logic and formal languages**]: Temporal logic; H.2.3 [**Database management**]: Languages—*Query languages*

General Terms

Theory, Algorithms, Languages

Keywords

Incremental evaluation, XML, temporal logic

1. INTRODUCTION

In this paper, we model an XML document as a finite unranked tree over a finite alphabet. Suppose that an XML document is modified by a sequence of local update operations. Each update adds, removes or relabels a node of the document. We want to know if these updates preserve some correctness constraint. This kind of problem is called incremental evaluation. Suppose, for instance, that the correctness constraint is given by a DTD, or more generally a regular language of unranked trees. This problem is solved by an algorithm of Balmin, Papakonstantinou and Vianu [4]. The algorithm maintains a data structure, and every update on the tree requires an update to the data structure that is done in time

$$poly(Q) \cdot \log^2(n)$$

where Q is the state space of the automaton for the correctness constraint and n is the size of the current document. If the correctness constraint is given by an XPath query, the translation from the query into a tree automaton can result in a state space Q that is exponential in the size of the XPath query. The problem has been addressed by [6], which provides algorithms that work directly with XPath queries.

A limitation of incremental evaluation, as described above, is that the property talks only about the current version of the XML document. In this paper, we study properties that compare versions of the document in different times. Here are some examples:

1. Every *order* node eventually gets an *approved* child. That is, if at some time i a node x has tag name *order*, then at some time $j \geq i$ node x has a child with tag name *approved*.

2. Every node with one child gets a second child in at most two steps. That is, if at some time i, a node x has one child, then node x has at least two children in any time $j \geq i + 2$.

To express these examples, we need a logic or formalism that is evaluated not in a single document, but in a sequence of documents

$$t_1, \ldots, t_k.$$

We use the name *document evolution* for such a sequence. In this paper we define a logic for document evolutions, which captures the two examples given above. We then study the evaluation problem for formulas φ of the logic:

- Input. A document evolution $t_1, \ldots, t_k$.

- Output. Does φ hold in the document evolution?

[*]We acknowledge the financial support of the Future and Emerging Technologies (FET) programme within the Seventh Framework Programme for Research of the European Commission, under the FET-Open grant agreement FOX, number FP7-ICT-233599.

As in incremental evaluation, the document evolution on the input is not an arbitrary sequence of documents, but a sequence where t_1 is an empty document and t_{i+1} is obtained from t_i by doing a local update that consists of adding, removing or relabeling a single document node. In this case, the size of document t_i is bounded by i. If the updates consist exclusively of adding nodes, then after time k the combined size of the documents $t_1, \ldots, t_k$ is quadratic in k.

We want an algorithm that works well for large XML documents, with millions of nodes or more. For documents of this size an algorithm that is linear in the combined size of the documents $t_1, \ldots, t_k$, and therefore quadratic in k, may be impractical. However, when the document evolution is a result of local updates, there is no reason to read the whole document t_i for every $i \in \{1, \ldots, k\}$, because this document is almost identical to t_{i-1}. The principal contribution of this paper is an algorithm for the evaluation problem that runs in time

$$O(k \cdot \log(n)),$$

where k is the duration of the document evolution and n is the maximal document size (of course $n \leq k$). We present the algorithm only for XML documents of bounded depth, although we believe it should work for documents of unbounded depth.

To the best of our knowledge, the problem of efficiently evaluating logics on document evolutions has not been studied before. In this paper, we try to optimize the data complexity of the problem, and we assume that the formula of the logic is fixed. Unfortunately, the query complexity of our algorithm is very bad: the constant hidden in the expression $O(k \cdot \log(n))$ is nonelementary in the size of the formula of the logic. That is why this paper is more like a proof of concept: even when the correctness property compares different versions of the document, it is still possible to have an algorithm with very good data complexity.

In this paper, we only talk about the tag names and tree structure of XML documents. That is, we model an XML document as an unranked tree over a finite and fixed alphabet (the tag names). Any additional data in the document, such as attribute values, is ignored. Logics and automata that talk about such additional data are a lively research topic, see the survey [13], and in the future we would like to extend our results to the richer logics. Note that for logics that depend on attribute values, such as XPath, the incremental evaluation problem seems to be difficult already for formulas that talk about only the current state of the document. In particular, we are not aware of any algorithm that would be significantly faster than simply reevaluating the XPath query on every new version of the document. By significantly faster we mean an algorithm that would require polylogarithmic time per update operation. Observe that in the presence of additional data, an evalution algorithm for XPath (without any time aspects, just evaluating a query in a given document) with linear data complexity has appeared only recently [8].

Related work. As already mentioned, [6] studies the problem of incrementally maintaining the result set of a XPath query on a changing XML document. Algorithms are provided for several fragments of XPath. The queries from [6] talk only about the current document, and cannot study the change of the structure of the document in time.

There have been efforts to extend the XPath query language to make it time-aware [9]. In this work we choose to work with a temporal logic to talk about different instants of the evolution of a document.

In a similar setup, there have been works on the incremental maintenance of the validity of regular languages [4, 5], where the validity of an XML Schema, a DTD or a specialized DTD is checked to be preserved throughout the document evolution.

Abiteboul, Herr and Van den Bussche [3] study the expressive power of some of the logics we work with.

The model of evolution of documents is also related to regular model checking [2]. In this field, the evolution of the document is dictated by a regular transducer, whereas here updates can occur anywhere and in any order, in an incremental way. In this context, [1] treats a logic similar to ours, LTL(MSO), where first and second order variables are interpreted over positions of the document, and tempral operators are used to navigate the word in time.

2. TWO LOGICS

In this section, we define the logics that we use to describe document evolutions. As presented in the introduction, the update operations are: adding and removing nodes, as well as relabeling. In order to simplify the complicated evaluation algorithm, and the definitions of the logics, for the most part of the paper we only use relabeling, and do not add or remove nodes. In particular, all documents in a document evolution will have the same nodes. In Section 7, we come back to the implementation of adding and removing nodes.

Fix an input alphabet A. We deal with finite, unranked, sibling-ordered trees with nodes labeled by A. The *domain* of a tree is the tree without the labels. A *document evolution* is a sequence of trees $t_1, \ldots, t_k$. The number k is the *duration* of the document evolution, and the number n of nodes in the domain is the *document size* of the evolution. We work with the assumption that all documents have the same domain. This assumption is made for technical reasons to simplify the algorithm, but this assumption can be lifted, as explained in Section 7. Throughout the paper, we will preserve the convention that n refers to the document size and that k refers to the duration. We use x, y, z to refer to nodes in the domain and variables i, j to refer to moments in time.

In this section we define two logics to describe document evolutions. The first logic is a variant of first-order logic. The second logic is a variant of temporal logic. The evaluation algorithms of this paper are for the temporal logic, and the first-order logic is described mainly to provide some background.

First-order logic. A document evolution $t_1, \ldots, t_k$ with domain X can be treated as a relational structure. The elements of the structure are pairs

$$(x, i) \in X \times \{1, \ldots, k\}.$$

The relational structure is equipped with the following predicates. For each letter $a \in A$ in the input alphabet, we have a unary predicate a, which holds for an element (x, i) if node x has label a in the document t_i. There are three binary relations:

- The *descendant order* $\leq_{desc}$ which ignores the time coordinate of its arguments and compares the nodes for descendant relationship.

- The *document order* $\leq_{doc}$ which ignores the time coordinate of its arguments and compares the nodes for document order relationship. This corresponds to the total order induced by the preorder visit of the tree.

- The *time order* $\leq_t$ which ignores the node coordinate of its arguments and compares the times.

Because the predicates above ignore one of the coordinates, they are not antisymmetric when $k \geq 2$ or $n \geq 2$. Using these predicates, we can write formulas of first-order logic to express properties of document evolutions. For instance, the following formula says that once a document node gets label a, none of its descendants ever have label b afterwards. (We use p, q for the variable names, because x, y, z are reserved for positions, and not space/time pairs.)

$$\forall p \forall q. \; (a(p) \wedge p \leq_t q \wedge p \leq_{desc} q) \Rightarrow \neg b(q) \qquad (1)$$

Two-dimensional temporal logic. We now define a logic with temporal syntax, with operators that travel in the time dimension and the space dimension. In particular, formulas of this logic will have no variables. We use the name *two-dimensional temporal logic* for this logic. This is the principal logic studied in the paper.

In the two-dimensional temporal logic, a formula is evaluated in a pair

$$(x, i) \in X \times \{1, \ldots, k\}$$

of a document evolution of document domain X and duration k. Instead of quantifiers, formulas use modal operators such G for Globally or U for Until. For instance the property from example (1) is stated as

$$\mathsf{G}_{desc}\mathsf{G}_t(a \Rightarrow \mathsf{G}_{desc}\mathsf{G}_t\neg b).$$

In the formula above, we begin in the root node in the first document. We then use the $\mathsf{G}_{desc}\mathsf{G}_t$ operators to say that $a \Rightarrow \mathsf{G}_{desc}\mathsf{G}_t\neg b$ occurs in all descendants in all later times, and likewise for the smaller formula.

We believe that when describing document evolutions, it is important to allow past operators in the space dimension (i.e. descendants and preceding nodes in document order). For example, consider an XPath unary query α, which selects a position x in a document if it has an ancestor with label a. In XPath syntax this query looks like this:

$$//a//*$$

One might want to say that for every document node x and time i, if node x has label b in time i, then at all later times the node x satisfies the XPath query α

$$\mathsf{G}_{desc}\mathsf{G}_t(b \Rightarrow \mathsf{G}_t\alpha).$$

In the particular example of α, we can write $\mathsf{F}_{desc}^{-1}a$ to search for an ancestor of the current node in the current document.

We now provide the formal syntax and semantics of the temporal logic. As remarked above, a formula of the logic is evaluated in a pair (x, i) of a document evolution $t_1, \ldots, t_k$. We fix this document evolution in the definition below.

- For every letter of the alphabet, a is a formula. This formula is true in (x, i) if node x has label a in document t_i.

- Boolean connectives are allowed, with the usual semantics.

- If φ, ψ are a formulas, then $\varphi\mathsf{U}_{desc}\psi$ is a formula, which is true in (x, i) if there exists a node $y >_{desc} x$ such that φ is true in all the pairs (z, i) with $x <_{desc} z <_{desc} y$ and ψ is true in the pair (y, i). Observe that we use the *strict until* operator, which does not use the current position. Often, one uses the *non-strict until*, which is defined by

$$\psi \vee (\varphi \wedge (\varphi\mathsf{U}_{desc}\psi)).$$

The strict until allows one to define all other operators as derived constructs:

$$\mathsf{X}_{desc}\varphi \stackrel{def}{=} \bot\mathsf{U}_{desc}\varphi \qquad \mathsf{F}_{desc}\varphi \stackrel{def}{=} (\top\mathsf{U}_{desc}\varphi) \vee \varphi$$
$$\mathsf{G}_{desc}\varphi \stackrel{def}{=} \neg\mathsf{F}_{desc}\neg\varphi$$

- If φ, ψ are formulas, then $\varphi\mathsf{U}_{desc}^{-1}\psi$ is a formula, which is the inverse of the U_{desc} operator. This operator is often called *since*. As in the previous item, we can define all sorts of derived operators.

- Let $\leq_{sib}$ be sibling order, where $x \leq_{sib} y$ if x and y are siblings, and x is to the left of y. If φ, ψ are formulas, then $\varphi\mathsf{U}_{sib}\psi$ and $\varphi\mathsf{U}_{sib}^{-1}\psi$ are formulas, defined in the same way as before, for the sibling order $\leq_{sib}$.

- Finally, we allow an until operator U_t that works in the time dimension, i.e. $\varphi\mathsf{U}_t\psi$ holds in (x, i) if there is a time moment $j > i$ such that φ is true in the pairs

$$(x, i+1), \ldots, (x, j-1)$$

and ψ is true in the pair (x, j).

Observe that we do not allow a since operator in the time dimension. Such a logic would make perfect sense, but we do not know how to extend our evaluation algorithm to cover a since operator in the time dimension. In fact, it seems that the two dimensional temporal logic with since and until is strictly more expressive than with only until, the witness property being "there is a time moment i such that $t_1 = t_i$".

As far as the space dimension is concerned, our logic behaves like two-way CTL. Two-way CTL is first-order complete, see [12]. We could even allow more powerful operations in the logic. This is because our evaluation algorithm represents the formula as an alternating automaton. Then, our algorithm works even if we make tests for any regular properties at fixed time moments.

3. EVALUATION

The subject of this paper is evaluation of logical formulas on document evolutions. We are not interested in the satisfiability problem, because it is undecidable for all the logics described here, by using a document evolution to describe a run of a Turing machine.[1]

The *evaluation problem* for a logical formula φ is stated as follows.

- Input. A document evolution $\bar{t}$.

---

[1] In fact, it has been shown that the two-dimensional temporal logic is undecidable even if we only allow future modalities in both dimensions [10].

- Output. Does the formula hold in $\bar{t}$?

When measuring the complexity of the problem, we use two parameters of the document evolution $\bar{t}$: the document size n and the duration k.

First-order logic. In this paper, we are mainly interested in the logics that are temporal in at least one of the two dimensions of space and time. Why not first-order logic where the variables range over space/time pairs? A document evolution of document size n and duration $n = k$ can encode any graph with n vertices, since it is essentially an $n \times k$ matrix. Therefore, evaluating first-order logic on document evolutions is the same as evaluating first-order logic on graphs, or arbitrary relational structures for that matter. The latter is a fascinating and widely studied topic, but it is not the topic of this paper.

An optimal algorithm for the two-dimensional temporal logic. There is a simple optimal algorithm for the two-dimensional logic.

THEOREM 1. *The evaluation problem for two-dimensional temporal logic can be solved in time $O(k \cdot n)$.*

PROOF. Suppose that X is the domain of the document evolution. By induction on the size of a formula φ, we show that the set of pairs

$$(x, i) \in X \times \{1, \ldots, k\}$$

in a document evolution $t_1, \ldots, t_k$ that satisfies φ can be computed in time

$$O(|\varphi| \cdot n \cdot k).$$

Suppose that we want to compute the pairs where $\varphi \mathsf{U}_t \psi$ is satisfied. For document node $x \in X$, we scan the document evolution from time k to time 1. Using the precomputed information on φ and ψ we can compute the bigger formula. A similar argument works for the other operators. For the space operators, one needs to do a bottom-up or top-down pass through the trees. $\square$

Observe that the algorithm above would also work if we allowed a since operator in the time dimension. The since operator will be a problem in our later algorithm.

If the document evolutions are arbitrary sequences of documents, with no restriction on small differences between consecutive documents, then this naive algorithm is optimal. All $n \cdot k$ positions of the document evolution must be read for some queries, e.g. the query "all nodes in all times have label a."

Incremental evaluation. The *incremental evaluation problem* is a variant of the evaluation problem, where we assume that the document evolution is the result of applying a sequence of local updates to an initially empty document. Here empty means that all nodes have the same blank label. Formally speaking, the input of the incremental evaluation problem consists of: a tree domain X, a duration $k \in \mathbb{N}$, an initial letter $a \in A$ and a sequence of pairs

$$(a_1, x_1), \ldots, (a_{k-1}, x_{k-1}) \in A \times X.$$

Given this input, we define a document evolution $t_1, \ldots, t_k$ as follows. The first document t_1 has all nodes labeled by a.

Once t_i has been defined, t_{i+1} is defined as t_i with position x_i changing label to a_i. A document evolution obtained from such a sequence of relabeling operations is called an *incremental document evolution*.

In the (general) evaluation problem, reading the input requires time $n \cdot k$. In the incremental evaluation problem, reading the input requires time k, so the simple lower bound of $O(n \cdot k)$ does not hold any more. The principal contribution of this paper is that the incremental evaluation problem can be solved more efficiently, as stated in the following theorem.

THEOREM 2 (MAIN THEOREM). *Fix a formula φ of the two-dimensional temporal logic. The incremental evaluation problem, on a document evolution of document size n and duration k can be solved in time $O(k \cdot \log(n))$.*

In the theorem above, the constant in the O notation depends on the formula φ. As a function of φ, the constant grows faster than any tower of exponentials. That is why this paper is intended more as a proof of concept, the concept being that the incremental evaluation problem can be done in time smaller than the obvious $O(n \cdot k)$.

4. AN AUTOMATON MODEL

In this section we define an automaton model that accepts or rejects document evolutions. This automaton can capture the two-dimensional temporal logic, and even some extensions. Our evaluation algorithm works with the automaton.

Regular queries. A regular tree language is like a boolean query for trees: it says yes or no to each tree. In this paper we also use unary queries, binary queries and so on. An m-ary query over trees, with input alphabet A, is a function f which maps every tree over alphabet A to a set of m-tuples of nodes in the tree. An example of a binary query is one that maps a tree to the set of all pairs of nodes (x, y) such that there is an even number of a's on the shortest path from x to y.

We will be using *regular queries*, which are queries that can be defined by formulas of MSO logic with free individual variables, see e.g. [11]. Regular queries can also be described in other ways, different than MSO formulas, e.g. by automata or monoids. The way we describe regular queries is not very important for our evaluation algorithm (actually, the algorithm uses monoids as its internal representation). In particular, the bad query complexity of our algorithm is not due to the use of MSO in the automaton, the algorithm would have nonelementary complexity even with regular queries represented in some less succint way, e.g. by monoids.

Document update processing automata. We now introduce the automaton model, which we call a *document update processing automaton*. Such an automaton, call it $\mathcal{A}$, is given by the following ingredients.

- An input alphabet A.

- A set of states Q, an initial state q_0 and a set of accepting states $F \subseteq Q$. The states are partitioned into $Q_\exists$ and $Q_\forall$. (This is a kind of alternating automaton.)

- A finite set Δ of transitions of the form (q, φ, p) where $q, p \in Q$ and φ is a binary regular query over input alphabet A.

An input for the automaton is a document evolution

$$\bar{t} = t_1, \ldots, t_k$$

with domain X, where the trees are over alphabet A. The automaton accepts the document evolution if player $\exists$ wins the following perfect-information, finite duration, two-player game, call it $G_{\bar{t}}^{\mathcal{A}}$. Positions of the game are triples of the form (q, x, i) where $q \in Q$ is a state of the automaton, $x \in X$ is a node, and $i \in \{0, \ldots, k\}$ is a moment in time. The interpretation of i is that we are about to read the tree t_{i+1}. The initial position is $(q_0, root, 0)$, i.e. the game starts in the initial state, in the root, and before reading the first tree in the document evolution. When in a game position (q, x, i) with $i < k$, the player who owns state q chooses a new game position $(p, y, i+1)$ such that

$$(q, \varphi, p)$$

is a transition of the automaton and φ selects the pair (x, y) in the document t_{i+1}. When a game position of the form (q, x, k) is reached, the game is finished, and player $\exists$ wins if q is accepting, otherwise $\forall$ wins. A position in the game is called winning for $\exists$ if he can win the game starting in that position.

From two-dimensional logic to dupa automata

PROPOSITION 3. *For every formula φ of the two-dimensional temporal logic there is a document update processing automaton that accepts the same document evolutions.*

PROOF. States of the automaton are subformulas, so the size of the automaton is quadratic in the formula. The translation is as usual when going from temporal logic to an alternating automaton. □

Ordered automata. We say a transition (p, φ, q) in a document update processing automaton is a *local transition* if the formula φ only selects pairs of the form (x, x) in every tree (in wich case, φ is essentially a unary query). An automaton is called *ordered* if there is a ranking function $\Omega : Q \to \mathbb{N}$ on its states such that performing any transition preserves or decreases the rank, and performing a non-local transition decreases the rank. It is possible that several states have the same rank, in which case the states can be connected only by local transitions. Observe that the automaton produced in Proposition 3 is an ordered automaton, the ranking function refers to the size of the subformula corresponding to the current state.

The principal technical result of this paper is that ordered document update processing automata can be evaluated efficiently.

THEOREM 4. *Fix an ordered document update processing automaton. Whether or not the automaton accepts a document evolution of duration k and tree length n can be tested in time $O(k \cdot \log(n))$.*

Thanks to Proposition 3, the theorem above also yields an evaluation algorithm for the two-dimensional temporal logic, of same complexity, as stated in Theorem 2.

The evaluation algorithm is described in Sections 5 and 6. Due to the complicated structure of the algorithm, we describe it for the case of words (which can be seen as the special case of trees with only one path). In Section 7 we comment on how to extend the algorithm for trees.

5. LOCAL ORDERED AUTOMATA

In this section we show how to evaluate a *local automaton*, which is a document update processing automaton where only local transitions are allowed. In the next section, the ideas on local automata are extended to the general case of ordered automata with non-local transitions.

As mentioned before, we describe the algorithm for words and not trees. In particular, the tree domain is now given by just specifying the *word length* n, in which case the domain is $\{1, \ldots, n\}$. We will prove the following theorem in this section.

PROPOSITION 5. *Fix a local automaton. The automaton can be evaluated on incremental document evolutions of word length n and duration k in time $O(k \cdot \log(n))$.*

Actually, we prove a slightly stronger result. We will create a data structure such that for every node $x \in \{1, \ldots, n\}$, one can tell in time $O(\log(n))$ if the automaton accepts the word if it begins in the initial state in node x. So, in a sense, we evaluate the local automaton for all nodes in the word simultaneously.

We fix for the rest of this section a local automaton. We also fix an input to the automaton, i.e. an incremental document evolution

$$w_1, \ldots, w_k \in A^n.$$

Our goal is to determine if the automaton accepts this word. In the algorithm, we will refer to the differences between successive words w_i and w_{i+1}, so we assume that the incremental document evolution is given by a sequence of relabeling operations.

Monoids for queries. In this section, we assume that all of the transitions are local, i.e. every transition is of the form

$$(p, \varphi, q)$$

where φ only selects tuples of the form (x, x) in every word. Therefore, we will simply treat φ as a unary query. Instead of MSO logic, we use monoids to describe regular queries. We describe the monoid approach to unary queries below.

Suppose that

$$\alpha : A^* \to M$$

is a monoid homomorphism. The unary α-type of a node x in a word $a_1 \cdots a_n$ is the triple

$$(\alpha(a_1 \cdots a_{x-1}), a_x, \alpha(a_{x+1} \cdots a_n)) \in M \times A \times M.$$

We say the homomorphism α recognizes a unary query $\varphi(x)$ if there is a set of triples

$$H \subseteq M \times A \times M$$

such that a node x is selected by the query φ in a word w if and only if the unary α-type of x in w belongs to H. For every unary MSO query there exists a monoid homomorphism that recognizes it. The monoid M might be nonelementary in the size of the query. (This translation of MSO into monoids is not the only reason for bad query complexity, our algorithm has nonelementary query complexity even when the monoids M are small.)

We fix a single monoid homomorphism $\alpha : A^* \to M$ that recognizes all the queries that appear in the transitions of the automaton. This can be done by using the direct product of all the monoids for all the queries. When referring to unary types, we omit the name of α, because it is the only homomorphism we use.

Zones. We begin by introducing some notation. We write x, y, z for positions in the words, i.e. for elements of $\{1, \ldots, n\}$. A zone is defined to be any connected set of positions, i.e. a zone is a set $\{x, x+1, \ldots, y\}$ for $1 \le x \le y \le n$. We write X, Y for zones, and we also allow an empty zone. If X is a zone and w is a word with n positions, then $w|X$ is the word obtained from w by only keeping positions from X. The *type* of a zone X in a word w is defined to be $\alpha(w|X)$. Zones $X_1, \ldots, X_m$ are called *consecutive* if the last node in zone X_1 is the predecessor of the first node in X_2, and so on until X_{m-1} and X_m.

The *environment* of a zone X inside a zone $Y \supseteq X$ is the difference $Y - X$. Such an environment is the union of two disjoint zones, the one to the left of X and the one to the right of X. The type of such an environment is the pair of types of these two disjoint zones. We write

$$Externals \overset{def}{=} M^2$$

for the set of possible types of such environments. The *external type* of a zone X is the type of its environment with respect to the set $\{1, \ldots, n\}$ of all word positions. We write τ, σ for external types. For $i = 1, 2$, we write $\tau(i)$ for the i-th coordinate of an external type τ. We can also insert one external type inside another

$$in_\sigma(\tau) \overset{def}{=} (\tau(1) \cdot \sigma(1), \sigma(2) \cdot \tau(2)) \in Externals.$$

The idea is that if $X \subseteq Y \subseteq Z$ and σ is the type of the environment $Y - X$, and τ is the type of the environment $Z - Y$, then $in_\sigma(\tau)$ is the type of the environment $Z - X$.

Histories. We write i, j for times, which are elements of $\{1, \ldots, k\}$. A time interval is defined like a zone, but for times. For a time $i \in \{1, \ldots, k\}$ we write

$$ext(X, i) \in Externals$$

for the external type of a zone X in the word w_i. Consider a zone X and a time interval $I = \{i, \ldots, j\}$. We define the *external history* of the interval X in time interval I, denoted $history(X, I)$, to be the sequence

$$ext(X, i), \ldots, ext(X, j)$$

of external types of X in the times from the interval I. Since we only talk about external histories, we simply write history from now on. We only use the value $history(X, I)$ when the zone X does not change labels in the time interval I. To underline this requirement, we assume that $history(X, I)$ is undefined otherwise. We write *Histories* for the set of possible histories, this set includes the undefined history $\perp$.

5.1 The history toolkit

We define some operations on histories. These operations will be used by the algorithm as a black box.

Monoid operations on histories. There is an empty history:

$$empty \in Histories \tag{2}$$

The simplest operation we can do on histories is concatenate them. When histories are represented as sequences of external types, this operation is simply sequence concatenation. Later, we represent histories in a more concise way, and the operation becomes less trivial, so we give it a name:

$$concat : Histories \times Histories \to Histories. \tag{3}$$

Applying a history to a node. For a node x and a time i, we define $P_{xi} \subseteq Q$ to be the set of states q such that the game position (q, x, i) is winning in the game $G_{\bar{w}}^{\mathcal{A}}$. Recall that (q, x, i) describes the situation between words w_i and w_{i+1}. The principal goal of our algorithm is to design an algorithm and data structure, so that after the algorithm terminates, each set P_{x0} can be computed in time $O(\log(n))$ by using the data structure.

Generally speaking, our algorithm will be processing the words in the time evolution in reverse order, beginning with w_k and ending with w_1. All the information gathered by the algorithm will be propagated from later times to earlier times. We say that a node x does not change label in time i if the label of x is the same in words w_i and w_{i+1}.

LEMMA 6. *Suppose that in the time interval $\{i, \ldots, j\}$, the label of a position x is constantly $a \in A$. Then the set $P_{x(i-1)}$ is uniquely determined by: the label a, the set P_{xj} and $history(\{x\}, \{i, \ldots, j\})$.*

PROOF. Consider first a history of length one, i.e. $j = i$. Let $history(\{x\}, \{i\})$ be (σ, τ). Then the α-type of x in w_i is (σ, a, τ). The set $P_{x(i-1)}$ contains the states q such that either

- q is owned by player $\forall$ and for every transition (q, φ, p), if (σ, a, τ) satisfies φ then $p \in P_{xi}$, or

- q is owned by player $\exists$ and there is a transition (q, φ, p) such that (σ, a, τ) satisfies φ, and $p \in P_{xi}$.

These conditions are necessary and sufficient for $(q, x, i-1)$ being an accepting position in the automaton's game.

For longer histories, the lemma is obtained by iterating the statement for histories of length one. $\square$

We denote the function that realizes the dependency from the above lemma by

$$apply : Histories \to A \times P(Q) \to P(Q). \tag{4}$$

That is, this function is defined so that, under the assumptions of the lemma, we have

$$P_{x(i-1)} = apply(history(\{x\}, \{i, \ldots, j\}))(a, P_{xj}).$$

Inheriting the history of a parent. Let Y be a zone that contains X. Suppose that in the time interval I, the input labels of $Y - X$ did not change, and therefore constantly had the same type $\sigma \in Externals$. In this case,

$$history(X, I) = in_\sigma(history(Y, I))$$

where the operation

$$in_\sigma : Histories \to Histories \tag{5}$$

is defined by $in_\sigma(\tau_1, \ldots, \tau_m) = in_\sigma(\tau_1), \ldots, in_\sigma(\tau_m)$.

5.2 The algorithm

We now present our algorithm. It uses a fairly natural divide-and-conquer approach (not for nothing there is $\log(n)$). The crux is an efficient implementation of operations on histories, which is described in later sections.

We define *logarithmic* zones as follows: the set of all positions of $\{1, \ldots, n\}$ is a logarithmic zone; and if X is a logarithmic zone of w and $x \in X$ is in the middle of X then $X \cap \{1, \ldots, x\}$ and $X \setminus \{1, \ldots, x\}$ are both logarithmic zones. The properties of these zones are: they are either disjoint or one is included in the other, each position is included in a logarithmic number of them, and there are linearly many of them. We write $parent(X)$ for the smallest logarithmic zone $Y \supsetneq X$ and *Logs* for the set of all logarithmic zones.

The history tree. We first define the data structure used by our algorithm. An instance D of the data structure consists of four labelings:

$$D.lastupdate : Logs \to \{0, \ldots, k\}$$
$$D.lastlabel : \{1, \ldots, n\} \to A \times P(Q)$$
$$D.history : Logs \to Histories$$
$$D.monoid : Logs \to M$$

Because the logarithmic zones have a tree structure, and because the component $D.history$ is the most important one, we use the name *history tree* for such an instance D.

We will first compute a history tree for time k, and then will compute it for times $k-1, k-2, \ldots, 0$. A history tree D is called *correct* at time moment $i \in \{0, \ldots, k\}$ if the following conditions hold. (The idea is that D describes the situation between words w_i and w_{i+1}.)

1. For every logarithmic zone X and its parent Y,

   $$D.lastupdate(X) \geq D.lastupdate(Y).$$

   In other words, zones intervals are more up to date than smaller zones. (Because the algorithm starts in k and progresses towards 0, information about a smaller time is more up to date.) We say a zone X is *up to date* (at moment i) if

   $$D.lastupdate(X) = i.$$

   We require that the root logarithmic zone $\{1, \ldots, n\}$ is up to date.

2. Labels cannot change between the current time i and the last update. That is, for every logarithmic zone, all of its input labels have stayed the same in the time interval

   $$\{i, \ldots, D.lastupdate(X)\}$$

3. For every logarithmic interval X, the value $D.monoid(X)$ stores the monoid element corresponding to X at the time of its last update:

   $$D.monoid(X) = \alpha(w_{D.lastupdate(X)}|X)$$

   In fact we have that $D.monoid(X) = \alpha(w_j|X)$ for every $i \leq j \leq D.lastupdate(X)$ since $w_j|X$ remains unchanged.

4. Suppose that X is a logarithmic interval, and Y is its parent. Then $D.history(X)$ stores the value

   $$history(X, \{D.lastupdate(Y), \ldots, D.lastupdate(X) - 1\}).$$

In the case when $D.lastupdate(Y) = D.lastupdate(X)$ the above history is empty.

5. Suppose that x is a node and let

   $$j = D.lastupdate(\{x\}) \quad \text{and} \quad (a, P) = D.lastlabel(x).$$

   Then the label of x in word w_j is a and $P_{xj} = P$. Together with condition 2 this means that the input label of x is a during the interval $\{i, \ldots, j\}$.

The algorithm. The algorithm begins with a history tree D_k that is correct and up to date for time moment $i = k$. Then for each time moment $i \in \{k-1, \ldots, 0\}$, the algorithm calculates a history tree D_i that is correct for time moment i. The algorithm that maintains this invariant will manipulate histories. In our complexity analysis, we will use the history operations

$$empty \quad concat \quad apply \quad in_\sigma$$

described in Section 5.1 as black boxes, with unit cost in the algorithm. Later, we will show how the operations can be implemented in constant time.

LEMMA 7. D_k *can be computed in time* $O(n)$.

It is safe to assume $k > n$, because otherwise our algorithm can ignore the positions where no labels are updated. Therefore, the $O(n)$ precomputation cost of D_k will be amortized by the algorithm's $O(k \cdot \log(n))$ complexity.

LEMMA 8. *Let* D_i *be a history tree that is correct for time* i. *Let* x *be a position. We can compute a history tree* D_i' *that is also correct for time* i *and which is up to date at the zone* $\{x\}$. *This computation can be done in time* $O(\log(n))$, *assuming the history operations have unit cost.*

PROOF. Consider the logarithmic zones that contain x:

$$\{x\} = X_0 \subsetneq X_1 \subsetneq \cdots \subsetneq X_m.$$

We will compute history trees

$$D^{(m)}, D^{(m-1)}, \ldots, D^{(0)} = D'$$

which are all correct for time i, and such that

$$D^{(r)}.lastupdate(X_r) = i \qquad \text{for } r \in \{0, \ldots, m\}.$$

Furthermore, a constant number of operations on the history tree $D^{(r)}$ are sufficient to compute $D^{(r-1)}$. The statement of the lemma then follows, because m is logarithmic in n.

For the induction base, we simply use $D^{(m)} = D_i$, because item 1 of the correctness conditions says that the root logarithmic zone is always up to date.

The rest of the proof is devoted to the induction step. Suppose we computed $D^{(r+1)}$ and we want to compute $D^{(r)}$. We simply make the zone X_r up to date in $D^{(r)}$ by setting

$$D^{(r)}.lastupdate(X_r) := i$$

and keeping the value of *lastupdate* unchanged for other logarithmic zones. What else do we need to change in $D^{(r)}$ to make this history tree correct for time i? We examine the conditions of correctness item by item.

1. Item 1 holds because the zones $X_{r+1}, \ldots, X_m$ are already up to date in $D^{(r+1)}$, and the root zone is unchanged.

265

2. We have decreased the value of $D^{(r)}.lastupdate(X_r)$, which makes item 2 even more true.

3. Let use j for the previously used time in X_r, i.e.

$$j = D^{(r+1)}.lastupdate(X_r).$$

We know from item 2 applied to $D^{(r+1)}$ that no positions have been changed in the zone X_r between the current time i and time j, so we can keep

$$D^{(r)}.monoid(X_r) := D^{(r+1)}.monoid(X_r).$$

4. For this item, we change the histories in at most three zones. For the history of X_r, we use the empty history, because X_r is now up to date:

$$D^{(r)}.history(X_r) := empty.$$

Suppose that $r > 0$. In this case, X_r has two children zones, call them Y_0 and Y_1 from left to right. (One of the children is X_{r-1}, but this plays no role in our argument.) The condition in item 4 could now be invalid for the two zones Y_0, Y_1, because we have changed the update time of their parent X_r. For $l \in \{0, 1\}$ let j_l be

$$D^{(r)}.lastupdate(Y_l) = D^{(r+1)}.lastupdate(Y_l).$$

To make the history tree $D^{(r)}$ correct, we should have

$$D^{(r)}.history(Y_l) = history(Y_l, \{i, \dots, j_l - 1\}),$$

so we need to compute the history on the right of the above equation. What we have from the history tree $D^{(r+1)}$ is two histories:

$$history(Y_l, \{j, \dots, j_l - 1\}) \quad history(X_r, \{i, \dots, j - 1\}).$$

However, we know that from time i to j the external type of Y_l inside X_r was the same, call this external type τ_l. The value of this external type is taken from the *monoid* part of the history tree:

$$\tau_0 = (1, D^{(r)}.monoid(Y_1)) \quad \tau_1 = (D^{(r)}.monoid(Y_0), 1).$$

By applying the in_{τ_l} operation, we can compute the history of Y_l between times j and i as follows:

$$history(Y_l, \{i, \dots, j - 1\}) = \\ in_{\tau_l}(history(X_r, \{i, \dots, j - 1\})).$$

Then, the value of $D^{(r)}.history(Y_l)$ should be set to

$$concat(D^{(r+1)}.history(Y_l), in_{\tau_l}(D^{(r+1)}.history(X_r))).$$

5. Let y be any position. If we have the equality

$$D^{(r)}.lastupdate(\{y\}) = D^{(r+1)}.lastupdate(\{y\}),$$

then no change in $D^{(r)}.lastlabel(y)$ is required preserve item 5, because of correctness of $D^{(r+1)}$. The only case when the equality above can fail is when $y = x$ and $r = 0$. We study this case below.

Let $j = D^{(1)}.lastupdate(\{x\})$. By correctness of $D^{(1)}$ we know that

$$D^{(1)}.lastlabel(x) = (a, P_{xj})$$

where a is the label of x in time j. To make item 5 true, we need to have

$$D^{(0)}.lastlabel(x) = (a, P_{xi}),$$

which requires knowing the set of states P_{xi}. By the previous item, we have the history

$$D^{(0)}.history(\{x\}) = history(\{x\}, \{i, \dots, j - 1\}).$$

Therefore, we can apply the history above to the pair (a, P_{xj}) and get the set P_{xi} from

$$apply(D^{(0)}.history(\{x\}))(D^{(1)}.lastlabel(x)). \quad \square$$

A similar proof yields the following lemma.

LEMMA 9. *Let x be the position where w_{i+1} differs from w_i. Let D'_{i+1} be a history tree that is correct for time $i + 1$ and up to date at x. We can compute a data structure D_i that is correct for time w_i. This computation can be done in time $O(\log(n))$, assuming the history operations have unit cost.*

By applying the two lemmas in alternation, we can compute successively data structures

$$D_k, D'_k, D_{k-1}, D'_{k-1}, \dots, D'_1, D_0.$$

This takes $O(k \cdot \log(n))$ time, and $O(k \cdot \log(n))$ history operations. If we implement histories in a naive way, by writing down a history as a list of pairs, each of the operations will take time linear in the length of the list. This will be a problem for the algorithm, which would run in time $O(k \cdot n \cdot \log(n))$.

The essence of the algorithm is to implement histories so that the operations can be done in constant time. This will be done in Section 5.3.

5.3 A constant time implementation of histories

History congruence. Recall the operations on histories that were used as black box operations in the algorithm from the previous section.

$$empty \in Histories$$
$$concat : Histories \times Histories \to Histories.$$
$$apply : Histories \to A \times P(Q) \to P(Q).$$
$$in_\sigma : Histories \to Histories$$

A *history congruence* is an equivalence relation $\sim$ on *Histories* that is a congruence with respect to all the above operations. Formally speaking, a history congruence must satisfy the following conditions whenever $h \sim h'$

$$concat(g, h) \sim concat(g, h') \quad \text{for all } g \in Histories$$
$$concat(h, g) \sim concat(h', g) \quad \text{for all } g \in Histories$$
$$apply(h) = apply(h')$$
$$in_\sigma(h) \sim in_\sigma(h') \quad \text{for all } \sigma \in Externals$$

If $\sim$ is a history congruence, then the history operations can be applied to equivalence classes of $\sim$. The family of equivalence classes together with the history operations on equivalence classes is denoted by $Histories/_\sim$.

LEMMA 10. *Suppose that $\sim$ is a history congruence. Then Histories can be replaced by $Histories/\sim$ in the algorithm, and the computed values for $D_i.lastlabel(\{x\})$ will be the same.*

PROOF. The algorithm accesses the histories only using the operations. $\square$

The constant time implementation of histories is based on the following lemma.

LEMMA 11. *There is a history congruence where the number of equivalence classes is finite and depends only on the automaton, and not its input (not on n or k).*

The idea of the proof is that two histories are considered equivalent if they induce the same mapping:

$$\tau \in Externals \quad \mapsto \quad apply(in_\tau(h)) : A \times P(Q) \to P(Q).$$

6. NON-LOCAL ORDERED AUTOMATA

In this section we generalize the algorithm from the previous section to deal with non-local transitions in an ordered automaton.

The difficulty in this section is a new notion of history. A history is still used to store information about environments of zones, but this information is now more complex.

6.1 Preliminaries

Fix an ordered document update processing automaton. Assume that the maximum rank given by the function Ω of the automaton is t. We define the sets of states

$$Q^1 \subseteq Q^2 \subseteq \cdots \subseteq Q^t \quad \text{where } Q^i \stackrel{def}{=} \{q \in Q \mid \Omega(q) \le i\}.$$

Binary types. The automaton now includes non-local transitions, which are of the form (q, φ, q') where φ is a binary regular query that may select nodes (x, y) of the word with $x \neq y$. As in the previous section, we use monoids to recognize queries. For unary queries, we use the notion of type of a node x as in the previous section. We write $Unarytypes_\alpha$ to denote the set of unary α-types, we omit the index α when the homomorphism α is clear from the context.

We extend the notion of type to pairs of nodes. Suppose

$$\alpha : A^* \to M$$

is a monoid homomorphism. We define the binary α-type of two nodes x and y in a word w as the element of

$$Binarytypes_\alpha \stackrel{def}{=} M \times A \times M \times A \times M \times \{<, >, =\}$$

containing the three types of the three infixes of the word $\{1, \ldots, i-1\}$, $\{i+1, \ldots, j-1\}$, $\{j+1, \ldots, n\}$, where $i = \min(x, y)$, $j = \max(x, y)$, and the labels of positions i and j. The last component says whether $x = y$, $x < y$ or $x > y$. We write $type_\alpha(x, y, w) \in Binarytypes_\alpha$ to denote the binary type of x and y on w. For every regular binary query φ there is a homomorphism α and a set $F \subseteq Binarytypes_\alpha$ that recognizes φ, that is, that (x, y) is selected on w by φ if and only if $type_\alpha(x, y, w) \in F$.

We fix a homomorphism α that recognizes all the binary queries in the transitions of the automaton. We omit the index α from the notation.

Node profiles. As in Section 5, the goal of the algorithm is to compute the sets P_{xi} for positions x and times i.

Suppose that a node x does not change its label between in times $I = \{i, \ldots, j\}$. Due to non-local transitions, it is not enough to know the sequence of external types of x in order to update it from P_{xj} to $P_{x(i-1)}$. There may be a state q in $P_{x(i-1)}$ that is triggered by some $q' \in P_{yi}$ via a non-local transition from some other node y. Due to these issues, we store more information in our data structures. We describe this information below, starting with the simplest brick: profiles of nodes.

Consider a node $x \in \{1, \ldots, n\}$, a time $i \in \{1, \ldots, k\}$ and a rank $l \in \{1, \ldots, t\}$. By induction on the rank l, we define *the rank l profile of node x in time i* to be the following information, which is denoted by $\pi_x^{l,i}$:

- The type of node x in the word w_i;
- the set of states in $P_{xi} \cap Q^l$;
- for every binary type $\tau \in Binarytypes$, the set of rank $l - 1$ profiles of nodes y in time i such that the binary type of x and y in w_i is τ.

When the rank l is not specified, it assumed to be the maximal rank $l = t$. Observe that the information in π_x^i also describes other nodes than x, due to the third item of the definition. Since the definition is recursive, a rank l profile can be seen a tree of depth t where edges correspond to $Binarytypes$ elements, and nodes with a subtree of depth l are described by the accepting states from Q^l. The data type where rank l profiles live is denoted by $Nodeprofiles_l$, and it is described below:

$$Nodeprofiles \stackrel{def}{=} Nodeprofiles_t$$

$$Nodeprofiles_1 \stackrel{def}{=} Unarytypes \times P(Q^1)$$

$$Nodeprofiles_{l+1} \stackrel{def}{=} Unarytypes \times P(Q^{l+1}) \times Neighbours_l$$

$$Neighbours_l \stackrel{def}{=} Binarytypes \to P(Nodeprofiles_l)$$

Note that from $\pi_x^{l,i}$ we can deduce $\pi_x^{l',i}$ for all $l' < l$, because $Q^{l'} \subseteq Q^l$. The size of the data type $Nodeprofiles_{l+1}$ is exponential in the size of $Nodeprofiles_l$, hence the nonelementary query complexity of our algorithm.

Zone profiles. We define the profile of a node x relative to a zone $X \ni x$ by taking $w_i|X$ as the whole word. All the elements from $Unarytypes$ and $Binarytypes$ are relative, and the neighbours are limited to the zone X. This profile is denoted by $\pi_{x \in X}^i$.

The profile of a zone X in time moment i is just the set of node profiles (relative to X) of nodes in X. We use the symbol Π to denote zone profiles. Following the same notation introduced before, $\Pi_X^{l,i}$ is the zone profile of the zone X at time moment i containing the information of the states from Q^l.

$$\Pi_X^{l,i} \stackrel{def}{=} \{\pi_{x \in X}^{l,i} : x \in X\} \in Zoneprofiles_l \stackrel{def}{=} P(Nodeprofiles_l)$$

$$\Pi_X^i \stackrel{def}{=} \Pi_X^{t,i} \in Zoneprofiles \stackrel{def}{=} Zoneprofiles_t$$

The following lemma shows that zone profiles are compositional with respect to union of consecutive zones.

LEMMA 12. *There is an associative concatenation operation on profiles $(\Pi_1, \Pi_2) \mapsto \Pi_1 \cdot \Pi_2$ such that for two consecutive zones X_1 and X_2, we have*

$$\Pi_{X_1 \cup X_2} = \Pi_{X_1} \cdot \Pi_{X_2}.$$

One step computation.

LEMMA 13. *Suppose that the nodes of the word are partitioned into three consecutive zones X_1, X, X_2. Suppose also that in time $i-1$ the labels of zone X do not change. For every node $x \in X$, the node profile $\pi_{x \in X}^{i-1}$ depends only on:*

$$\Pi_{X_1}^i \qquad \Pi_{X_2}^i \qquad and \qquad \pi_{x \in X}^i$$

Actually, the dependency is even a bit more fine grained. If we want to know the rank l profile $\pi_{x \in X}^{l, i-1}$, we only need the profile of the same rank in the current node, but profiles of smaller rank in the surrounding zones:

$$\Pi_{X_1}^{l-1, i} \qquad \Pi_{X_2}^{l-1, i} \qquad and \qquad \pi_{x \in X}^{l, i}.$$

The idea is that any dependency on nodes that are different from x requires using a non-local transition, which decreases the rank. However, since we do not need the more fine grained dependency, we use the dependency as stated in Lemma 13, which does not indicate ranks.

Observe that we do not need the profiles $\pi_{x' \in X}^i$ of other elements $x' \in X$ since all the information relevant to X is inside $\pi_{x \in X}^i$. Let us fix the term *Externalzoneprofiles* to name zone profiles of the environment of zones.

$$Externalzoneprofiles \stackrel{def}{=} Externalzoneprofiles_t$$

$$Externalzoneprofiles_l \stackrel{def}{=} Zoneprofiles_l \times Zoneprofiles_l$$

We define the *ext* function to work with *Externalzoneprofiles*.

$$ext(X, i) \stackrel{def}{=} (\Pi_{X_1}^i, \Pi_{X_2}^i) \in Externalzoneprofiles$$

for (X_1, X_2) the environment of X in w_i. By Lemma 13, there exists a function

$$update : Externalzoneprofiles \rightarrow Nodeprofiles \rightarrow Nodeprofiles$$

such that the following holds.

$$\pi_{x \in X}^{i-1} = update(ext(X, i), \pi_{x \in X}^i)$$

This function can be extended to zones

$$update : Externalzoneprofiles \rightarrow Zoneprofiles \rightarrow Zoneprofiles$$

by lifting the previous definition to sets of profiles, and we then have

$$\Pi_X^{i-1} = update(ext(X, i), \Pi_X^i).$$

6.2 Histories

We now generalize the notion of histories, as they were defined in Section 5, to the non-local case. Let $i \leq j$ be times and let X be a zone, with (X_1, X_2) its environment. Suppose that the labels of X do not change in times $i, \dots, j$ (and therefore they are the same as in the word w_{j+1}). We define the history of X between i and j, denoted by

$$history(X, \{i, \dots, j\}),$$

to be the following sequence:

$$ext(X, i), ext(X, i+1), \dots, ext(X, j) \in Externalzoneprofiles.$$

We write *Histories* for the set of possible histories. We next define the *apply* and *in* functions on *Histories*.

LEMMA 14. *Suppose that in time interval $\{i, \dots, j\}$, the labels of a zone X do not change. Then the zone profile Π_X^{i-1} is uniquely determined by Π_X^j and $history(X, \{i, \dots, j\})$.*

PROOF. By iterating the function

$$update : Externalzoneprofiles \rightarrow Zoneprofiles \rightarrow Zoneprofiles.$$

for each item on the list in the history. $\square$

Let the dependency in the above lemma be realized by the function:

$$apply : Histories \rightarrow Zoneprofiles \rightarrow Zoneprofiles$$

That is, under the assumptions of the lemma we have

$$\Pi_X^{i-1} \quad = \quad apply \quad (history(X, \{i, \dots, j\})) \quad (\Pi_X^j).$$

In the algorithm for local transitions from Section 5, one important part has to do with the possibility to compute, given the history h of a zone X in an interval $\{i, \dots, j\}$ (and assuming that there were no changes on X between times i and j), the history h' of a smaller zone $X_0 \subseteq X$ having as environment inside X the subzones X_1 and X_2. In the previous section, this was obtained simply with $in_\sigma(h)$ where $\sigma \in Externals$ corresponds to the types of (X_1, X_2). But here the operation is somewhat more complicated, since to obtain the history h' we need at the same time to update the zone profiles of X_1 and X_2 to the time $j-1$ (remember that a history element is from *Externalzoneprofiles*), then to time $j-2$ until we update it to time i. Thus, in some sense the *apply*() and in_σ() functions of the previous section are done simultaneously for the non-local automata. Another issue to solve is that in order to update the zone profile of, say X_1, we need the updated profiles of X_0, X_2. But these need at the same time the updated profile of X_1. However, this will not be a problem because of the *ordered* condition we impose to the automaton.

LEMMA 15. *Let Y be a zone partitioned into three consecutive zones X_1, X, X_2. Suppose that in time interval $\{i, \dots, j\}$ the labels of zone Y do not change. Then*

$$history(X, \{i, \dots, j\})$$

is uniquely determined by

$$history(Y, \{i, \dots, j\}) \qquad \Pi_{X_1}^j \qquad \Pi_{X_2}^j \qquad \Pi_X^j.$$

Let the operation that realizes the dependency of the above lemma be denoted by

$$in : Histories \rightarrow Externalzoneprofiles$$
$$\rightarrow Zoneprofiles \rightarrow Histories.$$

That is, under the assumptions of the lemma we have

$$history(X, \{i, \dots, j\}) =$$
$$in \quad (history(Y, \{i, \dots, j\})) \quad (\Pi_{X_1}^j) \quad (\Pi_{X_2}^j) \quad (\Pi_X^j).$$

6.3 The algorithm

The high level structure of the algorithm is the same as in Section 5. We keep a tree of histories and update one branch with each iteration, performing $O(\log(n))$ operations. The main difference is that we also retain the profiles of each of the logarithmic zones, which become necessary to transfer a history of a zone to a history of a smaller zone.

The history tree. We also maintain a structure as the one showed previously. An instance D of the data structure consists of the following labeling.

$$D.lastupdate : Logs \rightarrow \{0, \ldots, k\}$$
$$D.lastprofile : Logs \rightarrow Zoneprofiles$$
$$D.history : Logs \rightarrow Histories$$

Note that instead of using $D.lastlabel$ and $D.monoid$ we have a $D.lastprofile$ which contains the profile of the logarithmic zone. In particular it contains the label and external value for each node.

As before, we first compute a history tree for time k, then for times $k-1$ and so on, down to 0. We call a history tree *correct* at time moment $i \in \{0, \ldots, k\}$ if conditions 1, 2, and 4 of the previous definition of correctness hold (with the new notions of history) and

6. $D.lastprofile(X)$ is the updated zone profile of X, i.e., after applying $D.history(X)$ to it. Suppose that $X \in Logs$ and let

$$j = D.lastupdate(parent(X)) \quad \text{and}$$
$$\Pi = D.lastprofile(X),$$

then Π is equal to the zone profile Π_X^j of X in the time moment j. If X is the root, then it is the zone profile at time moment i: $D.lastprofile(X) = \Pi_X^i$.

Like with the algorithm of previous section we begin with a history tree D_0 that is correct for time moment $i = k$ and then for each time moment $i = k-1, \ldots, 0$ the algorithm calculates the history tree D_i that is correct for time moment i. The algorithm manipulates histories and zone profiles. Here we use as black boxes the following operations on histories that have unit cost in the algorithm.

$$empty \quad concat \quad apply \quad in$$

emtpy and *concat* have the exact same definition as in the previous section: the empty history and the concatenation of histories. *apply* and *in* follow the definitions seen in Section 6.2.

One states analogues of Lemmas 8 and 9 for the new setup, with the exact same statements, only with the new notion of history tree. Then, one proves that the history operations can be implemented in constant time, also using a history congruence.

7. IMPROVEMENTS

7.1 Off ine vs online

There are two ways of looking at the incremental evaluation problem, when the input is a document evolution

$$w_1, \ldots, w_k.$$

In the offline view, the algorithm begins its work once all of the document evolution is known.

In the online view, the words of the document evolution come one at a time, and the algorithm should do logarithmic processing for each word, without knowing the words that are going to come in the future.

Is our algorithm offline or online?

The answer depends on the order in which the words come, or equivalently stated, the direction of time in the temporal logic. As we had defined the temporal logic, time flows to the right, with the first time moment being 1 and the last time moment being k. As the reader will recall, our algorithm begins by analyzing time k, then $k-1$ and so on down to 1. An inspection of the algorithm reveals that operations of the algorithm when doing step i do not depend on the part of the document evolution $w_1, \ldots, w_{i-1}$. Therefore, our algorithm actually is an online algorithm, assuming that the flow of time in the logic or automaton works in the opposite direction as the development of the document evolution.

Summing up, our algorithm is online (i.e. it does a logarithmic computation per each new word of the document evolution, and the computation does not depend of the words that are about to come in the future) if the temporal logic uses past operators on the time dimension, and not future operators. Although future operators are more common in temporal logics (which is why we defined the logic with future operators), it seems that past operators might actually be a better idea for the application at hand.

7.2 Insertion and deletion

In our evaluation algorithm we dealt with only one kind of update operation: relabeling. In this section we show that the algorithm still works if we allow insertions and deletions.

In the presence of insertions and deletions, one has to take care to distinguish between a node and its distance from the beginning of the word. For instance, suppose that we start with a word a and then apply the operation "insert a node with label b before the first position". The resulting document evolution is a, ba. However, the first and only node in the word a corresponds to the second node in the word ba, and not the first one.

To solve the issue presented above, we redefine a word as a connected graph where every node has outdegree and indegree at most one, and the nodes are labeled by letters from the alphabet. This way, we can assume that every node has a unique identifier, and the identifier does not change even if the distance of the node from the beginning of the word changes as a result of an insertion or deletion. A document evolution is a sequence of such words, which share nodes with the same identifiers.

Using identifiers, we adapt the semantics of the temporal and first order logic to document evolutions that include insertions and deletions. In the first-order logic, the quantifiers range over pairs (identifier/time), and not (distance from beginning/time) pairs. In the temporal logic, a modality that stays in a node stays in an identifier. For instance, the formula $\neg X_t \top$ says that the current node will be deleted in the next time moment. Another example is the formula

$$G_t\big((\neg X_t \top) \Rightarrow a\big),$$

which says that the label of the current node is a just before it gets deleted (if it gets deleted).

Thanks to the insertion and deletion operations, we may assume that an incremental document evolution begins in an empty word.

THEOREM 16. *Suppose that, apart from label changes, we also allow insertions and deletions as update operations. For any fixed formula φ of the temporal logic, the incremental evaluation problem can be solved in time $O(k \cdot \log(k))$, where k is the number of updates.*

The same online/offline remarks as in the previous section

apply to the algorithm above. That is, it works online if the words are given in reverse order, or the temporal logic uses past instead of future operators in the time dimension. (But not both changes simultaneously.)

7.3 Trees

In the previous sections, we have described the evaluation algorithm for ordered document update processing automata, assuming input document evolution was a sequence of words. What about the trees?

Bounded depth trees. One solution is to reduce trees to words. For a tree t, we define its word representation $word(t)$, which is like the text representation of an XML tree. If the labels of t are A, then the labels of $word(t)$ are $\{open, close\} \times A$. Every node of t corresponds to two nodes in w, one with an opening tag and one with a closing tag. If the depth of the tree is known in advance, and can be encoded in the states of the automaton, then this representation can be decoded by document update processing automata, as stated in the following lemma.

LEMMA 17. *Fix $d \in \mathbb{N}$. For any document update processing automaton on trees $\mathcal{A}$, one can compute a document update processing automaton on words $\mathcal{A}_d$ such that $\mathcal{A}$ accepts a document evolution (consisting of trees)*

$$\bar{t} = t_1, \ldots, t_k$$

if and only if $\mathcal{A}_d$ accepts the document evolution

$$word(\bar{t}) = word(t_1), \ldots, word(t_k),$$

provided all the trees in $\bar{t}$ have depth at most d.

From the lemma above, it follows that all results on evaluation can be transferred from the bounded depth words to bounded depth trees.

Unbounded depth trees. We believe that, after some modifications, our algorithm can actually work directly on trees, without the need for the reduction $t \mapsto word(t)$. That is, we believe that Theorem 16 holds for trees, without any restriction on the depth. The idea is to use forest algebra [7], instead of monoids. Observe that this would improve the algorithm of Balmin, Papakonstantinou and Vianu [4] in two ways: first, a more general problem is considered, and second the data complexity per update is improved from $O(\log^2(n))$ to $O(\log(n))$. On the other hand, the query complexity of our algorithm is very bad.

8. CONCLUSIONS

We have designed an algorithm for evaluating a logic that inspects documents evolutions. The logic has operators that travel in the time dimension, and operators that travel in the space dimension. The algorithm works in time $O(k \cdot \log(k))$ where k is the length of the document evolution.

Below we list some topics for future work. We would like to investigate a logic with past and future operators on the time axis. We would also like to investigate a hybrid logic, where quantifiers are used for the space dimension and temporal operators are used for time dimension. Finally, we would like to improve the query complexity of the algorithm, possibly at the cost of using weaker logics.

9. REFERENCES

[1] Parosh Aziz Abdulla, Bengt Jonsson, Marcus Nilsson, Julien d'Orso, and Mayank Saksena. Regular model checking for LTL(MSO). In *CAV*, volume 3114 of *Lecture Notes in Computer Science*, pages 348–360. Springer, 2004.

[2] Parosh Aziz Abdulla, Bengt Jonsson, Marcus Nilsson, and Mayank Saksena. A survey of regular model checking. In *CONCUR*, volume 3170 of *Lecture Notes in Computer Science*, pages 35–48. Springer, 2004.

[3] Serge Abiteboul, Laurent Herr, and Jan Van den Bussche. Temporal connectives versus explicit timestamps to query temporal databases. *J. Comput. Syst. Sci.*, 58(1):54–68, 1999.

[4] Andrey Balmin, Yannis Papakonstantinou, and Victor Vianu. Incremental validation of XML documents. *ACM Trans. Database Syst.*, 29(4):710–751, 2004.

[5] Denilson Barbosa, Alberto O. Mendelzon, Leonid Libkin, Laurent Mignet, and Marcelo Arenas. Efficient incremental validation of XML documents. In *ICDE*, pages 671–682, 2004.

[6] Henrik Björklund, Wouter Gelade, Marcel Marquardt, and Wim Martens. Incremental XPath evaluation. In *ICDT*, pages 162–173, 2009.

[7] M. Bojańczyk and I. Walukiewicz. Forest algebras. In *Automata and Logic: History and Perspectives*, pages 107–132. Amsterdam University Press, 2007.

[8] Mikołaj Bojańczyk and Paweł Parys. XPath evaluation in linear time. In *PODS*, pages 241–250, 2008.

[9] Ghislain Fourny, Daniela Florescu, Donald Kossmann, and Markos Zacharioudakis. A time machine for XML: PUL composition. In *XML Prague*, 2010.

[10] David Gabelaia, Agi Kurucz, Frank Wolter, and Michael Zakharyaschev. Products of 'transitive' modal logics. *J. Symb. Log.*, 70(3):993–1021, 2005.

[11] Leonid Libkin. Logics for unranked trees: An overview. *Logical Methods in Computer Science*, 2(3), 2006.

[12] Bernd-Holger Schlingloff. Expressive completeness of temporal logic of trees. *Journal of Applied Non-Classical Logics*, 2(2), 1992.

[13] Luc Segoufin. Automata and logics for words and trees over an infinite alphabet. In *CSL*, pages 41–57, 2006.

Rewrite Rules for Search Database Systems

Ronald Fagin[*]   Benny Kimelfeld[*] Yunyao Li[*] Sriram Raghavan[†] Shivakumar Vaithyanathan[*]

fagin@almaden.ibm.com   {kimelfeld, yunyaoli}@us.ibm.com   sriramraghavan@in.ibm.com   shiv@us.ibm.com

ABSTRACT

The results of a search engine can be improved by consulting auxiliary data. In a search database system, the association between the user query and the auxiliary data is driven by rewrite rules that augment the user query with a set of alternative queries. This paper develops a framework that formalizes the notion of a rewrite program, which is essentially a collection of hedge-rewriting rules. When applied to a search query, the rewrite program produces a set of alternative queries that constitutes a least fixpoint (lfp). The main focus of the paper is on the lfp-convergence of a rewrite program, where a rewrite program is lfp-convergent if the least fixpoint of every search query is finite. Determining whether a given rewrite program is lfp-convergent is undecidable; to accommodate that, the paper proposes a safety condition, and shows that safety guarantees lfp-convergence, and that safety can be decided in polynomial time. The effectiveness of the safety condition in capturing lfp-convergence is illustrated by an application to a rewrite program in an implemented system that is intended for widespread use.

Categories and Subject Descriptors

H.3.3 [**Information Storage and Retrieval**]: Information Search and Retrieval—*search process*; F.4.2 [**Mathematical Logic and Formal Languages**]: Grammars and Other Rewriting Systems

General Terms

Algorithms, Theory

Keywords

Search database system, rewriting

1. INTRODUCTION

It is well known that an auxiliary database of concepts associated with the contents of a document collection can significantly

[*]IBM Research–Almaden, San Jose, CA 95120, USA.

[†]IBM India Research Lab, Embassy Manyatha Business Park Bldg D4, Bangalore 560045, India

improve the quality (precision and recall) of a keyword search engine [9, 10, 19, 22, 23]. The intuitive idea is that the auxiliary data enables the engine to better interpret the search query terms and retrieve documents matching the "intent" behind the query, as opposed to documents that merely contain physical matches for the query terms. For example, modern Web search engines are very good at interpreting and generating specially crafted results for queries referring to popular concepts such as movies, locations, weather, places, etc. Thus, a query such as "nyc map" brings back the map of New York City, a query such as "san jose weather" brings back the weather forecast for the city of San Jose, and so on.

At IBM Research–Almaden, we have developed a generic search engine with such "interpretation" capabilities that can be customized to different document collections by providing an appropriate auxiliary database. A central tool used for obtaining such an auxiliary database (to aid a search engine) is *information extraction* [2, 9, 12, 23, 26]. In earlier work, we developed the framework of a *search database system* [6] to formalize the approach taken by our engine. As we deployed this engine in large-scale production scenarios, we encountered the requirement to provide search administrators and domain experts with the ability to customize the process of generating interpretations.

For example, consider the scenario of intranet search. Administrators wished to express a rule that whenever a query involves the name of a person and a word such as "contact", "profile", "phone" or "email", the search engine should generate an interpretation that looks for the person's name within the company's internal employee directory. Similarly, any query of the form "download" or "install" followed by the name of some software should generate an interpretation that looks for the name of this software within the company's internal software download Web site. These examples illustrate how rules are used to direct the search engine towards specific subcollections or Web sites based on the concepts occurring in the search query. In our deployments, we encountered several other use cases for rules, such as dropping noise words (e.g., inside IBM, the query "ibm health insurance" should really be simply "health insurance") or handling under-specified queries (e.g., a vague query such as "travel"). In the latter case, the query "travel" might be augmented by a set of more specific queries. In all of these cases, the original query is augmented with a set of additional queries that should all be executed, with the results concatenated or interleaved in some manner, perhaps based on some quality measure of the queries (the details of how the result sets of the various queries are combined is beyond the scope of this paper).

To support these requirements, we enhanced our engine with support for *rewrite rules*. Rewrite rules govern how the input keyword query should be augmented by additional queries that should all be executed against the underlying search index. For example, assume that the user gives the query "laura haas number"; let us denote this query by $\mathbf{q}$. Assume that the system has the rules ρ_1, ρ_2, ρ_3 that are depicted in Figure 1(b). (We shall explain the syntax and semantics of these rules later; for now, we shall simply discuss their effect when the user query is $\mathbf{q}$.) Given the query $\mathbf{q}$, the rewrite rule ρ_1 would fire to associate "laura haas" with the concept of a "person". Thus, in Figure 2, the rewrite rule ρ_1 is applied to the search query $\mathbf{q}$ in the upper-left box to obtain the query h_1 in the upper-right box. Here $\overline{\text{person}}$ denotes the concept of a "person". This new query h_1 is a *hedge*, as we shall discuss later, which is why we use the letter h (we do not use bold letters as we did for $\mathbf{q}$, since we reserve bold letters for sequences of keywords). The rule ρ_2 would associate the $\overline{\text{person}}$ concept and the word "number" with a $\overline{\text{person}}$ concept and a $\overline{\text{phone}}$ concept that are tied together with a person-phone compound concept $\overline{\text{prph}}$. This gives the query h_2 in the bottom-right box in Figure 2. Finally, the rule ρ_3 implies that a query of the form of h_2 should generate another query that looks for the home page of the person, as in the bottom-left box in Figure 2. We are then left with the set $\{\mathbf{q}, h_1, h_2, h_3\}$ of queries, which should all be run with their results interleaved in some manner. Note that these queries might give quite different answers. For example the original query $\mathbf{q}$ might give many pages that each contain all of the words "laura" "haas", and "number" (and might not include the home page of Laura Haas, if her home page does not contain the word "number"), whereas the query h_3 might give back just the home page of Laura Haas.

Rewrite rules proved to be a powerful and effective mechanism in the hands of search administrators and quickly resulted in deployments where hundreds of such rules were registered with the search engine. However, this quickly pointed us to a major problem: the application of the rules to a search query may result in a non-terminating process that produces an infinite number of alternatives. As a simple example, an administrator may add a pair of rules: a rule ρ_1 to transform "almaden" to its common short form "arc", and a rule ρ_2 to transform "ibm arc" to "ibm almaden research". Given the query "ibm almaden", the rule ρ_1 creates the query "ibm arc"; the rule ρ_2 then creates the query "ibm almaden research"; the rule ρ_1 then creates the query "ibm arc research"; the rule ρ_2 then creates the query "ibm almaden research research", and so on. This process never ends, and we get infinitely many queries of the form "ibm almaden research $\cdots$ research", where "research $\cdots$ research" represents the word "research" repeated arbitrarily many times. Lacking effective tools that would detect and help avoid such combinations, we were forced (before the research in this paper) to make the ad hoc choice of limiting rule composition by applying each rule at most once, in some prescribed order.

The goal of this paper is to lay foundations for rewrite rules in a search engine, where the focus is on understanding the above problem of non-terminating rewriting, and guaranteeing that it is avoided in the set of rewrite rules at hand. Our formalism is within the framework of the *search database system* that we developed in previous work [6]. We show that the notion of rule introduced in that work essentially corresponds to a special type of rewrite rule that is more limited in expressivity but guaranteed to terminate. A more formal discussion of this phenomenon appears in Section 5.4.

A formal definition of a search database system is given in Section 2. The essence is as follows. The *schema* of such a system is a partially ordered set of *concepts* (e.g., $\overline{\text{person}}$ and $\overline{\text{phone}}$, which are subconcepts of $\overline{\text{prph}}$). In our examples, each concept is written with a bar over it. A *database* over the schema specifies instantiations of the concepts (e.g., "laura haas" instantiates $\overline{\text{person}}$) in the documents of the corpus, as well as relationships between these instantiations according to the schema (e.g., a $\overline{\text{prph}}$ association between

a person and her phone number). A query over the database is a hedge (ordered forest) where nodes are (labeled by) *terms* (which are essentially the words used as keywords) and concepts from the schema, such that the parent-child relationships between concepts are consistent with the schema $\mathbf{S}$; such a query is called an $\mathbf{S}$-*hedge*. Examples of $\mathbf{S}$-hedges, where $\mathbf{S}$ is depicted in Figure 1(a), appear in the rectangular boxes of Figure 2. The *search query* phrased by the user is an $\mathbf{S}$-hedge that contains only terms, as in the upper-left box in Figure 2.

A *rewrite rule* is, conceptually, a (possibly infinite) binary relation over the $\mathbf{S}$-hedges, where inclusion of the pair (h, h') in this relation means that the $\mathbf{S}$-hedge h is rewritten to the $\mathbf{S}$-hedge h'. The exact syntax that we use for specifying a rewrite rule is described in Section 3. Essentially, a rule has the form $E \Rightarrow F$, where E and F are $\mathbf{S}$-hedges that contain variables (in addition to terms and concepts). In terms of standard *rewriting systems* [25], our rules can be classified into the category of *hedge rewriting* [11], *context sensitive* [20] (actually, the full context is captured in each of the two sides of a rule), *linear* [25] (i.e., each variable has at most one occurrence in each of the two sides of a rule), and *conditional* [13] (i.e., the involved hedges need to conform to the schema). Examples are the rules $E_i \Rightarrow F_i$ (for $i = 1, 2, 3$) in Figure 1(b). Under this syntax, a rewrite rule should be *consistent* in the sense that every $\mathbf{S}$-hedge is indeed rewritten into an $\mathbf{S}$-hedge. We show that consistency of a rule can be decided in polynomial time, which we realize by a nontrivial algorithm. A *rewrite program* consists of a schema $\mathbf{S}$ and a finite set R of rewrite rules. When a rewrite program is applied to a search query $\mathbf{q}$, it maintains a set H of $\mathbf{S}$-hedges that is initially the singleton $\{\mathbf{q}\}$. This set grows by adding to it every $\mathbf{S}$-hedge h' such that an $\mathbf{S}$-hedge h in H can be rewritten using the rewrite rules into h'. We terminate when no such h' can be found, which means that the set H we reach is the *least fixpoint* (which we sometimes abbreviate as *lfp*) for $\mathbf{q}$. The *lfp-convergence* of a rewrite program means that this process always terminates, or in other words, the least fixpoint of every search query is finite. The notion of lfp-convergence is very similar to *weak termination* (or *quasi-termination*) of a rewriting system [8], except that we are restricted to rewritings that start with a search query (and not an arbitrary hedge).

We would like to be able to decide whether a given rewrite program is lfp-convergent. Unfortunately, it follows from known results [8] that this task is undecidable, even under strong restrictions on the rewrite program (e.g., no concepts are involved in the rewrite rules), and even if we fix *any* arbitrary schema. Due to this undecidability, the best one can hope for is a *safety condition* that is useful in practice. In Section 5, we present such a safety condition after making the case the vast literature on *proof techniques for termination* (e.g., [1, 3–5, 7, 14]) does not capture the special needs and features of lfp-convergence for our rewrite programs. We show that our safety condition indeed guarantees lfp-convergence. We show that safety can be decided in polynomial time, and we realize it by a nontrivial recursive algorithm that involves dynamic programming, linear programming, and graph theory.

We found our safety approach to be extremely useful for the management of the rewrite program used in an actual large-scale deployment of our search engine. Specifically, we were able to detect a small set of rewrite rules that cause non-termination (non-lfp-convergence), while the remaining part is lfp-convergent. Almost all of that remaining part of our program (more precisely, around 95% of the remaining part, which is around 90% of the original program) was found to be safe. (In Section 5.5 we provide more details, including some comments about how we dealt with the non-safe portion of the rules.) Hence, our experience shows that the safety condition is highly successful in capturing lfp-convergence in a practical rewrite program.

2. SEARCH DATABASE SYSTEMS

In this section, we give the formal definitions for the framework of a *search database system*. We begin with some preliminaries.

2.1 Preliminaries: Strings, Trees and Hedges

Let Σ be a set, which we refer to as an *alphabet*. We denote by Σ^* the set of all strings over Σ, that is, all the finite sequences $\sigma_1 \cdots \sigma_n$, where $\sigma_i \in \Sigma$ for $1 \leq i \leq n$. The length n of a string $\mathbf{s} = \sigma_1 \cdots \sigma_n$ is denoted by $|\mathbf{s}|$.

The trees we use in this paper are directed, ordered (i.e., the children of each node form a sequence), and node labeled. Formally, for a set Σ of labels, a *tree (over Σ)* is inductively defined as follows. If $\sigma \in \Sigma$ and $t_1, \ldots, t_n$ are trees over Σ (where n is a nonnegative integer), then $\sigma(t_1 \cdots t_n)$ is a tree over Σ. Intuitively, $\sigma(t_1 \cdots t_n)$ is a tree with a root labeled with σ, such that the subtrees under the root, from left to right, are $t_1, \ldots, t_n$. For convenience, we identify the symbol σ with the tree $\sigma()$ (hence, a symbol of Σ is a special case of a tree). A *hedge (over Σ)* is a sequence $h = t_1 \cdots t_n$ of trees over Σ. Special cases of a hedge include a tree, a symbol of Σ, and a string of Σ^* (including the empty string).

The choice of the above formalism for trees (i.e., as strings) is convenient in the sense that isomorphism is the same as equality (i.e., two trees are isomorphic if and only if they are equal). There is a straightforward translation of a tree in this formalism to the more standard formalism by means of *nodes* and *edges*,[1] and it is convenient for us to (implicitly) make this translation. In particular, we denote by nodes(h) the set of nodes of the hedge h, and we denote by edges(h) the set of edges of h. If (v, w) is an edge of h, then w is a *child* of v, which in turn is the *parent* of w. The label of the node v is denoted by label(v). A *leaf* of a hedge is a node without children, and a non-leaf node is an *internal node*. If a hedge h contains a directed path from node v to node w, then w is a *descendant* of v, which in turn is an *ancestor* of w. Note that every node is both an ancestor and a descendant of itself. For a tree t, the *root* of t, denoted root(t), is the unique node without a parent.

2.2 Concepts, Schemas and Instances

We fix an infinite set Cncpt of *concepts*. A *schema* is a finite *poset* (i.e., a partially ordered set) of concepts. More specifically, a schema $\mathbf{S}$ is a pair $(C, \prec)$, where C is a finite subset of Cncpt, and $\prec$ is a strict partial order over C (i.e., $\prec$ is an irreflexive, asymmetric and transitive binary relation over C). For a concept $\gamma \in C$, the set of *subconcepts* of γ, denoted $sc(\gamma)$, comprises all the elements $\delta \in C$, such that $\delta \prec \gamma$ and there is no $\gamma' \in C$, such that $\delta \prec \gamma' \prec \gamma$. A minimal concept $\gamma \in C$ (i.e., γ such that $sc(\gamma) = \emptyset$) is called an *atomic concept*, abbreviated *a-concept*. If $\gamma \in C$ is not atomic, then it is a *compound concept*, abbreviated *c-concept*. We usually abuse the notation and identify $\mathbf{S}$ with C, avoiding any mentioning of $\prec$; for example, we may write $\gamma \in \mathbf{S}$ when we actually mean $\gamma \in C$.

EXAMPLE 2.1. Figure 1(a) shows the schema $\mathbf{S}$ that we use in our running example. The concepts of $\mathbf{S}$ are $\overline{\text{person}}$, $\overline{\text{phone}}$, $\overline{\text{prph}}$ (which stands for "person-phone"), $\overline{\text{body}}$, and $\overline{\text{prhome}}$ (which stands for "personal home page"). As done here, throughout this paper we denote a specific concept by an over-lined word, in order to distinguish concepts from words of other roles (as we define below). Note that $\overline{\text{prph}}$ and $\overline{\text{prhome}}$ are c-concepts, with $sc(\overline{\text{prph}}) =$

[1]For a specific translation see, for example, [21].

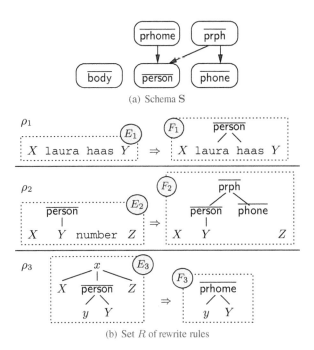

(a) Schema $\mathbf{S}$

(b) Set R of rewrite rules

Figure 1: Rewrite program $(\mathbf{S}, R)$ (running example)

$\{\overline{\text{person}}, \overline{\text{phone}}\}$ and $sc(\overline{\text{prhome}}) = \{\overline{\text{person}}\}$. The remaining three concepts of $\mathbf{S}$ are a-concepts. Intuitively, $\overline{\text{prph}}$ denotes an association between a person and her phone number, and $\overline{\text{prhome}}$ denotes the home page of a person. □

Next, we define the notion of a *database instance* over a schema. Throughout the paper, we fix two sets. First, we have a set URIs of *unique resource identifiers*, which are used for identifying documents. (We use the standard abbreviation *URI* for Unique Resource Identifier.) Second, we have an infinite set of *terms* that is denoted by Terms; a term can appear in a document, and it can be used as a keyword in a search query.

Let $\mathbf{S}$ be a schema. A *database instance* (or just *instance*) I (over $\mathbf{S}$) is a finite set of *records*, where each record r is associated with a unique concept $\gamma \in \mathbf{S}$ (thus, γ acts as a property of r). Every record r has a URI from the set URIs, and this URI is denoted by $uri(r)$. As for the rest of the content of a record, we distinguish between two types of records r, depending on whether the concept γ associated with r is atomic or compound.

- If γ is an a-concept, then r is called an *a-record*. Then, r has textual data, which is a string of Terms*. The textual data of r is denoted by $txt(r)$.

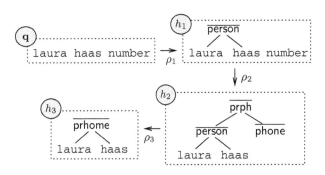

Figure 2: S-hedges

273

rec.	concept	uri	text
r_{lh}	person	doc1	laura haas
r_{wc}	person	doc1	william cody
r_{ph}	phone	doc1	+1(234)567-8910
r_{bd}	body	doc1	welcome to ibm research ...
s_{pr}	person	doc2	laura haas
s_{ph}	phone	doc2	+1(098)765-4321
s_{bd}	body	doc2	laura's home page ...

(a) The a-records of I

rec.	concept	uri	references
r_{pp}	prph	doc1	$r_{pp}[\text{person}] = r_{wc}, r_{pp}[\text{phone}] = r_{ph}$
s_{pp}	prph	doc2	$s_{pp}[\text{person}] = s_{pr}, s_{pp}[\text{phone}] = s_{ph}$
s_{hm}	prhome	doc2	$s_{hm}[\text{person}] = s_{pr}$

(b) The c-records of I

Figure 3: An instance I of schema S of Figure 1(a)

- If γ is a c-concept, then r is called a *c-record*. Then, for each subconcept $\delta \in sc(\gamma)$, the record r references a record $s \in I$ with the concept δ and with the same URI as r (that is, $uri(r) = uri(s)$); the record s is denoted by $r[\delta]$.

EXAMPLE 2.2. We continue with our running example. The tables of Figures 3(a) and 3(b) show the a-records and c-records, respectively, of an instance I over the schema S (Figure 1(a)). The top table (Figure 3(a)) contains the a-records and the bottom one (Figure 3(b)) contains the c-records. This instance represents two indexed pages with the URIs doc1 and doc2. Each row in the table describes one record. For example, the first row of the top table describes the a-record r_{lh}, and the first row of the bottom table describes the c-record r_{pp}. The column "concept" gives the concept of the record. For example, the concept of r_{lh} is person. The column "uri" gives the URI of the record; for example, $uri(r_{lh}) = \text{doc1}$. In the top table, the column "text" shows the textual data; thus, $txt(r_{lh}) = \text{laura haas}$ (which consists of the two terms laura and haas). In the bottom table, the column "references" shows the reference of each subconcept.

The body records of I can be produced by standard operations on Web pages (e.g., HTML-to-text conversion). Other records, however, are not explicitly specified in a Web page, and their production may require more complex (possibly heuristic) techniques. For example, the person records are obtained by identifying a person name in the document. Similarly, producing a phone record requires a mechanism for identifying that a substring of the document is a phone number, and producing a prph record entails identifying that a recognized person and a recognized phone number are semantically associated. Producing the record s_{hm} with the reference to a person requires understanding that the document is the person's home page (in addition to recognition of that person). These are typical tasks in *information extraction* [17, 24], which form a primary tool for the construction of a database instance. □

Let I be an instance, and consider the directed graph G that has the records of I as the set of nodes, and an edge (r_1, r_2) from record r_1 to record r_2 whenever $r_2 = r_1[\gamma]$ for some concept γ. A record r is a *descendant* of a record r' if G has a directed path from r to r'. Note that every record is a descendant of itself.

2.3 Queries

We assume the existence of a boolean *matching operator* $\propto$ of a term τ in a string $\mathbf{t}$ of terms (that is, $\propto$ is a subset of Terms $\times$ Terms*). For simplicity, in our examples we will always interpret $\tau \propto \mathbf{t}$ as (case-insensitive) membership of τ in the string $\mathbf{t}$. For example, america $\propto$ United States of America, but usa $\not\propto$ United States of America. The practical instantiation of this operator is irrelevant to this paper, and is discussed more in [6] (for example, in the practical implementation we are likely to have bill $\propto$ william, when the two terms refer to person names).

A *search query* is a string of terms, that is, a member $\mathbf{q}$ of Terms*. Every term of a search query is called a *keyword*. Let I be an instance, and let $\mathbf{q}$ be a search query. A URI u *matches* $\mathbf{q}$ if for every keyword τ of $\mathbf{q}$ there is an a-record $r \in I$ such that $\tau \propto txt(r)$ and $uri(r) = u$. As an example, consider the instance I of Figure 3, and let the search query $\mathbf{q}$ be laura haas number. We have that laura $\propto txt(r_{lh})$ and haas $\propto txt(r_{lh})$; hence, doc1 matches $\mathbf{q}$ if and only if $txt(r_{bd})$ contains the term number (hidden in the three dots). The same holds for doc2.

We generalize a search query by enriching it with structural constraints, in the context of a schema S, on the matched URIs and on the way keywords are matched. We call such a query an S-*hedge*. The formal definition is as follows.

DEFINITION 2.3. Let S be a schema. An S-*hedge* is a hedge h over S $\cup$ Terms such that for all edges (u, v) of h it holds that $label(u)$ is a concept, and $label(v)$ is either a term or a subconcept of $label(u)$. □

Note that the definition of an S-hedge implies that a node that is labeled with a term must be a leaf. The converse, however, is not true; a leaf can have any label of S $\cup$ Terms (i.e., a term, an a-concept, or a c-concept).

EXAMPLE 2.4. Consider again the schema S of our running example (Figure 1(a)). Figure 2 shows a search query $\mathbf{q}$ and three other S-hedges h_1, h_2 and h_3. For now, ignore the arrows between the hedges; these will be discussed later. Note that in each of these S-hedges, every term is a leaf, as is required by the definition. Also note that in h_2, the phone node is also a leaf, which is allowed. Finally, consider the edge from the prph node to the person node of h_3, and observe that, indeed, person $\in sc(\text{prph})$. □

Let I be an instance over a schema S, and let h be an S-hedge. A *match* of h in I is a mapping $\mu : nodes(h) \rightarrow I$, such that:

1. The image of μ consists of a single URI; that is, $uri(\mu(u)) = uri(\mu(v))$ for all nodes $u, v \in nodes(h)$. We denote this URI by $uri(\mu)$.[2]
2. For all nodes $v \in nodes(h)$, if $label(v)$ is a concept, then $label(v)$ is the concept of $\mu(v)$.
3. For all nodes $v \in nodes(h)$, if $label(v)$ is a term, then $label(v) \propto txt(\mu(v))$.
4. For all edges $(u, v) \in edges(h)$, if $label(v)$ is a concept γ, then $\mu(u)[\gamma] = \mu(v)$.
5. For all edges $(u, v) \in edges(h)$, if $label(v)$ is a term, then $\mu(v)$ is a descendant of $\mu(u)$.

Note that in the definition of a match μ, if an edge (u, v) of h is such that $label(u)$ is an a-concept (and so $label(v)$ is a term), then $\mu(u)$ and $\mu(v)$ must be the same; that holds due to Condition 5 and the fact that an a-record has no descendants other than itself. Also, if an edge (u, v) of h is such that $label(u)$ is a c-concept and $label(v)$ is a term (e.g., as in h_3 of Figure 2), then

---

[2]If h is empty, then $uri(\mu)$ is an arbitrary URI.

$\mu(v)$ should match the text of a descendant of $\mu(u)$ (that is, the descendant $\mu(v)$), since $\mu(u)$ itself is a c-record without text.

A URI u *matches* an **S**-hedge h if $u = uri(\mu)$ for some match μ of h in I.

EXAMPLE 2.5. Consider again the schema **S** of our running example (Figure 1(a)) and the instance I of Figure 3. We will illustrate the notion of a match by considering the **S**-hedge h_2 of Figure 2. Since every node of h_2 has a unique label, we will describe a match μ by means of mappings $\text{label}(v) \mapsto r$, where v is a node and r is a record. The following is a match μ of h_2 in I, such that $uri(\mu) = \texttt{doc2}$.

$$\overline{\text{prph}} \mapsto s_{\text{pp}} \quad \overline{\text{person}} \mapsto s_{\text{pr}} \quad \overline{\text{phone}} \mapsto s_{\text{ph}}$$
$$\texttt{laura} \mapsto s_{\text{pr}} \quad \texttt{haas} \mapsto s_{\text{pr}}$$

Consider Items 1–5 in the above definition of a match. Item 1 holds for μ since every record r in the image of μ is such that $uri(r) = \texttt{doc2}$ (hence, $uri(\mu) = \texttt{doc2}$). For Item 2, observe that each mapping $\gamma \mapsto r$, where γ is a concept, is such that γ is the concept of r. For Item 3, note that both $\texttt{laura}$ and $\texttt{haas}$ are mapped to s_{pr}, and $txt(s_{\text{pr}}) = \texttt{laura haas}$; hence $\texttt{laura} \propto txt(s_{\text{pr}})$ and $\texttt{haas} \propto txt(s_{\text{pr}})$ (under our specific interpretation of $\propto$ in the examples). For Item 4, note that the nodes of h_2 labeled $\overline{\text{prph}}$ and $\overline{\text{person}}$ (which are a parent and a child, respectively) are mapped to s_{pp} and s_{pr}, respectively, and indeed, $\overline{\text{person}}[s_{\text{pp}}] = s_{\text{pr}}$; the same holds for the nodes with the labels $\overline{\text{prph}}$ and $\overline{\text{phone}}$. Finally, for Item 5 observe that the nodes labeled $\overline{\text{person}}$, $\texttt{laura}$ and $\texttt{haas}$ are all mapped to the same record.

Since the match μ exists, we conclude that $\texttt{doc2}$ matches h_2. Note that $\texttt{doc2}$ also matches the **S**-hedge h_3; specifically, a proper match μ' is the following.

$$\overline{\text{prph}} \mapsto s_{\text{hm}} \quad \texttt{laura} \mapsto s_{\text{pr}} \quad \texttt{haas} \mapsto s_{\text{pr}}$$

Note that although $\texttt{doc1}$ contains the person $\texttt{laura haas}$ and a phone number, $\texttt{doc1}$ does not match h_2, since no phone number is associated with $\texttt{laura haas}$ (via the concept $\overline{\text{prph}}$). $\square$

We conclude this section with two remarks. First, the notions of a *database instance* and a *match* therein do not play any role in this paper, beyond providing the background that explains the meaning of an **S**-hedge within the search database system. Second, in some applications it may be desired that, for $\delta \in sc(\gamma)$, a γ-node of an **S**-hedge has at most one δ-child. For simplicity of presentation, we do not adopt this restriction; however, the results of this paper can be extended to allow it.

3. REWRITE PROGRAMS

In this section, we introduce the notion of a *rewrite program*, and give complexity results for testing properties of rewrite programs. We first give the definition of a rewrite program.

3.1 Definition

We fix an infinite set LVars of *label variables*, and an infinite set HVars of *hedge variables*. We assume that the sets Cncpt, Terms, LVars and HVars are pairwise disjoint.

DEFINITION 3.1. A *hedge expression* is a hedge E over Cncpt$\cup$ Terms $\cup$ LVars $\cup$ HVars, with the following properties.
1. Each variable of LVars$\cup$HVars has at most one occurrence in E (in the terminology of rewriting systems, E is *linear* [25]).
2. Each node of E with a label in HVars$\cup$Terms is a leaf of E.
We denote by LVars(E) and HVars(E) the sets of label variables and hedge variables, respectively, that occur in E. We also denote by Vars(E) the union LVars$(E) \cup$ HVars(E). $\square$

EXAMPLE 3.2. Figure 1(b), which is a part of our running example, shows the expressions E_i and F_i for $i = 1, 2, 3$. In all of the examples of this paper, hedge variables are represented by uppercase letters from the end of the Latin alphabet (e.g., X, Y and Z), and label variables are represented by lower-case from the end of the Latin alphabet (e.g., x, y and z). For the expression E_3, we have LVars$(E_3) = \{x, y\}$ and HVars$(E_3) = \{X, Y, Z\}$. $\square$

An *assignment* for a hedge expression E is a function α over Vars(E) that maps every label variable $x \in$ LVars(E) to an element $\alpha(x) \in$ Cncpt$\cup$Terms, and every hedge variable $X \in$ HVars to a hedge $\alpha(X)$ over Cncpt$\cup$ Terms. The *result* of the assignment α for E, denoted $\alpha(E)$, is the hedge that is obtained from E as follows.
- The label of every node v with $\text{label}(v) \in$ LVars is replaced with $\alpha(\text{label}(v))$.
- Every node v with $\text{label}(v) \in$ HVars is replaced with the hedge $\alpha(\text{label}(v))$; if v has a parent w in E, then w becomes the parent of each root node of $\alpha(\text{label}(v))$.

Let **S** be a schema, let E be a hedge expression, and let α be an assignment for E. We say that α is **S**-*consistent* if $\alpha(E)$ is an **S**-hedge. We also say that E is **S**-consistent if there exists an **S**-consistent assignment for E.

EXAMPLE 3.3. Consider again the expressions E_i and F_i (for $i = 1, 2, 3$) of our running example (Figure 1(b)). Let α be the assignment that maps x to $\overline{\text{prph}}$, y to $\texttt{laura}$, X to the empty hedge, Y to the (single-node) hedge $\texttt{haas}$, and Z to the (single-node) hedge $\overline{\text{phone}}$. Then $\alpha(E_3)$ is the hedge h_2 of Figure 2. As another example, let E be the hedge expression X $\texttt{number}$, and let α' be the assignment that maps X to the tree $\overline{\text{person}}(\texttt{laura haas})$. Then $\alpha'(E)$ is the hedge h_1 of Figure 2.

Recall the schema **S** of our running example (Figure 1(a)). Note that the above assignment α is **S**-consistent, since the hedge h_2 is an **S**-hedge. Hence, E_3 is **S**-consistent. It is easy to verify that each of the expressions of Figure 2 is **S**-consistent.

The reader may wonder what role the variable y plays in the expression E_3. The answer is that y guarantees that the string under $\overline{\text{person}}$ is nonempty, since every **S**-consistent assignment α maps y to a term. In contrast, an assignment for E_2 may place nothing under the $\overline{\text{person}}$ node, which happens when Y is mapped to the empty hedge. $\square$

The following theorem states that there is a polynomial-time algorithm for testing whether a given hedge expression is **S**-consistent. Our specific algorithm for realizing this result applies dynamic programming, based on a bottom-up traversal of the given expression.

THEOREM 3.4. *Testing whether a hedge expression E is* **S**-*consistent, given* **S** *and E, is in polynomial time.*

Next, we define a rewrite rule.

DEFINITION 3.5. A *rewrite rule* is an expression of the form $E \Rightarrow F$, where E and F are hedge expressions satisfying Vars$(F) \subseteq$ Vars(E). $\square$

Consider rule $E \Rightarrow F$, and let h be an **S**-hedge for some schema **S**. An assignment α for E, such that $\alpha(E) = h$, gives rise to the production of the hedge $\alpha(F)$.

EXAMPLE 3.6. Figure 1(b) shows the rewrite rules of our running example. Specifically, there are rewrite rules $E_i \Rightarrow F_i$, denoted ρ_i, for $i = 1, 2, 3$. Recall that the expressions E_i and F_i were discussed in Example 3.2. For ρ_3 we have that Vars$(F_3) = \{y, Y\}$

and $\mathrm{Vars}(E_3) = \{X, Y, Z, x, y\}$; hence, $\mathrm{Vars}(F_3) \subseteq \mathrm{Vars}(E_3)$, as required for a rewrite rule. Note that the variables x, X and Z appear in the left-hand side E_3 of rule ρ_3, but not in the right-hand side F_3. In particular, if ρ_3 is fired, then x is necessarily instantiated with either $\overline{\text{prhome}}$ or $\overline{\text{prph}}$, and rule ρ_3 says that we can then ignore the contents of X and Z and simply look for the relevant home page. $\square$

In terms of standard *rewriting systems* [25], our rules hold the following properties.

- *Hedge rewriting* [11] (i.e., they define a transformation of a hedge into another hedge).[3]
- *Context sensitive* [20]; actually, our rules are applied in a very special context: the full hedge (context) is captured in each of the two sides of a rule.
- *Linear* [25] (that is, every variable can have at most one occurrence in each side of the rule).
- *Conditional* [13]; this property means that the rule is applied to a hedge h only when h satisfies some condition, and here are condition is conformance to the schema **S**.

In addition, to the best of our knowledge the label variable (which is needed to express, e.g., non-emptiness of the assigned hedges) has not been used in hedge rewriting.

Among the rewrite rules that are used in our implemented system (developed at IBM Research–Almaden), many rules are what we call *replacement rules*. Intuitively, when such a rule is applied to an **S**-hedge $t_1 \cdots t_n$, it replaces a sub-hedge $h = t_k \cdots t_{k+i}$ with a new hedge h' in a context-free manner. Formally, a replacement rule has the form $X h Y \Rightarrow X h' Y$, where X and Y are hedge variables (as implied by the notation), and h and h' are hedges that contain no variables (that is, h and h' are hedges over $\mathsf{Cncpt} \cup \mathsf{Terms}$). As an example, in Figure 1(b) the rule ρ_1 is a replacement rule, but neither ρ_2 nor ρ_3 is a replacement rule (specifically, note that in each side of ρ_2 the hedge between X and Z contains a variable Y, and that cannot happen in a replacement rule). Furthermore, a replacement rule $X h Y \Rightarrow X h' Y$ is a *semi-Thue* rule [25] if h and h' are search queries (i.e., consist of only terms).

Next, we consider consistency of a rewrite rule with a schema.

DEFINITION 3.7. Let **S** be a schema. A rewrite rule $E \Rightarrow F$ is **S**-consistent if the following hold.

1. E is **S**-consistent (i.e., there exists an **S**-consistent assignment for E).
2. $\alpha(F)$ is an **S**-hedge for all **S**-consistent assignments α for E. $\square$

EXAMPLE 3.8. Consider again the schema **S** and the rules ρ_i (for $i = 1, 2, 3$) of our running example (Figure 1). Recall from Example 3.3 that each E_i (and each F_i) is **S**-consistent. We claim that each ρ_i is **S**-consistent, and we will prove that for ρ_2 (the proofs for ρ_1 and ρ_3 are similar or simpler). Let α be an **S**-consistent assignment for E_2. Then $\alpha(F_2)$ is an **S**-hedge if and only if $\alpha(Y)$ is a hedge that can be put under $\overline{\text{person}}$; since $\overline{\text{person}}$ is an a-concept, a $\overline{\text{person}}$ node can have only terms as children. But, it is guaranteed that $\alpha(Y)$ consists of only terms, because α is **S**-consistent for E_2, and in E_2 the Y node is a child of the $\overline{\text{person}}$ node.

Consider now the rule $E \Rightarrow F$, which we denote by ρ, of Figure 4. Clearly, both E and F are **S**-consistent. Nevertheless, ρ itself is not **S**-consistent, since there is an **S**-consistent assignment α that maps x to $\overline{\text{prhome}}$, and yet, $\overline{\text{phone}}$ (which occurs in F under x) is not a subconcept of $\overline{\text{prhome}}$. $\square$

---

[3]To the best of our knowledge, the vast majority of the literature on rewriting systems considers *term rewriting* and *string rewriting* that apply transformations to trees and strings, respectively.

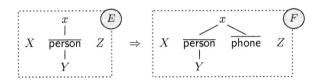

Figure 4: A rule ρ that is not S-consistent

Observe that if ρ is the replacement rule $X h Y \Rightarrow X h' Y$, then ρ is **S**-consistent if and only if both of its sides are **S**-consistent, which is equivalent to saying that both h and h' are **S**-hedges.

The following theorem states that there is a polynomial-time algorithm for testing whether a given rule $E \Rightarrow F$ is **S**-consistent. We have an interesting algorithm for realizing this result. Intuitively, our algorithm attempts to find labels that, if used instead of certain variables, would make F inconsistent while leaving E consistent; for these consistency tests, we use the algorithm of Theorem 3.4.

THEOREM 3.9. *Testing for the **S**-consistency of a rewrite rule ρ, given **S** and ρ, is in polynomial time.*

Finally, we define a *rewrite program*.

DEFINITION 3.10. A *rewrite program* is pair $(\mathbf{S}, R)$, where **S** is a schema, and R is a finite set of **S**-consistent rewrite rules. $\square$

EXAMPLE 3.11. For the schema **S** and the set R of our running example (Figure 1), the pair $(\mathbf{S}, R)$ is a rewrite program. Recall from Example 3.8 that each of the rules of R is **S**-consistent (hence, $(\mathbf{S}, R)$ indeed satisfies the definition of a rewrite program). $\square$

3.2 Semantics of a Rewrite Program

A rewrite program $(\mathbf{S}, R)$ is used within the execution of a search engine, having an instance I over **S**, and the rewrite program is applied as follows (at least conceptually). Given a search query **q** submitted by the user, each rule of R that is applicable to **q** is applied to **q**, generating new **S**-hedges h. We then further apply the rules of R to the generated **S**-hedges h, and continue doing so until no new **S**-hedge can be produced. (Later on, we will discuss the question of whether or not this process indeed terminates.) We then use the set of generated **S**-hedges, first for finding the URIs (of the instance I) that match the final set of hedges, and second for *ranking*, which we discuss briefly at the beginning of Section 4.

We now formally define the application of a rewrite program $(\mathbf{S}, R)$ to a search query **q**. For **S**-hedges h_1 and h_2, we denote by $h_1 \Rightarrow_R h_2$ the fact that there is a rule $E \Rightarrow F$ of R and an assignment α for E, such that $h_1 = \alpha(E)$ and $h_2 = \alpha(F)$. The $(\mathbf{S}, R)$-*graph* is a special case of the well-known notion of an *abstract rewrite system*, and is formally defined as follows.

DEFINITION 3.12. The $(\mathbf{S}, R)$-*graph*, denoted $\mathcal{G}(\mathbf{S}, R)$, is the infinite directed graph (V, E), where V is the set of all **S**-hedges, and E contains all the edges (h_1, h_2), such that $h_1 \Rightarrow_R h_2$. $\square$

We view $(\mathbf{S}, R)$ as a logic program that gets as input a single search string $\mathbf{q} \in \mathsf{Terms}^*$, and produces a set of **S**-hedges, such that this set forms a *least fixpoint* (which we often abbreviate as *lfp*). More precisely, let h be an **S**-hedge (e.g., a search query), and let H be a (possibly infinite) set of **S**-hedges. We say that H is a *fixpoint* for h if $h \in H$, and furthermore, for all **S**-hedges h_1 and h_2 with $h_1 \Rightarrow_R h_2$, if $h_1 \in H$ then $h_2 \in H$ as well. We say that H is a *least fixpoint* for h if H is a fixpoint for **q**, and $H \subseteq H'$ for all fixpoints H' for **q**.

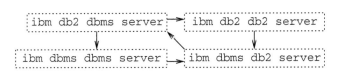

Figure 5: The subgraph of $\mathcal{G}(\mathbf{S}, R')$ that is reachable from `ibm db2 dbms server`

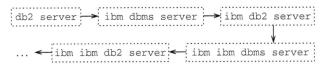

Figure 6: The infinite subgraph of $\mathcal{G}(\mathbf{S}, R'')$ reachable from `ibm db2 server`

By applying standard observations from fixpoint logic, it easily follows that a least fixpoint for a hedge h always exists, and is unique: it is exactly the set of $\mathbf{S}$-hedges that are reachable from h in $\mathcal{G}(\mathbf{S}, R)$. We denote by $lfp_R^{\mathbf{S}}(h)$ the least fixpoint for h. When R and $\mathbf{S}$ are clear from the context, we may write just $lfp(h)$ instead of $lfp_R^{\mathbf{S}}(h)$.

We can now formalize the application of a rewrite program to a search query (we informally discussed this notion at the beginning of this section). Given a search query $\mathbf{q}$ submitted by the user, *applying* $(\mathbf{S}, R)$ *to* $\mathbf{q}$ means generating the set $lfp(\mathbf{q})$ (and terminating if $lfp(\mathbf{q})$ is finite).

EXAMPLE 3.13. Consider the rewrite program $(\mathbf{S}, R)$ of our running example (Figure 1). Consider also the search query $\mathbf{q}$ of Figure 2 and the $\mathbf{S}$-hedges h_i (for $i = 1, 2, 3$) of Figure 2. When taking the arrows entering the h_i in Figure 2 as directed edges, the figure actually shows a path in (hence, a subgraph of) $\mathcal{G}(\mathbf{S}, R)$. Note that the rules ρ_i labeling the edges are not a part of $\mathcal{G}(\mathbf{S}, R)$; they are given only for convenience (i.e., to show the rule that gives rise to the edge). The reader can easily verify that $lfp(\mathbf{q}) = \{\mathbf{q}, h_1, h_2, h_3\}$. □

EXAMPLE 3.14. Let $\mathbf{S}$ be a schema. Consider the following set R' of three replacement rules, saying that a user can use `ibm db2` to refer to `ibm dbms`, `dbms server` to refer to `db2 server`, and `dbms db2` to refer to `db2 dbms`.

$$X \; \text{ibm db2} \; Y \Rightarrow X \; \text{ibm dbms} \; Y$$
$$X \; \text{dbms server} \; Y \Rightarrow X \; \text{db2 server} \; Y$$
$$X \; \text{dbms db2} \; Y \Rightarrow X \; \text{db2 dbms} \; Y$$

Figure 5 shows the subgraph of $\mathcal{G}(\mathbf{S}, R')$ that is reachable from the search query `ibm db2 dbms server`.

Now consider the set R'' that consists of the following two replacement rules:

$$X \; \text{db2} \; Y \Rightarrow X \; \text{ibm dbms} \; Y$$
$$X \; \text{dbms server} \; Y \Rightarrow X \; \text{db2 server} \; Y$$

Note that the rules of R'' are the first two rules of R', except that the left-hand side of the first rule is `db2` instead of `ibm db2`. Figure 6 shows the subgraph of $\mathcal{G}(\mathbf{S}, R'')$ that is reachable from `db2 server`. Note that this subgraph is an infinite path that contains every string of the form $\text{ibm}^n \; \text{db2 server}$ for $n \in \mathbb{N}$, where ibm^n is the string `ibm` repeated n times. □

We emphasize that, unlike the usual interest in rewriting systems, in our semantics there is no (a priori) importance to whether or not

a hedge h is a *normal form* (or *irreducible*, which means that no rule can be applied to h for producing a different hedge).

4. LFP-CONVERGENCE

Recall that when applying a program $(\mathbf{S}, R)$ to a search query $\mathbf{q}$, we would like to produce the set $lfp(\mathbf{q})$. From a practical point of view, having the set $lfp(\mathbf{q})$ at hand is important not only to identify the set of matching documents, but also for the crucial task of *ranking* (which is beyond the scope of this paper). Essentially, in our system hedges are ranked by reasoning about their properties (e.g., the concepts involved) and the set of rules involved in producing the hedges. For example, some rules are marked as "improving" the query, and when ranking matching documents such information is incorporated along with other measures (e.g., the extent to which keywords are matched, and the global quality of documents). Therefore, it is critical that the production of $lfp(\mathbf{q})$ will terminate on every search query $\mathbf{q}$ (and if that is not the case, then the program violates the intent of the developer phrasing the rules). A rewrite program with this property is said to be *lfp-convergent*. The formal definition follows.

DEFINITION 4.1. A rewrite program $(\mathbf{S}, R)$ is *lfp-convergent* if $lfp(\mathbf{q})$ is finite for all search queries $\mathbf{q} \in \text{Terms}^*$. □

EXAMPLE 4.2. Consider again the rewrite program $(\mathbf{S}, R)$ in Example 3.11 for our running example, and consider the sets R' and R'' defined in Example 3.14. In Section 5, we will show that the programs $(\mathbf{S}, R)$ and $(\mathbf{S}, R')$ are both lfp-convergent. However, the program $(\mathbf{S}, R'')$ is not lfp-convergent, since $lfp(\mathbf{q})$ is infinite when $\mathbf{q}$ is the search query `ibm db2 server` (as explained in Example 3.14). □

According to Definition 4.1, a rewrite program $(\mathbf{S}, R)$ is lfp-convergent if $lfp(h)$ is finite whenever the $\mathbf{S}$-hedge h is a search query. A closely related notion is *weak termination* (or *quasi-termination*) [8], which in our setting means that $lfp(h)$ is finite for *every* $\mathbf{S}$-hedge h (rather than for only those that are search queries). For clarity of presentation, here we call weak termination *strong lfp-convergence*. For instance, we will later show that the rewrite program $(\mathbf{S}, R)$ of our running example is strongly lfp-convergent. Clearly, strong lfp-convergence implies lfp-convergence; the other direction, though, is not true, as the following example illustrates.

EXAMPLE 4.3. Let $\mathbf{S}$ be the schema of our running example (Figure 1(a)), and consider the set R that consists of the following single replacement rule:

$$X \; \overline{\text{person}} \; Y \Rightarrow X \; \overline{\text{person}} \; \text{facebook} \; Y$$

Let h be the single-node $\mathbf{S}$-hedge $\overline{\text{person}}$. Clearly, $lfp(h)$ is infinite (as it includes the $\mathbf{S}$-hedge $\overline{\text{person}} \; \text{facebook}^n$ for all $n \in \mathbb{N}$), and hence, the system $(\mathbf{S}, R)$ is not strongly lfp-convergent. However, the one rule of R is not applicable to a search query $\mathbf{q}$ (since $\mathbf{q}$ does not contain the concept $\overline{\text{person}}$). That implies that $lfp(\mathbf{q}) = \{\mathbf{q}\}$ for all search queries $\mathbf{q}$, and in particular, $(\mathbf{S}, R)$ is lfp-convergent.

More interesting is the set R' with the following two rules:

$$\text{locate number} \; X \Rightarrow \overline{\text{phone}} \; \overline{\text{person}} \; X$$
$$\overline{\text{phone}} \; x \; Y \Rightarrow x \; \overline{\text{phone}} \; \text{whitepages} \; Y$$

Unlike the set R in the previous example, both rules of R' can fire. For example, the first rule rewrites `locate number laura` as $\overline{\text{phone}} \; \overline{\text{person}} \; \text{laura}$, which in then rewritten by the second rule as $\overline{\text{person}} \; \overline{\text{phone}} \; \text{whitepages} \; \text{laura}$. It is easy to see that for a search query $\mathbf{q}$, either none of the two rules is applicable (and then $lfp(\mathbf{q}) = \{\mathbf{q}\}$), or each of the two rules is applied exactly once (and then $lfp(\mathbf{q})$ has exactly three hedges). Therefore, $(\mathbf{S}, R')$ is lfp-convergent. However, $(\mathbf{S}, R')$ is not strongly lfp-convergent. For example, $lfp(h)$ is infinite for $h = $ phone phone; to see that, note that using just the second rule, h is transformed into phone phone whitepages, which is transformed into phone phone whitepages whitepages, and so on, so that $lfp(h)$ contains phone phone whitepages^n for all $n \in \mathbb{N}$. $\square$

Ideally, we would like to be able to verify that a rewrite program is lfp-convergent, and warn the developer if not. A typical use case of such verification is when a new rule is added to the program; if the program is non-lfp-convergent following this addition, then the developer is urged to modify (or avoid) the new rule, or to change rules that already exist in the program. One may desire a closely related verification at runtime: once a query $\mathbf{q}$ is submitted by a user, verify that $lfp(\mathbf{q})$ is finite before applying the program.

Unfortunately, the following theorem, which follows easily from the work of Guttag et al. [8] (specifically, their results on weak termination), implies that neither of the above two types of verification is possible in the general case. Specifically, the theorem states that lfp-convergence (or strong lfp-convergence) of a given rewrite program $(\mathbf{S}, R)$, as well as finiteness of $lfp(\mathbf{q})$ for a given search query $\mathbf{q}$, is undecidable. Furthermore, undecidability remains even if only replacement rules are allowed, and even if we fix *any* schema $\mathbf{S}$.

THEOREM 4.4. *Let $\mathbf{S}$ be a fixed schema. The following problems are undecidable.*
1. *Given a set R of $\mathbf{S}$-consistent replacement rules, determine whether $(\mathbf{S}, R)$ is (strongly) lfp-convergent.*
2. *Given a set R of $\mathbf{S}$-consistent replacement rules and a search query $\mathbf{q}$, determine whether $lfp(\mathbf{q})$ is finite.*

In the next sections, we devise tractable *safety conditions* that are sufficient (but not necessary) for lfp-convergence.

5. SAFETY CONDITION

Theorem 4.4 shows that it is impossible to determine automatically whether a given rewrite program is lfp-convergent. Still, we would like to have a tractable *safety condition*, which guarantees lfp-convergence, and which is robust enough to capture lfp-convergence in practical rewrite programs.

There is a vast literature on proof techniques for *termination* of rewrite systems (e.g., [1, 3, 4, 14]), especially for tree rewriting. In our terminology, usual termination means that the $(\mathbf{S}, R)$-graph has no infinite paths (e.g., cycles). These techniques find a *well-founded* order on the set of trees, such that the order is respected by the rules [18]. But recall that there is a major difference between termination and lfp-convergence (or weak termination). As a simple example, the program $(\mathbf{S}, R')$ of Example 3.14 is clearly non-terminating (see Figure 5), but is nevertheless (strongly) lfp-convergent as we show later. Examples like that are abundant in practical rewrite programs, since they include replacements among synonyms and similar terms, and such rules cause cycles.

There are also proof techniques for weak termination [5,7]. However, it is not at all clear to us how these existing techniques can be translated into efficient (i.e., polynomial-time) safety checking (rather than just proof techniques). More importantly, to the best of our knowledge none of the existing techniques for weak termination takes into account the special (key) properties of our rewrite programs, notably linearity and being an extreme case of context sensitive (i.e., the whole context is represented). Finally, to the

best of our knowledge, weak termination has not been studied for hedge rewriting. Therefore, in this section we propose a tractable safety condition. In Section 5.5, we will discuss the performance of the safety condition in our implemented search database system, where we found the condition to be highly successful in capturing lfp-convergence.

5.1 Definitions and Notation

We first need some definitions and notation. The principal new notions are those of an *invocation path*, an *invocation cycle*, and a *guarding potential*.

5.1.1 Invocation Paths and Cycles

Let $\mathbf{S}$ be a schema, and let E_1 and E_2 be two hedge expressions. We say that E_1 and E_2 are $\mathbf{S}$-*unifiable* if there are $\mathbf{S}$-consistent assignments α_1 and α_2 for E_1 and E_2, respectively, such that $\alpha_1(E_1) = \alpha_2(E_2)$. For example, an easy observation is that every two $\mathbf{S}$-consistent hedge expressions that start and end with hedge variables (e.g., expressions of the form $X \ E \ Y$ where E is $\mathbf{S}$ consistent) are $\mathbf{S}$-unifiable.[4] In particular, if $E_1 \Rightarrow F_1$ and $E_2 \Rightarrow F_2$ are replacement rules, then every two expressions in $\{E_1, F_1, E_2, F_2\}$ are $\mathbf{S}$-unifiable. Additional examples are given next.

EXAMPLE 5.1. Consider again the rewrite program $(\mathbf{S}, R)$ of our running example (Figure 1). The expressions F_2 and E_3 are $\mathbf{S}$-unifiable, since there are assignments α_2 and α_3 for F_2 and E_3, respectively, such that $\alpha_2(E_2) = \alpha_3(F_3) = h_2$, where the $\mathbf{S}$-hedge h_2 is depicted in Figure 2. Due to the remark preceding this example, every pair in $\{E_1, F_1, E_2, F_2\}$ is $\mathbf{S}$-unifiable (since each of them starts and ends with a hedge variable). It is easy to show that for all $E' \in \{E_1, F_1, E_2, F_3\}$, the expressions E_3 and E' are not $\mathbf{S}$-unifiable; similarly, for all $E' \in \{E_1, F_1, E_2, F_2, E_3\}$, the expressions F_3 and E' are not $\mathbf{S}$-unifiable. $\square$

Next, we define the notions of an *invocation path* and an *invocation cycle*.

DEFINITION 5.2. Let $(\mathbf{S}, R)$ be a rewrite program. An *invocation path* is a (finite or infinite) sequence $E_1 \Rightarrow F_1, E_2 \Rightarrow F_2 \ldots$ of rules of R, such that F_i and E_{i+1} are $\mathbf{S}$-unifiable for all i. A finite invocation path $E_1 \Rightarrow F_1, \ldots, E_n \Rightarrow F_n$ is an *invocation cycle* if F_n and E_1 are $\mathbf{S}$-unifiable. $\square$

Note that in an invocation path $E_1 \Rightarrow F_1, E_2 \Rightarrow F_2 \ldots$, the rules $E_i \Rightarrow F_i$ are not necessarily distinct. It is not hard to show that a cycle in the graph $\mathcal{G}(\mathbf{S}, R)$ (which was defined in Definition 3.12) implies the existence of an invocation cycle. However, the converse is not necessarily true. As a simple example of the failure of the converse, let R consist of the single rewrite rule ibm $X \Rightarrow X$, which might be a rule in an IBM intranet system where ibm is a noise word, and let p consist of this single rule. It is straightforward to verify that p is an invocation cycle of $(\mathbf{S}, R)$, but that there is no cycle in $\mathcal{G}(\mathbf{S}, R)$.

If p is an invocation path, we denote by rules(p) the set of all rewrite rules $E_i \Rightarrow F_i$ that participate in p. In the sequel, we may discuss an invocation path without mentioning the underlying rewrite program $(\mathbf{S}, R)$.

EXAMPLE 5.3. We consider again the rewrite program $(\mathbf{S}, R)$ of our running example (Figure 1). Recall that $\mathbf{S}$-unifiability among the E_i and the F_i is discussed in Example 5.1. It follows from

---

[4]This is true since if α and α' are assignments for E and E', respectively, then there are assignments for $X \ E \ Y$ and $X' \ E' \ Y'$ that produce $\alpha(E)\alpha(E')$.

the observations in Example 5.1 that the following are invocation paths:

- $p_1 : E_1 \Rightarrow F_1, E_2 \Rightarrow F_2, E_2 \Rightarrow F_2$
- $p_2 : E_1 \Rightarrow F_1$
- $p_3 : E_2 \Rightarrow F_2, E_3 \Rightarrow F_3$
- $p_4 : E_1 \Rightarrow F_1, E_2 \Rightarrow F_2, E_1 \Rightarrow F_1, E_2 \Rightarrow F_2, \cdots$

Note that p_1, p_2 and p_3 are finite invocation paths, while p_4 is infinite. Also note that p_1 is an invocation cycle, since F_2 and E_1 are **S**-unifiable. Similarly, p_2 is an invocation cycle, since F_1 and E_1 are **S**-unifiable. Finally, p_3 is not an invocation cycle, since F_3 and E_2 are not **S**-unifiable. □

Let E be a hedge expression. We denote by $\|E\|$ the number of nodes v of E, such that label(v) is not a hedge variable (i.e., label(v) is a term, a concept, or a label variable). Note that a term or a concept can be counted multiple times if it has multiple occurrences in E. Next, we define when a finite invocation path is *expanding*.

DEFINITION 5.4. An invocation path $E_1 \Rightarrow F_1, \ldots, E_n \Rightarrow F_n$ is said to be *expanding* if $\sum_{i=1}^{n} \|E_i\| < \sum_{i=1}^{n} \|F_i\|$; otherwise, $E_1 \Rightarrow F_1, \ldots, E_n \Rightarrow F_n$ is *nonexpanding*. □

For instance, consider the paths p_1 and p_3 of Example 5.3. For p_1 we have $\|E_1\| + \|E_2\| + \|E_2\| = 2 + 2 + 2 = 6$ and $\|F_1\| + \|F_2\| + \|F_2\| = 3 + 3 + 3 = 9$; hence p_1 is expanding. For p_3 we have $\|E_2\| + \|E_3\| = 2 + 3 = 5$ and $\|F_2\| + \|F_3\| = 3 + 2 = 5$; hence, p_3 is nonexpanding. Another example is given next.

EXAMPLE 5.5. Let **S** be a schema, and consider the set R that consists of the following three rules:

- X home $\Rightarrow X$ home page
- X home page $\Rightarrow X$ personal info page
- X page $\Rightarrow X$

Denote the first rule by $E_1 \Rightarrow F_1$, the second by $E_2 \Rightarrow F_2$, and the third by $E_3 \Rightarrow F_3$. Note that F_1 and E_2 are **S**-unifiable, and so are F_2 and E_3, and F_3 and E_1. Also **S**-unifiable are F_1 and E_3, and F_3 and E_i for all $i \in \{1, 2, 3\}$. Let p_1 be the invocation path $E_1 \Rightarrow F_1$. Since $\|E_1\| = 1$ and $\|F_1\| = 2$, the path p_1 is expanding. Now, consider the following two invocation cycles:

- $p : E_1 \Rightarrow F_1, E_2 \Rightarrow F_2, E_3 \Rightarrow F_3$
- $p' : E_1 \Rightarrow F_1, E_3 \Rightarrow F_3$

For p we have $\|E_1\| + \|E_2\| + \|E_3\| = 4$ and $\|F_1\| + \|F_2\| + \|F_3\| = 5$; hence, p is expanding. But for p' we have $\|E_1\| + \|E_3\| = \|F_1\| + \|F_3\| = 2$, and hence, p' is nonexpanding. □

5.1.2 Guarding Potentials

We call a member of Cncpt ∪ Terms a *constant*. Furthermore, if v is a node of a hedge expression E, and label(v) is a constant, then we call v a *constant node*. We denote by nodes$^{ct}(E)$ the set of all constant nodes of E; that is, nodes$^{ct}(E) = \{v \in \text{nodes}(E) \mid \text{label}(v) \in \text{Cncpt} \cup \text{Terms}\}$.

In this paper, a *potential function* (or just *potential* for short) is a numerical nonnegative function π over the constants; that is, $\pi : \text{Cncpt} \cup \text{Terms} \rightarrow [0, \infty)$. If E is a hedge expression and π is a potential, then we define:

$$\pi(E) \stackrel{\text{def}}{=} \sum_{v \in \text{nodes}^{ct}(E)} \pi(\text{label}(v))$$

Let π be a potential, let $E \Rightarrow F$ be a rule, and let R be a set of rewrite rules. We say that π is *(1) nonincreasing on* ρ if $\pi(E) \geq \pi(F)$, *(2) decreasing on* ρ if $\pi(E) > \pi(F)$, *(3) nonincreasing on* R if π is nonincreasing on every rule of R, *(4) weakly decreasing on* R if π is nonincreasing on R and decreasing on one or more

rules of R, *and (5) positive-nonincreasing on* R if π is nonincreasing on R and $\pi(c) > 0$ for all the constants c that appear in R. Lastly, we define a *guarding potential*.

DEFINITION 5.6. A *guarding potential* for a set R of rules is a potential π that is either weakly decreasing on R or positive-nonincreasing on R. A *guarding potential* for an invocation cycle p is a guarding potential for rules(p). □

EXAMPLE 5.7. Let **S** be a schema, and let R be the set of rules from Example 5.5. Consider again the invocation cycles p and p' of Example 5.5. Define the potential π by $\pi(\text{home}) = 1$ and $\pi(c) = 0$ for every other constant c. Note that π is nonincreasing on rules(p); for example, $\pi(E_1) = \pi(F_1) = 1$ and $\pi(E_3) = \pi(F_3) = 0$. Moreover, $\pi(E_2) = 1$ and $\pi(F_2) = 0$ (since home occurs in E_2 but not in F_2); hence, π is weakly decreasing on rules(p). Thus, π is a guarding potential for p.

Note that π is not a guarding potential for p', since π is neither weakly decreasing nor positive-nonincreasing on rules(p'). Actually, there is no guarding potential for p': if π' is such a potential, then $\pi'(\text{page}) > 0$ must hold; but then, $\pi'(E_1) < \pi'(F_1)$, as opposed to the fact that a guarding potential is nonincreasing. □

EXAMPLE 5.8. A common use of rewrite rules is to apply substitution among acronyms. Such a substitution is done by a set of replacement rules as in the following example:

- X nyc $Y \Rightarrow X$ new york city Y
- X new york city $Y \Rightarrow X$ big apple Y
- X big apple $Y \Rightarrow X$ nyc Y

Note that the three rules are replacement rules, which implies that every two of the hedge expressions are **S**-unifiable (for the underlying schema **S**). Consider an invocation cycle p that contains all three rules. An easy observation is that there is no potential that is weakly decreasing on rules(p). However, positive-nonincreasing on p is the potential π defined by the following assignments:[5]

- $\pi(\text{nyc}) = 1$
- $\pi(\text{new}) = \pi(\text{york}) = \pi(\text{city}) = \frac{1}{3}$
- $\pi(\text{big}) = \pi(\text{apple}) = \frac{1}{2}$

Observe that π is indeed positive-nonincreasing on p, and hence, π is a guarding potential for p. □

5.2 The Safety Condition

We can now present our safety condition for a rewrite program.

SAFETY CONDITION. *Every expanding invocation cycle has a guarding potential.*

A program $(\mathbf{S}, R)$ that satisfies the safety condition is said to be *safe*; otherwise it is *unsafe*. The following theorem states the correctness of the safety condition, that is, that its satisfaction guarantees lfp-convergence. Actually, even strong lfp-convergence is guaranteed. (Recall from Theorem 4.4 that strong lfp-convergence is undecidable, as is usual lfp-convergence.) The proof shows a contradiction to the existence of a simple infinite path of $\mathcal{G}(\mathbf{S}, R)$ which, by an argument similar to the proof of König's lemma [15], must be present in the absence of strong lfp-convergence.

THEOREM 5.9. *Every safe rewrite program* $(\mathbf{S}, R)$ *is strongly lfp-convergent.*

A simple example of a safe (hence, lfp-convergent) rewrite program is the program $(\mathbf{S}, R')$ of Example 3.14. There, $\|E\| = \|F\| = 2$ for each rewrite rule $E \Rightarrow F$, and therefore, every invocation cycle is nonexpanding. Next, we give additional examples.

[5]Here and in other places, we define a potential only on the constants used in the rewrite program at hand; the rest of the potential is irrelevant, and can be defined arbitrarily.

EXAMPLE 5.10. Let $\mathbf{S}$ and R be as defined in Example 5.5. We will now prove that $(\mathbf{S}, R)$ is safe. Later, we will give an efficient algorithm for testing safety; for now, the proof will be ad hoc. Consider the invocation cycles p and p' that are given in Example 5.5 and discussed in Example 5.7. In Example 5.7 we showed that p has a guarding potential π, and in the same way it is shown that π is a guarding potential for *every* invocation cycle that includes the rule $E_2 \Rightarrow F_2$. Hence, it suffices to consider invocation cycles p'_0 that use only $E_1 \Rightarrow F_1$ and $E_3 \Rightarrow F_3$. Let p'_0 be such a cycle. Suppose that p'_0 is $E'_1 \Rightarrow F'_1, \ldots, E'_n \Rightarrow F'_n$ (where each $E'_i \Rightarrow F'_i$ is either $E_1 \Rightarrow F_1$ or $E_3 \Rightarrow F_3$). Every occurrence of $E_1 \Rightarrow F_1$ adds 1 to $\sum_{i=1}^{n} \|E'_i\|$ and 2 to $\sum_{i=1}^{n} \|F'_i\|$. Every occurrence of $E_3 \Rightarrow F_3$ adds 1 to $\sum_{i=1}^{n} \|E'_i\|$ and 0 to $\sum_{i=1}^{n} \|F'_i\|$. An easy observation is that if $E'_1 = E_1$, then every occurrence of $E_1 \Rightarrow F_1$ is followed by an occurrence of $E_3 \Rightarrow F_3$, and if $E'_1 = E_3$, then every occurrence of $E_1 \Rightarrow F_1$ is preceded by an occurrence of $E_3 \Rightarrow F_3$. Hence, in both cases, p'_0 contains at least as many occurrences of $E_3 \Rightarrow F_3$ as of $E_1 \Rightarrow F_1$, which implies that $\sum_{i=1}^{n} \|E'_i\| \geq \sum_{i=1}^{n} \|F'_i\|$ (i.e., p'_0 is nonexpanding). $\square$

EXAMPLE 5.11. Consider again the rewrite program $(\mathbf{S}, R)$ of our running example (Figure 1). Let p be the invocation cycle $E_1 \Rightarrow F_1$ (consisting of one occurrence of ρ_1). Note that p is expanding, since $\|E_1\| = 2$ and $\|F_1\| = 3$. Moreover, the bag of constants of E_1 is strictly contained in the bag of constants of F_1, and this easily implies that there is no guarding potential for p. Hence, $(\mathbf{S}, R)$ is unsafe. However, as we discuss next, we will later show that $(\mathbf{S}, R)$ is lfp-convergent, and moreover, its lfp-convergence can be verified by a simple relaxation of the safety condition. $\square$

The rule ρ_1 of our running example (Figure 1) belongs to an important class of rewrite rules, which we call *Context-Free Grammar* (*CFG*) rules and discuss later in Section 5.4. We will show how to relax our safety condition to accommodate these rules. We will also show that the program $(\mathbf{S}, R)$ of Example 5.11 satisfies the relaxed safety condition, and hence, is (strongly) lfp-convergent.

Recall that safety is defined due to the inability to test for lfp-convergence. Of course, it would be useless unless safety checking is tractable. This tractability is not at all clear since, on the face of it, infinitely many invocation cycles need to be inspected. In the next section, we describe an algorithm that shows the surprising result that safety can be tested in polynomial time.

5.3 Algorithm for Safety Checking

In this section, we present a polynomial-time algorithm for testing the safety of a rewrite program. Our algorithm operates on the *expression graph*, which we now define.

Let $(\mathbf{S}, R)$ be a rewrite program, and let $E \Rightarrow F$ be a rule in R. We call E a *left expression* of R, and we call F a *right expression* of R. The *expression graph* of $(\mathbf{S}, R)$, denoted $\mathcal{X}(\mathbf{S}, R)$, is the directed and edge-weighted graph G that is defined as follows. First, for each left expression E of R there is a unique node v_E^l in G, and similarly, for each right expression F of R there is a unique node v_F^r in G. Second, G has an edge e from v_E^l to v_F^r if $E \Rightarrow F$ is a rule of R; in this case, the weight of e is $\|F\| - \|E\|$. Finally, G has an edge e from v_F^r to v_E^l if F and E are $\mathbf{S}$-unifiable; in this case, the weight of e is zero.

EXAMPLE 5.12. The left side of Figure 7 depicts the graph $\mathcal{X}(\mathbf{S}, R)$ of the rewrite program $(\mathbf{S}, R)$ of our running example (Figure 1). Note that there are three rightward edges that correspond to the three rules of R. The leftward edges go from every F_i to every E_j such that F_i and E_j are unifiable. Recall that unifiability among these rules is discussed in Example 5.1. The graph specifies the weights only for rightward edges, while the weights of the

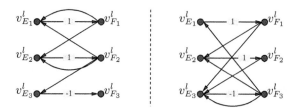

Figure 7: The expression graphs $\mathcal{X}(\mathbf{S}, R)$ of the rewrite programs $(\mathbf{S}, R)$ of the running example of Figure 1 (left) and Example 5.5 (right)

leftward edges are zero by definition. As an example, the weight on the edge from $v_{E_3}^l$ to $v_{F_3}^r$ is -1, since $\|F_3\| - \|E_3\| = 2 - 3 = -1$.

The graph $\mathcal{X}(\mathbf{S}, R)$ in the right-hand side of Figure 7 is that of the program $(\mathbf{S}, R)$ of Example 5.5. $\square$

We denote our algorithm for checking the safety of a rewrite program $(\mathbf{S}, R)$ by IsSafe$(\mathbf{S}, R)$, and the pseudo-code is given in Figure 8. Our algorithm operates on the expression graph. Of course, the expression graph can be constructed in polynomial time if $\mathbf{S}$-unifiability can be decided in polynomial time. Hence, the following lemma is needed.

LEMMA 5.13. *Testing whether two hedge expressions are $\mathbf{S}$-unifiable, given the expressions and $\mathbf{S}$, is in polynomial time. Hence, the expression graph can be constructed in polynomial time.*

The first step of the algorithm is based on the observation that $(\mathbf{S}, R)$ has an expanding invocation cycle if and only if $\mathcal{X}(\mathbf{S}, R)$ has a positive cycle (i.e., a cycle such that the weights on the edges sum up to a positive number). We abbreviate "positive-weight cycle" by simply "positive cycle." This means that lack of positive cycles in $\mathcal{X}(\mathbf{S}, R)$ implies safety. So, in lines 1–2 the algorithm tests whether $\mathcal{X}(\mathbf{S}, R)$ has a positive cycle, and if not, it terminates by returning **true**; otherwise, the algorithm continues to the next steps. Note that testing whether a graph has a positive cycle is in polynomial time (e.g., using the *Bellman-Ford* algorithm).

The next step of the algorithm is based on the observation that safety can be tested independently in each *strongly connected component* of $\mathcal{X}(\mathbf{S}, R)$. More formally, let $(\mathbf{S}, R)$ be a rewrite program, and let U be a subset of the nodes of $\mathcal{X}(\mathbf{S}, R)$. Recall that U is a *strongly connected component* (abbreviated *SCC*) if U is a maximal set of nodes in which $\mathcal{X}(\mathbf{S}, R)$ contains a path from every node to every other node. Note that the SCCs are pairwise disjoint. For example, in the left graph of Figure 7 the SCCs are the set $\{v_{E_1}^l, v_{F_1}^r, v_{E_2}^l, v_{F_2}^r\}$ and the singletons $\{v_{E_3}^l\}$ and $\{v_{F_3}^r\}$. In the right graph of Figure 7, $\mathcal{X}(\mathbf{S}, R)$ has exactly one SCC (namely, the one containing all six nodes), and in that case we say that $\mathcal{X}(\mathbf{S}, R)$ is *strongly connected*.

Observe that every cycle of $\mathcal{X}(\mathbf{S}, R)$ must be entirely contained in a single connected component. This observation implies that $(\mathbf{S}, R)$ is safe if and only if $(\mathbf{S}, \text{rules}(U))$ is safe for all SCCs U, where $\text{rules}(U)$ is the set of all the rules $E \Rightarrow F$ of R with both v_E^l and v_F^r in U. So, if $\mathcal{X}(\mathbf{S}, R)$ has two or more SCCs, then in Line 5 the algorithm terminates by recursively testing safety of each SCC.

In lines 6–11, the algorithm looks for a guarding potential π for R. Note that for the sake of safety checking, we care about the values of π only on the finite set of constants that actually appear in R; hence, we view π as a finite function (with a finite representation). In lines 6–7, the algorithm tests whether R has a positive-nonincreasing potential, and if so, it terminates by returning **true**. Correctness of this step follows from the fact that if π is a positive

280

Algorithm IsSafe($\mathbf{S}, R$)

1: **if** $\mathcal{X}(\mathbf{S}, R)$ has no positive cycles **then**
2:    **return true**
3: let $U_1, \ldots, U_k$ be the SCCs of $\mathcal{X}(\mathbf{S}, R)$
4: **if** $k > 1$ **then**
5:    **return** $\bigwedge_{i=1}^{k}$ IsSafe($\mathbf{S}, \text{rules}(U_i)$)
6: **if** R has a positive-nonincreasing potential **then**
7:    **return true**
8: **if** R has a weakly decreasing potential **then**
9:    $\pi \leftarrow$ a weakly decreasing potential for R
10:    $R' \leftarrow$ all rules $E \Rightarrow F$ in R, such that $\pi(E) = \pi(F)$
11:    **return** IsSafe($\mathbf{S}, R'$)
12: **return false**

Figure 8: Algorithm for Safety Checking

guarding potential for R, then π is a positive guarding potential for every invocation cycle of R.

In lines 8–11 the algorithm considers the case where R has a weakly decreasing potential π. In that case, let $R' \subseteq R$ be the set of rules $E \Rightarrow F$ with $\pi(E) = \pi(F)$, and let $R'' \subseteq R$ be the set of rules $E \Rightarrow F$ with $\pi(E) > \pi(F)$. Note that $R = R' \cup R''$. In Line 11 the algorithm returns the result of the recursive safety check on $(\mathbf{S}, R')$. Correctness of this step is due to the fact that π is a guarding potential for every invocation cycle that contains one or more rules of R'', and hence, $(\mathbf{S}, R)$ is safe if and only if $(\mathbf{S}, R')$ is safe. For a later use, we record this conclusion as a proposition.

PROPOSITION 5.14. *Let $(\mathbf{S}, R)$ be a rewrite program, let π be a potential that is weakly decreasing on R, and let R' be the set of rules $E \Rightarrow F$ of R with $\pi(E) = \pi(F)$. Then $(\mathbf{S}, R)$ is safe if and only if $(\mathbf{S}, R')$ is safe.*

Regarding the complexity of lines 6–11, the following lemma states that in polynomial time we can find a guarding potential or decide that none exists. The proof is by a straightforward translation of the problem of finding a guarding potential to that of finding a feasible solution to a linear program (LP), where each constant c gives rise to a variable X_c of the LP.[6]

LEMMA 5.15. *Deciding whether a set of rewrite rules has a guarding potential, and finding one if so, are in polynomial time.*

If the tests of lines 1, 4, 6, and 8 are all **false**, then $\mathcal{X}(\mathbf{S}, R)$ has a positive cycle (which means that R has an expanding invocation cycle), $\mathcal{X}(\mathbf{S}, R)$ is strongly connected, and R does not have a guarding potential. In this case, the algorithm terminates by returning **false** (declaring that $(\mathbf{S}, R)$ is unsafe). We now discuss the justification of this step.

If we reach Line 12, then R has an expanding invocation cycle p, and R does not have a guarding potential. But it may be the case that p has a guarding potential, since p can use only *some* of the rules of R. As an example, suppose that R is the set that contains the replacement rules $X \text{ a } Y \Rightarrow X \text{ b } \text{ c } Y$ and $X \text{ b } \text{ c } \text{ b } \text{ c } Y \Rightarrow X \text{ a } \text{ a } \text{ a } Y$, which we denote by ρ_1 and ρ_2, respectively. The rule ρ_1 forms an expanding cycle, but it clearly has a guarding potential

(e.g., $\pi(\text{a}) = 3$ and $\pi(\text{b}) = \pi(\text{c}) = 1$). So, on the face of it, it may seem like Line 12 can be wrong in declaring that $(\mathbf{S}, R)$ is unsafe. Nevertheless, by using the fact that $\mathcal{X}(\mathbf{S}, R)$ is strongly connected (due to lines 4–5), we can show that $(\mathbf{S}, R)$ is necessarily unsafe. For instance, in the above example an expanding cycle that has no guarding potential is ρ_1, ρ_1, ρ_2. Actually, in this example not only is $(\mathbf{S}, R)$ unsafe, it is non-lfp-convergent, since as the reader can verify, $lfp(\text{a a})$ is infinite.

The next lemma verifies the correctness of the algorithm returning **false** (declaring that $(\mathbf{S}, R)$ is unsafe), if the tests of lines 1, 4, 6, and 8 are all **false** (i.e., $\mathcal{X}(\mathbf{S}, R)$ has a positive cycle, $\mathcal{X}(\mathbf{S}, R)$ is strongly connected, and R does not have a guarding potential).

LEMMA 5.16. *Let $(\mathbf{S}, R)$ be a rewrite program, such that (1) $\mathcal{X}(\mathbf{S}, R)$ has a positive cycle, (2) $\mathcal{X}(\mathbf{S}, R)$ is strongly connected, and (3) R has no guarding potential. Then $(\mathbf{S}, R)$ is unsafe.*

We get the following theorem, stating the correctness and efficiency of IsSafe($\mathbf{S}, R$), and the resulting tractability of safety.

THEOREM 5.17. IsSafe($\mathbf{S}, R$) *returns* **true** *if and only if the program $(\mathbf{S}, R)$ is safe, and it terminates in polynomial time. Thus, safety checking for a rewrite program is in polynomial time.*

5.4 Weak Safety

As we describe later, our safety condition very well captures lfp-convergence in our implemented search database system. But to properly handle rules of our past research [6], a weakened safety condition is needed. Specifically, in our previous paper [6], we applied a different kind of rule to a search query in order to obtain an *interpretation*, which is essentially a special type of an $\mathbf{S}$-hedge. Those rules are captured by a special type of rewrite rules, which we call *CFG (Context-Free Grammar) rules*.[7] Unfortunately, our safety condition does not capture lfp-convergence of programs that constitute such rules. But we can handle CFG rules by a slight relaxation of our safety condition, as we briefly describe next.

For a set R of rewrite rules, we denote by $R{\downarrow}$ the set that is obtained from R by removing from each rule every node but the leaves of the expressions. A potential π is a *weakly guarding potential* for a set R of rules if π is a guarding potential for R, or it is the case that $R{\downarrow}$ is a rewrite program (i.e., in each rule, every variable occurs in the left side) and π is a guarding potential for $R{\downarrow}$. Then, we relax our safety condition by replacing "guarding potential" with "weakly guarding potential." That is, the weaker safety condition is "every expanding invocation cycle has a weakly guarding potential." We can show that the weaker safety condition is correct (i.e., guarantees strong lfp-convergence) and tractable (i.e., can be decided in polynomial time). One can easily show that every rewrite program that consists of only CFG rules satisfies the weaker safety condition. Furthermore, the rewrite program $(\mathbf{S}, R)$ of our running example satisfies the weak safety condition as well (and hence, is strongly lfp-convergent).

5.5 Practical Evaluation

We considered a rewrite program that is used in a search database system. This system was developed at IBM Research–Almaden, and is used internally within IBM. The rewrite program has 380 rules, and it is blatantly non-lfp-convergent. For example, 22 rules ρ are such that $\{\rho\}$ is non-lfp-convergent, like $X \text{ medical } Y \Rightarrow X \text{ medical plans } Y$. Therefore, instead of using the desired

---

[6] Linear programming has also been used, in a similar flavor, by Korovin and Voronkov [16] for a related problem of finding a special type of a *Knuth-Bendix order* [14] (for the sake of ordinary termination).

[7] To be precise, we note that [6] required each term of an $\mathbf{S}$-hedge to have a concept parent. We do not view this requirement as practically important, and we indeed avoid it here.

least-fixpoint semantics, in the past (before the research of this paper) each rule was applied at most once, in some arbitrary order.

Following the research of this paper, we essentially used the algorithm ISSAFE in an extended way, where the goal was to extract a significant part of the program that is lfp-convergent, and mark the remaining part (which includes the above 22 rules) as needing modification.[8] So, in the end we were left with an lfp-convergent rewrite program that is obtained from $(\mathbf{S}, R)$ by removing from R a subset Z of marked rules.

More specifically, recall that ISSAFE recursively partitions and reduces sets R of rules (e.g., by applying Proposition 5.14), until none of the tests of lines 1, 4, 6, and 8 is true (hence, $\mathcal{X}(\mathbf{S}, R)$ has no positive cycles and is strongly connected, and R has no guarding potential). For each such set R (where none of the tests is true) we manually tested whether R is lfp-convergent or not.[9] In all but two cases (that together consist of 13 rules, which are discussed below), we found that R is indeed non-lfp-convergent, in which case we moved one or more selected rules from R to Z, and continued.

At the end of the day, with the above process we extracted a safe program of 336 (out of 380) rules. Among the 44 remaining rules, 31 were in Z, marked as requiring modification, and we were left with an unsafe yet lfp-convergent program $(\mathbf{S}, R)$ such that R contains only 13 rules.

Following is an example of a rule ρ among the 13 rules, such that $\{\rho\}$ is unsafe, but is nevertheless strongly lfp-convergent.

$$X \; \texttt{publishing external} \; Y \Rightarrow$$
$$X \; \texttt{external web publishing process} \; Y$$

We handled this and the other 12 rules by extending the notion of a guarding potential from constants to strings (for example, we assign values to $\pi(\texttt{publishing external})$ rather than just to $\pi(\texttt{publishing})$ and $\pi(\texttt{external})$). A general discussion on this extension is beyond the scope of this paper.

Overall, we found our safety approach highly successful. In particular, we found that safety captures lfp- convergence very well in our system. Furthermore, it allowed us to extract a significant lfp-convergent part of our of program by eliminating problematic rules for justifiable reasons (they cause non-lfp-convergence).

6. CONCLUSIONS

We presented a framework that incorporates rewrite rules in a search database system. Specifically, a rewrite program is applied to a search query in a least-fixpoint manner. Our focus has been on lfp-convergence. Because lfp-convergence is undecidable, even under strong restrictions on the program, we presented a safety condition and showed that it guarantees lfp-convergence and that it is tractable. We also presented a weakened (less restrictive) version of the safety condition that better suits the CFG rules used in [6]. We believe that our safety condition (and the weakened one) well capture lfp-convergence in practice. As described in Section 5.5, we found this condition very successful when we applied it to a system being developed at IBM.

Several extensions of this work are desired to capture practical needs, and they will be the subject of future work. One such extension is the generalization of a guarding potential to strings and hedges (rather than just to constants), thereby broadening the notion of safety. Another extension will allow *regular expressions* in a rewrite rule, in order to qualify a restricted domain for a variable.

---

[8]There are simple ways of applying such modification, but a discussion on them is beyond the scope of this paper.

[9]To obtain small sets R, we used additional partitioning techniques that are not discussed in this paper.

Acknowledgments

The authors are grateful to members of the PODS 2011 Program Committee and their subreferees, and to Balder ten Cate, for their invaluable help with understanding and referencing the literature of rewriting systems.

7. REFERENCES

[1] T. Arts and J. Giesl. Termination of term rewriting using dependency pairs. *Theor. Comput. Sci.*, 236(1-2):133–178, 2000.

[2] J. Bear, D. J. Israel, J. Petit, and D. L. Martin. Using information extraction to improve document retrieval. In *TREC*, pages 367–377, 1997.

[3] A. B. Cherifa and P. Lescanne. Termination of rewriting systems by polynomial interpretations and its implementation. *Sci. Comput. Program.*, 9(2):137–159, 1987.

[4] N. Dershowitz. Orderings for term-rewriting systems. *Theor. Comput. Sci.*, 17:279–301, 1982.

[5] N. Dershowitz. Termination. In *RTA*, volume 202 of *Lecture Notes in Computer Science*, pages 180–224. Springer, 1985.

[6] R. Fagin, B. Kimelfeld, Y. Li, S. Raghavan, and S. Vaithyanathan. Understanding queries in a search database system. In *PODS*, pages 273–284. ACM, 2010.

[7] O. Fissore, I. Gnaedig, and H. Kirchner. A proof of weak termination providing the right way to terminate. In *ICTAC*, volume 3407 of *Lecture Notes in Computer Science*, pages 356–371. Springer, 2004.

[8] J. V. Guttag, D. Kapur, and D. R. Musser. On proving uniform termination and restricted termination of rewriting systems. *SIAM J. Comput.*, 12(1):189–214, 1983.

[9] M. A. Hearst. Direction-based text interpretation as an information access refinement. In P. S. Jacobs, editor, *Text-Based Intelligent Systems: Current Research and Practice in Information Extraction and Retrieval*, pages 257–274. Erlbaum, Hillsdale, 1992.

[10] P. S. Jacobs. Introduction: Text power and intelligent systems. In P. S. Jacobs, editor, *Text-Based Intelligent Systems: Current Research and Practice in Information Extraction and Retrieval*, pages 1–8. Erlbaum, Hillsdale, 1992.

[11] F. Jacquemard and M. Rusinowitch. Closure of hedge-automata languages by hedge rewriting. In *RTA*, volume 5117 of *Lecture Notes in Computer Science*, pages 157–171. Springer, 2008.

[12] E. Kandogan, R. Krishnamurthy, S. Raghavan, S. Vaithyanathan, and H. Zhu. Avatar semantic search: a database approach to information retrieval. In *SIGMOD Conference*, pages 790–792. ACM, 2006.

[13] S. Kaplan. Conditional rewrite rules. *Theor. Comput. Sci.*, 33:175–193, 1984.

[14] D. Knuth and P. Bendix. Simple word problems in universal algebra. In J. Leech, editor, *Computational Problems in Abstract Algebra*, pages 263–297. Pergamon Press, 1970.

[15] D. König. *Theorie der Endlichen und Unendlichen Graphen: Kombinatorische Topologie der Streckenkomplexe*. Akad. Verlag, Leipzig, 1936.

[16] K. Korovin and A. Voronkov. Orienting rewrite rules with the Knuth-Bendix order. *Inf. Comput.*, 183(2):165–186, 2003.

[17] R. Krishnamurthy, Y. Li, S. Raghavan, F. Reiss, S. Vaithyanathan, and H. Zhu. SystemT: a system for declarative information extraction. *SIGMOD Record*, 37(4):7–13, 2008.

[18] D. S. Lankford. On proving term rewriting systems are Noetherian. Technical report, Mathematics Department, Louisiana Tech. University, Ruston, 1979.

[19] D. D. Lewis. Text representation for intelligent text retrieval: A classification-oriented view. In P. S. Jacobs, editor, *Text-Based Intelligent Systems: Current Research and Practice in Information Extraction and Retrieval*, pages 179–197. Erlbaum, Hillsdale, 1992.

[20] S. Lucas. Context-sensitive computations in confluent programs. In *PLILP*, volume 1140 of *Lecture Notes in Computer Science*, pages 408–422. Springer, 1996.

[21] F. Neven. Automata theory for XML researchers. *SIGMOD Record*, 31(3):39–46, 2002.

[22] B. Pang and L. Lee. Using very simple statistics for review search: An exploration. In *Proceedings of COLING: Companion volume: Posters*, pages 73–76, 2008.

[23] Y. Qiu and H.-P. Frei. Concept based query expansion. In *SIGIR*, pages 160–169. ACM, 1993.

[24] F. Reiss, S. Raghavan, R. Krishnamurthy, H. Zhu, and S. Vaithyanathan. An algebraic approach to rule-based information extraction. In *ICDE*, pages 933–942. IEEE, 2008.

[25] Terese. *Term Rewriting Systems*, volume 55 of *Cambridge Tracts in Theoretical Computer Science*. Cambridge University Press, 2003.

[26] H. Zhu, S. Raghavan, S. Vaithyanathan, and A. Löser. Navigating the intranet with high precision. In *WWW*, pages 491–500. ACM, 2007.

Relational Transducers for Declarative Networking

[Extended Abstract]

Tom J. Ameloot[*]
Hasselt University &
Transnational University of
Limburg
Diepenbeek, Belgium
tom.ameloot@uhasselt.be

Frank Neven
Hasselt University &
Transnational University of
Limburg
Diepenbeek, Belgium
frank.neven@uhasselt.be

Jan Van den Bussche
Hasselt University &
Transnational University of
Limburg
Diepenbeek, Belgium
jan.vandenbussche@uhasselt.be

ABSTRACT

Motivated by a recent conjecture concerning the expressiveness of declarative networking, we propose a formal computation model for "eventually consistent" distributed querying, based on relational transducers. A tight link has been conjectured between coordination-freeness of computations, and monotonicity of the queries expressed by such computations. Indeed, we propose a formal definition of coordination-freeness and confirm that the class of monotone queries is captured by coordination-free transducer networks.

Coordination-freeness is a semantic property, but the syntactic class of "oblivious" transducers we define also captures the same class of monotone queries. Transducer networks that are not coordination-free are much more powerful.

Categories and Subject Descriptors

H.2 [**Database Management**]: Languages; H.2 [**Database Management**]: Systems—*Distributed databases*; F.1 [**Computation by Abstract Devices**]: Models of Computation

General Terms

languages, theory

Keywords

distributed database, relational transducer, monotonicity, expressive power, cloud programming

---

[*]PhD Fellow of the Fund for Scientific Research, Flanders (FWO). We acknowledge the financial support of the Future and Emerging Technologies (FET) programme within the Seventh Framework Programme for Research of the European Commission, under the FET-Open grant agreement FOX, number FP7-ICT-233599.

1. INTRODUCTION

Declarative networking [18] is a recent approach by which distributed computations and networking protocols are modeled and programmed using formalisms based on Datalog. In his keynote speech at PODS 2010 [15, 16], Hellerstein made a number of intriguing conjectures concerning the expressiveness of declarative networking. In the present paper we are focusing on the CALM conjecture (Consistency And Logical Monotonicity). This conjecture suggests a strong link between, on the one hand, "eventually consistent" and "coordination-free" distributed computations, and on the other hand, expressibility in monotonic Datalog (Datalog without negation or aggregate functions). The conjecture was not fully formalized, however; indeed, as Hellerstein notes himself, a proper treatment of this conjecture requires crisp definitions of eventual consistency and coordination, which have been lacking so far. Moreover, it also requires a formal model of distributed computation.

In the present paper, we investigate the CALM conjecture in the context of a model for distributed database querying. In the model we propose, the computation is performed on a network of relational transducers. The relational transducer model, introduced by Abiteboul and Vianu, is well established in database theory research as a model for data-centric agents reacting to inputs [6, 12, 13, 14, 20]. Relational transducers are firmly grounded in the theory of database queries [4, 5] and also have close connections with Abstract State Machines [10]. It thus seems natural to consider networks of relational transducers, as we will do here. We give a formal operational semantics for such networks, formally define "eventual consistency", and formally define what it means for a network to compute a conventional database query, in order to address the expressiveness issues raised by Hellerstein.

It is less clear, however, how to formalize the intuitive notion of "coordination". We do not claim to resolve this issue definitively, but we propose a new, nonobvious definition that appears workable. Distributed algorithms requiring coordination are viewed as less efficient than coordination-free algorithms. Hellerstein has identified *monotonicity* as a fundamental property connected with coordination-freeness. Indeed, monotonicity enables "embarrassing parallelism" [16]: agents working on parts of the data in parallel can produce parts of the output independently, without the need for coordination.

One side of the CALM conjecture now states that any database query expressible in monotonic Datalog can be computed in a distributed setting in an eventually consistent, coordination-free manner. This is the easy side of the conjecture, and indeed we formally confirm it in the following broader sense: any monotone query Q can be computed by a network of "oblivious" transducers. Oblivious transducers are unaware of the network extent (in a sense that we will make precise), and every oblivious transducer network is coordination-free. Here, we should note that the transducer model is parameterized by the query language $\mathcal{L}$ that the transducer can use to update its local state. Formally, the monotone query Q to be computed must be expressible in the while-closure of $\mathcal{L}$ for the above confirmation to hold. If Q is in Datalog, for example, then $\mathcal{L}$ can just be the conjunctive queries.

The other side of the CALM conjecture, that the query computed by an eventually consistent, coordination-free distributed program is always expressible in Datalog, is false when taken literally, as we will point out. Nevertheless, we do give a Datalog version of the conjecture that holds. More importantly, we confirm the conjecture in the following more general form: coordination-free networks of transducers can compute only monotone queries. Note that here we are using our newly proposed formal definition of coordination-free.

Finally, the present work also lead us to think about the computational power of the language Dedalus [8], the Datalog extension used by Alvaro and Hellerstein. We will show that this language is quite powerful by establishing a monotone simulation of arbitrary Turing machines.

This paper is organized as follows. Preliminaries are in Section 2. Section 3 introduces networks of transducers. Section 4 investigates the use of transducer networks for expressing conventional database queries in a distributed fashion. Section 5 discusses the issue of coordination. Section 6 looks into the CALM conjecture. Section 7 presents some further results. Section 8 compares our results to the language Dedalus. Section 9 is the conclusion.

In this extended abstract, proofs are mainly given on an informal level.

2. PRELIMINARIES

We recall some basic notions from the theory of database queries [1].

A *database schema* is a finite set $\mathcal{S}$ of relation names, each with an associated arity (a natural number). Assume some infinite universe **dom** of atomic *data elements*. An *instance* of a database schema $\mathcal{S}$ is an assignment I of finite relations on **dom** to the relation names of $\mathcal{S}$, such that when R has arity k then $I(R)$ is a k-ary relation. Equivalently, we can view an instance as a set of *facts* over $\mathcal{S}$, where a fact is an expression of the form $R(a_1, \ldots, a_k)$ with $a_1, \ldots, a_k \in$ **dom** and $R \in \mathcal{S}$ of arity k. The *active domain* of an instance I, denoted by $\mathrm{adom}(I)$, is the set of data elements occurring in I.

A *k-ary query over* $\mathcal{S}$ is a partial function Q mapping instances of $\mathcal{S}$ to k-ary relations on **dom** such that for each I on which Q is defined, the following two conditions hold: *(i)* $Q(I)$ is a k-ary relation on $\mathrm{adom}(I)$; and *(ii)* Q is also defined on the isomorphic instance $h(I)$, for each permutation h of **dom**, and $Q(h(I)) = h(Q(I))$. A query Q is *monotone* if for any two instances $I \subseteq J$, if $Q(I)$ is defined then so is $Q(J)$, and $Q(I) \subseteq Q(J)$.

We assume familiarity with *first-order logic (FO)* as a basic database query language. An FO formula $\varphi(x_1, \ldots, x_k)$

expresses the k-ary query defined by $\varphi(I) = \{(a_1, \ldots, a_k) \in \mathrm{adom}(I)^k \mid (\mathrm{adom}(I), I) \models \varphi[a_1, \ldots, a_k]\}$. Note that we evaluate FO formulas on instances under the active-domain semantics. The resulting query language is equivalent in expressive power to the relational algebra, as well as to recursion-free Datalog with negation.

We will also consider the query languages Datalog, stratified Datalog (with negation), and *while*. Datalog and stratified Datalog are well known; *while* is the query language obtained from FO by adding assignment statements and while-loops. Finally, we recall that there exist quite elegant *computationally complete* query languages in which every partial computable query can be expressed.

2.1 Relational transducers

A *transducer schema* is a tuple $(\mathcal{S}_{\mathrm{in}}, \mathcal{S}_{\mathrm{sys}}, \mathcal{S}_{\mathrm{msg}}, \mathcal{S}_{\mathrm{mem}}, k)$ consisting of four disjoint database schemas and an *output arity* k. Here, 'in' stands for 'input'; 'sys' stands for 'system'; 'msg' stands for 'message'; and 'mem' stands for 'memory'.

An *abstract relational transducer* (or just transducer for short) over this schema is a collection of queries $\{Q_{\mathrm{snd}}^R \mid R \in \mathcal{S}_{\mathrm{msg}}\} \cup \{Q_{\mathrm{ins}}^R \mid R \in \mathcal{S}_{\mathrm{mem}}\} \cup \{Q_{\mathrm{del}}^R \mid R \in \mathcal{S}_{\mathrm{mem}}\} \cup \{Q_{\mathrm{out}}\}$, where

- every query is over the combined database schema $\mathcal{S}_{\mathrm{in}} \cup \mathcal{S}_{\mathrm{sys}} \cup \mathcal{S}_{\mathrm{msg}} \cup \mathcal{S}_{\mathrm{mem}}$;

- the arity of each Q_{snd}^R, each Q_{ins}^R and each Q_{del}^R equals the arity of R; and

- the arity of Q_{out} equals the output arity k.

Here, 'snd' stands for 'send'; 'ins' stands for 'insert'; 'del' stands for 'delete'; and 'out' stands for 'output'.

A *state* of the transducer is an instance of the combined schema $\mathcal{S}_{\mathrm{in}} \cup \mathcal{S}_{\mathrm{sys}} \cup \mathcal{S}_{\mathrm{mem}}$. Intuitively, a state just consists of some input relations, some system relations (we will make these precise in the next section), and some stored relations that constitute the memory of the transducer.

A *message instance* is, plainly, an instance of $\mathcal{S}_{\mathrm{msg}}$. Such a message instance can stand for a set of messages (facts) received by the transducer, but can as well stand for a set of messages sent by the transducer. It will always be clear from the context which of the two meanings we have.

Let Π be a transducer. A *transition* of Π is a five-tuple $(I, I_{\mathrm{rcv}}, J_{\mathrm{snd}}, J_{\mathrm{out}}, J)$, also denoted as $I, I_{\mathrm{rcv}} \xrightarrow{J_{\mathrm{out}}} J, J_{\mathrm{snd}}$, where I and J are states, I_{rcv} and J_{snd} are message instances, and J_{out} is a k-ary relation such that

- every query of Π is defined on $I' = I \cup I_{\mathrm{rcv}}$;

- J agrees with I on $\mathcal{S}_{\mathrm{in}}$ and $\mathcal{S}_{\mathrm{sys}}$;

- $J_{\mathrm{snd}}(R)$, for each $R \in \mathcal{S}_{\mathrm{msg}}$, equals $Q_{\mathrm{snd}}^R(I')$;

- J_{out} equals $Q_{\mathrm{out}}(I')$;

- $J(R)$, for each $R \in \mathcal{S}_{\mathrm{mem}}$, equals

$$(Q_{\mathrm{ins}}^R(I') \setminus Q_{\mathrm{del}}^R(I'))$$
$$\cup (Q_{\mathrm{ins}}^R(I') \cap Q_{\mathrm{del}}^R(I') \cap I(R))$$
$$\cup (I(R) \setminus (Q_{\mathrm{ins}}^R(I') \cup Q_{\mathrm{del}}^R(I'))).$$

The intuition behind the instance I' is that Π sees its input, system and memory relations, plus its received messages.

The transducer does not modify the input and system relations. The transducer computes new tuples that can be sent out as messages; this is the instance J_{snd}. The transducer also outputs some tuples; this is the relation J_{out}. These outputs cannot later be retracted! Finally the transducer updates its memory by inserting and deleting some tuples for every memory relation. The intimidating update formula merely expresses that conflicting inserts/deletes are ignored [13, 20]. Note that an assignment $R := Q$ can be expressed by using Q for Q_{ins}^R and R for Q_{del}^R.

Note also that transitions are *deterministic*: if $I, I_{rcv} \xrightarrow{J_{out}} J, J_{snd}$ and $I, I_{rcv} \xrightarrow{J'_{out}} J', J'_{snd}$, then $J'_{snd} = J_{snd}$; $J'_{out} = J_{out}$; and $J' = J$.

An abstract relational transducer as defined above is just a collection of queries. If we want to write down a transducer then we will of course use some query language to express these queries. By default, we use FO as the query language. More generally, for any query language $\mathcal{L}$ we can consider the language of $\mathcal{L}$-*transducers* consisting of all transducers whose queries are expressed in $\mathcal{L}$. Because we are going to place transducers in networks, we can think of $\mathcal{L}$ as the language that individual peers use locally. For example, in the language Dedalus [8], the local language is stratified Datalog.

3. TRANSDUCER NETWORKS

Proviso 1. From now on we will only consider transducers where the system schema $\mathcal{S}_{sys}$ consists of the two unary relation names Id and All.

A *network* is a finite, *connected*, undirected graph over a set of vertices $V \subset \mathbf{dom}$. We refer to the vertices as *nodes*. Note that nodes belong to the universe $\mathbf{dom}$ of atomic data elements; indeed we are going to allow that nodes are stored in relations. We stress again that a network must be connected. This is important to make it possible for flow of information to reach every node.

A *transducer network* is a pair $(\mathcal{N}, \Pi)$ where $\mathcal{N}$ is a network and Π is a transducer. The general idea is that a copy of Π is running on every node. A database instance is distributed over the input relations of the different nodes. Relation Id contains the node identifier where the transducer is running, and relation All is the same at all nodes and contains the set of all nodes. When a node v sends a set of facts as messages, these facts are added to the message buffers of v's neighbors. Nodes receive facts one by one in arbitrary order; messages are not necessarily received in the order they have been sent. A similar situation can happen in the Internet with subsequent TCP/IP connections between the same two nodes, where an earlier connection might be slower than a later one. Moreover, nodes regularly receive a "heartbeat" message which allows them to transition even when no message is read.

We proceed to define the possible runs of a transducer network more formally. A *configuration* of the system is a pair $\gamma = (state, buf)$ of mappings where

- *state* maps every node v to a state $I = state(v)$ of Π, so that $I(Id) = \{v\}$, and $I(All) = V$ (the set of all nodes of $\mathcal{N}$).

- *buf* maps every node to a finite multiset of facts over $\mathcal{S}_{msg}$.

Thus, the system relations Id and All give the transducer knowledge about the node where it is running and about the other nodes in the network. We will discuss the use and necessity of these relations extensively.

A *general transition* of the system is the transformation of one configuration to another where some node v reads and removes some message instance I_{rcv} from its input buffer, makes a local transition, and sends the resulting message instance J_{snd} to its neighbors. Formally, a general transition is a tuple $\tau = (\gamma_1, v, I_{rcv}, J_{out}, \gamma_2)$, also denoted as $\gamma_1 \xrightarrow[v, I_{rcv}]{J_{out}} \gamma_2$, where $\gamma_i = (state_i, buf_i)$ for $i = 1, 2$ is a configuration, v is a node, and $I_{rcv} \subseteq buf_1(v)$ (multiset containment), such that:

- $state_2(v') = state_1(v')$ for every node $v' \neq v$.

- There exists J_{snd} such that
$$state_1(v), I_{rcv} \xrightarrow{J_{out}} state_2(v), J_{snd}.$$
We call J_{out} the *output* of the transition and denote it also by $out(\tau)$. Note that, since individual transducer transitions are deterministic, J_{out} and J_{snd} are uniquely determined by $state_1(v)$ and I_{rcv}.

- $buf_2(v) = buf_1(v) \setminus I_{rcv}$ (multiset difference).

- $buf_2(v') = buf_1(v')$ for every node $v' \neq v$ that is not a neighbor of v.

- $buf_2(v') = buf_1(v') \cup J_{snd}$ for every node v' that is a neighbor of v. Note we are using multiset union here.

We will, however, not use transitions in their most general form but only in two special forms:

Heartbeat transition: is of the form $\gamma_1 \xrightarrow[v, \emptyset]{J_{out}} \gamma_2$. So, some node v transitions without reading any message.

Delivery transition: is of the form $\gamma_1 \xrightarrow[v, \{f\}]{J_{out}} \gamma_2$. So, some node v reads a single fact f from its received message buffer.

We only consider these two forms because they appear to be the most elementary. We are not sure it is realistic to assume that entire message instances can be read in one transition. Therefore we limit message reading to a single fact. Heartbeat transitions ensure that nodes can transition even if their message buffer is empty.

For any two configurations γ_1 and γ_2 we simply write $\gamma_1 \to \gamma_2$ to denote that the system can transition from γ_1 to γ_2 either by some heartbeat transition or by some delivery transition. A *run* of the system now is an infinite sequence $(\tau_n)_n$ of heartbeat or delivery transitions such that for each n, if τ_n is $\gamma_n \to \gamma_{n+1}$ then τ_{n+1} is of the form $\gamma_{n+1} \to \gamma_{n+2}$. In other words, each transition τ_n with $n > 0$ works on the result configuration of the previous transition.

The *output* of a run ρ is then defined as $out(\rho) = \bigcup_n out(\tau_n)$. We note the following:

PROPOSITION 1. *For every run* $\rho = (\tau_n)_n$ *there exists a natural number* m *such that* $out(\rho) = \bigcup_{n=0}^m out(\tau_n)$. *The number* m *is called a* quiescence point *for* ρ.

Indeed, since the initial configuration contains only a finite number of distinct atomic data elements, and a local query cannot invent new data elements, only a finite number of distinct output tuples are possible.

In the language Dedalus [8], new data elements are invented in the form of increasing timestamps, so the above proposition does not hold for Dedalus. It would be interesting to investigate a version of transducer networks with timestamps, or with object-creating local queries.

4. EXPRESSING QUERIES WITH TRANSDUCER NETWORKS

What does it take for a transducer network to compute some global query? Here we propose a formal definition based on the two properties of *consistency* and *network-topology independence*.

An instance I of the input part of the transducer schema, $\mathcal{S}_{\mathrm{in}}$, can be distributed over the input relations of the nodes on the network. Formally, for any instance I of $\mathcal{S}_{\mathrm{in}}$, a *horizontal partition of I on the network $\mathcal{N}$* is a function H that maps every node v to a subset of I, such that $I = \bigcup_v H(v)$. The *initial configuration for H* is a configuration $(state, buf)$ such that:

- $buf(v) = \emptyset$ and $state(v)(R) = \emptyset$ for each node v and every $R \in \mathcal{S}_{\mathrm{mem}}$. So, each node starts with an empty message buffer and empty memory;

- For each node v, the restriction of $state(v)$ to the input schema $\mathcal{S}_{\mathrm{in}}$ equals $H(v)$.

A *run on H* is a run that starts in the initial configuration for H.

We also need the notion of *fair* run. A run is fair if every node does a heartbeat transition infinitely often, and every fact in every message buffer is eventually taken out by a delivery transition. We omit the obvious formalization.

We now say that a transducer network $(\mathcal{N}, \Pi)$ is *consistent* if for every instance I of $\mathcal{S}_{\mathrm{in}}$, all fair runs on all possible horizontal partitions of I have the same output. Naturally, a consistent transducer network is said to *compute* a query Q over $\mathcal{S}_{\mathrm{in}}$ if for every instance I of $\mathcal{S}_{\mathrm{in}}$ on which Q is defined, every fair run on any horizontal partition of I outputs $Q(I)$.

Example 1. Let us see a simple example of a network that is *not* consistent. Consider a network with at least two nodes (indeed if the network consists of a single node the transducer runs all by itself; no messages are delivered and there is only one possible run). The input is a set S of data elements. Each node sends its part of S to its neighbors. Also, each node outputs the first element it receives and outputs no further elements. This is easily programmed on an FO-transducer. When there are at least two nodes and at least two elements in S, different runs may deliver the elements in different orders, so different outputs can be produced, even for the same horizontal partition. $\square$

Example 2. For a simple example of a consistent network, let the input be a binary relation S. Each node outputs the identical pairs from its part of the input. No messages are sent. This network computes the equality selection $\sigma_{\$1=\$2}(S)$.

An example of a consistent transducer network that involves communication, computes the transitive closure of S in a distributed fashion in the well-known way [18]. We present here, a naive, unoptimized version. Each node sends its part of the input to its neighbors. Each node also sends all tuples it receives to its neighbors. In this way the input is flooded to all nodes. Each node accumulates the tuples it receives in a memory relation R. Finally, each node maintains a memory relation T in which we repeatedly insert $S \cup R \cup T \cup (T \circ T)$ (here $\circ$ stands for relational composition). This relation T is also output. Thanks to the monotonicity of the transitive closure, this transducer network is consistent. $\square$

We are mainly interested in the case where the query can be correctly computed by the distributed transducer program, regardless of the network topology. For example, the transitive closure computation from Example 2 is independent of the network topology (as long as the network is connected, but we are requiring that of all networks).

Formally, a transducer Π is *network-topology independent* if for every network $\mathcal{N}$, the system $(\mathcal{N}, \Pi)$ is consistent, and regardless of $\mathcal{N}$ computes the same query Q. We say that Q can be *distributedly computed* by Π.

Example 3. For a simple example of a transducer that is consistent for every network topology, but that is not network-topology independent, consider again as input a set S distributed over the nodes. Each node sends its input to its neighbors and also sends the elements it receives to its neighbors. Each node only outputs the elements it receives. On any network with at least two nodes, the identity query is computed, but on the network with a single node, the empty query is computed. $\square$

In order to state a few first results in Theorem 3, we introduce the following terminology.

Oblivious transducer: does not use the relations *Id* and *All*. Intuitively, the transducer program is unaware of the context in which it is running.

Inflationary transducer: does not do deletions, i.e., each deletion query returns empty on all inputs.

Monotone transducer: uses only monotone local queries.

LEMMA 2. *1. There is an inflationary FO-transducer such that, on any network, starting on any horizontal partition of any instance I of $\mathcal{S}_{\mathrm{in}}$, any fair run reaches a configuration where every node has a local copy of the entire instance I in its memory, and an additional flag Ready (implemented by a nullary memory relation) is true. Moreover, the flag Ready does not become true at a node before that node has the entire instance in its memory.*

2. There is an oblivious, inflationary, monotone FO-transducer that accomplishes the same as the previous one, except for the flag Ready.

3. A query is expressible in the language 'while' if and only if it is computable by an FO-transducer on a single-node network.

PROOF. For (1), a multicast protocol [9] is implemented. Every node v sends out all the facts in its local input relations, but each fact is tagged with the id of v in an extra coordinate (using relation Id). Every node also forwards all input facts it receives, and stores received facts in memory. Moreover, for every input fact received, every node sends an acknowledge fact, additionally tagged with its own identifier. Every node v keeps a record of for which of its local input facts it has received an ack from which node. When v has received an ack from v' for every local input fact, it sends out a message $done(v, v')$ meant for v'. When a node has received $done$ from every node (which can be checked using the relation All), it knows it is ready. No deletions are necessary.

For (2), the program is much simpler. All nodes simply send out their local input facts and forward any message they receive. In any fair run, eventually all nodes will have received all input facts. Relations Id and All are not needed.

For (3), on a one-node network there are only heartbeat transitions. A *while* program can be simulated by iterated heartbeats using well-known techniques [3]. Conversely, it is clear that a one-node transducer network can be simulated by a *while* program. The only difficulty is that the transducer keeps running indefinitely whereas the *while* program is supposed to stop. Using the technique described by Abiteboul and Simon [2], however, the program can detect that it is in an infinite loop. This implies that the transducer has repeated a state and will output no more new tuples. □

THEOREM 3.   *1. Every query can be distributedly computed by some abstract transducer. In particular, if $\mathcal{L}$ is computationally complete, every partial computable query can be distributedly computed by an $\mathcal{L}$-transducer.*

2. Every monotone query can be distributedly computed by an oblivious, inflationary, monotone abstract transducer. In particular, if $\mathcal{L}$ is computationally complete, every partial computable monotone query can be distributedly computed by an oblivious $\mathcal{L}$-transducer.

3. A query is expressible in the language 'while' if and only if it can be distributedly computed by an FO-transducer.

4. Every monotone query expressible in while can be distributedly computed by an oblivious FO-transducer.

5. A query is in Datalog if and only if it can be distributedly computed by an oblivious, inflationary, non-recursive-Datalog-transducer.

PROOF. For (1), to distributedly compute any query Q, we first run the transducer from Lemma 2(1) to obtain the entire input instance. Then we apply and output Q.

For (2), the idea is the same, but we now use the transducer from Lemma 2(2). We continuously apply Q to the part of the input instance already received, and output the result. Since Q is monotone, no incorrect tuples are output.

For (3) we only still have to argue the only-if implication. We first run the transducer from Lemma 2(1) to obtain the entire input instance. Then every node can act as if it is on its own, ignoring any remaining incoming messages and simulate the *while*-program.

For (4) the idea is the same as in (2). We receive input tuples and store them in memory. We continuously recompute the *while*-program, starting afresh every time a new input fact comes in. We use deletion to start afresh. Since the query is monotone, no incorrect tuples are output.

For (5) the idea for the only-if implication is again the same as in (2). We receive input tuples and apply continuously the T_P-operator of the Datalog program. By the monotone nature of Datalog evaluation, deletions are not needed, so the transducer is inflationary. The Datalog program for the if-implication is obtained by taking together the rules of all update queries Q_{ins}^R and the output query Q_{out}. The answer predicate of Q_{out} is the global answer predicate. The answer predicate of each Q_{ins}^R is replaced by R, so that we obtain a recursive program. □

The transducer from Lemma 2(1) can actually be implemented to use only unions of conjunctive queries with negation (UCQ¬). We omit the proof of this claim. By simulating FO queries by fixed compositions of UCQ¬, we then obtain: (proof omitted)

PROPOSITION 4. *Every (monotone) query that can be distributedly computed by an FO-transducer can be distributedly computed by an (oblivious) UCQ¬-transducer.*

To conclude, we remark that in a transducer network of at least two nodes, each node can establish a linear order on the active domain, by first collecting all input tuples, then sending out all elements of the active domain, forwarding messages and storing the elements that are received back in the order they are received. But such a transducer is not truly network-topology independent, as it does not work in the same way on a one-node network. At any rate, by the well-known characterization of PSPACE [1], we obtain:

COROLLARY 5. *On any network with at least two nodes, every PSPACE query can be computed by an FO-transducer.*

5. COORDINATION

The CALM conjecture hinges on an intuitive notion of "coordination-freeness" of certain distributed computations. For some tasks, coordination is required to reach consistency across the network. Two-phase commit is a classical example. The multicast protocol used in Lemma 2(1) also requires heavy coordination. Since coordination typically blocks distributed computations, it is good to understand precisely when it can be avoided. This is what the CALM conjecture is all about.

It seems hard to give a definitive formalization of coordination. Still we offer here a nontrivial definition that appears interesting. A very drastic, too drastic, definition of coordination-free would be to disallow any communication. Our definition is much less severe and only requires that the computation can succeed without communication on "suitable" horizontal partitions. It actually does not matter what a suitable partition is, as long as it exists. Even under this liberal definition, the CALM conjecture will turn out to hold.

Formally, consider a network-topology independent transducer Π and a network $\mathcal{N}$. We call Π *coordination-free on* $\mathcal{N}$ if for every instance I of $\mathcal{S}_{\text{in}}$, there exists a horizontal partition H of I on $\mathcal{N}$ and a run ρ of $(\mathcal{N}, \Pi)$ on H, in which a quiescence point (Proposition 1) is already reached by only performing heartbeat transitions. Intuitively, if the horizontal partition is "right", then no communication is required to correctly compute the query. Finally we call Π *coordination-free* if it is coordination-free on any network.

Example 4. Consider again the transitive closure computation from Example 2. When every node already has the full input, they can each individually compute the transitive closure. Hence this transducer is coordination-free.

The reader should not be lulled into believing that with a coordination-free program it is always sufficient to give the full input at all nodes. A (contrived) example of a coordination-free transducer that needs communication even if each node has the entire input is the following. The input, distributed over the nodes as usual, consists of two sets A and B, and the query is to determine if at least one of A and B are nonempty. If the network has only one node (which can be tested by looking at the *All* relation), the transducer simply outputs the answer to the query. Otherwise, it first tests if its local input fragments A and B are both nonempty. If yes, nothing is output, but the value 'true' (encoded by the empty tuple) is sent out. Any node that receives the message 'true' will output it. When A or B is empty locally, the transducer simply outputs the desired output directly. The transducer is coordination-free, since if we take care to have at least one node that knows A, and another node that knows B, but no node knows both, then the query can be computed without communication. When A and B are both nonempty, however, a run on the horizontal partition where every node has the entire input will not reach quiescence without communication. □

Example 5. A simple example of a transducer that is not coordination-free, i.e., requires communication, is the one that computes the emptiness query on an input set S. Since every node can have a part of the input, the nodes must coordinate with each other to be certain that S is empty at every node. Every node sends out its identifier (using the relation *Id*) on condition that its local relation S is empty. Received messages are forwarded, so that if S is globally empty, eventually all nodes will have received the identifiers of *all* nodes, which can be checked using the relation *All*. When this has happened the transducer at each node outputs 'true'. □

Coordination-freeness is undecidable for FO-transducers, but we can identify a syntactic class of transducers that is guaranteed to be coordination-free, and that will prove to have the same expressive power as the class of coordination-free transducers. Specifically, recall that an *oblivious* transducer is one that does not use the system relations *Id* and *All*. For now we observe:

PROPOSITION 6. *Every network-topology independent, oblivious transducer is coordination-free.*

PROOF. Let Π be a network-topology independent, oblivious transducer. Let Q be the query distributedly computed by Π. On a one-node network and given any input instance I, transducer Π reaches quiescence and outputs $Q(I)$ by doing only heartbeat transitions. Now consider any other network, any instance I over S_{in}, and the horizontal partition H that places the entire I at every node. Since Π is oblivious, nodes cannot detect that they are on a network with multiple nodes unless they communicate. So, by doing only heartbeat transitions initially, every node will act the same as if in a one-node network and will already output the entire $Q(I)$. □

6. THE CALM CONJECTURE

CONJECTURE 1. *(CALM conjecture [16]) A program has an eventually consistent, coordination-free execution strategy if and only if it is expressible in (monotonic) Datalog.*

It is not specified what is meant by "program" or "strategy"; here, we will take these terms to mean "query" and "distributedly computable by a transducer", respectively. The term "eventually consistent" is then formalized by our notions of consistency and network-topology independence. Under this interpretation, the conjecture becomes "a query can be distributedly computed by a coordination-free transducer if and only if it is expressible in Datalog".

Let us immediately get the if-side of the conjecture out of the way. It surely holds, and many versions of it are already contained in Theorem 3. That theorem talks about oblivious transducers, but we have seen in Proposition 6 that these are coordination-free.

As to the only-if side, the explicit mention of Datalog is a bit of a nuisance. Datalog is limited to polynomial time whereas there certainly are monotone queries outside PTIME. This continues to hold for queries expressible in the language Dedalus that Alvaro and Hellerstein use; we will show this in Section 8. We also mention the celebrated paper [7] where Afrati, Cosmadakis and Yannakakis show that even within PTIME there exist queries that are monotone but not expressible in Datalog.

We will see in Corollary 9(3) how a Datalog version of the CALM conjecture can be obtained. Datalog aside, however, the true emphasis of the CALM conjecture clearly lies in the monotonicity aspect. Indeed we confirm it in this sense:

THEOREM 7. *Every query that is distributedly computed by a coordination-free transducer is monotone.*

PROOF. Let Q be the query distributedly computed by the coordination-free transducer Π. Let $I \subseteq J$ be two input instances and let $t \in Q(I)$. We must show $t \in Q(J)$. Consider a network $\mathcal{N}$ with at least two nodes. Since Π is coordination-free, there exists a horizontal partition H of I such that $Q(I)$ is already output distributedly over the nodes, by letting the nodes do only heartbeat transitions. Let v be a node where t is output. Let v' be a node different from v and consider the horizontal partition H' of J where $H'(v) = H(v)$ and $H'(v') = H(v') \cup (J \setminus I)$. The partial run on H where v first does only heartbeat transitions until t is output, is also a partial run on H'. This partial run can be extended to a fair run, so t is output by some fair run of $(\mathcal{N}, \Pi)$ on H'. Since $(\mathcal{N}, \Pi)$ is consistent, t will also be output in any other fair run on any horizontal partition of J. Hence, t belongs to the query computed by $(\mathcal{N}, \Pi)$ applied to J. Moreover, Π is network-topology independent, so t belongs to $Q(J)$. □

COROLLARY 8 (CALM PROPERTY). *The following are equivalent for any query Q:*

1. *Q can be distributedly computed by a transducer that is coordination-free.*

2. *Q can be distributedly computed by a transducer that is oblivious.*

3. *Q is monotone.*

PROOF. Theorem 3 yields (3) $\Rightarrow$ (2); Proposition 6 yields (2) $\Rightarrow$ (1); Theorem 7 yields (1) $\Rightarrow$ (3). $\square$

Similarly we obtain the following versions of the CALM property:

COROLLARY 9. *Within each of the following three groups, the statements are equivalent, for any query Q:*

1. *Let $\mathcal{L}$ be a computationally complete query language.*

   (a) *Q can be distributedly computed by a coordination-free $\mathcal{L}$-transducer.*

   (b) *Q can be distributedly computed by an oblivious $\mathcal{L}$-transducer.*

   (c) *Q is monotone and partial computable.*

2. (a) *Q can be distributedly computed by a coordination-free FO-transducer.*

   (b) *Q can be distributedly computed by an oblivious FO-transducer.*

   (c) *Q is monotone and expressible in the language 'while'.*

3. (a) *Q can be distributedly computed by a coordination-free nonrecursive-Datalog-transducer.*

   (b) *Q can be distributedly computed by a nonrecursive-Datalog-transducer that is oblivious.*

   (c) *Q is expressible in Datalog.*

7. FURTHER RESULTS

It is natural to wonder about variations of our model. One question may be about the system relations Id and All. Without them (the oblivious case) we know that we are always coordination-free and thus monotone. What if we have only Id or only All? As to coordination-freeness, it is readily verified that the argument given in the proof of Proposition 6 still works in the presence of Id. It does not work in the presence of All, and indeed we have the following counterexample.

Example 6. We describe a transducer that is network-topology independent, does not use Id, but that is not coordination-free. The query expressed is simply the identity query on a set S. The transducer can detect whether he is alone in the network by looking at the relation All. If so, he simply outputs the result. If he is not alone, he sends out a ping message. Only upon receiving a ping message he outputs the result. Regardless of the horizontal partition, on a multiple-node network, communication is required for the transducer network to produce the required output. $\square$

So, coordination-freeness is not guaranteed when we use the relation All, but yet, monotonicity is not lost:

THEOREM 10. *Every query distributedly computed by a transducer that does not use the system relation Id, is monotone.*

PROOF. Let Π be a network-topology independent transducer and let Q be the query distributedly computed by Π. Let $I \subseteq J$ be two input instances and let $t \in Q(I)$. We must show $t \in Q(J)$. Consider the network $\mathcal{R}_4$ with four nodes 1–2–3–4–1 in the form of a ring. Let H be the horizontal

partition of I that places the entire I at every node. Consider now the following, fair, run ρ of $(\mathcal{R}_4, \Pi)$ on H. This particular run has a fifo behavior of the message buffers. We go around the network in rounds. The construction is such (proof omitted) that after each round, all nodes have the same state and the same fifo message buffer queue. In each round, we first let each node do a heartbeat transition. Then, if some (hence every) input buffer is nonempty, let each node do a delivery transition, receiving the first tuple in its message buffer. If the buffers are empty, we let each node do a second heartbeat transition. Since $t \in Q(I)$, we know that t is output during run ρ. Without loss of generality, assume node 1 outputs tuple t in round m during run ρ.

We now consider the modified network $\mathcal{R}'$ on the same four nodes, obtained by adding the shortcut 2–4 to $\mathcal{R}_4$. Consider the horizontal partition H' of J defined by $H'(1) = H'(2) = H'(4) = I$ and $H'(3) = J \setminus I$. Consider now the following prefix ρ' of a possible run of $(\mathcal{R}', \Pi)$ on H'. The idea is that run ρ is mimicked until round m, but we ignore node 3 completely. The construction is such (proof omitted) that after each round, nodes 1, 2 and 4 have the same state and the same fifo message buffer queue as after the same round in ρ. In each round i, we first let each node 1, 2 and 4 do a heartbeat transition. Then, if in the same round in ρ we made delivery transitions, then we make the same delivery transitions in ρ' but not for node 3. If in round i we did a series of second heartbeat transitions, we do the same in ρ' but again not for node 3.

The result is that t is also output by node 1 during any fair run that has ρ' as a prefix. Since Π is network-topology independent, we have $t \in Q(J)$ as desired. $\square$

As a corollary we can add two more statements to the three equivalent statements of the CALM Property (Corollary 8):

COROLLARY 11. *The following statements are equivalent for any query Q:*

1. *Q can be distributedly computed by an oblivious transducer.*

2. *Q can be distributedly computed by a transducer that does not use the Id relation.*

3. *Q can be distributedly computed by a transducer that does not use the All relation.*

To conclude this section we note that distributed algorithms involving a form of coordination typically require the participating nodes to have some knowledge about the other participating nodes [9]. This justifies our modeling of this knowledge in the form of the system relations Id and All. Importantly, we have shown that these relations are only necessary if one wants to compute a nonmonotone query in a distributed fashion.

8. DEDALUS

Dedalus [8] is the declarative language used by Alvaro et al. to model and program network protocols. The precise expressive power of Dedalus needs to be better understood. Here, we compare Dedalus to our setting and we also show that Dedalus can at least simulate arbitrary Turing machines in an eventually consistent manner.[1] By the time hierarchy theorem [19], it follows that eventually-consistent Dedalus programs are not contained in PTIME, let alone in Datalog.

Dedalus is a temporal version of Datalog with negation where the last position of each predicate carries a timestamp. All subgoals of any rule must be joined on this timestamp. The timestamp of the head of the rule can either be the timestamp of the body (a "deductive rule"), or it can be the successor timestamp (an "inductive rule"). The deductive rules must be stratifiable, thus guaranteeing modular stratification and a deterministic semantics through a unique minimal model. Note how this corresponds well to transducers using stratified Datalog as local query language.

Furthermore, Dedalus has a non-deterministic construct by which facts can be derived with a random timestamp, used to model asynchronous communication. In our transducer networks, the same effect is achieved by the semantics we have given, by which one node may send a message in its nth local step, whereas another node may receive the message in its mth local step where m can be smaller as well as larger than n. As long as a Dedalus program is monotone in the relations derived by asynchronous rules, the program remains deterministic, but there is no longer a simple syntactic guarantee for this.

The feature that makes Dedalus quite powerful is that timestamp values can also occur as data values, i.e., in other predicate positions than the last one. This feature, called "entanglement", is intriguing and makes Dedalus go beyond languages such as temporal Datalog [11]. Note that entanglement does not involve arithmetic on timestamps; it merely allows them to be copied in relations in a safe, Datalog-like manner.

Turing machine simulations in database query languages are well known [1, 3, 17], but the Dedalus setting is new, so we describe the Turing machine simulation in some detail. For any database schema $\mathcal{S}$ we can consider the database schema $\mathcal{S}^{\text{time}}$ with the same relation names as $\mathcal{S}$, but in $\mathcal{S}^{\text{time}}$ each relation name has an arity higher by one than in $\mathcal{S}$, in order to accommodate timestamps. Dedalus works with temporal database instances; these are instances over schemas of the form $\mathcal{S}^{\text{time}}$ in which the last coordinate of every fact is a natural number acting as timestamp. For any instance I over $\mathcal{S}^{\text{time}}$ and any timestamp value n, let $I|_n$ be the instance over $\mathcal{S}$ obtained from the facts in I that have timestamp n, and let $\hat{I}$ equal $\bigcup_n I|_n$.

Now let Σ be an arbitrary but fixed finite alphabet, and consider the database schema $\mathcal{S}_\Sigma$ consisting of relation names $Tape$ of arity two, $Begin$ and End of arity one, and a of arity one for each $a \in \Sigma$. Recall that any string $s = a_1 \ldots a_p$ over Σ can be presented as an instance I_s over $\mathcal{S}_\Sigma$. We consider only strings of length at least two. Then I_s consists of the facts $Tape(1, 2), \ldots, Tape(p-1, p), Begin(1), End(p), a_1(1), \ldots, a_p(p)$. Such instances, and isomorphic instances, are known as *word structures* [21].

For any Turing machine M, we define the boolean (0-ary) query Q_M over the class of temporal instances over $\mathcal{S}_\Sigma^{\text{time}}$ as follows.

- If $\hat{I}$ is a word structure representing string s, and M accepts s, then $Q_M(I)$ equals true (encoded by the 0-ary relation containing the empty tuple). If M does not terminate on s, then $Q_M(I)$ is undefined.

- If $\hat{I}$ contains a word structure, but is not a word structure (due to spurious facts), then $Q_M(I)$ also equals true.

- In all other cases $Q_M(I)$ equals false (encoded by the empty 0-ary relation).

The second item in the definition is there to ensure that Q_M is monotone; nevertheless, when we give Q_M a proper word structure as input, a faithful simulation of M is required. Hence, the computational complexity of Q_M is as high as that of the language accepted by M.

We say that a (deterministic) Dedalus program Π *expresses* a boolean query Q over temporal instances, if for every I such that $Q(I)$ is defined, $\Pi(I)$ contains a fact $Accept(n)$ for some n if and only if $Q(I)$ is true. Moreover, Π expresses Q in an *eventually consistent way* if for every I such that $Q(I)$ is defined, there exists n such that $\Pi(I)|_m = \Pi(I)|_n$ for all $m \geq n$.

THEOREM 12. *For every Turing machine M, the query Q_M is expressible by a Dedalus program in an eventually consistent way.*

PROOF. We only sketch the proof and assume some familiarity with Dedalus. The main difficulties to overcome are the following.

1. Detection of a word structure. Since input facts can arrive at any timestamp, they are persisted, e.g.,

   $$a(x, n+1) \leftarrow a(x, n) \qquad \text{for each } a \in \Sigma$$

   (Officially, this should be done using "pos-predicates" [8].) A word structure is detected at time n if there is a path in the *Tape* relation, beginning in an element in *Begin*, and ending in an element in *End*, where all elements on the path are *labeled*, i.e., belong to some a relation. This is readily expressed in Datalog.

2. Detection of spurious tuples. When a word structure is already detected, we can detect spurious tuples by checking for one of the following conditions, which can be expressed in stratified Datalog:

   (a) *Begin* and *End* contain more than a single element.

   (b) An element in the active domain is labeled by two different alphabet letters.

   (c) *Tape* is more than a successor relation from its begin to its end point, i.e., there is an element on the tape with out-degree or in-degree more than one, or there is an element on the tape that is not reachable from *Begin*.

   (d) There exists a phantom element, i.e., an element in the active domain that is not labeled, or that is not on the tape.

3. Turing machine simulation. When a proper word structure is discovered, without spurious tuples, the simulation of M is started. We copy the a predicates to

---

[1]This is not the same as saying that all computable queries can be expressed in Dedalus; we conjecture this is not the case.

a^{simul} predicates. This is necessary because a is persisted, which would cause the simulation to be overwritten. And we need to continue persisting a because new (spurious) a facts may still arrive after the simulation has already started. Each transition of M goes to the next timestamp. For each state q of M we use a predicate $q(x, n)$ that holds if M at time n is in state q with its head on position x. Timestamp values (entanglement) is used to extend the finite tape to the right. Care must be taken to do this only when necessary, to ensure eventual consistency. Moreover, we must avoid confusing timestamp values that may also already occur as input tape cells, with timestamp values that are used to build the tape extension. Thereto we use a separate predicate $TapeExt$ to represent the tape extension. For example, the first time that M extends the input tape, in some state q and seeing letter a at the last input position, is expressed by the following rules:

$$ExtNext(x, n) \leftarrow TapeExt(x, y, n)$$
$$TapeExt(x, n, n+1) \leftarrow q(x, n), a(x, n),$$
$$End(x, n), \neg ExtNext(x, n)$$

For positions on the extension tape, we use predicates q_{ext} instead of q and $a_{\mathrm{ext}}^{\mathrm{simul}}$ instead of a^{simul}.

$\square$

Distribution is not built in Dedalus but can be simulated using precisely one extra data value in each fact that serves as a location specifier. For a rule all subgoals must be joined on the location specifier and one can differentiate between rules depending on how the location specifier in the head relates to the location specifier in the body [8]. The above theorem can be extended to a distributed setting where different peers send around their input data to their peers. The receiving peer treats these messages as EDB facts. This works without coordination since the program is monotone in the EDB relations. More generally, it seems one can define a syntactic class of "oblivious" Dedalus programs in analogy to our notion of oblivious transducers: for each Dedalus rule disallow the projection of location variables in the body into positions of the head fact that are not used as the location specifier. Roughly speaking, that prevents a Dedalus program to reason about what nodes send what facts.

9. CONCLUSION

Encouraged by Hellerstein [15, 16], we have tried in this paper to formalize and prove the CALM conjecture. We do not claim that our approach is the only one that works. Yet we believe our approach is natural because it is firmly grounded in previous database theory practice, and delivers solid results.

Much further work is possible; we list a few obvious topics:

- Look at Hellerstein's other conjectures.

- Investigate the expressiveness of variations or extensions of the basic distributed computation model presented here.

- Understand the exact expressive power of the Dedalus language. Also, investigate the automated verification of Dedalus programs.

- Identify special cases where essential semantic notions such as monotonicity, consistency, network-topology independence, coordination-freeness, are decidable.

10. REFERENCES

[1] S. Abiteboul, R. Hull, and V. Vianu. *Foundations of Databases.* Addison-Wesley, 1995.

[2] S. Abiteboul and E. Simon. Fundamental properties of deterministic and nondeterministic extensions of Datalog. *Theoretical Computer Science*, 78:137–158, 1991.

[3] S. Abiteboul and V. Vianu. Datalog extensions for database queries and updates. *Journal of Computer and System Sciences*, 43(1):62–124, 1991.

[4] S. Abiteboul and V. Vianu. Generic computation and its complexity. In *Proceedings 23rd ACM Symposium on the Theory of Computing*, pages 209–219, 1991.

[5] S. Abiteboul and V. Vianu. Computing with first-order logic. *Journal of Computer and System Sciences*, 50(2):309–335, 1995.

[6] S. Abiteboul, V. Vianu, et al. Relational transducers for electronic commerce. *Journal of Computer and System Sciences*, 61(2):236–269, 2000.

[7] F.N. Afrati, S.C. Cosmadakis, and M. Yannakakis. On Datalog vs polynomial time. *Journal of Computer and System Sciences*, 51(2):177–196, 1995.

[8] P. Alvaro, W. Marczak, et al. Dedalus: Datalog in time and space. Technical Report EECS-2009-173, University of California, Berkeley, 2009.

[9] H. Attiya and J. Welch. *Distributed Computing: Fundamentals, Simulations, and Advanced Topics.* Wiley, 2004.

[10] A. Blass, Y. Gurevich, and J. Van den Bussche. Abstract state machines and computationally complete query languages. *Information and Computation*, 174(1):20–36, 2002.

[11] J. Chomicki and T. Imieliński. Finite representation of infinite query answers. *ACM Transactions on Database Systems*, 18(2):181–223, June 1993.

[12] A. Deutsch, R. Hull, F. Patrizi, and V. Vianu. Automatic verification of data-centric business processes. In *Proceedings 12th International Conference on Database Theory*, 2009.

[13] A. Deutsch, L. Sui, and V. Vianu. Specification and verification of data-driven Web applications. *Journal of Computer and System Sciences*, 73(3):442–474, 2007.

[14] A. Deutsch, L. Sui, V. Vianu, and D. Zhou. Verification of communicating data-driven Web services. In *Proceedings 25th ACM Symposium on Principles of Database Systems*, pages 90–99. ACM Press, 2006.

[15] J.M. Hellerstein. Datalog redux: experience and conjecture. In *Proceedings 29th ACM Symposium on Principles of Database Systems*, pages 1–2. ACM Press, 2010.

[16] J.M. Hellerstein. The declarative imperative: experiences and conjectures in distributed logic. *SIGMOD Record*, 39(1):5–19, 2010.

[17] N. Immerman. *Descriptive Complexity.* Springer, 1999.

[18] B.T. Loo et al. Declarative networking. *Communications of the ACM*, 52(11):87–95, 2009.

[19] C.H. Papadimitriou. *Computational Complexity*. Addison-Wesley, 1994.

[20] M. Spielmann. Verification of relational transducers for electronic commerce. *Journal of Computer and System Sciences*, 66(1):40–65, 2003.

[21] W. Thomas. Languages, automata, and logic. In G. Rozenberg and A. Salomaa, editors, *Handbook of Formal Languages*, volume 3, chapter 7. Springer, 1997.

A Rule-based Language
for Web Data Management[*]

Serge Abiteboul
INRIA Saclay
& LSV-ENS Cachan
fname.lname@inria.fr

Meghyn Bienvenu
CNRS
& Université Paris-Sud
meghyn@lri.fr

Alban Galland
INRIA Saclay
& LSV-ENS Cachan
alban.galland@inria.fr

Émilien Antoine
INRIA Saclay
& Université Paris Sud
emilien.antoine@inria.fr

ABSTRACT

There is a new trend to use Datalog-style rule-based languages to specify modern distributed applications, notably on the Web. We introduce here such a language for a distributed data model where peers exchange messages (i.e. logical facts) as well as rules. The model is formally defined and its interest for distributed data management is illustrated through a variety of examples. A contribution of our work is a study of the impact on expressiveness of "delegations" (the installation of rules by a peer in some other peer) and explicit timestamps. We also validate the semantics of our model by showing that under certain natural conditions, our semantics converges to the same semantics as the centralized system with the same rules. Indeed, we show this is even true when updates are considered.

Categories and Subject Descriptors

H.2.4 [**Information Systems**]: Database Management—*Systems, Distributed databases*

General Terms

Languages, Theory

Keywords

Datalog, Delegation, Distribution, Web

[*]This work has been partially funded by the European Research Council under the European Community's Seventh Framework Programme (FP7/2007-2013) / ERC grant Webdam, agreement 226513. http://webdam.inria.fr/

1. INTRODUCTION

The management of modern distributed information, notably on the Web, is a challenging problem. Because of its complexity, there has recently been a trend towards using high-level Datalog-style rules to specify such applications. We introduce here a model for distributed computation where peers exchange messages (i.e. logical facts) as well as rules. The model provides a novel setting with a strong emphasis on dynamicity and interactions (in a Web 2.0 style). Because the model is powerful, it provides a clean basis for the specification of complex distributed applications. Because it is simple, it provides a formal framework for studying many facets of the problem such as distribution, concurrency, and expressivity in the context of distributed autonomous peers.

In recent years, there has been renewed interest in studying languages in the Datalog family for a wide range of applications ranging from program analysis, to security and privacy protocols, to natural language processing, or multiplayer games. For references see [17] and the forthcoming proceedings of the Datalog 2.0 workshop [13]. We are concerned here with using rule-based languages for the management of data in distributed settings, as in web applications [2, 7, 14, 4], networking [21, 20, 16] or distributed systems [22]. The arguments in favor of using Datalog-style specifications for complex distributed applications are the familiar ones, cf. [17].

A main contribution of the paper is a new model for distributed data management that combines in a formal setting deductive rules as in Datalog with negation, cf. [12] (to specify intensional data) and active rules as in Datalog¬¬ [8] (for updates and communications). There have already been a number of proposals for combining active and deductive features in a rule-based language; see [19, 17] and our discussion of related work. However, there is yet to be a consensus on the most appropriate such language. We therefore believe that there is a need to continue investigating novel language features adapted to modern data management and to formally study the properties of the resulting new models.

The language we introduce, called Webdamlog, is tailored to facilitate the specification of data exchange between autonomous peers, which is essential to the applications we have in mind. Towards that goal, the novel feature we introduce is *delegation*, that is, the possibility of installing a rule at another peer. In its simplest form, delegation is essentially a *remote materialized view*. In its general form, it allows peers to exchange rules, i.e., knowledge beyond simple facts, and thereby provides the means for a peer to delegate work to other peers, in Active XML style [3]. We show using examples that because of delegation, the model is particularly well suited for distributed applications, providing support for reactions to changes in evolving environments.

A key contribution is a study of the impact of delegation on expressivity. We show that view delegation (delegation in its simplest form, allowing only the specification of materialized views) strictly augments the power of the language. We also prove that full delegation further augments it. These results demonstrate the power of exchanging rules in addition to facts.

A message sent from peer p, received at peer q, that starts some task at q, introduces a kind of synchronization between the two peers. Thus, time implicitly plays an important role in the model. We show that when explicit time is allowed (each peer having its local time), view delegation no longer augments the expressive power of the language.

Because of their asynchronous nature, distributed applications in Webdamlog are nondeterministic in general. To validate our semantics for deductive rules, we study two kinds of systems that guarantee a form of convergence (even in presence of certain updates). These are positive systems (positive rules and persistence of extensional facts) and strongly-stratified systems (allowing a particular kind of stratified negation [12] for restricted deductive rules and fixed extensional facts). We also show that both types of systems essentially behave like the corresponding centralized systems.

The language Webdamlog is used in the implementation of a Web data management system that we briefly discuss. We also discuss some known optimization techniques that render this technology feasible.

Related work. This work is part of the ERC project *Webdam* on the foundations of Web data management [30]. The project is motivated by the conviction that the management of distributed data is still missing a unified formal foundation, and that this is hindering progress in Web data management. This opinion seems to be increasingly shared [17].

The present work is motivated by the renewed interest in distribution of Datalog. To our knowledge, the first attempts to distribute Datalog on different peers are [18] and [26]. The first distributes a positive Datalog program on different machines after a compilation phase. The second adapts classical transformations of positive programs based on semi-joins to minimize distribution cost.

Perhaps the most interesting usage of Datalog-style rules for distributed data management came recently from the Berkeley and U. Penn groups. They used distributed versions of Datalog to implement Web routers [24], DHT [23] and Map-Reduce [9] rather efficiently. By demonstrating what could be efficiently achieved with this approach, these works were essential motivations for our own. The most elaborate variant of distributed Datalog used in these works is presented in [21] and formally specified in [25]. In both papers, the semantics is operational and based on a distribution of the program before the execution. In view of issues with this model, a new model was recently introduced in [17], based on an explicit time constructor. We found the

semantics of negation together with the use of time rather unnatural. In particular, time is used as an abstract logical notion to control execution steps and the future may have influence on the past. As a consequence, we found it difficult to understand what applications are doing as well as to prove results on their language. However, we have been influenced by this line of work.

We have also been influenced by previous work on Active XML [3], a model for distributed data intensive applications. Rules are used in Active XML [7], but they are different because the data are XML trees. Perhaps the work closest to that presented here is [1] that adapts query-subquery optimization [29] to a variant of positive distributed Datalog.

We are currently exploring a data model, called Webdam Exchange, for access control and distribution on the Web [5]. The model presented here is motivated to a large extent by the needs of Webdam Exchange applications.

Outline. The paper is organized as follows. We introduce the model in Section 2, first by means of examples and then formally. In the following section, we discuss some key features of the model and illustrate them with more examples. In Section 4, we compare the expressivity of different variants of our model. In Section 5, we discuss the convergence of Webdamlog systems and compare the semantics to the "centralized semantics", for the positive and strongly-stratified restrictions of the language. In Section 6, we mention an implementation and optimization techniques. The final section concludes with directions for future work.

2. THE MODEL

In this section, we first illustrate the model with examples, then formalize it. More examples and a discussion of key issues will be provided in the next section.

2.1 Informal presentation

Simple Webdamlog by example. We introduce with a first example the main concepts of the model: the notions of *fact* that captures both *local tuples* and *messages* between peers, *extensional* and *intensional* data, and *(Webdamlog) rule*.

Consider a particular peer, namely *myIphone*, with the relation *birthday* that gives the birthdates of friends and how to wish them a happy birthday (on which servers, with which messages). Examples of facts are:

birthday@myIphone("Alice", sendmail, inria.fr, 08/08)
birthday@myIphone("Bob", sms, BobIphone, 01/12)

Now the following [*Happy-Birthday*] rule is used to actually send birthday messages:

$message@$peer($name, "Happy birthday") :-
    today@myIphone($d),
    birthday@myIphone($name, $message, $peer, $d)

Observe that peer and message names are treated as data. The two previous *birthday*-facts represent pieces of local knowledge of *myIphone*. Now consider the fact :

sendmail@inria.fr(Alice, "Happy birthday")

This fact describes a message that is sent from *myIphone* to *inria.fr*.

As in deductive databases, the model distinguishes between extensional relations that are defined by a finite set of ground facts and intensional relations that are defined by rules. So for instance, the relation *birthday* on myIphone may be intensional and defined as follows:

    intensional birthday@myIphone(string, relation, peer, date)
    birthday@myIphone($n, $m, $p, $d) :-
        birthdates@myIphone($n, $d),
        contact@myIphone($n, $m, $p)

using extensional relations.

As usual, intensional knowledge is defined by rules such as the previous one, that we call *deductive* rules. Other rules such as the [*Happy-Birthday*] rule, that we call *active*, produce extensional facts. Such an extensional fact $m@p$ is received by the peer p (e.g. inria.fr and Bob's Iphone). During its next phase of local processing, this peer will consume these facts and produce new ones. By default, any processed fact disappears. Facts can be made persistent using persistence rules, illustrated next on the relation *birthdates@myIphone*:

    birthdates@myIphone($n, $d) :-
        birthdates@myIphone($n, $d),
        ¬ del.birthdates@myIphone($n, $d)

The rules state that a fact persists unless there is explicitly a deletion message (e.g. *del.birthdates*).

Delegation by example. In the model, the semantics of the global system is defined based on local semantics and the exchange of messages and rules. Intuitively, a given peer chooses how to move to another state based on its local state (a set of personal facts and messages received from other peers) and its program. A move consists in (1) consuming the local facts, (2) deriving new local facts, which define the next state, (3) deriving nonlocal facts, i.e., messages sent to other peers, and (4) modifying their programs via "delegations".

The derivation of local facts and messages sent to other peers are both standard and were illustrated in the previous example. The notion of delegation is novel and is illustrated next. Consider the following rule, installed at peer p:

    at p: m@q() :- m₁@p($x), m₂@p'($x)

where $m@q, m_1@p$ and $m_2@p'$ are all extensional. Its semantics is as follows. Suppose that we have a value a_1 such that $m_1@p(a_1)$ holds, then the effect of this rule is to install at p' the following rule:

    at p': m@q() :- m₂@p'(a₁)

The action of installing a rule at some other peer is called *delegation*. When p' runs, if $m_2@p'(a_1)$ holds, it will send the message $m@q()$ to q.

Now suppose instead that $m@q$ is intensional. When p' runs, if $m_2@p'(a_1)$ holds, the effect of this rule is to install at q the following rule:

    at q: m@q() :-

The intuition for the delegation from p to p' is that there is some knowledge from p' that is needed in order to realize the task specified by this particular rule. So, to perform that task, p delegates the remainder of the rule to p'. The

delegation from p' to q is somewhat different. Peer p' knows that $m@q$ (an intensional fact) holds until some change occurs. As q may need this fact for his own computation, p' will pass this information to q in the form of a rule (since as a fact, it would be consumed).

We next formalize the model illustrated by the previous example.

2.2 Formal model

Alphabets. We assume the existence of two infinite disjoint alphabets of sorted *constants*: *peer* and *relation*. We also consider the alphabet of *data* that includes in addition to *peer* and *relation*, infinitely many other constants of different sorts (notably, *integer*, *string*, *bitstream*, etc.). It is because *data* includes *peer* and *relation* that we may write facts such as those in the *birthday* relation. Similarly we have corresponding alphabets of sorted *variables*. An identifier starting by the symbol $ implicitly denotes a variable. A *term* is a variable or a constant.

A *schema* is an expression $(\Pi, \mathcal{E}, \mathcal{I}, \sigma)$ where Π is a (possibly infinite) set of peer IDs; $\mathcal{E}$ and $\mathcal{I}$ are disjoint sets, respectively, of *extensional* and *intensional* names of the form $m@p$ for some relation name m and some peer p; and the typing function σ defines for each $m@p$ in $\mathcal{E} \cup \mathcal{I}$ the arity and sorts of its components. Note because $\mathcal{I} \cap \mathcal{E} = \emptyset$, no m is both intensional and extensional in the same p. Considering Π to be infinite reflects the assumption that the set of peers is dynamic and of unbounded size just like data.

Facts and rules. Given a relation $m@p$, a (ground) (*p*-)*fact* is an expression $m@p(\overline{u})$ where $\overline{u}$ is a vector of data elements of the proper type, i.e., correct arity and correct sort for each component. For a set K of facts and a peer p, $K[p]$ is the set of *p*-facts in K. The notion of fact is central to the model. It will be the basis for both stored knowledge and communication. For instance, in the peer p, if we derive the extensional fact $r@p(1, 2)$, this is a fact p knows. On the other hand, if we derive the extensional fact $s@q(2, 3)$, this is a message that p sends to q.

A *(Webdamlog) rule* is an expression of the form

$$M_{n+1}@Q_{n+1}(\overline{U}_{n+1}) :\text{-} (\neg)M_1@Q_1(\overline{U}_1)...(\neg)M_n@Q_n(\overline{U}_n)$$

where each M_i is a relation term, each Q_i is a peer term and each $\overline{U}_i$ is a vector of data terms. We also allow in the body of the rules, atoms of the form $X = Y$ or $X \neq Y$ where X, Y are terms.

We require a rule to be *safe*, i.e.,

1. For each i, if Q_i is a peer variable, it must be previously bound, i.e. it must appear in $\overline{U}_j$ for some positive literal $M_j@Q_j(\overline{U}_j), j < i$.

2. Each variable occuring in a literal $\neg M_i@Q_i(\overline{U}_i)$ must be previously bound to a positive literal.

3. Each variable in the head must be positively bound in the body.

REMARK 1. *Observe that we treat differently peer and relation names. By (1), a peer variable has to be previously positively bound. We insist on (1) so that we control explicitly to whom a peer sends a message or delegates a rule.*

Note also that because of (1), the ordering of literals is relevant. One could define a variation of the language, namely peer-unguarded Webdamlog *by not imposing Constraint (1) and considering all orderings of the body literals (with the negative ones seen implicitly after all the others). When deriving new facts, we simply consider first the positive literals and never consider a literal if its peer is not instantiated. This variant would not differ much from the language we study here.*

We say that a rule is *deductive* if the head relation is intensional. Otherwise, it is *active*. Rules live in peers. We say that a rule in a peer p is *local* if all Q_i in all body relations are from p. It is *fully local* if the head relation is also from p. We will see that the following four classes of rules play different roles:

Local deduction Fully local deductive rules are used to derive intensional facts *locally*.

Update Local active rules are used for sending messages, i.e., facts, that modify the databases of the peers that receive them.

View delegation The local but not fully local deductive rules provide some form of view materialization. For instance, this rule results in providing at q a view of some data from p:

$$at\ p:\ r@q(\overline{U}) :\text{-} (\neg)r_1@p(\overline{U_1}), ...(\neg)r_n@p(\overline{U_n})$$

General delegation The remaining rules allow a peer to install arbitrary rules at other peers.

Peer and relation variables provide considerable flexibility for designing applications. However, observe that because of them, it may be unclear whether a rule is (fully) local or not, deductive or active. Using atoms such as $Q = p$, $Q \neq p$ for some constant peers and similarly for relations, one could remove the ambiguity and distinguish the nature of the rule. We omit the formal details. Note that in a real system, one can wait until a rule is (partially) instantiated at runtime to find what its nature is, and decide what should be done with it.

The semantics of Webdamlog is based on autonomous local computations of the peers. We consider this first, then look at the global semantics of Webdamlog systems.

Local computation. A local computation happens at a particular peer. Based on its set of facts and set of rules, the peer does the following: (1) some local deduction of intensional facts, (2) the derivation of extensional facts that either define its next state or are sent as messages, and (3) the delegation of rules to other peers.

(Local deduction) For local deduction, we want to rely on the semantics of standard Datalog languages. However, because of possible relation variables, Webdamlog rules are not strictly speaking proper Datalog$^\neg$ rules, since the relation names of atoms may include variables. So, to specify local deduction, we proceed as follows. We start by *grounding* the peer and relation variables appearing in the rules. More precisely, for each rule

$$M_{n+1}@Q_{n+1}(\overline{U}_{n+1}) :\text{-} (\neg)M_1@Q_1(\overline{U}_1)...(\neg)M_n@Q_1(\overline{U}_n)$$

of peer p, we consider the set of rules obtained by instantiating relation variables M_i with relation constants and peer

variables Q_i with peer constants. To ensure finiteness, we only use constants from the active domain of the peer, that is, that appear in some fact or rule in the peer state. We can now treat pairs $m@p$ of relation and peer constants as normal relation symbols in Datalog. Since for local deduction, we are only interested in fully local deductive rules, we will remove rules with a relation $m@q$ for $q \neq p$ or an extensional relation in the head. We must also remove rules that violate the arity or sort constraints of σ. The remaining rules are all fully local deductive rules which belong to standard Datalog.

Now, given a set I of facts and a set P_d of fully local deductive rules (obtained as in the preceding paragraph), we denote by $P_d^*(I)$ the set of facts inferred from I using P_d with a standard Datalog semantics. For instance, in absence of negation, the semantics is, as in classical Datalog, the least model containing I and satisfying P_d. When considering negation, one can use any standard semantics of Datalog with negation, say well-founded [27] or stable [15]. For results in Section 5.2, we will use a variant of stratified negation semantics [12].

(Updates) Given a set K of facts and a set P_a of local active rules, the set $P_a(K)$ of *active consequences* is the set of *extensional* facts $v(A)$ such that for some rule $A :\text{-} \Theta$ of P_a and some valuation v, $v(\Theta)$ holds in K, and $v(A), v(\Theta)$ obey the typing and sort constraints of σ. This is the set of *immediate consequences*. Note that it does not necessarily contain all facts in K.

Observe that for deductive rules, we typically use a fixpoint (based on the particular semantics that is used), whereas for active rules, we use the immediate consequence operator that is explicitly procedural.

(Delegation) Given a set K of facts and a set P of (active and deductive) rules in some peer p, the *delegation* $\gamma_{pq}(P, K)$ of peer p to $q \neq p$ is defined as follows.

If for some deductive rule $M@Q(\overline{U}) :\text{-} \Theta$ in P, there exists a valuation v such that $v\Theta$ holds in K, $v(Q) = q$, and the typing constraints in σ are respected, then

$$vM@vQ(v\overline{U}) :\text{-}$$

is in $\gamma_{pq}(P, K)$.

If for some active or deductive rule

$$A :\text{-} \Theta_0, (\neg)M@Q(\overline{U}), \Theta_1$$

in P (where Θ_0, Θ_1 are sequences of possibly negated atoms), there exists a valuation v satisfying σ such that $v\Theta_0$ contains only p-facts, $v\Theta_0$ holds in K, and $vQ = q(\neq p)$, then

$$vA :\text{-} (\neg)M@vQ(v\overline{U}), v\Theta_1$$

is in $\gamma_{pq}(P, K)$.

Nothing else appears in $\gamma_{pq}(P, K)$.

Observe that we do not produce facts that are improperly typed. In practice, a peer p may not have complete knowledge of the types of some peer q's relations. Then p may "derive" an improperly typed fact. This fact will be sent and rejected by q. From a formal viewpoint, it is simply assumed that the fact has not even been produced. Similarly, a peer may delegate an improperly typed rule, but that rule will never produce any facts, and so can safely be ignored.

We are now ready to specify the semantics of Webdamlog systems.

States and runs. A *(Webdamlog) state* of the schema $(\Pi,$ $\mathcal{E}, \mathcal{I}, \sigma)$ is a triple $(I, \Gamma, \tilde{\Gamma})$ where for each $p \in \Pi$, $I(p)$ is a finite set of extensional p-facts at p, $\Gamma(p)$ is the finite set of rules at p, and $\tilde{\Gamma}(p, q)$ $(p \neq q)$ is the set of rules that p delegated to q. For $p \in \Pi$, the $(p\text{-})move$ from $(I, \Gamma, \tilde{\Gamma})$ to $(I', \Gamma', \tilde{\Gamma}')$ (corresponding to the *firing* of peer p) is defined as follows. Let P_p be $\Gamma(p) \cup (\cup_q \tilde{\Gamma}(q, p))$, P_{pd} be the set of fully local deductive rules in P_p and P_{pa} the set of local active rules in it. Then the next state is defined as follows:

- (Local deduction) Let $K = P_{pd}^*(I(p))$.

- (Updates) $I'(p) = P_{pa}(K)[p]$; and
  (external activation) $I'(q) = I(q) \cup P_{pa}(K)[q]$ for each $q \neq p$.

- (Delegations) $\tilde{\Gamma}'(p, q) = \gamma_{pq}(P_p, K)$ for each q $\neq$ p; and $\tilde{\Gamma}'(p', q') = \tilde{\Gamma}(p', q')$ otherwise.

A *(Webdamlog) system* is a state $(I, \Gamma, \tilde{\Gamma})$ where $\tilde{\Gamma}(p, q) = \emptyset$. We will speak of the system (I, Γ) (since $\tilde{\Gamma}$ is empty). A sequence of moves is *fair* if each peer p is invoked infinitely many times. A *run* of a system (I, Γ) is a fair sequence of moves starting from (I, Γ).

Observe that $I(p)$ is finite for each peer and that it remains so during a run, even if the number of peers is infinite. Note also that deletions are implicit: a fact is deleted if it is not derived for the next state. We recall that facts can be made persistent using persistence rules of the form

$$r@p(\overline{U}) :\text{-} r@p(\overline{U}), \neg del.r@p(\overline{U})$$

In the following, such a rule for relation $r@p$ will be denoted *persistent r@p*.

REMARK 2. *It is important to observe a difference between the semantics of facts and rules. Observe that, if we visit twice peer p in a row, the fact-messages that p sends to q accumulate at q. On the other hand, the new set of delegations replaces the previous such set. Moreover, when we visit q, the messages of q are consumed whereas the delegations stay until they are replaced. These subtle differences are important to capture different facets of distributed computing, e.g., for capturing materialized views or for providing the expected semantics to extensional / intensional data.*

3. DISCUSSION

In this section, we present examples that illustrate the interest of our model for distributed data management, and make key observations about different aspects of the model.

We first consider two serious criticisms that could be adressed to the model, namely too much synchronization and too little local control. We show how both issues can be resolved.

Too much synchronization. Observe that moves capture some form of asynchronicity and parallelism. The peer that fires is randomly chosen and does (atomically) some processing. However, there is still some undesired form of synchronization. When we process peer p, messages from p to some peer q are instantaneously available in q. This is impossible to guarantee in practice. In a standard manner, when a more precise modeling is desired, one can introduce a peer acting as the network between p and q. Instead of going instantaneously from p to q, the message goes instantaneously from p to $network_{pq}$, waits there until $network_{pq}$

is fired, then goes instantaneously to q, and similarly for delegations. This captures more realistically what happens in practice, and does not require changing the model.

Too little local control. In the model we have defined, nothing prevents a peer p from modifying another peer q's relations or accessing q's data using delegation. In realistic settings, one would want a peer to be able to hold private information, which cannot be modified or accessed by another peer without its permission. This can be easily accomplished by extending the model with *local relations*. These relations can only appear in p's own facts and rules (i.e. $I(p)$ and $\Gamma(p)$), but not in any rules delegated to p (in practice, this means p would simply ignore any delegations using one of its private relations).

To illustrate, suppose that we want to control the access to a relation $r@p$ of peer p. We create for this purpose two local relations $read@p(\$r, \$q)$ and $write@p(\$r, \$q)$ that store who can read/write in p's relations. Note that the *read* and *write* relations are local, i.e., only p can specify the access rights in p. Relations $r@p$ and $del.r@p$ must also be local so that p control access to them. To obtain relation $r@p$, a peer q sends a message $get@p(r, q)$. The following rule controls whether q will receive the data it requested:

at p: send@\$q(\$r,\$x) :- get@p(\$r,\$q), read@p(\$r,\$q),
$\qquad\qquad$ \$r@p(\$x)

Insertions in $r@p$ (or deletions using $del.r@p$) are treated similarly. Access control is at the center of the work around WebdamExchange [5] that motivated the work presented here.

We next consider two subtleties of delegation.

Delegation and complexity. Consider the rule:

at p: m@q() :- m_1@p(\$q,\$x), m_2@\$q(\$x)

If there are 1000 distinct tuples $(p_i, 0)$ such that $m_1@p(p_i, 0)$ holds, then we have to install rules in 1000 distinct peers. So delegation is inherently transforming data complexity into program complexity.

Peer life and delegation. It is very simple in the model to consider that peers are born, die or hibernate. We simply have to insist that p can be fired (p-move) only if p is alive and not hibernating. We can assume that messages and delegations to dead peers are simply lost and that for hibernating ones, they are buffered somewhere in the network. A subtlety is that (with this variant of the model), if a peer dies without cleanly terminating, delegations from this peer are still valid. In practice, the system may realize that a particular peer is no longer present and terminate its delegations.

We conclude this section with three examples that illustrate different aspects of the language, communications, persistence services, and rule updates.

Multicasting. We can simulate channels, i.e., m-n communications with the following rules:

at q: persistent channelsubscribe@q
$\qquad$ channel@\$p(\$m,q,\$s) :- channelsubscribe@q(\$p,\$m),
$\qquad$ \$m@q(\$s)

The rules at peer q allows him to support channels. A peer p can subscribe to receiving all the messages from the channel m hosted by q by sending $channelsubscribe@q(p,m)$ to q. Then, whenever someone sends a message $m@q(s)$, p will receive $channel@p(m,q,s)$.

Database server replication. The following rule allows a database server to replicate relations from many peers:

    intensional export@db(relation,peer)
    at db: persistent tobeexported@db
        export@db($r,$p,$x) :- tobeexported@db($r, $p),
            $r@$p($x)

If a peer p wants his relation $r@p$ to be stored at db, then p simply needs to send q the message $tobeexported@db(r,p)$. Now, $export@db(r,p,\$x)$ is a copy of $r@p(\$x)$.

Rule updates and rule deployment. Observe that (to simplify) we assumed that the set of rules in a run is fixed, i.e., $\Gamma(p)$ is fixed for each p. It is straightforward to extend the model to support addition or deletion of rules. Furthermore, one might want to be able to control whether a particular rule is deployed on a particular peer. To illustrate this point, consider the two rules:

    at p: persistent server@p
        f@$p($u) :- server@p($p), f_1@$p($u_1),...,f_n@$p($u_n)

Sending the message $server@p(q)$ results in installing

    at q: f@q($u) :- f_1@q($u_1),...,f_n@q($u_n)

Note that if we send the message $del.server@p(q)$, the rule is removed.

4. EXPRESSIVITY

In this section, we study the expressive power of Webdamlog and of different languages that are obtained by allowing or restricting delegations. We also consider the expressive power of timestamps. More precisely, we consider the following languages for rules:

- WL (Webdamlog): the general language.

- VWL (views WL): the language obtained by restricting delegations to only view delegations.

- SWL (simple WL): the language obtained by disallowing all kinds of delegations.

At the core of view delegation, we find the maintenance of materialized views. To maintain views, we will see that timestamps turn out to be useful. More precisely, for time, we assume that each peer has a local predicate called *time* (with *time(t)* specifying that the current move started at local time t.) The predicate $<$ is used to compare timestamps. Note that each peer has its separate clock, so the comparison of timestamps of distinct peers is meaningless. To prevent time from being a source of nondeterminism, for t_1, t_2 two times at different peers, we have: $t_1 \not< t_2$ and $t_2 \not< t_1$. The languages obtained by extending the previous languages with timestamps are denoted as follows: WL^t, VWL^t, SWL^t.

Traces and simulations. To formally compare the expressivity of the above languages, we need to introduce the auxiliary notions of trace and simulation.

Let $r = (I_1, \Gamma_1, \tilde{\Gamma}_1), ...(I_n, \Gamma_n, \tilde{\Gamma}_n), ...$ be a run. Let M be a set of predicates and I a set of facts. Then $\Pi_M(I)$ is the set of facts in I with predicates in M. The M-*trace* of the run r for a set M of predicates is the subsequence of $\pi_M(I_{i_1}), ..., \pi_M(I_{i_n})...$ obtained by starting from $\pi_M(I_1), ..., \pi_M(I_n)...$ and removing all repetitions, i.e., deleting the $(k+1)$th element of the sequence if it is identical to the kth, until the sequence does not contain two identical consecutive elements. Given an initial state S and a set of predicates M, we denote by M-*trace*(S) the set of M-traces of runs from S. In some sense, it is what can be observed from S when only facts over M are visible.

Le α be a set of peers. An initial state $S = (I, \Gamma)$ can be α-*simulated* by an initial state $S' = (I, \Gamma')$ if $\Gamma(p) = \Gamma'(p)$ for all $p \in \alpha$ and S and S' have the same M-traces, where M is the set of relations of S. In other words, from the point of view of what is visible from S, S' behaves exactly like S. The set of peers α is meant to capture the part of the system (one or more peers) that we want to keep strictly identical.

Now, we say that a language L can be *simulated* by a language L', denoted $L \prec L'$, if there exists a translation τ from programs in L to programs in L' such that for each initial state (I, Γ) (with programs in L) and for each α, $(I, \overline{\tau}(\Gamma))$ α-simulates (I, Γ) where $\overline{\tau}$ is defined by: for each peer p,

- if $p \in \alpha$, $\overline{\tau}(\Gamma(p)) = \Gamma(p)$.

- otherwise, $\overline{\tau}(\Gamma(p)) = \tau(\Gamma(p))$.

Clearly, in the previous definition, the peers in α are not part of the simulation, they behave exactly as originally. In some sense, they should not even be aware that something changed.

Expressivity results. The expressive power of the different languages are compared in Figure 1. The containments are strict except for that of VWL^t inside WL^t where the issue remains open.

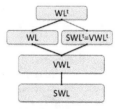

Figure 1: Expressive power of the rule languages (the inclusion is strict when the arc is in bold)

Our first result states that view delegation cannot be simulated by simple rules.

THEOREM 1 (NO VIEWS IN SWL). $VWL \not\prec SWL$.

PROOF. Intuitively, the difficulty is that the system may visit an arbitrary number of times the same peer p before visiting another peer q. Then q sees all the messages from

p at the same time and ignores in which order they were received.

Formally, consider a VWL system (I, Γ) consisting of three peers p_α, p, q. There are two facts that hold in the initial state: $true@p_\alpha()$, $true@p()$.

The set of active rules $\Gamma(p_\alpha)$ maintain the peer p_α in a permanent flip-flop between two modes:

$$at\ p_\alpha : r@p() :\text{-} true@p_\alpha()$$
$$false@p_\alpha() :\text{-} true@p_\alpha()$$
$$del.r@p() :\text{-} false@p_\alpha()$$
$$true@p_\alpha() :\text{-} false@p_\alpha()$$

Note that p_α keeps inserting then deleting the same proposition in p, namely $r@p()$. Peer p uses the following four rules:

$$at\ p : r@p() :\text{-} r@p(), \neg del.r@p()$$
$$true@p() :\text{-} false@p()$$
$$false@p() :\text{-} true@p()$$
$$s@q() :\text{-} r@p()$$

The first active rule maintains relation $r@p$. The next two active rules maintain p in a flip-flop between two modes. The last rule is a view delegation rule. It is because of this latter rule that the system is in VWL but not in SWL.

Finally peer q has one active rule:

$$at\ q : true@q() :\text{-} s@q()$$

Suppose for a contradiction that there is a p_α-simulation of this system in SWL, via some program translation function τ. As the set of peers is finite (namely 3), the initial state $(I, \tau(\Gamma))$ is finite. Thus, it includes a finite set of relation names and constants. This means that there is a finite number of distinct messages that can be sent during a run of this system. Now let r_1 be any run of $(I, \tau(\Gamma))$ such that the initial segment of activated peers is as follows: p_α, then p, then p_α, then p, etc., n times (for n to be fixed later in the proof), and then q. Let $I, I_1, I_2, ..., I_{2n-1}, I_{2n}, I'$ be the trace of r_1. Because of the two flip-flops, the trace has this size and it is clear from it which peer has been activated at each step.

Consider a second run r_2 which is defined like r_1 except that this time we visit p_α and p, $n+1$ times, then q. Let $I, I_2, I_3..., I_{2n-1}, I_{2n}, I_{2n+1}, I_{2n+2}, I''$ be the trace of r_2.

Observe that while p and p_α are being activated, q is simply accumulating messages. Recall that the set of messages that q may accumulate is finite. Thus we can choose n large enough so that $I_{2n+2}(q) = I_{2n}(q)$. Suppose that $I'(q)$ contains $true@q$. Then because the set of messages at q is the same in the second run, $I''(q)$ also contains $true@q$, a contradiction because the last iteration in p_α, p must have removed $r@p$. A similar contradiction occurs if $true@q$ is not produced. Thus such a simulation does not exist. □

Next we separate VWL and WL.

THEOREM 2 (NO GENERAL DELEGATIONS IN VWL). $WL \nprec VWL$.

PROOF. (sketch) Intuitively, peer q will use a general delegation to ask peer p to do something that is beyond the capability of the rules in p. This is not trivial because p may perform very complex operations with arbitrarily many complex rules. However, it turns out that there is a limit to what p can do. To prove it, we use the fact that with formulas using a bounded number k of variables, one cannot check whether a graph has a clique of size $k + 1$ (when an ordering of the nodes is not available).

Formally, consider a WL system (I, Γ) that consists of three peers p_α, p, q. Intuitively, peer p_α sends a sequence of updates to a graph that is originally empty and is stored at p. To do that, p_α has a persistent relation that stores a sequence of updates. More precisely, p_α has a set of tuples of the form: $upd@p_\alpha(i, o, a, b)$ where i in $[0, m]$ for some m and there is a single tuple for each i, o in { ins, del }, and a, b are data elements in a very large fixed set Σ (the identifiers of the graph g.) Peer p_α also has a persistent relation $next$ containing the tuples: $[0, 1], ... [m - 1, m]$. Finally, p_α has the fact $now@p_\alpha(0)$ in its initial state. The program of p_α consists of the following active rules:

$$at\ p_\alpha : g@p(\$x, \$y) :\text{-} now@p_\alpha(\$i), upd@p_\alpha(\$i, ins, \$x, \$y)$$
$$del.g@p(\$x, \$y) :\text{-} now@p_\alpha(\$i), upd@p_\alpha(\$i, del, \$x, \$y)$$
$$now@p_\alpha(\$j) :\text{-} now@p_\alpha(\$i), next(\$i, \$j)$$

Now p has the following active rule for maintaining the graph g :

$$at\ p : g@p(\$x, \$y) :\text{-} g@p(\$x, \$y), \neg del.g@p(\$x, \$y)$$

Finally, peer q has a rule delegation to p:

$$at\ q : clique@q() :\text{-} \wedge_{1 \le i, j \le n} g@p(\$x_i, \$x_j), \$x_i \ne \$x_j$$

which essentially requests p to send a message if there exists an n-clique in $g@p$. Peer q also has a flip-flop rule:

$$at\ q : true@q() :\text{-} false@q()$$
$$false@q() :\text{-} true@q()$$

Originally $true@q()$ holds.

Suppose for a contradiction that there is a p_α-simulation of this system in VWL. Consider the run of (I, Γ) beginning with a very long sequence $q(p_\alpha)^* p(p_\alpha)^* ... p$ where each time p is called, the graph oscillates between "there is a clique" and "there isn't". Note that the first time q is called, it installs the delegation.

Let k be the number of variables and constants that appear in a rule in $\tau(\Gamma(p))$. As the rules in p have less than k symbols, they can only evaluate formulas in FO^k. Choose $n > k$, so that formulas in FO^k cannot check for the presence of an n-clique in a graph. Choose also the set of graph identifiers Σ large enough. (Recall that the translation for the rules of p is independent from the program of q and p_α.) So, it is not possible for p to evaluate whether there is a clique. So q has to be called before each *clique* message to check the existence of a clique. Note that it is possible to do so: p pretends it has not been called and waits until q is called; then q sends a secret message to p to tell p whether there is a clique.

This is "almost" a simulation except that q has a bounded memory that depends essentially on Σ. Now consider a very long sequence of the WL system that never calls q. If the sequence is long enough, its simulation in VWL will visit twice the same state. Then by pumping, one can construct an infinite run of the VWL simulating system such that the flip-flop of q is never activated. This corresponds to a simulation of an unfair run of the WL system, a contradiction. Thus there can be no VWL simulation of the above WL system. □

We now consider timestamps. The next result compares the expressive power of WL and WL^t.

THEOREM 3 (TIMESTAMPS). *For a finite number of peers,*

1. *WL is in* PSPACE;

2. SWL^t *over a single peer can simulate any arbitrary Turing machine;*

3. *Thus,* $SWL^t \not\prec WL$ *and (a fortiori)* $WL^t \not\prec WL$.

PROOF. (sketch) For (1.), consider a fixed schema over a finite number of peers. Let (I, Γ) be an initial instance of size $n = |I| + |\Gamma|$. Let $(I_i, \Gamma, \widetilde{\Gamma}_i)$ be an instance that is reached during the computation. Because the schema is fixed, the number of facts that can be derived is bounded by a polynomial in n, and each fact is also of bounded size. So, $|I_i|$ can be bounded by a polynomial in n. Similarly, the size of $\widetilde{\Gamma}_i$ can be bounded by a polynomial in n, since a rule that is delegated is essentially determined by an instantiation of an original rule and a position in it. Thus we can represent $(I_i, \Gamma, \widetilde{\Gamma}_i)$ in polynomial space in n. Hence, WL is in PSPACE.

Now consider (2.). Let M be a Turing Machine. We can assume without loss of generality that it is deterministic and that it has a tape that is infinite only in one direction. The SWL^t system that simulates it is as follows. Its initial instance encodes the initial state of M. More precisely, it has a relation *input*, with initial value

$$\{ input(0,1,a_1), input(1,2,a_2), \dots input(n{-}1,n,a_n) \}$$

where $a_1 a_2 \dots a_n$ is the input of M. It also has a relation *tape* that is originally empty.

First, the SWL^t system copies the input on its tape using the timestamps $t_0, t_1, t_2 \dots$ to identify tape cells. More precisely, it constructs,

$$\{tape(t_0,t_1,a_1,s_0), tape(t_1,t_2,a_2,\bot), \dots, tape(t_{n-1},t_n,a_n,\bot)\}$$

where s_0 is the start state of M. Using rules from SWL^t, it is straightforward to simulate moves of M. The only subtlety is that at each step of the iteration, the tape is augmented so that there is no risk of reaching its limit. The fact that the cells are denoted with timestamps guarantees that no two cells will have the same ID.

Now, given the encoding of a word w, one can simulate the computation of TM on w. Thus (2), so (3). □

Note that the converse of (1) holds: any PSPACE query over an ordered database can be computed in SWL (hence WL) with a single peer. This can be shown by proving how to simulate in SWL with a single peer, the language Datalog$^{\neg\neg}$ that can express all PSPACE queries on ordered databases [8].

Next we see how to use timestamps to simulate view maintenance.

THEOREM 4 (VIEWS WITH TIMESTAMPS). $VWL^t \approx SWL^t$.

PROOF. (sketch) We illustrate with an example the simulation of view delegation by a program with timestamps.

Consider a VWL system with an extensional relation $s@q$ and the deductive rule at p: $r@p(\overline{U})$:- $s@q(\overline{U})$ that specifies that $r@p$ is a view of $s@q$. The simulation of the view delegation in SWL^t is as follows.

at q : persistent $past@q$
  $aux@p(\overline{U}, \$t)$:- $s@q(\overline{U})$, $time@q(\$t)$
  $past@q(\$t)$:- $time@q(\$t)$

$obsolete@p(\$t)$:- $past@q(\$t)$

at p : intensional $r@p$
  persistent $aux@p$, $obsolete@p$
  $r@p(\overline{U})$:- $aux@p(\overline{U}, \$t)$, $\neg$ $obsolete@p(\$t)$

Then the value of $r@p$ is that of $s@q$ when q was last visited, i.e., $r@p$ is a copy of $s@q$ at the last visit of q.

The above simulation is straightforwardly generalized to arbitary VWL systems, from which we obtain the desired $VWL^t \approx SWL^t$. □

It is still open whether $WL^t \not\prec VWL^t$.

5. CONVERGENCE OF WEBDAMLOG

Systems that converge to a unique state independently of the order of computation, i.e., some form of Church-Rosser property, are of particular interest. In this section, we consider two kinds of such systems: the positive and the strongly-stratified Webdamlog systems. Indeed, we show that such systems continue to converge even in presence of insertions of facts or rules. Finally, we show that for these two classes of systems, the distributed semantics can be seen as mimicking the centralized semantics.

5.1 Positive Webdamlog

Clearly, negation may explain why a system does not converge. However, the following example shows that even in absence of negation, convergence is not guaranteed because the order of arrival of messages matters:

EXAMPLE 1. *Consider the rules:*

at q: extensional $r1@q$, $r2@q$, $r@q$
    persistent $r@q$
    $r@q()$:- $r1@q()$, $r2@q()$
at $q1$: $r1@q()$:-
at $q2$: $r2@q()$:-

If we process the peers according to the order $q1, q, q2, q, q1, \dots$, then $r@q$ is never derived. If we consider instead the order $q1, q2, q, q1, q2, q, \dots$, then $r@q$ is derived and remains forever. The absence of convergence here is in fact a desired feature of the model: the extensional relations model events, so their arrival times matter.

On the other hand, note that, as we will see, if in the example $r1@q$ and $r2@q$ were intensional, the system would converge.

We now introduce the restricted systems we study in this section. A Webdamlog state or system is *positive* if the following holds:

1. Each of its rules is positive (no negation); and

2. Each extensional relation $m@p$ is made persistent with a rule of the form $m@p(\overline{U})$:- $m@p(\overline{U})$.

We will see that because of these restrictions, the states in runs of positive systems are monotonically increasing. For positive systems with a finite number of peers, there are only finitely many possible states, so monotonicity implies that runs converge after a finite number of steps. We will also show convergence for positive systems with infinitely many peers, except that in this case, we may converge only in the limit. This motivates the following somewhat complex definition of convergence.

A run $S_0, S_1, S_2, \ldots$ *converges* to a possibly infinite state $S^* = (I^*, \Gamma^*, \widetilde{\Gamma}^*)$ if for each finite $S' \subseteq S^*$, there exists $k_{S'}$ such that for all $k > k_{S'}$, $S' \subseteq S_k$ and if for each finite $S' \not\subseteq S^*$, there is $k_{S'}$ such as for all $k > k_{S'}$, $S' \not\subseteq S_k$. We say a system S *converges* if all its runs converge to the same state.

The following theorem states the convergence of (possibly infinite) positive systems.

THEOREM 5 (CONVERGENCE). *All positive Webdamlog systems converge.*

The previous theorem is still true if one allows the peers to insert facts and rules. One can show that the system will reach a stable state that does not depend on the points of insertion.

THEOREM 6 (UPDATES). *Given two positive Webdamlog systems (I,Γ) and (I',Γ'), for any run of the system (I,Γ), if for a given step, I' is added to the current set of facts and Γ' to the current set of rules, then the modified run converges to the convergence state of $(I \cup I', \Gamma \cup \Gamma')$.*

The previous theorem is straightforwardly extended to a series of updates. However, as illustrated by the following example, a more liberal definition of updates which also allows deletion of facts or rules in a system would compromise convergence.

EXAMPLE 2. *Consider the system defined as follows:*

at p: extensional@p, intensional r@p
  r@q() :- r@p()
  r@p() :- s@p()
  s@p() :- s@p()
  s@p().
at q: intensional r@q
  r@p() :- r@q()

This system converges to a state where $I^*(p) = \{s@p()\}$, $\widetilde{\Gamma}^*(p,q) = \{r@q():\text{-}\}$, $\widetilde{\Gamma}^*(q,p) = \{r@p():\text{-}\}$ Then removing the fact $s@p()$ or the rule $r@p():\text{-} s@p()$ after the convergence will not change $\widetilde{\Gamma}$ whereas $\widetilde{\Gamma}$ would be empty were the fact or the rule removed before beginning a run.

The previous example illustrates the difficulty of managing non-monotony. If we remove a fact or a rule, we need to remove as well all facts or rules that were deduced using this fact. This could be achieved using view maintenance techniques. We leave this to future work.

To further ground our semantics, we show that for positive systems, our semantics correspond to the standard centralized Datalog semantics.

Centralized semantics. In the positive case, we can compare with a "centralized" semantics, in which all facts and rules are combined into a single Datalog program. Such a comparison would not make sense in the general case since our semantics too closely depends on the order in which peers fire.

We associate to a positive Webdamlog state (I,Γ) the set $\cup_p(I(p) \cup \Gamma(p))$ composed of the facts and rules of all peers.

We can transform this set of facts and rules into a standard Datalog program by first instantiating the variable relations in the rules (as was done for local computation) and then removing those rules which violate the typing constraints in σ. We denote by $c(I,\Gamma)$ the Datalog program thus obtained.

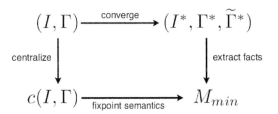

Figure 2: Link with centralized semantics

The following theorem (illustrated by Figure 2) demonstrates the equivalence, for the class of positive systems, of our distributed semantics and the traditional fixpoint semantics of Datalog. The result deals only with systems with finitely many peers to avoid having to extend Datalog to infinitely many relations.

THEOREM 7. *Let (I,Γ) be a positive system with a finite number of peers which converges to $(I^*, \Gamma^*, \widetilde{\Gamma}^*)$, and let M_{min} be the unique minimal model of the Datalog program $c(I,\Gamma)$. Then*

$$M_{min} = \cup_p P^*_{p,d}(I^*(p))$$

where $P_{p,d}$ is the set of fully local deductive rules in $\widetilde{\Gamma}^*(p) \cup \cup_q \Gamma^*(q,p)$.

5.2 Strongly-stratified Webdamlog

With negation, convergence is not guaranteed in the general case as illustrated by the following example.

EXAMPLE 3. *Consider the program that is stratified in the sense of Datalog with stratified negation:*

intensional s@p, r@p, r@q
at p: r@q() :- r@p()
  r@p() :- ¬s@p()
at q: r@p() :- r@q()
  s@p() :-

Any run of this system that begins with p converges to a state where p delegates $r@q():\text{-}$ to q and q delegates $r@p():\text{-}$ and $s@p():\text{-}$ to p. On the other hand, runs that begin with q converge to a state where p delegates nothing to q and q delegates $s@p():\text{-}$ to p.

As already mentioned for the non-monotone updates in the previous subsection, one may adapt methods of view maintenance to solve the problem. We develop in this section an alternative in which syntactic restrictions prohibit circles of false deductions, without having to deal with the complexity of view maintenance in presence of belief revision. Note that most of the examples of the paper belong to (or are easily adapted to) this restricted class.

A *stratification* σ' is an assignment of numbers to relations, i.e., to pairs $r@p$. If $\sigma'(r@p) = i$, we say that $r@p$ is in the ith stratum. The stratification is *strong* if for each i, all the relations in the ith stratum refer to the same peer. Given a strong stratification σ', an instantiated rule is σ'-stratified if all relation names of positive body atoms appear in a stratum smaller or equal to that of the head relation and all relation names of negative terms belong to a strictly smaller stratum. Note that a stratification for Example 3 would not be strong because $r@p$ and $r@q$ have to be in the same stratum, although they belong to different peers.

In our setting, we see a strong stratification σ' of $\mathcal{I}$ as an extra component of the system's schema. The strong stratification works much like the typing constraint σ in that it tells us whether a particular rule instantiation is legal. Specifically, a peer is only allowed to use instantiated rules which are σ'-stratified. Observe that our use of stratification is in the spirit of classical Datalog with stratified negation, namely preventing cycling through negation. However, the way stratification is enforced is somewhat different. In the centralized context, one analyzes the program and checks for the existence of a stratification. In the distributed case, this is not possible because no one has access to the entire program. Also, the use of relation and peer variables makes such a computation even less conceivable. So, instead, one assumes that a stratification is imposed and the computation is such that it prevents deriving facts with rule instantiations that would violate the strong stratification.

There is a subtlety with strong stratification arising from general delegation. Indeed, we will see that the result does not hold for WL. So the next result deals simply with view delegation, i.e., the language VWL. One of the advantages of VWL is that at the time a rule is delegated, it is possible to check that it does not violate the strong stratification. We consider systems with finitely many peers, where the extensional facts are fixed and only the intensional delegations vary. Formally, a Webdamlog system is said to be *strongly-stratified* if for some strong stratification σ':

1. its local computation is constrained by the stratification σ'.

2. Each extensional relation $m@p$ is made persistent with a rule of the form $m@p(\overline{U}) \text{ :- } m@p(\overline{U})$ and these are the only active rules in the system[1]. We say the system is *purely intensional*.

Observe that, by Condition (2), the set of extensional facts is fixed whereas it was increasing for positive systems. So Condition (2) here is more restrictive than for positive systems. Thus, strictly speaking the two classes are incomparable. Clearly, it would be interesting to consider classes that would include both.

We are now ready to present our results, following the same logic as in the previous section.

THEOREM 8 (CONVERGENCE). *All strongly-stratified VWL systems over a finite number of peers converge.*

This result does not hold if we allow general delegation instead of view delegation. This is because with general delegation, a peer p may delegate a partially instantiated rule to q. As the relation and peer terms of the rule may contain

---

[1] Technically speaking, if we want to use variable or peer relations in the rule heads, then we must forbid instantiations which yield extensional relations in the heads.

variables, peer p may not be able to decide whether the rule is σ'-stratified, and neither will q (or later peers) as they do not know which relations p used to launch the delegation. So enforcement of the stratification is not straightforward. This is illustrated by the following example.

EXAMPLE 4. *Consider the following program:*

intensional $m@p$, $s@q$, $r@q$
at p: $m@p(\$x) \text{ :- } m@p(\$x), r@q(\$x)$
$\quad\quad\quad m@p(\$x) \text{ :- } r@q(\$x), \neg s@q()$
at p': $s@q() \text{ :- }$
at q: $r@q(a) \text{ :- }$

Consider a run that starts by firing p, q, then p. Then the rule $m@p(a)\text{:- }$ is delegated by q to p and will remain forever. Now, consider a run that starts by firing p'. Then q will know $s@q()\text{:- }$. from the beginning and will never delegate $m@p(a)\text{:- }$.

Convergence also holds for strongly-stratified VWL systems in the presence of insertions as well as deletions.

THEOREM 9 (UPDATE). *Let (I,Γ) be a VWL system with strong stratification σ' over a finite number of peers. Consider $(I^+, I^-, \Gamma^+, \Gamma^-)$ where I^+, I^- are sets of extensional facts and Γ^+, Γ^- are sets of deductive rules. For each run of the system (I, Γ), if for some k a given state $(I_k, \Gamma_k, \widetilde{\Gamma}_k)$ is replaced by $(I_k \cup I^+ \setminus I^-, \Gamma_k \cup \Gamma^+ \setminus \Gamma^-, \widetilde{\Gamma}_k)$, then the modified run converges to the convergence state of the σ'-stratified system $(I \cup I^+ \setminus I^-, \Gamma \cup \Gamma^+ \setminus \Gamma^-)$.*

This theorem can obviously be generalized to any sequence of updates. The final theorem of this section shows that the set of facts computed by a σ'-stratified system corresponds to the set of facts in the minimal model of a centralized version of the system. As in the previous section, we associate a σ'-stratified Webdamlog system (I, Γ) with the set $\cup_p(I(p) \cup \Gamma(p))$ composed of the facts and rules of all peers. We then transform this set of facts and rules into a standard Datalog program by instantiating the variable predicates in the rules and removing rules which violate the typing constraints σ or the strong stratification σ'. We use $c_s(I, \Gamma)$ to refer to the resulting Datalog program.

THEOREM 10 (CENTRALIZED). *Let (I, Γ) be a σ'-stratified system with a finite number of peers and rules in SWL, which converges to $(I^*, \Gamma^*, \widetilde{\Gamma}^*)$, and let M_{min} be the unique minimal model of the Datalog program $c_s(I, \Gamma)$. Then*

$$M_{min} = \cup_p P^*_{p,d}(I^*(p))$$

where $P^*_{p,d}$ is the set of fully local deductive rules in $\widetilde{\Gamma}^*(p) \cup \cup_q \Gamma^*(q, p)$.

6. SYSTEM AND OPTIMIZATION

In this section, we briefly mention the system that motivated the present work and standard optimization techniques that make the approach feasible.

Webdam Exchange. In Webdam Exchange [5], data (XML documents, collections), access rights, secrets, localization, and knowledge about other peers, are all seen as logical statements. These statements can be communicated, replicated, queried, and updated, while keeping track of time and provenance. Localization statements guide the search for pieces of information to access or update. The same information may be supported by different peers. Each statement carries its own access control enforcement. It may be *authenticated*, in the sense that it is possible to verify the identity of the participant who created the statement and that this participant was indeed entitled to create it. Information content may also be *protected* in the sense that only participants with a particular secret (e.g., a decryption key or a login/password pair) can read it.

We have implemented a proof-of-concept system that handles all the components of the knowledge base. We also implemented a lighter system designed for smartphones. First versions of the systems are up and running and will be demonstrated at [10]. The entire system may be seen as a distributed knowledge base. Most of the effort so far has been dedicated to the local management of access rights and the verification of data. The reasoning to find data is hardwired in Java programs. We intend to replace these programs by some reasoning using the Webdamlog system we started implementing. In the new setting, each peer has its own logic (a set of rules) that depends on the particular application and on its resources and may acquire new rules by update or by delegation.

Optimization. To render the approach feasible, we have to rely intensively on some known optimization techniques. We briefly mention them next and see how they fit in the Webdamlog picture.

(Differential technique) Consider a peer p who has the rule $s@q(x, y)$:- $r@p(x, y)$ with $s@q$ an extensional relation. Suppose that $r@p$ is a very large relation that changes infrequently. Each time we visit p we have to send to q the current version of $r@p$, say a set K_n of tuples. This is a clear waste of communication resources. It is preferable to send the symmetric difference of $r@p$, i.e., send a set of updates Δ with the semantics that $K_n = \Delta(K_{n-1})$, since q already knows K_{n-1}. If $s@q$ is intensional, we face a similar issue; it is preferable to send the new set of delegation rules as Δ rather than sending the entire set.

(Seed-based delegation) Consider again the rule:

at p: m@q() :- m$_1$@p($x), m$_2$@p'($x)

Now suppose that $m_1@p(a_i)$ holds for $i = [1..1000]$. We need to install 1000 rules. However, in this particular case, we can install a single rule at p' and send many facts:

at p': m@q() :- seed$_{r,1,p}$@p'($x), m$_2$@p'($x)
at p': seed$_{r,1,p}$@p'(a_i). (for each i)

Note that it now becomes natural to use a differential technique to maintain delegation. In particular, if the delegation from p to q does not change, there is no need to send anything. If it does, one needs only to send the delta on $seed_{r,1,p}@p'$. Observe that we have replaced the task of installing and uninstalling delegation rules by that of sending insertion and deletion messages in a persistent extensional (seed) relation that controls a rule.

(Query-subquery and delegation) Consider the following example of a rule in BIP (Bob's IPhone), where photosAlice@BIP is intensional:

at BIP: photosAlice@BIP($X,$Y) :-
    photos@picasa(Alice,$X,$Y)

This rule says that to find the photos of Alice, one needs to ask Picasa. The formal semantics says that we install the following [*Upload*] rule at Picasa:

at Picasa: photosAlice@BIP($X,$Y) :-
    photos@picasa(Alice,$X,$Y)

which will result in uploading in BIP all the photos. However, observe that this has no effect on the state since *photosAlice* is only intensional. This uploading may therefore be considered a waste of resources. An optimizer may decide not to install the [*Upload*] rule at Picasa, i.e., not ask Picasa to upload anything. Now suppose that Bob asks his Iphone for the photos of Sue:

query@BIP($X) :- photosAlice@BIP($X, Sue)

where *query* is an extensional predicate. Now obtaining photos from Picasa changes the state. So the optimizer will install on Picasa the rule:

at Picasa: photosAlice@BIP($X,Sue) :-
    photos@picasa(Alice,$X,Sue)

Observe that the optimizer performed some form of resolution in the spirit of query-subquery [29] or rewriting in the Magic Set style [11] (see also [6]). Indeed, the entire management of delegation can be optimized using these techniques. Note that strictly speaking this may change the semantics of applications: the derivation of some facts may take a little longer than if we had installed all the delegations in advance.

7. CONCLUSION AND FUTURE WORK

We have introduced a new Datalog-style language for distributed data management. The main novelty is the notion of delegation that allows a peer to install rules at other peers. We have studied the expressivity of the language and of restrictions. We have also studied convergence properties for fragments of the language.

One should observe that the power of delegation critically depends on the exact definition of the model. The situation would be different, for instance, if we were to consider an asynchronous version of the model in which messages between peers are not instantaneous. A natural direction for future work is the extension of our study of the power of delegation and related issues (e.g. possibility of electing a leader) to different variants of the model.

We use in our model a rather strict notion of type based on fixed arity and fixed sort for each column. It would be interesting to be more tolerant and allow some form of polymorphism (e.g., relations with arbitrary arity) or recursive types (an email may include an email). Note that this is useful for the exchange of XML data (and our implementation in Webdam Exchange is based on XML).

The notion of provenance (also important for Webdam Exchange) is not considered in the model we presented here. We intend to study it and in particular to develop methods for tracing the origin of deduced facts.

As another possible direction for future work, Active XML considers intensional data of a very different form, namely functions that may be included in documents and are defined intensionally. It would be interesting to investigate the relationships between these two kinds of intensional data.

Acknowledgements. We thank David Gross-Amblard (Univ. Bourgogne), Yannis Katsis and Bruno Marnette (INRIA Saclay), Philippe Rigaux (CNAM, Paris), Marie-Christine Rousset (Univ. Grenoble) and Victor Vianu (UCSD) for discussions on this work.

8. REFERENCES

[1] S. Abiteboul, Z. Abrams, S. Haar, and T. Milo. Diagnosis of asynchronous discrete event systems: datalog to the rescue! In *PODS*, pages 358–367, 2005.

[2] S. Abiteboul, O. Benjelloun, and T. Milo. Positive active xml. In *PODS*, pages 35–45, 2004.

[3] S. Abiteboul, O. Benjelloun, and T. Milo. The active xml project: an overview. *The VLDB Journal*, 17:1019–1040, 2008.

[4] S. Abiteboul, M. Bienvenu, A. Galland, and M.-C. Rousset. Distributed datalog revisited. In *Datalog 2.0 Workshop*, 2010.

[5] S. Abiteboul, A. Galland, and A. Polyzotis. Web information management with access control. In preparation, 2011.

[6] S. Abiteboul, R. Hull, and V. Vianu. *Foundations of Databases*. Addison-Wesley, 1995.

[7] S. Abiteboul, L. Segoufin, and V. Vianu. Static analysis of Active XML systems. In *PODS*, pages 221–230, 2008.

[8] S. Abiteboul and V. Vianu. Datalog extensions for database queries and updates. *Journal of Computer and System Sciences*, 43(1):62–124, 1991.

[9] P. Alvaro, T. Condie, N. Conway, K. Elmeleegy, J. M. Hellerstein, and R. Sears. Boom analytics: exploring data-centric, declarative programming for the cloud. In *EuroSys*, pages 223–236, 2010.

[10] E. Antoine, A. Galland, K. Lyngbaek, A. Marian, and N. Polyzotis. Social networking on top of the WebdamExchange system. In *ICDE*, 2011.

[11] F. Bancilhon, D. Maier, Y. Sagiv, and J. D. Ullman. Magic sets and other strange ways to implement logic programs. In *PODS*, pages 1–15, 1986.

[12] A. K. Chandra and D. Harel. Horn clauses queries and generalizations. *J. Log. Program.*, 2(1):1–15, 1985.

[13] Proceedings of the Datalog 2.0 Workshop, Oxford, 2010.

[14] J. Field, M.-C. Marinescu, and C. Stefansen. Reactors: A data-oriented synchronous/asynchronous programming model for distributed applications. *Theoretical Computer Science*, 410(2-3):168–201, 2009.

[15] M. Gelfond and V. Lifschitz. The stable model semantics for logic programming. In *ICLP/SLP*, pages 1070–1080, 1988.

[16] S. Grumbach and F. Wang. Netlog, a rule-based language for distributed programming. In *PADL*, pages 88–103, 2010.

[17] J. Hellerstein. The declarative imperative: experiences and conjectures in distributed logic. *ACM SIGMOD Record*, 39(1):5–19, 2010.

[18] G. Hulin. Parallel processing of recursive queries in distributed architectures. In *VLDB*, pages 87–96, 1989.

[19] G. Lausen, B. LudÃd'scher, and W. May. *On Active Deductive Databases: The Statelog Approach*, volume 1472 of *Lecture Notes in Computer Science*, pages 69–106. Birkhauser Basel, 1998.

[20] C. Liu, Y. Mao, M. Oprea, P. Basu, and B. T. Loo. A declarative perspective on adaptive manet routing. In *PRESTO*, pages 63–68, 2008.

[21] B. T. Loo, T. Condie, M. Garofalakis, D. E. Gay, J. M. Hellerstein, P. Maniatis, R. Ramakrishnan, T. Roscoe, and I. Stoica. Declarative networking: language, execution and optimization. In *SIGMOD*, pages 97–108, 2006.

[22] B. T. Loo, T. Condie, M. N. Garofalakis, D. E. Gay, J. M. Hellerstein, P. Maniatis, R. Ramakrishnan, T. Roscoe, and I. Stoica. Declarative networking. *Commun. ACM*, 52(11):87–95, 2009.

[23] B. T. Loo, T. Condie, J. M. Hellerstein, P. Maniatis, T. Roscoe, and I. Stoica. Implementing declarative overlays. *SIGOPS Oper. Syst. Rev.*, 39:75–90, 2005.

[24] B. T. Loo, J. M. Hellerstein, I. Stoica, and R. Ramakrishnan. Declarative routing: extensible routing with declarative queries. In *SIGCOMM*, pages 289–300, 2005.

[25] J. Navarro and A. Rybalchenko. Operational semantics for declarative networking. In A. Gill and T. Swift, editors, *Practical Aspects of Declarative Languages*, volume 5418 of *Lecture Notes in Computer Science*, pages 76–90. Springer Berlin / Heidelberg, 2009.

[26] W. Nejdl, S. Ceri, and G. Wiederhold. Evaluating recursive queries in distributed databases. *IEEE Trans. Knowl. Data Eng.*, 5(1):104–121, 1993.

[27] T. C. Przymusinski. The well-founded semantics coincides with the three-valued stable semantics. *Fundam. Inform.*, 13(4):445–463, 1990.

[28] B. Rossman. On the constant-depth complexity of k-clique. In *STOC*, pages 721–730, 2008.

[29] L. Vieille. Recursive axioms in deductive databases: The query-subquery approach. In *Proc. 1st Int. Conf. on Expert Database Systems*, pages 179–193, 1986.

[30] ERC grant Webdam. http://webdam.inria.fr.

Querying Semantic Web Data with SPARQL

Marcelo Arenas
Department of Computer Science
PUC Chile
marenas@ing.puc.cl

Jorge Pérez
Department of Computer Science
Universidad de Chile
jperez@dcc.uchile.cl

ABSTRACT

The Semantic Web is the initiative of the W3C to make information on the Web readable not only by humans but also by machines. RDF is the data model for Semantic Web data, and SPARQL is the standard query language for this data model. In the last ten years, we have witnessed a constant growth in the amount of RDF data available on the Web, which have motivated the theoretical study of some fundamental aspects of SPARQL and the development of efficient mechanisms for implementing this query language.

Some of the distinctive features of RDF have made the study and implementation of SPARQL challenging. First, as opposed to usual database applications, the semantics of RDF is open world, making RDF databases inherently incomplete. Thus, one usually obtains partial answers when querying RDF with SPARQL, and the possibility of adding optional information if present is a crucial feature of SPARQL. Second, RDF databases have a graph structure and are interlinked, thus making graph navigational capabilities a necessary component of SPARQL. Last, but not least, SPARQL has to work at Web scale!

RDF and SPARQL have attracted interest from the database community. However, we think that this community has much more to say about these technologies, and, in particular, about the fundamental database problems that need to be solved in order to provide solid foundations for the development of these technologies. In this paper, we survey some of the main results about the theory of RDF and SPARQL putting emphasis on some research opportunities for the database community.

Categories and Subject Descriptors
H.2.3 [**Database Management**]: Query languages

General Terms
Algorithms, Theory

Keywords
SPARQL, RDF, RDFS, Semantic Web, Linked Data

1. INTRODUCTION

The Resource Description Framework (RDF) [26] is a data model for representing information about World Wide Web

resources. Jointly with its release in 1998 as Recommendation of the W3C, the natural problem of querying RDF data was raised. Since then, several designs and implementations of RDF query languages have been proposed. In 2004, the RDF Data Access Working Group, part of the W3C Semantic Web Activity, released a first public working draft of a query language for RDF, called SPARQL [37]. Since then, SPARQL has been rapidly adopted as the standard for querying Semantic Web data. In January 2008, SPARQL became a W3C Recommendation.

In the last ten years, we have witnessed a constant growth in the amount of RDF data available on the Web, which has motivated the theoretical study of some fundamental aspects of SPARQL, and the development of efficient mechanisms for implementing this query language. RDF and SPARQL have attracted interest from the database community. However, we think that this community has much more to say about these technologies, and, in particular, about the fundamental database problems that need to be solved in order to provide solid foundations for their development.

This paper is a compendium of the material to be presented in a tutorial about RDF and SPARQL, targeted to database researchers that are new to Semantic Web data management. Next, we briefly discuss the topics to be covered in this paper, putting an emphasis on the distinctive features that make the problem of querying Semantic Web data challenging.

RDF and SPARQL: An atomic piece of data in RDF is a *Uniform Resource Identifier* (URI), which is syntactically similar to a URL but identifies an abstract *resource* (which can be, literally, anything). For example, http://dbpedia.org/resource/Ronald_Fagin is the URI used by DBpedia (the Semantic Web version of Wikipedia [13]) to identify Ronald Fagin. In the RDF data model, URIs are organized in the form of so called RDF graphs, which are labeled directed graphs, where node labels and edge labels are URIs. Formally, an RDF graph is a finite set of *triples* of the form (*subject, predicate, object*). Figure 1 shows an example of an RDF graph that stores data from DBpedia [13] and an RDF representation of DBLP [24]. Shorthands for URIs prefixes are usually defined to avoid overcrowding RDF specifications and queries. In Figure 1, prefixes are shown at the top of the figure. For example, the following is a triple in the RDF graph in Figure 1:

(inPods:FaginLN01, dct:isPartOf, inPods:2001)

SPARQL is essentially a graph-matching query language. A SPARQL query is composed of: (1) a *body*, which is a

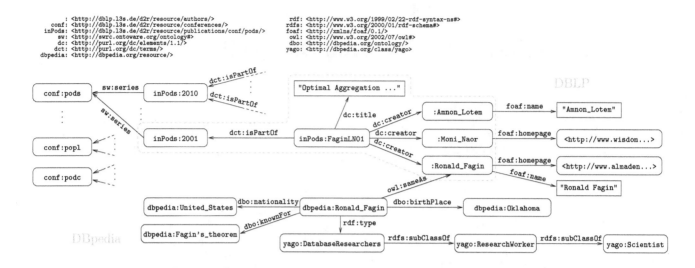

Figure 1: An RDF graph storing DBLP and DBpedia information.

complex RDF *graph pattern-matching expression*, and (2) a *head*, which is an expression that indicates how to construct the answer to the query. The following is an example of a simple SPARQL query that retrieves the authors that have published in PODS and were born in Oklahoma (prefixes are the same as in Figure 1). The body of the query is just a set of triples with variables, which are prefixed by the symbol ?, and the head is a projection (via a SELECT operator):

```
SELECT ?Author
WHERE {
  ?Paper      dc:creator    ?Author .
  ?Paper      dct:isPartOf  ?InPods .
  ?InPods     sw:series     conf:pods .
  ?DbpPerson  owl:sameAs    ?Author .
  ?DbpPerson  dbo:birthPlace dbpedia:Oklahoma . }
```

The evaluation of a query as the one shown above is done in two steps. First, values are given to variables in such a way that the triples in the body of the query match the triples in the queried graph. Second, the values assigned to the variables are processed to construct the answer. In this case, some variables are projected out to keep only the authors. According to the RDF graph in Figure 1, :Ronald_Fagin is an answer to this query. SPARQL also considers the possibility of adding optional information. For example, the following query retrieves the authors that have published in PODS, and their Web Pages if this information is available:

```
SELECT ?Author ?WebPage
WHERE {
  ?Paper    dc:creator    ?Author .
  ?Paper    dct:isPartOf  ?InPods .
  ?InPods   sw:series     conf:pods .
  OPTIONAL { ?Author foaf:homePage ?WebPage . } }
```

In our example graph, the answer to the query is:

?Author	?WebPage
:Ronald_Fagin	<http://www.almaden...>
:Moni_Naor	<http://www.wisdom...>
:Amnon_Lotem	

Notice that ?WebPAge is *unbounded* in the last answer. One distinctive feature of SPARQL is that one naturally obtains partial answers to queries. With SPARQL one can also make queries with complex join sequences. For example, the fol-

lowing query retrieves the authors that have published in PODS, PODC, and POPL conferences.[1]

```
SELECT ?Author
WHERE {
  ?Paper1   dc:creator    ?Author .
  ?Paper1   dct:isPartOf  ?InPods .
  ?InPods   sw:series     conf:pods .

  ?Paper2   dc:creator    ?Author .
  ?Paper2   dct:isPartOf  ?InPodc .
  ?InPodc   sw:series     conf:podc .

  ?Paper3   dc:creator    ?Author .
  ?Paper3   dct:isPartOf  ?InPopl .
  ?InPopl   sw:series     conf:popl . }
```

In Section 2, we give a formalization of RDF and SPARQL that follows the approach proposed in [32, 33], and we present some results regarding the complexity of evaluating SPARQL queries. In Section 3, we study the expressiveness of SPARQL and, in particular, we put forward the question of whether SPARQL is the right query language for RDF data. As opposed to the usual database applications, the semantics of RDF is open world, making RDF databases inherently incomplete. Nevertheless, SPARQL has adopted a semantics based on a closed world assumption. Thus, we explore in Section 3 the relationship between the open nature of RDF data and the closed-world semantics underlying SPARQL.

Vocabulary with predefined semantics: One of the distinctive features of the Semantic Web data is the existence of vocabularies with predefined semantics: the RDF *Schema* (RDFS [12]) and the *Ontology Web Language* (OWL [31]). Both languages can be used to derive logical conclusions from RDF graphs. For example, we have used some RDFS and OWL special URIs in Figure 1 [2]: rdf:type to denote that Ronald Fagin is a Database Researcher, and rdfs:subClassOf to denote that the class of Database Researchers is a subclass of Research Worker, which in turn is a subclass of Scientist. The RDFS semantics allows one to conclude from these explicit data that Ronald Fagin is a Scientist. Notice that we

---

[1] In fact, one can execute this query against real DBLP data at http://dblp.l3s.de/d2r/, and obtain 17 authors (among them, Philip Bernstein, Jeffrey Ullman, and Moshe Vardi).

[2] Under the prefixes rdf:, rdfs: and owl:.

306

have also used `owl:sameAs` to indicate that the URIs used by DBpedia and DBLP to represent Ronald Fagin denote the same resource. Consider now the following SPARQL query:

```
SELECT ?Author
WHERE {
    ?Author    rdf:type     yago:Scientist .
    ?Author    dbo:birthPlace dbpedia:Oklahoma .
    ?Paper     dc:creator   ?Author .
    ?Paper     dct:isPartOf ?InPods .
    ?InPods    sw:series    conf:pods . }
```

This query intuitively asks for scientists that were born in Oklahoma and that have published in PODS. When matching the body of the above query against the graph in Figure 1, one obtains no valid binding of the variables. In fact, there is no triple in the graph with `rdf:type` as predicate and `yago:Scientist` as object, thus no URI assigned to variable `?Author` could make the first triple in the query to match the graph. Nevertheless, if one considers the predefined semantics of RDFS and OWL (in particular, the semantics of `rdf:type`, `rdfs:subClassOf`, and `owl:sameAs`), then one obtains `:Ronald_Fagin` as an answer to the query. Evaluating queries considering the semantics of RDFS and OWL is challenging, and there is not yet consensus in the Semantic Web community on how to deal with this problem [39, 37, 35, 17]. In Section 5, we present a simple approach for querying RDFS data that was proposed in [18, 29, 34]. Dealing with queries that consider the OWL semantics is a very interesting topic of research [39, 17, 25], but it is out of the scope of this paper.

Navigating RDF graphs: As with any data model, a natural question is what are the desired features for an RDF query language. Among the multiple design issues to be considered, it has been largely recognized that navigational capabilities are of fundamental importance for data models with an explicit tree or graph structure (like XML and RDF). However, SPARQL only provides limited navigational functionalities, as recognized by the W3C and the working group behind the upcoming specification of SPARQL (SPARQL 1.1 [19]). In Section 5.2, we introduce the notion of *nested regular expression*, which was proposed in [34] as a language to specify how to navigate RDF data. Interestingly, these expressions allows one to pose many natural queries, which do not seem to be expressible even in classical path languages such as *Conjunctive Regular Path Queries* (CRPQs) [10, 14] or the recently proposed language of *Extended* CRPQs [5]. For example, there exists a nested regular expression that can retrieve from the graph in Figure 1 the complete network of co-authorship of PODS papers: the expression retrieves all the pairs (a_1, a_n) of authors for which there exists a list of authors $a_2, \ldots, a_{n-1}$ such that a_i is a co-author of a_{i+1} ($1 \leq i < n$) in a PODS paper (see Example 5.1 for details). Another interesting property of nested regular expressions is that they can be used to answer queries considering the semantics of RDFS by directly traversing the input graph. In fact, this was the motivation in [34] to propose nested regular expressions. We also discuss this issue in Sections 5.2 and 5.3, and present the language nSPARQL [34] which is obtained from SPARQL by including nested regular expressions.

Linked Data: Most of the research on RDF and SPARQL assumes a classical database perspective in which the RDF data reside in a single repository to which queries have full access. This assumption is becoming outdated with the advent of the *Web of Linked Data* [8]. The Web of Linked Data

is the materialization of a set of principles for publishing Semantic Web data [6]. Essentially, these principles state that each piece of data should be published as a Web-accessible URI in such a way that when this URI is accessed by some application, an RDF specification describing the URI should be provided, which in turn should point to other accessible URIs. URIs satisfying this principle are called *dereferenceable*. For example,

http://dblp.l3s.de/d2r/resource/publications/conf/pods/FaginLN01

is a dereferenceable URI currently published (April 2011) as Linked Data. In fact, its description contains the links inside the dashed area in Figure 1.

Linked Data poses many interesting research questions. In particular, there is still plenty of room for research on the foundations of querying Linked Data, although some progress has been made in the area [20, 21, 9]. One particular open issue is the definition of the right querying model for this highly distributed scenario, as it is not clear whether SPARQL can deal with the features of Linked Data. Scalability issues are also an imperative topic of research in this context. As of May 2009, the Web of Linked Data was estimated to contain more than 4.7 billion RDF triples interlinked by approximately 142 million RDF links [8]. Today, just the DBpedia project [13] describe more than 3.5 million things (URIs), which descriptions sum-up to more than 600 million RDF triples containing 6.5 millions of links to other RDF stores. In Section 6, we briefly describe Linked Data and some of the research opportunities in this area.

Most of the material of this paper is the result of a fruitful collaboration with our co-authors Claudio Gutierrez, Carlos Hurtado, Alberto Mendelzon, and Sergio Muñoz. We also want to thank Juan Sequeda for many insightful discussions about Linked Data. Arenas was supported by FONDECYT grant 1090565.

2. RDF AND SPARQL

The RDF specification considers two types of values: *resource identifiers* (in the form of URIs [7]) to denote Web resources, and *literals* to denote values such as natural numbers, Booleans, and strings. In this paper, we use $\mathbf{U}$ to denote the set of all URIs and $\mathbf{L}$ to denote the set of all literals, and we assume that these two sets are disjoint. RDF considers also a special type of objects to describe *anonymous resources*, called blank nodes in the RDF data model. Essentially, blank nodes are existentially quantified variables that can be used to make statements about unknown (but existent) resources. In this paper, we do not consider blank nodes, that is, we focus on what are called *ground* RDF graphs. Formally, an RDF triple is a tuple:

$$(s, p, o) \quad \in \quad \mathbf{U} \times \mathbf{U} \times (\mathbf{U} \cup \mathbf{L}),$$

where s is the *subject*, p the *predicate* and o the *object*. An RDF graph is a finite set of RDF triples.

Figure 1 shows an example of an RDF graph with data from DBpedia [13] and the RDF version of DBLP [24]. For example, the graph states that Ronald Fagin is the author of a paper with title "Optimal Aggregation Algorithms for Middleware" by using the triples:

```
(inPods:FaginLN01, dc:creator, :Ronald_Fagin)
(inPods:FaginLN01, dc:title, "Optimal Aggregation ...")
```

For simplicity, and when there is no ambiguity, we will omit the *prefixes* in URIs, and thus, we denote the last two triples simply as:

(FaginLN01, creator, Ronald_Fagin)
(FaginLN01, title, "Optimal Aggregation ...")

Jointly with the release of RDF in 1999 as Recommendation of the W3C, the natural problem of querying RDF data was raised. Since then, several designs and implementations of RDF query languages have been proposed [15]. In 2004, the RDF Data Access Working Group released a first public working draft of a query language for RDF, called SPARQL [37]. Currently, SPARQL is a W3C recommendation, and has become the standard language for querying RDF data. In this section, we give an algebraic formalization of the core fragment of SPARQL. Following [32, 33], we focus on the body of SPARQL queries, i.e., in its graph pattern matching facility.

2.1 Syntax of SPARQL graph patterns

The official syntax of SPARQL [37] considers operators OPTIONAL, UNION, and FILTER, and *concatenation* via a point symbol (.), to construct graph pattern expressions. The syntax also considers { } to group patterns, and some implicit rules of precedence and association. For example, the point symbol (.) has precedence over OPTIONAL, and OPTIONAL is left associative. In order to avoid ambiguities in the parsing, we present the syntax of SPARQL graph patterns in a more traditional algebraic formalism following [32, 33]. More specifically, we use binary operators AND (.), UNION (UNION), OPT (OPTIONAL), and FILTER (FILTER), and we fully parenthesize expressions making explicit the precedence and association of operators.

Let **V** be an infinite set of variables disjoint from **U** and **L**. In this paper, we assume that the elements from **V** are prefixed by the symbol ?. Then SPARQL graph patterns are recursively defined as follows:

1. A tuple from $(\mathbf{U} \cup \mathbf{V}) \times (\mathbf{U} \cup \mathbf{V}) \times (\mathbf{U} \cup \mathbf{L} \cup \mathbf{V})$ is a graph pattern (a *triple pattern*).

2. If P_1 and P_2 are graph patterns, then the expressions $(P_1$ AND $P_2)$, $(P_1$ OPT $P_2)$, and $(P_1$ UNION $P_2)$ are graph patterns.

3. If P is a graph pattern and R is a SPARQL built-in condition, then the expression $(P$ FILTER $R)$ is a graph pattern.

A SPARQL built-in condition is a Boolean combination of terms constructed by using equality (=) among elements in $(\mathbf{U} \cup \mathbf{L} \cup \mathbf{V})$, and the unary predicate bound over variables. Formally,

- if $?X$, $?Y \in \mathbf{V}$ and $c \in (\mathbf{U} \cup \mathbf{L})$, then bound($?X$), $?X = c$ and $?X = ?Y$ are built-in conditions; and

- if R_1 and R_2 are built-in conditions, then $(\neg R_1)$, $(R_1 \vee R_2)$ and $(R_1 \wedge R_2)$ are built-in conditions.

EXAMPLE 2.1. The following is a SPARQL graph pattern

$$(((?P, \text{creator}, ?A) \text{ AND } (?A, \text{name}, ?N))$$
$$\text{FILTER } (?N = \text{"Ronald Fagin"})). \quad (1)$$

Intuitively, it retrieves the papers of an author with name "Ronald Fagin". □

Given a graph pattern P, we denote by var(P) the set of variables occurring in P. In particular, if t is a triple pattern, then var(t) denotes the set of variables occurring in the components of t. Similarly, for a built-in condition R, we use var(R) to denote the set of variables occurring in R.

2.2 Semantics of SPARQL graph patterns

To define the semantics of SPARQL graph pattern expressions, we need to introduce some terminology from [32, 33]. A *mapping* μ is a partial function $\mu : \mathbf{V} \to (\mathbf{U} \cup \mathbf{L})$. Abusing notation, for a triple pattern t such that var(t) $\subseteq$ dom(μ), we denote by $\mu(t)$ the triple obtained by replacing the variables in t according to μ. The domain of μ, denoted by dom(μ), is the subset of **V** where μ is defined. Two mappings μ_1 and μ_2 are *compatible* when for all $?X \in \text{dom}(\mu_1) \cap \text{dom}(\mu_2)$, it is the case that $\mu_1(?X) = \mu_2(?X)$, i.e. when $\mu_1 \cup \mu_2$ is also a mapping. Intuitively, μ_1 and μ_2 are compatibles if μ_1 *can be extended* with μ_2 to obtain a new mapping, and vice versa. Note that two mappings with disjoint domains are always compatible, and that the empty mapping $\mu_\emptyset$ (i.e. the mapping with empty domain) is compatible with any other mapping.

Let Ω_1 and Ω_2 be sets of mappings. We define the join of, the union of and the difference between Ω_1 and Ω_2 as:

$$\Omega_1 \bowtie \Omega_2 = \{\mu_1 \cup \mu_2 \mid \mu_1 \in \Omega_1, \mu_2 \in \Omega_2 \text{ and }$$
$$\mu_1, \mu_2 \text{ are compatible mappings}\},$$
$$\Omega_1 \cup \Omega_2 = \{\mu \mid \mu \in \Omega_1 \text{ or } \mu \in \Omega_2\},$$
$$\Omega_1 \smallsetminus \Omega_2 = \{\mu \in \Omega_1 \mid \text{for all } \mu' \in \Omega_2,$$
$$\mu \text{ and } \mu' \text{ are not compatible}\}.$$

Moreover, we define the left outer-join as:

$$\Omega_1 \mathbin{\rtimes\mkern-5mu\bowtie} \Omega_2 = (\Omega_1 \bowtie \Omega_2) \cup (\Omega_1 \smallsetminus \Omega_2).$$

Intuitively, $\Omega_1 \bowtie \Omega_2$ is the set of mappings that result from extending mappings in Ω_1 with their compatible mappings in Ω_2, and $\Omega_1 \smallsetminus \Omega_2$ is the set of mappings in Ω_1 that cannot be extended with any mapping in Ω_2. The operation $\Omega_1 \cup \Omega_2$ is the usual set theoretical union. A mapping μ is in $\Omega_1 \mathbin{\rtimes\mkern-5mu\bowtie} \Omega_2$ if it is the extension of a mapping of Ω_1 with a compatible mapping of Ω_2, or if it belongs to Ω_1 and cannot be extended with any mapping of Ω_2. These operations resemble relational algebra operations over sets of mappings (partial functions).

We are now ready to define the semantics of graph pattern expressions as a function $[\![\cdot]\!]_G$ which takes a graph pattern expression and returns a set of mappings. For the sake of readability, the semantics of filter expressions is presented in a separate definition.

Definition 2.2 ([32, 33]) *The* evaluation *of a graph pattern P over an RDF graph G, denoted by $[\![P]\!]_G$, is defined recursively as follows:*

1. *if P is a triple pattern t, then $[\![P]\!]_G = \{\mu \mid \text{dom}(\mu) = \text{var}(t) \text{ and } \mu(t) \in G\}$.*

2. *if P is $(P_1$ AND $P_2)$, then $[\![P]\!]_G = [\![P_1]\!]_G \bowtie [\![P_2]\!]_G$.*

3. *if P is $(P_1$ OPT $P_2)$, then $[\![P]\!]_G = [\![P_1]\!]_G \mathbin{\rtimes\mkern-5mu\bowtie} [\![P_2]\!]_G$.*

4. *if P is $(P_1$ UNION $P_2)$, then $[\![P]\!]_G = [\![P_1]\!]_G \cup [\![P_2]\!]_G$.*

The idea behind the OPT operator is to allow for *optional matching* of graph patterns. Consider graph pattern expression $(P_1$ OPT $P_2)$ and let μ_1 be a mapping in $[\![P_1]\!]_G$.

If there exists a mapping $\mu_2 \in [\![P_2]\!]_G$ such that μ_1 and μ_2 are compatible, then $\mu_1 \cup \mu_2$ belongs to $[\![(P_1 \text{ OPT } P_2)]\!]_G$. But if no such a mapping μ_2 exists, then μ_1 belongs to $[\![(P_1 \text{ OPT } P_2)]\!]_G$. Thus, operator OPT allows information to be added to a mapping μ if the information is available, instead of just rejecting μ whenever some part of the pattern does not match. This feature of *optional matching* is crucial in Semantic Web applications, and more specifically in RDF data management, where it is assumed that every application have only partial knowledge about the resources being managed.

It is evident from the definitions of the operators AND and UNION that these two operators are associative and commutative, thus permitting us to avoid parenthesis when writing sequences of either AND operators or UNION operators. In the following sections, we show some other algebraic properties of graph patterns.

The semantics of filter expressions is defined as follows. Given a mapping μ and a built-in condition R, we say that μ satisfies R, denoted by $\mu \models R$, if (omitting the usual rules for boolean connectives): (1) R is bound($?X$) and $?X \in \text{dom}(\mu)$; (2) R is $?X = c$, $?X \in \text{dom}(\mu)$ and $\mu(?X) = c$; and (3) R is $?X = ?Y$, $?X \in \text{dom}(\mu)$, $?Y \in \text{dom}(\mu)$ and $\mu(?X) = \mu(?Y)$. Then we have that:

Definition 2.3 ([32, 33]) *Given an RDF graph G and a filter expression $(P \text{ FILTER } R)$,*

$$[\![(P \text{ FILTER } R)]\!]_G \;=\; \{\mu \in [\![P]\!]_G \mid \mu \models R\}.$$

From now on, we usually represent sets of mappings as tables where each row represents a mapping in the set. We label every row with the name of a mapping, and every column with the name of a variable. If a mapping is not defined for some variable, then we simply leave empty the corresponding position. For instance, the table

	$?X$	$?Y$	$?Z$
$\mu_1:$	a	b	
$\mu_2:$		c	

represents the set $\Omega = \{\mu_1, \mu_2\}$ where (1) $\text{dom}(\mu_1) = \{?X, ?Y\}$, $\mu_1(?X) = a$, and $\mu_1(?Y) = b$, and (2) $\text{dom}(\mu_2) = \{?Y\}$ and $\mu_2(?Y) = c$. Sometimes we also use notation $\{\{?X \to a, ?Y \to b\}, \{?Y \to c\}\}$ for the above set of mappings.

EXAMPLE 2.4. The following are examples of SPARQL graph patterns and their evaluations over the RDF graph in Figure 1.

$P_1 = ((\text{FaginLN01}, \text{creator}, ?A) \text{ AND } (?A, \text{name}, ?N))$

$?A$	$?N$
Ronald_Fagin	"Ronald Fagin"
Amnon_Lotem	"Amnon Lotem"

$P_2 = \big[((\text{FaginLN01}, \text{creator}, ?A) \text{ OPT } (?A, \text{name}, ?N))$

$\qquad\qquad \text{OPT } (?A, \text{homePage}, ?H)\big]$

$?A$	$?N$	$?H$
Ronald_Fagin	"Ronald Fagin"	http://www.almaden...
Amnon_Lotem	"Amnon Lotem"	
Moni_Naor		http://www.wisdom...

$P_3 = \big[(\text{FaginLN01}, \text{creator}, ?A) \text{ OPT }$

$\qquad\qquad ((?A, \text{name}, ?N) \text{ OPT } (?A, \text{homePage}, ?H))\big]$

$?A$	$?N$	$?H$
Ronald_Fagin	"Ronald Fagin"	http://www.almaden...
Amnon_Lotem	"Amnon Lotem"	
Moni_Naor		

2.3 The complexity of evaluating SPARQL

A fundamental issue in every query language is the complexity of query evaluation and, in particular, what is the influence of each component of the language in this complexity. In this section, we present a survey of the results on the complexity of the evaluation of SPARQL graph patterns. In this study, we consider several fragments of SPARQL built incrementally, and present complexity results for each such fragment. Among other results, we show that the complexity of the evaluation problem for general SPARQL graph patterns is PSPACE-complete [32], and that this high complexity is obtained as a consequence of unlimited use of nested optional parts.

As is customary when studying the complexity of the evaluation problem for a query language [40], we consider its associated decision problem. We denote this problem by EVALUATION and we define it as follows:

Input	:	An RDF graph G, a graph pattern P and a mapping μ.
Question	:	Does $\mu \in [\![P]\!]_G$?

Notice that the pattern and the graph are both input for EVALUATION. Thus, we study the *combined complexity* of the query language [40].

We start this study by considering the fragment consisting of graph pattern expressions constructed by using only the operators AND and FILTER. In what follows, we call AND-FILTER to this fragment [3]. This simple fragment is interesting as it does not use the two most complicated operators in SPARQL, namely UNION and OPT. Given an RDF graph G, a graph pattern P in this fragment and a mapping μ, it is possible to efficiently check whether $\mu \in [\![P]\!]_G$ by using the following simple algorithm [32]. First, for each triple t in P, verify whether $\mu(t) \in G$. If this is not the case, then return *false*. Otherwise, by using a bottom-up approach, verify whether the expression generated by instantiating the variables in P according to μ satisfies the FILTER conditions in P. If this is the case, then return *true*, else return *false*.

Theorem 2.5 ([32, 33]) EVALUATION *can be solved in time* $O(|P| \cdot |G|)$ *for the* AND-FILTER *fragment of SPARQL.*

We continue this study by adding the UNION operator to the AND-FILTER fragment. It is important to notice that the inclusion of UNION in SPARQL was one of the most controversial issues in the definition of this language. The following theorem shows that the inclusion of this operator makes the evaluation problem for SPARQL considerably harder.

Theorem 2.6 ([32, 33]) EVALUATION *is NP-complete for the* AND-FILTER-UNION *fragment of SPARQL.*

In [38], the authors strengthen the above result by showing that the complexity of evaluating graph pattern expressions

---

[3] We use a similar notation for other combinations of SPARQL operators. For example, the AND-FILTER-UNION fragment of SPARQL is the fragment consisting of all the graph patterns constructed by using only the operators AND, FILTER and UNION.

constructed by using only AND and UNION operators is already NP-hard. Thus, we have the following result.

Theorem 2.7 ([38]) EVALUATION *is* NP-*complete for the* AND-UNION *fragment of* SPARQL.

We now consider the OPT operator. The following theorem proved in [32] shows that when considering all the operators in SPARQL graph patterns, the evaluation problem becomes considerably harder.

Theorem 2.8 ([32, 33]) EVALUATION *is* PSPACE-*complete.*

To prove the PSPACE-hardness of EVALUATION, the authors show in [33] how to reduce in polynomial time the quantified boolean formula problem (QBF) to EVALUATION. An instance of QBF is a quantified propositional formula φ of the form $\forall x_1 \exists y_1 \forall x_2 \exists y_2 \cdots \forall x_m \exists y_m \, \psi$, where ψ is a quantifier-free formula of the form $C_1 \wedge \cdots \wedge C_n$, with each C_i ($i \in \{1, \ldots, n\}$) being a disjunction of literals, that is, a disjunction of propositional variables x_i and y_j, and negations of propositional variables. Then the problem is to verify whether φ is valid. It is known that QBF is PSPACE-complete [16]. In the encoding presented in [33], the authors use a fixed RDF graph G and a fixed mapping μ. Then they encode formula φ with a pattern P_φ that uses nested OPT operators to encode the *quantifier alternation* of φ, and a graph pattern without OPT to encode the satisfiability of formula ψ. By using a similar idea, it is shown in [38] how to encode formulas φ and ψ by using only the OPT operator, thus strengthening Theorem 2.8.

Theorem 2.9 ([38]) EVALUATION *is* PSPACE-*complete even for the* OPT *fragment of* SPARQL.

When verifying whether $\mu \in [\![P]\!]_G$, it is natural to assume that the size of P is considerably smaller than the size of G. This assumption is very common when studying the complexity of a query language. In fact, it is named *data complexity* in the database literature [40], and it is defined as the complexity of the evaluation problem for a fixed query. More precisely, for the case of SPARQL, given a graph pattern expression P, the evaluation problem for P, denoted by EVALUATION(P), has as input an RDF graph G and a mapping μ, and the problem is to verify whether $\mu \in [\![P]\!]_G$.

Theorem 2.10 ([33]) EVALUATION(P) *is in* LOGSPACE *for every* SPARQL *graph pattern expression* P.

3. IS SPARQL THE RIGHT QUERY LANGUAGE FOR RDF?

As we pointed out in the introduction, one of the distinctive features of RDF is the fact that its semantics is open world, making RDF databases inherently incomplete. More precisely, if we are given an RDF graph G, we know that all the tuples in G hold, but we have no information about the tuples that are not included in this graph. This gives rise to the following notion of interpretation of an RDF graph G: If H is an RDF graph such that $G \subseteq H$, then H is a possible *interpretation* of G as all the tuples in G also hold in H.

The open nature of RDF leads to an infinite number of possible interpretations for each RDF graph. However, the semantics of SPARQL proposed by the W3C [37, 32, 33], which is presented in Section 2, does not take into consideration these possible interpretations. Thus, it is natural to ask whether the semantics of SPARQL is appropriate for

the open-world semantics of RDF. In this section, we provide both positive and negative answers to this question, depending on what SPARQL operators are considered. In particular, we show in Section 3.1 that the semantics of SPARQL is appropriate for the open-world semantics of RDF if the OPT operator is not considered, and we show in Section 3.2 that the situation is completely different if OPT is used.

3.1 A positive answer: SPARQL without the OPT operator

As we mentioned above, the open nature of an RDF graph G leads to an infinite number of possible interpretations of G, which immediately raises the question of how a query can be answered over such a graph. The standard way to deal with this problem is to consider the answers to a query that hold in every such interpretation. Formally, given an RDF graph G and a SPARQL graph pattern P, define the set of certain answers of P over G as follows:

$$\text{CERTAINANSWERS}(P, G) \;=\; \bigcap_{H \,:\, G \subseteq H} [\![P]\!]_H.$$

According to the semantics of SPARQL defined by the W3C [37, 32, 33], the answer to a query over an RDF graph G should be computed by considering only the triples in G (without taking into account the possible interpretations of G). Thus, it is natural to ask what is the relationship of this semantics with the certain answers semantics defined above. Next we show that these two semantics coincide for the AND-FILTER-UNION fragment of SPARQL.

In order to prove the equivalence of the two semantics, we first provide a simple characterization of the notion of certain answers in terms of the notion of monotonicity of a query language. Following the usual database terminology, a SPARQL graph pattern P is said to be monotone if for every pair G_1, G_2 of RDF graphs such that $G_1 \subseteq G_2$, it holds that $[\![P]\!]_{G_1} \subseteq [\![P]\!]_{G_2}$. Then we have that:

Proposition 3.1 *A* SPARQL *graph pattern* P *is monotone if and only if* $[\![P]\!]_G = \text{CERTAINANSWERS}(P, G)$ *for every RDF graph* G.

It is straightforward to prove that every graph pattern in the AND-FILTER-UNION fragment of SPARQL is monotone.

Lemma 3.2 *Every graph pattern* P *in the* AND-UNION-FILTER *fragment of* SPARQL *is monotone.*

Thus, as a corollary of Proposition 3.1 and Lemma 3.2, we obtain the following result:

Theorem 3.3 *Let* P *be a graph pattern in the* AND-UNION-FILTER *fragment of* SPARQL. *Then for every RDF graph* G, *it holds that* $[\![P]\!]_G = \text{CERTAINANSWERS}(P, G)$.

That is, when the semantics of SPARQL is restricted to the AND-UNION-FILTER fragment, it properly handles the possible interpretations of an RDF graph. In fact, Theorem 3.3 tells one that in order to compute the certain answers of a graph pattern P in this fragment over an RDF graph G, it is enough to compute the answers to P over G according to the semantics proposed by the W3C.

3.2 A negative answer: The OPT operator

In the previous section, we show that the open-world semantics of RDF is properly handled by the semantics of SPARQL when restricted to the AND-UNION-FILTER fragment of this query language. This fact, which is shown in

Theorem 3.3, holds essentially because the AND-UNION-FILTER fragment of SPARQL is a positive query language; because of monotonicity, it cannot represent a difference operator between sets of mappings (like the MINUS operator of SQL). Thus, one may be tempted to think that a graph pattern including the OPT operator should also satisfy Theorem 3.3, as OPT is, at least conceptually, a positive operator. However, we show in this section that the inclusion of the OPT operator leads to a completely different scenario.

In the previous section, it was shown that the notion of monotonicity characterizes the equivalence of the certain answers semantics with the semantics of SPARQL proposed by the W3C. However, this notion of monotonicity is not appropriate for the OPT operator, as shown in the following example.

EXAMPLE 3.4. Assume that G_1 is the RDF graph shown in Figure 1, and let G_2 be a graph obtained by adding to G_1 the triple (Ronald_Fagin, email, ron@fagin.com). Moreover, let P be the following SPARQL graph pattern:

$$(\text{Ronald\_Fagin}, \text{homepage}, ?X) \text{ OPT}$$
$$(\text{Ronald\_Fagin}, \text{email}, ?Y). \quad (2)$$

The answer to this query in G_1 is $\{\mu_1\}$, where μ_1 is the mapping $\{?X \rightarrow <\text{http://www.almaden...}>\}$, while the answer to this query in G_2 is $\{\mu_2\}$, where μ_2 is the mapping $\{?X \rightarrow <\text{http://www.almaden...}>, ?Y \rightarrow \text{ron@fagin.com}\}$. Hence, we have that $[\![P]\!]_{G_1} \not\sqsubseteq [\![P]\!]_{G_2}$ (since $\mu_1 \notin [\![P]\!]_{G_2}$), from which we conclude that P is not monotone as $G_1 \subseteq G_2$. □

Graph pattern (2) in the previous example is not monotone. However, one can claim that this pattern is at least monotone in terms of the retrieved information; for the graphs G_1, G_2 given in Example 3.4, we have that the information in $[\![P]\!]_{G_1}$ is contained in the information in $[\![P]\!]_{G_2}$, as the latter set includes not only the homepage of Ronald_Fagin but also his email. This idea gives rise to a weaker notion of monotonicity that is more appropriate for the study of the OPT operator. Formally, given mappings μ_1 and μ_2, we say that μ_1 is subsumed by μ_2, denoted by $\mu_1 \preceq \mu_2$, if $\text{dom}(\mu_1) \subseteq \text{dom}(\mu_2)$ and $\mu_1(?X) = \mu_2(?X)$ for every $?X \in \text{dom}(\mu_1)$. Moreover, given sets of mappings Ω_1 and Ω_2, we say that Ω_1 is subsumed by Ω_2, denoted by $\Omega_1 \sqsubseteq \Omega_2$, if for every for every $\mu_1 \in \Omega_1$, there exists $\mu_2 \in \Omega_2$ such that $\mu_1 \preceq \mu_2$. Then a SPARQL graph pattern P is said to be *weakly monotone* if for every pair G_1, G_2 of RDF graphs such that $G_1 \subseteq G_2$, it holds that $[\![P]\!]_{G_1} \sqsubseteq [\![P]\!]_{G_2}$. For instance, graph pattern (2) is weakly monotone.

The notion of weak monotonicity captures the intuition that if some extra triples are included in an RDF graph, then the use of the operator OPT should allows one to extend some mappings without losing any information. Thus, in order to answer the question of whether the semantics of SPARQL properly handles the open-world semantics of RDF, and following the approach developed in Section 3.2, we now look for a notion of certain answers that is properly characterized by the notion of weak monotonicity. Formally, let P be a SPARQL graph pattern, G an RDF graph, Ω a set of mappings and Υ a family of sets of mappings. Then Ω is said to be a lower bound of Υ w.r.t the preorder $\sqsubseteq$ if $\Omega \sqsubseteq \Omega'$ for every $\Omega' \in \Upsilon$, and Ω is said to be a greatest lower bound of Υ w.r.t. $\sqsubseteq$ if Ω is a lower bound of Υ w.r.t. $\sqsubseteq$, and for every other lower bound Ω' of Υ w.r.t. $\sqsubseteq$, it holds

that $\Omega' \sqsubseteq \Omega$. In the following proposition, we show that there exists a tight connection between the notions of weak monotonicity and greatest lower bound w.r.t. $\sqsubseteq$.

Proposition 3.5 *A SPARQL query P is weakly monotone if and only if for every RDF graph G, it holds that $[\![P]\!]_G$ is a greatest lower bound of $\{[\![P]\!]_H \mid G \subseteq H\}$ w.r.t. $\sqsubseteq$.*

Proposition 3.5 gives us a natural definition of what it means for a SPARQL graph pattern to properly handle the open-world semantics of RDF: Given a SPARQL graph pattern P and an RDF graph G, $[\![P]\!]_G$ should be the largest set in terms of information content that is contained in the answer to P over every possible interpretation of G. Thus, we have a criteria to formally answer the question of whether the semantics of SPARQL is appropriate for the open nature of RDF. Unfortunately, the answer to this question is negative as shown in the following example.

EXAMPLE 3.6. Assume that G_1 is the RDF graph shown in Figure 1, and let G_2 be a graph obtained by adding to G_1 the triple (Ronald_Fagin, email, ron@fagin.com). Moreover, let P be the following SPARQL graph pattern:

$$\Big[(?X, \text{name}, \text{``Moni Naor''}) \text{ AND}$$
$$\Big((?Y, \text{name}, \text{``Ronald Fagin''}) \text{ OPT } (?X, \text{email}, ?Z)\Big)\Big] \quad (3)$$

Graph pattern P stores in variable $?X$ a URI with name "Moni Naor", in variable $?Y$ a URI with name "Ronald Fagin", and it optionally stores in $?Z$ the email of the URI stored in $?X$. The answer to this query in G_1 is $\{\mu_1\}$, where μ_1 is the mapping $\{?X \rightarrow \text{Moni\_Naor}, ?Y \rightarrow \text{Ronald\_Fagin}\}$. The answer to this query in G_2 is the empty set of mappings since (a) the answer to the triple pattern $(?X, \text{name}, \text{``Moni Naor''})$ over $G_2$ is $\{\nu_1\}$, where $\nu_1$ is the the mapping $\{X \rightarrow \text{Moni\_Naor}\}$, (b) the answer to the graph pattern $((?Y, \text{name}, \text{``Ronald Fagin''}) \text{ OPT } (?X, \text{email}, ?Z))$ over G_2 is $\{\nu_2\}$, where ν_2 is the mapping $\{?Y \rightarrow \text{Ronald\_Fagin}, ?X \rightarrow \text{Ronald\_Fagin}, ?Z \rightarrow \text{ron@fagin.com}\}$, and (c) ν_1 is not compatible with ν_2. Hence, we have that $[\![P]\!]_{G_1} \not\sqsubseteq [\![P]\!]_{G_2}$, from which we conclude that P is not weakly monotone as $G_1 \subseteq G_2$. □

The idea behind the OPT operator is to allow for optional matching of patterns, that is, to allow information to be added if it is available, instead of just rejecting whenever some part of a pattern does not match. However, this intuition fails in the simple graph pattern (3) given in Example 3.6, as this pattern is not weakly monotone. And not only that, it can also be shown that the intuition that SPARQL is a positive query language fails, as OPT can be used to express a difference operator between sets of mappings. More precisely, given SPARQL graph patterns P_1, P_2 and an RDF graph G, define operator MINUS as $[\![(P_1 \text{ MINUS } P_2)]\!]_G = [\![P_1]\!]_G \setminus [\![P_2]\!]_G$, where $\setminus$ is the difference operator between sets of mappings defined in Section 2.2. Then we have that:

Proposition 3.7 ([3]) *Let P_1 and P_2 be SPARQL graph patterns. Then $(P_1 \text{ MINUS } P_2)$ is equivalent to:*

$$\Big[\Big(P_1 \text{ OPT } (P_2 \text{ AND } (?X_1, ?X_2, ?X_3))\Big) \text{ FILTER } \neg \text{bound}(?X_1)\Big],$$

where $?X_1, ?X_2, ?X_3$ are fresh variables mentioned neither in P_1 nor in P_2.

In light of these negative results, we present in Section 4 a fragment of SPARQL that is defined by a syntactic restriction (proposed in [32]) over the scope of the variables used in the OPT operator. The graph patterns in this fragment are shown to be weakly monotone in Section 4 and, thus, the semantics of these patterns is appropriate for the open nature of RDF.

4. WELL-DESIGNED GRAPH PATTERNS

One of the most delicate issues in the definition of a semantics for graph pattern expressions is the semantics of the OPT operator. As we have mentioned before, the idea behind this operator is to allow for optional matching of patterns, that is, to allow information to be added if it is available, instead of just rejecting whenever some part of a pattern does not match. However, this intuition fails in some simple examples.

EXAMPLE 4.1. Let P_1 be the graph pattern:

$$((?X, \text{name}, \text{"Moni Naor"}) \text{ AND } (?Y, \text{name}, \text{"Ronald Fagin"})),$$

and P_2 be the graph pattern (3), which is obtained by replacing $(?Y, \text{name}, \text{"Ronald Fagin"})$ in P_1 by optional pattern $((?Y, \text{name}, \text{"Ronald Fagin"}) \text{ OPT } (?X, \text{email}, ?Z))$. Moreover, let G be the RDF graph obtained by adding the triple (Ronald_Fagin, email, ron@fagin.com) to the RDF graph in Figure 1. It is easy to see that $[\![P_1]\!]_G = \{\mu_1\}$, where μ_1 is the mapping $\{?X \to \text{Moni\_Naor}, ?Y \to \text{Ronald\_Fagin}\}$. On the other hand, although P_2 is obtained by adding optionality to P_1, it is shown in Example 3.6 that $[\![P]\!]_G$ is the empty set of mappings $\quad\square$

The graph pattern in the previous example is unnatural as the triple pattern $(?X, \text{email}, ?Z)$ seems to be giving optional information for $(?X, \text{name}, \text{Moni Naor})$ (they share variable $?X$), but in the graph pattern appears as giving optional information for $(?Y, \text{name}, \text{"Ronald Fagin"})$. In fact, it is possible to find a common pattern in the examples that contradict the intuition behind the definition of the OPT operator: A graph pattern P mentions an expression $P' = (P_1 \text{ OPT } P_2)$ and a variable $?X$ occurring both inside P_2 and outside P', but not occurring in P_1.

In [32], the authors focus on the AND-FILTER-OPT fragment of SPARQL and introduce a syntactic restriction that forbids the form of interaction between variables discussed above. Next we present this restriction, for which we need to introduce some terminology. A graph pattern Q is said to be *safe* if for every sub-pattern $(P \text{ FILTER } R)$ of Q, it holds that $\text{var}(R) \subseteq \text{var}(P)$.

Definition 4.2 ([32]) *Let P be a graph pattern in the* AND-FILTER-OPT *fragment of* SPARQL. *Then P is well designed if (1) P is safe, and (2) for every sub-pattern $P' = (P_1 \text{ OPT } P_2)$ of P and variable $?X$, if $?X$ occurs both inside P_2 and outside P', then it also occurs in P_1.*

For instance, pattern (3) in Example 3.6 is not well designed.

The condition of being well-designed imposes a natural restriction over the scope of variables in the OPT operator. In [32], the notion of being well designed was introduced in an attempt to regulate the scope of variables in the OPT operator and, in particular, to forbid some unnatural SPARQL graph patterns that violate the intuition

1. Sub-property:

   (a) $\dfrac{(\mathcal{A},\text{sp},\mathcal{B}) \quad (\mathcal{B},\text{sp},\mathcal{C})}{(\mathcal{A},\text{sp},\mathcal{C})}$

   (b) $\dfrac{(\mathcal{A},\text{sp},\mathcal{B}) \quad (\mathcal{X},\mathcal{A},\mathcal{Y})}{(\mathcal{X},\mathcal{B},\mathcal{Y})}$

2. Subclass:

   (a) $\dfrac{(\mathcal{A},\text{sc},\mathcal{B}) \quad (\mathcal{B},\text{sc},\mathcal{C})}{(\mathcal{A},\text{sc},\mathcal{C})}$

   (b) $\dfrac{(\mathcal{A},\text{sc},\mathcal{B}) \quad (\mathcal{X},\text{type},\mathcal{A})}{(\mathcal{X},\text{type},\mathcal{B})}$

3. Typing:

   (a) $\dfrac{(\mathcal{A},\text{dom},\mathcal{B}) \quad (\mathcal{X},\mathcal{A},\mathcal{Y})}{(\mathcal{X},\text{type},\mathcal{B})}$

   (b) $\dfrac{(\mathcal{A},\text{range},\mathcal{B}) \quad (\mathcal{X},\mathcal{A},\mathcal{Y})}{(\mathcal{Y},\text{type},\mathcal{B})}$

Table 1: RDFS inference rules.

behind the definition of the OPT operator. Next we show that this restriction also leads to weak monotonicity, thus showing that well-designed graph patterns are appropriate for the open-world assumption underlying RDF.

Theorem 4.3 *Every well-designed graph pattern is weakly monotone.*

Well-designed graph patterns also have good properties regarding the complexity of the evaluation problem. In [32, 33, 38], it was proved that the evaluation problem for SPARQL is PSPACE-complete, even if only the OPT operator is considered [38]. In these papers, the PSPACE lower bounds were proved by using graph patterns that are not well-designed. Thus, an immediate question is whether the complexity of evaluating well-designed graph pattern expressions is lower than in the general case. In [33], the authors showed that this is indeed the case.

Theorem 4.4 ([33]) EVALUATION *is coNP-complete for the fragment of* SPARQL *consisting of well-designed patterns.*

It is important to notice that it was also shown in [32, 33, 9] that well-designed patterns are suitable for reordering and optimization, demonstrating the significance of this class of queries from the practical point of view.

Well-designed patterns form a well-behaved fragment of SPARQL that we think deserves future investigation. In particular, given the result in Theorem 4.3, it would be interesting to explore whether weakly monotone graph patterns coincide with well-designed graph patterns. The question of whether an AND-FILTER-OPT SPARQL pattern is weakly monotone if and only if it is well designed, remains open. Notice that we are considering only AND-FILTER-OPT SPARQL patterns, since the notion of being well-designed is defined only for this fragment. Thus, an interesting subject to explore is how to extend this notion to patterns containing the UNION operator. A first proposal is presented in [36], but the study of fundamental properties such as weak monotonicity, complexity of evaluation, and optimization has not been carried out.

5. RDFS VOCABULARY AND A NAVIGATIONAL LANGUAGE FOR RDF

The RDF specification includes a set of reserved URIs (reserved elements from **U**) with predefined semantics, the RDFS vocabulary [12]. This set of reserved URIs is designed to deal with inheritance of classes and properties, as well as typing, among other features [12]. In Figure 1, we use two of these URIs, namely `rdf:type` and `rdfs:subClassOf`, when describing the resource `dbpedia:Ronald_Fagin`. Intuitively, it is possible to conclude from the graph in Figure 1 that "Ronald Fagin" is a "Scientist", as it is stated in the graph that "Ronald Fagin" is a "Database Researcher", which is a subclass of "Research Worker", which in turn is a subclass of "Scientist".

RDFS was designed to deal with the the kind of deductions shown in the previous paragraph. In this section, we present a formalization of RDFS taken from [18, 29], and then we study the problem of answering queries over RDFS data. In particular, we introduce the notion of nested regular expression in Section 5.2, which has shown to be appropriate to navigate RDF data [34], and then we introduce in Section 5.3 the query language nSPARQL, which extends SPARQL with nested regular expressions and has shown to be appropriate to deal with the RDFS vocabulary [34]. Interestingly, we also show that nSPARQL can be used to pose many interesting and natural queries over RDF data, which require of its navigational capabilities.

5.1 RDFS vocabulary

The semantics of RDFS was defined in [22] by borrowing some notions from mathematical logic. We consider here a simplified version of this semantics, which is obtained by focusing on the subset of RDFS consisting of the reserved URIs `rdf:type`, `rdfs:subClassOf`, `rdfs:subPropertyOf`, `rdfs:range`, and `rdfs:domain`. This fragment was studied in [29], where the authors provide a formal semantics for it, and show it to be equivalent to the semantics of RDFS defined in [22] (when restricted to the five keywords just mentioned).

From now on, we use shorthands `type`, `sc`, `sp`, `range`, `dom` for the reserved URIs `rdf:type`, `rdfs:subClassOf`, `rdfs:subPropertyOf`, `rdfs:range`, and `rdfs:domain`, respectively. The semantics of these keywords can be given in terms of the rule system shown in Table 1. In every rule, letters $\mathcal{A}$, $\mathcal{B}$, $\mathcal{C}$, $\mathcal{X}$, $\mathcal{Y}$ stand for *variables* to be replaced by actual terms. Formally, an *instantiation* of a rule is a replacement of its variables by elements of $(\mathbf{U} \cup \mathbf{L})$. Then an RDF graph G' is said to be obtained by an *application* of a rule r to G, if there is an instantiation $\frac{R}{R'}$ of r such that $R \subseteq G$ and $G' = (G \cup R')$. Moreover, an RDF triple t can be *inferred* from G, if there exists a graph G' that is obtained from G by successively applying the rules in Table 1 and such that $t \in G'$. In [29], it is proved that the rule system given in Table1 is sound and complete for the inference problem in the presence of the vocabulary `type`, `sc`, `sp`, `range` and `dom`.

When dealing with RDFS vocabulary, a particular property that separates RDF graphs from standard graphs comes into play: edge labels may also be considered as nodes in the graph. For example, consider the RDF graph in Figure 2, which stores information about transportation services between cities. It states that TGV provides a transportation service from Paris to Calais by using the triple (Paris, TGV, Calais). It also states that a TGV service is a sub-property of train_service by using the triple (TGV, `sp`, train_service). Thus, TGV is simultaneously acting as an edge label and as a node label in the graph of Figure 2.

The RDF graph in Figure 2 also contains RDFS annotations to describe the relationship between transportation services. For instance, (Seafrance, `sp`, ferry_service) states that Seafrance is a sub-property of ferry_service. Thus, by using this triple and (Calais, Seafrance, Dover), we can con-

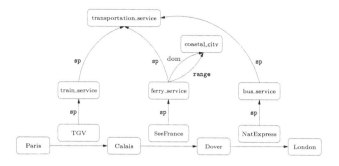

Figure 2: RDF graph storing information about cities and transportation services between cities.

clude that there is a ferry going from Calais to Dover. Formally, this conclusion can be obtained by a single application of rule (1b) to triples (Seafrance, `sp`, ferry_service) and (Calais, Seafrance, Dover), from which we obtain triple (Calais, ferry_service, Dover). Moreover, by applying the rule (3b) to this last triple and (ferry_service, `range`, coastal_city), we obtain triple (Dover, `type`, coastal_city) and, thus, we conclude that Dover is a coastal city.

For the RDFS vocabulary consisting of `type`, `sc`, `sp`, `range` and `dom`, it was shown in [29] that one can determine whether a triple is implied by a graph just by checking the existence of some paths in the graph. For example, a query that asks whether a resource A is a sub-class of a resource B can be answered just by checking the existence of a path from A to B in the graph where each edge has label `sc`. This observation has motivated the extension of SPARQL with path expressions [2, 34, 19], that allow the user to specify ways to navigate RDF graphs. For instance, in the query languages proposed in [2, 34, 19], an extended triple pattern of the form (A, sc^+, B) can be used to check whether A is a sub-class of B, as sc^+ is a path expression denoting paths of length at least 1 and where each edge has label `sc`. In the rest of this section, we present the query language nSPARQL that was introduced in [34], and which uses the notion of *nested regular expression* to specify how to navigate an RDF graph. More specifically, nested regular expressions are introduced in Section 5.2, and nSPARQL is introduced in Section 5.3.

5.2 Nested regular expressions

The query language proposed in [34] uses, as usual for graph query languages [28, 4], regular expressions to define paths on graph structures, but taking into consideration the special features of RDF graphs. In particular, the authors extend in [34] regular expressions by borrowing the notion of *branching* from XPath [11], to obtain the language of *nested regular expressions* to specify how to navigate RDF data.

The navigation of a graph is usually done by using an operator *next*, which allows one to move from a node to an adjacent node. In our setting, we have RDF "graphs", which are sets of triples, not classical graphs. In particular, the sets of node labels and edge labels of an RDF graph can have a nonempty intersection. The notion of nested regular expression proposed in [34] takes into account the special features of the RDF data model. In particular, nested regular expressions use three different *navigation axes* `next`, `edge` and `node`, and their inverses next^{-1}, edge^{-1} and node^{-1}, to move through an RDF triple. These axes are shown in Figure 3.

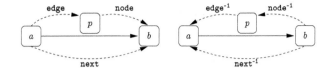

Figure 3: Axes for an RDF triple (a, p, b).

In the language of nested regular expressions, a navigation axis allows one to move one step forward (or backward) in an RDF graph and, thus, a sequence of these axes defines a path. Moreover, one can use classical regular expressions over these axes to define a set of paths that can be used in a query. Nested regular expressions also include an additional axis **self** that is used not to actually navigate, but instead to perform a test over a node in a path. Finally, the language also allows *nested expressions* that can be used to test for the existence of certain paths starting at any axis. The following grammar defines the syntax of nested regular expressions:

$$exp \quad := \quad \text{axis} \mid \text{axis}::a \ (a \in \mathbf{U}) \mid \text{axis}::[exp] \mid$$
$$exp/exp \mid exp|exp \mid exp^* \quad (4)$$

with axis $\in \{\text{self}, \text{next}, \text{next}^{-1}, \text{edge}, \text{edge}^{-1}, \text{node}, \text{node}^{-1}\}$.

Before introducing the formal semantics of nested regular expressions, we give some intuition about how these expressions are evaluated in an RDF graph. The most natural navigation axis is $\text{next}::a$, with a an element from $\mathbf{U}$. Given a graph G, the expression $\text{next}::a$ is interpreted as the *a-neighbor* relation in G, that is, the pairs of nodes (x, y) such that $(x, a, y) \in G$. The language also allows one to navigate from a node to one of its leaving edges by using the **edge** axis. Formally, the interpretation of $\text{edge}::a$ is the pairs of nodes (x, y) such that $(x, y, a) \in G$. The nesting construction $[exp]$ is used to check for the existence of a path defined by expression exp. For instance, when evaluating nested expression $\text{next}::[exp]$ in G, one retrieves the pairs of nodes (x, y) such that there exists z satisfying that $(x, z, y) \in G$ and there exists a path in G starting in z and conforming to expression exp.

The evaluation of a nested regular expression exp in an RDF graph G is formalized as a binary relation $[\![exp]\!]_G$, denoting the pairs of nodes (x, y) such that y is reachable from x in G by following a path that conforms to exp. The semantics of the language is shown in Table 2. In this table, G is an RDF graph, $a \in \mathbf{U}$, $\text{voc}(G)$ is the set of all the elements from $\mathbf{U}$ that are mentioned in G, "axis" represents any of the navigational axes in $\{\text{next}, \text{node}, \text{edge}\}$, and exp, exp_1, exp_2 are nested regular expressions. Notice that the semantics of our expressions considers only URIs (elements in $\mathbf{U}$), and not literals, as the navigation of an RDF graph has to be done through the actual nodes in the graph, and not through the data values. As is customary for regular expressions, given a nested regular expression exp, we use exp^+ as a shorthand for the expression exp/exp^*.

EXAMPLE 5.1. Let G be the graph in Figure 1, and consider the following nested regular expression:

next::isPartOf/**next**::series

The evaluation of this expression over G is the set of all pairs (x, y) such that x is a paper that was published in conference y. For example $(\text{FaginLN01}, \text{pods})$ is in the evaluation of

$[\![\text{self}]\!]_G$	$=$	$\{(x, x) \mid x \in \text{voc}(G)\}$
$[\![\text{self}::a]\!]_G$	$=$	$\{(a, a)\}$
$[\![\text{next}]\!]_G$	$=$	$\{(x, y) \mid \text{there exists } z \text{ s.t. } (x, z, y) \in G\}$
$[\![\text{next}::a]\!]_G$	$=$	$\{(x, y) \mid (x, a, y) \in G\}$
$[\![\text{edge}]\!]_G$	$=$	$\{(x, y) \mid \text{there exists } z \text{ s.t. } (x, y, z) \in G\}$
$[\![\text{edge}::a]\!]_G$	$=$	$\{(x, y) \mid (x, y, a) \in G\}$
$[\![\text{node}]\!]_G$	$=$	$\{(x, y) \mid \text{there exists } z \text{ s.t. } (z, x, y) \in G\}$
$[\![\text{node}::a]\!]_G$	$=$	$\{(x, y) \mid (a, x, y) \in G\}$
$[\![\text{axis}^{-1}]\!]_G$	$=$	$\{(x, y) \mid (y, x) \in [\![\text{axis}]\!]_G\}$
$[\![\text{axis}^{-1}::a]\!]_G$	$=$	$\{(x, y) \mid (y, x) \in [\![\text{axis}::a]\!]_G\}$
$[\![exp_1/exp_2]\!]_G$	$=$	$\{(x, y) \mid \text{there exists } z \text{ s.t. } (x, z) \in [\![exp_1]\!]_G$ and $(z, y) \in [\![exp_2]\!]_G\}$
$[\![exp_1|exp_2]\!]_G$	$=$	$[\![exp_1]\!]_G \cup [\![exp_2]\!]_G$
$[\![exp^*]\!]_G$	$=$	$[\![\text{self}]\!]_G \cup [\![exp]\!]_G \cup [\![exp/exp]\!]_G \cup \cdots$
$[\![\text{self}::[exp]]\!]_G$	$=$	$\{(x, x) \mid x \in \text{voc}(G) \text{ and there exists } z$ s.t. $(x, z) \in [\![exp]\!]_G\}$
$[\![\text{next}::[exp]]\!]_G$	$=$	$\{(x, y) \mid \text{there exist } z, w \text{ s.t. } (x, z, y) \in G$ and $(z, w) \in [\![exp]\!]_G\}$
$[\![\text{edge}::[exp]]\!]_G$	$=$	$\{(x, y) \mid \text{there exist } z, w \text{ s.t. } (x, y, z) \in G$ and $(z, w) \in [\![exp]\!]_G\}$
$[\![\text{node}::[exp]]\!]_G$	$=$	$\{(x, y) \mid \text{there exist } z, w \text{ s.t. } (z, x, y) \in G$ and $(z, w) \in [\![exp]\!]_G\}$
$[\![\text{axis}^{-1}::[exp]]\!]_G$	$=$	$\{(x, y) \mid (y, x) \in [\![\text{axis}::[exp]]\!]_G\}$

Table 2: Semantics of nested regular expressions.

the expression. One can use the **self** axis to test that the conference in the above expression is actually PODS:

$$exp_1 \quad = \quad \textbf{next}::\text{isPartOf}/\textbf{next}::\text{series}/\textbf{self}::\text{pods}$$

By using expression exp_1, it is easy to construct a nested regular expression that has as evaluation all the pairs (x, y) such that x and y are co-authors of a PODS paper:

$$exp_2 \quad = \quad \textbf{next}^{-1}::\text{creator}/\textbf{self}::[\,exp_1\,]/\textbf{next}::\text{creator}$$

Notice that $\textbf{next}^{-1}::\text{creator}$ is used to navigate from an author x to a paper p created by x, then the nested expression $\textbf{self}::[\,exp_1\,]$ is used to test that p is actually a PODS paper, and then $\textbf{next}::\text{creator}$ is used to navigate from p to one of its authors y. For example, the pair $(\text{Ronald\_Fagin}, \text{Moni\_Naor})$ is in $[\![exp_2]\!]_G$. Moreover, one can use the power of nested regular expressions to obtain the complete network of co-authorship of PODS papers as follows:

$$exp_3 \quad = \quad (\textbf{next}^{-1}::\text{creator}/\textbf{self}::[\,exp_1\,]/\textbf{next}::\text{creator})^+$$

This expression defines the set of all pairs (x_1, x_k) for which there exists a sequence $x_2, \ldots, x_{k-1}$ of authors such that x_i is a co-author of x_{i+1} $(1 \le i < k)$ in a PODS paper. $\square$

5.2.1 On the complexity and expressiveness of nested regular expressions

In [34], the authors study several properties of nested regular expressions. In the first place, they study the complexity of evaluating these expressions, and considered two problems. The first one is the standard decision problem considered when studying the complexity of a query language:

PROBLEM	:	Evaluation problem for nested regular expressions.
INPUT	:	An RDF graph G, a nested regular expression exp, and a pair (a, b).
QUESTION	:	Is $(a, b) \in [\![exp]\!]_G$?

The second problem considered in [34] is the following *computation* problem associated to nested regular expressions:

PROBLEM	:	Computation problem for nested regular expressions.
INPUT	:	An RDF graph G, a nested regular expression exp, and a node a.
OUTPUT	:	List all elements b s.t. $(a, b) \in [\![exp]\!]_G$.

It turns out that both problems can be solved efficiently.

Theorem 5.2 ([34]) *The evaluation and computation problems for nested regular expressions can be solved in time $O(|G| \cdot |exp|)$.*

In the second place, it is studied in [34] whether nested regular expressions are expressive enough to deal with the RDFS vocabulary. Interestingly, it is shown in [34] that this is indeed the case:

Theorem 5.3 ([34]) *There exists a function TRANS from $\mathbf{U}$ to the set of nested regular expressions such that, for every RDF graph G and triple $(a, p, b) \in \mathbf{U} \times \mathbf{U} \times \mathbf{U}$, it holds that (a, p, b) can be inferred from G according to the RDFS semantics if and only if $(a, b) \in [\![\text{TRANS}(p)]\!]_G$.*

Due to the lack of space, we do not reproduce here the complete definition of TRANS (see [34] for details), and we only show in an example the intuition behind this transformation.

EXAMPLE 5.4. Let G be the RDF graph in Figure 2, and consider the following nested regular expression:

$$exp = \texttt{next}::[(\texttt{next}::\texttt{sp})^*/\texttt{self}::\text{transportation\_service}]$$

A pair (x, y) is in the evaluation of the expression exp over G if there exists a triple (x, p, y) in G and a path from p to transportation_service where every edge has label $\texttt{sp}$. Thus, nested expression $[(\texttt{next}::\texttt{sp})^*/\texttt{self}::\text{transportation\_service}]$ is used to emulate the inferencing process in RDFS; it retrieves all the nodes that are *sub-properties* of transportation_service (rule (1a) in Table 1). Therefore, we have that the triple $(x, \text{transportation\_service}, y)$ can be inferred from G if and only if (x, y) is in $[\![exp]\!]_G$, which tells one that the evaluation of expression exp results in the set of pairs of cities that are connected by a transportation service (which can be a train service, ferry service, bus service, etc). In fact, in the example we have that (Calais, Dover) is in $[\![exp]\!]_G$.

We can also use nested regular expressions to obtain the pairs of cities such that there is a way to travel from one city to the other with any number of transportation services:

$$(\texttt{next}::[(\texttt{next}::\texttt{sp})^*/\texttt{self}::\text{transportation\_service}])^+$$

For example, the pair (Paris, London) is in the evaluation of this last expression over G. $\square$

The previous example shows the power of nested regular expressions not only to deal with the RDFS vocabulary, but also to express interesting and natural queries over RDF data (which require of navigational capabilities to be expressed).

5.3 nSPARQL

In this section, we give a brief overview of the query language nSPARQL, which was proposed in [34] as an extension of SPARQL with navigational capabilities, and was designed to be able to answer queries considering the semantics of the RDFS vocabulary.

Let the closure of a graph G, denoted by $cl(G)$, be the graph obtained from G by successively applying the rules in Table 1 until the graph does not change. Then the RDFS

evaluation of a SPARQL graph pattern P over an RDF graph G, denoted by $[\![P]\!]_G^{\text{rdfs}}$, is defined as $[\![P]\!]_G^{\text{rdfs}} = [\![P]\!]_{cl(G)}$.

As we have pointed out before, a SPARQL graph pattern P treats the RDFS vocabulary without considering its predefined semantics. Thus, we have in general that $[\![P]\!]_G \neq [\![P]\!]_G^{\text{rdfs}}$, which immediately raises the question of how the semantics of RDFS could be included into SPARQL. A simple approach to do this could be based on the materialization of the closure of a graph; once this closure has been computed, a query can be directly evaluated over it. Unfortunately, this approach has some practical drawbacks; among others, the closure of a graph can be of quadratic size thus making its computation and storage too expensive. In light of these limitations, it was proposed in [34] to replace triple patterns in SPARQL by patterns using nested regular expressions, which can be used to simulate the RDFS inferencing process without computing the closure of a graph (see Theorem 5.2). The resulting language was called nSPARQL in [34]. More specifically, nSPARQL is obtained by considering triple patterns with nested regular expressions in the predicate position. The evaluation of an extended triple pattern of the form $(?X, exp, ?Y)$ over an RDF graph G is defined just as the set of mappings $\mu = \{?X \to a, ?Y \to b\}$ such that $(a, b) \in [\![exp]\!]_G$. The language nSPARQL also includes the operators AND, FILTER, UNION and OPT, whose semantics is inherited from SPARQL. In [34], the authors showed that in order to evaluate a SPARQL graph pattern P over an RDF graph G according to the RDFS semantics, one does not need to materialize the closure of G, but instead one can just rewrite P into an nSPARQL pattern that is evaluated over the initial graph G. Formally, the following theorem is proved in [34]:

Theorem 5.5 ([34]) *Let P be a SPARQL graph pattern constructed by considering only triple patterns without a variable in the predicate position. Then there exists an nSPARQL pattern Q, that can be computed in linear time from P, such that for every RDF graph G: $[\![P]\!]_G^{\text{rdfs}} = [\![Q]\!]_G$.*

It should be noticed that Theorem 5.5 does not hold for the triple pattern $(?X, ?Y, ?Z)$ (which has a variable in the predicate position), as the evaluation of $(?X, ?Y, ?Z)$ over an RDF graph G according to the RDFS semantics would inevitably imply the computation of the closure of G, which is something that cannot be computed by using the navigational approach of nSPARQL [34].

6. A BIG CHALLENGE: LINKED DATA

We conclude the paper by pointing out some challenges for the database community that come from the Linked Data project [6]. Up to this point, we have modeled RDF data assuming a classical centralized database approach: the data resides in a single repository to which queries have full access. In fact, the normative specifications of RDF and SPARQL follow the same assumption [22, 37]. The *Web of Linked Data* [6, 8] is a shift towards a data model in which every piece of RDF information describes itself (describes its relations with other pieces of data) in a decentralized way. Linked Data is based on the following set of principles to publish Web data [6, 23]: (1) URIs should be used to identify *things*, (2) URIs should be Web-accessible so that people/machines can *look up* those URIs, (3) when someone/something looks up a URI, an RDF graph with *useful* information should be provided, and (4) the RDF graph should include links to other Web-accessible URIs so that more things can be *discovered*.

There are several issues posed by these principles that are not covered from a classical database point of view, among the most important: data is highly distributed and at a *fine grain*, any URI can make statements about (provide links to) any other URI, and anyone can publish anything about a resource. These issues together with the scalability issues faced when querying Web data and the distinctive features of RDF (such as the inherent incompleteness of the information in an RDF database, the graph structure of RDF and the use of vocabularies with predefined semantics) make Linked Data a very challenging scenario from a database point of view. Although there has been some work on querying Linked Data [20, 21, 9], little research has been pursued towards the fundamental problems of developing appropriate data models and query languages in this context. Linked Data can be benefited from the large body of work done in database areas such as semi-structured data [41], graph databases [4], Web data models [27, 1] and distributed databases [30]. Thus, we think that the database community has much more to say about the fundamental database problems that need to be solved in the context of the Linked Data project.

The amount of Web data published following the Linked Data principles has grown constantly since their proposal in 2006. With the advent of large projects such as `data.gov` and `data.gov.uk`, whose purposes are to increase public access to government data, we can only expect it to grow more in the future. Thus, we expect that the interest in managing highly-distributed large-scale RDF data will continue growing both in the Semantic Web and database communities.

7. REFERENCES

[1] S. Abiteboul and V. Vianu. Queries and computation on the Web. *Theor. Comput. Sci.*, 239(2):231–255, 2000.

[2] F. Alkhateeb, J.-F. Baget, and J. Euzenat. Extending SPARQL with regular expression patterns (for querying RDF). *J. Web Sem.*, 7(2):57–73, 2009.

[3] R. Angles and C. Gutierrez. The expressive power of SPARQL. In *ISWC*, pages 114–129, 2008.

[4] R. Angles and C. Gutiérrez. Survey of graph database models. *ACM Comput. Surv.*, 40(1), 2008.

[5] P. Barceló, C. A. Hurtado, L. Libkin, and P. T. Wood. Expressive languages for path queries over graph-structured data. In *PODS*, pages 3–14, 2010.

[6] T. Berners-Lee. Design issues: Linked Data. `http://www.w3.org/DesignIssues/LinkedData.html`, July 2006.

[7] T. Berners-Lee, R. Fielding, and L. Masinter. Uniform resource identifier (URI): Generic syntax. `http://www.ietf.org/rfc/rfc3986.txt`, 2005.

[8] C. Bizer, T. Heath, and T. Berners-Lee. Linked data - the story so far. *Int. J. Semantic Web Inf. Syst.*, 5(3):1–22, 2009.

[9] C. Buil-Aranda, M. Arenas, and O. Corcho. Semantics and optimization of the SPARQL 1.1 federation extension. In *ESWC*, 2011.

[10] D. Calvanese, G. De Giacomo, M. Lenzerini, and M. Y. Vardi. Containment of conjunctive regular path queries with inverse. In *KR*, 2000.

[11] J. Clark and S. DeRose. XML path language (XPath). W3C recommendation. `http://www.w3.org/TR/xpath`, November 2008.

[12] R.V. Guha D. Brickley. RDF vocabulary description language 1.0: RDF schema, W3C recommendation, February 2004.

[13] DBpedia. `http://dbpedia.org/`.

[14] A. Deutsch and V. Tannen. Optimization properties for classes of conjunctive regular path queries. In *DBPL*, pages 21–39, 2001.

[15] T. Furche, B. Linse, F. Bry, D. Plexousakis, and G. Gottlob. RDF querying: Language constructs and evaluation methods compared. In *Reasoning Web*, pages 1–52, 2006.

[16] M. R. Garey and David S. Johnson. *Computers and Intractability: A Guide to the Theory of NP-Completeness*. W. H. Freeman, 1979.

[17] B. Glimm and M. Krötzsch. SPARQL beyond subgraph matching. In *ISWC*, pages 241–256, 2010.

[18] C. Gutierrez, C. A. Hurtado, A. O. Mendelzon, and J. Pérez. Foundations of semantic web databases. *J. Comput. Syst. Sci.*, 77(3):520–541, 2011.

[19] S. Harris and A. Seaborne. SPARQL 1.1 query language. W3C working draft. `http://www.w3.org/TR/sparql11-query/`, October 2010.

[20] O. Hartig and A. Langegger. A database perspective on consuming Linked Data on the Web. *Datenbank-Spektrum*, 10(2):57–66, 2010.

[21] O. Hartig, J. Sequeda, J. Taylor, and P. Sinclair. How to consume Linked Data on the Web: tutorial description. In *WWW*, pages 1347–1348, 2010.

[22] Pat Hayes. RDF semantics, W3C Recommendation, February 2004.

[23] T. Heath and C. Bizer. *Linked Data: Evolving the Web into a Global Data Space*. Morgan & Claypool Publishers, 2011.

[24] D2R DBLP Bibliography Database hosted at L3S Research Center. `http://dblp.l3s.de/d2r/`.

[25] I. Kollia, B. Glimm, and I. Horrocks. SPARQL query answering over OWL ontologies. In *ESWC*, 2011.

[26] F. Manola and E. Miller. RDF primer, W3C recommendation, February 2004.

[27] A. O. Mendelzon and T. Milo. Formal models of Web queries. *Inf. Syst.*, 23(8):615–637, 1998.

[28] A. O. Mendelzon and P. T. Wood. Finding regular simple paths in graph databases. In *VLDB*, pages 185–193, 1989.

[29] S. Muñoz, J. Pérez, and C. Gutiérrez. Minimal deductive systems for RDF. In *ESWC*, pages 53–67, 2007.

[30] M. T. Özsu and P. Valduriez. *Principles of Distributed Database Systems, Third Edition*. Prentice-Hall, 2011.

[31] P. F. Patel-Schneider, P. Hayes, and I. Horrocks. OWL semantics and abstract syntax. W3C recommendation. `http://www.w3.org/TR/owl-semantics/`, February 2004.

[32] J. Pérez, M. Arenas, and C. Gutierrez. Semantics and complexity of SPARQL. In *ISWC*, pages 30–43, 2006.

[33] J. Pérez, M. Arenas, and C. Gutierrez. Semantics and complexity of SPARQL. *ACM Trans. Database Syst.*, 34(3), 2009.

[34] J. Pérez, M. Arenas, and C. Gutierrez. nSPARQL: A navigational language for RDF. *J. Web Sem.*, 8(4):255–270, 2010.

[35] A. Polleres. SPARQL1.1: New features and friends (OWL2, RIF). In *Rules and Reasoning*, pages 23–26, 2010.

[36] Axel Polleres. From SPARQL to rules (and back). In *Proceedings of the International Conference on World Wide Web (WWW)*, pages 787–796, 2007.

[37] E. Prud'hommeaux and A. Seaborne. SPARQL query language for RDF. W3C recommendation. `http://www.w3.org/TR/rdf-sparql-query/`, January 2008.

[38] M. Schmidt, M. Meier, and G. Lausen. Foundations of SPARQL query optimization. In *ICDT*, pages 4–33, 2010.

[39] E. Sirin and B. Parsia. SPARQL-DL: SPARQL query for OWL-DL. In *OWLED*, 2007.

[40] M. Y. Vardi. The complexity of relational query languages (extended abstract). In *STOC*, pages 137–146, 1982.

[41] V. Vianu. A Web odyssey: from Codd to XML. *SIGMOD Record*, 32(2):68–77, 2003.

Theory of Data Stream Computing: Where to Go

S. Muthukrishnan
Rutgers University
Piscataway, NJ
muthu@cs.rutgers.edu

Categories and Subject Descriptors

F.2 [**Theory of Computation**]: Analysis of Algorithms
and Problem Complexity

General Terms

Algorithms

Summary Computing power has been growing steadily,
just as communication rate and memory size. Simultaneously our ability to create data has been growing phenom-
enally and therefore the need to analyze it. We now have
examples of massive data streams that are

- created in far higher rate than we can capture and
  store in memory economically,

- gathered in far more quantity than can be transported
  to central databases without overwhelming the communication infrastructure, and

- arrives far faster than we can compute with them in a
  sophisticated way.

This phenomenon has challenged how we store, communicate and compute with data. Theories developed over past
50 years have relied on full capture, storage and communication of data. Instead, what we need for managing modern
massive data streams are new methods built around working with less. The past 10 years have seen new theories
emerge in computing (data stream algorithms), communication (compressed sensing), databases (data stream management systems) and other areas to address the challenges
of massive data streams. Still, lot remains open and new
applications of massive data streams have emerged recently.
We present an overview of these challenges.

Puzzle: One Word Median. We start with a puzzle.
This was posed by Mark Sandler. Items $i_1, i_2, \ldots$ arrive
in a stream, each generated independently and randomly
from some *unknown* distribution $\mathcal{D}$ over integers $[1, m]$. The
problem is to provide an estimate after every item i_j of the
median of the items $i_1, \ldots, i_j$. This is trivial to solve by
running a standard median finding algorithm after each i_j,
or more efficiently by maintaining the items in a balanced
search tree. What makes this a puzzle is that we are allowed
to store only one word (to be formal of size $\log n$ bits), and
not archive the stream seen thus far. Please contact the
author for the solution. The puzzle is also interesting if we
allow say 2 or 3 words to be stored, or if we know $\mathcal{D}$ *a priori*
but must provide accuracy guarantees with respect to the
empirical stream $i_1, \ldots, i_j$ (not an expected stream), and so
on. Again, contact the author for discussions. Previously,
puzzles have been used to illustrate data streams [1]. In that
spirit, the puzzle here is to illustrate certain new aspects of
data streams of current interest.

Background. We start with a quintessential application
that generates massive data streams.

- *IP Traffic Analysis.* Consider the data generated from
  IP networks at the level of each packet and its contents:
  each new packet is seen at a router and forwarded in
  a few nanoseconds and has 100's of bytes of header
  and payload information. Capturing all this information will need memory working at nanosecond response
  which is expensive, transporting them to central warehouses would need lot of communication infrastructure
  because of duplication in observation, and doing any
  analysis in the few nanoseconds before another packet
  arrives will limit computation to simplest tasks.

There are other examples from sensor networks to Homeland Security, scientific discovery and others where one or
the other of the computing, communication and storage infrastructure becomes the challenge because of the massive-
ness of the data.

This phenomenon has challenged how we store, communicate and compute with data. Traditional systems capture
all the data they can, communicate all the data between
storages, and compute sophisticated functions on the stored
data when needed. This in turn saw over half a century of
theory:

- Theory of Computing led to the notion of efficiency to
  be polynomial time algorithms based on the premise
  that all the data is stored and can be processed multiple times.

- Theory of Communication led to the notion of information content and the minimum number of bits needed
  to transfer data in entirety.

- Theory of Signal Processing developed under the premise that signal can always be sampled at the Nyquist rate for full reconstruction.

- Theory of Databases led to an algebra to process data that can be applied recursively to intermediate results and are provably correct on the state of the stored input and intermediate data.

The assumption that all data can be captured, moved and processed pervades all of computing, communication, data acquisition and ananlysis we have seen the past half century. Instead, in the new world of massive data streams, we need to ask what is the minimal amount of data that needs to be captured and stored, what is the minimal number of bits that need to be transferred for suitable analyses we need to do, what are algorithms that will support sophisticated analyses on whatever portion of data is available, and finally, what are suitable redesign of applications to work with this new world of storage, communication and computation.

The research community is beginning to address the above fundamental questions. In particular, they have developed *theory of streaming computation* that uses few passes over the data with only polylogarithmic storage and per-item processing time [1, 2]; database community has developed *data stream management systems* for dealing with operators for which data sources never end [3]; there are *specialized applications* for IP network analysis [4], financial stream, etc.; and, the signal processing community has developed *theory of compressed sensing* [5, 6] where signals can be sampled at sub-Nyquist rate for sparse signals. Altogther, these developments are already impacting Telecoms and have potential applications in Medical Imaging, Radar and many others [7]. Still, this world is nascent, comparable to early days of computing. Our ability to deal with massive data is still primitive despite the developments in the last 10 years in directions above. Massive data is real, and the last few years have convinced everyone from Scientists to Engineers, Industries and Governments that analyzing them is needed for security, operations and innovation.

Directions in Massive Data Streams Research. We describe some of the challenges research community needs to address to deal with massive data streams. We will use two new massive data applications to motivate our discussion.

- *Web Data Analysis.* The web is an information publication network that amasses text to conversations, friendships, video and images, growing in terabytes a day. Portions of the web can be gathered, stored and analyzed via traditional crawl based systems or as updates when information changes. Billions of dollar of Industry as well as telecom and Homeland Security application rely on analyzing such web information [9]. Such analyses can not be carried out easily with single machines, or traditional streaming systems.

- *Continual Security Monitoring.* Homeland Security and other security applications use not only on-demand query analyses for forming hypotheses, discovering evidence and finding connections, but need to monitor many data sources and sensors in a continual way, looking for pre-specified or emergence of patterns, and generate alerts and root causes, so possibly humans can investigate them. This requirement is not met by systems that do periodic analyses of all data because it is difficult to analyze all the data at sufficient time granularity to be useful for real time alerting. On the other hand, for many analyses we do not yet know how to compile them down to monitoring primitives on distributed sensors or sources so they can automatically trigger alerts as early as possible as threatening phenomenon emerges.

Inspired by these applications, we present a series of research directions.

- *Models of Massive Distributed Data.* While MapReduce [8] and its variants are being used for simple analyses of web data with massively distributed systems, often analysts in the field tend to change problems they need to solve into ones they can solve easily using known techniques and compromising on the end analysis. We need suitable new models to design and analyze algorithms for massively distributed systems going beyond streaming and MapReduce and they have to model energy concerns of using 1000's of processors. We need a theory to provide us new algorithmic design techniques as well as provide a framework to understand what are truly hard problems. We need notions of complexity classes beyond the traditional NC that captures the true tradeoff between communication, energy and computation in massively distributed systems, and will guide this area much as polynomial time computations did for 50+ years and polylog one-pass models have done for the past 10+ years. Preliminary work appears in [10, 11].

- *Continual Computation Theory.* For monitoring applications, we need a new framework of algorithm design that rather than quantifying the cost of solving a problem on the whole data in one shot, quantifies the incremental overhead of a computation as data is progressively seen. The crux here is to also model the cost of communicating the updates from distributed points. Recently, some progress has been made in defining such models [12], but a far deeper understanding and richer theory is needed. In particular, the underlying challenges are in developing a new, continual eversion of the well known Communication Complexity [13], and a time-varying extension of the well-known Slepian-Wolf [14] results to distributed networks for specific analyses of interest.

- *Graph and Matrix Data Analyses Problems.* The applications above need new kinds of analyses. In particular, web data has a variety of rich graph structures in them. The analyses of interest involves computing graph properties, finding substructures, learning properties of nodes and edges, as well as looking at them as suitable matrices and computing fundamental quantities like rank approximations, eigenvalues etc. While many of these problems have been studied in standard settings, scaling these solutions to applications above — massively distributed or continual monitoring — is a great challenge. The past few years have seen some progress on graph algorithms [16] and matrix methods [15], but far more is needed.

- *Stochastic Data Algorithms.* The applications above have uncertain data because of inaccuracies in sensing or malicious data from web. A large class of tasks with massive data is machine learning including classification, clustering, and labeling. Finally, nearly all problems of interest are hard in distributed or continual settings above in standard worst case models. Therefore we need principled methods for learning the stochastics and uncertainties of data and designing algorithms that tune to them, and a new theory of Stochastic Data Algorithms. There is some recent work in machine learning community on incremental machine over stochastic data, recent work in CS and OR community on stochastic online optimization and space-efficient tracking of sufficient statistics, emerging work in database community on processing uncertain data, etc. We need a far richer research program to truly have a suite of algorithms suitable for dealing with stochastics of massive data applications.

- *Cryptography and Privacy of Massive Data.* Data needs encryption, authentication and privacy, no matter what size. But the motivating applications for massive data including web data and security analsys bring many novel challenges to even traditional tasks. For example, well known Interactive proofs have to be expanded in novel ways for applications to stream verification [17]; privacy of data stream analyses needs new stringent notions including pan-privacy [18, 19]; and, continual computation needs new differential privacy [20]. We need a systematic research effort to extend and invent new cryptographic and privacy primitives for data access and computation for massive data applications such as the ones above.

- *Compressed Functional Sensing.* Streaming and compressed sensing brought two groups of researchers (CS and signal processing) together on common problems of what is the minimal amount of data to be sensed or captured or stored, so data sources can be reconstructed, at least approximately. This has been a productive development for research with fundamental insights into geometry of high dimensional spaces as well as the Uncertainty Principle [7]. In addition, Engineering and Industry has been impacted significantly with analog to information paradigm. This is however just the beginning. We need to extend compressed sensing to functional sensing, where we sense only what is appropriate to compute different functions and SQL queries (rather than simply reconstructing the signal) and furthermore, extend the theory to massively distributed and continual framework to be truly useful for new massive data applications above.

Conclusions. The directions above are substantial and require research across not only theoretical and applied areas of Computer Science, but also in Applied Mathematics (eg signal analysis) and beyond in Engineering (eg from telecoms to medical imaging, astronomy, Radar and more). The fledging research of the past 10 years on massive data streams has already generated new insights in Mathematics, new theories of Computing and Communication, as well as new Data Stream Systems for data analysis; it has also impacted industries of size in billions of dollars. New focused research agenda bringing these communities together on directions above will impact much more, and define fundamentally new ways software, hardware, analog and digital systems will be built in the future.

1. REFERENCES

[1] S. Muthukrishnan. *Data Streams: Algorithms and Applications.* In Foundations and Trends in Theoretical Computer Science, 2005.

[2] P. Indyk A tutorial on Streaming, Sketching and Sub-linear Space Algorithms. 2009 Information Theory and Applications Workshop, San Diego, 2009. `http://people.csail.mit.edu/indyk/ita-web.pdf`

[3] M. Garofalakis, J. Gehrke and R. Rastogi. *Data Stream Management: Processing High-Speed Data Streams,* 2007.

[4] C. Cranor, T. Johnson and O. Spatscheck. Gigascope: How to monitor network traffic at 5Gbit/sec at a time. `http://www2.research.att.com/~divesh/meetings/mpds2003/schedule/spatscheck.pdf`.

[5] David Donoho. Compressed sensing. *Technical Report,* 2004.

[6] E. Candes and T. Tao. Near-optimal signal recovery from random projections and universal encoding strategies. 2004.

[7] `http://dsp.rice.edu/cs`.

[8] J. Dean and S. Ghemawat. Mapreduce: Simplified data processing on large clusters. *Proc. OSDI,* 2004.

[9] `http://en.wikipedia.org/wiki/XLDB`.

[10] Jon Feldman, S. Muthukrishnan, Anastasios Sidiropoulos, Clifford Stein, Zoya Svitkina. On distributing symmetric streaming computations. em Proc. SODA 2008: 710-719.

[11] H. Karloff, S. Suri, S. and S. Vassilvitskii. A Model of Computation for MapReduce. Proc. ACM-SIAM SODA 2010.

[12] Graham Cormode, S. Muthukrishnan, Ke Yi. Algorithms for distributed functional monitoring. *Proc. SODA* 2008: 1076-1085

[13] Eyal Kushilevitz and Noam Nisan. *Communication Complexity,* 1997.

[14] `http://www.scholarpedia.org/article/Slepian-Wolf_coding`

[15] Kenneth L. Clarkson, David P. Woodruff. Numerical linear algebra in the streaming model. *Proc STOC.* 2009: 205-214.

[16] Kook Jin Ahn, Sudipto Guha. Graph Sparsification in the Semi-streaming Model. *ICALP* (2) 2009: 328-338.

[17] A. Chakrabarti, G. Cormode, and A. McGregor. Annotations in data streams. In International Colloquium on Automata, Languages and Programming (ICALP), 2009.

[18] C. Dwork, M. Naor, T. Pitassi, G. Rothblum, and S. Yekhanin. Pan-Private Streaming Algorithms. ICS, 2010.

[19] D. Mir, S. Muthukrishnan, A. Nikolov and R. Wright. Pan-Private Algorithms Via Statistics on Sketches. PODS, 2011.

[20] Cynthia Dwork. Differential Privacy in New Settings. *SODA,* 2010.

Author Index

www.ingramcontent.com/pod-product-compliance
Lightning Source LLC
Chambersburg PA
CBHW080352060326
40689CB00019B/3981